FIFTH EDITION

The Practice of Social Work

FIFTH EDITION

The Practice of Social Work

Charles Zastrow

University of Wisconsin—Whitewater

Brooks/Cole Publishing Company
Pacific Grove, California

I(T)P™ The trademark ITP is used under license.

 A CLAIREMONT BOOK

Brooks/Cole Publishing Company
A Division of Wadsworth, Inc.
© 1995, 1992 by Wadsworth, Inc., Belmont, California
94002. All rights reserved. No part of this book may be reproduced, stored in a retrieval system, or transcribed, in
any form or by any means—electronic, mechanical, pho-
tocopying, recording, or otherwise—without the prior
written permission of the publisher, Brooks/Cole Publishing Company, Pacific Grove, California 93950, a division of Wadsworth, Inc.

Printed in the United States of America
10 9 8 7 6 5 4 3 2 1

Library of Congress Cataloging-in-Publication Data
Zastrow, Charles.
    The practice of social work / Charles Zastrow.—5th ed.
        p.   cm.
    Includes bibliographical references (p.   ) and index.
    ISBN 0-534-23844-0
    1. Social service.   2. Social service—Psychological
aspects.   3. Counseling.   I. Title.
HV40.Z273   1994
361.3'2—dc20   94-8987
                                                       CIP

Sponsoring Editors: *Claire Verduin, Lisa Gebo*
Editorial Associate: *Gay C. Bond*
Production Editor: *Nancy L. Shammas*
Production Assistant: *Tessa A. McGlasson*
Manuscript Editor: *Robin Witkin*
Permissions Editor: *Catherine Gingras*
Interior Design: *Katherine Minerva*
Cover Photo: *Ed Young Photography*
Cover Design: *Lori Hughes Design*
Art Coordinator: *Lisa Torri*
Senior Photo Editor: *Larry Molmud*
Photo Researcher: *Sue C. Howard*
Indexer: *Do Mi Stauber*
Typesetting: *ColorType*
Cover Printing: *Phoenix Color Corporation, Inc.*
Printing and Binding: *Arcata Graphics/Fairfield*

THIS BOOK IS PRINTED ON ACID-FREE RECYCLED PAPER

TO GINNY AND VICKI

CONTRIBUTING AUTHORS

WALLACE J. GINGERICH, MSW, Ph.D.
Professor, Mandel School of Applied Social
Sciences
Case Western Reserve University
Cleveland, OH

GRAFTON H. HULL, JR., MSW, Ed.D.
Department Head and Professor
Department of Social Work
Southwest Missouri State University
Springfield, MO

KAREN K. KIRST-ASHMAN, MSW, Ph.D.
Professor, Social Work Department
University of Wisconsin—Whitewater
Whitewater, WI

DONALD NOLAN, MSSW, BCD
Clinical Social Worker
South Central Psychiatric Center
Janesville, WI

LLOYD G. SINCLAIR, MSSW, ACSW
Certified Sex Educator, Sex Therapist, and
Sex Therapist Supervisor
Midwest Center for Psychotherapy and Sex
Therapy
Madison, WI

CAROLYN WELLS, MSW, Ph.D.
Associate Professor, Social Work Program
Marquette University
Milwaukee, WI

JAMES P. WINSHIP, MSW, DPA
Associate Professor, Social Work
Department
University of Wisconsin—Whitewater
Whitewater, WI

CONTENTS

PREFACE

The Council on Social Work Education (CSWE) is the national organization in the United States that accreditates baccalaureate and master's degree programs in social work education. In 1992 CSWE adopted revisions in its curriculum policy statements for baccalaureate and master's degree programs. A major thrust of this edition of *The Practice of Social Work* is to present material that is consistent with the revisions in the social work practice content of these policy statements. Material is added in this fifth edition on social work values and ethics, diversity, promotion of social and economic justice, populations-at-risk, social work practice with organizations, the change process in social work, and feminist perspectives on intervention.

This text provides the theoretical and practical knowledge needed for entry levels of practice in social work. Material is presented covering generalist practice, social work values, confidentiality, principles of interviewing, contemporary theories of counseling, sexual therapy, social work with individuals, social work with groups, social work with families, social work with organizations, social work community practice, assessment, evaluation, general systems theory, cross-cultural social work, working within a bureaucratic system, burnout, and the frustrations and satisfactions of being a social worker. A number of case examples are included to illustrate the theory that is presented.

The Practice of Social Work, Fifth Edition, is designed for use in practice courses in social work at both the undergraduate and graduate levels. Social work practitioners will also find the text valuable as it describes a variety of approaches to social work practice, including sexual treatment techniques, hypnosis, biofeedback, relaxation approaches, mediation, neurolinguistic programming, milieu therapy, task-centered practice, systematic desensitization, family counseling concepts, feminist intervention, transactional analysis, reality therapy, rational therapy, and behavior therapy. An eclectic approach is used in presenting these diverse types of therapies. After each therapy approach is described, a critical review of the theory is presented to help the reader assess its merits and shortcomings.

This book is unique in that it combines the key components in existing practice texts, both traditional and contemporary, into one text. As much as possible, jargon-free language is used so the reader can more readily grasp the theory. Exercises for students are presented at the end of each chapter to illustrate key concepts and to help students learn how to apply the theoretical material to social work practice.

Plan of the Book

Part I is an introductory section with two chapters. The first chapter conceptualizes social work practice. It describes what social workers do, explains how social work is distinct from other professions, and summarizes the knowledge, values, and skills needed for beginning-level social work practice. This chapter also describes the goals of social work practice, gives a brief history of social work, indicates that social work is a multiskilled profession, and summarizes professional activities performed by social workers, including casework, case management, group work, group therapy, family counseling, and community organization. Various role models of social work practice are defined, including that of an enabler, broker, advocate, and activist. Generalist practice in social work is also defined and described.

The second chapter summarizes social work values. Values described include self-determination, individualization, confidentiality, belief in the institutional approach for the delivery of services, focus on family, advocacy for those being discriminated against, and accountability.

Part II has several chapters that describe social work practice. Social work with individuals, social work with groups, social work with families, social work with organizations, and social work community practice are covered in depth. Techniques for interviewing and counseling clients are given considerable attention. Eight stages of a problem-solving approach to counseling clients are presented. Guidelines are also provided on how to begin and end interviews, how to phrase interview questions, and how to take notes while interviewing. Chapters are also included on assessment, and on evaluating social work practice. Material is summarized on computer applications in social work practice, and on systems analysis. This part also covers material on changing the delivery system to serve clients better, and cross-cultural social work (for example, white workers and Native American clients).

Part III presents and critiques the prominent theories of counseling that are widely used in the helping professions: psychoanalysis, client-centered therapy, feminist intervention, transactional analysis, reality therapy, rational therapy, behavior therapy, sex therapy approaches, task-centered practice, and neuro-linguistic programming. A number of specific treatment techniques are also described, including assertiveness training, token economies, systematic desensitization, implosive therapy, covert sensitization, aversive techniques, milieu therapy, psychodrama, crisis intervention, parent effectiveness training, mediation, muscle relaxation approaches, deep-breathing relaxation, imagery relaxation, meditation, hypnosis, and biofeedback.

It is not necessary for the instructor to cover all of the theories of intervention presented in this text. Rather it is suggested that he or she (with the consultation of the other faculty in the program) decide which intervention theories are most important for students to learn in order to best serve clients in the school's geographic area. This part also has a chapter that analyzes and compares prominent theories of counseling.

Part IV focuses on taking care of self. To be of help to others, social workers must first take care of themselves. Suggestions are presented for resolving common concerns of students receiving professional training in social work. Techniques to manage stress and prevent burnout are described. This part concludes with a discussion of the importance for social workers (as well as other people) of developing a positive identity, and provides guidelines on how to develop a positive sense of self.

Acknowledgments

I wish to express my deep appreciation to the following people who made this book possible: the contributing authors; the artist Don

Baumgart for the whimsical line drawings; and Vicki Vogel, Ralph Navarre, and Diane Sonsthagen who assisted in conceptualizing various chapters and helped in a number of ways with the writing of this text. My thanks also go to the reviewers of this edition: T. Paul Furukawa, University of Hawaii—Manoa; Charlotte Goodluck, Northern Arizona University; Barbara King, Case Western Reserve University; and Ralph Pifer, Sauk Valley Community College.

Charles Zastrow

I

Introduction

1

Overview of Social Work Practice

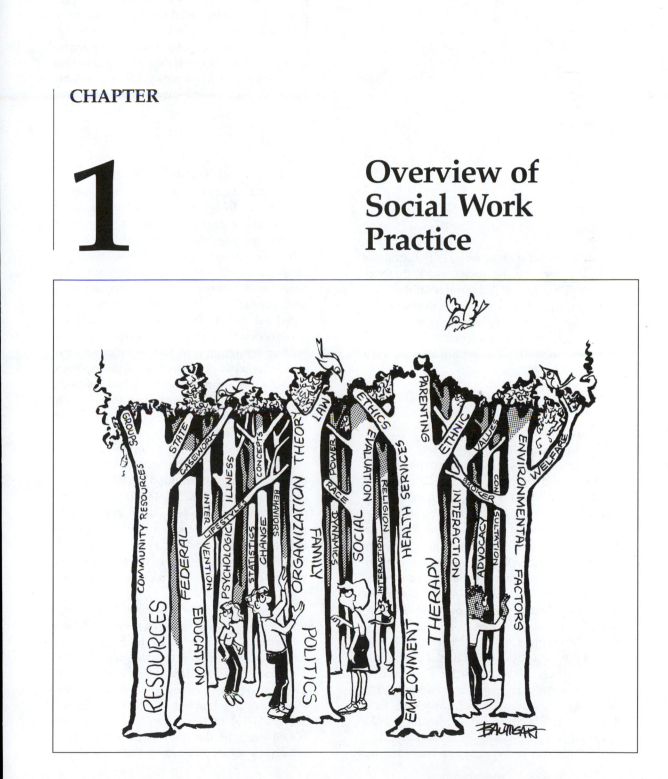

The *Practice of Social Work,* Fifth Edition, is intended for use in social work practice courses. The focus of this book is on the theoretical and practical knowledge that students need to do the tasks of a beginning-level social worker. This book is designed to be read by students preparing for, or already in, field placement.

The Purpose of This Chapter

What do social workers do? How is social work different from psychology, psychiatry, guidance and counseling, and other helping professions? What is the relationship between social work and social welfare? What knowledge, skills, and values do social workers need to be effective? Since there are hundreds of intervention techniques available, which ones should social workers learn? This chapter will address these questions. There have been a number of other efforts to address these same issues. (See Baer & Federico, 1978; Bartless, 1970; "Conceptual Frameworks II," 1981; Council on Social Work Education, 1982, 1992a, 1992b; Germain & Gitterman, 1980; Lowenberg & Dolgoff, 1971; National Association of Social Workers, 1973, 1976, 1981, 1982; Pincus & Minahan, 1973; "Special Issue on Conceptual Frameworks," 1977.) This chapter is largely an effort to inte-

grate these prior conceptualizations. Its purpose is to describe social work as a profession and thereby assist social workers and other interested persons in understanding and articulating what social work is and what is unique about the social work profession. We will begin by taking a brief look at the history of social work.

The History of Social Work

Social work as a profession is of relatively recent origin. To attempt to meet the needs of people living in urban areas, the first social welfare agencies were developed in the early 1800s. These agencies, or services, were private and were developed primarily at the initiation of the clergy and religious groups. Up until the early 1900s, these services were provided exclusively by the clergy and affluent "do-gooders" who had no formal training and little understanding of human behavior or of how to help people. The focus of these private services was on meeting such basic physical needs as food and shelter and on attempting to cure emotional and personal difficulties with religious admonitions.

An illustration of an early social welfare organization was the Society for the Prevention of Pauperism, founded by John Griscom in 1820 (Bemner, 1962, p. 13). This society investigated the habits and circumstances of the poor, suggested plans by which the poor could help themselves, and encouraged the poor to save and economize. One of the remedies used was house-to-house visitation (a very elementary type of social work).

By the latter half of the 1800s, a fairly large number of private relief agencies had been established in large cities to help the unemployed, the poor, the ill, persons with physical or mental disabilities, and orphans. Their programs were uncoordinated and sometimes overlapping. Therefore an English invention—the Charity Organization Society (COS)—caught the interest of a number of American cities (Cohen, 1958). Starting in

Buffalo, New York, in 1877, COS was rapidly adopted in many cities. In charity organization societies, private agencies joined together to (1) provide direct services to individuals and families—in this respect, they were the forerunners of social casework and of family counseling approaches and (2) plan and coordinate the efforts of private agencies to meet pressing urban social problems—in this respect, they were the precursors of community organization and social planning approaches. Charity organizations conducted a detailed investigation of each applicant for services and financial help, maintained a central client registration system to avoid duplication, and used volunteer *friendly visitors* extensively to work with those in difficulty. The friendly visitors were primarily "doers of good works," as they generally gave sympathy rather than money and encouraged the poor to save and to seek employment. Poverty was viewed as a personal shortcoming. Most of the friendly visitors were women.

Concurrent with the COS movement was the establishment of settlement houses in the late 1800s. Toynbee Hall was the first settlement house, established in 1884 in London; many others were soon formed in larger U.S. cities. Many of the early settlement house workers were the daughters of ministers. The workers, who were from the middle and upper classes, would live in a poor neighborhood to experience the harsh realities of poverty. Simultaneously, in cooperation with neighborhood residents, they sought to develop ways to improve living conditions. In contrast to friendly visitors, they lived in impoverished neighborhoods and used the missionary approach of teaching residents how to live moral lives and improve their circumstances. They sought to improve housing, health, and living conditions; find jobs; teach English, hygiene, and occupational skills; and change environmental surroundings through cooperative efforts. Settlement houses used change techniques that are now called social group work, social action, and community organization.

On the one hand, settlement houses placed their emphasis on "environmental reform" while "they continued to struggle to teach the poor the prevailing middle-class values of work, thrift, and abstinence as the keys to success" (Becker, 1968, p. 85). In addition to dealing with local problems by local action, settlement houses played important roles in drafting legislation and in organizing to influence social policy and legislation. The most noted leader in the settlement house movement was Jane Addams of Hull House in Chicago, who summarized what a settlement house was as follows:

> The Settlement, then, is an experimental effort to aid in the solution of the social and industrial problems which are engendered by the modern conditions of life in a great city. (Addams, 1959, pp. 125–126)

Settlement house leaders believed that by changing neighborhoods, they would improve communities; and through altering communities, they would develop a better society.

The first paid social workers were executive secretaries of charity organization societies in the late 1800s (Dolgoff & Feldstein, 1980, pp. 233–234). In the late 1800s charity organization societies received some contracts from the cities in which they were located to administer relief funds. In administering these programs, COS hired people as executive secretaries to organize and train the friendly visitors and to establish accounting procedures to show accountability for the funds received. To improve the services of friendly visitors, executive secretaries needed to establish standards and training courses. In 1898 a training course was first offered by the New York Charity Organization Society. By 1904 the New York School of Philanthropy offered a one-year program. Soon after, colleges and universities began offering training programs in social work. Initially, social work education focused on environmental reform approaches to meet social problems. (Environmental reform approaches focus on changing the system to better meet people's needs. The enactment in 1935 of the Social Security Act to meet the needs of the poor and the unemployed is an example of an environmental reform approach.)

Richard Cabot introduced medical social work into Massachusetts General Hospital in 1905 (Dolgoff & Feldstein, 1980, pp. 233–234). Gradually social workers were employed in schools, courts, child guidance clinics, and other settings.

In 1917 Mary Richmond published *Social Diagnosis*, a text that presented for the first time a theory and methodology for social work. The book focused on how the worker should intervene with individuals. The process is still used today and involves study (collecting information), diagnosis (stating what is wrong), prognosis, and treatment planning (stating what should be done to help clients improve). This book was important as it formulated a common body of knowledge for casework.

In the 1920s Freud's theories of personality development and therapy became popular. The concepts and explanations of psychiatrists appeared particularly appropriate for social workers, who also worked in one-to-one relationships with clients. The psychiatric approach emphasized intrapsychic processes and focused on enabling clients to adapt and adjust to their social situations. Therefore, social workers switched their emphasis from reform to therapy for the next three decades. In the 1960s, however, social workers expressed a renewed interest in sociological approaches, or reform. Several reasons account for this change. Questions arose about the relevance and appropriateness of talking approaches with low-income clients who have urgent social and economic pressures. Furthermore, the effectiveness of many psychotherapeutic approaches was questioned (Eysenck, 1961). Other reasons for the renewed interest included the increase in status of sociology and the mood of the 1960s, which raised questions about the relevancy of social institutions in meeting the needs of the

Prior to the twentieth century, relief agencies focused on meeting the basic needs of the poor, the unemployed, and the ill. Two engravings from *Harper's Weekly*—"For the Poor" and "Visiting the Sick"—present an admiring view of the roles played by the church and the upper class in ministering to the needy.

population. Social work at the present time embraces both the reform and the therapy approaches.[1]

Not until the end of World War I did social work begin to be recognized as a distinct profession. The Depression of the 1930s and the enactment of the Social Security Act in 1935 brought about an extensive expansion of public social services and job opportunities for

[1] *Note:* The author believes there is little difference between the terms *psychotherapy* and *counseling* (for emotional and behavioral problems), and therefore these terms will be used interchangeably in this text.

social workers. Since 1900 there has been a growing awareness by social agency boards and the public that professionally trained social workers are needed to provide social services competently. In 1955 the National Association of Social Workers was formed to represent the social work profession in this country. Its purpose is to improve social conditions and promote high quality and effectiveness in social work practice.

In recent years there has been considerable activity in developing a system of registration or licensing of social workers. Such a system helps assure the public that qualified personnel are providing social work services and also advances the recognition of social work as a profession. All states have now passed legislation to license or regulate the practice of social work.

Social work is a relatively young profession, but it is one of the most important professions in our society in terms of the number of people affected, the human misery treated, and the amount of money spent.

A Definition of Social Work

The National Association of Social Workers (NASW) has defined social work as follows:

> Social work is the professional activity of helping individuals, groups, or communities to enhance or restore their capacity for social functioning and to create societal conditions favorable to their goals.
>
> Social work practice consists of the professional application of social work values, principles, and techniques to one or more of the following ends: helping people obtain tangible services; providing counseling and psychotherapy for individuals, families, and groups; helping communities or groups provide or improve social and health services; and participating in relevant legislative processes.
>
> The practice of social work requires knowledge of human development and

behavior; of social, economic, and cultural institutions; and of the interaction of all these factors. [NASW, 1973, pp. 3–4]

The term *social worker* is generally applied to graduates of educational programs (either with bachelor's or master's degrees) in social work who are employed in the field of social welfare. A social worker is a *change agent*, a helper who is specifically employed for the purpose of creating planned change (Pincus & Minahan, 1973, p. 54). As a change agent a social worker is expected to be skilled at working with individuals, groups, families, and organizations, and in bringing about community changes.

The Relationship Between Social Work and Social Welfare

The goal of social welfare is to fulfill the social, financial, health, and recreational requirements of all individuals in a society. Social welfare seeks to enhance the social functioning of all age groups, both rich and poor. When other institutions in our society (such as the market economy and the family)—fail at times to meet the basic needs of individuals or groups of people, then social services are needed and demanded. Barker (1991) defined social welfare as follows:

> A nation's system of programs, benefits, and services that help people meet those social, economic, educational, and health needs that are fundamental to the maintenance of society. [p. 221]

Examples of social welfare programs and services are foster care, adoption, day care, Head Start, probation and parole, public assistance programs (such as Aid to Families with Dependent Children), public health nursing, sex therapy, suicide counseling, recreational services (Boy Scouts and YWCA programs), services to minority groups and veterans, school social services, medical and

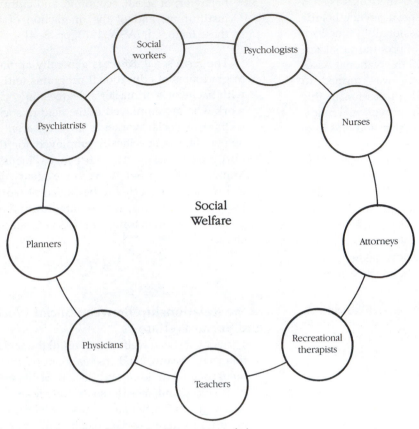

Professional people staffing social welfare services include attorneys
providing legal services to the poor; urban planners in social planning
agencies; physicians in public health agencies; teachers in residential
treatment facilities for the emotionally disturbed; psychologists, nurses,
and recreational therapists in mental hospitals; and psychiatrists in
mental health clinics.

Figure 1.1
Examples of professional groups within the field of social welfare

legal services to the poor, family planning services, Meals on Wheels, nursing home services, shelters for battered spouses, services
to persons with acquired immune deficiency
syndrome (AIDS), protective services for victims of child abuse and neglect, assertiveness
training, encounter groups and sensitivity
training, public housing projects, family
counseling, Alcoholics Anonymous, runaway services, services to people with
developmental disabilities, and sheltered
workshops.

Almost all social workers are employed in
the social welfare field. There are, however,
many other professional and occupational
groups working the field, as illustrated in
Figure 1.1.

What Is the Profession of Social Work?

The National Association of Social Workers
defines the social work profession as follows:

A social worker at a family adult shelter counsels a woman who has been battered by her partner. Counseling individuals is one of the important services provided by social workers.

The social work profession exists to provide humane and effective social services to individuals, families, groups, communities, and society so that social functioning may be enhanced and the quality of life improved. . . .

The profession of social work, by both traditional and practical definition, is the profession that provides the formal knowledge base, theoretical concepts, specific functional skills, and essential social values which are used to implement society's mandate to provide safe, effective, and constructive social services.[2]

Social work is thus distinct from other professions (such as psychology and psychiatry), because it has the responsibility and mandate to provide social services.

A social worker needs training and expertise in a wide range of areas to be able to effectively handle problems faced by individuals, groups, families, organizations, and the larger community. While most professions are increasingly becoming more specialized (for example, most medical doctors now specialize in one or two areas), social work continues to emphasize a generic (broad-based) approach. The practice of social work is analogous to the old general practice of medicine. A general (or family) practitioner has training to handle a wide range of common medical problems, while a social worker has training to handle a wide range of common social and personal problems. The case example on page 10 highlights some of the skills needed by social workers.

[2] Published 1982, National Association of Social Workers, Inc. Reprinted with permission, from *Standards for the Classification of Social Work Practice*, Policy Statement 4, p. 5. Copyright National Association of Social Workers, Inc.

Case Example
Rape

Dr. Richard Carr referred Kay Barber to Lakeside Counseling Center (a mental health center). Kay is 17 years old and a senior at West High School. The previous evening she had been raped by four males in a parking lot near West High. The rape had occurred after Kay left a school dance, about 1:00 A.M. The intake worker assigned the case to Karen Bowman, a social worker who in the recent past had counseled most of the agency's sexual assault cases. Ms. Bowman immediately met with Kay.

Kay was in tears, badly bruised, and still shaking from terror. She was angry, confused, and deeply hurt emotionally. In the next 50 minutes, she briefly described the details of the assault and some of her feelings. She was getting into her dad's car, alone, when she was grabbed by two youths and pulled into some bushes. Behind the bushes were two other youths, one of whom she recognized as the son of a college professor in the community. Following the assault, the youths warned her there would be serious trouble if she informed anyone. Hurt (emotionally and physically) and terrified, she returned home. Her mother was awake when she returned and immediately recognized that something had happened. Kay informed her parents. Kay's mother was horrified and angry, but attempted to comfort Kay. Kay indicated that her father was even more upset, and even today was talking about shooting the rapists if he could find out who they were (Kay had not as yet informed him that she knew one of the attackers for fear of what her father might do).

Kay indicated that on hearing of the assault her parents took her to the police station. There she was questioned by two male police officers. Kay indicated that she revealed only sketchy details of the rape to the police officers as she was in tears, still terrified, and on the defensive because she felt many of the officers' questions suggested she contributed to the rape. She also felt that the officers may not have even believed she was assaulted.

Earlier this morning her parents took her to the family doctor, Richard Carr, who provided medical attention and then referred the case to the counseling center.

Kay was especially confused about a number of issues. Should she seek to press charges against the youths, particularly the one she knew? If she pressed charges, would she have to appear in court? What might this do to her reputation if she went to court? If she didn't press charges, might not these youths rape others, or perhaps even herself in the future? In either case how would she face the other students in school who she felt would hear, one way or the other, about the attack? Why did the police officers doubt her story about being raped, and why did the officers imply she may have contributed to the assault? What were her chances of getting pregnant? If she were pregnant, what would she do then? (Ms. Bowman indicated that the medical services she received might well have prevented her from now being pregnant—and this could be checked with Dr. Carr.) Should she inform her father that she knew one of the assailants? If she did, what might be the consequences? How could she ever learn to deal with the terror she experienced? She also indicated that she felt she would never go out in the evening, alone or with anyone else, in the future, unless she went with a member of her family. And, she wondered why this had to happen to her.

Ms. Bowman listened attentively and conveyed warmth, empathy, support, and a sincere sense of caring. After Kay had ventilated her concerns, Ms. Bowman expressed her understanding that Kay had been deeply hurt and was now feeling overwhelmed by this situation. Ms. Bowman gradually informed Kay that something could be done about all of her present concerns. The way to proceed would be to take her concerns, one by one, and work on resolving them. Ms. Bowman asked Kay to indicate her most urgent concerns. Kay thought awhile and said they were whether to inform her parents that she knew one of the attackers, whether to press charges, and how to react to schoolmates who might make cruel remarks related to the rape.

Kay was then asked to elaborate her concerns in each of these three areas. Her concerns about telling her parents centered around what her father might do. Her concerns about pressing charges focused on wanting to know the procedures involved and what might be the consequences to her of a long drawn-out court trial. In regard to cruel remarks from others, Ms. Bowman suggested to Kay that they role-play how she might respond to such remarks. Ms. Bowman first played Kay's role to model a few assertive strategies to respond to cruel remarks. The roles were then reversed, with Ms. Bowman role-playing someone giving a crude remark, and Kay practicing responding to them.

After this initial hour and 40-minute meeting, Kay became a little more relaxed. Kay mentioned that she was really worried about what her father might do. Ms. Bowman suggested her parents (who were in the waiting room) might be brought in to discuss their concerns. Kay agreed. A rather lengthy meeting was then held with the Barbers. They began by ventilating a great deal of anger, wanting to find out who did this. Mr. Barber indicated he was going to shoot whoever did this. Ms. Bowman mentioned Kay was partially upset, now, by what her father might do if he found out, and asked Mr. Barber if he was aware of this. Following a lengthy discussion of the negative consequences of taking the law into one's own hands, Mr. Barber cried and acknowledged that he would not carry out his threats and that he was only making the threats because he felt so helpless. After Mr. Barber gave full assurance that he would not do anything illegal, he was informed that Kay thought she knew one of the attackers. The pros and cons of pressing charges were then discussed. The procedures involved were described. Another meeting was arranged for the next day with the Barbers to talk further, partially because they wanted additional time to think about what to do. Time was also set aside for Kay and Ms. Bowman to meet the next day to talk further about her concerns.

As indicated earlier, this case was only one of several sexual assault cases that Ms. Bowman was handling. These cases led her to conclude that the area she was living in (320,000 population) needed a well-publicized rape crisis center. She began by gathering data on the incidence of sexual assault in the community—from the police department (many cases go unreported) and from other social service agencies in the community. She then convinced the director of the counseling center to form a committee of representatives from other interested social service agencies in the community and from certain women's organizations in the community. After formation of the committee (of which Ms. Bowman was a

(continued)

member), a questionnaire to obtain further information on the incidence of sexual assault was constructed. Committee members distributed the questionnaire to women shoppers at a large shopping center (respondents in this way remained entirely anonymous). The results suggested less than one rape in ten was being reported to the police, which further documented the need for a rape crisis center that would be well publicized so that victims would know where help was available. Another proposed service of the center would be to provide speakers to schools and other organizations on how to avoid becoming a victim and on what to do if an assault occurred. The center would also work with the police department and the court system to "humanize" the reporting and processing of sexual assault cases. The committee then wrote a grant proposal. After 11 months of searching for funding, the proposal was funded for a three-year test period by the city and the United Way. Because of her capacities in this area, Karen Bowman was appointed assistant director of this rape crisis center.

This case illustration documents a wide range of knowledge and skills displayed by Ms. Bowman: interviewing skills, ability to effectively counsel individuals and families during a crisis, ability to work effectively with other agencies, research and grant-writing skills, public speaking capacities, program development and fundraising skills, and knowledge of how to handle ethical/legal issues that arise.

Perhaps the most basic skill that a social worker needs is to be able to counsel clients effectively. If an individual is not able to do this, he or she should probably not be in social work, certainly not in direct service. Another key skill is to be able to interact effectively with other groups and professionals in the area. Social workers need to learn a wide range of skills and intervention techniques that will enable them to intervene effectively with (1) the client's common personal and emotional problems and (2) the common social problems faced by groups, organizations, and the larger community.

Generalist Social Work Practice

There used to be an erroneous belief that a social worker was either a caseworker, a group worker, or a community organizer. Practicing social workers know that such a belief is faulty because every social worker is involved as a change agent in working with individuals, groups, families, organizations, and the larger community. The amount of time spent at these levels varies from worker to worker, but every worker will, at times, be assigned and expected to work at these three levels and therefore needs training in all of them.

The Council on Social Work Education (the national accrediting entity for baccalaureate and masters programs in social work) requires all bachelor's and master's level programs to train their students in generalist social work practice. (MSW programs, in addition, usually require their students to select and study in an area of specialization. They generally offer several specializations such as family therapy, administration, corrections, and clinical social work.)

A generalist social worker is trained to use the problem-solving process to assess and intervene in the problems confronting individuals, families, groups, organizations, and communities. Anderson (1981) identified three characteristics of a generalist social worker: (1) the generalist is often the first professional to see clients as they enter the social welfare system; (2) the worker must therefore be competent to assess their needs and to identify their stress points and problems; and (3) the worker must draw on a variety of skills and methods in serving clients.

Brieland, Costin, and Atherton (1985) defined and described generalist practice as follows:

> The generalist social worker, the equivalent of the general practitioner in medicine, is characterized by a wide repertoire of skills to deal with basic conditions, backed up by specialists to whom referrals are made. This role is a fitting one for the entry-level social worker.
>
> The generalist model involves identifying and analyzing the interventive behaviors appropriate to social work. The worker must perform a wide range of tasks related to the provision and management of direct service, the development of social policy, and the facilitation of social change. The generalist should be well grounded in systems theory that emphasizes interaction and independence. The major system that will be used is the local network of services. . . .
>
> The public welfare worker in a small county may be a classic example of the generalist. He or she knows the resources of the county, is acquainted with the key people, and may have considerable influence to accomplish service goals, including obtaining jobs, different housing, or emergency food and clothing. The activities of the urban generalist are more complex, and more effort must be expended to use the array of resources. [pp. 120–121]

Hull (1990) defined generalist practice as follows:

The basic principle of generalist practice is that baccalaureate social workers are able to utilize the problem solving process to intervene with various size systems including individuals, families, groups, organizations, and communities. The generalist operates within a systems and person-in-the-environment framework (sometimes referred to as an ecological model). The generalist expects that many problems will require intervention with more than one system (e.g., individual work with [a] delinquent adolescent plus work with the family or school) and that single explanations of problem situations are frequently unhelpful. The generalist may play several roles simultaneously or sequentially depending upon the needs of the client, (e.g.: facilitator, advocate, educator, broker, enabler, case manager, and/or mediator). They may serve as leaders/facilitators of task groups, socialization groups, information groups, and self-help groups. They are capable of conducting needs assessments and evaluating their own practice and the programs with which they are associated. They make referrals when client problems so dictate and know when to utilize supervision from more experienced staff. Generalists operate within the ethical guidelines prescribed by the NASW Code of Ethics and must be able to work with clients, co-workers and colleagues from different ethnic, cultural, and professional orientations. The knowledge and skills of the generalist are transferable from one setting to another and from one problem to another. [p. 7]

The crux of generalist practice involves a view of the situation in terms of the person-in-environment conceptualization (described in an upcoming section of this chapter) and the capacity and willingness to intervene at several different levels, if necessary, while assuming any number of roles. The case example on page 14 illustrates the approach

Case Example
Generalist practice involves options planning

Jack Dawson is a social worker at a high school in a midwestern state. Four teenagers are expelled (consistent with school board policy) for being caught drinking alcoholic beverages at the school during school hours. Mr. Dawson assesses the situation and identifies the following potential courses of action. He can serve as an advocate for the youths by urging the school board and the administration to reinstate the youths. Mr. Dawson is aware that the expulsions are upsetting not only to the youths and their parents but also to the police department and the business community (because expelled youths tend to spend the day on city streets). He can involve the four teenagers in one-to-one counseling about their expulsion and their drinking patterns. He can involve these youths (along with others having drinking problems) in group counseling at the school. He can function as a broker to have the youths receive individual or group counseling from a counseling center outside the school system. He can ascertain the willingness of the parents to become involved in family therapy and serve as a broker to link the interested families with a counseling center that offers family therapy. He can raise the issue (to parents, to the business community, to the police department, to the school administration, and to the school board) of whether expulsion from school for drinking alcoholic beverages is a desirable policy. (Perhaps a better school system policy, in cases like this, is to place the youths on "in-school suspension," where they are required to stay in a study room for a few days.) Expulsion is a drastic measure that may adversely affect the futures of these youths. Mr. Dawson can serve as an organizer and a catalyst to encourage interested parents and school staff to use the incident as a rationale for incorporating educational material on alcohol and other drugs into the curriculum. (The selected courses of action will depend on a variety of factors, including a cost-benefit analysis of each course.)

---

of responding at several different levels in a variety of roles.

This text should facilitate readers' learning a generalist practice approach in social work by describing a variety of assessment and intervention strategies. Through learning these strategies, readers can then select those approaches that hold the most promise in facilitating positive changes in clients (who may be individuals, groups, families, organizations, or communities).

The Change Process

A social worker uses a *change process* in working with clients. (Clients include individuals, groups, families, organizations, and communities.) The Council on Social Work Education (1992a, b), in its curriculum policy statements, identifies eight skills that are needed for social work practice:

1. Defining issues
2. Collecting and assessing data
3. Planning and contracting
4. Identifying alternative interventions
5. Selecting and implementing appropriate courses of action
6. Using appropriate research to monitor and evaluate outcomes
7. Applying appropriate research-based knowledge and technological advances
8. Termination

These eight skills, interestingly, provide an excellent framework for conceptualizing the phases of the change process in social work.

Phase 1: Defining Issues

Defining issues is the first step in the change process and often becomes fairly complex. Let's examine the case example on page 14, which involves four teenagers being expelled from high school for drinking beer at school during school hours. Jack Dawson, the school social worker, identifies a wide number of issues (questions/concerns/problems), including the following: Do the youths have a drinking problem? Were they disenchanted with the school system, and are they displaying their discontent by breaking school rules? What short-term and long-term adverse effects may the expulsions have on these students? Will the expulsions have an adverse labeling effect by labeling these youths as "troublemakers," and thereby be a factor that leads them to become further involved in delinquent behavior? How will the youths' parents react to the drinking and the expulsions? What effects will the expulsions have on other students at the school? (A possible positive effect is that the expulsions may be a deterrent to other students who are considering violating school rules; whereas a possible negative consequence is that the expulsions may encourage other students to violate school rules in order to also be expelled.) Since the expelled youths are now apt to spend their days on the street, will the expulsions create problems for merchants in the community? Is the school policy of expelling youths for drinking on school grounds a constructive or destructive educational policy? Does the school system have a responsibility to add an educational drug component to the curriculum? Are there aspects of the school system that encourage youths to rebel; if there are, should these aspects be changed?

The first step a social worker must take in a problematic situation is to identify the wide variety of issues raised. The issues serve as a guide for the next phase—data collection and assessment. (The Pincus-Minahan approach described in Chapter 3 provides a framework for using a systems approach to defining issues.)

During this initial phase, and during the other phases as well, the worker must establish and continue a working relationship with the client(s). To do so, the worker must reflect empathy, warmth, and genuineness. (See Chapter 5 for elaboration of the skills and processes to establish rapport.)

Phase 2: Collecting and Assessing Data

In this phase the social worker begins an in-depth collection and analysis of data to gain answers to the issues raised in phase 1. For some of the issues, useful information can be obtained directly from the clients (such as the youths in our example). For instance, the issue of whether the youths have a drinking problem can perhaps be answered by meeting individually with each one, forming a trusting relationship, and then inquiring how often the youth drinks, how much the youth consumes when drinking, and any problems the youth has encountered while drinking. For other issues raised in phase 1, useful information will need to be collected from other sources. For example, the question of the short- and long-term adverse effects that the expulsions are apt to have on the youths can perhaps be answered by researching the literature on this topic.

Assessment is the process of analyzing the data to make sense of it. The processes of collecting data and arriving at valid assessments are described in Chapter 3.

Phase 2 also involves an assessment of the degree of match, or fit, between the client's needs and the agency's eligibility requirements and resources. The service may be terminated for a lack of fit. The client may be referred elsewhere for service, perhaps because of the presumed superiority of some other agency's resources. Or, the fit may be deemed appropriate, and the social worker and the client then move on to the next phase.

Phase 3: Planning and Contracting

Planning includes formulating initial objectives (goals) and deciding which objectives to pursue. Will an objective be to explore with the youths whether they have a drinking problem? To have the youths reinstated in school? To change the expulsion policy to in-school suspension? To add educational material about alcohol and other drug abuse to the curriculum? Often a strategy, such as cost-benefit analysis (estimating resources being used and potential benefits), is used to decide which objective(s) to pursue. (Rarely, in real-life situations, are social workers able to pursue all worthy objectives—due to time and resource constraints.)

Contracting includes making arrangements with the client(s), or with the organizations providing funding for the client(s), about the services (often with a specification of the objectives) to be provided and the cost (with a specification of financial arrangements). (Planning and contracting are further described in Chapters 5, 6, 7, 8, 10, and 16.)

Phase 4: Identifying Alternative Interventions

As one of his objectives (in phase 3), Jack Dawson selects the preventive approach of adding educational material about alcohol and other drug abuse to the curriculum. Numerous questions related to this objective now arise for Mr. Dawson. What specific material should be covered in a drug education program? Which drugs should be included? (Mr. Dawson is aware that describing certain drugs, such as LSD, may cause parents to question whether educational material about seldom-used drugs actually encourages some youths to experiment with these drugs.) Where should the drug education component be added to the curriculum—in large assemblies with all students required to attend, in health classes, in social science classes? Will the school administration, teachers, school board, students, and parents support adding this component to the curriculum? What will be the most effective strategy to gain the support of these groups?

As a first step in this phase, Mr. Dawson meets with his immediate supervisor, Dr. Maria Garcia, Director of Pupil Services at the high school, to discuss these issues and to generate a list of alternative strategies for how to proceed. They discuss three strategies: (1) conduct an anonymous survey to obtain data on the extent of alcohol and other drug use and abuse among the high school students. Such survey results may document the need for a drug education program. (2) Appoint a committee composed of the professional staff in the Pupil Services Department to develop a drug education program. (3) Request that the school administration and school board appoint a committee—composed of representatives from the school board, school administration, teachers, students, parents, and Pupil Services—to explore the need and feasibility for a drug education program. (Identifying alternative interventions is described in further detail in Chapters 5, 7, 8, 10, and 19.)

Phase 5: Selecting and Implementing Appropriate Courses of Action

Mr. Dawson and Dr. Garcia decide the best way to obtain broad support for the drug education program is to pursue the third option listed in phase 4. Dr. Garcia meets with the high school principal, Mary Powell, who after some contemplation agrees that exploring the need for such a program is desirable. Ms. Powell asks the school board to support the formation of such a committee. The school board agrees. A committee is eventually formed, and it begins holding meetings. Mr. Dawson is appointed by Dr. Garcia to be Pupil Services' representative to the committee.

(Selecting and implementing appropriate courses of action is described in further detail in Chapters 5, 7, 8, 10, and 19.)

Phase 6: Using Appropriate Research to Monitor and Evaluate Outcomes

One of the first questions raised by some committee members during the initial deliberations concerns the specific drugs that would be discussed in a drug education program. As expected, some committee members are concerned that providing information about those drugs that are currently not being used by young people in the community may actually encourage their use. As a result, the committee asks the Pupil Services Department to survey high school students in order to identify the mind-altering drugs currently being used and the extent to which they are used.

A second, and related, issue is whether a drug education program has preventative value or whether it may actually promote illegal drug use. To obtain information on this issue, the Pupil Services Department staff research the literature on the preventative value of such programs nationally and on the most effective formats for drug educational programs.

After 14 months of planning and deliberation, the committee presents a proposal to the school board for a drug education program. The program is designed to become part of the curriculum in the school district's middle schools and high schools. One component of the proposal requires the Pupil Services Department to conduct an annual survey of a random sample of middle school and high school students to obtain information on the extent of drug use or abuse and feedback on the merits and shortcomings of the drug education program. Such a survey provides one way of monitoring and evaluating the outcomes of the program. (Research in social work practice is described in further detail in Chapters 5, 7, and 11.)

Phase 7: Applying Appropriate Research-Based Knowledge and Technological Advances

The drug education program that is added to the health class curriculum contains the latest research-based knowledge on the drugs commonly used by young people in the community. The information includes mind-altering effects, physical and psychological dependency characteristics, and withdrawal and long-term health effects. The curriculum also contains research-based information on the most effective treatment approaches, how to cope in a family where someone is abusing, how to confront a friend or relative who is abusing, dangers of drug use and driving, associations between drug use and sexually transmitted diseases (including AIDS), what to do if one has concerns about his or her own drug use, and how to say no to peer pressure to use drugs.

The technological advances for this drug education program are computers to research data bases of effective programs in other U.S. school systems, computers to process the annual drug use surveys conducted by the Pupil Services Department, and current films and videotapes containing drug education material for middle and high school students. (Additional information on research and the use of computers in social work is presented in Chapter 11.)

Phase 8: Termination

The committee that developed the drug education program has its final meeting after the school board approves the proposal. Most members experience mixed emotions at this meeting. They are delighted their task is successfully completed, but there is some sadness because the group that has become an important and meaningful part of their lives is now ending.

If a close working relationship has formed between the worker and the client, termination is often a painful process—especially for the client and sometimes also for the worker. In the change process, sensitive issues are often addressed, considerable effort is frequently made to make constructive changes, dependency may develop, and as a result the client is apt to experience a sense of loss when termination occurs. The client may also feel angry and rejected.

A final evaluation is usually a part of terminating. The final evaluation involves more than the assessment of what occurred during monitoring, because it places a value on the usefulness of the change process. The final evaluation is also extremely significant to the agency, because it provides information about whether, for this situation, the agency's services have been beneficial. Each agency needs composite evaluations of all their services to all clients in order to provide documentation to their funding sources of the extent to which their services are worthy of continued funding. (Termination and evaluation are described in Chapters 5, 6, 7, 8, 10, and 11.)

A Variety of Roles

In working with individuals, groups, families, organizations, and communities, a social worker is expected to be knowledgeable and skillful in filling a variety of roles. The particular role that is selected should (ideally) be determined by what will be most effective, given the circumstances. The following material identifies some, but certainly not all, of the roles assumed by social workers.

Enabler. In this role a worker *helps* individuals or groups articulate their needs, clarify and identify their problems, explore resolution strategies, select and apply a strategy, and develop their capacities to deal with their own problems more effectively. This role model is perhaps the most frequently used approach in counseling individuals, groups,

and families. The model is also used in community practice, primarily when the objective is to help people organize to help themselves.

This definition of the term *enabler* is very different from the definition used in the topic area of chemical dependency. There the term refers to a family member or friend who facilitates the substance abuser in continuing to use and abuse the drug of his or her choice.

Broker. A broker links individuals and groups who need help (and do not know where help is available) with community services. For example, a wife who is frequently physically abused by her husband might be referred to a shelter home for battered women. Nowadays even moderate-sized communities have 200 or 300 social service agencies/organizations providing community services. Even human services professionals are often only partially aware of the total service network in their community.

Advocate. The role of an advocate has been borrowed from the law profession. It is an active directive role in which the social worker is an advocate for a client or for a citizen's group. When a client or a citizen's group is in need of help and existing institutions are uninterested (and sometimes openly negative and hostile) in providing services, then the advocate's role may be appropriate. In such a role, the advocate provides leadership for collecting information, arguing the correctness of the client's need and request, and challenging the institution's decision not to provide services. The object is not to ridicule or censure a particular institution but to modify or change one or more of its service policies. In this role the advocate is a partisan who is exclusively serving the interests of a client or of a citizen's group.

Activist. An activist seeks basic institutional change; often the objective involves a shift in power and resources to a disadvantaged group. An activist is concerned about social injustice, inequity, and deprivation. Tactics involve conflict, confrontation, and negotiation. Social action is concerned with changing the social environment to better meet the recognized needs of individuals. The methods used are assertive and action-oriented (for example, organizing welfare recipients to work toward improvements in services and increases in money payments). Activities of social action include fact finding, analysis of community needs, research, dissemination and interpretation of information, organization of activities with people, and other efforts to mobilize public understanding and support on behalf of some existing or proposed social program. Social action activity can be geared toward a problem that is local, statewide, or national in scope.

Mediator. The mediator role involves intervention in disputes between parties to help them find compromises, reconcile differences, or reach mutually satisfactory agreements. Social workers have used their value orientations and unique skills in many forms of mediation between opposing parties (for example, divorcing spouses, neighbors in conflict, landlord-tenant disputes, labor-management disputes, and child custody disputes). A mediator remains neutral, not siding with either party in the dispute. Mediators make sure they understand the positions of both parties. They may help clarify positions, recognize miscommunication, and help the parties present their cases clearly.

Negotiator. A negotiator brings together those who are in conflict over one or more issues and seeks to bargain and compromise in order to arrive at mutually acceptable agreements. Somewhat like mediation, negotiation involves finding a middle ground that all sides can live with. However, unlike a mediator (which is a neutral role), a negotiator usually is allied with one of the sides involved.

Educator. The educator role involves giving information to clients and teaching them adaptive skills. To be an effective educator, the worker must first be knowledgeable. Additionally, the worker must be a good communicator so information is conveyed clearly and is readily understood by the receiver. Examples include teaching parenting skills to young parents, instructing teenagers in job-hunting strategies, and teaching anger-control techniques to individuals with difficulties in these areas.

Initiator. An initiator calls attention to a problem, or to a potential problem. A problem does not have to exist before attention can be called to it. For example, the approval of a proposal to renovate a low-income neighborhood by building middle-income housing units may dispossess the current low-income residents, because they may not be able to afford the cost of the middle-income units. Since calling attention to problems usually does not resolve them, the initiator role must often be followed by other kinds of work.

Coordinator. Coordination involves bringing components together in an organized manner. For example, in the case of a multiproblem family, several agencies must often work together to meet the complicated financial, emotional, legal, health, social, educational, recreational, and interactional needs of the family members. Frequently, one social worker needs to assume the role of case manager to coordinate the services from the different agencies to avoid duplication of services and conflicting objectives.

Researcher. At times, every worker is a researcher. Research in social work practice includes researching the literature on topics of interest, evaluating the outcomes of one's practice, assessing the merits and shortcomings of programs, and studying community needs.

Group facilitator. A group facilitator is a leader for some group experience. The group may be a therapy group, an educational group, a self-help group, a sensitivity group, a family therapy group, or a group with some other focus.

Public speaker. Social workers occasionally talk to a variety of groups (for example, high school classes, public service organizations such as Kiwanis, police officers, staff at other agencies) to inform them of available services or to advocate developing new services for clients whose needs are not being met. In recent years a variety of new services have been identified as being needed (for example, runaway centers, services for battered spouses, rape crisis centers, services for persons with AIDS, and group homes for youth). Social workers who have public speaking skills are not only better able to interpret services to groups of potential clients, but probably also earn a few thousand dollars more each year.

A Systems Perspective

Social workers are trained to have a systems perspective in their work with individuals, groups, families, organizations, and communities. A systems perspective emphasizes looking beyond the presenting problems of the client to assess the complexities and interrelationships of problems. A systems perspective is based on systems theory. The key concepts of general systems theory are wholeness, relationship, and homeostasis.

The concept of *wholeness* means that the objects or elements within a system produce an entity that is greater than the additive sums of the separate parts. Systems theory is anti-reductionistic; it asserts that no system can be adequately understood or totally explained once it has been broken down into its component parts. (For example, the central nervous system is able to carry out thought processes that would not occur if only the parts were observed.)

The concept of *relationship* asserts that the patterning and structuring among the elements in a system are as important as the elements themselves. For example, Masters and Johnson (1970) found that sexual dysfunctions primarily occur due to the nature of the relationship between husband and wife, rather than to the psychological makeup of the partners in a marriage system.

Systems theory opposes simple cause-and-effect explanations. For instance, whether a child will be abused in a family is determined by a variety of variables and the patterning of these variables: the parents' capacity to control their anger, relationships between the child and the parents, relationships between the parents, degree of psychological stress, characteristics of the child, and opportunities for socially acceptable ways for parents to ventilate anger.

The concept of *homeostasis* suggests that most living systems seek a balance to maintain and preserve the system. Jackson (1965), for example, noted that families tend to establish a behavior balance or stability and to resist any change from that predetermined level of stability. Emergence of the state of imbalance (generated either within or outside the marriage) ultimately restores the homeostatic balance of the family. If one child is abused in a family, that abuse often serves a function in the family as indicated by the fact that if that child is removed, a second child is often selected to be abused. Or, if one family member improves through counseling, that improvement will generally upset the balance within the family; and other family members will have to make changes (such changes may be adaptive or maladaptive) to adjust to the new behavior of the improved family member.

Ecological theory is a subcategory of systems theory. Ecological theory has become prominent in social work practice, as discussed in the next section.

The Medical Model Versus the Ecological Model of Human Behavior

The Medical Model

From the 1920s to the 1960s, most social workers used a medical model approach to assessing and changing human behavior. This approach, initiated primarily by Sigmund Freud, views clients as *patients*. The task of the service provider is first to diagnose the causes of a patient's problems and then to provide treatment. The patient's problems are viewed as being inside the patient.

The medical model conceptualizes emotional and behavioral problems as *mental illnesses*. People with emotional or behavioral problems are then given medical labels, such as schizophrenia, paranoia, psychosis, and insanity. Adherents of the medical approach believe the disturbed person's mind is affected by some generally unknown, internal condition. That unknown, internal condition is thought to result from a variety of possible causative factors: genetic endowment, metabolic disorders, infectious diseases, internal conflicts, unconscious uses of defense mechanisms, and traumatic early experiences that cause emotional fixations and prevent future psychological growth.

The medical model has a lengthy classification of mental disorders that are defined by the American Psychiatric Association. The major categories of mental disorders are listed in Exhibit 1.1. The *DSM-III-R* (American Psychiatric Association, 1987) defines numerous mental disorders. Psychosis and a variety of specific mental disorders are defined in the following section.

Psychosis. A major mental disorder of organic or emotional origin in which a person's ability to think, respond emotionally, remember, communicate, interpret reality, and behave appropriately is sufficiently impaired to interfere grossly with the capacity to meet the ordinary demands of life.

Schizophrenia. A large group of disorders, usually of psychotic proportion, manifested by characteristic disturbances of language and communication, thought, perception, affect, and behavior that last longer than six months.

Paranoia. A rare condition characterized by the gradual development of an intricate, complex, and elaborate system of thinking based on (and often proceeding logically from) misinterpretation of an actual event. A person with paranoia often considers himself or herself endowed with unique and superior ability or has systematized delusions of persecution.

Hypochondriasis. A chronic maladaptive style of relating to the environment through preoccupation with shifting somatic concerns and symptoms, a fear or conviction that one has a serious physical illness, seeking of medical treatment, inability to accept reassurance, and either hostile or dependent relationships with caregivers and family.

Bipolar disorder. A major affective disorder in which there are episodes of both mania and depression; formerly called manic-depressive psychosis. Bipolar disorder may be subdivided into manic, depressed, or mixed types on the basis of currently presenting symptoms.

Phobia. An obsessive, persistent, unrealistic, intense fear of an object or situation. A few common phobias are the following:

Acrophobia: Fear of heights
Algophobia: Fear of pain
Claustrophobia: Fear of closed spaces
Erythrophobia: Fear of blushing

Personality disorders. Deeply ingrained, inflexible, maladaptive patterns of relating, perceiving, and thinking of sufficient severity to cause either impairment in functioning or

Exhibit 1.1

Major mental disorders according to the American Psychiatric Association

Disorders usually first evident in infancy, childhood, or adolescence
These include, but are not limited to, mental retardation, attention deficit disorders (including hyperactivity), eating disorders (including anorexia), pervasive developmental disorders (such as infantile autism), and others.

Organic mental disorders
These can be induced by substances (alcohol, drugs) or can be organic brain syndromes (delirium, dementia, and so on).

Substance use disorders
This category includes abuse of alcohol, barbiturates, amphetamines, and so on.

Schizophrenic disorders
This category includes all forms of schizophrenia.

Delusional (paranoid) disorders
This category includes all forms of paranoia and persistent irrational delusions. Often there is a fear of persecution.

Mood disorders
These include emotional disorders such as depression or exaggerated mood swings, including manic behavior.

Anxiety disorders
These include phobias, panic, extreme anxiety, and stress from traumatic experiences (for example, battle shock).

Somatoform disorders
These are psychological problems that manifest themselves as symptoms of physical disease (for example, hypochondria).

Dissociative disorders
This category includes problems in which part of the personality is dissociated from the rest (for example, multiple personalities and amnesia).

Sexual disorders
These include sexually related problems such as transsexualism, exhibitionism, and inhibited sexual desire.

Sleep disorders
These include insomnia and other problems with sleep.

Disorders of impulse control
These disorders include the inability to control certain undesirable impulses (for example, kleptomania, pyromania, and pathological gambling).

Adjustment disorders
These involve difficulty in adjusting to stress created by such common events as unemployment or divorce.

Personality disorders
These are inflexible and maladaptive patterns of sufficient severity to cause either significant impairment in adaptive functioning or subjective distress.

SOURCE: American Psychiatric Association, *DSM-III-R (The Diagnostic and Statistical Manual of Mental Disorders, Third Edition, Revised)* (Washington, DC: American Psychiatric Association, 1987).

distress. Some personality disorders and their characteristics follow:

Antisocial: A lack of socialization along with behavior patterns that bring a person repeatedly into conflict with society; incapacity for significant loyalty to others or to social values; callousness; irresponsibility; impulsiveness; and inability to feel guilt or learn from experience or punishment.

Borderline: Instability in a variety of areas, including interpersonal relationships, behavior, mood, and self-image.

Compulsive: Restricted ability to express warm and tender emotions; preoccupation with rules, order, organization, efficiency, and detail; excessive devotion to work and productivity to the exclusion of pleasure; indecisiveness.

Narcissistic: Grandiose sense of self-importance or uniqueness; preoccupation with fantasies of limitless success; need for constant attention and admiration; disturbances in interpersonal relationships such as lack of empathy, exploitativeness, and relationships that vacillate between the extremes of over-idealization and devaluation.

Passive-aggressive: Aggressive behavior manifested in passive ways such as obstructionism, pouting, procrastination, intentional inefficiency, and obstinacy.

Schizoid: Manifested by shyness, oversensitivity, social withdrawal, frequent daydreaming, avoidance of close or competitive relationships, and eccentricity. Persons with this disorder often react to disturbing experiences with apparent detachment and are unable to express hostility and ordinary aggressive feelings.

The medical model approach arose in reaction to the historical notion that the emotionally disturbed were possessed by demons, were mad, and were to be blamed for their disturbances. These people were "treated" by being beaten, locked up, or killed. The medical model led to viewing the disturbed as in need of help, stimulated research into the nature of emotional problems, and promoted the development of therapeutic approaches.

The major evidence for the validity of this approach comes from studies suggesting that some mental disorders, such as schizophrenia, may be influenced by genetics (heredity). The bulk of the evidence for the importance of heredity comes from studies of twins. For instance, in a sample of over 15,000 twins, Hofer and Polin (1970) found a concordance rate (if one has it, both have it) for schizophrenia of 15.5 percent for identical twins and 4.4 percent for fraternal twins. Critics of such studies argue that the findings may be flawed, claiming that the physical similarity of identical twins leads their family and friends to treat them alike. However, some research (Kety, 1976) suggests a higher concordance rate for schizophrenia among identical twins even when they have been raised apart.

The Ecological Model

In the 1960s social work began questioning the usefulness of the medical model. Environmental factors were shown to be at least as important as internal factors in causing a client's problems. Research was also demonstrating that psychoanalysis was probably ineffective in treating clients' problems (Stuart, 1970).

In the 1960s social work shifted at least some of its emphasis to a *reform approach*, which seeks to change systems to benefit clients. The enactment of the antipoverty programs (such as Head Start) is an example of an effort to change systems to benefit clients.

In the past several years, social work has increasingly focused on an *ecological approach*.

This approach integrates both treatment and reform by conceptualizing and emphasizing the dysfunctional transactions between people and their physical and social environments. Human beings are viewed as developing and adapting through transactions with all elements of their environments. An ecological model gives attention to both internal and external factors. It does not view people as passive reactors to their environments, but rather as being involved in dynamic and reciprocal interactions with them.

This model tries to improve the coping patterns of people and their environments so that a better match can be attained between an individual's needs and the characteristics of his or her environment. One emphasis of the model is on the person-in-environment. The person-in-environment conceptualization is depicted in Figure 1.2.

As is evident in the figure, people interact with many systems. With this conceptualization, social work can focus on three separate areas. First, it can focus on the person and seek to develop his or her problem-solving, coping, and developmental capacities. Second, it can focus on the relationship between a person and the systems he or she interacts with and link the person with needed resources, services, and opportunities. Third, it can focus on the systems and seek to reform them to meet the needs of the individual more effectively.

The ecological model views individuals, families, and small groups as having transitional problems and needs as they move from one life stage to another. Individuals face many transitional changes as they grow older, like learning to walk, entering first grade, adjusting to puberty, graduating from school, finding a job, getting married, having children, having children leave home, and retiring.

Families also have a life cycle. The following are only a few of the events that require adjustment: engagement, marriage, birth of children, parenting, children going to school, children leaving home, and loss of a parent (perhaps through death or divorce).

Small groups have transitional phases of development as well. Members of small groups spend time getting acquainted, gradually learn to trust one another, begin to self-disclose more, learn to work together on tasks, develop approaches to handle interpersonal conflict, and face adjustments to the group eventually terminating or some members leaving.

The model's central concern is to articulate the transitional problems and needs of individuals, families, and small groups. Once these problems and needs are identified, intervention approaches are then selected and applied to help individuals, families, and small groups resolve the transitional problems and meet their needs.

An ecological model can also focus on the maladaptive interpersonal problems and needs in families and groups. It can seek to articulate the maladaptive communication processes and dysfunctional relationship patterns of families and small groups. These difficulties cover an array of areas, including interpersonal conflicts, power struggles, double binds, distortions in communicating, scapegoating, and discrimination. The consequences of such difficulties are usually maladaptive for some members. An ecological model seeks to identify such interpersonal obstacles and then apply appropriate intervention strategies. For example, parents may set the price for honesty too high for their children. In such families children gradually learn to hide certain behaviors and thoughts, and even learn to lie. If the parents discover such dishonesty, an uproar usually occurs. An appropriate intervention is to open up communication patterns and help the parents understand that if they really want honesty from their children, they need to learn to be more accepting of their children's thoughts and actions.

Two centuries ago people interacted primarily within the family system. Families

People in our society continually interact with many systems, some of which are listed in this figure.

Figure 1.2
Person-in-environment conceptualization

were nearly self-sufficient. In those days, the *person-in-family* was a way of conceptualizing the main system that individuals interacted with. Our society has become much more complex. Today, a person's life and quality of life are interwoven with and interdependent on many systems, as shown in Figure 1.2.

Goals of Social Work Practice

The National Association of Social Workers (1982) has conceptualized social work practice as having four major goals.

Goal 1: Enhance People's Problem-Solving, Coping, and Developmental Capacities

Using the person-in-environment concept, the focus of social work practice at this level is on the "person." With this focus a social worker serves primarily as an *enabler*. In this role the worker may take on the activities of a counselor, teacher, care giver (i.e., providing

supportive services to those who cannot fully solve their problems and meet their own needs), and behavior changer (i.e., changing specific parts of a client's behavior).

Goal 2: Link People with Systems That Provide Them with Resources, Services, and Opportunities

Using the person-in-environment concept, the focus of social work practice at this level is on the relationships between persons and the systems they interact with. With this focus a social worker serves primarily as a *broker*.

Goal 3: Promote the Effective and Humane Operation of Systems That Provide People with Resources and Services

Using the person-in-environment concept, the focus of social work practice at this level is on the systems people interact with. One role a worker may fill at this level is an *advocate*. Additional roles include:

Program developer: The worker seeks to promote or design programs or technologies to meet social needs.

Supervisor: The worker seeks to increase the effectiveness and efficiency of the delivery of services through supervising other staff.

Coordinator: The worker seeks to improve a delivery system through increasing communications and coordination between human service resources.

Consultant: The worker seeks to provide guidance to agencies and organizations by suggesting ways to increase the effectiveness and efficiency of services.

Goal 4: Develop and Improve Social Policy

Similar to goal 3, the focus of social work practice at this level is on the systems people interact with. The distinction between goal 3 and goal 4 is that the focus of goal 3 is on the available resources for serving people, while goal 4 focuses on the statutes and broader social policies that underlie such resources. The major roles at this level are *planner* and *policy developer.* In these roles workers develop and seek adoption of new statutes or policies and propose elimination of ineffective or inappropriate ones. In these planning and policy development processes, social workers may take on an advocate role and, in some instances, an activist role.

The Council on Social Work Education (1992) has recently formulated a closely related, but somewhat different, conceptualization of the purpose (which incorporates the goals) of social work practice. Formulated by the CSWE is the national accreditating body for social work education in the United States. It has defined the purpose of social work as follows:

The profession of social work is committed to the enhancement of human well-being and to the alleviation of poverty and oppression. The social work profession re-

ceives its sanction from public and private auspices and is the primary profession in the provision of social services. Within its general scope of concern, professional social work is practiced in a wide variety of settings and has four related purposes:

1. The promotion, restoration, maintenance, and enhancement of the functioning of individuals, families, groups, organizations, and communities by helping them to accomplish tasks, prevent and alleviate distress, and use resources.
2. The planning, formulation, and implementation of social policies, services, resources, and programs needed to meet basic human needs and support the development of human capacities.
3. The pursuit of policies, services, resources, and programs through organizational or administrative advocacy and social or political action, so as to empower groups at risk and promote social and economic justice.
4. The development and testing of professional knowledge and skills related to these purposes.[3]

This definition of the purpose of social work differs from NASW's definition of the goals of social work practice in the following important ways: (1) it emphasizes that social work has a commitment to "the enhancement of human well-being and to the alleviation of poverty and oppression"; (2) it identifies the client systems of social work practice as "individuals, families, groups, organizations, and communities"; and (3) it adds, in effect, two goals to NASW's listing of goals of social work practice—"to empower groups at risk and promote social and economic justice," and "development and testing of professional knowledge and skills." Readers of these two

[3]This material was first published by the Council of Social Work Education (1992a) in the *Curriculum Policy Statements for Baccalaureate Degree and Master's Degree Programs* and is reprinted here with the permission of the Council on Social Work Education.

definitions should not view them as being inconsistent, but as each identifying important goals or purposes that all social workers need to follow.

A Problem-Solving Approach

In working with individuals, families, groups, organizations, and communities, social workers use a problem-solving approach. Steps in the problem-solving process can be stated in a variety of ways. A simple statement of this process follows:

1. Identify as precisely as possible the problem or problems.
2. Generate possible alternative solutions.
3. Evaluate the alternative solutions.
4. Select a solution or solutions to be used, and set goals.
5. Implement the solution(s).
6. Follow up to evaluate how the solution(s) worked.

Another conceptualization of the problem-solving approach is the change process of social work practice, which was described earlier in this chapter.

Micro, Mezzo, and Macro Practice

Social workers practice at three levels: (1) *micro*—working on a one-to-one basis with an individual, (2) *mezzo*—working with families and other small groups, and (3) *macro*—working with organizations, communities or seeking changes in statutes and social policies.

The specific activities performed by workers include, but are not limited to, the following.

Social Casework

Aimed at helping individuals on a one-to-one basis to meet personal and social problems, casework may be geared to helping the client adjust to his or her environment, or to changing certain social and economic pressures that are adversely affecting an individual. Social casework services are provided by nearly every social welfare agency that provides direct services to people. *Social casework* encompasses a wide variety of activities, such as counseling runaway youths; helping unemployed people secure training or employment; counseling someone who is suicidal; placing a homeless child in an adoptive or foster home; providing protective services to abused children and their families; finding nursing homes for stroke victims who no longer need to be hospitalized, counseling individuals with sexual dysfunctions; helping alcoholics acknowledge they have a drinking problem; counseling those with a terminal illness; being a probation and parole officer; providing services to single parents; and working in medical and mental hospitals as a member of a rehabilitation team.

Case Management

Recently a number of social service agencies have labeled their social workers *case managers*. The tasks performed by case managers are similar to those of caseworkers. The job descriptions of case managers vary from service area to service area. For example, case managers in a juvenile probation setting supervise clients, provide some counseling, monitor clients to make certain they are following the rules of probation, link clients and their families with needed services, prepare court reports, and testify in court. On the other hand, case managers at a sheltered workshop are apt to provide job training, counseling, arrange transportation, discipline clients for unacceptable behavior, act as an advocate, and act as liaison with the people who supervise clients during their non-work hours (which may be at a group home, foster home, residential treatment facility, or their parent's home). Hepworth and Larsen (1986) described the role of a case manager as follows:

Case managers link clients to needed resources that exist in complex service delivery networks and orchestrate the delivery of services in a timely fashion. Case managers function as brokers, facilitators, linkers, mediators, and advocates. A case manager must have extensive knowledge of community resources, rights of clients, and policies and procedures of various agencies and must be skillful in mediation and advocacy. [p. 563]

Barker (1991) defined case management as follows:

A procedure to plan, seek, and monitor services from a variety of agencies and staff on behalf of a client. Usually one agency takes primary responsibility for the client and assigns a case manager, who coordinates services, advocates for the client, and sometimes controls resources and purchases services for the client. The procedure makes it possible for many social workers in the agency, or different agencies, to coordinate their efforts to serve a given client through professional teamwork, thus expanding the range of needed services offered. Case management may involve monitoring the progress of a client whose needs require the services of many different professionals, agencies, health care facilities, and human services programs. [p. 29]

Group Work

The intellectual, emotional, and social development of individuals may be furthered through group activities. In contrast to casework or group therapy, *group work* is not primarily therapeutic, except in a broad sense. Different groups have different objectives, such as socialization, information exchange, curbing delinquency, recreation, changing socially unacceptable values, and helping achieve better relations between cultural and racial groups. For example, through group activities a group worker at a neighborhood center may seek to curb delinquency patterns and change socially unacceptable values; or a worker at an adoption agency may meet with a group of applicants to explain adoption procedures and help applicants prepare for becoming adoptive parents. Activities and focuses of groups vary: arts and crafts, dancing, games, dramatics, music, photography, sports, nature study, woodwork, first aid, home management, information exchange, and discussion of such topics as politics, sex, marriage, religion, and selection of a career.

Group Therapy

Group therapy is aimed at facilitating the social, behavioral, and emotional adjustment of individuals through the group process. Participants in group therapy usually have emotional, interactional, or behavioral difficulties. Group therapy has several advantages over one-to-one counseling, such as the operation of the *helper therapy* principle, which maintains it is therapeutic for the helper (who can be any member of a group) to feel he or she has been helpful to others. In contrast to one-to-one counseling, group pressure is often more effective in changing individuals' maladaptive behavior, and group therapy is a time saver as it enables the therapist to treat several people simultaneously. For example, group therapy might be used for individuals who are severely depressed, have drinking problems, are rape victims, are psychologically addicted to drugs, have a relative who is terminally ill, are single and pregnant, are recently divorced, or have an eating disorder.

Family Therapy

A type of group therapy aimed at helping families with interactional, behavioral, and emotional problems, *family therapy* can be used with parent-child interaction problems, marital conflicts, and conflicts with grandparents. A wide variety of problems are dealt with in family therapy or family counseling, such as communication problems and disagreements between parents and youths on choice of friends, drinking and other drug use, domestic tasks, curfew hours, sexual values and behavior, study habits and grades received, and choice of dates.

Community Organization

The aim of *community organization* is stimulating and assisting the local community to evaluate, plan, and coordinate efforts to provide for the community's health, welfare, and recreation needs. Perhaps it is not possible to define precisely the activities of a community organizer, but they are apt to include encouraging and fostering citizen participation, coordinating efforts between agencies or groups, public relations and public education, research, planning, and being a resource person. A community organizer acts as a catalyst in stimulating and encouraging community action. Such specialists are apt to be employed in community welfare councils, social planning agencies, health planning councils, and community action agencies. The term *community organization* is now being replaced in some settings by *planning, social planning, program development, policy development,* and *macro practice.*

Barker (1991) defined community organization as:

An intervention process used by social workers and other professionals to help individuals, groups, and collectives of people with common interests or from the same geographic areas to deal with social problems and to enhance social well-being through planned collective action. Methods include identifying problem areas, analyzing causes, formulating plans, developing strategies, mobilizing necessary resources, identifying and recruiting com-

munity leaders, and encouraging interrelationships between them to facilitate their efforts. [p. 43]

Administration

Administration involves directing the overall program of a social service agency. Administrative functions include setting agency and program objectives, analyzing social conditions in the community, making decisions about what services will be provided, employing and supervising staff members, setting up an organizational structure, administering financial affairs, and securing funds for the agency's operations. Administration also involves setting organizational goals, coordinating activities to achieve the selected goals, monitoring and making necessary changes in processes and structure to improve the effectiveness and efficiency of processes that contribute to transforming social policy into social services. In social work, the term *administration* is often used synonymously with management. In a small agency, administrative functions may be carried out by one person, whereas several people may be involved in administrative affairs in a larger agency.

Other areas of professional activity in social work include research, consulting, supervising, planning, program development, policy development, and teaching (primarily at the college level). Social casework, case management, group work, group therapy, family therapy, and community organization constitute the primary professional activities that beginning-level social workers are apt to provide. All of these activities require social workers to have counseling skills. (Counseling involves helping individuals or groups resolve social and personal problems through the process of developing a relationship, exploring the problem(s) in depth, and exploring alternative solutions—this process is described in Chapter 5.) Caseworkers, case managers, group workers, group therapists, and family therapists obviously need a high level of counseling skills to work with individuals and groups. Community organizers need to be perceptive, and they need skills in relating to other people and in assessing problems and developing resolution strategies—skills that parallel or are analogous to counseling skills. Therefore, a major emphasis of this text will be on counseling.

Counseling skills, however, are not the only skills social workers need. For example, caseworkers also need to be able to do social histories and to link clients with other human services. Some agencies require skills in public speaking, preparing and presenting reports to courts and to other agencies, and teaching parents better parenting techniques. Research capacities to evaluate one's own practice and other programs are also important. The essential skills needed for social work practice are further described in the next section. As will be seen, generalist social workers are expected to have an extensive knowledge base and numerous skills and to adhere to a well-defined set of professional social work values.

The Knowledge, Skills, and Values Needed for Social Work Practice

Knowledge

The NASW has identified the knowledge needed for effective social work practice as follows:

Knowledge of casework and group work theory and techniques.

Knowledge of community resources and services.

Knowledge of basic federal and state social service programs and their purposes.

Knowledge of community organization theory and the development of health and welfare services.

Knowledge of basic socioeconomic and political theory.

Knowledge of racial, ethnic, and other cultural groups in society—their values and lifestyles and the resultant issues in contemporary life.

Knowledge of sources of professional and scientific research appropriate to practice.

Knowledge of the concepts and techniques of social planning.

Knowledge of the theories and concepts of supervision and the professional supervision of social worker practice.

Knowledge of theories and concepts of personnel management.

Knowledge of common social and psychological statistical and other research methods and techniques.

Knowledge of the theories and concepts of social welfare administration.

Knowledge of social and environmental factors affecting clients to be served.

Knowledge of the theories and methods of psychosocial assessment and intervention and of differential diagnosis.

Knowledge of the theory and behavior of organizational and social systems and of methods for encouraging change.

Knowledge of community organization theory and techniques.

Knowledge of the theories of human growth and development and of family and social interaction.

Knowledge of small-group theory and behavioral dynamics.

Knowledge of the theories of group interaction and therapeutic intervention.

Knowledge of crisis intervention theories and techniques.

Knowledge of advocacy theory and techniques.

Knowledge of the ethical standards and practices of professional social work.

Knowledge of teaching and instructional theories and techniques.

Knowledge of social welfare trends and policies.

Knowledge of local, state, and federal laws and regulations affecting social and health services.[4]

(In regard to the knowledge base of social work, this text summarizes a number of intervention approaches at the micro, mezzo, and macro levels of practice.)

The Council on Social Work Education (1992) has categorized the knowledge needed by social workers into ten broad content areas. Every accredited social work education program is expected to provide the following content, which is excerpted from the 1992 curriculum policy statements:

Liberal Arts Perspective

A liberal arts perspective enriches understanding of the person-environment context of professional social work practice and is integrally related to the mastery of social work content. The baccalaureate professional program in social work is built upon a liberal arts perspective.

A liberal arts perspective provides an understanding of one's cultural heritage in the context of other cultures; the methods and limitations of various systems of inquiry; and the knowledge, attitudes, ways of thinking, and means of communication that are characteristic of a broadly educated person. Students must be capable of thinking critically about society, about people and their problems, and about such expressions of culture as art, literature, science, history, and philosophy. Students must have direct knowledge about social, psychological, and biological determinants of human behavior and of diverse cultures, social conditions, and social problems.

Social Work Values and Ethics

Programs of social work education must provide specific knowledge about social work values and their ethical implications and must provide opportunities for students to demonstrate their application in professional practice. Students must be assisted to develop an awareness of their personal values and to clarify conflicting values and ethical dilemmas.

Diversity

Professional social work education is committed to preparing students to understand and appreciate human diversity. Programs must provide curriculum content about differences and similarities in the experiences, needs, and beliefs of people. The curriculum must include content about differential assessment and intervention skills that will enable practitioners to serve diverse populations.

Each program is required to include content about population groups that are particularly relevant to the program's mission. These include, but are not limited to, groups distinguished by race, ethnicity, culture, class, gender, sexual orientation, religion, physical or mental ability, age, and national origin.

Promotion of Social and Economic Justice

Programs of social work education must provide an understanding of the dynamics and consequences of social and economic injustice, including all forms of human oppression and discrimination. They must provide students with the skills to promote social change and to implement a wide range of interventions that further the achievement of individual and collective social and economic justice. Theoretical and practice content must be provided

---

[4] Published in 1982, National Association of Social Workers, Inc. Reprinted with permission, from *Standards for the Classification of Social Work Practice*, Policy Statement 4, p. 17. Copyright National Association of Social Workers, Inc.

about strategies of intervention for achieving social and economic justice and for combatting the causes and effects of institutionalized forms of oppression.

Populations-at-Risk

Programs of social work education must present theoretical and practice content about patterns, dynamics, and consequences of discrimination, economic deprivation, and oppression. The curriculum must provide content about people of color, women, and gay and lesbian persons. Such content must emphasize the impact of discrimination, economic deprivation, and oppression upon these groups.

Each program must include content about populations-at-risk that are particularly relevant to its mission. In addition to those mandated above, such groups include, but are not limited to, those distinguished by age, ethnicity, culture, class, religion, and physical or mental ability.

Human Behavior and the Social Environment

Programs of social work education must provide content about theories and knowledge of human bio-psycho-social development, including theories and knowledge about the range of social systems in which individuals live (families, groups, organizations, institutions, and communities). The human behavior and the social environment curriculum must provide an understanding of the interactions between and among human biological, social, psychological, and cultural systems as they affect and are affected by human behavior. The impact of social and economic forces on individuals and social systems must be presented. Content must be provided about the ways in which systems promote or deter people in the maintenance or attainment of optimal health and well-being. Content about values and ethical issues related to bio-psycho-social theories must be included. Students must be taught to evaluate theory and apply theory to client situations.

Social Welfare Policy and Services

Social welfare policy and services content must include the history, mission, and philosophy of the social work profession. Content must be presented about the history and current patterns of provision of social welfare services, the role of social policy in helping or deterring people in the maintenance or attainment of optimal health and well-being, and the effect of policy on social work practice. Students must be taught to analyze current social policy within the context of historical and contemporary factors that shape policy. Content must be presented about the political and organizational processes used to influence policy, the process of policy formulation, and the frameworks for analyzing social policies in light of the principles of social and economic justice.

Social Work Practice

At the baccalaureate level, professional social work education prepares students for generalist practice with systems of all sizes. Practice content emphasizes professional relationships that are characterized by mutuality, collaboration, and respect for the client system. Content on practice assessment focuses on the examination of client strengths and problems in the interactions among individuals and between people and their environments.

Social work practice content must include knowledge, values, and skills to enhance the well-being of people and to help ameliorate the environmental conditions that affect people adversely. Practice content must include the following skills: defining issues; collecting and assessing data; planning and contracting; identifying alternative interventions; selecting and implementing appropriate courses of action; using appropriate research to monitor and evaluate outcomes; applying appropriate research-based knowledge and technological advances; and termination. Practice content also includes approaches and skills for practice with clients from differing social, cultural, racial, religious, spiritual, and class backgrounds and with systems of all sizes.

Research

The research curriculum must provide an understanding and appreciation of a scientific, analytic approach to building knowledge for practice and for evaluating service delivery in all areas of practice. Ethical standards of scientific inquiry must be included in the research content.

The research content must include quantitative and qualitative research methodologies; analysis of data, including statistical procedures; systematic evaluation of practice; analysis and evaluation of theoretical bases, research questions, methodologies, statistical procedures, and conclusions of research reports; and relevant technological advances.

Each program must identify how the research curriculum contributes to the student's use of scientific knowledge for practice.

Field Practicum

The field practicum is an integral component of the curriculum in social work education. It engages the student in supervised social work practice and provides opportunities to apply classroom learning in the field setting.

The baccalaureate practicum must provide the student with opportunities for:

a. The development of an awareness of self in the process of intervention.
b. Supervised practice experience in the application of knowledge, values and ethics, and practice skills to enhance

the well-being of people and to work toward the amelioration of environmental conditions that affect people adversely.
c. Use of oral and written professional communications which are consistent with the language of the practicum setting and of the profession.
d. Use of professional supervision to enhance learning.
e. Critical assessment, implementation, and evaluation of agency policy within ethical guidelines.[5]

The curriculum at the master's level in social work must also be based on a liberal arts perspective. The statement of this perspective is very similar to the statement given previously for the liberal arts perspective at the baccalaureate level. The CSWE's *Curriculum Policy Statement* mandates that the master's level curriculum be composed of professional foundation content and concentration content in an area.

The professional foundation component includes content on social work values and ethics, diversity, promotion of social and economic justice, populations-at-risk, human behavior and the social environment, social welfare policy and services, social work practice, research, and field practicum. The description of these areas in the master's level *Curriculum Policy Statement* is nearly identical to the description in the baccalaureate level *Curriculum Policy Statement*, and therefore will not be repeated here.

The concentration content component includes knowledge, values, and skills for advanced practice in an identifiable area. Areas frequently offered by master's programs include fields of practice, problem areas, populations-at-risk, and intervention methods or roles.

[5] This material was first published by the Council on Social Work Education and is reprinted here with the permission of the Council on Social Work Education.

This text provides material primarily in the social work practice content area. It also includes material on social work values and ethics, diversity, promotion of social and economic justice, and populations-at-risk.

Core Practice Skills

There have been a number of efforts to articulate the essential skills for entry-level social work practice positions. A few of these conceptualizations will be presented to indicate contemporary thinking about core practice skills. Numerous similarities exist among these conceptualizations, but as yet there is *not* full agreement on these core skills.

Federico (1973, pp. 146–147) indirectly described social work skills by outlining roles and activities:

1. *Outreach worker*—reaching out into the community to identify need and follow up referrals to service contexts.
2. *Broker*—knowing services available and making sure those in need reach the appropriate services.
3. *Advocate*—helping specific clients obtain services when they might otherwise be rejected, and helping to expand services to cover more needy persons.
4. *Evaluator*—evaluating needs and resources, generating alternatives for meeting needs, and making decisions between alternatives.
5. *Teacher*—teaching facts and skills.
6. *Mobilizer*—helping to develop new services.
7. *Behavior changer*—changing specific parts of a client's behavior.
8. *Consultant*—working with other professionals to help them be more effective in providing services.
9. *Community planner*—helping community groups plan effectively for the community's social welfare needs.

10. *Care giver*—providing supportive services to those who cannot fully solve their problems and meet their own needs.
11. *Data manager*—collecting and analyzing data for decision-making purposes.
12. *Administrator*—performing the activities necessary to plan and implement a program of services.

Baer (1979, p. 106) identified the following ten competencies as being essential for successfully performing the responsibilities of entry-level positions:

1. Identify and assess situations in which the relationship between people and social institutions needs to be initiated, enhanced, restored, protected, or terminated.
2. Develop and implement a plan for improving the well-being of people, based on problem assessment and the exploration of obtainable goals and available options.
3. Enhance the problem-solving, coping, and developmental capacities of people.
4. Link people with systems that provide them with resources, services, and opportunities.
5. Intervene effectively on behalf of populations most vulnerable and discriminated against.
6. Promote the effective and humane operation of the systems that provide people with services, resources, and opportunities.
7. Actively participate with others in creating new, modified, or improved service, resource, or opportunity systems that are more equitable, just, and responsive to consumers of services; work with others to eliminate unjust systems.
8. Evaluate the extent to which the ob-

jectives of the intervention plan were achieved.

9. Continually evaluate one's professional growth and development through assessment of practice behaviors and skills.

10. Contribute to the improvement of service delivery by adding to the knowledge base of the profession as appropriate and supporting and upholding the standards and ethics of the profession.

These ten competencies were originally developed by Baer and Federico (1978).

The National Association of Social Workers has identified the following skills as being essential for social work practice:

Skill in listing to others with understanding and purpose.

Skill in eliciting information and in assembling relevant facts to prepare a social history, assessment, and report.

Skill in creating and maintaining professional helping relationships and in using oneself in relationships.

Skill in observing and interpreting verbal and nonverbal behavior and in using a knowledge of personality theory and diagnostic methods.

Skill in engaging clients in efforts to resolve their own problems and in gaining trust.

Skill in discussing sensitive emotional subjects in a nonthreatening supportive manner.

Skill in creating innovative solutions to clients' needs.

Skill in determining the need to end therapeutic relationships and how to do so.

Skill in interpreting the findings of research studies and professional literature.

Skill in mediating and negotiating between conflicting parties.

Skill in providing interorganizational liaison services.

Skill in interpreting or communicating social needs to funding sources, the public, or legislators.[6]

NASW has identified the following abilities, which are closely related to conceptualizing essential skills, as being needed for social work practice:

Ability to speak and write clearly.

Ability to teach others.

Ability to respond supportively in emotion-laden or crisis situations.

Ability to serve as a role model in a professional relationship.

Ability to interpret complex psychosocial phenomena.

Ability to organize a workload to meet designated responsibilities.

Ability to identify and obtain resources needed to assist others.

Ability to assess one's performance and feelings, and to use help or consultation.

Ability to participate in and lead group activities.

Ability to function under stress.

Ability to deal with conflict situations or contentious personalities.

Ability to relate social and psychological theory to practice situations.

Ability to identify the information necessary to solve a problem.

Ability to conduct research studies of agency services or one's practice.[7]

[6] Published 1982, National Association of Social Workers, Inc. Reprinted with permission, from *Standards for the Classification of Social Work Practice*, Policy Statement 4, pp. 17–18. Copyright National Association of Social Workers, Inc.

[7] Published 1982, National Association of Social Workers, Inc. Reprinted with permission, from *Standards for the Classification of Social Work Practice*, Policy Statement 4, p. 18. Copyright National Association of Social Workers, Inc.

In the *Curriculum Policy Statements* for both the baccalaureate and master's degree programs, the Council on Social Work Education (1992) mandated that social work programs must provide content on the following skills: (1) defining issues, (2) collecting and assessing data, (3) planning and contracting, (4) identifying alternative interventions, (5) selecting and implementing appropriate courses of action, (6) using appropriate research to monitor and evaluate outcomes, (7) applying appropriate research-based knowledge and technological advances, and (8) termination. (These skills were discussed earlier in this chapter.)

The acquisition of social work skills depends partly on innate ability and partly on learning experiences. Social work educational programs facilitate the learning of such skills by presenting theoretical material to students (such as material on how to interview), by monitoring and critiquing students who are practicing applying these skills (for example, videotaping students in simulated counseling situations), and by extensively supervising students in practicum courses.

Values

Should the primary objective of imprisonment be rehabilitation or punishment? Should a father committing incest be prosecuted with the likelihood of such publicity in the community leading to family breakup, or should an effort first be made, through counseling, to stop the incest and keep the family intact? Should a wife who is occasionally abused by her husband be encouraged to remain with him? Should an abortion be suggested as one alternative for resolving the problems of someone who is single and pregnant? Should youths who are claimed to be uncontrollable by their parents be placed in correctional schools? If a client threatens serious harm to some third person, what should the social worker do? If a client indi-

cates he or she is HIV positive and continues to persist in behavior that places a partner in danger of contracting the disease and refuses to warn the partner of the peril, what should the social worker do? All of these questions involve making decisions that are largely based on values. Much of social work practice depends on making decisions based on values.

The National Association of Social Workers has identified the following broad-based values as necessary for social work practice:

Commitment to the primary importance of the individual in society.
Respect for the confidentiality of relationships with clients.
Commitment to social change to meet socially recognized needs.
Willingness to keep personal feelings and needs separate from professional relationships.
Willingness to transmit knowledge and skills to others.
Respect and appreciation for individual and group differences.
Commitment to developing clients' ability to help themselves.
Willingness to persist in efforts on behalf of clients despite frustration.
Commitment to social justice and the economic, physical, and mental well-being of all in society.
Commitment to a high standard of personal and professional conduct.[8]

The Council on Social Work Education's (1992) *Curriculum Policy Statements* for both the baccalaureate and master's degree programs assert that

[8] Published 1982, National Association of Social Workers, Inc. Reprinted with permission, from *Standards for the Classification of Social Work Practice*, Policy Statement 4, p. 18. Copyright National Association of Social Workers, Inc.

Among the values and principles that must be infused throughout every social work curriculum are the following:

1. Social workers' professional relationships are built on regard for individual worth and dignity and are furthered by mutual participation, acceptance, confidentiality, honesty, and responsible handling of conflict.
2. Social workers respect people's rights to make independent decisions and to participate actively in the helping process.
3. Social workers are committed to assisting client systems to obtain needed resources.
4. Social workers strive to make social institutions more humane and responsive to human needs.
5. Social workers demonstrate respect for and acceptance of the unique characteristics of diverse populations.
6. Social workers are responsible for their own ethical conduct, the quality of their practice, and seeking continuous growth in the knowledge and skills of their profession.[9]

Because values play a key role in social work practice, it is essential that social work education programs (1) help students clarify their values and (2) foster the development of values that are consistent with professional social work practice. Social work values will be further discussed in Chapter 2.

Outcomes of Social Work Education

The Council on Social Work Education has specified outcomes for both baccalaureate and master's degree programs. (These outcomes highlight much of the knowledge, values, and skills needed for social work practice.) Baccalaureate graduates are expected to be prepared for beginning-level social work practice, while master's graduates are expected to be prepared for advanced-level social work practice.

In addition, the Council on Social Work Education's (1992a) *Curriculum Policy Statement* specifies that graduates of a baccalaureate social work program will be able to do the following:

1. Apply critical thinking skills within the context of professional social work practice.
2. Practice within the values and ethics of the social work profession and with an understanding of and respect for the positive value of diversity.
3. Demonstrate the professional use of self.
4. Understand the forms and mechanisms of oppression and discrimination and the strategies of change that advance social and economic justice.
5. Understand the history of the social work profession and its current structures and issues.
6. Apply the knowledge and skills of generalist social work to practice with systems of all sizes.
7. Apply knowledge of bio-psycho-social variables that affect individual development and behavior, and use theoretical frameworks to understand the interactions among individuals and between individuals and social systems (i.e., families, groups, organizations, and communities).
8. Analyze the impact of social policies on client systems, workers, and agencies.
9. Evaluate research studies and apply findings to practice, and, under supervision, evaluate their own practice

---

[9] This material was first published by the Council on Social Work Education, and is reprinted here with the permission of the Council on Social Work Education.

interventions and those of other relevant systems.

10. Use communication skills differentially with a variety of client populations, colleagues, and members of the community.

11. Use supervision appropriate to generalist practice.

12. Function within the structure of organizations and service delivery systems, and under supervision, seek necessary organizational change.[10]

The Council on Social Work Education's (1992b) *Curriculum Policy Statement* specifies the following competencies for graduates of a master's level program:

Graduates of a master's social work program are advanced practitioners who can analyze, intervene, and evaluate in ways that are highly differentiated, discriminating, and self-critical. They must synthesize and apply a broad range of knowledge as well as practice with a high degree of autonomy and skill. They must be able to refine and advance the quality of their practice as well as that of the larger social work profession. These advanced competencies must be appropriately integrated and reflected in all aspects of their social work practice, including their ability to:

1. Apply critical thinking skills within professional contexts, including synthesizing and applying appropriate theories and knowledge to practice interventions.

2. Practice within the values and ethics of the social work profession and with an understanding of and respect for the positive value of diversity.

3. Demonstrate the professional use of self.

4. Understand the forms and mechanisms of oppression and discrimination and the strategies and skills of change that advance social and economic justice.

5. Understand the history of the social work profession and its current structures and issues.

6. Apply the knowledge and skills of a generalist social work perspective to practice with client systems of all sizes.

7. Apply the knowledge and skills of advanced social work practice in an area of concentration.

8. Critically analyze and apply knowledge of bio-psycho-social variables that affect individual development and behavior, and use theoretical frameworks to understand the interactions among and between individuals and social systems (i.e., families, groups, organizations, and communities).

9. Analyze the impact of social policies on client systems, workers, and agencies and demonstrate skills for influencing policy formulation and change.

10. Evaluate relevant research studies and apply findings to practice, and demonstrate skills in quantitative and qualitative research design, data analysis, and knowledge dissemination.

11. Conduct empirical evaluations of their own practice interventions and those of other relevant systems.

12. Use complex communication skills differentially with a variety of client populations, colleagues, and members of the community.

13. Use supervision and consultation appropriate to advanced practice in an area of concentration.

[10] This material was first published by the Council on Social Work Education (1992a), and is reprinted here with the permission of the Council on Social Work Education.

14. Function within the structure of organizations and service delivery systems and seek necessary organizational change.[11]

These outcomes (or competencies) can be viewed as yet another way of stating the knowledge, values, and skills needed for beginning-level, and advanced-level, social work practice.

The Key Objectives of This Text

In regard to the knowledge, skills, and values needed for social work practice, this text uses an *integrative* approach that presents the prominent approaches to social work practice. In summary form, the key objectives of this text are to present material designed to accomplish the following:

- Provide content on social work practice, social work values and ethics, diversity, promotion of social and economic justice, and populations-at-risk that is consistent with the baccalaureate and master's level *Curriculum Policy Statements.*
- Help prepare students for generalist social work practice by informing them of the contemporary assessment and intervention strategies.
- Facilitate the development of students' interviewing and counseling skills and capacities so they can intervene effectively with individuals, families, and groups.
- Facilitate the development of students' macro practice skills and capacities in intervening with organizations and communities.
- Help students develop a philosophical value orientation that is consistent with social work practice.

[11] This material was first published by the Council on Social Work Education (1992b), and is reprinted here with the permission of the Council on Social Work Education.

- Facilitate the development of students' capacities to function effectively in a variety of social work roles, including enabler, broker, advocate, activist, mediator, negotiator, educator, initiator, coordinator, researcher, and group facilitator.
- Develop in students an awareness, understanding, and appreciation of how to intervene effectively with people of diverse racial, ethnic, cultural, social, and class backgrounds.
- Develop students' capacities to evaluate and modify human service programs and systems in order to make human services more equitable, humane, and responsive to consumers.
- Develop philosophical conceptual skills so graduates will be able to critically evaluate and further develop their own practice capacities throughout life.
- Help students develop a positive sense of self and an awareness and appreciation of the importance of continuing to evaluate their professional skills and professional growth.

Which Intervention Strategies Should Social Workers Learn?

Literally hundreds of intervention approaches have been developed at the micro, mezzo, and macro levels of practice. A partial list of available techniques that can be used at the micro and mezzo levels of practice appears in Exhibit 1.2.

It is impossible for any social worker to have an effective working knowledge of all these intervention approaches. What social workers should do, however, is continue throughout their careers to learn additional approaches and to learn to apply more effectively those approaches they already use. Social work agencies encourage this continual learning by offering in-service training and workshops, sending workers to conferences,

Exhibit 1.2

Partial list of intervention therapies at the micro and mezzo levels

Treatment Approach

Task-centered therapy	Gestalt therapy
Psychoanalysis	Assertiveness training
Client-centered therapy	Token economies
Transactional analysis	Contingency contracting
Feminist intervention	
Rational-emotive therapy	Systematic desensitization
Reality therapy	In vivo desensitization
Crisis intervention	Implosive therapy
Behavior modification	Covert sensitization
Provocative therapy	Aversive techniques
Radical therapy	Thought-stopping
Adlerian therapy	Sex therapy
Analytical therapy	Milieu therapy
Existential therapy	Play therapy
Encounter therapies	Parent effectiveness training
Ego psychology approaches	
Cognitive approaches	Muscle relaxation
General systems approaches	Deep breathing relaxation
Role theory approaches	Imagery relaxation
Time management	Meditation
Biofeedback	Hypnosis
Marathon groups	Self-hypnosis
Alcoholics Anonymous	Encounter groups
Weight Watchers	Sensitivity groups
Psychodrama	Parents Anonymous
	Neuro-linguistic programming

and encouraging workers to take additional college courses in the helping professions.

Workers should continue to learn a wide variety of intervention approaches so they can select from their "bag of tricks" the intervention approach that is apt to be most effective (given each client's unique set of problems and circumstances). Selection of an intervention approach is also based on a worker's personality. Workers soon become aware that their own personalities partially determine which intervention approaches

they are more comfortable with and effective in applying.

Because there are so many intervention techniques (as suggested in Exhibit 1.1), readers are apt to be bewildered about which intervention approaches to learn. It is therefore crucial that the faculty of social work education programs give direction to students by (1) making carefully thought-out decisions, as a group, regarding the intervention theories that are most useful for students in their geographic area to learn; (2) giving an overview of many of these theories so that students are familiar with a wide number of theories; and (3) conveying material on each theory's merits and shortcomings. Future chapters in this text summarize most of the intervention approaches listed in Exhibit 1.1. *The instructor of this course, along with the other social work faculty members, should decide which intervention approaches to cover in this class.*

After the student graduates and obtains employment, the work setting will also be a factor in focusing his or her attention on which intervention approaches to use. If a worker is working with shy or aggressive people, assertiveness training may be recommended. Alcoholics Anonymous may be recommended for people with drinking problems, rational therapy for people who are depressed, systematic desensitization for people who have phobias, and so on.

An effective social worker generally has a working knowledge of a variety of intervention approaches. In working with clients, the worker should focus on selecting the most effective intervention approaches to help clients solve their problem(s) rather than trying to redefine the problems in terms of the worker's favorite intervention approach.

Summary

Social work is the professional activity of helping individuals, families, groups, organizations, and communities enhance or restore their capacity for social functioning and create societal conditions favorable to their goals. The term *social worker* is generally applied to graduates of either bachelor's- or master's-level social work programs who are employed in the field of social welfare. A social worker is a change agent who is skilled at working with individuals, groups, families, organizations, and communities. Almost all social workers are employed in the field of social welfare.

The profession of social work is distinct from other helping professions because it has the responsibility and mandate to provide social services and it uses the person-in-environment concept. Social work has a number of goals, including: (1) to enhance the problem-solving, coping, and developmental capacities of people; (2) to link people with systems that provide them with resources, services, and opportunities; (3) to promote the effectiveness and humane operation of systems that provide people with resources and services; (4) to develop and improve social policy; (5) to empower groups at risk and promote social and economic justice; and (6) to develop and test professional knowledge and skills in social work.

A social worker needs training and expertise in a wide range of areas to effectively handle problems faced by individuals, groups, families, organizations, and the larger community. While most professions are becoming increasingly more specialized, social work continues to emphasize a generalist (broad-based) approach.

Social work uses a problem-solving approach. Social workers practice at three levels: micro, mezzo, and macro. Specific activities include social casework, case management, group work, group therapy, family counseling and family therapy, community organization, planning, program development, policy development, research, consulting, supervision, and administration. The knowledge, skills, and values needed for social work practice were summarized.

Literally hundreds of intervention approaches have been developed for social work practice. It is impossible for any social worker to have an effective working knowledge of all these theories. Educational programs have an obligation to provide social work students with an overview of the commonly used theories and to convey information on the merits and shortcomings of these approaches. Social workers have an obligation to continue throughout their careers to learn a variety of intervention approaches. In working with clients, a worker should focus on selecting the most effective intervention approaches to help clients solve their problems rather than trying to redefine the clients' problems in order to use the worker's favorite intervention approach.

Exercise
Breaking the ice

Goal: Starting a new class can be both exciting and anxiety producing for students and for the instructor. This exercise is designed to facilitate getting acquainted and to reduce anxiety.

Step 1: Explain the purpose of the exercise. Ask students to brainstorm about what they would like to know about other members of the class. Examples might include marital status, hometown, work or volunteer experience in social work, and most unforgettable experience. These characteristics should be written on the blackboard.

Step 2: Have each student answer the items listed on the blackboard.

Step 3: Ask the students what they would like to know about the instructor. The instructor should attempt to answer these questions.

Step 4: (This is an additional, optional step.) Divide the class into subgroups of two. Ask each member to share an experience that has had a profound effect on his or her life. Listeners should be encouraged to ask questions to seek clarification. After each person has had a chance to speak, reform the class and have the students report on what they learned about their partners.

2

Social Work Values

Value Dilemmas

Let's assume that you are a social worker and are assigned the following case. What would you do to help this family?

Mrs. Kehl is two months pregnant. She works part-time in a shoe factory and is paid at the minimum wage. Her husband is a janitor in a business office and earns only slightly more. They already have seven children and are living in substandard poverty conditions. They do not wish to have additional children and the pregnancy has resulted partially from a failure of the birth control method they were using. The family is Catholic and attends church regularly. On one hand, they want to have an abortion; they feel their family is already being hurt because of a lack of money. On the other hand, they believe having an abortion may be immoral because it may mean taking the life of an unborn child.

This case raises a number of questions about values. As a social worker, how would you help this family weigh their moral views against abortion with their values about wanting to limit their family size in order to improve living conditions?

This case is not unique. Most situations that clients face involve, at least partially, value dilemmas. A few more examples follow:

Mr. Ritter is 82 years old and has terminal cancer. He has lived a full life but now is in severe pain. He is rather depressed and is seriously considering taking his own life. Should he be allowed to?

Mr. and Mrs. Sinclair have a 2-year-old profoundly retarded child who needs extensive medical care. They have three older children. The family's emotional and physical resources are being severely drained, and family relationships are becoming increasingly tense. Yet the family feels the child will develop at a faster pace in their home than in an institution. What should they do?

Mr. and Mrs. Fedders have been married for six years and have two children. Their love for each other has been practically nonexistent for the past three years. Mr. Fedders recently discovered his wife has been having an affair. They both hold religious beliefs against divorce, but they are seriously considering terminating their marriage. How should a social worker help them?

Mr. Franzene is on probation for two years for theft. For the past 18 months he has stayed out of trouble. He inadvertently reveals to his probation officer that he took two pens from a discount store. Should his probation officer make a report on this?

LaVonne Hall recently left a mental hospital and was helped by her aftercare worker to obtain a filing job. While intoxicated and angry, Ms. Hall calls her worker and says that she has been fired. She then says that she is going to shoot her former employer and hangs up. What should the worker do?

Mr. Townsend's neighbors occasionally hear cries of anguish from Mr. Townsend's two children. The neighbors make a report to the public welfare department because they suspect abuse. A protective service worker investigates, and Mr. Townsend and the children report the cries are the result of spankings. How does the worker decide when harsh spanking should be considered abuse?

Mr. and Mrs. Stonek's only child was taken away two years ago and placed in a foster home because of neglect. The father drank excessively, and the mother was very depressed. Over the past two years, the Stoneks occasionally have made efforts to improve their lives but have always "slid back." For the past two months, Mr. Stonek has been involved in Alcoholics Anonymous and only occasionally has gotten drunk. Mrs. Stonek presently seems less depressed and feels having her son back would help make her life more meaningful. The Stoneks ask to have their child returned. Should the child be returned? How would you as worker arrive at a decision?

Mrs. Barta seeks counseling at a comprehensive mental health center. She states her husband is having intercourse with their 11-year-old daughter. The counselor arranges a joint meeting with the Bartas. Mr. Barta first denies the accusation, but then admits it after being confronted with what his wife has seen and heard. How should the worker attempt to help this family?

Mrs. Johnson is a caseworker at a public welfare agency in a rural county. She observes and collects evidence that the director makes a range of decisions that deny migrant workers in the area (most of whom are Mexican Americans) public assistance benefits for which they are eligible. Mrs. Johnson believes if she confronts the director with this evidence, she will be fired, or at least denied merit increases and promotions at work. What should she do?

Mrs. Gordon seeks counseling from a sex therapist. She indicates she is fairly content with her marriage and has an enjoyable sex life with her husband. Yet she feels substantial guilt about her desire and following through on her desire to masturbate. How can the therapist help her?

A community worker in an inner city is working with residents to organize a rent strike against a landlord who neglects making essential repairs. The building does not have adequate heat and has rats and roaches. The organizer wonders whether she should fully inform the residents of the risks involved in a rent strike (such as being evicted). She fears that if she fully informs the tenants of the risks, they probably will decide not to strike, which will mean essential improvements in living conditions will not be made. What should she do?

These examples highlight the fact that much of social work practice involves value dilemmas. Social work is both an art and a science. Because social work is partly an art, a worker frequently must make decisions based on values rather than on knowledge. It also means the change techniques workers use are often based on theory and value assumptions, rather than on proven intervention techniques.

One value assumption that is frequently useful in helping clients resolve value dilemmas is the principle of self-determination. This principle asserts that clients have the right to hold and express their own opinions and to act on them, as long as in so doing they do not infringe on the rights of others. When clients face a value dilemma, a worker can often proceed effectively by helping the clients first define their problems precisely and then examine fully the merits and shortcomings of each of the various alternatives to resolving the problem. After this is done, clients are then given the responsibility to decide which course of action they desire to pursue. This problem-solving format might be useful for many of the case situations listed above. For example, the Kehls who are considering having an abortion might make a list of all their reasons for and against having an abortion, and then make a decision. This same approach might also be useful in helping the Sinclairs make a decision about whether to place their profoundly retarded child in an institution and in helping the Fedders to decide whether to terminate their marriage.

Although this self-determination principle may be useful in some cases, *there are no absolutes in social work practice.* Guidelines are simply guidelines. What works in one situation may not resolve problems in others. Suppose, for example, that Mr. Ritter makes a list of the reasons for and against taking his life and decides that there is no rational reason for him to endure further pain. Such a decision may raise a value dilemma for the social worker regarding whether he should attempt to stop

Mr. Ritter from taking his life. Or, suppose the Bartas decide they do not want further counseling on the incestuous relationship between Mr. Barta and his daughter because they both conclude that delving into it further will break up their marriage and their family. What should the worker do then?

Much of social work practice depends on the worker's professional judgment. Directors of social welfare agencies frequently tell me that their best workers are those who have common sense and are able to "trust their guts" (that is, trust their feelings, intuition, and perceptions). This chapter will spell out value assumptions and principles of social work practice. *These guidelines (and all other guidelines presented in this text) are not to be applied as absolutes, but simply as concepts that may be useful in working with people.* An effective worker has an understanding of these guidelines and is then able to make a professional judgment of whether a guideline is, or is not, useful when working with particular people.

Knowledge and Values

It is important for workers to be able to distinguish between values and knowledge and to be aware of the role each plays in social work practice.

Pincus and Minahan (1973) concisely defined the difference between values and knowledge as follows:

> Values are beliefs, preferences, or assumptions about what is desirable or good for man [humans]. An example is the belief that society has an obligation to help each individual realize his fullest potential. They are not assertions about how the world is and what we know about it, but how it *should* be. As such, value statements cannot be subjected to scientific investigation; they must be accepted on faith. Thus we can speak of a value as being right or wrong only in relation to the particular belief system or ethical code being used as a standard.

What we will refer to as knowledge statements, on the other hand, are observations about the world and man [humans] which have been verified or are capable of verification. An example is that black people have a shorter life expectancy than white people in the United States. When we speak of a knowledge statement as being right or wrong, we are referring to the extent to which the assertion has been confirmed through objective empirical investigation. [p. 38]

The distinction between values and knowledge can be illustrated in some of the cases described earlier. First, let us take the abortion question. Suppose a person questions the abortion procedure because she feels it may be immoral. The person believes it means killing an unborn baby. Implicit in this value statement is the belief that life begins at or shortly after conception. Deciding whether life does in fact begin at conception is a belief that is not verifiable.

On the other hand, if a person has qualms about an abortion because she fears the risks of the medical procedure or fears there is a high probability of feeling remorseful after the abortion, then informational questions are raised. Knowledge, or empirical evidence, can in these situations be presented showing that the health risks of having an abortion are less than those of carrying the child to full term, and evidence can be presented showing that only a small percentage of women who have an abortion have severe remorse (Hyde, 1990).

Mrs. Gordon's guilt over masturbating may also be used as an illustration. If she feels guilty because she believes masturbating is immoral and sinful, she then obviously has a value system that asserts it is wrong to masturbate. For her to resolve this value dilemma would either involve having her change her belief system, or stop masturbating. On the other hand, if she feels guilty because she fears she is hurting herself physiologically or hindering her sex life with her husband, she could be shown that both of these beliefs are erroneous by pointing out that most married men and women masturbate, masturbation is highly recommended by sex therapists, and masturbation usually fosters rather than hinders a sexual relationship (Masters & Johnson, 1966).

As these case illustrations suggest, it is much easier to change a client's belief that conflicts with current knowledge. Changing a belief that is based on a value is much more difficult, because the "rightness" or "wrongness" of the belief cannot be determined with empirical evidence.

Value Dilemmas of Clients Versus Workers

Also, it is important (as will be discussed later in this text) for social workers to distinguish just who has the value dilemma. An important guideline in social work practice is not to become overly emotionally involved in a client's case. (If you find yourself frequently taking clients' problems home with you so that your dwelling on their problems interferes with your life, then you are overly involved.) If a client faces a value dilemma about whether to obtain a divorce, or have an abortion, or place a member of the family in an institution, it is important for you to be aware that it is the *client's* dilemma, and not yours. By being aware that it is not your dilemma, you will best be able to remain objective and thereby be most helpful to a client.

On the other hand, if you feel strongly that a client is doing something immoral (for example, if you believe abortions are unethical), then *you* face a value dilemma. In such situations it will be very difficult for you to remain objective.

When you face a value dilemma about what a client is doing, or planning to do, the following guidelines are sometimes helpful.

1. The first step in coping with such a value question is to recognize its existence. Such self-awareness is often difficult to ob-

tain. Ethical questions are often ambiguous and make us feel uncomfortable. Therefore, we like to avoid them.

2. Self-awareness is not enough unless it is put to use with clients. Kelman (1965) recommended that a worker should "label" his or her values for the client and allow the client to "talk back" in a sort of mutual influence situation. Such an approach *may* be useful in working with clients who are involved with drugs, or having extramarital affairs, or have been arrested for stealing, and so forth. However, there is a danger to this approach. The worker's values may not be in the client's best interest. By the worker sharing his or her values, he or she is influencing (and perhaps also manipulating) the client. For example, if a worker is morally opposed to abortions, sharing his or her values with a young unmarried and pregnant woman probably will influence her not to have an abortion, which may (or may not) be in this woman's best interest. In making a decision of when a worker should share his or her values, that worker has to make a professional judgment as to what will be most constructive and helpful for the client.

3. Clients should be encouraged to explore their own values and to relate alternative actions to their own value systems. Clients need protection against manipulation that would encroach on their freedom of choice. For example, if a worker is morally opposed to abortions, clients might well be encouraged to see (and referral arrangements be made to see) someone who views abortions as a viable alternative.

4. A useful moral code advanced by Glasser (1965) allows clients to fulfill their needs and to do what they want to do, as long as by so doing they do not deprive others of the ability to fulfill their needs. I have found this code very useful in counseling people considering abortions, and in a wide variety of other situations—counseling gays and lesbians, people involved in premarital relationships, and so forth. The code is also useful in working with adults

involved in child abuse, incest, and extra-marital affairs because those involved need to examine the effects of their actions on others. There is no one right moral code—what works for one person may not work for another, due to differences in lifestyles, life goals, and personal values.

Values underlying social work practice will be summarized in the following material.

Respect for the Dignity and Uniqueness of the Individual

Every human being is unique in a variety of ways—value system, personality, life goals, financial resources, emotional and physical strengths, personal concerns, past experiences, peer pressures, emotional reactions, self-identity, family relationships, and deviant behavioral patterns. In working with a client, a social worker needs to perceive and respect the uniqueness of the client's situation. *Individualization* is the ethical value in social work and other helping professions of viewing, and relating to, the client as a person or group rather than as one whose characteristics are simply typical of a class.

Individualization is relatively easy for a social worker to achieve when the worker is assisting clients who have values, goals, behavioral patterns, and personal characteristics similar to the worker's. Individualization is harder to achieve when a worker is assigned clients who have values or behavioral patterns that the worker views as disgusting. For example, a worker holding traditional middle-class values may have difficulty in viewing a client with respect when that client has raped a young girl, or is involved in an incestuous relationship, or has killed a member of his family, or has severely abused a child. A general guideline in such situations is that the worker should seek to accept and respect the client but not accept the deviant behavior that needs to be changed. If a worker is unable to convey acceptance of the client, a helping relationship will not be established. If such a relationship is not established, then the worker will have practically no opportunity to help the client change deviant behaviors. A second guideline is that if a worker views a client as being disgusting and is unable to establish a working relationship, then the worker should transfer the case to another worker. There should be no disgrace or embarrassment in having to transfer a case for such reasons; it is irrational for a worker to expect to like every client, or for every client to like the worker (Ellis & Harper, 1977b).

Social workers occasionally encounter "raw" situations. For a while I worked in a mental hospital for the criminally insane and had a variety of clients who had committed a wide range of asocial and bizarre acts including incest, rape, decapitation of a girlfriend, sodomy, sexual exhibitionism, and removing corpses from graves. I've worked in a variety of other settings and encountered other raw situations. Achieving an attitude of respect for people who commit bizarre actions is difficult at times to achieve, but rehabilitation will not occur unless it is achieved.

Social psychologists have firmly established the theoretical principle that people's images of themselves develop largely out of their interactions and communications with others. A long time ago Charles Cooley (1902) called this process the *looking glass self-concept*. The looking glass says that people develop their self-concept in terms of how other people relate to them, as if others were a looking glass or mirror. For example, if a person receives respect from others and is praised for positive qualities, he or she is apt to feel good about himself or herself, will gradually develop a positive sense of worth, will be happier, and will seek responsible and socially acceptable ways to maintain the respect of others.

On the other hand, if a person commits a deviant act and *then* is shunned by others, viewed as different, and treated with disrespect, that person will develop a *failure identity*. According to Glasser (1972), people with failure identities either withdraw from society, become emotionally disturbed, or express their discontent in delinquent and deviant actions.

For example, if a neighborhood identifies a youth as being a troublemaker (a delinquent), the neighbors are apt to relate to the youth as if she were not to be trusted, may erroneously accuse her of delinquent acts, and will label her semidelinquent and aggressive behavior as being delinquent. In the absence of objective ways to gauge whether she is, in fact, a delinquent, she will rely on the subjective evaluations of others. Thus, gradually, as she is related to as being a delinquent, she is apt to perceive herself in that way and will begin to enact the delinquent role.

Compton and Galaway (1975) expanded on the importance of social workers' attending carefully to their communications with clients:

Social workers and other professionals intervening in the lives of people are well advised to be constantly sensitive to the messages they are extending to others about their worth. Do we, in the little things we do, communicate to the other person that he is a unique individual to be highly prized? What, for example, is the message communicated when we safeguard time and provide a client with a specific time to be seen as opposed to a catch-me-on-a-catch-as-catch-can basis for visits? Do appointments in advance communicate to the client a higher sense of respect than unannounced visits or hurriedly arranged telephone appointments? And, speaking of telephoning, how about the all too frequently overlooked return call? What message does the client get from the worker in terms of the client's worth when the worker does not have the courtesy or good sense to return telephone calls promptly? How about the ability to listen to clients, to secure from them their own account of their situation, and to avoid prejudg-

ments? And does not privacy, both in terms of how the social worker conducts the interviews and how he treats the material gained from interviews, communicate something to clients about the esteem in which they are held? A worker attempting to operationalize the premise of individual uniqueness and dignity may find it useful to repeatedly inquire of himself, "What does this action on my part communicate to the client about my perception of his personhood?" [pp. 106–107]

The principle of individualization also plays a key role in social work treatment. Various problems, needs, goals, and values of clients involve different patterns of relationships with clients and different methods of helping. For example, consider the needs of a teenaged male who is placed in a group home for being beyond parental control. At times he may need an understanding but firm counselor who sets and enforces strict limits. At times he may need encouragement and guidance in how to perform better at school. If conflicts develop between the youth and other boys at the group home, the counselor may need to play a mediating role. If the youth is shy, counseling on how to be more assertive may be needed. If his parents are fairly ineffective in their parenting role, the counselor may seek to have the parents enroll in a Parent Effectiveness Training program (Gordon, 1970). If the youth is being treated unfairly at school or by the juvenile court, the counselor may play an advocate role and attempt to change the system. If the youth has behavior problems, the reasons need to be explored and an intervention program developed.

A thorny problem facing social workers involves striking an effective balance between classification and individualization. There is a need in all human service areas to generalize beyond individuals and to organize data on the basis of common characteristics. Classification is essential to make sense out of a mass of data and is an essential part of developing theories. The danger of classifying people into a particular category is that such a classification may lead social workers to respond to people as objects rather than as individuals. Compton and Galaway (1975) commented about the labeling process:

> The pitfalls of this process are being documented in a growing body of literature from sociologists studying deviance from a labeling perspective. Not only does labeling or classification lead to a distortion of individual differences, but, as labeling theorists and their supporting research are noting, a person labeled deviant, those doing the labeling, and the surrounding audience frequently respond to the deviant on the basis of the label rather than on the basis of individual characteristics. This creates conditions for the development of a self-fulfilling prophecy in which the person becomes what he has been labeled. [p. 107]

In the same vein, Hans Toch (1970) noted:

> Playing the classification game in the abstract, as is done in universities, is a joyful, exhilarating experience, harmless and inconsequential. Classifying people in life is a grim business which channelizes destinies and determines fate. A man becomes a category, he is processed as a category, plays his assigned role, lives up to the implications. Labeled irrational, he acts crazy; catalogued dangerous, he becomes dangerous or he stays behind bars. [p. 55]

This labeling process, most simply stated, occurs due to Cooley's *looking glass self* in which people define who and what they are in terms of how others relate to them. A person labeled as mentally ill, or a delinquent, or an ex-con, or a welfare mother is then apt to define himself or herself in terms of these labels and unfortunately begin playing these roles.

Social workers have to continue to be alert to the dangers of labeling and should interact with each client (or judge, attorney, professor, and so forth) as being a person rather than a label.

The Client's Right to Self-Determination

As indicated earlier, social workers believe that clients have the right to express their own opinions and to act upon them, as long as by so doing clients do not infringe on the rights of others. This principle is in sharp contrast to the layperson's views that a social worker seeks to "remold" clients into a pattern chosen by the worker. Instead, the workers' efforts are geared to enhancing the clients' capability to help themselves. Client self-determination derives logically from belief in the inherent dignity of each person. If people have dignity, then it follows that they should be permitted to determine their own lifestyles as far as possible.

Social workers believe that making all decisions and doing everything for a client is self-defeating, because it leads to increased dependency rather than greater self-reliance and self-sufficiency. In order for people to grow, to mature, to become responsible, they need to make their own decisions and take responsibility for the consequences. Mistakes and emotional pain will at times occur. But that is part of life. We learn by our mistakes and by trial and error. Respect for the clients' ability to make their own decisions is associated with the principle that social work is a cooperative endeavor between clients and workers (client participation). Social work is done *with* not *to* a client. Plans imposed on people without their active involvement have a way of not turning out well.

Four points should be made in operationalizing the principle of *client self-determination*. First, self-determination implies that clients should be made aware that there are alternatives for resolving the personal or social problems they face. Self-determination involves having clients make decisions—that is, making a choice selected from several courses of action. If there is only one course of action, there is no choice and therefore clients would not have the right of self-determination. As will be expanded on in later chapters, the role of a social worker in helping clients involves (1) building a helping relationship, (2) exploring problems in depth with clients, and (3) exploring alternative solutions, with clients then choosing a course of action. This third step is the implementation of the principle of self-determination.

Second, self-determination means that the client, not the worker, is the chief problem solver. Workers need to recognize that the client *owns* the problem and therefore has the chief responsibility to resolve the problem. This is an area in which social work differs markedly from other professions. Most professionals, such as physicians and attorneys, advise clients in terms of what they believe clients ought to do. Doctors, lawyers, and dentists are experts in advising clients. The client's decision making after receiving the expert's advice in such situations is generally limited to the choice of whether to accept the professional's advice.

In sharp contrast, social workers should not seek to establish an expert-inferior relationship, but a relationship between equals. The worker's expertise does *not* lie in knowing or recommending what is best for the client. Rather, the expertise lies in assisting clients to define their problems, develop and examine the alternatives for resolving the problems, maximize their capacities and opportunities to make decisions for themselves, and implement the decisions they make. In conjunction with this principle, Matthew Dumont (1968) noted:

> The most destructive thing in psychotherapy is a "rescue fantasy" in the therapist—a feeling that the therapist is the divinely sent agent to pull a tormented soul from the pit of suffering and adversity and put him back on the road to happiness and glory. A major reason this fantasy is so destructive is that it carries the conviction that the patient will be saved only through and by the therapist. When such a conviction is communicated to the patient, verbally or otherwise, he has no choice other than to rebel and leave or become more helpless, dependent, and sick. [p. 60]

Third, self-determination does not prohibit or restrict social workers from offering an opinion or making a suggestion. In fact, social workers have an obligation to share their viewpoints with their clients. Compton and Galaway (1975) noted:

> Workers have the obligations of sharing with clients their own thinking, perhaps their own experiences, not as a way of directing the clients' lives but rather as an additional source of information and input for the clients to consider in their own decision making. It is imperative, however, that the social workers' input be recognized as information to be considered and not an edict to be followed. [p. 111]

The key to implementing this principle is for the social worker to phrase the alternative as a suggestion rather than as advice. For example, if a client is worried about how her elderly mother, who is living alone, will be able to have her physical, emotional, and social needs met, the social worker should not advise: "The best thing for you to do is to place her in a nursing home." Instead the worker should offer a suggestion for the client to consider: "Have you thought about placing your mother in a nursing home?"

Fourth, client self-determination is possible and should be encouraged even in areas in which the social worker has the additional function to protect society. Three areas in social work for which the worker has this additional function are in protective services, in prisons, and in probation and parole. Compton and Galaway (1975) noted:

A probation agency, for example, may enforce the legal requirement that the probationer must report to the probation officer; this is not a matter for client self-determination. But the sensitive probation officer can allow for considerable client self-determination in the frequency of reporting, the length of the interviews, the time of reporting, and the content to be discussed during the interviews. [p. 112]

Actually probationers, in one sense, also can be informed that they even have a choice in reporting to the probation officer. In working with involuntary clients who are angry with the legal authority held by the social worker, it is often helpful for the worker to inform the clients that they do have a choice regarding whether they are willing to meet the minimum legal requirements. The consequences of not cooperating (such as being sent to prison, or having their children taken away in the case of abusive parents) are also made clear to them. This approach appears to be useful, because it reduces the clients' inclination to view the social worker as a parent or a cop. Instead of playing the game of how much they can get away with, this approach puts the responsibility for their future squarely on the clients. They are faced with the decision of reporting or suffering the consequences of not reporting; of deciding whether to stop abusing their children or of suffering the consequences of making no effort to refrain from abusing their children. In this connection Gerald O'Connor (1972) noted:

The recognition of man's [a person's] right to free choice guarantees that he may choose to run his life as he sees fit. This choice may run counter to society's welfare and even his own, yet essentially it is his choice and his prerogative. Society may censure, but it cannot take from him his right; nor should society strip him of his dignity by a censure. The criminal then has a right to say "crime is my choice and I am willing to pay the price. If you send me to prison, I am paying my debt to society and refuse to submit to your attempts to reform me." The principle of self-determination makes it incumbent upon society to honor such a plea. [pp. 485–486]

In working with involuntary clients whose actions have adversely affected other people in the past (for example, abusive parents), the worker's obligation is to outline the minimum legal requirements (for example, no further incidents of abuse) and specify the consequences if these clients decide not to meet these requirements. Even in such situations, clients have a choice in deciding whether they will meet the requirements. If they are not met by a client, then the worker must follow through on implementing the consequences to maintain credibility with the client. Often the consequences have therapeutic shock value as clients learn they can no longer manipulate the system and are responsible for the consequences they suffer.

Confidentiality

Confidentiality is the implicit or explicit agreement between a professional and a client that the professional will maintain the private nature of information about the client. An *absolute* implementation of this principle means that the professional will not share client disclosures with anyone else, except when authorized by the client in writing or required by law. Because of the principle of confidentiality, professionals can be sued if they disclose information that the client is able to document having a damaging effect.

One of the reasons confidentiality is important is that clients may not share their hidden secrets, personal concerns, and asocial thoughts and actions with a professional if they believe the information will be revealed to others. A basic principle of counseling is that clients must feel comfortable in fully revealing themselves to the professional without fear that their secret revelations will be used against them.

Confidentiality is absolute when information revealed to a professional is *never* passed on to anyone or anything in any form. Such information would never be shared with other agency staff, fed into a computer, or written in a case record. A student or beginning practitioner tends to think in absolutes and may even naively promise clients *absolute confidentiality.*

Absolute confidentiality is seldom achieved. Social workers today generally function as part of a larger agency. Much of the communication is written into case records and shared orally with other staff in the system as part of the service-delivery process. Social workers share details with supervisors, and many work in teams and are expected to share information. Therefore, instead of absolute confidentiality, it is more precise to indicate that a system of *relative confidentiality* is being used in social work practice (Wilson, 1978, p. 3).

Confidentiality is a legal matter, and there is a fair amount of uncertainty as to what is an unlawful violation. In addition, there have been few test cases in court to determine this issue. Let me provide a brief summary of how agencies are now handling issues related to confidentiality.

Practically all agencies allow (and in fact encourage) their workers to discuss a client's circumstances with other professionals employed at the same agency. At many agencies (such as a mental hospital) the input of many professionals (psychiatrist, psychologist, social workers, nurses, physical therapist, and so forth) is used in assessing a client and developing a treatment plan.

Many agencies feel it is inappropriate to share or discuss a client's case with a secretary. (Yet, the secretary does the typing and usually knows as much about each client as the professional staff does.)

Most agencies believe it is inappropriate to discuss a client's case with professionals at another agency unless the client first signs a release of information form (see Figure 2.1). (Yet, informally, professionals employed by different agencies do at times share information about a client without the client's authorization.)

Nearly all agencies share case information with social work interns. (Whether it is legally permissible to share information with student interns has not been determined.)

It is certainly permissible to discuss a case for educational purposes with others if no identifying information about the client is given. Yet, this is another gray area, because the person talking about the case will not be able to determine precisely when identifying information is being given. Take the following example:

Some years ago I was employed at a maximum security hospital for the criminally insane and had on my caseload a young male who had decapitated his 17-year-old girlfriend. Such a criminal offense is indeed shocking and rare. People in the client's local area will never forget the offense. If I were to discuss this case in a class at a university (which I occasionally do), I would never be fully assured that no one would be able to identify the offender. There is always the chance that one of the students may have lived in the client's home community and would recognize the offender.

A question that is sometimes raised in relation to confidentiality is whether clients have a right to see the agency's records on them. The 1974 Federal Privacy Act legislated that any agency receiving federal funds must allow clients to see their records. Furthermore, if a client requests a copy of the record, the agency must provide one. (It is probably a good idea not to put anything into a client's record that you do not want the client to see.)

Lakeside Counseling Center
Consent for Release of Confidential Information

_____ at Lakeside Counseling Center requests permission from _____
(Name of social worker)

_____ to release confidential information about _____. This information will be released to:
(Name of client)   (Name of client)

Name: _____   Address: _____

Position: _____   _____

Agency: _____

Material to be released: _____

_____

_____

Reason for this disclosure: _____

_____

_____

_____ must abide by the following limitations in their
(name of person and the agency receiving the information)

use of the information received: _____

_____

_____

My signature verifies that I know what information is being disclosed and have had the opportunity to correct the data to make certain it is accurate. I am aware that this consent can be revoked (in writing) at any time. I am also aware of the consequences that might occur as a result of signing this form or of my refusal to do so.

My signature means that I have read this form and/or have had it read and explained to me in language I can understand. I have checked this form, and upon signing it will receive a copy.

This consent form expires on _____ unless revoked by me in writing prior to that date.
(Date)

_____   _____   _____
(Client's signature or "X")   (Date signed)   (Witness)

_____   _____   _____
(Client's guardian—if applicable)   (Date signed)   (Witness)

_____   _____
(Lakeside Counseling Center representative)   (Date signed)

Figure 2.1

Release of information form (sample copy of a suggested format).   SOURCE: One of the sources from which this release of information form was adapted is Suanna J. Wilson, _Confidentiality in Social Work: Issues and Principles_ (New York: Free Press, 1978).

A number of voluntary agencies also now have policies to allow clients access to their records.

Another problematic area is the thorny question of when a professional should violate confidence and inform others. Again, many gray areas surround this question (Wilson, 1978).

Most state statutes permit or require the professional to inform the appropriate people when a client admits to a past or intended *serious* criminal act. Yet, the question of how serious a crime must be before there is an obligation to report it has not been resolved. On the extreme end of the severity continuum, it has been established that a professional *must* inform the appropriate people.

A precedent-setting case occurred in the case of *Tarasoff* v. *Regents of the University of California, 1974* (*University of Pittsburgh Law Review,* 1975). In this case a university student informed his psychiatrist that he was going to shoot his girlfriend. The psychiatrist informed the campus police of this threat but did not inform the intended victim or her parents. Campus security picked up and questioned the student and soon released him, concluding that he "appeared rational." Shortly afterward he murdered his girlfriend. Her parents sued the psychiatrist, and the Supreme Court ruled:

> When a doctor or a psychiatrist, in the exercise of his professional skills and knowledge, determines, or shall determine that a warning is essential to avert danger arising from a medical or psychological condition of his patient, he incurs a legal obligation to give that warning. [*University of Pittsburgh Law Review,* 1975, p. 159]

The court also concluded:

> The public policy favoring protection of the confidential character of patient-psychotherapist communication must yield in instances in which disclosure is essential to avert danger to others. The pro-

tective privilege ends where the public peril begins. [*University of Pittsburgh Law Review,* 1975, p. 161]

Thus, the court set a precedent holding that a professional is liable for failure to warn the intended victim. This precedent has continued to be upheld in recent court decisions involving a helping professional's obligation to inform the intended victim (Schwartz, 1989, pp. 225–226).

In regard to the question of how serious a crime must be before it is reported, Wilson (1978) noted:

> How serious must a crime be in order for the professional to take protective measures? Obviously, crimes involving someone's life are sufficiently serious. But what about destruction of personal property, theft, and the hundreds of misdemeanors that are so minor that they are rather easily overlooked? Unfortunately, there seems to be no clear-cut definition of what constitutes a serious crime, and it appears that this will have to be determined by the courts in individual case rulings. [pp. 116–117]

Without guidelines, professionals today must use their own best judgment of when a client's actions or communications warrant protective measures and what those measures should be. Student interns or beginning practitioners are advised to ask their supervisors when questions in this area arise.

Several years ago I was the faculty supervisor for a student in a field placement at a public assistance agency. The student intern had an unmarried AFDC mother (Aid to Families of Dependent Children Program) on his caseload. A trusting, working relationship between the intern and the mother was developed. The mother then informed the student she was dating a person who was sometimes abusive to her when he was drunk. The mother further indicated there was a warrant for the boyfriend's arrest in another state for an armed robbery charge. The student intern contacted me inquiring whether it was his obligation to inform the police, thereby violating confidentiality. My response was that he should discuss this with his agency supervisor to find out the agency's policy in regard to this question.

Wilson (1978) further concluded:

> In summary, a professional whose client confesses an intended or past crime can find himself in a very delicate position, both legally and ethically. There are enough conflicting beliefs on how this should be handled, so that clear guidelines are lacking. Social workers who receive a communication about a serious criminal act by a client would be wise to consult an attorney for a detailed research of appropriate state statutes and a review of recent court rulings that might help determine the desired course of action. [p. 121]

There are a number of other areas in which a professional is permitted, expected, or required to violate confidentiality.[1] These areas include the following:

> When a client formally (usually in writing) authorizes the professional to release information.
>
> When a professional is called to testify in a criminal case (state statutes vary regarding guidelines on what information may be kept confidential in such criminal proceedings, and therefore practitioners must research their own particular state statutes in this area).
>
> When a client files a lawsuit against a professional (for example, for malpractice).
>
> When a client threatens suicide and a professional may be forced to violate confidentiality to save the client's life. While

---

[1]An extended discussion of these areas is contained in Suanna J. Wilson, *Confidentiality in Social Work: Issues and Principles* (New York: Free Press, 1978).

the treating professional is encouraged to violate confidentiality in such circumstances, there is not necessarily a legal requirement to do so.

> When a client threatens to harm his or her therapist.
>
> When a professional becomes aware that a minor has committed a crime, when a minor is used by adults as an accessory in a crime, or when a minor is a victim of criminal actions. In such situations most states require that counselors inform the legal authorities. Again, the question arises of how serious the crime must be before it is reported.
>
> When there is evidence of child abuse or neglect. Most states require professionals to report the evidence to the designated child-protection agency.
>
> When a client's emotional or physical condition makes his or her employment a clear danger to self or others (for example, when a counselor discovers that a client who is an airplane pilot has a serious drinking problem).

In all these areas, professional judgment must be used in deciding when the circumstances justify violating confidentiality (for example, making a judgment as to when child abuse or neglect may be occurring).

Privileged Communication

Privileged communication is closely related to confidentiality, but is narrower in scope. *Privileged communication* refers only to the legal right that protects clients, under certain circumstances, from having their communication with a professional revealed in court without their permission. Bernstein (1975) defined privileged communication as follows:

> In states where certain professional groups are granted privileged communication, the client or his attorney has the privilege of preventing the professional from answer-

ing questions about their communication when called as a witness in court. [p. 521]

Privileged communication is a legal term dealing with the admission of evidence in a court, whereas confidentiality refers to the laws or rules of professional ethics that regulate the disclosure of information by a client to a professional.

In addition, privileged communication protects the client, and the right to exercise this privilege belongs to the client, not to the professional. Four fundamental conditions are necessary for the establishment of privilege against disclosure:

1. Communications must originate in the confidence that they will not be disclosed;
2. The element of confidentiality must be essential to the maintenance of the relationship between the parties;
3. The relation is one which in the opinion of the community ought to be fostered;
4. The injury that would inure to the relationship as a result of disclosure must be greater than the benefit gained in regard to the correct disposal of litigation. [Wigmore, 1961, p. 52]

These conditions represent the foundation for the determination of privileged communication by the judiciary. Every case that raises the issue of privileged communication is evaluated in terms of having met these conditions.

Many state statutes contain exceptions to privileged communication whereby the professional must testify in court. A listing of these exceptions is contained in Wilson (1978). Examples of such exceptions include the following:

- The client waives privilege.
- The client introduces privileged material into litigation.
- A communication does not meet Wigmore's four criteria.

- The social worker is called to testify in a criminal case.
- A client sues his counselor.
- A client commits or threatens a criminal act.
- A patient threatens suicide.
- A client threatens to harm his therapist.
- Physicians must report certain medical conditions and treatments.
- A minor is involved in criminal activity.
- Child abuse or neglect is suspected.
- A client is using certain types of drugs.
- A client's condition makes his employment hazardous to others.
- The court orders a professional examination.
- Involuntary hospitalization is needed for someone's protection.
- The client dies.
- A treating professional needs to collect fees for services rendered.
- Information is learned outside the professional treatment relationship.
- Information is shared in the presence of a third person.
- The federal government needs certain information.
- The right of privileged communication is not transferable from one state to another.
- Emergency action is needed to save a client's life.
- Legal action is needed for protection of a minor.
- A client engages in treasonous activities.
- A presentence investigation report is prepared.

In the past few decades, social workers have been successful in most states in attaining passage of state legislation that recognizes social worker–client privileged communication to avoid forced disclosures of confidential information in court. In states in which social workers are not granted privileged communication, they can be subpoenaed by any party to a court action, and thereby forced to testify in court fully and under oath all that transpired between the client and the social worker. If they fail to testify, they can be found in contempt of court by the judge and either fined, sent to jail, or both. Such court appearances can be detrimental to the client-worker relationship, and to future work with the client.

Social workers in recent years have been successful in all states in securing passage of legislation that licenses (or certifies) social workers. A section of such legislation usually contains a provision that recognizes social worker–client privileged communication. In various states a number of other professionals have been licensed and have secured recognition of privileged communication with clients. These professionals include attorneys, accountants, physicians, the clergy, guidance counselors, marriage counselors, nurses, psychiatrists, and psychologists.

Explaining Confidentiality to Clients

Given all the above material on confidentiality, how should a worker respond to clients' questions about confidentiality? Clients often wonder when they seek services how the information they reveal will be used. Clients need to be assured the information they divulge will be kept confidential; otherwise they are unlikely to share their secret concerns. Compare the following two explanations involving a question asked by a husband who is seeking marriage counseling for himself and his wife:

First response:

Husband: Will what we say here be told to others?

Worker: Our agency operates on a system of relative confidentiality. This means I may discuss certain aspects of your case with other staff members at this agency, but I will not discuss your case with anyone else outside the agency. There is one exception to this: if I am subpoenaed (which might happen if you decide to get a divorce and the divorce is contested), then I would have to reveal what we talked about. I

guess there might be one additional exception. Should the need arise for me to talk with professionals at other agencies (for example, your doctor), then I would first ask you to sign a release-of-information form allowing me to discuss your case.

Second response:

Husband: Will what we say here be told to others?

Worker: No, what you say here will be kept within this agency. I know when clients first come to an agency they often wonder how the information they reveal will be used. I assure you that what we talk about will be kept confidential.

The second response is probably the most desirable at agencies when the chances of subpoenas are unlikely. The first response, while more thorough, is apt to suggest to clients that there is a moderate chance that information they reveal will be used against them at some future time, which will inhibit them from sharing their "secret" concerns.

However, if a worker is providing services in an area with a moderate or high chance of court action, then clients should be informed about the limits of confidentiality. For example, a probation and parole officer should inform clients (early in the supervision period) about his or her obligations to the court if a client reveals a violation of the conditions of probation (for example, by committing another offense) as illustrated in the following excerpt from an interview:

Probation Officer: I'm here to help you in any way I can. If you have personal concerns and want to talk to someone, I'd be happy to talk with you. If you choose to talk with someone else, that's certainly OK with me. The important thing is that when you have personal concerns, you get them worked out. We all have personal concerns at times. If you choose to talk to me, it will be kept confidential. The only information that will not be kept confidential is a violation by you of the conditions of probation, which we have discussed and which you have a copy of. If you violate the conditions of probation, and I find out, either by your telling me, or in some other way, I am required to make a report to the court of the violation. Do you have questions about this?

Probationee: No.

Probation Officer: All right, if you have some concerns, now, or in the future, I'll be happy to talk with you.

Probationee: There is one concern I have. My girlfriend's parents as yet don't know I've been arrested and placed on probation. He's a minister, and his wife is a school teacher. I don't know what they will say when they find out I'm in trouble. How do you think I should handle this? [The interview continues—and a trusting, helping relationship begins to develop.]

Ethical Dilemmas About AIDS

The major social concerns and controversies encompassing AIDS are far too numerous to be addressed here, so the focus will be on a select few. The intent is to provide a perspective for how massive and complicated the issues are.

A core concern and one that has many offshoots is confidentiality. Once a person has been positively diagnosed as having antibodies to HIV and is, therefore, contagious, who else should have access to this information? Do social workers have an obligation to help protect the public health that outweighs their clients' interests? Is it ethically permissible for social workers to notify identifiable partners who are in danger of contracting the AIDS virus, if their clients refuse to change high-risk behaviors or to warn their partners? Where does a social worker's obligation to preserve client confidentiality end and duty to protect or warn another person begin?

Clients who are HIV-positive may be reluctant to inform their sexual partners for a variety of reasons. They may be concerned about the possibility of being abandoned. They may be angry that their partners may, in fact, have infected them. They may fear that their partners might tell others that they are HIV-positive.

The NASW's policy statement (Landers, 1993) on HIV/AIDS concerning whether there is a duty to inform is as follows:

> Practitioners and agencies may perceive a responsibility to warn third parties of their potential for infection if their spouses, other sexual partners, or partners in intravenous drug use are HIV-infected and the partners refuse to warn them. [p. 3]

In this HIV/AIDS policy statement, NASW refers to the "duty to warn" principle, which was established by the 1974 case *Tarasoff* v. *Regents of University of California* (*University of Pittsburgh Law Review*, 1975). In this precedent-setting case, the California Supreme Court ruled that psychotherapists have a duty to warn a potential victim when the professional believes there is a clear danger, even if this means breaching confidentiality. The court concluded: "The protective privilege ends where the public peril begins." Whether *Tarasoff* applies to AIDS cases has not been tested. All *Tarasoff* cases tested in court have involved threats with weapons or arson, not sexually transmitted diseases.

Another issue related to confidentiality is mandatory testing for antibodies to the AIDS virus. Who should be tested and what should be done with the results? Many other questions are involved before these issues can be resolved. Should all health care officials be required to be tested? Should public employees?

There are many ramifications to testing. People have lost jobs, been thrown out of residences and schools, and been denied services they desperately needed. For instance, some physicians and other health care professionals have refused to serve people with AIDS. Morticians have refused to prepare the bodies for burial. People with AIDS need to have their rights protected, including their right of free choice. Mandated testing does not guarantee protection from discrimination.

An important issue is the distinction between confidential testing (also called "name-associated testing") and anonymous testing. In *confidential testing*, the identity of the person being tested is recorded, although supposedly not made publicly known. Questions have been raised regarding who has (or should have) access to a person's positive results—those having access may include secretaries in testing sites, the state's communicable disease center, the person's physician, and even insurance companies. With confidential testing, there is a danger that those who have access to the test result may then discriminate against the person who tested positive; for example, an insurance company may find an excuse to cancel a health or life insurance policy. *Anonymous testing*, on the other hand, involves no identification. An individual goes in for testing, uses a code word or number, and returns approximately two weeks later to receive the results. Names are neither mentioned nor recorded. One drawback is that the state's communicable disease center is not informed of a positive test result and therefore is unable to contact and encourage the person's past and present sexual partners to also be tested.

A body of law is beginning to be established that extends the legal protection against discrimination (already available to those with a physical disability) to people with AIDS. However, most of these laws involve employment discrimination. Some involve housing. Fewer legal cases target the issues of "education, credit, and insurance." Therefore, people with AIDS are very often not protected from discrimination in these important parts of their lives.

Yet another issue concerning health care directly involves the providers of such care. A number of people in the health care professions either refuse to treat people with AIDS or treat them very differently from their other patients. For example, one medical attendant would talk to a person with AIDS only when wearing surgical clothing including gown, gloves, and mask. Under no circumstances would he touch or shake hands with a person having AIDS. How would such behavior make a person with AIDS feel? Such a person may already be feeling isolated and scourged. Such differential treatment could make anyone feel much like a leper must have felt in Biblical times.

Other health care issues involve nursing homes. Many such homes refuse to admit people with AIDS. Is this fair or right? What other alternatives are available to people with AIDS when their health is seriously fading and they need extensive care?

Solutions to the last two problems must involve educating people about AIDS and preparing them to work with people who have it. Health care professionals need to learn what is safe and what is not. They need to work on their own fears and personal conflicts. It is unlikely that making new laws and mandating to people how they must behave will be enough. Would you like to have a physician remove a cancerous brain tumor from your skull when she was forced to do the surgery totally against her will?

In 1991 the American public was shocked when it was revealed that Kimberly Bergalis had apparently contracted the AIDS virus from her dentist while receiving dental services. An extensive investigation concluded that four other dental patients had also contracted the AIDS virus from this same dentist. Exactly how these patients became infected is unknown. Nationwide, very few people have contracted the AIDS virus from health care workers, such as dentists, physicians, and nurses. Therefore, because so many patients are believed to have contracted the AIDS virus from the Florida dentist (who died of AIDS), some authorities have questioned whether he intentionally engaged in dental procedures that put his patients at risk (Findlay, 1991). The risk of contracting the AIDS virus from infected health care workers is minimal. Findlay (1991) noted:

> Even if the doctor is infected, most procedures, such as a routine checkup or blood-pressure reading, put patients at no risk. . . . Even in surgery, risk is minimal. Odds are between 1 in 42,000 and 1 in 417,000 of your picking up the virus from an infected surgeon who uses proper precautions, says the CDC [Centers for Disease Control]. In contrast, your chance of dying in a car accident this year is 1 in 5,300. . . . The CDC puts your chance of contracting HIV from an infected dentist at between 1 in 263,000 and 1 in 2,632,000. [p. 66]

The danger of patients becoming infected by health care workers has led the American Medical Association, the American Dental Association, and the Centers for Disease Control to recommend that HIV-infected health care workers (who know they are infected) stop performing certain at-risk procedures. The only time for concern is when a health care procedure exposes some of the patient's blood to the blood of the infected health care worker.

Actually, health care workers are at a greater risk of contracting the AIDS virus from infected patients than vice versa. (Drawing blood, for example, from an infected patient can result in an accidental needle prick, perhaps transmitting the AIDS virus.) Substantially more health care workers have contracted the AIDS virus from infected patients than the other way around (Findlay, 1991). The risk of transmission of the virus, however, has raised numerous complex questions. When (perhaps for what health care procedures) should patients be told that one of their health care providers has the AIDS virus? Are there circumstances or medical conditions that would warrant informing health care workers that their patient is HIV positive? Most patients and health care workers who are HIV-positive are unaware they are infected. Are there circumstances or medical

conditions for which HIV testing of either patients or health care workers should be mandated?

Many other issues have not even been mentioned here. There are opposing views regarding the conditions under which children with AIDS can go to school. Likewise, there are opposing views over whether free needles should be distributed to intravenous drug users. Will this procedure prevent them from sharing needles and thereby contracting AIDS, or will it only encourage their antisocial drug-abusing behavior? Another controversial issue is whether free condoms should be distributed to adolescents at school. Proponents say it helps prevent the spread of AIDS; opponents claim it promotes sexual promiscuity.

All of these matters merit serious attention and consideration, because people who contract this deadly disease deserve attention and compassion.

Other Values

Additional values and principles of social work practice will briefly be summarized in this section. You should also study the Code of Ethics of the National Association of Social Workers, and the Canadian Association of Social Workers' Code of Ethics (presented in Appendixes A and B), which summarize important practice ethics for social workers. The NASW is the largest professional association representing the social work profession in the United States, and the Canadian Association of Social Workers is the largest professional association representing the social work profession in Canada.

The Institutional Orientation

Currently there are two conflicting views of the role of social welfare in our society (Wilensky & Lebeaux, 1965). One view, which has been termed *residual*, promotes a gap-filling or first-aid role. This view holds that social welfare services should be provided only when an individual's needs are not properly met through other societal institutions, primarily the family and the market economy. Social services and financial aid should not be provided until all measures or efforts have failed, after the exhaustion of the individual's or the family's resources. In addition, this view asserts that funds and services should be provided on a short-term basis (primarily during emergencies) and withdrawn when the individual or the family again becomes self-sufficient.

The residual view has been characterized as being "charity for unfortunates" (Wilensky & Lebeaux, 1965, p. 14). Funds and services are seen not as a right (something to which one is entitled) but as a gift, with the receiver having certain obligations (for example, to receive financial aid the recipient may be required to perform certain low-grade work assignments). An associated belief holds that the causes of recipients' difficulties are rooted in their own malfunctioning (that is, recipients are brought to their predicament through their own fault, because of some personal inadequacy, or ill-advised activity, or sin).

Under the residual view, there is usually a stigma attached to receiving services or funds. The prevalence of the residual stigma can be shown by your asking yourself, "Have I ever in the past felt a reluctance to seek counseling for a personal or emotional situation that I faced because I was wary of what others might think of me?" For almost everyone the answer is yes, and the reluctance to seek help is due to the residual stigma.

The opposing point of view, which has been called the *institutional view,* holds that social welfare programs are to be "accepted as a proper, legitimate function of modern industrial society in helping individuals achieve self-fulfillment" (Wilensky & Lebeaux, 1965, p. 14). Under this view, there is no stigma attached to receiving funds or services; recipients are entitled to such help. Associated with this view is the belief that individuals' dif-

ficulties result from causes largely beyond their control (for example, a person is unemployed because of a lack of employment opportunities).

The residual approach characterized social welfare programs from our early history to the Depression of the 1930s. Since the Great Depression, both approaches have been applied to social welfare programs, with some programs being largely residual in nature while others are more institutional in design and implementation. Social workers believe in the institutional approach and strive to develop and provide programs with this orientation.

Establishment of Professional Boundaries with Clients

Is is appropriate for a social worker to have lunch or dinner with a client? Is it appropriate to attend a party (where alcoholic drinks are being served) where clients may be present? Is it appropriate to hug a client who is experiencing emotional distress? These are examples of boundary questions that arise in interactions with clients.

As the years have passed, I have seen a variety of boundary problems. A well-meaning male psychotherapist was charged by a female client for unethical conduct because he occasionally gave her hugs and because he overstepped (according to her) the boundaries of a professional relationship by giving her his room air-conditioner after he had central air installed in his home. In another case, a man charged a female psychotherapist with alienation of affection after the psychotherapist and the man's wife, who was a client of the female therapist, had dinner a few times and the wife became attracted to the therapist. Both male and female social work faculty members have dated social work students, and now universities across the country are questioning the propriety of such relationships. A power differential exists between students and faculty, and many campuses now view such dating relationships as evidence that the involved students could use to prove sexual harassment. A female social work intern at a group home for adolescent males was confronted by her agency supervisor because she sought to become friends with the residents. She frequently played pool with them and occasionally shared some of her "partying" stories, and one of the residents became infatuated with her. A male intern at a shelter for runaway youths occasionally related jokes that had some sexual connotations; one of the female residents charged that such behavior was evidence that the intern was making romantic advances toward her. A female intern was terminated at her field placement at a halfway house for chemically addicted correctional residents after she began dating one of the residents. A male intern at a shelter for battered women was confronted by his agency supervisor about the "provocative and revealing" clothes he tended to wear, which was a factor in some of the residents becoming infatuated with him.

Social workers have an obligation to establish appropriate boundaries in professional relationships with clients. The Canadian Association of Social Workers' Code of Ethics (1994) contains the following statements on these boundary issues:

A social worker shall not exploit the relationship with a client for personal benefit, gain or gratification. [p. 9]

A social worker shall not become involved in a client's personal affairs that are not relevant to the service being provided. [p. 10]

The social worker shall distinguish between actions and statements made as a private citizen and actions and statements made as a social worker. [p. 11]

The social worker shall not have a sexual relationship with a client. [p. 13]

The social worker shall not have a business relationship with a client, borrow money from a client, or loan money to a client. [p. 13]

The NASW Code of Ethics (1979) contains the following statements on boundary issues:

The private conduct of the social worker is a personal matter to the same degree as is any other person's, except when such conduct compromises the fulfillment of professional responsibilities.

The social worker should not participate in, condone, or be associated with dishonesty, fraud, deceit, or misrepresentation.

The social worker should distinguish clearly between statements and actions made as a private individual and as a representative of the social work profession or an organization or group.

The social worker should not exploit professional relationships for personal gain.

The social worker should not exploit relationships with clients for personal advantage.

The social worker should avoid relationships or commitments that conflict with the interests of clients. The social worker should under no circumstances engage in sexual activities with clients.

It is impossible to develop additional guidelines that will answer all the questions that may arise when social workers set boundaries with clients. The following guidelines may be useful in resolving some boundary dilemmas:

• In your professional *and* personal life, try to be a role model for the values and principles of the social work profession.

• In relationships with clients, try to gain their respect and to exemplify the values and principles of the social work profession, rather than establish a friend-to-friend relationship.

• Never try to meet your personal needs or wants in relationships with clients.

• Try to increase your awareness of your own needs, feelings, values, and limitations so you become increasingly aware of how such factors may impact client relationships.

• When questions arise about the appropriateness of certain interactions with a client (such as whether to go to lunch), try to arrive at an answer by gauging whether the interaction will have a constructive impact on the client and your relationship. If a concrete beneficial impact cannot be objectively specified, do not engage in the interaction.

• Constructive professional relationships with clients require a certain amount of distance. If you have questions abut whether contemplated social interactions will interfere with the boundaries of a professional relationship, consult your supervisor or a respected colleague.

• In your professional social work role with clients, be aware of any inappropriate behavior, verbal communications, and dress on your part. For example, sharing details of your "wild" parties with teenage clients is probably unprofessional.

Promotion of Social and Economic Justice

Social workers have an obligation to promote social and economic justice for those who are oppressed or victimized by discrimination. The Council on Social Work Education has identified populations-at-risk (that is, populations in the United States with a history of subjection to discrimination, economic deprivation, and oppression) to include, but not be limited to, people of color, women, gay and lesbian individuals, and those populations who are oppressed due to their ethnicity, culture, age, class, religion, or physical or mental ability.

The social work profession holds that society has a responsibility to all of its members to provide security, acceptance, and satisfaction of basic cultural, social, and biological needs. Only when individuals' basic needs are met, is it possible for them to develop their maximum potentials. Therefore, social workers have a special responsibility to protect and se-

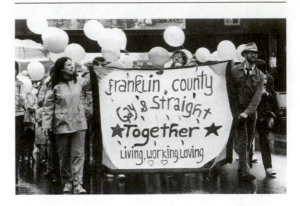

Gays and lesbians are frequently oppressed in our society because of their sexual orientation. Social workers have an obligation to promote social and economic justice for all groups who are oppressed or victimized by discrimination in our society.

cure civil rights based on democratic principles and a moral responsibility to work toward eradicating discrimination for any reason. Clients' civil rights need to be protected to preserve human dignity and self-respect.

In promoting social and economic justice for oppressed populations, social workers are expected to have an understanding of (1) the consequences and dynamics of social and economic injustice, including the forms of human oppression and discrimination, and (2) the impact of economic deprivation, discrimination, and oppression on populations-at-risk. Social workers have an ethical obligation to understand and appreciate human diversity. They are expected to have and use skills to promote social change that furthers the achievement of individual and collective social and economic justice.

Focus on Family

Often the focus of social work services is on the family. A family is seen as an interacting independent system. The problems faced by any person are usually influenced by the dynamics within a family, as illustrated in the following example.

A schoolteacher became concerned when one of her pupils was consistently failing, and she referred the child for psychological testing. Testing revealed a normal IQ, but failure was found to be due to a low self-concept (the girl was reluctant to do her academic work because she saw herself as being incapable of doing it). A school social worker met with the family and observed that the low self-concept was primarily a result of the parents' ridiculing and criticizing the child and seldom giving emotional support, encouragement, or compliments.

Since a family is an interacting system, change in one member affects others. For example, with some abusive families, the abused child is a scapegoat on which the parents vent their anger and hostility. If the abused child is removed from the home, another child within the family is at times selected to be the scapegoat (Leavitt, 1974).

Another reason for the focus on the family rather than on the individual is that the other family members are often needed in the treatment process. For example, other family members can put pressure on an alcoholic to have him or her acknowledge that a problem exists. The family members may also need counseling to help them cope with the person when he or she is drinking, and these family members may play important roles in providing emotional support for the alcoholic's efforts to stop drinking.

Accountability

Increasingly, federal and state governmental units and private funding sources are requiring that the effectiveness of service programs be measured. Gradually, programs found to be ineffective are being phased out. While some social workers view accountability with trepidation and claim the paperwork involved interferes with serving clients, members of the social work profession have

an obligation to funding sources to provide the highest quality services. Two hundred years ago, bloodletting was thought to be an effective treatment technique. Only a few decades ago, lobotomies were erroneously thought to be effective. Now the value of electroshock therapy, psychoanalysis, and some other therapy techniques is being questioned. Program outcome studies have also demonstrated that orphanages are not the best places to serve homeless children, long-term hospitalization is not the best way to help those who are emotionally disturbed, probation generally has higher rehabilitative value than long-term confinement in prison, the Job Corps program of the 1960s was too expensive for the outcomes achieved, children with a cognitive disability can be better served in their home communities through local programs than by confinement in an institution, and so on.

Social workers need to become skilled at evaluating the extent to which they are being effective in providing services. A wide variety of evaluation techniques are now available to assess effectiveness of current services and to identify unmet needs and service gaps. One of the most useful approaches is management by objectives (MBO). This technique involves specifying the objectives of a program, stating in measurable terms how and when these objectives are to be met, and then periodically measuring the extent to which the objectives are being met.

Management by objectives is perhaps also one of the most useful approaches that social workers can use to assess their effectiveness in providing services. Many agencies are now requiring each of their workers, *with the involvement of their clients*, to (1) identify and specify what the goals will be for each client—generally this is done together with clients during the initial interviews; (2) write down in detail what the client and the worker will do to accomplish the goals—deadlines for accomplishing these tasks are also set; and (3) assess, when treatment is terminated (and perhaps periodically during the treatment process), the extent to which the goals have been achieved.

If goals are generally not being achieved, the worker needs to examine the underlying reasons. Perhaps unrealistic goals are being set. Perhaps the program or the treatment techniques are ineffective. Perhaps certain components of the treatment program are having an adverse effect. Perhaps other reasons account for the low success rate. Depending on the reason, appropriate changes need to be made.

On the other hand, if the goals are generally being met, workers can use this information to document to funding sources and to supervisors that high-quality services are being provided.

Values Highlighted by the Council on Social Work Education

As identified in Chapter 1, the Council on Social Work Education (1992a, b) in its *Curriculum Policy Statements* for both baccalaureate and master's degree programs has made the following six statements about the values and principles that must be infused throughout every social work curriculum:

1. Social workers' professional relationships are built on regard for individual worth and dignity and are furthered by mutual participation, acceptance, confidentiality, honesty, and responsible handling of conflict.
2. Social workers respect people's rights to make independent decisions and to participate actively in the helping process.
3. Social workers are committed to assisting client systems to obtain needed resources.
4. Social workers strive to make social institutions more humane and responsive to human needs.
5. Social workers demonstrate respect for and acceptance of the unique characteristics of diverse populations.

6. Social workers are responsible for their own ethical conduct, the quality of their practice, and further study to seek continuous growth in the knowledge and skills of their profession.

The remainder of this section will address values that have not yet been discussed in this chapter.

Mutual participation and responsible handling of conduct. Mutual participation stems from the principle of mutuality. The Canadian Association of Social Workers Code of Ethics (1983) succinctly summarized the principle of mutuality:

The social worker's professional relationship with voluntary and involuntary clients will be developed on the principle of mutuality. This means that the helping process, where feasible, will involve shared control responsibilities between the client and the social worker toward the achievement of agreed to or acknowledged outcome goals. In the case of the involuntary client, mutual agreements may not exist at the outset of the relationship but the social worker's reasonable adherence to this principle is expected. Where the client is defined by statutory legislation, or where the rights of the community and others to protection are paramount and may be harmed by adherence to the principle, the latter may need to be modified or disregarded. The social worker will take care to reasonably manage all parameters of authority involved in social control responsibilities and act to protect clients from undue influence and abusive use of power or expert position. When it is apparent that clients, voluntary or involuntary, have misunderstood the achieved or intended interdependence of the professional relationship, the social worker will explain and renegotiate so that the client is fully advised of and encouraged to participate in an atmosphere of mutuality. [sec. 5.5]

Conflict resolution. Conflict, which is an antagonistic state or action involving divergent ideas or interests, is inevitable in human interactions. Many in our society have an erroneous belief that conflicts produce negative results and should be avoided. Conflict is erroneously seen as a cause of divorce, low work morale, deterioration of friendships, psychological trauma, violence, and social disorder. In reality, the cause of these destructive events is the ineffective and harmful management of conflict. Since people have divergent interests, beliefs, values, and goals, conflicts will inevitably occur in interpersonal relationships.

Conflicts are a natural part of any relationship. They are also often desirable because, when handled effectively, they have numerous payoffs. Conflicts may motivate the people involved to define issues more sharply, search harder for resolution strategies, and work harder in implementing solutions. Conflict can also lead to greater commitment, cohesion, communication, and cooperation and can revitalize stagnant groups. By expressing and working out their dissatisfactions, those involved can assess their beliefs, values, and opinions. Therefore, verbal conflicts can also lead to personal growth and encourage innovation and creativity.

There are basically two categories of approaches to resolving conflict: the win-lose approach and the no-lose problem-solving approach. In the *win-lose approach,* each side denies the legitimacy of the other's interests and concerns and attempts to sell its position without really listening to the other side. Each side attempts to force the other side into submission. The losing side is often angry and seeks to find a way to "even the score." In such an atmosphere, distrust increases, and communication becomes more limited and increasingly inaccurate.

A more effective approach to resolving conflicts is the *no-lose problem-solving approach.* This approach is based on two premises: all persons have the right to have their needs met, and what is in conflict between the two sides is almost never their *needs* but their *solutions* to those needs.

The six steps to the no-lose problem-solving approach are as follows:

1. Identify and define the needs of each opposing side.
2. Generate possible alternative solutions.
3. Evaluate the alternative solutions.
4. Decide on the best acceptable solution.
5. Work out ways of implementing the solution.
6. Evaluate how it worked.

The first step is by far the most difficult because the parties involved often view conflicts in terms of win-lose and attempt to identify and meet their own needs. When each side's needs are identified, however, what usually is in conflict are not the *needs* of each side, but their *solutions.* No-lose problem solving will generally lead to creative solutions, after *all* six steps are followed. A major advantage of this approach is that both sides fulfill their needs. The resentment, hostility, and subversive actions of a win-lose situation are also eliminated. (The win-lose approach and the no-lose problem-solving approach are described in greater detail in Chapter 7.)

Summary

Several values underlying social work practice and their implications for practice were presented. Social work is both an art and a science. Because social work is partly an art, a worker frequently must make decisions based on values rather than on knowledge. Change techniques used by workers are often based on theory and value assumptions rather than on proven therapy techniques.

Values were distinguished from knowledge. Values are beliefs, preferences, or assumptions about what is desirable or good for people. Knowledge statements are observations about the world and people that have been verified or are capable of verification. It is much easier to change a client's belief that conflicts with current knowledge than it is to change a belief based on values. Guidelines were presented for how a worker should handle a value conflict between the worker and the client.

An important value of social work is respect for the dignity and uniqueness of the individual. The importance of individualizing each client was discussed, and guidelines were presented on how to relate to clients whose behavior is viewed as disgusting by the worker. Involved in individualization is the ability to accept clients but not the deviant behavior to be changed, careful attendance to clients' communications, and the discreet use of labeling.

Self-determination is the clients' right to express their own opinions and to act on them, as long as clients do not infringe on the rights of others. Clients should be made aware that there are alternatives for resolving the personal and social problems they face. Self-determination means that the client, not the worker, is the chief problem solver, although the worker has an obligation to offer suggestions of resolution approaches that the client may not be aware of.

Confidentiality is the implicit or explicit agreement between a professional and a client to maintain the private nature of information about the client. In professional practice a system of *relative confidentiality* currently exists, rather than a system of *absolute confidentiality*. Numerous unresolved questions surrounding confidentiality were raised, and some guidelines on how beginning practitioners should handle these questions were presented. At times, circumstances arise in which a professional is permitted, expected, or required to violate confidentiality, and a number of these circumstances were listed—for example, when a client admits to a past or intended serious criminal act.

Other values of social work practice were summarized: belief in the institutional approach for the delivery of social services rather than the residual approach, establishment of professional boundaries with clients, promotion of social and economic justice for those being oppressed or discriminated against, focus on family instead of the individual in provision of services, and accountability.

In presenting guidelines for social work practice the reader was advised that such guidelines are not to be applied as absolutes, but simply as concepts that *may* be useful in working with people.

Exercises

1. Confidentiality

Goal: This exercise is designed to help students learn guidelines about when to uphold, and when to violate, confidentiality.

Step 1: State the purpose of the exercise. Divide the class into subgroups of about five students. Ask each subgroup to arrive at answers to questions raised in the following vignettes.

a. You're a social worker at a public school and have been working with a family that has multiple problems. Two of the children are in special education programs for the emotionally disturbed. The mother has occasionally been hospitalized for emotional problems. The father has been investigated for child abuse by protective services in the past. Mother and father are having marital problems and are presently separated. The father comes to your office and demands to see a copy of the school's records on his children and his family. As a social worker, would you show him a copy of these records?

b. You're a social worker at a mental health center and are working with a client who appears emotionally upset. He states he has heard that his girlfriend is seeing someone else. While saying this, he becomes enraged and says he intends to shoot her. He asks you not to tell anyone that he has said this. As you seek to discuss his threat, he continues to become more upset and walks out, stating, "I'll make sure she doesn't cheat on me." Should you violate confidentiality and inform someone? If you believe you should inform someone, who would you inform?

c. You're a social worker at a drug abuse treatment center and you're working with a 23-year-old female. You establish a good working relationship with her. She says something has been bothering her for a long time, but she states she won't discuss it unless you agree not to tell anyone. You assure her that what she reveals will be kept confidential. She then reveals that in the past she had an incestuous relationship with her stepfather that started when she was fourteen and lasted for nearly three years. She believes her unresolved feeling about this experience is one of the reasons she sometimes drinks too much. In a staffing that is held on this client would you reveal what she has said to the other staff at this agency?

Step 2: (Answers to these questions are found in the chapter and involve (1) the 1974 Federal Privacy Act, (2) the 1974 *Tarasoff* v. *Regents of the University of California* decision, and (3) guidelines about sharing information with other staff.) Ask the subgroups what they arrived at, and then provide the answers that are given in the text.

Step 3: Explain that in social work practice a system of relative rather than absolute confidentiality is used. Present the guidelines (outlined in this chapter) as to when to uphold and when to violate confidentiality.

2. Clarifying values

Goal: This exercise is designed to help students clarify their values in regard to a number of prominent issues in social work.

Step 1: State the purpose of this exercise. Explain that social workers need to be aware of their personal values and aware of professional values so that they know when they should take a nonjudgmental position in working with clients, and when they should seek to sell to clients (or enforce to clients) a particular set of values. Have the class form subgroups of three. Instruct each subgroup to arrive at answers, and reasons for their answers, to each of the following ten questions. (Distribute the following questions on a handout, or have the students read the questions from this text.)

a. Assume that you are a protective service worker and that you have evidence that a father is committing incest with his 10-year-old daughter. Would you seek to end the incest by (1) seeking to provide counseling services to all members of the family in order to keep the family intact, or (2) bringing legal charges against the father, or (3) seeking to do both at the same time?

b. Do you support a constitutional amendment to make abortions illegal?

c. Does a social worker have an obligation to preserve confidentiality if an HIV-infected client refuses to inform his or her sexual partner of the infection (while persisting in behavior that places the partner at risk), or does the social worker have an obligation to warn the partner about the peril?

d. Do you support affirmative action programs which assert that certain minority groups and women should be given preference in hiring over white males?

e. If an elderly person who is terminally ill and in intense pain wants to end his or her life, should physicians be allowed to provide assistance in helping this person end his or her life?

f. Do you believe our country should support an extensive program to develop the capacity to clone human beings?

g. Do you believe in capital punishment for certain crimes?

h. Do you think a gay or lesbian teacher should be allowed to teach in elementary and secondary schools?

i. If there were a war, do you think women in the military service should fight in combat?

j. Should condoms and other birth control contraceptives be provided to requesting students through health care clinics that are located in middle schools and high schools?

Step 2: After the subgroups have arrived at answers, take each question (one at a time) and have the subgroups present and discuss their answers. (Indicate that the purpose of this exercise is to help students clarify their values and not to sell any particular value system.)

Step 3: Have the students discuss their feelings about how they felt when others in class expressed views with which they strongly disagreed.

3. *New Frontier* to Rings of Fire

Goal: This exercise is designed to help students clarify their values about humanity.

Step 1: State the purpose of the exercise. Have the class form subgroups of about five. Read the following vignette to the subgroups.

The United States has recently completed building a remarkable spaceship, named *New Frontier,* that is capable of carrying 7 people to planets in other galaxies. *New Frontier* uses nuclear power and is guided by a new computer system that does not require a pilot to fly the spaceship.

Our government has recently discovered a new planet in a faraway galaxy that is very similar to our Earth's atmosphere and appears capable of supporting life. This planet has been named Rings of Fire as it has a red hue and several rings around it similar to those of Saturn.

Your subgroup has been chosen by the president of the United States to select the 7 people who will take the first flight. *New Frontier* is presently located on a remote Samoan island.

Suddenly a nuclear war breaks out in the Middle East, and the superpowers quickly enter the conflict. The bombs and the radioactive fallout will destroy civilization as we know it. The chief scientist frantically calls your group. She indicates there are 15 minutes available to select the 7 people to go on *New Frontier* to Rings of Fire. A country we are fighting in this war has sent a nuclear missile to this Samoan island to destroy *New Frontier*. There are 13 people close enough to board *New Frontier*. The chief scientist wants your subgroup to select the 7 people so that these 13 people do not begin fighting among themselves. If your subgroup does not select 7 people in 15 minutes, there is a danger the human race will cease to exist. The 7 people selected may well be the only hope for continuing the human race. Your subgroup has only the following information about the 13 people.

1. Chief scientist, 57 years old, has a husband and three children who are in Beaumont, Texas.
2. Male Korean medical student, 24 years old.
3. White male rabbi, 28 years old.
4. Female Samoan prostitute who has herpes, 35 years old.
5. White male professional baseball player, 26 years old and gay.
6. Protestant male child, 8 years old.
7. Ten-year-old white female who has a cognitive disability from not having enough oxygen at birth.
8. Twenty-seven-year-old white Catholic male who is unemployed and has cerebral palsy.
9. Thirty-four-year-old white male truck driver who has a history of not getting along with people and of getting into numerous fights.
10. Twenty-two-year-old Samoan farmer who has had a vasectomy.
11. Twenty-seven-year-old female Japanese stockbroker.
12. Thirty-five-year-old white female who is depressed and has a long history of being hospitalized for emotional problems.
13. Twenty-six-year-old white female who is a millionaire via inheritance and detests working.

Step 2: Distribute copies of this list to the subgroups. Give the subgroups 15 minutes to complete the task, and inform them when they have the following time remaining (in minutes): 10, 5, 3, and 1. Call time at the end of 15 minutes.

Step 3: Have each subgroup state its choices and the reasons for its selections. Seek to ask questions to reveal the values underlying the selections. End the exercise by asking the students their thoughts about the merits and shortcomings of this exercise.

II

Social Work Practice

3

Assessment

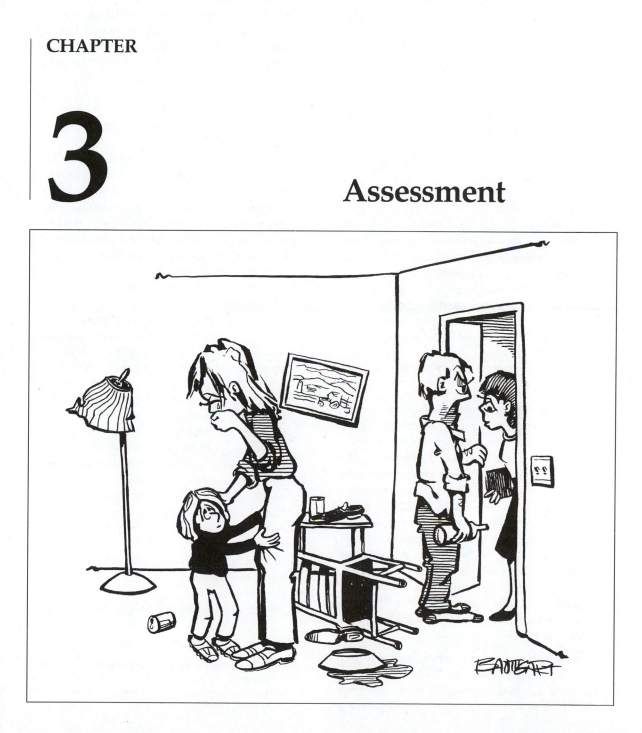

Assessment is a critical process in social work practice. The selection of goals and interventions depends largely on the assessment. An inaccurate or incomplete assessment will probably lead to inappropriate goals being set and inappropriate interventions being used. When an inaccurate or incomplete assessment is made, positive changes in the targeted client are unlikely to occur.

Hepworth and Larsen (1986) defined assessment as follows:

Assessment is the process of gathering, analyzing, and synthesizing salient data into a formulation that encompasses the following vital dimensions: (1) the nature of clients' problems, including special attention to the roles that clients and significant others play in the difficulties; (2) the functioning (strengths, limitations, personality assets, and deficiencies) of clients and significant others; (3) motivation of clients to work on the problems; (4) relevant environmental factors that contribute to the problems; and (5) resources that are available or are needed to ameliorate the clients' difficulties. [p. 165]

Assessment has sometimes been referred to as *psychosocial diagnosis* (Hollis, 1972). But the term *diagnosis* focuses on what is wrong with the client, family, or group that is being diagnosed—such as having a disease, dysfunction, or mental problem. Because diagnosis has a negative connotation, many other social work educators, myself included, prefer the term *assessment*. Assessment includes not only what is wrong with the client[1] but also the resources, strengths, motivations, functional components, and other positive factors that can be used in resolving difficulties, in enhancing functioning, and in promoting growth. In fact, assessment in its broadest sense is the base for the development of an intervention plan.

The nature of the assessment task varies significantly with the type of setting in which the social worker practices, although the process used in different settings is similar. A social worker in a nursing home who is assessing an applicant for potential placement will look at variables that are radically different from those examined by a social worker in a protective service setting who is assessing an allegation of child abuse.

In some settings (as in many protective services programs), the social worker makes an independent assessment. With independent assessments, the social worker may consult with colleagues or professionals in other disciplines on complicated cases. In other settings (for example, mental health clinics, schools, and medical hospitals), the social worker is apt to be a member of a clinical team that makes an assessment. Other team members may include a psychologist, psychiatrist, nurse, and perhaps professionals from other disciplines. With clinical teams, each team member has a circumscribed role in the assessment process, which is based on his or her special professional expertise. A psychologist, for example, would focus primarily on psychological functioning and would probably administer a variety of psychological tests

---

[1]The term *client* in this chapter will often be used in a generic sense to refer to an individual, family, group, organization, or community that a practitioner is working with.

(including personality and intelligence tests). A social worker would compile a social history that assesses family background, marital dynamics, environmental factors, and employment and educational background. In settings in which the social worker is the primary assessor, the assessment is generally completed in one, two, or three sessions. With a clinical team approach, the case is usually more complicated, and assessment by the various professionals may take a few weeks.

Assessment is sometimes a product and sometimes an ongoing process. As a product, an assessment is a formulation at a point in time regarding the nature of a client's difficulties and resources. An illustration is the completion of a mental status assessment at a psychiatric hospital. Such an assessment is first focused on determining whether the client is sane or psychotic. If the client is assessed as psychotic, a psychiatric label is assigned and a recommended treatment approach is then stated. Even when an assessment is a product, the assessment will usually have to be updated and revised months or sometimes years later. An assessment is, in essence, a working hypothesis of a client's difficulties and resources that is based on the current data. As time passes, the client will change and so will environmental factors that impact him or her. Based on such changes, assessments have to be updated and revised periodically.

Assessment can also be viewed as an ongoing process from the initial interview to the termination of the case. The length of time a client receives services may be weeks, months, or even years. During this time, the professionals working with the case are continually receiving and analyzing new information that gradually emerges. In the early stages of contact with a client, the focus is primarily on gathering information to assess the client's problems and resources. Once these are tentatively specified, the problem-solving phase has a greater emphasis—as resolution strategies are suggested, analyzed, and then one or more strategies are selected and imple-

mented. But even in the problem-solving phase, new information related to the client's difficulties and resources is apt to emerge, necessitating a revision of the assessment. In fact, as contact between a professional and a client continues, the client may disclose additional problems that need to be assessed and then resolved. It is common in initial contact for a client to withhold vital information from fear of condemnation by the professional. For example, a parent who is abusing a child is apt initially to deny that the abuse is occurring. As time passes, if the parent comes to trust the worker, the parent may disclose that she at times loses control and then hits the child. As new information is provided, the initial assessment needs to be revised.

Hepworth and Larsen (1986) noted that assessment continues to occur even during the termination phase:

> The process of assessment continues even during the terminal phase of service. During the final interviews, the practitioner carefully evaluates the client's readiness to terminate, assesses the presence of residual difficulties that may cause future difficulties, and identifies possible emotional reactions to termination. The practitioner also considers possible strategies to assist the client to maintain improved functioning or to achieve additional progress after formal social work service is concluded. [p. 166]

A Focus on Strengths

For most of the past several decades, social work and the other helping professions have had a primary focus on diagnosing the pathology, shortcomings, and dysfunctions of clients. One reason may be that Freudian psychology was the primary theory used in analyzing human behavior. (Freud's theories of personality development and psychopathology are summarized in Chapter 13.) Freudian psychology is based on a medical model and thereby has concepts that are geared to identify illness or pathology. It has very few concepts to identify strengths. As described in Chapter 1, social work is now shifting to a systems model in assessing human behavior. This model focuses on identifying both strengths and weaknesses.

It is essential that social workers include clients' strengths in the assessment process. In working with clients, social workers focus on the strengths and resources of clients to help them resolve their difficulties. To utilize clients' strengths effectively, social workers must first identify those strengths.

Unfortunately, Maluccio (1979) found that many social workers focus too much on clients' perceived weaknesses and underestimate or are blind to their strengths. Maluccio concluded:

> There is a need to shift the focus on social work education and practice from problems or pathology to strengths, resources, and potentialities in human beings and their environments. [p. 401]

There is a danger that a primary focus on weaknesses will impair a worker's capacity to identify the clients' growth potential. Social workers strongly believe that clients have the right (and should be encouraged) to develop their potentialities fully. Focusing on pathology often undermines this value commitment.

Another reason for attending to clients' strengths is that many clients need help in enhancing their self-esteem. Many have feelings of worthlessness, feelings of inadequacy, a sense of being a failure, and a lack of self-confidence and self-respect. Glasser (1972) noted that low self-esteem often leads to emotional difficulties, withdrawal, or criminal activity. To help clients view themselves more positively, social workers must first view their clients as having considerable strengths and competencies. Berwick (1980) underscored this point in working with neglectful parents of children who fail to thrive:

Self-esteem is already at a low ebb in many of the parents of these children, and the success of the hospital in nourishing a child when the mother has failed only serves to accentuate the pain of failure. . . . Even in the few cases that require foster care, the health care team's task is to seek strengths and to develop a sense of competence in both the parents and the child that will permit a synchronous nurturant relationship to emerge. [p. 270]

Sources of Information

Data used in making an assessment are derived from a variety of sources. The following are the primary sources.

The Client's Verbal Report

A client's verbal report is often the primary source and in some cases the only source of data. (For example, social workers in private practice sometimes obtain information only from the client.) A variety of information may be obtained in this way: description of the problems, feelings about the problems, views of his or her personal resources to combat the problems, motivations to make efforts to resolve the problems, the history of the problems, views of the causes, a description of what has already been done in attempting to resolve the problems, and so on.

Although clients are often fairly accurate in describing their difficulties and resources, workers should be aware that verbal reports are sometimes distorted by embarrassment, bias, distorted perceptions, and strong emotional feelings. For example, a married woman whose husband has left her for someone else may have such strong emotional reactions that she may not be objective about the role she played in the breakup of her marriage. In some settings clients deliberately try to conceal, or even distort, information. Abusive parents, for example, may deny they have abused their children. Alcoholics, because of the nature of the addictive process, are apt to deny they have a drinking problem. Correctional clients may try to conceal some of their illegal activities.

Clients' verbal reports should be respected as valid until additional information indicates otherwise. In some settings, as in protective services, it is often necessary to verify a client's denial that a problem exists by checking with other sources—such as neighbors, relatives, and school personnel.

Assessment Forms

Many agencies, before or after the first interview, ask clients to complete certain forms that request such information as name, address, telephone number, employer, years of school completed, marital status, description of problem, names of family members, and so on. Such information often is most efficiently collected by having the client fill out a form.

Several self-report forms can also be used in the assessment process. Some clients, particularly adolescents, may be more relaxed and potentially more truthful if they can answer questions on a form, while being assured that only helping professionals at the agency will see the answers. Examples of self-report forms for children and adolescents are the Piers-Harris Children Self-Concept Scale (Piers & Harris, 1969), and the Personal Problems Checklist for Adolescents (Schinka, 1985). Both of these instruments repeat questions in different ways so that the examiner can get a sense of reliability—that is, the extent to which the respondent answers the same question in the same way. These instruments also have validity indexes. There are also self-report instruments for adults, such as the Forty-Eight Item Counseling Evaluation Test: Revised (McMahon, 1971).

If a worker chooses to use a self-report instrument, he or she needs to become knowledgeable about the instrument and guidelines for its use. Research on its reliability and validity should be carefully studied in order to evaluate its value. Also, the worker needs to use common sense in interpreting the results. Like so many other parts of the assessment process, a test result is a starting point, not an end product.

Collateral Sources

Information is sometimes collected from a variety of collateral sources: friends, relatives, neighbors, physicians, other social agencies, teachers, and others who may be able to provide relevant information. In some cases, clients have received social services from a number of other agencies. Summary information about such clients is often obtained from these agencies.

Some workers overlook collateral sources; as a result, potentially valuable information is not collected. Less frequently, workers spend too much time gathering collateral information. In social work practice, a practitioner needs to exercise prudence in deciding what information is needed. In many circumstances, it is essential to get the client's verbal consent and have the client sign release-of-information forms before contacting collateral sources. (See Chapter 2 for a description of confidentiality and release-of-information forms.)

Psychological Tests

There are a variety of personality and intelligence tests. Most psychological tests are designed to be administered by psychologists. An exception, however, is the limited number of tests that Hudson (1982) has developed for clinical social workers. This package of tests gathers information on self-esteem, contentment, marital satisfaction, sexual satisfaction, parent's attitudes toward the child, child's attitudes toward the mother, child's attitudes toward the father, attitudes toward the family as a whole, and peer relations.

Caution should be used with psychological tests, because most tests are not designed to be administered or interpreted by social workers. Such administration and interpretation is the responsibility of psychologists. In addition, most personality tests have low validity and reliability and therefore should be used with extreme caution, if at all.

Nonverbal Behavior

Clients' nonverbal behavior provides a valuable source of information. As practitioners become more experienced, they give greater attention to and become more competent in identifying and interpreting nonverbal cues. These cues are invaluable in identifying what clients are actually thinking and feeling. There are a wide variety of nonverbal cues: gestures, posture, breathing patterns, tension in facial and neck muscles, facial color, eye movements, choice of clothes, physical appearance, eye contact, and tone of voice. Such cues give information about stress levels, kinds of feelings being experienced, and whether the client is telling the truth. For example, a client who folds his arms over his chest and frowns every time a worker brings up a particular topic is conveying valuable information about his feelings related to that topic.

Interactions with Significant Others and Home Visits

Observation of a client interacting with people who are important in her life reveals a lot of information. These significant others include family members, other close relatives, peers, friends, and neighbors. The way a client presents herself in an office may be dramatically different from the way she interacts at home. In an office setting, a client may seek to portray an image that is atypical for her. A home visit will provide information not only about how a client interacts with significant others but also on environmental factors that are impacting the client. For example, a home visit investigating a charge that a single mother is neglecting her children will reveal information about home cleanliness, available food and diet, presence of animals (including pets and rats), presence of cockroaches and insects, available clothing, possible drug abuse by the parent, home interactions between mother and children, interactions between the mother and neighbors, type of neighborhood, and financial circumstances.

Social work emphasizes the importance of assessing the person-in-environment. Home visits are an integral part of assessing the environmental factors that impact a client.

Remember that an office setting is an unnatural arena for family interaction. In an unnatural setting, families are less apt to interact as they do at home. As with any source of information, there are chances of errors in observing interactions. For example, the way a family interacts while being observed may be atypical for how they interact when they know they are not being observed.

Additionally, clients will often feel some discomfort if the worker is better educated and has a higher societal status. Since most people are more relaxed in their own home, a home visit may help such clients to feel more accepted and less anxious.

Worker's Intuition from Direct Interactions

A worker's reactions to the way a client interacts with him provides clues to how others react as well, because clients often manifest similar interactional patterns in their general social relationships. The way clients interact with a worker therefore provides clues to probable difficulties or successes in interactions with others. Some of the many ways in which a worker may experience clients are nonassertive, passive, submissive, aggressive, withdrawn, passive-aggressive, personable, caring, manipulative, highly motivated, insecure, and dependent. Such intuition may provide valuable information about problematic behavior facing a client. For example, I recently counseled a 22-year-old college coed who complained that her roommates used her as a "doormat" by frequently borrowing her car, failing to pay for gas, wearing her clothes without asking, and eating the food she bought without asking. In the interview she came across as nonassertive (with her verbal and nonverbal communication) and as making extraordinary efforts to please me. I pointed out these specific behaviors to her and asked whether she thought she had indirectly communicated through these kinds of behaviors that she would not object to her roommates' "using her things." She thought about it for a while and acknowledged that that assessment was probably accurate. She was then instructed in how to express her concerns assertively to her roommates. With role playing, she gradually acquired the confidence to confront her roommates about these concerns.

There are cautions and limitations to using intuition to assess an client's interactions with others. A client may interact atypically with a social worker because he may want to convey an atypical image. Just as some people change their patterns when interacting with a police officer, some clients seek to convey an atypical image when interacting with a worker.

Also the worker's personality may lead clients to interact atypically. For example, if a worker comes across as aggressive and highly confrontive, two reactions are common: one is the client either becomes passive and submissive or aggressive. Therefore, to use intuition effectively in assessing clients' behaviors, the worker must have substantial awareness of self and an awareness of how he or she tends to affect others during interactions. The worker must also convey a nonjudgmental attitude. For lasting change to occur, most clients need to feel competent. To feel competent, most clients need to value and believe in themselves.

Knowledge Used in Making an Assessment

An *extensive* knowledge of human behavior and the social environment is needed to have a high degree of accuracy in assessing the problems of a client system. Hepworth and Larsen (1986) noted:

> To assess the problems of a client system (individual, couple, or family) . . . requires extensive knowledge about that system as well as careful consideration of the multifarious systems (e.g., economic, legal, educational, medical, religious, social, interpersonal) that impinge upon the client system. Moreover, to assess the functioning of an individual entails evaluating various aspects of that person's functioning. For example, one must consider dynamic interactions among the biophysical, cognitive, emotional, cultural, behavioral, and motivational subsystems and the relationships of those interactions to problematic situations. [p. 172]

As identified by Hepworth and Larsen, conducting an assessment may require a broad array of knowledge about

- Multifarious systems
- Biophysical factors
- Cognitive factors
- Emotional factors
- Cultural factors
- Behavioral factors
- Motivational factors
- Family systems
- Environmental factors

At first glance learning about all these factors seems overwhelming, but such knowledge is obtained in college from a variety of social work courses. A key course in most social work programs that includes these factors is a course in human behavior and the social environment. Practice and policy courses also cover some of these areas. Other disciplines providing background information are sociology, psychology, anthropology, biology, political science, women's studies, ethnic studies, history, communication, philosophy, religious studies, and economics.

In addition, the overall purpose of an assessment adds considerable focus to what knowledge is needed. For example, a social worker doing an assessment of an elderly applicant for a placement at a nursing home would first need to know the criteria used by the nursing home for accepting applicants. Such criteria may include variables involving financial resources, medical conditions, physical strengths and impairments, emotional and behavioral patterns, special needs, level of cognitive functioning, and degree of willingness to enter a nursing home. Based on the nursing home's criteria, the social worker would then seek to obtain information from the client, from family members, from physicians, and from other relevant sources to determine the extent to which the client meets the criteria of the nursing home.

The purpose of an assessment *always* gives focus to the kinds of factors that are examined. For example, for a fourth-grade child who is performing considerably below his grade level in schoolwork, the following variables are apt to be examined: Does he have a learning disability? What is his I.Q. as measured by intelligence tests? Is he having some emotional difficulties? Does he have a low self-esteem that may be contributing to his low level of performance? Does he have a visual or hearing impairment, or other medical problems? Are there factors in his home and family life that may be influencing his school performance? What specific educational subjects and tasks is he doing fairly well at, and which is he having the most trouble with? How does he interact with peers and with teachers? Has he experienced significant traumas in the past that may still be affecting him? Is he involved in using and perhaps abusing drugs? Is he motivated to do his best in

school? How does he feel about his school performance?[2]

The theory or theories used by a practitioner have a major influence on what is examined when conducting an assessment. For example, Freudian psychology focuses on pathology, or unconscious processes, on fixations during a child's development, on sexuality, and on traumatic experiences during childhood. In contrast, rational therapy asserts that thinking patterns determine emotions and actions, and therefore the focus is on identifying clients' self-talk that leads to unwanted emotions and dysfunctional behaviors. (Chapter 22 summarizes rational therapy.) What a worker looks for in conducting an analysis also has a large effect on determining the outcome. For example, practically everyone has traumatic early childhood experiences—so it is not surprising that when an adherent of Freudian psychology does an assessment that she is apt to identify some traumatic early childhood experiences that are then hypothesized as being causes of the client's current problems. Similarly, all individuals talk to themselves in negative ways at times, so it is not surprising that a rational therapist will find evidence to support his

[2]There is additional material elsewhere in this text that may be valuable in conducting an assessment: Chapter 4, how to write a social history; Chapters 4 and 5, interviewing and counseling (helpful when gathering information from clients and from collateral resources); Chapters 6 and 7, group dynamics; Chapter 8, family functioning and family systems (useful in assessing families); Chapter 9, how to analyze social welfare organizations; Chapter 10, how to assess community needs and how to conduct a community needs assessment; Chapter 12, diversity and populations-at-risk; Chapters 13, 14, 15, 21, and 22, contemporary theories of personality development and psychopathology; Chapter 16, summary of learning theory approaches to conceptualizing behavioral dysfunctions; Chapter 17, a communicating model that has useful concepts in assessing human behavior; Chapter 18, assessing sexual dysfunctions; Chapter 19, gender-role stereotyping and the feminist perspective.

Social and physical environments have immense impacts on human development and behavior.

"theory" in an assessment. For example, adherents of Freudian psychology are much more apt to assess a person as psychotic (because they believe mental illness exists) than are adherents of reality therapy, who believe that mental illness is a myth. (Freudian psychology is summarized in Chapter 13, and reality therapy is described in Chapter 21.)

Most theories of human behavior have not been proven. Many practitioners make the mistake of assuming their favorite theory or theories are factual. When an assessment is based on a theory of human behavior, the practitioner should be aware that the results of the assessment rest on the accuracy of the theory, which has not yet been proven. Practitioners need to realize that their assessment of someone is not "gospel," but only a hypothesis based on unproven theories.

Environmental Systems Emphasis

As described in Chapter 1, social work is increasingly using an ecological perspective in assessing human behavior. The ecological perspective involves considering the adaptive fit of human beings and their environments; that is, the ecology of people in their "life space," which includes all the components of the social and physical environments that have an impact on them. An ecological perspective asserts the importance of assessing the person in the environment. Such an assessment therefore focuses not only on the person but also on the environmental systems that have an impact on him or her.

When assessing environment, the worker should limit his or her attention to those elements that are affecting (positively or negatively) the problem situation. In some cases the elements may be obvious (for example, substandard housing and serious financial problems). In other cases the elements may be subtle (for instance, having aloof parents who give little encouragement).

Although the assessment of environmental factors should be limited to those that impact the client's problematic situations, a number of basic environmental needs are universal. A partial list of these follows:

- Adequate housing
- Safety from hazards and safety from air, noise, and water pollution
- Opportunities for a quality education
- Adequate social support systems (for example, family and relatives, neighbors, friends, and organized groups)
- Access to quality health care
- Access to recreational facilities
- Adequate police and fire protection
- Adequate financial resources to purchase essential items for an acceptable standard of living
- Sufficient food and opportunities for a nutritional diet
- Adequate clothing
- Emotional support from significant others
- Support from significant others to be drug free

Some students majoring in social work have the misconception that a social worker sits in an office and counsels clients. True, counseling is one of the functions that social workers perform. But a worker has many more responsibilities, such as working with groups, working with families, working with organizations, assessing community needs, and working with a variety of groups to meet unmet needs. For most social workers, in-office counseling is only a small fraction of the total services provided. A major part of working with individuals, families, groups, organizations, and communities is assessing environmental systems and then trying to change those systems that are negatively impacting clients. To change environmental systems, a worker may use a variety of skills, such as brokering, advocacy, program development, mediation, research, enabling, and case management. The following are some examples:

- A protective service worker may remove a child from a family in which she is being sexually abused and place her in a foster home.
- A worker may arrange for visiting nurses and Meals on Wheels (home-delivered hot meals for homebound persons) to serve an elderly couple so they can continue to live independently.
- A worker may arrange for homemaker services for a single mother with three young children; such services may involve shopping, cleaning, budgeting, preparing balanced meals, doing the laundry, and teaching these same skills to the mother.
- A worker may get involved with a women's group to work toward developing a shelter for battered women and their children in the community.
- A worker may help a community develop local chapters of needed self-help groups, such as Alcoholics Anonymous, Narcotics Anonymous, and Parents Anonymous.
- For a family in which the husband has a terminal illness, a worker may make a referral to a hospice program.
- A practitioner may work with parents of children with special needs to establish closer collaboration with schoolteachers in order to enhance the children's functioning in school.
- A worker may join with other health professionals in seeking to raise the state's licensing standards for residential treatment centers, nursing homes, or day-care centers.

Assessing Problems

As indicated earlier, assessments are always focused on evaluating the clients' needs and problems. In assessing needs and problems, it is helpful to use the concept *problem system*. Hepworth and Larsen (1986) have defined a problem system as follows:

> The configuration of the client(s), other people, and elements of the environment that interact to produce the problematic situation are designated as the problem system. The problem system revolves around the client's concerns and is limited to those persons and factors directly involved in the client's ecological context. [p. 174]

The following 15 questions are useful guides for assessing problem systems:

1. *What specifically are the problems?* Many problems have several dimensions. It is crucial in an assessment to articulate the subproblems and dimensions of the problem as specifically and accurately as possible. For example, a 27-year-old wife with two children whose husband is killed in a traffic accident caused by a drunk driver may have a variety of needs and problems. She will probably undergo several emotional reactions to the death including denial of the tragedy, depression, anger at the drunk driver, possible guilt over unresolved conflicts she had with her husband, anger that the husband has left her with two children to raise alone, and nightmares. Since intensive grieving is highly stressful, she may come down with one or more stress-related illnesses (such as skin rashes, ulcers, or hypertension). She may seek to escape her problems by using drugs. She is apt to have financial difficulties caused by loss of her husband's income. She will need companionship and emotional support. Her children may have a variety of emotional reactions to the death, which they will need help in handling. She may need help in learning to take on the child care responsibilities that were previously performed by her husband. She may face a sharp reduction in her standard of living with the loss of her husband's income. She may be forced to seek a job (if she is not working) or to seek a higher-paying job. She may be forced to apply for AFDC benefits and have to cope with the embarrassment she may feel about being on welfare. She may need legal help in receiving any death benefits she is entitled to. At some point in the future, she may have to decide whether to begin dating again. For the social worker to do an accurate assessment, he or she must identify, prioritize, and specify these problems and subproblems. Those subproblems that are not identified in an assessment will not be combated in the problem-solving phase.

2. *How does the client view the problems?* The meanings that clients assign to negative events in their lives are often as important, or more important, than the negative events. For example, a woman may end a relationship with a man she has been engaged to for over a year. The man's view of the breakup will largely determine the problems he faces. Let's assume he tells himself the following: "Life is not worth living. My life is ruined forever. I might just as well end it right now." Such a person will be very depressed and perhaps suicidal. These are the problems he then needs help with.

On the other hand, let's assume he tells himself the following: "I'll miss her somewhat, but's probably best we end it now. The last three or four months we apparently grew in different directions. I'm somewhat relieved she broke up with me, as I was thinking about ending the relationship myself. It's easier with both of us wanting out of the relationship. I'll soon find someone else to date." In this case the man will probably be somewhat sad but also relieved that the relationship is over. With such views he may have little need for social services.

3. *Who is involved in the problem system?* The problem system includes all the people who are involved in producing the problematic situation. In the example where the husband was killed in a traffic accident, the problem system would definitely include the surviving wife and her two children. The problem system may also include others who are highly involved with this family, such as in-laws, other relatives, neighbors, friends, or employers. Such people may need help for the grief they are experiencing, and some may also be part of the intervention process by becoming a social support system for the wife and her children. Another problem system that may or may not be identified is the drunk driver and his close family members. The drunk driver and his family may need help for the

guilt and remorse they are experiencing, and the driver is probably also in need of help for his or her drinking problem.

4. *How are the participants involved?* In this aspect of the assessment process, the focus is on identifying the roles that each person plays in the problem system. Some systems become very complex. For example, a multi-problem family may require considerable analysis to determine the roles played by each member. In a multiproblem family, several problems need to be identified. For each problem, each family member may be playing one or more roles. Detailed information is needed about how each person affects and is affected by others and about consequences of events that tend to perpetuate problematic behavior.

5. *What are the causes of the problems?* Frequently, identifying the causes or determinants of problems will suggest ways to intervene. If a husband abuses his wife when he is angry, then instructing him in learning alternative ways to vent his anger (such as jogging or expressing his feelings in an assertive rather than an aggressive manner) may be constructive. If he abuses his wife when under stress, then instructing him in stress management techniques (such as relaxation techniques) may be useful. If he abuses his wife only when intoxicated, he is apt to have a drinking problem and may benefit from an alcohol treatment program.

In making an assessment, remember that all human behavior is purposeful. A powerful way of analyzing human behavior is in terms of

Antecedents → Thought Processes →

Behavior → Consequences

The following is an example:

Antecedent: John Shaw comes home from work intoxicated.
Mrs. Shaw's Thought Processes: "John is spending all of our money on booze.

This is awful. My evening is ruined. Now I'll have to listen to his foolish talk. I am angry at him, and he needs to feel as bad as I do."
Mrs. Shaw's Behavior: Yelling and screaming at her husband for coming home intoxicated.
Consequences: Mr. Shaw becomes defensive. He thinks the verbal abuse is unwarranted, so he decides to "put her in her place" by becoming verbally and physically abusive to her.

In this situation the wife may not be able to stop her husband from drinking or from coming home intoxicated. But she has the power to stop the physical and verbal abuse that she has been suffering when her husband comes home intoxicated. She can, for example, go shopping or make arrangements to stay with someone else whenever her husband comes home intoxicated. She can also decide to separate from her husband. Analyzing behavior in terms of this model often enables practitioners to suggest new response patterns to clients that will break dysfunctional cycles and reduce the damage generated by the problematic behaviors.

What each participant says and does during the problematic event needs to be determined, because the response of each participant is a stimulus to the other participants. Analyzing problematic behavior in terms of this model frequently identifies the stimuli that lead to problematic behaviors. Once the stimuli are identified, interventions can be made to change the stimuli in order to break the dysfunctional cycles.

6. *Where does the problematic behavior occur?* Problematic behavior tends to occur in certain locations and not in others. A child may throw temper tantrums at home, but not at school or when visiting relatives. Perhaps the child has learned that having a tantrum at home will manipulate his parents into giving him what he wants; perhaps he has also learned that throwing a tantrum else-

where will result in ridicule instead of getting what he wants. Identifying where problematic behavior does *not* occur is as important as identifying where it does occur—both may provide clues to identifying factors that trigger the problematic behavior and factors that prevent it from occurring. For example, a married couple may get into heated arguments when they visit the wife's parents but not when they visit the husband's parents. Perhaps there are factors that lead to increased tension when the couple visits the wife's parents—such as the husband's feeling he is being "put down" and not accepted by the wife's parents. An excellent way to determine why arguments occur at the wife's parents' home is to ask each spouse what the arguments were about and why they occurred.

7. *When does the problematic behavior occur?* Closely related to *where* the problematic behavior occurs is the question of *when* it occurs. The process of identifying when problematic behavior occurs and when it does not occur frequently reveals valuable clues to factors that trigger the behavior. If a client frequently becomes depressed at a certain time of year, she may be grieving about a serious loss that occurred at that time some years ago—such as the death of a loved one or a divorce—or she may be suffering from seasonal affective disorder (SAD). Identifying when serious arguments occur for a married couple may suggest factors that trigger the conflict: one or both drinking at a party, one having contact with someone she or he dated in the past, one spouse participating in activities that the other is excluded from, or a misbehaving child (the parents may disagree about discipline). A child may feign a headache or throw a temper tantrum when she has to go someplace she does not want to go, or when she is told to do something (such as studying her spelling words) that she views as unpleasant. A male in a romantic relationship may start talking abut taking his life whenever his woman friend suggests they stop dating. A person with a drinking problem may drink to excess whenever she has intense unwanted emotions, such as anger, frustration, depression, and feelings of insecurity. Once the antecedents that trigger the problematic behavior are identified, the intervention phase can then focus on making the kinds of changes that will reduce the frequency of the problematic behavior.

8. *What is the frequency, intensity, and duration of the problematic behavior?* Someone who becomes intoxicated once or twice a year may not have a drinking problem, whereas someone who becomes intoxicated once or twice a week probably does. Someone who becomes depressed for a day or two every three months probably does not have a serious problem with depression, but someone who is depressed daily certainly does.

Closely related to the frequency of the problematic behavior is its intensity. Someone who is mildly depressed is much more functional than someone who is so severely depressed that he sleeps 15 hours a day, cries frequently during his waking hours, and cannot think rationally. For many other problematic behaviors there are varying degrees of intensity, such as extent of intoxication, extent of violent behavior when angry, intensity of family arguments, and extent of overeating.

The duration of problematic behavior is also an important assessment variable. For example, when someone is intoxicated, how long does she continue to drink to maintain the intoxication? Or, if he is angry or depressed or under high stress, what is the typical duration of problematic behavior? A marital disagreement that lasts three weeks is obviously much more serious than one that lasts 20 minutes.

An assessment of the frequency, intensity, and duration of the problematic behavior helps specify its severity and clarify its impact on the client and members of his or her family.

9. *What is the history of the problematic behavior?* An assessment of the history of a problem often identifies the events that

originally acted as antecedents in triggering the dysfunctional behavior. For example, if an eighth-grade child develops a school phobia, an assessment of the history of the problem would first seek to identify when the phobia began to occur. Once identified, the assessment would focus on identifying what was happening in the child's life at this time that was making her fearful about going to school. Perhaps she was not getting the grades she hoped she would. Perhaps her classmates were making her life miserable. Perhaps her parents were having severe marital conflict and she may erroneously have believed that by staying home she could help ease the marital conflict. Perhaps it is part of a larger anxiety-related problem that has been developing for years. Identifying such antecedents may help in designing an intervention plan to reduce the frequency and severity of the problematic behavior.

However, identifying the antecedents that initially caused the dysfunctional behavior may not fully isolate the current factors that are maintaining the behavior. For example, a child may have developed a school phobia because two of his classmates were "bullying" him. It is possible that those two classmates may have moved to another city. Other factors may now be causing the child to want to stay home, such as being able to watch television, being able to play all day long, and not having any schoolwork to do.

For voluntary clients, it is also often revealing to seek out the *precipitating events* that led them to seek help. Often, their problems have existed for months, even years, and identifying the precipitating events yields valuable information. For example, a person who has been bulimic for two and one-half years sought help after she noticed blood in her vomit, which suggested she might have internal bleeding; she was referred to a physician who found that her esophagus was severely damaged. A married couple who had been arguing periodically for three years sought counseling after they had their first serious physical fight; both were fearful their feuding had entered a new phase that could potentially be life-threatening to both. The precipitating events can usually be identified by the practitioner's asking (and probing) clients to identify the reasons for seeking help at this time.

Involuntary clients usually have a crisis, or a series of crises, that results in their being seen by a practitioner. A practitioner needs to obtain as much information about these crises as possible (often from collateral sources) to determine why an involuntary client is being referred and what his problems are. Such information is also useful in confronting the involuntary client. (Involuntary clients frequently deny they have a problem.)

10. *What does the client want?* A key social work value is to start where the client is. In an initial interview with a client, whether voluntary or involuntary, it is crucially important to address any problems that the client identifies. Failure to do so may leave the client feeling either helpless or annoyed, both of which interfere with the eventual intervention effort. Additionally, too often assessment of problematic situations is made from the practitioner's perspective rather than the client's. An adult services worker for a public welfare department was assigned the following case. A 78-year-old man was living alone in a house on a farm where he had been born and raised. The house was a shambles; it was filthy and had no running water or toilet facilities. Dishes were washed (when they were washed) in rainwater. A small wood-burning stove in the kitchen was used to heat the house. The elderly man was mentally alert but suffered from a variety of minor medical problems: he was overweight and had gout and hypertension. The man drank to excess and also rolled and smoked his own cigarettes, which was a potential fire hazard especially when he was intoxicated. The worker decided it was best for the man to be placed in a nurs-

ing home where adequate care could be given. To the workers' surprise, the man refused and bluntly stated, "I was born and raised here, and I'm going to die here. If you would get a court order to place me in a nursing home, which I don't believe you will be able to get, I'll give up the will to live, and die quickly there." The worker was shocked. She discussed the case with her supervisor, and her supervisor pointed out that she may have been viewing the situation from what she wanted rather than what the client wanted. The worker agreed.

This example points out that what a worker views as being a problematic situation may not be viewed as a problem by a client. If the client chooses to live in a substandard living situation, that is *his* choice— and he has a right to do so, *as long as he is not hurting anyone else in the process.* If, for example, young children were living with this elderly man, then child neglect might have been occurring. In that case, changes in living conditions might need to be made, or the children might need to be removed from the home.

In any assessment it is crucial to accurately obtain the client's view of the problem and what the client wants. If the client's desires are realistic and obtainable, satisfying them should generally be a major goal of the helping process. If what the client wants is not realistic, the reasons that her desires cannot be fulfilled need to be tactfully explained to the client.

11. *How has the client attempted to handle the problem?* The ways in which clients have attempted to cope with their problems provide valuable information during an assessment. Clients may have tried some ways of resolving their problems that did not work. Those strategies can be eliminated from consideration in the problem-solving phase.

Perhaps clients have tried some strategies that were partially successful. Perhaps with increased effort or some modifications, they will work. For example, a client suffering from a high level of stress had learned in the past to relax by using imagery relaxation. However, she did not think of using the technique when she was highly anxious or frustrated. She was instructed to set aside 15 minutes every morning before going to work and 15 minutes in the evening, to practice the technique. (See Chapter 20 for a description of imagery relaxation.) Structuring imagery relaxation into daily activities proved to be a useful way of helping her combat the stress.

Examining the strategies that clients have used to try to resolve their problems may also reveal valuable information about their coping and problem-solving skills. If clients have marked deficits in problem solving, it may be helpful to instruct them in the no-lose problem-solving approach (see Chapter 20 for a description of this approach.)

Some clients may respond to interpersonal difficulties by becoming passive or nonassertive. Others may respond to interpersonal conflict by becoming aggressive. If either is the case, it may be desirable to instruct clients in using assertiveness to handle interpersonal conflict (see Chapter 16 for a description of assertiveness training).

Some clients have good problem-solving and interpersonal skills in some situations but not in others. For example, a schoolteacher was able to handle disruptive students in his classroom but was ineffective in dealing with his own children. A closer examination revealed that he was divorced and was fearful that if he disciplined his children they would want to live with his ex-wife. Through counseling he came to realize that his children would respect him more if he more clearly specified and enforced behavioral limits. Once this was accomplished, he was able to use the same child management skills he used in the classroom with his own children.

12. *What skills does the client need to combat the problem?* An assessment of a problematic situation should also identify the skills that clients need to resolve their difficulties. If a

parent is having difficulties with a child, specific skills that may be needed include listening, negotiating, setting limits, following through on consequences, and nurturing. If a couple is having marital conflicts, they may need problem-solving, communication, listening, and conflict management skills. (Sometimes helping such a couple learn these skills may be more productive in the long run than helping them resolve their present conflicts.) If a client frequently loses considerable sums of money while gambling, he may need to learn how to say no assertively when his friends ask him to play poker or go to the racetrack. If a client is depressed, she may need to learn what she can do to counter the depression (see Chapters 22 and 23 for some strategies).

13. *What external resources are needed to combat the problem?* An assessment should identify not only the skills that clients need to combat their problems but also the external resources they need. A single mother on AFDC may need day-care services, transportation, and job training to help her become employable. Someone addicted to gambling may need a self-help group, such as Gamblers Anonymous, to give him the emotional support and guidance he needs to combat his addiction. A bulimic may need medical attention to assess and treat physical damage from binging and purging, one-to-one counseling to stop the binge-purge cycle, support from a self-help eating disorders group, and instruction in what is a nutritious and well-balanced diet. Once an assessment is made, a social worker often acts as a broker or case manager in connecting clients with needed services and resources. Frequently, some or all of the needed services are not provided by the practitioner's agency and arrangements need to be made for the services to be provided by other agencies, organizations, self-help groups, and natural support systems (such as neighbors, family members, fellow workers, church groups, and social groups).

A Meals on Wheels volunteer delivers food to an elderly man. Meals on Wheels is an external resource that helps elderly people live independently.

14. *What are the client's resources, skills, and strengths?* As mentioned earlier in this chapter, a quality assessment also identifies the resources, strengths, and skills that clients already possess to combat their problems. The importance of identifying such strengths has been described. Sometimes problems are resolved by enabling clients to apply to their problematic behavior the resources and skills they already have. Clients who have frequent stress-related illnesses may learn, through counseling, that greater application of the following techniques will help them relax and reduce their high stress levels: positive thinking, problem solving rather than "awfulizing" about their problems, using social support systems, and being more assertive with significant others in expressing their feelings and concerns. A couple who has marital problems may find their relationship improving when they seek to treat each other with the same kind of respect that they give to strangers and acquaintances; many spouses use tact in communicating with acquaintances but not in communicating with each other. A person who is grieving about the death of a loved one may find that discussing her grief with

friends and relatives not only helps ventilate her grief but also helps in developing a social support system for putting her life back together.

15. *What are the recommended courses of action?* The recommended courses of action have also been called the *treatment plan* and the *intervention plan*. Once a client's difficulties and strengths have been assessed, the next step is to set goals and arrive at a course of action to accomplish the goals. Some authorities conceptualize goal setting and specifying recommended courses of action as a process that follows an assessment. However, in social work practice most assessments contain a recommended course of action; therefore, this process is discussed briefly here.

The goals should be jointly agreed to by the client and the worker and should be realistic and obtainable. The goals should be geared to resolving the identified problems and should be stated in such a way that they are operational and measurable. An *operational goal* can be directly translated into a course of action so the goal can be accomplished. For example, for a nonassertive client, an operational goal might be to learn to be assertive with significant others; assertiveness training can be used as the course of action to accomplish this goal. A *measurable goal* can be measured in its contribution to achieving the goal. One way to measure whether a client is making progress in becoming more assertive with significant others is for the client to record for two weeks the number of times he is assertive and nonassertive in interactions with significant others. The client is then given training in being assertive. After the training he again records for another two weeks the number of times he is assertive and nonassertive in interactions with significant others. If the proportion of being assertive after treatment is higher than before treatment, measurable progress toward accomplishing the goal has occurred.

The stated courses of action should be realistic and obtainable. They also should usually be agreed to by the client; if the client disagrees with these courses of action she is unlikely to carry them out. (With some involuntary clients, there are exceptions to this guideline. For example, a parolee may not agree with the parole officer's assessment that her violation of the rules of parole warrants a recommendation to the court for a return to prison.)

The stated courses of action should usually be selected through the following process. After a goal has been set, the client and the worker should generate a list of feasible courses of action to accomplish the goal. The strengths and shortcomings of each alternative should be considered. Then, the client and the worker should usually select the course of action.

In some settings the worker or the clinical team selects the recommended courses of action, with minimal input from the client. For example, when an assessment is done for an elderly person's admission application for a nursing home, the recommendation will usually be based on the extent to which the elderly person's characteristics meet the nursing home's criteria for admission.

A Systems Perspective: The Pincus-Minahan Model[3]

A systems perspective emphasizes looking beyond a client's presenting problems to assess the complexities and interrelationships of problems. Through a systems analysis of a case, the most effective intervention targets

---

[3]The material on a systems perspective was especially written for this text by Donald Nolan, M.S.S.W., BCD (Board Certified Diplomate in Clinical Social Work). Mr. Nolan is a clinical social worker in private practice.

and strategies can usually be identified. (A system is a regularly interacting or interdependent group of items forming a unified whole.) To understand how to use systems theory and systems analysis, one can work from many systems models. The most publicized systems model in social work literature is the Pincus-Minahan (1973) approach.

In 1973 Allen Pincus and Anne Minahan wrote *Social Work Practice: Model and Method*, which to many has become the primary way of applying systems analysis to social work practice. Their basic premise is that a *common core* of skills and concepts is essential to the practice of social work (Pincus & Minahan, 1973, p. xi). Assessment skills are part of the common core of skills needed by social work practitioners.

Pincus and Minahan theorized that there are four basic systems in social work practice: a change agent system, a client system, a target system, and an action system. The *change agent* system is composed of professionals who are employed specifically for the purpose of creating planned change. The employing organizations of the change agents (Pincus & Minahan, 1973, p. 54) are also part of this system. The term *employing organization* is important, because Pincus and Minahan viewed only *paid* individuals as change agents. A change agent, then, is a professional who is employed specifically for the purpose of creating planned change.

The *client system* is composed of the people who sanction or *ask* for the change agent's services, who are the expected beneficiaries of the service, *and* who have a working agreement or contract with the change agent (Pincus & Minahan, 1973, p. 56). *Client* is used here in a more limited sense than is often used by social workers, precluding the possibility of "doing things" for people or organizations without their knowledge or agreement.

The *target system* is composed of the people, agencies, and/or organizational practices that the worker wishes to change in some *measurable* way in order to reach the goals of

the change agent(s) (Pincus & Minahan, 1973, p. 59). Through analyzing the changes of the target system, the worker can measure effectiveness and provide a mechanism for accountability.

The last defined system is the *action system*. This term is used to describe those with whom the social worker works to accomplish the tasks and achieve the goals of the change effort (Pincus & Minahan, 1973, p. 61). The worker may need to involve numerous different action systems in different aspects of a planned change effort to accomplish all the different goals of the change agent(s). The concepts of strategies and outcome goals are also used to further differentiate how action systems and target systems are developed and utilized. Figure 3.1 displays the basic conceptualizations in the Pincus-Minahan model.

Although data assessment is formally displayed in this model as occurring within the target system, assessment also occurs within the client and the change agent systems. As noted earlier in this chapter, specifying the problem and its causes is a step in assessment. The assessment process also involves analyzing the client's perception of the problem and assessing who and how others are involved in the client system. In developing a target system, the practitioner must consider the history of problematic behavior as well as where and when it occurs. Assessing the frequency and intensity of problematic behavior and past attempts to solve the problem are also important in the development of goals within a target system. In addition, this systems approach helps a practitioner develop targets for change; it presents a framework for analyzing client needs and wants and the external resources that may have to be developed or modified. Changes that a client needs to make in order to improve also become targets for change through a comprehensive assessment. The information thus acquired is then put into an action plan through which recommended courses of action are developed. Ongoing assessment continues to oc-

Figure 3.1
The basic conceptualizations of the Pincus-Minahan model

cur in the implementation and evaluation phases.

The four systems presented in Figure 3.1 are not mutually exclusive but can and do overlap in many cases. Such overlap is illustrated in Figure 3.2.

The Pincus-Minahan model is illustrated by the case example on page 94.

Another example (page 98) demonstrates how systems analysis can be applied in a clinical setting. Psychiatric social work has long been seen as different or distinct from other types of social work practice: Its roots are more clinical and psychoanalytic than those of generalist social work practice. Also some authorities view a clinical approach as being more limited in scope (for example, social ac-

tion and macropractice approaches are seldom used in clinical practice) than a generalistic practice approach. The assessment process is similar in all settings, although comprehensiveness and specifics may be different. In this example the major focus of a systems analysis approach is on analyzing the client's presenting problem. This analysis is done by a social worker who has had extensive training in systems analysis and considerable experience in using the approach. The case example demonstrates that after a practitioner gains experience in using the approach she can do much of the analysis "in her head," rather than writing out the components in diagrams, as was done with the previous example.

Figure 3.2
Examples of the association and overlap between various systems in the Pincus-Minahan model

Case Example
In a school setting

Richard Thomas is a social worker in a school setting. He gets a referral from a teacher, Mr. Phillips, that one of his students, John Hecht, a third-grade boy, is not behaving well in class (not complying with teacher directions, not listening, and not completing assignments). The teacher asks Mr. Thomas to counsel the student to improve his attitude—a simple-enough referral, and one in which the problem could be seen as one of motivation or attitude. A number of counseling sessions could be beneficial; and given time limitations, this is often the way social workers would intervene in this case. The implicit assumption is that there is an identified problem (the student), and to solve this problem the student must change. However, by not analyzing the problem more fully, the worker may miss a number of other problems in this situation.

In using systems analysis as an approach to assess the problem, Mr. Thomas would first list the presenting problems and then decide who his client is in this situation. Using the prior definition of what determines a client, only the teacher and in some sense Mr. Thomas's employing organization can be defined as clients at this point. John or his parents may be potential clients in the future (see Figure 3.3).

The next phase of analyzing this case is to establish clear targets. Going back to Figure 3.1, this part of the analysis involves more thorough investigation and assessment of the data and then the development of long-range or outcome goals as the targets are identified. Exhibit 3.1 shows the beginning step in this assessment stage.

Within the data assessment phase, outcome goals need to be developed. Then targets must be established to accomplish these outcome goals. This continuing process of assessment is diagrammed in Exhibit 3.2 (page 96).

At this point, goals and targets have been identified and it is now necessary to develop an action system. The first part of this process, as seen in Figure 3.1, is the determination of strategies. (Determination of strategies is a later part of the assessment process.) These strategies must be linked to the targets and must be individualized to meet the needs of the target population. Systems analysis firmly requires that the intervention strategies that are applied should not be based on the worker's favorite techniques but on the worker's objective professional judgments about which strategies will most effectively meet the clients' needs. For example, a worker may desire to use small-group intervention skills at which she is particularly adept, but these skills would be applied only when systems analysis suggests such an approach is the best way to change a target and ultimately accomplish a goal. Exhibit 3.3 (page 97) shows the development of strategies as the first step in developing an action system.

Now that consistent outcome goals, targets, and strategies have been developed, the next step of applying systems analysis is to plan the *implementation stage* of the action system (see Figure 3.1). Often the social worker uses personal judgment as to what is practical and feasible at the time. Additionally, the worker prioritizes needs according to the most immediate and pressing needs of the client(s). Of course, the worker must also be prepared to reassess the strategies as intervention progresses, through observing the extent to which the desired *outcomes* are occurring. There may

(continued)

Presenting problems

John Hecht, a third-grade student, is:

a. not complying with teacher's directions.

b. not listening.

c. not completing assisgnments.

Client system

Actual:

The teacher (Mr. Phillips) has asked for help, expects to benefit, and has a contract through the school system for the social worker to provide help. The school system that employs Mr. Thomas is also a client.

Potential

John and/or his family may want to ask for help in the future. They may also be expected beneficiaries of help in the future. As yet, they have not contracted for help.

Chage agent system

a. School social worker, Mr. Thomas.

b. The school system that employs Mr. Thomas

Note: Additional change agents may be included later when the systems analysis approach is further developed.

Figure 3.3
The first steps of the systems analysis approach in the John Hecht case

Exhibit 3.1
Data assessment in the John Hecht case

The social worker, Mr. Thomas, seeks to develop a target system. He begins by collecting the following data:

A. The student's behavior in class is more complicated than originally reported. The student is often belittled by the teacher and frequently ignored when he asks for help. Additional in-class observations show that many other students also demonstrate inappropriate behavior. The teacher, Mr. Phillips, appears to have difficulty with classroom control. Also, conversations with him reveal that he has a pattern of negative comments toward low-income students.

B. The student's attendance is a matter of concern. Over the past two years, John has averaged approximately 25 percent nonattendance. He also is not completing much of his schoolwork, is not following directions, and is being disruptive. Further assessment shows that John is not relating very well to his peers.

C. On talking with John's mother, a single parent, Mr. Thomas finds a pattern of school absences by the other two children in the family and a home situation reflecting economic problems, family disorganization, and questionable knowledge of parenting skills. In discussions with other teachers that John has had, and other school faculty who "know of" the family, the social worker finds concerns about parental supervision at home, including the suspicion that John's mother has problems with alcohol abuse and is often not home.

Case Example

In a school setting *(continued)*

also be changes in client and change agent systems along the way as continuing assessment occurs. In this case the change agent system now includes not only the school social worker but also the school principal, the referring teacher as he alters his teaching style, the school guidance counselor, and social workers from the County Social Services Department in the areas of financial assistance, child management training, and protective services. In addition, some potential clients (such as John and his mother) may also become actual clients during the implementation phase of the action system.

In forming action systems that involve other agencies and other professionals, a key social work goal is to keep the process moving. Often the referring social worker should serve as an advocate of the client and of the outcome goals of the systems analysis. It is often necessary to restate these goals to others and to find ways to encourage other change agents to continue to provide services when "roadblocks" are encountered. In fact, monitoring or continuing to assess the progress should be expected; a systems analysis approach implies that there will be a group of people working *together* and thus there will be a need for coordination and direction.

It is also imperative to *evaluate* and stabilize the change effort after a prescribed amount of time. This evaluation (another part of overall assessment) should measure the extent to which the *initial outcome goals* of the target system are being accomplished.

Not all cases are as complicated as this one or involve as many targets and action systems. This case did in fact exist, and assessment and strategy were developed as described. However, many, and perhaps most, social work cases are complicated. As such, systems analysis can help the worker understand the complexities of the case and the overall complexities of assessment. Systems analysis can be applied by virtually all social workers.

Exhibit 3.2

Determination of outcome goals and of targets in the John Hecht case

Determination of Outcome Goals	*Determination of Targets*
(These goals represent the goals that were set in John Hecht's case, and relate to the three sets of problems identified in the beginning data assessment stage in Exhibit 3.1).	(These targets identify the focuses of the change effort.)
A. Improve the teacher's classroom control and attitude toward students.	A. Target: Mr. Phillips, the teacher 　1. Attitudes toward low-income students. 　2. Shortcomings in classroom control.
B. Improve John's behavior, attendance, and peer relationships in school.	B. Target: John Hecht 　1. Inappropriate attitudes and behaviors in school. 　2. Inadequate peer relationships. 　3. Frequent absences from school.
C. Bring more stability to John's home situation.	C. Target: The Hecht family 　1. Financial difficulties. 　2. Mrs. Hecht's lack of management skills and inadequate supervision of children. 　3. The possibility of alcohol abuse by Mrs. Hecht.

Exhibit 3.3
Determination of strategies in the John Hecht case

A. Target: Mr. Phillips, a third-grade teacher.
  1. Discuss concerns about Mr. Phillips's attitudes toward low-income students with the school principal and ask that the principal help by providing educational supervision in this area; that is, by arranging an in-service training session for teachers on (a) the societal conditions that contribute to the financial and family change problems that are occurring in the area, (b) the destructive effects on low-income students of teachers' negative attitudes, and (c) the benefits for low-income students of a nonjudgmental attitude by teachers. Ask that the principal help Mr. Phillips individualize more of his assignments for students so he can better recognize individual differences and can give students academic work that is at their individual grade level.
  2. Discuss the issues of classroom management with Mr. Phillips and provide material on behavioral strategies of positive and negative reinforcement. Explore with Mr. Phillips the benefits of developing some type of student charting system so John (and potentially other students) can work toward goals on a daily basis. Finally, consult with Mr. Phillips periodically about problematic behavior in his classroom, problem-solve these situations, and provide suggestions on more effective techniques for controlling disruptive student behavior.

B. Target: John Hecht.
  1. Provide supportive counseling to John on issues of developing more constructive ways of confronting others, developing goals as a learner, and developing responsibility for his actions. The need for supportive counseling is evident in order to develop rapport with John, to help John develop more effective problem-solving skills, and to demonstrate a positive adult role model.
  2. Talk to the school guidance counselor about the possibility of John's joining one of the small groups the counselor is currently leading, or joining one in the future. This could help John improve his relationships with other students. Additionally, discuss with the counselor the need for developing a classroom guidance program, perhaps for the entire school, directed toward improving human relations.
  3. Refer the problem of frequent absences to the Protective Services Unit of the County Social Services Department, as a case of unexcused absences or truancy. This referral will bring to the change effort the resources of another agency to help with the overall family difficulties. This referral also provides the County Social Services Department with an access point to the family.

C. Target: The Hecht family.
  1. Inform Protective Services of the family's economic difficulties and ask them to investigate whether the family is receiving all the financial assistance they are eligible for, and whether financial counseling is needed to better budget the family's resources.
  2. After assessing the seriousness of the home management difficulties, refer this matter to the County Social Services Department. Realistically, this difficulty will involve the same Protective Services worker (at least as a case manager) who received the referral for truancy and financial assistance. The Protective Services worker may well ask other workers to provide certain services to this family, such as involving the mother in a Parent Effectiveness Training class (see Chapter 20). It is important that timing the involvement of several workers not overwhelm the family. Together with Mrs. Hecht and the social workers from the County Social Services Department, develop a treatment plan to help Mrs. Hecht improve her knowledge of child development and parenting/behavioral practices. This plan may involve individual counseling, involvement in a parenting group, or demonstrating behavioral practices through modeling.
  3. Investigate the alleged alcohol abuse further and then decide whether to refer Mrs. Hecht for alcohol and other drug abuse assessment, which is provided by the County Social Services Department. Since Mrs. Hecht also appears somewhat depressed and lacking in energy, an adult psychiatric referral may also be considered in the future. Additionally, since alcohol problems are also not unidimensional, suggest that the County Social Services Department assist Mrs. Hecht in finding employment or in receiving job training. Also, it is likely that Mrs. Hecht will need some support (either through group or individual counseling) to help meet the demands of being a single parent.

Case Example
In a clinical setting

Jane Angell comes to a private mental health facility with vague concerns of unhappiness. She is referred by a friend. The psychiatric social worker explains that a thorough assessment needs to occur before a treatment plan can be developed. Ms. Angell is the client system at this point. Terra Montana (a social worker), and the clinic where she practices, compose the initial change agent system. Because there are complaints that suggest a possibility of depression, Ms. Montana needs to identify and examine Ms. Angell's symptoms as part of the assessment. Some types of depression are now viewed as having contributing factors that are considered "medical" in nature. Depression is an affective disorder with a number of distinguishing symptoms. Some current research suggests that depression is partly caused by chemical imbalances within the brain and central nervous system (Coryell et al., 1988; Rasmussen & Tsuang, 1986). Imbalances in chemicals called neurotransmitters that transmit messages from one nerve cell to another are theorized to cause problems with dysphoria (marked and persistent unhappiness, often without specific cause) as well as difficulties with concentration and often worry and guilt.[4] Environmental stressors also play a role and are often seen as "triggers" that may eventually lead to neurotransmitter imbalance in susceptible individuals. Ms. Montana, in assessing mental health issues in the client, needs to find out the following:

1. What is the client's current perception of her problems? What is the history of the depression including history of past treatment, successful or not?
2. Are there disturbances of sleep, including nightmares or night terrors, sudden awakening, early morning awakenings, insomnia, or excessive sleep? What is the overall quality and history of sleep behaviors?
3. Are there disturbances of appetite, including loss or lack of appetite, periods of binging or purging of food, and/or specific *avoidance* of certain foods?
4. Is there a history of headaches? If so, specifically when and how often do these headaches occur? Do the headaches cause accompanying nausea, fatigue, or difficulty going outside because of light sensitivity? Do they cluster together? Is there history of sinus trouble and if so has this been medically assessed?
5. Is there a history of stomachaches or other gastrointestinal difficulties, such as chronic constipation or diarrhea? Did these difficulties also occur in childhood?
6. Is there a history of somatic or physical complaints, such as backaches, joint or knee pains, a general feeling of malaise or not feeling well? Has the individual sought medical care? If so, is there history of "doctor hopping," perhaps because physicians cannot find medically diagnosable conditions?

[4]There are several excellent resources for a comprehensive discussion of depression: Nancy Andreasen, *The Broken Brain* (New York: Harper & Row, 1985), and Paul Wender and D. Klein, *Mind, Mood and Medicine* (New York: Meridian Publishers, 1968). Additionally, specific diagnostic criteria for depression are found in the American Psychiatric Association's *The Diagnostic and Statistical Manual of Mental Disorders*, 3rd ed., rev. (*DSM-III-R*), (Washington, D.C.: American Psychiatric Association, 1987).

7. Is there history of anxiety and/or worry? How dysfunctional is this? Are there specific phobias that interfere in the person's lifestyle? Is there history of panic behaviors; that is, a sudden feeling of intense anxiety and uneasiness often accompanied by rapid heartbeat, difficulties in breathing, intense perspiring, and at times fear?

8. How does the client perceive what are normally pleasant times, such as birthdays and holidays? Is there any seasonal nature to the depression?[5]

9. Are there difficulties in sexual functioning and/or desire? If there are, how does the client interpret these? Is there past history of rape or incest?

10. What is the client's prevalent mood? Is there history of fearfulness and crying, ruminating, worry, feelings of worthlessness, and/or thoughts of death or suicide? Has her mood generally been stable and predictable or are there substantial variations sometimes associated with excess energy or manic feelings?

11. Does the client have difficulty concentrating and remembering things?

12. How is the client functioning at home, at her job, and within her social context? Is she chronically tired? Does she feel "slowed down"? What are her family or friends telling her about her actions or moods? If married, what is the status of the marital relationship? If there are children in the family, how is the client relating to them?

13. Is there history of obsessive unwanted thoughts or compulsive actions, such as pacing or hand wringing?

14. Is there current alcohol or drug abuse, including abuse of prescription medications (such as Valium or other minor tranquilizers)? Is the client in denial of these problems? Is there any past history of treatment?

15. What is the client's history as a child and teenager and how does she view her parent(s)? Does she view her parent(s) as contributing or helping with past or current problems? Are there dysfunctional ways of thinking that were developed in childhood (for example, the client viewing herself as a "bad child" as a result of being an adult child of an alcoholic)?

16. How did the client function in school, including history of past learning problems or disabilities, social interactions, patterns of dealing with school stresses and pressures, and possible past feelings of failure?

17. What is the client's personal medical history including relevant illnesses, exposure to toxins, medications used, allergies, and accidents? Has specialized medical care or previous psychiatric consultation occurred? How does the client view medical practitioners? If female and previously pregnant, were there problems associated with postpartum depression or possible termination of pregnancies?

18. What is the client's genetic history? Since certain types of depression are often seen as biologically or genetically influenced, a very careful and thorough history is essential.

(continued)

---

[5]There is a condition called seasonal affective disorder that seems to coincide with winter seasons and corresponding low amounts of daylight.

Although this type of assessment is time-consuming, it is necessary in psychiatrically oriented social work practice. In developing change agent, client, target, and action systems for this case, information related to these areas is used in combination with information about environmental stressors and client strengths to develop a treatment plan. In this example, Ms. Angell is assessed as having many of the physical and emotional symptoms of depression. Since she has not seen her personal physician in some time, she needs a comprehensive physical. She will then need a psychiatric consultation to confirm a diagnosis of depression and to determine whether any medications may help in an overall treatment plan. Because current research indicates that some depression may be related to neurochemical imbalances, antidepressant medication may be necessary to restore the balance. Ms. Angell, who is married and has two young children, also is assessed to have difficulties in these family relationships. Family therapy will become part of the action system, with targets of her husband and children. Mr. Angell does not understand his wife's difficulties with depression. He is often angry with her and blames her for being depressed. He needs to understand better why she is depressed and to be aware of what he and the children can do to help alleviate the depression. The children have behavioral problems at home, and therefore he and his wife need to develop (together with the therapist) an agreed-on discipline plan. The couple also needs to increase their capacities to listen and to communicate with each other. Ms. Angell also has past feelings of worthlessness, derived in part from feeling that her parents viewed her as a failure. She needs individual therapy to counter and change her negative views of herself (see Chapter 22) and to improve her capacities to be assertive with her husband and her parents (see Chapter 16). Job stress also appears to trigger problems with depression. Ms. Angell may need to reconsider her job demands (or her vocation itself); she may even need career counseling. Thus, a presenting problem of generalized unhappiness becomes a system of interrelating difficulties and numerous targets. As targets and action strategies are developed, client and change systems are also more fully developed. The overall change effort with this case involves the development of a treatment plan that evolves from a systems analysis of Ms. Angell's problems and life circumstances.

Summary

Assessment is a critical process in social work practice. The selection of goals and interventions largely depends on the assessment. An assessment should include not only what is wrong with a client but also the client's resources, skills, and strengths that can be used in resolving difficulties and promoting growth. Too often, in the past, assessments have focused only on clients' shortcomings and pathology.

The nature of the assessment process varies significantly with the type of setting in which the social worker practices. In some settings the social worker makes an independent assessment, and in other settings the social worker is a member of a clinical team that makes an assessment. An assessment is, in essence, a working hypothesis of a client's difficulties and resources based on current data. As time passes, assessments have to be revised and updated as changes occur in the client and in his or her environment.

Data used in making an assessment are derived from various sources: the client's verbal report, assessment forms, collateral sources, psychological tests, the client's nonverbal behavior, home visits, observation of client interacting with significant others, and the worker's gut feelings from interacting with the client.

To do a quality assessment, a worker needs an extensive knowledge of human behavior and the social environment. An assessment may require knowledge about multifarious systems, biophysical factors, behavioral factors, motivational factors, family systems, and environmental factors. Such knowledge is obtained from a variety of courses that social work majors typically take in college. The purpose of an assessment is to give focus to the kinds of factors that are examined.

The theory or theories of human behavior that a practitioner uses in making an assessment will have a major influence on what is examined during the assessment. What a worker examines in conducting an assessment has a large effect on the outcome. Since most theories of human behavior have not been proven, practitioners need to be aware that their assessment of someone is only a hypothesis that is based on unproven theories.

Social work is increasingly using an ecological perspective to assess human behavior. An ecological perspective asserts that it is important to assess the person-in-environment. This chapter presented 15 questions that serve as guides for what to examine in conducting an assessment.

Systems theory is a way of conceptualizing problems and forming action/treatment plans. Through systems analysis of a situation, the social worker can attempt to understand the relative importance of the many influences in the client's life. As a way of expanding on a presenting problem, the social worker can conceptualize issues in terms of client, change agent, target, and action systems in order to determine goals and strategies in a planned change effort. A systems perspective highlights the importance of looking beyond the client's presenting problems in order to assess the complexities of his or her life. A dynamic balance exists between individuals and their environments. Assessment, using a systems analysis approach, seeks to understand this balance so compensating changes can improve the client's life within an environment of systems included in the change effort.

Exercises

1. Writing an assessment

> *Goal:* This exercise is designed to give students experience in writing an assessment.

> *Step 1:* Explain the purpose of the exercise. Summarize the 15 questions in the chapter as guides for information to focus on in writing an assessment. (As an alternative, the students may read these questions in the text.)

> *Step 2:* Ask a student to volunteer to come up with a *contrived* problem prior to the next class period. At the next class period, interview the volunteer about the contrived problem. The other students in the class should then independently write up an assessment that covers the following topics:

a. Specific problems.
b. Client's views of problems.
c. People involved in the problem system.
d. Roles of participants in problem system.
e. Causes of problems.
f. Where problematic behavior occurs.
g. When problematic behavior occurs.
h. Frequency, intensity, and duration of problematic behavior.
i. History of the problematic behavior.
j. Client's goals regarding this problematic behavior.
k. Strategies client has used to handle the problem.
l. Skills client needs to resolve the problem.
m. External resources needed to combat the problem.
n. Client's resources, skills, and strengths.
o. Recommended courses of action.

During the interview, ask questions that will provide the data to be written up for all the topics except the last. Then inform the students that they need to cover all of the above topics, with a significant percentage (perhaps 40 percent) of their grade for this assignment being based on the quality of their response to "Recommended courses of action."

Step 3: Have the students write up the assessment and turn in it at a later class period. Grade the papers. Before returning the papers, read one or two responses (without identifying the names of the writers) to the section "Recommended courses of action" in order to give the students one or two examples of a high-quality recommendation.

Step 4: End the exercise by having the students discuss the merits and shortcomings of this assignment.

2. Identifying client and change agent systems[6]

Goal: The purpose of this exercise is to give students practice in determining client and change agent systems.

Step 1: Explain the goal of this exercise and then review the definitions of client and change agent systems.

Step 2: In each of the following situations, have *students* individually write down who is part of the client system and of the change agent system. Students can identify actual and potential categories in each of these systems.

a. A mother and her son come to a social services agency seeking food and shelter.

[6]Exercises 2 and 3 were specially written for this text by Donald Nolan, M.S.S.W., BCD (Board Certified Diplomate in Clinical Social Work). Mr. Nolan is a clinical social worker in private practice.

b. A social worker employed by a public mental health center asks a psychiatrist for a consultation regarding whether a young woman the social worker has seen is clinically depressed.

c. A social worker in a hospital setting is asked by a nurse to talk with a single mother who has just given birth to her first child. The young woman's parents may also have some concerns and are presently visiting her.

d. A high school student is taken by his parents to a social worker in private practice because the parents are concerned with their son's violence and destructive behavior.

Step 3: Discuss each one of these situations with the class, asking students to share their answers. Use a blackboard if possible to write down the answers given by students.

Step 4: Discuss how each of these situations may change over time, thereby changing the elements in the client and change agent systems. Use the fourth situation to show this process by adding more data and a time sequence to the case.

3. Forming target and action systems

Goal: The purpose of this exercise is to give students practice in developing target and action systems.

Step 1: Review Figure 3.1 with the students, writing it on a blackboard if possible.

Step 2: Using the following situation, devise outcome goals, targets, and strategies. Remember that there should be some logical consistency between each outcome goal, the targets for that goal to be achieved, and the strategies to be used for achieving that goal (see Exhibits 3.2 and 3.3).

You are a social worker employed by a family services agency. Through your involvement with the juvenile court with a number of delinquency cases, a judge refers to you a group of teenagers who are required to attend weekly court-ordered counseling sessions. In your data-gathering or assessment process, you find out that these teenagers all come from the same large public housing complex in a low-income section of the city. This part of the city is considered a problem area by the police department because of high rates of crime and high unemployment among adults. Numerous social service and volunteer organizations are involved with this part of the community, but there seems to be no coordination among them. There is a neighborhood organization, but few people attend its meetings. The school is concerned about a high truancy rate and a high dropout rate. You have heard that the managers of the public housing complex in the area have generally discouraged the formation of tenant organizations, and there are serious problems in the maintenance of the apartments. As a result, there is a high rate of mobility in and out of the complex.

Step 3: Now go back and have the class identify the client systems and change agent systems in this situation.

4

Social Work with Individuals: Interviewing

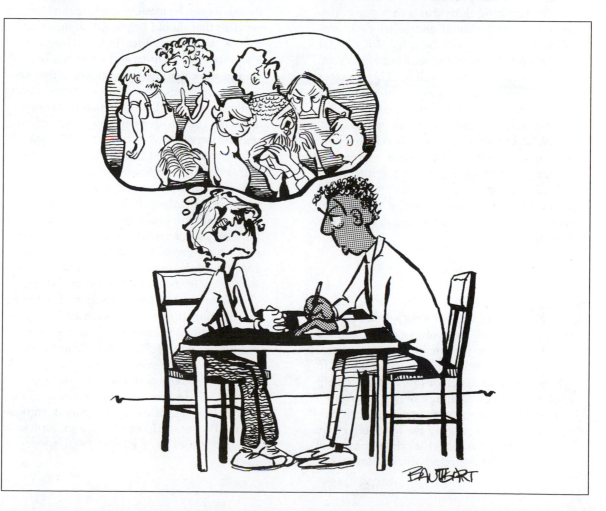

Social work practice with individuals is aimed at helping individuals on a one-to-one basis to meet personal and social problems. Perhaps the two most essential skills social workers need in working with individuals are interviewing and counseling. This chapter presents material on how to interview; the next chapter focuses on how to counsel. This chapter covers types of social work interviews, how to begin and close interviews, how to phrase questions, note taking, and use of audiotapes and videotapes while interviewing. Workers spend a great deal of their time interviewing, and much of what they are responsible for depends on what they learn from these interviews.

Three Types of Social Work Interviews

Most social work interviews can be classified as informational (to obtain data for a social study or for a social history), assessment (to arrive at an appraisal), or therapeutic (to help clients change). Often, there is overlap among these three types. For example, a protective services worker in the initial interview with a couple suspected of child abuse will often obtain background information about the family members and seek to arrive at an appraisal of whether child abuse has occurred. If abuse is occurring, the worker may also begin helping the families make changes to end further abuse. In spite of overlap, these three types of interviews differ in the way they are structured and conducted.

Informational or Social History Interviews

Informational interviews are designed to obtain background or life history material related to the client's personal or social problem. The purpose is not to learn all there is to know about a client's background but to seek information that will enable the worker (or agency) to better understand the client so that decisions can be made regarding the kinds of services that should be provided. Information that is sought includes both objective facts and subjective feelings and attitudes. In addition to the client, parents, friends, other relatives, employers, and other agencies having contact with the client (such as social service agencies, police departments, and schools) may be interviewed or contacted. The specific information desired in a social history varies somewhat from agency to agency. An adoption agency, for example, would be more interested in information about the child-rearing philosophies of potential adoptive parents as compared to a sheltered workshop, which would be more interested in the specific work capacities of potential clients. As the social history example in Exhibit 4.1 shows, a social history usually has fact sheet information (name, age, occupation, and so on) and then information about the presenting question or problem, early childhood experiences and development, family background, school performance, dating and marital history, employment history, contact with other agencies, and general impressions. The desired objectives and format of social histories vary greatly from agency to agency.

A few examples of informational interviews follow. A social worker at a mental hospital may seek background information to better understand the problems and social functioning of an inpatient. A probation officer may be asked to do a social investigation to guide the court in dealing with someone charged with a felony. A worker for a community welfare council may be asked to interview people in a multiproblem neighborhood to identify what they view as their most urgent unmet needs. A worker at a nursing home may do a social history on a new resident to obtain information on current social and personal problems and on special interests, so the resident can be better understood.

Assessment Interviews

Assessment or decision-making interviews are generally more focused in purpose than informational interviews. Assessment interviews differ from informational interviews in that the questions asked in assessment interviews are focused more on making *specific* decisions involving human services. Examples include the following. A protective service worker investigates a child abuse complaint to make a judgment about whether abuse is occurring. A public assistance worker interviews an unmarried woman who is pregnant to determine eligibility for a grant. A vocational rehabilitation counselor interviews a client with a developmental disability to determine eligibility for a range of services including financial assistance, vocational training, and sheltered workshop participation. A social worker at a residential facility for persons with developmental disabilities interviews the parents of a child with a severe cognitive disability to obtain decision-making information that will be used by the admissions committee to determine whether the child should be admitted. A director of a group home for adolescent boys interviews a youth on juvenile probation who is having se-

vere conflict with his parents to determine whether the youth might benefit from the group home, or perhaps needs to be placed in a correctional school.

Therapeutic Interviews

The purpose of therapeutic interviews is to help clients make changes, or to change the social environment to help clients function better, or both. Examples of the first type include the following. A shy parent may be counseled on how to be more assertive. A depressed, lonely, or suicidal client may be counseled on how to handle such problems better. A client on probation may be counseled on how to apply for and find a job. A couple having marital problems may be counseled on how to communicate and handle their problems better. A newly married couple distressed by the husband's premature ejaculation may be counseled on how to resolve such a dysfunction (Belliveau & Richter, 1970). A couple with problems disciplining their children might be given instructional sessions in Parent Effectiveness Training techniques (Gordon, 1970).

Other therapeutic interviews might be geared to changing the social environment to facilitate a client's social functioning. The spouse of a client with a drinking problem might be counseled on how to help the spouse stop drinking and develop a meaningful life separate from alcohol. Alfred Kadushin (1972, p. 19) gave other examples:

Interviews may have a therapeutic purpose but the person for whom the therapeutic change is sought may not be present. These include interviews with persons important in the client's life, where the social worker acts as a broker or advocate in the client's behalf. The social worker engaged in brokerage or advocacy may interview people in strategic positions in an attempt to influence them on behalf of the client. The purpose of the interview

Exhibit 4.1
Example of a social history

Wisconsin State Hospital
Social History

*Donald Cooper**

Birth date: June 30, 1965

Occupation: Accountant

Race: White

Religion: Unaffiliated

Marital status: Divorced, and currently engaged

Height: 5′10″

Weight: 180

Home Address: 2030 Lincoln Drive
Milwaukee, Wisconsin

Phone: (414) 726-4567

Presenting Problems: Mr. Cooper was committed to this hospital by Judge Cherwenka of Washington County for a 60-day observation period. Mr. Cooper was arrested on August 1 on the charge of sexually molesting a minor earlier in the day. The reported victim was an 8-year-old girl whom Mr. Cooper reportedly enticed into his car at the girl's school, and then fondled her genitals after driving to a secluded area.

Mr. Cooper has been arrested on three previous occasions for fondling young girls; each time the charges were dropped after Mr. Cooper consented to receiving psychiatric care. Besides minor traffic violations, he has no other arrest record.

Family Background and Early History: Mr. Cooper's father, Dave Cooper, has been a dairy farmer near Stevens Point all his life. His income has been marginal through the years. Dave Cooper gave the impression of being a meek, submissive person who reportedly has a drinking problem. Dave Cooper indicated he has no idea why his son would become involved in his current difficulties.

David Cooper's wife died when Donald was 8 years old, after being ill with cancer for a relatively short time. Dave Cooper mentioned this was a substantial blow to the children and to himself. He added that he has not as yet fully adjusted to his wife's death.

Donald has one sibling, Mary, who is one year older. She is currently married to a serviceman and they are now stationed in San Diego.

Dave Cooper reported his son's developmental milestones were normal, except he sometimes was enuretic until age 5. Dave Cooper reported Donald had a very close relationship with his mother, but seemed to adjust satisfactorily to his mother's death. Dave Cooper continued to provide and care for the two children after his wife died.

School Performance: Mr. Cooper received slightly above average grades in elementary and high school and received a two-year associate degree in accounting from Portage County Vocational School. Mr. Cooper reported he neither disliked nor liked school, and that he was somewhat of a loner during his school years.

General Health: Mr. Cooper reports his health has been good. He had a hernia operation at age 20 with no lingering complications.

Marital History: Mr. Cooper was married at age 19 to Nancy Riehle whom he met in high school. It was a forced marriage and ended after one year

*Names and other identifying information have been changed in this social history.

because of "incompatibility." His ex-wife was interviewed and had no explanation for his involvement in his current difficulties. She is currently receiving $290 per month in child support, and is currently a typist and caring for their 10-year-old daughter. The daughter has not been informed of her father's current confinement; she seldom has contact with her father. The ex-wife appeared to be very dominating and overly critical of Donald whom she views as "morally immature."

Mr. Cooper is currently engaged to Mary Gautier, and the marriage was planned for December 2 of this year. Miss Gautier indicated she is now reconsidering the upcoming marriage. She is a charming, attractive, petite person currently employed at Jones High School as a secretary. She mentioned she was shocked on being informed of her fiancé's arrest, and had not previously known about his prior arrests. She mentioned she still loves Donald, but feels that unless his reported involvement with young girls is discontinued, it would be better for them to break their engagement. She mentioned she has had sexual relations with Mr. Cooper about twice a week for the past six months, which she described as "satisfying" for her, and she also thought for her fiancé.

Employment History: Mr. Cooper has been employed as an accountant at Paul Realty Company for the past five years. His supervisor, John Namman, reported his work is reliable, that he associates well with other employees, but is sometimes "moody." Mr. Cooper reported he likes his current job and hopes he can return after his confinement.

Prior to this position, Mr. Cooper worked as an accountant for two other firms where his work was also reported as acceptable. While in high school and in vocational school, he helped his father on the farm.

Prior Contact with Social Agencies: Since Mr. Cooper's first arrest for fondling young girls six years ago, he has been seeing Dr. Timmer at Midwest Psychiatric Center occasionally.

Dr. Timmer reported Mr. Cooper's difficulty is due to the following past history. (Mr. Cooper also related these events in an interview.)

Mr. Cooper mentioned his family life was fairly normal until his mother died when he was 8 years old. His father then began drinking. When sober, his father was considerate, quiet, and an adequate family provider. However, when intoxicated, he was verbally, and sometimes physically, abusive to the children. The children became terrified when they knew their father was drinking. Therefore, when they heard him coming home, they learned to hide by crawling under a blanket. While under the blanket, in fear, they began fondling each other, which seemed to make them feel better. Now, Mr. Cooper mentioned when he feels "moody" or depressed, he seeks young girls to fondle, hoping to feel better again.

In treating Mr. Cooper, Dr. Timmer has been using a modified psychoanalytic approach, but he admits the therapy has as yet apparently not curbed Mr. Cooper's involvement with young girls.

General Impressions: In the interviews, Mr. Cooper appeared to be very concerned about his fondling behaviors with young girls and displayed motivation to curb the deviant behavior. He appears to have traditional middle-class values. He is fairly attractive, and has a pleasant personality.

Mr. Cooper, however, has had repeated incidents of involvement with young girls, even while under psychiatric care. The latest incident occurred at a time when Mr. Cooper is engaged; and as he reported, when he is having satisfying relations with his fiancée. His deviant behavior is apparently deeply entrenched. Sexual activities such as Mr. Cooper's are difficult to change. Perhaps covert sensitization, a form of behavior therapy, might be attempted.[†] Or, rational therapy might be used to teach him other ways of handling his emotions of depression and moodiness, instead of through seeking to fondle young girls.[‡] Also an arrangement might be made with the local mental health center to have Mr. Cooper call and receive immediate counseling (perhaps staying overnight at the center) whenever he has a strong urge to fondle young girls.

[†]See Chapter 16.
[‡]See Chapter 22.

is to change the balance of forces in the social environment in the client's favor. The school social worker may interview a teacher in order to influence her to show more accepting understanding of a client. The social worker at the neighborhood service center may interview a worker at the housing authority or at the local department of public welfare in order to obtain for his client full entitlement to housing rights or to assistance. Or a social worker may accompany an inarticulate client to an employment interview in an effort to influence the decision in the client's favor. In each instance the scheduled interview has a definite, and in these cases, therapeutic purpose on behalf of the client.[1]

Therapeutic interviews are the most common in social work, and therefore this text will focus mainly on this type.

The Place of the Interview

Social work interviews can take place anywhere—in the office, the client's home, on street corners, in restaurants, and in institutions. Office interviews permit control of the physical setting, usually make the interviewer comfortable, and can usually be arranged to assure privacy. Office interviews also reduce the worker's travel time between interviews.

Home visits have an advantage in helping the interviewer better understand the living conditions of the interviewee. Family interactions can also be observed. Some clients, such as those with severe disabilities, find it difficult or impossible to travel to an office; therefore, home visits are common in social work. Other clients find an office "foreign" to them and, therefore, are more comfortable in their home or in other settings.

The home visit also offers more opportunities for the worker to enter the life of the interviewee as a participant—opening a stuck door, moving furniture, holding a crying baby. However, there is also the chance that the interviewer may have to respond to conflict between family members if it occurs, and some clients may feel that a home visit suggests that the worker is spying on them. Distractions are also more apt to occur—for example, telephone calls, TV programs that other family members want to watch, friends dropping by to visit.

In practice I have found that while the physical setting may have an initial effect on the start of an interview, these effects can almost always be handled by a skillful interviewer. For example, on a home visit where there are a number of other people present, the worker can suggest to the client that they go to a restaurant where they can have a soda and talk in private. The interviewer's skills are almost always more important in determining the productivity of an interview than the setting.

Opening the First Interview

When Interviewee-Initiated

If someone has asked to see a counselor and has come, it is best to let that person state just what he or she is concerned about. The counselor should, of course, greet the client with something like "Hi, I'm Jane Bernes, and I'm a counselor at this agency." After the client has been seated, the client often begins indicating his or her concerns. If this does not

[1]Alfred Kadushin, *The Social Work Interview*. Copyright © 1972, Columbia University Press, New York. This and all other quotations from the same source are used with permission.

happen, the worker should say something brief and neutral (not to sidetrack the client) to help the client get started, such as: "You came in here to see me about something today."

Openings that are *not* as desirable are the following: (1) "I'm glad you came in this afternoon"—the client may know that you are being superficial and may not in fact be glad to hear what he or she has to say; (2) "In what way can I help you?"—the worker should not erroneously convey that he or she is the chief problem solver—the client owns the problem and is the primary problem solver; (3) "You have a problem?"—the word *problem* in a counseling situation may suggest to the client that the worker is viewing the client as a psychiatric case.

Benjamin (1974, p. 13) recommended the following about small talk at the beginning of an interview:

Sometimes at the outset there is room or need for small talk on the interviewer's part, something to help the interviewee get started. But we should attempt this only when we truly feel that it will be helpful. Brief statements such as the following may break the ice: "With traffic the way it is around here, you must have found it hard to get a parking place" or "It's nice to have a sunny day after all that rain, isn't it?"[2]

Kadushin (1972, pp. 130–131) gave the following suggestions on how to start an interview:

It is helpful if the interviewer can greet the interviewee by name. She invites her in, goes through the familiar social amenities—taking her coat, offering her a chair,

and demonstrating her concern that she is reasonably comfortable. The interviewer gives the interviewee a chance to get settled—to compose herself, to absorb first impressions, to get her bearings, to catch her breath. She needs a little time to get used to the room and the interviewer. . . .

It is helpful, particularly at the beginning and the end of the contact, to make general conversation rather than engage in an interview. . . . The preliminary chit-chat may be about the weather, parking problems, cooking, baseball, or the high cost of living.

This socializing is not a waste of time. It eases the client's transition from the familiar mode of conversational interaction into a new and unfamiliar role which demands responses for which he has little experience. The conversation has the additional and very important advantage of permitting the interviewee to become acquainted with and size up the interviewer as a person.

When Interviewer-Initiated

Whether talking to a client, or to a client's relatives, or to professionals at other agencies, the worker should indicate his or her role or position at the agency and then state the purpose of the interview. Thus a school counselor may say to a student who is receiving failing grades, "Hi, John. I'm Mr. Roberts, a social worker at this school. I asked that you see me today because I was looking at your grade report. It looks as if you are having difficulty in some of your courses. Perhaps we can talk about the reasons." A protective services worker might say, "Hi, I'm Mary Seely, a protective services worker with Rock County Social Services. Information that raises questions about the care your child is receiving has come to our attention. I realize there are always two sides to any such report, and therefore I would like to talk with you about this."

[2]Alfred Benjamin, *The Helping Interview*, 2nd ed. Copyright © 1974, by Houghton Mifflin Company. This and all other quotations from the same source are used with permission.

Closing an Interview

Closing is not always easy. Ideally, both the interviewer and the interviewee should accept the fact that the interview is ending, and the subjects being discussed should not be left hanging. Saying something like, "Well, you really have serious problems, but I've got to catch my ride. When can we talk further?" is too abrupt and unprofessional. Such abrupt endings are apt to be perceived by the interviewee as being discourteous and uncaring.

There are some useful guidelines on how to terminate an interview. Kadushin (1972, p. 207) recommended:

> Preparation for termination begins with the very beginning of the interview. The interviewee should be informed explicitly at the beginning that a definite period of time has been allotted for the interview, that she is free to use some, or all, of this time but that going beyond the time limit is clearly discouraged. Unless an unusual situation develops, it is understood that the interview will terminate at the end of the allotted time.

When the allotted time is nearly up, the interviewer may inform the interviewee by saying something like: "Well, our time is just about up. Is there anything you'd like to add before we look at where we have arrived, and where we now go from here?" It is often helpful to summarize what was discussed at the end of the interview. If the interview focused only on exploring problems that the client has, another interview should be set up for fuller exploration and to begin looking at alternatives.

I have found it helpful to give clients "homework" assignments between interviews. A couple who is having trouble communicating with each other, for example, might be encouraged to set aside a certain amount of time each evening to discuss their personal thoughts with each other. At the next interview this "homework" assignment is then reviewed.

Reid and Shyne (1969) have found that if an agency establishes a set, limited time period for contact with the client (including both the number of interviews and the length of each interview), both the worker and client make more productive use of the time as they mobilize their efforts to accomplish the tasks within the designated time.

Ideally, the interviewee should be emotionally at ease when the interview ends; therefore the interviewer should not introduce emotionally charged content at the end, but should seek a reduction in intensity of emotion.

If an interviewee displays a reluctance to end the interview, it is sometimes helpful to confront this directly by saying, "It appears to me that you wished we had more time." The reasons for the interviewee's reluctance can then be discussed, and perhaps another appointment can be made.

Just as it is sometimes advisable to begin an interview with small talk, a short social conversation at the end may be useful as it provides a transition out of the interview. There are many styles of closing. The style used will depend on the interviewer, the interviewee, and what was said during the interview.

At times an interview can be closed with a restatement of the way both the interviewer and interviewee agreed to proceed: for example, "I'm glad you have decided to have the pregnancy test. If it's positive, give me a call so we can arrange another time to further discuss the options we briefly talked about here."

At times the interviewer may make a more explicit summation of what was discussed, what decisions were arrived at, what questions remain to be resolved, and what actions will be taken. A somewhat different approach is to ask the interviewee to state what was discussed, what was learned from the interview, and plans for the future.

Sometimes in closing an interview, concerns that were alluded to but not fully discussed might be mentioned as topics that will be discussed at the next interview. I have found some clients will first reveal their most serious concerns at the end of the interview, perhaps because they are ambivalent about whether they are ready to fully explore these concerns with the interviewer. In such instances the interviewer has to make a professional judgment of whether to extend the interview beyond the allotted time or to set up another appointment to discuss these concerns.

Benjamin (1974, p. 32) observed:

Closing is especially important because what occurs during this last stage is likely to determine the interviewee's impression of the interview as a whole. We must make certain that we have given him full opportunity to express himself, or, alternatively, we must set a mutually convenient time for this purpose. We should leave enough time for closing so that we are not rushed, since this might create the impression that we are evicting the interviewee.

Questioning

Questions are asked for a variety of purposes—to obtain information, to help a client tell his or her story, to help build a relationship, to help a client look at alternative solutions, and to help a client select an alternative.

The tone in which the question is asked is often as important as the question itself. For a client who is depressed, an appropriate tone should indicate caring and understanding. For someone who is angry, the tone should imply recognition of the anger and a willingness to examine the anger. For someone anxious, the tone should convey reassurance.

In exploring both problems of clients and alternative solutions, usually a series of questions having an increasingly specific focus is advisable. Kadushin (1972, p. 149) expanded on this point.

The successive questions should act as a funnel, moving from general to more specific aspects of the content being discussed. As discussion of one area is completed at the more specific end of the funnel, the new content area introduced for discussion should start with another general, open-ended question. The movement is from "Could you tell me what it is like for you to live on an AFDC budget?" to "What did you do about food for the children the last time you ran out of money before the next check was due?"

"How do you feel about that?" is a common question that I find useful for a variety of situations: for example, when a client is pregnant or is involved in a failing romance. Another common question that I ask when a client has a problem that involves someone else is "Could you describe what kind of a person (*name*) is?" Such a question usually facilitates getting a rapid impression of the client's thoughts and feelings about the other person.

Probing questions are often used by skilled interviewers to help clients elaborate on the specific details of their concerns and to help clients look in greater detail at the merits, shortcomings, and consequences of possible resolution strategies. For example, probing questions with a client who feels her husband drinks too much include the following: "How much does he drink?" "How often does he drink?" "How does he act when intoxicated?" "What concerns you most about his drinking?" (Common concerns are his employer may fire him, embarrassment over his behavior, possible abuse to her or to their children, decline in sexual satisfaction, and fear of a driving accident.) The concerns she mentions also need to be explored in depth, using such probing questions as the following: "Given his drinking, how do you now feel about him?"

Exhibit 4.2
Phrasing questions

Errors in Phrasing Questions	*Most Desirable Neutral Formulation*
The loaded question: This question assumes an unknown action is occurring. "When did you last hit your wife?" "What are you going to do when John breaks up with you?"	"Have you ever hit your wife?" "Do you think John is considering breaking up with you?"
The suggestive, or leading, question: The interviewer suggests a "desired" answer. "Don't you think it's high time you stop drinking and shape up?" "You're really making good progress—aren't you?"	"Do you think you have a drinking problem?" "What progress do you think you're making?"
Yes-no question: Such questions do not encourage elaboration. "Do you ever do anything together with your husband?" "You really don't like Mary—do you?"	"What kinds of things do you and your husband do together?" "How do you feel toward Mary?"
Either-or question: The interviewee might prefer both or neither or a third. "Would you like to talk about your marriage or your job this morning?" "Have you and Tim decided to get married or have an abortion?"	"What would you like to talk about this morning?" "What alternatives have you and Tim talked about?"
Bombarding: The interviewer asks two or more questions at the same time. "How are you feeling today, and did you and your husband get a chance to further discuss what we talked about last week?" "What were your parents' reactions when you told them you were pregnant? Did they suggest getting an abortion? How do you now feel about having an abortion?" "Since graduating from high school have you found a job, a place to live, and are you still dating the same person?"	Such questions should be asked separately.
Garbled question: Such questions usually occur when the interviewer is unclear about what he or she wants to ask. "You've been considering, uh, what was it, oh yeah, something about what we talked about last time—now how do you feel about that?" "Have you thought about—no, that wouldn't work, another possible thing you could do is—I don't know. What were we talking about?"	The interviewer needs to be clear about what he or she wants to ask before speaking. Silence is better than asking garbled questions.

"Does he recognize he may have a drinking problem?" "Do you think he would be willing to come in to talk about these concerns?" Probes should not be used in a cross-examination fashion but in a manner that gradually permits the interviewer and the interviewee to see the situations more clearly.

There are a variety of errors that should generally be avoided in phrasing questions. A number of these are shown in Exhibit 4.2. The questions in the exhibit that are classified as "errors" should not be used unless a worker has a *specific, constructive* purpose for phrasing the question in that fashion.

Note Taking

Note taking is an integral part of counseling. Workers need notes to refresh their memory of past interviews, to record the contracts made with clients, to record information for social histories, to share important facts with professional colleagues, and to note what has been done or left undone.

Benjamin (1974, p. 58) observed:

In our culture, when note taking is discriminately handled, it is not resented. On the contrary, its absence may be looked upon as negligence or lack of respect. Usually no explanation of our recording practice is required. However, should an explanation be requisite because of the needs of either or both partners in the interview, it can be easily provided.

Note taking should be subordinate to interviewing. Don't let note taking interfere with the flow of the interview; for example, avoid saying or conveying, "I wish you would talk slower, I can't write that fast." Don't turn note taking into cross-examination; for example, "Let's see if I got it right, you state you sometimes think about getting a divorce because you find marriage confining." Convey that you are relaxed and comfortable with note taking; don't be secretive about taking notes; this may cause the client to become suspicious or anxious.

Note taking presents a possible distraction to interview interaction. When a worker breaks eye contact and then makes notes, there is a danger that the focus on the interview may shift from what is *being* said to what *has been* said. Ideally, workers should acquire the capacity to take notes unobtrusively without seeming to shift their attention from the client to what is being written.

At times it is important for a worker to record certain kinds of information in order to demonstrate an interest in the client; such expected information includes certain addresses, names, telephone numbers, contract goals, and tasks.

Kadushin (1972, p. 206) advised:

The effect of note taking needs to be assessed periodically during the interview. If at any point the interviewee appears to be upset or made hesitant by note taking, this should be raised for explicit discussion. If, despite the interviewee's stated assent, note taking appears to be a disruptive tactic, one might best forget it.

Note taking generally decreases in quantity as a worker gains experience. In recording, don't emphasize the importance of note taking by, for example, sitting with a pen and paper between you and the client, or by recording most of what clients say. Most experienced interviewers find that in therapeutic interviews they often do not need to make notes during the interview. Frequently, writing down a few key phrases and points after an interview will enable the worker to recall the important points that were discussed.

Benjamin (1974, p. 60) stressed the importance of honesty with clients in taking notes:

I am certain of one thing: we must be honest. If the notes taken are to be used for the purpose of research, we should state this at the outset. In the event that the information gathered cannot be kept confidential, we should frankly indicate this, too. Above all, we should not promise confidentiality if we are not certain that we can provide it.

Tape Recording and Videotaping

Audiotape and videotape recordings of interviews are increasingly being used. Both have the advantage over note taking because they provide a full recording of what was said. However, a worker can hardly refer to tapes as readily as to written notes. Tapes may be transcribed, but this usually is quite expensive.

Tape recordings and note taking are generally used for different purposes. They are used as a mirror to reflect either to the interviewer or to the interviewee exactly what was said and how. As such they have a *self-confrontation* or *sensitivity* value, because they reflect how a person interacts with others. Playing back tapes to clients can help show areas where clients have interactional problems (for example, shyness). For interviewers, tapes can be used for training purposes to help develop counseling and interviewing skills.

An initial concern of interviewers in deciding whether to use tape recordings is how the interviewee will react to being taped. I have used both audiotaping and videotaping extensively for the past several years and have found that clients soon forget the interview is being taped. A number of other authorities agree. Benjamin (1974, p. 62), for example, said:

I am firmly convinced that after the first few minutes he will not react to it at all for he will no longer notice it. It is my belief that, as a manner of ethics, the fact that the interview is being taped should not be concealed. If I tell him that it is my custom to record interviews to learn from them after-

wards and that the tape will be kept confidential, he will usually not object. He will not be uneasy unless he feels that I am. If I can say that he, too, may listen to the tapes to learn, so much the better. If after all this the interviewee still objects, it is probably best to respect his feelings. Some people are simply afraid or suspicious. In areas or cultures in which the tape recorder is seldom used or seen, for the interviewer to insist might prove harmful indeed. When one finds he is working with suspicious people, the wise thing to do is to get at the suspiciousness and leave the tape recorder alone for the time being.

Some counselors now routinely videotape interviews so clients can more fully grasp what was said and also gain valuable feedback on how they present themselves in interactions. Videotaping allows both the interviewer and the interviewee to study their verbal and nonverbal communication simultaneously.

Videotaping for Training Purposes

Most educational programs in social work and counseling now use videotaping of simulated counseling situations to help students develop and assess their interviewing and counseling skills. Our program (similar to a growing number of other programs) also uses videotaping as one approach to screen out those students who do not have the aptitude to be social workers.

It is our belief that an essential capacity social workers must possess is the ability to counsel and relate to people. We believe this capacity is necessary in social work practice with individuals, groups, families, organizations, and communities. The capacity to relate to people is a necessary component for performing competently in micro, mezzo, and macro practice.

Recording interviews on videotape is a tool that is frequently used in human service agencies and in social work educational programs for a variety of purposes, including the development of helping professionals' interviewing and counseling skills.

In the first practice course of our program, each student has to demonstrate a level of counseling and interviewing skills that will give field placement agencies substantial assurance that he or she will be able to counsel clients. Students are required to demonstrate their interviewing and counseling capacities via videotaped role playing. Each student in the class is videotaped in the role of a counselor while counseling someone else in the class who has a contrived problem. This videotape is later reviewed jointly by the student and the instructor. Students are graded on a pass/fail basis on this videotaped role play. They are permitted to videotape a role-playing situation as many times as they want. If they fail to make an acceptable tape, they are not allowed to pass the course and are encouraged to transfer to another major. This course, therefore, serves as a first step in "screening out"

students from the program. The emphasis of this requirement, however, is not on culling students from the program, but on helping them develop their interviewing and counseling techniques. If the student feels the instructor's review of the tape is unfair, an appeal process is available in which the student can take the tape to other social work faculty members for their review.

We have received some grants to study the effectiveness of using videotapes as a training tool and have found (Zastrow & Navarre, 1979) the following. At the beginning of the course, students were quite apprehensive (and some extremely apprehensive) about participating in the videotape role playing. This apprehensiveness was partially reduced by didactic material and discussions in class on "how to counsel," and by role-playing counseling situations in class (generally two students counseling two other students who have a contrived problem). Following the videotaped role playing, students expressed considerable increased confidence in their capacities to counsel and a substantial reduction in their apprehensiveness about being videotaped in the future.

The following responses by students of how videotaping was helpful are typical (Zastrow & Navarre, 1979):

> It helped make me comfortable in a counseling situation. I was able to test out different ways in helping a client and when reviewing the tape I saw what things I did well, and what I need to work on to become a better counselor.

> I became aware of my own voice, posture, and gestures and the importance they play in counseling.

> I was able to see an actual picture of myself, not what I thought I looked like, and was able to see where I made my mistakes and could have done something different.

> I feel that the best way to learn something is to actually do it, instead of just talking about it. I also thought it was useful to watch the tape and look for your mistakes. This is the best way to correct them.

> I became aware of exactly how I came across to the client and I noticed that I was suggesting things to him—which I didn't even realize before reviewing the tape.

> Made me more aware of my self-presence (mannerisms). Gave me the opportunity early in my academic career to have a slight taste of what counseling is about and what I might be in store for!

> I was not confident in my counseling skills at first. But after seeing the videotape I saw that I could do it. Videotaping is a good confidence builder. [pp. 201–202]

The benefits of using videotaped role playing to assess and develop counseling skills appear to be the following:

1. Students report it is a valuable tool in learning how to counsel.
2. Problems that students have in counseling and relating to people can be identified, shown to the student; then efforts can be made to make improvements.
3. Students whose capacities lie elsewhere can be identified early in their college career and counseled into some other major.
4. Videotaping links theory with practice and thereby makes the course more meaningful and relevant.
5. Students report videotaping provides considerable feedback on themselves and on how they relate to others.
6. Students report videotaping builds their confidence for counseling "real" clients in the future, and gives them an opportunity to test their skills and interpersonal behaviors in a relatively safe setting.
7. This laboratory approach helps students make the transition from having intellectual ideas of what should be done to trying out their ideas.
8. The approach provides assurance to field placement agencies that student interns will have an acceptable level of counseling capacities.

We also found that almost all students are able (sometimes after three or four attempts) to develop their interviewing and counseling skills to an acceptable level. It is interesting that the few students who have been identified with this approach not to have the aptitude for social work have, for the most part, voluntarily decided to switch to another major. They generally conclude after viewing their videotapes that they do not have the capabilities to be a social worker.

Summary

Most social work interviews can be classified as informational (to obtain data for a social study or for writing a social history), assessment (to arrive at an appraisal), or therapeutic (to help clients change). Often, there is overlap among these three types. Therapeutic interviews are the most common in social work. Their purpose is either to help clients make changes, or to change the social environment to help clients function better, or both.

Social work interviews can take place anywhere. Most commonly, they occur either in the interviewer's office or the client's home. Although the place does affect an interview, the interviewer's skills are almost always more important in determining the productivity of an interview.

Material on how to begin and how to end interviews was presented. In interviewee-initiated interviews, the beginning focus should be on helping clients become comfortable and start relating their concerns. In interviewer-initiated interviews, the beginning focus, after the introductions, is for the interviewer to state the purpose concisely and then begin the dialogue. There are a variety of ways to close interviews—the style used depends on the interviewer, the interviewee, and what was said during the interview. Ideally, both the interviewer and the interviewee should accept the fact that the interview is ending, and topics being discussed should not be left hanging. Most interviews end with either the interviewer or the interviewee summarizing what was said or what course of action is now planned.

Questions in interviews are used for a variety of purposes—to gather information, to help a client tell his or her story, to help a client look at alternative solutions, and to help a client select an alternative. The tone in which a question is asked is often as important as the question itself. Probing questions are common in social work practice. However, several types of questions should usually be avoided: loaded questions, suggestive questions, yes-no questions, either-or questions, clustered questions (bombarding), and garbled questions.

Note taking is an integral part of counseling, and should be done unobtrusively so it does not interfere with the flow of the interview.

Audiotape and videotape recordings are increasingly being used. They provide a full recording of what was said and are generally used for different purposes than note taking. For clients, reviewing tapes helps them grasp more fully what was said and gives them valuable feedback on how they present themselves in interactions. For counselors, reviewing tapes is particularly valuable in helping them assess and further develop their interviewing skills.

Exercise
Writing a Social History

Goal: The purpose of this exercise is to give students practice in writing a social history.

Step 1: At an earlier class session, inform the class there will be an exercise in a future session designed to teach them how to write a social history. Instruct them to read the material contained in this chapter on how to write a social history. Inform the students they may either use the format and subheadings contained in the case example of a social history in this chapter or an adaptation of it. Ask for a volunteer to develop a contrived story of (1) some unusual incident that has led him or her to become a client of an agency, and (2) background information covering the following material:

Birth date
Religion
Occupation
Marital status
Height
Weight
Address
Home phone
Why referred
    By whom
Early developmental history
    Toilet trained (what age)
    First walked (what age)
    First talked (what age)
    Relationship to parents, brothers, sisters
Education
    Kindergarten
    Grade school   } Places, grades, relationships to
    Junior high   other students, and attitudes
    High school   about these schools.
    College
Employment history
    Where worked
    How long
Health
Family life
    Dating
    Courtship
Prior contact with other social agencies

Inform the class that at a future session you will interview the "client" and that each student will have to write a social history based on this interview. (The volunteer may be excused from having to write the social history.) Inform the students that a significant part of their grade for this project will depend on their *realistic* recommendations on how to intervene effectively to help this "client." Indicate that bringing tape recorders to record the interview for the write-ups is acceptable.

Step 2: Interview the "client" at a future class session, covering the information contained in Step 1. In this interview explore problems, but end the interview before the client chooses specific courses of action to resolve the situation. A major focus of this exercise is to give students practice in arriving at recommendations for how to intervene. (Set a deadline for when students are to hand in their social histories.) After grading them, read to the class one or two (without naming the writers) that were particularly well done.

Social Work with Individuals: Counseling

Counseling someone with personal problems is neither magical nor mystical.[1] Although training and experience in counseling is beneficial, everyone has the potential of helping others by listening and talking through their difficulties. Counseling with a beneficial outcome can be done by a friend, neighbor, relative, the local barber, hairdresser, banker, and bartender, as well as by social workers, psychiatrists, psychologists, guidance counselors, and the clergy. This is not to say that everyone will be effective at counseling. Professional people, because of their training and experience, have a higher probability of being effective, but competence and rapport, rather than degrees or certificates, are the keys to desirable outcomes. The focus of this chapter is on how professional counseling should be done. Since all of us at one time or another counsel others, the closer

---

[1]This chapter is adapted from three other chapters written by this author: (1) "How to Counsel," in *The Personal Problem Solver,* edited by Charles Zastrow and Dae H. Chang, © 1977, pp. 267–274. Adapted by permission of Prentice-Hall, Inc., Englewood Cliffs, New Jersey; (2) "Self-Talk in Counseling," in *Talk to Yourself: Using the Power of Self-Talk* © 1979, pp. 266–279. Adapted by permission of Prentice-Hall, Inc., Englewood Cliffs, New Jersey; (3) "The Counseling Process," in *Introduction to Social Welfare Institutions,* 2nd ed. (Pacific Grove: Brooks/Cole, 1982), pp. 484–486.

the counseling (including friend-to-friend counseling) approaches professional counseling, the higher the probability of a successful outcome.

Counseling from the Helper's Perspective

Most simply stated there are three phases to counseling: (1) building a relationship, (2) exploring problems in depth, and (3) exploring alternative solutions with the client then selecting a course of action. (These phases are components of the problem-solving approach, described in Chapter 1.) Successful counseling gradually proceeds from one phase to the next, with some overlap. For example, in many cases, while exploring problems, the relationship between the counselor and the counselee continues to develop, and while they are exploring alternative solutions, the problems are generally being examined in greater depth. At the end of a series of counseling interviews, there is often the fourth phase of termination and evaluation. (Guidelines on the counselor's role in each of these phases are presented in the next section.)

Many times before the initial interview a counselor is unaware of the concerns (or problems) that new clients have. The question arises about what the counselor's objective should be in the first interview. In such initial interviews, the counselor should seek to build a helping relationship and to begin exploring the client's problems. The third phase—examining alternative solutions—may or may not be arrived at in the initial interview. Every interview has a goal or objective, and the counselor should use this goal to give focus to the interview.

On many occasions the first problem that clients present may not be the one that they are most concerned about. Clients sometimes initially present problems that they believe are more socially acceptable to test how objective, accepting, and helpful the counselor will be. I once had a client who mentioned six "presenting" problems before sharing the one she was most concerned about, which was the guilt she experienced over masturbating.

Counseling from the Helpee's Perspective

The counseling process can also be conceptualized from the client's point of view. For counseling to be successful, clients must arrive at a progressive series of "self-talk" statements (that is, clients must arrive at having certain thoughts and beliefs). These self-talk stages are as follows:

Stage I   *Problem awareness:* "I have a problem."

Stage II   *Relationship to counselor:* "I think this counselor has what it takes to help me."

Stage III   *Motivation:* "I want to improve my situation and am willing to put forth the effort to do so."

Stage IV   *Conceptualizing the problem:* "My problem is not overwhelming but has specific components that can be changed."

Stage V   *Exploration of resolution strategies:* "I see there are several courses of action that I might try in order to do something about my situation."

Stage VI   *Selection of a strategy:* "I think this approach might help and I am willing to try it."

Stage VII   *Implementation:* "This approach is helping me."

Stage VIII   *Evaluation:* "Although this approach takes a lot of my time and effort, it's worth it."

The advantage of this conceptualization of the counseling process is that it presents a framework for assessing and improving the effectiveness of counseling. When counseling is not producing positive changes in clients, this framework helps identify the reasons for a lack of progress. Once these reasons are identified, needed changes can then be made in the counseling process.

Stage I: Problem Awareness

At this initial stage counselees must say to themselves, "I have a problem—I need to do something about my situation." If people with problems refuse to acknowledge they have a problem, they will not be motivated to make the efforts needed to change. In some areas of counseling (for example, working with problem drinkers), it is sometimes difficult to have people acknowledge that they have a problem. Involuntary clients are particularly apt to deny a problem exists. Involuntary clients are clients who are forced to seek counseling. Social workers encounter involuntary clients in a variety of settings: protective services, corrections, certain public school settings, group homes, mental health facilities, nursing homes, and hospitals.

For people who deny a problem exists, constructive changes are not apt to occur unless the counselor finds a way to convince them that there is a problem. When a person denies the problem, counseling needs to focus on this denial by exploring why the counselee believes a problem does not exist and by gathering evidence to document the existence of the problem to the counselee. The client then needs to be confronted (in a tactful manner) with this evidence. If after such a confrontation the client still denies a problem exists, the counselor should be aware that the client *owns* the problem, and there is little more that the counselor can do constructively at this time, except perhaps to indicate he or she will be available in the future if the client wants to talk.

At times a person who acknowledges a problem exists may prefer to try to resolve it without receiving help from others. A person with a problem is the "owner" of the problem, and therefore has a right to decide how he or she wants to handle it. If the person decides to work on it alone, the counselor should respect this decision, but also indicate that he or she will be available in the future by saying something like, "If you do decide later that you'd like to talk further about it, my door will always be open."

Stage II: Relationship to Counselor

This stage overlaps the first stage and all other stages in the counseling process. For counseling to be effective, the counselee must arrive at the point where his or her self-talk is, "I think this counselor has what it takes to help me." If the counselee instead has the self-talk, "This counselor can't help me. I don't need a head shrinker. I just don't trust this counselor," counseling will fail unless a more positive relationship is established. Throughout the counseling process, and especially in the initial meetings, the counselor must be aware of and give attention to the kind of relationship that is developing with the counselee.

Eriksen (1979) emphasized the importance of a helping relationship being formed with clients:

> The relationship that develops between worker and client is the very cornerstone of helping. Through the helping relationship, the client and worker come together to unblock communication that is preventing problem solving. . . .
>
> Through the vehicle of the helping relationship, the client can communicate to the worker what she thinks, knows and feels about her problem. This kind of in-depth communication, when reinforced by effective responses by her worker, will strengthen the helping relationship itself and will soon open the door to problem solving. [p. 54]

The following guidelines focus on how to build a constructive relationship.

1. Try to establish a nonthreatening, comfortable atmosphere where the counselee feels safe to communicate fully his or her troubles while feeling accepted as a person.

2. In initial contacts with the counselee, you need to "sell" yourself, not arrogantly, but as a knowledgeable, understanding person who may be able to help and who wants to try.

3. Be calm, do not laugh or express shock when the counselee begins to open up about his or her problems. Emotional outbursts, even if subtle, will lead the counselee to believe that you are not going to understand these difficulties, and he or she will usually stop discussing them. Remaining calm is not always easy. I remember one interview with a client who had brutally murdered his estranged partner by decapitating her. It took 45 minutes for the client to explain his reasons for killing her and for recounting how he had planned and carried out this murder. Many details were shocking, but I had to continue to tell myself to take a professional approach, to remain calm, and to continue to maintain a nonthreatening atmosphere so that he would feel free to relate what occurred.

4. Generally be nonjudgmental, not moralistic. Show respect for the counselee's values and do not try to sell your own. The values that work for you may not be best for someone else in a different situation. For example, if the counselee is premaritally pregnant, do not attempt to force your values toward adoption or abortion, but let the counselee decide on the course of action after a full examination of the problem and an exploration of alternative solutions.

5. View the counselee as an equal. "Rookie" counselors sometimes make the mistake of thinking that because the client is sharing intimate secrets, the counselor must be very important, and they end up arranging a superior-inferior relationship. If counselees feel that they are being treated as inferiors, they will be less motivated to reveal and discuss personal difficulties.

6. Use a shared vocabulary. This does not mean using the same slang words and the same accent as the counselee. If the counselee sees the counselor as being artifi-

cial in use of slang or accent, it may seriously offend him or her. Use words that the counselee understands and that are not offensive.

7. The tone of your voice should convey the message that you empathetically understand and care about the counselee's feelings.

8. Keep confidential what the counselee has said. People unfortunately have nearly irresistible urges to share "juicy secrets" with someone else. If the counselee discovers that confidentiality has been violated, a working relationship may be quickly destroyed.

9. If you are counseling a relative or a friend, there is a danger that, because you are emotionally involved, you may get upset or enter into an argument with the other person. If that happens, it is almost always best to drop the subject immediately, as tactfully as possible. Perhaps after tempers cool the subject can be brought up again, or perhaps it may be best to refer the counselee to someone else. When counseling a friend or relative, you should be aware that when you find yourself becoming upset, further discussion will not be productive. Many professional counselors refuse to counsel friends or relatives because they are aware that they are emotionally involved. Emotional involvement interferes with the calm, detached perspective needed to help clients objectively explore problems and alternative solutions.

Stage III: Motivation

Counselees must come to say to themselves, "I want to improve my situation and am willing to put forth the effort in order to do so." Unless a counselee becomes motivated to change, constructive changes are not apt to occur. In counseling, the key variable in determining whether a client will improve his or her circumstances is the client's motivation to want to improve and put forth the necessary effort (Losoncy, 1977).

A counselor can best seek to motivate discouraged or apathetic people by being an encouraging person. According to Losoncy (1977), an encouraging person has the following characteristics:

1. Complete acceptance of the discouraged person, but not of the dysfunctional behavior that has to be changed. He or she conveys "I accept you exactly as you are, with no conditions attached."

2. A nonblaming attitude, so the discouraged person no longer feels a need to lie, pretend, or wear a mask.

3. Empathy. The counselor is aware and can to some extent feel what the discouraged person is feeling. Empathy occurs, as described by Kadushin (1972), when a counselor

feels with the client rather than for him. Feeling *for* the client would be a sympathetic rather than an empathic response. Somebody once said that if you have a capacity for empathy you feel squat when you see a squat vase and feel tall when you look at a tall vase. Empathy is entering imaginatively into the inner life of someone else. It is not enough simply to be empathically understanding; one needs to communicate to the client that one accurately perceives and feels his situation. [p. 52]

4. Genuine interest in the client's progress, conveying that the counselee is an important, worthwhile person.

5. Confidence in the capacity of the discouraged person to improve.

6. Sincere enthusiasm about the discouraged person's interests, ideas, and risk-taking actions. In order for discouraged persons to believe in themselves, they generally need an encouraging person who conveys they are important, worthwhile persons.

7. The capacity to be a nonjudgmental listener, so the discouraged person's real thoughts and feelings can be expressed freely, without fear of censure.

8. The ability to notice (reward) every small instance of progress (particularly during the beginning of the relationship)—for example, if the person is wearing something new, say "That's new, isn't it? It really looks good on you."

9. The ability to motivate. Motivating a discouraged person takes a long, long time. Discouraged people generally have a long history of failures. To reverse this trend requires having the time to spend listening and understanding this person as fully as possible.

10. A sincere belief in the discouraged person's ability to find a purpose in life.

11. The ability to allow the person to take risks without passing judgment.

12. The ability to reinforce *efforts* made by the discouraged person. The important thing is that one tries, not necessarily succeeds. By making efforts to improve, there is hope.

13. The ability to help the discouraged person see the falsehood and negative consequences of self-defeating statements (such as "I'm a failure"). Every person has skills and deficiencies, and every person should be encouraged to improve both strengths and weaknesses.

14. The capacity to recognize that all that can be done is to give one's best efforts in trying to motivate a discouraged person. Success in motivating such a client is not guaranteed. To give up hope of motivating means no longer being effective in working with this discouraged person.

15. The skill to look for uniquenesses and strengths in an individual. These uniquenesses should be communicated to the discouraged person so that he or she begins to realize he or she is special and worthwhile. This process leads to a sense of improved self-worth and strengthens the courage to take risks and change.

16. Awareness of the negative consequences of overdependency in a relationship. When the discouraged person is on the way to taking risks and making constructive changes, the counselor should start to help her develop self-encouragement, in which the counselee is encouraged to make and trust her own decisions and to take more risks.

(Note: these guidelines on motivating clients are also useful in building a relationship with them.)

Stage IV: Conceptualizing the Problem

For counseling to be effective, a client needs to recognize, "My problem is not overwhelming, but has specific components that can be changed." Many clients tend to view their situation initially as being so complex that they become highly anxious or emotional, and thereby are unable to see that their problem has a number of components that they can change in a step-by-step fashion. Several years ago I counseled a teenager who had missed her menstrual period for three months and was so overwhelmingly afraid of being pregnant that she was unable to figure out on her own that the first step was to have a pregnancy test. (When she finally took the test, the results showed she was not pregnant.) To help clients conceptualize their problems, the counselor needs to explore the problems together in depth with the client. The following guidelines focus on how to explore problems in depth:

1. Many "rookie" counselors make the mistake of suggesting solutions as soon as a problem is identified, without exploring the problem area in depth. For example, an advocate of abortions may advise this solution as soon as a single female revels that she is pregnant, without taking the time to discover whether this person is strongly opposed to abortions, really wants a baby, or intends to marry soon.

2. In exploring problems in depth, the counselor and counselee need to examine such areas as the severity of the problem, how long the problem has existed, what the causes are, how the counselee feels about

the problem, and what physical and mental capacities and strengths the counselee has to cope with the problem, before exploring alternative solutions. For example, if a single female is pregnant, the counselor and counselee need to explore the following questions: How does she feel about being pregnant? Has she seen a doctor? About how long has she been pregnant? Do her parents know? What are their feelings and concerns if they know? Has she informed her sexual partner? What are his feelings and concerns if he knows? What does she feel is the most urgent situation to deal with first? Answers to such questions will determine the future direction of counseling. The most pressing, immediate problem might be to inform her parents (who may react critically) or it might be to secure medical services.

3. When a problem area is identified, there are usually a number of subproblems that can be identified. Explore all of these; for example, deciding how to tell the father, obtaining medical care, obtaining funds for medical expenses, deciding where to live, deciding whether to leave school or stop working during the pregnancy, deciding whether to terminate the pregnancy, making plans for what to do after the child is delivered or the pregnancy is terminated.

4. In a multiproblem situation, the best way to decide which problem to handle first is to ask the counselee which problem he or she perceives as most pressing. If the problem can be solved, start with exploring that subproblem in depth and developing together a strategy for the solution. Success in solving a subproblem will increase the counselee's confidence in the counselor, and thereby further solidify the relationship.

5. Convey empathy, not sympathy. Empathy is the capacity to show that you are aware of and can to some extent feel what the counselee is saying. Sympathy is also a sharing of feelings, but it has the connotation of offering pity. The difference is subtle, but empathy is problem-solving-oriented

and sympathy is usually problem-prolonging. Giving sympathy usually causes the counselee to dwell on his or her emotions without taking action to improve the situation. For example, if one gives sympathy to a depressed person, that person will keep telling you the sad story over and over, each time having an emotional outpouring supported by your sympathy, without taking any action to improve the situation. Telling the story over and over only reopens old wounds and prolongs the depression.

Benjamin (1974, p. 47) further described how to be empathic:

> The empathic interviewer tries as much as he possibly can to feel his way into the internal frame of reference of the interviewee and to see the world through the latter's eyes as if that world were his own world. The words "as if" are crucial for although the interviewer is empathic, he never loses sight of the fact that he remains his own self. Knowing all the time that he is distinct from the interviewee, he tries to feel his way about in the internal world of thought and feeling of the other in order to come as close to him as possible, to understand with him as much as possible.[2]

The difference between sympathy and empathy can be shown in responses to the following statement by a client whose male friend has recently ended their three-year relationship, "How could he do this to me, after all I've done for him? He's hurt me so much."

Sympathic response by the interviewer: "Yes, he sure is a schnook. With what he did to you, I don't see how you can even face the world. You're probably going to be miserable for a long, long time."

Empathic response by the interviewer: "I know ending this relationship has deeply hurt you. You also appear confused about

[2]Alfred Benjamin, *The Helping Interview,* 2nd ed. Copyright © 1974, by Houghton Mifflin Company, used by permission.

why he said he wants to end the relationship. Have you discussed this with him?"

Keith-Lucas (1972) gave a cogent example separating sympathy, pity, and empathy:

Consider three reactions to someone who has told us that he strongly dislikes his wife. The sympathetic person would say, "Oh, I know exactly how you feel. I can't bear mine, either." The two of them would comfort each other but nothing would come of it. The pitying person would commiserate but add that he himself was most happily married. Why doesn't the other come to dinner sometime and see what married life could be like? This, in most cases, would only increase the frustration of the unhappy husband and help him to put his problem further outside himself, on to his wife or his lack of good fortune. The empathetic person might say something like, "That must be terribly difficult for you. What do you think might possibly help?" and only the empathetic person, of the three, would have said anything that would lead to some change in the situation. [pp. 80–81]

6. "Trust your guts." The most important tool that counselors have is themselves (their feelings and perceptions). Counselors should continually strive to place themselves in the client's situation (with the client's values and pressures). To use the earlier example, if the client is 17 years old, single, and pregnant, and has parents who are very critical of the situation and who want her to have an abortion, a competent counselor will continually strive to feel what she is feeling and to perceive the world from her perspective, with her goals, difficulties, pressures, and values. It probably never happens that a counselor is 100 percent accurate in placing himself or herself in the counselee's situation, but 70 to 80 percent is usually sufficient to gain an awareness of the counselee's pressures, problems, and perspectives. This information is very useful in helping determine what additional areas need to be explored, what he or she should say, and what might be possible solutions. Stated in a somewhat different way, a counselor should wonder "What is this person trying to tell me and how can I make it clear that I understand not only intellectually but empathically?"

7. When you believe that the client has touched on an important area of concern, further communication can be encouraged in the following ways:

• Nonverbally showing interest.
• Pausing. Rookie counselors usually become anxious when there is a pause and hasten to say something, anything, to have conversation continue. This is usually a mistake, especially when it leads to a change in an important topic. A pause will also make the counselee anxious, give him or her time to think about the important area of concern, and then usually continue conversation in that area.
• Neutral probing. "Could you tell me more about it?" "How do you feel about that?" "I'm not sure I understand what you have in mind."
• Summarizing what the client is saying. "During this past hour you made a number of critical comments about your spouse; it sounds as if some things about your marriage are making you unhappy."
• Reflecting feelings. "You seem angry" or "You appear to be depressed about that."

8. Approach socially unacceptable topics tactfully. Tact is an essential quality of a competent counselor. Try not to ask a question in such a way that the answer will put the respondent in an embarrassing position. Suppose, for instance, that you are an adult who has a good relationship with a teenager and you have reason to suspect that this person has concerns about masturbating. How would you tactfully bring up the subject? One possible approach is "When I was your age, I had a number of

concerns about masturbating. That was unfortunate. Most teenagers masturbate, and many have strong feelings of guilt or shame about it. Although masturbation has been stigmatized, it is in reality a natural outlet for sexual feelings and is not harmful. In fact, most sex therapists recommend masturbating as a way to release sexual tensions. I'm wondering if you may have some questions or concerns about masturbation that perhaps it would be helpful for us to discuss?" Informing the youth that you also had concerns about this subject personalizes it and informs the teenager that you have successfully dealt with similar concerns to those he or she is currently facing. Through this self-disclosing process, communication and relationship building are fostered.

A question occasionally arises as to when a counselor should self-disclose by sharing past experiences. There is a danger that when such experiences are shared the client may come to view the counselor as being in need of counseling. (The client is particularly apt to reach this conclusion if the counselor reveals, by nonverbal and verbal communication, that she still has unresolved issues surrounding these experiences.) Also when working in certain settings (for example, drug treatment centers) a statement by a counselor that she continues to engage in behaviors that the client needs to change (such as getting drunk or smoking pot) may be used as an excuse for the client to maintain problematic behaviors. A good rule to follow in deciding whether to self-disclose is for the counselor to first ask herself, "If I share these personal experiences, will they have a constructive effect?" If not, don't share the experience.

9. When pointing out a limitation that a counselee has, mention and compliment him or her on any assets. When a limitation is being mentioned, the counselee will literally feel that something is being laid bare or taken away. Therefore, compliment in another area to give something back.

10. Watch for nonverbal cues. A competent counselor will generally use such cues to identify when a sensitive subject is being touched on, as the client will generally become anxious and show anxiety by changing the tone of voice, fidgeting, tightening facial or neck muscles, yawning, assuming a stiff posture, or flushing. Some counselors even claim they can tell when a client becomes anxious by observing when the pupils dilate.

11. Be honest. An untruth always runs the risk of being discovered. If that happens, the counselee's confidence in the counselor will be seriously damaged, and perhaps the relationship will be seriously jeopardized. If a client asks an important question that the counselor cannot answer, it is usually best to say, "Unfortunately I do not know the answer to that important question, but let me check into it and I'll let you know by _____ (a specified time)." Being honest goes beyond not telling lies. The counselor should always tactfully inform the client of the shortcomings that the client has that are in vital need of attention. For example, if someone is being fired from jobs because of poor grooming habits, this fact needs to be brought to that person's attention. Or, if a trainee's relationship skills and intervention capacities are not suited for the helping profession, that trainee needs to be "counseled out" in the interest of clients and in the trainee's own best interests.

12. Listen attentively to what counselees are saying. Seek to view their words from their perspective, not from yours. Unfortunately, some counselors, at times, are caught up in their own interests and concerns and do not tune out those thoughts while the counselee is speaking. This guideline seems very simple, but it is indeed difficult for many to follow. Kadushin (1972, p. 188) expanded on why listening attentively is difficult:

The nature of spoken communication presents a special hazard, seducing the interviewer into an easy nonlistening. The hazard lies in the great discrepancy between the number of words that are normally spoken in one minute and the number of words that can be absorbed in that time. Thought is much more rapid than speech. The average rate of spoken speech is about 125 words per minute. We can read and understand an average of about 300–500 words per minute. There is, then, a considerable amount of dead time in spoken communication, during which the listener's mind can easily become distracted. The listener starts talking to herself to take up the slack in time. Listening to the internal monologue may go on side by side with listening to the external dialogue. More often, however, it goes on at the expense of listening to the external dialogue. The interviewer becomes lost in some private reverie—planning, musing, dreaming.[3]

Kadushin (1972, p. 190) gave the following suggestions on how to listen effectively:

Rather than becoming preoccupied as a consequence of the availability of the spare time between the slow spoken words, the good interviewer exploits this time in the service of more effective listening. The listener keeps focused on the interviewee but uses the time made available to the mind by slowness of speech to move rapidly back and forth along the path of the interview, testing, connecting, questioning: How does what I am hearing now relate to what I heard before? How does it modify what I heard before? How does it conflict with it, support it, make it more understandable? What can I anticipate hearing next? What do I miss hearing that needs asking about? What is he trying to tell me? What other meanings can the message have? What are his motives in telling me this?[4]

[3]Alfred Kadushin, *The Social Work Interview,* Copyright © 1972 Columbia University Press, New York. Reprinted by permission.
[4]Ibid.

Stage V: Exploration of Resolution Strategies

After (or sometimes while) a subproblem is explored in depth, the next step is for the counselor and the counselee to consider alternative solutions. In exploring alternative solutions, it is almost always best for the counselor to begin by asking something like "Have you thought about ways to resolve this?" The merits, shortcomings, and consequences of the alternatives thought of by the counselee should then be tactfully and thoroughly examined. If the counselee has not thought of certain viable alternatives, the counselor should mention these, and the merits and shortcomings of these alternatives should also be examined.

Each client is unique, and so are his or her problems. What works for one client may not be in the best interest of another. An abortion, for example, may be compatible with one client's values and circumstances, but may well be undesirable for another unmarried pregnant woman who has a different set of values and goals. If counseling is going to be effective, the client needs to say, "I see there are several courses of action that I might try in order to do something about my situation." Unless a client comes to realize there are some resolution strategies, counseling is apt to fail.

Stage VI: Selection of a Strategy

After the counselor and the client discuss the probable effects and consequences of possible resolution strategies, it is essential that the client conclude, "I think this approach might help me and I am willing to try it." If a client is indecisive or refuses to make an honest commitment to trying a course of action, constructive change will not occur. For example, if a client says to himself or herself, "I know I have a drinking problem, but am unwilling to take any action to cut down on my drinking," counseling probably will not be successful.

The counselee usually has the right to self-determination; that is, to choose the course of action among possible alternatives. The counselor's role is to help the counselee clarify and

At the hospital, a social worker, nurse, and patient explore alternatives. It is important to examine the merits and shortcomings of each alternative.

understand the likely consequences of each available alternative. It is generally not the counselor's role to give advice or to choose the alternative for the counselee. If the counselor were to select the alternative, there are two possible outcomes: (1) the alternative may prove to be undesirable for the counselee, in which case the counselee will probably blame the counselor for the advice and the future relationship will be seriously hampered, and (2) the alternative may prove to be beneficial for the counselee. This immediate outcome is desirable, but the danger is that the counselee will then become overly dependent on the counselor, seeking the counselor's advice for nearly every decision in the future and generally being reluctant to make decisions on his or her own. In actual practice, most courses of action have desirable and undesirable consequences. For example, if an unmarried mother is advised to keep her child, she may receive considerable gratification from being with and raising the child, but at the same time she may blame the counselor for such possible negative consequences as long-term financial hardships and an isolated social life.

The guideline of not giving advice does *not* mean that a counselor should not suggest alternatives that a client has not considered. On the contrary, it is the counselor's responsibility to suggest and explore all viable alternatives with a client. A good rule to follow is that when a counselor believes a client should take a certain course of action, this should be phrased as a suggestion, "Have you thought about . . . ?" rather than as giving advice, "I think you should . . ."

Counselees' rights to self-determination should be taken away only if the selected course of action has a high probability of seriously hurting others or themselves. For example, if it is highly probable that a parent will continue to abuse a child, or if the counselee attempts to take his or her own life, intervention by the counselor is suggested. For most situations, however, the counselee should have the right to select his or her alternative, even when the counselor believes that another alternative is a better course of action. Frequently, the counselee is in a better position to know what is best for him or her, and if the alternative is not the best, the counselee will probably learn from the mistake.

Stage VII: Implementation

Counseling will be successful only if the client follows through on his or her commitment to try a resolution approach and then concludes "This approach is beginning to help me." If the client follows through on the commitment, but instead concludes "I don't believe this approach is helping me," counseling again is failing. If this occurs, the reasons for no gain need to be examined, and perhaps another resolution strategy needs to be tried. The following are some guidelines on how to implement a resolution approach:

1. Attempt to form explicit, realistic "contracts" with counselees. When the counselee does select an alternative, he or she should clearly understand what the goals will be, what tasks need to be carried out, how to do the tasks, and who will carry out each of them. Frequently, it is desirable to write the

"contract" for future reference, with a time limit set for the accomplishment of each task. For example, if an unmarried mother decides to keep her child and now needs to make long-range financial plans, this goal should be understood and specific courses of action decided on—seeking public assistance, seeking support from the alleged father, securing an apartment within her budget, and so on. Furthermore, who will do what task within a set time limit should be specified.

When a contract is negotiated (and perhaps renegotiated in future interviews), it helps bring a focus to the interview. Client and counselor are less likely to get side-tracked by extraneous issues, and the interview's productivity can be sustained.

If client and the counselor differ in their expectations of desired goals, or in their expectations of who will do what tasks, the process of negotiating a contract will force the client and counselor to discuss and hopefully resolve their differences.

2. Counseling is done *with* the counselee, not *to* or *for* the counselee. The counselee should have the responsibility of doing many of the tasks necessary to improve the situation. A good rule to follow is that the counselee should take responsibility for those tasks that he or she has the capacity to carry out, while the counselor should attempt to do only those that are beyond the client's capacities. Doing things *for* counselees, similar to giving advice, runs the risk of creating a dependency relationship. Furthermore, successful accomplishment of tasks by counselees leads to personal growth and helps prepare them for taking on future responsibilities.

3. "Role play" certain tasks that the counselee lacks confidence or experience in carrying out. For example, if a pregnant single woman wants help in knowing how to tell her male friend about the pregnancy, role playing the situation will assist the woman in selecting words and developing a strategy for informing him. The counselor

can first play the woman's role and model an approach, with the woman playing the male role. Then the roles should be reversed so that the woman gains practice in telling her male friend.

Stage VIII: Evaluation

If constructive change is apt to be long lasting or permanent, the client must conclude, "Although this approach takes a lot of my time and effort, it's worth it." On the other hand, if he or she concludes, "This approach has helped a little, but it's really not worth what I'm sacrificing for it," then counseling will either be ineffective, or an alternative course of action needs to be developed and implemented.

When counselees meet commitments, reward them verbally or in other ways. Rewarding them increases their self-esteem and self-respect, and further motivates them to continue working on improving their circumstances.

One of the biggest reality shocks of new trainees entering the helping professions is that many clients, even after making commitments to improve their situations, do not carry out the steps outlined.

If a counselee fails to meet the terms of the "contract" that has been developed, generally do not punish. Punishment usually increases hostility without producing positive lasting changes. Also, do not accept excuses when commitments are not met. Excuses let people off the hook; they provide temporary relief, but they eventually lead to more failure and to a failure identity. Simply ask, "Do you still wish to try to fulfill your commitment?" If the counselee answers affirmatively, another time deadline acceptable to the counselee should be set.

Whether or not the counselee reaches all the goals that have been set, careful attention should be given to terminating the relationship. If the counselee still has unresolved problems that the counselor is unable to help with, a referral should be made to an appropriate agency or professional person. Care should be taken in terminating the contact so that the client does not erroneously conclude that the counselor is rejecting him or her. Also, the counselee should be asked whether there are additional concerns that he or she would like help with. If there are no concerns, the counselee should be informed the counselor's "door will be open" if help is needed in the future.

At the final interview, or a few weeks after termination, it is usually beneficial to ask the client (verbally or with a brief questionnaire) the following questions:

- Did the counseling help you? If yes, how? If no, why did it not help?
- What did the counselor do well?
- What were the shortcomings of the counseling that was received?
- What suggestions do you have for improving counseling services at this agency?
- Do you have some concerns for which you desire additional counseling?

Such information is very useful in improving the counseling process and in determining whether the counselee needs additional help.

The guidelines on counseling should not be followed dogmatically, as they will probably work only 70 to 80 percent of the time. The most important tool that a counselor has is herself or himself (feelings, perceptions, relationship capacities, and interviewing skills).

One final important guideline—the counselor should refer the counselee to someone else, or at least seek another professional counselor to discuss the case with, for any of the following situations: (1) if the counselor feels unable to empathize with the counselee, (2) if the counselor feels that the counselee is choosing unethical alternatives (such as seeking an abortion) that conflict with the counselor's basic value system, (3) if the counselor feels that the problem is of such a nature that he or she will not be able to help, or (4) if a working relationship is not established. A competent and secure counselor knows that it is possible to work with and help some peo-

ple but not all, and that it is in the counselee's and the counselor's best interests to refer those he or she cannot help to someone else who may be able to provide the counseling needed.

Clients' Reactions to Having a Personal Problem

In counseling clients there is another crucial area that counselors need to be aware of and learn to handle effectively: clients' emotional reactions to having a personal problem. The following example involving Lee Askew underscores the importance of this area. Mr. Askew has been an alcoholic for many years, and for most of these years his reaction to his drinking problem has been *denial*. Why? When Mr. Askew was first seen in counseling nearly three years ago, he had experienced a variety of problems related to his drinking. The following is a summary of the intake history of Mr. Askew:

Lee Askew is 43 years old and has been drinking heavily since he was 16 years of age. For the past several years, he has drunk an average of a quart of vodka each day. His second marriage is in trouble because his wife, Callie, claims their money is being spent on alcohol rather than on paying their bills. Also, his wife has informed him she can no longer tolerate his drunken behavior—nearly every evening he is in a drunken stupor and rambles on repeating himself until he finally falls asleep, often by passing out. Mr. Askew's first wife divorced him because of his drinking. When he is sober, he is friendly and enjoyable to be with. But as the day moves along, he increasingly becomes intoxicated and his behavior becomes intolerable. Five years ago he had serious automobile accident while intoxicated and was nearly killed. Three and one-half years ago he was again arrested for drunken driving.

(continues on page 140)

Case Example
Counseling principles

Our social work program (similar to social work programs at other universities) places students in social service agencies for an internship. As social work interns, students observe, and soon begin to do, the kind of work that social workers do. A frequent "reality shock" reported by interns is that many clients are apathetic, discouraged, and simply not motivated to improve. Often, the result is that clients do not "follow through" on commitments made during counseling sessions to make certain efforts to improve their circumstances.

Several years ago, at a county social services agency (county welfare department), I was supervising an intern who became quite surprised and frustrated when clients failed to follow through on commitments. The intern was working with a small caseload of AFDC mothers (Aid to Families of Dependent Children Program). The intern commented, "The case examples discussed in textbooks are always successes, and I as yet have seen no improvement in my cases." I reassured her that she was not at fault and that lack of improvements is more often the rule than the exception. I added that textbooks are very selective in that they usually present success cases, rather than typical cases, to illustrate theory. Yet, I cautioned that if she became discouraged and gave up being an "encouraging person," there would be *no* hope of her being effective in helping her clients improve. After further discussion she developed an approach in which she used the principles presented earlier. By the end of her internship, not all of the AFDC mothers she was working with showed substantial improvement. Yet she had formed a respected working relationship with all her clients, and some were making significant efforts to improve their circumstances. At the end of the semester, she wrote the following summary about her contacts with one of her clients:

I was assigned the case of Mrs. H. She was 33 years of age and had three children, ages 15, 11, and 7. She had been receiving AFDC assistance for the past six years, ever since her husband deserted her. During the past four years, the agency had made several efforts to get her a job, without success. The records showed Mrs. H did not want a full-time job, because she felt she was too busy taking care of her children. She applied for several part-time jobs but was not hired. Mrs. H felt she was not skilled, and the reality of the situation was that a low-paying job would result in a reduction of her AFDC check, with the end result being that financially a part-time job would hardly be beneficial.

I was assigned Mrs. H's case when she requested a social worker's help with a problem she was having with her 15-year-old son. Mrs. H had found some "pot" in her son's clothes drawer and didn't know how to handle the situation. I met with Mrs. H. Her home had a general unclean appearance. Mrs. H's physical appearance gave the impression she had been through a war. Her clothes were wrinkled and had what appeared to be food stains on several places. Her hair was greasy, she was quite obese, and she had few teeth left in her mouth. Dark circles were under her eyes, suggesting a great deal of fatigue and stress.

We met for about an hour and a half, and Mrs. H related much of her life history. She had never held a full-time job, having a "forced marriage," due to becoming pregnant, shortly after she graduated from high school. Her husband had been a road construction worker and had a drinking problem. She had not heard from him in six years. She felt if he did come back, she would not even want to see him. She had heard that when he left he moved to a distant state with another woman.

My aim in the first interview was to build a working relationship, obtain Mrs. H's trust, and help her explore what she saw as her problems. Her immediate problem appeared to be what to do about her discovery of "pot." We discussed to some extent the legalities of smoking marijuana and the effects and consequences of the drug. I also said I could bring over some brief reading material on the drug the next day, and she responded by saying she would very much appreciate receiving such material.

We then role-played how she might bring up the subject of smoking marijuana with her son. First I played her role to model a possible approach, and she played her son. Then we reversed roles to give her practice in trying out an approach. Before discussing the subject with her son, she mentioned she wanted to look at the reading material I had promised her. I dropped off this material the next day. We also set another meeting for the following week.

At our next appointment, Mrs. H indicated she had discussed smoking marijuana with her son. Her son responded first with some surprise and some displeasure that Mrs. H had gone through his clothes drawer. The son, Jerry, indicated he had tried smoking marijuana only twice and was not that interested in smoking in the future. Mrs. H added that her somewhat greater concern with Jerry appears to be his interest in occasionally drinking beer with some of his friends. She indicated that she and Jerry had had some moderate disagreements in this area, and they are working on it.

I asked if she felt she needed help from our agency for this issue. She responded, "No, not at this time." I then asked if she needed any other additional help from our agency. She thanked me for the help I had given and said she was not aware of other areas where she needed help. I could have left, but I thought since I had a good relationship established with her, and had been of some prior help, this might be an opportunity to have her take a look at her future.

I began by asking her what she would like to see herself doing ten years from now. She responded by saying, "I haven't given that much thought. I probably will be doing what I'm doing now." I asked if she was satisfied with her current life. She rather firmly said no, and went on at length about how difficult it is to live on an inadequate AFDC budget and to raise three children by herself. She was also critical of her husband, who placed her in this situation by deserting her.

I conveyed an understanding of her concerns and mentioned that it was certainly true that past events had led to her current circumstances. But I added that what she wanted for the present and the future was largely up to her. She asked what I meant.

I said, "Take your financial situation, for example. You have a choice between staying home or seeking a job. Now, I know at the present time that working would not improve your finances very much. But if you don't begin learning an employable skill now, and gradually working your way up in a job, what's going to happen in 10 years? In 10 or 11 years your youngest child will no longer be eligible for AFDC

(continued)

Case Example
Counseling principles (*continued*)

payments. Then what will you do? There are also other areas that we could work on; for example, dental care. But the choice is totally up to you. If you want to work on some of these areas, I'm very interested in working with you. If you aren't interested at the present time, there's little I can do to change your mind."

Mrs. H responded by indicating she was aware that her teeth needed attention, but added she didn't have the money to pay a dentist. I indicated the expenses were covered under her medical card (Medicaid Program). She expressed surprise, and indicated she would make an appointment with a dentist. She thanked me for the information, and I noted her face showed a spark of interest.

I then asked if she had thought about obtaining a job. She mentioned that would be nice, but then started citing a number of reasons she thought that it would not be possible. Many of these appeared to me to be "self-defeating self-talk." The following is a summary of her negative self-talk, along with a more positive view for each reason that I suggested to her.

Mrs. H's Reasons for Not Seeking a Job	*A More Positive View*
1. "I've tried finding a job several times in the past and was not able to obtain one."	1. "Having tried in the past and failed does not mean you can't obtain a job at this time. We could provide you with work training in an area that you were interested in, and also help you obtain a job after the training."
2. "Even if I worked, it would not significantly add to my total income, since my AFDC grant would be reduced."	2. "There is some truth in this. However, a job would add some money to your total income. Also, you need to start thinking about your future, because when your children become adults, you will no longer be eligible for AFDC. Having a job now will help you prepare for the future. Also, there are other benefits in working, such as the opportunity to get to know other people."
3. "I'm really not skilled at any job. Frankly, it is very embarrassing to be turned down when I apply."	3. "Nothing ventured, nothing gained. As far as not having a skill, we can enroll you in a work-training program. We can also help you find a job. You are not alone in being turned down for a job. I have a friend who applied to 67 teaching positions before being hired. This person was becoming quite discouraged but kept on trying. She finally found one and really liked it. The key is to keep on trying and hoping."
4. "I won't be able to work and also take care of my home and family."	4. "A working mother does have a lot to do and limited time to get it all done. However, many

mothers are able to do both." (At this point I asked if she would be interested in discussing this area with a friend of mine, Mrs. S. Mrs. S is also on AFDC and has four children, but now works full-time as a secretary. Mrs. S is an "encouraging" person. She got her job by first having work training, then volunteering at an agency to do clerical work. By volunteering she developed her typing skills, and after a year the agency hired her. Mrs. H indicated she would be interested in talking with Mrs. S.)

5. "Frankly, my personal appearance is such that I don't think that anyone would hire me."

5. "You're selling yourself short. Our agency can help you with dental care and in getting some new clothes. When you meet with Mrs. S, you will see she probably will not win a beauty contest but has an inner beauty (personality) that helped her get a job. I think with a more positive attitude, people would note an inner beauty on your part."

6. "I wouldn't, if I worked, be able to watch some of my favorite game shows and soap operas during the day. My present daily routine would be greatly altered."

6. "This is true. But you would be able to meet more people if you worked, and perhaps grow more as a person. Also, wouldn't your children be prouder of you if you worked? Are you really satisfied and contented with your present circumstances and current daily routine?"

7. "I don't own a car, and therefore don't have a way to get to a job even if I did get one."

7. "We can help you here by paying the cost of transportation and by helping you arrange for transportation. For example, we have volunteer drivers who would be able to provide transportation when you go for job interviews."

At this point I asked her to think over what we had talked about, and indicated that I would ask Mrs. S to contact her.

A week later I stopped by to see Mrs. H. She mentioned she had had an "inspirational" talk with Mrs. S. At that point she asked to be enrolled in our work-training program. I praised her decision. Within three months she had obtained a receptionist job for a new car dealer. Equally important, she appeared to have a renewed interest in living and had improved her personal appearance with increased grooming attention, some new clothes, and a set of dentures. For me as a student social work intern, this turned out to be a deeply rewarding, gratifying person to work with.

SOURCE: This case example is adapted from a case illustration that appeared in Charles Zastrow, *Talk to Yourself: Using the Power of Self-Talk,* © 1979, pp. 75–79. Adapted by permission of Prentice-Hall, Inc. Englewood Cliffs, New Jersey.

In the past ten years he has held a variety of sales jobs and been fired from three of these jobs for being intoxicated. Last night Mr. Askew physically abused his wife for the first time. This morning Mrs. Askew informed Lee that he must either seek help for his drinking or she will leave. Mr. Askew apologized for hitting his wife, claiming he had had a bad day at work. Lee, however, refuses to acknowledge he has a drinking problem.

Mr. Askew's denial of having a drinking problem is not unique. Clients display a variety of emotional reactions when confronted with evidence they have a personal problem. The effectiveness of counseling frequently depends on the counselor's understanding such emotional reactions in order to help clients recognize that they have a personal problem and need certain services.

In spite of the importance of understanding clients' emotional reactions to having a personal problem, there is a paucity of literature in this area.[5] An important contribution, however, has been made by Elizabeth Kübler-Ross. In *On Death and Dying*, Kübler-Ross (1969) presents five stages of dying that terminally ill people typically proceed through. These stages are not absolute, since not everyone goes through each one. But helping professionals who counsel the terminally ill have found this paradigm, when used in a flexible, insight-producing way, to be valuable in explaining why a patient may be behaving the way he or she is. The five stages are also typical of any individual's reaction when confronted with a serious personal problem of any kind.

The following section has three objectives.

1. Summarize Kübler-Ross's five stages of dying for the terminally ill. These five stages are in actuality five distinct emotional reactions that people display on being informed they have a terminal illness.

2. Suggest that these five stages are emotional reactions that are not unique to the terminally ill, but that clients typically display when confronted with evidence that they have a personal problem.

3. Show how a counselor's awareness of why clients are reacting as they are can be used to develop intervention approaches that will lead clients to acknowledge that they do have a personal problem and need services.

Kübler-Ross's Five Stages of Dying

Hans O. Mauksch (1975, p. 10) provided a concise summary of Kübler-Ross's five stages that terminally ill people typically proceed through:

1. *Denial:* "No, not me." This is a typical reaction when a patient learns that he or she is terminally ill. Denial, says Dr. Ross, is important and necessary. It helps cushion the impact of the patient's awareness that death is inevitable.

2. *Rage and anger:* "Why me?" The patient resents the fact that others will remain healthy and alive while he or she must die. God is a special target for anger, since He is regarded as imposing, arbitrarily, the death sentence.

3. *Bargaining:* "Yes, me, but . . ." Patients accept the fact of death but strike bargains for more time. Mostly they bargain with God—"even among people who never talked with God before." They promise to be good or to do something in exchange for another week or month or year of life. Notes Dr. Ross: "Why they promise is totally irrelevant, because they don't keep their promises anyway."

4. *Depression:* "Yes, me." First, the person mourns past losses, things not done, wrongs committed. But then he or she

[5]For several articles in this area, see Simos, 1977; Smith, 1978; and Wiseman, 1975.

enters a state of "preparatory grief," getting ready for the arrival of death. The patient grows quiet, doesn't want visitors. "Why a dying patient doesn't want to see you anymore," says Dr. Ross, "This is a sign he has finished his unfinished business with you, and it is a blessing. He can now let go peacefully."

5. *Acceptance:* "My time is very close now and it's all right." Dr. Ross describes this final stage as "not a happy stage, but neither is it unhappy. It's devoid of feelings but it's not resignation, it's really a victory."

In presenting these five stages, Kübler-Ross (1969) warns it is a mistake to expect that all terminally ill patients will methodically pass through all five stages. Some never reach the fifth stage of acceptance. Others may display reactions from two stages at the same time, for example, anger and denial. Still others may waver from one stage to another—reaching the depressed stage, and then returning to an earlier stage of denial or anger.

Kübler-Ross's Five Stages as Emotional Reactions

Kübler-Ross's five stages are common emotional reactions that clients have when they are confronted with evidence that they have a personal problem. Denial, rage and anger, bargaining, depression, and acceptance are, in my experiences, common reactions in the following situations: a husband is informed his wife is having an affair; a single teenager is informed she is pregnant; an employee is fired for incompetence; a woman is informed she has a malignant tumor in her breast; a woman informs her fiancé she is ending their engagement; a college coed is raped; a young couple is informed their youngest child has a cognitive disability; an elderly male discovers he is losing his sexual potency; a student intern is informed he does not have the capaci-

ties to become a competent counselor; a teacher is informed her contract will not be renewed for the next year. This list could perhaps be infinitely expanded, as it appears that clients are likely to have these emotional reactions to practically any personal problem.

Any time that a client first recognizes that he or she has a personal problem, a sense of loss occurs. The client feels or fears a loss of past, present, or future valued experiences. All of the aforementioned problems involve such a loss. Kübler-Ross's five stages are emotional reactions to losses. To illustrate, Lee Askew's case will be presented for each stage.

Stage 1: Denial ("No, not me."). For clients to admit they have a problem is difficult as they may often (erroneously) perceive themselves as weak, sinful, or irresponsible. Also, recognizing a problem exists means a client has to acknowledge that change is inevitable. When such change is inevitable, clients often mourn the loss of that which must be changed. For example, for alcoholics to admit they have a drinking problem generally means they will be expected to give up their drinking. This is especially difficult as their social activities and their lifestyles are centered around drinking. Unless clients have already developed an openness or reaching out pattern with others, it will be very difficult for them to share a new problem openly. Denial is often important and necessary, as it helps cushion the impact of the client's awareness that change is inevitable.

For people who are denying a problem exists, constructive changes are not apt to occur unless the counselor finds a way to convince them that there is a problem. When a client denies a problem exists, counseling needs to focus on the denial by exploring why the person believes there is no problem and by gathering evidence to document the existence of the problem to the client. The client then needs to be confronted in a tactful manner with this evidence by the counselor.

For over 20 years, Mr. Askew has been denying that he has a drinking problem. He believes that he needs alcohol to get through each day. He feels such a strong need for alcohol that he has allowed his drinking to end his first marriage, and he will not face reality that his drinking is also ruining his second marriage. Because he believes alcohol is such a necessity for him, he will not acknowledge that he nearly lost his life while driving when intoxicated, nor will he acknowledge that he has lost several jobs because of his drinking.

Mrs. Askew gave her husband an ultimatum—either he sees a counselor or she is leaving now. Mr. Askew reluctantly chose to see a counselor. In counseling Mr. Askew denied he had a drinking problem. He had excuses for everything that happened to him. His automobile accident resulted from slippery roads. He was fired because his employers did not like his suggestions for how to increase sales. He ended his first marriage because his wife was a "nag." He denied that he had more than a couple of drinks each day.

Stage 2: Rage and anger ("Why me?"). The client resents the fact that he or she has to make changes while others do not. Also, the client may be resentful that old friends, relatives, or society at large are doing the things that the clients must change. Anyone may be the target for the anger. Sometimes the anger is used to avoid discussing the issue at hand. At other times the client's anger may be directed at the counselor for confronting him or her with the reality of the "real problem."

The underlying reasons generating the client's anger need to be remembered during this stage. There are some therapeutic techniques that are often helpful during this stage. Allowing clients to ventilate their anger reduces its intensity; once this happens, they are better able to examine their difficulties realistically. Conveying empathy and emotional support helps create an atmosphere in which they feel more comfortable examining their difficulties. Often during this stage clients feel overwhelmed by their problems, which is a factor in their intensely felt "Why me?" If clients feel overwhelmed, they need to see that their problems are not overwhelming but can be broken down into subproblems that are resolvable in a gradual step-by-step fashion. During this stage it is also helpful for counselors to realize that when clients are angrily attacking them, the reason for the anger is probably being generated by the client's saying "Why me?" and should not be personalized by counselors. Reacting personally or angrily to the client's anger will only prolong the client's hostile behavior.

Lee Askew at times displayed anger while in counseling with Paul Decker. As indicated earlier, Mr. Askew at first denied he had a drinking problem. He had excuses for all the problems that were being caused by drinking. Mr. Decker knew counseling would not be productive unless this denial was broken through. Mr. Decker suggested that at the next session a joint meeting be held with the Askews to get both their perceptions of their marital problems. Mr. Askew reacted angrily to this suggestion, castigating his wife for making up stories about him, particularly his drinking. The counselor allowed Mr. Askew to ventilate his anger, and then asked, "Are you fearful of what your wife might say?" Mr. Askew stated "No," and agreed to a joint meeting.

Several meetings were jointly held with the Askews. Mr. Askew frequently continued to deny he had a drinking problem. These denials were countered by the counselor's asking Mr. Askew questions that served to confront Mr. Askew with his drinking problem. Such questions included how much he drinks each day, how he acts while drunk, how Mrs. Askew feels about seeing her husband intoxicated, whether his drinking has gotten him into trouble at work and with the police. At times Mr. Askew reacted angrily to such confrontations. (It appeared he was using anger to try to manipulate the counselor and his wife into refraining from forcing him to acknowledge that he has a drinking problem.) Mr. Decker let Mr. Askew "spit fire" and ventilate his anger. On a few occasions after Mr. Askew calmed down Mr. Decker would ask, "I wonder why you are reacting angrily to what is being said?" or "It appears we are touching a sensitive chord with you." Such questions were designed to help Mr. Askew gain an awareness of why he was reacting angrily.

At other times, Mr. Askew would go into a tirade about the fact that many of his friends drank and had a good time. He angrily wondered why his wife was putting pressure on him to stop drinking. He was clearly illustrating "Why me?" After allowing Mr. Askew to ventilate his anger, Mr. Decker pointed out that unlike social drinkers, his drinking was a serious problem for him because alcohol was controlling him; he was not in control of his drinking. Specific incidents of difficulties created when he was intoxicated were also tactfully mentioned.

On one occasion Mr. Askew, with his wife present, began castigating Mr. Decker for meddling in his family affairs. The counselor calmly listened, and then replied, "Are you feeling angry at me because I'm forcing you to see that you face a choice between giving up drinking or losing your wife?" Mr. Askew at first reacted angrily to this but later acknowledged the statement was true. Again, anger was Mr. Askew's reaction to being forced to face his drinking problem.

Stage 3: Bargaining ("Yes, me, but . . ."). During this stage clients are beginning to accept the problem but will bargain for such things as "just one more time." They promise to be good or to do something in exchange for another week or month before they use the alternatives presented to them to change. During this stage a counselor should confront clients with the reality of the circumstances and their bargaining efforts.

During the bargaining stage clients will usually try to change a few circumstances in their lives and they generally believe that if these circumstances change they can continue in their old ways. They are telling themselves that "if such and such changes, I can still continue to . . ." Bargaining is a common reaction. People who are urged to lose weight bargain for "strawberry shortcake"; smokers who are urged to quit bargain to smoke when tense; some spouses seek to preserve a marriage that is in trouble via a pregnancy.

Mr. Askew, in counseling, tried several bargaining efforts. At first he asked if he continued in counseling whether he could continue to drink socially. Both the counselor and Mrs. Askew doubted that Mr. Askew could quit after a few drinks and expressed their misgivings. Social drinking was tried for a week, and Mr. Askew became intoxicated on three occasions. At the next session Mrs. Askew again stated her ultimatum, "Stop drinking, or I'm leaving." Efforts were then made to supplement this counseling by getting Mr. Askew involved in Alcoholics Anonymous (AA) meetings. Initial results in AA were good. Then a wedding came up and Mr. Askew bargained with his wife (outside of counseling) that he would continue in AA if he could socially drink at special occasions such as the wedding. His wife struck the bargain on the condition that he quit after a few drinks. Mr. Askew became intoxicated at the wedding, and his actions (including wetting his pants) were immensely embarrassing to Mrs. Askew. At the next counseling session, Mrs. Askew again stated her ultimatum, "Stop drinking completely, or else I'm leaving." After a few other similar bargaining efforts, Mr. Askew was confronted by Mr. Decker with the statement that it appeared he was not committed to giving up drinking but was striking bargains to continue his drinking. Mr. Askew at first reacted angrily (back to the anger stage) but gradually acknowledged he was bargaining.

Stage 4: Depression ("Yes, me."). Clients at the depression stage usually become very quiet. They have, by now, stopped denying their problem. Their anger has subsided and they no longer try to bargain. They have gained insight into their particular problem and realize they must make changes in their lives. Alternatives, however, are not yet perceived as being viable solutions. They are blaming themselves in a "self-downing" manner for their problems and frequently mourn the loss of what they will have to change in their lives. During this stage counselors need to convey empathy and help clients see that their problems are not overwhelming. At this stage clients need to be given hope; frequently this can be accomplished by developing resolution strategies with them.

Mr. Askew and his wife had been coming to weekly counseling for three and one-half months. During this time Mr. Askew made some efforts to give up drinking. At times he would go for a week or two without drinking, but always returned to the bottle. In counseling sessions he often vacillated between making excuses for his drinking (denial) and displaying anger, or bargaining when confronted with the need to stop drinking. Generally at the counseling session following a drinking episode he would usually be depressed, acknowledging he was ruining his life by drinking. He would deprecate himself, and beg his wife to give him one more chance. When she did, a week or two later he would find an excuse to start drinking again.

After three and one-half months, Mr. Askew came into counseling one day a little hung over, and very depressed. He indicated he had gotten drunk the day before, and he and his wife had gotten into an argument. He wasn't certain, but he thought he may have slapped her face a few times. He added that afterward she packed a bag, indicated she was going to file for divorce, and left. Mr. Askew stated life was not worth living without his wife. He fully acknowledged he had a drinking problem and had to abstain completely. The counselor and Mr. Askew discussed various alternatives. Mr. Askew stated

with emotion that he would never take another drink, and that he would demonstrate this to his wife. He further decided to wait for two weeks before contacting her so that she could sort out her feelings and thoughts. Mr. Askew left the interview depressed, realizing that his drinking may now have ruined his marriage forever.

Stage 5: Acceptance ("I have a problem, but it's all right." "I can."). Clients now will make a concentrated effort at this stage to work out alternatives. Not only those suggested earlier in treatment but also some of their own. They have the attitude now of "I can do it." There is hope. A plan for rehabilitation can be presented if one was lacking or dismissed in the earlier stages. Fear is still present but very much reduced with the prospect of hope.

After two weeks Mr. Askew called his wife. They talked, and she agreed to attend the next counseling session. At this session, Mrs. Askew indicated she was ambivalent about ending her marriage, but she had totally had it with her husband's drunken behavior. They agreed to live apart for the next four months. If Lee participated in AA meetings and did not drink at all, they then would live together again, on the condition that he would never drink again.

That was over two years ago. Lee Askew has not had a drink, and he is active in AA helping other problem drinkers. He is also active in a speaker's bureau in which he talks to high school students and to businesses and organizations about the dangers of alcohol and about treatment programs. After three months of being separated, his wife returned, and both report their marriage and their careers are going well.

Summary

From the counselor's perspective, counseling can be divided into three phases: (1) building a relationship, (2) exploring problems in depth, and (3) exploring alternative solutions, with the client then selecting a course of action. Successful counseling gradually proceeds from one phase to the next, with some overlap of these stages. At the end of a series of counseling interviews, there is often the fourth phase of "termination and evaluation."

The counseling process can also be conceptualized from the client's perspective. In order for counseling to be successful, clients must give themselves a progressive series of "self-talk" (that is, clients must arrive at having certain thoughts and beliefs). These self-talk stages are listed below:

Stage I   *Problem awareness:* "I have a problem."

Stage II   *Relationship to counselor:* "I think this counselor has what it takes to help me."

Stage III   *Motivation:* "I want to improve my situation and am willing to put forth the effort to do so."

Stage IV   *Conceptualizing the problem:* "My problem is not overwhelming but has specific components that can be changed."

Stage V   *Exploration of resolution strategies:* "I see there are several courses of action that I might try in order to do something about my situation."

Stage VI   *Selection of a strategy:* "I think this approach might help and I am willing to try it."

Stage VII   *Implementation:* "This approach is helping me."

Stage VIII   *Evaluation:* "Although this approach takes a lot of my time and effort, it's worth it."

The advantage of this conceptualization of the counseling process is that it presents a framework for improving the effectiveness of counseling. This framework indicates when counseling is not helpful; the reasons for no progress can be identified by examining clients' self-talk about the counseling. Once these reasons are identified, needed changes can be made in the counseling process.

In counseling clients there is another crucial area that counselors need to be aware of and learn to handle effectively: clients' emotional reactions to having a personal problem. Material is presented demonstrating that Kübler-Ross's (1969) five stages are emotional reactions that are not unique to the terminally ill but are typical reactions that any client is apt to display when confronted with evidence of having a personal problem. Any time that a client first recognizes that he or she has a personal problem, a sense of loss occurs. Kübler-Ross's five stages are emotional reactions to loss. The five stages are denial, rage and anger, bargaining, depression, and acceptance. Only when clients reach the fifth stage of acceptance are they ready to work effectively on alternatives for resolving their problems. With a better understanding of these emotional reactions, counselors will be more effective in selecting appropriate intervention strategies.

Exercises
1. Understanding clients' reactions to having a personal problem

Goal: This exercise is designed to help students understand clients' reactions to having a personal problem.

Step 1: Explain the purpose of the exercise. Indicate that when a person acknowledges he or she has a personal problem, almost always that person experiences a loss of some kind. The loss may involve giving up something one has had (such as an alcoholic giving up drinking). Or, the loss may involve recognition that a desired goal is not obtainable (for example, parents who have a child with a cognitive disability may feel the loss of not having a child of normal intelligence). When a loss is experienced, the person almost always has the emotional reactions described by Kübler-Ross. Describe the following reactions to students: denial, anger and rage, bargaining, depression, and acceptance.

Step 2: Ask students to volunteer to describe a loss they have had, and have them comment on whether they experienced the five reactions described by Kübler-Ross.

Step 3: Explain that clients are frequently not ready emotionally to work on resolving a personal problem or a loss until they reach the fifth stage of acceptance. Ask the students who describe a loss if in fact they had to reach the stage of accepting their loss before they were able to make a concentrated effort to work on alternatives for resolving the problems.

2. Learning how to counsel through role playing

Goal: The purpose of this exercise is to help students develop their counseling skills through role playing counseling situations.

Step 1: Describe the goal of the exercise. Indicate that the counseling process from the counselor's view can be divided into five phases: (1) starting the interview; (2) building a relationship; (3) exploring problems in depth; (4) exploring alternative solutions with the client(s) then choosing one or more of the alternatives; and (5) ending the interview. (Material on these five phases is summarized in Chapters 4 and 5 of this text.) Briefly summarize guidelines on how a counselor should handle each of these phases.

Step 2: Ask two students to volunteer to role play being clients. Allow the "clients" to come up with their own contrived problems. Indicate the following as examples of possible problems:

a. Two college students are roommates. One believes the other has a drinking problem while the other refuses to acknowledge a problem exists.
b. Two siblings are concerned about their mother living alone. Her health is failing, and her husband has recently died. The siblings also believe they are unable to care for their mother as each is married and has a family, and the mother is not easy to live with.
c. A husband and wife both want children but the husband is infertile. The wife wants to become pregnant through artificial insemination. The husband objects to his wife getting pregnant using this means.

Step 3: Counsel the two students who have contrived problems in order to demonstrate the five phases of counseling. After the counseling is completed, have the class discuss the strengths and shortcomings of the counseling that was given.

Step 4: Ask four more students to volunteer—two as clients having contrived problems and two as counselors for the two "clients." (It is useful to have two people, at this early stage, volunteer to be counselors to offset the potential of one counselor becoming "stuck" by not knowing what to say.) Role play the interview.

Step 5: As an additional step, require each student in the class to role play as counselor and also as client (for some other student who role plays being a counselor). Ideally each student should be videotaped in the role of the counselor, and this videotape should then be played back so students can access the interview. (As described in Chapter 4, the videotaping may be used not only to help students develop their counseling skills but also as a screening device to counsel out students from the social work major if they are unable, after several tries, to make an acceptable videotape.)

Step 6: Show each videotape to the class; hold a brief class discussion after each tape is shown. This discussion should review the strengths and shortcomings of the counseling and also look at what else might be done. If each tape is shown to the class, it is helpful for each student to fill out the Interviewer Skills Rating Sheet on the following page, which is then given to the "counselor" for feedback purposes. (One advantage of showing each tape to the class is that students learn aspects of what should and should not be done in counseling from viewing tapes.)

Note: Role playing contrived counseling situations (and also videotaping of such situations) can be structured in a variety of ways. This exercise presents some ideas, but the instructor of course has the autonomy to structure the role-playing in ways that he or she believes will be most beneficial.

3. Responding effectively to critical statements from clients

Goal: This exercise is designed to help students learn how to respond more effectively to highly emotional and complex statements made by clients.

Step 1: Explain the purpose of the exercise. Then read the first client statement and ask the class for their suggestions on the most effective way for a counselor to respond. There are a variety of effective responses. (One way of responding to each of these statements is presented in Appendix C.) A class discussion of the merits and shortcomings of some of the students' suggested responses is apt to be a productive learning experience.

Step 2: After the class responds to and discusses the first statement, the instructor should read the second statement and again seek responses and discussion from the students. This process continues with the remaining statements.

Client Statements

1. *Male client* (fifth interview): "There's something that's been bothering me for the past few weeks (pause). I'm beginning to feel that you're not really

INTERVIEWER SKILLS RATING SHEET

Student _____ Date _____

Skills	Need Improvement	Satisfactory	Excellent
1. Opening remarks			
2. Explanation of counselor role			
3. Voice quality and volume			
4. Body posture			
5. Eye contact			
6. Behavioral congruence/facial expression (therapist's words match his/her outward appearance)			
7. Frequency of open-ended questions (not yes-no or multiple-choice questions)			
8. Amount of therapist's verbal activity			
9. Verbal following behavior (sequencing questions with client's answers preparing client for shift in subject matter)			
10. Clarity of questions			
11. Ability to confront client with inconsistencies			
12. Use of humor			
13. Warmth/ability to put client at ease			
14. Use of silence			
15. Ability to help client define problems			
16. Ability to have client specify goals			
17. Paraphrasing			
18. Reflection of client's feelings			
19. Summarization of client information			
20. Ability to answer client's questions—provide useful information			
21. Extent to which interviewer presented him/herself as a professional			
22. Extent to which necessary data about the problem was obtained			
23. Ending the interview/length of interview			
24. Completeness of interview			
25. Extent to which a helpful relationship was developed			
26. Extent to which alternative solutions to the problem were begun to be explored			

Positive Comments About Strengths Demonstrated During the Interview

Areas Needing Attention

interested in me as a person. I have the feeling that the only reason you're meeting with me is because you're getting paid to see me."

2. *Engaged female*, age 20: "I'm engaged to marry Kent. My uncle thinks he's terrific, but my parents are telling me I'm making the biggest mistake of my life to marry him. They dislike him and also think I'm too young to marry. I'm so confused about what I should do. Kent is putting a lot of pressure on me to elope."

3. *Juvenile probationee*, age 16, who is recognized as being a con artist—in required weekly visit with probation agent: "Your office is really cool. You've really got it made. I admire your taste in furnishing this office. You deserve what you've got in life. I admire you. Those are great photographs on the wall—Did you take them?" The probation officer is aware that students received their midterm grade reports this past week.

4. *Male client*, age 27 (fourth interview): "I'm feeling real tense today. I've got a lot on my mind (pause). I don't think we've made much progress in the last three meetings, although I am gradually coming to trust you (pause). I haven't been fully honest with you. You know the marital problems I've been having? Well, the main reason our marriage hasn't gone well, and Karen doesn't even know this, is because for the past few years I've been involved with someone else—who happens to be a male. Karen no longer turns me on because I guess I'm more attracted to males."

5. *African American client* from an inner city who has a white therapist: "You honkies don't know what life is really like for us who live in a ghetto. You say you want to help me, but I don't buy that jive. How can you possibly help me when you have no idea what it is like to be black and living in a ghetto?"

6. *Teenage male delinquent* caught with marijuana in his possession at a correctional institution: "Please don't report this. You know I've been doing really well here at school and have a clean record. If you report this, my stay will be extended. I was only holding the drugs for a friend here. I'm not using any of it myself. Give me a break—everyone needs one in life." The youth was involved with drugs when he committed the offenses for which he was sent to this correctional facility.

CHAPTER

6

Social Work with Groups: Types of Groups and Guidelines for Leading Them

The practice of social work in groups is not a new phenomenon.[1] The ideological roots of social group work can be traced most directly to the settlement houses, informal self-help recreational organizations (YMCA, YWCA), Jewish centers, and scouting, all of which developed during the first three decades of this century. During this period, many social workers found group-based methods of intervention effective and efficient for confronting a variety of personal and social problems. The last 60 years have witnessed a progressive interest in, and expansion of, group services in our society. The involvement of the social work profession in groups has broadened accordingly. Today it is not uncommon to find social workers as both group leaders and participants in a myriad of settings, helping solve or ameliorate human or social problems, and planning for and creating change. There are many reasons behind the attractiveness of groups for members and for practitioners. Hartford (1971) defined a group as

at least two people—but usually more, gathered with common purposes or like interests in a cognitive, affective, and so-

cial interchange in single or repeated encounters sufficient for the participants to form impressions of one another, creating a set of norms for their functioning together, developing goals for their collective activity, evolving a sense of cohesion so that they think of themselves and are thought of by others as an entity distinct from all other collectivities. [p. 26]

From this description we can see that the members of a group relate to one another within a context of sensing they form a distinct entity, that they share a common goal or purpose, and that they have confidence that together they can accomplish as much or more than would be possible were they to work separately. This commonality is characteristic of a wide variety of groups dealing with a multitude of societal problems. The beginning social worker is likely to be surprised at the diversity of groups in existence and excited by the challenge of practicing social work in groups. The period from 1960 to the present has witnessed an explosion in the number of groups and group-based techniques utilized by the social work profession. The following section describes a significant sample of the types of groups in which social workers may become involved. This listing is not exhaustive; only the creativity of the helping professional and the client group served will provide such limits.

Types of Groups

Recreation Groups

The objective of recreation groups is to provide activities for enjoyment and exercise. Often such activities are spontaneous and the groups are practically leaderless. The group service agency (such as YMCA, YWCA, or neighborhood center) may offer little more than physical space and the use of some equipment. Spontaneous playground activities, informal athletic games, and an open

---

[1]Material in this chapter is adopted from Charles Zastrow, "Social Work Practice with Groups," in *Introduction to Social Welfare Institutions*, 2nd ed. (Pacific Grove, CA: Brooks/Cole, 1982), pp. 507–529.

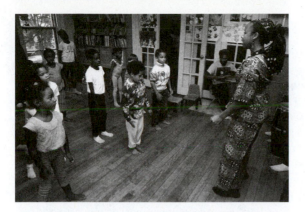

Instructing children in African-American culture is the focus of this educational group.

fessional person with considerable training and expertise in the subject area. Examples of topics include child-rearing practices, assertiveness training, techniques for becoming a more effective parent, preparing to be an adoptive parent, and training volunteers to perform a specialized task for a social service agency. Educational group leaders often function in a more didactic manner and frequently are social workers. These groups may resemble a class, with considerable group interaction and discussion being encouraged. The case example shows how assertiveness training can be taught in an educational group.

game room are examples. Some group agencies providing such physical space claim that recreation and interaction with others helps build character and prevent delinquency among youth by providing an alternative to the street.

Recreation-Skill Groups

The objective of a recreation-skill group is to improve a set of skills while providing enjoyment. In contrast to recreational groups, this group has an adviser, coach, or instructor; also there is more of a task orientation. Examples of activities include golf, basketball, needlework, arts and crafts, and swimming. Competitive team sports and leagues may emerge. Frequently such groups are led by professionals with recreational training rather than social work training. Social service agencies providing such services include YMCA, YWCA, Boy Scouts, Girl Scouts, neighborhood centers, and school recreation departments.

Educational Groups

The focus of educational groups is to help members acquire knowledge and learn more complex skills. The leader generally is a pro-

Task Groups

Task groups are formed to achieve a specific set of tasks or objectives. The following types of task groups are examples of task groups that social workers are apt to interact with or become involved in. A *board of directors* is an administrative group charged with responsibility for setting the policy governing agency programs. A *task force* is a group established for a special purpose and is usually disbanded after the task is completed. A *committee* of an agency or organization is a group that is formed to deal with specific tasks or matters. An *ad hoc committee,* like a task force, is set up for one purpose and usually ceases functioning after completion of its task.

Problem-Solving and Decision-Making Groups

Both providers and consumers of social services may become involved in groups concerned with problem solving and decision making. (There is considerable overlap between task groups and these groups; in fact, problem-solving and decision-making groups can be considered a subcategory of task groups.)

Providers of services use group meetings for such objectives as developing a treatment plan for a client or a group of clients, deciding

Case Example
Assertiveness training—an educational group

Assertiveness training in a group is an example of an educational group. There are several advantages of group over individual assertiveness training. A group provides a "laboratory" for testing or experimenting with new assertive behaviors. A group has a broader base for social modeling, since each person sees several others trying out a variety of assertive approaches. A wider variety of feedback is also offered. Furthermore, a group is generally understanding and supportive. Finally, group pressure and expectations motivate members to conscientiously develop and practice new assertive responses.

A typical format for an assertiveness training group is as follows: The size of such groups generally ranges from 5 to 20 members. The first session is devoted to a lecture presentation on the differences between assertive, nonassertive, and aggressive behavior. The specific steps in assertive training are then summarized. (These steps are presented in Chapter 16.) Several examples of typical situations are also given to illustrate that assertive responses are generally more effective than aggressive or nonassertive responses.

In the following sessions specific situations involving assertive responses are then examined. At first it may be desirable to begin with situations that are not brought forth by members of the group (group members may at first be reluctant to reveal personal situations they face). Alberti and Emmons (1975, pp. 183–184) suggested the following situations be practiced:

1. Starting a conversation with a small group of strangers who are already engaged in conversation at a party.
2. Saying "no" assertively when a roommate or friend asks to borrow something that you do not want to lend to others.
3. Returning faulty or defective items to a store.
4. Asking someone next to you to extinguish a cigarette.
5. Asking someone to turn down a stereo that is too loud, or not talk so loudly in the library, theater, and so forth.
6. Asking for a date/refusing a date on the telephone and face-to-face.
7. Expressing positive feelings; "soft assertions."
8. Responding assertively to a date or spouse who is giving you "put-down" comments.
9. Assertively refusing to take an alcoholic beverage from a friend when you prefer not to drink.

For each situation the following steps are used: (1) each member is asked to visualize (form a mental image of) his or her response, (2) one member is selected to role-play an assertive response, (3) the group briefly discusses the strategy after it is role-played, (4) if a more effective response is desired, a new assertive response is role-played by a member, and (5) the group then discusses the strategy.

Following this exercise, group members are encouraged to bring to the group real-life situations that are troubling them. These are often complicated and involve close, intimate relationships. Such situations may not have pat, simple resolutions. The following steps are recommended for group leaders in helping members become more assertive.

1. Help each group member identify the situations/interactions in which it would be to his or her benefit to be more assertive. Usually group members will bring up these situations themselves. Some members, however, may be reluctant to reveal problem interactions, or they may be unaware they could handle certain situations better by being more assertive. Considerable tact and skill by the leader is necessary in initiating problem areas of the latter type. (One approach that usually works is to have the members anonymously write the situations they want role-played on a note card.)

2. When a problem interaction is identified, each member of the group is asked to visualize a response silently. For complicated situations with no simple solutions, considerable discussion may arise about possible ways of resolving the matter.

3. A member (often someone other than the person with the problem situation) is asked to role-play an assertive response. The member with the problem may be asked to play the role of the person with whom he or she is having difficulty. The situation is then role-played.

4. The group briefly discusses the merits of the assertive strategy that was modeled in step 3.

If it is effective and the person with the problem is comfortable with it, that person is then asked to role-play the approach. If the group believes there may be a more effective approach, steps 3 and 4 are repeated. If the person with the problem is uncomfortable about using a strategy that is effective, the reasons for the discomfort are then explored. For example, for very shy people, certain attitudes, such as "don't make waves" or the "meek shall inherit the earth" may need to be dealt with.

5. The person with the problem is asked to rehearse an assertive strategy silently, thinking of what he or she will say and what the consequences may be.

6. The person with the problem is then asked to role-play an assertive strategy.

7. The group gives feedback about the merits of the strategy. Generally the person is praised for the effective aspects and coached on how to improve other aspects. This approach is practiced via role-playing until it is perfected and the person has developed sufficient comfort and self-confidence for the "real event." For feedback purposes, if possible, the approach is recorded on audiotape or videotape.

8. The person tries out the new response pattern in an actual situation.

9. The person describes at the next group meeting how the real-life test went. The person is complimented on the degree of success attained, and assistance is given on aspects that could be improved.

how to best allocate scarce resources, deciding how to improve the delivery of services to clients, arriving at policy decisions for the agency, deciding how to improve coordination efforts with other agencies, and so on.

Potential consumers of services may form a group to study an unmet need in the community and to advocate the development of new programs to meet the need. Data on the need may be gathered, and the group may be used as a vehicle either to develop a program or to influence existing agencies to provide services. Social workers may function as stimulators and organizers of such group efforts as well as participants (see Chapter 10 on social work community practice).

In problem-solving and decision-making groups, each participant normally has some interest or stake in the process and may gain or lose, depending on the outcome. Usually, there is a formal leader of some sort, although other leaders sometimes emerge during the process. There are three issues of importance to problem-solving and decision-making groups: group versus individual decision making, groupthink, and decision by consensus versus decision by majority vote.

Group versus individual decision making. Is group decision making superior to individual decision making? There is evidence that group decision making is usually superior to individual decision making (Johnson & Johnson, 1975, p. 60). This conclusion applies even when the individual decision is made by an expert.

There appear to be several reasons that group decision making is generally superior (Watson & Johnson, 1972). First, through group interaction the knowledge, abilities, and resources of each member are pooled. An individual acting alone often lacks some of the information, skills, or resources needed to arrive at the highest quality decision. Second, working in the presence of others motivates a person to put forth more effort, to be more careful, and to increase the quality of the work. Third, having more people working on a problem increases the probability that someone in the group will suggest the highest quality solution. Fourth, through group interaction the members can build on one another's ideas and develop a high-quality decision that is based on this building block approach. Fifth, through group discussion there is a greater chance of identifying the positive and negative consequences of each alternative. Therefore, the negative consequences of an inferior decision are more likely to be identified. Sixth, it is easier to identify other people's mistakes than it is to identify your own. Through group interaction we are more likely to identify the problem areas in the favorite alternatives of others, and others are more apt to identify the problem areas in our favorite alternative.

In general the effectiveness of group decision making is enhanced when there is high involvement by all group members in making decisions. High involvement increases the willingness of members to share their information and abilities in making a decision, increases their allegiance to the group, increases their commitment to implementing the decision, and increases their commitment to working for the group in the future. Most groups can become more effective by seeking to increase the involvement of all group members in making decisions.

There are only a few situations in which decisions might best be made by one or a few individuals: (1) when a decision has to be made so quickly it is not possible to have a meeting, (2) when the decision is relatively unimportant and the person making the decision follows precedents previously set by the group, and (3) when the decision is relatively unimportant, does not require committed action by most members of a group, and there is no reason to believe the group will object to the decision.

But there are some problems with group decision making that take place in real life. At times a subgroup will seek to "railroad" a decision that will benefit them but be counterproductive for the whole group or for certain people outside the group. (Hitler, for example, used many tactics to sway groups he worked with to begin World War II and to exterminate 6 million Jews.) Railroading tactics include pressuring a group to make a quick decision without giving the members time to analyze all the consequences, withholding information that is adverse to the desired decision, buying votes with promises, and suggesting there may be negative consequences for members who do not vote for the desired decision.

Another problem in group decision making is that friendships and paybacks for past favors sometimes lead members to vote for "the person" rather than for a decision based on thorough analysis of the consequences of the alternatives. Republicans and Democrats in Congress, for example, largely vote for the position taken by their party on issues.

Sometimes groups reach incorrect or ineffective decisions because of a phenomenon known as *groupthink.*

Groupthink. Irving Janis (1971) has identified groupthink as an unusual condition that can prevent effective problem solving. Janis studied groups who advised presidents of the United States and found that powerful social pressures were often exerted whenever a dissident began to voice objections to what otherwise appeared to be a group consensus. Groupthink is a problem-solving process in which proposals are accepted without a critical, careful review of the pros and cons of the alternatives, and in which considerable social pressure is brought to bear against expressing opposing points of view. Groupthink occurs partially because the norms of the group hold that it is more important to bolster group morale than to evaluate all alternatives critically. Another group norm that increases groupthink is that members should remain loyal to the group by sticking with the policies to which the group has already committed itself, although those policies are not having the intended effects, or are even having disturbing unintended consequences.

Janis (1971) listed a number of factors that promote groupthink. They include the following:

- Members have an illusion of being invulnerable, which leads them to become overly optimistic about their selected courses of action, to take extraordinary risks, and to fail to respond to clear warnings of danger.
- Members have an unquestioning belief in the group's moral rightness, which leads them to ignore the ethical consequences of their decisions.
- The group applies social pressures of disapproval on any member who momentarily questions the basic policies or who raises questions about a policy alternative favored by the majority.
- The group constructs rationalizations to discount warnings and other forms of negative feedback that would, if taken seriously, lead the members to rethink basic assumptions about policies that are not working out well.
- Group members hold stereotyped views of the leaders of opposing groups. These leaders are viewed as either being so evil that it would be a mistake to try genuinely to negotiate differences, or they are viewed as so stupid or so weak that they will not be able to prevent the group from attaining its objectives.
- Members sometimes assume "mind guard" roles in which they attempt to protect their leader and the group from negative information that might lead them to question the morality and effectiveness of past decisions.
- Members keep quiet about their misgivings and even minimize to themselves the importance of these misgivings. Through self-censorship members avoid deviating from what appears to be group consensus.
- The members believe practically everyone in the group fully agrees on the policies and programs of the group.

Case Example
Nominal group approach—A problem identification technique for problem-solving groups

The nominal group approach was developed by Delbecq and Van de Ven (1971) for use as a problem identification technique in social program development efforts. The approach involves meeting with potential users of a service. A *nominal group* is defined as "a group in which individuals work in the presence of others but do not verbally interact" (Van de Ven & Delbecq, 1971, p. 205). This need-identification approach emphasizes the importance of understanding clearly the view of the population that the group is trying to serve, and asserts that potential consumers of new services should articulate their needs, problems, and goals. The main orientation is to respond to consumers' needs rather than independently develop programs for them. To accomplish this objective, the nominal group approach is designed to receive input from all group members rather than just the more vocal or aggressive ones, as often happens in conventional group discussions. This technique has successfully been used in such applications as determining the housing difficulties of college students, reasons that have led delinquent youth into difficulty with police (Zastrow, 1973), and specific course topics wanted by students enrolling in social work courses (Zastrow & Navarre, 1977).

Research indicates that the nominal group approach is superior to brainstorming and to other types of interacting groups in generating information relevant to a problem situation. Both quantity and quality of suggestions are enhanced with this technique (Van de Ven & Delbecq, 1971). Several features appear to be involved in leading to this superiority. The approach has a game mystique that stimulates the interest of participants. Creative tension is stimulated by the presence of others, which fosters individual commitment to the task. Evaluation of items is avoided, which substantially reduces the pressure against expressing minority opinions or conventional ideas. Conflicting, incompatible ideas are tolerated. Furthermore, the approach appears to be "a time-saving process since it can be activated and concluded with greater rapidity than interacting group processes" (Van de Ven & Delbecq, 1971, p. 210).

The mechanics of conducting a nominal group are as follows:

1. Gather together a group of participants, any size, ranging up to about 100, and explain the nature of the study. Emphasize the importance of their ideas related to this topic. Care should be taken to obtain a representative cross-section of the populations of interest.

2. Randomly divide the participants into small groups ranging in size from 5 to 8. Seat each group around a separate table or in desks arranged in a circle.

3. Distribute to each participant a sheet of paper containing a question that must be answered. For example, the wording for determining desired course content might be

What specific subject topics do you want covered in this course?
PLEASE—NO TALKING

4. For 15 to 20 minutes, the participants privately list items they feel are in response to the question being asked; no talking is permitted during this period.

5. A round-robin listing technique is then used in which each individual in turn is given the opportunity to disclose one item at a time to the group. This listing is done

separately for each group with one of the members acting as a recorder. Ideas may be recorded on flip-chart paper or on a chalkboard. This round-robin listing continues until all members indicate they have no further ideas to share. Until this point is reached, there is no discussion or evaluation of ideas presented.

6. Following the listing of all ideas, the flip-chart sheets are posted on the wall with masking tape. There is a brief, informal discussion of the items, which is focused on clarifying what the ideas mean. There are two different approaches to reviewing the items: (1) all items are made known to all participants, or (2) each group briefly reviews only the items recorded for their group. Both approaches appear to work. For smaller-sized groups, the first is usually used; with larger groups, in which the total number of listed items becomes very large, the second approach is generally used.

7. Once the participants are familiar with the items listed, each is asked to write privately on index cards the five items he or she feels are the most important.

8. These selections are then tabulated and posted. The highest ranked problems or topics represent those considered most important by the group members.

Numerous poor decision-making practices result from groupthink. The group limits its discussion to only those courses of action that are consistent with past decisions and policies; as a result, more divergent strategies (some of which are viable) are not considered. The group fails to reexamine a selected course of action, even when they discover the risks, drawbacks, and unintended consequences that they had not previously considered. The group makes little effort to get cost-benefit information on possible strategies from experts who might be able to supply more accurate information. Members seek primarily to obtain facts and listen to opinions that support their preferred policy and tend to ignore facts and opinions that do not. The group fails to work out contingency plans to cope with foreseeable setbacks, and it spends little time considering how the chosen strategy might be sabotaged by political opponents or hampered by bureaucratic red tape.

Consensus versus majority voting. Decision making by consensus is usually the most effective approach for getting all mem-

bers to support and work for the decision. Consensus means that everyone is willing to go along with the decision, at least temporarily. This approach is also the most time consuming because the concerns of each member need to be dealt with. For many decisions, consensus is difficult to achieve because members are apt to have diverse opinions about what should be done.

To use consensus effectively, the group members need to have a certain mind-set, and the group has to have a trusting, cooperative atmosphere. For consensus to be arrived at, members need to feel free to present their views as clearly and logically as possible but to avoid blindly arguing their own individual views. They need to listen and respect the views of other members. Members should *avoid* going along with the group if they believe the majority opinion is a mistake. It is a mistake to yield to the majority if the only reason is to avoid conflict and appear united. Members, however, might yield to the majority opinion if that position appears to have merit and is a position they believe has a fair chance of having positive outcomes.

To make consensus work effectively, differences of opinion are sought out and respectfully dealt with. Disagreements and divergent views are advantageous because they increase the chances that all crucial aspects will be reviewed, that members will build on the views of others, and that viable decisions will be made.

With consensus, the participation of all members is encouraged. The emphasis is on finding the best solution that everyone can agree on and support. If a group becomes stalemated between two possible alternatives, a vote is not taken to allow one subgroup to win while the other loses. Instead, a third alternative is sought to incorporate the major desires of both subgroups.

There are a number of benefits to consensus. Since consensus resolves controversies and conflicts, it increases the group's ability to make future high-quality decisions.

If group members feel they have participated in the decision and support it, they are more likely to contribute their resources to implement the decision. Consensus is useful in making important, serious, and complex decisions in which the success of the decision depends on the commitment of all members.

There are some disadvantages to consensus. It takes a great deal of time and psychological energy. There is a danger that the pressure for group consensus may lead to groupthink. In this situation members go along with what they believe is the majority opinion, even when they have evidence or information (which they fail to share for fear of making waves) that the probable decision will be unproductive or even destructive. In addition, consensus will not work in many groups for a variety of reasons. A high level of trust may not exist in the group, thereby not allowing candor, honesty, and directness. Some members may try to dominate or manipulate the group rather than listen and support one another as individuals. Some members may see the slow process required to arrive at consensus as painful, aggravating, and a waste of time.

Most groups make decisions by simple majority vote. With this approach, issues are discussed until they are clarified and a simple majority of the members have arrived at an alternative. A vote is then taken.

There are several advantages to this type of decision making. Decisions are arrived at much faster than with the consensus approach. Most decisions in a group are not so important that full support of all members is necessary to achieve the objectives of the decision. Also, majority vote does not require, to as great an extent, the characteristics that are essential for consensus (such as trust, open communication, and willingness to give up one's favorite position).

There are also shortcomings of the simple majority approach. Minority opinions are not always safeguarded. Racial groups, women, certain ethnic groups, gay men and lesbians, and people with disabilities are minority groups that in the past have suffered from adverse decisions made by simple majority voting. Majority voting frequently splits a group into winners and losers, with the losers often becoming angry, frustrated, and apathetic. Sometimes the group of losers is nearly as large as the winners (such as having 49 percent of the vote), but they wind up feeling their concerns are receiving no attention. A large-sized minority that feels it has been outvoted may not lend its resources to implement the decision and may even work to subvert or overturn it. If the final vote alienates a minority, the group's future effectiveness is diminished. There is a danger that the majority rule approach may be interpreted by the minority as being an unfair means of control and manipulation by the majority. Therefore, to maintain effective group functioning, groups that use majority voting should seek to create a climate in which members feel they have had their day in court and have an obligation to go along with the group decision.

A compromise between consensus and simple majority is a high-percentage majority vote (such as two-thirds or three-fourths). This approach requires more time to arrive at a decision than a simple majority since more votes are needed. But it takes less time than consensus as not everyone has to be convinced or persuaded. A strong minority (such as 45 percent) can block a decision it dislikes, but a small majority cannot force its views on a strong minority. However, a small minority may still feel it is being controlled and manipulated by a high-percentage majority vote. A high-percentage majority vote will generally draw stronger support from group members than the simple majority approach, but it will not generate as much support as the consensus approach.

Self-Help Groups

Self-help groups are becoming increasingly popular and are often successful in helping individuals with certain social or personal problems. Katz and Bender (1976) provided a comprehensive definition of self-help groups.

> Self-help groups are voluntary, small group structures for mutual aid and the accomplishment of a special purpose. They are usually formed by peers who have come together for mutual assistance in satisfying a common need, overcoming a common handicap or life-disrupting problem, and bringing about desired social, and/or personal change. The initiators and members of such groups perceive that their needs are not, or cannot be, met by or through existing social institutions. Self-help groups emphasize face-to-face social interactions and the assumption of personal responsibility by members. They often provide material assistance as well as emotional support; they are frequently cause-oriented, and promulgate an ideology or values through which members may attain an enhanced sense of personal identity. [p. 9]

To convey the varieties and focuses of self-help groups that now exist (see Table 6.1), two different classifications of these groups are summarized in the following paragraphs. Katz and Bender (1976) classified self-help groups into the following five categories.

1. Groups that focus on self-fulfillment or personal growth. Examples include Alcoholics Anonymous, Recovery Inc. (for former mental patients), Gamblers Anonymous, and Weight Watchers.

2. Groups that focus on social advocacy. Examples include Welfare Rights Organizations, MADD (Mothers Against Drunken Drivers), and the Committee for the Rights of the Disabled. Katz and Bender (1976, p. 38) noted that the advocacy "can be both on behalf of broad issues, such as legislation, the creation of new services, change in the policies of existing institutions and so on, or it can be on behalf of individuals, families, or other small groups."

3. Groups that focus on creating alternative patterns for living. Examples include Gay Liberation and certain religious cults such as the Moonies.

4. *Outcast haven* or *rock-bottom* groups. Katz and Bender (1976) defined this type as follows:

> These groups provide a refuge for the desperate, who are attempting to secure personal protection from the pressures of life and society, or to save themselves from mental or physical decline. This type of group usually involves a total commitment, a living-in arrangement or sheltered environment, with close supervision by peers or persons who have successfully grappled with similar problems of their own. [p. 38]

Examples include Synanon, at least in its early years, and many other ex–drug addict organizations.

5. Groups of mixed types that have characteristics of two or more categories. One such group is Parents Without Partners, which promotes personal growth, advocacy, and social events for its members.

Organization	Service Focus
Abused Women's Aid in Crisis	For battered wives and other abused women
Adoptee's Liberty Movement Association	For adoptees searching for their natural parents
Alcoholics Anonymous	For adult alcoholics
American Diabetes Association	Clubs for diabetics, their families, and their friends
Brain Tumor Support Group	For persons with brain tumors or their loved ones
Burns Recovered	For burn victims
Caesarian Birth Association	For those expecting a caesarian birth
Candlelighters	For parents of young children with cancer
Checks Anonymous	For persons in debt
Concerned United Birthparents	For parents who have surrendered children for adoption
Depressives Anonymous	For depressed persons
Divorce Anonymous	For divorced persons
Emotions Anonymous	For persons with emotional problems
Emphysema Anonymous	For those with emphysema
Fly Without Fear	For people who are afraid of flying
Fortune Society	For ex-offenders and their families
Gam-Anon	For families of gamblers
Gray Panthers	An intergenerational group
Make Today Count	For persons with cancer and their families
Mensa	For persons with high IQs
Naim Conference	For widowed persons
The National Conference of Stutterers	For adult stutterers
National Organization for Women	For women's rights
Overeaters Anonymous	For overweight persons
Parents Anonymous	For parents of abused children
Phobia Self-Help Groups	For persons with phobias
Prison Families Anonymous	For family members of prisoners
Resolve	A support group for infertile people
Stroke Clubs	For those who have had strokes and their families
Survivors of Suicide Victims	For the relatives and friends of suicide victims
We Care	Support group for divorced and separated persons

Note: Alan Gartner and Frank Riessman in *Help: A Working Guide to Self-Help Groups* (New York: Franklin-Watts, 1980) describe more than 200 self-help groups.

Table 6.1
Examples of self-help groups

Powell (1987) classified self-help groups into the following five categories:

1. *Habit disturbance organizations:* These organizations focus on a problem that is specific and concrete. Examples include Alcoholics Anonymous, Smokestoppers, Overeaters Anonymous, Gamblers Anonymous, Take Off Pounds Sensibly (TOPS), Women for Sobriety, Narcotics Anonymous, and Weight Watchers.

2. *General purpose organizations:* These organizations address a wide range of problems and predicaments. Examples are Parents Anonymous (for parents of abused children), Emotions Anonymous (for persons with emotional problems), the Compassionate Friends (for persons who have experienced a loss through death), and GROW, an organization that works to prevent the hospitalization of mental patients through a comprehensive program of mutual aid. In contrast to habit disturbance organizations, general purpose organizations address a wider range of problems and predicaments.

3. *Lifestyle organizations:* These organizations seek to provide support for, and advocate for, the lifestyles of people whose members are viewed by society as being different (the dominant groups in society are generally indifferent or hostile to that difference). Examples of this category include Widow-to-Widow Programs, Parents Without Partners, ALMA (Adoptees' Liberty Movement Association), Parents/FLAG (Parents and Friends of Lesbians and Gays), National Gay and Lesbian Task Force, and the Gray Panthers, an intergenerational group that advocates for the elderly.

4. *Physical handicap organizations:* These organizations focus on major chronic diseases and conditions. Some are for people with conditions that are relatively stable, some for conditions that are likely to get worse, and some for terminal illnesses. Examples of this category include Make Today Count (for the terminally ill and their families), Emphysema Anonymous, Lost Chord clubs (for those who have had laryngectomies), stroke clubs, Mended Hearts, the Spina Bifida Association, and Self-Help for Hard of Hearing People.

5. *Significant other organizations:* The members of these organizations are parents, spouses, and close relatives of troubled and troubling persons. Very often, members of significant other groups are last-resort care givers. Significant others contend with dysfunctional behavior. Through sharing their feelings, they obtain a measure of relief. In the course of sharing, they may also learn about new resources or new approaches. Examples of such organizations include Al-Anon, Gam-Anon, Toughlove, and the National Alliance for the Mentally Ill.

Many self-help groups stress (1) a confession by members to the group that they have a problem, (2) a testimony by members to the group recounting their past experiences with the problem and their plans for handling the problem in the future, and (3) support—that is, when a member feels an intense urge of a recurrence (such as to drink or to abuse a child), a member of the group is called, and that member comes over to stay with the person until the urge subsides.

There appear to be several other reasons that such self-help groups are successful. The members have an internal understanding of the problems, which helps them help others. Having experienced the misery and consequences of the problem, they are highly motivated and dedicated to finding ways to help themselves and their fellow sufferers. The participants also benefit from the *helper therapy principle:* the helper gains psychological rewards by helping others (Riessman, 1965). Helping others makes a person feel good and worthwhile; it also enables the helpers to put their own problems into perspective as they see that others' problems may be as serious, or even more serious, than their own.

When people help each other in self-help groups, they tend to feel empowered as they are able to control important aspects of their lives. When help is given from the outside (from an expert or a professional), there is a danger that dependency may develop, which is the opposite effect of empowerment. Empowerment increases motivation, energy, personal growth, and an ability to help that goes beyond helping oneself or receiving help.

Some self-help groups advocate for the rights and lifestyles of people whose members are viewed by society as being different. One such group is the National Gay and Lesbian Task Force. Some self-help groups (such as the National Association for Retarded Citizens) raise funds and operate community programs. Many people with a personal problem use self-help groups in the same way others use social agencies. An additional advantage is that self-help groups generally are able to operate with a minimal budget. Hundreds of these groups are now in existence. Social workers often act as brokers in linking clients to appropriate self-help groups.

Case Example
Parents Anonymous—A self-help group[2]

Parents Anonymous (PA) is a national self-help organization for parents who have abused or neglected their children. PA was originally established in 1970 by Jolly K in California, who was desperate to find help to meet her needs. For four years prior to this time, she struggled with an uncontrollable urge to severely punish her daughter. One afternoon she attempted to strangle her daughter. Desperate, she sought help from the local child-guidance clinic. She was placed in therapy. When asked by her therapist what she could do about this situation, she developed an idea; as she explained (Zauner, 1974, p. 247), "if alcoholics could stop drinking by getting together, and gamblers could stop gambling, maybe the same principle would work for abusers, too." With her therapist's encouragement, she formed "Mothers Anonymous" in 1970, and started a few local chapters in California. Nearly every major city in the United States and Canada now has a chapter, and the name has been changed to Parents Anonymous (since fathers who abuse their children are also eligible to join).

PA uses some of the basic therapeutic concepts of Alcoholics Anonymous. PA is a crisis intervention program that offers two main forms of help: (1) a weekly group meeting in which members share experiences and feelings and learn better control of their emotions, and (2) personal and telephone contact among members during periods of crisis, particularly when a member feels a nearly uncontrollable desire to take their anger or frustration out on a child.

Parents may be referred to PA by a social agency (including protective services), or may be self-referrals of parents who are aware they need help.

Cassie Starkweather and S. Michael Turner (1975) described why some parents who abuse their children would rather participate in a self-help group than receive professional counseling.

It has been our experience that most (abusive) parents judge themselves more harshly than other more objective people tend to judge them. The fear of losing their children frequently diminishes with reassurance from other members that they are not the monsters they think they are.

Generally speaking, PA members are so afraid they are going to be judged by others as harshly as they judge themselves that they are afraid to go out and seek help. Frequently our members express fears of dealing with a professional person, seeing differences in education, sex, or social status as basic differences that would prevent easy communication or mutual understanding.

Members express feelings of gratification at finding that other parents are "in the same boat." They contrast this with their feelings about professionals who, they often assume, have not taken out the time from their training and current job responsibilities to raise families of their own. [p. 151]

PA emphasizes honesty and directness. In the outside world, parents who are prone to abuse their children learn to hide this problem because society finds it

---

[2]This description of Parents Anonymous is adapted from Charles Zastrow, "Parents Anonymous," in *Introduction to Social Welfare Institutions,* 2nd ed. (Pacific Grove, CA: Brooks/Cole, 1982), pp. 159–161.

difficult to stomach. In contrast, the goal of PA is to help parents admit and accept the fact that they are abusive. The term *abuse* is used liberally at meetings. PA has found that this insistence on frankness has a healthy effect. Parents are relieved because they've finally found a group of people who are able to accept abusive parents for what they really are. Furthermore, only when they are able to admit they are abusive can they begin to find ways to cope with this problem.

During PA meetings parents are expected actually to say they are beating their child or engaging in other forms of abuse, and the members challenge each other to find ways to curb such activities. Members also share constructive approaches that each has found useful, and efforts are made to help one another develop specific plans for dealing with situations that have in the past resulted in abusive episodes. Members learn to recognize danger signs and to then take necessary action to curb the potential abuse.

Leadership in the group is provided by a group member selected by the parents themselves. The leader, called a chairperson, is normally assisted by a professional sponsor who serves as resource and backup person to the chair and the group members. The social worker who becomes the sponsor must be prepared to perform a variety of roles including teacher-trainer, broker of community services needed by parents, advocate, consultant, and in some instances, behavior changer (Hull, 1978).

Riessman (1987, pp. ix–x) summarizes the distinctive characteristics of self-help groups as follows:

- A noncompetitive, cooperative orientation
- An anti-elite, antibureaucratic focus
  An emphasis on the indigenous—people who have the problem and know a lot about it from the inside, from experiencing it
- An attitude of do what you can, one day at a time (you can't solve everything at once)
- A shared, often revolving leadership
- An attitude of being helped through helping (the helper-therapy principle) . . .
- An understanding that helping is not a commodity to be bought and sold
- A strong optimism regarding the ability to change
- An understanding that although small may not necessarily be beautiful, it is a place to begin and the unit to build on
- A critical stance toward professionalism, which is often seen as pretentious, purist,

distant and mystifying. Self-helpers like simplicity and informality
- An emphasis on the consumer . . . The consumer is a producer of help and services
- An understanding that helping is at the center—knowing how to receive help, give help, and help yourself . . .
- An emphasis on empowerment

Socialization Groups

The objective of socialization groups generally is to develop or change attitudes and behaviors of group members to become more socially acceptable. Social skill development, increasing self-confidence, and planning for the future are other foci. Illustrations include working with a group of predelinquent youth in group activities to curb delinquency trends, a youth group of diverse racial backgrounds to reduce racial tensions, a group of pregnant young females at a maternity home to make plans for the future, a group of elderly residents at a nursing home to

Case Example
Socialization—A rap group at a runaway center

New Horizons is a private, temporary shelter care facility for runaways in a large midwestern city. It is located in a large house that was built over 80 years ago. Youth on the run can stay for up to two weeks. State law requires that parents must be contacted and parental permission received for New Horizons to provide shelter overnight. Services provided include temporary shelter care, individual and family counseling, and a 24-hour hotline for youths in crisis. The facility is licensed to house up to eight youths. Since the average stay is nine days, the population is continually changing. During the stay, intensive counseling is provided the youths (and often their parents), focusing on reducing conflicts between the youths and their parents and on making future living plans. The maximum stay at New Horizons is two weeks. This limit is used partially to convey to youths and their families, beginning with day one, that they must work on the reasons for leaving home.

Every evening at 7 P.M. a rap group meeting is held. All the residents and the two or three staff members on duty are expected to attend. This rap group has four main objectives. One is to serve as a vehicle for residents to express their satisfactions and dissatisfactions with the facilities and programs at New Horizons. Sometimes the rap group appears to be primarily a gripe session, but the staff make conscientious efforts to improve those aspects where the youths' concerns are legitimate. For example, the youths may indicate that the past few days have been boring, and staff and residents then jointly plan activities for the next few days.

Another objective is to handle interaction problems that arise between residents, and between staff and residents. A wide range of problems arise: a resident may be preventing others from sleeping, some residents may refuse to do their fair share of domestic tasks, there may be squabbles about which TV program to watch, some residents may be overly aggressive, and so forth. Since most of the youths face a variety of crises associated with being on the run, many tend to be anxious and under stress. In such an emotional climate, interaction problems are apt to arise. Staff are sometimes intensely questioned by residents about their actions, decisions, and policies. For example, one of the policies at New Horizons is that each resident must agree not to use alcohol or illegal drugs while staying at this shelter, with the penalty being expulsion. Occasionally a few youths use drugs and are caught and expelled. Removing a youth from this facility has an immense impact on the other residents, and at the following rap meetings staff are expected to clarify and explain such decisions.

A third objective of rap meetings is for staff to present material on topics requested by residents. Examples include sex; drugs; homosexuality; physical and sexual abuse (a fair number of residents are abused by family members); how to avoid being raped; AIDS; how to handle anger, depression, and other unwanted emotions; legal rights of youths on the run; how to be more assertive; how to explain running away to relatives and friends; and what other human services are available to youths in the community. During such presentations, considerable discussion with residents is encouraged and generally occurs.

The final objective of rap groups is to convey information about planned daily activities and changes in the overall program at New Horizons.

remotivate them and get them involved in various activities, and a group of boys at a correctional school to help them make plans for returning to their home community. Leadership of such groups requires considerable skill and knowledge in using the group to foster individual growth and change. These leadership roles are frequently filled by social workers.

Therapy Groups

Therapy groups are generally composed of members with rather severe emotional or personal problems. Leadership of such groups generally requires considerable skill, perceptiveness, knowledge of human behavior and group dynamics, group counseling capacities, and ability to use the group to bring about behavioral changes. Among other skills, the group leader needs to be highly perceptive regarding how each member is being affected by what is being communicated. Considerable competence is needed to develop and maintain a constructive atmosphere within the group. Similar to one-to-one counseling, the goal of therapy groups is generally to have members explore their problems in depth and then to develop one or more strategies for resolving them. The group therapist generally uses one or more therapy approaches as a guide for changing attitudes and behaviors; these approaches include psychoanalysis, reality therapy, learning theory, rational therapy, transactional analysis, client-centered therapy, and psychodrama.

Group therapy is being used increasingly in social work. It has several advantages over one-to-one therapy. The *helper* therapy principle, in which members interchange roles and sometimes become the helper for someone else's problems, is generally operative. In such roles, members receive psychological rewards for helping others. Groups also help members put their problems into perspective as they realize others have equally serious problems. Groups also help members who are having interaction problems test out new interaction approaches. Research has shown that it is generally easier to change the attitudes of an individual in a group than in one-on-one counseling (Lewin, 1952). Research on conformity has found group pressure can have a substantial effect on changing attitudes and beliefs. Furthermore, group therapy permits the social worker to help more than one person at a time, with potential savings in the use of professional effort.

In essence a group therapist uses the principles of one-to-one counseling (discussed in Chapter 5) and of group dynamics (see Chapter 7) to work with clients to change dysfunctional attitudes and behavior. Generally the group leader also uses the principles of certain treatment techniques (such as reality therapy, rational therapy, Parent Effectiveness Training, and assertiveness training) to help clients resolve personal and emotional problems. The selection of the techniques to use should ideally be based on the nature of the problems presented.

Encounter Groups

Encounter groups and sensitivity training groups (these terms are used somewhat synonymously) refer to a group experience in which people relate to each other in a close interpersonal manner, and self-disclosure is required. The goal is to improve interpersonal awareness. Jane Howard (1970) offered a typical description of an encounter group:

> Their destination is intimacy, trust, awareness of why they behave as they do in groups; their vehicle is candor. Exhorted to "get in touch with their feelings" and to "live in the here-and-now," they sprawl on the floor. . . . As they grow tired they rest their heads on rolled-up sweaters or corners of cot mattresses or each other's laps. [p. 3]

An encounter group may meet for a few hours or for as long a period as a few days. Once increased interpersonal awareness is achieved, it is anticipated that attitudes and

Case Example
Therapy group for spouses of adults with cancer

Eight years ago Linda Sonsthagen's husband was found to have cancer. Linda was a social worker, and her husband was a successful life insurance agent. They had two sons in grade school. Four and one-half years ago Mr. Sonsthagen died, after having gone through a variety of treatment programs and through considerable pain. He lost weight and his hair fell out. These years were extremely difficult for the Sonsthagens. Linda had to take a larger role in raising the children and had to be the primary care giver to her husband and to the children. During these years, the Sonsthagens found that relatives and friends shied away from them—it took several months before they became aware that the reason was that friends and relatives saw cancer as being something they didn't understand and wanted to avoid. Even more difficult was dealing emotionally with not knowing the course of the disorder, going through cycles of hope and then disappointment as different treatment approaches were tried. As her husband became more incapacitated, Linda found she had to assume more of the tasks that he had previously done—for example, home repairs, maintaining their two cars, disciplining the children, and doing more of the daily household tasks.

After her husband's death, Linda and the two children when through several months of mourning and grief. Linda also discovered it was somewhat awkward to go to social functions alone initially. Fortunately she had two single female friends with whom she increasingly socialized. These were very difficult years for Linda. She needed over two years after her husband's death to rebuild her life in such a way that she was again comfortable.

During these years she had received some financial help from the local chapter of the American Cancer Society. She also had met through this society another woman whose husband was dying of cancer. They were able to give each other emotional support and to share with each other useful ideas for handling the problems that arose.

Eighteen months ago Linda proposed to the local chapter of the American Cancer Society that she was willing to volunteer her time to start a group for spouses of those having cancer, and for spouses who are adjusting to a recent cancer death. The Cancer Society gave their approval and endorsement.

Linda initially started a group with nine members. The objectives were to give emotional support, to help members handle the new responsibilities they had to take on, and to help them deal with their emotional reactions. Linda used primarily a combination of reality therapy and rational therapy (see Chapters 21 and 22). Reality therapy was used to help the group members better understand and make decisions and plans for the problems they faced. For example, for the members whose spouses had cancer, one focus was how to inform and handle their friends' and relatives' reactions to the spouse's having cancer. For the survivors, a major focus was on making realistic decisions to rebuild their lives. Rational therapy was used to counter unwanted emotions. Such common emotions included depression, guilt, anxiety, the feeling of being overwhelmed, and anger (particularly resulting from "Why does this have to happen to me?"). Members were instructed on how to do a Rational Self-

Analysis (see Chapter 22) on their unwanted emotions, and members often shared and discussed these RSAs at group meetings.

Group members stated on several occasions that the group was very helpful. They mentioned that knowing others faced similar plights was beneficial in and of itself. Seeing how others handled difficult decisions inspired them and gave them useful ideas on how to handle crises they faced. When a member suffered a serious crisis (for example, the spouse being hospitalized for a serious operation), other members were available for telephone contact and to lend physical assistance.

After eight months the local chapter of the American Cancer Society was so encouraged by the results that they offered Linda a full-time position to run additional groups and to be available for individual counseling for people with cancer and their relatives. Linda gave up her part-time job as a counselor at the YWCA and took this position. Her first effort was to divide her group, which was growing, into two groups. The definition of eligible membership was also expanded: one group was for adults who have a family member with cancer, and the other for adults who are survivors. At this time Linda is leading one group of the first type and two groups of the second type.

---

behaviors will change. In order for these changes to occur, a three-phase process generally takes place: unfreezing, change, and refreezing.

Unfreezing occurs in encounter groups through a deliberate process of interacting in nontraditional ways. Our attitudes and behavior patterns have been developed through years of social experiences. Such patterns, following years of experimentation and refinement, have now become nearly automatic. The interpersonal style we develop through years of trial and error generally has considerable utility in our everyday interactions. Deep down, however, we may recognize a need for improvement but are reluctant to make the effort, partly because our present style is somewhat functional and partly because we are afraid to reveal things about ourselves. Unfreezing occurs when we decide certain patterns of our present behavior need to be changed, and we are psychologically ready to explore ways to make changes.

Stewart L. Tubbs and John Baird (1976) described the unfreezing process in sensitivity groups:

Unfreezing occurs when our expectations are violated. We become less sure of ourselves when traditional ways of doing things are not followed. In the encounter group, the leader usually does not act like a leader. He or she frequently starts with a brief statement encouraging the group members to participate, to be open and honest, and to expect things to be different. Group members may begin by taking off their shoes, sitting in a circle on the floor, and holding hands with their eyes closed. The leader then encourages them to feel intensely the sensations they are experiencing, the size and texture of the hands they are holding and so forth.

Other structured exercises or experiences may be planned to help the group focus on the "here-and-now" experience. Pairs may go for "trust walks" in which each person alternatively is led around with his eyes closed. Sitting face-to-face and conducting a hand dialogue, or a silent facial mirroring often helps to break the initial barriers to change. Other techniques may involve the "pass around" in which a person in the center of a tight circle relaxes and is physically passed around the circle. Those who have trouble feeling a part of the group are encouraged to break into or out of the circle of people whose hands are tightly held. With these experiences, most participants begin to feel more open to conversation about what they have experienced. This sharing of experiences or self-disclosure about the here and now provides more data for the group to discuss. [p. 48]

The second phase of the process is *change*. Changes in attitudes and behavior are usually facilitated in sensitivity groups by spontaneous reactions or feedback to how a person "comes across" to others. In everyday interaction we almost never get spontaneous feedback and we tend to repeat ineffective interaction patterns because we lack knowledge of our effect on others. But in sensitivity groups such feedback is strongly encouraged. The following set of interactions illustrates such feedback:

Carl: All right (*in a sharp tone*), let's get this trust walk over with, and stop dilly-dallying around. I'll lead the first person around—who wants to be blindfolded first?

Judy: Your statement makes me feel uncomfortable. I feel you're saying this group is a waste of your time. Also it's the third time tonight that you've ordered us around.

Jim: I feel the same way, like you're trying to tell us peons what to do. Even the tone of your voice sounds autocratic, and I get the message you're really down on this group.

Carl: I'm sorry, I didn't mean it to sound like that. I wonder if I do that outside the group too?

Such feedback provides us with new insights on how we affect others. Once problem interactions are identified, that member is encouraged to try out new response patterns in the relative safety of the group.

In trust walks, group members become more aware of themselves and their interactions with others.

The third and final phase is *refreezing*. Unfortunately this term is not the most descriptive as it implies rigidity with a new set of response patterns. The goal of this phase involves the attitude of experimenting with new sets of behaviors so that the person becomes a growing, continually changing person who increasingly becomes more effective in interacting with others. In terminating a sensitivity group, the leader may alert the participants that they have to be on guard, because former dysfunctional behavior patterns tend to creep back in.

Sensitivity groups usually generate an outpouring of emotions that are rarely found in other groups.

The goal of sensitivity groups provides an interesting contrast to that of most therapy groups (see Exhibit 6.1). In therapy, the goal is to have all members explore in-depth personal or emotional problems that they have, and then develop a strategy to resolve the problems. In comparison, sensitivity groups seek to foster increased personal and interpersonal awareness and then develop more effective interaction patterns. Sensitivity groups generally do not attempt to identify and change specific emotional or personal problems (such as drinking problems, feelings of depression, sexual dysfunctions, and so on). The philosophy behind sensitivity groups is that with increased personal and interpersonal awareness, people will be better able to avoid, cope with, and handle specific personal problems that arise.

In our society sensitivity groups are being used for a wide variety of purposes: to train professional counselors to be more perceptive and effective in interpersonal interactions with clients and with other professionals, to train people in management positions to be more effective in their business interactions, to help clients with overt relationship problems become more aware of how they affect others and to help them develop more effective interaction patterns, and to train interested citizens in becoming more aware and effective in their interactions.

Despite their popularity, sensitivity groups remain controversial. In some cases inadequately trained and incompetent individuals have become self-proclaimed leaders and have enticed people to join through sensational advertising. If handled poorly, the short duration of some groups may intensify personal problems; for example, a person's defense mechanisms may be stripped away without developing adaptive coping patterns. Many authorities on sensitivity training disclaim the use of encounter groups as a form of psychotherapy and discourage those with serious personal problems from joining such a group. Carl Rogers (1970) in reviewing his own extensive experience as leader/participant, echoed these concerns:

> Frequently the behavior changes that occur, if any, are not lasting. In addition, the individual may become deeply involved in revealing himself and then be left with problems which are not worked through. Less common, but still noteworthy, there are also very occasional accounts of an individual having a psychotic episode during or immediately following an intensive

Exhibit 6.1

Contrasting goals of therapy versus sensitivity groups

Therapy Groups

Step 1	*Step 2*
Examine problem(s) in depth.	Develop and select from various resolution approaches a strategy to resolve the problem.

Sensitivity Groups

Step 1	*Step 2*
Help each person become more aware of self and how he or she affects others in interpersonal interactions.	Help a person develop more effective interaction patterns.

group experience. We must keep in mind that not all people are suited for groups. [pp. 40–41]

In some cases the popularity of sensitivity groups has led some individuals to enter harmful groups with incompetent leaders where normal ethical standards have been abused. Shostrom (1969, pp. 38–39) has identified some means by which those interested in encounter groups can prevent exploitation: (1) Never participate in a group of fewer than a half-dozen members. The necessary and valuable candor generated by an effective group cannot be dissipated, shared, or examined by too small a group, and scapegoating or purely vicious ganging up can develop. (2) Never join an encounter group on impulse—as a fling, binge, or surrender to the unplanned. (3) Never stay with a group that has a behavioral ax to grind. (4) Never participate in a group that lacks formal connection with a professional on whom you can check.

After reviewing the research on the outcome of sensitivity groups, Lieberman, Yalom, and Miles (1973) provided an appropriate perspective for those interested in the intensive group experience:

> Encounter groups present a clear and evident danger if they are used for radical surgery to produce a new man [person]. The danger is even greater when the leader and the participants share this misconception. If we no longer expect groups to produce magical, lasting change and if we stop seeing them as panaceas, we can regard them as useful, socially sanctioned opportunities for human beings to explore and to express themselves. Then we can begin to work on ways to improve them so that they may make a meaningful contribution toward solving human problems. [p. 73]

How to Start, Lead, and Terminate Groups

The remaining part of this chapter focuses on guidelines for how to start, run, and terminate groups. This section covers homework, session planning, relaxing before a meeting, cues on entering the meeting room, seating arrangements, introductions, role clarification, agenda, additional guidelines for leading a group, and terminating a group. Many students fear taking a leadership role in groups. They are uncertain what a leader does, and they fear they do not have the qualities or traits to be a leader. Amazingly, the truth is that even the most fearful and anxious students have already taken leadership roles in many groups. Every student has in the past been a member of several groups and has performed some essential tasks for these groups. As we will see in Chapter 7, performing an essential task is simultaneously an effective leadership action.

Homework

Extensive preparation is the key to a successful experience for the group members (including yourself). Even experienced leaders have to prepare carefully for each group and for each meeting.

In planning a new group, the following questions need to be answered. What are the overall purpose and general goals of the group? What are possible ways in which these general goals can be accomplished? What are the characteristics of the members? Are some members apt to have unique, individual goals or needs? What resources do the members need to have to accomplish the general goals? What should be the agenda for the first meeting? The group members should have considerable input in suggesting and deciding on the specific goals of the group—how can this best be accomplished? When the group first meets, should an icebreaker exercise be used—if so, what? Should refreshments be provided? How should the chairs be arranged? What type of group atmosphere will best help the group accomplish its tasks? What is the best available meeting place? Why have you been selected to lead the group? What do the members expect you to do?

As you plan for the first meeting, it is very helpful to view the group as a new member would view it. Questions and concerns that a new member may have are the following. What are the goals of this group? Why am I joining? Will my personal goals be met in this group? Will I feel comfortable in this group? Will I be accepted by other members? Will the other members be radically different in terms of backgrounds and interests? If I do not like this group, can I get out of attending meetings? Will other members respect what I have to say or will they laugh and make fun of me? Through considering such concerns, the leader can seek to plan the first meeting in a way that will help the other members feel comfortable and will clarify the members' questions about the group's goals and activities.

It is *absolutely essential* for a group leader to identify the group's needs and expectations before the first meeting. The quickest way to fail as a leader is to try to have a group go in a direction different from what the members want. For example, I remember going to a workshop with other counselors that was entitled "Grief, Death, and Dying." The counselors expected material on how to counsel more effectively clients who were grieving about the death of a loved one. The presenter instead gave a historical review of how present-day funeral rituals had evolved since the Middle Ages. The audience was very disappointed because their expectations were unmet.

There are a variety of ways to identify what the members want. Prior to the first meeting, it may be possible to ask some members what their expectations are. If you are asked by someone to lead the group, it is essential to ask that person about the expectations for the group. The members should generally be asked at the first meeting to give their views as to what they desire to get out of the group. Another way (which needs to be done for preparatory reasons anyway) is to "scout" the following about the members:

1. How many members are expected?
2. What are their characteristics—ages, socioeconomic status, racial and ethnic backgrounds, sex mix, educational and professional backgrounds, and so on?
3. How knowledgeable and informed are the members about the topics the group will be dealing with?
4. What are apt to be the personal goals and agendas of the various members?
5. How motivated are the members to accomplish the purposes for which the group is being formed? This can partly be determined by examining how voluntary the membership is. Groups composed of involuntary members (for example, a group that is court ordered to attend because of conviction for driving while intoxicated) have little motivation, and may perhaps even be hostile that they are being forced to attend.
6. What are apt to be the underlying value systems of the members? A group of teenagers on juvenile probation is apt to dif-

fer significantly from a group of retired priests. (However, it is important to view the members as unique persons rather than as stereotypes.)

In planning for the first (and additional meetings) it is helpful to visualize (imagine) how you, as leader, want the meeting to go. For example, at the first meeting the following may be visualized:

The members will arrive at various times. I will be there early to greet them, to introduce myself, to assist them in feeling comfortable, and to engage in small talk. Possible subjects of small talk that are likely to be of interest to these new members are _____, _____, and _____.

I will begin the meeting by introducing myself and stating the overall purpose of the group. As an icebreaker exercise I will ask the group to give me a list of four or five facts they would like to know about the other members and have the members introduce themselves and give the four or five facts about themselves. I will also tell about myself and encourage the members to ask questions about me and the group.

After the icebreaker exercise, I will again briefly state the overall purpose of the group and ask if the members have questions about this. Possible questions that may arise are _____. If such questions arise, my answers will be _____.

We will then proceed to the items on the agenda (which has previously been mailed to the members). During the discussion of each of these items, the questions that may arise are _____. My answers to such questions, should they arise, are _____.

The kind of group atmosphere I will seek to create is democratic. Such an atmosphere is best suited for encouraging all members to accept the group goals and then to contribute their time and resources toward accomplishing them. I will seek to do this by arranging the chairs in a circle, by drawing out through questions those who are silent, by using humor, and by making sure that I do not dominate the conversation.

I will end the meeting by summarizing what has been covered and the decisions that have been made. We will set a time for the next meeting. I will finally ask if anyone has any additional comments or questions. Throughout the meeting I will encourage a positive atmosphere, partly by complimenting the members on the contributions they make.

If a group has met for one or more times, the leader needs to review the following kinds of questions. Have the overall goals been sufficiently decided on and clarified? If not, what needs to be done in this clarification process? Is the group making adequate progress in accomplishing its goals? If not, what are the obstacles that are slowing down the group that need to be confronted? Has the group selected adequate courses of action to reach its goals, or are there more effective courses of action that might be considered? What items should be placed on the agenda for the next meeting? What activities should be planned? Will successful completion of these activities move the group toward accomplishing its overall goals? If not, perhaps other activities need to be selected. Does each member seem sufficiently interested and motivated to help the group accomplish its goals, or are there some members who appear disinterested? If so, why do they appear disinterested, and what might be tried to stimulate their interests?

Session Planning

In planning a session, it is essential to be fully aware of the overall goals for the group. It is also essential to identify what the specific goals are for each session. It is critical to know exactly what you want to accomplish in each session and to make sure that all the items on the agenda relate to the goals you have set. The following are some suggestions.

1. *Select content that is relevant.* The material should be relevant not only to the specific goals for the session but also to the backgrounds and interests of the participants. For example, in a time management presentation, the time-saver tips you give to college students probably will be quite different from those for business executives. In the former the tips should probably focus on improving study habits while the latter should probably focus on improving work activities in an office setting. An excellent way to evaluate the relevance of your material is to define precisely how it will be valuable to the members of the group. Ask yourself, "If a group member asks why should I know this, can you give a valid reason?" If you are unable to come up with more than a vague answer, it may be best to consider discarding that material and selecting other, more relevant material.

2. *Use a number of examples.* Examples help illustrate key concepts. They also stimulate the participants' interest. People tend to remember examples much more than statistics. To illustrate, in a presentation on spouse abuse, a few vivid real-life stories of the drastic effects on a woman's life of continued battering by her husband will be remembered much longer than statistics on the extent of spouse abuse.

3. *Present materials in a logical order.* It is generally desirable to begin by summarizing the agenda items for the session. Ideally, one topic should blend into the next. If group exercises are used, they should be placed next to the related theoretical material.

4. *Plan for time.* Once you have the content of the session fairly well organized, estimate how long each segment will take. Accurate estimations will help you determine if you have too much or too little material planned for the allotted time. It is also a good idea to plan what you will do if the content is covered faster or slower than what you are estimating. (For example, if

the material is being covered more slowly than anticipated, you will be prepared to revise your agenda when you realize that you will not have time for everything.) You should also be prepared to cover extra material when the anticipated content is covered more quickly than you estimated. If you are planning to use a film, or have a guest speaker for part of the time, you should have plans for appropriate substitute material in case the film projector breaks, or the guest speaker fails to appear.

5. *Be prepared to be flexible with your agenda.* A variety of unexpected events may make it desirable to change the agenda during a session. The material may be covered much faster than anticipated, or interpersonal conflict may erupt between some members, which may take considerable time to process. Some members may bring up subjects related to the group's overall purpose that may be more valuable for the group to focus on than the prepared agenda.

6. *Occasionally change the pace.* People will be able to pay attention for longer periods if there is an occasional change of pace. Long, long lectures or discussions bore people. The pace can be changed in a variety of ways: use a group exercise, show a film, invite a guest speaker, take a break, have a debate, show slides, change topics, and so on. In group therapy sessions, one way to change pace is to switch from focusing on one member's problems to focusing on another's concerns. If you are presenting a lecture, you can increase attention in several ways:

• Speak extemporaneously rather than read the material.
• Occasionally walk around the room, rather than stand or sit in one place.
• Draw out the participants by asking questions.

(An excellent way to learn how to give more stimulating presentations is to observe the nonverbal and verbal communication patterns of dynamic speakers.) When you change pace it is critical to use appropriate transitions so the topics blend into one another rather than becoming choppy and confusing.

In changing pace, it is helpful to use a variety of methods. There are many methods of conveying information: lectures, discussions, role plays, films, exercises, slide presentations, diagrams, and so on. In selecting methods, be aware that people tend to remember longer information they receive actively (such as through an exercise) than information they receive passively (through listening).

Relaxing Before a Meeting

Before starting a meeting, you may be nervous about how the session will go. Some anxiety is helpful for you to be mentally alert and to facilitate your attending to what is being communicated during the meeting. Some leaders, however, have an excessively high level of anxiety, which reduces their effectiveness. If your anxiety is too high, you can reduce it by engaging in activities that you find relaxing. Relaxation techniques are highly recommended and are described at some length in Chapter 20. Other suggestions include taking a walk, jogging, listening to music you find relaxing, and finding a place where you can be alone to clear your mind. Effective group leaders generally learn they can reduce their level of anxiety by using one or more of these techniques. Practice in leading groups will also gradually build your confidence until you are an effective group leader.

Cues on Entering the Meeting Room

It is important for you as leader to be on time, and perhaps a little early. Being early allows you to see that everything is arranged as you planned. By being early, you'll be able to do what needs to be done—such as checking to see that refreshments are available (if refreshments are planned), erasing the chalkboard, arranging the chairs, and so on.

It will also allow you to observe the moods of the members. If it is a group you have not previously met, arriving early will give you an opportunity to gain information about the participants' interests by observing their age, gender, clothes and personal appearance, small talk, and the way they are interacting with one another. An effective leader notices such cues and generally finds a way to "join" the participants.

I was once asked to give a workshop on suicide prevention to a high school class. On arriving, I was informed by the teacher that one of the students in the class had recently committed suicide. Instead of beginning with my planned presentation, I acknowledged that I had just been informed about their former classmate, and I began by asking each of them anonymously to write down on a sheet of paper one or two concerns or questions that they had about suicide. After they turned in their sheets, we had a lively discussion related to these. Such a discussion was probably more valuable than the formal presentation (which was never given) because it focused on their specific questions and concerns.

Seating Arrangements

Seating arrangements are important for several reasons. They can affect who talks to whom and can have an influence on who is apt to play leadership roles. As a result, they can affect group cohesion and morale.

It is important in most groups for the members to have eye contact with one another. It is even more important for the group leader to be able to make eye contact with everyone, in order to obtain nonverbal feedback on what the members are thinking and feeling.

A circle is ideal for generating discussion, for encouraging a sense of equal status for each member, and for promoting group openness and cohesion. The traditional classroom arrangement (with the leader in front, and everyone facing that person while sitting in rows) has the effect of placing the leader in a position of authority. It also tends to inhibit communication, since members are generally able to make eye contact with only those closest to them.

Tables have advantages and disadvantages. They provide a place to write and to put work materials. Some members feel more comfortable at a table, since it gives them something to lean on. However, tables tend to restrict movement and may serve as a barrier between people.

The leader should consider carefully whether it is desirable or undesirable to have tables. If members are to sift through papers or are expected to take notes, tables should generally be used. In therapy groups tables are seldom used, because they tend to restrict movement and act as a barrier.

In many settings tables can be arranged to best meet the goals of the meeting. For example, arranging small tables in a circle tends to facilitate communication.

Tables influence the way group members interact with each other. If the table is rectangular, it is customary for the leader to sit at one end, which then is viewed as the "head" of the table. The person who is at the head of the table is often viewed as the "authority" and usually does more talking and has a greater influence on the discussion than other group members. If an egalitarian atmosphere is desired, it is helpful to use a round or square table. The "head of the table" effect can also be reduced by placing two rectangular tables together to make a square.

Tables also influence interactions by where people sit. People are most likely to talk to those who are sitting at right angles to them and then to those next to them. Those sitting directly across receive less communication, and those sitting anywhere else are even less likely to be addressed.

When a group meets for the first time (and often later), members are most likely to sit next to friends. If it is important for everyone in the group to interact with one another, it may be desirable to ask people to sit next to people they do not know, in order to counteract any cliquishness in the group and to encourage members to get to know each other.

Introductions

During the introduction, the leader's credentials should be summarized in such a way that members gain a sense of confidence that the leader can fulfill the expectations of the members. If the leader is being introduced by someone else, a brief and concise summary of the leader's credentials *for the expected role* is desirable. If the leader is introducing herself or himself, the important credentials should be summarized in a nonarrogant fashion. The summary should also be delivered in a way to create the desired atmosphere—whether it is informal or formal, fun or serious, and so on. An excellent way to handle the introduction is to use an icebreaker exercise, as described in Chapter 1.

In meeting with a group, it is highly desirable to learn the members' names as quickly as possible. This requires extra attention on the leader's part. Name tags facilitate this process for everyone. Members appreciate being called by name—it helps convey to them that they have importance.

If the group is small, it is generally advantageous for each member to introduce himself or herself—perhaps through using an icebreaker. It is often desirable during introductions for members to state their expectations for the group. This helps uncover hidden agendas. If a stated expectation is beyond the scope of the group, the leader should tactfully state and discuss it to pre-vent an unrealistic expectation from becoming a source of frustration or dissatisfaction for that member.

Role Clarification

As the leader of a group, you should be clear about your roles and responsibilities. If you are unclear, you may want to discuss with the group their expectations about the appropriate roles for the leader and for the other members. One way of doing this is for the group to select goals and then make decisions about the tasks and responsibilities that each member will have in working toward those goals. In most situations it is clearly a mistake for the leader to do the majority of the work. The group will generally be most productive if all members make substantial contributions. The more members contribute to a group, the more they are apt to feel a part of the group psychologically.

Even if you are fairly clear about what you would like your role to be, the other members may be confused about what your role is, or may have different expectations of you. If there is a realistic chance that the other members are unclear about your role, you should explain carefully what you perceive your role to be. If members indicate they have somewhat different expectations, the group should take the time to make decisions about who will do what.

In explaining what you perceive your role to be, it is generally desirable to be humble about your skills and resources. Generally, you will want to come across as a knowledgeable "human" rather than as an authority figure who has all the answers.

You should always be prepared to explain the reasoning behind the things you do. If you are doing an exercise, the group should generally be informed about the goals or objectives of that exercise. (If questions arise about whether the goals for the exercise are consistent with the overall goals for the group, you should be prepared to provide an explanation.)

The role that the leader should assume in a group will vary somewhat from situation to situation. For example, there are apt to be marked differences in responsibilities of the leader of a therapy group versus a Boy Scout troop.

Agenda

For most meetings, there should be an agenda. Ideally, all group members should have an opportunity to suggest items for the agenda. If possible, the agenda should be sent to the members several days before the meeting to give them an opportunity to prepare for the items that will be considered.

At the start of the meeting the agenda items should be briefly reviewed, before consideration of the first item. This review gives each member a chance to suggest additions, deletions, or other changes. In some meetings it may be appropriate for the group to discuss, and perhaps vote, on the suggested changes in the agenda.

Additional Guidelines for Leading a Group

This section briefly summarizes additional suggestions for effectively leading a group.

1. Remember that leadership is a shared responsibility. Every member at times will take on leadership roles. Designated leaders should not dominate a group, nor should they believe they are responsible for directing the group in all of its task functions and group maintenance functions. (These functions are described in Chapter 7.) In fact, productivity and group cohesion are substantially increased when everyone contributes.

2. Seek to use decision-making procedures that are best suited for the issues facing the group. (The merits and shortcomings of decision making by consensus and

by majority voting were discussed earlier in this chapter.)

3. Seek to create a cooperative group atmosphere rather than a competitive group atmosphere. (These two atmospheres are described in Chapter 7.)

4. View controversy and conflict as being natural and desirable for resolving issues and furthering discussion. In resolving conflicts and in handling the issues and problems facing the group, seek to use a problem-solving approach rather than a win-lose approach. (See Chapter 7.)

5. Try to create an atmosphere of open and honest communication.

6. You need to give attention to how to end a session. A few minutes before the session is scheduled to end, or when it appears the group has exhausted a subject, you may conclude with a summarization of the key points made by you and the other members. This summary should be brief. Such a summary emphasizes the major points to be remembered and leaves the group with a sense of achievement. It also signals that this portion of the session has come to a close.

Terminating a Group

Inherent in termination is separation from the group and from group members. Separation typically involves mixed feelings that vary in intensity according to a number of factors, several of which are mentioned here. The greater a member's emotional closeness and investment in a group, the greater will be the person's feeling of loss. The greater the feeling of success of members in accomplishing their goals through the group, the greater will be the feeling of "sweetness and sorrow"—sweetness from feeling that they have grown and had success, and sorrow from separation from the group that has come to be an important and meaningful part of their lives. The more emotionally dependent they have become on a group, the more members are apt to feel anger, rejection, and depression over termination. The more they have experienced difficulties in separating in the past from significant others, the more likely it will be that the separation will be experienced as difficult, as the pattern of reacting to separations is repeated.

There are several types of termination: (1) termination of a successful group, (2) termination of an unsuccessful group, (3) dropout, (4), transfer of a member, and (5) departure of the leader. Each of these types is discussed briefly.

Termination of a successful group. A successful group is one in which the group and its members have generally accomplished their goals. Termination of such a group is apt to generate the "sweetness and sorrow" reaction in members. They are likely to be delighted with their accomplishments, which will probably increase their levels of self-confidence and self-esteem. Members may also experience a feeling of loss (varying in intensity) because they are separating from a group in which they have become emotionally invested. Such a group may desire to have dinner together or have some other ceremony to commemorate and recognize the group and its accomplishments.

In terminating a successful group, it is essential that formal termination begin one or more meetings before the final one. Ideally, the date of the last meeting should be discussed and agreed on by the members well in advance. (For some groups the final meeting is scheduled even before the group begins to meet.) Sufficient time has to be allowed in terminating a successful group so that (1) progress made in accomplishing the tasks and goals of the group and its members can be evaluated, (2) plans can be made for continued work by the members on remaining problems, (3) work can be done on unresolved, last-minute issues, (4) the emotional reactions of members to terminating can be handled, and (5) the members have time to discuss whether they want to plan for a special social event for the group's ending.

While goodbyes are often sad, the negative feelings can be offset by emphasizing what members have given and received, the ways they have grown, the skills they have learned, and the accomplishments of the group. In some cases an extra session could be held to complete unfinished business items. The members may decide to have periodic "class reunions" or social get-togethers.

Termination of an unsuccessful group. An unsuccessful group is one in which most or all the goals of the group and its members are largely unmet. The reactions of members to the lack of progress may vary considerably: anger, frustration, disappointment, despair, guilt (for unproductive efforts or lack of effort), scapegoating, blaming, and apathy. In rarer cases, it is possible for an unsuccessful group to be fairly pleased and accepting of its efforts. For example, a group that is formed to write a grant (when there is limited hope of funding from the federal government) may be pleased with its efforts and with the new relationships with others that were formed; the members may be only mildly disappointed when they learn they were not funded.

The termination of an unsuccessful group is as important as the termination of a group that has achieved its goals. As with all groups, the plan for termination should have been made well in advance. The date of the last meeting should have been discussed and agreed on by the members long before the final meeting. Sufficient time for discussion must be allowed in terminating an unsuccessful group: (1) The reasons for the lack of progress need to be assessed and analyzed. (2) Alternatives by which the group and its members can reach their goals should be discussed. (Such alternatives may involve changing the format of the present group, referring members to other groups, and encouraging individual rather than group efforts.) (3) There must be time to handle the members' emotional reactions to terminating as well as to the lack of progress. (4) The members need time to work on unresolved, last-minute issues that are identified. (5) The members should have time to discuss whether they want to plan a special social event for the group's ending.

At times the ending of an unsuccessful group is chaotic and abrupt. A group that has been appointed to write a grant may be nearly finished when they are informed the funding organization has had a financial shortfall and is therefore withdrawing its request for funding proposals. Such a group may end abruptly in despair. Or, in a group of involuntary members (such as at a prison or at an adolescent residential treatment facility), the leader may decide that to continue the group is counterproductive because the members are continually " goofing off" and are not putting effort into achieving the group goals. In any case, the reasons for the group's ending should be fully explained and time should be given to handle the members' reactions to the closing. If there is insufficient time at the last meeting to deal with the tasks involved in ending a group, it is sometimes advisable either to have another session or for the leader to meet individually with each member to discuss his or her reactions to the group's failure to meet their goals, alternatives for reaching goals, reactions to the group's ending, and any unresolved concerns. When an unsuccessful group ends abruptly, some group members may be highly critical of the leader, of other group members, or of experiences that occurred in the group. If the leader contacts members to learn their thoughts about the group, he or she needs to be prepared to respond to highly critical feedback. One way of preparing is for the leader to "visualize" possible criticisms and then to formulate a positive and realistic response to each anticipated criticism.

Dropout.   When a member drops out, that member terminates even though the group continues on. A member may drop out for a variety of reasons. She may become disenchanted with the group and feel that neither she nor the group will accomplish the goals that have been set. He may have a disagreement with, or dislike, another group member. The member may be a parent who must now provide child care at the time the group meets or may have begun a new job with work hours that conflict with the meeting time. There are numerous other reasons.

When a member drops out without informing the group of the reasons, the leader should contact the member to learn why he or she decided to terminate. In some instances it is desirable for the leader to explain that deciding to leave is a major decision that should not be made abruptly and that the leader would like the opportunity to explore the reasons that led to the decision. If the member has a conflict with another group member, perhaps the conflict can be resolved so that the member will decide to return. Likewise, for other reasons, perhaps action can be taken to enable the member to return. If child care is a problem for a parent, perhaps child care arrangements can be made. If the member decides not to return, the reasons for leaving should be explored. Perhaps the member will raise legitimate concerns that may need to be dealt with so other members do not also become discouraged and leave. If the member drops out of a therapy group, sensitivity group, or an educational group and still has unresolved personal concerns, a referral to another group or to one-to-one professional help may be advisable. Whenever a member drops out, the leader needs to inform that member of his or her positive contributions to the group. Dropping out of a group is often viewed by that member as a personal failure, and therefore the leader needs to thank him or her for any positive contributions to help dispel the leaving member's sense of personal failure.

When a member drops out, the remaining members may experience a variety of emotions. Some may feel they failed this person. Some may feel guilt for what they said or did—or feel guilt for failing to do or say what they believe would have led the member to stay. Some may feel relief or joy; they may view the member as unworthy of the group or as an obstacle in the group's efforts to accomplish its goals. Some may feel sadness and be concerned that something tragic has happened to that member. Some members may be angry, feeling that the person who is leaving is abandoning the group. Some may feel personally rejected. Often, when a member drops out, erroneous rumors begin to circulate about the reasons. Therefore it is essential that the group be informed of the reasons for the member's leaving. When a member leaves, it can be devastating to group morale. If other members have also recently left, the group's survival may be jeopardized.

Ideally, the member who leaves should inform the group of the reasons, either in person or in writing. If the member does not, the leader or some other group member should contact the person who leaves to ascertain the reasons for leaving, and then soon afterward inform the group.

Transfer of a member. A transfer of a group member to another group or to some other type of professional services generally involves a planned arrangement between the group leader and the member. The transfer may occur for a variety of reasons. In a problem-solving group, the employing agency may decide the group member's talents and skills could be used better in some other capacity. In a therapy group, the leader and group member may jointly decide the member will be served better by receiving more specialized services in some other therapeutic format. A group member may be transferred in any kind of a group because of a conflict that cannot be resolved between the group member and other group members, especially when the conflict is severely interfering with goal accomplishment within the group. (For example, there may be a serious and insurmountable gap in mutual understanding and communication caused by differences in religious beliefs, values, or language.)

When a transfer occurs, the leader should do everything possible to keep it from being unexpected or abrupt. The member being transferred should clearly understand the reasons for the transfer and should ideally be accepting of it. In addition, the group should receive an explanation of why a member is transferring. The member should explain the reasons to the group. This would give the other group members an opportunity to wish the member well and to gain a sense of "closure" to the member's leaving.

Departure of the leader. Sometimes a group leader must terminate his or her work with a group because of reassignment, change of employment, health reasons, or family crises. The termination is often difficult for both the group leader and the members. Emotional reactions may be intense, and adequate time for working through these reactions may not be available. Members who feel vulnerable and depend on the leader may feel devastated. Some may erroneously personalize the leader's leaving as resulting from something they said or did. Some may feel anger and betrayal over having made a commitment to the group, confiding and trusting in the leader, and then feeling rejected by the leader who leaves when their goals and the group's goals are only partially accomplished.

The leader, too, may experience intense emotions, including guilt, for not being able to follow through on the implicit commitment to lead the group until its goals are accomplished and it ends.

When a leader leaves, he or she should encourage the members to express their feelings. The leader may want to initiate this expression by explaining fully why he or she is leaving, giving the members positive comments about the group, and stating his or her feelings of sadness and guilt over leaving. Prior to leaving, the group or the leader should select a new leader. If the new leader is not a member of the group, the one who is leaving should inform (outside of a group meeting) the new leader about the goals, the characteristics of members, current tasks and difficulties in the group, and progress toward goals that the group has made. The new leader should be introduced to the group by the departing leader. A smooth transition should be the goal in shifting responsibilities from the former to the new leader.

Evaluating a Group

In the past few decades, accountability has become a major emphasis in social welfare. Funding sources demand research evidence that the funds allocated are having a beneficial effect. An essential component of accountability is evaluation.

In broad terms, evaluation is designed to assess whether the services provided were effective and efficient. Services provided in which goals and objectives are unmet are neither effective nor efficient. In evaluating the services provided by a group, there are two dimensions of evaluation: process evaluation and outcome evaluation.

Process Evaluation

Process evaluation is an assessment, generally by group members, of the aspects of the group that were useful or detrimental. Feedback about techniques and incidents that blocked or enhanced process is of immense value to the group leader. With this information, the leader can hone certain skills, eliminate some materials, and give direction for approaches and materials to add. Such feedback can aid confidence. If the feedback is highly critical, it can be humbling and even devastating. It is far better to make changes suggested by the evaluation than to reject and "deny" the feedback and repeat the same mistakes in future groups. Group leaders need to welcome criticism and be prepared to respond to it constructively, which is the way that social workers expect clients to take constructive criticism.

Process evaluation can be conducted orally by asking the group members to discuss the aspects, techniques, materials, and incidents that were constructive and those that were counterproductive. An advantage of such an oral evaluation is that most members enjoy a verbal discussion. A disadvantage is that some members may be inhibited from giving negative feedback verbally because there is a social norm in such situations to focus on the positives.

Process evaluation can also be accomplished using a brief questionnaire that includes these three key areas:

1. Summarize the group's strengths. (Cite specific materials and incidents. Also cite skills and techniques used by the leader.)
2. Summarize the group's shortcomings. (Cite specific materials and incidents. Also cite skills and techniques used by the leader.)
3. Briefly outline your specific suggestions for changes.

In process evaluations, group members typically cite positive factors more than negative ones (Hepworth & Larsen, 1986, p. 590). Such positive feedback not only has a "stroking value" but also enables leaders to be more aware of their strengths, so they are apt to increase the use of these strengths in the future.

Negative feedback is as valuable as, and often more valuable than, positive feedback. It informs the leader of aspects that need improvement, which the leader can then attend to.

Another way of evaluating process is by *peer review,* a form of quality control. Peer review is conducted by having one or more "peers" (usually other group leaders) periodically sit in on a group.(Some agencies have one-way mirrors so the group can be unobtrusively observed.) Before a peer review, the agency or organization should agree on a set of principles or criteria that reflect quality group leadership. A peer review is a review of a small portion of the total functioning of the group. That small portion may be typical, or atypical, of the total functioning of the group. (Many colleges and universities use a peer review process in which tenured faculty in a department sit in on some of the classes of recently hired faculty.)

A variation of the peer review process is taping (either audio or video) a meeting. That tape is played back and reviewed by the leader and a peer (or by the leader's supervisor). Before taping a meeting, the leader should explain the reasons for wanting to tape the meeting, indicate who will view the tape, and then ask the members for their permission to tape the session.

Outcome Evaluation

Outcome evaluation involves assessing the extent to which the goals that were formulated when the group began have been accomplished. Specific approaches to measure goal attainment are: single-subject design, task achievement scaling, and satisfaction questionnaire.

Single-subject design. Single-subject design has become increasingly popular in the helping professions in the past two decades. There are more than a dozen variations of single-subject design, some of which are very complex and rigorous. Fortunately, the simpler designs can be used by entry-level social workers in many direct practice situations. Single-subject design is described in considerable detail in Chapter 11.

Task achievement scaling. The objective of this approach is to gauge the degree to which group members and the leader have completed agreed-on intervention tasks. In this approach, work toward the goals of the members and of the group is broken down into many separate actions or tasks. The tasks are selected by mutual agreement, and each member is assigned or selects specific tasks to reach his or her goal and the overall goal of the group. Usually, a deadline is set for the completion of each task. *Task achievement scaling* refers to a procedure for rating the degree to which each agreed-on task has, in fact, been achieved.

Reid and Epstein (1972), in using this approach, used a 4-point scale to record progress on each task: 4 = completely achieved; 3 = substantially achieved, action is still necessary; 2 = partially achieved, considerable work remains to be done; and 1 = minimally achieved or not achieved. Where appropriate, they have a fifth rating: No for "no opportunity to work on task." With this approach, only results are rated—not effort, motivation, or good intentions. The appealing features of this approach are its simplicity and the fact that it can be used when more rigorous procedures are not feasible because of insufficient time, insufficient data, or difficulties in finding a suitable way to measure changes in the target behavior. The approach also has limitations.

If the tasks are erroneously conceptualized to be constructive in resolving the client's problems, then completing the tasks may have little effect on resolving the client's problems.

Satisfaction questionnaire. Still another way to assess the outcome of a group is to have group members fill out a questionnaire that measures level of satisfaction. An example of such a questionnaire is the Group Member Satisfaction Questionnaire shown in Exhibit 6.2.

Such a questionnaire is a relatively simple and inexpensive way to measure the members' level of satisfaction with the group. The questionnaire can be filled out at the group's last meeting or can be mailed to members some time after the last meeting. Questions that evaluate process (described earlier in this chapter) can be added to this questionnaire.

Such satisfaction questionnaires have limitations, however. Responses are affected by the mood of the respondent. In addition, dissatisfied members are less likely to fill out the questionnaire than satisfied ones, particularly if it is administered by mail (Sheafor, Horejsi, & Horejsi, 1988, p. 390).

A few concluding comments follow about the personal benefits you will receive in leading

Thank you for taking a few minutes to evaluate your experiences in our group. Your answers to this brief questionnaire will help us improve future groups. Feel free to offer your comments. To assure anonymity, please do not sign your name.

1. Did you accomplish what you expected when you joined the group?
    _____ Yes, completely
    _____ Mostly
    _____ No real progress
    _____ Worse off now than before
    Comments _____

2. Do you feel the group accomplished its goals?
    _____ Yes, completely
    _____ Mostly
    _____ No real progress
    _____ The group was an utter failure
    Comments _____

3. How do you feel about the group leader?
    _____ Very satisfied
    _____ Satisfied
    _____ No feelings one way or another
    _____ Dissatisfied
    _____ Very dissatisfied
    Comments _____

4. How do you feel about the other members in the group?
    _____ Satisfied with everyone
    _____ Satisfied with some, and dissatisfied with others
    _____ No feelings one way or another
    _____ Dissatisfied with most of the other members
    _____ Dissatisfied with all of the other members
    _____ Very dissatisfied with all of the other members
    Comments _____

groups. Through learning how to lead effectively, you will become more aware of yourself, grow as a person, become more self-confident, feel good about yourself, develop highly marketable skills that employers are seeking, learn to improve interpersonal relationships, and help yourself and other members accomplish important tasks. Leaders are not born. They are trained. You have the potential to become an effective group leader. You can do it!

Summary

Social group work's historical roots were in the informal recreational organizations—the YWCA and YMCA, scouting, Jewish centers, settlement houses, and 4-H Clubs. Now almost every social service agency provides some group services. Most undergraduate and graduate social work programs provide practice courses to train students to lead groups, particularly socialization, educational, and therapeutic groups. The focus of social work groups has considerable variation including recreation, recreation-skill development, task focused, problem solving and decision making, self-help, socialization, therapy, education, and encounter.

With problem-solving and decision-making groups, group decision making is usually superior to individual decision making. Problem-solving groups have the danger of groupthink, which may lead a group to make ineffective and even destructive decisions. Making decisions by simple majority voting may also alienate the minority.

Socialization groups generally have the objective of developing or changing attitudes and behaviors of group members in some socially accepted direction. Social skill development, increasing self-confidence, and planning for the future are other foci.

The goal in therapy groups is generally to have each member explore in depth personal or emotional problems and then to develop a strategy to resolve the problems. A group therapist uses principles of one-to-one intervention and group dynamics to assist members in achieving positive changes in attitudes and behaviors. In contrast, sensitivity groups seek to foster increased personal and interpersonal awareness and to develop more effective interaction patterns.

The chapter concluded with guidelines on how to start, lead, and terminate groups. Aspects included homework, planning a session, relaxing before starting a meeting, cues on entering the meeting room, seating arrangements, introductions, clarifying roles, agenda, terminating a group, and evaluating a group.

Exercises

1. Assertiveness training

Goal: Demonstrate to the class how to run an educational group by illustrating how to run an assertiveness training group.

Step 1: Indicate the purpose of this exercise. Describe nonassertive, aggressive, and assertive behaviors (see Chapter 16 for descriptions).

Step 2: Distribute a handout that describes the 12 steps of assertiveness training (contained in Chapter 16). Summarize these steps.

Step 3: Ask for volunteers (two for each situation) to role-play assertively the situations that you give them, such as

a. asking someone who is smoking next to you to put out a cigarette;
b. asking for a date and refusing a date;
c. indicating to your objecting father that you want to live with the person you are dating.

After a situation is role-played, have the class discuss the assertiveness strategy.

Step 4: Ask students to write anonymously on a note card one or two situations involving assertiveness that they are struggling with and that they would like others in the class to role-play.

Step 5: Collect these note cards and select some situations for volunteers to role-play. After a situation is role-played, have the class discuss the assertiveness strategy.

2. The nominal group

Goal: This exercise is designed to have the class learn how a nominal group is conducted.

Step 1: The steps of how to run a nominal group are described in this chapter. Ask a question for the nominal group to consider such as "What do you see as the shortcomings of our social work program (do not mention the names of faculty members)?" Then follow the steps for conducting a nominal group as described in this chapter.

3. Trust walk

Goal: This exercise is designed to demonstrate an approach—the trust walk—that is frequently used in sensitivity groups. A trust walk helps students get in touch with aspects of themselves that they are unaware of.

Step 1: Inform the class of the purpose of the exercise. Have the students form groups of two. (If a member is without a partner, the instructor can be a partner.) Have a member of each subgroup close his or her eyes and instruct him or her to keep eyes closed during the first part of this exercise. The "seeing" partner then is instructed to lead the "blind" partner down corridors, around the room, and perhaps outside. The "seeing" partner can lead the "blind" partner with verbal directions and by taking a hand. The "seeing" person has the responsibility to watch that the "blind" partner does not run into objects, fall, stumble, or get hurt in any way. (Inform the students to be very careful going up and down stairs.)

Step 2: After eight to ten minutes have the partners reverse roles and continue the exercise for another eight to ten minutes.

Step 3: Have the students then discuss their feelings about doing this trust walk. Ask questions such as the following. Did you occasionally open your eyes when you were the "non-seeing" partner? Did you have trust in your partner? Did you feel you would run into objects and hurt yourself? Were you afraid? If yes, how did you handle these fears? Did you become aware of feelings or thoughts about yourself that you previously were unaware of? If yes, what thoughts and feelings?

Social Work with Groups: Concepts and Skills

This chapter presents key group dynamic concepts and summarizes guidelines for leading therapeutic groups.[1] We begin by reviewing the following ideas that are important in understanding group process: Membership and reference groups, stages in group development, task and maintenance roles, leadership theory, social power bases in groups, personal goals and group goals, conformity, idiosyncratic credits, competitive and cooperative groups, controversy and creativity, the win-lose approach versus the problem-solving approach, handling disruptive behavior, and group size. Then we discuss starting, leading, and ending therapy groups.

Membership and Reference Groups

A membership group is any group to which a person belongs. In a sense membership in a group is clearly defined—either a person belongs to a group or does not belong. Membership is thus a boundary condition.

Some people are marginal members of a group. For example, everyone who is enrolled at your campus is a member of the student body, but some students are only margi-

<hr>

[1]Material in this chapter is adapted from Charles Zastrow, "Social Work Practice with Groups," in *Introduction to Social Welfare Institutions*, 2nd ed. (Pacific Grove, CA: Brooks/Cole, 1982), pp. 507–529. Grafton H. Hull, Jr. was a contributing author to this chapter.

nal members since they do not get involved in any campus activities. Tim Kelly at this campus only attends classes. He works nearly full-time in the evening and does not live on campus. He identifies primarily with the people with whom he works. The other students influence him very little. He comes to campus only for his classes and leaves almost immediately afterward.

Full psychological membership in a group occurs only when a person is positively attracted to being a member and is positively accepted as a member. Tim Kelly, for example, has limited psychological membership with the student body, since he has only a small identification with the campus. The more a person is attracted to a group, the greater will be that person's commitment toward accomplishing the goals of the group.

Aspiring members include those who are seeking admission to a group but as yet have not been admitted. They are not members but act as if they are. For example, students who aspire to be admitted to a fraternity or a sorority will seek to act like members to increase their chances of being admitted. Aspiring members are psychologically identifying with the group even though they are not as yet formally admitted.

There is also a difference between voluntary membership and involuntary membership. Voluntary membership occurs when an individual deliberately chooses to belong to a certain group, such as a fraternity or athletic team. In other situations a person may have little or no choice over becoming a group member. Social workers often work with groups whose membership is involuntary as in prison settings, mental hospitals, residential treatment facilities, group homes, programs for people arrested for driving while intoxicated, and school settings. Involuntary group members are likely (at least initially) to be uninterested in participating and are sometimes hostile and disruptive.

Reference groups are those groups whose influence we are willing to accept. They are the ones with which we most closely identify.

| A monk leads the prayers for the Cambodian New Year. Places of worship are reference groups.

In the example given earlier, Tim Kelly is a member of a student body and his work group. Since he primarily identifies with his work group, the work group is a reference group for him while the student body, for all practical purposes, is not.

The groups we use as a reference have two distinct functions. First, the members' behavior, attitudes, and other characteristics represent standards or comparison points that we use in making judgments and evaluations. Second, reference groups have a normative function in that we seek to conform to the standards for behavior and attitudes of our reference groups.

In a given group there are only some members who are referents for us. The referents are the people who influence us and who we, in turn, seek to influence. In a large group we normally have only a small subgroup of refer-

ents. These referents make sense to us, or they seem in contact with reality, or they are people we identify with, or they have most of the power. The other members we tend to "tune out" and interact with less.

Stages in Group Development

Garland, Jones, and Kolodny (1965) developed a model that identifies five stages of development in social work groups. This model seeks to describe the kinds of problems that commonly arise as groups begin to form and continue to develop. Understanding of these problems, it is theorized, enables the designated leader to anticipate and respond to the reactions of group members more effectively. The conceptualization of Garland and his colleagues (1965) appears particularly applicable to socialization groups, therapy groups, and encounter groups. To a lesser extent, the model is also applicable to self-help groups, problem-solving and decision-making groups, educational groups, recreation-skill groups, and task groups.

Closeness (that is, the question of how near group members will allow themselves to become to one another emotionally) is the central focus of the model. The question of closeness is reflected in *struggles* that occur at five levels of growth of the group: preaffiliation, power and control, intimacy, differentiation, and separation.

In the first stage, *preaffiliation,* members are ambivalent about joining the group. Interaction is guarded. Members test out, often through approach and avoidance behavior, whether they really want to belong to the group. New situations are often frightening, and the members try to protect themselves from being hurt or taken advantage of in such new situations. They attempt to maintain a certain amount of distance and to get what they can from the group without risking much of themselves. Individuals are aware that group involvement will make demands that may be frustrating or even painful. On the other hand, members are also attracted to the group because they generally have had prior rewards and satisfying social experiences in other groups, and this group offers the hope of similar rewards. In the first stage the leader should seek to increase the attractions toward the group "by allowing and supporting distance, gently inviting trust, facilitating exploration of the physical and psychological milieu, and by providing activities if necessary and initiating group structure" (Garland & Frey, 1973, p. 3). The first stage gradually ends when members come to feel fairly safe and comfortable with the group and view the rewards as being worth a tentative emotional commitment.

The second stage, *power and control,* emerges as the characteristics of the group begin to develop. Patterns of communication within the group emerge, alliances and subgroups begin to appear, members begin to take on certain roles and responsibilities, norms and methods for handling group tasks develop, and membership questions arise. Such processes are necessary for the group to conduct its business. However, these processes lead to a struggle as the members establish their places within the group. Each member seeks power, partly for self-protection and partly to attempt to gain greater control over the gratifications and rewards to be received from the group. In this struggle, the group leader is a major source of gratification. The leader is perceived as having the greatest power to influence the direction of the group and to give or withhold emotional and material rewards. At this point members realize that the group is becoming important to them.

The second stage is a transitional stage with certain basic issues needing to be resolved: Does the group or the leader have primary control over the group's affairs? What are the limits of the power of the leader and of the group? To what extent will the leader use his or her power?

This uncertainty results in anxiety among and considerable testing by group members to gauge the limits and establish norms for the power and the authority of both the group and the group leader. Rebellion is not uncommon, and the dropout rate in groups is often highest at this stage. During this struggle the leader should (1) seek to help the members understand the nature of the power struggle, (2) give emotional support to weather the discomfort of uncertainty, and (3) help the group establish norms to resolve the uncertainty. It is very important that group members develop trust in the leader so the leader will maintain a safe balance of shared power and control. When this trust is achieved, group members make a major commitment to become involved in the group.

In the third stage, *intimacy,* the loves and dislikes of intimate relationships are expressed. The group becomes more like a family, with sibling rivalry arising between members and the leader sometimes even being referred to as a parent. Feelings about the group at this stage are more openly expressed and discussed. The group is now viewed as a place where growth and change take place. Individuals feel free to examine and make efforts to change personal attitudes, concerns, and problems. Group tasks are also worked on, and there is a feeling of "oneness" or cohesiveness within the group. Struggle or turmoil during this stage leads the members to explore and make changes in their personal lives, and to examine "what this group is all about."

During the fourth stage, *differentiation*, there is increased freedom for members to experiment with new and alternative behavior patterns. There is a recognition of individual rights and needs and a high level of communication among members. At this stage the group is able to organize itself more efficiently. Leadership is more evenly shared and roles are more functional. Power problems are now minimal, and decisions are made and carried out on a less emotional and more objective basis. Garland and Frey (1973) noted:

> This kind of individualized therapeutic cohesion has been achieved because the group experience has all along valued and nurtured individual integrity. . . .
>
> The worker assists in this stage by helping the group to run itself and by encouraging it to act as a unit with other groups or in the wider community. During this time the worker exploits opportunities for evaluation by the group of its activities, feelings, and behavior. [p. 5]

The differentiation stage is analogous to a healthy functioning family in which the children have reached adulthood and are now becoming successful in pursuing their own lives; relationships are more between equals, members are mutually supportive, and members are able to relate to each other in ways that are more rational and objective.

The final stage is *separation*. The purposes of the group have been achieved, and members have learned new behavioral patterns to enable them to move on to other social experiences. Termination is not always easily accomplished. Members may be reluctant to move on and may even display regressive behavior in an effort to prolong the safety of the group. Members may also express anger over ending the group or even psychologically deny the end is near. Garland and Frey (1973) suggested the leader's (or worker's) role should be the following:

> To facilitate separation the worker must be willing to let go. Concentration upon group and individual mobility, evaluation of the experience, help with the expression of the ambivalence about termination and recognition of the progress which has been made are his major tasks. Acceptance of termination is facilitated by active guidance of members as individuals to other ongoing sources of support and assistance. [p. 6]

It is common for leaders just beginning their work with groups to expect a smooth transition from one stage to another and to be disappointed if this does not come about. Additionally, many new practitioners, lacking experience and trust in the group process, tend to force the group out of one stage and into another. Experience will demonstrate the futility of such efforts. Barring unforeseen circumstances, each group will move at its own pace and will eventually arrive at the same destination. Groups that skip stages or whose development is otherwise thwarted will often return to a previous stage where business is yet unfinished. The leader can best facilitate group life by recognizing this and by allowing the natural process to evolve. While groups do sometimes become mired in one stage, these occurrences are less common than feared.

Task and Maintenance Roles

All groups (whether organized for therapeutic reasons, for problem solving, or for other objectives) rely on the performance by members of a variety of roles. The group's needs generally require that both task roles and group-building roles be performed satisfactorily. Task roles are those that are needed to accomplish the specific goals set by the group, whereas maintenance roles include those that serve to strengthen social/emotional aspects of group life (Pfeiffer & Jones, 1976).

David and Frank Johnson (1975, p. 26) summarized these roles as follows:

Information and opinion giver: Offers facts, opinions, ideas, suggestions, and relevant information to help group discussion.

Information and opinion seeker: Asks for facts, information, opinions, ideas, and feelings from other members to help group discussion.

Starter: Proposes goals and tasks to initiate action within the group.

Direction giver: Develops plans on how to proceed and focuses attention on the task to be done.

Summarizer: Pulls together related ideas or suggestions and restates and summarizes major points discussed.

Coordinator: Shows relationships among various ideas by pulling them together and harmonizes activities of various subgroups and members.

Diagnoser: Figures out sources of difficulties the group has in working effectively and the blocks to progress in accomplishing the group's goals.

Energizer: Stimulates a higher quality of work from the group.

Reality tester: Examines the practicality and workability of ideas, evaluates alternative solutions, and applies them to real situations to see how they will work.

Evaluator: Compares group decisions and accomplishments with group standards and goals.

The Johnsons (1975, p. 27) also identified *group maintenance roles,* which strengthen social/emotional bonds within the group:

Encourager of participation: Warmly encourages everyone to participate, giving recognition for contributions, demonstrating acceptance and openness to ideas of others, is friendly and responsive to group members.

Harmonizer and compromiser: Persuades members to analyze constructively their differences in opinions, searches for common elements in conflicts, and tries to reconcile disagreements.

Tension reliever: Eases tensions and increases the enjoyment of group members by joking, suggesting breaks, and proposing fun approaches to group work.

Communication helper: Shows good communication skills and makes sure that each group member understands what other members are saying.

Evaluator of emotional climate: Asks members how they feel about the way in which the group is working and about each other, and share own feelings about both.

Process observer: Watches the process by which the group is working and uses the observations to help examine group effectiveness.

Standard setter: Expresses group standards and goals to make members aware of the direction of the work and the progress being made toward the goal and to get open acceptance of group norms and procedures.

Active listener: Listens and serves as an interested audience for other members, is receptive to others' ideas, goes along with the group when not in disagreement.

Trust builder: Accepts and supports openness of other group members, reinforcing risk taking and encouraging individuality.

Interpersonal problem solver: Promotes open discussion of conflicts between group members in order to resolve conflicts and increase group togetherness.

Hersey and Blanchard (1977) developed a situational theory of leadership that serves as a guideline for when effective leaders should focus on task behaviors, when they should focus on maintenance behaviors, and when they should focus on both. In essence, the theory asserts that when members have low maturity in terms of accomplishing a specific task, the leader should engage in high-task and low-maintenance behaviors. Hersey and Blanchard refer to this situation as *telling*, since the leader's behavior is most effective when he or she defines the members' roles and tells them how, when, and where to do needed tasks. The task maturity of members increases as their experience and understanding of the task increases. For moderately mature members, the leader should engage in high-task and high-maintenance behaviors. This combination of behaviors is referred to as *selling*, since the leader should not only provide clear direction as to role and task responsibilities, but should also use maintenance behaviors to get the members to psychologically buy into the decisions that have to be made.

Also, according to Hersey and Blanchard, when group members' commitment to the task increases, so does their maturity. When members are committed to accomplishing the task and have the ability and knowledge to complete the task, the leader should engage in low-task and high-maintenance behaviors, referred to as *participating*. Finally, for groups in which members are both willing and able to take responsibility for directing their own task behavior, the leader should engage in low-task and low-maintenance behaviors, referred to as *delegating*. Delegating allows members considerable autonomy in completing the task.

Leadership Theory

There are at least four major approaches to leadership theory: trait, position, style, and distributed functions. Each of these approaches is briefly summarized in the following paragraphs.

The Trait Approach

Aristotle observed, "From the hour of their birth some are marked for subjugation, and others for command" (Johnson & Johnson, 1987, p. 39). As implied by this comment, the trait approach to leadership has been in existence for centuries. This approach assumes that leaders have personal characteristics or traits that make them different from followers. It also implies that leaders are born, not made, and that leaders emerge naturally rather than being trained. The trait approach has also been called the *great person* theory of leadership.

Krech, Crutchfield, and Ballachey (1962) reviewed research studies on the traits needed by a leader. Their results suggested a leader needs to be perceived as (1) being a member of the group he or she is attempting to lead, (2) having to a special degree the norms and values that are central to the group, (3) being the most qualified group member for the task to be accomplished, and (4) fitting the members' expectations about how he or she should behave and what functions he or she should serve.

Research on personality traits indicates leaders, compared to followers, tend to be better adjusted, more dominant, more extroverted, and more assertive; they often have greater interpersonal sensitivity. Other traits such as intelligence, enthusiasm, self-confidence, and equalitarianism are also frequently found to characterize leaders (Hare, 1962).

Although potential leaders tend to have more of all positive attributes than any of the members in the group, they cannot be so extreme that they become deviates. In one study, for example, Davie and Hare (1956) found that "B" students were the campus leaders, while the more intelligent "A" students were considered "grinds" who occasionally were treated as outcasts for being "curve wreckers." Also, the person who does most of the talking has been found to win most of the decisions and become the leader, unless he or she talks too much and antagonizes the other group members (March, 1956).

Two postulated leadership traits that have received considerable attention are charisma and Machiavellianism. We will take a brief look at each of these traits.

Charisma. Johnson and Johnson (1987, p. 43) defined charisma as "an extraordinary power, as of working miracles." Johnson and Johnson (1987) gave the following definition of a charismatic leader:

> The charismatic leader must have a sense of mission, a belief in the social-change movement he or she leads, and confidence in oneself as the chosen instrument to lead the movement to its destination. The leader must appear extremely self-confident in order to inspire others with the faith that the movement he or she leads will, without fail, prevail and ultimately reduce their distress. [p. 44]

Some charismatic leaders appear to inspire their followers to love and be fully committed to them. Other charismatic leaders offer their members the hope and promise of deliverance from distress.

Charisma has not been precisely defined and its components have not been fully identified. The qualities and characteristics that any charismatic leader has will differ somewhat from those of other charismatic leaders. The following leaders all have been referred to as charismatic, yet they differed substantially in personality characteristics: John F. Kennedy, Martin Luther King, Jr., Julius Caesar, General George Patton, Confucius, Gandhi, and Winston Churchill.

One difficulty with the charisma approach to leadership is that people who are viewed as charismatic tend to express this quality in a variety of ways. A second difficulty is that many leaders do well as leaders without be-

ing viewed as having charisma. For example, many group therapists are very effective in leading groups, even though they are not viewed as charismatic.

Machiavellianism. Niccolò Machiavelli (1469–1527) was an Italian statesman who advocated that rulers use cunning, craft, deceit, and duplicity as political methods for increasing their power and control. (Machiavelli was not the originator of this approach; earlier theorists conceptualized leadership in terms of manipulation for self-enhancement. However, the term *Machiavellianism* has become associated with the notion that politics is amoral and that any unscrupulous means can justifiably be used in achieving political power.) Machiavellian leadership is based on the concepts that followers (1) are basically fallible, gullible, untrustworthy, and weak; (2) are impersonal objects; and (3) should be manipulated for the leader to achieve his or her goals.

Christie and Geis (1970) concluded that Machiavellian leaders have four characteristics: (1) They have little emotional involvement in interpersonal relationships, since it is emotionally easier to manipulate others when viewing them as impersonal objects. (2) They are not concerned about conventional morality and take a utilitarian (what they can get out of it) rather than a moral view of their interactions with others. (3) They have a fairly accurate perception of the needs of their followers, which facilitates their capacity to manipulate them. (4) They have a low degree of ideological commitment; they focus on manipulating others for personal benefit rather than for achieving long-term ideological goals.

While a few leaders may have Machiavellian characteristics, most do not. Very few groups would ever function effectively or efficiently with Machiavellian leaders.

In recent years the trait theory of leadership has declined in popularity. Studies on the importance of leadership traits have often been inconclusive. The characteristics, for example, needed to be a good leader (such as a colonel or general in the military service) differ markedly from characteristics needed in many other leadership positions, such as being a good therapy group leader. Though such qualities as high intelligence and being well adjusted may have some correlation with leadership, many highly intelligent persons never attain top leadership positions, and some leaders (such as Adolf Hitler and certain kings) have been emotionally unstable.

Trait research has shown that characteristics of leaders have also been found in followers, and that different leadership positions may require different leadership traits. The best rule for leader selection appears to be to select those individuals who have the necessary skills and who are motivated to help the group accomplish its goals.

The Position Approach

Most large organizations have several levels of leadership, such as president, vice-president, manager, and supervisor. The position approach defines leadership in terms of the authority of a particular position and has focused on studying the behavior of people in high-level positions. At times, the training and personal background of leaders have also been examined.

Studies using the position approach, however, have revealed little consistency in how people assume leadership positions. Obviously, some individuals may become leaders with little related training (in family businesses, for example), whereas others spend years developing their skills. Also, individuals in different leadership positions have been found to display a variety of appropriate behaviors. For example, a drill sergeant in basic military training is not expected to be empathetic, but a sensitivity group leader is. It is difficult to compile a list of leadership traits using this approach. Not surprisingly, the position approach has shown that what consti-

tutes leadership behavior depends on the particular requirements of the position.

It is also difficult to define which behavior of a designated leader is leadership behavior and which is not. Certainly not all of the behavior of a designated authority figure is leadership behavior. For instance, an inexperienced individual in a position of authority can mask incompetence with an authoritarian attitude. Also, the leadership behavior among group members who are not designated leaders is often difficult to clarify. An experienced supervisor who has joined a new firm, for example, may categorize her staff members according to guidelines set for specific positions by her former employer. If the positions are not interchangeable, a communication problem may develop and the supervisor's leadership abilities or those of her staff will be questioned.

The Style Approach

Because research on the trait approach was turning out contradictory results, Lewin, Lippitt, and White (1939) focused on examining leadership styles. These researchers described and studied three leadership styles: authoritarian, democratic, and laissez-faire.

Authoritarian leaders have more absolute power than democratic leaders. They alone set goals and policies, dictate the activities of the members, and set major plans. They are the purveyors of rewards and punishments, and they alone know the succession of future steps in the group's activities. In contrast, democratic leaders seek maximum involvement and participation of every member in all decisions affecting the group. They seek to spread responsibility rather than to concentrate it.

Authoritarian leadership is generally efficient and decisive. One of the hazards, however, is that group members may do what they are told out of necessity and not because of any commitment to group goals. The authoritarian leader who anticipates approval from subordinates for accomplishments achieved may be surprised to find backbiting and bickering common in the group. Unsuccessful authoritarian leadership is apt to generate factionalism, behind-the-scenes jockeying and maneuvering for position among members, and lead to a decline in morale.

Democratic leadership, in contrast, is slow in decision making and sometimes confusing but frequently proves to be more effective because of strong cooperation that generally emerges with participation in decision making. With democratic leadership, interpersonal hostilities between members, dissatisfactions with the leader, and concern for personal advancement all become issues that are discussed and acted on. The danger is that the private, behind-the-scenes complaining of the authoritarian approach becomes public conflict in a democratic approach. Once this public conflict has been resolved in a democratic group, a strong personal commitment develops that motivates members to implement group decisions rather than to subvert them. The potential for sabotage in an authoritarian group is high, and therein lies the advantage of the democratic style.

The democratic leader knows that some mistakes are inevitable, and that the group will suffer from them. Yet, such mistakes require the leader's ability to stand by without interfering because to do otherwise might harm the democratic process and impede the progress of the group in developing the capacity to make decisions as a group.

In some situations authoritarian leadership is most effective, whereas in others democratic leadership is most effective (Hare, 1962). As in any situation, the group will be more effective when members' expectations about the behavior appropriate for that situation are met. Where group members anticipate a democratic style, as they do in educational settings, classrooms, or discussion groups, the democratic style is usually found to produce the most effective group. When members anticipate forceful leadership from their superiors, as in industry or military service, a more authoritarian form of leadership results in a more effective group.

In the *laissez-faire* style, there is very little participation by the leader. The group members are primarily left to function (or flounder) with little input by the designated leader. There are a few conditions where group members function best under laissez-faire style (when the members are committed to a course of action, have the resources to implement it, and need a minimum of designated leader influence to work effectively). Because different leadership styles are required in different situations (even with the same group), research interest in recent years has switched to the distributed functions approach.

The Distributed Functions Approach

With this approach leadership is defined as the performance of acts that help the group reach its goals and maintain itself in good working order (Johnson & Johnson, 1975). Leadership functions include setting group goals, selecting and implementing tasks to achieve goals, and providing resources to accomplish goals. Leadership functions also include the group maintenance tasks of improving the group's cohesion and seeking to assure that individual members are satisfied. The functional approach to leadership seeks to discover what tasks are essential to achieve group goals under various circumstances and how different group members should take part in these actions.

This approach disagrees with the great person theory of leadership. It asserts that any member of a group will at times be a leader by taking actions that serve group functions. With this approach, leadership is viewed as being specific to a particular group in a particular situation. For example, telling a joke may be a useful leadership function in certain situations if it relieves tension, but telling a joke when other members are revealing intense personal feelings in a therapy group may be counterproductive and therefore not be a leadership function.

The functional approach defines leadership as occurring whenever one member in a group influences other members to help the group reach its goals. Because at times all group members influence other group members, each member in a group exerts leadership. A difference exists in most groups between being a designated leader (such as a president or chairperson) and engaging in leadership behavior. A *designated leader* has certain responsibilities (such as calling meetings and leading the discussion), whereas the term *leadership* means one member is influencing other group members to help the group reach its goals.

The functional approach asserts that leadership is a learned set of skills that anyone with certain minimal requirements can acquire. Responsible membership is the same thing as responsible leadership; both involve doing what needs to be done to help the group maintain itself and accomplish its goals. This approach asserts that people can be taught the skills and behaviors that help the group accomplish its tasks and maintain good working relationships. The implication for a social work practice course is that practically everyone in the class can learn to be an effective leader.

Like any member of a group, the designated leader may be called on or may be forced to adopt one or more of the task specialist or maintenance specialist roles discussed earlier in this chapter. Indeed, the leader has a special obligation to be alert for such occasions and to assume or assist others to assume whichever roles are timely and appropriate. The leader's contribution to the group is not limited, however, by the assumption of specified roles. Each leader is responsible for a variety of functions that range from the performing of intake to the planning for termination. The needs and developmental stage of a group may at different times require a leader who can assume any of the previously described roles as well as those that follow:

- Executive (being the top coordinator of the activities of a group).
- Policymaker (establishing group goals and policies).
- Planner (deciding the means by which the group will achieve its goals).
- Expert (serving as the source of readily available information and skills).
- External group representative (being the official spokesperson for the group).
- Controller of internal relations (controlling the structure as a way to control in-group relations).
- Purveyor of rewards and punishments (determining promotions, demotions, and assigning pleasant or unpleasant tasks).
- Arbitrator and mediator (acting as both judge and conciliator with the power to reduce or to increase factionalism within the group).
- Exemplar (serving as a model of behavior to show what the members should be and do).
- Ideologist (serving as the source of the beliefs and values of the members).
- Scapegoat (serving as the target for ventilating members' frustrations and disappointments).

Social Power Bases in Groups

French and Raven (1968) developed a framework for understanding the extent to which one member of a group has influence or power over another. Five bases of power are identified: reward, coercive, legitimate, referent, and expert. Each of these power bases will be more fully described. This framework allows group leaders to analyze the source of their power and also presents suggestions on when, and when not, to use their power to influence others.

Power is often erroneously viewed negatively in human interactions. But all human interactions involve power. In groups it is natural and generally desirable that every member seeks to influence other members to accomplish both personal goals and group goals.

Reward power is based on the perception of B (one member) that A (another member, or the entire group) has the capacity to dispense rewards or remove negative consequences in response to B's behavior. The power will be greater the more the group members value the reward, and the more that members believe they cannot get the reward from anyone else. Rewards include such things as promotions, pay increases, days off, and praise. Group members will usually work hard for someone who has high reward power, will usually like the person, and will communicate effectively with him. But reward power can backfire if group members feel they are being conned or bribed into going along, which can lead to dislike of the high reward person. If reward power is used by A in a conflict situation with B, B is apt to feel he is being bribed and controlled.

Coercive power is based on B's perception that A can dispense adverse consequences or remove positive consequences. Coercive power stems from the expectation of B that he will be punished by A if he fails to conform to her wishes. The ability to fire a worker if he falls below a given level of production is a common example. The distinction between reward and coercive power is important. French and Raven noted that reward power will tend to increase the attraction of B toward A, while coercive power will decrease this attraction. If A uses coercive power to attempt to settle a conflict, it often increases B's hostility, resentment, and anger. Threats often lead to aggression and counterthreats. Thus, coercive power may exacerbate the conflict by leading both A and B to trust each other less and to seek to retaliate against each other. Therefore, whenever possible, coercive power should not be used in a conflict situation.

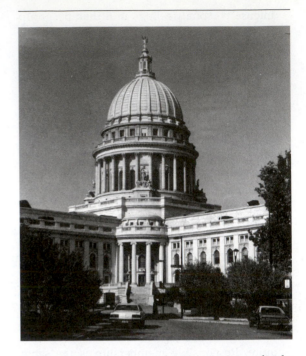

The electoral process is a legitimizing agent for the people who enact the laws in our society.

(Unfortunately, it often is, with the result that the conflict is exacerbated. For example, military threats often increase conflict between rival countries.)

Legitimate power is based on B's perception that A has a legitimate right to prescribe behavior for him, and that B has an obligation to accept this influence. Legitimate power is probably the most complex of the five power bases. Legitimate power is based on some internalized value or norm. There are several bases for legitimate power. Cultural values constitute one common basis for legitimate power and include such things as intelligence, age, caste, and physical characteristics. For example, in some cultures the aged are highly respected and granted the right to prescribe behavior for others. Acceptance of a social structure is another basis for legitimate power; for example, legitimate power in a formal organization is largely a relationship between positions rather than between persons.

(An illustration in a factory would be the perceived right of a supervisor to assign work.) A third basis for legitimate power is a legitimizing agent; for example, the process of electing a group leader is a common method of legitimizing a person's right to a position that already has a legitimate range of power associated with it.

The areas in which legitimate power may be used are generally specified (for example, in a job description), along with the designation of that power. The attempted use of power outside the range of legitimate power will decrease the legitimate power and attractiveness of the authority figure.

Referent power is based on B's identification with A. Identification in this context means either a feeling of oneness with A or a desire for such an identity. The stronger the identification of B with A, the greater the attraction to A and the greater the A's referent power. A verbalization of referent power is "I am like A, and therefore I will believe or behave as A does," or "I want to be like A, and I will be more like A if I believe or behave as A does." In ambiguous situations B will seek to evaluate his thoughts, beliefs, and values in terms of what A thinks, believes, and values. In ambiguous situations B is likely to adopt the thoughts, beliefs, values of the individual or group with which he identifies. French and Raven noted that B is often not consciously aware of the referent power that A exerts.

Expert power is based on the perception that A has some special knowledge or expertise. Accepting a physician's advice in medical matters is a common example of expert influence. Another would be accepting directions from a service station owner when in a strange city. For expert influence to occur it is necessary for B to think that A has the right answer, and for B to trust that A is telling the truth. A client accepting a counselor's suggestion is another example of expert power. The range of expert power is more limited than that of referent power, since the expert is seen as having superior knowledge or ability in very specific areas. French and Raven (1968)

noted that the attempted exertion of expert power outside the perceived range of that power will reduce it, as an undermining of confidence seems to take place.

French and Raven (1968) theorized that for all five types, the stronger the basis of power, the greater the power. Referent power is thought to have the broadest range of power. Any attempt to use power outside the prescribed range is hypothesized to reduce the power.

Personal Goals and Group Goals

A goal is an end toward which an individual or a group of people are working. It is an ideal or a desired end point that people value. A personal goal is a goal held by a member. A group goal is one held by enough members of a group that the group can be said to be working toward its achievement.

All groups have goals, and every person who joins a group has personal goals. Groups generally have both short- and long-range goals. The short-range goals should be stepping stones to reaching the long-range goals.

There are several reasons that it is very important to set group goals. The effectiveness and efficiency of the group (and group procedures) can be measured by the extent to which goals are achieved. Goals are guides that give direction to groups and to their members. Goals direct the group's programs and efforts. Conflicts of opinions between members are often resolved by making judgments about which opinion is most helpful in achieving group goals. Group goals are a motivating force that stimulates members to work toward achieving these goals. Once members make a commitment to achieve a certain goal, they will feel an obligation to put forth their abilities, efforts, and resources to attain this end.

The members' motivation to work toward accomplishing group goals is increased by involving group members in setting the goals. Through involvement members will (1) have a greater chance of having their personal goals for joining the group become a component of the group goals, (2) have an increased awareness of the importance of choosing these goals, and (3) feel a greater commitment to providing their resources to achieve the goals because they have had input in selecting the goals.

The more congruence there is between the members' personal goals and the group's goals, the more attracted to the group the members are likely to be and the more willing to provide their resources and energies to achieve the goals of the group. The members' personal goals can be heterogeneous (different) or homogeneous (alike). The more homogeneous personal goals are, the more likely members are to agree on group goals and to work together toward achieving them. They also tend to be happier with the group when personal goals are homogeneous.

When members have heterogeneous personal goals, hidden agendas are more likely to develop. A *hidden agenda* is a personal goal held by a member that is unknown to the other group members and that interferes with the group's accomplishing its group goals. Hidden agendas can be very destructive. For example, I have participated in groups where an individual sought to observe the comments and actions of others in order to obtain evidence to bring legal harassment charges. Usually, however, hidden agendas are less destructive. For example, a lonely person who enjoys talking may slow down a group in reaching its goals by monopolizing the "air time" with insignificant small talk.

Because hidden agendas can severely hamper a group, it is important that a group seek to set group goals that incorporate the members' personal goals. With such a focus, hidden agendas are likely to be minimized.

Still, all groups work on two levels: the surface task and the hidden needs and motivations. Although hidden agendas siphon off energy, they are a reflection of individual needs and may (or may not) even be known to the person who holds them. All members join groups with the intention of meeting their personal needs. Sometimes after initial needs are met, other, less obvious needs surface. Such needs are normal and expected. The real issue is the effect these needs have on the rest of the group. The important question is whether meeting A's needs will prevent B (or the rest of the group) from satisfying his needs. The goal is to find a means to legitimize the individual's needs in ways that allow for effective problem solving.

Managing hidden agendas requires that members and the designated leader be on the lookout for them and support members who try to bring hidden agendas to the surface. One such approach might involve the leader's saying "I wonder if we've said all that we feel about this idea. Perhaps we should go around the room once more and see whether anyone has anything to add." At the same time, the leader and other members should be aware that some hidden agendas might best be left hidden. Frequently it is best not to criticize a member for having a hidden agenda, since doing so often creates defensiveness and inhibits problem solving.

Conformity

Some classic studies have examined conforming behavior. Sherif (1936) examined what has been called the "autokinetic effect." In this experiment subjects are first placed in a darkened room and asked to judge how far a dot of light moves. Although the light appears to move (the autokinetic effect), it actually does not. Each subject sees the dot of light and makes a series of individual judgments about how far the light moves. The subjects are then brought together in groups of about three to judge again how far the light moves. In this situation, their judgments tend to converge to a group standard. Later, when they again view the light alone, they tend to retain the group standard and give that answer. The essential finding is that when a situation is ambiguous and there is no objective way of de-

Standard   Comparison lines

Figure 7.1
Cards in Asch conformity studies

termining the "right" answer, members rely on the group to help define reality. In real life this means membership in a group determines for individuals many of the things they will see, learn, think about, and do.

Asch (1955) also examined conforming behavior. Asch investigated what happens when an individual's judgment conflicts with the judgments of other group members. The experiments were designed as follows. There were two sets of cards, as shown in Figure 7.1. Subjects from psychology classes who volunteered for the experiment were arranged in groups of seven to nine. They were seated at a table and asked to state in turn, starting at the left, which line was closest in length to the standard. In the control groups practically all the subjects chose line two. The experimental groups, however, were the ones of greatest interest. In the experimental groups all of the group members, except for one subject, were accomplices of the experimenter. The subject was always seated at the end of the line (or near the end of the line) for giving his or her judgment. The accomplices all chose the same incorrect line. When it came to the subject's turn, he or she was then faced with relying on individual judgment or conforming to what the group was erroneously saying. In a variety of similar studies, Asch found that over one-third of the subjects conformed to the group judgment. Such a large conformity is amazing because there was no overt group pressure to conform, the situation was not ambiguous, and the subjects did not know each other. In addition, there was no promise

of future favor or advancement, nor was there any threat of ostracism or punishment.

Conformity is the yielding to group pressure. For there to be conformity, there must be conflict—conflict between the influences exerted by the group and those forces in an individual that tend to lead a person to value, believe, and act in some other way. For a member experiencing such conflict, there are two available options: announce his or her own independent decision, or conform by announcing agreement with the group's position. Conforming can take two forms: The expedient conformer outwardly agrees but inwardly disagrees. The true conformer both outwardly and inwardly comes to agree with the group.

A number of conclusions have arisen from conformity research (Krech, Crutchfield, & Ballachey, 1962, pp. 509–512).

1. Considerable amounts of yielding are produced by group pressure, even when the bogus group consensus to which the person conforms is obviously wrong. In one study, for example, a sample of 50 military officers were asked to indicate which of two figures, a star and a circle presented side by side, were larger in area. The circle was clearly about one-third larger, but under group pressure 46 percent of the men agreed with the bogus group consensus.

2. Many people can be pressured into yielding on attitude and opinion items, even those having significant personal implications for them. For example, 50 military officers were asked privately and then later under bogus group consensus the question: "I doubt whether I would make a good leader." In private none of the officers expressed agreement, but under unanimous group pressure, 37 percent expressed agreement.

3. Yielding is far greater on difficult, subjective items than on easy, objective ones.

4. There are extremely large individual differences in yielding. A few people yield on almost all items; a few yield on

none; most people yield on some and not on others.

5. When people are retested individually and privately on the same items some time later, a major part of the yielding effect disappears as the person tends to revert to his or her own unchanged private judgment. Yet, a small part of the yielding effect does remain, indicating group pressure does have a lasting effect on changing attitudes.

6. As a group increases in size, the pressure for yielding increases, and more yielding occurs. When a person is opposed by a single other person, there is very little yielding.

7. Yielding is markedly reduced when a person has the support of one other person (a partner) in the group. Apparently a dissident opinion has a tremendous effect in strengthening the independence of like-minded people.

In a dramatic study involving conformity, Milgram (1963) demonstrated that subjects in an experimental situation would administer electric shocks of dangerous strength to another person when instructed to do so by the experimenter. (The other person, who was unknown to the subject, did not actually receive the electrical shocks.) Most of the subjects complied with the experimenter's commands, even when they were instructed to give increasingly strong shocks to the victim, in spite of the victim's protests and cries of anguish. This series of studies on obedience demonstrated that people will yield to "authoritative" commands even when the behavior is incompatible with their own moral, normal standards of conduct. Milgram suggested his studies help us understand why the German people complied with the unethical commands of Hitler. Group pressures, especially when viewed as authoritative, have a tremendous effect on a person's actions, attitudes, and beliefs.

Stanley Schacter (1959) developed a theory of social comparison. Schacter assumed that everyone has a need to evaluate the "rightness" of his or her feelings, opinions, values, and attitudes. He also assumed that everyone has a need to evaluate the extent of his or her abilities. Schacter then theorized and conducted studies to demonstrate that in the absence of objective, nonsocial means of evaluation, a person will rely on other people as comparison points of reference. To a large extent, the groups we belong to define social reality for us. For most of our opinions, values, beliefs, and abilities, there is no objective, nonsocial way to evaluate ourselves, so we rely on others.

Idiosyncratic Credits

Every member of a group gains credits (and status) by showing competence and by conforming to the expectations applicable to his or her time. Eventually these credits allow a person to break the group's norms and rules without being chastised. To some extent, after credits have been accumulated, nonconformity to general procedures or expectations serves as a confirming feature of one's status. Yet there is a limit on the number of earned idiosyncratic credits. Nonconformity beyond this limit will result in a dramatic decrease in status and perhaps even rejection by the other group members (Hollander, 1958).

Competitive and Cooperative Groups

Groups basically have either a cooperative or a competitive group atmosphere. In a cooperative group there is open and honest communication, trust, pooling of resources, and cohesion. Research has found a number of positive consequences for a cooperative group atmosphere in problem-solving groups. Cooperation among members increases creativity, coordination of effort, division of labor, emotional involvement in group accomplishment, helping and sharing, interpersonal skills, cooperative attitudes and values, positive self-attitudes, liking among group members, positive attitudes toward the group and tasks, divergent thinking, acceptance of individual and cultural differences, and problem-solving skills (Johnson & Johnson, 1975, p. 88).

A cooperative group atmosphere results when the members' personal goals are perceived to be compatible, identical, or complementary. An example of a highly cooperative group is a successful basketball team in which the main goal of each member is to win, and the main goal of the team is to win. In a cooperative group, each member seeks to coordinate his or her efforts with those of other group members to achieve the goals of the group. In establishing a cooperative atmosphere, rewards to members must be based on the quantity and quality of group performance rather than on individual performance.

In contrast, a competitive atmosphere can be very detrimental and destructive. A competitive atmosphere exists when the members perceive their personal goals to be incompatible, different, conflicting, or mutually exclusive. In a highly competitive group, a member can achieve his or her goal only if the other group members fail to obtain their goals (Deutsch, 1949). An example of a group that is structured to be competitive is a group interview that is held for several applicants for a position vacancy. In a competitive group each member seeks to accomplish his or her goals, while seeking to block other group members from accomplishing their goals. The consequences of competition in problem-solving groups are numerous. Competition decreases creativity, coordination of effort, division of labor, helping and sharing, and cohesion. Competition promotes ineffective communication, suspicion and mistrust, high anxiety about goal accomplishments, competitive values and attitudes, negative self-attitudes, dislike among group members, and negative attitudes toward the group and

its tasks. Competition encourages rejection of differences of opinion, divergent thinking, and cultural and individual differences. A competitive atmosphere leads to low effectiveness in solving complex problems (Johnson & Johnson, 1975, p. 97).

Kelly and Stahelski (1970) examined the question of what happens when a competitive person joins a group that has a cooperative atmosphere. Since cooperative groups are much more effective in problem solving than competitive groups, the question is significant. Three consequences were found to occur: (1) the competitive behavior of the new member leads the other members to behave competitively, (2) the competitive person views the former cooperative members as having always been competitive, and (3) the former cooperative members are generally aware their competitive behavior is largely a consequence of the new member's competitiveness. Thus, it appears that one competitive person can change a cooperative group into a competitive group. Why does a competitive person have such a strong, destructive effect? Apparently, the cooperative members realize the competitive person will, if given a chance, take advantage of their cooperativeness and use it to his or her own advantage. In many situations their only recourse to prevent exploitation is to also become competitive. Thus it appears that while cooperation is by far the most effective atmosphere in problem-solving groups, it takes only one competitive person to change the atmosphere of the group to a competitive one. If a cooperative group is to survive, it is important that new members have an orientation compatible with that of the other members.

Controversy and Creativity

Controversy is a debate, dispute, or discussion involving differences in beliefs, information, opinions, ideas, or assumptions. Controversy in groups is natural. If handled constructively, controversy will increase creativity, increase members' involvement, and lead to high-quality decisions. Emotional reactions to controversy may be positive (curiosity, affinity for other members, excitement, exhilaration, stimulation, involvement, commitment) or negative (frustration, disgust, anger, fear, resentment, rejection, distrust, apathy, paranoia), depending on how the group handles the controversy.

People react differently to controversy. Some people shy away from it. Others take a difference of opinion personally and become hurt or angered. Others find controversy stimulating and fun; they hope to find a little each day. Still others view controversy as a way for each side to express itself, ventilate concerns, and work out differences.

Controversy has many values for a group. When handled effectively, controversy encourages inquiry, stimulates interest and curiosity, sharpens analysis, and promotes objectivity. It also increases the members' commitment to the group and improves the problem-solving processes. Controversy stimulates members to search for new and better alternatives and to synthesize suggested alternatives into higher quality decisions. Through controversy members often reassess and clarify their values and beliefs and grow as people. Through learning how to resolve interpersonal conflicts, members may also learn how to become better managers of their internal conflicts.

On the other hand, some groups do not manage controversy well. Ineffective groups tend to suppress and withdraw from controversy. They have group norms that urge members to suppress conflicts and to agree outwardly even when some members believe the group is making a serious mistake. When controversy does arise in ineffective groups, the members are apt to view the opposing positions in terms of "right versus wrong" or "we versus they."

The Win-Lose Approach Versus the Problem-Solving Approach

Ineffective groups are apt to view resolutions of controversy between opposing positions as being *win-lose situations*. We live in a very competitive society where in many fields (such as sports, business, and politics) individuals or teams are pitted against each other. In groups, destructive controversies are often cast in the "win-lose" mold. Members interrupt each other to sell their positions without really listening to what the other person is saying. Power blocs are formed to support one position against proponents of another. The group's original goals and objectives may fade into the background as seeking to win on issues becomes the objective of the warring sides.

In win-lose situations, each side denies the legitimacy of the other side's interests and concerns. Each side is concerned only about its own needs. Each side seeks to muster support and power for its position in order to defeat the other side.

In win-lose situations the group often winds up losing in terms of failing to achieve its long-range goals and objectives. The side that loses on an issue has little motivation to provide its resources to carry out the actions of the winning side. It resents the winner and may continue to seek to reverse the decision or to impede the implementation of the decision. Distrust increases among opposite sides, communication becomes more limited and inaccurate, and cohesion or togetherness decreases. Often members develop unresolved feelings (or gunnysacks full of grievances) that result in biased judgments and actions. In win-lose situations members frequently refuse to vote for a good idea because they dislike the person who suggested it. Conflict in win-lose situations leads to the denial or distortion of unpleasant facts and information. It leads to blind spots in which members misinterpret the ideas and actions of members perceived as being opponents. It leads to disagreement being interpreted as personal rejection by some or all group members. It leads to decisions that are of low quality and often incorrect. It increases group tension.

A more effective approach to use in resolving conflicts is the *problem-solving approach*. Effective groups generally use this approach. With a problem-solving approach, members attempt to find a mutually satisfying course of action. Members tend to listen to each other, to recognize the legitimacy of one another's interests, and to influence one another with rational arguments. Instead of a competitive orientation, the problem-solving approach functions in an atmosphere of cooperation among group members.

The steps in the problem-solving approach can be summarized as follows:

Step 1: The needs of each person or subgroup are identified and defined.

Step 2: Alternative solutions are generated.

Step 3: The alternative solutions are evaluated.

Step 4: A highly evaluated solution that is acceptable to practically everyone is selected.

Step 5: The solution is implemented.

Step 6: There is follow-up to evaluate how well the selected solution is working.

Adjusting win-lose situations so that the outcome is win-win is the goal of members and leaders committed to effective problem solving. It is very difficult for any one person to redirect a win-lose situation and usually a significant segment of the membership is needed to accomplish this goal. There are several means to this end. First it is important to have clear goals that all members understand and agree to. Issues that arise in a win-lose situation should be tested against the goals to determine whether they really are relevant to the group's functioning. Being on the alert for win-lose situations is important also.

When a member feels that he or she is being attacked by others or feels as if he or she is lining up support for a particular position, the likelihood is that a win-lose situation is developing.

Of course, active listening (see Chapter 20) often is effective in these situations. The listener can be empathic, listen to the other's reasoning (and perhaps be persuaded), and at least understand the other's position. When responding to other members' positions, it is better to suggest alternatives than say, "This is the only intelligent way to do this." As we have seen in the preceding chapter, arriving at decisions through a consensus model rather than majority-minority voting tends to be more effective and reduces the win-lose nature of some group debates. Finally, it is important to test whether compromises or consensus agreements actually are accepted by all members. This is best determined by polling all group members in turn, asking whether they have anything they would like to add to the discussion. The key for resolving win-lose situations is to try for a solution that is best for all members rather than attempting to get one's own way.

A cooperative, problem-solving atmosphere in a group has a number of payoffs. It increases the chances of finding a high-quality solution. It increases the commitment of all the group members to support and implement the group's decisions. It increases trust and reduces hostility among group members. It increases communication and cohesion. It increases each member's satisfaction with the group. It increases the chances of the group's achieving its long-range goals and objectives. It leads group members to interact together with fewer inhibitions. It sets up an atmosphere in which members can freely express and work out their frustrations and concerns. (If such frustrations are not expressed, they often fester and snowball, resulting in increased apathy and disengagement from the group.) The problem-solving approach keeps arguments focused on the present, as past conflicts have been worked out. It improves relationships with other group members and leads to greater understanding of self and others.

A cooperative, problem-solving approach in a group promotes creativity. Creativity is a process of bringing something new into existence. Creativity results from productive controversy, as the problem is viewed from new perspectives, new alternatives are suggested, and a new synthesis of alternatives is formulated for resolving the problem.

Handling Disruptive Behavior

There may be hostile or disruptive members in any group, even in groups whose members come voluntarily. Hostile or noncooperative members, however, are more likely to be found in involuntary groups. Involuntary groups are those whose members are forced to come. Involuntary members often (at least at the initial meetings of the group) wish they were a thousand other places rather than in the group. They may be angry because they are forced to come and may believe the time spent in the group will be a "complete waste of time."

There are various settings where social workers encounter involuntary clients: corrections, protective services, mental health facilities, certain public school settings, group homes, residential treatment facilities, nursing homes, and hospitals. In such settings, groups may be established that unwilling clients are required to attend and social workers are expected to lead. Disruptive behavior includes being aggressive, competing, fooling around, sympathy seeking, and failing to finish tasks on time.

There are three main ways a designated leader might handle hostile and disruptive behavior: (1) allow members to continue to be disruptive while seeking to ignore or minimize the effects of the disruptive behavior,

(2) confront members about their disruptive behavior, and (3) have other group members confront the disruptive members. Each of these ways will be briefly discussed. The approach chosen should be based on a judgment as to which will be most helpful to the group in handling the disruptive behavior.

1. Allowing the member to continue to express the disruptive behavior is often effective. Such expression has a ventilating effect, so the member may become less disruptive as time goes on. When a member is disruptive, it is often helpful to tactfully ask the member to express concerns that he has.

Tactfully asking the member probing questions about his concerns, and modeling good listening skills while reflecting the feelings expressed by the person often helps defuse a disruptive situation. In certain instances there may be benefit in using a role reversal in which the disrupter is asked to argue the alternate point of view with the designated leader taking the disrupter's position. Whenever possible disruption should be dealt with as a group issue, and the group may, in fact, decide to deal with at least some of the disrupter's concerns, especially those that are legitimate. Through resolution of some of these concerns, the disruptive group member may become less unhappy and begin to see that the group has some payoffs for him.

2. The designated group leader may assertively confront the member about how her behavior is disrupting the group. This confrontation may take place with other group members present or the group leader may meet privately with the disruptive member. The choice of whether to confront privately or with other members present should be based on a judgment of which will be most beneficial. If other members are present, they may be able to help by elaborating on the ways in which the member's behavior is proving disruptive. Also, having others present emphasizes the seriousness

of the problem. A disadvantage of confrontation when others are present is that the hostile member may feel ganged up on and may be more inhibited in fully expressing what she is unhappy about. In some instances simply indicating to the member in private that you are concerned about her behavior and are considering opening it up as a matter of discussion for the entire group will help the member reconsider whether the disruptions are accomplishing the desired purpose.

3. The third approach is to have a member other than the designated leader do the confronting. There are certain situations in which the confrontation is best handled by someone other than the leader. For example, another member may have better rapport with the disruptive member than the designated leader, and therefore the disruptive member may be more responsive if the confrontation comes from the neutral member.

Any of these approaches may prove fruitful. It is important to realize that conflict and differences in opinion are not uncommon or unnatural in groups, and may, in fact, be healthy.

Group Size

The size of a group has effects on members' satisfactions, interactions, and output per member. Smaller groups are often rated more favorably (Hare, 1962). Larger groups tend to create more stress, have more communication difficulties, and although successful in some tasks because of the greater number of skills available, are generally less efficient or productive. In larger groups each person has less opportunity to talk, and some people feel inhibited and reluctant to talk. In discussion groups it has been shown that as the size of the group increases, the most frequent contributor assumes an increasingly prominent role in the discussion. The bigger the group, the greater the gap in amount of participation between the most frequent contributor and other members of a group.

Slater (1958) found in one study that groups of five persons were considered most satisfactory by group members themselves. Observations of the interactions of groups smaller than five indicated the members were inhibited from expressing their ideas through fear of alienating one another and thereby destroying the group. Above the size of five, members felt restrictions on participating.

Groups of two members tend to avoid expressing disagreement and antagonism. This size also has high-tension levels because each member is more "on the spot," as each is forced to react to what the other says. If a dispute arises in such a group, it becomes deadlocked as there is no majority and the group may break up.

Groups of even size tend to have higher rates of disagreement and antagonism than odd-size groups, apparently because of the possible division of the group into two subdivisions of equal size.

Groups of three members have problems of the power of the majority over the minority; that is, a two to one split leaves the minority feeling isolated.

To sum up, it appears probable that for any given task there is an optimal group size. The more complex the task, the larger the optimum size to assure the greater number of needed abilities and skills.

Starting, Leading, and Ending Therapy Groups[2]

Extensive preparation is needed for leading therapeutic groups. The leader should have considerable training in (1) assessing human

[2]Material in this section is adapted from Charles Zastrow, "Starting and Leading Therapy Groups: A Beginner's Guide," *Journal of Independent Social Work,* 4, no. 4, 1990, pp. 7–26. Adapted by permission of the Haworth Press.

behavior and human problems; (2) comprehensive therapeutic intervention approaches—such as reality therapy, behavior therapy, rational therapy, transactional analysis, and client-centered therapy (see Chapters 14, 15, 16, 21, and 22); (3) specialized therapeutic intervention techniques—such as assertiveness training and relaxation techniques (see Chapters 16 and 20); (4) interviewing and counseling; and (5) principles of group dynamics—such as cohesion, task roles, social-emotional roles, and effects of authoritarian versus democratic styles of leadership. Baccalaureate and master's programs in social work generally provide considerable material on these areas. For any therapy group, the leader also needs to study the literature on the causes of the problems that the members are experiencing, the most effective intervention strategies for these problems, the prognosis for positive changes, and expectations as to the length of time the intervention strategies need to be applied to induce positive changes.

This section summarizes a number of guidelines for starting, leading, and ending therapy groups. Chapter 6 covered substantial material on the following aspects of leading groups: preparation and homework, relaxing before starting a session, cues on entering the meeting room, seating arrangements, introductions, and clarifying roles. This material is directly applicable to therapy groups and will not be repeated here. (Students learning how to lead therapy groups should review this material.) This section will focus on building rapport, exploring problems in depth, exploring alternative solutions, ending a session, and ending a group.

Building Rapport

In group therapy, as in individual therapy, there are two types of members: voluntary and involuntary. In voluntary groups, the therapist can take a more casual, less directive approach to begin with. In such groups the therapist can take a more casual, less directive approach to begin with. In such groups the therapist may begin by involving members in small talk. This preliminary chitchat may be about the weather, parking problems, baseball, something currently in the news, and so on. Such casual conversation has the advantage of letting group members become acquainted with the therapist and the other group members.

In involuntary groups, the therapist may begin by introducing himself or herself and making a formal statement about the purpose of the group. Then members may be asked to introduce themselves. Generally, in involuntary groups, less is left up to the members themselves since they have less motivation for being there and less commitment to the group itself.

Sometimes with both voluntary and involuntary clients, it is helpful (after introductions) to begin a session with providing some factual information. This can be done by a brief presentation by the group leader, or by showing a short film or videotape. For example, if the group members are involuntary clients who have been convicted of operating a motor vehicle while intoxicated, the leader may choose to show a film that vividly demonstrates that as alcohol consumption increases, reaction times slow and the chances of serious accidents occurring dramatically increases. Such factual information is designed not only to provide educational material, but to also serve as a trigger to ignite a discussion. Sometimes after factual information is presented, it is useful to involve the group members in an exercise related to the material.

When members are forced to attend a group they do not want to attend, as is the case with involuntary clients, the group leader may begin by saying something like, "I know most of you really don't want to be here, and I wouldn't either if I were forced to come. I wonder if we might begin by talking about your anger and unhappiness about being here?" Then the leader should attempt to convey the purposes of the group, what is going to happen, and how the members can satisfy the minimal requirements of "passing." The group leader should mention that each member can (1) choose to participate actively and get as much out of the group as possible, (2) remain silent and listen to what others have to say, (3) vent their anger and unhappiness in disruptive ways (which will probably anger and alienate others in the group), or (4) refuse to come, which will have certain consequences. The group leader may then indicate that he or she can in no way control their behavior, so the choice among these alternatives is up to each member. Such an approach almost always leads the involuntary clients to choose either the first or second alternative, perhaps because such an approach leads these clients to conclude that the leader is understanding of their anger—and they then focus on making the most constructive choice.

If the group has met previously, the leader may choose to begin by bringing up for discussion a topic that was not fully discussed at the last meeting. Or, if homework assignments were given to some members, the leader may begin by saying, "Jim, at the last meeting you indicated you were going to do (such and such). How did that work out?"

The therapist should try to establish a non-threatening group atmosphere in which the members feel accepted and safe enough to communicate their troubles fully. During the initial contacts, the therapist needs to "sell" himself or herself (but not arrogantly) as a knowledgeable, understanding person who may be able to help and who wants to try. The tone of the therapist's voice should convey the message that he or she understands and cares about group members' feelings. The therapist should be calm and never laugh or express shock when members begin to open up about problems. Emotional outbursts, even if subtle, will lead group members to believe that the therapist is not going to understand or accept their difficulties, and so they will usually stop discussing them.

A therapist should view group members as equals. New therapists sometimes make the mistake of thinking that because someone is sharing her intimate secrets with them, they must be very important, and end up assuming a superior position vis-à-vis their clients. If members feel that they are being treated as inferiors, they will be less motivated to reveal and discuss personal issues.

The therapist should use a "shared vocabulary" with the members. This does not mean that the therapist should use the same slang and the same accent as group members. If clients perceive the therapist is mimicking their speech patterns, they may feel seriously offended. In order to communicate effectively, the therapist should use words that members understand and do not find offensive.

The therapist (and other members) need to keep what members say confidential. Unfortunately, many people have nearly irresistible urges to share "juicy secrets" with someone else. If a group member discovers that confidentiality has been violated, that member's trust in the group will be quickly destroyed. It is essential that the therapist explain the importance of "what is said in the group, remains in the group."

Exploring Problems in Depth

In exploring a member's problems in depth, the therapist and group members need to examine such areas as the extent of the problem, how long the problem has existed, what the causes are, how the member feels about the problem, and what physical and mental capacities and strengths the member has to cope with the difficulty, before exploring alternative solutions.

A problem area is often multidimensional; that is, there are usually numerous problems that are involved. Explore all these. A good way to decide which problem to handle first is to ask the group member which problem she perceives as most pressing. If it can be solved, start with exploring that problem in depth and together develop a solution. Success in solving one problem will increase each group member's confidence in the leader, and thereby further solidify rapport.

Therapists should convey empathy, not sympathy, and encourage group members to do so, too. Empathy is the capacity to understand and to share in another person's feelings. Sympathy also involves sharing feelings, but it results in offering pity. The difference is subtle, but empathy usually encourages problem solving, while sympathy usually encourages group members to dwell on their problems without taking action to improve the situation. For example, if a leader offers sympathy to a person who is frustrated and angry about someone ending a romantic relationship with him, that person will keep telling his sad story over and over, each time having an emotional outpouring reinforced by the leader's sympathy, without taking any action to improve the situation. Telling the story over and over only reopens old wounds and prolongs the anger and frustration.

Therapists should "trust their guts." The most important resources that a therapist has are her own feelings and perceptions. A therapist should continually strive to place herself in members' shoes, understanding that their values and pressures may be different from her own. It probably never happens that a group leader is 100 percent on target in her appraisal of a client's pressures, problems, and perspectives, but 70 to 80 percent is usually sufficient to allow the therapist to be helpful. Empathizing is very useful in helping the therapist determine what additional areas may need to be explored, what she should say, and what the possible solutions are.

When a therapist believes that a client has touched on an important area of concern, further communication can be encouraged in a number of ways. Showing interest nonverbally (by making and continuing eye contact, leaning forward, and raising eyebrows slightly) encourages further sharing. Allowing for pauses is important. New therapists usually become anxious when there is a pause and hasten to say something—anything—to have conversation continue. This is usually a mistake, especially when it leads to a change in the topic. Although a pause will often make the group member anxious, it gives him time to think about what areas of concern are most important and then usually motivates him to continue conversation in that area.

Neutral probes that do not control the direction of conversation but encourage further communication are helpful. For example, "Could you tell me more about it?" "Why do you feel that way?" and "I'm not sure I understand what you have in mind" all ask for further information, but just what kind is left up to the member. Reflecting feelings—for example, "You seem angry" or "You appear to be depressed about that"—works that same way. Summarizing what a group member is saying not only shows that you are listening but also that you have received the same message the group member sent. An example is, "During this past hour, you made a number of critical comments about your spouse; it sounds like you're fairly unhappy about certain aspects of your marriage."

Socially unacceptable topics should be approached tactfully. Tact is an essential quality of a competent therapist. Try not to ask a question in a way that the answer will put the respondent in an embarrassing position.

When pointing out a limitation that a group member has, mention and compliment him or her on any assets. When a limitation is being mentioned, the person will literally feel that something is being laid bare or taken away. Therefore, give a compliment in another area to give something back.

A competent therapist will generally watch for nonverbal cues and use them to identify a sensitive subject, as the client will generally display anxiety by a changing tone of voice, fidgeting, yawning, stiff posture, or a flushed face.

The therapist should be honest. An untruth always runs the risk of being discovered. If that happens, the group member's confidence in the therapist will be damaged and the relationship seriously jeopardized. But being honest goes beyond not telling lies. The therapist should always point out those shortcomings that are in the group member's best interest to correct. For example, if a father's negative comments to his son are a factor in the son developing a negative self-concept (which is partly responsible for the son receiving failing grades at school), this should be brought to the father's attention.

Exploring Alternative Solutions

After a problem is explored in depth, the next step is for the therapist and group members to consider alternative solutions. The therapist's role is generally to begin by asking something like "Have you thought about ways to resolve this?" The merits, shortcomings, and consequences of the alternatives thought of by the member should then be tactfully and thoroughly examined. Next, the therapist should seek to involve other group members by asking them if they are aware of other alternatives that may work for this situation. Those members who suggest alternatives temporarily assume a "helper" role. In such a role the helper therapy principle is operating as a member receives psychological rewards from helping others. If the therapist has additional viable alternatives to suggest, he or she should mention these at this time. The merits, shortcomings, and consequences of the alternatives suggested by other group members and by the therapist should then be thoroughly explored.

Group members usually have the right to self-determination; that is, to choose a course of action among possible alternatives. The therapist's role is to help each individual clarify and understand the likely consequences of each available alternative but generally not to give advice or choose the alternative. If the therapist were to select the alternative, there are two possible outcomes: (1) the alternative may prove undesirable for the group member, in which case he or she will probably blame the therapist for the advice and their future relationship will be seriously hampered, or (2) the alternative may prove to be desirable for the person involved. This imme-

diate outcome is advantageous, but the danger is that the group member will then become overly dependent on the therapist, seeking the therapist's advice for nearly every decision in the future and generally being reluctant to make decisions on his or her own.

Group therapy is done *with* group members, not *to* or *for* them. Each member should have responsibility for doing many of the tasks necessary to improve a situation. A good rule to follow is that each member should take responsibility for those tasks that he has the capacity to carry out. Doing things *for* group members, similar to giving advice, brings with it the risk of creating a dependent relationship. Furthermore, successful accomplishments of tasks by clients leads to personal growth and better prepares them for taking on future responsibilities.

A group member's right to self-determination should be taken away only if the selected course of action has a high probability of seriously hurting the client or others. For example, if it is highly probable that a group member may attempt to take his life, the therapist should intervene (for example, making arrangements for the member to receive inpatient psychiatric care if the risk of suicide is high), even if the intervention is a course action that the group member objects to. For most situations, however, the group member should have the right to select an alternative, even when the therapist believes that another course of action is better. Frequently, a client is in a better position to know what is best for himself, and if it turns out not to be the best, he will probably learn from the mistake.

When a group member does select an alternative, he should clearly understand what the goals will be, what tasks need to be carried out, how to accomplish the tasks, and who will do them. Frequently, it is desirable to write a "contract" for future reference, with a time limit set for the accomplishment of each task.

If a group member fails to meet the terms of a contract, the therapist should not criticize him or accept excuses. Excuses let people off the hook; they provide temporary relief, but they eventually lead to more failure and to a failure identity. Simply ask, "Do you still wish to try to fulfill your commitment?" If the person answers affirmatively, another time deadline acceptable to the member should be set.

Perhaps the biggest single factor in determining whether a group member's situation will improve is his motivation to carry out essential tasks. A therapist should try to motivate apathetic group members. One way to increase a member's motivation is to clarify what will be gained by meeting a goal. When individuals meet commitments, therapists should reward them, verbally or in other ways. Never criticize members for failing. Criticism usually increases hostility and rarely leads to positive lasting change. Also, criticism serves as only a temporary means of obtaining different behavior; when a person no longer believes that he is under surveillance, he will usually return to the dysfunctional behavior.

If a group member lacks confidence or experiences, it may be helpful to role-play a task before actually attempting it. For example, if a male member wants help in telling his partner that he no longer is "in love" with her and wants to end the relationship, role-playing the situation within the group will assist the male in selecting words and developing a strategy for informing his partner. The therapist or another group member can first play the male's role and model an approach, letting the male play the partner's role. Then, the roles should be reversed so that the male practices telling his partner.

Ending a Session

Ending is not always easy. Ideally, the therapist and group members should accept the fact that the session is ending and subjects being discussed should not be left hanging in the middle. Abrupt endings are apt to be perceived by the group members as being discourteous and rejecting.

There are some useful guidelines on how to terminate a therapy session. Preparation for ending the session should be initiated at the very beginning of the session. The members should be explicitly informed of the time the session will end. Unless an unusual situation develops, the leader should assertively seek to terminate at the end of the scheduled time.

When the allotted time is nearly up, the therapist may so inform the group members by saying something like "I see our time is just about up. Is there anything you'd like to add before we look at where we've come to, and where we go from here?" At the end of the session, it is often helpful to summarize what was discussed. If this session focused only on exploring problems that the members have, another one should be set up for fuller exploration and to begin looking at alternatives for resolving the problems.

It is very helpful to give members "homework" assignments between sessions. A couple who is having trouble communicating with each other might, for example, be encouraged to set aside a certain amount of time each evening to discuss their personal thoughts with each other. At the next session this "homework" assignment may then be reviewed.

Ideally, the group members should be emotionally at ease when the session ends, and therefore the therapist should not introduce emotionally charged content at the end but should reduce the intensity of emotion. Just as it is sometimes advisable to begin a session with small talk, a short social conversation at the end may provide a transition out of the session. If a group member displays a reluctance to end a session, it is sometimes helpful to confront this directly by saying, "It appears to me that you wished we had more time." The reasons for the person's reluctance can then be discussed.

At times a group session can be ended with a restatement of the way both the therapist and group agreed to proceed. Or, a more explicit summation may be made by the group leader of what was discussed, what decisions were arrived at, what questions remain to be resolved, and what actions will be taken.

A somewhat different approach is to ask each group member to state one item that was discussed or learned from the session, and what he or she now plans to do. Some therapy groups end by having each member state a "bad" feeling he or she intends to now get rid of, and then state a good feeling to replace the bad one that he or she intends to act on during the week.

Sometimes concerns that were alluded to but not fully discussed might be mentioned in closing as topics that will be taken up at the next session. Some members will reveal their most serious concerns for the first time at the end of a session, perhaps because they are ambivalent about whether they are ready to explore these concerns fully with the group. In these instances the therapist has to make a professional judgment about whether to extend the session beyond the allotted time, to set up an appointment to discuss these concerns privately, or to wait until the next group session.

Sometimes it is helpful to end a group session with the therapist leading the group in a relaxation exercise. (Relaxation exercises are described in Chapter 20.) A relaxation exercise not only helps members relax but also reduces their level of stress so they can view their problems more objectively and work on resolving them after they leave.

Closing is especially important because what occurs during this last phase is likely to determine the members' impressions of the session as a whole. Group leaders should leave enough time for closing so the members do not feel rushed, which might create the impression that they are being evicted.

Ending a Group

The ending phase of a group frequently offers the highest potential for powerful, important work. Group members may feel a sense of urgency as they realize there is little time left; this can lead them to reveal their most sensitive and personal concerns. Because the work remaining to be done is usually clearly identified at this point, members can focus on completing it. However, the relationship dynamics are also heightened in this phase as the members prepare to move away from each other, and the termination of the group may evoke powerful feelings.

If group members have grown emotionally close, the ending of a group will be interpreted as a loss and produce a variety of emotions. Kübler-Ross's (1969) stages of emotional reactions that people display when terminally ill resemble reactions to other important losses, including the ending of a successful and cohesive group. Members may display denial (by ignoring the imminent end of the group), anger and rage, or sadness and depression. They may attempt to bargain for an extension of the group in various ways, such as urging that the group deal with additional problems. Ideally, members will ventilate and work through such feelings and gradually come to accept the ending of the group. (Kübler-Ross's stages are more fully described in Chapter 5.)

Other emotions may also be displayed. Some members may feel guilty because of adverse comments they made or because they believe they failed to take certain actions that would have benefited themselves or other members of the group. If a member left prematurely, some members may feel the group let him or her down. Members may want to share their feelings about the support system they will lose when the group ends. If certain members want the group to continue, they may interpret the ending as a personal rejection. On the other hand, members who feel that the group was very successful may want to have a celebration to give recognition to the successes and to say goodbye.

In many ways the concluding sessions are the most difficult for the therapist and the group members. Strong emotions are often generated and should be ventilated and worked through. It is painful to terminate a group when members have formed relationships to share their most personal and important concerns and feelings. Our society has done little to train us to handle such separations; in fact, some segments in our society have a general norm of being "strong" and not expressing feelings.

The therapist can help members accept the ending of a group in a number of ways, and the process of terminating a group should, in fact, begin during the early stages of the group. This guideline is particularly relevant for time-limited groups. The therapist should attempt to prevent the formation of dependency relationships between the members and the therapist. The goal is independence and better functioning, and this should be reiterated whenever appropriate during group sessions.

The therapist may summarize the emotional reactions that people have to group endings, and an appropriate point for a discussion may occur when some members display denial, anger, guilt, bargaining, or sadness. When discussing these feelings, the therapist should share his or her personal feelings and recollections, since the ending of the group has meaning for the therapist as well. The therapist can, in effect, provide a model that may help members express their positive and negative concerns about ending the group. A problem-solving approach can be used to alleviate concerns; for example, if a group member is apprehensive about future problems, the therapist might suggest several other counseling resources.

The ending process should provide enough time for the therapist and the members to sort out their feelings and use the ending productively. A sudden ending will cut short necessary work and may not allow enough time to work through feelings and complete the remaining tasks. Sometimes, members will indirectly express their anger by being late, appearing apathetic, being sarcastic, or battling over minor issues. In these situations the therapist should respond directly to the indirect cues by saying something like, "I wonder if your recent critical remarks are related to your anger that this group is ending? I know you have invested a lot in this group and may dislike the idea that our meetings are coming to an end." By helping members recognize and articulate their feelings, a therapist can help them express and work through those feelings. Once such feelings are dealt with, members will be more productive during the remaining time.

At or near the end of some groups, members may test new skills and do things independently. They may report having tackled a tough problem or dealt with an issue by themselves. The therapist should acknowledge their independence and make positive remarks about the members' ability to "go it alone."

At times, the therapist may be the person leaving the group, perhaps to take a job elsewhere. In these situations the therapist should create a smooth transition, and if appropriate, the members should be involved in selecting the new leader. At times it is helpful for the former leader and the new leader to be co-leaders for a brief period.

The ending of a group is always a transition to something else. The important element during the ending phase is to work with all members to help them develop a game plan so that the transition will enable them to work toward higher goals. The transition should not work to stifle members but to help them progress. Life is full of transitions and passages: from early childhood to kindergarten, from kindergarten to elementary school, from childhood to puberty, from puberty to dating, from school to the work world, from being single to being married, from having responsibility only for self to becoming a parent, from working to retirement, and so on. In a transition phase we have the potential to control our future; the choices we make and the efforts we put forth will determine whether the transition will be constructive or destructive for us. Helping each member make productive, realistic plans for the future is a goal of the ending phase of many groups.

During the process of terminating a group, the therapist must obtain feedback on how to improve future groups by having members fill out a brief evaluation at the last (or next-to-last) session. This evaluation should be done anonymously by the members. The following questions will apply to a variety of therapy groups. For the first seven questions, use the following scale: (1) Strongly disagree, (2) disagree, (3) neutral or uncertain, (4) agree, (5) strongly agree.

1. I am very satisfied with what this group accomplished.
   1   2   3   4   5
2. My personal goals in this group have been attained.
   1   2   3   4   5
3. I truly enjoyed being a member of this group.
   1   2   3   4   5
4. The therapist has done a superb job in leading the group.
   1   2   3   4   5
5. This has been one of the most rewarding groups I have participated in.
   1   2   3   4   5
6. I have grown extensively as a person through participating in this group.
   1   2   3   4   5
7. I have made substantial progress in resolving those personal problems that led me to join this group.
   1   2   3   4   5

The next three questions are open-ended.

8. The strengths of this group are
9. The shortcomings of this group are
10. My suggestions for changes in this group are

At the final session it is also desirable for the members to discuss what they got out of the group, the merits of the group, and suggestions for improving it. They should be given a chance to bring up unfinished business. In some cases an extra session may be held to complete unfinished business items.

The therapist should refer an individual to another group or therapist, or at least discuss the case with another professional therapist, if (1) the therapist feels unable to empathize with that group member, (2) the therapist has extreme personal difficulty in accepting the fact that a member is choosing alternatives (such as continuing to abuse his spouse) that the therapist finds disgusting, (3) the member's problems are of such a nature that the therapist feels unable to provide therapeutic help, (4) a working relationship is not established with the member, and (5) the member is such a disruptive force in the group that he or she is preventing other members from constructively working on their problems. A competent therapist knows that he or she can work with and help some people but not all, and that when the latter arises, it is in the individual's and the therapist's best interests to refer the person to someone who can help.

Summary

This chapter summarizes key group dynamic concepts and presents guidelines on how to lead therapy groups. A membership group is a group to which a person belongs, whereas a reference group is one whose influence a person is willing to accept.

Most social work groups have the following stages of development: preaffiliation, power and control, intimacy, differentiation, and separation. All groups have task roles and maintenance roles that need to be performed by members. Task roles are needed to accomplish the specific goals set by the group; maintenance roles strengthen the social or emotional aspects of group life.

The theory of leadership highlighted in this chapter is distributed functions. With this approach, leadership is defined as the performance of acts that help the group reach its goals and maintain itself in good working order. Leadership occurs when one member influences other members to help the group reach its goals. Because all group members at times influence other group members, each member in a group exerts leadership.

French and Raven (1968) identified the following five bases of power in which group members influence each other: reward, coercive, legitimate, referent, and expert. Each power base has different effects on those being influenced.

Personal goals and group goals should be identified soon after a group is formed. The more congruent personal goals are with group goals, the more effective the group is apt to be. Conformity studies have found that a group has considerable influence on members' opinions and attitudes.

Groups are more apt to be effective with a cooperative group atmosphere than with a competitive atmosphere. If handled constructively, conflict and controversy can have numerous beneficial effects on a group, including increasing creativity. The problem-solving approach is much more effective in resolving controversy than the win-lose approach. Hostile or disruptive members should generally be confronted by the designated leader or by other group members.

It appears probable that for any given task there is an optimal group size. The more complex the task, the larger the optimum size to assure the greater number of needed abilities and skills.

This chapter concluded with guidelines on how to lead therapy groups. Aspects discussed included building rapport, exploring problems in depth, exploring alternative solutions, ending a session, and ending a group.

Exercises

1. The autokinetic effect

> *Goal:* This conformity exercise is designed to demonstrate that in ambiguous situations students will usually rely on the group to help define reality.
>
> *Step 1:* Explain that this exercise is a study to measure students' capacities to judge how far a dot of light will move in the dark. Have the students sit in back of the classroom. Inform the students they will need a pen and paper to record their answers. Turn off all lights (the room has to have all lighting removed). Place a small flashlight that will produce a dot of light in front of the room in a position where it can't move. Turn the flashlight on for about 30 seconds, and then turn it off. Ask the students to record on a sheet of paper how far the light moved. Ask the students not to share their answers with others. Repeat the turning on and off of the flashlight for 30 seconds for a second and third time. Each time have the students record their answers as to how far the light moves. (Do not let the students see that the flashlight is stationary.)
>
> *Step 2:* Have the students form subgroups of about four, and have them continue to sit in back of the room. Turn the classroom lights off, and turn the flashlight on for 30 seconds, and then off for three more trials. After each time the flashlight is turned off, have the subgroups discuss and record their answers about how far the light moved.
>
> *Step 3:* Indicate that for the final three trials the students will again have to record individually how far the dot of light has moved, without talking to each other. For

the final three trials, turn the flashlight on again for 30 seconds and then off, and have students record their answers.

Step 4: Ask several volunteers to write their answers to the nine trials on the chalkboard. Discuss whether the results are similar to previous studies that have found that the final three judgments tend to converge to the subgroup standard in trials four, five, and six.

Step 5: Summarize the results of conformity studies described in this chapter.

2. Power bases

Goals: This exercise is designed to help students learn how to analyze influence efforts in terms of the bases of power identified by French and Raven (1968).

Step 1: Inform the students of the purpose of this exercise. Indicate that it is natural and desirable for group members to seek to influence each other. Briefly describe the following five power bases: reward, coercive, legitimate, expert, and referent.

Step 2: Ask the students to form subgroups of five students each. Ask each subgroup to answer the following questions. (Write the questions on the chalkboard.)

a. What kinds of power does the instructor have in this class?
b. For each type of power that is identified, what are specific ways in which the instructor has sought to use this power?
c. How do the students feel about the instructor's use of each of these different power bases?
d. What power bases do students have in this class?

Step 3: Have the subgroups share with the class their answers to the four questions.

3. Task and maintenance roles

Goal: This exercise is designed to help students identify task and maintenance roles.

Step 1: Inform the students of the purpose of the exercise. Describe task and maintenance roles, which are discussed in this chapter. Indicate for the purposes of this exercise that the class can be assumed to be a group.

Step 2: Ask the class to form subgroups of four or five students. Ask the subgroups to identify task functions and specific maintenance functions performed by the instructor and by students in this class.

Step 3: Have the subgroups share and discuss their conclusions.

4. Group therapy in action

Goal: This exercise is designed to give class members an experiential awareness of being in a group therapy session.

Step 1: Indicate that at the next class period a simulated group therapy session will be conducted, with the purpose stated. Each student is given the "homework" assignment of identifying one or two personal problems that a friend or relative currently has. Students are told that they should not reveal the identity of the person having the problem and that the personal problem should be that of a friend or relative (and not their own).

Step 2: At the next class period, begin by stating the following ground rules. "Today we will have a simulated group therapy session to give you an experiential awareness of being in group therapy. Because this is a class, I strongly request that you do not reveal any personal information about any dilemmas or difficulties you are experiencing. Instead, I ask you to describe one or two complicated personal dilemmas that a friend or relative is currently facing. For confidentiality reasons, please do not reveal the identity of the person whose problems you talk about. Remember, for reasons of confidentiality, what is said here, stays here. Are there any questions about what we are going to do, or about the ground rules?" If there are questions, answer them.

Step 3: Ask students to begin sharing the concerns. If the class is reluctant, initiate the process by asking a normally vocal student to begin. When a student is sharing, encourage other students to probe with questions in order to explore the problem further and suggest realistic and creative courses of action to resolve the problem. (In group therapy sessions, each member at times takes on the role of a therapist.)

Step 4: After the dilemma revealed by one student is fully discussed and problem-solved, have other students share the dilemmas they've brought. Continue until the end of the class period, or until no one has anything further to share. At the end of the exercise, ask students their thoughts about the benefits and shortcomings of the exercise and their suggestions for changes in the format of the exercise when it is again used.

Comment: During the exercise, one or more of the students may begin talking about a personal problem. At this point make a judgment about whether to let the student continue. Do not allow any students to divulge personal information that they are apt to regret later.

Social Work
with Families

Often the focus of social work services is on the family. A family is an interacting interdependent system. The problems faced by any person are usually influenced by the dynamics within a family. Because a family is an interacting system, change in one member affects others. For example, the abused child is at times a scapegoat on whom the parents vent their anger and hostility. If the abused child is removed from such a home, another child within the family is apt to be selected to be the scapegoat (Kadushin, 1980).

Another reason for the focus on the family rather than on the individual is that the other family members are often needed in the treatment process. For example, other family members can put pressure on an alcoholic to have her or him acknowledge that a problem exists. The family members may also need counseling (or support from a self-help group) to assist them in coping with the alcoholic when she or he is drinking, and these family members may play important roles in providing emotional support for the alcoholic's efforts to stop drinking.

Diversity of Family Forms

The family is a social institution that is found in every culture. The family has been defined by Coleman and Cressey (1990, p. 125) as "a group of people related by marriage, ancestry, or adoption who live together in a common household." This definition does not cover a number of living arrangements in which the members consider themselves to be a family. Some of these arrangements are as follows:

- A husband and wife raising two foster children who have been in the household for several years
- Two women, lesbians in a loving relationship, raising children born to one of the partners while in a heterosexual marriage that ended in divorce
- A family unit in which one of the spouses is living away from home—perhaps because of military service in a foreign country or because of incarceration
- A family unit in which one of the children who is severely and profoundly retarded is living in a residential treatment facility
- A man and a woman who have been living together for years in a loving relationship but who have never legally married

A wide diversity of family patterns exist in the world. Families in different cultures take a variety of forms. In some societies, husband and wife live in separate buildings. In others, they are expected to live apart for several years after the birth of a child. In many societies, husbands are permitted to have more than one wife. In a few countries, wives are allowed to have more than one husband. Some cultures permit (and a few encourage) premarital and extramarital intercourse.

Some societies have large communes where adults and children live together. There are communes in which the children are raised separately from adults. In some cultures without communes, surrogate parents (rather than the natural parents) raise the children. Some societies encourage certain types of homosexual relationships, and a few recognize homosexual as well as heterosexual marriages.

Case Example
Sex-role expectations are culturally determined

In the classic study *Sex and Temperament in Three Primitive Societies*, Margaret Mead demonstrated that sex-role expectations are culturally rather than biologically determined. The study further showed that family socialization patterns are immensely influenced by the larger culture. The study was conducted in three tribes in New Guinea in the early 1930s. Mead found that many characteristics that Americans classify as typically feminine or masculine are classified differently in these tribes.

Both sexes among the Arapesh would seem feminine to us. Both men and women are gentle, nurturant, and compliant. The personalities of males and females in this society are not sharply differentiated by sex. Both girls and boys learn to be unaggressive, cooperative, and responsive to the needs and wants of others. Relations between husband and wife parallel the traditional mother-child relations in our society, with the Arapesh husband often seeing his role as providing training to his much younger wife.

In contrast, among the Mundugamors, both sexes would see masculine to us. Both are headhunters and cannibals, are nonnurturant and aggressive, and actively initiate sexual involvement.

The most interesting society studied was the Tchambuli. This society virtually reverses our traditional sex-role expectations and stereotypes. The men spend much more time than the women in grooming and decorating themselves. Also, the men spend much of their time in painting, carving, and practicing dance steps. In contrast, the women are efficient, impersonal, unadorned, managerial, and brisk. The women are the traders and have most of the economic power.

SOURCE: Margaret Mead, *Sex and Temperament in Three Primitive Societies* (New York: Morrow, 1935).

In many cultures, marriages are still arranged by the parents. In a few societies, an infant may be "married" before birth (if the baby is of the wrong sex, the marriage is dissolved). Some societies do not recognize the existence of romantic love. Some cultures expect older men to marry young girls. Others expect older women to marry young boys. Most societies prohibit the marriage of close relatives. Yet, a few subcultures encourage marriage between brothers and sisters or between first cousins. Some expect a man to marry his father's brother's daughter, while others insist that he marry his mother's sister's daughter. In some societies, a man, on marrying, makes a substantial gift to the bride's father, whereas in others the bride's father gives a substantial gift to the new husband.

There are indeed substantial variations in family patterns. People in each of these societies generally feel strongly that their particular pattern is normal and proper, and many feel the pattern is divinely ordained. Suggested changes in their particular form are usually viewed with suspicion and defensiveness, and are often sharply criticized as being unnatural, immoral, and a threat to the survival of the family.

In spite of these variations, sociologists have noted that most family systems can be classified into two basic forms: the extended family and the nuclear family. An *extended family* consists of a number of relatives living together, such as parents, children, grandparents, great-grandparents, aunts, uncles, in-laws, and cousins. The extended family is the predominant pattern in preindustrial societies. The members divide various agricultural, domestic, and other duties among themselves.

A *nuclear family* consists of a married couple and their children living together. The nuclear family type emerged from the extended family. Extended families tend to be more functional in agricultural societies where many "hands" are needed; the nuclear family is more suited to the demands of complex, industrialized societies, as its smaller size and potential geographic mobility enable it to adapt more easily to changing conditions—such as the need to relocate to obtain a better job.

Although the nuclear family is still the predominant family form in the United States, Canada, and many other industrialized countries, it is a serious mistake for social workers and other helping professionals to use the nuclear family as the ideal model that individuals in our society should strive to form. There are many other family forms that are functioning in our society, such as the following:

- A married couple without children who are the primary care givers for the wife's mother who has Alzheimer's disease and who is residing with the couple
- Two men who are gay in a committed relationship, each of whom has joint custody of two children with his former wife
- A childless married couple who have decided not to conceive children
- A single parent with three young children
- A blended family in which the husband and wife procreate children in the marriage, and each spouse has children from earlier marriages who are also living in the household
- An unmarried young couple living together in what amounts to a "trial marriage"

In the past few decades there has been a trend in the United States for greater diversity in marital arrangements and family forms. There are increasing numbers of transracial marriages, marriages between spouses of diverse ages, transracial adoptions, single-parent families, and blended families. Although some social workers may personally judge a few of these types to be "wrong," it is essential that they not allow their personal beliefs to reduce the quality or quantity of professional services that are provided to these family units.

As the material suggests, family patterns and forms are substantially affected by the culture (larger system) in which they are located. In our culture, for example, women have traditionally been brought up to be passive, nurturing, and maternal, while males have traditionally been reared to be aggressive, competitive, outgoing, and nonexpressive. (In recent decades such sex-role socialization patterns have been undergoing major changes in our society.)

Societal Functions of Families

Families in modern industrial societies perform the following essential functions that help maintain the continuity and stability of society:

1. *Replacement of the population.* Every society has to have some system for replacing its members. Practically all societies consider the family as the unit in which children are to be produced. Societies have defined the rights and responsibilities of the reproductive partners within the family unit. These rights and responsibilities help maintain the stability of society, although they are defined differently from one society to another.

2. *Care of the young.* Children require care and protection until at least the age of puberty. The family is a primary institution for

the rearing of children. Modern societies have generally developed supportive institutions to help in caring for the young—for example, medical services, day-care centers, parent training programs, and residential treatment centers.

3. *Socialization of new members.* To become productive members of society, children have to be socialized into the culture. Children are expected to acquire a language, learn social values and mores, and dress and behave within the norms of society. The family plays a major role in this socialization process. In modern societies, a number of other groups and resources are involved in this socialization process. Schools, the mass media, peer groups, the police, movies, and books and other written material are important influences. (Sometimes these different influences clash by advocating opposing values and attitudes.)

4. *Regulation of sexual behavior.* Failure to regulate sexual behavior would result in clashes between individuals due to jealousy and exploitation. Unregulated sexual behavior would probably result in the birth of large numbers of children outside of marriage—children whom no fathers could be held responsible for raising. Every society has rules that regulate sexual behavior within family units. Most societies, for example, have incest taboos, and most disapprove of extramarital sex.

5. *Source of affection.* Spitz (1945) demonstrated that humans need affection, emotional support, and positive recognition from others (including approval, smiles, encouragement, and reinforcement for accomplishments). Without such affection and recognition, a person's emotional, intellectual, physical, and social growth would be stunted. The family is an important source for obtaining affection and recognition, because family members generally regard each other as among the most important people in their lives and gain emotional and social satisfaction from family relationships.

Family Problems and the Nature of Social Work

An infinite number of problems may occur in families. Exhibit 8.1 is a list of some of these problems.

When problems arise in a family, social services are often needed. The types and forms of services that social workers provide to troubled families are extremely varied. These services require the social worker to perform a variety of roles (for example, broker, educator, advocate, supporter, mediator). The following examples illustrate the diverse nature of social work with families.

• Ray Falk, age 56, is diagnosed as having a malignant brain tumor that is inoperable. The prognosis is that Mr. Falk has only a few more months left to live. He leaves the hospital and moves in with his daughter and her husband. Mary Brey, medical social worker at the hospital, serves as a broker for Mr. Falk and his care givers to receive respite care, counseling, and other services from the hospice program in the community.

• Mark Schwanke, age 32, is diagnosed as having AIDS. Betty Seely, a social worker with the AIDS Support Network in the community, serves as a case manager in providing a variety of services to Mark, his wife, who is HIV positive, and their two children. These services include medical information and care, housing, counseling, emotional support services, and financial assistance. Because of frequent discrimination against persons with AIDS and persons with the AIDS virus, Betty Seely often must be an advocate on the family's behalf to assure that family members receive the services they need.

• Beth Roessler, age 15, is adjudicated to be delinquent for committing six burglaries. Steve Padek, a juvenile probation officer and social worker, is assigned as Beth's juvenile probation officer. Mr. Padek provides the following services to Beth and her mother who is divorced: holding weekly supervision meetings with Beth to monitor her school performance and leisure activities, linking Beth's mother with a Parents Without Partners group, and conducting several counseling sessions with Beth and her mother to mediate conflicts in their relationship.

• Cindy Rogerson, age 27, has three young children. She is badly battered by her husband, and contacts the House of Hope, a shelter for battered women and their children. Sue Frank, a social worker at the shelter, assists in making arrangements for shelter for Mrs. Rogerson and her children. The oldest child is attending school, so Ms. Frank makes arrangements for him to continue attending school. Ms. Frank at the shelter provides one-to-one counseling to Ms. Rogerson to help her explore her options and to inform her of potential resources which she may not be aware of. Ms. Frank also leads groups at the shelter for residents and nonresidents which Mrs. Rogerson is required to attend while at the center. After two and one-half weeks Mrs. Rogerson decides she is interested in returning to live with her husband. Ms. Frank convinces Mrs. Rogerson to give her husband an ultimatum prior to returning—he must receive family counseling together with her from the Family Service agency in the community and must attend a group for batterers in the community. Mrs. Rogerson reluctantly agrees. Mrs. Rogerson, at the urging of Ms. Frank, only then returns to live with her husband, with the understanding that she will leave immediately if he hits her again or if he drops out of either family counseling or the group for batterers.

• Luke Harder, age 12, is failing the sixth grade and appears apathetic. He is referred for an M-team assessment. (An M-team is a multidisciplinary team that consists of a school psychologist, school nurse, speech and hearing specialist, and the social worker, Patrick Riesen.) Mr. Riesen's beginning responsibility is to do a social study of

Exhibit 8.1
A sampling of family problems

Divorce	Mental retardation of
Alcohol or drug	one or more
abuse	members
Unwanted pregnancy	Incarceration or
Bankruptcy	institutionalization
Poverty	of one or more
Terminal illness	members
Chronic illness	Compulsive
Death	gambling by one
Desertion	or more members
"Empty-shell"	Victim of a crime
marriage	Forced retirement of
Emotional problems	a wage earner
of one or more	Care giver for an
members	elderly relative
Behavioral problems	Involvement of a
of one or more	child in delinquent
members	and criminal
Child abuse	activities
Child neglect	Illness of a member
Sexual abuse	who acquires
Spouse abuse	AIDS
Elder abuse	A runaway teenager
Unemployment of	Sexual dysfunctions
wage earners	of one or more
Money management	members
difficulties	Infidelity
Injury from serious	Infertility
automobile	
accident involving	
one or more	
members	

the Harder family. He arranges to meet with Mr. and Mrs. Harder at their home. When Mr. Riesen arrives at the Harders, Mrs. Harder is present and explains that her husband has chosen to go to a tavern instead of meeting with the social worker. Mrs. Harder appears depressed and intensely frustrated with her family's plight. She explains that her husband may well be an alcoholic. She is overwhelmed with anger that he is spending most of his paycheck at the bar, that he is not helping to rear their children, and that he is very disruptive when he comes home intoxicated. Mr. Riesen asks Mrs. Harder if she thinks her husband would be interested in attending some joint sessions to discuss further what might be done. Another meeting, this time at school, is arranged, but again only Mrs. Harder attends. Three additional sessions are held with Mrs. Harder to discuss various options. Mr. Riesen encourages Mrs. Harder to join Al-Anon, which she does. After some meetings at Al-Anon, Mrs. Harder gives her husband an ultimatum that he must either stop drinking and enter family counseling with her, or she'll leave with the children. Mr. Harder stomps out in a rage. When he comes home he is physically abusive. He has been drinking again. Fortunately he passes out before causing serious physical injury. Mrs. Harder flees the house, taking the children. She spends the night with her parents. The next morning she calls Mr. Riesen, who arranges to meet her immediately. His first role is to provide emotional support to this distraught, frightened woman. Then various options are discussed. Mrs. Harder appears committed to her decision to divorce her husband. Mr. Riesen refers her to the Department of Social Services which assists her in getting financial assistance through the AFDC programs, assists her in finding an apartment, and refers her to an attorney in order to start divorce proceedings. The son, Luke, continues to fail in his courses during this family turmoil. At the end of the school year, he is required to repeat the sixth grade. During the summer Mrs. Harder and her children have time to begin adjusting to a new life. Life as a single parent for Mrs. Harder and the children is not easy, but it is a lot better than living with an abusive alcoholic. When Luke returns to school in the fall, he is more relaxed, settled, and motivated to do better academically. He does not want to repeat the sixth grade again, and therefore he works hard to raise his school performance to the "satisfactory" range.

• Katy Hynek, age 76, has Alzheimer's disease. She has been living alone in her house since her husband died three years ago. Her physician contacts Adult Services of the Department of Social Services and requests that an assessment of living arrangements be conducted. Linda Sutton, social worker, does an assessment and determines that Katy Hynek can no longer live alone. Katy's son Mark and his wife Annette agree to have Katy move in with them. During the next 19 months, Ms. Sutton has periodic contact with the Hyneks. As is common with this disease, Katy Hynek's physical and mental condition continue to deteriorate. Ms. Sutton listens to Mark and Annette's concerns and seeks to answer their questions about the disease. She also provides suggestions to help them cope with the changes in Katy's condition. As Katy's condition deteriorates, Ms. Sutton makes arrangements for Katy to attend an adult daycare center during the daytime, partly for respite care for Mark and Annette. At the end of 19 months, Mark and Annette request a meeting with Ms. Sutton to discuss the possibility of placing Katy in a nursing home, since her condition has so deteriorated that she now needs 24-hour care. (For example, she gets up in the middle of the night and gets lost in closets; she is also now incontinent.) The pros and cons of placing Katy in a nursing home are identified and discussed. Making the decision is exceedingly emotional and agonizing for Mark and Annette. With a careful discussion of the entire situation with Ms. Sutton, Mark and Annette decide they have no choice but to seek a nursing home placement. Ms. Sutton gives them the names of three nursing homes, which they visit, and then proceed to select one.

Family Assessment

The two areas in social work practice with families that have received the most attention are family assessment and family therapy. This section will focus on family assessment, and the next section on family therapy.

There are a variety of ways to assess families. Conducting a social history of a family and its members is a widely used approach (see Chapter 4). In regard to family assessment, however, two techniques that have received considerable discussion in recent years are eco-maps and genograms. Both of these techniques will be described here.

The Eco-Map

The eco-map is a paper-and-pencil assessment tool used to assess specific troubles and plan interventions for clients. The eco-map, a drawing of the client family in its social environment, is usually drawn jointly by the social worker and the client. It helps both parties achieve a holistic or ecological view of the client's family life and the nature of the family's relationships with groups, associations, organizations, and other families and individuals. The eco-map has been used in a variety of situations, including marriage and family counseling and adoption and foster-care home studies. It has also been used to supplement traditional social histories and case records. The eco-map is a shorthand method for recording basic social information. The technique helps clients and practitioners gain insight into the clients' problems by providing a "snapshot view" of important interactions at a particular point in time. Ann Hartman (1978) is the primary developer of this tool.

A typical eco-map consists of a family diagram surrounded by a set of circles and lines used to describe the family within an environmental context. The eco-map user can create her or his own abbreviations and symbols, but the most commonly used symbols are shown in Figure 8.1.

First, a circle (representing the client's family) is drawn in the center of a large blank sheet of paper (see Figure 8.2). The composition of the family is indicated within the circle. Numerous other circles are then drawn in the area surrounding the family circle. These circles represent other systems—that is, the

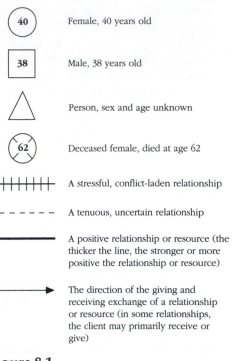

Figure 8.1
Commonly used symbols in an eco-map

groups, other families, individuals, and organizations—with which the family ordinarily interacts.

Different kinds of lines are then drawn to describe the nature of the relationships that the members of the client family have with these other systems. The directional flow of energy (indicating giving and/or receiving of resources, and communication between the client family members and the significant systems) is indicated by the use of arrows. A case example of the use of an eco-map follows on page 228.

A major value of an eco-map is that it facilitates both the worker and the client viewing the client's family from a systems and an ecological perspective. Sometimes, as happened in the Wilbur case example, the drawing of the eco-map helps clients and practitioners gain greater insight into the social dynamics of a problematic situation.

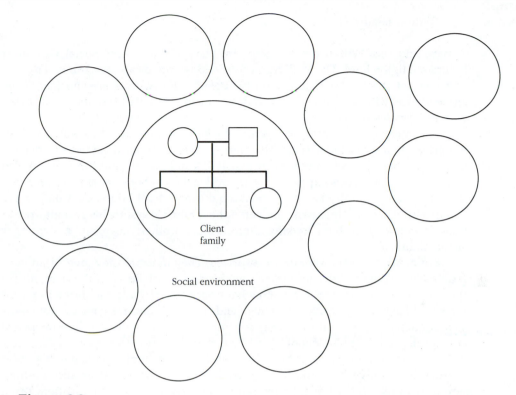

Client
family

Social environment

Figure 8.2
Setting up an eco-map

The Genogram

The genogram is a graphic way of investigating the origins of a client's or client family's presenting problem by diagramming the family over at least three generations. The client and the worker usually jointly construct the family genogram, which is essentially a family tree. Murray Bowen is the primary developer of this technique (Kerr & Bowen, 1988). The genogram is a useful tool for the worker and the family members to examine problematic emotional and behavioral patterns in an intergenerational context. These patterns tend to repeat themselves; what happens in one generation will often occur in the next. Genograms help family members identify and understand family relationship patterns.

Figure 8.4 shows commonly used genogram symbols. Together, the symbols provide a visual picture of a family tree, for at least three generations, including: who the members are; their names, ages, and gender; marital status; sibling positions, and so on. When relevant, additional items of information may be included, such as emotional difficulties, behavioral problems, religious affiliation, ethnic origins, geographic locations, occupations, socioeconomic status, and significant life events. The use of the genogram is illustrated in the case example on page 231.

The eco-map and the genogram have a number of similarities. With both techniques, users gain insight into family dynamics. Some of the symbols used in the two approaches are identical. There are differences, however. The eco-map focuses attention

Case Example
Using an eco-map: The Wilbur family

Barb and Dick Wilbur are contacted by Mary Timm, School Social Worker at Jefferson High School. The Wilburs' second-oldest son, Brian (age 16), had a knife in his jacket at school and liquor on his breath. The Wilburs are shocked. They agree to meet with Ms. Timm the next day to further discuss these incidents. Brian will also be present.

At the meeting Ms. Timm asks Brian why he brought a knife to school. At first, he refuses to respond. Ms. Timm also notes that records show he used to receive mainly B's, but his grades are now primarily D's and F's. Mr. and Mrs. Wilbur also sternly ask Brian what is happening. They add that the school system has informed them that he apparently has been drinking during school hours. Gradually tears come to Brian's eyes. He says no one cares about him. He asserts his parents are too busy at work and too busy looking after his older brother, Steve, and his younger sister, Shannon.

At first, Mr. and Mrs. Wilbur are suprised. They indicate they love Brian very much. Gradually they disclose they have been so involved with the demands of their other two children that they may have been "shortchanging" Brian in recent months. Shannon, age 13, has Down's syndrome and requires considerable individual attention, especially with her coursework. (Shannon is enrolled in special education courses at her school.)

Brian is asked where he obtained the knife. He hesitantly indicates his older brother, Steve, gave it to him for "protection." Brian adds that he sees nothing wrong with carrying a knife; Steve frequently carries a pistol. In addition, Brian says Steve urged him to take the knife to school, because some people who are unhappy with Steve have said they may come after Brian.

Ms. Timm asks Mr. and Mrs. Wilbur if they know anything about this. Barb and Dick suggest it may be best if Brian is excused at this point. Ms. Timm sets up a later meeting with Brian, and he leaves.

Both Barb and Dick then become teary-eyed. They indicate they are nearing their wit's end. Both work full-time, and in recent years Steve and Shannon have required so much of their attention that they now no longer are able to spend any time with their former friends. In addition, they have been arguing more and more. They are feeling increasingly that their family is disintegrating and that they are "failing" as parents. They also disclose that Steve is addicted to both alcohol and cocaine and has been for several years. He has been in for inpatient treatment three times, but always goes back to using soon after leaving treatment. They do not know where Steve is getting the money for his cocaine habit. They fear he may be dealing. He has not been able to hold a full-time job. He is usually terminated because he shows up for work while under the influence. Currently, he is working part-time as a bartender.

Mr. and Mrs. Wilbur fear that unless something is done soon, Brian may follow in Steve's footsteps. They add they have contemplated asking Steve to leave, but are reluctant to do so, since they feel it is their parental obligation to provide a house for their children as long as the children want to stay.

At this point Ms. Timm suggests it may be helpful to graphically diagram their present dilemma. Together the Wilburs and Ms. Timm draw the eco-map shown in Figure 8.3.

While drawing the map, Ms. Timm asks whether providing housing for Steve is helping him or whether it may be a factor in enabling him to continue his drug use and his irresponsible behavior. The eco-map helps Barb and Dick see that as a result of working full-time and spending the remainder of their waking hours caring for Shannon, Steve, and Brian, they are gradually becoming too emotionally and physically exhausted to cope. During the past few years, they have gradually stopped socializing. The Wilburs ask Ms. Timm to explain what she means by "enabling" Steve to continue his drug use and his irresponsible behavior. Ms. Timm explains enabling and indicates that a "tough love" approach may be an option. (In this case a tough love approach would involve the Wilburs' demanding that Steve live elsewhere if he continues to abuse alcohol and cocaine.) Ms. Timm also gives them some pamphlets that describe enabling and tough love. They make an appointment for the next week.

(continued)

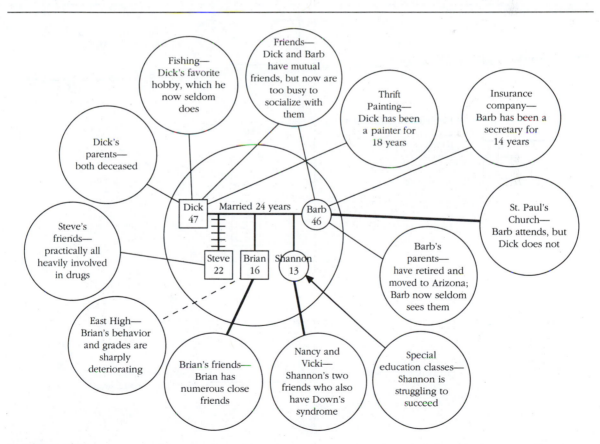

Figure 8.3
Sample eco-map: The Wilbur family

Case Example
Using an eco-map: The Wilbur family *(continued)*

For the next several weeks Ms. Timm continues to have weekly meetings with Mr. and Mrs. Wilbur and individual sessions with Brian. The Wilburs eventually decide to use a tough love approach with Steve. Steve leaves, but continues to use alcohol and cocaine. However, living on his own does appear to be somewhat beneficial, since he now works full-time at a maintenance job to pay his bills. With Steve out of the house, Barb and Dick Wilbur are able to spend more time with Brian and Shannon, and they begin to socialize again with some of their former friends.

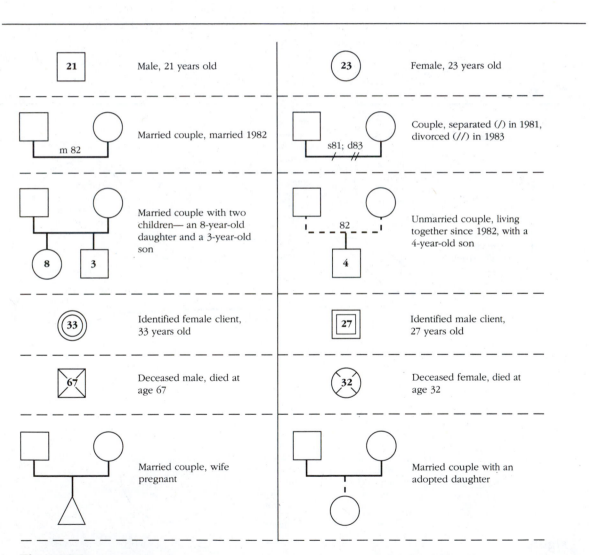

Figure 8.4
Commonly used genogram symbols

Case Example

Using a genogram: The Kull family

Jim Kull is referred by Rock County District Attorney's Office to the Rock County Domestic Violence Program. He was arrested two nights ago for an incident in which his wife, Diane, received several severe bruises on her body and her face. Kris Koeffler, a social worker has an intake interview with Mr. Kull. Mr. Kull is an involuntary client and is reluctant to discuss the incident. Ms. Koeffler informs Mr. Kull he has a right not to discuss it, but if he chooses not to, she is obligated to inform the district attorney that he refused services. She adds that in such cases the district attorney usually files a battery charge with the court, which may lead to jail time.

Mr. Kull reluctantly states he and his wife had a disagreement, which ended with her slapping him, and he defending himself by throwing a few punches. He adds that yesterday, when he was in jail, he was informed she left home with the children and is now staying at a women's shelter. He is further worried she may contact an attorney and seek a divorce.

Ms. Koeffler inquires about the specifics of the "disagreement." Mr. Kull indicates he came home after having a few beers, his dinner was cold, and he "got on" Mrs. Kull for not cleaning the house. He adds that Mrs. Kull then started "mouthing off," which eventually escalated into them pushing and hitting each other. Ms. Koeffler then inquires whether such incidents had occurred in the past. Mr. Kull indicates "a few times," and then adds that getting physical with his wife is the only way for him to "make her shape up." He indicates he works all day long as a carpenter, while his wife sits home watching soap operas. He feels she is not doing her "fair share"; he states the house usually looks like a "pigpen."

Ms. Koeffler asks Mr. Kull if he feels getting physical with his wife is justifiable. He responds with "sure," and adds that his dad frequently told him "spare the rod, and spoil both the wife and the kids." Ms. Koeffler asks if his father was at times abusive to him when he was a child. He indicates that he was and adds that to this day he detests his dad for being abusive to him and to his mother.

Ms. Koeffler then suggests that together they draw a "family tree," focusing on three areas: episodes of heavy drinking, episodes of physical abuse, and traditional versus modern gender stereotypes. Ms. Koeffler explains that a traditional gender stereotype includes the husband as the primary decision maker and the wife as submissive to him and primarily responsible for domestic tasks. The modern gender stereotype involves an equalitarian relationship between husband and wife. After an initial reluctance (related to his expressing confusion as to how such a "tree" would help get his wife back), Mr. Kull agrees to cooperate in drawing such a "tree." The resulting genogram is presented in Figure 8.5.

The genogram helps Mr. Kull see that he and his wife are products of family systems that have strikingly different values and customs. In his family the males tend to drink heavily, have a traditional view of marriage, and tend to use physical force in interactions with their spouse. (Mr. Kull further adds his father also physically abused his brother and sister when they were younger.) On questioning, Mr. Kull mentions he frequently spanks his children and has struck them "once or

(continued)

Case Example

Using a genogram: The Kull family *(continued)*

twice." Ms. Koeffler asks Mr. Kull how he feels about repeating the same patterns of abuse with his wife and children that he despises his father for using. Tears come to his eyes, and he says "not good."

Ms. Koeffler and Mr. Kull then discuss courses of action that he might take to change his family interactions, and how he might best approach his wife in requesting that she and the children return. Mr. Kull agrees to attend Alcoholics Anonymous (AA) meetings as well as a therapy group for batterers. After a month of attending these weekly meetings, he contacts his wife and asks her to return. Mrs. Kull agrees to return *if* he stops drinking (since most of the abuse occurred when he was intoxicated), *if* he agrees to continue to attend group therapy and AA meetings, and *if* he agrees to go to counseling with her. Mr. Kull readily agrees. (Mrs. Kull's parents, who have never liked her husband, express their disapproval.)

For the first few months, Mr. Kull is on his best behavior, and there is considerable harmony in the family. Then one day, on his birthday, he decides to stop for a few beers after work. He drinks until he is intoxicated. When he finally arrives home, he starts verbally and physically to abuse Mrs. Kull and the children. For Mrs. Kull, this is the last straw. She takes the children to her parents' house, where they stay for several days, until they are able to find and move into an apartment. She also files for divorce and follows through in obtaining one.

In many ways this case is not a "success." In reality, many social work cases are not successful. The genogram, however, is useful in helping Mr. Kull realize that he has acquired, and is now acting out, certain dysfunctional family patterns. Unfortunately, he is not ready to make lasting changes. Perhaps in the future he will be more committed. At the present time he has returned to drinking heavily.

---

on a family's interactions with groups, resources, organizations, associations, other families, and other individuals. The genogram focuses attention on intergenerational family patterns, particularly those that are problematic or dysfunctional.

Family Therapy in Systems Perspective

One of the many social services provided to families is family therapy (also called family counseling). A substantial amount of literature about family therapy has been developed in social work. The remainder of this chapter will focus on describing family therapy. Although social work with families involves many approaches and services in addition to

family therapy, the importance of family therapy in social work practice necessitates an extended discussion of this approach.

Family therapy: What is it? Strictly speaking, family therapy is a subset of the broader classification of group therapy that is aimed at helping families with whatever interactional, behavioral, and emotional problems that may arise in the course of everyday living. Problems include marital conflicts, parent-child interactional problems, and conflicts with grandparents or other relatives. A wide variety of problems are dealt with in family therapy, such as domestic violence, communication problems, and disagreements between family members on drug use and abuse, curfew hours, school performance, money management, sexual values and behavior, perfor-

Figure 8.5
Sample genogram: The Jim and Diane Kull family

mance of domestic tasks, and methods of disciplining the children.[1]

The Whitlock family walked into the therapist's office in an orderly fashion, the oldest son looking annoyed and bored, the younger children looking scared. Mrs. Whitlock introduced the group to the therapist immediately, saying that she was sure nothing was wrong with her family, yet the younger daughter had been crying all the time lately and had been doing very poorly in school of late; she was also obese. The mother said she was sure

[1]The remainder of this chapter was especially written for this text by Carolyn Wells, Ph.D. Dr. Wells is associate professor of social work at Marquette University, Wisconsin, and is a practicing family therapist.

the daughter would grow out of these problems, but when the little girl's teacher had called and said the child was talking about suicide, the mother was persuaded to seek help for the girl. The only reason the rest of the family were here, she announced, was because the therapist had requested that everyone be present at the interview to contribute ideas about what the trouble was with the younger daughter.

The father stood by the door while the mother was talking, and no one sat down. The therapist noted that the older daughter stood close to the father, and the younger son stood alone looking at the floor. The older son moved over to the window and looked out, whistling to himself. When the mother, holding her younger daughter's hand, finished her rapid-fire introductory speech, the therapist took advantage of the moment to invite the family to be seated. She asked each person present to introduce himself or herself. She noted that the older daughter had difficulty with that request; she stuttered badly and could not utter the first sound of her name.

Fortunately, not every family is as troubled as the Whitlocks. Some parents rear their children with minimum discomfort and maximum growth for all involved. Family therapy is a practice or activity to help those other families who are hurting, overtly or covertly. Families enter into therapy because they are hoping to reduce their pain and increase their happiness, as individuals and as a group. Families that hurt internally are also likely to find their standing in the community diminished because one or more of the children exhibit embarrassing behavior in public, perhaps delinquent behavior. The family self-image of happiness and tranquility is likely to be shattered by angry, rebellious, or destructive behavior within the home. Crises precipitated by the children's behavior are likely to precipitate flare-ups of old marital stresses and arguments. People suffer, and their self-esteem and personal growth are inhibited.

Virginia Satir was a noted social worker who worked with many troubled families. Satir (1972) believed that four factors differentiate troubled and untroubled families: level of felt self-worth, pattern of communication, type of family rules, and the way the family members relate to people and institutions outside the family (their pattern of linkage to society). She found that in the troubled families she worked with self-worth was low; communication was indirect, vague, and dishonest; rules were rigid and nonnegotiable; and the linkage to society vacillated between being fearful, placating, or blaming (Satir, 1972, pp. 3–4). By contrast, in nurturing families self-worth tended to be high; communication was clear, specific, and honest; rules were appropriate and flexible; and the linking to society was open.

Family therapy deals with a wide variety of problems and with diverse family types. Here a single-parent family is counseled.

Obviously, troubled and untroubled families stand at opposite ends of a continuum. Probably most families stand somewhere along the continuum. It takes a great deal of effort and energy to enter an activity like family therapy, and usually a family has to be far along the continuum toward the troubled end before it will make the move to seek help. Often the family is troubled for a long time before any effort is made to reach out for assistance. A particular event such as the clash of a family member, often a child, with an outside authority (such as the school or the police) may precipitate the seeking of help. Perhaps the sudden desertion of a spouse or the running away of a child brings about a great enough crisis that the family will seek professional help. At any rate, members of middle-class American culture, who have been exhorted to solve their own problems and lift themselves up by their own bootstraps, tend to enter therapy well after external intervention would have been useful. Often the family member who finally reaches out will be female, since males in our society are traditionally reared to erroneously believe it is a sign of weakness to seek help for individual and family problems. Unfortunately, seeking professional help for reasons of emotional adjustment will usually be perceived by the family as an admission of dependency and failure

Case Example
School phobia

A system inherently attempts to maintain a dynamic balance, or homeostasis, in order to maintain the particular arrangement or ordering of parts that was successful in the past and resulted in the establishment of the system. As an example of how problematic behavior in a family member may help maintain the family homeostasis (balance of the system so the system can continue), let us discuss a school phobia that arose in a little girl in a Jefferson County, Wisconsin, elementary school. The school phobia arose apparently spontaneously, but the school social worker discovered on her first home visit that the little girl was almost mute with strangers (at least with the social worker herself), and in fact ran out onto the yard rather than cope with a new person. The mother would not fetch the daughter ("she's too frightened of strangers") and offered only the most broad and general information about the child's development. On the other hand, the mother wanted to talk about herself; she listed a variety of stresses in her life unrelated to the daughter, in particular her aloof husband and her boring job. It became increasingly clear that this mother resented the time and attention her daughter was receiving; she wanted some attention herself. Yet the only reason she was receiving any attention from her husband was due to the daughter's phobia. The husband had to talk to the lonely woman fairly often because of the little girl's problematic behaviors (in the home the child would often stay in her room, or refuse her supper, and so forth). Because of the girl's school phobia, the mother got to stay home from her disliked job and to talk with her husband.

A combination of family therapy to help create a genuine relationship between the marital pair without the assistance of the daughter's problematic behaviors, plus reduction in the mother's work hours, helped reduce this family's need for a problematic daughter. At school, during the initial stages of the family therapy, the little girl was placed in a special class with an empathic and firm teacher. The father was assigned the task of taking his daughter to school. The mother was to accompany them but not take responsibility. Fortunately, the father was a well-meaning person and faithfully carried out his responsibility, which strengthened his relationship with the child and thus his investment in the family system as a whole. After successfully getting the child to school, the father and the mother would discuss their success, strengthening their own communication and increasing their appreciation of one another. The school phobia disappeared within a few weeks.

---

rather than as an assertive action in the direction of constructive problem solving, an act that would be more permissible for a male.

When a family does consult a therapist for help in reducing their family pain, there is hope. The act of seeking help itself is a positive indication that the family is capable of at least one innovative act in helping itself.

However, the family will usually enter therapy using an identified client as a sort of ticket for admission. Very often, in fact, the family will perceive that this identified client really is their only problem. If the therapist can only fix this person, the family will be just fine. An example of such a circumstance is the Whitlock family, described earlier. The younger daughter, obese and talking about suicide, is the family's identified client. At least within the first interview as described so far, there seems to be no indication from the family members that they think anything else is wrong. The rest of the family is dutifully tagging along to the interview to contribute ideas about what is wrong with the little girl.

The family therapist will perceive the identified client as serving an important function in the family system. Like all systems, a family has an overall purpose, In the case of the family, its purpose is to provide for the physical and emotional needs of the adults and to procreate new people. The interrelated parts of this system are the family members themselves. These parts establish a certain working order; for example, communication patterns, rules, levels of self-esteem. Energy to keep the system going is supplied by food, water, housing, and so forth, plus certain empowering beliefs regarding the emotional, intellectual, social, and spiritual lives of the family members and how one fits in with another (Satir, 1972, pp. 113–119). Like all systems, each family system is bounded, in that communication patterns within the family have special forms and a special significance and purpose (for example, continuation of the family). However, the boundary around the family is permeable to varying degrees. In a healthy family system, new information can flow into and out of the family through the boundary and the family is thus characterized as an open system. In this open system, rules are related to communication and change is considered normal. The members' self-worth is granted higher importance than the maintenance of a fixed power structure. On the other hand, in a relatively closed system, family members cling to the familiar even when it is painful and does not foster growth. Where self-worth is low, pain is at least familiar and thus preferable to the unknown. Self-worth is relegated to a secondary position below fixed authority, change is resisted, and relationships are regulated by force (at the whim of the person on top). Information from outside

the system is resisted, because there is just one "right way."

To repeat, when a family comes to therapy, they generally do so to have the therapist "fix" a particular family member so that their system can maintain itself as before, only without the stress that the particular identified client has been recently exerting. The perspective of the systems-oriented family therapist is that the identified client developed problematic behavior to help maintain the family system in some way. Now the problematic behavior has become severe enough that the family views it as a problem. So when the referral for therapy is made by a family member or outside institution (for example, school), the therapist will insist on the involvement of all family members, even very young children. The therapist will want to determine from direct observation what function the problematic behavior of the identified client plays in maintenance of the family system, and how and why it has now become stressful.

The possibility of family therapy is ultimately limited by the family itself. As mentioned before, when a family seeks help there is hope, because it indicates that the family is capable of innovative action. But the family may be willing to go only so far to have the identified client "cured" by the therapist. At this point the therapist can explain as simply and clearly as possible the obvious advantage of working with many different sources of information to solve this important problem. The therapist may be successful with this sort of persuasion. But if the family refuses, the therapist has the choice of working with the identified client alone, or of refusing service (in the latter case, the therapist should, of course, refer the patient to a different kind of agency). Many family-oriented therapists will refuse services if the family will not participate in treatment. However, if a significant subsystem of the family will involve itself (perhaps the mother and the child), the therapist may consider beginning therapy with part of the system with the hope that the rest will enter in later. This decision is a delicate one and every therapist will gradually evolve criteria for choosing when to refer and when to start with a subsystem only. More research data on significant criteria would be helpful in making such discriminations. Therapists also have to decide whether they will or can work with certain families who seek their services involuntarily. Perhaps a court has ordered the family to enter therapy as an alternative to a jail sentence for a child whose behavior is continually delinquent. In these cases the purposes and potential of family therapy must be carefully explained to the family, and their option of taking the alternative course should be clarified.

Four Approaches to Family Therapy

Several noted family therapists have contributed to the growing theory and practice of family therapy. Here we will briefly describe the theoretical frameworks of Virginia Satir, Salvador Minuchin, Jay Haley, and Ivan Boszormenyi-Nagi. All these theorists use a systems perspective, but they apply it in different ways.

Virginia Satir

Satir stressed clarification of family communication patterns in her work. She noted, in particular, that communication patterns among troubled families tend to be vague and indirect. In other words, rather than speaking clearly for themselves, the marital pair tends to avoid talking with each other about their needs and desires; or they talk to each other through their children. Children are thus maneuvered into the stressful position of speaking for, and therefore allying with, one parent or another, precipitating fear of loss of the other parent.

In Satir's view, indirect communication in the troubled family begins with courtship of the marital pair (if not before), due to the low self-esteem of the individuals involved. Each spouse-to-be feels worthless, but hides the feeling of worthlessness by acting confident and strong. Neither person talks about these feelings of worthlessness for fear of driving the potential mate away. So each sees in the other a strong person who will take care of him or her, and essentially marries to gain an extension of the self, but a stronger self who will be able to meet all felt needs; in other words, each marries to "get" (Satir, 1967, pp. 8–10).

Unfortunately, after marriage some of the illusions must fall away. Each spouse is forced to realize at some level that the other spouse is not just an extension of the self. One insists on using a separate toothbrush, for example, while the other wants to share the same one. Such incidents force perceptions of difference, and difference is experienced as bad because it leads to arguments. A desire for fusion and to be cared for conflicts with the other's different felt needs. Facing difference feels frightening—it might lead to arguments and that could result in the other's leaving.

Hence each frightened spouse with low self-esteem and high need for the other tries to mask differences as much as possible, attempting to please the other on one level to keep him or her, while fearing and resenting expressed needs from the other that may be experienced as undesirable. Since both spouses are in the same uncomfortable position of resenting differences yet needing the other, interpersonal communication gradually becomes more and more indirect. Rather than risk a clear statement such as "I'd like to get a dog," the spouse desiring a pet might state something like "Aunt Matilda likes dogs." The hope will be that the other spouse will mind-read the intended message and then spontaneously agree to get a dog for the family. However, the receiver of this particular message will more likely communicate a return response dealing with Aunt Matilda, bringing disappointment to the speaker. The speaker isn't able to negotiate the desired dog with this type of communication and is left with angry feelings toward the spouse and a sense of unfulfilled needs, but this state of affairs is experienced as being preferable to risking a point-blank denial. Meanwhile, the receiver of the message may become aware of the disappointment or anger of the speaker through nonverbal channels but have no idea what caused the anger or disappointment. If the spouse is also afraid to deal with conflict, he or she will not ask the reason for the apparent upset. So the misunderstanding and tension builds.

Satir also notes that communicating involves far more than the literal meaning of any words used. First of all, she notes that much communication is nonverbal—gestures, facial expressions, voice tone, posture, and the like. If nonverbal communication matches the meaning of any words used (if, for example, the words "I am sad" are accompanied by tears and a downturned mouth), then Satir considers the communication *congruent*. The receiver is not likely to misunderstand the meaning of this message because the verbal and nonverbal components agree. However, messages sent are often *incongruent*. For example, the statement "I am sad" may be accompanied by a grin. Which message should the receiver believe: the words or the facial expression? The receiver is likely to make a mistaken interpretation unless he or she explicitly asks the sender to explain. But the person who feels safe only with indirect communication is not likely to ask. Moreover, the sender who becomes skilled at sending incongruent communication for self-protection may even be unaware of the action and will be unable to explain if asked. Satir believes that incongruent communication can lead to misunderstanding in troubled families. Mother, for example, may say to her spouse in words, "I am angry with you." However, since she fears rejection if she sends this message too forcefully, she smiles sweetly as she says it. The spouse may then choose to believe the smile, not to take his spouse's words seriously, and continue the very behavior that made her use the word *angry*. This is likely to make her angrier, but she

may not feel safe enough to express the feeling more congruently, and the communication driving the spouses apart goes on.

While incongruent communication is one example of a double message, another type of double message may place the receiver in a *double bind*, where no matter how he or she responds, the sender will criticize. This type of situation can occur in a family where father says, on the one hand, that all good children should keep their toys picked up, and yet on the other tells his son that all "real" boys are messy. The boy who receives both these messages will be unable to please his father whether he keeps his toys neat or messy. He may solve the problem by refusing to listen at all. At the extreme, he may pull away from reality to such a degree that he may develop a severe emotional disturbance.

Satir's therapeutic goals and techniques are based on her assumption that people have the inherent ability (even drive) to grow and to mature. She felt that people can choose to take responsibility for their own lives and actions and that the mature person will

1. Manifest himself clearly to others.
2. Be in touch with signals from his internal self, thus letting himself know openly what he thinks and feels.
3. Be able to see and hear what is outside himself as differentiated from himself and as different from anything else.
4. Behave toward another person as someone who is separate and unique.
5. Treat the presence of differentness as an opportunity learn and explore rather than as a threat or signal of conflict. [Satir, 1967, p. 92]

To help the members of a troubled family differentiate from one another and learn to own their special unique beings, Satir patiently taught each person to speak for himself or herself and to send "I-messages."[2] She served as an active, directive, loving role model. She taught that differentness is nor-

[2]"I-messages" are described in Chapter 20.

mal and should be viewed as a catalyst for growth. She pointed out incongruent messages and double binds, and taught family members to send clear, congruent messages instead. She used touch and other nonverbal means, such as family sculpturing, to help illustrate to families the unverbalized assumptions they operate by, and in this way took the burden of labeling off the identified client and revealed his or her symptomatic behavior as a product of the family system as a whole. She analyzed rules in the family and helped clarify them in the context that some rules may be bad, but the people setting the rules or bound by them are not. She taught that bad rules can be changed and had the family members negotiate new ones as she insisted that each member be heard in her presence, thus teaching respect for each person and point of view.

Clearly, then, Satir viewed the family as a system and worked with the family as a whole as the means of relieving the distress of the identified client, or of the family itself due to the previous dysfunctional behavior of the identified client. Her major emphasis in intervention with the family as a system was to clarify the family communication patterns and to help them become direct and congruent. Basically, Satir's therapeutic goal of improving methods of communication involves three outcomes: (1) Each member should be able to report congruently, completely, and obviously on what he or she sees and hears, feels, and thinks about himself or herself and others. (2) Each person should be related to his or her uniqueness so that decisions are made in terms of exploration and negotiation rather than in terms of power. (3) Differentness should be openly acknowledged and used for growth (Okun & Rappaport, 1980, p. 93).

Salvador Minuchin

Like Satir, Minuchin and Fishman (1981) operated from a systems perspective in their work with families. In short, this means that if a particular person is referred for therapy due to certain undesirable symptoms, Minuchin will assume that this behavior is generated and maintained by needs of the family as a whole, so that intervention with the family will be necessary for effective alleviation of the problems of the identified client.

Unlike Satir, however, Minuchin's major emphasis in therapy is not clarification of communication patterns per se but restructuring of the major subsystems within the family (spouse, parental, sibling) so each may accomplish its appropriate functions. Because of this emphasis, Minuchin is considered a member of the *structural* school of family therapists. In restructuring the family, Minuchin may certainly work with communication patterns in the family, just as in clarifying communication patterns, Satir restructured the family subsystems into a more functional relationship. However, the theoretical perspective on the importance of clear, direct communication versus a functional family structure is clearly different for the two therapists. Minuchin, for example, may actually choose to bypass direct cognitive understanding by a family of its communication patterns in order to restructure the family subsystems; for example, he may use a paradoxical suggestion in working with a resistant family. He chooses to do so only in highly selected circumstances where direct explorations and clarifications of family communication patterns and behavior in therapy have failed to change the dysfunctional aspects. Minuchin described an illustration of a systemic paradox:

A systemic paradox is used in treatment of the Allen family, in which an eight-year-old boy is failing in school. The therapist determines that the symptom serves the function of keeping the mother's disappointment focused on her son, Billy, rather than her husband. The husband is failing in business and, rather than redoubling his efforts, is sinking into apathy, leaving the mother to shoulder much of the financial burden. He gives off signals that he would collapse if confronted openly with this issue and the mother collaborates in protecting him. Whenever she becomes angry at his lack of ambition, she nags Billy to straighten out and make something of himself, do his homework, practice his violin, or clean up his room. The mother and Billy end up fighting, and the father retires to the den to watch television. Both parents deny there is a marital problem, the wife stating, "My husband doesn't like to fight and I've accepted this."

The therapist tells the mother it is important for her to continue to express her disappointment in Billy, because otherwise she might begin to express her dissatisfaction with her husband. This would be risky, as her husband might become depressed, and since Billy is younger and more resilient than her husband, he can take it better. Billy is advised to continue to protect his father by keeping the mother's disappointment focused on him, and the father is commended for his cooperation. The mother has an immediate recoil, saying, "You're suggesting I fight with my eight-year-old son instead of my husband, a grown man? Why should I damage my son to protect my husband?" thus defining her own predicament. The husband supports the therapist, saying he thinks her suggestion is a good one "because Billy bounces right back. With him it doesn't last for a long period of time, and he doesn't get depressed as I do. Besides, we can't know for sure if it's doing him any damage." The mother is outraged at her husband and proceeds to fight with him. The conflict is refocused onto the parents, and Billy is released from his middle position. Defining and prescribing their system in a way that is both accurate and unacceptable makes it impossible for them to continue it. [Minuchin & Fishman, 1981, p. 247]

In this example, by the use of paradoxical suggestion Minuchin clarified the boundaries around the spouse subsystem in such a way that the son is appropriately excluded. Solving the problems of the spouse subsystem has now been squarely placed back within the boundaries of the spouse subsystem. The wife's disappointment with her husband is not "cured" nor is the apathetic behavior of the husband toward his failing business, but the wife's dissatisfaction with her spouse is now appropriately expressed within the boundaries of the spouse dyad, where it can be dealt with directly. Prior to use of this therapeutic technique, 8-year-old Billy was being pulled in between the spouses to divert them from fighting. Billy's inappropriate inclusion by the parents in their spouse subsystem might temporarily work to keep the family together for a longer period, but the cost to Billy is unacceptable. In the long run, using Billy this way will not work for the spouses either, for their problems obviously cannot be solved by Billy's failing in school.

In Minuchin's structural perspective, every family contains multiple interacting systems, including each particular individual and the various dyads, but three major subsystems are of particular importance in families with children. These are the spouse, the parental, and the sibling subsystems. Each has different major functions that must be fulfilled if the family is to survive as a healthy unit. The spouse subsystem must be able to protect itself as a unique entity with clear boundaries if the spouses' long-term psychological needs are to be met. This will involve certain rules of interaction with other significant subsystems, such as in-laws or children, that reinforce rather than interfere with the rights and needs of the spouses to interact as spouses. Once children are born, a parental subsystem then comes into being. The parental subsystem is likely to interfere with the spouse subsystem, because when one parent bonds closely with a newborn child then the primacy of the relationship with the other spouse is threatened. Moreover, in-laws may demand parental rights that conflict with the wants and needs of the biological parents.

Later on, older children may be asked to take on parental functions that interfere with their own needs to be nurtured and protected as they learn and grow. Finally, the sibling subsystem is of particular importance because this is the context in which children first learn what the world is all about for them: initially, how to interact and deal with peers and hierarchies. Minuchin points out that families continue to develop and change as children are added, grow, leave home—so that constant adaptational changes are required for every family. The family has both to maintain itself and to change with the changing conditions. Sometimes professional intervention is required to help troubled families cope successfully.

In working with a given family, Minuchin analyzes its structure to determine whether the boundaries of the major subsystems are clear and defined, or too enmeshed (too close, as when a parent and a child are emotionally closer than the two members of the spouse subsystem) and/or too disengaged (as when two spouses communicate with each other only through their children). Minuchin may draw a hypothetical structural diagram of the family, noting positions and types of boundaries as they exist when the family is referred. He may then rediagram the subsystem boundaries as new information emerges or as they change throughout the therapeutic process. His goal is to restructure the family so there is (1) a functioning spouse subsystem with a clear boundary differentiating it from other subsystems; (2) a parental subsystem with clear executive functions that may or may not involve other persons besides the spouses, but where at any rate the channels of authority are clear; and (3) a sibling subsystem that is free from enmeshment with both the spouse and the parental subsystems so the siblings may develop and grow under the protection, guidance, and appropriate authority of the parents.

To achieve these objectives, Minuchin has developed a creative variety of techniques ranging from direct education of the family members all the way to the occasional use of paradoxical suggestion, where the family interactional patterns are restructured within appropriate subsystem boundaries without the members' conscious understanding of how it happened. Minuchin uses himself actively and directly within the therapy sessions according to his assessment of the requirements of the situation. He may move people physically around his office or out of the office, and move himself physically as well to demonstrate and enact appropriate and inappropriate subsystem boundaries.

Minuchin cautions against preoccupation with therapeutic techniques—he believes that they should be studied with care and then consciously forgotten, so the educated practitioner can spontaneously meet the requirements of each unique therapeutic situation. He describes his own restructuring techniques in family therapy as belonging to three major categories: boundary making, unbalancing the current dysfunctional family structure, and complementarity (changing perceptions of hierarchical relationships within the family) (Minuchin & Fishman, 1981, p. 145).

Jay Haley

Like Satir, Jay Haley, a leading advocate for the approach generally known as *strategic*, was an early student of communication theory. He actively participated in the research that developed the concept of the double bind in interpersonal communication theory, described earlier in this section on Satir (Bateson et al., 1956). Like both Satir and Minuchin, Haley is an adherent of the family systems approach. Rather than search for intrapsychic causes for behavioral symptoms, he looks instead for interpersonal meanings of symptomatic behavior. For example, Haley views symptoms (such as certain illnesses, alcoholism, or phobias) as creative means for the sufferer to exert control in a relationship. Such unhealthy means for control would surely arise as a last resort and outside of the consciousness of the sufferer. Nevertheless, these symptoms constitute important interpersonal tactics for control in a relationship; the sufferers would not be able to give them up without meeting the need for control in some other way.

For example, a woman whose husband is engaging in a series of affairs may develop a severe physical illness that eludes exact diagnosis, but which forces the husband to come home at night to take care of her physical needs. The philandering husband's time is now required for shopping, housecleaning, and meal preparation. He no longer has enough time to conduct his extramarital affairs. The wife thus is able to regain control in her marital relationship. The cost to her is her health, a price she may be more than willing to pay to reclaim her husband. However, both she and her husband will be puzzled about the nature of the illness and concerned that she does not seem to be getting well. Doctors may call her a hypochondriac.

While Haley, in his strategic model of therapy, is interested in family communication patterns, his particular interest involves communication specifically in the present. How does current communication, both verbal and nonverbal, maintain the status quo (homeostasis) in the family? Haley consciously focuses narrowly on the presenting problem as it is brought to him by the family. He feels that this is the most powerful point of entry for family therapy. He works actively with the whole family to help them define the presenting problem clearly and distinctly. Then, he develops a specific plan to change the particular behavior that has been described as problematic. He uses directives or tasks to get the family to move beyond the present functioning that is maintaining the problem behavior. For example, one family's presenting problem was bedwetting by a young daughter. The father sided with the daughter against the mother—he felt that the mother should be more understanding. So the therapist assigned the father the task of washing the sheets every time his daughter wet the bed (Haley, 1963, p. 60).

Many systems-oriented therapists argue against "just curing a symptom" in family therapy. They argue that after one symptom is cured, another will crop up to fill the same function (maintaining the family homeostasis, or status quo) that the first symptom served. Haley's point of view, however, is that if the therapist can get a family to experience positive change, the family members will learn from the results of their actions. The learning can then be applied to further systems change. For example, in the case just mentioned, Haley's immediate strategy was to end the bedwetting. But the reason Haley believed the intervention would work involved a structural perspective. According to Haley's observation of the current interactions within this family, the father and daughter formed a subsystem that was "tighter" than either the parental subsystem (father and mother) or the spousal subsystem (husband and wife). By assigning the father the task of washing wet sheets, Haley assumed that the father would soon tire of the daughter's symptomatic behavior and would join with the mother in defeating it. To do so, the father would have to disengage from the daughter. This disengagement could then become the basis for further work, in which different tasks could be assigned to help the father and mother strengthen their own subsystems (parental and spousal). Work with the marital pair could then remove the need for the development of further symptomatic behavior by the daughter.

Even more than Minuchin's structural model, Haley's strategic therapy utilizes paradoxical directives in helping families change symptomatic behavior. The paradoxical approach is normally used only with families who consciously wish to change but who resist control by the therapist. They resist because unconsciously, the change they think they want is threatening to them in some way. Yet they have contracted for help. The therapist might find, for example, that for some apparently inexplicable reason a given family does not carry out the therapist's directives as assigned. In such a circumstance, Haley might experiment with paradoxical directives. Supposing, in the case above, the father forgets that his task is to wash his daughter's wet sheets, or the mother forgets that the father is supposed to do it and does the washing herself before he gets the chance. Haley might then *reframe* the bedwetting to the family as something the daughter is doing to help the parents in some way. Reframing is a therapeutic technique in which the meaning of problem behavior may be redefined as somehow good for the family system as a whole. (Reframing changes the conceptual and/or emotional setting or viewpoint in relation to which a situation is experienced and places it in another frame that fits the "facts" of the same concrete situation equally well, or even better, and thereby changes its entire meaning.)

In this case, the therapist might suggest that the daughter be encouraged to wet her bed because the bedwetting might just be the most important thing the couple has to talk about at the end of the day. The therapist might even tactfully suggest that if the girl were cured, the couple might grow bored with each other and split apart. This would be a terrible thing, and so the parents should be advised not to do anything to change the bedwetting behavior.

According to the theory behind paradoxical interventions such as these (actually, this is double-bind theory applied to the therapeutic intervention itself), if the family were to follow Haley's instructions as given, the bedwetting would continue; yet the parents cannot consciously consent to this directive. The parents cannot consciously let themselves think that the daughter's bedwetting is important to the preservation of their marriage. But to continue to resist the therapist's directives, as they have been doing so far, the parents have to cure the bedwetting! When the bedwetting is cured, the therapist must act puzzled and complimentary, saying that he doesn't know how the family has managed

to bring about this important change. (This helps stabilize the results.)

Ivan Boszormenyi-Nagi

Ivan Boszormenyi-Nagi's influence as a family therapist has been growing in recent years. In his early practice, he was not a systems-oriented theorist. Born in Hungary, Boszormenyi-Nagi was educated as a psychiatrist and psychoanalyst. Because of their medical training, psychiatrists tend to look for biological origins for symptomatic behavior. Psychoanalysts, on the other hand, are trained to look for intrapsychic origins of symptomatic behavior, believing that symptoms are manifestations of unconscious conflicts within the individual. Both models (medical and psychoanalytic) place heavy emphasis on the individual as the appropriate unit for analysis to understand symptomatic behavior.

Boszormenyi-Nagi emigrated to the United States in 1948. Several years later he began studying the origins of schizophrenia at the Eastern Pennsylvania Psychiatric Institute, which he founded in 1957. Given his medical background, Boszormenyi-Nagi originally searched for biological causes for the illness. When this research did not produce significant results, he gradually began to pay attention to the role of family dynamics in the development and maintenance of the disease.

Boszormenyi-Nagi was influenced by Erik Erikson's (1963) emphasis on the importance of trust in normal human psychological development (Erikson's "trust versus mistrust" developmental stage) and Martin Buber's (1958) emphasis on accountability in human interaction (Buber's I–Thou relationship). He began paying attention not only to families in their various nuclear and extended forms but also to multigenerational issues and themes, particularly those dealing with trust and accountability.

While remaining psychoanalytic in his basic orientation, Boszormenyi-Nagi began to view families from a systems perspective as well, appreciating the family as an organic whole composed of interacting parts, each one affecting all others—not only at a given time but over many generations.

Boszormenyi-Nagi (see Goldenberg & Goldenberg, 1991, pp. 103–108) identified a new dimension in family therapy that he believed was crucial to facilitate normal child development and healthy human behavior: the ethical dimension. He named his new approach *contextual therapy* to highlight that what happens in terms of ethical behavior in one generation affects the next. He believed that, whenever possible, therapy should be conducted with at least three generations present to help work out unaddressed issues of fairness and to reconcile family members of each generation.

From his research, Boszormenyi-Nagi believes that every family has a sense of who owes what to whom—a sort of multigenerational "family ledger." The family's bookkeeping system isn't strict or exact, but it does affect the "context" of daily life. For example, if the mother has put the father through medical school, there will be agreement in the family on some level that the father "owes" her. If he pays his debt via loyalty to the mother over the years, and perhaps even puts her through law school later, the ledger will be "balanced" and family members will have a sense of well-being. If he treats her badly, however—for example, abandons her emotionally on the excuse that she is no longer his intellectual equal—a sense of imbalance in the ledger may affect the next generation and beyond. Regardless of whether the source of psychological discomfort is known by later generations, Boszormenyi-Nagi believes that unresolved feelings of injustice may result in symptomatic behavior later.

Unresolved intergenerational issues may explain otherwise inexplicable incidents of symptomatic behavior. Boszormenyi-Nagi theorizes that every person experiences that family ledger as an assortment of unsettled accounts—accounts in which each individual owes or is owed. These accounts are funda-mentally psychological in nature. Among important accounts to be settled (debts and entitlements) are issues of family loyalty and obligations to maintain significant relationships. Family legacies may include the obligation to mistrust significant others, to fail at one's work, or to excel at all costs. The purpose of therapy is to uncover these legacies and free oneself by consciously "balancing the ledger." All family relationships must be reassessed in the process.

Problem-Solving Stages

Family therapy can be viewed as a process of problem solving in a systems context, and from this perspective can be seen to consist of different stages, although in the actual interview session these stages may not appear to be distinct and may actually take place at the same time. However, for the best cognitive understanding of the process, distinguishing the stages is helpful. The stages of the problem-solving process can be conceptualized as follows:

1. Initial information gathering
2. Assessing information
3. Defining the problem
4. Planning for action
5. Developing an explicit contract for action
6. Carrying out the action plan
7. Evaluating results; modifying action plan if necessary
8. Terminating when appropriate

At the initial interview, the anxious family may spill out the entire problem as they see it; or, at the opposite extreme, they may be unable to speak coherently at all. The initial session may be spent largely in helping the family feel comfortable in this new environment so that they can function more or less in their own normal manner. Of primary importance is building a relationship between the therapist and family that will involve essential trust and goodwill. The therapist can help by making sure that the physical office and furnishings are comfortable and pleasing to the eye, eliminating frightening barriers such as the huge desk that some professionals seem to feel safer thrusting between themselves and their clients. A desk, if needed, can be pushed into a corner and chairs can be placed so that other physical objects do not come between them (unless used for the therapeutic purposes, for example, to demonstrate visibly the invisible barriers that may separate family members). The therapist can also help build a trusting relationship by modeling a reachable, personal, and informal style of communication. The beginning part of the initial interview is usually a social session in which all participants get a feel for each other. An atmosphere of hope and goodwill can make the therapy session much less threatening. Virginia Satir (1967) suggested taking a structured family history during the initial interview or interviews. Since questions on a family history are reasonably predictable, this procedure may help the family members feel safer and more in control, while they reveal important information about themselves. For example, Satir asked couples how and when they met, and how and why they decided to marry each other in particular. She asked each spouse what his/her family of origin was like, including parents, siblings, and lifestyle. She asked what each spouse expected to get from marriage, and what early married life was actually like. She asked each spouse how their expectations of marriage, gleaned from their respective families of origin, affected their present marriage in its early stages. Satir continued to question each spouse about his or her significant experiences in marriage up to the present, so a smooth transition to present problems was usually possible (Satir, 1967, p. 135). Tactics for building trusting relationships are not fixed, and different therapists develop their own techniques over time.

As explained previously, when the therapist feels that the family is ready to enter into the problem-solving process, he or she will ask for initial information regarding the family's perception of the problem and why they have come for help. It is likely that the family members will then talk about their concern for or frustration with a particular member—the identified client. The therapist with a systems orientation will recognize that the problematic behavior of an identified client manifests strains involved in the effort to maintain the family system as it exists. Since maintaining the family system requires at least one of the members to develop behavioral problems, the therapist will hypothesize that "fixing the patient" alone won't work. Rather, the family interactional system itself, which has led to the development of the identified client's problem, will be the real target of any change effort. Family therapists have argued for years whether it is legitimate to contract with the client system to work on reducing the problems of the identified client. Since the therapist knows that the problems of the identified client cannot be modified for any significant period without change in the interaction and communication patterns of the entire family system, some family therapists argue that it is not legitimate to make an initial contract with a family to work on the problems of the identified client alone. Rather, these therapists believe that the family must be convinced to include their entire family pattern of interaction as a target for therapy from the very beginning.

Social workers as a profession, however, historically have taken the point of view that the most effective problem-solving interventive efforts can be achieved by "starting where the client is." If the family states that its problem is the identified client alone and wants help in problem reduction, a legitimate initial contract between family and therapist is working on the reduction of the client's problems. To accomplish problem reduction, change in the family system will have to be implemented anyway; and to maintain problem reduction, the change in the interaction patterns among members of the family system will have to be maintained. However, developing a family's understanding of its interactional patterns as a system takes time and demonstration, so the working out of a so-phisticated contract between therapist and family in the initial stages of therapy would probably be unwise anyway. The family would be unlikely to understand what they had agreed on and might submit to a contract involving change in family interactional patterns only under the influence of the therapist's authority, which they might then resent. It is legitimate to develop a limited initial contract involving problem reduction in an identified client as long as the family will agree that the entire family will take part in the therapy sessions, as sources of information, helpers, spectators, or whatever role initially appeals to the family members to get them there. When the family is together and trying to help solve the presenting problem, the therapist can begin to observe the family system at work and identify and understand the factors that led to the development of the problematic behavior.

Regardless of the content of the therapeutic contract, it is important to take time to discuss and establish a contract in the problem-solving process. The contract specifies the respective roles of the participants in therapy and is an initial working agreement, which can be renegotiated later as new facts shed light on a need for new contract terms. The contract specifies the "problem for work" as well as more mundane agreements such as fees, frequency, place of interviews, and so forth. The role of the therapist in any therapeutic contract is that of change agent. Skill will be essential in locating and manifesting the strains in the maintenance of the family system and in working out ways to teach and demonstrate to the family members the maladaptive elements in their communication patterns and new, healthier patterns. The therapist must be particularly careful not to get "sucked into" the family system, becoming in fact another member of the family who contributes to the maintenance of the pain-producing system (Minuchin & Fishman, 1981, pp. 161–162).

It may become apparent with time that other persons besides nuclear family members need to be included in some of the therapy sessions. A divorced spouse or a grandparent may wield strong influence that is not understood at the beginning of the family interviews. As described before, the family therapist will strongly attempt to have all family members included in the sessions, although very young children, approximately 3 years of age or younger, may not be included by some therapists except at the initial sessions and then on occasion later. Any disruptive behavior exhibited by the children during the family sessions provides valuable on-the-spot clues as to family rules, patterns of communication, and respective levels of self-esteem. Family interviews in the home setting can be extremely important in terms of understanding the meaning of certain patterns of family communication and behavior.

Beginning the Counseling Process

Let us return to the Whitlocks. Due to non-verbal cues of spatial position in the office, the family therapist has already formulated some initial hunches about family alliances. These hunches are based on visual data and hence are worth investigating, although only some will prove true. For example, the physical separation of the husband and wife, with the husband barely within the office, and the wife well inside, might tend to indicate an emotional distance between the two and indicate the relative positions of the marital pair within the family, one at the center and one on the way out, so to speak. The location of the older daughter (Pat, 14) close to the father and also near the door, might indicate that they form a coalition of some sort. The mother's holding the younger daughter's hand (Susan, 10) might indicate a similar close bond. Both sons maintain positions alone, and each further separates himself from family contact in a physical way—the younger son, George, 7, by staring at the floor and the older son, Lacey, 16, by looking out of the window and whistling. These cues also signal to the therapist the presence of family pain, felt in different ways and probably to different degrees by each member. It is likely that this family does not experience much closeness among its members as a total group; however, it is also possible that anxiety relating to this interview alone is precipitating the separation of various members of this family group.

An initial interview for family therapy is not a normal situation for the family, and hence their behaviors will not be normal; most likely "company manners" or anxiety will be exhibited.

When the therapist seats the family and asks the members to introduce themselves, even though the mother has already taken charge and done so for everyone, the therapist is structuring a new communication style that is important in family therapy to break old and unsatisfying patterns. Each family member needs to be permitted and needs to learn how to speak for himself or herself to minimize the amount of mind reading the other family members must do (so often inaccurately) and also to reduce the tendency of the family communication system to relegate a family member to a fixed position in the family structure that is not necessarily the one he or she wants.

When Pat Whitlock attempted to introduce herself, she found *p* a difficult sound to pronounce. After a second or two of stuttering, Mother broke in. "Now Pat, take a deep breath and speak slowly or you'll never learn to stop stuttering," Mother said in a loud, impatient voice. She turned to the therapist and explained: "Pat doesn't need to stutter. She never stutters when she takes a deep breath first and slows down. She just tries to say everything so fast." "We'll come back to Pat when she's ready," the therapist commented. "Pat, you tell me when you are ready," the therapist continued. And then the therapist went around to each member of the family

and asked for names. The therapist checked with Pat visually and learned that Pat was not yet ready to speak. She had a hunch that Pat needed to feel safe in order to use her tongue effectively. The therapist then turned to Mr. Whitlock. "Mr. Whitlock, I'm wondering what it is that you hope will change for you and your family." The statement by the therapist contains an embedded question that assumes that the father has hopes for change, which may not necessarily be the same as the mother's. The question is aimed intentionally at Mr. Whitlock because all too often in the American family, the male is excluded from important family transactions, partly because his primary work is considered to take place outside of the home. So much of virtually any American father's actual time is in fact spent outside of the home that his sporadic presence may actually be experienced as uncomfortable by other family members. Systematic adjustments will be made to maintain the normal interactional system as if the father were in fact still absent, which socially erases him. However, a wife and an absent husband do not form an intact marital pair, and the stability of the family system is endangered. The family may fall apart unless primary contact between the marital pair can be reestablished in some way. There is real danger that the father will actually continue his drift out of the mainstream of the family system until he formalizes the reality with desertion, divorce papers, perhaps even alcoholism, or in some instances "accidental" death.

Mr. Whitlock responded that the problem as he saw it was out of the province of the therapist to help. His daughter was having problems in school as his wife said, but he knew that she was an intelligent girl and she was just a little lazy this year. Lots of children go through periods of being lazy. That was the same reason she was fat—she just lacked self-discipline. She'd outgrow it. He wasn't really very concerned. What did bother him was his health. His stomach constantly bothered him. But, he repeated, he certainly didn't expect a family therapist to be much help with that. Moreover, he hated his job, and the therapist couldn't do anything about that either. These children all had to get to college, and the first one would start in two years. Time was passing too fast, and the savings account looked pretty inadequate to put four children through college. However, if his wife thought that therapy was important for Susan, and the agency said he had to come too, he wouldn't object. But he sure was upset about the cost. (Mr. Whitlock was already demonstrating potential for change—he was unhappy, he knew it, and when given an opportunity to express himself, words came out like a flood. But his attitude, while overtly cooperative, came across like that of a self-perceived martyr, who was good enough to sacrifice himself but who would let his family know subtly that he was being wronged.)

"Now, Daddy," interrupted Mother, "you know you're just being a hypochondriac about your stomach. The doctor says there's nothing wrong with you. And you've got a good job. We can afford whatever is important. You just always find something wrong with your boss, no matter who he is. And we're lucky all our children are bright and college material."

Mr. Whitlock spills out his words when elicited, the therapist notes, but Mrs. Whitlock has just cut him off. Is this by coincidence, or is it an ongoing pattern? This is something to check out over time.

The therapist now asks the oldest son what he experiences as a problem in the family. "The family's OK," he responds, "only Dad's always afraid I'm going to screw my girlfriend, and Mom doesn't like her because of her religion . . ."

"And," interrupts Mother, "she is skinny as a beanpole and she'll grow up to look worse, you can tell by what her own mother looks like. I can't imagine marrying a woman like that—that's why I keep my figure, so that the boys who date my girls can see that I'm . . ."

"But Mother," interrupts her son, "Who says that I'm going to marry her?"

"It's not a matter of wanting to marry her," Mother responds. "She just isn't the kind of girl who wouldn't try to trap you, just trap you—you're too young to understand . . ."

"I understand exactly what you mean," Lacey replies angrily. "You think she's going to seduce me. That's crazy. Anything I do I'll do of my own choosing."

"Well," says Mother, looking vacant. Silence ensues.

Older son can stop mother, the therapist notes. Father is silent and fidgeting.

Both parents are apparently worried about their older son's sexuality. How satisfactory is their own sexual relationship?

"How do you feel about Susan's problem?" the therapist asks Lacey. "She's OK, just a little too fat," he replies. "She'll be a knockout someday." "Anything else?" probes the therapist. "No, not particularly," responds Lacey.

The therapist turns to Pat and asks how she feels about the family situation. Pat begins to respond, "Susan isn't v-very happy when k-k-kids t-tease her. K-kids are mean, and I tr-try to k-k- . . ."

"Now Pat, take a deep breath . . ." says Mother.

The therapist intervenes, "Let Pat keep going. I'm interested in what she has to say. You find that kids are mean sometimes, Pat, and what do you try to do about it?" "Tr-try to k-k-keep to myself a lot. The gym t-t-teacher lets me run on th-the t-track by m-m-myself whenever I want t-t-to, and I run alone during study halls and by m-myself a lot after school. I hate school." Pat has said that she hates school clearly and effectively.

"You hate school, but you stay there when school is out in the afternoon?"

"Well, M-M-Mom w-w-won't let us stay in the house . . ."

Mother breaks in. "She just drives me crazy when she's home. All she does is sit in her room with the door closed and the radio blaring. Children need fresh air to stay healthy. I make her go out in the afternoon for her own good. All of the children have to keep out of the house to get their air after school. That's my job, to keep them healthy until they know better. They'll thank me someday. A woman's place is in the home."

"I see," responds the therapist. "But I don't believe that Pat is finished. Pat, go on."

"W-W-Well" says Pat, "th-th-that's ab-b-bout i-i-it."

Pat has been effectively silenced by Mother, notes the therapist. And she seems to stutter a little worse after each interruption.

"George," says the therapist, "Please feel free to share with us what you think hurts in your family."

"Aw," says George looking at his toes, and then he starts to cry. "George," says Father, "don't act like a baby." George drops his head and shoulders further.

Father has not scolded Pat, his apparent ally, for her stuttering. Mother has. But Father has ordered his youngest son to hide his feelings, just as Mother has ordered father to hide his own feelings. Is it possible that Father tries to maintain his self-esteem by putting down his youngest son?

"He-he-he-he's n-n-not acting l-l-like a b-baby," says Pat. Interestingly, Pat, although apparently part of a coalition with the father, is now allying herself with George, with considerable personal effort.

George stops crying but continues to look at his toes with an almost theatrically tragic look on his face. Even with encouragement by the therapist, he will not say a word. He does look up at the therapist once or twice with big moist eyes, a pathetic, almost dog-like expression warping his features.

"Susan," asks the therapist, "what makes you feel unhappy at times? I understand that sometimes you talk about being very unhappy, and that is why the family came here tonight." "Oh, not at home," gasps Susan. "I never say anything at home. My teacher told on me. I thought she wouldn't tell; she said she wouldn't ever get me in trouble with

Mom. And then she went and called Mom and she must have told her everything I said. I'm not going to talk to anybody anymore. People can't keep a secret. Nothing's the matter with me except I wish I weren't so fat. But Mom says sometimes she's so upset she might as well commit suicide, and nobody cares."

At this point Mother begins to cry loudly and insistently. "Now everybody's going to blame me for everything," she sobs, "and I'm only trying to help as best I know how. Here I work hard trying to get everybody in here for this appointment, and nobody here has even asked me what I think the problem is even though I tried to explain right when I got here. And now everybody's going to think everything is all my fault. Just listen to her, saying that I've threatened to commit suicide, like it was all my idea. Susan, you know I never meant it, and you are a very naughty child for talking about that here." (The session is overtaken by several minutes of loud sobbing by Mother. The therapist gets a box of tissues.)

Mother has now effectively shut off Susan, as she has shut off Father, George, and Pat. Only Lacey has been able to gain the upper hand with her in this session, but Lacey's life is clearly far from his own. Now is not the time to bring this communication pattern to the attention of Mother and the family. Mother, although she is effectively manipulating (controlling everyone's attention and silencing others), is genuinely hurting. At this time she will not be able to assimilate any information the therapist has already learned about the functioning of this family system and the roles the various members are playing that help maintain rather than alleviate family pain. The communication pattern within this family system, which inhibits the growth of most of its members, will need to be demonstrated over time by a therapist who can remain outside of its control. The family will have to be taught now to change its pattern of communication and personal interaction, with opportunities for concrete practice of the new patterns.

The usual introductory social phase of an initial interview has been virtually omitted in this particular session, because Mother immediately attempted to control the input of information to the therapist. The therapist has had to intervene immediately to model and elicit new communication patterns, asking for information from each family member directly rather than permitting that information to come through Mother. However, the phase of problem exploration and family interaction has yielded rich data for the therapist. Since, on this occasion, the therapist estimates that the family has already undergone as much stress as is a good idea in the initial interview (for the family may choose not to return to therapy if more fearful than hopeful), she will utilize the break in communication precipitated by Mother's crying to decrease the situational stress. The therapist's goal at this point, in recognizing a genuinely troubled family, is to enable the family to make a decision to return. Kleenex tissues, and reassurance of the mother that she is demonstrably capable, having produced four admirable children, will mollify Mother and reestablish her position of family dominance, which will return the family to its normal homeostasis. In future interviews the task will be instead to upset this same homeostasis, since it manifestly inhibits self-expression and personal growth in every member of the family. The therapeutic goal for the future will be to restructure the rules and interactional patterns of the family system into a more satisfying and growth-enhancing system, with higher rather than low morale or self-esteem among the members.

The basic purpose of an initial session is beginning problem definition, at least to the stage of the presenting problem; basic fact finding related to the presenting problems, which one hopes will reveal clues about contributing underlying systemic factors; and helping the family to begin to trust the therapist. The therapist and family also need to work out a tentative initial contract, defining the initial "problem for work," the respective roles of the therapist and family, specification of who will be included in the interviews, fees, places of meeting, frequency and time of appointments, and so forth.

In the latter part of this initial interview, the therapist will help reduce the family's (particularly the Mother's) fear of family therapy by helping them see the therapist's role as that of helper rather than judge. She can reassure the family that when there is pain present, it is reasonable and normal to seek outside consultation to gain relief. Many families have indeed been able to benefit by working on their problems together, she will point out, and she has noted many family strengths that make their particular situation look hopeful as far as potential for improvement is concerned. The therapist will list these strengths: intelligence, caring, ability to work hard, sense of responsibility, ability to present thoughts verbally (and the clear potential for those less comfortable with speaking, Pat and George, to develop the ability to do so).

The therapist will then help the family develop an initial commitment to therapy. Is the family willing to invest the time and effort necessary to make their family circumstances better? Can the family afford the fee (perhaps a sliding scale is available to alleviate worries about cost). If the family is willing to enter into a contract to meet with the therapist for general improvement of family functioning, this is a useful and open-ended agreement. If the family is willing to meet with the therapist only on the more limited problem of learning how to help Sue, this is a valid contract also. If the entire family will agree to meet together regarding how to help Sue, then Sue becomes the key to working with the family. Later, the therapist may recontract with the parents: for example, "It is becoming clearer that Sue's unhappiness has something to do with the fact that you, Mr. Whitlock, and you, Mrs. Whitlock, are not very happy yourselves, and that you sometimes are not happy about certain things concerning each other. I think it would be a good idea to talk about you and your relationship together. How about it?" When Mr. and Mrs. Whitlock have come to trust the therapist and her concern for them, they will more likely be willing to admit that they have a problem between themselves.

The Whitlocks clearly have the capacity for change, but there are indications that change will be difficult. For one thing, commitment to therapy is low. Mr. Whitlock indicates feelings of hopelessness and he believes the important things that are stressing his life (the pain in his stomach, the endless need to earn money, his dissatisfaction with his job) cannot possibly be changed through family therapy. He believes therapy can only cause him more pain (it costs money). Mr. Whitlock has said that he isn't worried abut Sue. From his point of view at the commencement of therapy, therapy is only an unnecessary new financial pressure.

Mrs. Whitlock is threatened by therapy, because already in the first interview her preferred patterns of family communication have been disturbed. She is the controlling member of the family. Yet she has felt a bigger threat from outside. That threat is her fear of loss of social standing if one of her products (her child, Sue) should be labeled defective by a highly visible outside institution, the school. So Mrs. Whitlock's commitment to therapy does not initially involve a desire to bring about any change in herself or her lifestyle; rather, she wants to have her daughter straightened out.

Continuing the Counseling Process

For a therapist to work effectively with the Whitlock family (or any family), he or she will have to create a safe setting for interaction, a setting in which all members will be able to reduce their fearfulness and will recognize that their attempts at communication will be received empathetically and nonjudgmentally. Reducing fear reduces the need for defensiveness. The therapist will need to structure the interviews with certain rules that will help decrease the threat for all members, from very basic ones such as "no hitting," to more complex ones such as "each person here speaks for herself or himself." The therapist needs to demonstrate for the family that difficult material will be treated with care, and that privacy, when any family member feels the need, will be respected. This means that some counseling sessions may be held with only certain family members or subsystems present, if there is a clear need and purpose. The therapist needs to know how to ask for information in such a way that the person is enabled to answer. Questions that a family member may not feel safe to answer early in therapy may be necessary and possible later when trust is firmer. Techniques such as the use of embedded questions, which clearly verbalize the therapist's question without demanding or otherwise putting the client "on the spot," are helpful as are questions that ask for a description or clarification rather than a simple yes or no answer (although the simple yes or no question can be very helpful with fearful clients before rapport is established, because these questions require less energy, and generally clients feel they are safer to answer).

A feeling of safety in the therapeutic setting can also be enhanced by the therapist's demonstrating that he or she is not afraid of discussing or observing issues that are emotion laden and by offering support to family members as they experience the fears, stresses, and strains of life itself and of the experience of therapy. The therapist must also be able to demonstrate that he or she will not be sucked into the family system with its destructive operational patterns. Use of a cotherapist on occasion can be very helpful in avoiding the pitfall of becoming too intimate a part of the family system rather than a change agent for the system. Also useful is a one-way mirror through which a consultant may watch the session as it happens. The interview can be taped or videotaped so that the therapist, the family, or both can study it later.

Family interactional patterns and rules will resist change. This is the nature of systems, as discussed earlier in this chapter. Merely "diagnosing" the nonfunctional behavior patterns and communication systems and telling the family members about them will not be sufficient to create change. The family needs more than an intellectual grasp of their respective roles in maintaining dysfunctional family patterns. However, the therapist must understand the patterns and rules of the ongoing family system if he or she is to select appropriate intervention techniques to change the system. Hence the therapist will need to observe how the family interacts, so he or she will insist that the family members talk with each other in the sessions. Where an identified client or scapegoat is present, the therapist will try to understand the function of that individual in maintaining the system.

Often, the term *scapegoat* is used in a more limited sense than the term *identified client*. A child identified as a scapegoat is usually a child *blamed* by the family for a series of misdemeanors that make the family angry at him or her: bad behavior, instigating family arguments, and so forth. The term *identified client* includes the scapegoat, but may also include children whom the family do not apparently blame for creating problems for anybody except themselves. They merely see the child as having embarrassing or self-destructive problems, such as obesity, suicidal tendencies, and anorexia nervosa.

In the Whitlock family, Susan is clearly the identified client, but why Susan, and what function does she perform? There are other persons in the family who seemingly could have been presented as the identified client: Pat, for one, because of her stuttering and extreme social discomfort, and Father, for another, because of his feelings of hopelessness and his physical problems, which appear to be psychosomatic in origin (that is, largely caused by stress). It is probable that Sue became the identified client in this case because she is manifesting Mother's own fantasies, "committing suicide."

If the model used for therapy with this family were purely strategic as in Jay Haley's approach, in the first session Susan's symptoms would have been highlighted more specifically as the immediate problem for work. Susan's presenting symptomatic behaviors would have been more deeply explored and outlined in detail: staying at home during many school days, doing poor work at school, overeating, and talking about suicide. A specific plan to change these behaviors would have been developed. For example, the therapist might have directed Susan to stay home from school every day for the first week between sessions; Susan might have been directed to talk about suicide with Mother every day, but only between the hours of 9 and 10 A.M. The therapist would be acting on the theory that this would allow Susan to stay home. Then, as a part of expected behavior, she would be practicing obedience. The fearful pull of suicide would be reduced by getting that topic right out into the open, yet discussion of suicide would be confined to one hour per day. Mother, as a responsible parent, would feel constrained to tell Susan that she herself had no intention of committing suicide; Mother would come up with all sorts of reasons to persuade Susan that Mother would not really do such a thing, and that Susan should not consider doing such a thing either. Under close scrutiny, the "pull" of suicide as a means of problem solving (gaining attention) would be exposed as inadequate (the perpetrators wouldn't be around to enjoy the attention they would receive).

Under the strategic therapy model, how the task was carried out (and the results) would be discussed in detail at the next family therapy session. Further tasks would then be assigned as needed to interrupt Susan's symptomatic behaviors. The therapist would hope that this type of work would lead into therapy with the married couple, Mr. and Mrs. Whitlock.

The Whitlocks' therapist does not use a purely strategic model, however. She chooses to begin with a structural approach combined with techniques derived from the communication model. She chooses to study patterns of interaction within the family as a whole to determine what factors are helping maintain Susan's symptomatic behavior. Further interviews reveal that Mother feels very stressed and unappreciated within the family, even though she clearly occupies the position of dominant parent, and in that role is the key to the family pain. Mother can make the decisions in this family. But what factors led to this situation?

Mother, the only child of elderly parents, learned when she was young that she could get anything she wanted by making enough noise about it. When a direct request was often ignored—because her parents tended to be tired or involved in community issues—asking, insisting, tears, and finally temper tantrums always worked if carried on long enough. Hence Mother learned to get the attention she needed by demanding it, and her demands were effective for her in that setting. Father, on the other hand, was a middle child in a large family controlled by a very dominant male parent. Father wasn't able to get what he wanted, either materially or in terms of affection, no matter what he did, and so he tended to withdraw and feel hopeless during much of his childhood. He made the most gains with his own father when he was visibly obedient, so Father tended to repeat the role of the good child within his family of procreation because they worked best for him as a child. But it didn't meet his needs very well in either situation, and as an adult he still feels helpless and hopeless. From the perspective of Boszormenyi-Nagi's contextual approach, Father feels that he was shortchanged as a child in terms of appreciation and nurturing, and that these are due, and owed to him, now. Because they are not forthcoming, either from his parents or his wife, he tends to play a martyr role.

The combination of a demanding, blaming wife and a withdrawn, compliant, and placating husband developed into an increasingly rigid system within the Whitlock family. Mrs. Whitlock kept right on demanding, and on the surface of things, she got everything she wanted; Mr. Whitlock did her bidding. He was able to send effective messages to his wife, however, that he did not appreciate how he was treated, that he did not deserve the treatment, and that he did not like Mrs. Whitlock very much because of how she treated him. Mr. Whitlock felt used and unappreciated, but Mrs. Whitlock felt lonely and misunderstood. A new family system developed in which everyone's self-esteem remained low and rules were rigid (set by the mother). In the family rules for communication that developed, everything had to go through Mother and be approved by her before communication was considered valid. This type of system tended to feminize all the members of the family (speaking in terms of feminine sex-role training as culturally tending to be in the direction of impulse control, inhibition, passivity, and dependence on the parents, in this case the mother). All males in the Whitlock family, at the time of entrance to therapy, were responding by withdrawing in one way or another, and, in fact, Pat was also. Only Susan was emotionally bonded with Mrs. Whitlock.

It is interesting to note how the cultural norms for expected male and female gender role behaviors and means for achieving personal happiness have affected the Whitlocks' life and emotions, helping produce some of the unhappiness and confusion of various family members. Mother is not happy but she cannot openly admit her unhappiness to herself and thus examine the causes, because she is doing exactly what she has been taught she should want to do: be a wife and a mother. Mother has also had exactly the number of children she thought she wanted (two more than her husband wanted). A bright woman, she has read most of the literature circulated among her generation of mothers, which extolled the virtues of bright young women bearing large families, to maintain the quality of the population. The children she produced are all bright and physically attractive. She thinks she ought to feel happy, and spends a lot of energy telling herself and everybody else how happy she is and what a fine family she has. Happiness and a fine family are important status symbols to Mother because her culture says that these products are her means of achieving personal importance. However, when the children or husband try to defy her strong will, she feels desperate and deserted and breaks into tears, threatening to commit suicide because "nobody cares about me around here." Since four children and one husband add up to five against one, even with Mother the very dominant and controlling personality, incidents of defiance do occur with reasonable regularity. However, Mother's tears, angry words, and accusations usually bring her the desired results. She wins each battle at the price of standing alone—nobody dares to get emotionally near to her. All defend themselves against her. Mother's closest emotional bond is with her 10-year-old daughter, Sue, who feels her mother's loneliness. Sue becomes fearful of leaving Mother (does poorly in school, stays home from school a lot), talks about suicide with her teacher when she does attend school (the environment in which she consciously feels the most stressed), and overeats. Sue's problem then has the function of manifesting Mother's unhappiness as well as her own. Moreover, Sue does not feel especially wanted by her father. She does not think her father likes her very much and knows her existence is a financial burden to him.

Sue's problems are the ones recognized within the family quite simply because Mother is the parent with the power to recognize them. She is the dominant parent and thus can make the decision to take Sue to therapy when virtually nobody else wants to go. Mother will want to help Sue because she feels a bond with Sue. She will not necessarily recognize that Sue's problems reveal her own distress, although this realization comes very close to the surface in the first interview.

Further interviews reveal that Mr. Whitlock consciously feels alienated from and an-

gry with his wife. He feels she has put him in an impossible position. He hates his work but knows he has to work to support his family. Society teaches him that monetary support of the family is up to him, or he is a failure. He feels responsible to support his children now that they are born, but he wishes they hadn't been born, particularly Sue and George, because he felt overburdened already after the birth of the first two. He feels stuck, and because Mrs. Whitlock made him have a large family, everything is her fault. To do his duty to his family, he will have to continue to do work he dislikes forever. He is extremely resentful about it, toward his wife and the children too. He cannot express his resentment toward his wife overtly because she is too powerful—she verbally puts him down whenever he tries to express his resentment, or she bursts into tears and threatens suicide. Besides, she can make him feel very guilty about his wish to have had fewer children. How can he not want George and Sue? Sometimes Mr. Whitlock expresses his resentment toward his children in subtle ways—by criticizing Lacey's relationship with his girlfriend or George's hypersensitivity. Mr. Whitlock is also developing somatic problems—taking out on his own body what he cannot express against the significant others in his life. This happens because his constant tension affects his body chemistry.

Continued therapy sessions reveal clear coalitions or subsystems within the family: Father and Pat, Mother and Susan, Mother and Lacey (not as strong), Pat and George, which occasionally conflicts with Pat and Father. Father has little or no relationship with Lacey, because of competition for influence with the mother. Lacey can get his way with Mother more than Father can. Mother respects Lacey more than Father as Lacey is a successful leader at school and a social success, although she disapproves of all the girls he dates. Father avoids George and Susan; he feels too tired to play with them when he comes home from work, and they are still little enough that at times they ask for his attention. Mother has little or no relationship with Pat, except to criticize her social awkwardness, her stuttering, and her appearance. Mother does not think Pat is a very good family showpiece. She is obviously awkward.

The normal *natural* subsystems do not manifest themselves in this family. The husband-wife, or spouse, subsystem exists only minimally—Father brings home the income and Mother takes care of the housework and the children. Emotionally they do not satisfy each other's basic needs, and each feels resentful about what he or she is not getting (appreciation, love, and so forth). To use Boszormenyi-Nagi's perspective, each feels unjustly treated, and the ledger is not balanced. However, Mr. and Mrs. Whitlock are also both fearful of completely losing each other, the only scrap of adult sustenance they have. Once Mother did run off with Sue to her father's home, terrifying Mr. Whitlock that he would be left having to hire a babysitter to take care of George. She came home, however, and no one spoke of the incident thereafter until it finally came up in therapy. Mrs. Whitlock had hoped that her leaving would make Mr. Whitlock more attentive, but after the first stir, nothing changed. Mr. Whitlock felt he was already doing more than could be reasonably expected of him in terms of holding up his end of the family bargain. Only Mr. Whitlock's fear of the unknown and his strong conservative values kept him from leaving his family. He felt he did not love Mrs. Whitlock any longer, although he didn't admit it to her. He had not attempted a sexual relationship for years; she demeaned him as being impotent. In fact, anger and fear of another pregnancy created Mr. Whitlock's main sexual problem. Being ignored sexually, of course, effectively communicated to Mrs. Whitlock her husband's displeasure with her.

The children do not form a normal subsystem, either. Only Pat and George have even a minimal bond between them, and this is actually a substitute parent bond. Neither Mr. nor Mrs. Whitlock feels close to George—each has other favorites. George is alone ex-cept for Pat; their relationship has to be parental in nature as Pat is seven years older. However, she cannot provide George with much protection, since no one can stand up to Mother's anger except Lacey. The isolation is frightening for the little boy, and when he began therapy he was effectively speechless. Mother's dominance had, in fact, kept all the children separate. She would not permit the children to have any sort of conflict in her presence, which developed an emotional separation among all the children. Rather than help the children solve problems of conflict together, so they could learn how to communicate and to resolve their differences constructively, she separated them and punished them individually for taking part in a quarrel. She also would not permit the children to stay inside the house during the day except to do chores, because they irritated her. The children actually did not have much time together. Mr. Whitlock, although he often disapproved of his wife's parenting when he was present to observe it, rarely offered any parenting of his own, corrective or otherwise. Lacey had no strong relationship with any sibling, nor did Susan. It was every child for himself or herself.

Restructuring the Family System

In this household full of relatively isolated individuals, the family subsystems need restructuring. The husband-wife bonds needs to be strengthened and made primary to provide the protection and nurturance the children need. The lopsided dominance relationship between Mr. and Mrs. Whitlock needs to be more of a relationship of equals. While the cultural mores call for the male to be dominant, and Mr. Whitlock's suffering in his subordinate position in this family is only increased due to the perceived gap in what he sees as his reality and the cultural ideal, the family need is not male dominance. What is needed is a relationship in which the needs of both parents are more nearly equally met. Each spouse needs to feel treated in a just, ethical manner by the other. By apparently meeting all the dominance needs of Mrs. Whitlock and none of those of the father, both parents are isolated and both are suffering, along with the children. Mr. Whitlock's essential feelings of suffering revolve around hopelessness and helplessness and being stuck as an overburdened economic provider. Mrs. Whitlock's essential feelings of suffering revolve around loneliness and the sense of not being loved or appreciated.

The parent subsystem has been truncated in this family so it effectively consists of Mother only. Father has withdrawn into his depression and somatic complaints. The parent subsystem needs restructuring and strengthening so it includes both parents.

Moreover, the boundary between the spouse subsystem and the sibling subsystem is enmeshed. Mrs. Whitlock and Lacey, and Mr. Whitlock and Pat, are more involved emotionally than the two spouses themselves are with each other. Such a lack of boundary between the spouse subsystem and the sibling subsystem can only be frightening and confusing to the children and to the marital pair as well.

The children could benefit by a strengthening of their subsystem as well. If the bonds among the children were stronger, or their bonds with peers outside the family were stronger, their dependence on the emotional situation between their parents would not be so profound.

Restructuring a family system is a difficult task. Certain techniques can help a family prepare for change, however. Family members can watch themselves interact on videotape, which can sensitize them to how they come across to other people. Even an audiotape recording can be very helpful for this purpose. Virginia Satir (1972) suggested problem-solving vignettes are relatively nonthreatening because they describe the problems of other people, and each family member is asked to choose a solution independently. Then the family members must compare their responses and come to an agreement on a group approach. In this way family coalitions are revealed but the family also has the opportunity to observe their own coalitions explicitly and can learn how to compromise effectively in a situation where nobody is going to lose anything perceived as vital.

Family members can also be separated from the rest of the family and allowed to observe family interaction patterns from behind a one-way mirror. Or, a subgroup can sit behind the rest of the family as they interact, in the role of observers. At the end of the specified interaction, the persons in the subgroup can provide feedback to the family on the communication patterns they observe.

The therapist can have various members of the family group reenact conflicts through role play. Role play brings the conflicts right into the therapy room. But in role-play situations, there is opportunity to reconstruct the scenes. The therapist may choose to model more constructive ways of handling conflict, or may instruct the family members to reenact the scene but perform different or reversed roles. The therapist may have a child play the role of a parent in instances where discipline is an issue, may have the respective parent play the child, and so forth. Role play offers the possibility of practicing new and more constructive methods of conflict resolution and of developing empathy for the other person's point of view.

In the therapy sessions, the therapist may choose to escalate stress in order to break a nonproductive stalemate in a family conflict. Escalation of stress can temporarily break an unhealthy pattern of interaction. For example, in the Whitlock family situation, the therapist can choose to side with Father on every issue until Mother explodes; the therapist can then deal with the function of tears and threats, and discuss and demonstrate other means of conflict resolution. The therapist may choose to side with the mother on every issue until the father is goaded into changing his habitual pattern of being the placater and martyr and will finally become angry enough to defend himself. The therapist can then observe his method of expressing angry feelings and will be able to learn why they are normally so ineffective in the particular family. New methods of self-assertion may be discussed, demonstrated, and practiced (Minuchin & Fishman, 1981, p. 179).

The therapist may take on an educator's role with the family, explaining how apparent success at dominating and getting what a person wants in the short run can rob him or her of the goodwill of significant others, eventually resulting in isolation (no one left to dominate), as was happening between Mr. and Mrs. Whitlock. However, to fortify the intellectual understanding, simulation and role play games can be utilized.

Virginia Satir (1972), for example, used family structuring and communication games in which she had appropriate members of the family model the stance and non-verbal gestures of the placater, the blamer, the computer, and the distractor (Satir, 1972, pp. 59–79). With the Whitlock family, Mrs. Whitlock would initially be assigned the role of the blamer. The therapist would help her position her body so that the nonverbal symbols of blaming would be highlighted and magnified—the pointed finger, twisted face, and so forth. Mr. Whitlock would be arranged as the placater, kneeling, open hand upward, and so forth. Lacey could be assigned the role of distractor, looking off in an irrelevant direction, whistling, and so on, and Pat the computer (stiff body, upright spine). The next step is to act out the corresponding roles. Satir suggested role playing the communication stereotypes in triads, keeping sessions to approximately five minutes in length. The family is to choose the problem to communicate about, but each role player must stick to his or her role in a given role-play situation. The blamer must blame, physically and verbally. The placater must apologize for anything and everything and agree with the blamer that he or she is unworthy of living. The distractor must toss in irrelevant words and gestures. The computer must mouth logical positions irrelevant to the emotional components of the situation. After five minutes, roles should be shifted. The game should continue until every family member has played all the roles. This may take hours, depending on family size, but Satir felt that this is an excellent and intensive way of demonstrating to family members how the various roles feel, how to shift to a new method of interaction, and what that feels like.

The very humor of some of the games, and the surprises revealed through observing themselves on audiotape or videotape, can help loosen the rigid defenses of the individual family members and break up the rigidity of the old communication patterns. For example, among the Whitlocks, a communication pattern existed in which Mrs. Whitlock played blamer, Mr. Whitlock placater, and the children shifted between the placater and the distractor roles in the real family situation. Through practice and demonstration, they were able to loosen these patterns toward the more ideal interaction pattern that Satir called "leveling" or "telling like it is."

In the case of the Whitlock family, Mother also created a typical double-bind situation for all family members. She told them that people shouldn't speak unless they had something pleasant to say. She also told them people worth their salt were honest and should be frank, like herself. If she then asked a family member to express an opinion on something she had done (which she often did: "Look at the new dress I made; what do you think of it?") in order to get some needed attention, she placed the person she addressed in a double bind if that person did not like the dress. If the person lied and said the dress was lovely, then that person was worthless. If the person was frank, Mother would feel unappreciated and would become angry. If was a "damned if you do, damned if you don't" communication system.

Because Mrs. Whitlock so often placed the other family members in a double-bind situation, the other family members had learned to avoid attempting real communication with her. They became experts at evasiveness ("I'm sure you must have worked hard on it, Mother"), or at disappearing, either through silence, stuttering, or through activities away from home. Lacey generally chose the latter by remaining as uninvolved as possible. The toll was great, even on Lacey, because he lost the nurturance and protection a family should provide. Moreover, Mother was openly critical of all his friends, and Lacey couldn't silence her all the time. Mother recognized that Lacey preferred his friends to her.

The toll was also great on Mother. Nobody leveled with her and she knew it, driving her to distress. She had no idea she created double binds and thus had no idea of her own role in driving her family away. She could learn to identify the setup, however, through the use of audiotapes, videotapes, and role-play, and she could then decide which she really wanted most—a real relationship with her family or placation and rote obedience. Mother will need courage and persistence to break her patterns of relationship. It is hard to change, and besides, a dominant role provides a lot of immediate rewards.

The therapist was also able to identify a destructive family communication "loop" involving Mother. Mother usually had to initiate verbal exchange if she wanted verbal communication, due to the various types of withdrawal of the rest of the family system. But then when Mother succeeded in eliciting a response, she would criticize it, precipitating a new withdrawal response. The new withdrawal response would anger Mother, and she would further criticize, usually couched in language of "I'm only telling you this because I love you." Her words were of love, but her voice tone and facial expression were of anger. Family members generally believed the visual communication cues rather than the verbal, and responded as if attacked: Lacey by attacking in return, the others by further withdrawal, precipitating a new destructive communication loop, with Mother forcing a new response to try to maintain con-

tact, being displeased with the response, and criticizing it. Pat and George effectively solved this problem by being unable to speak in their own various ways, so it was harder for Mother to "hook" them. Not surprisingly, Mother felt closer to Lacey and Susan.

To break the loop, all family members had to recognize it intellectually. Then they had to practice new patterns of communication, using techniques of role-play and modeling by the therapist. Mrs. Whitlock's control of the communication process had to be blocked. The process took a great deal of energy and commitment from the family. The person for whom new self-assertion was hardest was Mr. Whitlock, because he honestly felt he was being "a good guy" by letting Mrs. Whitlock run her show the way she thought she wanted it. He had to understand that she was in pain too before he could permit himself to alter his placater role. Moreover, he had never successfully attempted any other role in his life. He had to begin to believe that his own feelings were important, that he wasn't being a good guy, but rather dishonest and lazy by withdrawing from the household, and that he wasn't totally stuck with his unsatisfactory life. He could make a change. (He had to learn emotionally to understand that Mrs. Whitlock's control over him was not as truly invincible as his father's had been when he was a small boy.)

The therapist assigned tasks to Mr. Whitlock and Mrs. Whitlock that they were to do together without the children to strengthen their marital bond. Lacey was old enough to baby-sit, so the parents were instructed to go away together on several different weekends, all by themselves, leaving Lacey in charge.

The therapist was able to engage the couple in a discussion of their lengthy sexual abstinence, and brought the factor of fear of pregnancy out into the open. Fear of pregnancy was discussed early in the therapeutic process, and Mr. and Mrs. Whitlock were able to agree on sharing responsibility for birth control. Fortunately they did not have to cope with negative religious values in this area.

Some sexual activity resumed. Later in the therapeutic process, as part of discussions of the functions of sex in the marriage as a means of communicating approval or disapproval, Mr. Whitlock was able to realize that he was equally responsible with his wife for procreating four children. Gradually he was able to let go of most of his resentment toward his wife for "insisting" on having the children. In fact, Mr. Whitlock had chosen to go along with her desires and could instead have exerted the energy to refuse to participate in conception. In the case of the Whitlocks, the wife had never deliberately deceived her husband through, for example, "forgetting" to use her means of contraception and "accidentally" conceiving children. She had been emotionally powerful enough to secure her husband's voluntary (if grudging) cooperation. It was later on that Mr. Whitlock's growing resentment manifested itself in sexual abstinence. (In family therapy, some therapy sessions may be scheduled with particular family subsystems if there is a special purpose. Most of Mr. and Mrs. Whitlock's therapeutic sessions surrounding their sexual lives together were conducted with the husband-wife subsystem.)

Lacey's baby-sitting responsibilities involved him more closely with the sibling system without bringing him in competition with Mrs. Whitlock. Attention from Lacey was pleasing to all the children and helped strengthen the sibling system. Another related task the therapist assigned was for Mrs. Whitlock to take time outside of her family system without her children, leaving Mr. Whitlock in charge, strengthening his bond with the children and weakening her total dependence on child rearing as her only meaning in life. The therapist also met with Sue and her teacher (as soon as possible after the commencement of the family counseling) to discuss means for overcoming her fear of school. A "big sister," who also acted as a tutor, was found for her.

The family as a whole discussed with the therapist their various future hopes for themselves. It became clear that Pat in particular was not excited about going to college but would prefer to work in a music store for a while. She thought she might want to go to college someday but was willing to save some money in advance for it. However, she had been certain her parents would insist on college attendance right after high school and hence resented rather than appreciated her parents' real financial sacrifice in her behalf as they tried to save ahead for her college expenses. George and Sue were too young to know what they thought about college, but Mr. and Mrs. Whitlock were able to recognize that their preoccupation with college for their children was more their own expectation (reflecting a societal status symbol) than a necessity. Lacey did want to go to college right after high school but was willing to pay some of his own expenses. He enjoyed the idea of contributing to his own support. He hadn't wanted his father to pay for his college expenses anyway, even before coming to therapy, because he had felt so alienated from his father, whom he perceived as an unhappy and ineffective man. However, Lacey hadn't been able to tell anybody about these feelings before. Now that the children could talk about their feelings in a safe place, and could work out ways of dealing with them, they could release themselves from their restrictive and rigid roles in their destructive family myth—that everybody had to do what was expected, from saying the right things on command to going to college when and where expected.

None of the children wanted Father to continue working at a job he hated so much. They felt responsible for his misery and helpless to change it. Mother was also able to recognize that Father's unhappiness more than canceled out the benefits of his reliable and adequate income. Moreover, Mrs. Whitlock was able to recognize that she did not enjoy being in the home all day herself, that maybe her place wasn't totally in the home, and that perhaps she could better utilize her time and energy by helping provide part of the family income. Once Mrs. Whitlock could recognize her irritation with child rearing without guilt, the family could make some shifts in its linkage with the economic market. Mr. Whitlock changed to a lesser paying job that allowed him more freedom and personal creativity, which he craved. Mrs. Whitlock took on a part-time job, which both demanded and provided emotional energy, thus reducing her demands on her children to supply her meaning in life. She was also able to help reduce the financial pressures in the family through producing her own income. Now the family ledger was more evenly balanced; each spouse was clearly receiving as well as giving. The children began to understand that seemingly hopeless circumstances could indeed be changed and that they could influence their own futures. They began to take themselves seriously, and the family began to pull together.

Maintenance of Gains and Termination of Counseling

While family therapy can often be effectively completed in a few weeks, the problems of the Whitlocks required a longer time to resolve. Therapy for the family continued for approximately a year, until Mr. Whitlock was established in a new job and Mrs. Whitlock was working part-time and able to release her rigid control on the family system. Important changes had taken place and were being maintained. Lacey was working part-time, saving for college, and Pat was seriously visiting music stores with an eye toward future employment. She still stuttered somewhat but was no longer being reprimanded for it. Susan was attending school regularly, doing average work scholastically, and no longer talking of suicide. George was talking, at least occasionally. Mr. and Mrs. Whitlock regularly took time to do things as a couple, and while they still disagreed with each other frequently, they could talk with each other about their feelings and work out compromise solutions. At this point, termination of therapy became appropriate.

Termination itself requires preparation, so that the family system will not revert to its old patterns of interaction, brought on by distress precipitated by the withdrawal of the person (the therapist) who has been actively intervening to restructure the system. Discussion of termination must begin well in advance of its actual occurrence. Mutual evaluations by the family members of where they came from at the beginning of therapy, where they are now, and where they would like to be ideally can be helpful. Assurance by the therapist of continued availability should the family feel the need is also helpful. A gradual tapering off of interview sessions—for example, from once a week to once every two weeks, with a final meeting a month or so later may help reduce regression. (For further information on termination and evaluation, see Chapters 6, 7, and 11.)

Summary

This chapter describes social work practice with families. A wide diversity of family patterns exists in the world. Although the nuclear family is still the predominant family form in our society, it is a serious mistake for social workers to use the nuclear family as the ideal model that individuals should strive to form. There are many other family forms that are functioning well and that deserve respect.

Family patterns and forms are substantially affected by the culture (larger system) in which they are located. Families in our society perform the following functions that help maintain the continuity and stability of society: replacement of the population, care of the young, socialization of new members, regulation of sexual behavior, and provision of affection.

An infinite number of problems may occur in families. When there are problems in a family, social services are often needed. There is extensive variation in the types and forms of services that are provided by social workers to troubled families.

The two areas in social work practice with families that have received the most attention are family assessment and family therapy. Two assessment techniques are described: eco-maps and genograms. An eco-map provides a snapshot view of important family interactions at a particular point in time. A genogram, which is essentially a family tree, is a graphic way of investigating the origins of family problems over at least three generations.

One of the many social services provided to families is family therapy. In this chapter family therapy is defined. Characteristics of open and closed family systems are described. Coalitions and alliances between subsystems and members of subsystems are discussed, as well as ideas of how and why certain subsystems are formed and how behaviors of particular subsystems affect behaviors in others. The role of the identified client and/or scapegoat in helping maintain unhealthy family homeostases and in serving as somewhat socially acceptable tickets of admission to therapy is explored and discussed in detail.

Four approaches to family therapy are described and compared: those of Satir, Minuchin, Haley, and Boszormenyi-Nagi. Satir stressed clarification of family communication patterns. Satir pointed out incongruent messages and double binds to family members and taught family members to send clear, congruent messages instead. She analyzed rules in the family and helped clarify them in the context that rules may be bad but the people setting or bound by them are not. She taught family members how to change bad rules and insisted each member be heard in her presence, thus teaching respect for each person and each point of view. She em-

phasized that differentness between family members should be openly acknowledged and used for growth.

Minuchin's major emphasis in therapy is restructuring the major subsystems (spouse, parental, and sibling) within the family so that each may accomplish its appropriate functions. Minuchin is considered a member of the *structural* approach to family therapy. According to Minuchin, the parental, the spouse, and the sibling subsystems have different major functions that must be fulfilled if the family is to survive as a healthy unit. In restructuring the family Minuchin may seek to have members consciously understand and improve communication patterns. Or, he may bypass direct cognitive understanding by a family of its communication patterns and instead use a paradoxical suggestion.

Haley's approach involves clear definition and description of the presenting problem and the assigning of specific tasks or directives to solve the presenting problem. With resistive families, paradoxical directives may be used, with the therapist choosing to act "puzzled" when the presenting problem is alleviated.

Boszormenyi-Nagi introduces an ethical dimension to family therapy, calling his approach contextual therapy. He believes that every family keeps a kind of "ledger" of debts and entitlements that must be reasonably well balanced within and across generations. If not, a sense of injustice may lead to symptomatic behavior by various family members.

The chapter also examines the role of the social worker as change agent in the guise of family counselor or therapist, utilizing the perspective of family counseling and therapy as a particular example of the problem-solving process in the systems perspective.

Exercises
1. An eco-map of my family

> *Goal:* This exercise is designed to help students comprehend this family assessment technique and to gain insight into the dynamics of their family.

Step 1: Before the class period in which students will draw an eco-map of their family, assign the material on eco-maps in this chapter.

Step 2: Distribute large sheets of paper (such as flip-chart paper) and broad-tip markers to the students. Have the symbols for an eco-map visually available, either on the chalkboard or with the text. Instruct the students to draw an eco-map of their family.

Step 3: Ask for volunteers to share and describe their eco-maps. After a student describes his or her eco-map, inquire whether he or she gained some insight into the family dynamics.

Step 4: End the exercise by asking students their thoughts about the problems encountered and the merits and shortcomings of drawing an eco-map of one's family. Describe how eco-mapping may be used by a social worker in working with clients and families.

2. A genogram of my family

Goal: This exercise is designed to help students comprehend the value of a genogram and to gain insight into the dynamics of their family and its history.

Step 1: Before the class period in which students will draw a genogram of their family, assign the material on genograms in this chapter.

Step 2: Distribute large sheets of paper (such as flip-chart paper) and broad-tip markers to the students. Have the symbols for a genogram visually available, either on the chalkboard or with the text. Instruct the students to draw a genogram of their family.

Step 3: Ask for volunteers to share and describe their genogram. After a student describes her or his genogram, inquire whether he or she gained insight into the family's dynamics and history.

Step 4: The exercise can end in a variety of ways. Ask students their thoughts about the problems encountered and the merits and shortcomings of drawing a genogram. Or describe how a genogram may be used by a social worker in working with clients and families. Or briefly compare and contrast an eco-map and a genogram.

3. The application of systems theory concepts to a family's interaction[3]

Goal: This activity is designed to illustrate systems theory principles in a meaningful manner. Student volunteers are asked to assume specific roles in a family. The family is presented with various situations and then family members are

---

[3]This exercise was written by Karen K. Kirst-Ashman, Ph.D., professor in the social work department, University of Wisconsin—Whitewater.

asked to describe their reactions. Following each situation is a brief total class discussion focusing on the identification of various systems concepts to describe family interactions.

Objectives: On completion of this exercise, students will be able to

1. Describe some systems theory concepts and apply them to a family's interactions.
2. Examine the effects of various problem and crisis situations on families.

Step 1: Name and define the following family systems concepts:

- *System:* A set of elements so arranged and so interrelated that change in any one of the parts of the system activates reaction and change in all the other parts.
- *Homeostasis:* The dynamic balance and particular ordering of parts that was successful in the past for maintaining the system and that the system strives to maintain.
- *Boundaries:* The repeatedly occurring patterns of behavior that characterize the relationships within a system and give that system a particular identity.
- *Open system:* A system that tends to exchange new information relatively easily across the system's boundaries and can develop a new homeostasis that incorporates new information.
- *Closed system:* A system that tends to inhibit any flow of new information across the system's boundaries. A closed system tends to become rigid and atrophy.
- *Subsystem:* A secondary or subordinate system within the larger system.

Step 2: Describe the following family roles to the entire class and solicit volunteers to play each role:

Rob: husband and father
   age 41
   calm, level-headed
   makes most of the family's decisions
   works as an accountant
   makes an upper-middle-class income

Laura: wife and mother
   age 35
   pleasant, attractive, warm
   typically follows Rob's lead
   does not work outside the home

Benji: 15-year-old son
   quiet, private, likes to spend time alone
   has a few friends who tend to have a history of minor delinquencies
   maintains a B– average in school

Susie: 10-year-old daughter
   outgoing, personable
   has numerous friends and interests
   maintains an A average in school

Step 3: Have the volunteer family assemble in a group before the class. Tell them that you will be presenting three different situations that will happen to the family. Ask them each to discuss their personal reactions to each situation. After the family's reactions, ask the class to discuss which system's concepts apply to the family.

Step 4: Present the following situation, ask for family members' reactions, and ask the class to discuss how the family system might be affected:

Situation: Rob loses his job and the family is in serious financial difficulty.

Family members' reactions: The following are some potential reactions:

    a. Stress due to economic conditions may cause Rob and Laura to have marital conflict. The spouse subsystem may be weakened.
    b. Benji and Susie may be confused and worried about the future.
    c. All family members might be angry at the lack of funds for personal use.

Systems theory applications: The class may focus on the following possible applications of systems concepts.

    a. Homeostasis within the system is disrupted.
    b. Change affecting Rob affects the entire family system.
    c. The system may change from being an open system with easy interchange of information across system boundaries to a closed system under stress. New information and input may no longer be easily assimilated.

Step 5: Using the procedure described earlier, present the following situation:

Situation: Rob finds another comparable job. However, Laura has also found a full-time job as a receptionist at a law firm. She decides she likes the additional income and the feeling of competence and independence that the job provides.

Family members' reactions: The following are some potential reactions:

    a. Rob may resent Laura's newfound sense of independence. The spouse subsystem may be further disrupted.
    b. The children may resent not having a mother doing things for them at home more regularly.
    c. All family members may feel more pressure to participate in household tasks when they are at home.

Systems theory applications: The class may focus on the following potential applications of system concepts.

    a. The parental subsystem may be disturbed as a result of the change in roles.
    b. Boundaries within the system may change. Rob, Benji, and Susie may form a new subsystem in reaction to Laura's absence.

Step 6: Once again, using the same procedure, present the following situation:

Situation: The school vice-principal calls and complains that Benji was found falling asleep in his class several times, and that a bottle of Southern Comfort was found in his school locker.

Family members' reactions: Family members may have the following reactions:

a. Rob and Laura are shocked and worried about what to do.
b. Benji may feel isolated and become even more withdrawn.
c. Susie may become very worried about Benji and approach him to offer any help she can give.

Systems theory applications: The following applications to systems theory may be discussed:

a. Homeostasis within the family system has been disturbed.
b. The parental subsystem may be strengthened to combat this newly defined problem.
c. The sibling subsystem may be strengthened if Benji and Susie form an alliance.
d. The entire family system may have to become a more open system to work with outside resources to solve the problem. The school, a counselor or therapist, or Alcoholics Anonymous may become involved in problem solving.

Social Work
with Organizations

An organization is defined here as a collectivity of individuals gathered together to serve a particular purpose. The types of purposes (or goals) that people organize to achieve are infinite in number, ranging from obtaining basic necessities to eliminating the threat of worldwide terrorism or attaining world peace. In each case an organization exists because people working together can better accomplish tasks and achieve goals than one individual can.

Etzioni (1964) described the importance of organizations in our lives:

> We are born in organizations, educated by organizations, and most of us spend much of our lives working for organizations. We spend much of our leisure time paying, playing, and praying in organizations. Most of us will die in an organization, and when the time comes for burial, the largest organization of all—the state—must grant official permission. [p. 1]

The importance of organizations for social work practice has been summarized by Netting, Kettner, and McMurtry (1993):

> As social workers, our roles within, interactions with, and attempts to manipulate organizations define much of what we do. Clients often come to us seeking help because they are not able to obtain help from organizations that are critical to their survival or quality of life. In turn, the resources we attempt to gain for these clients usually come from still other organizations. . . . Social workers with little or no idea of how organizations operate, how they interact, or how they can be influenced and changed from both outside and inside are likely to be severely limited in their effectiveness. [p. 123]

Many disciplines (including business, psychology, political science, and sociology) have produced a prodigious amount of theory and research on organizations. However, in spite of the importance of organizations to social work practice, the amount of social work literature devoted to organizations is limited. One significant reference in this area is *Social Work Macro Practice* (Netting, Kettner, & McMurtry, 1993).

This chapter provides an introduction to social work practice with organizations. Several theories are presented, which provide a variety of perspectives for viewing and analyzing organizations. These theories of organizational behavior include the autocratic model, the custodial model, the scientific management model, the human relations model, theory X, theory Y, the collegial model, theory Z, and management by objectives. The impacts of value orientations in decision-making processes in organizations are also covered. Two diverse value orientations that have major impacts on human services— liberalism and conservatism—are also summarized. The chapter ends with a presentation of guidelines for helping professionals survive, and thrive, in a bureaucracy.

Models of Organizational Behavior

The Autocratic Model

The autocratic model has been in existence for thousands of years. During the Industrial Revolution, this model was the prominent model of how an organization should function. The model depends on *power.* Those who are in power act autocratically. The message to employees is "You do this—or else," meaning that an employee who does not follow orders is penalized, often severely.

An autocratic model uses one-way communication—from the top to the workers. Management believes that it knows what is best. The employee's obligation is to follow orders. Employees have to be persuaded, directed, and pushed into performance, and this is management's task. Management does the thinking, and the workers obey the directives. Under autocratic conditions, the workers' role is *obedience* to management.

The autocratic model does work in some settings. Most military organizations throughout the world are formulated on this model. The model was also used successfully during the Industrial Revolution; for example, in building great railroad systems and in operating giant steel mills.

The autocratic model has a number of disadvantages. Workers are often in the best position to identify shortcomings in the structure and technology of the organizational system, but one-way communication prevents feedback to management. The model also fails to generate much of a commitment among the workers to accomplish organizational goals. Finally, the model fails to motivate workers to put forth effort to further develop their skills (skills that often would be highly beneficial to the employer).

The Custodial Model

Many decades ago when the autocratic model was the predominant model of organizational behavior, some progressive managers began to study their employees and soon found that the autocratic model often caused the employees to be filled with insecurity, frustration, and feelings of aggression toward management. Since the employees could not directly express their discontent, it was expressed indirectly. Some employees vented their anger on their families and neighbors,

and the entire community suffered. Others sabotaged production. Davis and Newstrom (1989) described sabotage in a wood-processing plant.

> Managers treated workers crudely, sometimes even to the point of physical abuse. Since employees could not strike back directly for fear of losing their jobs, they found another way to do it. They *symbolically* fed their supervisor to a log-shredding machine! They did this by purposely destroying good sheets of veneer, which made the supervisor look bad when monthly efficiency reports were prepared. [p. 31]

In the 1890s and 1900s some progressive employers thought that if these feelings could be alleviated, employees might feel more like working, which would increase productivity. To satisfy the employees' security needs, a number of companies began to provide welfare programs. Examples include pension programs, child-care centers at the workplace, health insurance, and life insurance.

The custodial approach leads to employee dependence on the organization. According to Davis and Newstrom (1989, p. 31), "If employees have ten years of seniority under the union contract and a good pension program, they cannot afford to quit even if the grass looks greener somewhere else!"

Employees working under a custodial model tend to focus on their economic rewards and benefits. They are happier and more content than under the autocratic model, but they do not have a high commitment to helping the organization accomplish its goals. They tend to give *passive cooperation* to their employer. The model's most evident flaw is that most employees are producing substantially below their capacities. They are not motivated to advance to higher capacities. Most such employees do not feel fulfilled or motivated at their place of work. In summary, contented employees (which the custodial model is designed to generate) are not necessarily the most productive employees.

The Scientific Management Model

One of the earliest and most important schools of thought on the management of functions and tasks in the workplace was based on the work of Frederick Taylor (1947). Taylor was a mechanical engineer, an American industrialist, and an educator. He focused primarily on management techniques that would lead to increased productivity. He asserted that many organizational problems in the workplace involved misunderstandings between managers and workers. Managers erroneously thought that workers were lazy and unemotional, and they mistakenly believed they understood workers' jobs. Workers mistakenly thought that managers cared most about exploiting them.

To solve these problems, Taylor developed the *scientific management model*, which focused on the need for managers to conduct scientific analyses of the workplace. One of the first steps was to conduct a careful study of how each job could best be accomplished. An excellent way to do this, according to Taylor, was to identify the best worker for each job and then carefully study how he or she effectively and efficiently did the work. The goal of this analysis was to discover the optimal way of doing the job—in Taylor's words, the "one best way." Once this best way was identified, tools could be modified to better complete the work, workers' abilities and interests could be fitted to particular job assignments, and the level of production that the average worker could sustain could be gauged.

Once the level of production for the average worker was determined, Taylor indicated the next step was to provide incentives to increase productivity. His favorite strategy for doing this was the piece-rate wage, in which workers were paid for each unit they produced. The goals were to produce more units, reduce unit cost, increase organizational productivity and profitability, and provide incentives for workers to produce more.

Taylor's work has been criticized as having a technicist bias, since it tends to treat workers as little more than cogs in a wheel.

No two workers are exactly alike, so the "one best way" of doing a job is often unique to the person doing it. In fact, forcing the same work approach on different workers may actually decrease both productivity and worker satisfaction. In addition, Taylor's approach has limited application to human services. Since each client is unique—with unique needs, unique environmental impacting factors, and unique strengths and capacities—each human services case has to be individualized, and therefore it is difficult (if not impossible) to specify the "one best way" to proceed.

The Human Relations Model

In 1927 the Hawthorne Works of the Western Electric Company in Chicago began a series of experiments designed to discover ways to increase worker satisfaction and worker productivity (Roethlisberger & Dickson, 1939). Hawthorne Works manufactured telephones on an assembly-line basis. Workers needed no special skills and performed simple, repetitive tasks. The workers were not unionized, and management sought to find ways to increase productivity. If job satisfaction could be increased, employees would work more efficiently and productivity would increase.

The company tested the effects on productivity of a number of factors: rest breaks, better lighting, changes in the number of work hours, changes in the wages paid, improved food facilities, and so on. The results were surprising. Productivity increased, as expected, with improved working conditions; but it also increased when working conditions worsened. This latter finding was unexpected and led to additional study.

The investigators discovered that participation in the experiments was extremely attractive to the workers. They felt they had been selected by the management for their individual abilities, and so they worked harder, even when working conditions became less favorable. In addition, the workers' morale and general attitude toward work improved, since they felt they were receiving special attention. By participating in this study, the workers were able to work in smaller groups and became involved in making decisions. Working in smaller groups allowed them to develop a stronger sense of solidarity with their fellow workers. Being involved in decision making decreased their feelings of meaninglessness and powerlessness about their work.

In sociological and psychological research, the results of this study have become known as the "Hawthorne effect." In essence, when subjects know they are participants in a study, this awareness may lead them to behave differently and substantially influence the results.

The results of this study, and of other similar studies, led some researchers to conclude that the key variables impacting productivity are social factors. Etzioni (1964, pp. 34–35) summarized some of the basic tenets of the human relations approach:

- The level of production is set by social norms, not by physiological capacities.
- Noneconomic rewards and sanctions significantly affect the behavior of the workers and largely limit the effect of economic incentive plans.
- Workers do not act or react as individuals but as members of groups.
- The role of leadership is important in understanding social factors in organizations and this leadership may be either formal or informal.

Numerous studies have provided evidence to support these tenets (Netting, Kettner, & McMurtry, 1993, p. 131). Workers who are capable of greater productivity often will not excel because they are unwilling to exceed the "average" level set by the norms of the group, even if this means earning less. These studies have also found that attempts by management to influence workers' behavior are often more successful if targeted at the group as a whole, rather than at individuals. Finally, the studies have documented the im-

portance of informal leadership in influencing workers' behavior in ways that can either amplify or negate formal leadership directives. This model asserts that managers who succeed in increasing productivity are most likely responsive to the workers' social needs.

One criticism of the human relations model is (surprisingly) that it tends to manipulate, dehumanize, oppress, and exploit workers. The model leads to the conclusion that management can increase productivity by helping workers become content, rather than by increasing economic rewards for higher productivity. The human relations model allows for concentrated power and decision making at the top. It is not intended to empower employees in the decision-making process or to assist them in acquiring genuine participation in the running of the organization. The practice of dealing with people on the basis of their perceived social relationships within the workplace may also be a factor in perpetuating the "good old boys" network; this network has disadvantaged women and people of color over the years. Another criticism of the human relations approach is that a happy work force is not necessarily a productive work force, because the norms for worker production may be set well below the workers' levels of capability.

Theory Y: Internal Rewards

Douglas McGregor (1960) developed two theories of management. He theorized that management thinking and behavior are based on two different sets of assumptions, which he labeled Theory X and Theory Y.

Theory X managers view employees as being incapable of much growth. Employees are perceived as having an inherent dislike for work and attempting to evade work whenever possible. Therefore, X-type managers believe they must control, direct, force, or threaten employees to make them work. Employees are also viewed as having relatively little ambition, wishing to avoid responsibilities, and preferring to be directed.

Theory X managers therefore spell out job responsibilities carefully, set work goals without employee input, use external rewards (such as money) to force employees to work, and punish those who deviate from established rules. Because Theory X managers reduce responsibilities to a level at which few mistakes can be made, work usually becomes so structured that it is monotonous and distasteful. These assumptions, of course, are inconsistent with what behavioral scientists assert are effective principles for directing, influencing, and motivating people. (Theory X managers are, in essence, adhering to an autocratic model of organizational behavior.)

In contrast, *Theory Y managers* view employees as wanting to grow and develop by exerting physical and mental effort to accomplish work objectives to which they are committed. These managers believe that the promise of internal rewards, such as self-respect and personal improvement, are stronger motivators than external rewards (money) and punishment. They also believe that under proper conditions, employees will not only accept responsibility but seek it. Most employees are assumed to have considerable ingenuity, creativity, and imagination for problem solving. Therefore, they are given considerable responsibility to test the limits of their capabilities. Mistakes and errors are viewed as necessary phases of the learning process, and work is structured so employees have a sense of accomplishment and growth.

Employees who work for Y-type managers are generally more creative and productive, experience greater work satisfaction, and are more highly motivated than employees who work for X-type managers. Under both management styles, expectations often become self-fulfilling prophecies.

The Collegial Model

A useful extension of Theory Y is the collegial model, which emphasizes the team concept. It involves employees working closely together and feeling a commitment to achieve a common purpose. Some organizations—such as university departments, research laboratories, and most human services organizations—have a goal of creating a collegial atmosphere to facilitate achieving their purposes. (Sadly, many such organizations are unsuccessful in creating such an atmosphere.)

Creating a collegial atmosphere is highly dependent on management building a feeling of partnership with employees. When such a partnership develops, employees feel needed and useful. Managers are then viewed as joint contributors rather than as bosses. Management is the *coach* who builds a better team. Davis and Newstrom (1989) described some of the approaches to developing a team concept:

> The feeling of partnerships can be built in many ways. Some organizations have abolished the use of reserved parking spaces for executives, so every employee has an equal chance of finding one close to the workplace. Some firms have tried to eliminate the use of terms like "bosses" and "subordinates," feeling that those terms simply create perceptions of psychological distance between managers and nonmanagers. Other employers have removed time clocks, set up "fun committees," sponsored company canoe trips, or required managers to spend a week or two annually working in field or factory locations. All of these approaches are designed to build a spirit of mutuality, in which every person makes contributions and appreciates those of others. [p. 34]

If the sense of partnership is developed, employees produce quality work and seek to cooperate with co-workers, not because management directs them to do so, but because they feel an internal obligation to produce high-quality work. The collegial approach thus leads to a sense of *self-discipline*. In this environment, employees are more apt to have a sense of fulfillment, to feel self-actualized, and to produce higher-quality work.

Theory Z

William Ouchi described the Japanese style of management in his 1981 best-seller *Theory Z*. In the late 1970s and early 1980s, attention in the U.S. business world became focused on the Japanese approach to management, as markets long dominated by American firms (such as the automobile industry) were taken over by Japanese industries. Japanese industrial organizations had rapidly overcome their earlier reputation for poor quality work and were setting worldwide standards for quality and durability.

Theory Z asserted that the theoretical principles underlying Japanese management went beyond Theory Y. According to Theory Z, a business organization in Japan is more than the profitability oriented entity that it is in the United States. It is a way of life. It provides lifetime employment. It is enmeshed with the nation's political, social, and economic network. Furthermore, its influence spills over into many other organizations, such as nursery schools, elementary and secondary schools, and universities.

The basic philosophy of Theory Z is that involved and committed workers are the key to increased productivity. Ideas and suggestions about how to improve the organization are routinely solicited and implemented, where feasible. One strategy for accomplishing this is the *quality circle*, where employees and management routinely meet to brainstorm about ways to improve productivity and quality.

In contrast to American organizations, Japanese organizations tend not to have written objectives or organizational charts. Most work is done in teams and decisions are made by consensus. The teams tend to function without a designated leader. Cooperation within units, and between units, is emphasized. Loyalty to the organization is also emphasized, as is organizational loyalty to the employee.

Experiments designed to transplant Japanese-style management to the United States have resulted in mixed success. In most cases American organizations have concluded that Theory Z probably works quite well in a homogeneous culture that has Japan's societal values, but some components do not fit well with the more heterogeneous and individualistic character of the United States. In addition, some firms in volatile industries (such as electronics) have difficulty balancing their desire to provide lifetime employment with the need to adjust their work forces to meet rapidly changing market demands.

Management by Objectives

Fundamental to the core of an organization is its purpose; that is, the commonly shared understanding of the reason for its existence.

Management theorist Peter Drucker (1954) proposed a strategy for making organizational goals and objectives the central construct around which organizational life is designed to function. In other words, instead of focusing on employee needs and wants, or on organizational structure, as the ways to increase efficiency and productivity, Drucker proposed beginning with the desired outcome and working backward. The strategy is first to identify the organizational objectives or goals and then to adapt the organizational tasks, resources, and structure to meet those objectives. This management by objectives (MBO) approach is designed to focus the organization's efforts on meeting these objectives. Success is determined, then, by the degree to which stated objectives are reached.

This approach can be applied to the organization as a whole, as well as to internal divisions or departments. When the MBO approach is applied to internal divisions, the objectives set for each division should be consistent and supportive of the overall organization objectives.

In many areas, including human services, the MBO approach can also be applied to the cases being serviced by each employee. Goals are set with each client, tasks to meet these goals are then determined, and deadlines are set for the completion of these tasks. The degree of success of each case is then determined at a later date (often when a case is closed) by the extent to which stated goals were achieved.

An adaptation of the MBO approach, called strategic planning and budgeting (SPB), has become popular in the 1990s. The process involves first specifying the overall vision or mission of an organization, then identifying a variety of more specific objectives or plans for achieving that vision, and finally adapting the resources to meet the specific high-priority objectives or plans. Organizations in the 1990s often hire outside consultants to assist in conducting the SPB process.

One major advantage of the MBO approach for an organization (or its divisions) is that it produces clear statements (made available to all employees) about the objectives and the tasks that are expected to be accomplished in specified time periods. This type of activity tends to improve cooperation and collaboration. The MBO approach is also useful because it provides a guide for allocating resources and a focus for monitoring and evaluating organizational efforts.

An additional benefit of the MBO approach is in the area of diversity in the workplace. Prior to this approach, those responsible for hiring failed to employ women and people of color in significant numbers. As affirmative action programs were developed within organizations, the MBO approach was widely used to set specific hiring goals and objectives. The result has been significant changes in recruitment approaches that have enabled a number of women and other minorities to secure employment.

Summary Comments About Models of Organizational Behavior

Any of these models can be successfully applied in some situations. The question of which model to apply in order to obtain the highest productivity depends on the tasks to be completed and on employee needs and expectations. For example, the autocratic model will probably work well in military operations, where quick decisions are needed to respond to rapidly changing crises and where military personnel expect autocratic leadership. However, this model does not generally work well in human services organizations in which employees are anticipating the Theory Y style of managers.

In addition, some of these models or approaches can be applied simultaneously. For example, the management by objectives approach can be used at the same time that an organization is using any of the other models described.

Value Orientations in Organizational Decision Making

In theory, the task of making decisions (on objectives and goals) within organizations should follow a definite rational process, including identifying the problems, specifying resource limitations, weighing the advantages and disadvantages of proposed solutions, and selecting the resolution strategy with the fewest risks and the greatest chance of success. In practice, however, subjective influences (particularly on value orientations) can impede the rational process.

Most people tend to believe that decisions are made primarily on the basis of objective facts and figures. However, values and assumptions form the bases of most decisions, and facts and figures are used only in relation to these values and assumptions. Consider the following list of questions. What do they indicate about how we make our most important decisions?

- Should abortions be permitted or prohibited during the first weeks following conception?
- Should homosexuality be viewed as a natural expression of sexuality?

- When does harsh discipline of a child become child abuse?
- Should the primary objective of imprisonment be rehabilitation or retribution?

Answers to these questions are usually not based on data uncovered after careful research; they are based on individual beliefs about the value of life, personal freedom, and protective social standards. Even everyday decisions are based largely on values.

Practically every decision is also based on certain assumptions. Without assumptions, nothing can be proved. Assumptions are made in every research study to test any hypothesis. In a market survey, analysts assume that the instruments they use (such as a questionnaire) will be valid and reliable. It cannot even be proved the sun will rise in the east tomorrow without assuming that its history provides that proof.

Every decision maker in an organization brings not only his or her objective knowledge and expertise to the decision-making process, but also his or her value orientations, unique attitudes, feelings, biases, and vested interests.

Value orientation means an individual's own ideas about what is desirable and worthwhile. Most values are acquired through prior learning experiences in interactions with family, friends, educators, organizations such as the church, and anyone else who has made an impression on a person's thinking.

The philosopher Edward Spranger (1928) believed that most people eventually come to rely on one of six possible value orientations. While it is possible for a person to hold values in all six orientations, each person tends to lean more heavily toward one type in the decision-making process. The six value orientations are theoretical, economic, aesthetic, social, political, and religious.

Theoretical: A person with a theoretical orientation strives toward a rational, systematic ordering of knowledge. Person preference does not count as much as being able to classify, compare, contrast, and interrelate various pieces of information. The theoretical person places value on simply knowing what is—and why.

Economic: An economic orientation places primary value on the utility of things, and practical uses of knowledge are given foremost attention. Proposed plans of action are assessed in terms of their costs and benefits. If the costs outweigh the benefits, the economic-oriented person is not likely to support the plan.

Aesthetic: An aesthetic orientation is grounded in an appreciation of artistic values, and personal preferences for form, harmony, and beauty are influential in making decisions. Since the experience of single events is considered an important end in itself, reactions to aesthetic qualities will frequently be expressed.

Social: A social orientation is an empathetic one that values other people as ends in themselves. Concern for the welfare of people pervades the behavior of the socially oriented decision maker, and primary consideration is given to the quality of human relationships.

Political: A political orientation involves a concern for identifying where power lies. Conflict and competition are seen as normal elements of group activity. Decisions and their outcomes are assessed in terms of how much power is obtained and by whom, since influence over others is a valued goal.

Religious: A person with a religious orientation is directed by a desire to relate to the universe in some meaningful way. Personal beliefs about an "absolute good" or "higher order" are employed to determine the value of things, and decisions and their outcomes are placed into the context of such beliefs.

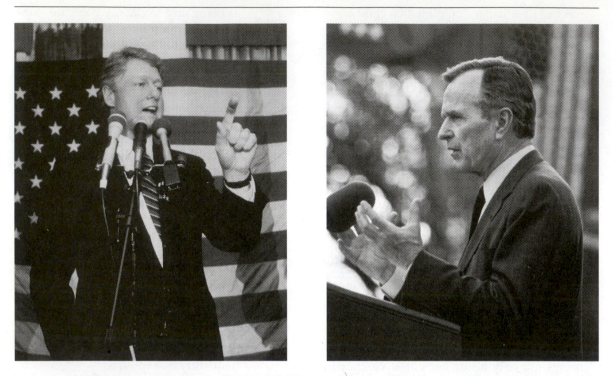

In the 1992 Presidential election campaign, Bill Clinton adhered to liberalism and George Bush adhered to conservatism.

Liberalism Versus Conservatism

In regard to value orientations, two diverse views that have major impacts on human services organizations are liberalism and conservatism. Politicians and decision makers often make their decisions on human service issues in terms of whether they adhere to a liberal philosophy or to a conservative philosophy. The Republican party is considered to be relatively conservative, and the Democratic party is considered to be relatively liberal. (However, some Democrats are primarily conservative in ideology, and some Republicans are primarily liberal in ideology.)

Conservatives (derived from the verb "to conserve") tend to resist change. They emphasize tradition and believe that rapid change usually results in more negative consequences than positive ones. In economic matters, conservatives feel that government should not interfere with the workings of the marketplace. They encourage the government to support (for example, through tax incentives), rather than regulate, business and industry in society. A free-market economy is thought to be the best way to ensure prosperity and fulfillment of individual needs. Conservatives embrace the old adage that "government governs best which governs least." They believe that most government activities constitute grave threats to individual liberty and to the smooth functioning of the free market.

Conservatives generally advocate a residual approach to social welfare programs (see Chapter 2 for a fuller description of the residual and institutional approaches to social welfare programs). They believe that dependency is a result of personal failure and that it is natural for inequality to exist among humans. They assert that the family, the church, and gainful employment should be the primary defense against dependency. Social welfare should only be a temporary function that is used sparingly, because prolonged social welfare assistance will lead recipients to become permanently dependent. Conservatives believe that charity is a moral virtue, and that the "fortunate" are obligated to help the "less fortunate" become productive, contributing citizens in a society. If governmental funds are provided for health and social welfare services, conservatives advocate that such funding should go to private organizations that are thought to be more effective and efficient than public agencies in providing services.

In contrast, liberals believe that change is generally good, as it usually brings progress. Moderate change is best. They view society as needing regulation to ensure fair competition among various interests. In particular, a free-market economy is viewed as needing regulation to ensure fairness. Government programs, including social welfare programs, are viewed as necessary to help meet basic human needs. Liberals advocate government action to remedy social deficiencies and to improve human welfare. They feel that government regulation and intervention is often necessary to safeguard human rights, to control the excesses of capitalism, and to provide equal chances for success. They emphasize egalitarianism and the rights of minorities.

Liberals generally adhere to an institutional view of social welfare. They assert that because modern society has become so fragmented and complex and because traditional institutions (such as the family) have been unable to meet emerging human needs, few individuals can now function without the help of social services (including work training, job location services, child care, health care, and counseling).

Surviving in a Bureaucracy

There are basic structural conflicts between helping professionals and the bureaucratic systems in which they work. Helping professionals place a high value on creativeness and changing the system to serve clients. Bureaucracies resist change and are most efficient when no one is "rocking the boat." Helping professionals seek to personalize services by conveying to each client that "you count as a person."Bureaucracies are highly depersonalized, emotionally detached systems that view every employee and every client as being a tiny component of a large system. In a large bureaucracy employees *don't* count as "persons," but only as functional parts of a system. Additional conflicting value orientations between a helping professional and bureaucratic systems are listed in Exhibit 9.1.

Any of these differences in value orientations can become an arena of conflict between helping professionals and the bureaucracies in which they work. Knopf (1979) summarized the potential areas of conflict between bureaucracies and helping professionals:

> The trademarks of a BS (bureaucratic system) are power, hierarchy, and specialization; that is, rules and roles. In essence, the result is depersonalization. The system itself is neither "good" nor "bad"; it is a system. I believe it to be amoral. It is efficient and effective, but in order to be so it must be impersonal in all of its functionings. This then is the location of the stress. The hallmark of the helping professional is a highly individualized, democratic, humanized, relationship-oriented service aimed at self-motivation. The hallmark of a bureaucratic system is a highly impersonalized, valueless (amoral), emotionally detached, hierarchical structure of organization. The dilemma of the HP (helping person) is how to give a personalized service to a client through a delivery system that is not set up in any way to do that. [pp. 21–22]

Exhibit 9.1
Value conflicts between a helping professional and bureaucracies

Orientations of a Helping Professional	Orientations of Bureaucratic Systems
Desires democratic system for decision making.	Most decisions are made autocratically.
Desires that power be distributed equally among employees (horizontal structure).	Power is distributed vertically.
Desires that clients have considerable power in the system.	Power is held primarily by top executives.
Desires a flexible, changing system.	System is rigid and stable.
Desires that creativity and growth be emphasized.	Emphasis is on structure and the status quo.
Desires that focus be client-oriented.	System is organization-centered.
Desires that communication be on a personalized level from person to person.	Communication is from level to level.
Desires shared decision making and shared responsibility structure.	A hierarchical decision-making structure and a hierarchical responsibility structure are characteristic.
Desires that decisions be made by those having the most knowledge.	Decisions are made in terms of the decision-making authority assigned to each position in the hierarchy.
Desires shared leadership.	System uses autocratic leadership.
Believes feelings of clients and employees should be highly valued by the system.	Procedures and processes are highly valued.

Numerous helping professionals respond to these orientation conflicts by erroneously projecting a "personality" onto the bureaucracy. The bureaucracy is viewed as being "red tape," "officialism," "uncaring," "cruel," "the enemy." A negative personality is sometimes also projected onto the officials, who may be viewed as being "paper shufflers," "rigid," "deadwood," "inefficient," and "unproductive." Knopf (1979) stated:

The HP (helping person) . . . may deal with the impersonal nature of the system by projecting values onto it and thereby give the BS (bureaucratic system) a "personality." In this way, we fool ourselves into thinking that we can deal with it in a personal way. Unfortunately, projection is almost always negative and reflects the dark or negative aspects of ourselves. The BS then becomes a screen onto which we vent our anger, sadness, or fright, and while a lot of energy is generated, very little is accomplished. Since the BS is amoral,

it is unproductive to place a personality on it. [p. 25]

A bureaucratic system is neither good nor bad. It has neither a personality nor a value system of its own. It is simply a structure developed to carry out various tasks.

A helping person may have various emotional reactions to these conflicts in orientation with bureaucratic systems.[1] Common reactions are anger at the system, self-blame ("It's all my fault"), sadness and depression ("Poor me"; "Nobody appreciates all I've done"), and fright and paranoia ("They're out to get me"; "If I mess up I'm gone").

[1]This description highlights a number of negatives about bureaucratic systems, particularly their impersonalization. In fairness, an advantage of being part of a large bureaucracy is that the potential is there for changing a powerful system to the clients' advantage. In tiny or nonbureaucratic systems, the social worker may have lots of freedom but little opportunity or power to influence large systems or mobilize extensive resources on behalf of clients.

Knopf (1979) identified several types of behavior patterns that helping professionals choose in dealing with bureaucracies. The *warrior* leads open campaigns to destroy and malign the system. A warrior discounts the value of the system and often enters into a win-lose conflict. The warrior generally loses and is dismissed.

The *gossip* is a covert warrior who complains to others (including clients, politicians, and the news media) how terrible the system is. A gossip frequently singles out a few officials for criticism. Bureaucratic systems often make life very difficult for the gossip by assigning distasteful tasks, refusing to promote, giving very low salary increases, and perhaps even dismissing.

The *complainer* resembles a gossip, but confines complaints to other helping persons, to in-house staff, and to family members. A complainer wants people to agree in order to find comfort in shared misery. Complainers desire to stay with the system, and generally do.

The *dancer* is skillful at ignoring rules and procedures. Dancers are frequently lonely, often reprimanded for incorrectly filling out forms, and have low investment in the system or in helping clients.

The *defender* is scared, dislikes conflict, and therefore defends the rules, the system, and bureaucratic officials. Defenders are often supervisors and are viewed by others as "bureaucrats."

The *machine* is a "bureaucrat" who takes on the orientation of the bureaucracy. Often a machine has not been involved in providing direct services for years. Machines are frequently named to head study committees and policy groups and to chair boards.

The *executioner* attacks persons within an organization with enthusiasm and vigor. An executioner usually has a high energy level and is impulsive. An executioner abuses power by indiscriminately attacking and dismissing not only employees but also services and programs. Executioners have power and

are angry (although the anger is disguised, denied). They are not committed to either the value orientation of helping professionals or to the bureaucracy.

Knopf (1979) listed 66 tips on how to survive in a bureaucracy. A number of the most useful suggestions are summarized here:

1. Whenever your needs, or the needs of your clients, are not met by the bureaucracy, use the following problem-solving approach: (a) Precisely identify your needs (or the needs of clients) that are in conflict with the bureaucracy; this step is defining the problem. (b) Generate a list of possible solutions. Be creative in generating a wide range of solutions. (c) Evaluate the merits and shortcomings of the possible solutions. (d) Select a solution. (e) Implement the solution. (f) Evaluate the solution.

2. Obtain a knowledge of how your bureaucracy is structured and how it functions. This knowledge will reduce fear of the unknown, make the system more predictable, and help in identifying rational ways to best meet your needs and those of your clients.

3. Remember that bureaucrats are people who have feelings. Communication gaps are often most effectively reduced if you treat them with as much respect and interest as you treat clients.

4. If you are at war with the bureaucracy, declare a truce. The system will find a way to dismiss you if you remain at war. With a truce, you can identify and use the strengths of the bureaucracy as an ally, rather than having the strengths being used against you as an enemy.

5. Know your work contract and job expectations. If the expectations are unclear, seek clarity.

6. Continue to develop your knowledge and awareness of specific helping skills. Take advantage of continuing education opportunities (for example, workshops, conferences, courses). Among other advantages, your continued professional development

will assist you in being able to contract from a position of competency and skill.

7. Seek to identify your professional strengths and limitations. Knowing your limitations will increase your ability to avoid undertaking responsibilities that are beyond your competencies.

8. Be aware that you can't change everything, so stop trying. In a bureaucracy, focus your change efforts on those aspects that most need change and that you have a fair chance of changing. Stop thinking and complaining about those aspects you cannot change. It is irrational to complain about things that you cannot change or to complain about those things that you do not intend to make an effort to change.

9. Learn how to control your emotions in your interactions with the bureaucracy. Emotions that are counterproductive (such as most angry outbursts) particularly need to be controlled. Doing a rational self-analysis on unwanted emotions (see Chapter 22) is one way of gaining control of your unwanted emotions. Learning how to respond to stress in your personal life will also prepare you to handle stress at work better.

10. Develop and use a sense of humor. Humor takes the edge off adverse conditions and reduces negative feelings.

11. Learn to accept your mistakes and perhaps even to laugh at some of them. No one is perfect.

12. Take time to enjoy and develop a support system with your co-workers.

13. Acknowledge your mistakes and give in sometimes on minor matters. You may not be right, and giving in sometimes allows other people to do the same.

14. Keep yourself physically fit and mentally alert. Learn to use approaches that will reduce stress and prevent burnout (see Chapter 24).

15. Leave your work at the office. If you have urgent unfinished bureaucratic business, do it before leaving work or don't leave.

Extensive paperwork may lead to burnout.

16. Occasionally take your supervisor and other administrators to lunch. Socializing prevents isolation and facilitates your involvement with and understanding of the system.

17. Do not seek self-actualization or ego-satisfaction from the bureaucracy. A depersonalized system is incapable of providing this. Only you can satisfy your ego and become self-actualized.

18. Make speeches to community groups that accentuate the positives about your agency. Do not hesitate to ask after speeches that a thank-you letter be sent to your supervisor or agency director.

19. If you have a problem involving the bureaucracy, discuss it with other employees; focus on problem solving rather than on complaining. Groups are much more powerful and productive than an individual working alone to make changes in a system.

20. No matter how high you rise in a hierarchy, maintain direct service contact. Direct contact keeps you abreast of changing client needs, prevents you from getting stale, and keeps you attuned to the concerns of employees in lower levels of the hierarchy.

21. Do not try to change everything in the system at once. Attacking too much will overextend you and lead to burnout. Start small and be selective and specific. Double-check your facts to make certain they accurately prove your position before confronting bureaucratic officials.

22. Identify your career goals and determine whether they can be met in this system. If the answer is no, then (a) change your goals, (b) change the bureaucracy, or (c) seek a position elsewhere in which your goals can be met.

Summary

An organization is a collectivity of individuals gathered together to serve a particular purpose. This chapter presents a number of theories that provide a variety of perspectives for viewing and analyzing organizations. The theories covered include the autocratic model, the custodial model, the scientific management model, the human relations model, Theory X, Theory Y, the collegial model, Theory Z, and management by objectives. These models are not exhaustive of the large number of models that have been developed. Any of these models can be applied successfully in some situations. Some of these models can be applied to organizations while other models are being used.

Values and assumptions (rather than facts and figures) form the bases of most decisions in organizations. Spranger (1928) identified six value orientations that frequently impact decision making: theoretical, economic, aesthetic, social, political, and religious.

Two diverse value orientations that have major impacts on human services organizations are liberalism and conservatism. Politicians and decision makers often make their decisions on human services issues in terms of whether they adhere to a liberal or conservative philosophy. Conservatives generally advocate a residual approach to social welfare programs, whereas liberals generally follow an institutional view of social welfare.

Knopf (1979) noted that there are numerous potential areas of conflict between bureaucracies and helping professionals. Helping professionals want bureaucratic systems to individualize interactions with clients and employees, to be humanized, to be democratic in decision making, to be relationship-oriented, and to quickly change to meet emerging needs. On the other hand, bureaucratic systems are generally depersonalized, autocratic, procedures- and process-oriented, emotionally detached, and resistive of change. Such differences in orientations can become arenas of conflict between helping professionals and the systems they work in. A number of suggestions are given on how to survive in a bureaucracy.

Exercises
1. Hard choices—Funding social programs

   Goals: This exercise is designed to help students understand that most decisions are based on values and assumptions and to realize that setting budgets for social programs involves hard choices because of scarce resources.

   Step 1: Explain that funding sources (such as the federal, state, and local governments and United Way) have to make difficult choices about how much money to allocate to diverse social programs. Financial resources to fund all social programs are simply unavailable, and some people suffer greatly because they do not receive the needed services and funds.

Step 2: Divide the group into subgroups of five or six members each. Tell each subgroup that it is the funding source for a local community and that it has $10 million to allocate for the following social programs, which need a total of $15 million. Each subgroup has the task of deciding how much money to allocate to each agency. No subgroup can go over the $10-million limit. (Distribute the following information in a handout or have the students read this material directly from the text.)

The Center for Developmental Disabilities needs $1.5 million to care for severely and profoundly retarded adults. These adults are so retarded that they are unable to walk. It costs $35,000 a year to care for each adult. If the center does not receive its requested funds, some of these clients may not receive necessary medical care and may die.

The Anti-Poverty Agency needs $3.5 million to maintain families at an income level of only 80 percent of that defined as the poverty line. It costs $10,000 per year to maintain a family of three (generally a single parent with two children). If the agency does not receive its requested funds, many of these families will go hungry, have inadequate shelter, and lack essential clothing for winter.

Protective Services needs $1 million to combat abuse, neglect, and incest. If the agency does not receive all of its needed funds, a number of children will continue to be exposed to abuse, neglect, or incest, which could severely affect them for the rest of their lives.

The Mental Health Center needs $2.5 million to help clients with severe emotional problems, some of whom are so depressed they are suicidal. If the center does not receive all of its needed funds, inadequate services will be provided to clients and the problems of many clients will intensify. A few may even take their own lives.

The Alcohol and Drug Abuse Treatment Center needs $2 million to help chemically dependent clients and their families. If the center does not receive all of its needed funds, inadequate services will mean the problems experienced by the clients and their families are apt to intensify. Since alcohol and drug abuse is a contributing factor to many other problems (such as poverty, mental illness, and family violence), these problems will also intensify.

The Shelter for Battered Women, which is located in a house in a residential area, is requesting $500,000. If funds are cut back, the shelter staff assert they will have to turn away some of the battered wives and their children who request shelter and other services.

Group Homes for Youths runs four group homes: two for young women and two for young men. It needs $500,000. If needed funds are cut back, this agency will have to reduce the number of youths it is serving. Some will be transferred to more expensive residential treatment programs, some returned to an unhealthy home environment, and some will simply run away.

The Red Cross needs $1 million for its blood bank and for disaster relief. If funds are cut back, there will be an insufficient supply of blood available for transfusions, and many of the families who are hit by disasters (such as tornadoes and floods) will not be served.

The Sheltered Workshop provides work training and sheltered work to clients with a variety of physical or mental disabilities. It needs $2 million, or it will be forced to turn away clients. If clients are turned away, they will lose hope of becoming productive and perhaps self-supporting, and will also end up requesting assistance from the Mental Health Center and from the Anti-Poverty Agency.

Equal Rights is an agency providing a wide range of services to people of color in the area: work training, job placement, and housing location. It also investigates and takes legal action against employers and landlords charged with racial discrimination. The agency needs $500,000. If funds are cut back, discrimination against people of color will increase.

Step 3: Have each subgroup share with the class its decisions for allocating funds. (The cuts that are made can be summarized on the chalkboard by having the leader list the names of the agencies, and then having a representative from each subgroup list the amount of money that was cut—totaling $5 million—from the requested allocations.) Ask each subgroup to state its reasons for making its cuts in funding. Help the students recognize that most of these reasons are based on values. Ask the students to discuss how they felt making such funding decisions that would (in real life) have significant adverse impacts on potential recipients of services. Ask the class if the exercise helps them understand that making funding decisions for human services involves hard choices caused by scarce resources.

2. Analyzing a human services organization

Goals: This exercise is designed to show students how to analyze a human services organization by such an analysis.

Step 1: Require each student to visit (perhaps in groups of two or three) a human services agency and write a report covering the following information. (Some agencies may not have information or data on one or more questions. If the information is unavailable, the students should indicate this is in their reports.) Instruct the students to call their agency to arrange a meeting. Also, ask them to include the name and telephone number of the person they met with in their report. (If you have questions about material presented in a report, you can then communicate with the agency contact person.)

a. What is the agency's mission statement?
b. What are its clients' major problems?
c. What services does the agency provide?
d. How are client needs determined?
e. What percentage of clients are people of color, women, gays or lesbians, elderly, or members of other at-risk populations?
f. What was the total cost of services for the past year?
g. How much money is spent on each program?
h. What are the agency's funding sources?

i. How much and what percentage of funds are received from each source?
j. What types of clients does the agency refuse?
k. What other agencies provide the same services in the community?
l. What is the organizational structure of the agency? For example, is there a formal chain of command?
m. Is there an informal organization (that is, people who exert a greater amount of influence on decision making than would be expected for their formal position in the bureaucracy)?
n. How much decision-making input do the direct service providers have on major policy decisions?
o. Does the agency have a board that oversees its operations? If yes, what are the backgrounds of the board members?
p. Do employees at every level feel valued?
q. What is the morale among employees?
r. What are the major unmet needs of the agency?
s. Does the agency have a handbook of personnel policies and procedures?
t. What is the public image of the agency in the community?
u. In recent years what has been the rate of turnover among staff at the agency? What were the major reasons for leaving?
v. Does the agency have a process for evaluating the outcomes of its services? If yes, what is the process, and what are the outcome results?
w. What is the student's overall impression of the agency? For example, if the student needed services that this agency provides, would she or he want to apply at this agency? Why, or why not?

Step 2: Request that the reports be handed in and inform the class that they will be graded. As a resource person for providing suggestions for agencies to visit in the community, devise a procedure for different students to visit different agencies—to prevent a few agencies from becoming inundated with requests for interviews.

3. Understanding and applying models of organizations

Goal: This exercise is designed to increase students' knowledge of organizational models and to teach them how to apply the models.

Step 1: Summarize the models of organization described in this chapter: the autocratic model, the custodial model, the scientific management model, the human relations model, Theory X, Theory Y, the collegial model, Theory Z, and management by objectives. (As an alternative, assign the students to read this material in the text.)

Step 2: Ask the students to form subgroups of about five members. Ask each subgroup to decide which models are currently most applicable to describing organizational behavior within the organization of social work faculty in the program.

Step 3: Have the members of each subgroup state their views on which models are most applicable and the reasons for their decisions.

Step 4: Summarize your views about which models are currently most applicable and what changes (including in resources) are needed to improve the efficiency, effectiveness, and productivity of the department.

CHAPTER

10

Social Work Community Practice

In the words of one of the pioneers of social work, Bertha Reynolds, social work's unique place is "between client and community" (Hartman, 1989).[1] Throughout the range of fields of practice and agencies in which social workers are employed, social workers are more effective when they have the knowledge and skills of *community practice.*

The great majority of social work students envision themselves working with individuals and/or with groups when they graduate—as juvenile probation officers, as adult protective service workers, or as social workers in nursing homes, for example. They do not see themselves as being integrally involved in community practice, and the topic may seem to be as irrelevant as other unpopular course areas, like research or biology.

In a sense, they are correct. Especially for BSW graduates, most will not be working exclusively in macropractice. In the undergraduate social work program in which I teach, only a handful of the 100-plus graduates in the last two years are working totally in this area.

The lack of interest by students often intersects the reality of agency life. A recent study

found that frontline child welfare workers in Canada, mostly BSW graduates, were mostly uninvolved in change activities that would improve the situation of children. Neither as part of the workers' jobs nor in their activities outside their job roles were these social workers active in advocacy or community practice (Herbert & Mould, 1992).

Yet the functions and roles of macropractice are ones that all social workers can be involved in, either as part of the employing agency's tasks or in one's role as a citizen and professional concerned about how societal institutions treat people. To be more effective, social workers who are providing one-on-one service have recently been urged to expand their repertoire of skills and techniques; among the roles suggested are those of advocate, program developer, and organization reformer (Weissman, Epstein, & Savage, 1987).

These suggestions mirror the realities of the ways in which social workers are involved in their communities. The following examples illustrate the ways social workers are involved in macropractice.

• Workers in an agency serving people with developmental disabilities learn how to communicate effectively with politicians and residents to obtain community support for group homes being located in residential neighborhoods and get around the NIMBY (Not In My Back Yard) Syndrome (Hogan, 1986).

• Foster care and adoption workers work with African American churches, civic, and social organizations to promote the "community ownership" of children in foster care, and thereby dramatically increase the number of African American foster parents and adoptive parents in these communities (Washington, 1987).

• A mental health center worker, aware of the lack of services for Vietnam War veterans in this area, arranges for space and publicity and helps start a support group for Vietnam vets dealing with post-traumatic stress syndrome.

---

[1]This chapter was especially written for this text by James Winship, M.S.W., D.P.A. Dr. Winship is an associate professor in the social work department at the University of Wisconsin—Whitewater.

• Social workers and other professionals have become concerned about the loneliness, fearfulness, and boredom of latchkey children, who are home alone in the afternoon after school until a parent or parents come home from work. "Warmlines" have been established in a number of communities, where volunteers provide contact with children who need information, support, or assistance (Nichols & Schilit, 1988).

• A foster care worker in a rural community is concerned because payments to foster parents do not cover some expenses that the foster parents incur—school fees and eyeglasses, for example. With the help of a local civic club, fund-raising events are organized to set up a fund to pay for those kinds of expenses.

• A social worker working in a community support program for individuals with schizophrenia who have been deinstitutionalized helps organize a local group of Recovery Inc., a self-help group for former mental patients.

• A social worker hears through his practice about a number of grandparents (and one set of great-grandparents) who have become the primary caretakers for their grandchildren because their children are not doing an adequate job of parenting because of alcohol and drug problems and other concerns. He works to get funding for providing parenting classes especially designed for custodial grandparents.

• A social worker in an agency that serves people with physical disabilities hears a number of horror stories about how physically inaccessible the community is. She meets with a group of individuals with disabilities and works with them to publicize their case through the local media, to lobby the city council for sidewalk curb cuts, and to persuade local restaurants and theaters to make their facilities accessible.

These examples involve various kinds of activities—fund-raising, group skills, publicity, lobbying, political skills, communication,

and more. What they have in common is that they involve more than an individual or a family; in a sense, *the community is the client*. The focus is not just on helping an individual or a relatively few individuals through group therapy but to benefit the community. If the workers in these scenarios are successful in their endeavors, not only individuals but also the community would benefit. A community that offers more opportunities for people with developmental disabilities to live in the community, that provides a greater number of options for people who need support or self-help groups, and that works actively to recruit foster parents and other care givers is, by the standards of the social work profession, a better community.

A commonality in these examples is that the workers involved are all people whose jobs are not primarily in macropractice, but who are willing to become active on that level when the need arises.

Personal Problems and Community Problems

Some of the problems that the clients of social workers face are almost as old as the sibling rivalry of Cain and Abel; others are ones that a decade ago were not considered problems, at least in some communities. AIDS, homelessness, and youth gangs are examples of social problems that are no longer "new" on the American scene. However, in many rural areas and small cities, the number of individuals in their communities living with AIDS has increased in recent years, seeing the homeless on the streets is no longer an uncommon event, and parents in areas once considered safe from gangs are concerned about their children's gang involvement. Consequently, the social worker whose client has a "new problem" for that community may be dealing with both the client's personal problem and the broader problem of inadequate community response or support for those needing help in this area.

Local communities have had to take leadership roles in response to the emerging problems caused by AIDS. In rural areas, social workers can be active in creating an AIDS task force, in educating the community, and in developing an AIDS services network (Rounds, 1988).

The homeless, who number between 1 and 3 million, have problems that are difficult for the social worker and community to address. How do you provide for continuity of schooling for children of homeless parents when there is a limited amount of time (often three to six weeks) that families can stay in one shelter before they have to move? How can you help individuals find low-income housing in areas where the low-income housing stock is dwindling? (There are twice as many low-income families as available housing units.) How do you help a community develop more affordable housing or supports for low-income families seeking the "American Dream" of home ownership? The difficulties of the emerging problems facing the "new American poor" have prompted one book's authors to describe their efforts as "working under the safety net" (Burghardt & Fabricant, 1987).

Generalist Practice Skills and Macropractice

The differences between *macro-* (large-scale) practice, *micro-* (one-on-one), and *mezzo-* (group) practice will become evident in this chapter. Macropractice is an integral part of social work practice, and many of the skills and much of the training for micro- and mezzopractice are also applicable to macropractice.

Working on a scale larger than one-on-one or group still involves working with people, and the interpersonal and communication skills are indispensable in this area. Especially in rural areas, the ability of a social worker to communicate effectively with others and be accepted as a person may be as significant in

getting approval or cooperation for a project as the worth of the project itself (Davenport & Davenport, 1982; Falck, 1966). Showing empathy and respect are not confined to counseling sessions.

In their article on planning in social work, Googins, Capoccia, and Kaufman (1983) also stressed the importance of the interactive aspects of planning as well as the analytic or cognitive dimensions. The social worker's ability to use himself or herself is crucial in being more effective in facilitating and integrating the efforts of all the people involved in the planning process.

Problem-solving skills are also as appropriate on the macro level as they are at the micro and mezzo levels. The ability to help people clarify issues and problems, decide which of these are the most important to work on, set feasible goals, evaluate the options for action, decide on the most appropriate actions, implement the plan, and then evaluate it are as important in working with citizen groups and community projects as in individual work.

It is the author's experience that well over half the attempts by groups of people to address community problems (for example, a group of people concerned over the lack of recreational facilities for youth) are not successful. In many cases, people who come to meetings with an interest in doing something are stymied by unorganized discussions or fragmented planning. Thirty-three people may come to the first meeting, 19 to the second, and only 5 to the third. These 5 complain to one another about the apathy in the community, unaware that if someone had served as a facilitator in the meetings, the group might have made the kind of progress that would have kept people's interest.

Related to this is the need for skills in working with groups. In working to help people form a self-help group, the social worker will use group work skills, including the skills of being an enabler and catalyst for the individuals interested in the group. At the beginning, to attract potential members, the social worker may use information networks as well as the media. As the group becomes estab-lished, the role becomes more of working with process-oriented issues to help group members express themselves, work out dif-ferences, question the movement of the group, and so on (King & Meyers, 1981).

The skills of relationship formation and communication, problem solving, and work-ing with groups are as important in macro-practice as they are in working with individ-uals and groups. However, just as there are specific intervention techniques and knowl-edge appropriate for these levels, there are also specific skills and knowledge useful in macropractice. The following sections sum-marize material on the importance to social workers of knowing their community as well as information on essential macropractice skills.

Knowledge Necessary for Macropractice

Knowledge of the Community

Given the agency and client base of the worker, it is useful to know not only "the community" but also the community as per-ceived by newcomers to the area, by mem-bers of minority groups, by those with differ-ing sexual orientations, and so on. Different groups have preference for the kinds of help they would seek or use. Farm families, ac-cording to one study, are more likely to go to clergy, family, or friends than to social service agencies when problems arise (Martinez-Brawley & Blundall, 1989). Pregnant teen-agers in one urban area also demonstrated a preference for their informal supports (fami-lies and friends) over formal organizations (Bergman, 1989).

Too often social work educators talk about how social services and financial assistance programs meet human needs in general terms—for example, "home health care ser-vices can be started in communities, which will be useful in helping the elderly stay in

their homes." While the statement is an accu-rate reflection of the worth of that service, it also leaves the impression that all commu-nities are essentially alike—what will work in Midland, Texas, will work in Midland, Michigan. In actuality, many characteristics of regions and communities will work for or against the success of a project. For this rea-son, it is essential to be aware of the services, governmental structure, the values, and other characteristics of the community.

In a locality that is not ethnically homoge-neous, it is essential to begin to understand the values and economic and political real-ities of the ethnic communities. A lack of un-derstanding can lead to an identification of erroneous concerns that are inappropriate for members of ethnic minority groups (Rivera & Erlich, 1992). This lack of understanding can also lead to the development of programs or approaches that are not ethnically sensi-tive. One study of patterns on family inti-macy yielded wide variations in practices of bathing practices, sleeping arrangements (where children slept), and physical intimacy between African Americans, Cambodians, Caucasians, Hispanics, Koreans, and Viet-namese. The authors of the study fault sexual abuse prevention programs that are not sen-sitive to the values and customs of the groups with which they are working (Ahn & Gilbert, 1992).

How does a citizen's local government, or a department of it, work now? Who is to blame when it seems not to work? What are the long-range problems? Which are short term? Does the failure to resolve these prob-lems result from the lack of money and capa-ble people? Is the failure because of conflict-ing or overlapping responsibilities? Is the problem one that can't be handled by the city but needs to be treated regionally, or by the neighborhood? Is the system itself set up wrong? Does it not work because of the kinds of people in charge, or from not having enough people, or from poor management?

The average citizen (if unable to get help with a problem) may in frustration want to change the system. But he or she can't make much of a start without knowing something about "the system," or at least about the part needing to be changed. A little digging may show that it isn't the system but the people in charge who are at fault. Or the citizen may find that the local government wants to do certain things but can't—because the state constitution or the state legislature won't let it raise the money or provide the services.

A citizen who wants to bring about change in community government should first analyze how the existing apparatus is meant to work, what limits there are on the department that concerns him or her and who imposes them, and how each part fits into the rest of the system.

Beyond the correction of particular problems, social workers and other citizens have a tremendous stake in finding workable solutions to the ever-increasing demands on governments. Future problems as well as current ones need to be taken into account. If people are to make intelligent proposals for change, they first need to analyze their present government, its structure, its functions, what it can do now, and what it is unable to do. They should also analyze neighborhood governments and the more comprehensive systems of which their local government is a part, because the actions of these systems will affect their local community.

The questionnaire presented in Exhibit 10.1 is a useful tool in obtaining the kind of specific information that is invaluable in planning for services (or just functioning as a social worker in the community).

Knowledge of Organizations

The social worker who is getting involved in macropractice will need information on how organizations function in general, and specific knowledge on the social worker's employing organizations. For example, if a social worker in protective services is interested in starting a Parents Anonymous group for sin-

gle mothers, one important issue is that of permission and approval. Does the supervisor approve of this involvement? Does this approval extend to the worker's being involved in this undertaking on agency time? Is the worker acting as a representative for the agency or just as an individual? Does the supervisor (or other administrators) see any potential conflicts as a result of this activity? These questions are best answered before the worker becomes too involved. Otherwise, he or she could find herself in the position of the Saturday morning cartoon character who is walking out on a tree limb and hears the sound of a saw.

I was once employed by a private social services agency in a midwestern city. Not long after I was hired, the director asked me to represent him at a meeting of people interested in expanding area mental health services. After the meeting, I enthusiastically reported to the director that I was serving on one of the task forces. He became irate, informing me that my purpose was to go and observe and not to become involved in a project about which he had reservations. What I didn't know how to do at that time was to get clarification on my purpose and ask what behaviors would be supported.

Another important concept is that of organizational memory. Individually, each of us may have positive or negative associations with a particular object or event because of past memories. A friend of mine does not eat bananas because he once was violently ill with intestinal flu after eating them. While he knows cognitively that the bananas did not cause the flu, the association is such that bananas are not palatable.

Similarly, some organizations or governing bodies may be unwilling to become active in certain areas if past efforts were unsuccessful. If the worker and others are interested in starting a program that would provide jobs and/or training for teenagers, it is important to know whether anything in this area has been attempted before. It may be that five years ago a program was funded but was poorly supervised. Youths were paid for standing around, and in some instances, even when they weren't there. Armed with this knowledge, the worker would realize that many people would have reservations about any youth employment program and would be careful in talking with people to point out the specific ways that the proposed program is different from the failed effort.

The worker also needs to be cognizant about the realities of organizational change. As Robert Pruger (1978) pointed out, much of the discussion of organizational change is not applicable or relevant to the situation of most social workers:

> Organizational change is an attractive subject to many students and faculty. Consequently, it is likely to come up in classroom discussions even where the formal curriculum seems to allow no place for any consideration of bureaucratic phenomena. The problem here is that most treatments are not helpful. They are ideological in character, rather than oriented to skill building. In class, as in the literature, the matter is too often addressed as if the central problem of change is to convince people to be for it. Though it is difficult to identify anyone who has directly opposed change, somehow there is an endless supply of able advocates seeking opportunities to cross swords with this invisible enemy. The results of these efforts are as morally satisfying as they are intellectually dulling. Through them, audiences regularly experience an invigorating, personal commitment to change. Unfortunately, such vicarious experience is no substitute for the patient observation, hard-headed analyses, and consistent behavior required to effect real change. [p. 161]

For the social worker interested in changing his or her employing organization or others in the community, the following organizational characteristics are relevant:

1. All organizations change. Just as an individual is not the same person he or she was a year ago, neither is an organization. Changes in funding or funding priorities, changes in societal values or trends, occurrences within the community, and changes in personnel all affect an organization's actions and policies.

2. The perceived risks and benefits of the proposed change to the organization need to be assessed and communicated to others in the organization as part of the change strategy. Identifying these can lead to understanding the sources of support and resistance to a proposed change (Frey, 1990).

3. The social worker who realizes that change within an organization is a continuous process can be prepared to attempt to influence organizational policies and politics when the opportunity arises. The juvenile probation worker who believes that his or her agency in general does an inadequate job of working with clients who are ethnic minority members can develop documentation to support this. If the present director and staff do not share the concern, the case can then be made if a new director is hired, or new training funds become available, or if other changes in the organization or community occur that allow the issue to be raised again. To the organized go the spoils.

4. As change occurs slowly in organizations and communities, individuals who "stick around" are more likely to be able to contribute to change than persons who "parachute" into a community and then leave a year or two later. The image of a community organizer that many people have is that of a Saul Alinsky-type (see the section, "Models of Community Practice" later in this chapter) who comes into a community, helps people right wrongs, and then rides off like the Lone Ranger. While outside resource people, like Alinsky-trained organizers, can be useful in winning battles, wars are won and lost by the people who have staying power in organizations and communities.

Exhibit 10.1
Your community—its background

A. Community characteristics
   1. What are the major population characteristics; for example, what percentage is white? Foreign-born? African American? Mexican American? Chinese? Indian? Puerto Rican? What are the principal ethnic and religious groups? What is the age composition? How do the population characteristics compare to state and national averages?
   2. What are the principal economic characteristics of the community? Principal types of employment? Major industries? What other sources of wealth are there? Have there been recent changes in the economic life? (Moving in or out of industry? Substantial industrial or other expansions? Diversification?)
   3. What is the unemployment rate? Its characteristics; that is, largely African American, Latino, young people, and so on? Have there been recent changes in this rate? If so, to what can the changes be attributed? Are there sections of your community where the rate is appreciably higher than the average?

      What is the median family income? If only average per capita income figures are available, assess in terms of these questions: Is the average skewed because of large numbers of wealthy people? Large numbers of poor? How does it compare to the national average? (Caution: even if it is lower, or higher, it may not reflect, in either case, wide variations or a skewed range in your community.)
   4. What are the housing patterns: Percentage of residential property that is high cost, moderate, low? Condition of housing; for example, mostly new? Well kept or maintained? Deteriorating? What is the pattern of rental property; that is, range of rents? Availability of moderate- and low-cost housing? Is the community dependent on a large metropolitan area for employment? For housing of those who work in your community?
   5. To what degree are "outsiders" accepted by the "insiders" who have always lived there? To what degree do "newcomers" and "old-timers" use the same services and facilities?
   6. What are the norms regarding the role of the church in helping? Do the churches help out their own members who are having difficulties or are in need? Do they help other community members who are not church members? If so, what kinds of persons are aided?
   7. What are the norms regarding conformity to community values regarding individual conduct? Which norms seem to be strongest? How are people treated who violate these norms?
B. Community life
   1. How many newspapers are there? (If more than one, are they independently owned?) Radio stations? Television stations? Are radio and/or television stations owned by newspapers? Is news of your community carried on a regular basis in a metropolitan newspaper? What are the principal out-of-town media influences? How does one learn about local governmental activities? Hearings? Meetings? Community cultural activities?
   2. What are the voluntary welfare organizations? Is there a community welfare council? Joint fund raising, such as United Way? If more than one overall fundraising effort, why?
   3. What are principal communitywide civic and service organizations? Fraternal groups? Labor organizations? Business organizations? Cultural groups? Do they work together on communitywide problems? Are there coalitions among these groups on common interests? Ad hoc? Of longer standing? Which groups are more likely to be aligned? On what kinds of issues? Are there neighborhood groups? If so, what are they organized around—cultural, school, political interests, other?
   4. How successful is the community in resolving disputes among various groups or over issues such as schools and zoning? Is there high participation in local decision

making (as measured by voter turnout?) Are the elected officials and local leaders committed to long-term local services, or are they "training" for statewide office?

Public welfare/Social services

A. Administration

1. What governmental agencies (town, county, state, federal) are involved in administration of public welfare or social services in your community?
2. Is there a public welfare board? If so, what is its composition? How are members selected? Are there legal requirements for their selection? What are the terms of office? Salaries? Duties?
3. What employees are engaged in public welfare or social service activities? How are they selected? What qualifications are required? What are the salaries? Are any jobs available in public welfare or social service functions for those on public assistance?

B. Interagency cooperation

1. What cooperative programs exist between public welfare agencies and the juvenile court, probation officers, schools, day-care centers, nursing homes, public health, other agencies?
2. What cooperation is there with private social services agencies, if any exist? If there are any, what are they? Is there exchange of information? Joint planning?

C. Programs and facilities

1. Noninstitutional care

a. What agency or agencies administer services for children—neglected, abandoned children without parents or relatives to care for them? Are foster homes used? What is the rate of pay to foster homes? How are such homes chosen? Supervised?

b. What money is available for aid to families with dependent children? General assistance? How much comes from state? Federal government? Local sources? What is the average amount available for each child? What is the caseload per worker? What type of care is provided? Are there efforts to help parents find jobs? If so, what kind? Are there adequate day-care centers?

c. Is there an adoption service?

2. Other public assistance programs

a. What programs are there for needy blind persons? Permanently disabled? Partially disabled? Elderly who don't qualify for social security?

b. What other assistance programs exist? Temporary assistance, special and corrective needs, exceptional needs (fares, emergencies, and so on), employment services, legal services, others? What money is available for such assistance? From what sources is it available? How do individuals apply for such assistance? How is information about such special assistance made available to the people?

c. Are special assistance programs administered by a public department? If so, what agency or agencies?

3. Institutional care

a. Are there public institutions for individuals with a physical or mental disability? The elderly? Orphaned? Delinquent? Emotionally disturbed? Needy persons? If private institutions are used, how? On a contracting-for-services basis? Cost sharing? Are county, regional, or state institutions used? If so, on what basis?

b. How are public institutions administered? What are the procedures and requirements for admission?

c. What kind of services (educational, recreational, training, and so on) are provided in each public institution? Do any community groups or individuals provide services? If so, what kinds?

d. What is the cost per resident per day? What is the average stay? Do any of the users pay? On what basis? Do these institutions operate on a budget or a given amount per day per patient?

e. Are there standards for public institutions—inspections, licensing, state supervision, and so on?

(continued)

Exhibit 10.1

Your community—its background *(continued)*

f. How many persons from your community are in state institutions? What is the cost to your local government per patient? What is the procedure for admission? Average length of stay by case type?

g. Do any of the local institutions provide outpatient services? What kinds?

4. Self-help groups and voluntary associations

a. Are there self-help groups for persons seeking to work with others in similar situations? Are there local meetings of Alcoholics Anonymous, Narcotics Anonymous, and Recovery, Inc. (for persons with chronic mental illness), as well as of local (nonnationally affiliated) groups?

b. Are there voluntary associations, such as churches and civic organizations that are important sources of support and leadership, especially within neighborhoods or ethnic communities?

SOURCE: This guide was adapted from League of Women Voters, *Know Your Community*. Copyright 1972, pp. 6, 7, 35–37. Adapted by permission of League of Women Voters of the United States.

Knowledge of Funding Sources and Funding Cycles

As was stated earlier in this chapter, social workers often become involved in helping people or groups to organize in order to develop services for unmet community needs. In some cases, such as self-help groups, money may not be needed. In many other cases, funds will be needed to put the ideas or plans into operation.

Three questions are important in this area:

1. *Where is the money?* One interpretation of the golden rule is "the person who has the gold, rules."

Many times organizations and communities are able to do only what the state or federal government is funding at that time. A knowledge of those funding sources is important, as is an awareness of other sources of funding. In many states where funding has been decentralized, county governments make most of the decisions on how mental health, mental retardation, and juvenile corrections services will be provided.

Additionally, local foundations in some areas will provide "seed" money for services or organizations in their first year or two of operation. United Way or United Givers may be another source of funds for new or expanded services.

Another option for securing money is fund raising, which will be covered later in the chapter.

2. *What is the funding cycle of the governmental unit or organization with the money?* Every level of government—city, county, state, federal—and every formal organization has a defined fiscal year. For the federal government, it is October 1–September 30. For many state and local governments, it is July 1–June 30. Some organizations use the July 1–June 30 fiscal year, and some use the standard calendar year. Depending on the fiscal year used, decisions on how money will be spent are made at different times by different governmental bodies. For example, a county government that would be able to fund a Youth Diversion Project (which would treat youthful offenders in their home community) may be on a July 1–June 30 calendar. Budget hearings and deliberations are generally held in March and April for the coming year. By June 1 at the latest, all funding decisions for the coming year will have been made. If a community group approached the county on that date, the county's reply would most likely be "wait until next year."

3. *How "real" is the money?* At times there is an announcement of a new source of funds that gets people excited about the prospect of doing something about unmet needs. Often, it turns out that the "new program" is simply a relabeling of an already existing program that supports service programs, and no additional money is available. I was working in Georgia in 1976 when Title XX funding for social services was introduced. Public hearings were held all over the state to help the state government decide how the $300 million plus was to be spent. Hundreds of people came to hearings in rural counties, advocating their interest. (In reality, the hearings probably measured the effectiveness of individual agencies' transportation systems in busing their clients to the meetings rather than measuring community opinion.) What people discovered at the hearings was that there would be no additional money, and if they wanted funding for new services, this would require reduced funding for the day-care centers, senior citizen programs, and so on, that had been funded in the past years.

Social work students generally learn about governments and the mechanisms by which they fund programs in social welfare policy courses. While the information may seem dry and somewhat irrelevant at that time, it becomes useful when they are working in a community with unmet needs.

When social workers and the people they are working with are familiar with the political process, they are more likely to see political change as possible; when they are unfamiliar with change processes, they tend to avoid them (Rubin & Rubin, 1992). Social workers who are getting involved in political processes also need to be aware of the informal as well as the formal political processes. Individuals with economic or other kinds of power may have great influence in local or statewide decision making, although they never run for political office (Fellin, 1987).

Skills for Macropractice—Group Decision-Making Skills

In addition to specific information and knowledge that are applicable to macropractice, there are also a number of skills and techniques that are useful in certain situations. Some of these, like the decision-making techniques described later, are also used in group work. Others, such as fund raising and community awareness, are used primarily in macropractice.

Brainstorming

One excellent technique for use in groups that are looking for ways to accomplish a goal is brainstorming (Maier, 1970; Osborn, 1963). One common definition of *brainstorming* involves generating ideas about an issue. However, the term also denotes a *specific technique* for generating ideas, possibilities, or alternate courses of action. In using brainstorming, one tries to identify as many different ways of achieving a goal as possible. Brainstorming was developed by Alex Osborn (1963), who outlined the following ground rules.

1. Brainstorming can last anywhere from about one minute to half an hour.
2. The session continues as long as ideas are being generated.
3. Each session is to be freewheeling and open.
4. The quantity of ideas counts, not the quality. A greater number of ideas will increase the likelihood that usable ideas will be suggested.
5. Members are encouraged to build on the ideas of other members whenever possible, so that thoughts are expanded and new combinations of ideas are formulated.
6. The focus is on a single issue or problem. Members should not skip from problem to problem, or try to brainstorm a multiproblem situation.

7. A relaxed, congenial, cooperative atmosphere should be promoted.
8. All members (no matter how shy and reluctant to participate) should be encouraged to contribute.
9. It is often advisable to limit members to one idea at a time so that less vocal individuals feel encouraged to say their ideas.
10. For new members unfamiliar with brainstorming, the rationale and rules for brainstorming should be explained.
11. If groups are being formed specifically for brainstorming, it is helpful to seek members having some diversity of opinion and background.
12. After the brainstorming session is over, the group then selects the best ideas (or a synthesis of these ideas) related to the issue or problem.

Brainstorming has a number of advantages:

1. It increases involvement and participation by all members.
2. It reduces dependence on a single authority figure.
3. It provides a procedure for obtaining a large number of ideas in a relatively short period.
4. It reduces the pressure to say the "right things" in order to impress others in the group.
5. It makes the meeting more interesting, fun, and stimulating.
6. It encourages an open sharing of ideas.
7. It helps create a nonevaluative climate.
8. The ideas of one member can build on those of others so that creative and unique combinations are suggested.

Some shortcomings of brainstorming should be noted. For many people brainstorming is a strange experience and may lead to an initial sense of discomfort. To a restricted, self-conscious group, brainstorming may actually hinder participation as it forces members into new patterns of behavior.

Conversely, in some situations brainstorming can be used as an icebreaker to open up a stuffy and inhibited group. Whether brainstorming will have an inhibiting effect or an opening-up effect will depend partially on the leader's skills and timing in using the approach.

One example of a situation in which brainstorming was useful is that of a group of residents in a part of a town where there were no recreational facilities for children. A group of the residents negotiated with the city to turn a city-owned lot in the area into a park. The city council agreed to let the residents use the area indefinitely as a park and to have city maintenance personnel keep the area mowed. However, the residents would have to raise the money for the playground equipment.

A social worker met with the group and acted as facilitator for a brainstorming session. The 23 neighborhood residents were initially skeptical about the process, but "got into it" as the ideas started rolling in. A total of 46 ideas were generated and then categorized. The two major categories were fund raising and looking for playground equipment not presently being used. After some discussion, the residents decided to hold a carnival on the proposed site and to use that as a focus for the fundraising effort. A group of residents volunteered to work on that project. Another small group then volunteered to make inquiries as to the possibilities of locating unused playground equipment.

Nominal Group Technique

The process for using this technique has been explained in Chapter 6. It can be a useful approach to help groups attempt to reach consensus or at least to give group members information on the thoughts of the other members.

Several years ago I was asked by an interagency council in a medium-size southern county to help them define their priorities.

The interagency council was well attended by representatives of health and social service agencies in that county, and the council leadership believed that the group could influence both the United Way and the county commission if they were to speak with one voice. The problem, as always with service providers, was that each member tended to think that his or her area of concern (the elderly, juveniles, people with developmental disabilities, and so on) was most deserving of support.

I met with 40 or more human services professionals representative of all the service providers in a one-day planning session. By using the nominal group technique (and asking the participants at each step to identify *two* groups that they considered to be especially in need of services and at a later stage of the process to list *two* specific kinds of services that should be started or strengthened), the individual biases of the participants toward their own services canceled out. By the end of the day, the participants had agreed on two specific service areas that they later proposed to the funding bodies.

As this example indicates, nominal group techniques can provide members of a task force or planning group with information about their own priorities. As such, it can also be considered a needs assessment technique. This concept is explained in the next section.

Needs Assessment

Needs assessment (NA) is a term that has acquired wide usage and a variety of meanings. It has been used in referring to a statewide comprehensive appraisal of problems and needs. It has also been used on a smaller scale to refer to assessment of a community's needs or assessment by an agency in a community of its clients' needs. For example, a youth services agency in a community may conduct a needs assessment of its clientele. On a large or small scale, needs assessment refers to efforts of acquiring and making sense out of information so it can be used as an aid in making decisions.

Defining needs. One can begin to define needs by differentiating among four different kinds of needs: felt, expressed, proscribed, and comparative. *Felt needs* are those that are perceived by the person with the need. For example, you perceive your need for water when you are thirsty or for shelter if you are homeless. However, we use the same term to refer to *wants:* "I need a red Porsche so people will notice me." Gerard Egan (1985) pointed out that people may also have unfelt needs; for example, they may need medical care or dental care without realizing it. *Expressed needs* are the felt needs that are communicated to others, because people do not automatically express the needs they feel. Part of the social worker's role may be to help people voice their needs in a way that others will hear them. *Proscribed needs* or normative needs are those that some expert or formal organization perceives to be needed in a given situation. In a class, a professor may write on a student's paper, "You need to write more clearly," although the student may not feel that this is a need or problem. In a family, a protective services agency may see a need for the parents to reduce the intensity and frequency of harsh disciplining of their children, even though the parents feel the discipline is justified and appropriate. Similarly, in a community, those outside the community may see that there is a need for youth programs or parenting classes, while the residents may not feel that need. *Comparative needs* arise when we compare one area or community or part of town to another, and notice a discrepancy. If one section of town receives few police patrols and another more affluent area has more police cars patrolling the streets, we can speak of a comparative need. The capacity to distinguish among these kinds of needs is essential for good community practice. We need to be clear who is defining the need, so one set of values is not blindly imposed on community residents by others (Egan, 1985).

Social workers involved in macropractice can find themselves in situations where they have no information on which to make decisions, or at other times they may have an overabundance of data and have difficulty sorting out the pertinent information from the rest. When a needs assessment study is being designed, the following questions help sharpen its focus.

Why do we want the information? An NA may be conducted for various reasons. A sponsoring group may be aware of the existence of a need, but without documentation it is difficult to convince decision makers and others of the necessity for action. In the same vein, an NA can serve to increase the visibility of an issue, condition, or subpopulation (Center for Social Research and Development, 1974).

An agency or organization may conduct an NA to determine whether its efforts are addressing the needs that are most critical. Especially when new money is involved, an NA is a procedure that can be used to gain information about various problem areas in order to determine which area most needs attention.

Another impetus for conducting an NA is that it is frequently required by a funding agency. Various governmental and private funding organizations have policies that include a needs assessment as part of the proposal development process.

Needs assessment can also be used as a consciousness-raising device. Based on the work of Paolo Freire, who combined adult literacy with politicization in working with the poor in Latin American countries, needs assessments can be designed with low-income community members so the NA is a vehicle for discussion of empowerment and community needs as well as a data collection and analysis technique (Marti-Costa & Serrano-Garcia, 1987).

One general rule is that if you cannot clearly answer the "why" question, you are probably better off not conducting an NA at this time. Information that is collected without a clear purpose rarely is used.

Who will use the data? In the early stages of drawing up an NA, it is essential to identify and involve the decision makers who will eventually use the data. Allowing the potential consumers of the data to define the NA's scope, focus, and content is required if the findings are to have an impact on their concerns (Center for Social Research and Development, 1974, p. 58).

What kind of information do we want? Many different types of information may be appropriate for a given local needs assessment. Exhibit 10.2 summarizes some of the types of information used in needs assessment.

Where do we get the data? There are two broad categories of data used in NAs. One is already existent information and the other is information that needs to be generated.

Among the sources of existent information for every community are census records, state labor department and health department statistics, and agency records and reports. These data can serve as statistical indicators of the extent of problems or conditions. Another potential source of existent information might be studies conducted at some previous time for a different purpose.

One good source of information may be the regional planning commission that serves the given geographical area. In addition to possessing certain statistical information, individuals at a planning commission may be helpful in directing one to other sources. In areas where there are city and county planning units, these can be valuable sources of information.

Exhibit 10.2

Types of information used in needs assessments

A. *Profile of community characteristics:* A profile gives an overview of the demographic characteristics of a community; for example, age structure, ethnic and racial composition, length of residence, and so on.

B. *Profiles of domains of living:* These profiles provide data on the incidence of a problem and the social patterns of the population. This can include the following:
   1. Economic data, including income levels, expenditures analysis, money management, and credit patterns.
   2. Employment data, including occupational levels, work history, occupational aspiration levels, and vocational needs.
   3. Family patterns, such as parent-child relationships, adjustment problems of children, marriage problems, and divorce rate.
   4. Educational patterns, including educational attainment and needs of adults, school adjustment of children, school dropout rate, and educational attainment.
   5. Housing, such as density, condition of dwelling units, and overcrowding.
   6. Physical and mental health, including long-term disability, causes of death, incidence of diseases, and environment conditions.
   7. Home management, including housekeeping problems, nutrition, home maintenance, and child care.
   8. Recreational patterns, including leisure activities, sports and athletics, and cultural activities.
   9. Criminal justice, including adult crime and juvenile delinquency rates, fear of crimes, and so on.
   10. Life satisfaction, such as community solidarity and self-appraisal.

C. *Knowledge and utilization of services:* Persons needing a service often are unaware of existing services or resources. Before making decisions, it is important to discover whether this lack of knowledge among those needing services is one cause of the problem's persistence.

D. *Barriers to service utilization:* Individuals who need services may be aware of them and still not use the services because of barriers to utilization. The following types of barriers can be identified in a needs assessment:
   1. Physical barriers, such as inadequate transportation or distance of the agency from target population.
   2. Negative attitudes of the staff, as perceived by the clients or potential clients.
   3. Feelings that a social stigma is attached to service usage.
   4. Fee for usage, which is beyond the means of those needing services.
   5. Actual or perceived restrictive eligibility criteria.

E. *Existing community information system:* Before a service can be utilized, the potential service recipients must be aware of its existence. A needs assessment can identify the formal and informal channels by which a given group is most likely to be reached.

F. *Resource assessment:* Identification of existing and potential resources available for utilization should occur before planning or allocating decisions are made.

G. *Political resources assessment:* The potential mobilization of political and community leaders and the population at large is necessary, since decisions are generally made in the political arena.

There are times when information that is not presently available will need to be generated. This can be done in many ways. A community forum is one way of obtaining information. Interviews with selected individuals, community leaders, frontline workers, or clients can yield valuable data.

One commonly used approach in generating data is the survey. Three techniques used in surveys to gather information are (1) the telephone interview; (2) the mailed questionnaire; and (3) the person-to-person interview.

A survey of a number of people can yield useful information that cannot be obtained in other ways. The obvious advantage of using a survey is that information directly relevant to the problem under consideration is collected.

The drawbacks to using a survey are that it requires substantial time, substantial effort, survey research expertise, and usually money. The way in which a survey is designed and conducted will influence the results. While the question "When did you stop beating your wife?" is laughable, there are questions in surveys that produce results almost as slanted.

It is a good idea to bring in someone with expertise or special knowledge about surveys to assist with the preparation or implementation. Potential sources of expertise might be found in the state office of human services departments, local colleges, or the business community.

Agency frontline workers can be an excellent source of information for determining needs, especially for expanded services. In Hamilton County, Ohio (which includes Cincinnati), 90 case managers were asked to review the records of over 1,400 clients and report on what kinds of needs, met and unmet, their clients had. They were able to determine that among the top priorities were unmet needs for ways to monitor medications and provide therapy, for socialization, and for subsidized apartments (Ford et al., 1992).

Who else needs to be involved? As well as involving the potential users of the data, it may also be appropriate to enlist the cooperation of other organizations, agencies, and prominent individuals in the needs assessment planning. This involvement may be advisable because the NA may indicate problem areas that the sponsoring agency may not be involved in. Also, if other agencies are involved in the collection and preparation of information, they are more likely to use it in their planning and decision making. A third reason is that at times the information will be more favorably received in a community if certain key individuals are involved in the NA process.

What information is necessary on an ongoing basis? Some of the information yielded in an NA becomes obsolete within a short time. One thing that agencies may discover in conducting an NA is that certain types of information need to be collected or updated periodically to be useful. Also, a process of needs assessment often indicates what information is not available; this in itself, is an important finding.

A needs assessment may involve a long, complex, and costly process, or it may be a relatively simple procedure. The process should mirror the need assessment's purpose—designed to yield most fully the information needed by those making decisions.

Public Relations Skills and Communicating with the Public

Social workers are aware of the lack of knowledge and the amount of misinformation that the public has about human services and those who use them. They also know the powerful influence that the media have. Yet, as a profession, we are ill prepared to use the media to get our message across. Skills in public education and public relations are not generally a part of social work curricula.

Brawley (1983) believed that a number of barriers to effective use of the media exist:

Many of the barriers that exist to the achievement of positive media treatment of human service topics are primarily psychological in nature. We think that the media are entirely out of sympathy with or disinterested in our causes; we think that prevailing "news values" that stress conflict, immediacy, sensationalism, personalities, and the like present hopeless obstacles to the proper understanding and reporting of human service issues; or we view the domain of radio, television, and newspapers as alien territory that we enter only at considerable risk.

Other barriers are more concrete. The typical human service practitioner simply does not know enough about the workings of the news media to know what opportunities exist for positive action and does not possess the tools needed to undertake activities in this area with confidence that his or her efforts will be productive. [p. 13]

For the social worker who wants to use the media, either to publicize a new service on a one-time basis or to spotlight a community problem as part of a larger change process, it is necessary to develop relationships with the media and to acquire the skills to utilize them.

Relationships with Media Representatives

The first step in getting coverage for your program is to get to know, personally, those who report the news in your community. Introduce yourself to the editor of a county weekly paper or the reporter for a daily paper that would cover your story. The persons in charge of news at local radio and television stations are also important to know. When working with the media, you should follow some basic rules.

1. Be honest at all times. This includes not only being truthful but also not leaving out important facts about a situation or issue. Media representatives will forgive mistakes if they trust you, so don't do anything that would damage the trust.

2. Know the deadlines of newspapers and those of the radio or television news show. Nothing is as irritating for an editor as someone walking in with a news article two hours after the deadline or five minutes before the deadline.

3. Know the orientation of the newspaper. Are they pro–social services or do they have axes to grind?

4. Know the staff of the newspaper. To whom do you address your story?

5. Do not complain about a story unless a serious error has been made, and then first call the reporter who handled the story. Do not go to his or her boss unless it is absolutely necessary.

6. Do not heckle newspeople by constantly asking them why a story you submitted was not used. It is all right to ask your contact if there was something wrong that you can correct next time. But there are many reasons your story might have been thrown out at the last minute to make room for something the editor considered more newsworthy.

7. Do not forget to say "thank you." It pays big dividends to let members of the press know you appreciate their efforts. When someone does a particularly good job of reporting about your program (on one occasion or over the space of several months), a short, simple thank-you note will always be appreciated and remembered. And if you are thanking a reporter, write to the editor with a copy to the reporter.

8. Every newspaper is run differently. General rules of how newspapers operate are just that—general. To know the specifics of each paper, you should ask for a copy of its *style sheet*. This is a list of news article rules that editors usually give to beginning reporters. If a small newspaper does not have a style sheet, the editor will probably refer you to a sample article or articles as a guide to how articles should be written.

9. There are distinct differences in the editorial content of a daily versus a weekly newspaper. Although a daily typically has a larger audience, a weekly places more stress on local issues and is therefore more closely targeted to the immediate needs of the readers. This is especially true in a rural area. Dailies usually have larger staffs than weeklies, so weekly editors may have a need for well-written news stories for their papers.

Skills for Media Utilization

Familiarization with the rules of the media is one step toward getting good coverage, but this doesn't automatically get your story in print or on the air. The social worker who doesn't have the skills to write newspaper articles or public service announcements (PSA) for the radio can follow one of several approaches.

1. *Find out whether the media will do the actual work.* Some newspapers do all of their own writing. If you want a feature on a client who has established a self-help program for others, a feature writer will come out and do the story. Similarly, some radio and television stations have people on staff who will develop public service information.

2. *Find community volunteers to do publicity.* People enjoy doing what they do well. In all communities, there are people with expertise in drawing, writing, design and layout, and so on. Some of these people will be interested in helping your agency, either for one project or on an ongoing basis. Journalism and public relations classes at nearby colleges and universities are also a good resource.

3. *Develop the skills.* A number of excellent books on using the media have detailed explanations on writing news articles, getting your message on television, and so forth (Brawley, 1983; Church, 1980; MacShane, 1979). Writing or designing community awareness materials is a skill. Like riding a bicycle or interviewing, you get better at it the more you do it.

Fund Raising

People who are involved in helping others are aware of the limitations of governmental funding. For some programs, there's just not enough money. The money can only be used for certain purposes and not for others. Regulations on how dollars are to be spent are designed to prevent waste and target the money, but they also restrict flexibility on how program dollars can be spent.

For new or small agencies and community groups, it may be difficult to get any or sufficient governmental help. There may not be any "new" money available, or the agency or group may not have the expertise or time to write a complicated, 250-page grant proposal. In all these cases, fund raising may be an answer.

In addition to the obvious benefit of having the money when you do fund raising, there are other advantages:

1. You gain credibility when you can show that local people support you.

When Kate Bradley was raising money for the Petros, Tennessee, health clinic, she learned the railroad was going to sell the land around its unused tracks. She wrote the president of the railroad and asked for the first option to buy the land for the clinic building. Then the politicians in Morgan County learned the land was for sale and tried to outbid her. It was clear they could double or triple her offer. Coal companies in Tennessee are used to getting their own way by using county and state politicians. Kate drove 175 miles to Nashville to meet with the railroad president and the representatives of the coal companies. When she walked into the meeting, she was the only woman in the room.

The president said, "You must be Mrs. Bradley."

"I am," she said, looking him straight in the eye. Without waiting to be asked, Kate Bradley spoke her piece to the older man:

"Sir, I know you are going to honor your letter giving the health clinic the right to buy your land in Petros. I know these politicians can give you a lot more money. But I just want you to know that our money comes from cupcakes. We've had a rummage sale every Saturday, and held dinners and bake sales. Everyone in the community has given me a quilt, or a jar of beans, or put up some preserves to sell for the clinic. That's where my bid comes from."

The railroad president sold her the land, and adjourned the meeting. [Flanagan, 1977, pp. 16–17]

2. It looks good to other funding sources if you have raised a significant amount of money. A women's center raised $2,500 its first year of operation through a raffle and solicitation of donations. They were able to use this as a demonstration of public support when they went to a United Way for support.

3. It creates favorable publicity for the agency or group. When people buy tickets for a raffle, attend a benefit concert, or buy a cupcake, they have some contact with the sponsoring organization. This can be a time for informing the public, one at a time, about the organization.

A number of excellent books and pamphlets explain the "how-to's" of fund-raising (Clifton & Dahms, 1980, chap. 3; Flanagan, 1977; Grubb & Zwick, 1976; Leibert & Sheldon, 1972). In deciding what to do and carrying it out, the following principles can be useful:

1. Be creative. One shelter for abused women in Wisconsin created and copyrighted a logo with the phrase "Women— You Can't Beat Them." They sell T-shirts, bags, and other items with that logo locally and nationally, and support most of their activities with the proceeds.

2. Work on your fears, and the fears of those working with you, of asking people for money.

Money is like sex. Everyone thinks about it, but no one is supposed to discuss it in polite company. Everyone has a lot of inhibitions about money, especially asking for money; think of all the cartoons of the officer worker afraid to ask for a raise. In our society fears about money are normal.

Most people are afraid to ask someone else for money. They are afraid they will

fail and afraid they will lose face. A few admit they are afraid, but others will give a lot of excuses: I can't make calls at the office; I don't know anyone rich; I can't get a baby-sitter. Or they postpone forever: I can't do it until after the kids are back in school, the holidays, the election, the tennis season, the vacation, the promotion. Volunteers often make asking for money sound like a bothersome chore, like taking out the garbage. It is not a chore; it is a challenge. Asking for money is like going out to beat up a bear. The larger the amount, the more frightening it becomes because you have to beat up a bigger bear.

One of the jobs of a good fund-raiser is to teach volunteers how to conquer their fear of the unknown. The first step is understanding that each person comes complete with his or her own set of fears and hang-ups, and the package of inhibitions usually includes a fear of asking for money. The second step is realizing this is normal and nothing to be ashamed of. The third step is working with the volunteers so they can get control of their own fears.

It is imperative that you understand and appreciate your volunteer's real feelings, because when members succeed at fund-raising they do more than bring in money for the organization. They have also overcome their own fear. When they raise money, they have won a personal victory, they have conquered the bear. When people can raise money, they can do anything. [Flanagan, 1977, p. 38]

3. Make the fundraising activity appropriate for your community. A benefit concert may not work in a small town where few people go out at night to hear music. Some churches have admonitions against gambling, which includes raffles. In a community where many people attend such churches, a raffle may not work.

4. Make it fun. When people work together on a project, they can develop camaraderie and develop or strengthen

friendships. An atmosphere that allows the social as well as the work aspect of a fund-raising project (coffee, doughnuts, and fruit at work meetings, for example) helps people to feel good about what they're doing. After a fund-raising effort is finished, a get-together allows the participants a chance to celebrate what they have accomplished.

Political Activity and Lobbying

Chauncey Alexander stated that "the social work profession, from its inception, has had a love-hate relationship with politics" (1982, p. 15). Partly because their interests and much of their interaction is on a one-to-one basis, and partly because of a lack of skills in the area, social workers have shied away from the political arena. Yet, because of their work "in the trenches," social workers have a greater knowledge of inequities and inadequate legislation than most people.

Recently, in the social work profession there has been a growing acceptance of the need to understand the political process and to work with it. Social workers are active in issues that affect the profession—such as lobbying—and that affect clients.

The whole arena of social work and politics is too large to cover in this chapter. Examples of the way social workers can be politically active include writing and introducing legislation, guiding it through the legislative process, and helping elect candidates. At various times, social workers will be involved in these activities. On a regular basis, however, social workers and human services agencies can attempt to influence local, state, and federal elected officials.

Attempting to influence elected officials, or lobbying, is an activity that we usually associate with high-powered, high-paid lobbyists in expensive suits. Yet, it is something that all social workers can do effectively. The following principles are useful:

1. Get to know your legislators. Agencies can invite elected officials to meet with staff to share information and concerns at a time when the legislature is not in session. My experience has been that breakfast is a good time for this. It's before the elected official's schedule is too busy, and it can be more relaxed than a meeting sandwiched between other appointments. Often, legislators don't know much about the nuts and bolts of what social workers and human services agencies do, and they appreciate the knowledge.

2. Contact your legislators not only when you want them to do something but also when you approve of what they've done. Elected officials don't get a lot of fan mail. They appreciate it and will remember it.

3. Never write anyone off. A lobbyist I know says, "There are no permanent friends or permanent enemies, only permanent issues." People who oppose your position may change eventually, especially if you don't treat them as if they are the enemy. The social work values of treating people as individuals worthy of respect is applicable to people in public life as well as to clients.

Community Practice—
A Problem-Solving Process

One of the dilemmas of teaching social work practice is that reality is not always as sequential as we make it out to be. For example, in micropractice we talk of problem identification, followed by problem assessment or clarification, followed by goal setting. What may happen in working with a client is that the client discovers or reveals during goal setting that there are more urgent concerns.

Similarly, in macropractice, things do not often go as smoothly as the following process indicates. Yet, a knowledge of the ideal is helpful. In the following section, a description of how the problem-solving process can be used in macropractice is presented.[2]

Planning, according to Meryl Ruoss (1970), is organized foresight. From the time a problem or opportunity arises until some action is taken, the persons involved in the decision making will in some manner gather information, look at alternatives, and make a decision. This may be done in an organized fashion or the principals may just be "muddling through."

Many efforts, such as involving citizens in an advisory committee or designing a telephone reassurance system, seem overwhelmingly large at first sight. A man once was invited to dinner, and when he arrived, was seated at a table where an immense elephant, cooked in its entirety, was laid out before him. When he confusedly asked how he was supposed to eat something so big, the host calmly replied, "One bite at a time."

In this section, the planning process is presented one bite at a time. The various steps are grouped into three stages:

Preplanning: Questions to ask	Why is the planning being done? Who is the sponsor? Who is to do the planning? Are varying points of view included?
Planning: Plans to make	Problem assessment Problem clarification Goal setting Objective setting Examination and decision among alternatives Determination of strategy
Impact: Steps to take	Implementation of strategy Monitoring Evaluation

This sequence is intended to serve as a guide for those involved in a planning process. The process includes ten steps, each of which needs to be considered. The amount of time and effort spent on each step will vary depending on the situation.

The agency setting, the time frame, the resources to be utilized, and other factors will determine (and should determine) how much effort is expended in each step. You don't call the Army Corps of Engineers to build a sandbox. Similarly, an extensive needs assessment or prolonged search for all the alternatives may be unnecessary if the outcome of the planning process will be a relatively minor program change.

Preplanning: Questions to Ask

The first of the three stages is that of preplanning. This includes all the activities that go on before a decision is made to confront actively a problem or opportunity.

The question "Why is the planning being done?" must be answered first. Generally, planning is done because someone perceives a problem or an opportunity.

The existence of a problem or an opportunity is not in itself sufficient reason to begin planning. In the case of a problem, John De-Boer (1970, p. 75) listed four questions that persons should ask themselves before beginning to plan, in order to check the validity of the problem and the assumptions on which it is based. They are the following:

1. Is this concern *our* concern, or some other individual's or group's concern?
2. Is this concern our concern *alone,* or should it be shared with others?
3. Is this a concern that is important to us *now,* or would be better to postpone consideration to a later time?

[2]This section is adapted from James R. Shimkus and James P. Winship, *Human Service Development: Working Together in the Community,* Athens: University of Georgia Printing Department, 1977, pp. 8–17. Adapted by permission of the copyright owners.

4. Is the apparent concern the *real concern,* or a symptom of a deeper underlying problem—or of a different but related problem?

Sometimes the "why" is answered for you. Legislation or administrative mandates may indicate that you begin planning to comply with legislation or administrative policy by a certain date. Although there may be some latitude in these instances, thorough examination of these questions is important before moving on to the next step.

From the beginning, the agency or organization sponsoring the human services development effort must be clearly identified. The organizational base often influences the nature of the effort. For example, a task force composed of professionals from many agencies and cities looking at the needs of youth will likely come up with a plan that is different from one developed by a single agency.

Another reason for clarifying sponsorship of an effort is to sanction those working on the effort. Planning on the local level is linked to service delivery, and if the agency involved is to deliver the service, the administrator may be the person doing the planning. If the administrator is not the chief planner, the person who is the planning manager still needs to have the active support of the administrator in order to conduct the planning and to ensure that the results are implemented.

There may be times in a planning process when the administrator is the appropriate person to initiate contacts; if the administrator is not "on board" with the process and is not willing to take appropriate actions, it may falter. At times, the administrator may also need to have the sanction of his or her division or board before tackling a project.

The other component of the "who" question deals with the composition of the group doing the planning. A "planner" formulating a "plan" in an office separated from an agency's activities will produce a far different outcome than a task force composed of staff, representatives from other agencies, consumers, and other interested citizens.

Preplanning includes persuasion; the project should be formulated with regard to the known philosophies of those who must approve what is to be done. Involving key persons who may have differences at an early stage affords them the opportunity to voice their ideas, and the final product is less likely to be rejected by those who participated in it.

At times, influential individuals will register initial opposition to an effort and refuse to participate in it. In these situations it is important that the planning group formulates its strategy in a way that recognizes and adjusts to the expected opposition.

Planning: Plans to Make

The first step in the planning sequence is the problem assessment. As used here, problem assessment includes needs assessment, problem identification, problem causal analysis, and resource assessment.

Needs assessment involves the gathering, ordering, and analyzing of information pertinent to the problem.

George Bernanos (1970) once stated that "the worst, the most corrupting of lies, are problems poorly stated." Problem identification is concerned with ascertaining whether the problem under consideration is the appropriate problem, and how well the problem is stated.

The difficulty in problem identification lies in the subjective nature of "problems"—a problem is what somebody or something perceives as a problem. The nature of the problem is determined by the manner in which it is perceived (Cartwright, 1973).

The perceptions of what the problem is are shaped by data, attitudes, and value judgments. A merchant and a juvenile court worker may interpret the same data on juvenile delinquency quite differently.

Because of the difficulty in defining a problem, determining who is to do the planning is very important. If the problem under consideration is a controversial one, such as juvenile delinquency, it is inevitable that at some point there will be conflict about what the problem is and what the solution should be. If the planning process is carried out by relatively few people, when the results are released or the program is to be implemented, there likely will be considerable conflict. The proposed program may be rejected, or be so embroiled in controversy that it is not fully effective.

This may be because the omission of certain persons in the planning process has caused the planning group to overlook vital information about conditions, resources, or attitudes.

Whenever the problem under consideration is controversial or will affect a large number of people, conflict will arise. It can be postponed but not avoided. What can be done is to attempt to involve the principals in the planning process, starting with problem identification. If persons can agree on the problem, there is more likelihood that they will be able to agree on goals, objectives, alternatives, and strategies. If a number of people are involved, they are more likely to advocate the action or plan in the larger community.

As the dimensions of the problem are revealed, the next move is to clarify them. Three measures that are helpful in this process relate to the problem's identity (exactly what is it?), its location (where is the problem under consideration?), and its magnitude (what is the extent of the problem?). For example, a group working on housing might define the problem as deteriorating housing (what) in a 14-block neighborhood, south of the downtown area (where), which has 37 percent substandard housing according to the last census, compared to 23 percent in the previous census (to what extent).

In clarifying a problem, it also helps to identify what is *not* the problem. In the previous example, the problem is not defined as the sidewalks, the streets, or the storm sewers.

After identifying the problem, the next component of problem assessment is to attempt to analyze its causes. In doing this, it is necessary to look at the forces that contribute to the problem—economic factors, political pressures, institutionalized values, and attitudes.

Another reason for conducting a causal analysis is that the analysis may reveal that the problem under consideration was not the "real problem," and it is necessary to backtrack and redefine the problem. For example, several decades ago it was thought that people who committed crimes did so because they were mentally retarded. This theory led to the notion that the crime problem could be solved by developing approaches to prevent and treat mental retardation. However, intelligence testing of prison inmates found that most inmates were of normal intelligence. The mental retardation theory of criminal behavior was then discarded. Discarding this theory forced criminologists to change their conceptualizations of criminal behavior.

An integral part of problem assessment is resource assessment. This involves cataloging all actual and potential resources for dealing with the problem. It may include a compilation of agencies and community groups involved in or sympathetic to the problem, a listing of potential funding sources, and a determination of the amount of advocacy around this problem present in the community. In the case of funding sources, it is important to ascertain the limitations under which the money may be spent. In many instances, "form follows financing."

The next step in the planning process is that of establishing goals. Goals are the long-term aims of the project and may be expressed in general terms. They are statements about a desired condition, and they may not be attainable. In the example of the neighborhood housing, the goal of the project might be to bring every housing unit in the neighborhood up to code-enforcement standards.

In writing goals, it is helpful to express them in terms of generally accepted standards whenever possible. In the example, the state or local housing code regulations serve as a standard. In describing adequate or satisfactory conditions in other areas, such as child-care or homemaker services, state agencies or private accrediting groups will have standards against which to measure the adequacy of a program.

After establishing the goals, the next step is to set specific objectives. These should relate directly to the goals, but they are different in that they describe outcomes that the planners realistically expect to meet instead of expressing an ideal condition.

Objectives are quantifiable. An objective is measurable both in relation to what is to be done and within what time period it is to be done. The use of the standards and measures in the objectives should also reflect the quality desired.

In the housing example, specific objectives might be the following:

1. Conducting a housing inspection of every house in the neighborhood within the first three months.
2. Rehabilitating 20 housing units in the first year that are structurally sound but do not presently meet code regulations.
3. Beginning proceedings to condemn and demolish all vacant houses judged not structurally sound.

There are two types of objectives. There will be some objectives that must be reached if the project is to be a success. Other objectives are desirable but not essential. The three objectives mentioned would be essential objectives. In this case, an example of a desirable objective might be:

4. The planting of trees along four residential streets.

Clear, specific objectives are necessary for several reasons. The consideration of alternatives and the selection of the strategy are based on the objectives. As computer operators say, "Garbage In, Garbage Out."

Furthermore, it is extremely difficult to evaluate a program if it does not have quantifiable objectives. Without good objectives, one can evaluate a program only by personal biases.

In the sport of archery there is one sure way for beginners to hit the bull's-eye on the side of the barn every time—paint the bull's-eye after the arrow has landed. A program that is launched without a clear statement of goals is like such an arrow; though wide of the mark intended by its launchers long ago, it may be dubbed on target by anyone who can paint a convincing bull's-eye (DeBoer, 1970, p. 108).

After the objectives are set, the next step is to examine and choose among various alternative approaches. In most cases there will be more than one way to meet the objectives.

The bases on which the alternatives are judged will vary with the circumstances. In selecting among alternative approaches, factors such as cost resources, technical feasibility, and political feasibility will be considered. The length of time in which a program has to prove itself is a consideration. If it is funded for only one year and then must find alternative sources of support, an approach that will give short-term results must be chosen.

When selecting among alternatives, one must guard against the practice of selecting the approach that seems most manageable or more interesting or convenient for the staff rather than the one that best meets the objectives.

When the approach that best meets the objectives has been selected, the next step is to determine strategy. The process of identifying the problem, setting the goals and objectives, and choosing among alternatives has indicated *what* needs to be done. In determining the course of action, the question of *how* it is to be done and *who* will do it are addressed.

In this step, one is packaging the plan of action. Parts of the strategy will have become apparent in the previous steps, but one can easily ignore some important factors unless a thorough examination of the proposed course of action is undertaken.

Realism is imperative. Further refinements of the selected approach may be necessary. When considering who is to implement the plan and how it is to be done, the participants may discover that there are not sufficient resources to implement the approach fully; and some hard decisions about modifying the approach will need to be made.

In setting the strategy, it is also necessary to build in procedures that will facilitate implementation, monitoring, and evaluation. If money is to be secured for a new program, and if there are civil service or state merit systems to work with, preparing the positions should be done before the money is received in order to cut down on the start-up time. Similarly, one can begin informally to look for staff before the hiring process can officially begin.

The mechanisms for monitoring and evaluation need to be decided on at this time. If an evaluation of the effects of the actions on a target population is desired, then data on that population's characteristics need to be gathered before the program is implemented.

Impact: Steps to Take

The final stage of the planning process is the impact stage, which covers implementing the strategy, monitoring it, and evaluating it. In all these steps, especially implementation, the actual situation will determine what actions need to be taken.

The last two steps are too often left out. Planning is done, a program is launched, and then there is a inclination to neglect monitoring (that is, the process of continually gaining information about the program's performance) and evaluation until such time as a review is called for.

The procedures and instruments for monitoring activities might include reporting forms for fiscal transactions, personnel, training, and participant intake in a program; site visits by the appropriate persons; and mechanisms for permitting client feedback.

Monitoring serves many important purposes. It provides information for guidance while the program is in operation. If the administrator receives up-to-date information, he or she can make adjustments and correct program flaws before they become major.

Monitoring will also provide information for periodic evaluations. Two requisites for effective evaluation are clear objectives against which to measure performance and accurate data that reflect the performance.

The importance of evaluation cannot be overstated. In the planning process itself, the participants should continually check to see whether the objectives meet the problem and whether the strategy addresses the problem and objectives. The participants should also concern themselves with periodically evaluating how well they are working together.

Values and Macropractice

In Chapter 2, the topic of values in social work practice was discussed. In this section, the application of values to macropractice will be addressed. Exhibit 10.3 illustrates the importance of recognizing and adhering to community values.

The vignette in Exhibit 10.3 was designed to illustrate the barriers to social workers' using natural helping networks; in this case, Sally's and Jim's attitudes hinder the effective involvement of Mrs. Worthington in meeting community needs. It also shows how disregard for community values can thwart the efforts of social workers to secure or improve services for their clients. Because Sally Meanwell acquired a reputation as being a violator of community values, she received a negative reception from the board when she advocated expanded services. (Incidentally, the authors

Exhibit 10.3

Sally Meanwell and Jim Goodheart (*As you read this, try to identify which community values Sally and Jim are violating.*)

Sally and Jim are employed by a small human services agency in Gusty, Wyoming, a ranching-farming community about 50 miles from Cultureville, a city of 100,000. Sally was unable to find a job in her native Chicago and accepted employment in Gusty a little over a year ago. Jim, a native of New York, plans to return to the East but views his present employment as a "good experience," akin to the Peace Corps or Vista. He has been in Gusty for two years. It is Friday afternoon and they are taking a coffee break.

Jim slumps back in his chair and exclaims, "What a week; I'll sure be glad to get into Cultureville!"

"What have you got planned?" asks Sally.

"Oh," Jim replies, "I think I'll take in a play at the university, but first I better get my hair cut and styled. It's getting pretty long again and a few people have made comments. And I sure don't want Johnson to butcher it again. These locals don't keep up with anything. Anyway, last time I was in there, I started talking about a beef boycott to protest high beef prices, and he and a couple of ranchers in there really got into it with me. I think one of them even tore my "Question Authority" bumper sticker off when he left."

"I know what you mean," said Sally. "Johnson wouldn't even let me put up a family planning poster in there. He's a Mormon and you know how they are. Guess I'll be glad to escape Gusty, too. I need to pick up some groceries at the new mall. They have a better selection than Bick's [the local grocer]. Anyway, I don't feel like supporting Bick. He butchers deer for hunters and I think hunting should be outlawed. At the very least, they should let the poor deer grow up to be elk."

"By the way," Jim interjected, "Worthington wants you to call her before five. I think it's about the O'Connell family."

"Oh, yeah," responded Sally, "the O'Connell kid has cancer and the family can't afford all the expenses. Mrs. Worthington has been trying to help them. She means well, but I think she's getting too involved."

"She doesn't have any education or training in helping people, does she?"

Sally shook her head, "No, she's done some volunteer work for us, but she didn't seem very sure of herself. Anyway, she's talking about getting some community groups to help the O'Connells. It sounds good, but I'm not sure she can pull it off. I'm willing to help if I can, but I don't know much about organizing."

"Neither do I," replied Jim. "My background is all clinical. I did have a course in c.o., but it was dry as hell and I cut it a lot. Say, wouldn't confidentiality be a problem here? You just can't tell the whole community a lot of personal stuff about the family."

"That is a problem," nodded Sally. "Perhaps I should tactfully discourage Mrs. Worthington."

"I meant to ask you," said Jim, "how did your board meeting go?"

"You would ask!" said Sally, with a negative countenance. "It was the pits. I had the new budget request all ready and I was ready to answer any possible questions. But most of them didn't seem to be all that interested in expanded services. Baldwin really gave me a rough time."

"Isn't Baldwin the guy with all the sheep?"

"Yeah," replied Sally, "I think he found out I signed that 'Save the Coyotes' petition. He claims they killed thirty-seven of his sheep in one day, but everyone knows they only kill for food. Hell, the coyotes were here first."

"Sure," said Jim, "anyway, people eat too much meat for their own good. Why don't you suggest that Baldwin go on a macrobiotic diet?"

"Don't kid, Jim. I was halfway joking once when I suggested a Marxist perspective on county problems. He's had it in for me ever since."

"Well, what about Reverend Gebhart? Wasn't he really pushing for extra services?"

"He sure was," said Sally, "but he's been a little cool lately. You know, he lives down the street from you, and he must know we sometimes spend the night together. He sure knows that neither one of us goes to any church. He was lukewarm toward the new budget, and the board voted to table the request until further study. I'm not too optimistic about it."

"Too bad," said Jim; "it's a hell of a note when people don't separate our personal lives from professional ones. Not much we can do about that, though. It's a good excuse to have a few drinks in Cultureville, though."

"Sounds good, Jim. Why don't we take off now. I can call Mrs. Worthington Monday."

SOURCE: This vignette is adapted from Judith Davenport and Joseph Davenport, III, "Utilizing the Social Network in Rural Communities," *Social Casework*, February 1982, pp. 109–110. Permission to use this material has been received from the publisher, Families International, Inc.

state that although the dialogue is exaggerated, they have either committed or observed every ill-considered action in the account.)

Social workers in macropractice are also confronted with other value issues. One of these goes back to the assertion at the start of the chapter that the client is the community, and that the community benefits if human needs are met better than they were before. This assertion is a value statement that is not shared by everyone. Some people believe that social welfare benefits and services should be eliminated or severely curtailed, either because they believe that people should "make it on their own" or because they do not want to support governmental helping programs with their taxes. Others may not share these values when it comes to particular actions or programs. Public or community education efforts in sex education are opposed by some people because they believe that information on sexuality will lead to increased promiscuity among teenagers. Within their value framework, the community would not be worse off if such community education efforts were carried out.

Another value issue that can be raised is whether social work and social welfare institutions are "part of the problem or part of the solution." Galper (1980) stated that "conventional social work community organization practice is as likely to serve a co-optive role, or to function as a commonly based approach to social control, as it is to operate as a vehicle for progressive change" (p. 151). From the perspective of Galper and other radicals, much of what is advocated in community organization and other macropractice approaches has two basic aims. One is to give people who participate in planned change activities a sense of belonging, of not being powerless or isolated from society. In their opinion, the sense of power may not reflect reality. A second goal is to make minor changes in programs or practices that do not have an impact on the major societal forces that oppress the poor, persons of color, and others (Galper, 1975).

All social workers in practice must question the goals of any effort they are involved in. They must also question the means they are using, especially in working with people who are culturally or ethnically different. It may be that what you envision as feasible may not seem so to the people you are working with.

A number of the activities previously discussed (lobbying, publicity, fund-raising, group decision making) may not be within the range of behaviors of many people. For example, many Asian Americans come from a culture in which one does not question authority, so pressuring a local official is not an activity in which they feel comfortable. It has been my experience that Appalachian whites do not participate easily in community meetings in which a variety of persons are present. There are cultural values that discourage "opening up," especially in front of strangers.

What the social worker needs to do, in Saul Alinsky's words, is to "never go outside the experience of your people. When an action or tactic is outside the experience of the people, the result is—confusion, fear, and . . . a collapse of communication" (1972, p. 127).

The social worker can look for culturally sensitive or culturally acceptable methods of achieving goals. For example, one traditional Native American ritual, the Talking Circle, has been used with a number of Northwest tribes in the United States as a means for group decision making and communication (Stephenson 1983).

Models of Community Practice

Up to this point, this chapter has discussed macropractice from the perspective of the worker who is involved with it as a part of his or her job duties or personal conviction, not from the perspective of the full-time macropractice social worker. In this section, that aspect will be explored largely relying on the work of Jack Rothman.

Rothman (1979) stated that there are three major orientations or models to planned or deliberate change in contemporary American communities. He identified them as locality development, social planning, and social action. In this conceptual framework, he referred to community efforts of a continuing nature with paid staff who are responsible for sustained actions or involvement.

Model A, the *locality development approach* (also called *community development*), asserts that community change can best be brought about through broad participation of a wide spectrum of people at the local community level. The model seeks to involve a broad cross section of people (including the disadvantaged sector and the power structure) in identifying and solving their problems. Model A emphasizes democratic procedures, a consensus approach, voluntary cooperation, development of indigenous leadership, and self-help.

The roles of the community practitioner include enabler, catalyst, coordinator, and teacher of problem-solving skills and ethical values. The approach assumes that conflicts that result between various interest groups can be creatively and constructively handled. It encourages people to express their differences freely, but assumes they will put aside their self-interests to further the interests of their community. Model A also assumes people will put aside their self-interests through appeals to altruism. The basic theme is "Together we can figure out what to do and do it." The model seeks to use discussion and communication between different factions to reach consensus about the problems to focus on and the strategies or actions to resolve these problems. An example of locality development is the Peace Corps in village-level work in overseas community development programs. Peace Corps workers try to bring together residents in a village to identify and then work on solving their most urgent community needs.

Model B, the *social planning approach,* emphasizes a technical process of problem solving. The approach assumes that community change in a complex industrial environment requires highly trained and skilled planners who can guide complex change processes. The role of the expert is stressed in this approach to identifying and resolving social problems. The expert or planner is generally employed by a segment of the power structure, such as an area planning agency, city or county planning department, mental health center, United Way board, community welfare council, and so on. Because the social planner is employed by a segment of the power structure, there is a tendency for the planner to serve the interests of the power structure. Building community capacity or facilitating radical social change is generally not an emphasis.

The planner's roles include gathering facts, analyzing data, and serving as program designer, implementer, and facilitator. Community participation may vary from little to substantial, depending on the community's attitudes toward the problems being addressed. For example, an effort to design and obtain funding for a community center for the elderly may or may not result in substantial involvement by interested community groups, depending on the politics surrounding such a center. Much of the focus of the social planning approach is on identifying needs and on arranging and delivering goods and services to people who need them. The change focus of this approach is "Let's get the facts and take the next rational steps" (Rothman, 1979, p. 33).

Model C, the *social action approach*, assumes there is a disadvantaged (often oppressed) segment of the population that needs to be organized, perhaps in alliance with others, in order to pressure the power structure for increased resources or for treatment more in accordance with democracy or social justice. Social action approaches at times seek basic changes in major institutions or in basic policies of formal organizations. Such approaches often seek redistribution of power and resources. Unlike the vision of a unified community held by locality developers, the power structure or opposition is the target of action. Perhaps the best-known social activist was Saul Alinsky (1972, p. 130) who advised, "Pick the target, freeze it, personalize it, and polarize it." An example of his approach is illustrated in Exhibit 10.4.

The roles of the community practitioner include advocate, agitator, activist, partisan, broker, and negotiator. Tactics used in social action projects include protests, boycotts, confrontation, and negotiation. The change strategy is "Let's organize to overpower our oppressor" (Rothman, 1979, p. 34). The client population is viewed as being a "victim" of the oppressive power structure. Examples of the social action approach include boycotts during the civil rights movement in the 1960s, strikes by unions, protests by antiabortion groups, and protests by African American and Native American groups.

The social action model is not widely used

Exhibit 10.4
Social action tactics should be enjoyable to the people in the movement

Saul Alinsky, one of our country's most noted organizers, describes a tactic used by students at a private college to change the college's restrictive policies on social activities:

> I was lecturing at a college run by a very conservative, almost fundamentalist Protestant denomination. Afterward some of the students came to my motel to talk to me. Their problem was that they couldn't have any fun on campus. They weren't permitted to dance or smoke or have a can of beer. I had been talking about the strategy of effecting change in a society and they wanted to know what tactics they could use to change their situation. I reminded them that a tactic is doing what you can with what you've got. "Now, what have you got?" I asked. "What do they permit you to do?" "Practically nothing," they said, "except—you know—we can chew gum." I said, "Fine. Gum becomes the weapon. You get 200 or 300 students to get two packs of gum each, which is quite a wad. Then you have them drop it on the campus walks. This will cause absolute chaos. Why, with 500 wads of gum I could paralyze Chicago, stop all the traffic in the Loop." They looked at me as though I was some kind of a nut. But about two weeks later I got an ecstatic letter saying, "It worked! It worked! Now we can do just about anything so long as we don't chew gum."

SOURCE: Saul Alinsky, *Rules for Radicals* (New York: Random House, 1972), pp. 145–146.

by social workers at present. Many workers find that being involved in social action activities may lead their employing agencies to penalize them with unpleasant work assignments, low merit increases, and refusal to grant promotions. Many agencies will accept minor and moderate changes in their service delivery systems but are threatened by the prospect of radical changes that are often advocated by the social action approach.

The chart in Table 10.1 illustrates the similarities and differences in the three approaches of locality development, social planning, and social action.

One role that social workers may perform that is not covered by the Rothman models is that of broker. A broker links individuals and groups who need help (and do not know where help is available) with community services. Today even moderate-sized communities have 200 or 300 social service agencies or organizations providing community services. Even human resource professionals are frequently only partially aware of the total service network in their community. As in the fields of finance and real estate, social service brokers serve the function of negotiating, for their clients, a complex network of social institutions about which clients are uninformed and with which they are inexperienced in dealing. Grosser (1973) described this role:

> Like his commercial counterparts, the social broker is primarily committed to "consummating the deal"; his function is not fulfilled unless the social-service institution is in fact providing service to the beneficiary. The broker works directly neither for the recipient nor for the service institution; in a sense, his client is the transaction itself. And it is on behalf of the transaction that he expends his energies and develops his strategies. Community obstacles to the transaction have to be removed or circumvented; policies of the service institution that inhibit the transaction have to be altered; attitudes or misinformation that prevent the recipient from completing the transaction have to be dealt with. The broker is "kept honest," however, by the fact that he must keep the parties to the potential transaction in a common relationship. Because his commitment is to the deal, he enjoys a neutrality that enables both the beneficiary and the institution to relate to him with special confidence. Each party can accept his actions in that they favor neither side; he is committed merely to effecting an exchange of service. [p. 176]

A protest is a commonly used social action tactic, as for this father with a disability and his son demonstrating against state budget cuts in Boston.

Often all that is required to perform this linkage function is to provide information that puts people in contact with resources. However, if difficulties arise, collective action (a community organization effort) may be needed to effect the exchange. (For example, a broker may suggest to welfare recipients that needed benefits may be provided if they *collectively* request the local public assistance department to reexamine certain of its eligibility policies.) Through such brokerage activity, changes in policies may occur that affect whole classes of persons.

A few agencies (such as some mental health clinics, neighborhood centers, community action agencies, agencies serving the

	Model A (Locality Development)	Model B (Social Planning)	Model (Social Action)
1. Goal categories of community action	Self-help; community capacity and intergration (process goals)	Problem solving with regard to substantive community problems (task goals)	Shifting of power relationships and resources; basic institutional change (task or process goals)
2. Assumptions concerning community structure and problem conditions	Community eclipsed, anomie; lack of relationships and democratic problem-solving capacities; static traditional community	Substantive social problems; mental and physical health, housing, recreation	Disadvantaged populations, social injustice, deprivation, inequity
3. Basic change strategy	Broad cross section of people involved in determining and solving their own problems	Fact gathering about problems and decisions on the most rational course of action	Crystallization of issues and organization of people to take action against enemy targets
4. Characteristic change tactics and techniques	Consensus: communication among community groups and interests; group discussion	Consensus or conflict	Conflict or contest: confrontation, direct action, negotiation
5. Salient practitioner roles	Enabler-catalyst, coordinator; teacher of problem-solving skills and ethical values	Fact gatherer and analyst, program implementer, facilitator	Activist-advocate: agitator, broker, negotiator, partisan
6. Medium of change	Manipulation of small task-oriented groups	Manipulation of formal organizations and of data	Manipulation of mass organizations and political processes
7. Orientation toward power structure(s)	Members of power structure as collaborators in a common venture	Power structure as employers and sponsors	Power structure as external target of action: oppressors to be coerced or overturned
8. Boundary definition of the community client system or constituency	Total geographic community	Total community or community segment (including "functional" community)	Community segment
9. Assumptions regarding interests of community subparts	Common interests or reconcilable differences	Interests reconcilable or in conflict	Conflicting interests which are not easily reconcilable; scarce resources
10. Conception of the public interest	Rationalist-unitary	Idealist-unitary	Realist-individualist
11. Conception of the client population or constituency	Citizens	Consumers	Victims
12. Conception of client role	Participants in an interactional problem-solving process	Consumers or recipients	Employers, constituents, members

SOURCE: This chart is reprinted from J. Rothman, "Three Models of Community Organization Practice," in *Social Work Practice* (New York: Columbia University Press, 1968), pp. 24–25. Reprinted with permission from *Social Work Practice*, published for the National Conference on Social Welfare by Columbia University Press.

Table 10.1
Three models of community organization practice according to selected practice variables

elderly) employ "community outreach workers" whose function is to inform residents about available services, identify individuals and families with problems, and link such families with available services.

A number of governmental agencies (particularly in human services, education, health, and housing) now employ one or more staff persons to work part-time or full-time with citizens, educating them to the problems the agency is dealing with and eliciting their ideas to make changes in the delivery system to better serve consumers. This broker function acts as a consciousness-raising device to show people what the system is really like and to make the system more responsive to the needs of consumers.

Summary

Community practice (also called macropractice) is a term that describes social work activities in which the client is the community, where the focus of the change effort is larger than an individual, family, therapy group, or organization. Practitioners are usually involved in this as one part of their work and lives.

There are similarities between community practice and work with individuals, families, groups, and organizations. Skills in communicating and forming relationships, skills in working with groups, and problem-solving skills are as applicable in this realm of practice as in the others.

To be effective, however, the social worker needs to have knowledge of communities and organizations in general, and of the specific community and organization(s) for which he or she works. For some efforts, knowledge of funding sources and funding cycles is essential.

Depending on the kind of macro effort in which the social worker is involved, the following techniques can be utilized: group decision-making techniques, community awareness or publicity approaches, fundraising techniques, and lobbying strategies.

The problem-solving model can be used in addressing community problems. The various steps in a community problem-solving model were summarized in the following three stages:

Preplanning: Questions to ask	Why is the planning being done? Who is the sponsor? Who is doing the planning? Are varying points of view included?
Planning: Plans to make	Problem assessment Problem clarification Goal setting Objective setting Examination and decision among alternatives Determination of strategy
Impact: Steps to take	Implementation of strategy Monitoring Evaluation

In using this or other macro approaches, value issues such as community values, the role of social welfare in society, and ethnic or cultural sensitivity have to be considered.

Models of macropractice include community development (or locality development), social planning, social action, and community brokering.

Exercises
1. Community assessment

> *Goal:* This exercise is designed to instruct the class in how to conduct a community assessment.

Step 1: State the purpose of the exercise. Ask the students to form subgroups of about five members. Inform the subgroups that one of the major class assignments will be for them to conduct a community needs assessment. Inform the subgroups they need first to select a community, and then use the questions in Exhibit 10.1 as a basis for conducting the community assessment.

Step 2: As the course moves along, periodically allow the class time to discuss questions and obstacles that the subgroups encounter.

Step 3: Grade the completed assessments and return them. Have the students discuss what they learned from this exercise.

Note: As an alternative approach to this exercise, have the entire class assess one community, with subgroups focusing on different subtopics to assess. Or, as another alternative, assign each student individually to choose and assess a community.

2. Needs assessment and proposal development

Goal: The purpose of this exercise is to give students experience in conducting a needs assessment and in developing proposals to meet the needs that are identified.

Step 1: Explain the purpose of this exercise. Instruct the students to form subgroups of five or six members. Inform the subgroups their tasks are to conduct a needs assessment of an issue on the campus or in the surrounding community and then to develop a proposal to meet the needs that are identified. (Background material on how to conduct a needs assessment is contained in this chapter.)

Note: This assignment may be a major course assignment. Or, as an alternative, instruct the subgroups to make as much progress as they can in a class period to conduct a needs assessment and develop a program proposal. For example, if the latter approach is used the subgroups may be asked to arrive at answers to the following questions:

  a. What are the most urgent, unmet needs of our social work program?
  b. What evidence or documentation is there that these are urgent, unmet needs?
  c. What additional information needs to be sought to determine fully whether these needs are urgent and unmet?
  d. What specific, realistic proposals do you have for meeting the needs that have been identified?

Step 2: Have the subgroups present their needs assessments and proposals in verbal or written form. Provide feedback to the subgroups.

3. Identifying violations of community values

   Goal: This exercise is designed to help the class recognize violations of community values.

   Step 1: Explain the purpose of the exercise. Ask for a volunteer to read a vignette with you. (If you are a female, ask for a male volunteer to read a male's part. If you are a male, ask for a female volunteer.) Inform the class the two of you will read a vignette and that the task of each student is to identify the specific attitudes and specific behaviors that are apt to be violations of the values in a rural community in Wyoming.

   Step 2: Together with the volunteer, read the Sally Meanwell and Jim Goodheart vignette presented in Exhibit 10.3.

   Step 3: Ask the students to state the violations of community values that they have identified. End the exercise by stating the importance of identifying community values, and discuss with students whether they are willing to make possible adjustments in their personal lives in order to live up to community expectations. Indicate that a balance sometimes has to be found between living the way you want to live, and meeting community expectations in order to maintain credibility.

4. Identifying community values

   Goal: This exercise is designed to help students examine the values of their home communities.

   Step 1: Indicate that community values influence the types of services that are publicly available and supported by a community. Instruct the class to form subgroups of three or four. Ask students in each subgroup to discuss their home communities' reactions to the following community activities. (These activities can either be written on a chalkboard or read from this text.)

   a. High school students seek to establish a clinic in their school that dispenses contraceptive materials.
   b. An avowedly lesbian woman launches a campaign to seek election to a local political office (such as to the city council).
   c. A group of working parents requests the local school system to establish an all-day kindergarten, partially to meet the needs of working parents.
   d. An AIDS support group seeks authorization to use the public meeting room of the library for its weekly meetings.
   e. A local organization seeks the establishment of an additional (or the first) shelter for the homeless in your neighborhood.

   Step 2: Ask a representative from each subgroup to summarize to the class what was discussed. Or end the exercise by making some summary statements about community values that underlie community reactions (that were discussed) to these activities.

11

Evaluating Social Work Practice

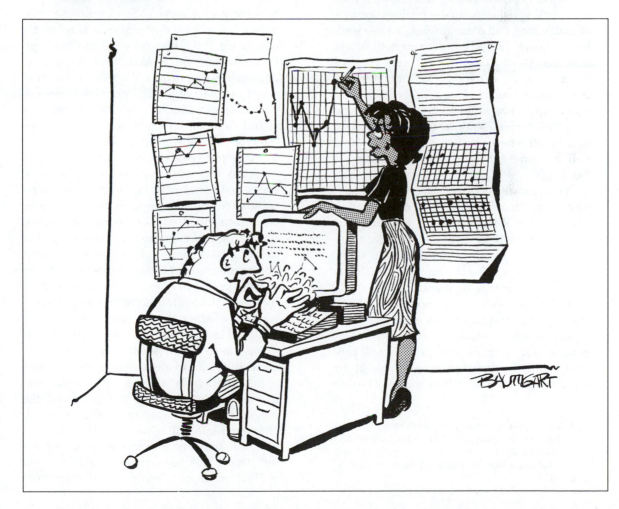

To this point, you've learned about social work with individuals, families, groups, organizations, and communities.[1] You've studied systems analysis, and you will study psychoanalysis (Chapter 13) and transactional analysis (Chapter 15), and you will read about half a dozen other therapies. You're probably eager to try out your new knowledge, confident that you can be of help to your prospective clients. But wait! How will you know if your choice of therapy is working?

As a professional social worker, you'll want to be accountable to your clients and to yourself. You'll want to know whether your clients achieve their goals and, if so, whether it is because of your interventions. In short, you'll want to evaluate your practice. That is what this chapter is all about.

Although most social workers evaluate their practice implicitly, few approach evaluation as systematically as they might. Systematic evaluation of your practice will provide you with reliable information about the achievements of your clients and may lead to

[1]This chapter was especially written for this text by Wallace J. Gingerich, MSW, Ph.D. Dr. Gingerich is a professor in the Mandel School of Applied Social Sciences at Case Western Reserve University, Cleveland, OH.

improved practice. Good evaluation will also help you avoid jumping to unwarranted conclusions about your work.

What Is Evaluation?

Evaluation, as we shall use the term here, refers to the use of research techniques to assess the outcome of social work interventions. As Thomas (1984) has suggested, there are two types of evaluation: outcome evaluation and evaluative research. As we shall see, these two types of evaluation address different but related objectives.

Outcome evaluation asks whether the intended outcome was achieved. Simply put, was the goal achieved? Since outcome evaluation has a limited objective, it is relatively easy to do. It requires minimal methodological know-how, and it doesn't impose rigid requirements on practice. Outcome evaluation should be part of normal practice. However, outcome evaluation does not provide a sound basis on which to conclude whether the intervention was effective.

Evaluative research also asks whether the outcome was achieved, but in addition it seeks to determine if the outcome can be attributed to your intervention. In other words, was treatment effective? Evaluative research is like traditional experimental research in that causal relationships are the focus of study. You might think of evaluative research as research applied to questions of practice effectiveness. Although it is relatively easy to determine whether the intended outcome was achieved (outcome evaluation), inferring that it was due to the intervention is considerably more difficult. Evaluating the effectiveness of interventions is important. If we know that it was our intervention that produced the outcome, we will want to continue using it. On the other hand, if we know the intervention had little or no impact, we should stop using it and look for something better. Good evaluative research enables us to contribute to the knowledge base of our profession and is mandated by our professional code of ethics.

Although both types of evaluation are important for social work practice, the main focus of this chapter is outcome evaluation. Outcome evaluation has become an essential part of ordinary practice; you and your client will always want to know if the desired outcome was achieved. Outcome evaluation does not interfere with practice, but may enhance and improve it (Gingerich, 1983b). On the other hand, rigorous evaluative research is not a requirement of ordinary practice (Gingerich, 1990b). The additional controls and measurements needed to conduct evaluative research may conflict with service objectives (Thomas, 1978). We are required as a profession to conduct scientific research to improve our knowledge of practice effectiveness; however, in many instances evaluative research is best left to trained researchers who can implement the rigorous controls and measurements required for inferring causality.

Just as social work practice may be carried out at various levels of intervention (individuals, groups, families, organizations, and communities), evaluation is also carried out at different levels. Evaluation at the level of individuals, families, and groups has sometimes been referred to as *clinical evaluation*, while evaluation at the level of program development and community practice has been called *program evaluation*. The main focus of this chapter is on evaluation at the level of individuals, families, and groups. As we shall see, many of the concepts and methods underlying clinical evaluation apply to program evaluation as well.

Until recently, evaluating practice usually meant that one would use some form of an experimental control group research design (Bloom, 1983). Such designs assign subjects randomly to two groups: one group gets the intervention and the other does not (or gets a different intervention). After intervention, the groups are compared on some measure of the desired outcome. Assuming all else was equal, differences between the two groups are attributed to the intervention the experimental group received. Although experimental control group designs are a useful research strategy, they are often not practical for evaluating day-to-day social work practice.

During the 1970s a new approach to evaluating practice began to emerge, based on the earlier work of clinical psychologists who were trained in research (Bloom, 1983). This approach, known as *single-subject* or *single-system* research, took a rather different approach to evaluation, an approach that was much more compatible with clinical practice. Instead of comparing randomly assigned groups of clients on some outcome measure after intervention, the single-system approach observes a single client (or client system) repeatedly before, during, and after intervention, and notes changes in the outcome measure that coincide with the intervention. In this way it is possible to determine whether the outcome was achieved and, perhaps, whether the change was due to the intervention.

While single-system designs are not as rigorous methodologically as classical control group designs, they are much more compatible with most social work practice. Furthermore, they are adequate in most instances for purposes of outcome evaluation. Thus, the single-system approach to evaluation is the one taken here.

The Single-System Evaluation Approach

Much has been written about how to evaluate practice (Jayaratne & Levy, 1979; Bloom & Fischer, 1982; Barlow, Hayes, & Nelson, 1984; Barlow & Hersen, 1984; Blythe & Tripodi, 1989; Alter & Evens, 1990). As a result, the procedures for evaluating practice are well defined. They may be described generally as follows:

1. Specify the goal.
2. Select suitable measures.
3. Record baseline data.
4. Implement the intervention and continue monitoring.
5. Assess change.
6. Infer effectiveness.

If these steps sound familiar, that is because they parallel very closely the steps one follows in social work practice (Jayaratne & Levy, 1979). Evaluation is based on the problem-solving process, just as social work practice is. The difference is one of emphasis, and it is a slight difference at that. While the main purpose of practice is to produce a desired outcome, the main purpose of evaluation is to assess whether in fact the outcome was achieved.

Specify the Goal

The first step in single-system evaluation is to specify the goal of your work with your client. The goal should reflect the information obtained in the social work assessment and should state in concrete terms what will be different at the end of treatment. Usually the goal involves a change in behaviors, thoughts, or feelings, or perhaps a change in social relationships or the environment. The goal should reflect the needs and wishes of your client and what is realistic to achieve, but it also must be an outcome that can be defined specifically and measured.

Select Suitable Measures

Evaluation requires that the desired outcome be measurable in some reliable way. Measurement means that the outcome must be quantifiable. At a minimum you must be able to tell whether it has occurred or not; but you may also be able to rate the level of the outcome using a scale or some other procedure.

Although some outcomes may seem to defy measurement, it would be irresponsible to intervene if one has no way to know if the outcome has occurred (Hudson, 1978). Neither you nor your client could tell if things were getting better. When practitioners say they cannot measure their clients' outcomes, they usually mean the outcomes are difficult to measure directly, or they are too complicated and multifaceted to measure quantitatively. Numerous advances have been made in the field of measurement in recent years and there are many available measuring instruments and procedures.

Measurement Methods

There are three main methods for measuring client outcomes: direct observation, self-anchored rating scales, and standardized measures (Bloom & Fischer, 1982).

Direct observation. Many client outcomes are behavioral. Simply put, clients want to *do* something different. When the outcome can be stated in behavioral terms, direct observation by the client or someone else is usually the measurement method of choice. Direct observation requires a clear, objective definition of the behavior. *Clear* means that two people using the definition agree on occurrences of the behavior. *Objective* means that the behavior is directly observable; that is, it requires little or no inference by the observer.

Examples of typical behavioral outcomes are playing cooperatively, completing assigned homework, having fewer headaches, and discussing disagreements calmly. Even some seemingly nonbehavioral outcomes such as improved self-esteem or reduced depression can be stated in behavioral terms. Clients can often give specific behavioral indicators of internal states when asked; for example, when asked what they will be doing (or not doing) when they have improved self-esteem, clients may indicate such behaviors as initiating conversations, making positive self-statements, or working more productively. Although it is not always possible to specify outcomes in behavioral terms, it is useful to attempt to do so. From a therapeutic standpoint, the client (and you) will have a more concrete idea of the actual desired outcome. From an evaluation standpoint, direct observation is generally considered the most reliable and direct measurement method. By the way, specifying behavioral outcomes does not imply that you must, or even should, use behaviorally based interventions. It simply means that the outcome you and the client are interested in is behavioral.

Behaviors may be observed and counted using a variety of methods (Barlow, Hayes, & Nelson, 1984). The most common method is a *frequency count.* Here, you simply record the number of times the behavior occurs during a specified time interval. For example, you might record the number of temper tantrums a child has each day, or the number of problems a child solves correctly during math class. Frequency counts work well for discrete behaviors (behaviors that have clear beginnings and endings) that do not occur too frequently to make counting impractical.

A related method of observation is counting *discriminated operants.* These are behaviors that occur only in the presence of clearly specified antecedents. For example, a child can comply only when the parent makes a request, or a husband and wife can resolve differences only when they have a disagreement. In such cases, rather than report the absolute frequency of occurrence, you would report the percentage of times the desired behavior occurred following the antecedent.

Continuous (no clear beginnings or endings) or high-frequency behaviors can be observed using *time-sampling* methods. In time-sampling the observation period is divided into short intervals (usually 5 to 15 seconds) during which you record the behavior as occurring or not. Usually this is done on an all-or-none basis, with the results presented as a percentage. For example, you might observe whether a psychiatric patient attends to the therapy group discussion during a 10-minute period using 15-second intervals. If the patient was observed to attend for 35 of the 40 intervals, you would report that she or he attended 88 percent of the time. Because of its nature, time-sampling is almost always done by someone other than the client, usually a staff member or perhaps a parent.

Several other observational methods are sometimes used. *Latency* measures the elapsed time between a particular event and the behavior; for example, the times it takes a child to get into bed after being told to do so. *Duration* measures how long the behavior lasts, such as how many minutes the child spends doing homework, or how long a headache lasts.

General procedures for observing behaviors, as well as specific definitions, codes, and recording systems for observing many predetermined behaviors are described in detail by Bellack and Hersen (1988) and Ciminero, Calhoun, and Adams (1986).

Self-anchored rating scales. Not all desired outcomes can be stated in behavioral terms. Sometimes the outcome is a change in an internal state (for example, thought, feeling, belief) such as becoming more self-confident, less anxious, or less depressed. In such cases, it would not make sense to try to define the outcome behaviorally if the client truly views the problem as an internal state. Accordingly, when the desired outcome is an internal state, the most direct method of measurement is of necessity some form of self-report.

One of the best methods of measuring internal states is to develop a self-anchored rating scale (Bloom, 1975). A self-anchored scale is a rating scale you and your client develop specifically to measure your client's outcome (Gingerich, 1979). To construct a self-anchored scale, begin with a 5- or 7-point rating scale (see Figure 11.1). Give the scale the name of the outcome you and your client have agreed on; for example, you might call it a "feeling good" scale.

Next, develop anchors for the low end of the scale by having your client imagine a recent time when she did not feel good at all. After she has begun to visualize the situation,

Figure 11.1
Self-anchored scale

as her to recall (1) what she was doing, (2) any recurrent thoughts she was having, and (3) what she was feeling. Behaviors sometimes occur along with internal states; for example, your client may stay in bed all day, not answer the phone, cry frequently, and overeat on a bad day. Your client may also experience recurrent thoughts or self-statements such as "no one likes me," "I am ugly," or "life is not worth living." Feelings are more difficult to elicit but often are expressed best in word pictures such as "feeling blue," "my stomach is tied up in knots," or "I'm down in the dumps." In any case, the behaviors, thoughts, and feelings the client experiences when at the low point on the scale become the anchors for that point.

Once you have anchored the low point, ask your client to imagine a recent time when she was feeling very good. This time you will elicit anchors for the high end of the scale. You should proceed to develop anchors for other points of the scale as well; ideally at least alternate points of the scale should be anchored.

If you have developed the anchors carefully, the completed scale should be a sensitive measure of your client's outcome as she uniquely experiences it. Since self-anchored scales are client-specific, you must develop a new one for each new client and each new outcome.

Because self-anchored scales are subjective (they measure the client's internal state), they have sometimes been criticized on meth-

odological grounds. Their reliability cannot be assessed directly, and they are always potentially reactive (more about these measurement issues later). On the other hand, self-report measures are the most direct measure of internal states, and there is little evidence that self-reports are any less adequate methodologically than many other types of measures (Bloom & Fischer, 1982). For purposes of outcome evaluation, self-anchored scales are often useful, and sometimes they are the only direct measure of the outcome.

Standardized measures. In most cases the preferred method of measuring client outcomes is direct observation of behavior or self-anchored ratings of internal states. That is because these methods are likely to provide the most direct and sensitive measures of outcome. Occasionally, however, standardized measures may exist that would provide a suitable measure of outcome. Furthermore, it is often a good idea to use standardized measures, in addition to behavioral and self-report measures, to provide a basis of comparison with known groups, or to be sure that you are measuring what you think you are.

Standardized measures include tests, questionnaires, rating scales, inventories, and checklists. These measures have three characteristics. First, they have uniform procedures for administration and scoring so everyone who uses the instrument uses it in the same way. Second, standardized measures must meet minimal standards of methodological adequacy (namely, reliability and validity). Third, most standardized measures have established norms; that is, they have guidelines for interpreting test scores based on the scores of known groups who have completed the measure or some independent standard of performance.

Standardized measures fall into two broad categories: published and unpublished. Published measures (commercially published) are described in the *Ninth Mental Measurements Yearbook* (Mitchell, 1985). Published measures have met accepted standards of reliability and validity, so you can use them with assurance that they will in fact measure what you think they will. The publishers of these measures require a fee, however, and some of them are available only to psychologists or other qualified professionals.

Unpublished measures have been developed and used in research and practice situations but are not published commercially. There is no one source or listing of unpublished measures; however, several collections have particular value for social work practice. Hudson (1982) and Nurius and Hudson (1993) have developed more than 20 scales designed for use in social work practice. Sample scales include self-esteem, marital satisfaction, child's attitudes toward parents, and generalized contentment. All of these scales are scored and interpreted in the same way, making them easy to use in daily practice. A computer-administered version of the scales is also available (Nurius & Hudson, 1993). It permits the client to complete the scale on the computer, with the computer scoring the scale and graphing the results.

Corcoran and Fischer (1993) have compiled a collection of over 125 measures that they refer to as *rapid assessment instruments*. Instruments are included for children, adults, and couples and cover a broad range of psychological, behavioral, and interpersonal problems. The sourcebook includes a description of each measure, its norms and scoring procedures, and reliability and validity data. In addition, each measure is reproduced in the book so you can decide for yourself whether it would be suitable for your clinical application.

In addition to these two collections, a wide range of standardized measures may be found in Bellack and Hersen (1988); Ciminero, Calhoun, and Adams (1986); Freedman and Sherman (1987); Gibson and Ottenbacher (1988); Grotevant and Carlson (1987); Hersen and Bellack (1988), and Touliatos, Perlmutter, and Straus (1990).

General Issues in Measurement

At times we have referred to the reliability and validity of measurement. These are terms that describe the methodological adequacy of measures. *Validity* refers to what the measure measures, and *reliability* refers to how well it measures it. If a measure is not reliable, it will not give consistent and accurate readings. Thus, when observing behavior, for example, it is important that the description of the behavior be clear and objective so the observer will record it consistently from day to day. If a measure is not valid, it will not measure what you think it measures. That is why, when developing self-anchored scales, for example, you should be sure that the anchors the client gives are real indicators of the outcome for each scale point.

In addition to reliability and validity, you also want a measure to be *sensitive* to the changes you expect a client to make. Direct observation of client behavior and self-anchored rating scales are sensitive measures of most client outcomes. On the other hand, standardized scales frequently are not since they have been developed to measure personality traits which, by definition, are relatively fixed and are not likely to change significantly during intervention.

Another requirement of measurement in single-case evaluation is that the measure be suitable for *repeated use* (at least weekly) during treatment. This is true for most behavioral observation measures and self-anchored scales but is often not true for standardized scales. The scales described by Hudson (1982)

Nurius and Hudson (1993), and Corcoran and Fischer (1993) are exceptions.

Finally, it is important to consider the *reactivity* of your measure. Since in most instances clients will be recording their own behavior, the measurements process itself will likely have some impact on the behavior it is reporting. For example, if you ask a mother who complains of her child's temper tantrums to count the tantrums, it is likely that she will notice some new things about her child's behavior as well as her own, and her behavior and that of her child may change as a result.

Because reactivity influences the behavior the measure is meant to measure, it is difficult to sort out how much behavior change is due to the intervention and how much is due to reactivity. Researchers generally try to minimize this problem by using unobtrusive measures (having someone else observe the client, for example), so they can be more sure of the exact impact on the intervention. However, from a practice point of view, reactivity may actually benefit the client. This is especially true if you are helping someone learn problem-solving strategies in which observing and altering one's own behavior are explicit goals of treatment.

Reactivity is a very complex process and its effect is difficult to gauge. Generally, however, you should have your clients record *positive* behaviors or internal states rather than negative ones, since the effect of reactivity (all else being equal) is apt to increase response rates rather than decrease them. For example, rather than recording an unwanted behavior such as eating snacks between meals, you could have your client record the number of times he thought of snacking but refrained. Koop (1988) provided an excellent discussion of the factors involved in estimating the reactivity of self-monitoring and how you can use it for your client's benefit.

Measurement of client outcomes is a crucial step in evaluating practice. Conclusions about whether the outcome has been achieved will be valid and trustworthy only if appropriate measures are used, so care and thoughtfulness are advised. You have also probably noticed the parallels between measurement as we have talked about it here and assessment as it has been discussed in Chapter 3. We have been talking about the same process from different perspectives: in the present discussion of measurement the emphasis has been on *how* to assess, whereas in Chapter 3 the emphasis was on *what* to assess. Clearly, you will want to pay careful attention to both aspects of assessment in your practice.

Record Baseline Data

After the selection of the measure or measures, the next step is to collect the data for a period of time before you implement the intervention. This is called *baselining,* meaning that you are establishing the base rate of the outcome measure before intervention occurs and the expected change takes place. The main purpose for baselining is to provide a basis of comparison for the data collected during and after treatment. If the treatment data show a different level or pattern from the baseline data, you may reasonably conclude there has been a change. If you collected data only after treatment, you would have no way of knowing whether there had been a change.

Since you may not implement treatment during the baseline period, an important question is, How long should you baseline? Barlow, Hayes, and Nelson (1984) made several recommendations. First, you should collect baseline data for a *minimum of three data points.* At least three points are required to begin to assess the level, trend, and stability of the data. (More about these properties later when we discuss assessing change.) Although three data points constitute a minimum, in normal practice baselines are often taken for a week or more. Some statistical aids for assessing change require a minimum of ten baseline observations. Second, you should continue baselining until the data

Figure 11.2
A simple graph

form a *stable pattern*. Frequently there is some fluctuation or trend in evidence during baseline; for example, there may be four or five tantrums one day and none the next, or the number of tantrums may seem to be decreasing. The idea is to baseline long enough that the pattern of behaviors becomes clear and consistent and (ideally) there is no upward or downward trend.

To be able to see the patterns contained in your data, you should always graph the data (see Figure 11.2). Not only is this helpful for you, but graphs are a very effective way to provide feedback to your clients (and others such as parents and third-party funders). Using lined graph paper, begin by drawing a vertical line on the left side and a horizontal line at the bottom. The vertical axis is always used to represent the outcome, and the horizontal dimension represents time units. Thus, you might record self-anchored ratings of "feeling good" on the vertical axis and days on the horizontal axis. Drawn in this way, the pattern of the client outcome over time can readily be seen. Other considerations in graphing are discussed in more detail in Bloom and Fischer (1982) and Parsonson and Baer (1978).

Conceptually, baselining parallels the assessment phase of treatment when the worker gathers information about the level of the client's problem, and when and where it happens. Seen in this way, baselining usually does not require you to delay the start of intervention any longer than you normally would. From a practice standpoint, it is unwise to begin intervening until you have a clear description of the problem or desired outcome and have reliable information about its current level. Occasionally, however, there will be situations (crises, for example) when it will be impossible to baseline before intervening. In such situations you may be able to reconstruct a baseline from archival data, or ask the client to estimate how often the identified outcome occurred during the previous week. Without any baseline data whatsoever, you will be severely hampered later on in determining whether there has been change in the outcome.

Implement the Intervention and Continue Monitoring

Once you have established a baseline, it is time to implement the intervention. The most important consideration from the point of view of evaluating practice is to specify and describe clearly just what the intervention consists of. Assuming your client improves, you will want to know what you did so you can do it again and can describe it to other professionals as well.

While this step sounds easy, it is perhaps the most difficult aspect of evaluation. In fact, there is ongoing debate in the literature regarding the extent to which interventions can be described and replicated (Frank, 1973). The helping process is a complex, multi-faceted activity that can probably never be described completely. The practical goal, however, is to describe the intervention with sufficient clarity and completeness that someone else can replicate it and obtain similar results (Blythe & Tripodi, 1989). Furthermore, it is assumed that although your actions from the start may be generally therapeutic, you will implement a *specific intervention* at the conclusion of baseline.

In addition to describing your intervention, you should verify that you have actually implemented it. Planning to do something does not necessarily mean it will happen. Occasionally, research studies on practice effectiveness have failed to produce positive results but on closer examination reveal that the intervention was never implemented as planned. This is important to know since it prevents you from mistakenly concluding that the intervention was unsuccessful when in fact it was never implemented.

Once you have implemented intervention, you should continue the same measurement procedure established during baseline (Figure 11.2). It is important that there be no changes in the definitions, times of measurement, or measurement procedures because such changes could affect the data you obtain. If you keep the measurement procedure exactly the same as baseline, changes in the data during treatment will reflect changes in the outcome itself, not the measurement procedure.

Assess Change

After you have collected data on your outcome measure during the baseline and treatment phases, the next step is to assess whether there has been any change. Actually, the issue is whether any significant change has occurred from a statistical or clinical standpoint (Kazdin, 1977a). Statistical or *experimental* change refers to actual change in outcome between phases. It is assessed on purely statistical and logical grounds. Clinical or *applied* change refers to change that is sufficient, desirable, or meaningful from a clinical or practical standpoint.

The first task is to determine whether there has been experimental change; that is, whether there has been any real change in the outcome during intervention. This task is sometimes made difficult because of some of the unique characteristics of time-series data (Jones, Vaught, & Weinrott, 1977; Kratochwill, 1978). Time-series data may be characterized by their level, trend, variability, and autocorrelation. *Level* refers to the central tendency or location of a set of data. When there is no trend, level is equivalent to the mean of observations in the baseline or treatment phase. *Trend* refers to a deterministic change in the level of the data over time; that is, a continuing upward and downward trend. *Variability* refers to the extent to which the data vary around the trend line. The more fluctuation around the trend line, the greater the variability of the data. Finally, *autocorrelation* refers to the possibility that the value of one observation may be related to previous observations. This is a complicated statistical phenomenon, which in practical terms means that most of the usual statistical techniques (which assume independence of observations) may not be suitable for assessing change in time-series data.

There are two general approaches for assessing change in time-series data: visual analysis and statistical analysis. We shall place most emphasis on visual analysis since it is fairly straightforward and easy, and it is one procedure you should do routinely. The following discussion of visual analysis is based heavily on the work of Parsonson and Baer (1978).

Visual analysis simply means that you look at the graphed data and, applying rules of analysis, conclude whether there has been change in the client outcome from phase to phase. The standard of significance for visual analysis is "clearly evident and reliable"; that is, the change must be clear and unmistakable (Parsonson & Baer, 1978, p. 112).

The first step in visual analysis is to graph the baseline and treatment data following the suggestions noted earlier. The data within phases should be connected by a solid line, and the phases should be divided by a vertical line.

Ideally, in visual analysis, you would want to see little or no overlap between phases, with no clear trend in the data (see Figure 11.3a). In such cases it is clear there has been a change. Also, the more immediate the change and the greater its magnitude, the easier it is to conclude there has been real change.

Sometimes the baseline data may contain a trend; that is, the outcome measure seems to be on a continuing increase or decrease.

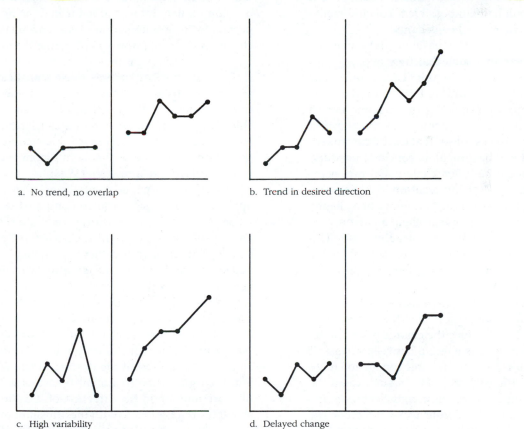

a. No trend, no overlap

b. Trend in desired direction

c. High variability

d. Delayed change

Figure 11.3
Visual analysis of graphed data

When this happens, you should make every effort to extend the period of baseline to see whether the trend will taper off and stabilize around a constant level. If not, you must analyze change cautiously. If the trend is in the opposite direction of desired change, then it will have little impact on assessing change. However, if the trend is in the desired direction, assessment of change will be ambiguous (Figure 11.3b). From a practice standpoint, it may be wise not to intervene in such cases since the desired change appears to be happening already. If you must intervene, and if intervention produces a large and immediate increase in outcome or a change in slope, you might cautiously conclude there has been change. However, in most situations where there is a trend in the desired direction, it will be difficult if not impossible to conclude reliably that there has been change.

On occasion the baseline data may be highly variable such that they overlap with the treatment data (Figure 11.3c). Again, your first strategy should be to try to reduce the variability by extending the baseline period or observing extraneous events affecting your client's responses that can be controlled. If not, it will be difficult to conclude unequivocally there has been change. On rare occasions the goal of intervention may be to increase or decrease the variability of a client's behavior (for example, to help a person with mood swings maintain a steadier state). Unfortunately, there are no readily available techniques for assessing change in variability of time-series data.

It is not uncommon in social work practice for client change to be delayed or gradual (Figure 11.3d). Since the change is not immediate and there is overlap between phases, it is difficult to reach a reliable conclusion (Gibson & Ottenbacher, 1988). In such cases the best thing to do is continue the intervention and continue observing to see whether the behavior eventually stabilizes around a new level. If so, you can be relatively confident there has been change in the outcome.

Ideally, our interventions would be so effective that visual analysis of graphed data would be sufficient to reach reliable conclusions about change. Of course, we know that this doesn't always happen. Sometimes there appears to be some change, but the change doesn't strictly meet the criteria of "clearly evident and reliable." What then? Some writers have suggested that if change is not clearly evident the intervention is simply not potent enough to be of interest, so we should abandon it altogether rather than try to sort out whether there was significant change. This argument is very persuasive from a practical standpoint. On the other hand, some of the outcomes we are interested in change slowly, and change may not be very immediate or dramatic. Furthermore, when developing new interventions it may be important to know whether there is even a small change, so we can improve and refine the intervention to the point that it may be of practical value. In cases such as these statistical and quasi-statistical techniques may be needed to determine whether there has been a reliable change in outcome. Although such techniques are beyond the scope of this chapter, good discussions are available in Bloom and Fischer (1982) and Gingerich (1983b).

In contrast to experimental significance, applied (clinical) significance compares the amount of change that has occurred with the amount of change thought necessary or desirable. This is often a difficult judgment to make since individuals disagree on what is necessary or desirable.

Kazdin (1977a) discussed a number of approaches for assessing applied significance. One of these, the *aim-star technique*, simply places an *aim-star* on the graph at the level and day that represent the desired outcome. You then graph the treatment data to see if they are moving in the direction of the aim-star. If the data coincide with the aim-star you have achieved applied significance. *Goal attainment scaling* offers a similar approach conceptually (Kiresuk & Lund, 1978). Both procedures are admittedly subjective, although they probably better reflect what our clients consider significant change than does experimental significance.

Kazdin discussed several additional ways to evaluate applied significance. One of these, *social comparison*, compares the client's performance in the target area with that of "normal" peers. For example, you decide what a reasonable standard of cooperative play is by observing "normal" children in the natural setting. Another approach for assessing applied significance is called *subjective evaluation*. Here you would poll qualified individuals such as teachers, social workers, or probation officers to determine what a reasonable standard of performance would be. For a more detailed discussion of applied significance see the articles by Kazdin (1977a) and Gingerich (1983b).

In practice, you should always attempt to assess change using both experimental and applied criteria. At the minimum, you should perform visual analysis of graphed data, and perhaps use some of the statistical techniques available if visual analysis is ambiguous. In addition, you should always specify before intervention what the goal of intervention is. You may express this verbally or graphically using the aim-star technique.

These five steps constitute the necessary steps for carrying out outcome evaluation as defined earlier. Your measure should indicate in quantitative terms what the desired outcome is; data should show what the baseline level was and whether there was change during intervention; and finally your analysis should tell you whether the change was significant. As we said earlier, practice evaluation should be a regular part of normal social work practice.

You may notice, however, that we have said almost nothing up to now about intervention effectiveness—that is, whether the intervention was responsible for producing the change. The question of effectiveness leads us into evaluation research per se, in which we must use research designs to develop a logical and empirical basis for making inferences about treatment effectiveness. Although it is not the goal of this chapter to make you a skilled researcher, a brief review of research designs and design issues will help you begin to think about effectiveness and, perhaps more important, deter you from making assertions about effectiveness that go beyond your data.

Infer Effectiveness

To infer that your intervention was effective, you must show logically and empirically that the intervention is the only plausible explanation for the observed change in client outcome. To put it a bit differently, you must rule out other possible explanations for the observed change.

The primary criterion for inferring causality is *concomitant variation;* that is, the observed change in client outcome must occur at (or soon after) the time the intervention is implemented. If change begins before intervention, logically we would have to conclude that something other than the intervention was responsible for the change. Likewise, if change occurs too long after intervention, other possible explanations take on more credence.

Threats to Validity

Concomitant variation alone is not sufficient to establish causality; it is only suggestive of a causal relationship. We must also rule out other possible (and plausible) explanations for why the client changed. These competing explanations fall into several categories, which have been called threats to validity (Cook & Campbell, 1979). *Validity,* as the term is used here, refers to the best available approximation of truth regarding the cause of client change. The following discussion includes several of the more important threats to validity.

Case Example
Treatment of obsessive-compulsive disorder

The following case example is based on a study by Cooper (1990), in which she used behavioral interventions to help a client reduce her ritualizing behavior. Cooper also noted improvement in depression and anxiety.

1. *Specify the goal.* This study involved a woman in her late twenties who displayed at intake pervasive ritualistic behavior, social isolation, depression, and anxiety. She had been in psychotherapy for the previous five years. The specific goals for this study were to reduce three behaviors: ritualistic opening and shutting of her makeup case, excessive rinsing in the shower, and ritualistic counting of belongings.

2. *Selecting suitable measures.* The measure used was client self-monitoring of the three behaviors on a 3 × 5 note card. The client recorded the number of times she opened and closed her makeup case, the minutes spent rinsing after soaping in the shower, and the percentage of times she counted her belongings when carrying them. In addition to these target behaviors, Cooper also asked her client to complete the Spielberger State-Trait Anxiety Inventory and the Beck Depression Inventory.

3. *Record baseline data.* Cooper implemented a modified form of the multiple baseline design in which each behavior was recorded for a variable period prior to the start of treatment. Baselines ranged from 13 days for opening and closing the makeup case to six weeks for counting belongings while carrying them.

4. *Implement intervention and continue monitoring.* The intervention consisted of behavior modification techniques (including modeling and response prevention). It was directed first toward the makeup case ritual, then the excessive rinsing, and finally the counting of belongings. The order of target behaviors was determined by client ratings of each on an anxiety hierarchy. Cooper continued to monitor each target behavior during the intervention period.

5. *Assess change.* Each target behavior was monitored during intervention (just as in baseline) and placed on a time-series graph. The results for the opening and closing of the makeup case are shown in Figure 11-4. It is clear from visual analysis that there was significant change during intervention—there was no overlap across phases and behavior changed abruptly when treatment was started. Cooper did a celeration line test that confirmed her visual analysis. The other two target behaviors showed similar reductions. Pre and post measures on the State-Trait Anxiety Inventory and the Beck Depression Inventory showed no significant change. Anxiety scores began high and continued high, and depression scores began low and remained so throughout. Cooper did three-month and six-month follow-ups, which verified that changes the client made during treatment continued.

6. *Infer effectiveness.* This study used a modified multiple baseline design to evaluate the impact of behavioral intervention on three ritualistic behaviors. In each case, introduction of treatment was followed immediately by a reduction in the target behavior. These results were confirmed using the celeration line. The fact that treatment was begun at different points in time for the three different

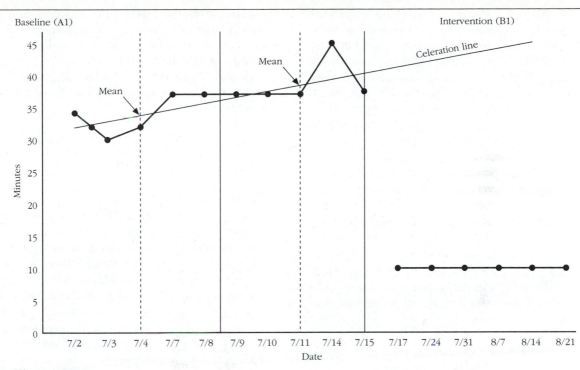

Figure 11-4

Number of twists, presses, and clicks of makeup case by client each morning at baseline (7/2 to 7/15) and after intervention (7/17 to 8/21)

target behaviors and was followed by immediate change lends credibility to the hypothesis that treatment produced the change, not historical events, maturation, and some other factor. Thus, we can be fairly safe in concluding that the intervention produced the observed changes in target behaviors. Intervention did not appear to influence general anxiety or depression.

This study is a good example of the extent to which a fairly rigorous single-subject evaluation design can be implemented in direct practice. It used clear, concrete measures of the target behaviors. The modified multiple baseline design is able to rule out most competing explanations for the observed change in target behavior. Although realities of the practice situation did not permit an exact implementation of the multiple baseline design, it could be closely approximated, which adds considerably to the therapist's ability to infer the effectiveness of the intervention. Even if the multiple baseline design could not have been implemented, a simple AB design (baseline-intervention) on any one of the target behaviors would have provided valuable information about change.

SOURCE: Marlene Cooper, "Treatment of a Client with Obsessive-Compulsive Disorder," *Social Work Research and Abstracts*, 26 (1990), pp. 26–32.

History. History refers to any event that may have occurred during the time the intervention was implemented that could also account for the change. Examples are events such as getting a promotion, getting a new classroom teacher, or having a birthday. Observed improvements in the client's functioning may result from such historical events rather than the intervention. Simple baseline-intervention designs (AB designs) do not permit us to rule out the effects of history. Other more advanced designs are needed.

Maturation. Maturation includes any processes within the client that operate as a function of the passage of time, such as growing up, becoming senile, or becoming tired. Maturation generally becomes more of a threat the longer it takes for the intervention to have an impact.

Statistical regression. Usually clients come to social workers for help when things have gotten worse; that is, they are in an extreme state. However, chances are good that things will look better at the next observation simply because of the random fluctuations of the behavior. This threat to validity is called statistical regression. The best way to control statistical regression is to take an adequate baseline. If the baseline shows an upward or downward trend, or an unusual amount of variability, you should continue to baseline to see whether the data stabilize or the pattern of normal variability becomes clear. The point is to not mistake normal variation in your client's behavior for a real change in behavior.

Multiple intervention interference. When a client receives more than one intervention at a time, there is no empirical basis for knowing which intervention produced the change. This is a common problem, particularly in institutional settings where clients may participate in a variety of groups, receive individual therapy, and perhaps take medication. Again, simple AB designs are inadequate to control for this threat. Other designs, such as multiple baseline designs, are useful in ruling out multiple intervention interference.

Although these are the most common and obvious threats to the validity of single-system evaluation, others are discussed by Cook and Campbell (1979) and Kratochwill (1978).

Single-System Designs

The Basic AB Design

Up to now we have discussed only the simplest of single-system designs, the baseline-intervention, or AB design. It is the most basic design because it provides the information necessary for determining that there has been change, and it suggests the possibility that the intervention produced the change. Since AB designs are not able to control for many of the threats to validity mentioned earlier, they are generally not adequate for inferring causality or intervention effectiveness. More advanced single-system designs are needed to control for such threats.

Withdrawal Designs

Withdrawal designs are characterized by repeated occasions in which the intervention is implemented and then withdrawn. The rationale underlying withdrawal designs is that the causal inference is stronger when there are more occasions on which client outcome can be shown to vary concomitantly with intervention. Common examples are the ABA and ABAB designs (see Figure 11.5). In the former, treatment is withdrawn after it has been implemented, and in the latter treatment is implemented again. Withdrawal designs are useful for controlling threats due to history, maturation, and statistical regression, among others. Withdrawal designs are often difficult to implement in day-to-day practice, however, because they require withdrawal of intervention, even when it appears to be working. This is one example in which the goals of research (demonstrating causal-

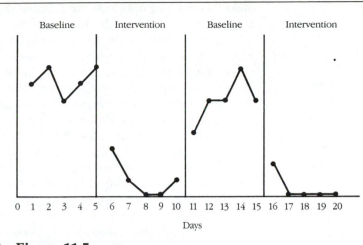

| Baseline | Intervention | Baseline | Intervention |

Days

Figure 11.5
Withdrawal design

ity) may conflict with the goals of service (providing effective treatment).

It is important to be careful to distinguish between withdrawal phases and follow-ups. In withdrawal designs the objective is for the client outcome to return to the pretreatment level in order to demonstrate repeatedly that it is under the control of the intervention. In follow-ups, however, the objective is to show that change is permanent and that it lasts even after treatment has been discontinued. You should be clear in your own mind about which objective you are addressing so you will know how to interpret the data.

Multiple baseline designs. In multiple baseline designs several outcomes of interest are identified and baselined simultaneously. The intervention is then implemented on each outcome at staggered intervals (Figure 11.6). This type of design is stronger than simple AB designs because it provides for several occasions on which outcome can vary concomitantly with intervention. Further, it avoids the practical and ethical problems of withdrawing treatment as in ABA and ABAB designs.

There are still other advanced single-system designs that should be considered if

the objective is to infer causality. The texts by Jayaratne and Levy (1979), Bloom and Fischer (1982), and Barlow and Hersen (1984) offer a more detailed discussion of single-system research designs.

Evaluating Programs

Most of the discussion up to now has assumed that we are evaluating social work practice with individuals, groups, and families. There is nothing inherent in the single-system approach that limits it to clinical evaluation, however. Some of the first applications of single-system designs were to evaluate the impact of policy, such as a change in speed limits or a change in monetary policy. Single-system designs can easily be applied to the evaluation of policy and program interventions. The basic designs are the same; the primary differences are the conceptualization of the intervention and outcome, and the selection of suitable measures.

In program evaluation, the policy or program becomes the intervention. Such interventions include providing incentives for able-bodied welfare recipients to obtain employment, instituting a token economy to

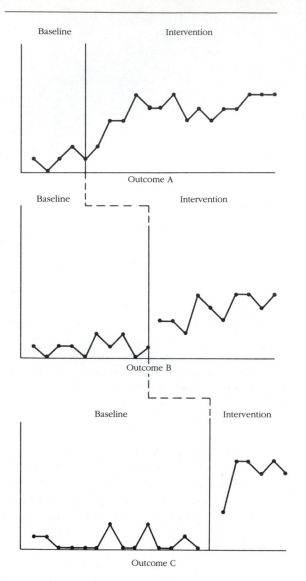

Figure 11.6
Multiple baseline design

reward good behavior in a group home, or starting a new procedure whereby staff ignore the obnoxious noises of children but give positive attention for appropriate talk.

Likewise, in program evaluation the desired outcome has to do with the behavior of the targets of the policy or program change, usually a group of people. Accordingly, the measures must be ones that are suitable for all individuals. This usually rules out client-specific measures such as self-anchored scales. Frequently, the desired outcomes are observable behaviors, such as getting a job, cooperative play in the cottage, or appropriate table conversation. In program evaluation you must be careful to define outcomes in sufficiently general terms so that the definitions will be relevant for all individuals in the target group. When the desired outcome is an internal state, you may need to use some of the standardized measures or rapid assessment instruments mentioned earlier.

Program evaluation, then, is no different conceptually from clinical evaluation. The main difference is that the intervention is a policy or program rather than a therapeutic technique, and the outcome is reflected in the behaviors of a target group of individuals rather than a single individual or therapy group.

The single-system approach to evaluation has much to recommend it. Single-system designs are compatible with most of social work practice, and they provide a beginning basis for inferring that our interventions are effective. Single-system designs, including the more advanced designs, are not always sufficient, however. They cannot always rule out all threats to validity. Some social work interventions, particularly policy and program changes, cannot be implemented abruptly, and other interventions sometimes have a delayed effect on outcome. In both cases it is difficult empirically to relate changes in outcome to the intervention. In such cases, traditional group designs may be justified.

The requirements of group designs—random assignment to groups, relatively large numbers of clients, and uniform treatment of all subjects within groups—make them costly and difficult to implement in normal practice settings. Frequently, the potential benefits of doing a group evaluation do not justify the costs involved. There are times, however, when group designs are warranted, particularly when single-system evaluation has provided cumulative evidence of effectiveness and a more rigorous test is desired. Group evaluation is a rather technical undertaking for which research expertise is advised. Texts by Weiss (1972); Rossi, Freeman, and Wright (1979); Posavac and Carey (1980); and Kaufman and Thomas (1980) are recommended for further reading in this area.

The Ethics of Evaluation

Most of the discussion in this chapter has assumed that we are conducting outcome evaluation as a part of normal practice. That is, we identify goals, select measures of them, and monitor change to verify that the desired goals have been achieved. Outcome evaluation is integral to practice because it tells us if we are making progress and when we can terminate the helping process. Because it is a part of normal practice, outcome evaluation as a process is treated no differently than any other aspect of practice. Accordingly, the usual ethical requirements of confidentiality, client self-determination, and client access to records discussed in earlier chapters apply.

When we undertake evaluative research to infer causality and advance our knowledge of effective practice, however, additional ethical guidelines are required to protect our clients as research subjects. The distinction between evaluation as a practice activity, and evaluative research as a knowledge-building activity is often not ambiguous. As a general rule, however, if the primary purpose of your activity is to develop the knowledge base of the profession rather than deliver a service to your client, you are engaging in research. If you plan to present your results to a professional meeting or publish them in a journal, you are probably engaged in research rather than practice. If in doubt, consider the activity to be research.

When we ask clients to participate in research activities, additional ethical standards apply. We must be sure that clients will not be subjected to undue risk as a consequence of their participation in the research activity. Furthermore, clients must be fully *informed* of the nature of the activity, both the intervention itself and the measurement and design requirements of the research component. Finally, clients' participation must be completely *voluntary*, with no adverse consequence if they decide not to participate in the research. The principle of voluntary informed consent is a fundamental ethical requirement for all research activity and must be carefully followed and documented at all times.

Computer Applications in Social Work Practice

At several points in our discussion of evaluation, the use of computers was mentioned. Computers have been used for some time in evaluation and research, and they are beginning to have an impact on many other aspects of social work practice as well. This brief summary introduces some of those applications and suggests how you may be using computers in your practice in the near future.

The rapid development of computer technology in the last several decades has been due to advances in miniaturization of computers and tremendous strides in the economics of production. Today it is possible to obtain in a desktop computer (costing about a thousand dollars) the computing capacity of the large mainframe computers of a decade or two ago (which cost hundreds of thousands of dollars). These trends are expected to continue. Comparable computing capacity will likely be available soon in machines the size of hand-held calculators costing perhaps only hundreds of dollars.

What does all this mean for social work practice? Well, for one thing, it means that the capacity to process large amounts of data at high speed with little or no error will be widely available. Consequently, the computer will be called on more and more to do the repetitive data processing tasks that until recently had to be done by people. Advances in the design of computing machines will make it possible for computers to handle symbolic processing tasks such as understanding human language and simulating human vision. With developments occurring so rapidly, it is impossible to predict just how computing technology will be applied even several decades from now, but it is certain to change significantly the ways in which social workers will do their work.

Computers come in all sizes, from small lap-top computers the size of notebooks to large mainframe computers that fill entire rooms. Today, social workers are most likely to use personal computers, computers that fit on a desk, cost from $1,000 to $3,000, are easy to use, and have a wide range of software available. In "computerese," *hardware* refers to the machine itself and the related peripheral equipment such as printers and monitors, and *software* refers to the programs the machines use to do tasks.

Typical software programs include word processing programs, which allow you to use your computer much like an electronic typewriter; database programs, which turn your computer into an electronic filing system; and spreadsheets, which instruct your computer to function as an accountant's ledger for use in budgeting and accounting. There are many additional types of software for computers, with new applications being added every day. One of the best ways to become familiar with the new computing technology is to read some of the magazines available on newsstands or the books available in the computer section of your local bookstore.

The most common computer applications in social work fall into the areas presented in the following paragraphs.

Office Management

The two most common office management applications are word processing and accounting. Word processing is used for routine correspondence, case notes, and reports; but is most useful for repetitive tasks such as individualized form letters or documents composed of standard subsections. Most word processing software includes the capability to manage mailing lists—useful for maintaining lists of clients, volunteers, contributors, and staff. The day will soon come when no office, even small human services agencies, will be able to justify being without word processing capabilities.

The other common office management function is accounting. Many social work agencies already use computers for keeping the general ledgers, accounts receivable, accounts payable, and payroll. Sometimes these functions are performed on the agency's own equipment, and sometimes they are contracted out to firms that specialize in providing such services.

Client Information Systems

Client information systems are computerized database systems that contain information about each client, the services received, and outcomes achieved. Comprehensive systems may also include appointment scheduling, community resource directories, and billing functions. The primary function of client information systems is to generate routine reports on the clients served and the services provided. Frequently client information systems focus mainly on serving the needs of agency managers.

Decision Support

If client information systems are designed properly, they can also be used to monitor client progress in treatment, to guide case managers and line workers in the design and implementation of treatment, and to evaluate the impact of agency services (Corcoran & Gingerich, in press; Vafeas, 1991). For example, the system may be able to identify those clients who are making satisfactory progress toward their goals and should be preparing for termination. Likewise, clients who are not making progress can be identified, so ·the treatment team can reassess and revise treatment as needed. Finally, well-designed systems permit analysis of which interventions seem to work best with which kinds of problems. These are referred to as decision support functions because the information generated by the computer is used to assist decision makers as they do their work.

One of the newest applications of computers in social work practice is *expert systems* (Gingerich, 1990a). An expert system is a computer program that contains the facts and rules of thumb a human expert uses to solve a given problem. For example, expert systems are being developed to advise social workers on the risk of child abuse, or which intervention to use in family therapy. Expert systems have the potential to make scarce and highly specialized expertise widely available to practicing professionals at negligible costs.

Another important decision support function is provided by spreadsheet programs. These popular programs, which are electronic versions of the accountant's spreadsheet, permit "what if" analysis of alternative courses of action. When used effectively, spreadsheets can help managers analyze cash flow, determine optimal agency fees, analyze patterns in intakes, or plan the most effective use of agency resources.

Clinical Assessment

One of the earliest uses of computers in mental health settings (along with computerized client records) was clinical assessment. Initially, this consisted of inputting standardized psychological tests so the computer could administer and perhaps score the test (Nurius & Hudson, 1993). Recently, assessment applications have expanded to having the computer administer social history interviews and write up narrative reports, or conduct diagnostic interviews.

One application of computer technology is in computer-administered psychological assessment.

Direct Intervention

Computers are just beginning to be used to actually deliver interventions. Programs have been developed to teach relaxation techniques, modify depression, and treat couples' sexual problems. In some cases, computer-delivered intervention appears to be as effective as intervention delivered by human therapists. Because of the importance of human involvement in social work practice, however, computers are not expected to have a large impact on direct intervention in the near future.

Electronic Networking

Computers can be connected to the telephone system and in this way access any other computer in the world. This capability is opening up many new possibilities for computer use in social work. The most common application of telecommunications to date is electronic mail—sending and receiving messages electronically. *E-mail*, as it is called, provides the capability for social workers to send messages, documents, and reports almost instantaneously at very low cost. Some agencies use electronic networking to maintain up-to-date listings of available resources. The Computer

Use in Social Services Network (see "Resource Materials" at the end of this chapter) maintains an electronic network to provide information and computer-related assistance to human service professionals.

Education and Training

Computers are also beginning to be used in the education and training of social workers. Some schools offer computer simulations of social work situations as a learning experience. Simulations may involve problems, such as managing a waiting list or developing a budget, or how to handle a variety of interviewing situations. In one agency the computer was combined with videodisc technology to provide training to new staff on how to determine eligibility for services. It was found in this case that the computer-delivered training took half the time of the usual classroom training, and the results appeared to be superior.

Research and Information Retrieval

One of the oldest applications of computers in social work is to analyze data for research purposes. Computers are accurate and very fast when it comes to numerical computations. It is now possible to do routine computations such as factor analyses, which previously required weeks for a human to do. On a more practical level, computers can be used to do some of the statistical analyses described earlier for assessing change in client outcomes or even graphing the client's behavior. Graphs can be printed out and made a part of the client's record.

A related application is to access large data bases such as bibliographic services. It is now possible, and economically feasible in many cases, to dial up some of the social work–related bibliographic services to obtain a listing of professional publications that deal with a particular topic. (*Social Work Research and Abstracts* is available on-line through several bibliographic services, and is also available on CD ROM.) You might ask for references on group homes for the hearing impaired, or treatment approaches for agoraphobia, for example.

Issues in Computer Applications

Computer applications such as these have raised some important questions that you should consider carefully before using this new and glamorous technology (Cwikel & Cnaan, 1991). For example, does the lack of a human interacting with the client reduce or limit the impact of services? How does being interviewed by a computer affect the client? What are the threats to maintaining confidentiality? What functions can the computer serve best? What functions should the computer not do? There are no clear answers to many of these questions. Initial research does indicate, however, that some clients prefer to be interviewed by the computer, especially when personal information such as illegal or sexual behavior is discussed. In some cases, clients actually give more accurate and complete information to the computer! When using computers, however, it is essential that we be sensitive to our clients' reactions to the computer and use computers only when it clearly seems to improve services to the client. Additional resource materials on computer applications to social work practice are listed at the end of this chapter.

Summary

Outcome evaluation asks whether the desired client outcome was achieved, and evaluative research asks whether the observed change was due to the intervention. Because it is an inherent part of the problem-solving approach to interventions, outcome evaluation should be done with all clients. Evaluative research requires more rigorous controls, and therefore it is more difficult to carry out and often requires research expertise.

The single-system approach to evaluation consists of the following six steps. First, you must specify the outcome you and your client are interested in. Second, you must select a suitable measure of the outcome, one that is adequate methodologically and is sensitive to the changes you expect your client to make. Third, you should record baseline data on the outcome measure until the pattern of behavior before intervention is clear. Fourth, you must implement your intervention and continue to monitor the outcome. Fifth, you must analyze your data to decide whether there is significant change in the outcome. Sixth, if you have used an appropriate research design, you may be able to infer whether your intervention produced the change.

Although it uses research techniques to assess change and infer treatment effectiveness, the single-system approach to evaluation is compatible with most social work practice. In treatment you ordinarily make informal judgments about whether your client is get-
ting better and whether your intervention is working. Evaluation simply makes the process more systematic and rigorous with a view to improving your information and making your conclusions more reliable. The goal of evaluation is to improve our information about outcomes and thereby improve our practice. Furthermore, several studies show that clients may actually prefer to work with practitioners who evaluate their practice (Campbell, 1988, 1990).

The chapter concludes with a summary of computer applications in social work practice. Not only have computers been used in evaluation and research, but they are beginning to have an impact on many other aspects of social work practice as well. The most common computer applications in social work fall into the following areas: office management, client information systems, decision support, clinical assessment, direct intervention, electronic networking, education and training, and research and information retrieval.

Exercises

1. Selecting a suitable outcome measure

Goal: This exercise is designed to help students consider alternative ways of measuring client outcomes and become aware of the advantages and disadvantages of each.

Step 1: Describe the purpose of this exercise. Explain that client outcomes may be expressed in observable behaviors, or in internal feelings or thoughts. Sometimes even though the outcome is an internal event, such as feeling depressed, it may be preferable to define constructive change in terms of observable behaviors such as socializing with friends, going to work, or expressing one's feelings directly. Review the three major measurement strategies: direct observation, self-anchored rating scales, and standardized measures.

Step 2: Ask students to form groups of three or four members. Then ask each group to recruit one of its members voluntarily to identify an outcome that will become the focus for this exercise. The outcome should be a real one that would be desirable for the student, although it need not be a personal one. For example, a student may identify "improving study habits," "feeling more confident in my field placement," or "settling disagreements with my roommate" as possible outcomes.

Step 3: Ask the other students in each group to interview the volunteer to find out more about the desired outcome. How would the volunteer like things to be? What will he or she be doing differently when the outcome is achieved?

Step 4: Now ask the students to identify at least two possible measurement strategies to measure the outcome. For the sake of this exercise, encourage them to use direct observation and a self-anchored scale. They may also want to select a standardized measure with which they are familiar. Students should describe each measure in detail. What would the anchors on the self-anchored scale be, for example? Or what specific behavior would they observe or ask their volunteer to observe?

Step 5: Have the students ask the volunteer to estimate what data he or she would have collected during the past week had they used each measure. What would the data be like when the problem has been solved?

Step 6: Next, ask each group to discuss the pros and cons of each measure they developed. They should consider these questions: (a) How reliable (accurate and consistent) would the measurement data be? (b) How valid would the data be— that is, would the behavior counts or self-ratings be good indicators of the outcome the volunteer is hoping to achieve? (c) Will the measure be sensitive to changes the volunteer would like to see? Do you really expect to see changes in the measures you have selected? (d) Which measure does your volunteer think is best? Why?

Step 7: Ask each group to discuss the practical value of identifying outcomes and measuring them. How do they think this will benefit their work with their clients? How could it interfere? If they do not plan to collect measurement data, how will they know if there is any change?

Step 8: Ask each group to report briefly to the entire class what outcome their group worked with, the measures they developed, and what they concluded in their discussion.

2. Threats to inferring causality

Goals: This exercise is designed to make students aware of the problems involved in inferring causality and to help them avoid making assertions about treatment effectiveness that cannot be supported by data.

Step 1: Describe the purpose of this exercise. Review briefly the concept of concomitant variation as the primary empirical basis for inferring causality. Then summarize the threats to validity (categories of other explanations for why the client might have changed): history, maturation, statistical regression, and multiple intervention interference. Mention that the purpose of a research design is to provide a logical and empirical basis for inferring that the intervention, not something else, produced the change in outcome.

Step 2: Ask students to imagine they have conducted the following evaluation of their work. Your client, a mother of two children (ages 5 and 8), comes in complaining that her 8-year-old, Joey, clings to her too much and doesn't play with other children his age. You and she agree that the desired outcome is for Joey to play with neighbor children his own age. Mother agrees to record the number of 15-minute periods each evening after supper and before bedtime that Joey plays nicely with his peers. She dutifully collects baseline information as shown below.

After a week of baselining, you instruct the mother to invite a neighbor child over to play with Joey each evening to get the children started in an activity appropriate to their age level. Once the activity has started, she is to give specific praise to the children for their play and to continue to praise every 5 or 10 minutes as it seems appropriate. Also, she is instructed to ignore Joey when he clings to her dress and whines. After role-playing some situations in your office, you are convinced that she understands the intervention and is able to carry it out. Mother returns the next week for her appointment. You review the data and refine and rehearse again the intervention. The next week Mother reports the following data:

During the interview, she reports the following additional information. She has begun to think that Joey is a nice kid after all. Last week when she took him to the park to play they had a really good time. Joey seemed to get along well with the other children on the playground, too. Mother also mentioned that Joey seemed to enjoy his last two weekend visits with his dad. In general, Joey seems to be getting back to his good old self.

Step 3: Now ask students to decide first whether they agree with Mother that there has been a change in Joey's behavior. Is the standard of "clearly evident and reliable" met? What are their doubts about whether the change is experimentally or clinically significant?

Step 4: Next, ask students to enumerate all the other possible explanations for why Joey's behavior has changed. What is the likelihood of each other explanation? Does the simple AB design used allow you to rule out these explanations?

Step 5: Based on the discussion in steps 3 and 4, ask the students whether they think their intervention was successful. How confident are they of the conclusion? If they are not completely convinced, does the intervention seem promising enough to continue using it and observing the results?

Resource Materials on Computer Applications to Social Work Practice

ADMINISTRATION IN SOCIAL WORK 5, nos. 3–4. Fall/Winter 1981. Special issue devoted to computer applications in social work administration.

COMPUTER USE IN SOCIAL SERVICES NETWORK, DICK SCHOECH, COORDINATOR. University of Texas at Arlington, P.O. Box 19129, Arlington, TX 76019. (quarterly newsletter, $10.00/year—$5.00 for students)

COMPUTERS IN HUMAN SERVICES. New York: Haworth Press. A new journal devoted exclusively to computer applications in the human services.

DEITEL, HARRY M., & BARBARA DEITEL, 1985. *Computers and Data Processing.* Orlando, FL: Academic Press.

GEISS, GUNTHER R., & NARAYAN VISWANATHAN, eds. 1986. *The Human Edge: Information Technology and Helping People.* New York: Haworth Press.

NASW PRACTICE DIGEST 6, no. 3. Winter 1983. Special issue devoted to computers in social work practice.

SCHOECH, RICHARD J. 1990. *Human Service Computing: Concepts and Applications.* New York: Haworth Press.

————. 1982. *Computer Use in Human Services.* New York: Human Science Press.

SCHWARTZ, MARC D., ed. 1984. *Using Computers in Clinical Practice.* New York: Haworth Press.

For more information on the computer programs in this chapter, write the author of the programs:

WALLACE J. GINGERICH
Mandel School of Applied Social Sciences
Case Western Reserve University
11235 Bellflower Road
Cleveland, OH 44106

CHAPTER

12

Social Work Practice with Diverse Groups

The social work profession has long prided itself on its recognition of the importance of ethnic, cultural, racial, and sexual differences.[1] Social workers were involved in early efforts to establish the National Association for the Advancement of Colored People (NAACP) and the National Urban League (Garvin & Cox, 1987, p. 36). The National Association of Social Workers' (NASW) *Code of Ethics* specifically prohibits discrimination against others based on race, color, sex, sexual orientation, age, religion, national origin, marital status, political belief, and other factors (see Appendix A). More recently, the 1990 Delegate Assembly adopted a resolution calling on the Council on Social Work Education to strengthen its standards on sexual orientation. On the basis of public pronouncements at least, one would expect that social workers would perform admirably when working with people from among these groups. Unfortunately, this benign view is not necessarily accurate. Mizio (1972, p. 82) noted that "all Americans are products of a racist system," the influence of which is

---

[1]Most of this chapter was specially written for this text by Grafton H. Hull, Jr., Ed.D. Dr. Hull is Department Head, Department of Social Work, Southwest Missouri State University. The section entitled "Macro Strategies to Promote Social and Economic Justice" was written by the text's primary author.

inescapable. Romero (1977, p. 217) claimed that "implicit and explicit biases have been incorporated in the foundation of the recognized knowledge and competence of the profession." Gilligan's (1982) work on women has underscored that much of what we have assumed about human development is based on a male perspective. Clearly, there is evidence that social workers face a difficult task understanding and working with clients whose background differs from their own.

In this chapter we will consider some barriers inherent in worker-client differences and attempt to point out reasons for the problematic nature of cross-cultural relationships. In the second section we will identify conditions that facilitate more effective relationships, discussing in particular self-knowledge and knowledge of the client group to be served. In the third section, specific techniques and approaches to be used (or avoided) will be suggested focusing on social work practice with Native Americans, African Americans, Latinos, women, gays and lesbians, and rural clients. The fourth and final section summarizes macro strategies for promoting social and economic justice. While much of this chapter is written from the perspective of a white male (the author), many of the examples and points raised are applicable to other workers as well.

Problems and Barriers

Clearly the social work profession needs to recognize the reality of practice in a culturally diverse environment. A variety of studies have demonstrated that social workers and other helping persons share many of the prejudices and misperceptions of the general society. Brown and Hellinger (1975), for example, found that social workers in general lag behind psychiatric nurses in holding contemporary attitudes toward women; and male workers, in particular, tend to hold relatively traditional views of females when compared to their sister therapists. Rauch (1978) cited multiple examples of sexism in the social work knowledge base. It has been asserted that "unless the therapists are . . . sensitive to feminist issues or committed to feminism, a certain amount of bias will exist in their therapy no matter how humanistic they view themselves" (Thomas, 1977, p. 450). Romero (1977) argued that sex biases are often in operation in the practice of social casework. If "male counselors share cultural values, for instance, that consider women to be less effective and more likely to have difficulty coping with life situations," the effectiveness of the worker is definitely compromised (Hook, 1979, p. 63). For example, males working with depressed women may simply recreate old relationships between the dependent woman and the controlling male, relationships counter to the goals of intervention.

The tendency to use one's own cultural, social, or economic values as the norm poses additional dangers for the well-meaning practitioner. The ease with which many workers confuse a healthy adaptation to a sick environment with pathology points up the difficulty. Both the habit of misreading strengths as deficits and the assumption that African Americans and other minorities are culturally deprived arise from the use of norms derived from the dominant white middle class (Thomas & Sillen, 1972). Medina and Reyes (1976, p. 515), viewing Latino counselors working with other Latinos, added that Spanish-speaking counselors "are subject to the same cultural characteristics as are their clients." The problematic nature of cross-cultural counseling does not, however, preclude its effectiveness. Some white workers, for instance, can establish viable working relationships with minority clients, while in other instances, minority workers are less effective with others of the same race or culture (Williams et al., 1975; Logan, 1990). The following excerpt illustrates this point quite well.

In answering the question of whether a white middle-class psychiatrist can treat a black family, I cannot help but think back over my own experiences. When I first came to New York and decided to go into psychotherapy I had two main thoughts: (1) that my problems were culturally determined, and (2) that they were related to my Catholic upbringing. I had grown up in an environment in which the Catholic Church had tremendous influence. With these factors in mind, I began to think in terms of the kind of therapist I could best relate to. In addition to being warm and sensitive, he had to be black and Catholic. Needless to say, that was like looking for a needle in a haystack. But after inquiring around, I was finally referred to a black Catholic psychiatrist.

Without going into too much detail, let me say that he turned out to be not so sensitive and not so warm. I terminated my treatment with him and began to see another therapist who was warm, friendly, sensitive, understanding and very much involved with me. Interestingly enough, he was neither black, nor Catholic. As a result of that personal experience, I have come to believe that it is not so much a question of whether the therapist is black or white but whether he is competent, warm, and understanding. Feelings, after all, are neither black nor white. [Sager, Brayboy, & Waxenberg, 1970, pp. 210–211]

Though this view may seem somewhat sanguine given the vast differences that sometimes separate client and worker, there is every reason to believe that the perception is accurate. Logan (1990, p. 33) concluded that "ethnicity and class are important variables in service delivery and should not serve as barriers to effective client-worker relationships." Despite rather disparate backgrounds and experiences, many social workers and clients do develop productive relationships. This is not to say there are not difficulties in intercultural relationships. Lewis and Ho (1975, p. 382) recognized this when they noted "it is impossible for a social worker always to know precisely how to respond to a . . . given client or group." The problem becomes increasingly complex when we focus on some of the major barriers to effective cross-cultural social work practice. The next section will review selected characteristics of a sample of diverse groups with whom a social worker is likely to interact and will identify some of the potential dangers facing the unwary helper. These issues are intended only to sensitize the social worker to the upcoming task and are not designed to cover all possible situations. They should be viewed accordingly.

Native American Clients

A social worker working with a Native American client could readily assume that the client's quietness indicates either an uncooperative attitude or, conversely, that the worker and client are on the same wavelength (Locklear, 1972). Unfortunately it is possible that neither assumption is appropriate. In fact, a Native American may not correct or challenge a worker who is off the track because to do so would be to violate a basic tenet of Native American culture: noninterference (Good Tracks, 1973). Noninterference in practice is similar, but not identical, to the social work value of self-determination. It requires the Native American to meet unwanted attempts at intervention or intrusion with withdrawal— emotional, physical, or both. In other cases, this may take the form of changing the subject or pretending not to hear the offending words. Even the most well-intentioned worker may be perceived as a coercive authority figure whose efforts are resisted passively but firmly. As Ferris and Ferris (1976, p. 388) noted, "The aggressive probings of many contemporary methodologies conflict with such tribal values as nonverbal passivity, decision making by consensus and noninterference." The Native American as a consequence is perhaps less likely to assert himself or herself than might be true of members of other protected classes. Assuming that clients will give feedback if the worker is off target is only one of several beliefs the worker must unlearn to practice effectively in a cross-cultural environment.

Another response pattern of social work practitioners that frequently proves counterproductive is direct eye contact. Many Native Americans consider such face-to-face eye contact rude and intimidating (Lewis & Ho, 1975). Kadushin (1990) noted that ethnic differences in eye contact have been acknowledged by other writers and that Native Americans in particular find eye contact disrespectful. Avoiding eye contact is a way of showing deference in this culture. Obviously, a white worker who plans to practice in a Native American community needs to be cognizant of these factors if he or she is not to exacerbate the already tenuous relationship that exists between cultures. Lacking a thorough knowledge of Native American culture often results in a failure to recognize its complexity and a worker does this at his or her peril.

African American Clients

With African American clients the picture is somewhat similar; workers frequently misread the meaning of client behavior with resultant deleterious consequences. For example, the adaptive behavior of many African Americans, which includes "guardedness or assuming a strong sense of identity," may be seen by whites as threatening or rejecting (Pinderhughes, 1979). Grier and Cobbs (1968) suggested that a certain level of cultural paranoia on the part of the African American client may intrude on the client–white worker relationship and Gilbert (1974) added that African American youths in particular lack trust in traditional social service agencies. With these factors in mind, it is easy to understand why some writers and others feel that only a worker from the client's cultural background can effectively work with minority clients. At times a non–African American worker may attempt to overcompensate for these differences by unrealistic empathicness. This reaction is understandable since, as Mizio (1972, p. 84) noted, "working with minority clients arouses acute anxiety" for some whites. To counter this, some workers ascribe all the emotional and social difficulties experienced by the African American client to a racist society. This, in effect, denies the client his or her humanity and similarities with other human beings, a result that is, of course, unintended.

Language differences may also serve as barriers to communication. Wofford (1979) estimated that 80 percent of African Americans use what he terms *Ebonics*. Ebonics is a verbal communication system that includes not only rate and rhythm, but also syntax, word choice, and nonverbal communication. The result is that words may have different meanings to the speaker and to the listener. Wright and Isenstein (1975, p. 13) cited an example of this communication when they noted that "I don't know what page you are on" means "I don't understand what you are saying." The result of these language differences may affect both oral communication and performance on psychological tests and pose difficulties for the novice social worker.

Latino Clients

As noted earlier, even workers who share common characteristics with minority clients sometimes experience comparable difficulties to those described earlier. Bilingual white practitioners, for example, who work in a predominantly Latino community do not necessarily possess the requisite skills to understand all aspects of the language. The special language of the barrio in particular is not easily understood unless one has some shared experience with the actual culture. Both the meaning of words and their usage differ, sometimes significantly (Norton, 1978). As a consequence the worker who does speak Spanish must be acutely sensitive to the possibility that words may have other meanings. Enhancement of one's ability to perceive accurately the intended "communication is fostered by a knowledge of the range of lifestyles or circumstances of the group with which one is working" (Norton, 1978, p. 21). Aguilar (1972, p. 186) added that "each minority group has its own problems and personality derived from long existing cultural and moral values, language, patterns of behavior, socioeconomic conditions, ethnic background, and many other factors." While bilingualism may not be a sufficient condition for successful practice with Latinos, it is often necessary or helpful.

Lest a worker become discouraged at this point about the difficulties inherent in cross-cultural social work, even counselors of the same background are not guaranteed freedom from problems. Medina and Reyes (1976) noted that even Chicano counselors may actually be hindered by the culturally supported bias regarding women that undermines the client's confidence in a female therapist's ability.

Gay and Lesbian Clients

It has been estimated that approximately 10 percent of the adult population is primarily homosexual (Berger, 1987, p. 797). This fact, combined with the usual family constellation, suggests that a large number of people will be directly affected by the issue of homosexuality. Humphreys (1983, p. 60) estimated that the lives of almost half of all Americans will be touched by homosexuality. Berger (1987, p. 797) concluded that "virtually everyone, whether self-identified as homosexual or heterosexual, has a close relationship with a gay man." Woodman (1987) suggested that the actual incidence of homosexuality may be greater than estimates.

Unfortunately, homosexuality traditionally has been viewed variously as deviant, criminal, an illness, an emotional disturbance, and, among some groups, a sin. The result has been an irrational fear of homosexuality, often called homophobia, that has become as serious a problem as other forms of prejudice, such as sexism and racism.

Helping professionals are as likely to be

affected by these prejudices as the general public. Lack of knowledge, acceptance of stereotypes, and fear of the unknown are not limited to the layperson. Whereas many social work practitioners may have been exposed to minority group members, the stigma associated with gay and lesbian lifestyles has kept a large number of homosexuals from sharing this information with others. As a result, social workers who come in contact with gay and lesbian clients are often no better prepared to help these groups than is the general public. The tendency to stereotype homosexual clients flies in the face of what is known about the differences and similarities among human beings. Loewenstein (1980, p. 31) argued, for example, that "lesbian women are extremely diverse in personality, family constellation, and developmental experiences, and categorizing them as a group becomes as meaningless as categorizing all heterosexual women." The same can likely be said for gay men.

The social worker who works with gay and lesbian clients can start with the information on diversity and yet still recognize common difficulties experienced by homosexuals in our society. The barriers and discrimination encountered by gays and lesbians should be acknowledged for their impact on the client's life as well as for their effect on the relationship between helper and client.

As a beginning, it is helpful to recognize that debate over causation of homosexuality is irrelevant to efforts to help. A focus on etiology does not assist the client with present functioning and tends to obscure the multiple problems resulting from societal reaction to gays and lesbians. Attempts to focus on cause have not been beneficial in coping with stereotypes and in fact have led to homosexuals' being mistreated in order to correct for some presumed deficit in early life experiences. Furthermore, few gays and lesbians can be identified either by appearance or mannerisms. This, coupled with the risks in coming out (publicly identifying oneself as homosex-

ual), has resulted in a lack of attention to the needs of gay and lesbian clients. As Berger noted, "This has especially been true of older homosexuals who have been all but ignored by the social work profession" (1982, p. 236). Later in this chapter we will suggest several means by which social workers can assist lesbian and gay clients by recognizing and dealing with the specialized needs of this group.

Rural Settings

Like practitioners in a biracial environment, social workers who work predominantly with clients of their own race or ethnic group may not be spared the necessity of adjusting their practice style. For example, the worker who is practicing in a basically rural environment must also be aware of a multiplicity of factors that impinge on effectiveness. The following case illustrates the risks inherent in ignoring the norms of a rural area.

> The Vistas packed their belongings the next day, after being asked to move. Before they left, they asked the man from whom they had purchased groceries if he had heard anything said about them.
>
> He told them that a woman customer had told him that Mary Newman had told her the Vistas had "dirty picture magazines" and "loads of beer cans" lying around the house. Mary Newman had said that the Vistas "hadn't shown proper respect for her dead mother by treating her house this way."
>
> The Vistas did recall a single copy of *Playboy* and one occasion when two empty beer cans were left on the table for two days. [Council on Social Work Education, 1968, p. 13]

This episode suggests the greater visibility experienced by the rural worker and, of course, the consequences of failing to be sensitive to community expectations.

Such seemingly innocuous factors as style of dress and model of car may set the social worker in a rural community apart (Buxton, 1976). In addition, the worker in a rural area may discover that events of the past still affect the behavior of residents today. For example, long-standing family and church conflicts may exist and create barriers to getting community members together to work on a problem or issue. The fact that many rural social workers lack exposure to the rural environment before beginning their practice can create additional difficulties. The worker's attitude and ideas regarding rural communities may be outdated or even quite negative. This attitude may affect his or her interaction with residents just as strongly as would racial bias in a minority community. The struggle to survive in a rural setting under these conditions may explain the relatively common problem of burnout experienced by the in-migrant practitioner.

Feminist Social Work

Increasing sensitivity to the impact of gender on the development, definition, and amelioration of social and personal problems has helped identify another barrier to effective social work practice—sexism. There is greater recognition today that many of the difficulties experienced by both men and women in society are related to gender inequality, specifically in the areas of privileges, power, and access to resources. The enormous role played by gender provides some limitations to social work practice and suggests ways in which the worker's own sex may become a contributing problem. Van Den Bergh and Cooper (1987, p. 610) identified some of the situations, for example, where a male worker may be less appropriate than a woman practitioner:

1. all-female groups, which may reinforce stereotypic dependencies or set up competition for male attention;
2. women who are hostile to men unless they work as a cotherapist in the therapeutic process;

3. women who relate to male therapists primarily in a seductive manner;
4. extremely dependent, inhibited women who equate femaleness with passivity and docility;
5. women who are in the midst of a divorce crisis and who may, as a result of intense transference feelings, see the male therapist as a surrogate spouse.

As will be shown later, these limitations do not mean that gender always must be a delimiting factor in social work practice. They do mean, however, that both male and female social workers must be aware of ways in which gender can have a major impact on a client's problems and the ways in which help can and should be provided. The significant consideration is the extent to which gender-related oppression encompasses all aspects of society—economic, social, religious, and political—and the fact that gender itself plays no less a role in social work practice than is true for race, sexual preference, and location. The difficulty in overcoming the bondage of sexism provides a challenge as great as dealing with the pressures that perpetuate racism and homophobia. Some methods of providing effective intervention within the context of nonsexist practice will be described later. (See also Chapter 19 for a discussion of the feminist perspective on therapy.)

Other Examples

There are many elements that can potentially separate worker and client and undermine the empathic quality of the relationship. We have identified some of the cultural, racial, and sexual differences that create this gulf. Kadushin (1990) described additional worker-client characteristics that may affect the outcome of the relationship. The age difference between a younger worker and an older client, for instance, may prove a barrier because of differences in values, perceptions, or physiological factors. At the same time, workers attempting to establish relationships with children will find that as adults they are potentially contaminated by their association with parents, a state of affairs that may have to be overcome if the child is to develop trust in the counselor.

Even something as individual to the counselor as a "preference for brief or short-term treatment may be antagonistic to the needs of minority clients or others whose situational conditions are nonsupportive and whose problems will be chronic until structural conditions are changed" (Norton, 1978, p. 22).

Clearly the role of a social worker can be complex. The critical and fundamental issues affecting the counselor's practice, however, are generally categorized into four areas: ignorance of the culture or characteristics of those with whom one is working, retention of stereotypic perceptions of the target group, lack of self-knowledge, and reliance on standard counseling techniques and approaches without regard to their implications for the client group. Each of these areas can be overcome, providing the worker is willing and able to make the necessary adaptations. The task is not necessarily an easy one since, as Montiel (1973) noted, much of the research available to the interested social worker paints an inaccurate picture of minority groups, misjudging such salient areas as family structure and lifestyle characteristics.

Part of the problem experienced in gathering factual data, of course, is that much of the research is based on the perceptions of white middle-class investigators. Despite this handicap, the worker who has a significant intercultural practice must seek appropriate information on the groups with which he or she intends to interact. However, this knowledge is only the beginning, since cross-cultural social work demands a high degree of self-knowledge and self-awareness on the part of the worker. Unlike sociological, psychological, and anthropological data, which is obtained with reasonable ease, self-knowledge is perhaps the most difficult to obtain since

it can be anxiety-producing for the worker. "An individual may deny his racist feelings because they conflict with his self-image as a humanitarian and a liberal. However, even if he does admit his prejudices and tries to work them through, it is impossible to reverse them completely" (Mizio, 1972, p. 82). And therein lies the dilemma. The worker must expect to practice in a somewhat prejudiced world as a result, though this should not prevent effective intervention.

Knowledge Needed for Cross-Cultural Work

Knowledge of Self

There is no substitute for self-awareness on the part of the social work practitioner. The ability to be responsive to one's own senses, feelings, behavior, and thoughts is a prime requisite for effective practice in the helping professions. This includes a thorough recognition, knowledge, and acceptance of one's value system. "It is especially crucial for the social worker to . . . possess . . . an understanding of the extent that his professional behavior contributes to the oppression or freedom of" minorities in general (Gilbert, 1974, p. 94).

In some cases, workers' feelings about racism and the plight of minorities or other groups suffering from discrimination may effectively block their functioning by generating guilt, depression, or a sense of being overwhelmed. This process can be averted by recognizing the likelihood of growing up prejudiced and by being willing "to be more ready to listen, less ready to come to conclusions, more open to guidance and correction of . . . presuppositions" (Kadushin, 1983, p. 304) that have arisen as a function of growing up in a racist society. The ability to correct one's own tendencies toward racist thinking obviously requires a sensitive worker willing to put forth the effort. "A white social worker cannot help a minority client unless he can accept the ugliness of racism without being overwhelmed by guilt" (Mizio, 1972, p. 84). To do so requires workers to be willing to make fundamental changes in their thinking patterns, attitudes, and behavior. Still, such growth in self-knowledge (of and by itself) is insufficient without a concomitant growth in awareness of the uniqueness of the client group.

Knowledge of Differences

It has long been asserted that similar needs exist in all cultures, but the molding and shaping of those needs is culturally relative. Thus, while a basic acceptance of the worth and dignity of each human being is required, the worker intending to practice with any of a variety of diverse groups must enhance this acceptance with hard facts. While we believe ourselves to be grounded in reality, our reality is nevertheless only a function of our perception of the real world. An individual who comes to a counseling situation from a different cultural background, especially one who has experienced racist or sexist behavior, may have a different reality. Therefore, the worker must be cognizant of the ways in which cultural and other background factors affect perceptions and feelings and the expression of these qualities. For example, Rauch (1978, p. 391) argued that many of the problems experienced by female clients are actually bio-psychosocial in origin. "Teenage and unwanted pregnancy, postpartum depression, and sexual dysfunction . . . vulnerability to wife abuse and rape . . . the empty nest syndrome," incest, and displaced homemaker status are a sample of the specific gender-related problems that women may experience. As Kravetz (1982, p. 46) pointed out, "Women's personal concerns, experiences, and problems are intricately related to their social, economic, legal, and political condition." The institutionized prejudice against women presents the worker with additional problems. Thus, the profeminist worker must

be aware of the unique difficulties to which women are especially vulnerable, the absence of coping resources experienced by many women, and the stereotypist tendencies of much of society.

Also beneficial is some knowledge of the history and language of the group to be worked with. A familiarization with common phrases or vocabulary would be helpful even if the worker is not bilingual. This background should also include a solid knowledge base in minority lifestyles so the client's strengths and ability to adapt are not ignored or branded as abnormal behavior. For example, the minority client who appears hostile or suspicious of a white worker may be expressing a quite reasonable reaction based on past experiences with well-meaning professionals or other representatives of "helping" agencies.

The growing incidence of ethnoviolence (conflict and violence motivated by prejudice) experienced in the United States over the past ten years is testimony to the continued difficulties experienced by members of minority groups (Weiss, 1990). It has also helped underscore the earlier observation of Thomas and Sillen (1972, p. 63) that "in order to judge what is healthy or morbid in an individual's psychological functioning, one must be aware of what is appropriate within his cultural milieu." Living with racism, prejudice, discrimination, and violence are going to have important consequences for a client's feelings, thoughts, and behaviors. Workers cannot ignore this reality.

Even the same behavior may carry a variety of meanings to persons from different cultures. The ability to understand and "work constructively with norms, family patterns, leadership patterns, community organizations and other cultural patterns of minority groups" is essential, yet more uncommon than common (Turner, 1972, p. 115). The knowledge of how a given group responds to authority, to stress, and to dependency is invaluable since a worker may easily mistake a given reaction as inappropriate without a sound grasp of the culture. This grounding could ideally come from living in a minority area, taking part in community activities, such as council meetings, powwows, and neighborhood get-togethers. Certainly, these activities should be pursued by any social worker serving a given population. Obviously a background of direct experience with minorities would perhaps be ideal, but most social workers who begin practice do not have this base. As a result, it behooves the worker to take advantage of some of the excellent bibliographic material available on the subject, some of which is listed at the end of this text in the bibliography. A worker, for example, who intends to work with Native Americans should carefully study the unique cultural heritage of this group. There are many Native American cultures, and each tribe has its own history, traditions, customs, and environment. This makes it a bit more difficult to generalize from tribal group to tribal group. However, there are some important similarities. For example, the fact that the Native American father plays a stronger disciplinarian role in the family may suggest to the unknowing worker that child abuse is occurring, when in fact the Native American family is perhaps less dependent on corporal punishment than the average non–Native American family. The failure to recognize cultural factors such as this will inevitably result in misunderstanding and frustrations for the erring worker. Awareness of the principal values of the Native American and an understanding of the cultural context in which the Native American exists will lessen this possibility.

The Native American tradition of sharing is another area that confuses white workers unaccustomed to this kind of hospitality. Even if resources are meager, the Native American is willing to allow other family and friends to partake of what there is. Although this may appear to be nonfunctional to many whites, the value is intrinsic to the Native American heritage. To do otherwise would be to ignore part of a value system that has

This Eskimo family is involved in a food preparation activity that might be unfamiliar to a social worker who has limited knowledge of the Eskimo culture. Social workers have an ethical obligation to become knowledgeable about the cultures of the diverse groups they work with.

helped the culture survive over 400 years of racism.

Even the Native American use of time can be a subject of confusion to the non–Native American, as the following account suggests (Hall, 1959):

> I can still remember a Christmas dance I attended some twenty-five years ago at one of the pueblos near the Rio Grande. I had to travel over bumpy roads for forty-five miles to get there. At seven thousand feet, the ordeal of winter cold at one o'clock in the morning is almost unbearable. Shivering in the still darkness of the pueblo, I kept searching for a clue as to when the dance would begin.
>
> Outside everything was impenetrably quiet. Occasionally there was the muffled beat of a deep pueblo drum, the opening of a door, or the piercing of the night's darkness with a shaft of light. In the church where the dance was to take place, a few white townsfolk were huddled together on a balcony, groping for some clue which would suggest how much longer they

were going to suffer. "Last year I heard they started at ten o'clock." "They can't start until the priest comes." "There is no way of telling when they will start." All this punctuated by chattering teeth and the stamping of feet to keep up circulation.

Suddenly an Indian opened the door, entered and poked up the fire in the stove. Everyone nudged his neighbor: "Maybe they are going to begin now." Another hour passed. Another Indian came in from outside, walked across the nave of the church, and disappeared through another door. "Certainly now they will begin. After all, it's almost two o'clock." Someone guessed that they were just being ornery in the hope that the white man would go away. Another had a friend in the pueblo and went to his house to ask when the dance would begin. Nobody knew. Suddenly, when the whites were almost exhausted, there burst upon the night the deep sounds of the drums, rattles, and low male voices singing. Without warning the dance had begun. [pp. 21–22]

Though some might suggest otherwise, Native Americans are not unaware of time, but rather they do not allow themselves to become captive to its tyranny as many whites have done. Punctuality is not a preeminent concern, a fact that confounds many time-conscious helping professionals. The time-bound worker may also misperceive the related Native American value of patience as evidence of laziness or lack of motivation. Respect for and appreciation of the Native American culture is essential if the worker is not to become an obstacle to an effective relationship.

Similarly, the Latino experience will be sufficiently new to most workers that a dedicated effort must be made to replace ignorance with knowledge. As in the case of Native Americans, the family unit of Latinos is more likely to be characterized as extended. This expanded family network is another indica-

tion of the adaptability of Latinos. The worker therefore needs to be alert for the boundaries of the family system so he or she does not exclude or overlook pertinent members. The fact that the elderly have an important role to play and must be included in planning places a special burden on the practitioner. The significance of religion in Latino life is more commonly known to most non-Latinos, as is the importance of the male role. Although there is some evidence that the cross-cultural differences in these areas may be exaggerated in the literature, the worker needs to be aware of the significance of these factors in Latino life. The worker "must be bicultural enough to be able to perceive, model and encourage behaviors that are not only more psychologically adaptive but are more suitable to the client's particular type of barrio [neighborhood] and familia [family]" (Boulette, 1975, p. 404).

The diversity of cultural backgrounds found within the Native American culture is duplicated within Latino culture. The tendency to see any culture as unidimensional fails to recognize the diversity within cultures. For instance, the term *Latino* encompasses Mexican Americans, Puerto Ricans, Colombians, Brazilians, and others whose ancestry can be traced to Spanish or Portuguese beginnings. The term also masks the degree of mixed-racial background found among, for example, Puerto Ricans, a situation that has created "intragroup divisiveness" (Solomon, 1987, p. 859).

Like Latinos, Asian Americans are such an extraordinarily diverse group that attempts to characterize them by identifying commonalities is difficult. For example, comparisons among Hmong, Laotian, and Japanese clients are most difficult. The recent immigrant experiences of the Hmong and other Southeast Asian groups, coupled with cultural differences between these groups and others who have been here for several generations, make it unlikely that one set of guidelines would ever be helpful. In addition, the tendency to lump these groups together has been criticized, because it does not specifically address the unique needs of individual Asian cultures (Magner, 1993). Special programs involving interpreters, language classes, and other efforts aimed at helping new immigrants learn about American culture are needed for recent immigrant groups. Such programs are one means of promoting social and economic justice for populations-at-risk. That immigrant groups such as the Hmong and Cambodians are at risk is evident from the fact that less than 25 percent of the Hmong and less than 45 percent of the Cambodians in the United States complete high school. This compares with around 75 percent for other Asian Americans (Magner, 1993, p. A34). The Hmong and Cambodians in the United States often speak little English, hold very low-paying jobs, and struggle with overt discrimination more often than more traditional third- or fourth-generation Asian Americans. In one sense, their experiences are more like those of immigrants in the 19th and early 20th centuries. For example, one community used program innovations in the school to help ensure that Hmong students and parents felt a part of the educational system. This included using bilingual aides to talk to parents about school programs, explain homework assignments, confirm parent-teacher conference times, and invite parents to participate in school programs (Alexander, 1993). The result of such programs has been almost 100 percent participation by parents in conferences and children in after-school programs. Such programs are examples of the kind of innovative efforts needed to reach at-risk populations.

Though the client group and community may not be ethnically or racially different from that of the worker, the practitioner who works in a rural environment must also possess a certain knowledge base to be effective. He or she must be aware of the network of nontraditional services often available in these areas. Service clubs and church groups, for instance, may assume greater import than in larger, more metropolitan communities. Likewise, the existence of natural support systems can be a real asset, but workers must know about them before they can use them effectively. Knowledge of the local power structure is perhaps more crucial than for the urban worker, since the worker's effectiveness may be seriously impaired without the necessary sanction and cooperation. As in the case of other diverse groups, ignorance of values, beliefs, and attitudes of the rural client system is inexcusable and likely to be counterproductive. If this need to be alert to, and operate within, local norms is seen as onerous by the worker, then he or she should consider moving elsewhere.

As discussed earlier, age differences between worker and client may also affect the worker's practice. Kadushin (1983) suggested, for example, that the worker must be aware of the effect that the physical condition of the elderly can have on the interview. Among other factors, lack of energy and hearing difficulties may impair the aged client's ability to participate in the relationship. The competent worker, thus, must have a firm foundation in human behavior and development as well as sensitivity to the nuances of communication within a helping relationship.

It is common for social workers to identify and build on clients' strengths. Assessment of these strengths, however, requires recognizing the clients' vast and diverse experiences. Too often, one of the strengths that is overlooked is the spiritual element. Spiritualism takes many forms, especially among the diverse groups in our society. A social worker might consider whether a client regularly attends church or belongs to a particular religious organization. Such activities often serve as a source of support in tough times and may also prove to be both an emotional and economic resource. Religious values may dictate appropriate behavior toward other family members and nonfamily members, as well as how the client expresses pain and suffering. In addition, in Caribbean, Hispanic, and some Asian cultures (Ortiz, 1993), spiritualism is used to explain a variety of physical and emotional problems. As Ortiz pointed out, the importance of spirituality is relevant for understanding human behavior, affects social work practice, and impacts social policy and research.

Application of Knowledge: Techniques of Intervention

Once a sufficient knowledge base is acquired, workers must incorporate this into practice to increase the effectiveness of their interventive activities. In this section we will review some specific approaches and techniques of intervention designed to enhance the worker's capabilities. The material presented is not intended to be exhaustive, and obviously there is no substitute for direct experience. The worker whose practice encompasses any of these areas must do more extensive reading (and, it is hoped, receive formal training) than is presented here.

Basic to any relationship, according to Truax and Mitchell (1971), is empathy, clearly communicated to the client, plus warmth and genuineness. Workers in a bicultural relationship must pay special heed to this advice, since authenticity is even more crucial when differences are greater between client and helper. Moreover, workers must use their own patterns of communication and avoid the temptation to adopt the client's vocabulary and speech. A worker who does not follow this stricture may find clients either withdrawing from the relationship or attacking the helper for lack of sincerity. In many cross-cultural relationships, there is a greater need on the part of the client to know the worker as a person (Kadushin, 1983). A helper who is uncomfortable stepping outside the professional role probably should avoid either working with many minority clients or practicing in a rural environment since a greater informality is expected in both settings.

There are clear limits to the time and place for informality in intercultural counseling. Generally the kind of informality that marks

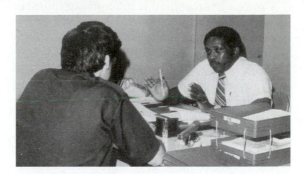

For workers in bicultural or biracial relationships, empathy and authenticity are crucial aspects of counseling.

the effective relationship does not occur immediately. For example, in the initial interview, Kadushin (1983) recommended using all the formalities associated with culturally prescribed displays of respect. This should include use of the client's proper full name, title (Mr., Miss, Mrs., Ms., Dr.), greeting with a handshake, and the other courtesies usually extended. Workers must also be upfront with clients about the reasons for their presence. For example, if the contact was worker-initiated, the worker should give identification, state the reasons for the meeting, and avoid placing the client in the position of having to guess the purpose.

> The helping relationship is in itself a power relationship in which the dynamics of power and lack of power are operating. The expertise of the worker and the neediness of the client place them in positions of power and lack of power, respectively. The cross-racial and cross-ethnic helping encounter compounds the consequences of this power differential. Power issues related to differences in ethnicity, class, sex, age, and other social markers may exaggerate the power inherent in the helping role in a way that causes the worker to misperceive the client [Pinderhughes, 1979, p. 315].

Workers in an empathic relationship must be alert to the power differential engendered by race and other differences and strive to reduce or eliminate this differential. The use of proper protocol is an aid in this effort.

Awareness of these differences and a degree of sensitivity to the subtle impact of racial prejudice should help the counselor avoid the related trap of color blindness that often confuses the novice. To avoid appearing prejudiced, the new worker may decide to adopt the strategy of color blindness and ignore the client's race or ethnic background. While well-intended, color blindness is ineffective because of the tendency it creates for separating "the black person's internal problems from his color" (Burgest, 1973, p. 23). According to Thomas and Sillen (1972), color blindness ceases to be a "virtue if it means denial of differences in the experience, culture and psychology of black Americans and other Americans . . . (p. 58) To gloss over race in a racist society may in itself be a capitulation to racism" (p. 143). It is understandable if on occasion the worker's feelings about racism get in the way of the relationship; guilt, depression, or a sense of being overwhelmed are not uncommon reactions, yet the helper must reject sympathy when empathy is required. Conversely, while some impact of racism may almost always exist, its impact on the presenting problem may be greater or less. It may be a contributing factor in the client's problem, the cause of the problem, or entirely unrelated to the issues at hand. The worker should not automatically attribute all difficulties to racism.

Like the culturally sensitive worker, an agency can be equally dedicated to providing services to different client groups. The agency's responsiveness can be demonstrated through relatively simple measures such as establishing hours that coincide with the needs of the groups to be served. This may include evening hours to avoid the need for some clients, already economically marginal, to lose time from the job, and it could ex-tend to weekend hours and walk-in arrangements, as Kadushin (1983) suggested. The fact that the poor are frequently afflicted by crises requires that there be more flexible means of dealing with immediate client needs and greater accessibility to services for the here-and-now, present-oriented client. Logically, the immediacy of the situation coupled with the economic and political existence of many minority clients suggest that first-level needs must be attended to on a priority basis. This orientation is basic to the social work principle of starting where the client is. It is most unlikely that the client whose housing needs are imminent will tolerate a worker who insists on focusing on the dynamics of the marital interactions. Clients from all cultures reject an incompetent and insensitive social worker.

Within the relationship, the counselor will have to judge the need to be more or less active. As we shall see later, a high level of intervention on the part of the worker dealing with a Native American family may well prove less productive than with a client from another cultural or racial group. Kadushin (1983) recommended that the focus in the relationship be on specific problems and behaviors, whereas other authors state that "particularly inadequate is the school of psychology called behaviorism which de-emphasizes the very patterns that distinguish ethnic strategies while publicizing merely obvious behaviors" (Southwestern Cooperative Educational Laboratory, 1968, p. 157). This issue likely cannot be resolved for all cases, and the social worker must therefore adopt the approach that fits most naturally with his or her helping style. Certainly, attempting to use a method of intervention in which one is uncomfortable or only marginally competent would be a serious error.

African American Client—White Worker

African Americans can easily be defined as a historically oppressed group. The patterns of discrimination they have encountered since colonial times and their history, intertwined with the institution of slavery, have combined to create a population-at-risk. For over three centuries, racism and mistreatment have enveloped the experiences of individuals and families. There is a tendency in our society to assign African Americans to inferior roles (for example, in employment) and to erroneously view them as having a lower status (Blassingame, 1972; Gutman, 1976; Greene, 1969). This has often placed African Americans in a disadvantaged position relative to community institutions, including social welfare agencies. Fortunately, most of the guides to practice discussed earlier are directly applicable to the relationship between the non–African American worker and the African American client. In addition, however, Hopkins (1973) stressed the need to avoid placing the African American client in a position of dependency. The power discrepancy described earlier in this chapter is often the result when this is neglected. Both workers and agencies serving the African American client, according to Hopkins (1973), must recognize the value of supporting African American manhood as well as efforts aimed at maintaining the male's role in the family. This may require that the agency arrange to have male social workers available in situations where a sex differential would be counterproductive to the goal of supporting African American males as males. While same-sex workers are by no means required in all cases, the agency should be sensitive to the possibility that individual cases may necessitate using a worker of the client's gender.

In the area of group services to minority clients, Davis (1979) recommended that membership be selected so that no one race vastly outnumbers the others represented and that biracial leadership may have a benign effect if members tend to be more open with workers of the same race. As always, if the worker is alert and responsive to the client's feelings and reactions, needed adjust-

ments in the intervention approach can be made and the use of standard formulas for success can be tempered by the practitioner's judgment.

Since the client's exposure to and experience with professional therapeutic relationships may be very limited, Kadushin (1983) pointed out that there may be a need to educate the client about the processes of counseling. The use of unambiguous jargon is the best means for conveying this information and, in fact, should be the rule for most worker-client interaction. Also suggested is the promotion of concrete activities by worker and client, including greater use of role playing, gaming, and simulations to supplant or supplement, as appropriate, more verbal techniques. Clients from lower socioeconomic backgrounds may better understand and appreciate direct action on the part of the worker.

Some general guidelines for practice with African Americans include the following:

1. Assume nothing about the client. For example:
   a. Don't assume he or she wants to talk to someone of the same race.
   b. Don't assume you understand completely the experiences of African American clients.
   c. Don't assume that the client's beliefs, actions, behaviors, or speech will match those of other African Americans you have known.
2. Don't comment on the client's clothes, hair, or other personal characteristics.
3. When assessing client strengths, consider such often-overlooked resources as spiritual or religious values. For example, the church has played a major role in the African American community over the centuries and is a significant source of support for many individuals and families.

These practice suggestions should help increase the likelihood that an intervention will not be marred by inappropriate or stereotyped behaviors on the part of the social worker.

Latino Client—Non–Latino Worker

With Latino clients, as with other groups, the verbal tradition of social work may need to be supplemented by other means of communication. The worker must bear direct responsibility for communicating when language difficulties compound the situation and the need for an interpreter is apparent. Lest the worker err by commission, however, certain rules apply to the use of such individuals. First, "bilingual children of the family are not suitable interpreters" (Norton, 1978, p. 22). Respect for the individual and for the family relationships dictate that children maintain their culturally established place. Serving as conduits for sensitive family information is not an acceptable role for children to play and places an unfair and unpleasant burden on them. In addition, children lack an adult's knowledge base, a fact that further reduces their value as interpreters. This prohibition on the use of children applies equally to other ethnic groups, including Asian Americans. Described in the following paragraphs is a situation in which a probation officer has ignored some of the basic caveats of relationship building with unfortunate consequences for the client.

> The purposes in mind for this first interview were accomplished, to meet Mr. and Mrs. X personally and to establish a comfortable relationship that would lead to a partnership once they were able to share their problems with the social worker. The next step would be to share a common purpose, in this case, helping Freddy.
> Mr. X was included in the helping process from the beginning. Had he been left out, it would have meant that Mrs. X was assuming an improper role, that Mr. X was being put down by her, and that his role as head of the household plus his macho role were being jeopardized.
> The following day Mr. and Mrs. X came a little late to the meeting and were reluctant to talk about their conference with the probation officer. Mr. X just kept silent, looking down. Mrs. X, red-eyed, finally said, "I am very ashamed. You should have heard what the probation officer said about us. He blamed us for all the troubles with Freddy and said that if we were not able to speak English we should go back to Mexico. Perhaps worst of all, our daughter heard all of this because she had to translate for us."
> It was suggested that they arrange to meet with the probation officer the next time at the center; there the social worker could translate for them and make the necessary interpretations. Thus the harmful effect of the probation officer's prejudices against them would be minimized. Mr. and Mrs. X were assured that they had certain legal and moral rights that had to be respected—among them the right to be treated as human beings. Major differences between the systems of law in the United States and Mexico were explained, as were the functions of the probation department and the role of its officers.
> Mr. and Mrs. X then seemed somewhat relieved and looked less tense and fearful. Mrs. X thanked the social worker and, looking at her husband, said: "We are not ignorant and dumb. We just did not understand anything about what was happening." [Aguilar, 1972, p. 189]

A second guide to the use of interpreters is equally important. The worker must at all times relate and talk to the client, not to the interpreter. To address the translator diverts attention from the client and places him or her in the position of a bystander to, rather than a central figure in, the relationship. The opportunity to enhance the client's personal dignity and individual autonomy should be vigorously pursued, since the same goal of helping the client to help himself or herself is applicable both between and within cultures. Whether termed "empowerment, liberation or consumerism" (Norton, 1978, p. 23), or self-determination, the effect is similar.

Workers beginning a relationship with Latino clients should be prepared for a longer assessment period and should be more leisurely, warm, personal and informal, and more low key than otherwise might be the case (Aguilar, 1972). Directness is considered rude and should not be utilized in these situations if possible. Boulette (1975) suggested that a behavioral approach would be an appropriate methodology to employ in working with Mexican Americans from a low-income background, coinciding with Kadushin's (1983) belief. Aguilar (1972) noted that obstacles faced by Mexican American families include prejudice, ignorance, fear of formal social and legal systems, and a reluctance to deal with them. This would suggest some areas to which workers could direct their attention during the early stages of the relationship. Mexican Americans often make decisions more quickly than is typical of Anglo clients. Once alternatives have been explored, the worker should be prepared for a decisive response from the client.

Successful intervention with Latino families, however, requires greater knowledge of their culture. Ghali (1982) provided some helpful guidance in this matter, focusing on the Puerto Rican culture. She noted that close family ties exist in this culture and stressed that these ties are a source of pride. Anglo culture, on the other hand, values independence from the family. She also pointed out that practices that are frowned on in American society are more readily accepted among many Puerto Ricans. Examples include common-law marriages among those with low incomes, the bearing of a child by a teenager which often accords the mother the status of adulthood, and the relatively supreme position of the father in the family. Ghali acknowledged that many Puerto Rican values need to be changed to reflect the reality of living among the dominant culture, pointing to the subservient role of the woman as an example.

Ghali (1982) correctly identified the special dilemma of Puerto Ricans who have two countries, two languages, and two cultures. The role confusion that this can entail, the resultant family problems, and the value conflicts inherent in this duality must be recognized. She suggested that the worker keep these in mind during the interview. Other suggestions include the following:

- Determine how important the client's ethnic values are, and whether the values are a source of conflict. (This could be ascertained by asking which, if any, of the old traditions, like holidays, are still observed.)
- Focus on the short-term benefits and on strengthening the worker-client relationship.
- Recognize that some measure of client dependence is likely.
- Demonstrate competence, respect, and warmth toward the client.
- Share some personal experience.
- Respect the role of the father in the family.
- Ask "What do you see as the problem here?" rather than "How do you feel about this?"
- Be alert to nonverbal cues to feelings, such as facial expressions and tone.
- Be prepared to explain the therapeutic process to the client.
- Begin and end the session with a handshake (the man extends his hand to the woman first).
- Use formal greetings to convey respect.
- Accept food or drink offered in the client's home (not doing so may offend the host).
- Recognize that the client may verbally agree with the worker to show respect for authority but may not follow through.
- Remember that the Puerto Rican culture does not look favorably on laughing at

oneself so humor must not be of the self-depreciatory type.

- Remember that strangers do not touch little girls, even to be friendly.
- Place signs in both Spanish and English in the agency.

Ghali's recommendations are very appropriate and should serve as a model for practice with Puerto Rican families.

Delgado and Humm-Delgado (1982) suggested other ways of providing assistance to Latino families. The use of natural support systems is one of their recommendations. Natural support systems include family and friendship groups, local informal care givers, volunteer service groups, and mutual or self-help groups (Baker, 1977). Delgado and Humm-Delgado (1982, pp. 83–84) identify four types of such resource systems important for Latino clients: extended family, folk healers, religious institutions, and merchants' and social clubs. Included in the category of extended family are the family of origin, nuclear family members, others related by marriage or blood or custom including "adopted relatives" and *"como familia"* (nonfamily members who are considered to be like family) (Delgado & Humm-Delgado, 1982, p. 84). Godparents also become an important resource for Latino children in the event that anything befalls the natural parents.

Folk healers include a variety of individuals including spiritists and *santeros* who focus on emotional and interpersonal problems, herbalists and *santiguadors* who deal primarily with physical ailments, and the *curanderos* whose interventions include both emotional and physical realms. In Mexican American, Cuban, and Puerto Rican communities any one of the five, or a combination, may exist. The *santero* is more common in the Cuban community, while the *curandero* is found frequently in Mexican American communities (Delgado & Humm-Delgado, 1982, pp. 84–85). Some of the folk healers use treatments that blend natural healing methods

with spiritual or religious beliefs. The latter is not surprising given the importance of religion, particularly Roman Catholicism, in Latino life.

Religious institutions that serve as a resource include the Roman Catholic church as well as such denominations as the Jehovah's Witness, Seventh-Day Adventist, and Pentecostal. Among the services offered are pastoral counseling, housing and job-locating assistance, emergency money, and specialized programs in areas such as drug abuse (Delgado & Humm-Delgado, 1982, p. 85).

Finally, the merchants' and social clubs provide such items as herbs and native foods, credit and information, referrals to other resources, recreation, prayer books, and the services of healers. Table 12.1 identifies the types of needs served by these various resource systems in the Latino community.

Natural support systems are highly significant. They ensure "maintenance of the Hispanic tradition and language," provide "warm, personal helping relationships," and include acceptance of those who are emotionally disturbed without stigmatizing the person (Delgado & Humm-Delgado, 1982, pp. 85–87). Formal agencies that provide services to Latinos should benefit from the availability of these additional community resources. The reluctance of some clients to come to the formal agency could be reduced if the agency staff made greater use of the natural support system and made increased attempts at reaching the targeted population. Outreach can be done at the merchants' and social clubs, at churches, through radio and newspaper ads or public service announcements, and through notices on barrio grocery bulletin boards (Watkins & Gonzales, 1982, pp. 68–73). Agencies should consider developing community resource directories in both English and Spanish and including nontraditional resources within the directory.

The worker who chooses to work in the Latino community must be much more alert to the unique resources available as well as to

Needs Served	Natural Support Systems			
	Extended Family	Folk Healers	Religious Institutions	Merchants' and Social Clubs
1. Accessibility to community	X	X	X	X
2. Communication in Spanish	X	X	X	X
3. Continuation of cultural traditions	X	X	X	X
4. Crisis intervention	X	X	X	X
5. Emotional support for interpersonal problems	X	X	X	X
6. Friendship, companionship, trust	X	X	X	X
7. Identification with Hispanic role models, leaders, or experts	X	X	X	X
8. Information and referral	X	X	X	X
9. Care and treatment of the disabled or aged	X	X	X	
10. Financial aid or credit	X		X	
11. Medical care and pharmaceutical products	X	X		X
12. Recreation	X		X	X
13. Translation or interpretation	X		X	
14. Advocacy	X		X	
15. Physical and emotional rehabilitation		X	X	
16. Religious or spiritual affiliation		X	X	
17. Baby-sitting, day care, respite care, foster care, or adoption	X			
18. Child rearing and parent education	X			
19. Educational alternative to public school			X	
20. Housing	X			

SOURCE: Reprinted from Melvin Delgado and Denise Humm-Delgado, "Natural Support Systems: Source of Strength in Hispanic Communities," *Social Work*, 27, no. 1 (January 1982). Table 1, p. 87. Copyright 1982, National Association of Social Workers, Inc. Reprinted with permission.

Table 12.1

Needs served by Latino natural support systems

the many cultural issues that impinge on social work practice with what has become the fastest-growing minority group in the United States.

Native American Client—Non–Native American Worker

"Any kind of intervention is contrary to the Indian's strict adherence to the principle of self-determination" (Good Tracks, 1973, p. 30). With this statement in mind, the well-meaning worker might respond, "Well, how can I help if I can't intervene?" The difficulty of this dilemma is at the heart of the problems faced by many non–Native American social workers. Native Americans will request in-

tervention only infrequently and the white worker must develop patience and wait for the necessary acceptance. How long this will take varies from client to client. During this period the non–Native American should be available and may offer assistance as long as there is no hint of coercion accompanying the offer. Once help is accepted, the worker's competence will be tested, and, if found wanting, the word will spread. Conversely, the worker's ability to do what he or she says will spread equally fast. The results of the former will be a cessation of clients; in the latter case, just the opposite is true. The situation described in the following extract indicates noninterference with a Native American family:

The Redthunder family was brought to the school social worker's attention when teachers reported that both children had been tardy and absent frequently in the past weeks. Since the worker lived near Mr. Redthunder's neighborhood, she volunteered to transport the children back and forth to school. Through this regular but informal arrangement, the worker became acquainted with the entire family, especially with Mrs. Redthunder, who expressed her gratitude to the worker by sharing her homegrown vegetables.

The worker sensed that there was much family discomfort and that a tumultuous relationship existed between Mr. and Mrs. Redthunder. Instead of probing into their personal and marital affairs, the worker let Mrs. Redthunder know that she was willing to listen should the woman need someone to talk to. After a few gifts of homegrown vegetables and Native American handicrafts, Mrs. Redthunder broke into tears one day and told the worker about her husband's problem of alcoholism and their deteriorating marital relationship.

Realizing Mr. Redthunder's position of respect in the family and his resistance to outside interference, the social worker advised Mrs. Redthunder to take her family to visit the minister, a man whom Mr. Redthunder admired. The Littleaxe family, who were mutual friends of the worker and the Redthunder family, agreed to take the initiative in visiting the Redthunders more often. Through such frequent but informal family visits, Mr. Redthunder finally obtained a job, with the recommendation of Mr. Littleaxe, as recordkeeper in a storeroom. Mr. Redthunder enjoyed his work so much that he drank less and spent more time with his family. [Lewis & Ho, 1975, p. 381]

White workers who are working with Native Americans can expect that the interview will also be a new experience. Periods of silence at the start of the interview, for example, are not uncommon. Neither is the practice of some clients of switching from English to their native tongue and back as they address other members of the family. The use of the Native American language is not necessarily meant to keep the message from the worker but rather indicates that this is the easiest way to translate a particular idea.

The establishment of intervention objectives should also be consistent with the environment of the Native American client, as must the specific techniques to be used. Approaches that are culturally repugnant will not succeed regardless of the good intentions of the worker. Transactional analysis is an example of one approach that will likely prove ineffective since it ignores "differences in culture and background between client and worker" (Lewis & Ho, 1975, p. 381). Any type of manipulation is likely to fail also, though the provision of alternative choices from which the Native American client may choose is generally acceptable. Lewis and Ho (1975, p. 380) emphasized that "techniques based on restating, clarifying, summarizing, reflecting and empathizing" are more likely to be successful with Native Americans. Certainly, a low-key, nondirective, permissive, and nonthreatening relationship can be effective and gratifying for both client and worker (Palmer & Pablo, 1978).

Lewis and Ho (1975) discuss the use of group approaches for treating Native Americans as a natural approach, though group composition needs to be more racially homogeneous than might be true for many other groups, notably Latinos (Boulette, 1975). The use of both indirect and extra group means of influence is particularly recommended. For example, the careful planning and implementation of program activities is preferred to more direct and unwelcome techniques. The use of group pressure on an individual would be a tactic to avoid if the worker and setting are not to appear coercive. Also recommended are self-help groups and other family support networks that are group based and are consistent with the values and culture of Native American clients.

Female Client—Male Worker

Continued evidence shows that women are at risk from a number of forces. Women's salaries continue to lag behind men's, and the concept of the "glass ceiling," which limits upward mobility of women, is discussed often in the media. Women constitute almost three-quarters of the elderly poor, while they account for only 59 percent of the elderly population (Stone, 1989). According to Stone, almost twice as many elderly women live in poverty as men. The statistics for elderly women of color are even worse. Factors accounting for such discrepancies include family obligations (women as primary care givers) and employment histories (often affected by job discrimination). If it were not for the success of the Social Security system, the rate of impoverishment among women would be much greater. Until 1983, even private pension plans were allowed to pay women lower retirement benefits than men.

Women are also more likely to shoulder the burden for caring for elderly family members, with devastating economic consequences when this comes at the expense of employment. When these factors are coupled with their concentration in low-paying jobs with few fringe benefits, women are clearly a population-at-risk. These factors reflect an institutional sexism, which can impede cross-sex social work interventions and challenge the worker-client relationship.

Although it is generally conceded that a difference in gender between client and worker is not an insurmountable barrier to an effective relationship, there are some points to be considered when such differences exist. According to Davenport and Reims (1978, p. 308), a clinician's sex has a decided influence on attitudes toward women's roles and, as a result, "anyone preferring a therapist with contemporary attitudes toward women would more likely be successful with a female therapist." Kravetz (1982, p. 44) has argued that most social workers hold "traditional and stereotypic views of women" and that such views have detrimental effects on women's health and their treatment by the systems of our society. Certainly, counselors of the same sex may be more of an aid in modeling new behaviors or when client identification with the worker is a major part of the change effort (Hook, 1979). Some authors feel that a female social worker engages in more modeling for women clients and is more likely to take the client's problems seriously. Some topics may be more comfortably discussed with a counselor of the same sex, and workers and agencies must not overlook this possibility. However, as in many other situations where dissimilarities between client and worker exist, the relationship can usually transcend the differences.

Because the sexist nature of much of society has in part contributed to the problems experienced by women, Thomas (1977) and Berlin (1976) provided a useful set of guides for work with women clients. First, the nature of the relationship between males and females in our society tends to be characterized by the same sort of power disparity noted in cross-cultural relationships; therefore, reduction of this power differential should be one goal of the therapeutic process. The suggestions discussed earlier in regard to this issue are equally applicable here. Second, the worker who can comfortably engage in greater levels of self-disclosure and use of self and of his or her own experience should aid in reducing this power differential. Third, the use of contracts with specified goals assists in involving the client in her own treatment effort. Fourth, a greater emphasis on problem solving and action should assist in achieving a degree of self-mastery for which the client can feel justifiably proud. Fifth, the assessment period should involve a thorough analysis of the client's "strengths, frustrations, wants and satisfactions" (Berlin, 1976, p. 493). This requires separating the client's needs, feelings, and beliefs from those of significant others, such as parents and husband. This may be accomplished through the use of a journal detailing the day's significant events, as illustrated in the following example:

Since early childhood, Jill had tried hard to be what she thought people wanted her to be. Despite her efforts to be sweet and compliant, the stored-up resentment and anger sometimes emerged. Her parents strongly objected to these outbursts and shamed her for them. To be "good" in the eyes of her parents—and later her male friends—Jill suppressed her "selfishness," her own thoughts, views, and feelings, until she felt like a nonentity. When she came in for counseling, Jill said that she no longer knew what she liked and didn't like or who she was. She was living with a boyfriend but felt distant from him. At the age of twenty-four, her life had already taken on a bland, weary quality.

At her counselor's suggestion, Jill began keeping a journal in which she recorded the events of her day and her different responses to them. During each counseling session these details were reviewed to reveal that Jill did indeed have specific likes and dislikes: she liked gardening; she liked being alone in the house; she liked to read, draw, and visit with a particular friend. She didn't like the routine nature of her job. Particularly, although she was afraid of standing up for herself, she didn't like herself to be closed or passive with her boyfriend, other friends, and her mother. She disliked not having a room of her own and resented it when her boyfriend pursued his own interests without telling her when he would be away. Jill found that there was a whole range of thoughts, talents, and behaviors that made her an identifiable and specific person. Moreover, she learned to pinpoint which of these aspects she wanted to cap-

italize on. Eventually Jill decided to move into her own apartment. She left her job and got a new one in a plant nursery. She began practicing more assertive, honest responses to the people in her life. [Berlin, 1976, pp. 493–494]

Sixth, the client should be assisted to recognize alternatives and to choose among them rather than feel limited or constrained unnecessarily. The following case example illustrates this guideline:

Ellen had lived through an almost unendurable number of personal crises—the death of two children, the subsequent divorce from her husband, a second brutal marriage, financial problems, the loss of custody of her third child, and a second divorce. Her reaction to all these events was flight, the abuse of amphetamines, and just plain helplessness.

As a girl, Ellen had been brought up to sparkle and to make others laugh. It was assumed that she would find a clear-headed, stable man who could make the hard decisions and manage the details of living. Ellen didn't know how to take care of herself and didn't think she could. Her solution to loneliness—spending binges, reckless driving, instant intimacy with strangers—only brought more problems and more guilt. Each time she was called on to take a stand and protect herself, Ellen would capitulate. The situations were too much for her and she felt victimized by them.

The counselor's approach to this situation was a relatively simple and basic one. She tried to help Ellen perceive different alternatives—to see that there were some things she could do differently if she wanted to. In addition to realizing that she had some choices, Ellen needed to decide what she wanted to do and to acquire the skills and confidence to do it. She had to be made aware that she didn't lose control, but that she stopped exercising it; that she wasn't being punished for being a bad person, but that she associated with people who were disrespectful and abusive. Ellen is now finding what she can do to make her life less frantic and destructive. She wants to continue her education, to clear up her debts, and to achieve equality in her relationships with other people. [Berlin, 1976, p. 494]

The worker should encourage action on the options that are available and can aid the client by posing questions such as "What choices do you see yourself as having?" "Do you know what you like about this particular alternative?"

Seventh, the use of behavioral rehearsal and practice in decision making can be extremely effective in building the necessary skills essential for choosing and implementing choices. The following client illustrates this guideline:

Cynthia came for counseling in a state of panic because the woman she loved and was living with was considering ending the relationship. Although there was little she could do to persuade her partner to stay, Cynthia did have considerable latitude in deciding how she wanted to behave and the way in which she could influence other facets of the terminating relationship.

Realizing that she still had considerable choice was a partial antidote to Cynthia's sense of helplessness. Instead of waiting silently and miserably for her friend to leave, Cynthia practiced certain responses with the counselor until she felt able to cope with the reality of the situation. She explained to her partner her feelings regarding the relationship—that she valued it, was aware that both of them needed to make some specific changes in order for it to stay viable, and that she herself was willing to make certain accommodations. She acknowledged that her friend would be the one to decide whether to stay or leave, but Cynthia wanted the decision made within the week—she didn't want to be tortured by uncertainty. To this extent,

Cynthia ceased to be the victim. She felt strengthened by her new position of influence and control over her circumstances. [Berlin, 1976, p. 495]

Eighth, a client who exhibits fears and a poor self-concept needs to be helped to evaluate these perceptions realistically. The worker must press the client for concrete examples the client believes exemplifies the perceived self-worthlessness and expose them to a rigorous objective analysis. The likelihood is that under this sort of scrutiny the client's behavior will indicate more evidence of self-worth than the client has been led (or had led herself) to believe.

The counselor who maintains a focus on assisting the client increase her control over her own life can be "profoundly helpful to . . . women by encouraging them to value their own ideas and interests, by helping them decide what they want, by urging them to develop the necessary skills and by letting them know they are not alone in their efforts" (Berlin, 1976, p. 497). Kravetz (1982, p. 46) has suggested additional guidelines that seem appropriate.

1. Problem assessment and goals must not be based on culturally prescribed sex-role behaviors. Alternative lifestyles, lesbianism, and other behaviors that do not meet cultural expectations should not be viewed as pathological or deviant.

2. It is growth-producing for women to understand the influence of social factors on their personal lives. Therefore work with women should incorporate a sex-role analysis, encouraging women to evaluate the ways in which social roles and norms and structural realities influence their personal experience, and to explore solutions that transcend traditional ones.

3. Women's lack of social power can generate passivity, dependence, and submissiveness. Therefore intervening should encourage female clients to be assertive, autonomous, and self-directed.

Profeminist social work can be practiced by both men and women. It does require a commitment to challenging the oppression that pervades much of our society and to empowering clients to act in their own behalf. It means being willing to alter everything from the client-worker relationship to the larger institutions of society. On a one-to-one basis, it includes reducing client-worker distance and power differentials and encouraging clients to redefine experiences to recognize oppression they have encountered. It also means recognizing sexist assumptions regarding appropriate gender behavior; encouraging assertive, independent client behavior; building on client strengths; encouraging woman-to-woman bonding rather than competition between women; and advocating equalitarian rights for women. While this stance does not necessarily mean that a worker must develop an entire new intervention model, it does require a recognition that some traditional approaches are inconsistent with a profeminist stance. Psychoanalytic social work is largely inappropriate because of its focus on the intrapsychic and its failure to take into account environmental influences. Humanistic practice approaches, problem-solving interventions, and systems perspectives are largely functional if used by a worker who also recognizes that many problems develop precisely because of the systemic inequities structured within society (Van Den Bergh & Cooper, 1987, pp. 613–614).

In summary, a profeminist worker will be more sensitive to ecological factors in the etiology of problems, oriented to prevention whenever possible, and supportive of client empowerment strategies. This approach is consistent with good social work practice, in keeping with the values of the profession, and will help ensure that the worker does not perpetuate gender-based oppression of women.

Gay and Lesbian Clients

The bigotry of some homophobic elements of society, in conjunction with the ignorance and fear of many Americans, produces another population-at-risk; namely, gay men and lesbian women. This perspective has been carefully documented by Hidalgo, Peterson, and Woodman (1985); Pierce (1993); and others. Some evidence suggests that social workers as a group may be more homophobic than other groups of helping professionals (DeCrescenzo, 1985). This evidence, coupled with the need to educate all social workers about sexual orientation, helped lead the Council on Social Work Education to require content on gay and lesbian people in all social work programs (Council on Social Work Education, 1992).

Pierce (1993, p. 5) identified four person-in-environment issues that gay and lesbian workers must face. These include the unusual situation of being part of a group yet remaining invisible in terms of sexual orientation, facing a potential of physical violence and harassment, dealing regularly with discrimination and prejudice, and living within a society that characterizes homosexuality as "bad." These experiences must be considered when one begins to work with lesbian and gay clients and recognized as affecting the lives of one's colleagues as well.

The recent debates about gays and lesbians in the military are evidence of the high degree of ignorance and homophobia that exist. Arguments against allowing gay and lesbian persons in the military mirror similar arguments made against allowing African Americans to serve with whites several decades ago. Social workers have an obligation to help gay and lesbian clients with the same degree of professionalism accorded to other clients and to work in the political process to overturn homophobia-based barriers that hinder gays and lesbians from enjoying the same rights and privileges as other Americans.

In individual worker-client relationships, the role of social work in providing assistance to gay and lesbian clients is clear. The worker's responsibility is to help clients meet their basic human needs and provide linkages with resources that further these goals. The problems of homosexual clients are often similar to those of heterosexuals. In other situations the problems are unique to gays and lesbians. For younger homosexuals, the stress associated with identity confusion regarding their sexuality may be a source of difficulty requiring intervention. The worker can assist here by "making the client aware of the incongruence between ways of acting, thinking, and feeling and the client's self-image" (Berger, 1983, p. 134). The goal of such help is self-acceptance by the client. The worker can also help with finding peer support if the client has decided to adopt or maintain his or her identity as a homosexual. Such a decision may also necessitate dealing with the client's parents, employers, and friends. Here again, the social worker can be of help. These significant others can be worked with individually or in groups to assist them in dealing with their own feelings and reactions.

For older gays and lesbians, the tasks and problems may be considerably different. Berger (1982) has identified four problem areas facing the elderly homosexual: institutional, legal, emotional, and medical. The older gay may find that institutional rules prohibit visits to a hospitalized patient by anyone but a member of the immediate family, thus excluding a lover of many years. Similarly, medical decisions in case of emergency often require consent by next of kin, thus ignoring the gay or lesbian partner completely. While services to the grieving spouse are common, there are almost no efforts made to provide similar help to the partner of the deceased homosexual. The need for companionship and dealing with loneliness in old age are also problems confronting many gays and lesbians that can be ameliorated by professional assistance. The worker can help clients prepare relationship contracts and encourage them to make other arrangements, such as wills.

The difficulties of the older gay may differ somewhat from those of younger homosexuals. For instance, the task of coming out may be easier when one is older because the most common problem of dealing with one's parents often no longer exists. At the same time, older gays may prefer not to address the issue of sexual orientation directly and the worker would be advised to follow suit. This requires a worker who is open to the client's needs but who feels no compulsion to press the client into coming out or openly communicating his or her sexuality.

For some homosexual clients, homophobia may indeed be a problem requiring assistance. The stigma associated with sexual orientation sometimes creates self-loathing among homosexuals themselves. Such a reaction is at odds with the goal of self-acceptance and can be dealt with accordingly. Social workers should be aware of local support groups and should encourage the development of such organizations when absent. Likewise, agencies that provide specialized services to gays or that are especially sensitive to their needs can be supported by referrals and by other means.

On another level, there are equally concrete activities in which the social worker can engage. Support for legislation to decriminalize same-sex acts would help reduce the psychological risks of being gay or lesbian, and civil rights protection would help ensure that discrimination in employment and housing would be avoided. Currently, many cities and states have adopted such laws removing yet another unnecessary burden to those whose sexual orientation is gay or lesbian.

Adequate sex education in schools, churches, and within the family can also be encouraged (Gramick, 1983). In-service training for agency staff on the topic of homosexuality and multi-agency efforts to combat prejudice and discrimination toward gays and lesbians can also be undertaken. Gramick (1983) also suggested refusing to accept homophobic behavior from colleagues and argued that such actions should be pointed out as a violation of the NASW Code of Ethics.

Certainly, to be of help to gay and lesbian clients, we must become more comfortable with the topic of homosexuality and begin to deal with our own homophobic tendencies. Just as in other areas of practice, ignorance and confusion about sexual orientation must be dealt with directly and openly.

Rural Settings

Social workers who elect to practice in a rural setting are likely to discover that a multiplicity of differences exists in the way they conduct business. For example, the social worker who comfortably assumes the role of advocate in a nonrural setting will quickly find that this is more difficult now. A rural advocate risks losing the trust of the community that he or she nurtured so carefully in such other roles as broker, mediator, and problem solver. The fact that workers become more a part of the area they serve means that there is a greater informality and less professional detachment than would be true in an urban setting. The need to have relationships with and the support of community power sources makes it more difficult to pursue changes that threaten those interests. Workers, especially in-migrant practitioners, are often perceived as outsiders and it takes time for the community to develop trust and confidence in the worker's competence. Thus, to advocate strongly for anything under these conditions is not recommended if other equally effective alternatives can be pursued. The greater autonomy of the rural worker is an asset but it also carries additional responsibilities. The worker needs to develop the ability to form relationships quickly because the geographical distance to be covered means less time can be devoted to long-term projects. Making each contact with a client count is essential since those contacts are more infrequent than would otherwise be the case. Knowledge of natural and informal rather than formal support systems is crucial, as is the ability to work with other professionals and nonprofessionals in achieving change. The rural worker must also be patient, however, since changes, when they come, can be exceedingly slow. Any "attempt

to change beliefs or practices can cause dislocations, anxiety, and resistance against the change agent" (Buxton, 1976, p. 37). As we described earlier, the worker must be knowledgeable about local norms and especially conscious of local etiquette. Moreover this awareness must be matched by "greater conformity with conventional norms" (Southern Regional Education Board, 1976, p. 42). Workers may need to adjust their personal lifestyles to the community and to the job to be done, and clearly not every social worker will be willing or able to accomplish this. It follows from what we have indicated previously that any existing cultural or ethnic differences may complicate understanding of, and practice in, the rural community.

Social workers new to rural areas and small towns sometimes ignore the many ways their private actions affect the way they are seen as professionals. For example, workers finding higher prices in smaller communities have often resorted to shopping in nearby communities that are larger. Purchases of groceries, automobiles, clothes, and other items are often made without regard to how this affects the local community. While this pattern of shopping may result in a lower price paid for goods and services, the net result may be that the worker is not seen as a member of the community. Shopping in the community where one practices helps link the worker with that community, supports the local economy, and gives the practitioner an opportunity to talk regularly with business people and leaders in the area. This entrée makes it easier to approach community leaders later on when the worker is pursuing a change opportunity.

Similarly, participating in local community activities helps ensure that the worker is seen as a member of the community. Workers who work in a community and do not live there, shop there, or participate in community activities will have greatly diminished ability to exert influence within that setting. In smaller communities, becoming part of the community is key to influencing local events.

Workers are encouraged to attend the local chicken dinners sponsored by church or civic groups, participate in the volunteer fire department fund-raising effort, serve on the centennial committee, and accept membership in local service organizations. Other ways of becoming involved include volunteering to work on special projects (such as the historical museum renovations, tree planting, and community beautification efforts). In the long run, the worker who is seen as part of the community will be better able to influence the course of events within that community.

Other Differences Affecting Practice

A variety of potential and actual differences between client and worker can impinge on the relationship and affect the outcome of interventive efforts. Age differences, as mentioned earlier, will dictate certain adaptations to the worker's usual style. When working with older clients, for example, the worker should exercise greater patience and understanding of the problems of the aged, and if feasible, elect to conduct the interview out of the office, in a location more suitable to the client. Home interviews are suggested when possible.

Similar care should be used when the worker is engaged in a practice with young children. The worker, as an adult, may need to place some distance between himself or herself and the child's parents to gain the youngster's confidence. While children are more open in many ways, they are also quick to tune out questions, thus reducing the worker's reliance on standard verbal techniques. The child's medium is play, and the worker would be advised to utilize such activities in the helping process. While adult rules of conversation are more strict, an interview with a child may appear both random and disorganized (Kadushin, 1983). This places a special responsibility on the practitioner to be sensitive to the unspoken aspects of the interview and to stay attuned to the bits and pieces of information that are generated in these situations. Though the process will be somewhat disjointed, in the author's view the rewards are substantial.

Some General Observations

This chapter has focused extensively on the unique differences among various groups, such as minorities of color, women, and gay and lesbian individuals. While the emphasis has been on characteristics that help to differentiate these groups and social work practice as it relates to the groups, there are some important commonalities that affect our efforts to help. In this section we will attempt to highlight some of these similarities.

Any intervention effort that is ethnically sensitive should take into account those individuals affected by the problem. Social workers, for example, who plan to work with minority families should be certain they understand "who the appropriate actors are" (Devore & Schlesinger, 1981, p. 179). This might include nuclear family members as well as other relatives and friends who are "like family." Most minorities of color evidence a sound respect for elders and seek their advice and opinion. In addition, most are also tolerant of other ethnic groups to a degree not found among the dominant majority. While each group's religious orientations and spiritual beliefs may differ markedly, each is likely to be characterized by some degree of religiosity or belief in a supreme being (Burgest, 1983).

People of color also share their commonality of color, their oppression, and their victimization by white society. Most have experienced conflict with this society ranging from colonization to slavery to economic bondage (Burgest, 1983). The result of this conflict has been a distrust of traditional social service institutions, a pride of and reliance on one's own kind, and a sense of impotence when dealing with the typical governmental agency.

To provide competent social services within the framework outlined earlier, the worker must attend to a variety of issues. First, it is helpful to keep in mind that feelings, emotions, and thoughts are all shared. Differences most often lie in how we choose to express them. Our own culture influences us to the extent that some say we are culture bound. As a result, feelings, thoughts, and ideas we felt were firmly under control or previously resolved may become aroused during one-on-one encounters with those of a different race. It is healthier to recognize this possibility than to be surprised at an inopportune time. Our attempts to provide sensitive and effective social work intervention can be enhanced by observing the following guidelines:

1. Avoid color blindness. (This issue was addressed earlier.)
2. Avoid jargon and clichés, such as referring to clients as culturally deprived.
3. Concentrate on building the relationship first and showing sensitivity to the client's culture and difficulty.
4. Consider client behavior as functional/ dysfunctional rather than normal/abnormal based on an a priori standard.
5. Recognize and accept that client distrust is likely to be the norm.
6. Accept the limits of your own knowledge.
7. Acquire some familiarity with the clients' language whenever possible.
8. Recognize that culture is fluid, not static.
9. Acquire and maintain a sound working knowledge of programs, services, agencies, and workers providing specialized assistance to diverse groups.
10. Keep abreast of new rules and laws affecting diverse groups.
11. Support training and education for agency staff related to diverse groups.
12. Take active steps to combat discrimination within your own agency and programs.

13. Place greater emphasis in your practice on developing community-based alternatives to reduce the discriminatory reliance on institutional placements for people of color.

Macro Strategies to Promote Social and Economic Justice

To this point, this chapter has primarily focused on micro and mezzo strategies to promote social and economic justice for populations-at-risk. This section will summarize a variety of macro strategies; it is not an exhaustive list of available strategies, only examples. (As noted in Chapter 1, social workers have an obligation to employ micro, mezzo, and macro strategies to promote social and economic justice for individuals and groups who are victimized by discrimination and oppression.)

The strategies described here include social programs, mass media appeals, civil rights laws, activism, school busing, affirmative action programs, human relations programs, confrontation of jokes and discriminatory actions, and grass-roots approaches to improve inner cities.

Social Programs

Thousands of social programs have been enacted at national, state, and local levels to promote social and economic justice for a variety of populations-at-risk. A few examples will be presented in this section.

The 1935 Social Security Act initiated a variety of programs for several populations-at-risk. Aid to the Blind provided financial assistance to low-income people of any age whose vision is 20/200 or less with correction. Aid to the Disabled provided financial assistance to low-income people, ages 18 through 65, who had a permanent disability. Old Age Assistance provided financial assistance to the low-income elderly (ages 65 and older). Aid to Dependent Children provided financial assistance to low-income mothers with children under age 18 and no father in the home.

In the 1960s Lyndon Johnson declared a War on Poverty. A variety of antipoverty programs were created, including Head Start, Medicare, and Medicaid. (Medicare helps the elderly pay the high cost of health care; Medicaid primarily provides medical care for recipients of public assistance.)

In 1975 the U.S. Congress passed the Education for All Handicapped Children Act. This legislation mandates that all school districts identify students with physical, developmental, learning, and social-emotional problems that hamper their education. Once the children are identified, school districts are then required to develop specialized programs to meet their needs.

In 1990 the U.S. Congress passed, and President Bush signed into law, the Americans with Disabilities Act. This act prohibits discrimination against persons with a disability either in employment or by limiting access to public accommodations (such as restaurants, stores, museums, and theaters). The law requires that new public buildings must be accessible to persons with a disability and requires that barriers in existing public buildings be removed, if the changes can be accomplished without much difficulty or expense.

Social workers have an obligation to be involved in enacting and implementing social programs to meet the needs of individuals and groups who are subjected to discrimination and oppression. Some of the ways that social workers can participate in the enactment of needed social programs include running for political office, calling and writing to political officials to express their views about needed programs, campaigning for persons running for office who support the enactment of needed social programs, lobbying for needed programs, and joining and becoming active in groups that support the enactment of needed social programs.

Mass Media Appeals

Newspapers, radio, and television at times present programs designed to explain the nature and harmful effects of prejudice and to promote social and economic justice for populations-at-risk. Mass media are able to reach large numbers of people simultaneously. By expanding public awareness of the existence of discrimination and its consequences, the media may strengthen control over highly prejudiced people. But mass media have limitations in changing prejudiced attitudes and behaviors; they primarily provide information and seldom have a lasting effect in changing deep-seated prejudices through propaganda. Broadcasting such platitudes as "all people are brothers and sisters" and "prejudice is un-American" is not very effective. Highly prejudiced people are often unaware of their own prejudices. Even if they are aware, however, they generally dismiss mass media appeals as irrelevant to them or as propaganda. The mass media probably have had a significant impact in reducing racial discrimination by showing nonwhites and whites working harmoniously in commercials, on news teams, and on TV shows.

Civil Rights Laws

In recent decades equal rights laws have been legislated in certain areas (such as employment, voting, housing, public accommodation, and education) for a variety of populations-at-risk. A few of these populations for which federal civil rights laws have been enacted include people of color, women, persons with disabilities, and the elderly. Civil rights laws prohibit overt discrimination in certain specified areas. For example, in 1986 the U.S. Congress outlawed most mandatory age retirement policies. Passage of this law prohibited overt discrimination of forced retirement against the elderly, which is age related.

The passage of a civil rights law protects the population-at-risk in only the area or areas that are specified in the law. It does not provide protection in areas that are unspecified. Subtle discrimination often continues to exist because it is hidden and therefore difficult to document.

A key question is "How effective are laws in curbing discrimination and reducing prejudice?" Proponents of civil rights legislation make certain assumptions. The first is that new laws will reduce discriminatory behavioral patterns. The laws define what was once "normal" behavior (discrimination) as now being "deviant" behavior. Through time, it is expected that attitudes will change and become more consistent with the forced nondiscriminatory behavior patterns.

A second assumption is that the laws will be used. Civil rights laws enacted after the Civil War prohibited discriminatory behavior against African Americans. However, such laws were seldom enforced and gradually eroded. It is also unfortunately true that some officials will find ways of evading the intent of the law by eliminating only the extreme, overt symbols of discrimination without changing other practices. Thus, the enactment of a law is only the first step in the process of changing prejudiced attitudes and practices. However, as Martin Luther King Jr. noted, "The law may not make a man love me, but it can restrain him from lynching me, and I think that's pretty important."

Activism

The strategy of "activism" attempts to promote social and economic justice through direct confrontation of policies involving discrimination and oppression. Activism has three types of politics: the politics of creative disorder, the politics of disorder, and the politics of escape (Johnson, 1973, pp. 374–379).

The *politics of creative disorder* operates on the edge of the dominant social system and includes school boycotts, rent strikes, job blockades, sit-ins (for example, at segregated restaurants), public marches, and product boycotts. This type of activism is based on the concept of nonviolent resistance. A dramatic illustration of nonviolent resistance began on December 1, 1955, when Rosa Parks, an African American of Montgomery, Alabama, refused to give up her seat on a bus to a white person. (Alabama and many other southern states at that time had Jim Crow laws that were designed to enforce segregation. One such law required African Americans to sit in the backseats of buses.) Mrs. Parks refused to get up and move to the back because her feet were hurting. She was arrested and unintentionally began the famous Montgomery Bus Boycott. The boycott lasted for a year and resulted in a U.S. Supreme Court ruling that declared ordinances that required segregated seating on public conveyances to be unconstitutional. The boycott had an even more important psychological impact; it suggested that people of color had rights equal to those of whites and that united nonviolent resistance could overturn discriminatory laws (Cummings, 1977, p. 197).

The *politics of disorder* reflects alienation from the dominant culture and disillusionment with the political system. In this type, those being discriminated against resort to mob uprisings, riots, and other forms of violence.

In 1969 the National Commission on Causes and Prevention of Violence reported that 200 riots had occurred in the previous five years, when our inner cities erupted (Johnson, 1973, p. 376). In the early 1980s, there were again some riots in Miami and in some of our other inner cities. In 1992 there were devastating riots in Los Angeles, following the acquittal of four white police officers, who had been charged with using excessive force in arresting Rodney King, an African American; the brutal arrest had been videotaped. The focus of most of these riots has been aggression by people of color against white-owned property.

The *politics of escape* engages in passionate rhetoric about how oppressed populations are being victimized. But because the focus is not on arriving at solutions, the rhetoric is not productive, except perhaps for providing an emotional release.

The principal value of activism or social protest seems to be the stimulation of public awareness of certain problems. The civil rights protests in the 1960s made practically all Americans aware of the discrimination to which nonwhite groups were being subjected. With this awareness, at least some of the discrimination has ceased, and race relations have improved. Continued protest beyond a certain (although indeterminate) point, however, appears to have little additional value (Sullivan et al., 1980).

School Busing

School busing is a strategy that has been used to increase integration among whites and people of color. Housing patterns in many large metropolitan centers have led to "de facto" segregation; that is, African Americans and certain other people of color live in one area and whites live in another. This segregation has affected educational opportunities for people of color. Nonwhite areas have fewer financial resources, and as a result, the educational quality is often substantially lower than in white areas. In the past two decades, courts in a number of metropolitan areas have ordered that a certain proportion of nonwhites must be bused to schools in white areas and that a certain proportion of whites must be bused to schools in nonwhite areas. The objectives are twofold: to provide equal educational opportunities and to reduce racial prejudice through interaction. In some areas school busing has become accepted and appears to be meeting the stated objectives. In other areas, however, the approach is highly controversial and has exacerbated racial tensions. Busing in these areas is claimed (1) to be highly expensive; (2) to destroy the concept of the "neighborhood school" as a recreational, social, and educa-

tional center of the community; and (3) to result in lower-quality education. A number of parents in these areas feel so strongly about busing that they are sending their children to private schools. In addition, some have argued that busing increases "white flight" from neighborhoods where busing has been ordered (Sullivan et al., 1980). In 1970, William Raspberry, a columnist for the *Washington Post*, commented about the effects of busing in Washington, D.C.: "We find ourselves busing children from all-black neighborhoods all the way across town to schools that are rapidly becoming all-black" (p. 11).

There have been additional concerns expressed about busing. It is argued that busing children a long distance is very costly and uses funds that could otherwise be used to improve the quality of education. Busing lessens local control and interest in schools, and it makes it less practical for parents to become involved in school affairs because the school is less accessible.

In certain communities, busing may also intensify racial tensions. For example, in Boston in 1975, a federal judge ordered school busing to counter housing segregation patterns. The Irish and Polish descendants of South Boston (who saw themselves as oppressed ethnic minorities) violently opposed the busing, and racial tensions intensified for several years. Sociologists also voice concern that school busing in an atmosphere of hostility may reduce the quality of education and increase racial prejudices and tensions.

School busing to achieve integration was vigorously pursued by the court system and the Justice Department in the 1970s. In 1981 the Reagan administration stated it would be much less active in advocating that busing be used as a vehicle to achieve integration. In the past decade, there has been less emphasis in many communities on using busing to achieve integration. In 1991 the U.S. Supreme Court ruled that busing to achieve integration, when ordered, is not forever. The ruling allows communities to end court-ordered busing by convincing a judge they have done everything reasonable to eliminate discrimination against African Americans.

Affirmative Action Programs

Affirmative action programs provide for preferential hiring and admission requirements (for example, admission to medical schools) for minority applicants. Affirmative action programs cover minority groups, including women, many groups of color, and persons with a disability. (Women—though in the majority in the United States—are considered a minority group because for generations they have been subjected to discrimination and have been denied equal opportunities.) Affirmative action programs also require that employers must (1) make active efforts to locate and recruit qualified minority applicants and (2) in certain circumstances, have hard quotas under which specific numbers of minority members must be accepted to fill vacant positions (for example, a university with a high proportion of white, male faculty may be required to fill half of its faculty vacancies with women and members of other minority groups). Affirmative action programs require that employers must demonstrate, according to a checklist of positive measures, that they are not guilty of discrimination.

A major dilemma with affirmative action programs is that preferential hiring and quota programs involve reverse discrimination, in which qualified majority-group members are sometimes arbitrarily excluded. There have been several successful lawsuits claiming reverse discrimination. The best-known case to date has been that of Alan Bakke, who was initially denied admission to the medical school at the University of California, Davis in 1973. He alleged reverse discrimination because he had higher grades and higher scores on the Medical College Admissions Test than several minority applicants who were admitted under the university's minorities quota policy. In 1978 his claim was upheld by the U.S. Supreme Court in a precedent-setting decision (Sindler, 1978). The Court ruled that strict racial quotas were unconstitutional, but the Court did not rule out the use of race as one among many criteria in making admissions decisions.

Supporters of affirmative action programs assert there is no other way to make up rapidly for past discrimination against minorities, many of whom may presently score slightly lower on qualification tests simply because they did not have the opportunities and the quality of training that the dominant group members have had.

Affirmative action programs raise delicate and complex questions about achieving equality through giving preferences in hiring and admissions to minorities. Yet, no other means has been found to end obvious discrimination in hiring and admissions.

Gaining admission to educational programs and securing well-paying jobs are crucial elements in working toward integration. The history of immigrant groups who "have made it" (such as the Irish, the Japanese, and the Italians) suggests equality will be achieved only when minority group members gain middle- and upper-class status. Once such status is achieved, the minority group members become an economic and political force with which to be reckoned. The dominant groups are then pressured into modifying their norms, values, and stereotypes. For this reason, a number of authorities have noted that the elimination of economic discrimination is a prerequisite for achieving equality (Featherman & Hauser, 1976). Achieving educational equality is also crucial because low educational attainments lead to less prestigious jobs, lower incomes, lower living standards, and the perpetuation of inequalities from one generation to the next.

Human Relations Programs

A number of school systems are developing human relations programs, which are designed to alleviate prejudice and discrimination. The program developed by the public

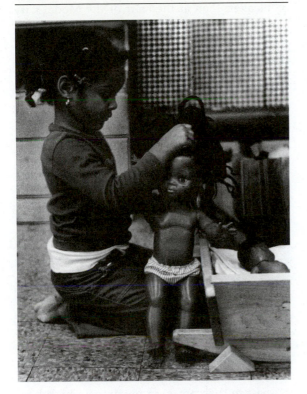

Self-esteem and personal development are facilitated when children have dolls and and other playthings that are positive symbols of their ethnic and racial cultures.

school system in Madison, Wisconsin, will be briefly described for illustrative purposes. (Buchanan & Cummings, 1975). The goal is to help children gain a better awareness of themselves as individuals and a better understanding of, and respect for, individual differences in others.

The program has several steps, along with some suggested activities, books, and other helpful hints for parents and teachers to use with their children. Some of the key concepts are:

• Each person is unique, with all people having common needs.

• Each person can do some things better than other things. It is a serious mistake to use yourself as a yardstick to measure others' abilities or to use others as a yardstick to measure yours. Words such as *stupid* or *dumb* hurt deeply, especially when one is doing one's best.

• Each person has different attitudes, ideas, beliefs, and values. Although the beliefs of others may differ from one's own, they are no less important.

• Prejudice differs from a dislike. Prejudice is defined broadly as "when you are against someone you do not know because of some/one of their differences" (Buchanan & Cummings, 1975, p. 13).

The program assists children in learning about some of the differences found in people and how a lack of understanding about these differences can be related to prejudice. The program explains that melanin is the pigment responsible for light and dark skin-color differences. The more melanin you have, the darker you are; but melanin, of course, in no way governs a person's personality or behavior. Suntanning occurs because the skin produces more melanin to protect it from the hot sun; yet tanning does not change the inner "self," only the outside wrapping. Besides skin-color differences, students are given an understanding of other individual differences (such as cognitive disabilities, religious differences, epilepsy, hearing impairments, and so on) so they can be more respectful of such differences. The program also assists students in learning about and appreciating cultural and ethnic differences.

Such human relations programs offer considerable promise of being a highly effective strategy in alleviating discrimination in the following areas: race, gender, ethnic or cultural differences, religious or political differences, and physical or mental disabilities.

Confrontation of Jokes and Discriminatory Actions

Jokes and sarcastic remarks related to people of color, women, persons with a disability, and other populations-at-risk help shape and perpetuate stereotypes and prejudices. It is important that we all seek to tactfully but assertively indicate that we do not view such remarks as being humorous or appropriate. We must also tactfully and assertively point out the inappropriateness of discriminatory actions by others against populations-at-risk. Such confrontations make explicit that jokes and discriminatory actions involving populations-at-risk are harmful; this has a consciousness-raising effect. Gradually, such confrontations will reduce prejudices and discriminatory actions.

Grass-Roots Approaches to Improving Inner Cities

Ghettos are a national disgrace. The United States is the richest and most powerful country in the world, yet we have been unable to improve living conditions in our inner cities.

Our country has tried a variety of approaches to improve ghetto living conditions. Programs and services provided include work training, job placement, financial assistance through public welfare, low-interest mortgages to start businesses, Head Start, drug and alcohol treatment, crime prevention, housing, rehabilitation, day-care services, health care services, and public health services.

One of the most comprehensive undertakings to assist inner cities was the Model Cities Program, which was part of the War on Poverty in the 1960s. Several inner cities were targeted for this massive intervention. The program involved tearing down dilapidated housing and constructing comfortable living quarters. Salvageable buildings were renovated. In addition, these Model City projects had a variety of programs that provided job training and placement, health care services, social services, and educational opportunities. The results were more than depressing. The communities have again become slums, and living conditions are as bleak, or

bleaker, than at the start of the Model City interventions (Weltner, 1977).

To date, practically all programs that have tried to improve inner cities have had, at best, only short-term success. No other conclusion can be made. Ghettos continue to have abysmal living conditions. In the 1980s, and extending into the 1990s, the federal government appears to have given up trying to improve living conditions; federal programs for inner cities have either been eliminated or sharply cut back.

Ghetto living is becoming a way of life. Poverty and dependency on welfare are becoming a lifestyle in ghettos, and this lifestyle is being passed on from one generation to another.

Our society, for better or worse, is materialistic. The two main legitimate avenues for acquiring material goods are by getting a good education and obtaining a high-paying job. It appears that many ghetto residents realize the prospects are bleak for them getting a good education (when only inferior schools exist in their areas) or obtaining a high-paying job (when they have few marketable job skills). As a result, many turn to illegitimate ways to get material goods (shoplifting, drug trafficking, robbery, and con games). Many have also turned to immediate gratification (including sex and drug highs). A value system is developing that includes being resigned to being dependent on the government through welfare for a substandard lifestyle.

One promising approach to improving inner cities is grass-roots organizations. These organizations can sometimes effect positive, long-lasting changes in a variety of settings, including inner cities. Grass-roots organizations are community groups, composed of community residents who work together to improve their surroundings. (It may be that lasting changes can be made only in neighborhoods whose residents are inspired to improve their community.) Following is a description of a successful grass-roots effort in Cochran Gardens in St. Louis, Missouri (Boyte, 1989).

Cochran Gardens was once a low-income housing project typical of many deteriorating housing projects in large urban areas. It was filled with rubbish, graffiti, and broken windows, and its residents were plagued by frequent shootings, crime, and drug trafficking.

Bertha Gilkey grew up in this housing project. Had it not been for her, this neighborhood might have continued to deteriorate. As a youngster, Gilkey believed the neighborhood could improve if residents worked together. As a teenager she attended tenant meetings in a neighborhood church. When she was 20 years old, she was elected to chair this tenant's association. The neighborhood has since undergone gradual, yet dramatically positive, changes.

Gilkey and her group started with small projects. They asked tenants what realistically achievable things they really wanted. There was a consensus that the housing project needed a usable laundromat. The project's previous laundromats had all been vandalized, and the only working laundromat in the projects had no locks. In fact, the entry door had been stolen. Bertha and her group requested and received a door from the city housing authority. The organization then held a successful fund-raiser for a lock. The organization next held a fund-raiser for paint, and that too was a success. The organization then painted the laundromat. The residents were pleased to have an attractive, working laundromat, and its presence increased their interest in joining and supporting the tenants' association. The association then organized to paint the hallways, floor by floor, of the housing project. Everyone who lived on a floor was responsible for being involved in painting their hallway's floor. Gilkey stated:

Kids who lived on the floor that hadn't been painted would come and look at the painted hallways and then go back and hassle their parents. The elderly who couldn't paint prepared lunch so they could feel like they were a part of it too. [Boyte, 1989, p. 5]

The organization continued to initiate and successfully complete new projects to spruce up the neighborhood. Each success inspired more and more residents to take pride in their neighborhood and to work toward making improvements. While improving the physical appearance of this housing project, Gilkey and the tenants' organization also reintroduced a conduct code for the project. A committee formulated rules of behavior and elected monitors on each floor. The rules included no loud disruptions, no throwing garbage out of the windows, and no fights. Slowly, residents got the message, and living conditions improved, one small step at a time.

The building was renamed Dr. Martin Luther King Jr. Building. (Symbols are important in community development efforts.) The organization also held a party and a celebration for each successfully completed project.

Another focus of Gilkey's efforts was to reach out to children and adolescents. The positives were highlighted. The young people wrote papers in school on "What I like about living here." In art class they built a cardboard model of the housing project that included the buildings, streets, and playground. Such efforts were designed to build the self-esteem of the young people and to instill a sense of pride in their community.

Today, Cochran Gardens is a public housing project with flower-lined paths, trees, and grass—a beautiful and clean neighborhood filled with trusting people who have a sense of pride in their community. The high-rise buildings have been completely renovated. There is a community center, and there are tennis courts, playgrounds, and townhouse apartments to reduce density in the complex. Cochran Gardens is managed by the tenants. The association (now named Tenant Management Council) has ventured into owning and operating certain businesses: a catering service, day-care centers, health clinics, and a vocational training program.

The Cochran success has been based on the principles of self-help, empowerment, responsibility, and dignity. Gilkey stated:

> This goes against the grain, doesn't it? Poor people are to *be* managed. What we've done is cut through all the bullshit and said it doesn't take all that. People with degrees and credentials got us in this mess. All it takes is some basic skills. . . . If we can do it in public housing, it can happen anywhere. [Boyte, 1989, p. 5]

Such successes suggest that it is desirable for our federal, state, and city governments to seek to improve inner-city conditions by encouraging and supporting (including financially) grass-roots efforts. Social workers can use their macropractice skills as catalysts in the formation of grass-roots organizations. Once such organizations are formed, social workers can provide invaluable assistance by helping them identify community needs and then plan and implement interventions to meet these needs.

Summary

This chapter reviews some of the barriers inherent in worker-client differences and discusses some of the factors that are obstacles in workers' forming relationships with clients who differ in terms of race, culture, age, gender, or sexual orientation. The chapter also provides information on how such obstacles and barriers can be overcome. The final section provides specific techniques and approaches that can be used (or should be avoided) in social work practice with Native Americans, African Americans, Latinos, women, gays and lesbians, children, and rural clients.

Generally the difficulties that workers experience can be attributed to four fundamental issues: (1) ignorance of the culture or characteristics of those with whom one is working; (2) retention of stereotypic perceptions of the target group; (3) insufficient knowledge of self; and (4) a tendency to rely on standard interventive techniques without regard to their appropriateness for the client group.

The existence of these barriers may give the reader the impression that client and worker differences present obstacles that only superhuman effort on the part of the helper can overcome. In actuality, the similarities between helper and client often outweigh the dissimilarities. Workers can deemphasize some of the differences that do exist through those mechanisms that are important to all relationships. A belief in (and practice consistent with) respect for the worth and dignity of the client is significant. A worker who is genuinely interested in the problems and situation of the client and who gives hope for improvement will assuage much of the division caused by racial, ethnic, cultural, or sexual orientation differences. Adhering to the values of the profession, while not a panacea, increases the likelihood that the worker in these situations will be accepted and accorded the status of a competent and sensitive professional. When coupled with a thorough knowledge of the client group, a depth of self-understanding, and a repertoire of culturally relevant techniques, the applied values of the profession provide an effective means to this end.

The chapter concluded with a presentation of macro strategies to promote social and economic justice for populations-at-risk. The strategies included social programs, mass media appeals, civil rights laws, activism, school busing, affirmative action programs, human relations programs, confrontation of jokes and discriminatory actions, and grass-roots approaches to improving inner cities.

Exercises

1. Diversity self-assessment

Goal: This exercise is designed to encourage students to recognize and understand their attitudes toward various diverse groups.

Step 1: Provide each student with a copy of the diversity checklist.

Step 2: Explain the purpose of the exercise and allow about ten minutes for completion.

Step 3: When all students have completed the checklist, provide each with two copies of the self-assessment guide and allow another ten minutes or so for completing these sheets. The sheets are to be completed in duplicate. The student's name should be placed on only one of the two copies, leaving one without a name.

Step 4: Break the class into small groups of six to eight persons to discuss the exercise, focusing on things each student learned about himself or herself while completing the exercise. At the same time collect one copy of the self-assessment guide (without any identifying information), and use the small-group time to prepare a profile of the class that can be placed on the board.

Step 5: Reassemble the class and ask students to share their reactions to the small-group sessions. Review the class profile and ask students to react to the profile and discuss the implications of their own self-assessment of their ability to work with diverse groups. Finally, ask students to consider ways in which they might deal with prejudices and attitudes that interfere with their ability to be effective social workers.

Diversity Self-Assessment Checklist

The following table lists a number of individuals with whom you may come in contact in your role as a social worker. In addition, there are questions listed that should be answered with reference to each of the individuals mentioned. Please keep in mind that the exercise will work best if you are as honest in your answers as you can be. Your individual responses will not be revealed to anyone else.

Instructions

a. Answer only one question at a time. When you have answered the question about the first individual, go on to the second individual. Continue through the list until you have answered the first question for each individual listed. Then proceed to question two and so on.

b. Place an X in the correct column for any individual for whom you answered no. Also place an X if you have to hesitate before answering yes.

Question 1: Would I be able to greet this person in a warm and sincere manner?

Question 2: Would I be sufficiently comfortable interviewing this person to be able to listen to his or her problems?

Question 3: Would I feel comfortable trying to help this person deal with the problems that brought him or her to me?

Individuals	Question Number		
	1	2	3
1. Asian American			
2. Mexican American			
3. Jew			
4. Gay male			
5. Native American			
6. Senile senior citizen			
7. Ku Klux Klan member			
8. Prostitute			
9. Blind person			
10. Alcoholic			
11. Drug pusher			
12. Farmer			
13. African American			
14. Lesbian			
15. Puerto Rican			
16. Person in a wheelchair			
17. Cerebral palsied person			
18. Jehovah's Witness			
19. Pimp			
20. Person with a badly disfigured face			

Diversity Self-Assessment Guide
The purpose of this guide is to help you recognize areas of potential difficulty when working with various diverse groups. The individuals listed on the checklist can be

divided into subgroups: ethnic or racial, lifestyle, religious or spiritual, mental or physical disability, and political.

You should be alert to any concentration of Xs under any of these categories, since they may indicate potential barriers to your efforts to work with certain diverse groups. Transpose your answers from the Diversity Self-Assessment Checklist to this guide.

Categories	Question Number		
	1	2	3
Ethnic or Racial			
1. Asian American			
2. Mexican American			
5. Native American			
13. African American			
15. Puerto Rican			
Lifestyle			
4. Gay male			
8. Prostitute			
10. Alcoholic			
11. Drug pusher			
12. Farmer			
14. Lesbian			
19. Pimp			
Religious or Spiritual			
3. Jew 18. Jehovah's Witness			
Mental or Physical Disability			
6. Senile senior citizen			
9. Blind person			
16. Person in a wheelchair			
17. Cerebral palsied person			
20. Person with a badly disfigured face			
Political			
7. Ku Klux Klan member			

2. The Billy Martin case

Goal: This exercise is designed to help students clarify their values toward homosexuality and foster care.

Step 1: State the purpose of this exercise. Have the students form subgroups of about five persons. Read the following vignette to the subgroups.

Billy Martin has been in foster care for the past three years. At age 14 he was thought too old to be adopted, and his worker expected he would remain with Julie and Ed Saunders until he turned 18. A typical teenager, Billy has begun to act up and assert his independence, challenging the Saunderses on almost every issue. Mrs. Saunders is having a difficult time coping with Billy, but is willing to try since Billy really has no other alternative.

Last week, Billy's older brother, Glenn, who is 24 and works as a repairman for the telephone company, offered to take Billy to live with him. Glenn is now living with another man and is active in the movement to have the city adopt an ordinance prohibiting discrimination against gays and lesbians. He is also involved with the Gay Task Force and a strong advocate for rights for homosexuals. Billy would miss the Saunderses but wants to live with his big brother. Glenn is economically able to care for Billy, but the case manager, Mr. Walton, has some strong reservations.

Step 2: Instruct the subgroups to arrive at answers to the following questions (these questions should be written on the chalkboard).

a. Would you let Billy live with his brother? Why or why not?
b. Should Billy be moved to another foster home if the Saunders are no longer able to handle him?
c. How much should the sexual orientation of a person affect decisions on such issues as suitability for raising children?

Step 3: Reassemble the class. Have the subgroups share and discuss their answers to these questions.

3. The Mary Mills case

Goal: This exercise is designed to help students clarify their values toward the roles of women and men in our society.

Step 1: State the purpose of the exercise. Have the students form subgroups of about five persons. Read the following vignette to the subgroups.

Mary Mills is angry. Her husband has been arguing with her about the time her new job takes and the fact that she is not home to vacuum and clean, as she was before. The Millses have been married for seven years and have no children. During the first years of marriage, Mary remained at home because her husband felt he should be the breadwinner. After she became bored with this routine, Mary decided to get a part-time job working as a clerk in the local supermarket. While they do not need the money, Mary enjoys the chance to meet people and do something different. After six months on the job, the manager offered Mary a chance to become her assistant. The new job is full-time, and Mary was very excited about the possibility of this position. Mr. Mills is opposed to her taking the position. Her best friend, a social worker named Allison Goetz, suggested she should not take the job because it would cause more difficulty in the Mills's marriage. Instead, she suggested Mary begin to do some volunteer work at the local hospital. This would give her a chance to get out of the house and would not be opposed by her husband.

Step 2: Instruct the subgroups to arrive at answers to the following questions (these questions should be written on the chalkboard):

    a. Is Mary better off to stay at home and not risk her marriage?
    b. Is Allison right in her opinion that Mary should quit her job and do volunteer work of which her husband approves?
    c. Does it make any sense for Mary to take a full-time job with important responsibilities if her husband objects so strongly?
    d. If you had been Allison, what would you have recommended?

Step 3: Reassemble the class. Have the subgroups share and discuss their answers to these questions.

4. Racial and ethnic prejudices[2]

Goal: This exercise is designed to help students identify their racial and ethnic prejudices and to demonstrate that practically everyone has racial and ethnic stereotypes.

Step 1: Reproduce and distribute to the class the following questionnaire:

Selecting a Spouse
Assume you are single. Place an X by the following groups that you would be hesitant to marry a member of. Do not write your name on this sheet so that you will remain anonymous.

____ Russian		____ Arab
____ Cuban		____ Israeli
____ French		____ Chinese
____ Mexican		____ Japanese
____ African American		____ Filipino
____ Native American		____ Eskimo
____ Puerto Rican		____ Brazilian
____ Italian		____ Hungarian
____ German		____ Vietnamese
____ Polish		____ Pakistani
____ Norwegian		____ Korean
____ Samoan		

[2]This exercise was written by Charles Zastrow.

Step 2: Ask the students to fill out the questionnaire. After they have finished this part, instruct them to write the reasons they would be hesitant to marry a member of each of the racial and ethnic groups they have checked. In writing their reasons, instruct them to go beyond general reasons (such as "Parents would disapprove" or "I don't like members of such groups") to give specific reasons why parents would disapprove or why they dislike members of certain groups.

Step 3: After the students have finished writing their reasons, collect the questionnaires. Then read to the class some of the derogatory statements made.

Step 4: Seek to elicit a class discussion on the following questions:

a. Does this exercise suggest that practically everyone has racial and ethnic stereotypes and prejudices?
b. How do such stereotypes and prejudices develop in people?
c. How would you feel if you were a member of a racial or ethnic group that was being disparaged by others?
d. How can such stereotypes and prejudices be eradicated?

Comment: Some students may write down some harsh, negative statements. If this occurs, confront such stereotypes in a tactful way. One way is to respond, "We are all members of racial and ethnic groups. How would you feel if the group of which you are a member was viewed in such a degrading manner?"

PART

Contemporary Theories of Counseling

CHAPTER

13 Psychoanalysis

An effective social worker needs to have a knowledge of comprehensive counseling theories[1] and specialized treatment techniques to be able to diagnose precisely what problems exist and how to intervene effectively. There are a number of contemporary comprehensive counseling approaches, including psychoanalysis, client-centered therapy, rational therapy, behavior modification, reality therapy, and transactional analysis. These therapy approaches generally present theoretical material on (1) personality theory, or how normal psychosocial development occurs; (2) behavior pathology, or how emotional and behavioral problems arise; and (3) therapy, or how to change disturbed behavior.

An effective counselor generally knows several treatment approaches and, depending on the unique set of problems being presented by the client, is able to pick and choose from a "bag of tricks" the intervention strategy apt to have the highest probability of success. In addition to comprehensive counseling approaches, there are a number of specialized treatment techniques for specific problems: assertiveness training for people who are shy

[1]A comprehensive counseling theory is a counseling approach that the theorist proposes as being applicable in treating practically all personal problems.

or overly aggressive; muscle relaxation training for people under stress or suffering from a variety of psychosomatic problems; and parent effectiveness training for parent-child relationship difficulties. An effective worker strives to gain a working knowledge of a wide variety of treatment techniques to increase the likelihood of being able to help clients.

This chapter and the next several chapters summarize contemporary approaches to counseling and illustrate with case examples how each is used. It is practically impossible for a social worker to acquire a working knowledge of all the comprehensive and specialized intervention approaches that are available. These chapters present an overview of the most widely used approaches. As indicated in Chapter 1, instructors (in conjunction with the other program faculty) are urged to select and cover those intervention theories that are most useful for students in their geographic area to learn.

Sigmund Freud

The founder of psychoanalysis was Sigmund Freud (1924). His theories have had an immense impact on the helping professions, including psychiatry, psychology, and social work.

Freud was born in Moravia, May 6, 1856, and died in London on September 23, 1939. For over 70 years, however, he lived in Vienna and left that city only when the Nazis overran Austria. He developed his theories primarily between 1895 and 1925, which was the end of the Victorian age (an era of sexual oppression). Every personality theorist's hypotheses (and definitely Freud's) are partially related to societal concerns and to internal concerns. Freud's emphasis on sexuality is a reflection of Europe's sexual oppression at this time and also of some of Freud's personal struggles.

Freud graduated from the medical school of Vienna, was married, and had six children. He conducted a searching self-analysis that

Sigmund Freud (1856–1939)

The Mind

Freud's (1924) conception of the mind was two-dimensional, as indicated in Figure 13.1. One dimension of the mind consisted of the conscious, the preconscious, and the unconscious. The second dimension consisted of the id, the superego, and the ego.

Emphasis on the Unconscious

Freud thought that the mind was composed of thoughts (ideas), feelings, instincts, drives, conflicts, and motives. Most of these elements were thought to be located in the unconscious or preconscious. Elements in the preconscious area had a fair chance of becoming conscious, whereas elements in the unconscious were unlikely to arise to a person's conscious mind. The small "conscious cap" at the top of Figure 13.1 indicates Freud's theory that a person was aware of only a fraction of the total thoughts, drives, conflicts, motives, and feelings in the mind.

The "repressed" area was a barrier under which disturbing material (primarily thoughts and feelings) had been placed by the defense mechanism of repression. Freud thought that repression was the defense mechanism that caused the most problems psychologically. Repression is a process in which unacceptable desires, memories, and thoughts are excluded from consciousness by sending the material into the unconscious under the "repressed" barrier. Once material has been repressed, Freud thought that material has energy and acts as an unconscious irritant, producing unwanted emotions and bizarre behavior, such as anger, nightmares, hallucinations, and enuresis.

The Id, Superego, and Ego

The *id* is the primitive psychic force in the unconscious. At birth a child's mind is thought to be entirely composed of the id. As the child grows older, the ego and superego develop

began in the 1890s and continued throughout his life, had personal conflicts with his parents, and suffered in his later years from cancer of the jaw. Freud had considerable charisma that enabled him to "market" and gain adherents to his views. He also had trouble interacting with colleagues who questioned aspects of his theories; these interactions often resulted in intense disagreements and a discontinuance of further communication.

A number of authorities have recognized Freud as being one of the greatest contributors to humanity in the 20th century. Although adherence to psychoanalysis is now waning, between 1920 and 1950 social workers, psychiatrists, and certain psychologists largely believed and adopted Freud's approach to therapy.

out of, and become differentiated from, the id. The id contains biological instincts. Many of these instincts are viewed as immoral or asocial and need to be controlled by the individual and the larger society. The id is governed by the pleasure principle; that is, the instincts within the id seek to be expressed regardless of the consequences.

The *superego* normally develops sometime between the ages of 3 and 5, and consists of the traditional values and mores of society that are interpreted to a child by the parents. The superego's main function is to decide whether something is right or wrong. The superego is considered to contain a person's conscience and also his or her self-ideal (what that person wants to become). When an instinctual demand strives for expression and the superego disapproves, the superego sends a signal of anxiety to the ego as a warning to prevent the expression of the instinct. The emotion of guilt is said to originate from the superego.

The *ego* begins to develop from the id through experience shortly after birth. The ego acts as the coordinator of the personality, with its major function being to find the least painful balance between meeting the desires or demands of the id, the superego, and the outside world. It operates on the basis of the reality principle, which is to achieve a balance between id instincts, the demands of the superego, and the demands of society.

An example may help illustrate how the id, superego, and ego function. Suppose a sex instinct seeks expression from the id of a teenager. The superego will note the instinct is seeking to be expressed and will send a signal of anxiety to the ego to inform it that an "evil" instinct is seeking expression. This will alert the ego that such expression will lead to condemnation from the superego. The ego is then in a crisis and usually functions defensively to handle the instinct. On one hand the ego has severe pressure from the id to allow the instinct to be expressed; on the other it is aware that a direct expression will lead to condemnation from the superego and probably

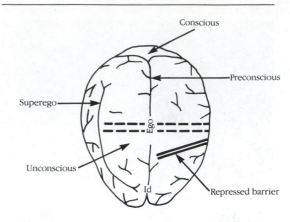

Figure 13.1
Freud's conception of the mind

also from the outside world. The ego has to choose between various options. These options include letting the instinct be directly expressed (for example, through intercourse or self-stimulation), which will probably lead to condemnation from the superego and society. Another option is for the ego to do nothing; the result is that the energy from the sexual instinct (which in this case is not allowed to be expressed) is then transformed into anxiety. (Freud thought anxious people were generally sexually frustrated.) A third option is to use a defense mechanism (see Exhibit 13.1 for a listing of common defense mechanisms). For example, the ego might use *sublimination*, the mechanism whereby consciously unacceptable instinctual demands are channeled into acceptable forms for gratification—in this case the sexual instinct might be expressed by channeling the energy of the sexual instinct into athletic activity. Or, the mechanism of repression might be used whereby the sexual instinct is sent down deep into the unconscious under the "repressed" barrier.

The libido. The energy of the biological instincts is called the *libido*, which is conceived as being primarily sexual energy. The libido is the unit that gives energy to a per-

Defense mechanism: Any *unconscious* attempt to adjust to painful conditions, such as anxiety, frustration, and guilt. Defense mechanisms are measures through which a person preserves self-esteem and softens the blow of failure, deprivation, or feelings of guilt.

Compensation: Making up for a real or fancied defect or inferiority by creating a real or fancied achievement or superiority. A common example is an effort to achieve success in one field after failure in another.

Repression: Mechanism through which unacceptable desires, feelings, memories, and thoughts are excluded from consciousness by being sent down deep into the unconscious.

Sublimation: Mechanism whereby consciously unacceptable instinctual demands are channeled into acceptable forms for gratification. For example, aggression can be converted into athletic activity.

Denial: Mechanism whereby a person escapes psychic pain associated with reality by unconsciously rejecting reality. For example, a mother may persistently deny that her child has died.

Identification: Mechanism through which a person takes on the attitudes, behavior, or personal attributes of another person whom he or she has idealized (parent, relative, popular hero).

Reaction formation: Development of socially acceptable behavior or attitudes that are the opposite of repressed unconscious impulses. Reaction formation is apparent in individuals who turn anal impulses into scrupulous cleanliness.

Regression: Acting in a more childish fashion. This mechanism involves a person's falling back to an earlier phase of development in which he or she felt secure. Some adults when ill, for example, will act more childish and demanding with the unconscious goal of having others around them give them more care and attention.

Projection: Mechanism through which a person unconsciously attributes his or her own unacceptable ideas or impulses to another. For example, a person who has an urge to hurt others may turn it around and consciously feel that others are trying to hurt him.

Rationalization: Mechanism by which an individual, faced with frustrations or with criticism of her actions, finds justification for them by disguising from herself (as she hopes to disguise from others) her true motivations. Often this is accomplished by a series of excuses that the person believes. For example, a student who fails an exam may blame it on poor teaching, having to work, and so on, rather than consciously acknowledging the real reasons.

Undoing: Mechanism whereby when a person feels guilty about some act or wish, he or she acts or speaks in a manner reflecting the reverse of some act or wish. For example, a spouse who has been unfaithful may react by being overly attentive to his mate.

Isolation: The separation of an object (idea, experience, or memory) from the emotions associated with it, resulting in the person's showing no emotion to the object. This mechanism makes it possible for an individual to avoid the pain of anxiety, shame, or guilt. For example, a person uses this mechanism when she is able to discuss a violent act she has committed without showing any emotion.

Fantasy formation: Involves using fantasy to dull the pain of reality. For example, an unhappy child in an adopted family may fantasize that his natural parents are exalted, loving people who will one day rescue him.

son's personality. In various writings Freud vacillated between locating the libido in the ego and locating it in the id. For Freud, the location of the libido was a vexing dilemma: if he claimed the libido was located in the ego, he could not explain where the id obtained its energy, and vice versa.

Eros and Thanatos. In his early writings Freud thought that humans primarily had only sexual instincts (also called Eros). Unable to explain sadism (pleasure from hurting others) and masochism (pleasure from being hurt), Freud in his later writings identified a second type of instinct (Thanatos), which he indicated was the death instinct. He was then able to explain masochistic and sadistic behavior in terms of fulfilling the death instinct's focus on seeking to return to an inorganic state, either by hurting oneself or by seeing others hurt.

Emphasis on sexuality. Partly because of the oppression of sexual expression in Freud's time, he came to realize that many people had sexual conflicts. He made sexuality a focus of his theories and defined most emotions and behaviors as being primarily sexual in nature. Freud thought sexuality included physical love, affectionate impulses, self-love, love for parents and children, and friendship associations. Freud believed sexual excitement originates from diverse sources: stimulation of an erogenous zone (an erogenous zone could be located on any part of the body—an example would be "tingling sensations" on an ear), expression of an impulse (such as laughing), muscular activity (like running), emotional excitement (such as fear or happiness), and intellectual work. (As can be seen from these examples, Freud had an exceedingly broad definition of the components of human sexuality.)

Psychosexual Development

Freud's theory of psychosexual, or personality, development included five stages: oral, anal, phallic, latency, and genital.

Oral Stage

This phase, which extends from birth to approximately 18 months, is called *oral* because the child's primary activities are centered around feeding and the organs (mouth, lips, and tongue) connected with that function. Feeding is considered an important area of conflict, and a child's attention is focused on receiving and taking. People fixated at this stage are thought to have the most severe personality disorders, such as schizophrenia or psychotic depression. (By the term *fixated*, Freud meant that a person's personality development is largely, though not completely, halted at the specified stage.)

Anal Stage

Between ages 18 months to 3 years, a child's activities are mainly focused on giving and withholding, primarily connected with retaining and passing feces. Bowel training is an important area of conflict. People fixated at this stage have such character traits as messiness, stubbornness, rebelliousness; or they may have a *reaction formation* and have such opposite traits as being meticulously clean and excessively punctual.

Phallic Stage

From the third through the fifth year, the child's attention shifts to the genitals. Prominent activities of the child are pleasurable sensations from genital stimulation, showing off one's body, and looking at the bodies of others. Also, a child's personality becomes more complex during this stage. Although still self-centered, the child wants to possess those who give him or her pleasure. The child becomes more curious, wants to love and be loved, and seeks to be admired. Character traits that are apt to develop from fixation at this stage are pride, promiscuity, and self-hatred.

Boys and girls experience separate complexes during this stage. Boys encounter an Oedipus complex. (Freud took many of his terms from Greek mythology. *Oedipus Rex* was a Greek drama in which Oedipus, who had been raised by foster parents, unwittingly kills his father, marries his mother, and then undergoes severe psychological trauma when he discovers what he has done.)

The *Oedipus complex* refers to the dilemma faced by every son at this stage when he falls sexually in love with his mother and has antagonism toward his father, whom he views as a rival for her affections. As the intensity of these relationships mounts, the son increasingly suffers from castration anxiety; that is, he fears his father is going to discover his "affair" with his mother and then remove his genitals. Successful resolution of the Oedipus complex occurs through defense mechanisms. A typical resolution is for the son to first *repress* his feelings of love for his mother and his hostile feelings toward his father. Next, the son has a *reaction formation* in which he stops viewing his father negatively, but now turns this around and has positive feelings toward his father. The final step is for the son to *identify* with is father, and thereby seek to take on his attitudes, values, and behavior patterns. Freud also asserted that the resolution of this complex results in the formation of the superego. (Precisely how the resolution of this complex results in the formation of the superego has not been clarified.)

Girls undergo an *Electra complex* during this phallic stage. (Freud, as you will see, would not be very popular with the feminist movement if he were advancing his theories at the present time.) The name *Electra* was taken from a Greek drama. Electra assisted her brother in avenging their father's death by slaying their mother—this mother had conspired with her lover to murder her husband.

Freud believed girls fall sexually in love with their father during this stage and also view their mother with antagonism. Because of these relationships, girls also suffer from castration anxiety, but the nature of this anxiety is different from that for boys. Castration anxiety in a girl results from the awareness that she lacks a penis. She then concludes she was castrated in infancy and blames her mother for this. Freud went on to theorize that because girls believe they have been castrated, they come to regard themselves as inferior to boys (have penis envy). From this point on, they perceive their role in life to be submissive and supportive of males. Freud did not identify the precise processes for resolution of the Electra complex.

Latency Stage

This stage usually begins at the time when the Oedipus/Electra complexes are resolved, and ends with puberty. The sexual instinct is relatively unaroused during this stage. The child can now be socialized and becomes involved in the educational process and in learning skills.

Genital Stage

This stage occurs from puberty to death. It involves mature sexuality and the person reaching this stage is fully able to love and to work. Again, we see Freud's emphasis on sexuality and on the work ethic, which was part of the Protestant ethic and highly valued in Freud's era.

Psychopathological Development

In his analysis of psychopathological development, or the development of emotional and behavioral problems, Freud theorized that disturbances can arise from several sources. One source is traumatic experiences that a person's ego is not able to cope with directly and thereby strives to resolve using such defense mechanisms as repression. The problem with using repression is that there is energy associated with the repressed material that then unconsciously acts as an irritant. Breuer and Freud (1895) provide an example of a woman named Anna O. who developed a psychosomatic paralysis of her right arm. Anna O. was sitting by her father's bedside (her father was gravely ill), when she dozed off and had a nightmare that a big black snake was attacking her father. She awoke terrified and hastily repressed her thoughts and feelings about this nightmare for fear of alarming her father. During the time she was asleep, her right arm was resting over the back of a chair and became "numb." Freud theorized that the energy connected with the repressed material then took over physiological control of her arm, resulting in psychological paralysis.

In addition to unresolved traumatic events, Freud though that internal unconscious processes could also cause disturbances. There is a range of possible sources. An unresolved Electra or Oedipal complex could lead to a malformed superego or to a variety of sexual problems—such as frigidity, promiscuity, sexual dysfunctions, excessive sexual fantasies, and nightmares with sexual content. Unresolved internal conflicts (for example, an unconscious liking and hatred of one's parents) may be another source that causes such behavioral problems as hostile and aggressive behavior and such emotional problems as temper tantrums. Fixations at early stages of development are additional sources that largely prevent development at later stages and lead the person to display such undesirable personality traits as messiness or stubbornness. (Freud thought that traumatic experiences are important contributing factors in leading to internal conflicts and fixations.)

As indicated earlier, the main source of anxiety is thought to be sexual frustration. Freud believed that anxiety arises when a sexual instinct seeks expression, but the ego blocks its expression. If the instinct is not then diverted through defense mechanisms, the energy connected with sexual instincts is transformed into anxiety.

Obsessions (a recurring thought such as a song repeatedly on one's mind) and compulsions (such as an urge to step on every crack of a sidewalk) are thought to be mechanisms through which a person works off energy connected with disturbing unconscious material.

For all types of mental disorders, unconscious processes (including fixations, internal conflicts, and defense mechanisms) are thought to be the causes. These disturbing unconscious processes are almost always connected with traumatic experiences, particularly traumatic experiences during childhood that are repressed.

Psychoanalysis

The goal of psychoanalysis, the theory of therapy, is to discover the disturbing unconscious processes and bring them into the conscious part of the patient's mind so that the unconscious emotion (or energy) can be expressed (and thereby dissipated) and the disturbing unconscious ideas (now conscious) can be "worked through" (dealt with). Often, Freud thought, emotional disturbances are the result of pent-up, undischarged emotional tension connected with the repressed memory of a traumatic childhood sexual experience.

Psychoanalysis is a long process, generally because a chain of traumatic events stemming deep into the past is believed to be the determinant of each symptom. To treat a patient, it is necessary to bring the memory of these traumatic experiences to the conscious part of the patient's mind in order to bring about an emotional catharsis (release of pent-up energy) and to allow the person to consciously handle the disturbing ideas connected with the trauma. For example, in the case of Anna O., Freud (Breuer & Freud, 1895) asserted that her arm became psychologically paralyzed due to the repression of the nightmare of a snake attacking her father. The paralyzed right arm was viewed as a *symptom* of unconscious processes that stemmed deep into Anna O.'s past. Freud asserted that the paralysis of the right arm disappeared when Anna, through psychoanalysis, remembered the nightmare, had an emotional catharsis, and was able to then consciously deal with having such a nightmare. However, Freud asserted that only the symptom (paralyzed arm) of her emotional disturbance was treated by remembering this event. Freud believed Anna was still rather severely disturbed as the underlying unconscious processes that had caused this symptom still remained. Therefore the aim of psychoanalysis is to treat not only the symptoms but also the unconscious processes that are viewed as causing the symptoms. These disturbing, unconscious processes generally stem from traumatic experiences that occurred far back in a person's past. The goal with Anna O., as with other patients, was to bring the unconscious memory of each of these traumatic events to her conscious mind so an emotional catharsis can occur and, through such an awareness or insight, she can consciously handle the disturbing ideas. In Anna's case, Freud believed that her nightmare indicated an unresolved Electra complex. Freud believed that snakes in dreams are a symbol for the male sex organ. Anna's nightmare involving a snake suggested to Freud that Anna had sexual conflicts, probably stemming from repressed childhood sexual traumas. Freud thus sought with all his patients to have them become aware of (gain insight into) these traumatic experiences. The case example on page 400 discusses treating multiple personality with psychoanalysis.

To discover such unconscious processes, Freud (1924) used four main techniques: hypnosis, free association, dream analysis, and transference.

Hypnosis

Freud used *hypnosis* early in his career; however, he soon discarded it because many of his patients could not be hypnotized. Also, even for those patients who could be hypnotized, Freud usually did not know the exact date and time a traumatic event had occurred so he did not know where to direct a patient's attention. (Hypnosis is further described in Chapter 20.)

Free Association

A second technique that Freud used was *free association*. In free association a patient is instructed to say whatever comes to mind, no matter how trivial the thought or association may seem. It is thought that if patients can let their mind associate while relaxed, their defenses will also be relaxed; therefore, disturbing unconscious material will have a much

greater chance of coming into their conscious mind. To facilitate this relaxed state, patients usually lie on a couch without looking at the analyst. They then make free associations with dreams, traumatic experiences, thoughts, feelings, fantasies, anything that comes to mind. At times patients remember traumatic events that occurred far back in their past, have an emotional catharsis, and together with the analyst "work through" the disturbing ideas. Usually after about 45 minutes of associating, and occasionally during this time, the analyst helps the patient gain insight into the meaning of some associations by attempting to interpret the psychological significance in terms of the psychoanalytic framework of what was being said—for example, pointing out that dreaming of clambering out of water is a symbol for the birth process (Freud, 1924, p. 160). During the association, the analyst listens to the patient and unobtrusively observes emotional reactions such as signs of distress or resistance to the treatment.

Dream Analysis

A third technique Freud used was *dream analysis*. He believed the focus of dreams centered around unfulfilled wishes. (If you received a grade on an exam that you were satisfied with, you would not be apt to dream about it; but if you strongly desired a higher grade, you would tend to dream about it.) Freud thought dreams were a royal road to the unconscious, because a person's defenses against allowing unconscious material into the conscious part of the mind are relaxed while dreaming. Freud believed there are two distinct types of content in dreams: manifest content and latent content. The dream as remembered on awakening is the manifest content. Psychologically, the manifest content is not the significant portion of the dream, since in the process of becoming conscious, it has undergone considerable distortion to make it more acceptable to the dreamer's conscious self. The latent or hidden content is much

Case Example
Sybil

Perhaps the most widely known case treated by psychoanalysis in recent years was that of Sybil Dorsett (Schreiber, 1973). (Sybil's name is a pseudonym.) Sybil was a young woman living in New York City who exhibited 16 different personalities, most of whom were unaware the other personalities existed. The main personality was Sybil, who was fairly depressed, quiet, nonassertive, and plain-looking. Fifteen other personalities were occasionally exhibited. Only a few will be mentioned. Vicky was a self-assured, sophisticated, attractive blonde. Peggy Lou was an assertive, enthusiastic, and often angry pixie with a pug nose and a Dutch haircut. Vanessa was a very attractive redhead who was intensely dramatic. Mike, one of Sybil's two male selves, had dark hair and was a builder and carpenter. Clara was intensely religious and highly critical of Sybil.

The reason Sybil developed these multiple personalities was explained as being the only way she could give expression during her childhood years to different aspects of herself. Also, the analyst states that Sybil would probably have become mentally ill had she not developed these different personalities.

Sybil had a very traumatic childhood. She was born and raised in a small midwestern town and had parents who were prominent and wealthy. Her father was described as religious, weak, and nonassertive. The main source of Sybil's problems stemmed from her mother, Hattie. In outward appearance Hattie presented an image of being deeply religious and proper. But her private life and her interactions with Sybil were startling. A few of Hattie's bizarre actions in Sybil's childhood years will be mentioned. On some summer evenings, Hattie would take Sybil for a walk and occasionally defecate with perverse pleasure on the lawns, behind bushes, of other wealthy people. Hattie also occasionally baby-sat for children in the neighborhood. With some of the girls, she played "horsey" and put her finger in their vaginas while yelling, "giddyap." With some of the young boys, she held and moved them between her hips stimulating her genitals. She was at times very abusive to Sybil. She forced objects such as a flashlight and a dinner knife into Sybil's genitals. She filled her rectum at times with water, and pressed a hot flatiron on Sybil's hand. At times she put Sybil in a trunk in an attic, closed the lid, and let her lie there for a while in order to show her what it was like to be dead. At another time she threatened to put Sybil's hand in a meat grinder. A favorite ritual of Hattie was to tie up Sybil, suspend her from the ceiling, and then fill her urethra and bladder with cold water. Hattie abused Sybil in many other ways—for example, by not allowing her to go to the bathroom and then beating her when she soiled herself. Another time Hattie tied a scarf around Sybil's neck until she gasped for breath. There were other times when Hattie stuffed a damp washrag down Sybil's throat and put cotton in her nose until Sybil lost consciousness. At other times Hattie was warm and loving toward Sybil and gave the neighbors the impression she was a model mother. Many times Hattie preached to Sybil and admonished her to behave in a prudish and puritanical manner. In such an environment it was hypothesized that Sybil developed multiple personalities as a way of coping with these abuses, as a way of giving expression to her wishes and desires and to different aspects of herself, as a way of developing and growing, and as a way to avoid becoming mentally ill.

Sybil was in analysis for 11 years. The analyst used hypnosis, dream analysis, free association, and transference to assist Sybil in recollecting these traumatic experiences that had been repressed into her unconscious. She also used sodium pentothal, a barbiturate drug, which helped enable Sybil to remember the experiences. The aim of analysis was to help Sybil relive these traumas. Reliving each of these experiences released the energy or emotion of these painful experiences and also led to increased insights. Delving into the past in this manner enabled the analyst, Dr. Cornelia Wilbur, to understand the reasons that each of these personalities emerged. The process of integrating all these personalities into one integrated personality (the new Sybil) was largely accomplished through hypnosis. Dr. Wilbur first gradually suggested to each of the personalities, individually, that they were growing older and older until each became 37 years old (Sybil's age at that time). Then Sybil was placed in a deep hypnotic sleep, and each of the different personalities (over several months) was introduced to her and she was given the suggestion that she would remember each and that each would become part of her. The reintegration into one personality was fraught with resistance from some of the personalities and required a few more years of analysis. Gradually a new, integrated Sybil emerged. After the integration of her personalities, Sybil continued her education, graduated from college, and eventually secured a college teaching position.

---

more important and must be discovered by searching deep below the surface of the manifest content.

This depth analysis is accomplished in two ways. The first way is to have the patient free-associate around elements within the dream. Presumably the elements have some hidden significance that may be uncovered by the patient as she free associates about her thoughts and feelings related to these elements.

The second method for discovering the latent content is symbol analysis. Since the meaning of many symbols in dreams varies from individual to individual, the meaning of symbols must be determined in relation to the psyche of the individual dreamer. Yet there are certain symbols that have similar meanings for nearly everyone. The majority of symbols in dreams are sexual. Parents appear in dreams as king and queen, or as other exalted personages. Clothes and uniforms stand for nakedness. The male sex organ appears in the form of poles, sticks, steeples, snakes, or some other pointed object. The female genitals are symbolized as trunks, caves, enclosed places, and pocketbooks. Children and sisters and brothers are symbolized by little animals or vermin. Dying is indicated by setting out on a journey or traveling by train (Freud, 1924).

Transference

Another approach that Freud used to discover disturbing unconscious processes was *transference*. In psychoanalysis analysts seek to be unobtrusive and neutral; they do not reveal themselves. Freud noted that when a patient is in analysis, he or she will transfer to the analyst feelings and thoughts relating to significant people (usually parent figures) of an earlier period of life. The patient, for example, may react as if he is a small child and the analyst is his father. Transference came to be recognized as an important area of insight, since the analyst would observe the transfer and gain an awareness of the patient's unconscious feelings and thoughts about significant people in the patient's past. This insight would then be interpreted to the patient and further discussed.

When the analyst gains insight into the patient's traumatic events, unconscious conflicts, and fixations, the process of "working through" begins. Working through involves interpretation to the patient of his or her difficulties and is a long process involving repetition, elaboration, and amplification. One or two experiences of insight into the nature of one's conflicts are usually not sufficient to bring about changes. The analysis is continued many times and in many different ways so the patient increasingly gains insight into the disturbing unconscious. Once insight is achieved, it is expected that the patient will be better able to function.

Evaluation

Freud is to be credited as the person who was most instrumental in developing a worldwide recognition that people who have emotional problems are in need of psychological help. Before Freud's time many disturbed people were looked on as "malingerers" and given little support or understanding. Freud also formulated a theory of personality development that is fairly comprehensive and is still widely used in assessing human behavior. When Freud began formulating his theories, there was little interest or support for psychological understanding and help for people with personal problems. Freud demonstrated the importance of helping people through "talk" therapy and inspired a wide range of other theorists to develop counseling techniques to help people.

Freud believed dreams are a royal road to the unconscious, as illustrated in *Charles Dickens' Dream.*

There are, however, a number of shortcomings in his theories:

1. Most of his concepts are difficult to operationalize (test out), so his hypotheses are difficult to prove or disprove. For example, there is no way to determine scientifically whether the following hypothesized concepts ever exist: the death instinct, Oedipal complex, penis envy, castration anxiety, Electra complex, superego, libido, fixation at the phallic stage of development, and unconscious conflict.

2. Research has shown that patients undergoing psychoanalysis have a *lower* rate of improving than people with comparable problems who receive no treatment (Eysenck, 1965)! This startling result has been found in a number of reviews of outcome studies on psychoanalysis (Stuart, 1970; Arlow, 1989). The reason for these discouraging results may be that when a person has a problem, such as being depressed, undergoing psychoanalysis may not focus the person's attention on how to handle the personal problem better but instead may lead a person to become more disturbed by worrying about having some of the mystical problems implied by psychoanalysis, such as an anal fixation, an unresolved Electra complex, castration anxiety, a death instinct, or an unconscious desire to retaliate against one's parents (Stuart, 1970).

3. Freud gives little attention to personality development beyond puberty. Other authorities have noted that personality development and changes occur throughout life (Hall & Lindzey, 1957). In another area, theorists have noted conscience development occurs throughout life, rather than between the third and fifth year as Freud suggests (Maddi, 1968).

4. Psychoanalytic theory is somewhat culture bound, particularly Freud's emphasis on sexuality. He lived in an era of sexual oppression, a time when many people had sexual concerns. Other theorists have noted that factors in addition to sexual instincts are driving forces in personality development. Rogers (1951), for example, discussed a self-actualization motive that strives to develop one's capacities to the fullest. Glasser (1972) indicated that the need to form an identity is a primary factor in personality development.

5. Psychoanalysis is time-consuming and expensive. A complete analysis takes several years with the patient seeing the analyst once or twice a week. Who can afford the time and the money (usually over $150 per hour) to see an analyst?

A few final comments will be made about the case of Sybil.[2] Multiple personality cases are very rare. Sybil's life was indeed startling, and the book and the TV movie that followed were engrossing. The psychoanalytic interpretation was indeed fascinating. But is it accurate? And is it the only interpretation of the case that can be made? Certainly other interpretations are possible. Sybil was in analysis for 11 years, a very long time. This writer can only raise some questions. Being in analysis for such a long time certainly gave Sybil considerable emotional support for her concerns. This writer wonders whether Sybil did not develop at least some of her different personalities to attempt to keep her analyst interested and to continue the therapy she was receiving. In reading the book, I wondered whether Sybil was not in fact aware of the other personalities, but played these different *roles* to get attention and to try to meet certain psychological needs that she had. (This writer has worked with a number of people who developed elaborate contrived stories— and if they received positive responses from enacting these roles, they continued to play these roles.) Also, if Sybil was truly unaware of the other personalities within her, would not a more effective treatment approach have been to videotape the different personalities and then play it back to her? Such an approach would have confronted her directly with the other personalities. Also it might have been helpful to videotape the transformations from

[2]The author is presenting this alternative explanation of Sybil's problematic behavior to convey that the same facts can often be explained in very different ways. Which explanation is more accurate—the psychoanalytic or the author's—is unknown. In fact, other explanations could probably be presented. Research is needed on counseling theories to determine which framework is more accurate. As will be seen in this case example, different explanations suggest radically different intervention approaches by therapists.

one personality to another (changing hair-dos, clothes, and makeup takes time). This videotape could be played back to her and discussed. It would have been useful, it would seem, to get her thoughts on why she was switching to another personality, and to get her views on when one personality loses recognition and another is emerging.

It is very difficult to believe that Sybil was not aware of the other personalities within her. Some had long hair, while others had short hair. Some were blonde, some were red-heads, and some had dark hair. Each personality dressed differently. Sybil must have had an apartment full of different clothes and wigs. How could she not be aware there were other personalities when she could see all these clothes and wigs? A more logical inter-pretation would seem to be that Sybil inten-tionally played different roles, and knew ex-actly what she was doing.

In reviewing this case I question whether Sybil had a loss of memory of her other per-sonalities. I remember supervising a student for a field placement in a probation and pa-role setting who was assigned a woman ar-rested for theft. The woman claimed to have no memory of taking things. She added that she occasionally "blanked out," and when she "reconnected with reality," she at times would have additional possessions in her home. The student asked for advice on how to handle this case. I suggested the woman's so-called loss of memory might be a "con act" to have people feel sorry for her. My sugges-tion was to inform this woman that if she claimed she didn't remember taking things, the judge would probably find her "mentally ill" and send her to a mental hospital for an indefinite period. The student intern tried this, and within a few minutes, the woman indicated she was aware she had taken the items for which she was arrested. She added she initially denied taking the items as she thought the court may go "easier" on her if she pretended that another personality within her (that she supposedly was unaware of) had taken the items.

Summary

Psychoanalysis was developed primarily by Sigmund Freud. Freud theorized that we pass through the following psychosexual de-velopment stages: oral, anal, phallic, latency, and genital.

For all types of mental disorders, he thought that unconscious processes (includ-ing fixations, internal conflicts, and defense mechanisms) were the causes. These disturb-ing unconscious processes were almost al-ways connected with traumatic experiences, particularly traumatic experiences during childhood that were repressed.

The goal of psychoanalysis is to discover the disturbing unconscious processes and bring them into the conscious part of the pa-tient's mind so that the unconscious emotion (or energy) can be expressed and so the dis-turbing unconscious ideas (now conscious) can be dealt with or worked through by the patient.

Psychoanalysis is a long process, as gener-ally a chain of traumatic events stemming far back into the past is believed to be the determi-nant of each symptom. To treat a patient it is necessary to bring the memory of these trau-matic experiences to the conscious part of the patient's mind, to bring about an emotional catharsis, and to allow the person consciously to work through the disturbing thoughts con-nected with the trauma. In order to bring such unconscious material to the conscious part of the mind, psychoanalysis uses the treatment techniques of hypnosis, free association, dream analysis, and transference.

Freud played a major role in developing a worldwide recognition that people who have emotional problems are in need of psycho-logical help. Although Freud's concepts and theories about human behavior are still fre-quently used by some social workers in as-sessing human behavior, very few social workers now use psychoanalysis in counsel-ing clients. A description of psychoanalysis was included in this text because of its histor-ical significance.

Exercises

1. Analyzing unusual behavior

Goal: This exercise is designed to help students analyze unusual human behavior in terms of psychoanalytic concepts.

Step 1: Instruct the students to read this chapter and indicate the purpose of this exercise. Assign a book to read or have the students watch a TV program or movie (such as *Sybil*) that seeks to explain why someone does something unusual.

One possible assignment is to have the students read newsmagazines in order to psychoanalyze why John W. Hinckley shot President Ronald Reagan on March 30, 1981. At the next class session have the students present their psychoanalytic interpretations about why the selected character did something unusual.

Step 2: Ask the students to suggest alternative explanations for why this selected character did something unusual. If the students are unable to present alternative explanations, suggest one or more. End the exercise by asking the students their thoughts on the merits and shortcomings of using psychoanalytic theory to assess human behavior.

2. Word association

Goal: This exercise is designed to demonstrate word association, which is a form of free association.

Step 1: Ask for a volunteer to say the first word that comes to mind for a variety of words that you will say.

Step 2: State a word, and then have the volunteer respond with the first word that comes to mind. Examples of words you might use include:

chair	pepper	salt
room	spoon	fork
grave	love	mountain
blue	red	romance
window	fire	sky
book	lamp	table
sex	relationship	pencil
green	death	money
picture	vacation	stress
gift	college	plant
mother	grief	car
brother	grandmother	summer
marriage	sister	winter

(In saying these words, interchange neutral words, such as *chair*, with words that are more apt to have emotional connections, such as *death*.)

Step 3: Explain that psychoanalysis uses word association to identify possible areas that a person may have conflicts about. Indicate that psychoanalysts believe possible conflicts are suggested if (a) the respondent takes longer than usual to respond to a word; (b) the respondent gives an unusual response, such as responding with "death" to the word *vacation;* and (c) the respondent signals with nonverbal cues that a sensitive area may have been touched on. After the word association game is over, indicate that a psychoanalyst would then probe further into possible areas of conflict with the patient.

Step 4: Do not seek to psychoanalyze the volunteer's responses, but in a positive fashion discuss with the students their thoughts about word association.

Client-Centered Therapy

Carl Rogers (1902–1987)

The founder of client-centered therapy is Carl Rogers.[1] Born in Oak Park, Illinois, in 1902, Carl Rogers was the fourth of six children. During most of his childhood years, he lived on a farm in Wisconsin. In 1931 he received a doctorate in clinical psychology from Columbia University (New York City) in a highly Freudian atmosphere. Following graduation he was employed for 12 years in a community guidance clinic in Rochester, New York. His work was to diagnose and plan for delinquent and underprivileged children who were referred by the courts and agencies. During these years Rogers was exposed to a variety of therapy approaches, including psychoanalysis and Otto Rank's functional approach. In 1940 he was offered a full professorship at Ohio State University where he remained for five years. During this time he realized he had developed a distinctive point of view in psychotherapy. In 1942 he published *Counseling and Psychotherapy*, which brought the term *nondirective* (later replaced by *client-centered*) into use. He later published a number of other books, and taught at other campuses, including the University of Chicago and the University of Wisconsin. In 1968 Rogers and some colleagues established their own Center for the Studies of the Person in La Jolla, California. Rogers died in 1987.

Rogers's views have found their way into psychiatry, psychology, social work, and guidance counseling. His contributions to psychotherapy are perhaps most noteworthy in delineating the type of relationship between therapist and client that is conducive to positive therapeutic changes. His emphasis on such concepts as "empathy," "nonjudgmental attitude," "acceptance," and "nonthreatening atmosphere" is prevalent in social work literature.

Rogers was a world figure in humanistic approaches to therapy. (*Humanism* is a philosophy that emphasizes the dignity and worth of people and their capacity for self-realization through reason.) Rogers also became highly involved in trying to inspire humanistic changes in business, education, and marriage.

---

[1]Rogers and his colleagues now prefer the term *person-centered* therapy to *client-centered*; they believe this term more accurately describes the human values their way of working incorporates.

Carl Rogers: Central Concepts

The central hypothesis of client-centered therapy, as stated by Meador and Rogers (1979, p. 131), is that

> the growth potential of any individual will tend to be released in a relationship in which the helping person is experiencing and communicating realness, caring, and a deeply sensitive nonjudgmental understanding. [p. 131]

Meador and Rogers (1979), further add:

> The basic theory of person-centered therapy can be stated simply in the form of an "if-then" hypothesis. If certain conditions are present in the attitudes of the person designated "therapist" in a relationship, namely, congruence, positive regard, and empathetic understanding, then growthful change will take place in the person designated "client." [p. 131]

To understand client-centered therapy, it is essential to understand certain terms used by Rogers. Client-centered therapy rests squarely on the assumption that everyone has a *self-actualization motive*. This motive is defined as the inherent tendency of every person (and all organisms) to develop his or her capacities in ways that maintain or enhance the person (Rogers, 1959). If this assumed motive does not exist, then client-centered therapy's main focus on being *nondirective* would be called into question. Rogers believed a therapist should not make suggestions or interpretations in therapy, because the actualizing motive will best guide a client. If this motive does not exist, then there is no rationale for a therapist to be nondirective.

In contrast to Freud, who viewed the basic nature of humans as being "evil" (having immoral, asocial instincts), Rogers viewed the basic nature of humans as inherently good. Rogers further believed that if a person remains relatively free of influence attempts from others, that person's self-actualization motive will lead him or her to become a sociable, cooperative, creative, and self-directed person.

The following are definitions of other key concepts in client-centered therapy:

Self-concept—One's conception of who one is.

Ideal self—The self-concept that one would like to possess; what one would like to be.

Incongruence between self and experience—A discrepancy that exists between one's self-concept and what one experiences. Example: an individual may perceive herself as outgoing, attractive, and sociable; but when she is with others, she may generally feel ignored. When such a discrepancy exists, she will feel tension, internal confusion, and anxiety.

Psychological maladjustment—Condition in which a person denies or distorts to awareness, significant experiences. A psychologically maladjusted person has an incongruence between self and experience.

Congruence, congruence of self and experience—Condition in which one's concept of self is consistent with what one experiences.

Need for positive regard—Need to be valued and held in esteem by others.

Need for self-regard—Need to value oneself.

Conditions of worth—Conditions of worth result from the introjection of others' values that are inconsistent with one's self-actualization motive. A person has conditions of worth when he feels his worth as a person is judged conditionally on certain behaviors. Those behaviors that he feels valued low on will be avoided. The result is that some behaviors, which are not actually experienced as satisfying, are regarded positively; whereas other behaviors, which are not actually experienced as unsatisfying, are regarded negatively.

Empathy—The capacity to perceive the internal frame of reference of another with accuracy *as if* one were the other person. Example: to sense the hurt or the pleasure of another as that person senses it. Also involved is the capacity to convey to the other person that you are sensing what that person is feeling.

Unconditional positive regard—To feel unconditional positive regard toward another; to "prize" him or her. This means to value another, irrespective of the differential values that one might place on his or her specific behaviors. In therapy this attitude comes in part form the therapist's belief in the inner wisdom of the self-actualization motive, which asserts that the client is best able to decide what courses of action are most advantageous. Showing unconditional positive regard means to communicate respect, warmth, acceptance, liking, caring, and concern for a client, all of which are *not* conditional on what the client says or does.

Genuineness or congruence of the therapist— A therapist's being her own self in the therapeutic relationship. To be genuine or congruent, the therapist has to read her own inner experiencing and to allow the quality of this inner experiencing to be apparent in the therapeutic relationship. Meador and Rogers (1979) stated:

> Congruence in the therapist's own inner self is his sensing of and reporting his own felt experiencing as he interacts in the relationship. The therapist trusts his own organismic responses in the situation and conveys those feelings of his that he intuitively believes have relevance in the relationship. [p. 153]

Being genuine or congruent is being "real" in a relationship; it is the absence of phoniness and defensiveness. Being genuine means the therapist does not put up a professional front or personal facade.

Theory of Personality Development and Psychopathology

Developing a theory of personality has not been a primary focus of client-centered theorists. Rogers was more interested in investigating the manner in which personality *changes* come about than in identifying the *causes* of present personality characteristics.

Client-centered theorists see the driving force in personality development as the "self-actualization motive," which seeks to optimally develop a person's capacities. As an infant grows, the infant's self-concept begins to be formed. The development of the self-concept is highly dependent on the individual's *perceptions* of his or her experiences. The person's perceptions of experiences is influenced by the "need for positive regard" (to be valued by others). The need for positive regard is seen as a universal need in every person (Rogers, 1959). Out of the variety of experiences of frustration or satisfaction of the need for positive regard, the person develops a "sense of self-regard"—that is, a learned sense of self that is based on the perception of the regard he or she has received from others.

Emotional and behavioral problems develop when the child *introjects* (takes on) those values of others that are inconsistent with his or her self-actualizing motive. Introjecting values inconsistent with one's self-actualizing motive results in "conditions of worth." For example, a child may introject values from his parents that sex is dirty or that dancing is bad. Rogers added that a child is apt to be influenced by others because of the need for positive regard.

When a person has conditions of worth, the result is that some behaviors are regarded positively (for example, avoiding all sexual activity) by the person even when they are not internally experienced as unsatisfying. Meador and Rogers (1979) then stated:

> What happens to the actualizing tendency as conditions of worth develop in the self-regard system? The actualizing tendency remains the basic motivation for the individual. However, a conflict develops between his organismic needs and his self-regard needs, now containing conditions of worth. The individual, in effect, is faced with the choice between acting in accord with his organismic sense or censoring the organismic urging and acting in accord with the condition of worth he has learned. [p. 144]

Such conditions of worth lead to an "incongruence between self and experience." For example, a person may feel morally righteous and view herself as being a value setter for refusing to dance or date; however, her peers may consider her a prude with archaic values. When a discrepancy exists between one's self-concept and one's experiences, that person will feel tension, anxiety, and internal confusion.

A person then responds to this "incongruence" in a variety of ways. One way is to use various defense mechanisms. A person may *deny* that experiences are in conflict with his or her self-concept. Or the person may *distort* or *rationalize* the experiences so they are then perceived as being consistent with his or her self-concept. If a person is unable to reduce the inconsistency through such defense mechanisms, he or she is forced to face the fact directly that incongruencies exist between self and experiences, which will lead the person to feel unwanted emotions (such as anxiety, tension, depression, guilt, or shame.)

If a person has a large or significant degree of incongruence between self and experiences with which the defense mechanisms cannot cope, "disorganization of self" generally occurs (that is, a "psychotic" breakdown).

Theory of Therapy

Client-centered therapy asserts that the following three therapist attitudes are necessary and sufficient conditions to effect positive change in the client: empathy, positive regard, and genuineness or congruence. It is theorized that whenever a therapist displays these three attitudes toward a client, the actualizing potential of the client will begin to change and grow.

Empathy is the capacity of the therapist to "put himself or herself in the shoes" of the client so the therapist is able to understand what the client is thinking and feeling. Empathy also involves communicating this understanding to the client.

Unconditional positive regard means that the therapist fully accepts the client and conveys a genuine caring for the client. Involved in positive regard is a nonjudgmental attitude. Also, the therapist does not express approval or disapproval, does not make interpretations, and does not probe unnecessarily. The therapist conveys that she or he fully trusts the client's resources for increased self-understanding and positive change. With this attitude the client concludes (Meador & Rogers, 1979, p. 152): "Here is someone who repeatedly tells me in one way or another that he believes in my ability to find my way in the process of growth. Perhaps I can begin to believe in myself."

Genuineness or *congruence* is the therapist's capacity to "trust his or her gut reactions," and then convey those feelings or reactions that the therapist believes have relevance in the relationship. This willingness to be real and to express what she or he is thinking and feeling provides the client with a reality base that the client can trust. It also takes away some of the risk of sharing hidden secrets with another.

For Rogers the *nature* of the relationship between client and therapist is seen as *the* key variable in producing positive changes. Rogers (1961) stated:

> The more the therapist is perceived by the client as being genuine, as having an empathetic understanding, and an unconditional regard for him, the greater will be the degree of constructive personality change in the client. [p. 32]

Rogers indicated that two conditions are necessary before therapy can occur. First, the client needs to be uncomfortable or anxious because of incongruencies between self and experiences. (Client-centered therapy will not work well with clients who deny that a problem exists or who are unmotivated to change.) Second, a therapist must create a nonthreatening atmosphere in which the client feels he or she is being fully accepted and understood, and that the therapist genuinely cares for the client.

In such a relationship a client feels free (perhaps for the first time) to explore incongruencies between self and experiences. (For example, a client begins to examine the inconsistency between believing that sex is sinful while organismically her experiences do not agree.) The client then comes face to face with the awareness that there is this incongruence. The client begins to examine this incongruence and to think about what it would mean if other values were held (for example, having a value that responsible sexual experiences are desirable). During this process the client usually experiences feelings that have in the past been denied, repressed, or otherwise kept from consciousness. (Similar to Freud, Rogers believed the person in therapy should become aware of unconscious feelings and ideas, and deal with them in the conscious part of the mind.) If and when this occurs, the concept of self becomes reorganized to include those experiences that in the past have been kept from consciousness. In addition, one's concept of self becomes increasingly congruent with one's experiences, and also more consistent with the self-actualizing processes.

The therapist's role is best characterized as *nondirective*. The therapist creates a permissive, nonthreatening psychological atmosphere in which the client feels accepted and feels free to explore his defenses and the incongruencies between self and experiences. If growth of the individual is to occur, it is postulated that each person must assume responsibility for her actions, decisions, and behavior. Change that is significant and enduring, Rogers postulated, must be self-initiated. Therefore, complete responsibility for the direction of treatment sessions rests with the client. A client-centered therapist does *not* bring up subjects to discuss, give advice, make interpretations, or provide suggestions. A person's self-actualization motive best knows what courses of action a person should take, and therefore the focus of client-centered therapy is to help the client gain insight into values that are inconsistent with this motive, and then to allow the self-actualizing processes to make decisions and determine future directions.

During therapy, a client-centered therapist seeks to help the client clarify personal thoughts and feelings. The following three types of statements are primarily, and continually, used in the interview.

Clarification, or Reflection of Feeling

For example, if a client begins an interview by making critical statements about his boss, his wife, and the weather, the therapist might help the client better understand what he is feeling by saying something like "you seem angry today" or "you're really upset about something today."

When client-centered therapists reflect feelings, they at times add to the reflection by expressing their own feelings at the moment, as indicated in the following excerpt (Meador & Rogers, 1979, p. 157):

Client: I think I'm beyond help.

Therapist: Huh? Feel as though you're beyond help. I know. You feel just completely hopeless about yourself. I can understand that. I don't feel hopeless, but I can realize that you do. Just feel as though nobody can help you and you're really beyond help.

The focus of a therapist in reflecting feelings is not simply to repeat the feelings expressed by the client but to reflect their intensity and meanings (that is, how the client feels) about the feelings he or she is expressing.

Restatement of Content

For example, if a wife goes on a 20-minute outburst about how her husband is not supporting the family, nor being affectionate, and is frequently coming home intoxicated, the therapist might say, "You're pretty unhappy with the way your husband is treating you and the children"—which is designed to help the wife take an overall look at her marriage. The focus of a therapist in restating content is to express to the client the therapist's view of the meanings of the content being expressed by the client.

Simple Acceptance

For example, the therapist might respond with "I see" or "M-hm" to something the client has said, with the therapist's words being said in a tone that conveys that the therapist understands and fully accepts what the client has said.

The theoretical objective of therapy is for the client to become fully functioning. A fully functioning person is a mature individual who has achieved complete congruence, and hence, is psychologically adjusted. This individual is not in a static state but is a person in process, a person who is continually changing (Rogers, 1959). Therapy frees clients of their faulty learning so they can be what they are innately meant to be. That is not to say that therapy will produce an optimally adjusted person, but the therapeutic experience can help start the development of a new pattern of adjustment.

The fully functioning person presents an ideal that Rogers believed the vast majority of people do not fully become—even with the benefit of extensive therapy. The main characteristics of a fully functioning person include the following:

1. Is open to all experiences
2. Does not use defenses to distort or deny experiences
3. Has a self-concept congruent with experiences
4. Has a locus of evaluation; that is, she or he determines what choices are best, and these decisions are based on his or her judgments of what is desirable or undesirable, rather than on what others say
5. Has unconditional positive regard for self
6. Enjoys others because of the reciprocal positive regard
7. Generally is socially effective and approved by significant others

Evaluation

Rogers can be praised for the outstanding contributions he has made in articulating the components of a therapeutic relationship. He has emphasized the importance of the following concepts in building a helping relationship: nonthreatening atmosphere, nonjudgmental attitude, empathy, genuineness, unconditional positive regard, and client as problem solver. Rogers has also developed techniques involving the therapist's responses that have facilitated the development of a constructive relationship: clarification (or reflection) of feeling, restatement of content, and simple acceptance. The relationship between the social worker and the client, partly due to Rogers's emphasis, has become

Case Example
Gloria

In 1964, Carl Rogers interviewed for 30 minutes a client named "Gloria" for a film series, *Three Approaches to Psychotherapy*. This film is available for purchase or rental (Rogers, 1965). Rogers believed this film was an excellent example of client-centered therapy. Meador and Rogers (1979, p. 180) stated: "The quality of this interview is like a piece of music, which begins on a thin persistent note and gradually adds dimension and levels until the whole orchestra is playing."

Gloria is a 30-year-old divorcee. Her presenting problem involves how she recently responded to her 9-year-old daughter, Pammy, when Pammy asked whether she had made love with any man since her divorce. She indicated to Rogers she lied by telling her daughter no. She feels guilty about this, because she feels she has always been honest with Pammy. She also wonders whether she should tell Pammy the truth—that she lied. Furthermore she wonders how she should respond in the future if Pammy again raises this question and whether the truth will affect Pammy adversely.

At the beginning of this interview Gloria asks, "I want you to tell me if it would affect her wrong if I told her the truth, or what?" On two later occasions, Gloria directly asks for Rogers's opinion to this question. On all three occasions Rogers's responses convey that he understands her dilemma, and that Rogers feels that is a question that she can best answer by herself. At one point Gloria shows her frustration in not getting an opinion by saying: "You're just going to sit there and let me stew in it, and I want more." Rogers replies, "No, I don't want to let you just stew in your feelings, but on the other hand, I also feel this is the kind of very private thing that I couldn't possibly answer for you. But I sure as anything will try to help you work toward your own answer."

Throughout the interview Rogers primarily uses the three types of statements mentioned earlier: clarification or reflection of feeling, restatement of content, and simple acceptance. In the interview, Rogers conveys empathy, positive regard, and congruence. The main focus of the interview is to help Gloria examine the dilemma of what to tell her daughter, while conveying that *she* has the resources to decide what to do, and then to carry out her decisions. After a while Gloria realizes that Rogers is not going to give his opinion or suggestions on how to handle this. She further realizes that Rogers believes she has the ability to find the answer within herself. Gloria goes on to discuss some other concerns, including the fact that she has never felt very close to her father.

Rogers is able to form a very close relationship with Gloria in this interview. Near the end Gloria says:

All of a sudden while I was talking to you, I thought, Gee, how nice I can talk to you and I want you to approve of me and I respect you, but I miss that my father couldn't talk to me like you are. I mean, I'd like to say, Gee I'd like you for my father. I don't even know why that came to me.

Rogers responds:

> You look to me like a pretty nice daughter. But you really do miss that fact that you couldn't be open with your own father.

Since the making of this film, Rogers (1984) noted that Gloria continued to write to him, once or twice a year for 15 years until her untimely death. Rogers (1984) added:

> I am awed by the fact that this fifteen-year association grew out of the quality of the relationship we formed in one thirty-minute period in which we truly met as persons. It is good to know that even one half-hour can make a difference in a life. [pp. 423–425]

---

recognized as the keystone of social work practice (Simon, 1970).

Fischer (1978) reviewed a large number of studies conducted on the three attitudes hypothesized by Rogers as being necessary and sufficient conditions for producing positive changes in clients—the three attitudes of empathy, genuineness, and positive regard or warmth. He concluded:

> The findings from these studies have been remarkably consistent. Taken together, this research strongly supports the view that the level of therapist or helper empathy, warmth, and genuineness and associated interpersonal skills is related to positive change in client personal and social functioning. Practitioners who are relatively high on these core conditions of interpersonal helping tend to be effective practitioners. These findings hold with a wide variety of types of practitioners regardless of training, background, or theoretical orientation. [Fischer, 1978, p. 207]

These findings dramatically suggest that regardless of a counselor's theoretical orientation, a successful outcome of counseling is highly dependent on conveying empathy, warmth, and genuineness!

Rogers is also to be credited for emphasizing the importance of evaluation studies. Client-centered therapy is one of the most extensively researched approaches to counseling in existence (Prochaska, 1979).

In spite of these strengths there are some limitations of client-centered therapy.

1. Eysenck (1965) reviewed outcome studies conducted on the effectiveness of contemporary psychotherapy approaches, including that of client-centered therapy. The results are not encouraging for client-centered therapy, because the studies of this approach *fail* to demonstrate that clients receiving this therapy will improve at a higher rate than control groups of people with similar problems. Although the results are complex and subject to different interpretations, studies generally show that about two-thirds of clients receiving "insight" counseling improve, which is the same rate of improvement for people with personal problems who receive no counseling. (Client-centered therapy is an "insight" approach to counseling. Insight approaches seek to increase the client's awareness and understanding of his or her problems, without focusing on ways to resolve those problems. See Chapter 23.)

Why these rather discouraging results? It

would seem that although developing a helping relationship and helping clients gain insight into their problems are an essential part of counseling, these elements do not constitute the total counseling process. As indicated in Chapter 5, clients not only need to gain an understanding of the nature and causes of their problems; they also need to be made aware that there are various courses of action that they can take to resolve the problem. Client-centered therapists do not inform clients of available resolution strategies, because they believe it is the clients' responsibility to figure this out for themselves. Many other therapists, such as Glasser (1965), have pointed out the importance of having the counselor suggest various alternatives, of helping clients explore the merits and consequences of these alternatives, and then having clients make commitments (contracts) to try one of these alternatives.

Examples of the importance of exploring alternatives are easily listed. People who are depressed may understand why they are depressed (for example, a broken romance) but may not know how to resolve the depression. A person who knows he has a drinking problem, or is addicted to narcotic drugs, or is a chain smoker, may be unaware of the various programs and approaches to resolve these addictions. A mother who is aware she is an ineffective parent may be unaware of what she can do to be more effective. A person who knows he is shy or aggressive may be uninformed about specific assertiveness training techniques that he can use to express himself more effectively. A person who has a phobia (for example, high test anxiety) knows a problem exists but is often unaware of how to resolve the fear and anxiety. Gloria, the client in the film discussed earlier, was in a dilemma about what to tell her daughter when asked if she had made love since her divorce—and was given no specific strategies for responding to such a question.

In the session with Gloria, for example, the therapist may have suggested that the next time her daughter asks if she has ever made love with another man, Gloria might respond with something like, "Let's sit and talk. I sense that you are concerned about something. Could you tell me what your concerns are?" The 9-year-old daughter could be concerned about a variety of things. She may want to ask questions about the facts of life. She may be wondering if her mother is intending to remarry soon. She may be concerned that she will have to establish a relationship with a male friend of her mother. It is hoped that such suggestions will provide a useful alternative for Gloria in handling her dilemma.

While empathy, warmth, and genuineness may well be an essential part of counseling, Prochaska (1979, p. 137) noted that Rogers "seems to have gone too far and concluded that what may be necessary conditions for therapy to proceed are also sufficient conditions for therapy to succeed."

2. Rogers claimed to be nondirective. He indicated that a therapist should not bring up topics to discuss, nor make suggestions, nor make interpretations. Rogers believed that the direction an interview takes should be the sole responsibility of the client. Truax (1966) has, however, shown that client-centered therapists in fact do subtly direct clients with nonverbal communication (for example, by showing greater interest in certain topics) and by selectively choosing which topics to respond to (for example, discouraging further communication by not saying anything when a client talks about his job, and encouraging further communication by reflecting feelings when a client talks about how she feels about her spouse).

3. Client-centered therapy does not provide much useful material on personality development, or on how emotional and behavioral problems arise. For example, the

theory does not help very much in explaining why depression, grief, and shyness occur, or why an individual may display such behavioral problems as enuresis, problem drinking, aggressive behavior, and acts of crime and violence.

4. Rogers assumed with his emphasis on therapists being "genuine" with clients, that therapists will like all their clients. (It would not be very therapeutic for a therapist to say, "You know, I really don't like you.") In reality, it is highly unlikely that a therapist will like all clients, as practically every person knows at least a few people who he or she dislikes.

5. Prochaska (1979) provided an intriguing interpretation of client-centered therapy from a learning theory perspective. He asserted that whatever positive effects occur from this therapy occur due to extinction—that is, by gradually reducing the client's concerns through having the client repeatedly talk about his or her concerns in an environment free of positive or negative consequences. Prochaska (1979) noted:

Beneath all the rhetoric, Rogers is advocating a treatment that is apparently based on a fuzzy form of extinction. Theoretically, troubled responses are assumed to have been conditioned by the contingent love and regard of parents. The therapist is supposed to reverse the process by establishing a social learning environment in which there are no contingencies, no conditions for positive regard. The client is allowed to talk on and on about troubled behavior without being reinforced or punished. Eventually the absence of contingencies leads to an extinction of talking about troubles. Of course, we cannot determine from this verbal extinction paradigm alone whether the client's troubled behavior itself has changed or whether the client has just quit talking about such problems.

But why rely on extinction when it is unnecessarily lengthy and can lead to complications such as the spontaneous recovery of the extinguished responses? Furthermore, when only extinction is used, there is no way of telling which new behaviors will be learned in place of the maladaptive responses that are being extinguished. [p. 136]

Summary

Client-centered therapy was formulated primarily by Carl Rogers. The approach postulates that every person has a self-actualization motive. The focus is to help clients become aware of incongruencies between their self-concept and their experiences. Once this insight is achieved, the self-actualizing motive fosters a reorganization of the self-concept to be more congruent with experiences. Because of this self-actualizing motive, client-centered therapists are nondirective. They do not even suggest possible resolution approaches to clients.

Client-centered therapy asserts that three therapist attitudes are necessary and sufficient conditions to effect positive changes in clients: empathy, positive regard, and genuineness or congruence. It is theorized that whenever a therapist displays these three attitudes toward a client, the actualizing potential of the client will begin to change and grow. During therapy, a client-centered therapist seeks to help the client clarify her or his thoughts and feelings by using primarily three types of statements: clarification or reflection of feeling, restatement of content, and simple acceptance.

Client-centered therapy has made outstanding contributions in identifying the components of a therapeutic relationship. A shortcoming of the approach appears to be that client-centered therapists do not suggest viable alternatives when clients are unaware of strategies to resolve their difficulties.

Exercise

Goal: This exercise is designed to help students understand the merits and short-comings of client-centered therapy.

Step 1: Before explaining client-centered therapy, ask for two volunteers to come up with a contrived problem that they jointly have (for example, a "wife" wants to become a surrogate mother, and her "husband" doesn't want her to). Ask for two students to volunteer to be counselors. Instruct the "clients" to go out in the hallway to select and develop their contrived problem. While the "clients" are out in the hallway, inform the counselors they can only use statements that clarify or reflect feelings, restate content, or convey simple acceptance. Briefly give examples of these statements. Inform the "counselors" that they should not ask questions, make interpretations, or provide suggestions. Indicate that in theory, client-centered therapists use only the three types of statements.

Step 2: Ask the "clients" to return, and have the "counselors" then counsel the "clients."

Step 3: After the counseling is completed, ask the "counselors" to discuss their feelings about being limited to these three types of statements. Ask the "clients" and the other students in class to discuss their thoughts about this type of counseling.

Step 4: Explain the principles of client-centered therapy.

15

Transactional Analysis

best-seller. The popularity of TA grew dramatically. Several other books, written by other TA authors, such as *I'm OK—You're OK* (Harris, 1969), have also become best-sellers.

Prochaska (1979) noted that Berne was an unlikely person to establish and market a new psychotherapy system. He was rather shy and lacking in the charisma that tends to characterize many leaders. However, he was highly creative, articulate, and hard working. His personal life was sacrificed for his professional life; he spent most of his time writing, doing therapy, consulting, or conducting seminars.

The founder of transactional analysis was Eric Berne (1910–1970). Like many other psychotherapy innovators, Berne was formally trained in classical psychoanalysis. He received his M.D. at McGill University in 1935 and did his psychiatric residency at Yale from 1936 to 1941. He then began his training as a psychoanalytic candidate in New York, but his training was interrupted by service in the army during World War II from 1943 to 1946. In the army he became excited about using group therapy and began moving away from the strict one-to-one format of psychoanalysis.

After the war he settled in Carmel, California, and resumed his psychoanalytic studies. In 1956 he applied for membership in the Psychoanalytic Institute. He was turned down on the basis that he was not doing orthodox analysis. Berne agreed with this reason and disassociated himself from psychoanalysis. A year later he presented his first paper on transactional analysis (TA). Although this marked the formal beginning of TA, Berne had been developing his system for several years. Beginning in the early 1950s, he formed a seminar group in Carmel in which he began presenting his emerging theory and having it critiqued by the professionals who attended.

In 1964 he published *Games People Play*, which was written primarily for professionals interested in TA. The book became a national

Eric Berne: Theory of Personality Development

Personality Structure

The basic premise of transactional analysis is that human personality is structured into three separate ego states—Parent, Adult, and Child. The definition of these ego states varies somewhat among TA authorities—this text will present Dusay and Dusay's (1979) definitions, which appear to be the most consistent and understandable. TA authorities assert that these ego states are not theoretical constructs but are actual realities that are readily identified by anyone trained in TA concepts.

The Parent ego state is basically composed of attitudes and behaviors that are copied through identification with parents and other authority figures. Although much of the Parent is learned during childhood, it can be modified throughout life as the person copies new authority figures. The Parent is the limit-setting, controlling, and rigid rule maker of the personality. It expresses one's morals, value systems, and beliefs. The Parent uses such words as *ought, should, must,* and *you'll be sorry*. Certain gestures, like pointing a finger, also characterize the Parent. The Parent's attitudes and behaviors may promote growth

Halloween is one of many occasions that encourage adults to enter the Child ego state. Here a male dressed as a female nurse and his ghoulish partner enjoy Halloween.

in others as well as being critical and controlling. The Parent may be judgmental and opinionated as well as protective and nurturing.

The *Parent* ego state has two forms: the Critical Parent and the Nurturing Parent. The *Critical Parent* is the part of one's personality that finds fault and criticizes. It also is directing and assertive; it sets rules, enforces one's value system, and stands up for one's rights. Too much Critical Parent is dictatorial. The *Nurturing Parent* is empathic, acts out of

genuine concern for others, and is warm, supportive, and protective. It usually promotes growth in others, but too much Nurturing Parent leads to overprotection, overinvolvement, and may be smothering. A classic example of a Nurturing Parent is a warm, friendly, parental, yet firm police officer.

The *Child* ego state is considered the best part of the personality, because it is the only part that can truly enjoy life. People in the Child state speak, stand, think, perceive, and feel as they did in childhood. Behavior is impulsive rather than restrained by reason. Some typical expressions include daydreaming, fantasizing, throwing temper tantrums, being irrational or irresponsible, having fun, and being creative.

The Child has two types: Free Child and Adapted Child. The *Free Child* is impulsive, creative, curious, playful, fun-loving, free, and eager. Too much Free Child leads to the person's becoming uncontrollable. The *Adapted Child* is compromising, conforming, adapting, compliant, and easy to get along with. A person with too much Adapted Child may display a variety of personal problems: being depressed, guilty, robotlike, or prone to temper tantrums.

The *Adult* ego state is factual, nonemotional, precise, nonjudgmental, and accurate. The Adult essentially acts like a computer, an unfeeling aspect of the personality that gathers and processes information for making predictions and decisions. The Adult accurately evaluates the environment and assesses the demands and emotions of the Parent and of the Child.

Each of these three ego states has adaptive functions—when used in the appropriate situation.[1] The Parent is ideally suited when control is needed, for example, in disciplining

---

[1]Berne appears to have been influenced by Freud in developing his Child, Adult, and Parent ego states. The Child has similarities to the id. The Adult has similarities to the ego. The Parent has similarities to the superego.

children. The Child is best when creative solutions to problems that appear unresolvable arise. The Child is also most adaptive for parties, celebrations, and other fun situations. The Adult is best suited for making important decisions, for example, making a career decision or deciding whether to marry. The well-adapted personality, then, switches from one ego state to another depending on the circumstances.

Harris (1969) described "a great moment in psychotherapy" involving a client in therapy, which was significant in leading Berne to conclude the existence of the Parent, Adult, and Child ego states:

> A thirty-five-year-old lawyer, whom he was treating said, "I'm not really a lawyer, I'm just a little boy." Away from the psychiatrist's office he was, in fact, a successful lawyer, but in treatment he felt and acted like a little boy. Sometimes during the hour he would ask, "Are you talking to the lawyer or to the little boy?" Both Berne and his patient became intrigued at the existence and appearance of these two real people, or states of being, and began talking about them as "the adult" and "the child." Treatment centered around separating the two. Later another state began to become apparent as a state distinct from "adult" and "child." This was "the parent" and was identified by behavior which was a reproduction of what the patient saw and heard his parents do when he was a little boy. [p. 39]

Psychosocial Drives

While ego states provide the structure of the personality, the motivation for behavior comes from fulfilling basic human needs (food, shelter, sex) and from psychosocial drives. Berne (1966) identified the following psychosocial drives: stimulus hunger, recognition hunger, structure hunger, and excitement hunger.

Stimulus hunger is the need to be stimulated. Stimulus deprivation studies have demonstrated that human beings will become highly disturbed when they are deprived of adequate amounts of physical stimulation (Hebb et al., 1961; Solomon et al., 1961; Spitz, 1945). One of the most important forms of stimulation is by receiving "strokes." The basic motivating force for all human social behavior is one's lifelong hunger for human recognition, which TA terms as seeking "strokes." In young children Spitz (1945) demonstrated that stroking needs to be in the form of direct physical contact that comes from being cuddled, held, and soothed. Without such direct physical contact, the emotional and physical development of children will be severely stunted.

Although direct physical contact is the most nourishing form of stimulation, adults generally are able to fulfill their *recognition hunger* by being recognized or attended to by others. Positive recognition through such strokes as greetings, smiles, approval, cheers, and applause is highly valued. However, if such strokes are not received, negative strokes are then sought, because they are considered better than no strokes. Such negative strokes include cold looks, disapproval, criticism, and frowns. Dusay and Dusay (1979, p. 388) noted, "Habitual criminals with high recidivism rates illustrate that negative strokes are better than no strokes at all." This principle is also illustrated by those battered women who choose to continue to live with their abusive husbands rather than living alone and receiving no strokes. As can be seen by this discussion, stimulus hunger is closely related to recognition hunger. Stimulus hunger is a broader term that encompasses recognition hunger. It is possible to receive stimulation from the environment (for example, being caught in a thunderstorm) that is not a form of recognition.

Structural hunger is the need to structure time, and develops out of the dilemma of what to do with 24 hours a day, 168 hours per week, 8,736 hours per year. This dilemma is heightened in societies such as ours in which people have surplus time. Preferred ways of structuring times are those that are most exciting.

Excitement hunger is the desire to avoid boredom and to have interesting and exciting things to do. Among the most interesting ways of structuring time are those involved in getting strokes from others and those involved in exchanging strokes with others.

Types of Transactions

A transaction is a unit of social intercourse. A transaction is composed of a transactional stimulus (verbal and nonverbal messages sent by one individual) and a transactional response (verbal and nonverbal messages by another individual who is reacting to a transactional stimulus). The following is an example of a transaction:

Husband: What are we going to have for dinner tonight?
Wife: I don't know—whatever you'd like to make.

Structure hunger, excitement hunger, and recognition hunger motivate humans to participate in transactions. TA identifies five types of transactions:

1. *Ritual:* The safest form of interaction is a ritual, which is a stereotyped transaction programmed by external social forces. Informal rituals include greetings such as "Hi, how are you?" "Fine, thank you." Examples of formal rituals include weddings and funerals, which are highly structured and predictable. Rituals are basically signs of mutual recognition and convey very little information.

2. *Activity:* Activities structure time. Common activities include studying for exams, doing the dishes, mowing the lawn, building a house, and doing projects at work. Activities may be satisfying in and of themselves or they may lead to satisfactions in the future through receiving strokes. During the time of the activity there may, or may not be, involvement with another person. Some people use their work activity to

avoid intimate involvement with others. (Critics of TA have questioned whether activities are transactions.)

3. *Pastime:* Pastimes are semiritualistic and are usually shared with people who have mutual interests—for example, a softball team, ham radio operators, poker players. Pastimes allow people to structure their time in fairly interesting ways but are also structured to minimize the possibility of incidents that are threatening or too emotional. Small talk at social gatherings is a typical example of a pastime.

4. *Intimacy:* Interactions that are entirely spontaneous and direct are intimate transactions. Such transactions may be exciting but also may be threatening and overwhelming. Such free and unstructured exchanges are generally avoided in favor of some structured and safer interactions.

5. *Game:* A game is a set of transactions with a gimmick (that is, a hidden scheme for attaining an end). In a game one or more participants are consciously or unconsciously striving to achieve an ulterior outcome by using a hidden scheme.

There are two levels of communication involved in games: social and psychological. The social level is the overt or manifest; the psychological level is the covert or latent.

Prochaska (1979) gave an example of these two levels of communication in a game:

For example, if a woman asks a man, "Why don't you come by my place to see my collection of sculpture?" and the man responds "I'd love to. I'm really interested in art," they may be having a simple, candid interchange between two adults beginning to share a pastime. In a game, however, both players are also communicating a message at a different level, such as Child-to-Child messages like "Boy, I'd really like to get you alone in my apartment" and "I'd sure love to look at your curves." [pp. 237–238]

This game is diagrammed in Figure 15.1.

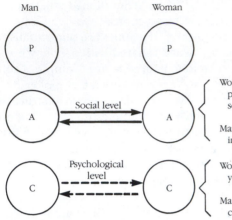

Woman: "Why don't you come by my place to see my collection of sculpture?"

Man: "I'd love to. I'm really interested in art."

Woman: "I'd really like to get you alone in my apartment."

Man: "I'd sure love to look at your curves."

P = Parent ego state
A = Adult ego state
C = Child ego state

Figure 15.1
A game diagram

For a game to progress, at least one of the participants has to pull a switch, as further described in Prochaska's (1979) example:

> For the payoff to occur, one of the players has to pull a switch. In this case, after fixing drinks and sitting close on the couch examining a reproduction of Rodin's *The Kiss,* the woman still seems to be sending a seductive communication. The man's vanity convinces him to proceed, and he puts his hand on her leg, only to be rebuffed by a slap on the face and an irate "What kind of a woman do you think I am?"
>
> The couple has just completed a heavy hand of RAPO.[2] Besides gaining mutual recognition, excitement, and some structured time together, there is also a strong emotional payoff for each. The woman is able to proudly affirm her position in life that she is OK, while feeling angry toward men for not being OK, just as her mother

always said. The payoff for the man is to feel depressed and thereby reaffirm his conviction that he is not OK. [p. 238]

People who are attempting to achieve a hidden outcome may or may not be aware of their intentions—or aware of the gimmick they are using. For instance, a husband who has a vague fear his wife may desert him may not be aware he is playing a game when he says to her, "Honey, why don't you quit work and stay home to take care of the house? I can earn enough to support both of us."

Although some games may lead to substantial financial loss or mental anguish for some participants, not all games are necessarily undesirable. For instance, an individual having a strong need for social approval may perform many "altruistic" and "charitable" deeds.

A game may also be repeated over and over. A few people, for instance, continually play "One Up." For some, playing a certain game may become so much a part of their personality that it can aptly be called their

[2]Berne (1964) defined RAPO as being "Kiss Off" or "indignation."

style of life. A male alcoholic who denies to himself and to others he has a drinking problem is an example of this. (The alcoholic's payoffs for denying his drinking problem are the rewards he receives from drinking—such as feeling high and a way to temporarily escape facing his problems.)

The "alcoholic" game also illustrates another aspect of games—several people may be involved. In the traditional alcoholic game described by Berne (1964), there may be a nagging, masochistic wife who literally drives her husband to drink so he will abuse her when inebriated. This wife receives two sets of payoffs. The abuse is a form of recognition or attention. The second reward the wife receives is that the day after a drunken episode the wife has ammunition to belittle and berate her husband and to get him to do things for her to atone for his behavior. The alcoholic is also apt to have companions who frequently invite him to "Let's go have a drink—a drink will be good for you." Their payoff is the fun and partying they have. Then there may also be a sympathetic listener to the alcoholic—perhaps a bartender who listens in order to get the alcoholic to spend his money.

Some people are involved in playing games that have destructive outcomes for themselves and for others. Often, people are unaware a destructive game is being played. For example, family members of an alcoholic may make elaborate efforts to keep the drinking problem hidden from others without realizing they are continuing to make it possible for the alcoholic to drink.

Common Games

Eric Berne listed a large number of psychological games in *Games People Play* (1964). People tend to have a repertoire of favorite games, and many base their social relationships on finding suitable partners to play the corresponding opposite roles. The following are common games.

In the game "Why Don't You? Yes, But . . . ," a person consistently asks for suggestions or advice and then consistently rejects any that are offered. The other participants in this game assume that the principal player is attempting to solve a real problem in a concrete manner so they offer suggestions. The principal player in this game is able to get at least two payoffs—one is attention from other people and the other is a payoff that comes from being able to put others down by implying "That's really a dumb suggestion." The other participants may get a payoff through telling themselves "I must be a warm, caring person, because this person respects and trusts me enough to share this problem with me."

In the "One Up" game, one person seeks to top whatever someone else says. If the conversation is about big fish, the One Upper always has a story about how he caught this mammoth fish. If the topic is about bad grades received, the One Upper seeks to amaze everyone with how bad her grades are. If jokes are being told, the One Upper begins by saying, "I've got one that'll top that. Have you heard about . . ."

"Wooden Leg" is a game in which people attempt to manipulate others to not expect too much from them because of such wooden legs as having a disability, being raised in a ghetto, having had a tragic romance, and having emotional problems such as being depressed. Closely related, "If it weren't for . . ." is a cop-out game in which players seek to rationalize not succeeding at a variety of tasks and goals.

A person who plays "Poor Me" is seeking sympathy and may at times try to get others to do things for him. Closely related is someone who plays "Ain't It Awful" by taking a negative view of events. Such a person is usually seeking attention and sympathy. In "There I Go Again," the player seeks to excuse away her ineffective behavior without taking responsibility.

Some clients enjoy playing "Confession" when they seek to tell all their personal and interpersonal troubles in the hopes of receiving recognition and help from others. Some unhappily married men get together and enjoy discussing "Wives Are a Pain" as a way of ventilating their unhappiness. Some unhappily married wives enjoy discussing "Men Aren't Worth It" as a way of ventilating their frustrations. Parents enjoy discussing "Look How Hard I've Tried" when a home situation is particularly uproarious and hostile as a way to relieve their frustrations that the goals for their family have not been achieved. Many people seek to avoid assuming responsibility for their failures and shortcomings by playing "It's All Them."

Some individuals who have received few positive strokes end up seeking a lot of negative strokes, which to them is better than receiving no strokes. One game that is played to receive negative strokes is "Kick Me," in which the player seeks to do things that elicit negative reactions from others.

People who enjoy creating trouble for others are apt to play "Let's You and Him Fight."

People who receive psychological rewards in analyzing others and in giving advice often play "Psychiatry." A person who seeks to see how many different sexual relationships he can have often seeks to play "Love 'Em and Leave 'Em." Men are socialized in our society to play "Mr. Macho" and women are socialized to play "Miss America."

"Monday Morning Quarterbacks" seek to make themselves feel important by telling you what you should have done differently *after* things have not turned out well for you.

The number of different games that can be played is best described as infinite.

Life Scripts

Every person has life scripts (plans) that are formed during childhood and are based on early beliefs about oneself and others. These plans are developed from early interactions with parents and others and are largely determined by the pattern of strokes that are received.

Scripts (as in a play in a theater) are plans we learn and then carry around in our heads.

These scripts enable us to conceptualize where we are in our activities and are plans for directing what we need to do to complete our activities and to accomplish our goals. Scripts are also devices for helping us remember what we have done in the past.

Many details of a life script are supplied by parental opinions, suggestions, and encouragements. Examples include: "She's such a cute girl, everyone loves her," "He's stupid and will never amount to much," "She'll be famous some day," "He's sure nutty," "All the girls will want to date him." Fairy tales, myths, TV shows, early life experiences, and children's stories are also important sources of life scripts. Although parental influences and fairy tales are important contributing factors, the life script is still the creation of a young child. One's life script may be either winning or losing, being a success or a failure, exciting or banal. Each script also includes specific roles, such as heroes and heroines, villains, persecutors, innocent bystanders, and victims.

Harris (1969) identified four general life scripts that a person chooses based on how a person views herself in comparison with others. These four positions are (1) I'm OK—You're OK; (2) I'm OK—You're not OK; (3) I'm not OK—You're OK; and (4) I'm not OK—You're not OK.

People who decide "I'm OK—You're OK" tend to be productive, law-abiding people who are successful and who have positive, meaningful relationships with others.

People who decide "I'm OK—You're not OK" predispose themselves to exploit, cheat, and rob others or succeed at the expense of others. This type of person may be a criminal, a ruthless business executive, or a destructive lover who loves them and leaves them.

People who decide "I'm not OK—You're OK" feel inferior in the presence of those they judge as superior. Such a life script frequently leads to withdrawal from others to avoid being reminded of not being OK. Withdrawal is not the only alternative. The person can write a counterscript based on lines borrowed from

Popular culture often reinforces traditional sex role expectations. In the situation comedy *Leave It to Beaver*, June Cleaver was the perfect wife and mother—domestic, conforming, and in the end forever deferring to her husband Ward, whose highly moral, fatherly lectures always seemed to rescue the Beaver in the nick of time.

early authority figures: "You can be OK if . . ." The person is then driven to achieve the "if" contingencies—for example, making huge sums of money, being submissive, being entertaining by making others laugh, and so on. Such a person then strives to meet these contingencies in order to receive strokes and approval from others.

People who decide "I'm not OK—You're not OK" tend to be the most unhappy and disturbed. Prochaska (1979) stated:

The extreme withdrawal of schizophrenia or psychotic depression is their most common fate. They may regress to an infantile

state in the primitive hope that they may once again receive the strokes of being held and fed. Without intervention from caring others, these individuals will live out a self-destructive life of institutionalization, irreversible alcoholism, senseless homicide, or suicide. [p. 241]

Decisions about life scripts are generally made early in childhood. James and Jongeward (1971) provide an incident in the life of a 43-year-old client that led her to conclude "I'm not OK and men are not OK either."

My father was a brutal alcoholic. When he was drunk he would hit me and scream at me. I would try to hide. One day when he came home, the door flew open and he was drunker than usual. He picked up a butcher knife and started running through the house. I hid in a coat closet. I was almost four years old. I was so scared in the closet. It was dark and spooky, and things kept hitting me in the face. That day I decided who men were—beasts, who would only try to hurt me. I was a large child and I remember thinking, "If I were smaller, he'd love me" or "If I were prettier, he'd love me." I always thought I wasn't worth anything. [p. 35]

Based on this script, she married an alcoholic at age 23, and for the next 20 years had been living her life drama of feeling worthless and living with a "beast."

One of the areas where our behavior is largely guided by scripts is sexual behavior. Sexual scripts result from elaborate prior learning in which we acquire an etiquette of sexual behavior. Scripts tell us who are appropriate sexual partners, what sexual activity is expected, where and when the sexual activity should occur, and what should be the sequence of the different sexual behaviors.

Scripts vary greatly from one culture to another. Powdermaker (1933) provided the following description of a script about female masturbation generally held by the Lesu of the South Pacific.

A woman will masturbate if she is sexually excited and there is no man to satisfy her. A couple may be having intercourse in the same house, or near enough for her to see them, and she may thus become aroused. She then sits down and bends her right leg so that her heel presses against her genitalia. Even young girls of about six years may do this quite casually as they sit on the ground. The women and men talk about it freely, and there is no shame attached to it. It is a customary position for women to take, and they learn it in childhood. They never use their hands for manipulation. [p. 241]

A life script and a theatrical script have many similarities. Each has a cast of characters, dialogue, themes and plots, acts and scenes; generally both move toward a climax. Often, however, a person is unaware or only vaguely aware of the life scripts he or she is acting out. Public stages on which people act out their scripts include home, social gatherings, church, school, office, and factory. As Shakespeare noted, "All the world's a stage."

Most life scripts are learned at an early age. As children grow they learn to play roles—villains, law enforcers, heroes, heroines, victims, and rescuers—and seek others to play complementary roles. Through playing roles, children integrate new themes and parts into their roles and gradually develop their life scripts. The particular scripts that are developed are substantially influenced by the reactions they receive from significant people in their lives.

Individuals follow scripts, and so do families and cultures. Cultural scripts are expected patterns of behavior within a society. In our culture, for example, only men are expected to fight in military conflict whereas in Israel both sexes are expected to fight wars. In regard to cultural scripts, James and Jongeward (1971) noted:

Script themes differ from one culture to another. The script can contain themes of

suffering, persecution, and hardship (historically the Jews); it can contain themes of building empires and making conquests (as the Romans once did). Throughout history some nations have acted from a "top-dog" position of the conqueror; some from an "under-dog" position of the conquered. In early America, where people came to escape oppression, to exploit the situation, and to explore the unknown, a basic theme was "struggling for survival." In many cases this struggle was acted out by pioneering and settling. [p. 70]

Historically, women are socialized in our society to have life scripts different from those of men. American women traditionally are expected to be affectionate, passive, conforming, sensitive, intuitive, dependent, and "sugar and spice and everything nice." They are supposed to be concerned primarily with domestic life, to be nurturing, to instinctively love to care for babies and young children, to be deeply concerned about their personal appearance, and to be self-sacrificing for their family. They should not appear to be ambitious, aggressive, competitive, or more intelligent than men. They are expected to be ignorant and uninterested in sports, economics, or politics. In relationships with men they should not initiate forming a relationship and are expected to be tender, feminine, emotional, and appreciative.

There are also a number of traditional sex-role expectations for males in our society. A male is expected to be tough, fearless, logical, self-reliant, independent, and aggressive. He should have definite opinions on the major issues of the day, and is expected to make authoritative decisions at work and at home. He is expected to be strong, to be a sturdy oak, never to be depressed, vulnerable, or anxious. He is not supposed to be "sissy" or feminine. He is expected not to cry or openly display so-called feminine emotions. He is expected to be the provider, the breadwinner, to be competent in all situations. He is supposed to be physically strong, self-reliant, athletic; to have a manly air of confidence and toughness; to be daring and aggressive; to be brave and forceful; always to be in a position to dominate any situation; to be a Clint Eastwood. He is supposed to initiate relationships with women and is expected to be dominant in relationships with them. (The women's movement has now made changes in these sex-role scripts.)

In our society (as well as in other large and complex societies) there are a number of subcultures, and each subculture has its own scripts. Street gangs, Chicanos, Texans, Presbyterians, Jews, professional baseball players, dentists, farmers, and college students each have their own subcultural scripts. For example, common aspects of scripts for college students include cramming at the last moment for exams, procrastination, partying, idealism, shortage of money, and expectation of success and happiness following graduation.

Families also have scripts. These scripts provide a set of directions for family members. Examples include the following:

We Winships have always been pillars of the community.
We Navarres have always been rowdy.
The men in our family have always held political offices in our community and the women have always been active in the church.
We Hubbards have always been in trouble with the police.
We Schomakers have always been gamblers.
We Collinses have always taken a long vacation each year.
We Hepps have never had to ask for a handout from anyone.
We Watsons have all gone to college.
We Rices have always been Democrats.
The men in our family have all been coal miners who are active in union activities.

If a family member does not live up to the script expectation, he or she is often viewed as a "deviant" or as a "black sheep."

Berne (1966) emphasized the importance of scripts in determining human behavior:

Nearly all human activity is programmed by an ongoing script dating from early childhood, so that the feeling of autonomy is nearly always an illusion—an illusion which is the greatest affliction of the human race because it makes awareness, honesty, creativity, and intimacy possible for only a few fortunate individuals. For the rest of humanity, other people are seen mainly as objects to be manipulated. They must be invited, persuaded, seduced, bribed or forced into playing the proper roles to reinforce the protagonist's position and fulfill his script. [p. 310]

The number of script themes is infinite. A few of the more common themes are the following:

I must be loved by everyone.
I've got to be perfect.
I've got to be the best at what I do.
My purpose in life is to save sinners.
When people tell me their problems, I have to rescue them.
I will take my life some day.
To be noticed I must play tricks on people.
People will only love me if I make them laugh.
I'll also be a victim.
I'm a martyr.
I can always get what I want by being pushy.
I'll eventually go crazy.
My life will always be one big party.
I'm cut out to be a leader.
I'm a failure and always will be.
I'll never get anywhere.
I've got to save for a rainy day.
If I acquire a lot of money, I'll be popular.
I'm always the life of a party.

I'm always miserable.

Life has always shortchanged me.

I should always be silent; it is wrong to
rock the boat.

Men are assholes.

I will never let anyone get the best of me.

I'm headed for fame and fortune.

James and Jongeward (1971) provided the following example of how a life script is played:

A woman who had taken the position, "Men are bums," marries a sequence of "bums." Part of her script is based on "Men are not OK." She fulfills her own prophecy by nagging, pushing, complaining, and generally making life miserable for her husband (who has his part to play). Eventually, she manipulates him into leaving. Then she can say, "See, I told you. Men are bums who leave you when the going gets rough." [pp. 84–85]

Often people play games as part of their life scripts. A person who has a script of being a Casanova plays the game "Love 'em and leave 'em." A person who has a script of "I won't let anyone get the best of me" is apt to play "One-Up." A person who has a script of being an adviser to others is apt to play "Monday Morning Quarterback." A person who has a script of "I'll always find a way to seduce people into helping me" is apt to play "Poor Me."

Theory of Psychopathology

According to transactional analysis, personal problems involve either problems within the personality or between personalities, or both.

Intrapsychic problems may result from several sources. One source that has already been described is having a self-defeating life script, such as "I'm a failure" or "I'm not OK and neither are you."

Another intrapsychic problem is rigidly holding to one ego state and shutting out the other two. As indicated earlier, having a balance of the three ego states is healthy. A "workaholic" spends too much time in the Adult ego state and thereby is unable to enjoy his or her family and to have fun. I've known athletes (jocks) who have spent their years in college playing games and partying, giving little attention to anything else. When their four years of eligibility for athletic competition were gone, they were far from graduating and untrained for any skilled employment. During their college years, they had been in their "Child" state at the expense of the other two states. I've also known people who were too much "Parent" in romantic relationships by constantly giving advice and by smothering the other person by trying to do things for, rather than with, the other person.

Another intrapsychic problem is being in an inappropriate ego state for what the circumstances warrant—for example, clowning around (being in the Child) when one should be studying for an exam or completing an urgent project at work.

TA has a unique approach to describing and understanding interpersonal problems. It focuses attention on how different individuals tend to communicate (both verbally and nonverbally) with one another. There are three rules of communication.

The first rule of communication is "Communication will proceed smoothly as long as transactions are *complementary*." Complementary transactions are those in which the arrows are parallel (see Figure 15.2).

The second rule of communication is "Communication on the specific topic ceases immediately whenever a crossed transaction occurs." A *crossed transaction* is one in which the arrows are not parallel, as illustrated in Figure 15.3.

The third rule of communication applies to *psychological games*. The rule is "Behavior cannot be predicted by attention to the social

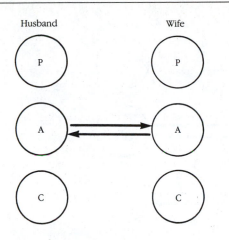

Husband: "Do you know where my cuff
  links are?"
Wife: "Yes, they're in my jewelry box."

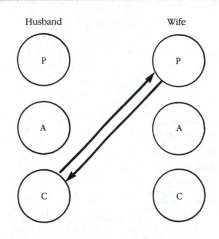

Husband: "I feel terrible today. Could you
  call the office and tell them I can't make it,
  and also get me two aspirin."
Wife: "I surely will. You just stay in bed. I'll
  call in sick also so that I can get whatever
  you need today."

Figure 15.2
Two examples of complementary transactions

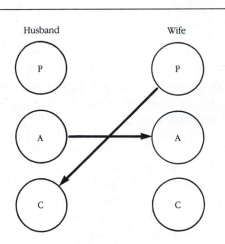

Husband: "Do you know where my cuff
  links are?"
Wife: "When are you ever going to learn
  to take care of your things—you lose
  everything."

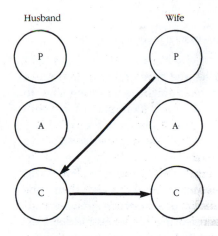

Husband: "Let's call in sick to work today,
  and go fishing."
Wife: "You're so irresponsible. You know it
  isn't right to do that."

Figure 15.3
Two examples of crossed transactions

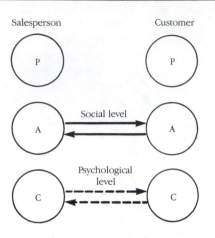

Social level

Salesperson: "This is a better product, but I don't think you can afford it."

Customer: "I'll take it!"

Psychological level

Salesperson: "I'll motivate this person to buy the expensive item."

Customer: "I'll show this salesperson I'm as good as anyone else."

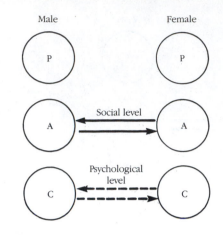

Social level

Male: "That dress really looks attractive on you."

Female: "Well, thank you. I like people who notice positive things about me."

Psychological level

Male: "If I say something nice, maybe I'll find out if she's interested in getting something going between us."

Female: "This fellow appears interested in me, and I'll indirectly indicate that I'm interested in him."

Figure 15.4

Two examples of psychological games

message alone; the psychological message is key to understanding the meaning and to predicting behavior." Examples of psychological games are presented in Figure 15.4.

Psychological games may be constructive or destructive. If the payoffs in games help people, then they are constructive. For example, people who volunteer to give their time and resources at social services agencies usually are volunteering for some hidden personal reasons and usually receive such payoffs as feeling worthwhile and good about themselves. In some cases boredom and loneliness are also curbed. At the same time such volunteers perform useful services for others. Other games, because of the payoff, tend to be undesirable. Some people continually play "One-Upmanship," where they are overly competitive, even to the point of continually disparaging others and trying to stop every story that others tell them.

Theory of Therapy

Simply stated, therapy seeks to have clients first become aware of the intrapsychic and/or interpersonal problems they face. In the process of helping clients gain insight into their problems, clients are educated in using the terms of TA. This instruction occurs in therapy (either one-to-one or in groups) and by giving clients reading such as *Games People Play* (Berne, 1964), *I'm OK—You're OK* (Harris, 1969), and *Born to Win* (James & Jongeward, 1971). Early in this instructional process, clients are taught *structural analysis*; that is, how to identify their Parent, Adult, and Child ego states. They also learn how to analyze problematic transactions through diagramming the transactions, and they learn the concepts of analyzing games and life scripts. If TA classes are offered in the client's community, clients may be urged to take a course in TA before or during therapy. As clients become educated in the TA approach and more aware of their own ego states, they often are able to teach others how to analyze themselves. Prochaska (1979, p. 243) stated: "The client's work is usually a pattern of going from student to self-analyzer to teacher of others."

To encourage clients to analyze their communications in terms of the TA format, the therapist frequently asks, "Which ego state is talking now?" If clients are confused or disagree with the therapist's or group's analysis of their ego states, the therapist may audiotape or videotape the clients' interactions and then play the tape back to let them see and hear how they are interacting.

Clients' problems are then analyzed in terms of TA concepts so clients gain insight into their personal problems. Such problems include those discussed in the prior section: being in an appropriate ego state for the situation, playing destructive games, having a destructive life script, and interpersonal difficulties created by crossed transactions. Much of the therapist's work is helping clients to become aware, often through confronting them, of the ways in which they are contributing to their intrapsychic and interpersonal problems. For example, clients may be confronted with how they are playing certain destructive games, including demonstrating the payoffs in such games.

Game Analysis

Two treatment techniques that are increasingly being used in transactional analysis are game analysis and script analysis. *Game analysis* is a treatment technique in which a thera-pist enables a client to gain insight into some of his or her interactions through the use of game concepts. Game analysis focuses on those kinds of games that lead to undesirable outcomes for the client or for others.

The therapist has several roles in analyzing games: (1) Teach clients the terminology of game analysis. This perhaps can best be accomplished at the first occasion in which a therapist helps a client gain insight into a game. (2) Point out to the clients that playing games is not necessarily undesirable. This may be therapeutically valuable; some clients may feel it is wrong to play games because games have an exploitative connotation. This feeling may cause resistances to examining games. These resistances may be reduced by informing clients that everyone plays games; some games have beneficial outcomes while others have undesirable outcomes. (3) Help clients recognize those games that are destructive for them or for other players, and also enable them to gain insight into how these games are being played. (4) Encourage clients to explore new ways of responding after they are aware of how their role in a game leads to undesirable consequences. (5) Help clients specifically assign names to those undesirable games they are playing. Using colloquial names for games is often acceptable and advantageous, because they may be more precise and have more meaning for clients. (6) Teach people the kind of games they need to play to achieve their goals. Some people have goals considered beneficial for themselves and society but do not know what they have to do to achieve these goals. Often such people can be instructed on what to do, using game concepts. For example, a person seeking a job may need to learn how to play "How to Get an Interview" and "How to Sell Yourself in an Interview." Or, a couple who is frequently feuding may need to learn "How to Fight Fairly" and "How to Give in a Relationship to Get What You Want."

Game analysis appears to be a useful therapeutic approach for three reasons: (1) One of the important functional values of naming something (in this case a certain kind of game) is that it increases clients' capacities to recognize similar transactions when they occur in the future. Once clients recognize and have insight into a game that is causing them difficulty, they are in a better position to cease their destructive behavior and to explore alternative modes of behavior. (2) Analyzing behavior in terms of games is apt to intrigue clients and, therefore, may lead to greater personal involvement in therapy and increase their motivation to resolve their difficulties. (3) Game analysis provides clients with a method of analyzing certain problematic interactions. After learning how to analyze such interactions, clients should be better able to analyze other problematic games beyond those specifically discussed in counseling.

Script Analysis

Script analysis can be defined as a treatment technique in which a therapist enables clients to gain insight into the scripts they are acting out through the use of script concepts. The types of scripts that are the primary focus of script analysis are those that lead to undesirable outcomes for clients or for others.

The therapist has the following role in analyzing scripts: (1) Teach clients the terminology of script analysis. (2) Point out to clients that everyone is playing a variety of scripts, and that scripts largely determine human behavior. Indicate that some scripts have beneficial outcomes while others have undesirable outcomes. (3) Help clients recognize those scripts that have undesirable outcomes. (4) Help clients assign names to the scripts they are playing, so they can be more readily identified when they are acted out in the future. (5) Help clients develop new, desirable scripts to act out, and encourage and teach clients more effective ways of responding.

Within transactional analysis, game analysis and script analysis can be used with fami-

lies and with small-sized groups as well as with individuals.

TA therapists emphasize personal responsibility. They believe, as does Ellis (1962), that clients are responsible for their emotions, their thoughts, and their behaviors (this concept will be more fully described in Chapter 22). If a client says "I can't think today," the TA therapist will confront him with "You mean you have decided not to think today." Or, if a client says "She makes me feel bad," the TA therapist will say "You know that you are choosing to feel bad—in response to her." Or, if a client says "He made me steal," the therapist will say "You mean you chose to steal."

After clients become aware of their personal problems and how they are contributing to their problems, various courses of action to resolve the problems are explored. Each client then usually makes a contract specifying what the client will do (and perhaps also what the therapist will do) to attempt to resolve the problem. A workaholic, for example, might make a contract limiting the number of hours per day she will spend on work and also be given homework assignments to become involved in fun activities (for example, joining a social group, going to movies, gardening).

The types of TA therapy may differ widely. Berne originally used TA as an adjunct to psychoanalysis. TA has also been combined with reality therapy and rational therapy. Other TA therapists restrict their practice to the TA approach. Transactional analysis is used individually, with groups, with families, with couples, in marathons, in prison, in outpatient and inpatient wards, and in business and industry settings.

In group therapy a variety of techniques may be used to help clients gain an awareness of their destructive transactions. One approach in game analysis involves psychodrama, which was originally developed by Moreno (1946). Dusay and Dusay (1979) described using psychodrama by having the cli-

Case Example
Game analysis and script analysis

James and Jongeward (1971) indicated that three common life scripts or roles are Persecutor, Victim, and Rescuer. Often a person will play a variety of games in conjunction with one of these life scripts. A person who plays a Victim role may also be persecuting those around her or him, and occasionally may shift directly to the Persecutor role. James and Jongeward (1971) provided the following example showing how transactions between a married couple can be analyzed in terms of games and life script concerns:

Ted and Mary came into counseling complaining about the failure of their second honeymoon. Each claimed to have been victimized by the other. He shouted, "You had the gall to take your mother along. She even shared our motel room." She retorted, "And you were very rude and embarrassed me." After a number of hostile exchanges, they were asked to tell about their first honeymoon. Ted challenged, "What does that have to do with us now?" Mary retorted, "I'll tell you what. You took your parents along on our honeymoon fifteen years ago. You said, 'They never get a chance to go anywhere.' You've been taking advantage of me ever since." [p. 89]

Mary had assumed the role of victim all these years. She had played the games of "Poor Me" and "See How Hard I Tried," and finally got even by assuming the role of Persecutor herself. Her favorite game became "Now I've Got You, You S.O.B." For 15 years the theme of their marriage drama had been "Getting Even."

---

ent play the director. In this role the client-director instructs other group members in how he or she is playing a destructive game. Dusay and Dusay (1979) noted:

By using this type of psychodrama, the client is able to step outside of his own game system; in this view he can view, think and direct his own part in the game. . . . Through these maneuvers, the client will gain a new awareness and experiment with corrective procedures. [p. 403]

Psychodrama is further described in Chapter 20.

Evaluation
Transactional analysis has grown remarkably in acceptance and popularity since its formu-

lation by Eric Berne in the 1950s. Dusay and Dusay (1989) provided reasons for its popularity:

Because of its easily understood vocabulary and because of the willingness of therapists to share ideas with clients, TA rapidly became a popular psychotherapy. As such, TA has been used not only by psychiatrists, psychologists, social workers, and other traditional therapists, but also by paraprofessionals who found that the theoretical aspects of TA were easy to learn and had direct applicability to their concerns. Indeed, street workers and prison inmates have become outstanding TA therapists. Effort for the TA therapist is in practical applications rather than in decoding mystical jargon. [p. 448]

The popularity of such books as *Games People Play* (Berne, 1964), *Scripts People Live* (Steiner, 1974), and *I'm OK—You're OK* (Harris, 1969) suggests that readers find such concepts as the following helpful in resolving personal problems: game analysis, life script analysis, complementary transactions and crossed transactions, seeking strokes, and personal responsibility for emotions and actions.

Another positive feature of TA is to borrow techniques (such as psychodrama) from other therapy approaches that are useful in producing therapeutic change. Transactional analysis is an "open" therapeutic approach that actively encourages experimentation with new techniques.

In contrast to most other therapy approaches, TA is perhaps more enjoyable to participate in for both clients and therapists. The approach uses a number of experimental exercises, such as role playing. In addition, analyzing personal problems in terms of games and life scripts has a game mystique that facilitates interest.

However, some criticisms can also be made:

1. There have been very few studies on the outcome of transactional analysis. In a review of TA, Merkel (1975) was able to locate only two studies and the results were inconclusive regarding whether TA is effective. Prochaska (1979) was quite critical of the lack of outcome research:

> Twenty years after TA was first practiced, it has yet to be evaluated for its clinical effectiveness. The best evidence that Holland could provide in 1973 was that Berne's patients had traveled further to get to therapy than did the patients of any other therapist in the Carmel area, an average of twelve miles. What a terrific criterion for the effectiveness of a therapy! [p. 258]

In a review of research conducted on TA, Dusay and Dusay (1989, pp. 438–439) cite only a few outcome studies—none of which provides convincing evidence that TA is effective.

2. The concepts of TA explain some aspects of human behavior but certainly not all. For example, what causes grief, depression, anger, love, happiness, and other emotions? How are such emotions perpetuated? What causes burglaries, alcoholism, crimes of violence, or such positive action as helping others in need? Game analysis and script analysis may provide some of the reasons but not all of them.

3. There is a danger in analyzing the personality into the three separate ego states of Parent, Adult, and Child. Most authorities on human behavior emphasize the importance of the personality's functioning as an integrated "whole." The danger of a tripartite personality approach is that it may encourage clients to function in separate roles as a Parent, Adult, and Child rather than as an integrated individual. For example, TA indicates the Adult ego state is best suited for work activities. But being a rational computer at work will lead a person to miss out on the "fun" activities at work and probably lead to ostracism by fellow employees who will find an Adult to be boring, especially during slack times. Even when things are hectic, humor is often useful in relieving some of the tension.

4. I have participated in some transactional groups and have found it difficult at times to determine which ego state a transaction is coming from. I have asked leaders of groups to identify the ego state producing certain communications and have gotten different answers. For example, I've asked, "If a male student intern in field placement decides to greet his first client as his father greets a stranger, and the father is very effective in interacting with people, which ego state is such a transaction coming from?" TA group leaders have given me three different answers: Parent, Adult, and Child. My concern is that the counseling process can get bogged down in a long, fruitless discussion of which ego state is the source

of a transaction rather than focusing on exploring and resolving clients' personal problems.

In raising this concern I am aware that Thompson (1972) found in a study that ego states are observable, that trained TA experts have a high degree of agreement in rating which ego state is in operation in a given client, and that naive observers can be trained to correctly identify ego states (Thompson is an advocate of TA).

Part of my concern results from the observation that there are *substantial* differences among TA authorities in defining the PAC ego states. Berne (1964) stated the Parent ego state has two forms—Direct Parent and Indirect Parent—while the Child has two forms—Adapted Child and Natural Child. Dusay and Dusay (1979) stated that the Parent ego state has two forms— the Critical parent and the Nurturing Parent— while the Child's two forms are Adapted Child and Free Child. James and Jongeward (1971) stated the two Parent forms are the Nurturing Parent and the Prejudicial Parent, while the Child ego state has three forms— Natural Child, Adapted Child, and Little Professor.

Whereas Berne (1964) divided the PAC ego states into five different forms (Direct Parent, Indirect Parent, Adapted Child, Natural Child, Adult), Steiner (1974) divided the PAC states into 27 forms!

I also find the distinction between Berne's Indirect Parent and his Adapted Child to be confusing. Berne (1964, p. 26) defined the Indirect Parent as follows: "When it is an indirect influence, he responds the way they wanted him to respond." Berne (1964, p. 26) defined the Adapted Child as ". . . one who modifies his behavior under the Parental influence. He behaves as father (or mother) wanted him to behave." It appears to me these two definitions are practically identical.

The considerable variation among TA authorities on how the PAC ego states are defined adds to the confusion of trying to identify the ego state in which a specific transaction is originating.

Summary

Eric Berne was the primary developer of transactional analysis. The basic premise of transactional analysis is that the human personality is structured into three separate ego states: Parent, Adult, and Child. Basic human needs and psychosocial drives (for example, recognition hunger) are motivational forces. Intrapsychic problems arise from a variety of sources, including adopting self-defeating life scripts, rigidly holding to one ego state while shutting out the other two, and being in an inappropriate ego state for the circumstances.

Interpersonal problems also arise from a variety of sources, including playing destructive psychological games and crossed transactions while communicating.

Transactional analysis seeks to have clients become aware of the intrapsychic and interpersonal problems they have. These problems are then analyzed and interpreted to clients in terms of TA concepts. Once their problems are analyzed, clients make a contract to take specific courses of action to resolve them. TA emphasize the importance of clients' taking personal responsibility for their thoughts, emotions, and actions, and uses a number of experiential techniques (such as psychodrama) to help clients understand and work out their problems. Two treatment techniques that are increasingly being used are game analysis and script analysis.

A number of concepts developed by TA appear useful in helping clients resolve personal problems: game analysis, script analysis, complementary transactions and crossed transactions, seeking strokes, and personal responsibility for emotions and actions. TA theorists need to work toward increased consistency in defining the Parent, Adult, and Child ego states. There is also a need for researchers to conduct outcome studies on the effectiveness of this approach.

Exercises

1. Life script analysis

Goal: This exercise is designed to help students identify and describe destructive life scripts and to examine how to change such scripts.

Step 1: Describe the purpose of this exercise. Define what life scripts are and summarize several examples of common life scripts (see the material in this chapter).

Step 2: Ask each student to write on a sheet of paper as fully as possible a destructive life script. Read the following example to illustrate the kind of description that is desired.

Mrs. H has been married for 22 years. She was brought up to believe that a woman's role was to be supportive of her husband and to do the domestic tasks involved in raising children. She and her husband, Paul, have two children. The oldest, Kelly, is a senior in college, and Jason is a freshman. Both children are no longer living at home.

The first several years of their marriage were fairly happy but a financial struggle. Paul was a life insurance salesman, so it took several years to get a large enough number of clients to make a decent standard of living. Mrs. H helped out by doing paperwork and answering the phone at home.

After they became more financially secure, they were able to take an occasional vacation and to travel some. About seven years ago, Mrs. H discovered her husband had for the previous five years been occasionally having extramarital affairs. When Mrs. H confronted her husband, there was considerable conflict. Mrs. H considered a divorce, but she did not know how she would be able to support herself and the children, particularly because she had few job skills. She decided to stay with her husband, particularly after he apologized and stated he would never "stray" again.

Paul, as Mrs. H discovered 18 months later, did not live up to his word. He has continued to have occasional affairs. Mrs. H has continued to remain married and has tried to make the best of it. She has not been sexually involved with her husband since the time she first discovered he was being unfaithful. Their marriage has become an empty shell marriage. The children have now left home, and Mrs. H has very little to do. She is becoming increasingly depressed. She has in recent years felt considerable tension. Her husband and her doctor have stated her medical concerns border on hypochondria. Her role of raising children has been completed. Her life plans of having a satisfying, happy marriage have long since disappeared. Her husband is now earning enough that if she stays in the marriage she can live comfortably financially. But she is increasingly depressed about her circumstances. Having few job skills, she believes living independently from her husband would be very difficult. Being a strict Catholic, she is morally opposed to a divorce. She is in a severe dilemma about what she should do.

Step 3: Have the students form subgroups of three and share the scripts they wrote. After a member reads a script, have the other members discuss what might be done to help the person who is playing this destructive life script.

Step 4: Form a circle and ask the students if anyone has questions about how to change any of the life scripts that were discussed. End the exercise by having the students discuss the merits and shortcomings of analyzing problematic interactions in terms of script analysis.

2. Game analysis

Goal: This exercise is designed to help students identify and describe destructive games and to examine how to stop such games from being replayed.

Step 1: Begin by stating the goal of this exercise. Then define what a game is and give examples of commonly played games. (This chapter identifies a number of games that can be used as examples.)

Step 2: Ask each student to describe on a sheet of paper one or more destructive games that he or she has played or has seen friends or relatives play.

Step 3: Have the class form subgroups of three and have the students share what they have written. (Inform the students that they have a right to privacy, and therefore they can, if they desire, choose not to share what they have written.) After a member shares what he or she has written, ask the subgroups to discuss what might be done to stop the destructive games from being replayed.

Step 4: Have the class form a circle and ask whether the students have questions about how to stop any of the destructive games they discussed. End the exercise by asking students to discuss the merits and shortcomings of analyzing interpersonal difficulties in terms of game concepts.

3. Analyzing your own life scripts

Goal: This exercise is designed to help students identify and reflect on some of their life scripts.

Step 1: Explain what life scripts are and give examples.

Step 2: Explain that life scripts are generally formed at a young age, and ask students to think about what their childhood years were like. Have each student write down one or two phrases or sentences in regard to what their parents said about the following. (Read each of the following, giving students time to write down their responses.)

Your health	Your friends
Your worth	Your sexuality
Your intelligence	Your abilities
Your morals	Your future
Your looks	

Step 3: Ask the students to reflect on whether their current assessments of themselves in these areas are consistent or inconsistent with what their parents told them.

Step 4: Have the class discuss the merits and shortcomings of this exercise.

16

Behavior Therapy

No one person is credited with the development of behavioral approaches to psychotherapy. Behavior therapists vary considerably in both theory and technique. The main assumption of this therapy system is that maladaptive behaviors are acquired primarily through learning and can be modified through additional learning.

Founders

Historically, learning theory has been the philosophical foundation for behavior therapy even though there has never been agreement as to which learning theory is the core of behavior therapy. A number of authorities have advanced somewhat different theories of how people learn. Pavlov, a Russian who lived between 1849 and 1936, was one of the earliest. Other prominent learning theorists include E. L. Thorndike (1913), E. R. Guthrie (1935), C. L. Hull (1943), E. C. Tolman (1932), and B. F. Skinner (1938).

A large number of behavior therapists have achieved international recognition for developing therapy approaches based on learning principles. Some of these therapists are R. E. Alberti and M. L. Emmons (1970), A. Bandura (1969), B. F. Skinner (1948), J. B. Watson and R. Rayner (1920), and J. Wolpe (1958).

In spite of the wide variation in behavioral therapy approaches and techniques, there are some common emphases. One is that the maladaptive behavior (such as bed-wetting) is the problem and needs to be changed. This approach is in sharp contrast to the psychoanalytic approach that views the problematic behavior as a *symptom* of some underlying, unconscious causes. While psychoanalysts assert the underlying causes must be treated to prevent the substitution of new symptoms or the return of old symptoms, behavior therapists assert that treating the problematic behavior will not result in symptom substitution.

Another common emphasis of behavior therapists is the assertion that therapy approaches must be tested and validated by rigorous experimental procedures. Such a focus requires that the goals of therapy be articulated in behavioral terms that can be measured. Baseline levels of problematic behaviors are established before therapy to measure whether the approach is producing the desired change in the rate or intensity of responding.

The use of behavior therapy approaches in counseling has increased dramatically in the past 30 years. Behavior therapy intervention techniques are now among the most widely used techniques in counseling and psychotherapy (Wilson, 1989).

Among behavior therapists little attention has been devoted to the development of a behavioral model of personality. Behaviorists generally believe that environmental conditions or experiences are of much greater influence in controlling behavior than are internal personality traits. Consequently, we shall omit the section on personality development. Because of the wide range of behavioral therapy techniques, the focus of this chapter is on describing the best-known and most-used approaches.

Types of Learning Processes

Before presenting the prominent behavioral therapy techniques, the three major types of learning processes—operant conditioning, respondent conditioning, and modeling—postulated by learning theory will be briefly described.

Operant Conditioning

Much of human behavior, according to learning theory, is determined by positive and negative reinforcers. A *positive reinforcer* is any stimulus that, when applied following a behavior, increases or strengthens that behavior. Common examples include food, water, sex, attention, affection, and approval. The list of positive reinforcers is inexhaustible and highly individualized. Praise, for example, is a positive reinforcer when, and only when, it maintains or increases the behavior with which it is associated (for example, efforts to improve one's writing skills).

A synonym for negative reinforcer is aversive stimulus. A *negative reinforcer* (or aversive stimulus) is any stimulus that a person will terminate or avoid if given the opportunity. Common examples include frowns, electric shock, and criticism. (The same stimulus—for example, the smell of Limburger cheese—can be a positive reinforcer for one person and a negative reinforcer for another.)

There are four basic learning principles involving positive reinforcers and aversive stimuli:

1. If a positive reinforcer (for example, food) is presented to a person following a response, the result is positive reinforcement. With positive reinforcement, the occurrence of a given behavior is strengthened or increased.

2. If a positive reinforcer is withdrawn following a person's response, the result is punishment.

3. If an aversive stimulus (for example, an electric shock) is presented to a person following a response, the result is punishment. (As can be seen, there are two types of punishment.)

4. If an aversive stimulus is withdrawn following a person's response, the result is negative reinforcement. In negative reinforcement, a response (behavior) is increased through removing an aversive stimulus (for example, fastening one's seat belt to turn off the obnoxiously loud and annoying buzzer).

In sum, positive and negative reinforcements increase behavior, and punishment decreases behavior. Principles of operant conditioning are used in several behavioral techniques described in this chapter, including assertiveness training, token economies, contingency contracting, and aversive techniques.

Respondent Conditioning

Respondent learning has also been called classical or Pavlovian conditioning. A wide range of everyday behaviors are considered respondent behaviors—perspiring, salivating, and, more important, many anxieties, fears, and phobias. A key concept in respondent learning is "pairing"; that is, behaviors are learned by being consistently paired over time with other behaviors or events. To explain respondent conditioning, we will begin by defining the following key terms:

- *Neutral stimulus (NS):* A stimulus that elicits little or no response.
- *Unconditioned stimulus (UCS):* A stimulus that elicits an unlearned or innate response.
- *Unlearned or innate response (UR):* A response that is innate; for example, the response of salivating to having food in the mouth.
- *Conditioned response (CR):* A new response that has been learned.
- *Conditioned stimulus (CS):* An original neutral stimulus that, through pairing with an unconditioned stimulus, now begins to elicit a conditioned response.

Respondent learning asserts that when a neutral stimulus (NS) is paired with an unconditioned stimulus (UCS), the neutral stimulus will also come to elicit a response similar to that being elicited by the UCS. That new response is called a conditioned response (CR) because it has been learned; the originally neutral stimulus, once it begins to elicit the response, becomes the conditioned stimulus (CS). Thus, it is possible for an event that originally elicited no fear whatsoever (for example, being in the dark) to elicit fear when it is paired with a stimulus that does elicit fear (for example, horrifying stories about being in the dark). This learning process is indicated in the following paradigm:

1. *UCS* (horrifying stories about being in the dark) → elicits *UR* (fear)
2. *NS* (being in the dark)
   ↓
   (paired with)
   UCS → elicits → *CR* (fear)
3. *NS* becomes *CS* → elicits *CR* (fear)

The *CS* → *CR* bond can be broken by respondent extinction or by counterconditioning. *Respondent extinction* involves continuing presentation of the conditioned stimulus without any further pairing with the unconditioned stimulus. Respondent extinction gradually weakens, and eventually eliminates, the CS-CR bond. Implosive therapy, soon to be discussed, is based on this principle.

Counterconditioning is based on the principle that the CS-CR bond can be broken by using new responses that are stronger than and incompatible with old responses that are elicited by the same stimulus. For example, it is possible to teach a person to relax (new response) instead of becoming anxious (old response) when confronted with a particular stimulus (for example, the prospect of flying in a small plane). Systematic desensitization and in vivo desensitization (to be discussed later in this chapter) are based on counterconditioning. Another technique to be discussed, covert sensitization, is based on establishing new CS-CR connections to eliminate problematic behavior.

Modeling

Modeling refers to a change in behavior as a result of the observation of another's behavior—that is, learning by vicarious experience or imitation. Much of everyday learning is thought to take place through modeling—using both live models and symbolic models (such as films). Modeling has been used in behavior modification to develop new behaviors that are not in a person's repertoire—for example, showing a youngster how to swing a bat. Modeling has also been used to eliminate anxieties and fears—for example, using a model in assertiveness training. Anxieties and fears are reduced or eliminated through modeling by exposing fearful observers to modeled events in which the model performs the feared activity without experiencing any adverse effects and even enjoys the process.

Theory of Psychotherapy

Behavior therapy is based on the assumption that all behavior occurs in response to stimulation, internal or external. The first task of the behavior therapist is to identify the probable stimulus-response (S-R) connections that are occurring for the client. This part of the therapy process is called the behavioral or functional analysis. The following is an illustration of an S-R connection: For a person who has a fear of heights, the stimulus (S) of flying in a small plane would have the response (R) of intense anxiety and avoidance of the stimulus.

Prior to and during the time the therapist is doing the behavioral analysis, he or she is also attempting to establish a working relationship. (The characteristics of a working relationship have been described in Chapter 5.) In regard to this emphasis on establishing a working relationship, Chambless and Goldstein (1979) stated:

Although behaviorists are often portrayed as cold and mechanical, a study of recordings of therapy sessions yields a different picture. When measured on variables used in the study of client-centered therapy, behavior therapists showed high warmth and positive regard for their clients (equal to other psychotherapists in the study) and higher empathy and self-congruence than the other therapists (Sloane, Staples, Cristol, Yorkston, and Whipple, 1975). [p. 243]

During the behavioral analysis, the therapist attempts to determine the stimuli associated with the maladaptive responses. Through this analysis, both the client and the therapist arrive at an understanding of the problem and generally how it developed. This insight, although it does not treat the problem, is useful because it reduces some of the client's anxiety and he or she no longer feels possessed or overwhelmed by unknown, mysterious forces. Errors about hypothesized S-R connections at this diagnostic stage usually lead to ineffective treatment, since the treatment will then be focused on treating S-R connections that are *not* involved in perpetuating the maladaptive behavior.

A behavioral analysis begins with the therapist taking a detailed history of the presenting problem, its course, and particularly its association with current experiences. In making such an analysis, it is crucial to obtain specific, concrete details about the circumstances in which the presenting problem arises. If, for example, a client is shy in some situations, it is important to identify the specific interactions in which the client is shy. Furthermore, it is important to determine the reasons the client is shy: Is it because he does not know how to express himself, or is it because he has certain fears? The treatment chosen depends on such information. If the client does not know how to express himself, a *modeling* approach through role playing might be used. On the other hand, if the client has the response potential but is inhibited by certain fears, a desensitization procedure (described later in this chapter) to reduce these fears might be used.

The objective in doing a behavioral analysis is to identify the antecedent stimuli that are generating the maladaptive responses. Once the therapist identifies these connections, he or she discusses them with the client to help the client gain insight and to obtain the client's feedback on possible erroneous connections. The client and the therapist then agree on the goals for the treatment. The process of how therapy will proceed (along with the techniques to be used) are described to the client. This provides the client with an idea of his role in treatment. Orne and Wender (1968) found that this knowledge fosters positive outcomes and reduces the dropout rate.

Chambless and Goldstein (1979) described the sources of information for making a behavioral analysis:

The behavior therapist may base the functional analysis on interviews with the client and important people in the client's life or on information gained by having the client keep a journal. Questionnaire data are often useful. Interpersonal problems may be more clearly defined if the therapist and client role play interactions with which the client reports difficulty. When the therapist has a difficult time making the analysis, observing the client in the situation where the problem occurs may lead to a wealth of information. Obviously, there are times when this would be impossible or in poor taste, but direct observation is used much less frequently than it should be. [pp. 244–245]

The remainder of this chapter is focused on presenting some of the most commonly used behavior therapy techniques.

Assertiveness Training

Assertiveness training has become the most frequently used method in modifying unadaptive interpersonal behavior. It is particularly effective in changing both timid behavior and aggressive behavior. Wolpe (1958) originally developed this approach, and it has been further developed by a variety of authors, including Alberti and Emmons (1970) and Fensterheim and Baer (1975).

In recent years interest has grown enormously, sparked by the recognition that sex-role stereotyping has led to a general lack of assertiveness in women. Assertiveness-training groups are now widely offered. During the past several years an increasing number of men are also getting involved, either individually or through groups, in assertiveness training. Outcome research on assertiveness training has found the approach to be effective in assisting participants to become more assertive (Cormier & Cormier, 1991).

Overview of Assertiveness Training[1]

Do you handle put-down comments well? Are you reluctant to express your feelings and opinions openly and honestly in a group? Are you frequently timid in interacting with people in authority? Do you react well to criticism? Do you sometimes explode in anger when things go wrong, or are you able to remain calm? Do you find it difficult to maintain eye contact when talking? If you are uncomfortable with someone smoking near you, do you express your feelings? Are you timid in arranging a date or social event? If you have trouble in any of these situations, there is, fortunately, a useful technique—assertiveness training—that enables people to become more effective in such interpersonal interactions.

Assertiveness problems range from extreme shyness, introversion, and withdrawal to inappropriately flying into a rage that results in alienating others. A nonassertive person is often acquiescent, fearful, and afraid of expressing his or her real, spontaneous feelings in a variety of situations. Frequently, resentment and anxiety build up, which may result in general discomfort, feelings of low self-esteem, tension headaches, fatigue, and perhaps a destructive explosion of temper, anger, and aggression. Some people are overly shy and timid in nearly all interactions. Most of us, however, encounter occasional problems in isolated areas in which it would be to our benefit to be more assertive. For example, a bachelor may be quite effective and assertive in his job as store manager but still awkward and timid when attempting to arrange a date.

There are three basic styles of interacting with others: *nonassertive, aggressive,* and *assertive.* Characteristics of these styles have been summarized by Alberti and Emmons (1975):

> In the *nonassertive* style, you are likely to hesitate, speak softly, look away, avoid the issue, agree regardless of your own feelings, not express opinions, value yourself "below" others, and hurt yourself to avoid any chance of hurting others.
>
> In the *aggressive* style, you typically answer before the other person is through talking, speak loudly and abusively, glare at the other person, speak "past" the issue (accusing, blaming, demeaning), vehemently expound your feelings and opinions, value yourself "above" others, and hurt others to avoid hurting yourself.
>
> In the *assertive* style, you will answer spontaneously, speak with a conversational tone and volume, and look at the other person, speak to the issue, openly express your personal feelings and opin-

---

[1]This material on assertiveness training is adapted from Charles Zastrow, "How to Become More Assertive" in *The Personal Problem Solver,* edited by Charles Zastrow and Dae H. Chang © 1977, pp. 236–243. Adapted by permission of Prentice-Hall, Inc., Englewood Cliffs, New Jersey.

ions (anger, love, disagreement, sorrow), value yourself equal to others, and hurt neither yourself or others. [p. 24]

Simply stated, *assertive behavior* is being able to express yourself without hurting or stepping on others.

Assertiveness training is designed to lead a person to realize, feel, and act on the assumption that she has the right to be herself and to express feelings freely. Assertive responses generally are not aggressive responses. The distinction between these two types of interactions is important. If, for example, a wife has an overly critical mother-in-law, aggressive responses by the wife would include ridiculing the mother-in-law, intentionally doing things that she knows will upset the mother-in-law (not visiting, serving the type of food the mother-in-law dislikes, not cleaning the house), urging the husband to tell his mother to "shut up," and getting into loud verbal arguments with the mother-in-law. On the other hand, an effective assertive response would be to counter criticism by saying, "Jane, your criticism of me deeply hurts me. I know you're trying to help me when you give advice, but I feel when you do that you're criticizing me. I know you don't want me to make mistakes, but everyone has to make some mistakes and learn from them. If you want to help me the most, let me do it myself and be responsible for the consequences. The type of relationship I'd like to have with you is a close, adult relationship, not a mother-child relationship."

Examples of nonassertive, aggressive, and assertive behavior: You are a social worker driving in a car with an associate to a conference in another city. The associate lights up a pipe; you soon find the smoke irritating and the odor somewhat stifling. What are your choices?

1. *Nonassertive response:* You attempt to carry on a "cheery" conversation for the three-hour trip without commenting about the smoke.

2. *Aggressive response:* You increasingly become irritated until exploding, "Either you put out that pipe or I'll put it out for you—the odor is sickening."

3. *Assertive response:* In a firm, conversational tone, you look directly at the associate and state, "The smoke from your pipe is irritating me. I'd appreciate it if you put it away."

At a party with friends, during small-talk conversation, your husband gives you a subtle "put-down" by stating, "Wives always talk too much." What do you do?

1. *Nonassertive response:* You don't say anything, but feel hurt and become quiet.

2. *Aggressive response:* You glare at him and angrily ask, "John, why are you always criticizing me?"

3. *Assertive response:* You carry on as usual. On the drive home, you calmly look at him and say, "When we were at the party tonight, you said that wives always talk too much. I felt you were putting me down when you said that. What did you mean by that comment?"

Steps in Assertiveness Training[2]

This section contains 12 self-training steps.

Step 1: Examine your interactions. Are there situations that you need to handle more assertively? Do you at times hold opinions and feelings within you for fear of what would happen if you expressed them? Do you occasionally blow your cool and lash out angrily at others? To study your interactions, keep a diary for a week or longer, recording the situations

[2]These self-training steps are a modification of assertiveness training programs developed by Robert E. Alberti and Michael L. Emmons, *Your Perfect Right* (San Luis Obispo, CA: Impact Publishers, 1970), and by Herbert Fensterheim and Jean Baer, *Don't Say Yes When You Want to Say No* (New York: Dell Publishing Co., 1975).

in which you acted timidly, those in which you were aggressive, and those that you handled assertively.

Step 2: Select those interactions in which it would be to your benefit to be more assertive. They may include situations in which you were overly polite, overly apologetic, timid, or allowed others to take advantage of you while you were harboring feelings of resentment, anger, embarrassment, fear of others, or self-criticism for not having the courage to express yourself. Overly aggressive interactions in which you exploded in anger or walked over others also need to be dealt with. For *each* set of nonassertive or aggressive interactions, you can become more assertive, as shown in the next steps.

Step 3: Concentrate on a specific incident in the past in which you were either nonassertive or aggressive when you wanted to be assertive. Close your eyes for a few minutes and vividly imagine the details, including what you and the other person said, and how you felt at the time and afterward.

Step 4: Write down and review your responses. Ask yourself the following questions to determine how you presented yourself:

a. Eye contact—did you look directly at the other person in a relaxed, steady gaze? Looking down or away suggests a lack of self-confidence. Glaring is an aggressive response.

b. Gestures—were your gestures appropriate, free flowing, relaxed, and used effectively to emphasize your messages? Awkward stiffness suggests nervousness; other gestures (such as an angry fist) signal an aggressive reaction.

c. Body posture—did you show the importance of your message by directly facing the other person, by leaning toward that person, by holding your head erect, and by sitting or standing appropriately close?

d. Facial expression—did your facial expression show a stern, firm pose consistent with an assertive response?

e. Voice tone and volume—was your response stated in a firm, conversational tone? Shouting may suggest anger. Speaking softly suggests shyness, and a cracking voice suggests nervousness. Tape recording and listening to one's voice is a way to practice increasing or decreasing the volume.

f. Speech fluency—did your speech flow smoothly, clearly, and slowly? Rapid speech or hesitation in speaking suggests nervousness. Tape recording assertive responses that you try out in problem situations is a way to improve fluency.

g. Timing—were your verbal reactions to a problem situation stated at a time closest to the incident that would appropriately permit you and the other person time to review the incident? Generally, spontaneous expressions are the best, but certain situations should be handled at a later time—for example, a challenge to some of your boss's erroneous statements should be made in private rather than in front of a group in which she is making a presentation.

h. Message content—for a problem situation, which of your responses were nonassertive or aggressive and which were assertive? Study the content and consider why you responded in a nonassertive or aggressive style. (At this point it is very helpful to identify the self-talk that led you to act nonassertively or aggressively, and to challenge this self-talk with rational, assertive self-challenges—see Chapter 22.)

Step 5: Observe one or more effective models. Watch the verbal and nonverbal approaches that are assertively used to handle the types of interactions with which you are having problems. Compare the consequences between their approach and yours. If possible, discuss their approach and their feelings about using it.

Step 6: Make a list of various alternative approaches for being more assertive.

Step 7: Close your eyes and visualize yourself using each of the alternative approaches. For each approach, think through what the full set of interactions would be, along with the consequences. Select an approach, or combination of approaches, that you believe will be most effective for you to use. Through imagery, practice using this approach until you feel comfortable that it will work for you.

Step 8: Role-play the approach with someone else, perhaps a friend or counselor. If certain segments of your approach appear clumsy, awkward, timid, or aggressive, practice modifications until you become comfortable with the approach. Obtain feedback from the other person as to the strengths and shortcomings of your approach. Compare your interactions to the verbal and nonverbal guidelines for assertive behavior in step 4. It may be useful for the other person to model through role-playing one or more assertive strategies, which you would then, by reversing roles, practice using.

Step 9: Repeat steps 7 and 8 until you develop an assertive approach that you believe will work best for you and that you are comfortable with.

Step 10: Use your approach in a real-life situation. The previous steps are designed to prepare you for the real event. Expect to be somewhat anxious when first trying to be assertive. If you are still too fearful of attempting to be assertive, repeat steps 5 through 8. For those few individuals who fail to develop the needed confidence to try being assertive, seeking professional counseling is advised—expressing yourself and effective interactions with others are essential for personal happiness.

Step 11: Reflect on the effectiveness of your effort. Did you remain calm?[3] Considering the nonverbal guidelines for assertive behavior discussed in step 4, what components of your responses were assertive, aggressive, and nonassertive? What were the consequences of your effort? How did you feel after trying out this new set of interactions? If possible, discuss how you did in regard to these questions with a friend who may have observed the interactions.

Step 12: Expect some success, but not complete personal satisfaction, with your initial efforts. Personal growth and interacting more effectively with others is a continual learning process. Quite appropriately "pat yourself on the back" for what you did well—you earned it. But also note the areas in which you need to improve, and use these steps for improving your assertive efforts. These steps systematically make sense but are not to be followed rigidly. Each person has to develop a process that works best for herself or himself.

Helping Others Become More Assertive

Either as a friend or as a counselor, you can be very helpful in assisting another person to become more assertive. The following guidelines are suggested.

1. Together identify the situations or interactions in which the person needs to be more assertive. Get information about such interactions from your observations and knowledge about the person, and from discussing in depth the interactions in which the person feels a need to be more assertive.

---

[3]Getting angry at times is a normal human emotion, and it needs to be expressed. However, the anger should be expressed in a constructive, assertive fashion.

Role playing is a useful technique in preparing one to be assertive.

You may also ask the person to keep a diary of interactions in which he or she feels resentment over being nonassertive, and those interactions in which he or she was overly aggressive.

2. Develop together some strategies for the person to be more assertive. Small assignments with a high probability of successful outcomes should be given first. A great deal of discussion and preparation should take place between the two of you in preparing for the "real event." For a person who is generally shy, introverted, and nonassertive in all interpersonal relationships, it probably will be necessary to explore and explain in great detail the connection between nonassertive behavior and feelings of resentment or low self-esteem. In addition, for very shy people, certain attitudes, such as "don't make waves" or the "meek will inherit the earth," may need to be dealt with

before developing strategies for the person to be more assertive.

3. Role playing is a very useful technique in preparing for being assertive. The helper first models an assertive strategy by taking the shy person's role. The shy person concurrently role plays the role of the person with whom he or she wants to be more assertive. Then the roles are reversed; the person role plays himself or herself and the helper plays the other role. An example may make this clearer. Using the illustration cited earlier in which a wife has problems interacting with an overly critical mother-in-law, the helper would play the role of the wife first, modeling an assertive strategy. The wife would concurrently play the role of the mother-in-law. Then the roles would be reversed, the wife practicing various assertive strategies with the helper playing the mother-in-law. The technique is practiced

until the wife becomes comfortable with it and develops sufficient self-confidence for the "real event." In addition to the above-mentioned benefits of modeling and practice experience, role playing has the added advantage of reducing the anxiety that the shy person has about attempting to be assertive. For feedback purposes, if possible, record the role playing on audio or videotape.

4. Explain the 12 steps described earlier that the person can use on his or her own to handle future problem situations involving assertiveness. If possible, provide reading material on these steps.

Although each person must be able to express himself or herself in an individual style, there is an additional guideline that is often useful. A good rule is to start sentences with "I feel" rather than making threatening or aggressive statements (I-messages are further described in Chapter 20). Frequently, in our fast-paced society we simply do not take the time to express our real feelings to others; as a result we end up creating serious misunderstandings, hurt feelings, and verbal fights that take ten times as long to work through. Consider the following example of two busy people, a working mother and her 15-year-old son.

Mother: John, please do the dishes for me tonight.
John: I can't, I'll do them tomorrow.
Mother: [*Getting angry.*] You never do anything for me.
John: I said I'll do the dishes tomorrow.
Mother: And you always forget. I asked you to clean your room two weeks ago, and you still haven't done that. [*Now angry.*] I just don't know what I'm going to do with you. Just for that you can't go camping this weekend.

And the argument has ignited. Contrast this to the following approach:

Mother: John, I feel very tired this evening. I had a bad day at work, and I still have to do all the washing and ironing tonight. Could you please help me out by doing the dishes?
John: I'm sorry you had a bad day. I'm supposed to be at basketball practice in five minutes. I'll be back at eight-thirty, would it be all right if I did them then?
Mother: Yes, if you don't forget.
John: I won't.

The structure of the technique in assertiveness training is relatively simple to comprehend. Considerable skill (common sense and ingenuity), however, is needed to determine what will be an effective strategy when a real-life situation arises. The joy and pride obtained from being able fully to express oneself assertively is nearly unequaled.

Token Economies

Tokens are symbolic reinforcers, such as poker chips or points on a tally sheet, that can later be exchanged for items that constitute direct forms of reinforcement, such as candy or increased privileges (for example, an adolescent in a group home being allowed to go to movies). An economy involves an exchange system that specifies exactly what the tokens can be exchanged for and how many tokens it takes to get particular items or privileges. The economy also specifies the target behaviors (such as going to school or making a bed) that can earn tokens and the rate of responding that is required to earn a particular number of tokens. For example, attending school every day for two weeks earns ten tokens at an adolescent group home, and ten tokens can be exchanged for attending a sports event.

Token economies have been successfully used in a wide variety of institutional settings, including mental hospitals, training schools for delinquents, classrooms for students with emotional problems, schools for individuals with a cognitive disability, sheltered workshops, and group homes for adolescents.

There is considerable evidence to support the effectiveness of token economies (Kazdin, 1977b). Token economies have been used to effect positive changes in a wide variety of behaviors, including personal hygiene, social interactions, job attendance and performance, academic performance, domestic tasks such as cleaning, and personal appearance.

At times, token economies are arranged in which clients not only earn tokens for desired behaviors but also lose tokens for undesired behaviors (for example, instigating a fight).

Effective token economies are much more difficult to establish than it appears at first glance. Prochaska (1979) summarized some of the most important factors that need to be given attention in establishing a token economy:

> Some of the more important considerations include staff cooperation and coordination, since the staff must be more observant and more systematic in their responses to clients than in a noncontingent system. A variety of attempts at establishing token economies have failed because the staff did not cooperate adequately in monitoring the behavior of residents. Effective token economies must also have adequate control over reinforcements, since an economy becomes ineffective if residents have access to reinforcements by having money from home or being able to bum a cigarette from a less cooperative staff member. Problems must be clearly defined in terms of specific behaviors to be changed in order to avoid conflicts among staff or patients. Improving personal hygiene, for example, is too open to interpretation by individuals, and patients may insist that they are improving their hygiene even though staff members may disagree. There is much less room for misunderstandings if personal hygiene is defined as clean fingernails, no evidence of body odor, clean underwear, and other clear-cut rules. Specifying be-

haviors that are positive alternatives to problem behavior is very critical in teaching residents what positive actions they can take to help themselves rather than relying on just a negative set of eliminating responses. Perhaps most important for more lasting effectiveness of token economies is that they be gradually faded out as problem behaviors are reduced and more adaptive responses become well established. Obviously the outside world does not run according to an institution's internal economy, and it is important that clients be prepared to make the transition to the larger society. Using an abundance of social reinforcers along with token reinforcers helps prepare clients for the fading out of tokens, so that positive behaviors can be maintained by praise or recognition rather than by tokens. Also encouraging patients to reinforce themselves, such as by learning to take pride in their appearance, is an important step in fading out tokens. Some institutions use transitional wards where clients go from token economies and learn to maintain adaptive behaviors through more naturalistic contingencies, such as praise from a fellow patient. In such transitional settings, backup reinforcers are available if needed, but they are used much more sparingly than in the token economies. Without the use of fading, token economies can become nothing more than hospital management procedures that make the care of patients more efficient without preparing patients to live effectively in the larger society.[4]

Contingency Contracting

Closely related to token economies is contingency contracting. Contingency contracts provide the client with a set of rules that govern the change process. Contracts may be

[4]James O. Prochaska, *Systems of Psychotherapy*, (Pacific Grove, CA: Brooks/Cole, 1979), pp. 324–325.

unilateral; that is, a client may make a contract with herself or himself. For example, a person with a weight problem may limit himself to a certain calorie intake, with a system of rewards being established for staying within the calorie limit and negative consequences being set for going over the calorie limit. Contracts may also be bilateral and specify the obligations and the mutual reinforcements for each of the parties.

Kanfer (1975, p. 321) noted that a good contingency contract should contain the following seven elements:

1. A clear and detailed description of the required instrumental behavior should be stated.

2. Some criterion should be set for the time or frequency limitations that constitute the goal of the contract.

3. The contract should specify the positive reinforcements, contingent on fulfillment of the criterion.

4. Provisions should be made for some aversive consequence, contingent on nonfulfillment of the contract within the specified time or with the specified frequency.

5. A bonus clause should indicate the additional positive reinforcements obtainable if the person exceeds the minimal demands of the contract.

6. The contract should specify the means by which the contracted response is observed, measured, recorded; and a procedure should be stated for informing the client of his or her achievements during the duration of the contract.

7. The timing for delivery of reinforcement contingencies should be arranged to follow the response as quickly as possible.

Helping professionals are increasingly finding it very useful to develop contingency contracts (also called *behavioral change contracts*) with clients. Such contracts specify the desired goals, the tasks to be performed to meet these goals, the tasks that will be done by the client and those that will be carried out by the therapist, and the deadline for completing these tasks.

Kanfer (1975) indicated that marriage counseling is one area in which contingency contracts are increasingly being used. In such a contract each spouse agrees to change behaviors that irritate the other, with a specified system of reinforcements and consequences that will be applied according to the extent to which the contract provisions are met.

Formulating contracts with clients in both one-to-one settings and in group settings has a number of advantages. The contracts guide clients in terms of the specific actions they need to take to improve their problematic situations. Contracts tend to have a motivational effect because when people commit to the terms of a contract, they usually feel a moral obligation to follow through. In addition, reviewing whether commitments made in contracts are being met provides therapists and clients with one method for measuring progress. If commitments are generally fulfilled, it suggests that positive changes are occurring; if commitments are generally unfulfilled, it suggests that positive changes are not occurring.

Systematic Desensitization[5]

A useful technique for a person who is unduly anxious about a specific stimulus is systematic desensitization. Most of us have extreme anxiety reactions (phobias) to one or more of the following stimuli: taking exams, snakes, rats, making love, being alone, fire, heights, walking alone, injections, medications, being in a small place or a crowded place, locked doors, steep stairways, the unknown, death, nightmares, traffic, thunder

---

[5]This material on systematic desensitization is excerpted from Charles Zastrow, "Systematic Desensitization," in *Talk to Yourself: Using the Power of Self-Talk*, © 1979, pp. 190–193. Reprinted by permission of Prentice-Hall, Inc., Englewood Cliffs, New Jersey.

and lightning, talking to authority figures, sexual dysfunctions, speaking in public, criticism, and losing one's mind.

Systematic desensitization was developed by Joseph Wolpe (1969). The basis for this approach is the scientific fact that a person cannot be simultaneously anxious and relaxed. Wolpe used "relaxation" as a counterconditioner to the feared stimulus. *Systematic desensitization* involves three phases: training in deep muscle relaxation, the construction of anxiety hierarchies, and counterpoising through imagery the anxiety-evoking stimuli and relaxation.

For training in deep muscle relaxation, a modification of Jacobson's (1934) procedures is used. The client, under the instruction of a therapist, is taught how to relax by tensing and then relaxing progressive groups of muscles. This phase is completed when the client is able to relax the muscles through imagery.[6]

The second phase is the construction of anxiety hierarchies. In a series of interviews the therapist seeks to discover the stimulus situations that elicit fear or anxiety. Suppose that a woman has an unreasonable fear of heights. There are apt to be several themes in which the fear arises: being in tall buildings, high-altitude driving, flying in a small plane, amusement park rides. For each theme, a set of stimuli about that theme are ranked according to how fear-producing they are, from the last frightening to the most. For example, rankings of stimuli about flying in a small plane might be the following:

Thinking about having to fly in a small plane some time in the future.
Knowing that in two weeks you have to fly in a small plane.
Knowing that next week you will have to fly in a small plane.
Thinking about flying in a small plane tomorrow.

[6]Muscle relaxation approaches are more fully described in Chapter 20.

Knowing you will have to fly in a small plane today.
Driving to the airport to fly.
Buying a ticket at the airport to fly.
Seeing your luggage put on the plane.
Walking toward the plane.
Getting into the small plane.
Fastening the safety belt.
Hearing the motor start.
Listening to the pilot getting clearance to fly.
Feeling the plane taxi down the runway.
Takeoff.
Feeling the plane gaining altitude.
Looking out the window while gaining altitude.
Reaching the plane's cruise height.
Looking out the window at cruising height.
Encountering a thunderstorm while flying.
Looking out the window during a thunderstorm.

Wolpe indicated that the construction of anxiety hierarchies is the most difficult phase of the desensitization technique.

The third phase is the counterpoising, with imagery, of relaxation and anxiety-evoking stimuli from the hierarchies. The objective of this phase is to replace the fear of each stimulus with relaxation. This is done by having the client imagine each fear-producing stimulus while in a relaxed state. The specific procedures of this phase are these:

1. The client is told that she will be asked to imagine (think about) various scenes from her anxiety hierarchies. The themes are worked on separately, beginning with the least-frightening stimulus situation in each theme.
2. The client is told that if she becomes anxious while imagining a stimulus situation, she should raise an index finger.
3. Taking a theme, the client is then asked to imagine the least-frightening stimulus situation in that theme. The client is asked to think about it, then told to relax,

then asked to think about it, then told to relax, and so on. The scene and relaxation are counterpoised several times.

4. If the client indicates no anxiety arises, the next scene in the anxiety hierarchy is presented and counterpoised with relaxation. Gradually the client and therapist work their way up the anxiety hierarchy in this manner. If the client indicates anxiety with any stimulus, the therapist instructs the client to relax. After the client is relaxed, a scene lower in the hierarchy is presented and the therapist and the client gradually start working their way up the anxiety hierarchy again.

The advantage of desensitization through imagination is that the appearance of the feared stimulis can be regulated. The client, by encountering the feared stimuli in a stepwise hierarchy in her imagination, will be unlikely to become overly anxious.

As a clinical technique, systematic desensitization has been found to be highly effective in substantially reducing anxieties, fears, and phobias that are attached to specific conditions (Paul, 1969).

There is also some evidence that systematic desensitization can be used as a self-modification procedure—that is, by a person who is not under the supervision of a therapist (Kahn & Baker, 1968; Migler, 1968; Rardin, 1969). Watson and Tharp (1972) cautioned that self-desensitization "should be discontinued if the course of anxiety-reduction is not relatively smooth and *it should be immediately discontinued if any increase in anxiety is noted*" (p. 179).

Self-desensitization involves the same stages as systematic desensitization: learning to relax through imagery after learning a muscle relaxation technique, construction of anxiety hierarchies; and counterpoising the anxiety-evoking stimuli with relaxation. (Learning to relax with muscle relaxation techniques is described in Chapter 20.)

In constructing anxiety hierarchies, Watson and Tharp (1972) advised that each feared situation be listed on a separate card, and then hierarchies with themes be constructed. For example, phobias of certain animals may include themes of snakes, rats, and dogs. In constructing the themes, various types of hierarchies may be used. For example, if a person has a fear of taking exams, hierarchy types might include distance in time before the feared event occurs, importance of the exam, and the exam taker's acquaintance or comfortableness with the anticipated content of the exam.

Desensitization occurs through counterpoising the anxiety-eliciting stimuli with relaxation. A theme is selected and, while deeply relaxed, you present to yourself the lowest fear-producing item in the theme by looking at the card on which it has been written. Keep counterpoising through imagery the item and relaxation. When you feel completely relaxed while imagining the item, you are ready to go on to the next.

In Vivo Desensitization[7]

In vivo (from the Latin "in life") desensitization refers to a real-life desensitization process in which a person gradually approaches an actual feared event or stimulus while being in a relaxed state. To carry out in vivo desensitization, the following three steps should be taken:

1. Make a ranked list of fear-producing situations, arranging items from least to most anxiety-producing. (This step is identical to the construction of anxiety hierarchies in systematic desensitization.)
2. Learn to produce or achieve relaxation, perhaps by meditation, muscle relaxation,

[7]This material on in vivo desensitization is excerpted from Charles Zastrow, "In Vivo Desensitization," in *Talk to Yourself: Using the Power of Self-Talk*, © 1979, pp. 195–196. Reprinted by permission of Prentice-Hall, Inc., Englewood Cliffs, New Jersey.

deep breathing relaxation, or imagery relaxation.[8]

3. Gradually approach an actual feared event while remaining relaxed.

A 22-year-old male college student used this approach in overcoming several situations (themes) connected with a fear of heights. He first became skilled at producing the relaxation response by imagery of his ideal relaxation place. (His ideal relaxation place was lying on the beach in Acapulco. With practice he became skilled at relaxing himself by fully focusing his thinking on relaxing in Acapulco.) He then gradually approached feared situations while remaining in a relaxed state with his imagery of Acapulco. For example, he countered his fear of tall buildings by looking out the window in the lower floors and gradually moving upward while thinking about being relaxed in Acapulco. He also used this approach to overcome his fears of taking amusement park rides and of flying in small planes.

Watson and Tharp (1972) indicated that in vivo desensitization is an effective method in eliminating fear and anxiety reactions associated with specific stimuli (events).

Implosive Therapy

Like systematic desensitization, implosive therapy has the client imagine (think about) anxiety-provoking material. Unlike systematic desensitization, relaxation training is not required or used.

Implosive therapy was developed by Stampfl and Levis (1967). The approach is based on *extinction*. As used by Stampfl and Levis, extinction refers to the gradual reduction in the occurrence of an anxiety response as a result of the continuous presentation of the fear-producing stimulus situation in the

absence of the reinforcement that perpetuates the fear.

In using the implosive therapy, the therapist first constructs an Avoidance Serial Cue Hierarchy. On the basis of interviews with the client, the therapist develops a ranking of important cues involved in the client's fear. For example, if a person has a fear of flying, a cue low on the hierarchy might be driving to the airport, while a cue high on the hierarchy might be taking off in a plane during a thunderstorm. In developing the hierarchy the therapist seeks primarily to include cues thought to be capable of producing a *maximum* level of anxiety in the client. An example of this type of hierarchy is described by Hogan and Kirchner (1967):

> Fear of rats
>
> Imagine that you are touching a rat in the laboratory. . . . It begins nibbling at your finger . . . and then runs across your arm. The rat suddenly bites you on your arm, and then you feel it run rapidly over your body. . . . It begins biting your neck and swishing its tail in your face . . . then it claws up your face into your hair . . . clawing in your hair . . . you try to get it out with your bloody arm, but you can't. It then goes for your eyes . . . you open your mouth and it jumps in and you swallow it. . . . It then begins to eat away at various internal organs—like your stomach and intestines, causing you great discomfort and pain . . . , etc. [p. 109]

After the hierarchy is developed, the therapist describes implosive therapy to the client. The client is then presented with the scenes, and asked to make every effort to imagine the scenes as vividly as possible, and encouraged to "live" the scenes with emotion.

The objective of implosive therapy is to extinguish fears through having the client produce in her mind frightening experiences of such magnitude that, in the absence of reinforcement, they will *lessen* the fear of the particular situation. Stampfl and Levis (1967) stated:

---

[8]All of these techniques to achieve relaxation are described in Chapter 20.

An attempt is made by the therapist to attain a maximal level of anxiety evocation from the patient. When a high level of anxiety is achieved, the patient is held on this level until some sign of spontaneous reduction in the anxiety-inducing value of the cues appears . . . the process is repeated, and again, at the first sign of spontaneous reduction of fear, new variations are introduced to elicit an intense anxiety response. This response is repeated until a significant diminution in anxiety has resulted. [p. 500]

Sessions end after 30 to 60 minutes, generally after the client experiences a reduction in anxiety to the implosive scenes. Between sessions the client is encouraged to practice imagining the implosive scenes at home to help her realize she can effectively handle the fears.

Morris (1986) indicated that few outcome studies have been conducted on implosive therapy, with the studies showing mixed results. There is a danger that implosive therapy may *increase*, rather than lessen, the fear of the particular situation (Morris, 1986). Because of this possibility, the technique should be used only by clinicians who have received extensive training.

Covert Sensitization

Covert sensitization is an aversive counter-conditioning approach that was first developed by J. R. Cautela (1967). Instead of inhibiting anxiety with relaxation as in systematic desensitization, covert sensitization is used to elicit anxiety in certain problematic situations. The technique is claimed to be particularly appropriate for treating such behavioral excesses as sexual deviations, alcoholism, stealing, overeating, and drug addiction (Anant, 1967, 1968; Ashem & Donner, 1968; Sundel & Sundel, 1975).

The first step in covert sensitization is to instruct the client in how to relax—for example, by using a muscle relaxation technique. (Relaxation techniques are described in Chapter 22.) The next step is to have the client imagine (visualize) becoming involved in his problematic behavior while imagining extremely distasteful consequences.

Jehu (1972) described how covert sensitization is used with people who have a drinking problem:

The patient is relaxed and asked to imagine a sequence of scenes leading up to the performance of the problem behavior; for example, looking at a glass containing his favorite alcoholic drink, holding the glass in his hand and bringing it to his lips. At this point he signals and the therapist tells the patient to imagine that he begins to feel sick and is vomiting in his drink and all over himself and his companions. He is then asked to visualize the whole sequence and final scene by himself, and to actually feel nauseous as he prepares to drink. Alternate scenes are presented in which the patient imagines himself abstaining from drinking and then "rushing out into the fresh clean air," or "home to a clean invigorating shower." The presentation of such relief scenes constitutes an escape and avoidance training component in the procedure. After several trials with the therapist, the patient is instructed to repeat the whole procedure on his own and immediately to imagine the vomiting scene whenever he is tempted to drink alcohol. [pp. 57–58]

Prochaska (1979) described using covert sensitization with a man who was having homosexual relationships with children:

A thirty-year-old pedophiliac was asked to imagine approaching a ten-year-old boy to whom he was attracted. As he approaches the boy to ask him to come up to his apartment, he feels his stomach become nauseous. He feels his lunch coming up into his esophagus, and just as he goes to speak to the boy he vomits all over himself and the boy. People on the street are staring at him and he turns away from the boy and immediately begins to feel better. He begins walking back to his apartment feeling better and better with each step he takes. He gets back to his apartment, washes up, and feels great. After teaching this man the covert scene we had him practice it overtly, including making vomiting noises and gestures. To make the scene even more vivid we had him sit in his apartment window, and when he saw a boy on the street that he would like to approach sexually, we had him go to the bathroom and stick his finger down his throat and vomit as he imagined propositioning the young boy. Within two months this chronic offender was no longer feeling the urge to approach young boys and he had followed through on our assertiveness techniques for forming adult homosexual relationships. [p. 30]

A word of caution—covert sensitization should be used only by skilled therapists with extensive training in this technique. There is a danger that improper application of this approach may create anxiety reactions in clients (and perhaps lead to other adverse side effects), without accomplishing the goal of eliminating the intended problematic behavior such as overeating or sexual deviation.

Aversive Techniques

An aversive stimulus is any stimulus that an organism (person) will avoid or terminate if given the opportunity. Examples of such stimuli include electric shock and unpleasant imagery. Covert sensitization is an example of an aversive technique in which the client imagines unpleasant consequences in conjunction with the maladaptive behavior. Covert sensitization results in diminished interest in the formerly desirable stimuli.

In a review of aversive methods, Sandler (1986) found aversive therapy has been used in treating self-injurious behavior (such as head banging and self-biting), enuresis, sneezing, stuttering, alcoholism, cigarette smoking, overeating, gambling, sexual deviations (for example, fetishes and transvestism), and aggressive behavior. The following are some illustrations of aversive techniques.

Vogler, Lunde, Johnson, and Martin (1970) served cocktails to alcoholic clients in a simulated lounge arrangement. Each time a client took a drink, he or she was given an electric shock and the shock was maintained until the client spat out the drink. The investigators did a follow-up and concluded the treatment led to abstinence.

Corte, Wolf, and Locke (1971) treated four adolescents with a cognitive disability who exhibited self-injurious behavior (including eye poking, self-slapping, scratching the skin, and hair pulling). Each time one of these adolescents displayed a self-injurious response, he was given an electric shock. The authors report this approach sharply reduced such self-injurious behaviors.

Bancroft, Jones, and Pullan (1966) treated a male pedophile (child molester) whose sexual deviancy was so serious that he was being considered for brain surgery. The treatment procedure simulated the natural conditions in which the child molesting occurred. In the treatment procedures an instrument called a penile plethysmograph, which measures penile volume, was used to gauge penile erection. Pictures of young girls were presented to the client and when an erection occurred the client was given a painful shock to the arm. The shock was continued until there was a reduction in the response. Treatment lasted for eight weeks with the treatment procedures being used several times a day. In addition, on every fourth trial the shock apparatus was disconnected and the client was presented with photographs of adult women and encouraged to engage in normal sexual fantasies. Although the results were not a complete success, there was a marked reduction in child-molesting activities and an increase in adult-adult heterosexual behavior.

In regard to the use of aversive techniques, Chambless and Goldstein (1979) cautioned:

When reporting on behavior therapy, the popular press emphasizes such techniques and often gives the impression that punishment is the behaviorist's major tool. On the contrary, punishment is used quite infrequently by behavior modifiers even though many clients initially ask for help via punishment in curbing unwanted behavior. To begin with, no behavior should be punished if no alternative behavior is available. For example, if a client complains of sexually deviant behavior, the first therapeutic intervention is usually directed toward reducing any inhibitions about normal sexual contact. This may be accomplished by a combination of desensitization procedures and training in appropriate expression. Generally the unwanted urges decrease when anxieties about "normal" sex, that is, sex with a consenting partner, diminish.

Such an approach is dictated not only by the moral imperative to employ the least painful method when there is a choice but also by the experimentally demonstrated futility of eliminating behavior through punishment when no alternative modes of satisfaction are available. Opening up alternatives is important in most cases in which punishment might otherwise be used. [p. 252]

Positive reinforcement (reward) approaches are generally more effective than those based on punishment. Punishment is often counterproductive as it can lead to the client's becoming hostile about the treatment procedures. Also, punishment may have only temporary effects. When clients realize they are no longer under surveillance, they may return to engaging in the dysfunctional behavior.

Cognitive Behavior-Modification Techniques

A major trend in behavior therapy in the past three decades has been toward a recognition of the role of cognition (thinking processes) in human behavior. Following the observations of cognitive therapists such as Albert Ellis (1962) and A. T. Beck (1976), cognitive behavior therapists have accepted the notion that changing thoughts will often change feelings and behavior.

The traditional paradigm of behavior therapy has been S (stimulus) $\rightarrow R$ (response). Cognitive behavior therapists insert an additional step in this paradigm:

$$S \text{ (stimulus)} \rightarrow O \text{ (cognitions of organism)} \rightarrow R \text{ (response)}[9]$$

This section summarizes the following techniques that have been developed to change cognitions: thought stopping and covert assertion, diversion techniques, and reframing.

Thought Stopping and Covert Assertion

Thought stopping is used for clients whose major problems involve obsessive thinking and ruminations about events that are very unlikely to occur (such as worrying that a plane they will be taking in two weeks will crash or that they are becoming mentally ill).

In thought stopping the client is first asked to concentrate on and express aloud her obsessive, anxiety-inducing thoughts. As she begins to express those thoughts, the therapist suddenly and emphatically shouts "Stop." This procedure is repeated several times until the client reports that her thoughts are being successfully interrupted. Then the

[9]The paradigm of cognitive behavior therapists [S (stimulus) $\rightarrow O$ (cognitions of organism) $\rightarrow R$ (response)] is very similar to the following paradigm of rational therapists [Events $\rightarrow$ Self-talk $\rightarrow$ Emotions and Actions]. See Chapter 22 on rational therapy.

responsibility for the intervention is shifted to the client, so that the client now tells herself "Stop" out loud when she begins to think about the troubling thoughts. Once the overt shouting is effective in stopping the troubling thoughts, the client begins to practice saying "Stop" silently to herself whenever the troubling thoughts begin.

Rimm and Masters (1974) supplemented the thought-stopping technique with a *covert assertion* procedure. In addition to having the client learn to interrupt the obsessive thoughts with saying "Stop," the client is encouraged to produce a positive, assertive statement that is incompatible with the content of the obsession. For example, a client who worries about becoming mentally ill (when there is no basis for such thinking) may be encouraged to add the covert assertion "Screw it! I'm perfectly normal" whenever he interrupts the obsessive thinking with "Stop."

Mahoney (1973) successfully used thought stopping and covert assertion as part of a comprehensive program for overweight clients. Mahoney first instructed the clients to become aware of such self-statements as, "I just don't have the will power" and "I sure can taste eating a strawberry sundae." The clients were then trained to use thought stopping and covert assertion to combat these thoughts.

Diversion Techniques

Diversion techniques are used to treat clients who have strong unwanted emotions such as loneliness, bitterness, depression, frustration, and anger. As indicated in Chapter 22, unwanted emotions stem primarily from negative and irrational thinking. When clients with unwanted emotions become involved in physical activity, work, social interactions, or play, they will usually switch their negative cognitions to different cognitions related to their new diversion activities. Once they focus their thinking on the diversion activities that they are finding meaningful and enjoyable, they will experience more pleasing emotions.

Diversion techniques are used in both rational therapy (see Chapter 22) and cognitive behavior therapy. Rational therapy and cognitive behavior therapy are closely related. In fact, rational therapy is sometimes classified as a cognitive behavioral approach.

Reframing

Reframing involves assisting a client to change those cognitions that are causing unwanted emotions or dysfunctional behaviors. As the following material describes, there are several categories of cognitions that may be reframed.

One focus of reframing is on *positive thinking.* When unpleasant events occur (such as receiving a lower grade on an exam than anticipated), we always have the choice of thinking positively or negatively. If we take a positive view and focus on problem solving, we are apt to identify and initiate actions to improve the circumstances. On the other hand, if we think negatively, we are likely to develop unwanted emotions (such as depression and frustration) and fail to focus on how to solve the problem. With negative thinking, we generally do not do anything constructive and may even engage in destructive behavior.

When a client is thinking negatively, a therapist can use reframing to assist the client in realizing he is thinking negatively. At times it is helpful to remind the client that both negative and positive thinking often become self-fulfilling prophecies (see Chapter 22). Then, by asking the client to identify some positive aspects of the situation, the therapist seeks to assist the client in thinking more positively. (If the client is unable to identify any positives, the therapist may suggest some.) The client may then be encouraged to tell herself "Stop" whenever she begins to think negatively and instead to focus on telling herself positive aspects of the situation. Some people take a negative view of most events that happen to them; for such people, reframing through using positive cognitions is more difficult and time-consuming. However, if they are successful in learning to think positively, they often make substantial gains.

A second closely related way in which reframing is used is *deawfulizing*. When distressing events occur, most of us tend to awfulize—we exaggerate the negatives. Think about your reactions when someone with whom you were romantically involved broke up with you, or when you received a parking or speeding citation. Did you awfulize and as a result feel angry, hurt, or depressed? When we awfulize we focus only on the negatives and do not identify constructive actions to improve the situation. When a client is awfulizing, a therapist can usually help the person identify such thought processes by simply inquiring, "I wonder if you're awfulizing?" The therapist can then assist the client, as described in the material on reframing with positive thinking, to give himself cognitions that are more positive and oriented toward problem solving.

When a client is awfulizing about distressing events that occurred, it is also helpful for the counselor to attempt to reframe the awfulizing by relating stories, such as "Good luck? Bad luck? Who knows?" (De Mello, 1978):

There is a Chinese story of an old farmer who had an old horse for tilling his fields. One day the horse escaped into the hills and when all the farmer's neighbors sympathized with the old man over his bad luck, the farmer replied, "Bad luck? Good luck? Who knows?" A week later the horse returned with a herd of wild horses from the hills and this time the neighbors congratulated the farmer on his good luck. His reply was, "Good luck? Bad luck? Who knows?" Then, when the farmer's son was attempting to tame one of the wild horses, he fell off its back and broke his leg. Everyone thought this very bad luck. Not the farmer, whose only reaction was, "Bad luck? Good luck? Who knows?" Some

weeks later the army marched into the village and conscripted every able-bodied youth they found there. When they saw the farmer's son with his broken leg, they let him off. Now was that good luck? Bad luck? Who knows? [p. 140]

Distressing events often are crises, which frequently lead those involved to make positive changes in their lives.

A third reframing focus involves *decatastrophizing* (Beck & Weishaar, 1989). This technique is used when clients are catastrophizing over anticipated feared events. Decatastrophizing involves continually asking clients "what if" an anticipated, undesired consequence occurs. The following is a dialogue with a 21-year-old college student who fears expressing his thoughts and feelings in class:

Therapist: What do you think will happen if you begin expressing your views in your classes?

Client: My voice may crack and the others may laugh at me.

Therapist: It is unlikely that your voice will crack. But even if it does, and the students happen to laugh a little, is that really worse than your anger and frustration over not sharing your thoughts?

Client: I don't know.

Therapist: Which is worse when you're asked a question in class? Shrugging your shoulders and appearing tongue-tied, or responding as well as you can even though your voice may crack?

Client: I hear what you're saying.

Therapist: What other negative consequences might occur if you begin expressing yourself in class?

Client: (pause) None that I can think of.

Therapist: What positives may come from your speaking up in class?

Client: I'd probably get more out of the class and feel better about myself. Enough of this. I get the message loud and clear. I will commit myself to speaking up at least once a week in each of my classes.

People who catastrophize usually exaggerate the anticipated feared consequences. De-catastrophizing is designed to demonstrate to clients that even if feared consequences occur (which they seldom do), those consequences are not as severe as feared.

A fourth focus of reframing is to assist clients on *separating positive intents from negative behaviors* so the positive intents then become linked to new positive behaviors. A parent who is physically abusive to a child has the positive intent of raising her child well, but when she is under stress and the child is misbehaving, that parent may not be aware that she has a number of other options that are much more constructive than physically beating her child. A therapist can assist such a parent by helping her reframe her thinking so that when the child misbehaves in the future she focuses her thinking processes on alternative responses, such as asking her husband to handle the child's misbehavior when she is under stress or by punishing the child with a timeout. (This type of reframing is described further in Chapter 17.)

Redefining is a fifth focus of reframing that is used for clients who believe a problem is beyond their personal control (Beck & Weishaar, 1989). A bored person who believes "Life is boring" may be encouraged to think, "The only reasons I'm bored is because I don't have special interests and because I'm not initiating activities. It's not life that is boring; it's my thinking processes that are leading me to feel bored. What I'm going to do is get involved in activities I enjoy and initiate interactions with people I like." Redefining is accomplished by the therapist first demonstrating that emotions, such as being bored, stem primarily from thoughts (see Chapter 22). The therapist next demonstrates that if the client thinks more positively and realistically, he will feel better. Together, the client and the therapist then identify the client's negative thinking patterns that are causing him to be-

lieve the problem is beyond his personal control. Finally they identify cognitions that the client makes a commitment to use to counter the cognitions that are (in actuality) causing his unwanted emotions and ineffective behaviors.

Decentering is a sixth focus of reframing that is used with anxious clients who erroneously believe they are the focus of everyone's attention (Beck & Weishaar, 1989). Reframing occurs by having such clients observe the behaviors of others rather than focusing on their own anxiety; thereby they come to realize they are not the center of attention. Beck and Weishaar (1989) gave an example:

> One student who was reluctant to speak in class believed his classmates watched him constantly and noticed his anxiety. By observing them instead of focusing on his own discomfort, he saw some students taking notes, some looking at the professor, and some daydreaming. He concluded his classmates had other concerns. [p. 310]

Additional cognitive change methods are being developed and hold considerable promise for behavior therapists to become increasingly involved in changing unwanted emotions and maladaptive behaviors of clients through changing their troubling thoughts (Hepworth & Larsen, 1986).

It is somewhat difficult to specify what is and what is not a cognitive-behavioral technique. In addition to the techniques described here, Cormier and Cormier (1991) identified the following as cognitive-behavioral techniques: role playing, problem-solving efforts, meditation, muscle relaxation, and paradoxical suggestions (see Chapter 8 for a description). In Chapter 22 it is asserted that changing irrational and negative cognitions may be the key psychotherapeutic change agent. Since practically all effective psychotherapeutic techniques change cognitions, then in a broad sense, practically all psychotherapeutic techniques can be considered cognitive-behavioral techniques.

Evaluation

It is difficult to make an overall evaluation of behavior therapy. Behavior therapy is composed of a wide range of therapy techniques, some of which are more effective than others. Also, behavior therapy is based on a variety of different learning theories, and there has never been agreement among behavior therapists about which learning theory should be the main focus of behavior therapy. Particularly controversial among behavior therapists is the learning approach being advocated by cognitive behavior therapists that states that emotions and actions are largely determined by our thoughts. Cognitive techniques are incompatible with the traditional principles of behaviorism, which has ignored cognitive processes because these thought processes cannot be measured and tested. Traditional behaviorism has sought to explain all behavior in terms of stimuli-response connections.

In the past 40 years behavior therapy has had a dramatic growth in the development of new treatment techniques and in the adoption of these techniques by members of the helping professions. Two books that inspired this development were *Science and Human Behavior* (Skinner, 1953) and *Psychotherapy by Reciprocal Inhibition* (Wolpe, 1958). Numerous books have since been published on behavior therapy. Behavior therapists have developed, and are continuing to develop, more treatment techniques than are emerging in any other psychotherapeutic area. One area that has not yet been mentioned but which has been heavily influenced by using behavior therapy techniques is sex therapy. (Chapter 18 describes sexual counseling and sex therapy in considerable detail.)

Behavior therapy is to be highly commended for its emphasis on testing the effectiveness of the treatment techniques that are developed. Such an emphasis is consistent with the demand by the public for human services to be accountable. With this emphasis on rigorous testing of therapy techniques, behavior therapy has discarded a number of techniques that have been found to be ineffective. Approaches that have shown effectiveness and are increasingly being used include assertiveness training for people who are shy or aggressive, contingency contracting with clients having a broad range of problems, token economies to change maladaptive behaviors of residents in institutional settings, and systematic desensitization with clients having irrational fears.

The future for behavior therapy is indeed bright. It is anticipated that helping professionals (psychologists, psychiatrists, social workers, guidance counselors, psychiatric nurses) will increasingly be trained in using behavior techniques.

There are also some criticisms that can be made of behavior therapy:

1. The research that has been conducted on many of the techniques has been on applying the techniques to the kind of problems that are readily tested in laboratory situations. Often successful results have been found. However, the kinds of problems that have been treated in laboratory situations are not the kinds of problems that clients commonly face. Prochaska (1979) has elegantly phrased this problem:

> So what if desensitization can reduce a college coed's fear of white rats? Does that have anything to do with the devastating problems that therapists are confronted with daily in their clinical practices? Whoever sees a snake phobic in a clinic? Most behaviorists would do themselves justice when planning a study if they asked the key clinical question for any outcome research—the so-what question. So what if having college students imagine vomiting in their lunches leads to a loss of a pound a week? So what if some of the loss lasts for four months? There is plenty of evidence that eighty-five percent of the people who lose weight through any means regain it within two years. How come only a tiny

fraction of their studies use a two-year follow-up? Are the authors more concerned with completing a thesis quickly or rushing to publish than with establishing a really useful therapy? [p. 354]

2. Many of the problems that clients face in the real world involve arriving at some decision. Should a pregnant 17-year-old teenager have an abortion or carry the pregnancy to full term? Should a husband and wife who have been married for 21 years and have fallen out of love with each other continue living together or seek a new life on their own? How should a recently divorced mother with three children try to support her family? How do you get a person with a drinking problem to admit he has a problem and make a decision to seek help? Should sons and daughters of an elderly parent seek to place him in a nursing home? How do you try to help a suicidal person make a decision not to take her life? How do you get a delinquent to make a decision to stop delinquent acts? How do you help a teenager who has run away from home make future plans about where to live? Behavior therapy does not have techniques for helping to arrive at such decisions. The focus of behavior therapy is on changing maladaptive behavior, not at arriving at decisions.

3. The punishment principles of behaviorism have occasionally been used in human services to justify cruel and inhuman treatment. Inmates in some prisons have been placed in isolation for several weeks at a time in environments lacking sensory stimulation. Adolescents in residential treatment centers and patients in mental hospitals have been placed in arm and leg restraints for several days at a time. Flogging has been used extensively in some situations. Aggressive residents at institutions for persons with a developmental disability have been placed in straitjackets during their waking hours for several months at a time. All these practices have been justified by the program directors as being part of a behavior modification program. However, well-trained behaviorists are highly critical of such inhumane uses of punishment.

Summary

The main assumption of behavior therapy is that maladaptive behaviors are acquired primarily through learning and can be modified through additional learning. Behavior therapy is based on learning theory. A number of somewhat different learning theories have been developed, and there has never been a consensus among behaviorists about which learning theory should be the basis of behavior therapy.

The main trend in behavior therapy in the past two decades has been toward a recognition of the role of cognition in human behavior. Some behavior therapists are now identifying themselves as cognitive behavior therapists and have accepted the notion that changing thoughts will often change feelings and behaviors. These theorists are now developing new techniques such as thought stopping, covert assertion, and reframing.

There are some common focuses among behaviorists. One is that maladaptive behavior is the problem and attention needs to be directed at changing the behavior rather than focusing on some unknown underlying causes. Behavior therapists assert that treating the maladaptive behavior will not result in symptom substitution. Another focus is the testing of therapy techniques by rigorous experimental procedures. Baseline levels of maladaptive behaviors are established before therapy to determine whether the therapy approach is producing the desired change in the rate or intensity of responding.

Behavior therapy is based on the assumption that all behavior occurs in response to stimulation, internal or external. The first task in the therapy process is for the therapist to do a behavioral analysis, which involves identifying the probable stimulus-response connections of the maladaptive behavior that are occurring for the client. Prior to and during the time the therapist is doing the behavioral analysis, the therapist is also attempting to establish a working relationship. Once the behavioral analysis is completed, the findings are discussed with the client, and the client and the therapist agree on the goals for the treatment. The treatment procedures and techniques are then described to the client.

This chapter summarizes some of the most commonly used behavior therapy techniques: assertiveness training, token economies, contingency contracting, systematic desensitization, in vivo desensitization, implosive therapy, covert sensitization, aversive techniques, and cognitive behavior-modification techniques. Most of these techniques (particularly systematic desensitization, in vivo desensitization, implosive therapy, covert sensitization, and aversive techniques) should be used only by skilled therapists with extensive training because improper application may intensify the problematic behavior or create undesired side effects.

Exercises

1. Contingency contracting

Goal: This exercise is designed to demonstrate the principles of contingency contracting by having students apply the principles to their own behavior.

Step 1: Describe the goal of this exercise and also explain the principles of contingency contracting.

Step 2: Ask each student to prepare a contract about an area of behavior he or she would like to change. The behavior may involve an area such as eating less, drinking less, exercising more, ending procrastination, studying more, or increasing contact with parents and other relatives. In preparing the contract, ask the students to write on a sheet of paper answers to the following questions. (Indicate that they will not be required to reveal what they wrote.)

    a. What behavior do you want to change? (Be as specific as possible.)
    b. What is your behavior goal?
    c. What specifically will you do to achieve this goal?
    d. What are your deadlines for doing these tasks?
    e. How will you reward yourself for doing the tasks necessary to reach this goal?
    f. What adverse consequences will you apply to yourself if you fail to do the tasks?

Step 3: Ask for volunteers to share what they wrote. Have the class discuss the merits and shortcomings of writing such a contingency contract.

Step 4: As an added component of the exercise, students may discuss whether they want to attempt to fulfill the conditions they have written into their contracts. If the class decides to do this, a future date (such as four weeks later) may be set for them to describe their successes and failures in fulfilling the conditions of their contract.

2. Learning to be assertive

Goal: This exercise is designed to help students learn how to be assertive in problematic interactions where in the past they were either nonassertive or aggressive.

Step 1: Describe the purpose of this exercise. Explain the differences between nonassertive, aggressive, and assertive behavior. Indicate that everyone is nonassertive or aggressive in some situations in which it would be more constructive to be assertive. Ask students to silently identify a situation in the past in which they wished they had been assertive, rather than being aggressive or nonassertive. Give some examples such as the following: The situation may involve being told to do something you did not want to do. Or, perhaps someone was smoking a cigarette near you, which bothered you. Or, perhaps someone made a put-down comment about you. Or, perhaps you're unable to express what you feel about certain situations to your parents, or to someone you're dating. Before proceeding further, ask whether the students have identified such a situation in which they wished they had been assertive. Do not proceed to the next step until everyone has identified a situation.

Step 2: State the following: "We will now do a visualization exercise that is designed to help you learn to be more assertive in the situation you identified. There will be no tricks in this exercise. Close your eyes and keep them closed during this exercise. Get as comfortable as possible in your chair, and slowly take a couple of deep breaths to become relaxed.

"Focus on a specific incident in your past when you wanted to be assertive, but instead were either nonassertive or aggressive. Visualize all the details of what happened. (*Pause a few seconds after asking each of the following questions.*) What was said to you? What did you fail to say that you wanted to say? What did you say that you didn't want to say? How did you feel about what was said? How do you now feel about this incident? Your nonverbal communication is as important in being assertive as is verbal communication. Think about your nonverbal communication. What did you communicate with your facial expressions? What did you communicate with your body posture? Did you look down or away from the other person? Did you glare at the other person? What did your gestures communicate? What was your voice tone and volume like? Did your voice crack? Did you yell or speak softly? Did you speak rapidly or with hesitation? During this incident which of your verbal and nonverbal communications were nonassertive? Which were aggressive? Which were assertive?

"Now, let's turn to focus on how to handle this situation more assertively when it arises again. Continue to keep your eyes closed. What might you say that would assertively handle this situation? (*Pause.*) What changes do you need to make in your nonverbal communication to present yourself more assertively? (*Pause.*) Is there someone you know who would be good at handling this situation assertively? (*Pause.*) If there is someone, what would this person say or do? (*Pause.*) Does this assertive model give you some ideas on how you might assertively handle this situation? (*Pause.*)

"Continue to visualize various approaches that might work for you. Also, visualize yourself using each of these approaches. For each approach, imagine the full set of interactions that would occur if you were to use the approach. (*Pause.*)

"Now, seek to select an assertive approach that you believe would best work for you when the nonassertive or aggressive situation arises again in the future. Are you now sufficiently prepared and confident to use this approach in a real-life situation? If not, you may want to visualize further what you might say or do to increase your confidence. Or, you may want to select another approach that you would be more comfortable in using. Or, you may want to role-play your approach with a friend so that you become more comfortable in using the approach. (*Pause.*)

"The real test will come when you try out your assertive approach in a real-life situation. The next time your problematic situation arises, seek to use your assertive approach. After trying it out, analyze how it turned out. Pat yourself on the back for what you did well. Identify aspects of your nonverbal and verbal communication that you need to improve in order to express yourself more assertively. Visualize ways in which you might more assertively express yourself in the areas you need to work on.

"Above all, congratulate yourself on your efforts to become more assertive. You've earned feeling good about yourself. Learning to express yourself in situations that you're comfortable in is one of the greatest thrills you'll ever experience. OK, gradually open your eyes, and take a little while to relax."

Step 3: Ask whether there are any questions or comments about the exercise. Then ask whether there are any situations they would like to see others in the class role-play. If students suggest some situations, have other students role-play these. If no situations are suggested, ask for volunteers to role-play situations you suggest, such as these:

a. Asking someone to put out a cigarette that is bothering you.
b. Refusing to accept an alcoholic drink that a friend wants to buy for you when you prefer not to drink any more alcoholic beverages that day.
c. Saying no when someone asks to borrow something you don't want to lend, such as a sweater.

3. Expressing anger assertively

Goal: The purpose of this exercise is to help students learn assertive and constructive ways to express their anger.

Step 1: Describe the goal of this exercise. Indicate that many people have not learned to express their anger assertively for a variety of reasons. Some of us have been brought up to believe it is wrong to get angry, so we seek to deny our anger. Some of us, through modeling, have learned to express our anger aggressively, thereby lashing out and hurting others. Indicate that we have a right to all our emotions. It is normal to become angry at times. Others do not have a right to try to convince us that we should not be angry when we are angry.

When anger is not expressed assertively, it is often expressed destructively. We may aggressively hurt others. Or, we may try to deny we are angry, and instead turn the anger inward and become depressed. Or, we may recognize the anger, but fail to express it, which can result in anxiety. Or, anger may lead to guilt if we punish ourselves for getting angry when we erroneously believe we should not get angry. Or, we may seek to relieve our angry feelings through excessive drinking or eating.

Step 2: Explain that there are assertive and constructive ways to express anger. These ways include the following:

a. Expressing angry feelings assertively so no one is hurt in the process. When expressing anger assertively, it is advisable to use nonblaming "I-messages" rather than "You-messages." (See Chapter 20 for a description of I-messages.)

b. Expressing angry feelings at the time we become angry so we do not "stew" about it. If we delay expressing anger, the hostility may built and we may explode and lash out at others.

c. Admitting to ourselves when we are angry, so that we do not try to hide our anger from ourselves. Through acknowledging our anger, we are better able to focus on finding constructive ways to express our anger.

d. Blowing off steam nondestructively through such physical activities as jogging, hitting a pillow or punching bag, taking a walk, or lifting weights, whenever it is counterproductive to express our anger or when we feel we are apt to explode.

e. Seeking to counter negative and irrational self-talk by writing out a rational self-analysis (see Chapter 22).

Step 3: Ask each student to complete the following three statements on a sheet of paper:

a. Three or four things that make me angry are
b. I usually express my anger by
c. Things that I can do to better handle and express my anger are

Step 4: Have the students form subgroups of three people each to share what they wrote and to receive additional suggestions on how to express their anger more effectively. (Indicate that students have a right to privacy, and therefore they do not have to self-disclose what they want to keep private.)

Step 5: Form a circle and ask the students whether they have any questions or comments about the exercise or about what was discussed in the subgroups.

4. Reframing

Goal: This exercise is designed to demonstrate to students how to reframe cognitions involving "awfulizing."

Step 1: Describe the concepts of "reframing" and "awfulizing." Illustrate the process of awfulizing by giving a few examples of occasions when you have awfulized in the past.

Step 2: Instruct each student to record his or her responses to the following questions and instructions on a sheet of paper. Indicate that students will not be required to reveal their responses.

a. Briefly describe a distressing event that occurred to you over which you awfulized.
b. Specify the awfulizing cognitions that you gave yourself about this distressing event.
c. For each awfulizing cognition, specify a more positive and realistic cognition that you could give yourself about this event. (Ideally, many of these countering cognitions should also facilitate problem solving.)
d. Indicate the approximate length of time that you awfulized over this event.
e. Are you still awfulizing about this event?
f. Do you believe countering the awfulizing cognitions with more positive and realistic cognitions would have shortened the time you spent awfulizing?

Step 3: Ask for volunteers to share their responses to these questions. End by asking the students to indicate their thoughts on the merits and shortcomings of using reframing in therapy.

17

Neuro-Linguistic Programming

Neuro-Linguistic Programming (NLP) is a recently developed model of communication that promises to have substantial application in assessing human behavior, in developing rapport, in influencing others (in education, public speaking, and sales), and in changing behavior (psychotherapy).[1] NLP was developed by John Grinder, Richard Bandler, and several other authorities (Lankton, 1980).

Practically all the psychotherapeutic treatment approaches described in this text were developed by psychiatrists and clinical psychologists. In contrast, NLP was developed primarily by specialists in communication and linguistics. The roots of NLP can be traced to Gregory Bateson, an anthropologist. Bateson conducted a broad range of research in anthropology, psychiatry, and communication patterns among dolphins. One of Bateson's interests was to synthesize cybernetic ideas with anthropology. *Cybernetics* is the science of communication and control theory; it focuses primarily on the compara-

[1]Material in this chapter is adapted from Charles Zastrow, Virginia Dotson, and Michael Koch, "The Neuro-Linguistic Programming Treatment Approach," *Journal of Independent Social Work* 1, (Fall 1986), pp. 29–38. Permission to adapt this material was received from The Haworth Press, Inc.

tive study of automatic control systems—such as comparing the human central nervous system with mechanical-electrical systems.

In 1952 Gregory Bateson received a grant from the Rockefeller Foundation to investigate communication in hypnosis, ventriloquism, animal training, popular moving pictures, the nature of play, humor, schizophrenia, neurotic communication, psychotherapy, family systems, and family therapy. The staff in this project consisted primarily of communication analysts and psychiatric consultants. As this communication research continued, other funding sources provided grants: the Macy Foundation, the Foundations Fund for Research in Psychiatry, and the National Institute of Mental Health (Haley, 1963).

In the 1970s John Grinder and Richard Bandler, specialists in communication and linguistics, became involved in these research projects. Using an approach similar to that of Bateson and his associates, Grinder and Bandler studied the nonverbal and verbal communication patterns between prominent therapists and their clients. The therapists included Salvador Minuchin (see Chapter 8), Virginia Satir (see Chapter 8), and Milton Erickson (a leading practitioner of medical hypnosis, which is described in Chapter 20.)

Grinder and Bandler's special genius is the ability to observe the communication patterns of prominent psychotherapists and then to describe in detail what they do, what cues they respond to, and how they go about helping clients make positive changes. Such descriptions, theoretically, make it possible for others to learn how to repeat the same procedures and get similar results.

Numerous texts are now appearing that describe the applications of the NLP communication model to business, sales, education, and psychotherapy (Haley, 1973; Bandler & Grinder, 1975, 1976, 1979, 1982; Lankton, 1980; Laborde, 1984). NLP is primarily a model of communication. NLP does not provide a theory of personality development or of psychopathology. The remainder of this chapter will focus primarily on NLP's applications to counseling and psychotherapy.

NLP Defined

Neuro-linguistic programming is the study of the structure of subjective experience (Lankton, 1980, p. 13). It makes explicit patterns of behavior and change that have previously been only intuitively understandable. The components of the term *neuro-linguistic programming* refer to the following:

neuro: nervous system through which experience is received and processed via the five senses.
linguistic: language and nonverbal communication systems through which neural representations are coded, ordered, and given meaning.
programming: ability to organize our communication and neurological systems to achieve specific desired outcomes.

NLP is a model, rather than a theory, of human behavior. A theory is a hypothesis that attempts to explain or interpret the *reasons* things relate as they do. A model, in contrast, is a copy or pattern of already existing phenomena, which, as designed, can be imitated or re-created. A model deals only with what can be observed. For example, a theory of what causes psychotherapeutic changes would seek to specify key variables that lead to positive changes in clients (such as clients being motivated to change). A model, in contrast, would formulate a framework. A framework might be formulated that seeks to represent the verbal and nonverbal communication between people. The framework might then be observed to determine the kinds of verbal and nonverbal messages from a therapist that lead to improved or desired responses from clients.

Representational Systems

Before reading further, take a few minutes to identify what you remember most about the following:

The last grocery store you were in.
What you did on your last birthday.
Your high school days.
Your most enjoyable sexual experience.
Your most enjoyable vacation.

Everyone has, at most, five sensory systems through which they contact physical reality. These senses are the eyes (visual), ears (auditory), skin (kinesthetic), nose (smell), and tongue (taste). For each of these questions, you probably responded with remembrances involving only one or two senses. Taking the grocery store question, you may have had an *image* of fresh fruits and vegetables, or *heard* the hustle and bustle of the activity, or remember *feeling* the Charmin™ bathroom tissue, or remember *smelling* the pleasant aromas of the fresh flowers, or remember *tasting* the free samples of freshly cooked pizza.

Anytime a person interacts with the external world, he or she does so through sensory representations. Your sensory contact with a grocery store is apt to be quite different from that of your closest friend. The same applies for everyone. Your most enjoyable sexual experience may be a visual one, while your partner's may be auditory or kinesthetic.

We operate out of our sensory representations of the world, and not in "reality" itself. Our sensory representations provide us with a *map* of the territory. But the map is *not* the territory.

According to NLP, to assess another's actions accurately, it is important to identify the sensory representational system being used by that person. If we are able to identify the other's representational system and "join with" that system in our interactions with that person, communication is apt to flow

Case Example
Sensory representational systems

A married couple sought counseling as they felt their sexual relationship was deteriorating rapidly. After rapport had been established, the counselor asked each, "What tends to turn you on sexually?" The husband mentioned it was hearing romantic things said to him while the wife mentioned it was being softly touched in a variety of areas. Not too surprisingly, the husband was trying to excite his wife by saying romantic things (without touching his wife much), while the wife was seeking to excite her husband by touching him while remaining silent. A simple description of the importance of "joining" with the other's representational system greatly enhanced their love life with the husband spending much more time in tenderly caressing his wife and the wife romantically talking to her husband.

much more smoothly and rapport is enhanced. On the other hand, if two people are not able to "join" together with the same representational system, communication is apt to be tangential and rapport will be adversely affected. The importance of this point is immense. Successful salespersons, educators, and therapists are able to identify and "join" with the representational systems of the persons they are seeking to influence. Once a person (customer, student, or client) has joined with the influencer, the influencer is able to lead the person in the direction she or he chooses. To a large extent the process of therapy, education, and sales can be defined as involving two steps: (1) the influencer's finding a way to join with the person to be influenced, and (2) the influencer's leading the person in a new (and, one hopes, positive) direction.

There are several ways for an influencer to join with the person to be influenced. These ways include (1) joining with the person's representational system, (2) talking knowledgeably with the person about subjects that interest the person, and (3) mirroring (without the person being consciously aware of the mirroring) the person's nonverbal communication—such as posture, gestures, and breathing patterns.

In discussing influencing, it is intriguing to note that there are some remarkable similarities between social workers and salespeople (see Exhibit 17.1).

Representational System Predicates

The adverbs, adjectives, and verbs that people select while speaking reveal the sensory system they are most conscious of at that point in time. NLP calls these words *predicates*.

In our culture people use primarily the visual, auditory, and kinesthetic systems. (A few other cultures in other countries place greater emphasis on smell and taste.) Unless the listener is aware of the sensory representational system the speaker is using, the listener may misinterpret what the speaker is intending. For example, when a client says "I understand you," the intended message depends on the representational system he or she is in:

Visual: "That looks really good to me."
Auditory: "I hear you clearly."
Kinesthetic: "What you are saying feels right to me."

Exhibit 17.1
Social workers and salesworkers: similarities and differences

There are several striking similarities in the essential characteristics of competent social workers and successful salesworkers. I am aware that some social work purists will find it degrading to compare the characteristics of social workers (who seek to enable people to achieve self-fulfillment and social well-being) to the characteristics of salesworkers (who are viewed as being guided primarily to sell more for personal financial gain). In response to such criticism, I urge that such pursuits reflect on the similarities and differences between these two endeavors. There is considerable evidence that social workers frequently need to "sell" themselves and the services they provide (Lankton, 1980). It appears that component social workers must possess extensive selling skills.

Contrasting Goals Between Sales and Social Work

There are wide differences between the goals of salesworkers and social workers. The salesworker's primary goal is to sell products and services. A successful salesworker receives a high salary and substantial commissions because she or he is very successful in selling products and services. A social worker is a "change agent"—a helper who is employed specifically for the purpose of creating planned change. As a change agent a social worker is expected to be skilled at working with individuals, groups, organizations, and families and at bringing about community changes.

In spite of these wide differences in goals, the following material suggests that several characteristics needed by social workers to accomplish their goals have remarkable similarities to the characteristics needed by salesworkers to accomplish their goal. Theorists who developed neuro-linguistic programming have identified the following common characteristics.

Capacity to Influence Is a Key Skill

NLP theorists assert that an essential capacity needed by social workers, salesworkers, psychotherapists, educators, and public speakers is the capacity to influence others.

NLP notes that the process of influencing another involves two steps: (1) the influencer finds a way to "join" with the person to be influenced, and (2) the influencer then leads the person in a new (and preferably positive) direction. Once the influencee (customer, client, or student) has joined with the influencer, the influencer is better able to lead the influencee in the direction desired. The concepts advanced by NLP have considerable power in enabling influencers to influence people more effectively.

The Process of "Joining" Involves Forming a Relationship

According to NLP, the first step in influencing someone involves the influencer's forming a relationship with the influencee. This process has also been called establishing rapport.

A number of guidelines have been developed for social workers to use in establishing rapport with clients. Many of these guidelines are summarized here.

- The social worker should seek to establish a nonthreatening, comfortable atmosphere in which the client feels safe to communicate his or her needs or wants while feeling accepted as a person.
- To identify better the client's needs and wants, the social worker should observe closely his or her nonverbal and verbal communication.
- In initial contacts with the client, the social worker should "sell" himself or herself—not arrogantly but as a knowledgeable, understanding person who may be able to help and who seeks to find ways to meet the client's needs or wants.
- The social worker should not laugh or express shock when the client begins to talk about his or her needs or wants. Emotional outbursts, even if subtle, will lead the client to believe the social worker is not going to understand his or her problems.

(continued)

- The social worker should generally be nonjudgmental, not moralistic. The social worker should show respect for the client's values and should not try to sell his or her values to the client.
- The beginning of a relationship is often facilitated if the social worker engages in small talk with the client. Such informal conversation sometimes provides information to the social worker about the needs and wants of the client.
- The social worker should not seek to establish a superior-inferior relationship with the client. Instead, the social worker should convey that the client is a worthy, "equal" person in the relationship. If the client feels he or she is being treated as an inferior, he or she will be less motivated to reveal wants and needs.
- The social worker should generally not use high-pressure techniques designed to force the client to choose an option he or she may not want. Instead, the social worker should make a variety of options available, help the client assess the merits and shortcomings of each option, and convey that the client has the right and responsibility to make his or her own decision.
- The social worker should use a "shared vocabulary" with the client. This does not mean that the social worker should use the same slang words and the same accent as the client. If the client perceives the social worker's speech as artificial, she or he may be seriously offended. The social worker should use words that the client readily understands and that are not offensive.
- The tone of the social worker's voice and his or her nonverbal communication should convey that the social worker empathetically understands the client's wants and needs, and cares about the client's feelings.
- The social worker should convey that the client is an important, worthwhile person.
- The social worker is a good listener who has skills in identifying the client's needs and wants.

The similarities between essential characteristics needed by social workers and salesworkers can be demonstrated by noting that salesworkers also need to "join with" customers. It is interesting that the guidelines for salesworkers in establishing rapport with customers are remarkably similar to the guidelines for social workers in establishing rapport with clients. This is easily demonstrated by noting that exchanging the words "social worker" for "salesworker" and "client" for "customer" in the guidelines above will provide guidelines salesworkers can use to establish rapport with customers.

As noted earlier, social workers are skilled at working with individuals, groups, families, and organizations. They function in roles that include counselor, broker, advocate, and consultant. They also work with administrators, public officials, board members of funding sources, and helping professionals at other agencies. In practically all this work, the essence of bringing about positive change involves the social worker's establishing rapport and then seeking to lead the person or persons to be influenced in a new direction.

Differences Between Social Workers and Salesworkers

It would be a serious mistake, however, to conclude that because of these similarities social workers can also be viewed as salesworkers. There are substantial differences between social workers and salesworkers. These differences include the following:

- Social workers have the responsibility of helping people find ways to meet their social, financial, recreational, and health needs. Salesworkers, on the other hand, focus on selling products or services. Salesworkers are much more guided by the profit motive.
- Social workers receive substantially more training in the following areas: human behavior, intervention techniques, research, social policy, social problems, and social services. Salesworkers receive more training in product knowledge and in sales techniques. Some sales techniques are practically never used by

social workers, such as lavishly entertaining a customer (client) in the hopes that she or he will be more inclined to make a large purchase.

• Social workers focus on improving the lives of people. One of the highest rewards and satisfactions in social work comes from seeing people grow and develop from services that are provided. Salesworkers focus on selling products and services. A major reward for salesworkers is to sell more in order to earn more money.

• Laborde (1984) in *Influencing with Integrity* made an important distinction between "influencing with integrity" and manipulating." In manipulating, the influencer seeks to lead a person in a direction that is in the influencer's self-interest. "Influencing with integrity" involves leading an influencee in a direction that is in the influencee's best interests. Some salesworkers have the image of seeking to influence customers in the salesworker's self-interests (that is, of seeking to sell products or services so that the salesworker will benefit financially). On the other hand, social workers have a strong ethical obligation to influence with integrity.

• Social workers focus on helping clients assess and identify their personal, social, emotional, health, and financial needs. Once such needs are identified, the role of the social worker is to help clients explore alternatives for meeting these needs. Salesworkers generally do not become involved in assessing and identifying their clients' social-emotional needs. Their focus is on identifying the customers' purchase desires, and then informing customers of products or services they are selling that may meet those desires. Sometimes salesworkers seek to stimulate a purchase desire in customers.

• The focus of the relationship between a social worker and client is to create a nonthreatening atmosphere in which the client is expected to communicate his or her personal concerns, some of which are highly charged emotionally. In a salesworker-customer relationship, the customer is expected to share his or her purchase desires. It is generally considered inappropriate for the customer to share highly charged personal concerns.

Usefulness of Comparing Social Workers and Salesworkers

Why is it important to compare the nature of the work performed by social workers to that performed by salesworkers? The primary benefit of this comparison is to emphasize that in establishing relationships with clients a social worker must nonarrogantly "sell" himself or herself as a warm, caring person who has expertise and who may be able to assist clients with difficulties they are experiencing. In this process of establishing a relationship, social workers need to present themselves in a way that has remarkable similarities to the ways in which successful salesworkers present themselves to customers.

This comparison also emphasizes the conceptualization (advanced by NLP) that an essential characteristic needed not only by social workers and salesworkers but also by educators and public speakers is the capacity to influence others. This influencing process involves two steps: "joining with" the influencee, and "leading" the influencee in a new (preferably constructive) direction. In this influencing process the influencer has to give attention not only to verbal communication but also to nonverbal communication so the optimal conditions will be created for the prospective influencee to want to "join with" the influencer. Aspects of nonverbal communication that the influencer needs to pay attention to include posture, body orientation (the extent to which the influencer faces toward or away from the influencee with head, body, and feet), facial expressions, eye contact, gestures, clothing and personal appearance, and appearance of the office (Mehrabian, 1981).

Social workers have an ethical obligation to seek to influence clients with integrity rather than for personal gain. Some readers may dislike viewing social workers as influencers. They may assert that clients have a right to self-determination and that social workers therefore should not seek to influence them.

In reality, social workers *must* seek to influence clients in constructive directions. If that was not their objective, then their role would be empty and meaningless. Conceptualizing social workers as influencers is *not* inconsistent with clients' rights to self-determination. The right to self-determination holds that clients have a right to express their own opinions and to act on them, as long as they do not infringe on the rights of

(continued)

others. In a salesworker-customer relationship it is clearly recognized that the customer retains the right to decide what he or she will purchase, even though the salesworker functions as an influencer. Similarly, in a social worker–client relationship the client retains the right to express his or her opinions, and to make his or her own decisions. A social worker acts as an influencer by using a problem-solving process. The steps in this process include these:

1. Helping clients identify their problems and needs.
2. Helping clients identify alternatives for meeting these difficulties and needs.
3. Helping clients assess the merits and shortcomings of these alternatives.
4. Urging clients to select and implement one or more of these alternatives.
5. Helping clients evaluate the outcomes of the strategies implemented, after the strategies have been implemented for a reasonable length of time.

SOURCE: This material is adapted from Charles Zastrow, "Social Workers and Salesworkers: Similarities and Differences," *Journal of Independent Social Work* 4, no. 3, 1990, pp. 7–16.

In the course of growing up, people learn to favor particular representational systems for particular events. People are not totally visual or auditory or kinesthetic. The sense in use depends on the situation, the context. It appears, though, that people tend to have a primary mode, in that they tend to use more of the one mode than the others (Laborde, 1984, p.57).

Exhibit 17.2 identifies a number of visual, auditory, and kinesthetic "predicates." Mismatched predicates interfere with communication and rapport, as indicated by the following example:

Client: I *feel* so awful! The IRS has just audited me and I just can't *handle* it!
Counselor: I *hear* you. It *sounds bad, but tell* me what it is that's so bad.
Client: I just can't *lift* this *feeling*. It's so *heavy!*
Counselor: Yes, but I don't *hear* what the problem is. *Listen* to me and *tell* me what's so bad!

In this illustration, the client is apt to end up viewing the counselor as being insensitive. An example of matched predicates in this situation is the following:

Exhibit 17.2

Predicates to identify sensory representational systems

Visual	Auditory	Kinesthetic
Appear	Audible	Back away
Clear	Buzz	Break down
Colors	Double talk	Bounce
Farsighted	Earshot	Caress
Foresee	Echo	Catch
Glance	Hear	Cold
Hindsight	Hear from	Dig in
Horizon	In tune with	Feel
Illustrate	Listen	Firm
Image	Loud	Grasp
In the dark	Muffled	Handle
Look	Noisy	Hard
Observe	Pronounced	Hold
Overview	Quiet	Iron out
Picture	Resound	Press
Resemble	Rings a bell	Rack your
Scan	Roar	brains
See	Rumbling	Run through
Show	Screech	Sensitive
Tint	Sound	Sensuous
Vague	Sound off	Stumble upon
Vision	Thundering	Toss around
Watch	Whispering	Touch
		Vibes

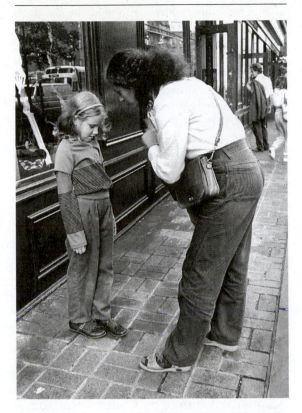

Contrary to popular belief, a child looking down while being scolded is not an indication the child is trying to ignore the parent but rather is a sign that she is feeling bad.

Client: I *feel* so awful! The IRS has just audited me and I just can't *handle* it!

Counselor: You *feel* as if you're *breaking down* because of the *heaviness* of the audit.

Client: That's exactly it. I'm *stumbling,* but yet *grasping to hold on.*

Counselor: What do you *feel* you need to *hold* on?

Client: *Support* and understanding from my wife, my tax accountant, and you.

In this example the counselor phrases her responses to be consistent with the client's representational system, which leads to better understanding and increased trust and rapport.

Eye-Accessing Cues

Listening to the predicates in another's speech is one reliable way to determine which representational system is dominant at a given time. Eye-accessing cues is another way. Generally the sensory system can be identified by eye-accessing cues as displayed in Figure 17.1.

As always with rules, there are exceptions: for example, some left-handers' kinesthetic representational system is eyes down and to the left, with the eyes down and to the right being their auditory representational system. To test out this information, the reader should ask friends or acquaintances questions such as "What do you remember most about your last vacation?" to watch how the eye-accessing cues are apt to be consistent with responses that are either visual, kinesthetic, or auditory.

A simple example will illustrate the importance of recognizing eye-accessing cues. When parents are scolding their children, it is common in our society for parents to become additionally angry when the children are looking down. Those parents who become additionally upset are erroneously assuming their children are ignoring what they are saying when they are looking down. They may even yell, "Look at me when I'm talking to you!" In actuality, the eyes being down is a sign that the children are feeling bad about their misbehavior—which is the feeling that parents want their children to have in such situations.

The Four-Tuple

The four-tuple is a way of representing a person's sensory experience at a moment in time. Its general form is V, K, A, O. These capital letters are abbreviations for the major sensory channels: *Visual, Kinesthetic, Auditory,* and *Olfactory / Gustatory.*

Visual	Eyes up right	Eyes up left	Eyes straight ahead defocused
Auditory	Eyes level right	Eyes level left	Eyes down left
Kinesthetic	Eyes down right		

Figure 17.1
Eye-accessing cues

It is also useful to distinguish between experiences that are internally generated (remembering or imagining a visual image, feeling, sound, or smell), and those that are externally generated (sights, sensations, sounds, or smells that we receive from the external world). Therefore, the superscript e is used to refer to external cues and the superscript i to internal cues. The experience of someone whose senses are fully turned outward is V^e, K^e, A^e, O^e. Someone attending fully to an internal event, oblivious of the immediate surroundings is V^i, K^i, A^i, O^i.

Most of us, at any point in time, are generally in a mixed state in which some of our senses are outwardly attending and some of our experiences are remembered or imagined. Also, many times one or more of the sensory systems will not be in use. The following example shows how this notational system can be used. Whenever Mrs. Worth *hears* about the Christmas season, she *visualizes* being at her husband's funeral several years ago, two days before Christmas day. (He was killed in an automobile accident.)

She remembers how depressed she *felt* afterwards. These cues in sequence are: A^e, V^i, K^i.

The usefulness of this concept can be readily demonstrated. Think about the last time you said something to someone and received an unusual response. Undoubtedly what happened was that your intended message led the listener to remember auditory, visual, kinesthetic, or olfactory events from the past, which then led the listener to respond primarily in terms of the internal cues. NLP makes an important point by asserting: *The meaning of a communication is the response it elicits, regardless of the intent.*

In therapy, an NLP counselor frequently seeks to identify the patterns of the thought processes that are destructive or disturbing to clients and then seeks directly or indirectly to change their patterns. Two of the techniques that are used in this process are metaphors and reframing.

Causing Change by Communicating in Metaphor

NLP uses the term *metaphor* to refer to the use of anecdotes, puns, analogies, and stories in therapy. Metaphors are particularly useful for clients who tend to resist direct suggestions. Metaphors also stimulate the interest of clients. One of the most recognized experts in the use of metaphors was Dr. Milton Erickson, a psychiatrist. (John Grinder and Richard Bandler studied Erickson's techniques extensively while developing the NLP approach.)

Haley (1973) provided the following example of Erickson's use of metaphors in working with a married couple who are embarrassed about discussing directly a conflict over their sexual relationship.

He will choose some aspect of their lives that is analogous to sexual relations and change that as a way of changing the sexual behavior. He might, for example, talk to them about having dinner together and draw them out on their preferences. He will discuss with them how the wife likes appetizers before dinner, while the husband prefers to dive right into the meat and potatoes. Or the wife might prefer a quiet and leisurely dinner, while the husband, who is quick and direct, just wants the meal over with. . . . He might end such a conversation with a directive that the couple arrange a pleasant dinner on a particular evening that is satisfactory to both of them. When successful, this approach shifts the couple from a more pleasant dinner to more pleasant sexual relations without their being aware that he has deliberately set this goal. [pp. 27–28]

I have used storytelling (with some stories being real and others contrived to fit the clients' circumstances) with a variety of clients. The following are some examples. A 21-year-old male college student was thinking of taking his life because his woman friend had left him to date someone else, he was not receiving the grades he desired, and he did not know what he wanted to major in. I asked him to visualize the following scene.

Let's assume you slit your wrists this evening and no one discovers you until you're dead. There will be blood all over. Tomorrow morning your younger brother or someone else will discover you in this pool of blood. For months and years afterward, this person will have nightmares about this scene. Eventually he may seek to end his nightmares in the same way you did—that happens! After they find you, a funeral director will be called and he will embalm you, which involves a variety of unpleasant procedures. Your parents will be shocked, and will forevermore be searching for why you did what you did—and feeling guilty that they had failed you. Your former woman friend will be temporarily shocked, but she will experience a sense of relief that you will no longer be able to seek to manipulate her by threaten-

ing suicide. She'll move on with her life and eventually marry someone else. People will come to your funeral and say a variety of things, including the statement that you didn't have the courage to face life's problems. In this funeral scene of mental anguish and confusion, the cover of the coffin will then be closed. You will be taken to the cemetery. Perhaps it's raining and chilly. You will be lowered into the ground, and slowly your body will deteriorate. If there is an air leak in the coffin, you will deteriorate much faster—perhaps worms may enter. Is this what you want?

Most people who are contemplating suicide think only about the pain and difficulties they are facing. The preceding story helps them see that what happens after suicide may be worse than their present agony. In this case the male student stopped thinking about taking his life and started focusing on resolving the problems he faced.

For a 21-year-old woman who was dating a married man (the married man refused to come into counseling), I vividly told a detailed story about another client who had a miserable life for seven years while dating a married man; that man refused to leave his wife for financial reasons and because he did not want to disappoint his children. This story helped the woman give her male friend an ultimatum—either you leave your wife in 30 days or our relationship is over. In this case the man refused to leave his wife and the woman ended the relationship.

For a 15-year-old adolescent female who thought her life would improve if she became pregnant and then had a child who would love her, I arranged for a single working mother (in her twenties) to talk about the following: young children *take* love and affection; they *give* very little in return; the financial costs of raising a child are enormous; being a mother is a full-time job that interferes with dating, partying, forming a relationship with a male, and developing a career. After this talk, the 15-year-old decided to wait for several years before wanting to again try to become a parent.

Reframing

Reframing involves turning clients' negative behavior, thoughts, and feelings into resources. The function of the problem part is simply altered for the clients' benefit to get them what they want more effectively. (See the following case example.)

NLP asserts that it is enduringly useful to presuppose a positive intent behind all behavior. The focus of reframing is to separate the positive intent from the negative behavior so that the positive intent then becomes linked to new positive behavior.

According to NLP "The cure lies within" the client. Clients already have the resources they need to resolve their difficulties. Clients who are in problematic situations are generally making undesirable choices. Reframing is a way to help clients make more constructive choices. (Reframing is also described in Chapter 16.)

Therapeutic Change Often Occurs Without Knowing the Cause of the Problem

Counselors who use traditional psychotherapeutic approaches spend considerable time trying to assess the causes of the problematic behavior. NLP asserts that positive changes can occur without intense attention being directed at the causes. Instead, the focus is on first identifying what the client wants and then on helping the client to identify the ways and the resources he or she already has to achieve his goals.

A college student walked into my office at the start of a spring semester. She stated she was very depressed, and her slumped posture, downcast eyes, and sad facial expressions verified this assessment. She started rambling on about how she had received a speeding ticket over vacation and that she was also sad about seeing a former male friend dating someone else.

The following transactions then occurred:

Counselor: Can you now do anything constructive about these two situations?
Client: No.
Counselor: Do you realize that dwelling on them will only make you more depressed?
Client: Yes.
Counselor: We need instead to focus on what you now want. Do you know what you now want?
Client: Yes, to be happy and face this semester with an optimistic outlook.
Counselor: Good, now we're getting someplace. Tell me about some of the things you could do in the next few hours that are enjoyable for you and that will also get your mind off upsetting things that you can't change.

The client at this point began talking about a variety of things she could do—taking a walk, calling some friends to get together for lunch, and listening to her stereo. The more she talked about these things, the more relaxed she became. After about ten more minutes of talking, she smiled, said good-bye, and proceeded to get involved in her enjoyable activities.

Evaluation

Neuro-linguistic programming is indeed rich in new concepts. Those described here are some of the more prominent NLP principles, but are only a small subset of the tenets of NLP. The interested reader is encouraged to read further in texts (such as those referenced in this chapter) and attend NLP training institutes (a number of such institutes are being offered in various regions of the country).

The concept of studying the verbal and nonverbal communication patterns between prominent therapists and their clients to identify what causes positive changes has consid-

Case Example
Reframing

A 28-year-old woman came into treatment because she wanted her husband to stop drinking so much. She indicated that one or two nights a week her husband would stop off at a bar with other construction workers. She added that he would usually be two or three hours late for dinner and would be quite intoxicated when he arrived home. She would then chastise him for being late, for spending their scarce money on alcohol, and for ruining her evening by his "foolish talk." The husband generally reacted by calling her names and verbally abusing her in other ways. The wife added that there were generally problems in the marriage only when her husband was drinking. She also stated that her husband denies he has a drinking problem and refuses to join her in counseling. The counselor reframed the positive intent of her behavior in the following manner:

> It appears that both you and your husband get along well except when he's been drinking. When he comes home drunk, you definitely want to make the best of the situation. Up until now, your wanting to do so has led you to respond by verbally getting on his case for drinking. At that point he probably feels a need to defend himself and a "blow-up" occurs. Since you want to avoid the heated exchanges with him when he's drunk, I'm wondering if there aren't other actions you can take—such as taking a walk by yourself, going shopping, or going to visit someone when he is intoxicated?

The wife thought about this for a while and concluded that such suggestions might well work. In the next session a month later she reported that the strategy of leaving home when her husband came home intoxicated was working out well. Since she realized she did not have the capacity to stop her husband from drinking, she stated that reducing the difficulties the drinking created was her next best choice.

---

erable merit. NLP includes a number of concepts that are useful in explicating how a person (therapist, teacher, salesperson, public speaker) can influence another. Many of these concepts (such as joining with the client's representational system to build rapport) are described in this chapter.

The concepts advanced by NLP have considerable power in enabling influencers to influence people more effectively. There are also some criticisms that can be made about NLP:

1. Little research has been conducted on NLP to test its principles and concepts.
2. NLP is not a theory of human behavior, and therefore it does not have sufficient

concepts that can be used independently to assess the causes of emotional and behavioral difficulties. The principles and concepts of NLP are perhaps best viewed as being useful adjuncts to other theories in assessing and changing human behavior.

3. One of NLP's stated goals is to identify the key psychotherapeutic change agents that result in positive changes for clients undergoing therapy. NLP includes a number of concepts in this area, including the therapist's finding a way to "join" with the client and then "leading" the client in a positive direction. "Joining" and "leading" may well be essential components in the process of influencing. However, I question whether "joining" and "leading" are the key

psychotherapeutic change agents for treating emotional and behavioral problems. (Chapter 22 presents an alternative explanation, which asserts that restructuring thinking patterns is the key psychotherapeutic change agent.) With its focus on only what is observable, NLP largely ignores thinking patterns—and thereby may fail to focus on the key component to changing unwanted emotions and dysfunctional behaviors (see Chapter 22 for an elaboration).

Summary

NLP was developed by John Grinder, Richard Bandler, and several other authorities. It is a model of communication that has substantial application in assessing human behavior, in influencing others (in education, sales, and public speaking), and in psychotherapy. Grinder and Bandler studied the communication patterns of prominent psychotherapists with their clients to identify the kinds of patterns that lead to positive changes in clients. This research led to the development of NLP.

NLP is the study of the structure of subjective experience. It makes explicit patterns of behavior and change that have previously been only intuitively understandable. NLP has advanced a number of concepts and techniques that are useful in assessment, building rapport, and treating clients. These concepts and techniques include sensory representational systems; the map is not the territory; joining with the client's representational system builds rapport; influencing someone involves the influencer joining and then leading the influencee; predicates identify representational systems; eye-accessing cues; four-tuples; use of metaphors in counseling; reframing; and therapeutic change often occurs without knowing the cause of the problem. The principles and concepts of NLP appear to be useful ideas that can be used as adjuncts to other theories in assessing and treating emotional difficulties and dysfunctional behavior.

Exercises

1. Eye-accessing cues

> *Goal:* This exercise is designed to demonstrate that visual, auditory, and kinesthetic representational systems can be identified by eye-accessing cues.

> *Step 1:* Before using this exercise, carefully study the position of the eyeballs in Figure 17.1 that identify visual, auditory, and kinesthetic representational systems. Begin the exercise by asking for two volunteers. Then sit somewhere with the rest of the class and have the volunteers sit facing the class. (None of the students should be informed about eye-accessing cues.) Ask the two volunteers to answer silently to themselves the questions that follow:

> What do you remember most about
> a. the last grocery store you were in?
> b. what you did on your last birthday?
> c. the last time you were really angry?
> d. what you did on New Year's Eve?
> e. your most romantic experience?

> After asking each question, pause for the volunteers to arrive at their answers. Record the position of the eyeballs—suggesting which representational

system is being used. It is likely that some students may use more than one representational system (such as both visual and auditory) in answering a question. When this happens, record the two or more positions of the eyeballs.

Step 2: After asking the questions, (for the eye-accessing cues that are fairly identifiable) ask questions of the volunteers according to the following code.

    a. Visual—Did you have a visual image or picture of your answer to question _____?

    b. Auditory—Did you hear some sounds in your answer to questions _____?

    c. Kinesthetic—Did you have a feeling experience in your answer to question _____?

Step 3: (In all probability, you will be fairly accurate in identifying the representational systems through these eye-accessing cues.) Next ask the class for their ideas on how these representational systems were identified. Then describe eye-accessing cues.

Step 4: As an optional step, assign the students to ask a friend the same, or similar questions, outside of class, requesting the friend to answer silently. The students should then seek to identify (using the same procedures used in steps 1, 2, and 3) the sensory representational systems that were used by their friends. The experiences of the students in using eye-accessing cues can then be discussed at the next class period.

2. Joining

Goal: This exercise is designed to help students learn how to build better rapport with strangers (and future clients).

Step 1: Begin by describing the purpose of the exercise. Explain that NLP asserts that rapport with others is enhanced by (a) using predicates that are consistent with the other person's representational system; (b) mirroring, in a nonnoticeable way, the gestures, posture, and breathing patterns of the other person; and (c) talking knowledgeably about topics that are of interest to the other person. Practically everyone is aware of the last-mentioned method.

Step 2: Assign the students the tasks of starting conversations with three different strangers (or three people they do not know very well.) Ask them to try to use predicates during these conversations that are consistent with the strangers' representational systems and to mirror the strangers' gestures, posture, and breathing patterns in a nonnoticeable manner.

Step 3: At the next class period, discuss the following: (a) What were the results of the students' efforts? (b) Did the students have difficulty using predicates that were consistent with the strangers' representational systems? (c) Did the students have difficulty mirroring behavior? Do the students think these techniques are useful in building rapport?

18

Sex Counseling
and Therapy

What is sexuality?[1] To many people, this word connotes a man and a woman, preferably married to each other, having intercourse. To me, sexuality includes many things:

- How we feel about ourselves as boys or girls, men or women
- Masturbation
- Having a baby
- Affection
- Deciding whether to terminate a pregnancy with abortion
- Persons in parental roles using children for their own sexual arousal
- Romantic love
- A person being biologically of one gender and feeling psychologically of the other gender
- "Dirty old men"
- Using a condom to reduce the likelihood of transmitting HIV
- Babies discovering that touching their genitals gives them pleasure
- Rape
- Pornography
- The wedding night
- Erectile dysfunction

- Intimacy
- A 17-year-old male realizing he is sexually attracted to other males and not to females
- Jealousy
- Getting sexual aroused by erotic thoughts
- Predictable physiological responses in our bodies
- That warm, goosey feeling we get when we're touched by someone who arouses us
- An 85-year-old man making love with an 81-year-old woman
- And many, many more thoughts, feelings, and experiences.

Very few social workers become sex therapists, but most social workers with counseling responsibilities are frequently presented with clients' sexual concerns. Remember a simple adage, "The answers you get depend on the questions you ask." If you're perceived as "askable"[2] by your clients—being comfortable talking about sex, having some knowledge, being sensitive and receptive to clients' sexuality—you will be asked questions about sex. Clients are both perceptive and self-protective—if you're uncomfortable, don't worry. Nobody will bring it up.

This author has been told by many clients who were suffering from sexual problems that in dozens of sessions of previous psychotherapy, the therapist *never asked* them any questions about sex. Or, following a serious injury or illness, the subject of resuming one's sex life was never addressed by helping professionals. These clients were very eager to talk about sex, but "it never came up."

The goals of this chapter are (1) to encourage you to see the legitimacy of professional intervention in the sexual area of people's lives, (2) to teach you some basic sex counseling skills, (3) to help you examine and broaden your own comfort and knowledge in this sensitive area, and (4) to teach you some

---

[1]This chapter was especially written for this text by Lloyd G. Sinclair, A.C.S.W. Mr. Sinclair is a Certified Sex Educator, Sex Therapist, and Sex Therapy Supervisor at Midwest Center for Psychotherapy and Sex Therapy in Madison, Wisconsin.

[2]The concept of "askable" was developed by Sol Gordon, Ph.D., an Emeritus Professor at Syracuse University, Syracuse, New York. Dr. Gordon has written numerous books and articles on various aspects of adolescence and sexuality.

evaluation techniques which can be helpful in determining when it might be appropriate to intervene and when referral to a specialist is indicated.

Why is it so important and necessary for social workers to be able to intervene in the area of sexuality? The most compelling reasons are (1) because sexuality is an extremely important aspect of the human personality, indeed a driving biological force; and (2) because many other professionals who *should* be helpful to people with sexual concerns, such as physicians and psychotherapists, often are not. The legitimacy of scientific study of and professional intervention in persons' sexual lives has received widespread recognition only in the very recent past. Consequently, only professionals who have received training in the last 10 or 15 years (either toward a degree or as continuing education) are likely to have acquired skills to assess, treat, or refer persons with sexual problems. The others are sexuality "experts" based solely on their personal experiences which, even if the professionals are pretty "experienced," is woefully inadequate. So don't blame the other professionals for not being helpful to persons with sexual concerns—chances are they were never taught these skills. But don't *assume* they are trained either, to use as an excuse for you to ignore the area.

Let's turn our attention now to some important concerns specific to counseling people about sex-related matters.

Knowledge

The first prerequisite to effective counseling in the area of sexuality, as well in any area, is knowledge. The information necessary to help persons with sexual problems goes well beyond the scope of this chapter. In addition to other resources listed in the footnotes of this chapter, there are two excellent comprehensive surveys of human sexuality: William H. Masters, Virginia E. Johnson, and Robert C. Kolodny, *Masters and Johnson on Sex and*

Human Loving (Boston: Little, Brown and Company, 1986), and Ira R. Reiss, *Journey into Sexuality* (Englewood Cliffs, N.J.: Prentice-Hall, 1986).

Assumptions

Perhaps more than in any other area, counselors should be extremely careful to avoid making assumptions when clients raise issues about sex. Because people express their sexuality in such a wide variety of ways, because people tend not to talk about their sexual experiences, and because so many people lack good sex education, it is easy to assume that everyone expresses their sexuality like you express yours.

There are basically two dangers in making assumptions. The first is that you can easily draw the wrong conclusions if you don't persevere to determine that your understanding is correct. For example, if your client talks about masturbation, don't assume every man pleasures himself sexually by rubbing his penis with his hand, and every woman by rubbing her clitoris. Some people masturbate by rubbing against objects, with vibrators, or under streams of water. Some people tie themselves up when they masturbate. Others need to cross-dress (dressing in clothes of the other gender) or to exhibit their genitals to strangers to feel aroused. If you assume everyone does it the same way, you may draw too-hasty conclusions based on inadequate information.

The second reason to carefully avoid making assumptions is that you risk not being perceived by your client as "safe" to ask questions of. For example, if a man comes to you and says, "Lately I've had trouble getting an erection with my partner," and you ask, "How does *she* feel about it?" you have effectively slammed the door on that client if he happens to be gay. Oh, he'll probably smooth it over nicely and you'll never know you made the mistake, because gay people frequently deal with heterosexual assumptions. But you will not be perceived as a person who is sensitive to the range of human sexual expression. And you will, consequently, counsel only those people who fit *your* stereotypes.

Words

Another important consideration is the vocabulary used by the sex counselor. Most counselors develop a vocabulary that is most comfortable for them. It is important to know the scientific language (*coitus, fellatio*) to understand much of the technical information about sexual response. But the English language contains many more "street" words for sexual expression than any other variety. Many clients are familiar only with those words. You will want to know the meaning of these terms (for example, *gettin' it on, blow job*) so you will understand them when clients use them and won't express shock when you hear them.

You will probably want to find words that describe in a straightforward manner (for example, does sleeping together mean having intercourse, or just sleeping?), in as value-free a way as possible, what you are trying to say (for example, intercourse, oral-genital sex).

Many counselors attempt to hide their own discomfort with talking about sex by using medical language. The greatest danger in using words that are unnecessarily scientific is that you are likely not to be understood. Clients are often embarrassed to admit they don't know the meaning of certain words, so they may pretend they do. And if you're not communicating, you're not helping.

Some counselors attempt to hide their discomfort by going to the other extreme—by using street terms to appear "with it." The problem here is that street terms are usually value laden. To some people, the word *fuck* simply means intercourse. But to others, *fuck* is a demeaning, sexist, aggressive, and filthy word.

Another extremely important concept to remember is that, in all likelihood, persons who have a cognitive disability do not use the same sophisticated language about sexuality that we may take for granted. So you may need to be especially graphic in order to be understood. A sensitive counselor may try her vocabulary first, but with the slightest hint of the client's lack of comprehension, she may need to stop talking about "masturbation" and instead talk about "rubbing your penis 'til the white stuff comes out," or "rubbing your privates 'til you feel extra good."

One method useful in becoming more comfortable with words that clients might use is to practice saying "street" words out loud, either by yourself or with a friend. If you blush when you say words you were taught to feel uncomfortable about, your client is likely to feel embarrassed too. With practice at desensitizing yourself, you can learn to use these words comfortably.

Levels of Intervention

When a client expresses a sexual concern to a social worker, it is important for the professional to make some preliminary evaluation regarding what the client needs to resolve his or her problem: a sentence or two of reassurance, or 12 weeks of intensive sex therapy?

Jack S. Annon has developed an extremely useful conceptual scheme to help professionals make this determination.[3] He believed that very few persons with sexual problems need intensive sex therapy. Rather, they need intervention at the levels he identifies as permission, limited information, and specific suggestions.

Permission describes the process of professional reassurance, letting clients know they

---

[3]Jack S. Annon, *Behavioral Treatment of Sexual Problems: Brief Therapy* (New York: Harper & Row, 1976); *Behavioral Treatment of Sexual Problems: Volume 2, Intensive Therapy* (Honolulu: Enabling Systems, Inc., 1975).

are normal. The client reports, "My wife and I hear a lot about oral sex. We just aren't interested in doing that. Do you think there's something wrong with us?" The counselor can give permission: "Sex is best when you're doing things you *both* want to do, not because of somebody else's expectations. I would encourage you to do what you both like, and if at some point you want to try oral sex, fine. But if you don't, that's fine too. Enjoy."

While the largest number of people would benefit from intervention at the level of permission, a significant but smaller number need *limited information* to alleviate their sexual concern. A client reports, "I'm happily married, we have a good sex life, but I still find I masturbate a couple of times a week. Do you think there's something wrong with me?" The counselor might respond with limited information:

> You might be interested in knowing a couple of things. First, it's a myth that masturbating indicates there's something wrong with you sexually. In fact, studies show that people who feel good about themselves sexually engage in a larger number of sexual activities of all kinds, including partner sex *and* masturbation, than people who have a lower sexual self-image. And studies also show that most people masturbate with some frequency throughout their lives. It's simply not true that being in a sexual relationship means all your sexual needs and desires will automatically be met. If you enjoy masturbation, and it's not used as a weapon in your relationship to try to coerce your partner into being sexual with you, then it can do you no harm. Enjoy![4]

The third level of psychotherapeutic intervention is *specific suggestions*. Annon suggested that to make responsible and potentially helpful suggestions, the counselor should take a sexual problem history. This is not a full social-sexual history, but rather data related solely to the specific problem.

First, the counselor must obtain a *description of the current problem:*

Counselor: Sally, what brings you to the office today?

Sally: I'm concerned because when Bill and I have intercourse, it hurts me.

Counselor: Can you describe the pain more specifically for me? Is it sharp or dull, shallow or deep?

Sally: It's more like a chafing pain—not really sharp, but it's sure uncomfortable. And sometimes it's deep, too, almost like he's banging into something deep inside me.

The counselor then asks about the *onset and course of the problem:*

Counselor: Has intercourse always been painful to you?

Sally: No, not always. At first it was a little, but I think that was just because we were new at it. But then for a few years, I wasn't having any pain. But in the past several months, it's hurt.

Counselor: Has it been painful every time you've had intercourse in the past few months?

Sally: No, and that confuses me. Sometimes, particularly when I initiate sex, it doesn't hurt.

Next, the counselor inquires about the *client's concept of the cause and maintenance of the problem:*

Counselor: Do you have any ideas about why you're having this problem?

Sally: Well, not really. I thought for a while that maybe I was just overtired, or maybe I was making the pain up because sometimes Bill is much more interested in intercourse than I am, but I don't think so. I really don't know.

---

[4]The counselor might also want to suggest some reading about male sexuality to this client. An excellent book is Bernie Zilbergeld's *Male Sexuality* (Boston: Little, Brown, 1978).

The counselor explores with the client any *past treatment and outcome:*

Counselor: Have you tried anything to alleviate the pain besides coming to see me to talk about it?

Sally: Yes. I asked my gynecologist about it during my last pelvic exam. He said I was fine. And I've talked with Bill about it a lot, but neither of us knows what to do.

Finally, the counselor is interested in learning the client's *current expectancies and goals of treatment:*

Counselor: What would you consider to be a satisfactory resolution of this problem, Sally?

Sally: I just want intercourse to stop hurting. I used to enjoy it a lot more, and I'm starting to avoid it 'cause it hurts.

The counselor determines from this sexual problem history that intervention at the level of permission alone, or even at the level of limited information, would probably not alleviate the problem. She decides to give some permission, some limited information, and follow up with some specific suggestions:

Counselor (Permission): I'm really glad, Sally, that you had the courage to come in here today to explore this with me. I know that sex is difficult for most people to talk about, and it's especially difficult when you're having a problem with it. And you know, lots of women believe that it's natural for intercourse to hurt, almost as if that's a woman's lot in life. I'm sure glad you're not of that opinion.

Let me ask you one more question. Do you feel aroused, turned on, ready for intercourse when Bill is ready?

Sally: No, he seems to be ready for intercourse much more quickly than I am. I could never be as fast as he is.

Counselor (Limited information): That's a pattern I hear from lots of couples. For whatever reason, the man often gets an erection and is ready for intercourse to begin long before the woman is adequately aroused. When you're turned on, your vagina will lubricate and your cervix, at the base of your uterus, will move up and out of the way of the penis. If you're not sufficiently aroused, Bill's penis doesn't slide in easily and it bumps your cervix, which may be that deeper, sharper pain you talked about.

Sally: So would an artificial lubricant help?

Counselor: Oh, it might help a little, but it wouldn't really solve the problem. What needs to happen is for you to be adequately aroused before you attempt intercourse. It's just as inappropriate for the two of you to be having intercourse if you're not lubricated as it is to attempt to have intercourse when Bill doesn't have an erection.

Sally: What can we do about this?

Counselor (Specific suggestions): I would suggest that you spend more time concentrating on what *you* like in the sex play prior to intercourse. Maybe you could tell Bill more about what is particularly arousing to you. Try to stay away from hurrying sex—lots of women need a good deal of time before they're adequately aroused and therefore lubricated, and there's nothing wrong with that. Perhaps if you take more initiative in directing the sexual encounter, you can do the things that are most arousing to you. I suspect one of the reasons you tend *not* to experience pain when you initiate sex is because you are likely to be more aroused then instead of being sexual according to Bill's rhythms. And most important, don't go ahead with intercourse until you're really ready.[5]

---

[5]The counselor might also want to suggest three books by Lonnie Garfield Barbach to this client to help her understand more about women's sexuality. They are Lonnie Garfield Barbach, *For Yourself: The Fulfillment of Female Sexuality* (New York: New American Library, 1975); *For Each Other: Sharing Sexual Intimacy* (Garden City, NY: Anchor Press/Doubleday, 1982); and *Pleasures* (New York: Harper & Row, 1984).

The final level of therapeutic intervention described by Annon is *intensive therapy*. Intensive sex therapy is discussed later in this chapter under "Sexual Problems."

Sex Offender Counseling[6]

As indicated in the case example, sexual assault has become a public mental health problem due to the enormous incidence of the violations. Historically, sex offenders have been incarcerated, which addresses society's need to punish them, but the mental health aspect of their problem has been largely ignored. More recently, social workers have been in the forefront of the development of innovative and effective treatment methods that have been proven effective in reducing sex offenses. These methods significantly depart from typical treatments for other mental health problems. They include

1. Breaking confidentiality in some circumstances between the client and the counselor (for example, the counselor may inform the police of the sexual offenses that the offender relates), because confidentiality promotes the secrecy frequently abused by the sex offenders.
2. Increasing victimization awareness, assisting the client to recognize the full extent of harm his or her sexual assaults cause.
3. Implementing behavioral interventions, to reduce deviant sexual arousal while promoting nondeviant (adult, consenting) arousal, and helping the client pair

inappropriate sexual impulses with their consequences.
4. Providing assertiveness training, to reduce anger (a motivation for rape) or passivity (a motivation for seeking children as sexual targets).
5. Clarifying sexual values, to address confusion clients may have about sexual thoughts and behavior.
6. Giving information on preventing sexual dysfunction, to help clients feel more confident in appropriate sexual encounters.
7. Reducing the rationalizations sex offenders use to justify their behaviors.
8. Preventing relapse, to assist the client in understanding the thoughts and behaviors that preceded previous offenses and recognize these patterns to avoid future assaults.

Recent social scientific studies have also advanced our knowledge of which sex offenders are most likely to reoffend. These data are critical in determining which clients need sex offender treatment, and which ones require incarceration and treatment. An excellent review of studies examining the factors associated with reoffense among known sex offenders is Robert J. McGrath's article, "Sex-Offender Risk Assessment and Disposition Planning: A Review of Empirical and Clinical Findings," in the *International Journal of Offender Therapy and Comparative Criminology*.

[6]Many of the ideas presented in this section are based on the author's clinical experience and are amplified in Anna C. Salter, *Treating Child Sex Offenders and Victims* (Newbury Park, CA: Sage Publications, 1988). Two books on the subject of sexual abuse of children are Sandra L. Ingersoll and Susan O. Patton, *Treating Perpetrators of Sexual Abuse* (Lexington, MA: Lexington Books, 1990), and Ellen Bass and Laura Davis, *The Courage to Heal* (New York: Harper & Row, 1988).

AIDS

AIDS and the Sexual Revolution
Decades of sexual conservatism emphasizing heterosexuality, marriage, and monogamy gave way to the sexual revolution of the 1970s. During this period many persons questioned traditional values and experimented with a variety of sexual behaviors and lifestyles. While some found this sexual revolution to be liberating, others were distressed at

Case Example
Patty—Counseling for sexual abuse

Incest is increasingly being recognized as a major problem in our society. Usually when incest becomes known, the family breaks up. The following case example was selected because it illustrates a recent trend to keep such families intact.

Fourteen-year-old Patty was referred by her teacher to the school social worker because her grades and interest had fallen below her abilities and previous academic record. The social worker, Ms. White, discussed these concerns one morning with Patty. Patty alluded vaguely to "pressure at home," and after a good deal of gentle probing, she finally revealed to Ms. White that her father had been having intercourse with her since she was 11.

Patty was understandably very upset, and yet relieved. She had considered telling someone but had not been able to bring herself to talk about it before. Her father had told her many times not to tell anyone, yet she felt the situation had become intolerable.

Ms. White assured Patty that she would help her and her family. Since they lived in a state that had a mandatory reporting law for suspected cases of child abuse and neglect, Ms. White telephoned the County Social Service Agency, which in turn notified the police. Social Services sent a social worker, Ms. Fox, their agency specialist in this area, to talk with Patty. Ms. Fox and Ms. White spoke with Patty together.

Both social workers were fully aware that, until a short time ago, incest was considered to be extremely rare in American society. Most people believed that it occurred only in large, rural, economically deprived families. Recent statistics, however, indicate this stereotype of child sexual abuse to be very inaccurate. Sexual abuse is not a rare phenomenon, perhaps because more people are seeking help since more help is available, and perhaps because there has been more publicity about sexual abuse recently, and perhaps because there are many more "blended" families. Indeed, current studies suggest that between one-fourth and one-third of adult women in the United States were sexually abused as children by someone in an authority position. Whether it is technically incest (a biological tie) or not often makes little difference. The critical issue is that the parent or parent surrogate is using his or her authority to engage in sexual acts *for the pleasure of the adult.* By emotional and legal definition, no child can give consent for sexual contact with an adult because of the differences in power between them.

Ms. Fox and Ms. White were also aware that sexual abuse in families almost invariably results in severe trauma for the victims, including the inability to trust others or himself or herself. The violation of the important sexual boundary that should exist between generations destroys normal family roles. When father and daughter cease to be father and daughter to become lovers, how can they comfortably switch back and forth? What about mother? What about other children, who feel the favoritism from Dad to daughter, or who may be being sexually abused by him as well?

The typical scenario with a family when sexual abuse becomes known is that the daughter or son is placed in a foster home "for protection." Dad, whose reputation in the community plummets, generally is jailed briefly and released (pending trial), and is prohibited from seeing his family; the legal process often takes months.

Mother tries to hold the rest of the family together under tremendous economic, social, and emotional strain. And the son or daughter ends up feeling responsible and therefore terribly guilty for destroying the family—"if only I had kept my mouth shut, stayed 'til I was eighteen, and left." With this typical sequence of events, it is easier to comprehend why child sexual abuse can remain "the family secret," sometimes even known or at least suspected by the mother, for years.

Patty told Ms. Fox and Ms. White that she was extremely scared, mostly of what her father might do now. She said she had tried to tell her mother, but she just couldn't come right out and say it, so the secret was never broken. Ms. Fox explained that they would do whatever they could to protect her, to help her father, and to keep the family together—as long as the sexual abuse stopped. Ms. Fox arranged to meet with Patty's father shortly after he had been arrested. This mixture of the law (represented by police, the courts, prosecuting and defense attorneys—with an emphasis on guilt or innocence) and the helping professions (represented by social workers and other psychotherapists—with an emphasis on mental health) makes for a powerful combination of legal enforcement of mental health improvement. Outcome studies indicate that without the clout of the law, reversal of sexually assaultive behavior is less likely to occur. And most enlightened police officers, judges, and district attorneys are well aware that conviction leading solely to incarceration in prison is often not the most helpful course for any of the parties involved. While this may take the father away from the children so further sexual abuse won't occur, it also takes him and all his *positive* contributions from the family as well. Sexual assault is a criminal violation, so a legal response is appropriate. However, the behavior will generally not change from punishment alone; specific sex offender treatment is required as well.

Mr. Reed, Patty's father, retained an attorney. While he acknowledged having intercourse with Patty ("for a few months"), he denied having forced or even encouraged her. She had been seductive with him, and, he reasoned, "It was better for her to learn about sex at home, the right way, from a man who's had a vasectomy so she won't get pregnant, than from some kid on the street who doesn't care about her. So we went progressively from touching to fondling to intercourse. But don't worry, I've decided to stop and not do it any more."

Once the charges were filed, the district attorney met with Mr. Reed, his attorney, and Ms. Fox. The district attorney agreed to suspend his prosecution of this case if the following conditions were met: (1) Mr. Reed moved out of the family home until his therapist felt he could safely return, and he was not to be alone with Patty (or any other minor children) under any circumstances until treatment had occurred. (The purpose of this is to protect Patty, of course, but also to reinforce Patty's mother's role as parent in the household.) (2) Mr. Reed participated in individual, couple, and family therapy over a period of not less than one year. If either of these conditions were not met, the district attorney would proceed with prosecution and probably gain a conviction.

Mr. Reed was evaluated by a social worker who specializes in the treatment of sex offenders, Mr. James. He knew that some persons who molest children are fixated pedophiles; that is, persons, generally men, whose primary and often exclusive sexual interest is in children, usually boys. In other words, fixated

(continued)

pedophiles aren't sexually interested in adults. They often go to great lengths to place themselves with boys by pursuing occupations or hobbies, such as being newspaper carrier supervisors or baseball team coaches, to gain sexual access to them. But many child molesters are heterosexually oriented men who are married and are sexually aroused by children as well as adults. These men sometimes seek to replace a conflictual adult relationship with involvement with a child. Mr. James believed Mr. Reed was this latter type of offender. He suggested the following goals in the treatment which ensued from the revelation of sexual abuse: (1) Mr. Reed was to take full and complete responsibility for all his deviant sexual behavior; (2) he was to end all sexual abuse; (3) he must understand the emotional and environmental precursors to his sexual assaults and begin to view them as warning signals, thereby changing his thoughts and behaviors early in his abusive cycle; (4) he must strengthen the marital relationship between himself and his wife; (5) he must provide a forum for Patty to express her feelings honestly to her parents; (6) Mr. Reed must make the necessary lifestyle changes to promote his developing relationships with people that are based on mutuality and reciprocity, not manipulation and deception; (7) he must manage the compulsive aspect of his sexual assaults of Patty; and (8) he must assist in rebuilding the family with each family member assuming her or his appropriate role.

The issue of seductiveness often comes up in these cases. In an effort to reduce guilt feelings on the part of the perpetrator of sexual abuse, he can rather easily deceive himself in placing the blame on the victim. The point is that children *are* seductive—for attention, not sexual interaction. Most children learn to attract the attention of significant adults in their lives by whatever means is effective. So an adult who interprets these advances as *sexual* can easily shift the blame to the child. Most counselors believe that it is absolutely necessary for the adult to acknowledge this deception, take full responsibility for his behavior, and say so to the child. This is seen as important primarily to (1) encourage the adult to see himself as in control, not a victim of circumstances, and therefore in control of *stopping* the behavior; and (2) unburdening the child of her guilt for "being seductive" and perhaps becoming aroused by the sexual interactions.

Mr. Reed was seen in group sex offender treatment and in various therapy combinations of father-daughter, husband-wife, and family treatment. Therapy occurred twice weekly for several months, then once weekly, and eventually monthly. Patty saw her own therapist to help her resolve her feelings of guilt, anger, and confusion. Mr. James also organized a self-help group of sexual abusers and their families to encourage mutual sharing and growth. No further incidents of sexual abuse were reported.

the departure from the value that sexuality should be expressed only within marriage.

The 1990s have given way to a sexual revolution of a far greater scope, growing not from a social movement but from the fear of the sexually transmitted disease Acquired Immunodeficiency Syndrome (AIDS). AIDS is an infectious disease in which a virus, the human immunodeficiency virus (HIV), attacks the body's immune system, leaving victims susceptible to a wide variety of cancers and other diseases. The virus can also have degenerative effects on the brain, regardless of whether the immune system has been compromised. Although new drugs are being used to alleviate some of the symptoms (and thereby prolong lives), there is no cure or immediate hope of discovering a vaccine to inoculate people against HIV. The social, economic, medical, and political consequences of this disease pose an unprecedented challenge to social workers in the 1990s and beyond.

The 1984 National Association of Social Workers' Delegate Assembly adopted a policy statement indicating how social workers can pursue action in six areas related to AIDS (Leukenfield & Fimbres, 1987, p. ix):

1. Basic epidemiological and clinical research on AIDS.
2. The distribution of accurate information on treatment and the medical, financial, and psychosocial resources that are available.
3. The provision of comprehensive psychological and social supports to help persons with AIDS, their families, children, spouses, and loved ones.
4. The development of a comprehensive service delivery system to respond to the AIDS crisis, including suitable housing, home health care, and transportation services.
5. The protection of the civil rights and right to confidentiality of persons who are diagnosed as having AIDS or AIDS-related complex (ARC).
6. The protection by the helping professionals and appropriate licensing authorities of the eligibility for and receipt of benefits by persons with AIDS.

There is a great deal of misunderstanding about AIDS. As misunderstanding, combined with fear, often results in prejudice and even panic, it is incumbent on social workers to be informed about AIDS.

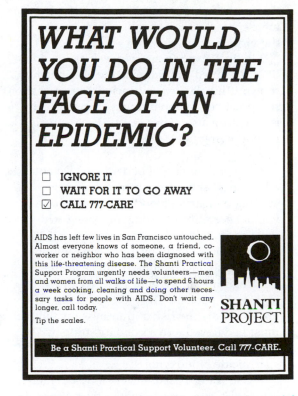

AIDS raises numerous critical issues for social workers and for society in general. An ad for the Shanti Project in San Francisco encourages volunteers to enroll in its practical support program.

Transmission of HIV

The virus that has been identified as the cause of AIDS is the human immunodeficiency virus. The first known death from AIDS occurred in England in 1959, and the disease is believed to have entered the United States in 1977. The only way to contract AIDS is for the virus to enter one's bloodstream. The four main ways this occurs are (1) through sexual contact, (2) by sharing an infected hypodermic needle, (3) by receiving AIDS-infected blood through transfusion or injection, and (4) by an infected mother transmitting it to her baby before or at birth and through breast milk. Although low levels of HIV have been found in saliva, "dry" kissing has not been demonstrated to transmit the virus. Less intimate contact will not result in transmission of the virus.

Medical experts have developed guidelines designed to minimize the likelihood of transmitting HIV. They include using safer sex practices and refraining from illicit, injected drug use. Safer sex practices involve the following:

- No exchanging of body fluids. Do not allow another person's semen, blood (including menstrual blood), urine, feces, or vaginal secretions to come in contact with your body.
- Use latex condoms for all types of intercourse (oral, anal, vaginal), but be aware that condom failure with HIV may be as high as 17 percent. Therefore, condoms will not eliminate the risk of transmission and must be viewed as a secondary strategy. The most effective condoms are treated with the spermicide Nonoxynol 9.
- Use water-based, never oil-based, lubricants with condoms to reduce the risk of breakage.
- Never mix alcohol or other drugs with sexual activity; drugs may impair your judgment and reduce your ability to make wise decisions.
- Develop a relationship of trust with any person with whom you are going to have sexual contact, and learn as much as you can about his or her sexual history.
- Avoid having sex with multiple partners.
- Choose lower-risk sexual activities.

Symptoms

There may be no overt symptoms of AIDS for several years or more after HIV infection. Typical symptoms resemble influenza ("flu") and may include recurrent fever and night sweats; persistent swollen glands in the neck, armpits, and groin; unexplained weight loss; recurrent diarrhea; persistent coughing; persistent debilitating fatigue; loss of appetite; unusual oral sores; blotches and bruised areas on the skin that do not go away; a series of infections and illnesses.

Testing for AIDS

There is no actual AIDS test. Rather, a blood test can only register the presence of HIV antibodies, which indicates exposure to the virus that causes AIDS. Therefore, a positive result on the HIV antibody test indicates exposure, not AIDS infection, and that the person is apt, at some time in the future, to develop AIDS. A diagnosis of AIDS is made when a patient's constellation of symptoms reaches a defined medical level. A person who is HIV-positive can infect others with the virus. The average length of time between HIV infection and onset of AIDS symptoms is approximately 10 years. However, this time period is highly variable from person to person. The HIV antibodies generally take 6 to 12 weeks to develop, and sometimes longer, following infection. This means that a person who was recently infected with HIV may show an inaccurate "false negative" test result.

There is a great deal of controversy surrounding the testing of persons for the HIV antibodies. Some believe that for certain populations, such as prisoners, persons seeking to immigrate to the United States, or those seeking marriage licenses, the test should be mandatory. Others fear that such widespread compulsory testing will lead to discrimination if results are not kept secret, as well as great emotional upheaval in the lives of individuals who are fearful and confused about the meaning of their test results. Indeed, advertent or accidental public disclosure of positive tests has led to the loss of insurance, marriage and family ties, and housing for certain individuals. Some states require health care providers to report the names of those who test positive for the virus, so previous sexual contacts might be notified of their risk. At the same time, people's fears of testing

Exhibit 18.1
Basic facts about AIDS

Once infected with the AIDS virus (HIV), you are infected *for life*. There is no cure, as yet, for the disease.

Anyone infected with the AIDS virus can transmit the virus to a partner via anal, oral, or vaginal intercourse, or by sharing drug needles.

It takes between three and four months for the HIV to be detectable in one's blood. This means you can carry the virus even though your blood test is negative (that is, okay). On rare occasions, it can take up to three years for the HIV to be detectable in blood.

Even though the HIV antibodies are not yet detectable in his or her blood, an infected person can transmit HIV to someone else.

Latex rubber condoms are very effective in preventing the spread of HIV. They should be put on prior to any sexual activity. A space should be left at the tip to accommodate ejaculation, and water-based lubricants and spermicides should be used as well. Condoms, however, are not a fool-proof method.

You cannot get AIDS by donating blood.

It is extremely unlikely that you could become infected with the AIDS virus by receiving a blood transfusion.

You cannot get AIDS by casual contact such as by working or attending school with persons with AIDS, or by sharing eating utensils, toilets, or towels.

Two people who do not have the HIV and who do not use intravenous drugs have *no risk* of contracting AIDS through sexual contact with each other.

---

positive for the HIV antibodies have led some to avoid the health care system, refusing help and trying to live a normal life as a symbol of hope. To circumvent discrimination while increasing people's likelihood of learning their HIV status and accessing health care services as needed, many medical clinics offer anonymous HIV testing. An enormous public policy issue looms: How can the public health and well-being be protected while still maintaining individual rights?

Who Are the Persons with AIDS?

Over 300,000 people in the United States have been diagnosed with AIDS, and over 60 percent of them have died. Almost half of those diagnosed with AIDS are African Americans and Hispanics. While AIDS is clearly not a gay disease, the majority of persons with AIDS in the United States have been homosexual or bisexual males or intravenous drug users. Some have confused this fact by viewing homosexuality as somehow the cause of AIDS, when, in fact, it is homosexuals who have so far suffered the most illness and death. Worldwide, the greatest transmission

of the HIV is via heterosexual contact. In the United States, women and adolescents are the groups sharing the largest incidence of new infections. Heterosexual intercourse is especially hazardous for women; one study found women who have sexual intercourse with HIV-infected men are 14 times more likely to contact the virus than are men who have sex with infected women (see Turner, Miller, & Moses, 1989). AIDS will soon exceed all other causes of deaths, except accidents, for men between the ages of 25 and 44.

Perhaps most tragically, AIDS is increasingly striking groups in the United States who already benefit the least from this society and are the most difficult to help: the poor, minorities, drug abusers, and those with little education.

The health care costs for each individual AIDS patient from the time of diagnosis to death are, on average, about $75,000. Understandably, a diagnosis of AIDS quickly plunges many sufferers into poverty. AIDS thereby presents a challenge of unprecedented magnitude to the U.S. health care system. It has been said that the measure of a society is determined by how well it cares for

Child with AIDS.

its least-advantaged members. Social workers have been and will continue to be advocates for these very disadvantaged members of our society.

AIDS has changed the social and sexual habits of many people. There has been an increase in sex education programs in institutions as well as in homes. The use of condoms is more widely accepted, and they are being advertised in places where previously they were banned. Legislation requiring travelers to certify that they do not carry HIV antibodies is being passed in some countries. There are indications that monogamy and celibacy have increased, particularly in the gay community, and the divorce rate is expected to continue to decline in the heterosexual community.

Social workers have many significant roles to play in the challenges posed by AIDS: developing services; conducting research about social consequences; individual, group, couple, and family counseling; serving the needs of orphans resulting from parental deaths caused by AIDS; training; educating; planning curricula—the list goes on and on. Indeed, AIDS raises every relevant social issue social workers have been taught to face. The values of the profession—respect for all people, the importance of self-determination, the

commitment to community service, ethical responsibility to society, an individual's right to confidentiality, freedom from bigotry and discrimination, and the rights of all persons to adequate physical and mental health care—will serve social workers as they define their individual roles in helping alleviate the effects of AIDS.[7]

Sexual Problems

Why do people develop sexual dysfunctions? This author believes that typical patterns of child rearing in America virtually guarantee sexual problems in adulthood. In other words, if you grew up in the United States and learned your lessons well, you'll likely have some sexual problems in adulthood. A little farfetched? Let's look at the evidence.

Young girls in America are encouraged to be sexy (become a cheerleader, attract boys) but certainly not sexual (nice girls don't . . .). They are taught that boys are naturally interested in sex (studs) but girls shouldn't be (because if you are, you're a whore, or at least an

[7]For further reading about AIDS, the following books are recommended: Ted Eidson, ed., *The AIDS Caregiver's Handbook* (New York: St. Martin's Press, 1993); Robert Searles Walker, *AIDS Today, Tomorrow* (Atlantic Highlands, NJ: Humanities Press, 1992); Spencer A. Rathus and Susan Boughn, *AIDS, What Every Student Needs to Know* (Forth Worth: Harcourt Brace & Co., 1993); Heather G. Miller, Charles F. Turner, and Lincoln E. Moses, eds., *AIDS: The Second Decade* (Washington, DC: National Academy Press, 1990); Judith Landau-Stanton and Colleen D. Clements, *AIDS, Health and Mental Health* (New York: Brunner/Mazel, 1993); Charles Turner, Heather Miller, and Lincoln Moses, eds., *AIDS: Sexual Behavior and Intravenous Drug Use* (Washington, DC: National Academy Press, 1989); Sasha Alyson, ed., *You Can Do Something About AIDS: New Edition* (Boston: The Stop AIDS Project, 1990); and Gary Anderson, ed., *Courage to Care* (Washington, DC: Child Welfare League of America, 1990). A source of excellent, up-to-date pamphlets on AIDS is the Sex Information and Education Council of the United States, 32 Washington Place, New York, NY, 10003: phone (212) 673-3850. For information about AIDS, contact the National AIDS Hotline at (800) 342-AIDS.

easy make). They are taught to attract boys but always to maintain a safe distance, giving sexual favors in a safe progression, always maintaining control.

A woman telephones the sex therapist, stating:

> I've been married for five years, I love my husband, we have a delightful child and a happy home. But when we get together sexually I turn on to a point and then, I just go numb. I don't feel anything.

This woman learned to control her sexual feelings so effectively in her earlier experiences that later, when it was no longer functional for her to maintain such control, her body responds, almost reflexively, by shutting down.

Boys, on the other hand, are often taught to "sow their wild oats," to have many sexual experiences. Adolescent boys may view their virginity as a curse, a condition that must never be admitted. They also learn a contradictory message, however: Don't get caught, by the police, her parents, a pregnancy, or a sexually transmitted disease. And not incidentally, if you don't "perform" at all (if you don't get an erection), you'll be safe.

A man tells the sex therapist:

> I love my wife. We've been happily married now for ten years. But my problems don't go away. Oh, at first I thought we just needed to get to know each other better. But even now, after all this time, I sometimes don't get an erection and when I do and enter her vagina, I come to orgasm right away. We're both pretty frustrated by that.

This man learned to associate anxiety with sex and to reach orgasm quickly. He later became a victim of his own, previously functional, pattern.

Under normal circumstances, two people who are sexually attracted to each other will, if they pursue sexual contact, respond well together. This means they will experience erotic feelings that will cause many physio-logical changes in their bodies and eventually move to high levels of arousal culminating in orgasm for each. But this is the ideal. What happens if:

The man is so concerned about his partner's performance that he watches himself and therefore blocks incoming sexual stimulation?

The woman doesn't like her partner, and her sexual value system requires liking someone as a prerequisite to sexual feelings?

The man wants to have intercourse but doesn't know how it is done, nor does his partner?

The woman is with a man, but her sexual orientation is toward women—she is not aroused by men?

The only way the woman can be aroused is when she is physically violent with her partner?

The only people the man is aroused by are children?

The woman is so angry at the man's insensitivity to her needs that she withholds sexual feelings to punish him and maintain her self-esteem?

So you can see that normal, ideal circumstances are often not a couple's norm at all. And just as nothing succeeds like success in sex, nothing fails like failure. In other words, a sexual experience that is seen by the couple as a failure often causes them to watch themselves, fearing the worst. And the worst can rapidly become a self-fulfilling prophecy.

Sexual Dysfunctions Defined

Sexual dysfunctions can be defined on two levels: specific, behaviorally measurable functional disorders; and general, often relationship-oriented problems. Problems often occur on both levels.

The specific functional disorders for men are (1) premature ejaculation, the inability "to exert voluntary control over his ejaculation reflex, with the result that once he is sexually aroused, he reaches orgasm very quickly" (Kaplan, 1974, p. 187); (2) erectile dysfunction, the inability to experience erection either at any time or, more commonly, when one is desired for a sexual experience with a partner (usually intercourse); (3) orgasmic dysfunction, the inability to reach orgasm voluntarily at any time, or, more commonly, when one is desired for a sexual experience with a partner (usually intercourse); and (4) dyspareunia—painful intercourse.

The specific functional disorders for women are (1) orgasmic dysfunction, the inability of the woman to experience orgasm voluntarily at any time or when with a partner, (2) dyspareunia, painful intercourse, (3) vaginismus, an anxiety response resulting in the involuntary tightening of the vaginal musculature to prohibit vaginal penetration.

The general dysfunctions include (1) problems of desire and arousal, lack of desire for a certain partner and/or failure to experience arousal with that partner; (2) problems related to aging, physical illness, or disability[8]; (3) fears of intimacy, inability or unwillingness to become close enough to a partner to risk "letting go" sexually; (4) power struggles, aggression with, or withholding of, sex to maintain power in a relationship; (5) communication difficulties, unwillingness or inability to state sexual needs and desire; and (6) lack of an interested and interesting partner.

Treatment of Sexual Dysfunction

The traditional view of sexuality and sexual problems was largely based on the ideas of the father of psychotherapy, Sigmund Freud (Strachey, 1962). (Freudian theory is also de-

scribed in Chapter 13 of this text.) Freud believed that sexuality was an extremely important life force and that sexual problems occurred because one's personality development was incomplete at some life stage. Intervention, therefore, involved the therapist's guiding the client back into that incomplete life stage, gaining *insight* into herself or himself, and therefore completing the development of the personality. And with a fully developed personality, full sexual function would occur.

Perhaps because the theory is faulty, or perhaps because it accounts for only some people's problems, or perhaps because it doesn't adequately account for all problems, including sexual problems, this "traditional" intervention method often failed to help people resolve their sexual problems. So the pendulum swung.

An opposing view of treating sexual problems was first introduced by William Masters, M.D., and Virginia Johnson, in 1970.[9] They suggested that sexual problems can be just sexual problems—that they may have nothing to do with incomplete life stages or any other personality defect. Instead, sexual problems may be solely the result of faulty learning about sex and consequently poor experiences, repeated over and over again. So the intervention dictated by their theory was very much oriented to the present (as opposed to the past). They, therefore, departed from the traditional focus on the *individual* and instead defined and treated the *relationship* as the client, to help persons (1) understand their sexual histories, sexual values, and physical responses more fully; (2) learn what is more interesting and arousing to them sexually and to communicate these things to their partner; (3) reduce goal- and performance-oriented sexual expression, concentrating more fully on the pleasure of

---

[8] Books on sexuality and aging, and physical illness and disability include Edward M. Brecher, *Love, Sex and Aging* (Boston: Little, Brown, 1984); Armando De-Moya, Dorothy DeMoya, Martha E. Lewis, and Howard R. Lewis, *Sex and Health* (New York: Stein & Day, 1983); Alex Comfort, *Sexual Consequences of Disability* (Philadelphia: George F. Stickley Co., 1978); and Thomas H. Walz and Nancee S. Blum, *Sexual Health in Later Life* (Lexington, MA: Lexington Books, 1987).

[9] An excellent synopsis of this medical text, written in lay persons' language, is Fred Belliveau and Lin Richter, *Understanding Human Sexual Inadequacy* (New York: Bantam Books, 1970).

the experience rather than on the goal of intercourse and orgasm; and (4) reduce their anxiety during sexual experiences.

Masters and Johnson treated people, often with very long-standing sexual problems, in a two-week intensive therapy program. This was the beginning of *sex therapy*.

By definition, "sex therapy differs from other forms of treatment for sexual dysfunctions in two respects: first, its goals are essentially limited to the relief of the patient's sexual symptom and second, it departs from traditional techniques by employing a combination of prescribed sexual experiences and psychotherapy" (Kaplan, 1974, p. 187).

In the 1990s there seems to be a decided trend among sex therapists nationwide that might be defined as the pendulum swinging back toward the center. In the past, the pendulum swung from treating sexual problems by "traditional" methods (that is, by helping the client gain insight into her or his personality and not directly talking about sex) to using a very programmed, behavioral approach. The former method was generally unsuccessful, while the latter frequently led to improvement—but sometimes only to a point. Some people start to "get better" and then their improvement plateaus, short of their goals. To help clients progress beyond this plateau, sex therapists have increasingly borrowed other methods of intervention frequently used in relationship therapy.[10] A case example is presented in the following section.

Sex Therapy

Steve telephoned the sex therapy clinic and spoke with a male therapist. Steve explained that he had lately become increasingly upset

---

[10] Sex therapists have also become much more knowledgeable about diagnosing and treating sexual disorders. Books that describe the present state of this knowledge include David M. Schnarch, *Constructing the Sexual Crucible* (New York: Norton, 1991); Helen Sanger Kaplan, *The Evaluation of Sexual Disorders* (New York: Brunner/Mazel, 1983); John Money, *Venuses Penises* (Buffalo: Prometheus Books, 1986).

about his marital and sexual problems and, after a particularly heated argument with his wife the previous evening, he realized something must be done. So he talked with his physician, who suggested he call the sex therapy clinic.

The therapist arranged an appointment to see Steve and his wife, Joan, together with his cotherapist. A principle subscribed to at this clinic is that since women and men grow up with such different messages about sex, and since there are obvious physical differences, women can best relate therapeutically to women and men to men. So couples seen at the clinic are seen by a male-female, cotherapy team.

The Intake

At the initial appointment, the therapists asked each person about the nature of the problems occurring in the marriage.

Joan described her general dissatisfaction with the relationship as well as her specific sexual complaints. She felt Steve was preoccupied with his work and generally insensitive to her needs. She felt frustrated at her inability to get him to share his feelings with her. In the past couple of years, she admitted to basically "shutting down" to him and had given up trying to draw him out. She sought and received most of her intimacy needs from their two children. Their sex life had suffered greatly; she professed very little interest in being sexual with Steve or by herself.

Steve, on the other hand, was angry at Joan because he felt he fulfilled his principal role in the relationship—that of breadwinner—and was increasingly being asked to participate in duties around the house and with the children. At the same time, Joan was denying him a sexual relationship. He felt she was unfair in her expectations of him, and he had become increasingly more withdrawn.

The therapists learned further that sex, early in the relationship, had been good for Steve and Joan. Lately, however, their lives had become more complicated: by having children, by additional stresses from Steve's job, and by Joan's increasing lack of satisfaction in her role as housewife. Therefore, the quality and quantity of their sexual intimacy had progressively deteriorated. Intercourse occurred about twice a month now, and there was little physical affection in the relationship outside the sexual encounters.

The therapists felt the couple was motivated to change. Each was frightened by the intensity of their dissatisfactions, but they were committed to each other and seemed eager to learn ways to improve the relationship.

The therapists discussed with Steve and Joan what their entering therapy would mean. They would meet once a week for therapy sessions and would additionally be expected to get together, in the privacy of their own home, three times a week for home experiences prescribed by the therapists. Sex therapy generally lasts for 12 to 18 sessions. The focus would be on intimacy—how to rebuild, through sexually intimate interactions, the strength of the marriage. There would be no demonstration or observation of sexual behavior in the sex therapy clinic.

Some areas of emphasis for Steve and Joan would be (1) improving verbal communication skills; (2) increasing their knowledge about sex; (3) helping each person individuate, or learn and act on what each wants rather than largely reacting to the other; (4) exploring each person's history to help them understand themselves better, with particular emphasis on parental role models; and (5) exploring the history of the relationship to better understand how the problems developed as they did and to discourage them from developing again.

The therapists encouraged Joan and Steve to discuss, after this initial session, whether they wanted to enter therapy.

The "chicken and egg" question often comes up with sexual problems—that is, has the sexual relationship deteriorated because the marriage is in trouble, or is the marriage in trouble because the sexual relationship has deteriorated? It probably makes little differ-

ence. If successful intervention is made in the sexual area—the couple learns to talk honestly about their needs and desires, they learn to cooperate, and so on—improvement in the remainder of the relationship generally occurs. This is because, for most people, sexual intimacy is a microcosm of their entire relationship. They often play out their power struggles, their fears of getting close, their anger, in bed. Intervening in sexuality, furthermore, can be very specific. When a couple is given an assignment to get together for an experience touching each other, the therapists can learn a great deal about motivation, cooperation, communication, ability to give and receive pleasure, and so forth. This promotes the efficiency of therapy by giving a rather concrete focus.

Joan telephoned the therapists two days later to say they had discussed therapy and decided to get started. They scheduled the next appointment.

At the next treatment session, the therapists separated the couple, the male therapist meeting with Steve and the female therapist meeting with Joan.[11] This was for history taking and would be the only time they would meet separately. Each therapist took an extensive, two-hour social/sexual history.[12]

The History

The purpose of the history-taking session is to enable each therapist to empathize with and understand as effectively as possible the client she or he will be representing. It also gives the same-gender therapists and clients

[11]This case history illustrates the method used most commonly by the author when seeing a couple in intensive sex therapy. Many sex therapists use similar treatment methods, based on principles and techniques originally introduced by Masters and Johnson, *Human Sexual Inadequacy*.

[12] Outlines of sexual histories can be found in Joseph LoPiccolo and Leslie LoPiccolo, eds., *Handbook of Sex Therapy* (New York: Plenum Press, 1978), pp. 103–113, and in Masters and Johnson, *Human Sexual Inadequacy*, pp. 34–51.

a better opportunity to get to know each other, facilitating openness and trust.

In taking a sexual history the therapists probed each client for her or his goals of therapy, childhood and adolescent experiences (including sexual assault victimization), sexual value systems, the history of the sexual problems, strengths and weaknesses in the marriage, descriptions of typical sexual experiences, and a great deal of other information helpful to the therapists in representing their same-sex client accurately and developing the treatment plan.

During the history-taking session, the therapists were particularly careful to ask specific questions and press for specific, detailed answers. A very important rule for sex counselors and therapists to observe is to avoid *assuming* anything. Because specific, personal sexual experiences are not something people tend to talk about, particularly if there is a sexual problem involved, persons often assume their behaviors are similar to everybody else's. The thorough, careful therapist will avoid serious pitfalls that would have sabotaged the success of therapy had they not been noticed.

The Roundtable

Joan and Steve met the next week for the subsequent therapy session, the roundtable. In this meeting, each therapist reviewed the significant contributions each partner makes to the strengths and weaknesses of their relationship. The areas of misunderstanding resulting from patterns of faulty communication were especially emphasized. The focus was not on whose fault the problems were, or who should feel guilty, but rather what was *dysfunctional* in their unique interactions with each other.

Sexual problems almost never develop in relationships because of some conscious, malicious intent. Instead, they are due to patterns of interaction that, as a whole, are dysfunctional. Each piece, taken out of context, might be done with the best of intentions. For example, Steve and Joan had fallen into a pattern of quick sex. This was largely because Steve knew Joan was not particularly enjoying their sexual experiences, so he hurried to get them over with. Unfortunately this exacerbated the problem because Joan was less likely to become aroused, and therefore enjoy sex, in a hurried encounter. The therapists pointed this out, along with many other patterns, to Joan and Steve.

At the end of the roundtable session, they were asked to abstain from intercourse and were given the following instructions, which were discussed verbally and were also contained in a handout:

Touching Experiences
For many persons, the idea of body touching is thought of only as a preliminary to orgasm. Thinking of touching in this way often causes the touching to become less valued for its own sake. Although the entire body may be pleasant to touch and to have touched, emphasis is usually placed on the breasts and vaginal area or on the penis and testicles. Touching need not be explicitly genital or goal-oriented to be pleasurable. Touching, by yourself or with a partner, can be a joyful expression of discovery and exploration, of giving and getting.

Plan ahead and prepare, together, a quiet and private, warm and comfortable place. Create an atmosphere that is pleasant for you. It may include soft, even colored lights or candles and music or other things that help you relax. Remove your clothing and assume positions that will permit comfort during long periods of touching. Give yourselves a lot of time. Slowly become very familiar with your partner's entire body. Remember, this experience is not one of trying to sexually arouse one's partner. It is designed to give you time to explore your own feelings about touching and being touched. Touch, stroke, squeeze, and caress your partner to explore what you feel. The feeling you receive need not be an arousing one. You will feel something; get in touch with whatever that feeling is.

You may wish to shower together, using pleasant soaps on one another's body, or try to shower in the dark (you must then rely on touch). Try a pleasant tasting, non-alcohol based lotion or oil, or a baby powder. These facilitate the movement of skin on skin and reduce friction. Oils or lotions should first be poured in your hands to be warmed or otherwise warmed beforehand.

Use your fingers, fingertips, your palms, and your full hand to touch and caress in different ways. This is not a massage. Massage is designed primarily to give pleasure to the other person. Remember, the major purpose of this touching experience is to discover feelings for yourself through touching your partner. It may be helpful to close your eyes while touching so you can "get into" your own feelings without observing your partner's response. Try a joyful fantasy, if you like; or pretend you've lost the use of your sight for a while and must rely on touch alone. The person being touched has only to lie there and concentrate on his or her own feelings of being touched. Sometimes, too, you may want to explore your partner's body visually while you are touching and would feel more comfortable if your partner were to close his or her eyes. If so, ask your partner to do so. If you would like to comb your partner's hair, do so.

Since you are touching your partner for yourself, you need not concern yourself about your partner's reaction, unless it is one of discomfort or pain (if so, your partner must tell you). After each touching experience discuss your feelings with one another; not in a directive or accusatory fashion but with an effort toward understanding each other's feelings about touching and being touched. Do not make assumptions about your partner's feelings. Use "I" language to express your feelings.

(See the next section.)

We ask you to have "nongenital touching experiences" a minimum of three times during the first week to reinforce comfortable feelings. We will discuss with you which partner should initiate the first touching experience. After the "initiator" has fully explored his or her feelings from touching the partner's body, change off, the person who was touching will then become the one who is touched. During this first week we do not want the man to touch his partner's breasts, nipples, or vaginal area; nor do we want the woman to touch her partner's nipples, penis, or testicles. Touching should be done only with the hands during this week period. (Much later you may wish to try touching your partner with other parts of your body: your feet, lips, face. etc.) [Midwest Therapy Center; Sinclair & Zastrow, 1993, p. 235]

Steve and Joan were also given the following instructions to improve their verbal interactions:

Self-Representation: The Use of "I-Language"[13]
Most sexually intimate couples think they know considerably more about each other's feelings, attitudes, and behaviors than they, in fact, really do know. They take pride in "outguessing" and in "predicting" their partner's responses without ever really communicating with each other. They believe "since he/she loves me—he/she *knows* how I feel."

Responsibility for self. We are each responsible for our own sexuality. We should not wait for someone else to discover it for us. We need to explore, dis-

---

[13]"I-language" is a verbal communication technique suggested by many therapists. It was developed by Thomas Gordon, *Parent Effectiveness Training* (New York: Peter H. Wyden, 1970). I-language, also called I-messages, is further described in Chapter 20.

cover, and understand our own sexual responses. We are then free to share or not to share our sexuality with another person. If we decide to share our sexuality, we need to be willing to communicate with our partner what we have learned about ourselves . . . to be open . . . to be vulnerable . . . to risk. We also need to be willing to learn about our partner's sexuality *from our partner*. We cannot make assumptions about his/her needs, feelings, etc., without asking. Too often our guesses are wrong. In order to share a sexual experience on an equal basis we must both have and express knowledge, comfort, and responsibility for our own sexuality. This "responsibility" is necessary to take ownership for our own feelings, attitudes, and ideas as well as our behaviors.

Representation of self. Once we are responsible for our own sexuality and have made a decision to share our sexuality with another person, we need to learn the best way of representing ourselves clearly to our partner.

"I-language." It begins with "I," taking responsibility for ourselves, and is followed by a feeling. "I appreciate your tenderness." "I'm upset because you're late, and I've had to delay a fine meal." "I would like to go to that new movie tonight and am curious if you would like to go with me." "I wonder what it would feel like if you touched me like this."

The purpose of "I" language is not to promote agreement but rather to promote accurate communication and understanding. Only with accurate understanding can you ever know whether you agree or disagree. When you use "I" language you must first be aware of your own feeling, attitude, idea, before you can clearly state it to your partner. Thus, the use of "I" language helps you to get in touch with your own feelings first. All feelings are real for you; they may not always be rational, yet you have them. It is your responsibility to represent your feelings—not your partner's feelings. Do not expect your partner

to know your feelings clearly unless you represent them clearly. Through the use of "I" language you minimize putting your partner in a defensive position. You also optimize opening further communication. You speak for *you*, not for someone else. By openly expressing your feelings you encourage your partner to do the same. Openness often seems risky when used with someone we care about, but the alternative may be years of misinformation. The following are examples of "you" language, succeeded by more effective "I" language:

a. "You make me so angry when you don't pick up your clothes." (An accusatory statement that is most likely to place your partner on the defensive.)

b. "I'm angry because in addition to picking up my own clothes I feel I have to pick your clothes up too." (Permits further communication and represents your feelings.)

a. "Let's go out to dinner." (A confused message that takes over your partner's response.)

b. "I'd like to go out to dinner and wonder if you would like to also." (Much better.)

a. "You're too clumsy when you touch my breasts." (Another accusatory message likely to shut down communication—not open it up.)

b. "I get turned off when you touch my breasts that way because it hurts; I'd like to show you what kind of touch feels good."

a. "Do you want to go to the movies tonight?" (Answer: "I don't know, do you?" Next response—"I don't know, I asked you first." Result: confusion.)

b. "I would like to see _____ tonight, and wonder if you would also like to see that film." [Midwest Therapy Center; Sinclair & Zastrow, 1993, p. 236]

Finally, Steve and Joan were instructed to take some time, each by himself/herself to

Sex therapy can help couples learn to talk honestly about their needs and desires and can lead to improvement in the remainder of the relationship.

explore their bodies through whole-body touching and masturbation. Since masturbation to orgasms was something each of them had done many times before, this was not expected to be difficult. However, talking about masturbation had been awkward before, and each felt some relief to get permission from the therapists and each other to self-pleasure.

The Physiology Session

The next therapy session focused on feedback Steve and Joan shared about their touching experiences.

Both reported feelings awkward at first, but after they got over the feeling that they were touching strictly for the therapists, they enjoyed each session a great deal. Joan felt much more relaxed than she had for some time. Since she wasn't expected to get aroused, she felt unburdened by expectations and was able to enjoy the sessions unencumbered by performance demands. Steve was encouraged; Joan initiated two of the three touching experiences they had that week. He had stated, when giving his history, his belief that if *he* never initiated sex, it wouldn't ever happen.

Both had used some "I-language" in discussing issues that came up throughout the week. Steve, particularly, said he needed to remind himself to use it more.

The therapists explored, very specifically, the touching experiences with Joan and Steve, encouraging them to give each other as much feedback as possible. The emphasis on touching for the pleasure of the active partner, rather than to "turn her/him on," was further emphasized. The assignment for the next week was the same, except touching of breasts and genitals was now permitted. Joan and Steve were encouraged not to place too much emphasis on genital touching, however. They were to integrate genital touching with other touching, to learn and explore, not to arouse. If arousal took place, that was fine; it was *not*, however, the purpose of the experience.

Joan and Steve were further encouraged to continue their private self-stimulation sessions.

In the second half of this therapy session, the therapists reviewed significant information about the physiology of human sexual response, described as follows:

The male therapist explained the genital response in the male, using slides and models to illustrate the physical changes. In the first stage of sexual response, excitement, blood flows into the erectile tissue of the penis (vasocongestion), resulting in erection. The scrotum (the sac surrounding the testicles) becomes thicker, more wrinkled, and the testicles move up closer to the body.

The plateau stage of sexual response is characterized by the continuation of erection, although it often waxes and wanes during sex play with a partner. The testicles become fully elevated, rotate toward the front, and become blood-engorged, causing expansion in their size. The Cowper's gland secretes a small amount of clear fluid which comes out of the tip of the penis. The purpose of this fluid is generally thought to be to cleanse the urethra of urine, thereby neutralizing the chemical environment for the passage of sperm.

The orgasm stage in men consists of two phases. The first is ejaculatory inevitability, a short period during which stimulation sufficient to trigger orgasm has occurred, and the resulting ejaculation becomes inevitable. The second phase, ejaculation, results from rhythmic contractions (myotonia) forcing sperm and semen through the urethra. Simultaneous with this is the very pleasant physical sensation of orgasm.

The final stage, resolution, represents a return to the unstimulated state. In resolution, the penis loses its erection, and the testicles lose their engorgement and elevation.

In women, the excitement stage of sexual response ushers in many changes. The process of vaginal lubrication begins. This response is analogous to the male erection; it is caused by sexual stimulation and is, physiologically, a blood engorgement response. The uterus and cervix begin to move up and away from the vagina. The clitoris and labia minora enlarge and the labia majora spread. Breast size increases slightly and the nipples may become erect.

In the plateau stage, the uterus continues in its movement up and back, the vagina lengthens and balloons at the rear, and the outer third of the vagina contracts, causing a gripping effect. The clitoris retracts under its hood, making it seem to disappear.

At orgasm, the uterus and vagina become involved in wavelike muscular contractions. This response, as well as the subjective pleasure of orgasm, are very similar to the experience of the male.

In resolution, the cervix and uterus drop to their normal positions, the outer third of the vagina returns to normal, followed by the inner two thirds. The clitoris and the breasts also return to normal.

The therapists also discussed the many involuntary extragenital physical responses in men and women. These include muscle tension responses such as facial grimace, spastic contractions of the hands and feet, and pelvic thrusting. Extragenital blood engorgement responses include sex flush, blood pressure and heart rate increases, and perspiration on soles of feet and palms of hands.

Finally, the therapists discussed how aging affects sexual response. They emphasized that persons are capable of experiencing pleasurable sexual response throughout life; while their bodies may slow down, they do not need to stop. [Sinclair & Zastrow, 1993, pp. 237–238]

Subsequent Treatment Sessions

Joan and Steve saw the therapists weekly for nine more sessions. They were gradually instructed to try new sexual behaviors, with the option to proceed at their own pace. Therapy progressed well until the fifth week.

The fifth, sixth, and seventh therapy session saw Joan reporting sexual interest and sexual arousal, but her progress plateaued. At first, the therapists interpreted the lack of progress as simply rough spots in the process of change. However, after three weeks, deeper exploration was indicated.

During a very intense seventh treatment session, therapists identified a power struggle existing in the relationship that was hampering further progress. Basically, Joan felt *she* was being asked to change for Steve much more than he for her. Since being sexual was what he wanted more than anything from her, and sharing his feelings was what she wanted from him—something she felt he was doing very little of—she was not willing to give further. This was probably an unconscious choice, a way for Joan to protect herself from being fully dominated by Steve. The therapists tested this hypothesis by explaining this power relationship to Steve and working with him to open his feelings more to Joan. Subsequent weeks saw great improvement in this area and the sexual relationship in general.

Therapy was terminated by agreement of clients and therapists, when the couple found that the sexual relationship, as well as the relationship in general, had improved greatly.

In addition, they had learned skills to foster further improvement in the months and years to come.

Summary

Any social worker who interacts with clients is presented with opportunities to be helpful in the area of sexuality. Since sex typically elicits concern and anxiety in people in this society, it is incumbent on social workers to examine their own feelings in this area and to become knowledgeable. Furthermore, they need to recognize the legitimacy and importance of their professional intervention in this area.

The first prerequisite to effective counseling in the area of sexuality is knowledge, and therefore social workers need to acquire accurate information. Counselors should be aware that it is a mistake to assume that everyone expresses sexuality in the same way. Social workers also need to learn the technical words involving sexuality and to become desensitized to the expression of "street" words in counseling.

Sexual dysfunctions are defined and the various dysfunctions (such as orgasmic dysfunction) are identified. Jack S. Annon developed a useful conceptual scheme of intervention levels: permission, limited information, specific suggestions, and intensive therapy. The largest number of clients benefit from intervention at the level of permission. Each of these levels is described.

Intensive sex therapy differs from other forms of treatment for sexual dysfunctions in two respects. First, its goals are essentially limited to the relief of the patient's sexual symptom. Second, it departs from traditional techniques by employing a combination of prescribed sexual experiences and psychotherapy. Intensive sex therapy is described in some depth. The stages of intensive sex therapy include problem definition, history gathering, physical examination, information dissemination, prescribed sexual and communication experiences, and ongoing evaluation.

We have explored some basic counseling skills that are helpful in working with clients. We have examined, through case examples, many areas of knowledge and treatment methodologies that are useful to the social worker. And we hope that we have encouraged you to think about, recognize, and explore your own areas of discomfort. The challenge is yours. Will you further the age-old "conspiracy of silence" in this sensitive area, or will you learn, explore, and help your future clients enrich this important area of their lives?

Exercises

1. Tell your neighbor

Goal: Give students an experiential appreciation for the difficulty people have in talking about their own sexuality, even for those who can easily talk about sex in general.

Step 1: Have each student pick a partner for the exercise. The person sitting closest is fine; the relationship between the partners is not important. If there is an odd number of students, one group can consist of three members. Be certain all students have partners before proceeding to step 2.

Step 2: Give the following task: "Turn to your partner and tell her or him about a sexual problem *you* have."

Step 3: Interrupt students after a brief period (not to exceed 30 seconds) by saying "Stop" loudly. Explain that the purpose of the exercise is not to elicit class members' sexual problems, but rather to have them experience their own uneasiness when they are expected to reveal some sexual vulnerability of their own.

Step 4: Lead the class in a discussion of what occurred when they were faced with the previous task. Typically, students will report they discussed who was going to say their problem first, with each hoping the partner would go first. Other students will likely say they searched their minds for a "safe" problem, one that would not be too threatening to reveal and one that would not be too embarrassing to disclose. The relationship between the partners (whether they are unacquainted or friends, members of the same or the other gender, whether there is a perception on the part of one partner that the other can be trusted with a confidence or will be helpful) has great bearing on how much one is willing to reveal. This exercise should lead students to a heightened awareness of the difficulty faced by a client who must discuss a sexual problem and the qualities they might strive to possess to elicit disclosure from clients.

2. The word game

Goals: (a) Begin desensitizing students to words with which they feel uncomfortable so this discomfort doesn't block their helpfulness with a client. (b) Help students identify a functional language that is comfortable and acceptable to use in a professional setting. (c) Help students learn new words that may be part of a client's vocabulary and hence should be familiar. (d) Help students realize that the vast majority of words associated with sex are street language and, therefore, many clients are familiar only with those words.

Step 1: Explain the four types of words used when talking about sex: scientific, childhood, common discourse, and street or slang. As described in the text of this chapter, scientific words, such as *coitus* and *fellatio,* are very specific. However, they are not commonly used by most people because they have a clinical connotation. Professionals sometimes hide behind these words as a way to diminish their discomfort. (As discussed in the chapter, if you're not communicating, you're not helping.)

Childhood language, such as words like *peepee* and *bottom,* is usually used by anxious parents who are searching for a nonthreatening (to the parents) way to convey their message to their child. When used by adults with each other, they sound ridiculous. Common discourse words and phrases, such as *making love* or *having sex,* are most comfortable for many people. Slang or street words, such as *fuck* or *pussy,* provide graphic descriptions, often laden with hostility. These words are "loaded"; that is, they can mean very different things to different people, depending on the intonation of the voice, the context, the relationship of the people, and other factors. While they are the most commonly used words to express sexual content in this culture, they are also the most powerful and, hence, the most potentially hazardous for a professional to use with a client.

Step 2: Divide the class into two groups, usually by making an aisle down the middle of the room.

Step 3: Write a word, such as *intercourse, breasts, penis,* or *masturbation,* on the chalkboard. Instruct one group to call out as many words as they can think of that have the same meaning as the word on the board. Then write the words on the board as they are being called out and stop the group after 60 seconds have elapsed.

Step 4: Count the words and write the total number on the chalkboard.

Step 5: Challenge the other group to generate a larger number of words than the first group. Write a new word on the board and repeat this exercise.

Step 6: If appropriate, give each group another word and repeat the exercise.

Step 7: In a debriefing discussion, note how many of the words fall into each category, discuss the gender bias to particular words, such as those that describe masturbation, and urge the students to practice saying these and other sexually descriptive words to increase their comfort in preparation for their presentation from a client.

3. Answer the question

Goals: Help students (a) experience the difficulty in answering a client's questions about sex, even when the answer is known to the students; (b) confront their sexual values as they attempt to respond to the needs of a young person; and (c) realize the most commonly asked questions by adolescents about sex are not ones that can be answered factually; rather, they relate to values and are therefore open to many answers.

Step 1: Tell the class that you are going to role-play an inquisitive adolescent, the age and gender of whom will vary with each phase of the exercise. The class is to role-play social workers with whom the adolescent has a trusting relationship.

Step 2: Adopt an insecure and immature affect and ask the first question. Typical questions frequently asked by adolescents include these:

Why do you sometimes get a stiff when you're not thinking about sex?
How tough is that hymen thing?
Will playing with yourself cause problems in intercourse?
How old do you have to be to have intercourse?
How many boys do it? How often? Do girls ever? How would they do it?
Do you automatically know how to have intercourse when you marry?
How do two females have sex together?
Can I use tampons if I'm a virgin?
How do you know if your girlfriend says no when she really means yes?
Why do boys like intercourse more than girls?
If you don't want to have sex before marriage, how far should you go?
Do people have control over their type of sexual behavior, and over how they feel? Is it biological or in your mind?
What does an orgasm feel like?

Instruct the class to respond to the questions and to the adolescent's clarifying questions. As the role play evolves, encourage class members to help each other respond to the young person's concerns.

Step 3: When the first question has been exhausted, lead the class in a discussion of the experience. What was difficult? Where did class members differ with each other on how to handle sensitive matters? How were values dealt with? What reluctances did people have to discuss certain specific areas?

Step 4: Repeat the exercise with a new question, playing a slightly different role. As the role play progresses, encourage the students to try to determine what the adolescent is really searching for, such as permission to have intercourse or permission *not* to have intercourse.

19

A Feminist Perspective on Therapy

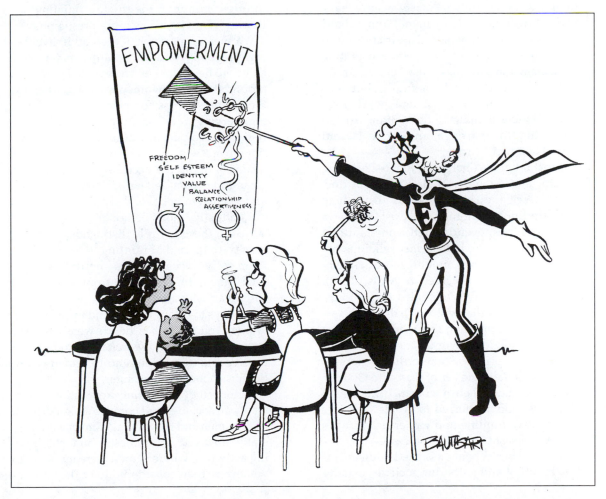

A History of Sex Roles and Sexism

In almost every known society women have had a lower status than men. Women have been bound by more social restrictions and have consistently received less recognition for their work. They have also been regarded differently, not only biologically, but also emotionally, intellectually, and psychologically. Double standards have often existed for dating, for marriage, and for social and sexual conduct.

Most religions (including Judeo-Christian, Hindu, and Islam) in their traditional doctrines ascribe an inferior status to women. This tradition continues to exist today in most countries, even though women attend church more often, hold firmer religious beliefs, pray more often, and are more active in church programs (Fichter & Mills, 1972). Many societies have concluded that it is divinely ordained that women shall play a secondary and supportive role to men. In many Christian religions, women cannot become ministers or priests. Some orthodox Jewish men offer a daily prayer of thanks to God for not having made them a woman. In almost all churches, God is referred to as "He."

Primitive hunting and gathering societies provide insight into the processes that resulted in women being assigned a lower status. Hunting and gathering societies usually lived in small tribes consisting of several married couples and their dependents. Men generally were the hunters, and women were the gatherers of nuts, plants, and other foods. There are several explanations for this differentiation. Males, it has been suggested, were better suited to hunting because they were physically stronger and could run faster. Also the infant mortality rate was very high in these tribes, so it was necessary for the women to be pregnant or nursing throughout most of their childbearing years to maintain the size of the tribe. The need to tend to children largely prevented women from leaving the camp for days at a time to hunt large game. Even though women often gathered more food than men were able to obtain through hunting, the male's hunting activities were viewed as more prestigious.

Women spent much of their adult lives being pregnant, nursing infants, and raising children. Because they were forced to remain around the home, women were also assigned the less prestigious "domestic tasks" of cooking, serving, and washing. Once these sex roles became part of tradition, these distinctions were not only recognized as practical means of doing the necessary work, but also came to be seen as "natural" ways for men and women to behave.

Gradually, more behavior patterns were added to these sex-role distinctions. Because men were trained at hunting, these skills led them to be recognized as the defenders of their tribe in case of attack from other tribes. Childrearing patterns were developed to teach boys to be aggressive and to be leaders. Women, on the other hand, were assigned supportive roles and were taught to be more passive and dependent and to provide emotional support for their men.

Before the Industrial Revolution, practically all societies had come to assign distinct roles to men and to women. Women were generally involved in domestic and childrearing activities, whereas men were involved in what were then considered to be the productive[1] (such as hunting and economic support) and protective functions for the family. In preindustrial societies women were also often involved in food producing and economic support, such as making clothes, growing and harvesting garden crops, and helping on the farm. But their specific responsibilities were often viewed as inferior and requiring fewer skills.

The 19th-century Industrial Revolution brought dramatic changes in sex roles. Instead of working on a small farm, men went outside the home to work in a factory or other setting to provide economic support. The economic role of women declined, since they were less likely to be performing economically productive tasks. Their roles became increasingly defined as childrearing and housework. But the amount of time required to perform these roles declined for several reasons. Families had fewer children. With mass education, older children went to school. Gradually, labor-saving devices reduced the need for women to perform time-consuming domestic tasks such as baking bread, canning vegetables, and washing. As traditional roles began to change, some women began to pursue activities (for example, outside employment) that had traditionally been limited to men. With these changes, sex roles began to blur and to become less clear-cut.

The struggle for women's rights in America has been going on for nearly two centuries. In the early part of the 19th century, women who were working for the abolition of slavery became aware that they too were denied such rights as voting. (An 1840 anti-slavery conference even refused seats for women while the male delegates gave impassioned speeches about the moral right of ending slavery.)

[1]The use of the term *productive* indicates the higher status that was assigned to men's roles. In actuality, women's roles were often as "productive," or more so, in completing the essential tasks that needed to be performed.

In 1848 two feminists, Susan B. Anthony and Elizabeth Stanton, organized the first women's rights caucus, which was held in the state of New York. These early leaders demanded suffrage (the vote for women) and the reform of many laws that were openly discriminatory toward women. It took over 70 years, until 1920, to pass the 19th Amendment to the Constitution, which gave the vote to women. The suffrage movement was marked by jailings of feminist militants and fierce controversy. The huge struggles and number of years spent in getting this amendment passed led many women leaders to believe that the right to vote went hand in hand with sexual equality. After the 1920 passage, the "women's movement" was nearly dormant for the next 40 years.

In the early 1900s, some modern birth control techniques became available. Through this advance women gained greater freedom from the traditional roles of childrearing and housework.

During World War II large numbers of women were employed outside the home for the first time to take the places of men who had been drafted into the military. At this time over 38 percent of all women 16 years of age and over were employed, causing a further blurring of traditional sex roles (Blaire, 1979, p. 272).

In the 1960s, there was a resurgence of interest in sex-role inequality for a variety of reasons. The civil rights movement had a consciousness-raising effect in that people became more aware of and concerned about inequalities. The civil rights movement to curb racial discrimination also served as a model, suggesting to a number of concerned women that sexual discrimination could also be alleviated through social action. More women attended college and thereby became more informed about inequalities. As women moved into new occupational positions, they became increasingly aware of discriminatory practices. Finally, there was an explosion of research suggesting that sex-role differences were not innately determined but were in fact the result of socialization patterns and that the effects of such sex roles were often discriminatory toward women.

Betty Friedan, in her 1963 book *The Feminine Mystique,* provided the ideological base for the resurgence of the women's movement. With the term *feminine mystique,* Friedan referred to the negative self-concept, lack of direction, and low sense of self-worth among women. The book served as a rallying point for women and led Friedan and others to form the National Organization for Women (NOW) in 1966. Today NOW is the largest women's rights group in the country and an influential political force. NOW and other women's groups have been working to end sexual discrimination, to achieve sexual equality, to end sexual double standards, and to improve the self-identity of women.

The Civil Rights Act of 1964, primarily intended to end racial discrimination, also prohibited discrimination on the basis of sex. A variety of statutes designed to prevent sex discrimination have been passed. The federal Equal Pay Act of 1963 and a number of similar state laws require equal pay for equal work. As mentioned earlier, the Civil Rights Act of 1964 outlaws discrimination on the basis of race, color, sex, or religion. Executive Order 11246, as amended by Executive Order 11375 on October 13, 1967, forbids sex discrimination by federal suppliers and contractors and provides procedures for enforcement. In addition, numerous court decisions have set precedents establishing the illegality of sex discrimination in hiring, promotions, and rates of pay. The Equal Credit Act of 1974 bars discrimination on the basis of marital status or sex in credit operations. A number of states have passed laws prohibiting discrimination against pregnant women in hiring, training, and promotion.

Affirmative action programs apply to women as well as to certain racial minorities. Women are considered a minority group because for generations they have been subjected to discrimination and have been denied equal opportunities. The following employers are required to have affirmative action programs: government contractors and suppliers, recipients of government funds, and businesses engaged in interstate commerce. Affirmative action primarily applies to job vacancies. Employers must demonstrate active efforts to locate and recruit minority applicants (defined to include women), demonstrate positive efforts to increase the pool of qualified applicants (for example, special training programs for minorities), give preference to hiring minority applicants, and in some cases set hard quotas that specify numbers of minority members that must be accepted to fill vacant positions. The clout of affirmative action programs is the threat of loss of government funds if employers do not have such programs effectively in place.

Women's Current Issues

In spite of the passage of federal and state statutes designed to protect women's rights, sexual discrimination continues to occur. This section summarizes the problems that women experience in our society. The statistical data is taken from Kirst-Ashman and Hull (1993):

- In the United States women who work full-time are paid only two-thirds of what men earn who are employed full-time. Eighty percent of women work in only one-quarter of all possible occupations, and these occupations generally pay less and offer fewer opportunities for advancement.
- Women are twice as likely to be poor within their lifetime.
- Single female–headed households are four times as likely to be poor as single male–headed households. The increase in one-parent families in recent years has led to an increase in the feminization of poverty.

- Approximately one-fourth to one-third of all women are raped sometime during their lifetime.
- One out of four to one out of two wives will be battered by their husbands. Extremely severe repeated violence occurs against women in almost 7 percent of all marriages.
- Women are much more likely to be subjected to sexual harassment than men. (Sexual harassment may be defined as repeated and unwanted sexual advances.)
- Women hold fewer than 10 percent of the nation's elective offices and fewer than 1 percent of the top-management positions in American corporations.

In addition to these specific problems, Collier (1982, pp. 57–77) has identified eight personal issues that women frequently bring to counseling situations:

1. *Sense of powerlessness:* Women who have been socialized to be passive and dependent often feel that no matter what they do, they cannot improve their life situation.

2. *Limited behavioral and emotional options:* Because of gender-role expectations, women often do not see the variety of alternatives open to them. For example, a battered wife who has been raised to believe that marriage is a permanent commitment may not view leaving her husband as an option.

3. *Anger:* Many women experience deep-seated anger because of the way they are treated at work or at home. Some women turn their anger inward, blaming themselves for their predicaments; this results in depression.

4. *Failure to nurture self:* Women who have devoted themselves to nurturing and caring for others may feel unfulfilled and unsure of who they are.

5. *Inability to balance independence with interdependence:* Many women struggle with being overly dependent on someone else. Other women struggle with finding a balance between being independent (that is, not needing anyone for anything, including emotional support) and interdependent (that is, feeling confident enough to function autonomously, yet acknowledging that interactions with other people are important).

6. *Lack of trust in self-direction:* Women who have low self-esteem and little experience in taking independent action generally have difficulty trusting their own judgment on how to proceed.

7. *Inadequate communication skills:* Some women feel they do not have the right to express their thoughts and feelings, due largely to adherence to traditional gender-role expectations. Other women who have been raised to be passive and nonassertive may not know to express themselves assertively.

8. *Old rules and expectations:* A woman who is seeking an egalitarian relationship with a man will encounter major problems if she becomes romantically involved with a man who has traditional gender-role expectations. Conflicts are likely to arise in a variety of areas, including her choice of careers, division of domestic tasks, and decision making (such as what type of car to buy and how to spend leisure time).

The Feminist Perspective

Women have been highly involved in the development of social work and social welfare programs. One of the founders of modern social work was Jane Addams (see Exhibit 19.1).

Approximately two-thirds of current social workers are female (Bureau of the Census, 1992, p. 398). Female social workers have held numerous leadership positions as deans of graduate schools, chairs of undergraduate social work programs, directors of agencies, and presidents of national, state, and local social work organizations. Women have also written a vast number of social work texts and professional journal articles.

Exhibit 19.1
Jane Addams: A prominent founder of social work

Jane Addams was born in 1860 in Cedarville, Illinois, the daughter of a successful couple who owned a flour mill and a wood mill. Jane graduated from Rockford Seminary (a college in Rockford, Illinois). She briefly attended medical school but was forced to leave because of illness. She then traveled for a few years in Europe, perplexed abut what her life work should be. At the age of 25 she joined the Presbyterian Church, which helped her find a focus for her life—religion and humanitarianism and, in particular, serving the poor. (Later in her life she joined the Congregational Church, now known as the United Church of Christ.) Addams heard about the establishment of Toynbee Hall in England and returned to Europe to study this approach. Its staff was composed of college students and graduates, mainly from Oxford, who lived in the slums of London to learn conditions firsthand and to contribute to the improvement of life in the slums with their own financial and personal resources.

Addams returned to the United States and rented a two-story house (later called Hull House) in an impoverished neighborhood in Chicago. With a few friends, she initiated a variety of group and individual activities for the community. Group activities included a literature reading group for young women, a kindergarten, and groups with the following foci: social relationships, sports, music, painting, art, and discussion of current affairs. Hull House also provided services to individuals who came asking for immediate help, such as food and shelter and information and referral for other services. A Hull House Social Science Club was formed, which studied social problems in a scientific manner and then became involved in social action efforts to improve living conditions. One of its successful efforts was to work for passage of Illinois legislation to prevent the employment of children in area sweatshops. Addams also became interested in the various nationality groups in the neighborhood. She was fairly successful in bringing the various nationalities together at Hull House, where they could interact and interchange cultural values.

The success of Hull House served as a model for the establishment of settlement houses in other areas of Chicago and in many other large cities in the United States. Settlement house leaders believed that by changing neighborhoods, they would improve communities, and through altering communities, they would develop a better society. For her extraordinary contributions, Jane Addams received the Nobel Peace Prize in 1931.

SOURCE: Herb Stroup, "Jane Addams," in *Social Welfare Pioneers* (Chicago: Nelson-Hall, 1986), pp. 1–29.

The feminist perspective on social work intervention has been developed by a number of authors; no one is specifically recognized as being its founder. However, authors Nan Van Den Bergh and Lynn Cooper (1987) have made extensive contributions.

Feminism is a multifaceted concept that is difficult to define accurately. In *The Social Work Dictionary*, Barker (1991, p. 82) defined *feminism* as "the social movement and doctrine advocating legal and socioeconomic equality for women. The movement originated in Great Britain in the 18th century." He then defined *feminist social work* as "the integration of the *values*, skills, and knowledge of social work with a feminist orientation to help individuals and society overcome the emotional and social problems that result from *sex discrimination* (1991, p. 83; italics added).

He further defined *feminist therapy* as follows:

A psychosocial treatment orientation in which the professional (usually a woman) helps the client (usually a woman) in individual or group settings to overcome the psychological and social problems largely encountered as a result of *sex discrimination* and sex-role stereotyping. Feminist therapists help clients maximize potential, especially through *consciousness-raising*, eliminating sex stereotyping, and helping them become aware of the commonalities shared by all women. [1991, p. 83; italics added]

Kirst-Ashman and Hull (1993) defined *feminism* as follows:

. . . the *philosophy of equality* between women and men that involves *both attitudes and actions,* which infiltrates virtually *all aspects of life,* which often necessitates providing *education and advocacy* on the behalf of women, and which appreciates the existence of *individual differences* and personal accomplishments regardless of gender. [p. 427; italics added]

Let's discuss the five emphasized components of this definition. The *philosophy of equality* between men and women does not mean that women should adopt behaviors that are typically masculine. It means that women and men should have equal or identical rights to opportunities and choices and that both women and men should not be discriminated against on the basis of gender.

The second component embodies *both attitudes and actions.* By attitudes, feminism emphasizes the importance of viewing other people in a fair, objective perspective and of avoiding stereotyping. By actions, feminism involves a commitment to act on one's beliefs involving gender equality. For example, a supervisor (male or female) who asserts that he or she believes in feminism has an obligation to confront a male supervisee who tells sexist jokes or who treats women according to traditional gender-based stereotypes (for example, by making demeaning comments about female social workers being too emotionally involved with their clients).

In the third component, *all aspects of life,* equality does not just apply to equal opportunity to attain a specific job or promotion, it involves many other aspects of life, such as: freedom to have opinions on political, social, and religious issues; freedom to ask another person out for a date; freedom to decide what to do with leisure time; freedom to attend, or not to attend, college; freedom to choose to become involved in competitive sports; and freedom to choose to have a sexual encounter.

The fourth component is the frequent need to *provide education and advocacy* on behalf of women. Feminism involves valuing equal op-portunities for women as well as for men. Since women have been subjected to sex-role stereotyping and gender-based discrimination, a person who values feminism has an obligation to provide education and advocacy on behalf of women. For example, the male employee who is telling sexist jokes at work needs to be educated about sexual harassment. He also needs to be informed about the negative impact such jokes have on women and that adverse consequences will result if he continues to make sexist remarks. Feminist advocacy involves speaking out for (or championing the rights of) those women who need help. These women are usually in positions of lesser power and opportunity.

The fifth component is the appreciation of *individual differences.* The feminist perspective places a high value on empowering women by emphasizing individual qualities and strengths.

Principles of Feminist Therapy

Van Den Bergh and Cooper (1987), Van Den Bergh (1992), and Kirst-Ashman and Hull (1993) have identified nine principles of feminist intervention.

1. A client's problems should be viewed "within a sociopolitical framework" (Kirst-Ashman & Hull, 1993, p. 613). Feminist intervention is concerned with the inequitable power relationship between women and men and is opposed to all "power-over" relationships, regardless of gender, race, class, age, and so on. Such relationships lead to oppression and domination. Feminism is concerned with changing all social, economic, and political structures based on the relationships between the haves and the have-nots. The problems of the have-nots are often rooted in a sexist social and political structure. Another way of stating this principle is that "personal is political." According to Van Den Bergh (1992):

This principle maintains that what a woman experiences in her personal life is directly related to societal dynamics that affect other women. In other words, an individual woman's experiences of pejorative comments based on sex and of blocked opportunities are directly related to societal sexism. For ethnic minority women, racism and classism also are factors that affect well-being. [p. 103]

A primary distinguishing characteristic of feminist treatment is to help the client analyze how her problems are related to systematic difficulties experienced by women in a sexist, classist, and racist society.

2. Traditional sex roles are pathological, and clients need encouragement to free themselves from traditional gender-role bonds. Traditionally, American women are expected to be affectionate, passive, conforming, sensitive, intuitive, dependent; in other words, "sugar and spice and everything nice." They are supposed to be primarily concerned with domestic life, to be nurturing, to instinctively love to care for babies and young children, to be deeply concerned about their personal appearance, and to be self-sacrificing for their family. They are raised to not appear to be ambitious, aggressive, competitive, or more intelligent than men. They are expected to be ignorant about and uninterested in sports, economics, or politics. They are not supposed to initiate relationships with men and are expected to be tender, feminine, emotional, and appreciative in these relationships. Women are put in a double bind due to *femininity achievement incompatibility*. There is a traditional view in our society that a woman cannot be both feminine and an achiever. Achievement somehow reduces a woman's femininity, and the truly feminine female is thought to be someone who does seek to be an achiever. Traditionally, women have been socialized to fill a "learned helplessness" role. Van Den Bergh (1992) described the effects of such sex-role stereotyping:

Sex-role stereotypes suggest that women should be submissive, docile, receptive, and dependent. The message is one of helplessness; that women cannot take care of themselves and are dependent upon others for their well-being. This sets up a dynamic in which a woman's locus of control is external to her self, preventing her from believing that she can acquire what she needs on her own in order to develop and self-actualize. In other words, oversubscription to sex-role stereotypes engenders a state of powerlessness in which a woman is likely to become involved in situations where she becomes victimized. . . . For example, because young girls are socialized to be helpless, when they become women they tend to have a limited repertoire of responses when under stress; e.g., they respond passively. [p. 101]

In feminist treatment, clients are helped to see how their difficulties may be related to oversubscription to traditional sex-role stereotypes. They are shown that by internalizing traditional sex roles, women are inevitably set up to play passive, submissive roles and to experience low self-esteem and self-hatred. The feminist approach asserts that clients need encouragement to make their own choices and to pursue the tasks and achievements they desire, rather than being constrained by traditional sex roles.

3. Intervention should focus on client empowerment. Van Den Bergh (1992) described the empowerment process:

Helping women to acquire a sense of power, or the ability to affect outcome in their lives, is a crucial component of feminist practice. Empowerment means acquiring knowledge, skills, and resources that enhance an individual's ability to control her own life and to influence others.

Traditionally women have used indirect, covert techniques to get what they want, such as helplessness, dependency, coyness, and demureness. [p. 104]

Empowerment is fostered in a variety of ways: (1) by helping the client define her own needs and clarify her personal goals so she can derive a sense of purposefulness; (2) by providing the client with education and access to resources; (3) by helping the client see that the direction and ability to change lie within herself (that is, alterations in her life will result only from her own undertakings); and (4) by focusing on the identification and enhancement of the client's strengths rather than on her pathologies. Women need to be empowered so they can increase their ability to control their environments in order to get what they need.

4. Clients' self-esteem should be enhanced. Self-esteem and self-confidence are essential for empowerment. Self-esteem can be enhanced in a variety of ways. The worker should try to be an encouraging person, as described in Chapter 5. The worker should help clients identify and recognize their unique qualities and strengths. Many clients with a low self-esteem tend to blame themselves for everything that is wrong. For example, a battered woman typically tends to blame herself for being battered. These clients need to look more realistically at those areas in which they are blaming themselves and feeling guilt. They need to distinguish where their responsibility for dysfunctional interactions ends and other individuals' responsibility begins.

5. Clients should be encouraged to develop their identity (sense of self) on the basis of their own strengths, attributes, qualities, and achievements. It is a serious mistake for a woman to develop her identity in terms of her spouse or dating partner. Women need to develop an independent identity that is not based on their relationships with others.

6. Clients need to value and develop social support systems with other women. In a society that devalues women, it is all too easy for some women to view other women as insignificant. With social support systems, women can ventilate their concerns and share their experiences and the solutions they've found to similar problems. They can serve as brokers in identifying resources and can provide emotional support and nurturance to one another.

7. Clients needs to find an effective balance between work and personal relationships. Feminist intervention encourages both women and men to share in the nurturant aspects of their lives and in providing economic resources.

8. The nature of the relationship between practitioner and client should approach equality as much as possible. Feminist practitioners do not view themselves as experts in resolving clients' problems, but as catalysts whose role is helping clients empower themselves. Feminist practitioners try to eliminate dominant/submissive relationships. In regard to an egalitarian relationship, Van Den Bergh (1992) noted:

Obviously, there is an innate power differential between practitioner and client because the former has expertise and training as an "authority." However, the feminist admonition is to avoid abusing that status; "abuse" in this sense might be, for example, taking all credit for client change, or using terminology and nomenclature that are difficult for the client to understand. [p. 104]

9. Many clients can benefit from learning to express themselves assertively. The steps in assertiveness training are described in Chapter 16. As indicated earlier, many women are socialized to be passive and nonassertive, and as a result, they have difficulty expressing themselves assertively. Clients can be helped through individual and group counseling.

Case Example
Marge Corcoran

Marge Corcoran came into therapy feeling hopeless and helpless. She indicated she had been mildly depressed for many years. She was brought up to believe that a marriage vow should never be broken, no matter how difficult the situation may become. Ms. Corcoran has a number of scripts associated with this view: (1) it is the wife's role to do the domestic tasks around the home, (2) she has the main responsibility for raising the children, (3) it is her duty to cover up for her husband's drinking, (4) God will reward her in the afterlife for her trials and tribulations in this present life, (5) it is her duty to work outside the home to meet financial needs, and (6) she should put up with the abuse that her husband dishes out. With these scripts, this woman is now in her sixties and has been married for 34 years. She has raised three children and has worked as a nurse all the years of her marriage. Her husband is an alcoholic. He was a construction worker but has not worked for the past 19 years because he has cirrhosis and has had one stroke.

He continues to drink. Throughout their marriage, he has been verbally and physically abusive. She recently retired. The three children moved away from home several years ago and now have families of their own. The husband comes home drunk three or four times a week and is now incontinent. Ms. Corcoran is becoming increasingly frustrated, angry, and depressed about having to be nursemaid to her husband who continues to berate her. He has been in numerous alcoholic treatment programs, including Alcoholics Anonymous, but nothing has curbed his drinking. He now needs extensive health attention, currently provided by his wife. She does not want to place him in a nursing home, because this expense would wipe out the money that she has worked hard to save for retirement. She is also at her wit's end about being nursemaid to an abusive, incontinent alcoholic.

The social worker, Nicole Felber, began by establishing rapport with Ms. Corcoran. She complimented Ms. Corcoran on a number of her strengths: raising three children, having a career in a very important profession, being the main breadwinner in the family, going to unbelievable lengths to try to make her marriage work, and doing most of the domestic tasks.

Then Ms. Felber began asking a number of probing questions.

Ms. Felber: Do you still love your husband?
Ms. Corcoran: No, not for many years.
Ms. Felber: Do you feel marriage entitles a husband to abuse his wife?
Ms. Corcoran: Certainly not.
Ms. Felber: Do you feel you have a right not to be abused?
Ms. Corcoran: Yes.
Ms. Felber: Then why are you continuing to live in an abusive relationship?
Ms. Corcoran: That's a good question. I don't have a good answer.
Ms. Felber: Are you feeling fulfilled and contented in your retirement?

Ms. Corcoran: No, not at all. My feelings are better described as being angry for having to take care of an abusive alcoholic. At times I am depressed and have a feeling of being trapped in a situation I can't get out of.

Ms. Felber: Are you really trapped?

Ms. Corcoran: Yes, I think so. I don't see any other options.

Ms. Felber: Are you aware there are other options?

Ms. Corcoran: No.

Ms. Felber explained that one option was divorce. Ms. Felber mentioned she was aware that Ms. Corcoran had a value that a marriage commitment was forever. Ms. Felber asked Ms. Corcoran to speculate what her life would be like if she continued to remain married to Mr. Corcoran. Ms. Corcoran rambled for a while and finally concluded that her husband's health would continue to deteriorate, her "living hell" of a life would only get worse, and her husband would eventually have to be placed in a nursing home, which would deplete all her savings. She added that an even worse scenario would be her dying first from stress-related illness.

Ms. Felber asked Ms. Corcoran to think about, until they next met, what her life might be like if she pursued getting a divorce. Ms. Felber added that as far as finances were concerned, the divorce laws in their state would require equal splitting of any assets. Ms. Corcoran replied, "Unreal—if I stay married, all my assets will probably go to paying for his care in a nursing home. If I get a divorce, he immediately gets half of the assets I acquired." Ms. Felber indicated that was a fairly accurate summary. Ms. Corcoran remarked that she might be judged harshly in the afterlife if she divorced her husband. Ms. Felber suggested she discuss this with her pastor (a Lutheran minister), whom she has known for years.

Ms. Corcoran came back the next week. She indicated that she had thought for hours about what life might be like if she sought a divorce. She said she had also talked to her minister, who had informed her that in his view God probably sees her as being a saint for all the abuse she has taken; that God is "all-good" and "all-knowing," and such a God would want her to have her remaining years be as enjoyable and contented as possible. She said she had made her decision to get a divorce last night when her husband came home intoxicated again and became verbally and physically abusive. She showed Ms. Felber a big bruise on her shoulder where he had hit her. Ms. Felber complimented her on making a responsible decision and asked if she had an attorney to process the divorce. Ms. Corcoran indicated she had contacted one earlier in the day.

Ms. Felber continued to see Ms. Corcoran biweekly for several months. She did secure a divorce, and Mr. Corcoran moved in with his brother, who lived alone. Ms. Corcoran became more active in her church and, at Ms. Felber's suggestions, she began doing volunteer work at a local shelter for battered women. Her sharing of the course of her domestic relationship has helped a number of women at the shelter decide to get out of their abusive relationships. On termination of therapy, Ms. Corcoran was happier, more contented, and fulfilled.

Clients who learn to express themselves assertively will experience increased self-confidence and self-esteem. They will be better able to communicate their thoughts, feelings, and opinions. Also, learning to express oneself assertively is an important component of empowerment.

Many women feel considerable anger over being victimized by sex discrimination and gender stereotyping. Some of these women turn these feelings inward, resulting in depression. Assertiveness training can help these women recognize their right to be angry and also help them identify and practice constructive ways to express their anger (for example, expressing their anger assertively, rather than aggressively).

Evaluation

The feminist perspective to therapy can be, and usually is, used in conjunction with other theoretical approaches. Therapists who have a feminist perspective almost always have training in and use other psychotherapeutic approaches—such as behavior therapy, reality therapy, rational therapy, and transactional analysis. They also often use a number of specific treatment approaches—such as assertiveness training, parent effectiveness training, mediation, meditation, sex therapy, and relaxation techniques.

Since the feminist perspective is almost always used in conjunction with other therapeutic approaches, it is extremely difficult to conduct evaluative studies that test its effectiveness.

Van Den Bergh and Cooper (1987) emphasized that the feminist perspective is consistent with the core values of social work practice, including equality, respect for individuals, and promotion of social and economic justice for populations-at-risk. They concluded that "a feminist social work practice is a viable way to accomplish the unique mission of social work, to improve the quality of life by facilitating social change" (p. 617).

While most contemporary approaches to psychotherapy look for the causes of a client's problems inside the client (for example, internal conflicts, repressed feelings, and early childhood traumas), the feminist perspective emphasizes viewing a client's problems in terms of the social, political, and economic systems that impact the client. This perspective is consistent with social work's emphasis on the person-in-environment, a systems approach, and an ecological approach.

The feminist perspective has also been helpful in identifying and conceptualizing numerous structural problems in our society. For example, feminists who practiced in the mental health field in the early 1970s began to view traditional psychotherapy as an agent of social control that maintained traditional sex roles by encouraging women to "adapt" (Van Den Bergh, 1992). Feminists have asserted that women need to be recognized as having the right to their reproductive capacities (including the right to choose to terminate a pregnancy); otherwise their lives would be largely controlled by the men who impregnate them, since raising a child requires a commitment of at least two decades. Feminists have also drawn attention to the sociopolitical forces that have led to an increase in the feminization of poverty in our society.

An extremely positive aspect of the feminist perspective is the view that all social workers have an obligation to identify inequalities in our social, economic, and political systems and then use macropractice techniques to confront these inequalities. Sometimes feminist social workers may involve clients in changing systems. Van Den Bergh (1992) noted:

The social worker should model her concern for changed societal conditions that eliminate institutionalized inequalities by working on some social change projects, such as abortion rights, comparable worth, anti-apartheid activism, or environmental protection. Clients can be encouraged to

The women's movement is effecting changes in gender roles in our society. Gradually, many men are moving toward equalitarian relationships with their spouse, where domestic responsibilities are shared.

engage in social activism themselves, as the experience of collective action can help to validate one's sense of self, personal worth, and power to change. However, judgment will have to be used as to whether this is appropriate, based on the client's current level of functioning and willingness to take risks. [p. 105]

Feminism is concerned with ending oppression and discrimination in our society and throughout the world.

The women's movement is bringing about a gender-role revolution in our society. Men and women are becoming aware of the negative effects of gender-role distinctions. More and more women are entering the labor force. Women are becoming more involved in athletics. Women are pursuing a number of professions and careers that previously were all male. Changes are also occurring in human interactions; more women are being assertive and seeking out equalitarian relationships with men. To some extent, men are (more slowly) beginning to realize the negative effects of gender-role distinctions. They are gradually realizing that the stereotypical "male" role limits their opportunities in terms of emotional expression, interpersonal relationships, occupations, and domestic activities.

A limitation of the feminist perspective is that a number of uninformed persons reject feminism in reaction to erroneous stereotypes. Apparently feminism has had some difficulties in informing segments of the general public about its basic tenets and principles. In this regard, Kirst-Ashman and Hull (1993) stated:

Some people have extremely negative reactions to the word "feminism." The emotional barriers they forge and the resulting resistance they foster makes it very difficult even to approach the concept with them. Others consider feminism a radical ideology which emphasizes separatism and fanaticism. In other words, they think feminism involves the philosophy adopted by women who spurn men, resent past inequities, and strive violently to overthrow male supremacists. Still others think of feminism as an outmoded tradition that is no longer relevant. [p. 427]

Summary

Sexism, sexual discrimination, and gender-role stereotyping continue to be serious problems. Women have been highly involved in the development of social work and social welfare programs. The feminist perspective on social work intervention has been developed by numerous authors.

Feminism is the philosophy of equality between women and men that involves both attitudes and actions, that infiltrates virtually all aspects of life, that often necessitates providing education and advocacy on behalf of women, and that appreciates the existence of individual differences and personal accomplishments of gender (Kirst-Ashman & Hull, 1993, p. 427).

Principles of feminist intervention in social work include the following. A client's problems should be viewed within a socio-political framework. Traditional sex roles are pathological, and clients need encouragement to free themselves from these gender-role bonds. Intervention should focus on client empowerment. Clients' self-esteem should be enhanced. Clients should be encouraged to develop their identity based on their strengths, attributes, qualities, and achievements. Clients need to value and develop social support systems with other women. Clients need to find a balance between work and personal relationships. The nature of the relationship between practitioner and client should approach equality as much as possible. Many clients can benefit from learning to express themselves assertively.

The feminist perspective to intervention is often used in conjunction with other intervention approaches. The feminist perspective is consistent with the core values of social work practice. An extremely positive aspect of this perspective is the view that all social workers have an obligation to identify inequalities in our social, economic, and political systems and then use macropractice techniques to confront them.

Exercises

1. The feminist perspective in counseling

> *Goal:* This exercise is designed to assist students in applying the feminist perspective to counseling.
>
> *Step 1:* Either describe the principles of the feminist perspective to therapy, or have the students read the material in this chapter.
>
> *Step 2:* Ask for a volunteer to role-play the feminist perspective in a simulated counseling situation. Ask for a second volunteer (probably a female) to role-play a situation in which the feminist perspective might be useful. Possible examples include:
>
> a. A woman discovers her partner has had three affairs since they began dating four years ago.
> b. A woman is frequently verbally abused by her partner.
> c. A wife is physically abused by an alcoholic husband; she feels she cannot leave him because she has three young children and is not employed outside the home.
> d. A female employee is being sexually harassed by her male employer; for financial reasons, she needs to continue working.
>
> *Step 3:* Instruct the two volunteers to role-play this simulated counseling situation. After the role playing, ask the class to discuss (a) what the "counselor" did well in applying the feminist perspective to counseling, and (b) what else the "counselor" might have done to apply the feminist perspective to this counseling situation.
>
> *Step 4:* If time permits, repeat steps 2 and 3 with a different "client problem."

2. Are you a feminist?

Goal: This exercise is designed to help students access the extent to which they have a feminist perspective and identify some key tenets of the feminist perspective.

Step 1: Instruct the students to answer "true" or "false" to each of the following statements on a sheet of paper. Inform them that their responses will remain anonymous and that they should not write their name on the paper. Read each statement slowly, giving the students an opportunity answer.

Statements
1. Men make better supervisors than women.
2. Men maker better leaders than women.
3. A woman would not do as good a job as president of this country.
4. Women should have the primary responsibility for raising children in our society.
5. In a heterosexual couple, the man should be the head of the household.
6. A male and a female living together should share the housework equally (for example, cleaning the bathroom, washing dishes, cooking, doing the laundry, cleaning, grocery shopping, taking out the garbage).
7. Women and men living together tend to share housework equally in our society.
8. Women should have the same access to jobs and social status as men.
9. A man who frequently relates jokes that are degrading to women in a work setting where women are present is guilty of sexual harassment.
10. I am willing to advocate on behalf of women (for instance, poor women or women who have been sexually assaulted).
11. Our society is generally structured politically, socially, and economically by and for men.
12. In heterosexual couples, the male has the obligation to be the primary breadwinner.
13. It is generally inappropriate for a woman to ask a man out on a date.
14. A male has a right to expect sexual gratification after dating a woman several times.

Step 2: Write the numbers of the statements on the chalkboard. Ask the students to hand in their responses. Ask for volunteers to tally the responses on the board.

Step 3: After the responses are tallied, reread each statement. Discuss the results, encouraging students to make comments or raise questions about the issues.

Step 4: End the exercise by indicating that those students who answered true to statements 6, 8, 9, 10, 11 and false to statements 1, 2, 3, 4, 5, 7, 12, 13, 14 probably have a belief system that is consistent with the feminist perspective.

3. Double standards

Goal: This exercise is designed to help students identify and examine double standards for male and female interactions.

Step 1: Ask the males to form subgroups of four or five, and the females to form subgroups of four or five. Ask each subgroup to identify double standards in dating relationships, marital relationships, and sexual behaviors between males and females. For example, society generally allows males to be more aggressive and to use more vulgar language; and males are expected to ask females for dates, but females traditionally have been raised to believe they should not ask males for dates. For each double standard, the subgroup should decide whether the double standard is desirable or undesirable. (Males are separated from females in this exercise, because they may have differing views about the desirability of the double standards that are identified.)

Step 2: After the subgroups have completed their work, ask a representative from each subgroup to summarize the double standards the group identified and its views on the desirability of these double standards. Class discussion may well ensue. End the exercise by summarizing the items identified and the differences between males and females regarding the desirability of such double standards.

20

Prominent Specific Treatment Techniques

Earlier chapters in this text have presented treatment techniques that are components of such comprehensive theories of psychotherapy as behavior therapy, transactional analysis, and psychoanalysis. This chapter summarizes a variety of other treatment techniques that have been used to treat clients who have emotional or behavioral problems. These treatment approaches were developed independently of (were not a part of) a comprehensive theory of psychotherapy; for lack of a better term, the techniques are referred to in this chapter as *specific treatment approaches.*

The therapy techniques covered in this chapter include milieu therapy, psychodrama, play therapy, parental education, crisis intervention, task-centered practice, meditation, relaxation, deep breathing and imagery, mediation, hypnosis, and biofeedback. Social workers have used crisis intervention, milieu therapy, play therapy, parental education, and psychodrama for many years. Mediation is a technique that has existed for some time, but only a few social workers used the technique until recently. The approach is increasingly being used to help resolve conflicts between two or more people. Relaxation approaches, meditation, hypnosis, and biofeedback have been around for a long time but have been used infre-

quently by social workers. With the recognition that stress (and resulting stress-related illnesses) is our nation's number one health problem (Rice, 1987), however, there has been a rising interest in training social workers to use these approaches.

Milieu Therapy

Milieu therapy involves the creation of a learning/living environment that systematically uses the events that occur in day-to-day living as formats for treating emotional and behavior problems. The theory behind the use of a therapeutic milieu is that the person's environment has an immense impact on behavior and can be structured to have a beneficial effect on changing deviant behavior as well as antisocial norms and values.

There are several models of milieu treatment. Milieu programs have been based on a wide variety of intervention approaches including reality therapy, behavior therapy, rational therapy, client-centered therapy, and psychoanalysis. Some milieu programs emphasize using individual therapy as part of the milieu, while others place heavy emphasis on changing behavioral and emotional problems in a group context. A token economy (described in Chapter 16) is one type of a milieu treatment program. Milieu programs typically include a team approach of professional staff members, such as social workers, psychiatrists, psychologists, special education teachers, occupational and physical therapists, and psychiatric nurses.

Although the components of milieu programs vary widely, there are some common focuses. Programs are usually formed on such principles as being democratic, permissive, and humanistic and having reality-oriented living experiences. Milieu programs assume that lasting changes are more likely to take place through group interactional experiences. The community (including the professional staff, nonprofessional staff, and

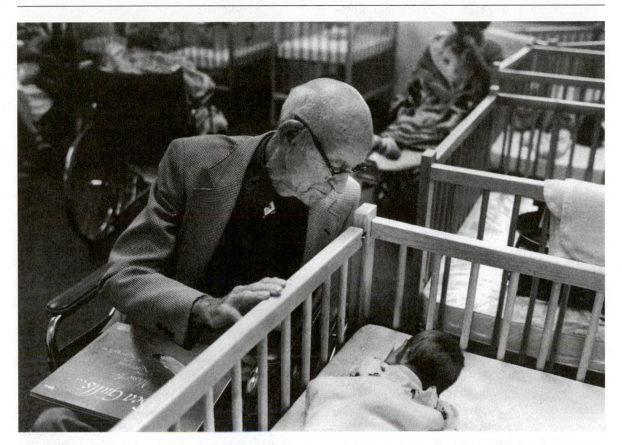

Milieu therapy: A combination nursing home for the elderly and day care center for infants can have benefits for both age groups.

residents) meet and interact regularly, often discussing common problems. An underlying philosophy is that personal problems primarily involve faulty interactions with others, and that an examination of these difficulties through discussion can lead to understanding and resolution. Usually the traditional pyramid of authority is flattened in milieu programs. Generally there is frequent reevaluation of staff roles and ways of functioning (Black, 1977).

Milieu programs have been used with a variety of client populations, including juvenile delinquents, mental patients, children and adults with a cognitive disability, the elderly, alcoholics and drug abusers, emotionally disturbed children, and correctional clients. These programs have been used in mental hospitals, day hospitals for the emotionally disturbed, halfway houses, residential treatment centers, day-care programs for disturbed children, nursing homes, group homes, correctional institutions, therapeutic communities for alcohol and drug abusers, and sheltered workshops.

The therapeutic community is one of the treatment programs that is often selected in treating drug addiction in this country. The theory is that drug addiction is a form of behavior that is encouraged by a particular subculture and that therapeutic communities will provide group support to help a person give up his or her commitment to the drug subculture and also pressure the person to replace previous norms and values with those acceptable to the general society.

Psychodrama

The primary developer of psychodrama was J. L. Moreno (1946). Its objective is to assist a client or client group to overcome personal problems through role playing, drama, or action therapy. Through these media, clients are helped to express feelings of conflict, anger, aggression, guilt, and sadness. Moreno thought, as did Freud, that the expression of pent-up emotions had a cathartic effect (eliminated emotional complexes by bringing them to consciousness and allowing the emotional energy to be expressed).

Moreno also thought psychodrama was therapeutic because a person who wants to change maladaptive behavior is presented with feedback about her or his behavior and allowed to try out and practice new behaviors. Psychodramas can be arranged to have other people model alternative behaviors and then to have the client practice new behaviors that are designed in a particular sequence to ensure success. Thus, the client can practice new behaviors in small bits until she incorporates them into her role repertoire and gains mastery through practice.

Psychodrama is a group therapy approach. Whittaker (1974) provided a brief description of psychodrama:

Psychodrama uses four major instruments: the stage, which is both the psychological and physical living space for the subject or client; the director, or worker; the staff of "auxiliary egos," or therapeutic aides; and the audience. Both the auxiliary egos and the audience are made up of other group members. The strategy is to enable the subject to project himself into his own world and draw responses from fellow group members. Below are several commonly used techniques:

1. Self-presentation. The client presents himself or a figure who is significant in his life.
2. Direct soliloquy. The client steps out of the drama and speaks to herself or to the group.
3. Double technique. An auxiliary ego acts with the client and does everything the client does and at the same time.
4. Mirror technique. An auxiliary ego acts in place of the client as clearly as he can. The client watches from the audience to see himself as others see him.
5. Role reversal. The client assumes the role of her antagonist and an auxiliary ego plays the client's part. [p. 230]

The director or worker functions as the producer and as the therapist. As the producer he selects and arranges the scenes and also directs the psychodrama action. The scenes are selected to reflect the client's problem, perhaps an emotionally charged situation for the client or one in which the client is behaving ineffectively or inappropriately. As the therapist, the worker provides the actors with support and clarification; at times he makes interpretations (often with the help of the other group members) of the play action.

Psychodrama presently is used by practitioners who subscribe to a variety of psychotherapeutic theories. Psychodrama has been used in marital therapy, with children, with drug and alcohol abusers, with people having emotional problems, in prison settings, in training psychiatric residents, in training people with physical and mental impairments, in business and industry, and in education and decision making. Fine (1979) noted:

We have all had experience with psychodrama. As children, one way we tested and mastered the world was to play roles. Lori put a coronet in her hair and became a queen and her girlfriend became her ladyin-waiting. Gary built satellites and took elaborate interstellar space explorations in his room. Children's play is an enactment of their fantasies in which they practice the social roles of their culture. The action and enacting world of the child is full of energy, excitement, and social learning. . . .

Modern psychodrama is an extension of life in which catharsis and insight are available not only to the audience but to the players as well. [p. 487]

Barocas (1972) illustrated one use of psychodrama. He used the technique to train police officers to handle family crises more effectively. Domestic fights have become a serious hazard to many metropolitan police officers, as the "family disturbance call" has become the single most frequent source of officer injury and death. Barocas hired trained actors and actresses to perform skits that were developed from actual family fights reported by police officers. These simulated fights involved arguments around such themes as child abuse, alcoholism, incest, unemployment, and infidelity. After the actors developed the basic fight, the police officer trainees intervened. These psychodrama skits were videotaped and other police officer trainees observed the intervention approach, which was then discussed in a group. The trainees who role-played were also shown the videotape and their performance was then critiqued further. Barocas concluded that this approach was effective in improving the way police officers handled family disputes.

Play Therapy

Play therapy is used with young children. Play is seen as a young child's most natural vehicle for self-expression and is therefore viewed by play therapists as a method for relating to and communicating with young children. Play therapy may serve many purposes: making a diagnosis, forming a relationship, ventilating feelings by the child, working

Play therapy capitalizes on children's natural means of self-expression.

through unwanted emotions, teaching the child desired new behaviors, and providing a format for modeling alternative behavior.

Play therapists vary on a continuum from almost totally nondirective to highly directive. Play therapy can be used by therapists with widely diverging orientations including psychoanalysis, client-centered therapy, reality therapy, rational therapy, transactional analysis, and behavior therapy.

Whittaker (1974) described play therapy as follows:

The therapist may use initial play sessions for diagnostic purposes to observe such things as relationship, attention span, areas of preoccupation, areas of inhibition, direction of aggression, wishes and fantasies, and self-perception. Depending upon orientation, the therapist typically encourages free play with a variety of available materials (paints, dolls, punching bags, puzzles, clay), interprets the child's affect to him ("You seem to be angry at the doll"), and finally offers insights into the child's behavior. The child may experience some regression to earlier levels of functioning while in the play situation and also may practice newly acquired skills and try on new behaviors. A central notion of play

Case Example
Play therapy

Dawn, age 7, was a second-grader who was referred by her teacher to a school social worker. Academically and socially she was functioning far behind her peers, even though tests showed she was of normal intelligence. The social worker observed her in her play interactions with peers. She was withdrawn and tried to avoid competitive game situations. Forced to participate, she would quit whenever she fell behind. When the social worker discussed Dawn's behavior with her teacher, the teacher indicated that Dawn shied away from doing her assignments and seldom completed any. Dawn was observed for a few sessions in a playroom at school. At one point Dawn held the mother doll and called the baby girl "stupid" and stated, "You'll never be able to do what your brother does." The social worker felt that Dawn's academic and social problems were resulting from Dawn's having such a low self-concept that she had virtually given up trying. Dawn's interactions with the dolls suggested her mother might be contributing to her low self-concept by disparaging her. Several meetings were then held with Dawn's parents, with Dawn present for two of these. The social worker observed that the mother was highly critical of Dawn without ever praising her. Dawn was placed in a special educational program for the next 18 months; here she received close attention and considerable praise for her academic and social efforts. The worker also counseled the parents on how they were contributing to her low self-concept and how they needed to praise Dawn for her efforts and to get her more involved in interests she had. On three separate occasions Dawn, her parents, Dawn's brother, and the social worker met in a playroom. The family members were encouraged to play together in various games, and the parents were instructed to praise Dawn whenever she made efforts to participate positively. Also, Dawn's mother was encouraged to refrain from disparaging Dawn. After this intensive program, Dawn was able to rejoin her class at the start of the fourth grade and had become much more outgoing and self-confident.

SOURCE: In the classic *Play Therapy*, Axline (1947) provided a number of other case examples in which play therapy has been used for diagnostic purposes, for helping children to understand themselves and their problems better and to resolve their problems.

therapy is that the child is expressing symbolically through play the conflicts he is experiencing in the outside world. In the relative safety of the play situation, these conflicts can be worked through and—so the theory goes—transferred to the child's real-life situation. [p. 225–226]

Play therapy generally takes place in a playroom, with only the child and the therapist present. At times other children are pres-

ent, which helps a child learn to interact more effectively with others. Occasionally parents attend the play therapy sessions, which helps them have a better understanding of their child and learn more effective interaction approaches with their child. Play materials include such items as a variety of dolls (usually composing a doll family), puppets, clay and finger paints, crayons, a sandbox, toy animals, soldiers and weapons, and cutting-out materials. In play therapy children are generally allowed to express themselves as freely as they desire. Usually minimal limits are set: establishing the duration of the play sessions, forbidding the willful destruction of play materials, and forbidding the child from physically attacking others in the playroom.

In recent years a number of protective services programs have used anatomically correct dolls to gather information from young children who are suspected victims of sexual abuse. A worker first forms a relationship with a child and then asks the child to show, with the dolls, what the alleged perpetrator did. In some jurisdictions this process is videotaped and is available for court use if formal charges are brought against the alleged perpetrator. This use of the dolls is primarily for investigative purposes.

Parental Education: Parent Effectiveness Training

The primary goal of parental education programs is to help parents understand child behavior and develop childrearing skills. Most programs are based on the assumption that rearing children is a difficult and complex task for which society ill prepares young people. A number of theoreticians have developed somewhat different educational programs: Dreikurs (1964), Ginott (1965), Gordon (1970), Patterson (1971), and Spock (1957). These programs use a variety of educational formats: short courses, small discussion groups, and programmed self-instruction.

Probably the most popular program is Parent Effectiveness Training (PET), developed by Thomas Gordon (1970). The basic concepts of this approach are presented, partly because some of the techniques, such as active listening, I-messages, and no-loss problem solving, can be used by any person to interact more effectively with others.

Parent Effectiveness Training (PET) courses are now being offered in hundreds of communities throughout this country and have been endorsed by numerous public and private agencies serving parents and youth. The PET system has been found to work effectively with children of all ages. The program leads to warmer and more harmonious relationships between parents and their children, and children learn to become more responsible. The principles are applicable not only for parents and parent surrogates (such as teachers, principals, counselors, and youth leaders) but for anyone who wants to improve interactions with others.

Parents Are People, Not Gods

Gordon urges parents to be "real" in their relationships with children. "Realness" is much more important than the impossible guidelines of always being consistent in displaying feelings, putting up a "united front," and being unconditionally tolerant and accepting. In a close relationship, it is impossible to hide one's true feelings. It is normal and real for parents to be accepting of some behaviors of their children and nonaccepting of other behaviors. Parents should recognize their true feelings and not attempt to convey false acceptance when they dislike what their children are doing. It is normal and real for one parent to be more accepting than the other, and one parent may feel accepting and the other nonaccepting of the same behavior. Being honest and human in interacting with children will improve a relationship substantially more than trying to convey false acceptance or trying always to be consistent.

Who Owns the Problem?

PET asserts that appropriate parental responses depend on the question "Who owns the problem?" A person owns a problem only when the situation affects the person's ability to get her or his needs met in a concrete and tangible way. If the *child* is the owner of a problem, then *active listening* is an appropriate technique for a parent to use. If the *parent* owns the problem, then *I-messages* are appropriate for the parent to use. If the situation involves a conflict between the parent and the child in meeting the needs of both, then *no-lose problem solving* is an appropriate technique. If the situation involves a conflict in values between the parent and the child, Gordon provides guidelines for *resolving collisions of values*.

PET Techniques

Active Listening

When a 16-year-old son announces "I hate school and I'm going to drop out," parents can respond in a variety of ways: ordering him to stay in school, warning him that he will be sorry if he drops out, moralizing by saying it would not be proper or right, giving advice by saying he should discuss it with the high school counselor, and so forth. Such approaches are generally not effective or productive in helping children express their feelings, explore their problems, and arrive at a comfortable solution.

Active listening, PET asserts, is a much more effective way of interacting. The following steps are involved in active listening: (1) the receiver of a message tries to understand what the sender's message means or what the sender is feeling; and (2) the receiver then puts this understanding into her own words and returns this understanding for the sender's verification. In using this approach, the receiver does *not* send a message of her own—such as a question, advice, her feelings, or an opinion. The aim is to feed back only what she feels the sender's message meant. Active listening is a difficult skill to learn and takes practice to master.

This approach is illustrated below in a set of interactions, with the parent consistently using the active listening technique.

Youth: I hate school, and I'm going to drop out.
Parent: You're fed up with school and thinking about leaving.

Youth: Yes I am! My teachers are really bummers this year.
Parent: You're disappointed with your current teachers.
Youth: Especially with my Spanish teacher. He asks us questions in Spanish and expects us to be able to understand what he's saying. All I hear is words that I can't understand.
Parent: You're having trouble understanding your Spanish teacher when he speaks in Spanish.
Youth: On written exams I've been getting A's and B's, but most of the other students in class appear to understand Spanish better when it is spoken.
Parent: Your grades show that you are doing well in Spanish, but you have trouble understanding Spanish when it is spoken.
Youth: Yes, I wonder what I could do to learn to understand people better when they speak in Spanish.
Parent: You're wondering how you can better learn to hear and speak in Spanish.
Youth: Perhaps I could talk to my teacher about this. He might have some ideas.

Gordon listed a number of advantages for using the active listening technique. It facilitates problem solving by the child, which fosters the development of responsibility. By talking a problem through, a person is more apt to identify the root of the problem and arrive at a solution than by merely thinking about a problem. When a child feels that his parents are listening to him, a by-product is that he will be more likely to listen to their point of view. In addition, the relationship between parent and child is likely to improve, because when the child feels he is being heard and understood by another person, he is apt to feel warmth toward the listener. Finally, the approach helps the child to explore, recognize, and express personal feelings.

Gordon noted that a parent needs to have certain attitudes in order to use the technique effectively. The parent must view the child as a separate person with his or her own feelings. The parent must be able to accept the child's feelings, whatever they may be. The parent should genuinely want to be helpful and must want to hear what the child has to say. And the parent must trust the child's capacities to handle personal problems and feelings.

There are some common mistakes that parents make initially in using the technique. One mistake is to use the technique with the intention of guiding the child's behavior or thinking toward what the parents think the child should do. If parents have this intention, children are likely to feel they are being manipulated and the approach may be counterproductive. A second mistake is to parrot back the words rather than the intended meaning or feeling. For instance, if a daughter yells at her father "you stupid jerk," an appropriate response geared to the message would be "you're angry with me," rather than parroting the words "you think I'm a jerk." A third mistake is to use active listening at the wrong time. If a child does not want to talk about her feelings, or is simply too tired, the parent should respect the child's right and need for privacy.

I-Messages

Active listening is used when the child has the problem. However, many occasions arise when the child causes a problem for the parent: for example, a child is talking loudly in church, or getting too close to a precious glass vase, or is about to walk on a new carpet with muddy shoes, or is recklessly driving an auto. In such cases entirely different communication skills are required. Confronted with such situations, many parents send either a *solution message* (they order, direct, command, warn, threaten, preach, moralize, or advise) or a *put-down message* (they blame, judge, criticize, ridicule, or name-call). Solution and put-down messages can have devastating effects on a child's self-concept and are generally counterproductive in helping a child become responsible.

Solution and put-down messages are primarily you-messages: "you do what I say," "don't you do that," "why don't you be good," "you're lazy," "you should know better."

PET advocates that parents should instead send *I-messages* for those occasions when a child is causing a problem for the parent. For example, if a child is walking on a clean carpet with dirty shoes, instead of saying, "John, get off that carpet, you're a pig!" PET urges parents to use an I-message: "I shampooed the living room rug today, and want to keep it clean as long as possible."

I-messages, in essence, are nonblaming messages that communicate only how the sender of the message believes the receiver is adversely affecting the sender. I-messages do not provide a solution nor are they put-down messages. It is possible to send an I-message without using the word *I*, as the essence of I-messages involves sending a nonblaming message of how the parent feels the child's behavior is affecting the parent. For example, a parent, riding in a car driven by the 17-year-old son who is exceeding the speed limit, may say, "Driving fast really terrifies me."

You-messages are generally put-down messages that convey to children either that they should do something or that they are bad. In contrast, I-messages communicate to children much more honestly the effect of the behavior on the parent. I-messages are also more effective because they help children learn to assume responsibility for their own behavior. An I-message tells children that the parent trusts them to respect the parent's needs, that the parent is leaving the responsibility with them, and that the parent is trusting them to handle the situation constructively.

You-messages frequently end up in a struggle between parent and child, while I-messages are much less likely to produce an argument. I-messages lead to honesty and openness in a relationship and generally foster intimacy. Children, as well as adults, often do not know how their behavior affects others. I-messages produce startling results as parents frequently report that their children express surprise on learning how their parents really feel.

For illustrative purposes, the following are some examples of you-messages and I-messages:

You-Messages	I-Messages
1. Don't you ever kick me again; you're a real pain.	Ouch! That kick really hurt me.
2. John, you stop pestering me now!	John, I am very tired today, and I just do not have the energy to play with you this evening.
3. You're a reckless driver and someday you'll kill someone.	I'm afraid to drive with you when you drive so fast.
4. You didn't mow the lawn today as you promised. You're so lazy and never help with the work around here.	I'm upset that the lawn didn't get mowed today. We're having company this evening, and I'm embarrassed about how the lawn looks.

No-Lose Problem Solving

In every parent-child relationship, there are inevitable situations in which the child continues to behave in a way that interferes with the needs of the parent. Conflict is part of life and is not necessarily bad. Conflict is bound to occur because people are different and have different needs and wants, which at times do not match. What is important is not how frequently conflict arises but how the conflicts get resolved. Generally in a conflict between parent and child, a power struggle is created.

In many families the power struggle is resolved by one of two *win-lose* approaches. Most parents try to resolve the conflict by having the parent win and the child lose. Psychologically, parents almost always are recognized as having greater size, greater

authority. When the parent wins it creates resentment in the child toward the parents, leads to low motivation for the child to carry out the solution, and does not provide an opportunity for the child to develop self-discipline and self-responsibility. Such children are likely to react by becoming either rebellious and aggressive or dependent and withdrawing.

In other families (fewer in number) the win-lose conflict is resolved when parents give in to their children out of fear of frustrating their children or fear of conflict. In such families children come to believe their needs are more important than anyone else's, and they generally become self-centered, selfish, demanding, impulsive, and uncontrollable. They are viewed by others as being spoiled, they have difficulty in interacting with peers, and also they do not have respect for property or feelings of others.

Of course, few parents use either approach exclusively. Oscillating between the two approaches is common. There is evidence that both approaches lead to the development of emotional problems in children (Gordon, 170, p. 161).

The two win-lose approaches are illustrated in the following situation:

Parent wins—child loses:

Mother: Since I'm now working, we need to divide the work tasks around the house. I'll continue to do most of the work, but from now on I'd like you to wash the dishes in the evening.

John: But I don't like washing dishes.

Mother: Well, I don't like cooking, and washing and ironing clothes, but have to do them. We all have to do things we don't like to do.

John: Washing dishes is for girls.

Mother: Look, I'm not going to argue with you about this. You're now old enough to help out. In this family we all have to contribute. If you don't do the dishes you won't receive your allowance. In fact, from now on, every evening you do not wash dishes, fifty cents will be deducted from your weekly allowance.

Child wins—parent loses:

Mother: Since I'm now working, we need to divide the work tasks around the house. I'll continue to do most of the work, but from now on I'd like you to wash the dishes in the evening.

John: But I don't like washing dishes.

Mother: Why?

John: Washing dishes is for girls.

Mother: But many boys help their mothers with the dishes.

John: Tom and Gary don't help their mothers. What would they say about me washing dishes?

Mother: You may be right. Could you instead help me with washing clothes, or dusting, or cleaning your room?

John: Aw—Mom, those things are for girls, too.

Mother: (*Dejectedly.*) Well, OK, I'll try to do these things while also working.

Gordon seriously questioned whether power is necessary or justified in a parent-child relationship. As a child grows older, he or she becomes less dependent and parents gradually lose their power. Rewards and punishments that worked in younger years become less effective. Children resent those who have power over them, and parents frequently feel guilty after using power. Gordon believed that parents continue to use power because they have had little experience in using nonpower methods of influence.

PET suggests a new approach, the *no-lose approach*, to solving conflicts. The approach is to have each parent and child solve their conflicts by finding their own unique solutions acceptable to both.

The following example illustrates this approach:

Mother: Since I'm now working, I will have less time to do the work that needs to be done around the house. I would appreci-

ate it if you would help me out with some of the things that need to be done.

John: I suppose I could help—what needs to be done?

Mother: The meals need to be cooked, dishes washed, the house cleaned, grocery shopping done, and the garbage taken out.

John: Let's see. I'd be willing to vacuum the floor and dust. Will my allowance be increased? I'd like to get a new bike.

Mother: Yes, since we'll have some more money now that I'm working, we could increase your allowance, with the increase dependent on how much additional work you do.

John: In addition to helping to clean the house, I'd be willing to wash the clothes if you show me what to do. I also could carry out the garbage.

The no-lose approach is simple to state: each person in the conflict treats the other with respect, neither person tries to win the conflict by the use of power, and a creative solution acceptable to both parties is sought. There are two basic premises to no-lose problem solving: (1) that all people have the right to have their needs met, and (2) that what is in conflict between the two parties involved is not their *needs* but their *solutions* to those needs.

Gordon (1970, p. 237) listed the six steps to the no-lose method:

Step 1: Identifying and defining the needs of each person.

Step 2: Generating possible alternative solutions.

Step 3: Evaluating the alternative solutions.

Step 4: Deciding on the best acceptable solution.

Step 5: Working out ways of implementing the solution.

Step 6: Following up to evaluate how it worked.

There are several advantages to this approach. It motivates children to carry out the solution because they participated in the decision. It develops the children's thinking skills and also develops responsibility. It requires less enforcement, eliminates the need for power, and improves relationships between parents.

Resolving Collisions of Values

Collisions of values are common between parents and their children, particularly as the children become adolescents and young adults. Likely areas of conflict include values about sexual behavior, clothing, religion, choice of friends, education, plans for the future, use of drugs, hairstyles, and eating habits. In these areas emotions run strong and parents generally seek to influence their offspring to follow the values the parents hold as important. Teenagers, on the other hand, often think their parents' values are old fashioned and stupid, and declare that they want to make their own decisions about these matters.

Gordon asserted there are three constructive ways in which parents and teenagers can seek to resolve these conflicts. (For the sake of simplicity, we will use the term *mother* in describing what should be done—a father or a teenager can also use these same techniques.)

The first way a mother can influence her offspring's values is to model the values she holds important. If she values honesty, she should be honest. If she values responsible use of drugs, she should exhibit a responsible model. If she values openness, she should be open. She needs to ask herself if she is living according to the values she professes. If her values and behaviors are incongruent in certain areas, she needs to change either her values or her behavior in the direction of congruency. Congruence between behavior and values is important if she wants to be an effective model.

The second way she can influence her teenagers' values is to act as a consultant to them. There are some do's and don'ts of a good consultant. First, a good consultant finds out whether the other person would

like her consultation. If the answer is yes, she makes sure she has all the available pertinent facts. She then shares these facts—once—so the other person understands them. She leaves the other person the responsibility for deciding whether to follow the advice. A good consultant is neither uninformed nor a nag; otherwise she is not apt to be used as a consultant again.

The third way for a mother to reduce tensions over values issues is to modify her values. By examining the values held by her teenagers, she may realize their values have merit, and she may move toward their values or at least toward an understanding of why they hold them as values.

In summary, PET concepts are designed to improve relationships between parents and children and to develop the concept of responsibility within children. A large number of parents who have participated in PET courses, or read Gordon's *Parent Effectiveness Training,* have found them to be effective. In recent years, these PET concepts have been found useful not only in improving relationships between parents and children but also in improving interactions and communication between people involved in practically any type of transaction.

The techniques advanced by PET will generally work if the influencee (person to be influenced) respects the influencer and wants a positive relationship with him or her. If the influencee neither respects nor wants a positive relationship with the influencer, then these techniques are not apt to work.

Crisis Intervention

Crisis intervention (CI) postulates that in a crisis situation current levels of functioning may be disrupted and previously manageable internal psychological difficulties stirred up. CI views the emotional disturbances presented by people facing crisis as being the result of (1) the stressful situation that a person faces, and (2) underlying emotional dispositions that come to the surface only in crisis situations. CI postulates that underlying emotional difficulties are ingredients of all personalities. People are viewed as being fairly normal in their general adjustment, with the crisis being a major cause of a person's emotional difficulties.

Figure 20.1 shows graphically the importance to people of successfully resolving crises that arise.

Crisis intervention postulates that a person is most vulnerable to change (either in a constructive or destructive direction) at the point of crisis, and therefore it is at this point that services (such as, counseling) are needed most and have the highest probability of having a positive effect. Proponents emphasize the importance of providing services when crises arise and are strongly opposed to agencies' placing people on waiting lists for services.

Golan (1979) described the typical efforts made by a person to resolve a crisis and the emotional reactions to a prolonged crisis:

First, he tries to use his customary repertoire of problem-solving mechanisms to deal with the situation. If this is not successful, his upset increases and he mobilizes heretofore untried emergency methods of coping. However, if the problem continues and can neither be resolved, avoided, nor redefined, tension continues to peak. . . .

As the crisis situation develops, the individual may perceive the initial and subsequent stressful events primarily as a *threat*, either to his instinctual needs or to his sense of autonomy and well-being; as a *loss* of a person, an attribute (status or role), or a capacity; or as a *challenge* to survival, growth, or mastery.

Each of these perceptions calls forth a characteristic emotional reaction that reflects the subjective meaning of the event to the individual: threat elicits a heightened level of anxiety; loss brings about feelings of depression, deprivation, and

A. Before a crisis a person is functioning in a groove; that is, he has a relatively routine, stable kind of living with only minor changes.
B. A crisis arises (for example, being fired from a job) that places a person in an unfreezing position. This unfreezing position is emotionally charged, and the person's lifestyle is highly vulnerable to change. In such a crisis, a person may either take the constructive (C) path or the destructive (D) path.
C. This constructive path has the person (perhaps with the assistance of others) gaining an awareness of why the crisis arose. The person develops adaptive ways of handling the crisis, and thereby grows through acquiring problem-solving skills that will enable her to solve future crisis situations.
D. If the destructive path is followed, the person does not satisfactorily resolve the crisis. Unsolved aspects of the crisis remain, and the person is apt to develop maladaptive coping patterns. She remains in an emotionally charged situation and is less able to face future crises that arise. Problems may well begin to snowball (for example, when a single, pregnant woman denies the pregnancy and makes no effort to begin making decisions that she will have to face).

Figure 20.1
The effects of a crisis

mourning; challenge stimulates a moderate increase in anxiety plus a kindling of hope and expectation, releasing new energy for problem solving. [p. 500]

Usually within four to six weeks after the onset of the crisis, a new state of equilibrium is reached. This state may be better than, the same as, or worse than the precrisis level of functioning, depending on how well the person has mastered the cognitive, emotional, and behavioral tasks inherent in the crisis. During the reorganization phase, new adaptive coping styles may develop to enable the individual to deal more effectively with future crises. However, maladaptive patterns may also emerge, which result in decreased ability to cope in the future.

Case Example
Crisis intervention

John Franzene (age 28) went to work intoxicated one day and was promptly informed by his supervisor that he was fired. John became incensed and yelled obscenities at his supervisor. He then went to a local tavern and drank until he passed out. A friend took him home. When his wife found out that John had been fired from his job as a janitor, she packed her bags that evening and took the two children to live with her mother. She indicated this was the "last straw."

John is an alcoholic and drinks an average of eight bottles of beer and a pint of whiskey every day. He has been drinking excessively for the past decade. Three years ago his wife separated from him because he was abusive to her and the children, both physically and verbally, when intoxicated. At that time John promised to stop drinking if his wife would only return; she did, and three weeks later he again began drinking. Five years ago he lost his position as an elementary school teacher because of his drinking and his frequent absenteeism. Two years ago he lost his driver's license for driving while intoxicated. In the past five years, he has lost three other jobs because of his drinking.

The next day John went to his mother-in-law's home to try to talk his wife into returning home. She refused to speak to him. John, feeling sorry for himself, went to a local tavern and again got drunk. He blamed his supervisor for his current difficulties. While intoxicated he decided to "straighten this matter out." He went to the office where he had been fired and got into a physical fight with his supervisor. He was arrested. While in jail he got the "DTs" (delirium tremens), which really scared him. He was transferred to a hospital. The doctor at the hospital explored his interest in receiving help for his drinking problem. John indicated he was willing to talk about it to someone, and he was referred to Tom Halaska, the hospital social worker.

For the first time in his life, John acknowledged that he had a drinking problem and needed help. Mr. Halaska met with John on several occasions during the next four days. The ways that alcohol was affecting his life (including his job and his family life) were traced and John gained an awareness that he got into trouble only when he was drinking. Mr. Halaska explored the reasons John drank, and it became clear that he drank excessively either when he was with male friends in a tavern or when he sought to relieve unwanted emotions of feeling tense, moody, or depressed. John appeared at this time to be sincerely committed to giving up drinking. Mr. Halaska suggested that one of the things he would have to do to give up drinking was to stop getting together with his friends at a tavern. John indicated that saving his marriage meant more to him than getting together with his male friends. Mr. Halaska arranged a meeting between John and his wife. His wife agreed to return if John would first go one month without drinking, promise never to drink again, and actively participate in AA meetings. John agreed. Mr. Halaska referred him to an AA group and also referred him to the outpatient treatment unit of the mental health center. Among other services, this outpatient treatment service provided marriage counseling services to John and his wife and helped him explore other job opportunities.

John occasionally stops by the hospital to visit Mr. Halaska briefly. It has now been 14 months since he had a drink. He is a sales clerk at a clothing store and is seeking a teaching position. He reports that he and his wife are getting along better than they ever have.

Note: Additional case examples using crisis intervention are presented in Parad (1965).

Because a person is in an unfreezing position when a crisis arises, crisis intervention services often have a dual opportunity: to resolve the current crisis and to resolve problems that the person has previously been denying or ignoring. For example, if a person is fired from a job because of drinking problems, services might be focused not only on helping a person obtain another job but also on breaking down the denial that a drinking problem does in fact exist and needs to be dealt with. Golan (1979, p. 500) noted that at the point of crisis "a minimal effort . . . can produce a maximal effect; a small amount of help, appropriately focused, can prove more effective than extensive help at a period of less emotional accessibility."

Crisis intervention services are generally brief and provided primarily when the client is emotionally in desperate need. The specific treatment techniques used in crisis intervention are borrowed from other approaches. A few examples are presented here. Role playing may be used to help a pregnant single woman gain confidence in how to inform her parents and to inform her sexual partner. Confrontation may be used to help a person arrested three times for drunken driving acknowledge that he does have a drinking problem. A person whose three-year engagement has been broken may be instructed on how to counter unwanted emotions by doing a rational self-analysis. A young woman who has been raped may be given immediate medical attention and counseling on legal implications and also on her thoughts and feelings about the assault. A counselor may use the active listening technique in counseling someone who is threatening suicide.

Whittaker (1974) provided a summary of crisis counseling services:

Requisite worker skills include the ability to function effectively and efficiently in an emotionally tense atmosphere and to give support and direction while at the same time helping the client to develop autonomous coping skills.

Crisis intervention generally progresses in the following manner: (1) An attempt is made to alleviate the disabling tension through ventilation and the creation of a climate of trust and hope. (2) Next the worker attempts to understand the dynamics of the event that precipitated the crisis. (3) The worker gives his impressions and understanding of the crisis and checks out these perceptions with the client. (4) Client and worker attempt to determine specific remedial measures that can be taken to restore equilibrium. (5) New methods of coping may be introduced. (6) Finally, termination occurs—often after a predetermined number of interviews—when the agreed-upon goals have been realized. [p. 212]

Crisis intervention services are provided in a wide variety of traditional and nontraditional settings, including runaway centers, rape crisis centers, "hot lines," hospital emergency rooms, mental health clinics, suicide prevention services, neighborhood centers, crisis hostels, halfway houses, detention facilities and self-help groups such as Parents Anonymous. Crisis intervention services are provided not only by professionals but also by paraprofessionals and volunteers.

Task-Centered Practice

The primary developers of task-centered practice are William J. Reid and Laura Epstein, social work faculty members of the School of Social Service Administration at the University of Chicago. Task-centered practice is described in Reid and Epstein (1977).

In the initial interview with a client, the counselor seeks to elicit, explore, and clarify the client's problems. During this interview the counselor may point out problems the client has not recognized, or the consequences of allowing significant problems to go unattended. In the first or second interview, the counselor and the client explicitly agree on the problems to be dealt with. The problems are defined in terms of specific circumstances to be changed. The counselor and the client also agree on the duration and amount of service to be given. There are usually 6 to 12 interviews over a two- to four-month time span. The kinds of services agreed on and the number of interviews to be held form the basis of the service contract, which may be modified by additional agreements as service proceeds.

The counselor and the client then identify tasks the client may undertake to alleviate specific problems. These tasks may be general in nature in that they give the client a direction for action but do not precisely specify the expected behavior—for example, client Jim K will seek to establish a better relationship with his parents. Or, tasks may be very specific—for example, Jim K will inform his parents how much he appreciates their financial support in sending him to college.

During the discussion of the tasks, the counselor may help the client structure the tasks to increase their chances of being accomplished. If the client is unable to arrive at alternatives for resolving the problems, the counselor may suggest various possibilities. The counselor's primary roles in this change process are to help the client identify target problems, to help the client identify tasks for resolving these problems, and to then carry out agreed-on tasks together with the client. The general tasks of clients, in this model, become the clients' own goals for change. In this change process the counselor uses relationship skills (which are discussed in Chapter 5) and a variety of resolution approaches suggested by contemporary theories of counseling, such as contingency contracting, assertiveness training, and game analysis.

During the treatment process, a substantial amount of the counselor's efforts goes into structuring communication during interviews to keep the client's attention and efforts focused on the tasks. There are a number of efforts to enhance the client's awareness of his or her problems and to help the client understand obstacles to task performance. The client is given substantial encouragement about constructive actions he or she is contemplating or is undertaking. The client may also be given suggestions or directions on how to proceed with the task.

Usually in the treatment process there is an emphasis for the counselor to help the client break down general tasks into more specific, operational tasks that he or she is then expected to carry out before the next treatment session. Incentives for task accomplishment are usually identified. Actions called for by the tasks are rehearsed or practiced (for example, through role playing). This task-centered approach has been used not only with individual clients but also with families and with groups (Reid & Epstein, 1977).

There are additional distinctive features of this approach. Treatment is short term by plan. It is theorized that when a contract is made with a client for a set number of interviews (usually 6 to 12), the client will work hard to resolve his or her problems during this brief time period.

Another emphasis is to focus treatment sharply on target problems and resolution tasks; that is, there is an emphasis on specifying problems and tasks in operational and measurable terms. With this emphasis, both counselor and the client are more aware of precisely what needs to be done and what progress is being made during the treatment process in resolving the problems.

A final emphasis is the use of explicit agreements or contracts between the counselor and the clients specifying problems, goals, and tasks to be worked on during the treatment process. The contract is formed in the first or second interview and guides the treatment process. This contract may be oral or written; it may be modified later if both parties agree to changing it.

A number of case examples of task-centered practice are given in Reid and Epstein (1977). The task-centered approach has many similarities to the counseling process described in Chapter 5 and to reality therapy described in Chapter 21.

Mediation

In the past two decades, mediation has been used increasingly to resolve conflicts between disputing groups. As far back as 1913, the federal government established the use of federal mediators to help resolve issues between employers and employees (Moore, 1986, p. 21). Mediated settlements were expected to prevent costly strikes or lockouts and to protect the welfare and safety of Americans. Federal use of mediation in labor disputes has set a precedent, encouraging many states to pass laws and to train a cadre of mediators to handle intrastate labor conflicts.

Mediation is currently being used in a variety of ways. The Civil Rights Act of 1964 created the Community Relations Service of the U.S. Department of Justice to use mediation to resolve disputes relating to discriminatory practices based on race, color, or national origin (Moore, 1986, pp. 21–22). Diverse private agencies, civil rights commissions, and state agencies now use mediation to handle charges of sex, race, and ethnic discrimination. The federal government funds Neigh-borhood Justice Centers that provide free or low-cost mediation services to the public to resolve disputes, informally, inexpensively, and efficiently (Moore, 1986, p. 22). Disputes settled through mediation are resolved much more efficiently and creatively than those resolved in court. Mediation is also used in schools to resolve issues between students, between students and faculty, between faculty members, and between faculty and administration. The criminal justice system uses mediation to resolve disputes in correctional facilities—for example, for prison riots, hostage negotiations, and institutionalized grievance procedures.

Mediation is also used extensively in family disputes involving child custody and divorce proceedings, disputes between parents and children, conflicts involving adoption and the termination of parental rights, and domestic violence situations. Moore (1986, p. 23) stated: "In family disputes, mediated and consensual settlements are often more appropriate and satisfying than litigated or imposed court outcomes."

Mediation is used to settle disputes between business partners, private individuals, government agencies and individuals, landlords and tenants, businesses and customers, and disputants in personal injury cases.

Many professionals now occasionally act as mediators to help people or groups in conflict resolve their concerns. Such professionals include attorneys, social workers, psychologists, and guidance counselors. A few social workers, attorneys, and other professionals work full-time as mediators—often in public or private mediation agencies.

Moore (1986) defined mediation as follows:

Mediation involves the intervention of an acceptable impartial and neutral third party who has no authoritative decision-making power to assist contending parties in voluntarily reaching their own mutually acceptable settlement of issues in dispute. . . . Mediation leaves the decision-making power in the hands of the people in conflict. Mediation is a voluntary process in that the participants must be willing to accept the assistance of the intervenor if the dispute is to be resolved. Mediation is usually initiated when the partners no longer believe that they can handle the conflict on their own and when the only means of resolution appears to involve impartial third-party assistance. [p. 6]

There are various models of the mediation process (Moore, 1986). As an illustration, the one developed by Joan Blades (1985) is summarized. Blades viewed the mediation process as involving five stages:

1. *Introduction/commitment:* This first stage usually is accomplished in a one- to two-hour session. The mediator sets ground rules, describes mediation, answers questions, discusses fees, and seeks to gain a commitment to the process from the two parties. The mediator also seeks to develop an understanding of the more pressing issues, gains a sense of the personal dynamics of the two parties, and tries to ascertain whether they are ready and willing to mediate. If one or both of the parties are not willing to mediate, then the mediation probably should not proceed. If one or both of the parties are hesitant to proceed, the mediator usually describes the alternatives to mediation—such as a lengthy and expensive court battle.

2. *Definition:* The two parties, with the mediator's assistance, define the areas in which they already agree and disagree. At this stage certain disputes, such as divorce mediation, require a considerable amount of information.

3. *Negotiation:* Once the two parties agree on the issues in conflict and relevant factual information on these issues is obtained, the two parties are ready to begin negotiating. At this stage the mediator seeks to have the parties focus on one issue at a time. A problem-solving approach is used in which the needs of each party are first identified

and alternatives are generated. The mediator recedes into the background when discussions are proceeding well and steps in when emotions intensify or when the two parties are overlooking creative solutions that will meet their needs.

4. *Agreement:* Once alternatives are generated and related facts are evaluated, the two parties are ready to begin making agreements on the issues. The role of the mediator is to maintain a cooperative atmosphere and to keep the two parties focused on a manageable number of issues. The mediator summarizes areas of agreement and provides legal or other information necessary to a discussion. The mediator helps the two parties examine the merits and shortcomings of the options. During this stage the mediator praises the parties for the progress they are making and gets them to praise themselves for progress made. The mediator seeks to create a positive atmosphere.

5. *Contracting:* In this final stage of mediation the two parties review the agreements and clarify any ambiguities. The agreements are almost always written in the form of a contract, which is available for future reference. Either party, the mediator, or everyone together may write the contract. The contract expresses what each party agrees to do, may set deadlines for the diverse tasks to be completed, and may specify consequences if either party fails to meet the terms of the contract. Mediators seek to have specific agreements stated in concrete form to prevent future controversies. The ultimate goal of mediation is a contract in which no one is a loser and by which both parties willingly abide.

One of the major techniques a mediator uses is a caucus (Moore, 1986). At times a mediator, or either party, may stop the mediation and request a caucus. In a caucus the two parties are physically separated from each other and there is no direct communication between them. The mediator meets with one of the parties or with both parties individually. There are many reasons for calling a caucus: to vent intense emotions privately, to clarify misperceptions, to reduce unproductive or repetitive negative behavior, to clarify a party's interests, to provide a pause for each party to consider an alternative, to convince an uncompromising party that the mediation process is better than going to court, to uncover confidential information, to educate an inexperienced disputant about the processes of mediation, or to design alternatives that will later be brought to a joint session.

Some parties are willing in a caucus to express privately possible concessions. Usually such concessions are conditional on the other party's making certain concessions. By the use of caucuses, a mediator can go back and forth relaying information from one party to the other and seek to develop a consensus.

Relaxation Approaches

The relaxation response can be achieved by muscle relaxation approaches, deep-breathing techniques, and by imagery relaxation methods.

Muscle Relaxation Approaches[1]

There are now a number of muscle relaxation programs available, described in detail in a review by Bernstein and Borkovec (1973). Muscle relaxation approaches stem from Jacobson's (1934) pioneering work in teaching people to help themselves deal with stress and anxiety. *Stress* is a state of bodily and mental tension resulting from physical, chemical, or emotional stressors; for example, stress is the state resulting from having a job that is perceived as being filled with "high pressure." (See Chapter 24 for a fuller description of stress and its effects.)

Anxiety has long been recognized as an emotion that accompanies stress. Anxiety is generally described as uncomfortable feelings of tension, apprehension, and dread.

Jacobson's investigations led him to the well-established fact that people are able to regulate certain effects of the automatic nervous system through their own efforts. Specifically, he discovered that anxiety is associated with the sensation of tension experienced when muscle fibers are shortened or contracted as they are during stress. Jacobson developed an approach to counteract anxiety by muscle relaxation. He demonstrated that anxiety can be sharply reduced by relaxing muscles. The specific approach he developed is an elaborate system for teaching people to progressively tighten and then relax the major muscles of their body. He also demonstrated that anxiety will not exist in the presence of complete muscle relaxation (Jacobson, 1938a).

Jacobson (1934, 1938b, 1959, 1964, 1973) published many popular books on how to relax, how to handle fatigue, how to sleep well, how to relax while having a baby, and how to help school children relax in the classroom.

His approach to relaxation consists of teaching people to relax 20 major muscle groups. Each group is tensed and relaxed in several different ways during a 60-minute period, practiced every day until the person becomes skilled in the procedure. Jacobson's method is thorough but time-consuming.

Muscle relaxation is a very effective approach in reducing and eliminating both stress and anxiety (Brown, 1977). Practically anyone can learn to reduce both anxiety and stress using muscle relaxation. In recent years shorter programs of muscle relaxation have been developed.

Learning to relax via muscle relaxation is accomplished by having a person first tighten and then relax a set of muscles. When relaxing muscle groups, the person is instructed to

[1]This material on muscle relaxation approaches is adapted from Charles Zastrow, "Muscle Relaxation Approaches," in *Talk to Yourself: Using the Power of Self-Talk*, © 1979, pp. 179–183. Adapted by permission of Prentice-Hall, Inc., Englewood Cliffs, New Jersey.

think about the relaxed feeling while noting that the muscles are more relaxed than before they were tensed. The following excerpt provides an illustration of the instructions for muscle relaxation.

Instructions for Muscle Relaxation[2]
Preparation: Spend a little time getting as comfortable as you can. While you are finding a good position, you will also want to loosen any tight clothing. Loosen your belt or tie if they are not already loose. If your shoes feel tight, you may wish to take them off. Your legs and arms should be slightly apart.

Slowly open your mouth and move your jaw gently from side to side. . . . Now let your mouth close, keeping your teeth slightly apart. As you do, take a deep breath . . . and slowly let the air slip out.

While you tighten one part of your body, try to leave every other part limp and loose. Keep the tensed part of your body tight for a few seconds and then relax and let it go. Then take a deep breath, hold it, and as you breathe out, silently say, "Relax and let go." In time, this will be a technique you can use to produce rapid relaxation. Now begin your relaxation practice.

Total body tension: First, tense every muscle in your body. Tense the muscles of your jaws, eyes, arms, hands, chest, back, stomach, legs, and feet. Feel the tension all over your body. . . . Hold the tension briefly and then silently say, "Relax and let go" as you breathe out. . . . Let your whole body relax. . . . Feel a wave of calm come over you as you stop tensing. Feel the relief.

[2]Reprinted with permission of Atheneum Publishers, an imprint of Macmillan Publishing Company, from *Stress Management: A Comprehensive Guide to Wellness* by Edward A. Charlesworth and Ronald G. Nathan, pp. 63–71. Copyright © 1984 by Edward A. Charlesworth and Ronald G. Nathan.

Gently close your eyes and take another deep breath. . . . Study the tension as you hold your breath. . . . Slowly breathe out and silently say, "Relax and let go." Feel the deepening relaxation. Allow yourself to drift more and more with this relaxation. . . . As you continue, you will exercise different parts of your body. Become aware of your body and its tension and relaxation. This will help you to become deeply relaxed on command.

Head and face: Keeping the rest of your body relaxed, wrinkle up your forehead. Do you feel the tension? Your forehead is very tight. Briefly pause and be aware of it. . . . Now, relax and let go. Feel the tension slipping out. Smooth out your forehead and take a deep breath. Hold it. (Briefly pause.) As you breathe out, silently say, "Relax and let go."

Squint your eyes as if you are in a dust storm. Keep the rest of your body relaxed. Briefly pause and feel the tension around your eyes. . . . Now, relax and let go. Take a deep breath and hold it. (Briefly pause.) Silently say, "Relax and let go" as you breathe out.

Open your mouth as wide as you can. Feel the tension in your jaw and chin. Briefly hold the tension. . . . Now, let your mouth gently close. As you do, silently say, "Relax and let go." Take a deep breath. Hold it. (Briefly pause.) As you breathe out say, "Relax and let go."

Close your mouth. Push your tongue against the roof of your mouth. Study the tension in your mouth and chin. Briefly hold the tension. . . . Relax and let go. Take a deep breath. Hold it. (Briefly pause.) Now, silently say, "Relax and let go" as you breathe out. When you breathe out, let your tongue rest comfortably in your mouth, and let your lips be slightly apart.

Keep the rest of your body relaxed, but clench your jaw tightly. Feel the tension in your jaw muscles. Briefly hold the tension.

. . . Now relax and let go, and take a deep breath. Hold it. (Briefly pause.) Silently say, "Relax and let go" as you breathe out.

Think about the top of your head, your forehead, eyes, jaws, and cheeks. Make sure these muscles are relaxed. . . . Have you let go of all the tension? Continue to let the tension slip away and feel the relaxation replace the tension. Feel your face becoming very smooth and soft as all the tension slips away. . . . Your eyes are relaxed. . . . Your tongue is relaxed. . . . Your jaws are loose and limp. . . . All of your neck muscles are also very, very relaxed.

All of the muscles of your face and head are relaxing more and more. . . . Your head feels as though it could roll from side to side, and your face feels soft and smooth. Allow your face to continue becoming more and more relaxed as you now move to the other areas of your body.

Shoulders: Now shrug your shoulders up and try to touch your ears with your shoulders. Feel the tension in the shoulders and neck. Hold the tension. . . . Now, relax and let go. As you do, feel your shoulders joining the relaxed parts of your body. Take a deep breath. Hold it. (Briefly pause.) Silently say, "Relax and let go" as you slowly breathe out.

Notice the difference, how the tension is giving way to relaxation. Shrug your right shoulder up and try to touch your right ear. Feel the tension in your right shoulder and along the right side of your neck. Hold the tension. . . . Now, relax and let go. Take a deep breath. Hold it. (Briefly pause.) Silently say, "Relax and let go" as you slowly breathe out.

Next, shrug your left shoulder up and try to touch your left ear. Feel the tension in your left shoulder and along the left side of your neck. Hold the tension. . . . Now, relax and let go. Take a deep breath. Hold it. (Briefly pause.) Silently say, "Relax and

let go" as you slowly breathe out. Feel the relaxation seeping into the shoulders. As you continue, you will become loose, limp, and relaxed as an old rag doll.

Arms and hands: Stretch your arms out and make a fist with your hands. Feel the tension in your hands and forearms. Hold the tension. . . . Now, relax and let go. Take a deep breath. Hold it. (Briefly pause.) Silently say, "Relax and let go" as you slowly breathe out.

Push your right hand down into the surface it is resting on. Feel the tension in your arm and shoulder. Hold the tension. . . . Now, relax and let go. Take a deep breath. Hold it. (Briefly pause.) Silently say, "Relax and let go" as you slowly breathe out.

Next, push your left hand down into whatever it is resting on. Feel the tension in your arm and shoulder. Hold the tension. . . . Now, relax and let go. Take a deep breath. Hold it. (Briefly pause.) Silently say, "Relax and let go" as you slowly breathe out.

Bend your arms toward your shoulders and double them up as you might to show off your muscles. Feel the tension. Hold the tension. . . . Now, relax and let go. Take a deep breath. Hold it. (Briefly pause.) Silently say, "Relax and let go" as you slowly breathe out.

Chest and lungs: Move on to the relaxation of your chest. Begin by taking a deep breath that totally fills your lungs. As you hold your breath, notice the tension. Be aware of the tension around your ribs. . . . Silently say, "Relax and let go" as you slowly breathe out. Feel the deepening relaxation as you continue breathing easily, freely, and gently. (Briefly pause.)

Take in another deep breath. Hold it again and again feel the contrast between tension and relaxation. As you do, tighten your chest muscles. Hold the tension. . . .

Silently say, "Relax and let go" as you slowly breathe out. Feel the relief as you breathe out and continue to breathe gently, naturally, and rhythmically. Breathe as smoothly as you can. You will become more and more relaxed with every breath.

Back: Keep your face, neck, arms, and chest as relaxed as possible, arch your back up (or forward if you are sitting). Arch it as if you had a pillow under the middle and low part of your back. Observe the tension along both sides of your back. Briefly hold that position. . . . Now, relax and let go. Take a deep breath. Hold it. (Briefly pause.) Silently say, "Relax and let go" as you breathe out. Let that relaxation spread deep into your shoulders and down into your back muscles.

Feel the slow relaxation developing and spreading all over. Feel it going deeper and deeper. Allow your entire body to relax. Face and head relaxed. . . . Neck relaxed. . . . Shoulders relaxed. . . . Arms relaxed. . . . Chest relaxed. . . . Back relaxed. . . . All these areas are relaxing more and more, becoming more deeply relaxed than you thought possible.

Stomach: Now, begin the relaxation of the stomach area. Tighten up this area. Briefly hold the tension. . . . Relax and let go. Feel the relaxation pour into your stomach area. All the tension is being replaced with relaxation, and you feel the general well-being that comes with relaxation. Take a deep breath. Hold it. (Briefly pause.) Silently say, "Relax and let go" as you slowly breathe out.

Now, experience a different type of tension in the stomach area. Push your stomach out as far as you can. Briefly hold the tension. . . . Now, relax and let go. Take a deep breath. Hold it. (Briefly pause.) Silently say, "Relax and let go" as you slowly breathe out.

Now, pull your stomach in. Try to pull your stomach in and touch your backbone. Hold it. . . . Now, relax and let go. Take a deep breath. Hold it. (Briefly pause.) Silently say, "Relax and let go" as you breathe out.

You are becoming more and more relaxed. Each time you breathe out, feel the gentle relaxation in your lungs and in your body. As you continue to do these exercises, your chest and stomach area will relax more and more. Check the muscles of your face, neck, shoulders, arms, chest, and stomach. Make sure they are still relaxed. If they are not, then tense and release them again. Whatever part is still less than fully relaxed is starting to relax more and more. Soon you will be able to tell when you have tension in any part of your body. You will learn that you can always relax and let go of the tension you may find in any part of your body.

Hips, legs, and feet: Now, begin the relaxation of your hips and legs. Tighten your hips and legs by pressing down the heels of your feet into the surface they are resting on. Tighten these muscles. Keep the rest of your body as relaxed as you can and press your heels down. . . . Now, hold the tension. . . . Relax and let go. Feel your legs float up. Take a deep breath. Hold it. (Briefly pause.) Silently say, "Relax and let go" as you breathe out. Feel the relaxation pouring in. Notice the difference between tension and relaxation. Let the relaxation become deeper and deeper. Enjoy the relaxation.

Next, tighten your lower leg muscles. Feel the tension. Briefly hold the tension. . . . Now, relax and let go. Take a deep breath. Hold it. (Briefly pause.) Silently say, "Relax and let go" as you breathe out.

Now, curl your toes downward. Curl them down and try to touch the bottom of your feet with your toes. Hold them and feel the tension. . . . Relax and let go. Wiggle your toes gently as you let go of the tension. Let the tension be replaced with relaxation. Take a deep breath. Hold it. (Briefly pause.) Silently say, "Relax and let go" as you breathe out.

Now, bend your toes back the other way. Bend your toes right up toward your knees. Feel the tension. Try to touch your knees with your toes. Feel the tension. Hold the tension. . . . Relax and let go. Feel all the tension slip right out. Take a deep breath. Hold it. (Briefly pause.) Silently say, "Relax and let go" as you slowly breathe out. Feel the tension leaving your body and the relaxation seeping in.

Body review: You have progressed through all the major muscles of your body. Now, let them become more and more relaxed. Continue to feel yourself becoming more and more relaxed each time you breathe out. Each time you breathe out, think about a muscle and silently say, "Relax and let go," . . . Face relax. . . . Shoulders relax. . . . Arms relax. . . . Hands relax. . . . Chest relax. . . . Back relax. . . . Stomach relax. . . . Hips relax. . . . Legs relax. . . . Feet relax. . . . Your whole body is becoming more and more relaxed with each breath.

Spend a few more minutes relaxing, if you would like. If, during your day, you find yourself getting upset about something, remember the relaxation you have just experienced. Before you get upset, take a deep breath, hold it, and as you breathe out, silently say, "Relax and let go." With practice, you will be able to use this technique to relax whenever you begin to feel the stress of everyday living.

With continued practice of such a muscle relaxation technique, a person is generally able to relax whenever anxious simply by *visualizing* (that is, thinking about) muscles re-

laxing. The procedure is to think about the tension progressively leaving the various muscle groups. A brief example of this procedure is from Brown (1977):

> Think of your lower arm, elbow, and upper arm, all the way up to your shoulders. Picture all the tension just melting away. . . . Think about your stomach and chest, up to your throat and neck. As you continue breathing more deeply, just imagine all the tension flowing out and you are relaxing more and more.
>
> Now think about your throat, neck, and head, feeling limp and relaxed. Relax your facial muscles. Drop the jaw, parting the lips and teeth. Picture yourself completely relaxed. [pp. 261–262]

In recent years physicians, psychiatrists, psychologists, social workers, and other counselors have increasingly explored and used muscle relaxation approaches to reduce both stress and anxiety (Charlesworth & Nathan, 1984). Muscle relaxation is also being used to bring relief to sufferers of both tension headaches and migraine headaches (Goleman, 1976b). Suinn (1976) demonstrated that relaxation is useful in helping athletes and others reduce stress before participating in important events. It is also useful in reducing hypertension (Shoemaker & Tasto, 1975). Relaxation training is used as a technique in its own right and is also used in conjunction with such other therapy approaches as self-hypnosis, biofeedback, and systematic desensitization.

Deep-Breathing and Imagery Relaxation Approaches

In addition to muscle relaxation approaches, the relaxation response can be achieved by deep-breathing techniques and by imagery of being in a relaxing place. Brown (1977) described the deep-breathing technique:

Relaxation technique: deep breathing (five minutes)

1. Select a comfortable sitting position.

2. Close your eyes and direct your attention to your own breathing process.

3. Think about nothing but your breath, as it flows in and out of your body.

4. Say to yourself something like this: "I am relaxing, breathing smoothly and rhythmically. Fresh oxygen flows in and out of my body. I feel calm, renewed and refreshed."

5. Continue to focus on your breathing as it flows in and out, in and out, thinking of nothing but the smooth, rhythmical process of your own breathing.

6. After five minutes, stand up, stretch, smile, and continue with your daily activities.[3] [p. 259]

Brown (1977) presented a relaxation approach using imagery of being in a relaxing place:

Relaxation technique: mental relaxation place (five to ten minutes)

1. Select a comfortable sitting or reclining position.

2. Close your eyes, and think about a place that you have been before that represents your ideal place for physical and mental relaxation. (It should be a quiet environment, perhaps the seashore, the mountains, or even your own backyard. If you can't think of an ideal relaxation place, then create one in your mind.)

3. Now imagine that you are actually in your ideal relaxation place. Imagine that you are seeing all the colors, hearing the sounds, smelling the aromas. Just lie back, and enjoy your soothing, rejuvenating environment.

4. Feel the peacefulness, the calmness, and imagine your whole body and mind being renewed and refreshed.

5. After five to ten minutes, slowly open your eyes and stretch. You have the realization that you may instantly return to your relaxation place whenever you desire, and experience a peacefulness and calmness in body and mind.[4] [pp. 259–260]

Practice in using any of these relaxation approaches gradually increases the proficiency of achieving the relaxation response. Developing the capacity to achieve the relaxation response is a highly effective approach to alleviating anxiety and stress, and thereby experiencing more pleasing emotions, maintaining health, preventing or coping better with stress-related disorders, and probably also extending the number of years you can expect to live. Counselors are increasingly using relaxation approaches to help clients relax in order to reduce anxiety and stress.

Meditation[5]

Recorded accounts of meditative practice date back over 2,000 years among Zen monks, Indian yogis, Judaic spiritual leaders, and Christian monks. The earliest known Christian meditators were hermits who lived during the fourth century A.D. in the most isolated areas of the Egyptian desert. Like present-day Indian yogis in the Himalaya Mountains, they sought isolation to communicate with God, free from worldly distractions. The meditative practices of these earliest Christian monks were strikingly similar to practices of Hindu and Buddhist meditators in India at that time (suggesting a cultural exchange). These Christian meditators

---

[3]From *Stress and the Art of Biofeedback* by Barbara B. Brown. Copyright © 1977 by Barbara B. Brown. By permission of Bantam Books, New York. All rights reserved.

[4]Ibid.

[5]This material on meditation is adapted from Charles Zastrow, "Meditation," in *Talk to Yourself: Using the Power of Self-Talk,* © 1979, pp. 185–189. Adapted by permission of Prentice-Hall, Inc., Englewood Cliffs, New Jersey.

Meditation has been found to have a number of positive effects.

repeated quietly or silently a selected phrase from the Scriptures. The most popular phrase or *mantra* was "Lord Jesus Christ, Son of God, have mercy on me, a sinner." Many of these monks repeated the short form of this mantra, "Kyrie eleison," silently for hours each day. Today, this form of meditation is no longer practiced among Christians in the West but still survives in some Eastern orthodox monasteries (Goleman, 1977).

There are numerous meditation approaches being practiced today. Goleman (1977) described the following:

Hesychasm: Christianity's Yoga
Kabbalah: Hidden Judaism
Sufism: Muslim Mysticism
Transcendental Meditation: Hinduism for Americans
Patanjali's Yoga Sutras
Bhakti: The Hindu Path of Devotion
Swami Muktananda's Kundalini Yoga
Tantra's Left-Handed Path
The Buddha's Middle Way
Tibetan Buddhism
Zen
Gurdjieff
J. Krisnamurti's Methodless Method

Practically all the approaches seek to achieve a meditative state by having a person concentrate on and/or repeat an object: word, phrase, chant, sound, spiritual value, imagery of an exquisite painting, and so forth. Different approaches use different rituals, different objects, have somewhat different goals to be achieved through meditation, and seek to produce somewhat different meditative experiences.

Transcendental meditation (TM) is used here for illustrative purposes since it is the most popular meditation approach in this country and is one of the most widely practiced forms of meditation in the world. TM first gained popularity in the 1960s when it was practiced by such widely known celebrities as the Beatles and Mia Farrow. TM, developed by Maharishi Mahesh Yogi, a guru (Hindu spiritual leader), is a simple Yogic technique.

In TM a meditator lets a mantra repeat itself over and over in her mind. The mantra is a Sanskrit word or sound that is given to meditators by TM instructors. The mantras themselves are not special to TM but come from Sanskrit sources used by many Hindus. Two examples of mantras are *Shyam* (a name of Lord Krishna) and *Aing* (a sound sacred to the divine mother). The goal of TM is "passage through a series of advanced spiritual states ending in union with God" (Goleman, 1977, p. 58). Meditators are advised to meditate 20 minutes in the morning, usually before breakfast, and 20 minutes in the evening, usually before dinner.

There is considerable evidence that the reduction of stress and anxiety through meditation derives from a simple set of general procedures that can be learned without elaborate rituals or large expenses (Goleman, 1976a). A strong advocate of this view is Herbert Benson, a Harvard cardiologist who has carefully reviewed the contemporary meditation approaches. Benson (1975) identified the following four elements as being key to eliciting the relaxation response in any meditation approach:

1. *Being in a quiet environment* that facilitates tuning out external distractions and internal stimuli.

2. *Being in a comfortable position,* such as sitting or lying down. The position should be one in which the meditator can feel comfortable for at least 20 minutes.

3. *Having an object to dwell on,* which also facilitates tuning out thoughts about day-to-day concerns. Examples of suitable objects include one's breathing, a word or phrase chanted to oneself, an audiotape of ocean waves, a symbol to be gazed at steadily, or the sights and sounds of a relaxing place, visualized with one's eyes closed.

4. *Having a passive attitude,* in which the meditator "lets go" of day-to-day concerns. A passive attitude appears to be the key element in eliciting the relaxation response; people become relaxed when they focus their cognitions on relaxing thoughts and stop thinking about everyday problems. If day-to-day concerns drift into the meditator's awareness, he or she should allow them to pass on as effortlessly as possible.

An example of a simplified, noncultic, nonreligious, meditation approach is as follows:

1. Find a quiet environment, such as a quiet room, where you will not be interrupted.

2. Sit quietly in a comfortable position.

3. Close your eyes.

4. Breathe in and out through your nose at a relaxed, natural pace. As you breathe out, silently say the word *Relax* slowly to yourself.

5. Continue this process for 10 to 20 minutes: Slowly breathe in, and then as you exhale slowly say "relax" to yourself.

6. Do not focus your thoughts on day-to-day concerns, and do not worry whether you will achieve a deep level of relaxation. Deep levels of relaxation are gradually achieved with continued practice. The state of being relaxed comes slowly as you let go of your worries and concerns. When distracting thoughts enter your mind, allow them to drift away as effortlessly as possible. Focusing your thoughts on your breathing and on silently saying "relax" as you exhale will facilitate your "letting go" of your worries and concerns.

7. When you finish, sit quietly for several minutes, first with your eyes closed and then with your eyes open. Practice this technique once or twice daily. With practice, you will gradually achieve more rapid and deeper levels of relaxation. A word of caution: walk around for 15 or more minutes before attempting to drive a car or some other vehicle, as you are apt to be lethargic, with your response reaction time being lengthened considerably.

In reviewing meditation approaches, note that meditation and relaxation approaches are closely relaxed. Both techniques are therapeutic because they produce the relaxation response. In addition, certain components of the muscle relaxation and deep breathing relaxation approaches are used by some meditation approaches to aid in producing the relaxation response. Finally, imagery relaxation has characteristics similar to those of meditation and can in fact be considered a meditation approach.

Research has demonstrated that meditation is physiologically and psychologically more refreshing and energy-restoring than deep sleep (Wallace, 1970). Many meditators, in fact, have reported that they needed less sleep after they began meditating, which suggests that a regenerative process occurs during meditation (Bloomfield, Cain, & Jaffe, 1975). Meditation has been used successfully in the treatment of many stress-related disorders including hypertension (Benson, Rosner, & Marzetta, 1973) and asthma (Honsberger & Wilson, 1973). It has also been effective in decreasing the use of drugs, alcohol, and cigarette smoking (Benson, 1975); alleviating sleep disorders; and accelerating the bodily healing process (Bloomfield, Cain, & Jaffe, 1975).

Meditation has also been found to have a number of other positive effects. It is useful in treating phobias (Boudreau, 1972) and in treating people with emotional problems (Bloomfield, Cain, & Jaffe, 1975). Regular practice of the technique improves learning ability (Abrams, 1974), perceptual motor performance (Blasdell, 1974), ability to recover from stress (Orme-Johnson, 1973), perceptual acuity (Pelletier, 1974), work productivity and job satisfaction (Frew, 1974), and creativity (Bloomfield, Cain, & Jaffe, 1975). Meditation improves psychological health (Shelly, 1973); heightens self-awareness (Bloomfield, Cain, & Jaffe, 1975); increases self-actualization (Ferguson & Gowan, 1974); reduces anxiety, depression, and aggression (Ferguson & Gowan, 1974); reduces reaction time (Shaw & Kolb, 1974); increases recall ability (Abrams, 1974); and improves academic performance (Heaton & Orme-Johnson, 1974).

Meditation's potential medical value in eliciting the relaxation response is dramatically described by Benson (1975):

The prevention of stress-related diseases carries with it enormous significance, certainly for the individual and his family in terms of their own physical and mental well-being, and for society as a whole through huge dollar savings in health expenditures. It is possible that the regular elicitation of the Relaxation Response will prevent the huge personal suffering and social costs now being inflicted on us by high blood pressure and its related ailments. [pp. 156–157]

Note: A word of caution. If and when you use meditation (or any relaxation technique) you should walk around for several minutes before driving, because you may be so relaxed that you will have difficulty concentrating on your driving.

Hypnosis and Self-Hypnosis[6]

Many people erroneously believe that the effects produced by hypnotism are the result of some mystical, magical power of the hypnotist. Authorities on hypnotism, however, are in full agreement that the effects result from the thinking processes and imaginative processes of the hypnotized person (Caprio & Berger, 1963; Freese, 1976; Lecron, 1964; White & Watt, 1973).

Being hypnotized involves entering a mental state of aroused concentration so intense that everything else is ignored and the hypnotized person goes into a trance. Freese (1976) defined hypnosis as follows:

To understand hypnosis, the trance state, one must always keep in mind this picture of aroused intense concentration. When we concentrate deeply on a book and become completely absorbed in its contents, we're not asleep even though we don't move a muscle, don't hear a thing going on about us.... In short, hypnosis is a normal state into which we will slip readily during our everyday lives. It's what happens to us every time we become entranced (note that

[6]The material on hypnosis is adapted from Charles Zastrow, "Hypnosis and Self-Hypnosis" in *Talk to Yourself: Using the Power of Self-Talk,* © 1979, pp. 197–203. Adapted by permission of Prentice-Hall, Inc., Englewood Cliffs, New Jersey.

word) by a movie or mind-blowing experience, a TV show or a work of art or even a conversation. It's the daydreamer lost in her or his vivid imagery. [pp. 37–38]

Caprio and Berger (1963) noted that all hypnosis is self-hypnosis. People who become hypnotized, hypnotize themselves by thinking and concentration. If a person does not wish to be hypnotized, it is almost impossible for a hypnotist to put that person in a hypnotic state. According to Caprio and Berger:

> Hypnotists do not possess any unusual or mystic powers. A hypnotist is a person who knows that his subject actually hypnotizes himself. The hypnotist is merely a person who has learned or perhaps mastered the science and art of *effective suggestion*. He teaches the subject how to bring about or self-induce the hypnotic state. Hypnotism has sometimes been called the "manipulation of the imagination." ... The hypnotic state is similar to becoming completely absorbed in a movie or a book. In other words, it represents a concentration of attention. [pp. 15–16]

Almost anyone can be hypnotized. It takes imagination, a willingness to cooperate with the hypnotist, and a willingness to accept suggestions. Caprio and Berger (1963) added:

> To be hypnotized, (1) you must *want* to be hypnotized; (2) you must have confidence in the hypnotist; (3) you must train your mind to *accept* suggestion. [p. 17]

While under hypnosis a person will not do anything contrary to his or her moral code. Those hypnotized have the power to select the suggestions they are willing to accept, and they will reject improper or unethical suggestions. The hypnotized person also has the power to terminate the hypnotic state at will. There has never been a case in which the hypnotized person did not return to the waking state. Hypnotized people are never in anybody else's power. They won't go into a trance unless they want to. They won't do anything unless they want to. They have the power to come out of a trance whenever they want to (Caprio & Berger, 1963). Caprio and Berger further described hypnosis and its medical value:

> All hypnosis is self-hypnosis. In hypnosis the subject responds to the suggestions of the hypnotist. The subject *permits* the hypnotist to bring about a state of calmness and relaxation because he, the subject, *desires* this mental state.
>
> Hypnosis involves (1) motivation, (2) relaxation and (3) suggestion.
>
> In self-hypnosis, the relaxation is self-induced, followed by the hypnotic state. It is the influence of our own minds over our bodies. By including our own hypnotic state, we heighten our suggestibility and are then capable of influencing our body functions. . . .
>
> The phenomena of hypnosis and self-hypnosis explain many of our publicized miracles of faith cures. Self-hypnosis is really a form of *psychic healing* accomplished through the voluntary *acceptance and application of one's own suggestions*. [p. 19]

Hypnotists use many techniques to induce a trance. One technique is relaxation: the hypnotist's voice gradually becomes monotonous (like a lullaby) as he or she keeps suggesting relaxation until the hypnotic state is reached. Another technique is arm levitation, in which the hypnotist suggests that the person's arm, fingers, or hand are gradually becoming lighter and lighter, until they "lift by themselves."

In the repetitive movement technique, the hypnotist keeps suggesting relaxation and then takes an arm and moves it back and forth while (in a monotonous voice) suggesting that the person perform this movement. A trance state is indicated when the person automatically begins to perform the movement.

The direct stare technique is the oldest and perhaps most famous technique but is rarely used today. With this technique, the hypnotist stares into the person's eyes and seeks to induce the trance state by using a dominant "Hollywood-style" stare.

Freese (1976) documented that over the centuries thousands of different rituals have been used for trance induction. Such rituals include chants or dances of witch doctors, a simple flashing light or a swinging pendulum, or a monotonous beat of a *metronome* (an instrument designed to mark exact time by a regularly repeated tick).

Whatever technique is used to induce a trance, all hypnosis is self-hypnosis in which a state of aroused intense concentration is achieved because the hypnotized person cooperates with the hypnotist and desires to enter this mental state.

The mechanics of how to induce self-hypnosis and how to help yourself with self-hypnotic suggestions will now be briefly described. The first step is to decide what you would like to use self-hypnosis for: losing weight, cutting back on drinking alcoholic beverages, overcoming anger, eliminating jealousy, combating insomnia, relieving a pain, stopping smoking, reducing a phobia, learning to relax in certain anxiety-producing situations—whatever.

The next step is to become very relaxed. Such relaxation can be achieved using one of the following approaches that have previously been described: muscle relaxation, deep breathing relaxation, imagery relaxation, or meditation. Such relaxation approaches are effective if (and only if) they shift a person's thinking from focusing on day-to-day problems to focusing on calming, monotonous, or relaxing thoughts. This relaxation phase of hypnosis and self-hypnosis is very important because it facilitates the hypnotized person's capacity to accept and follow through on hypnotic suggestions.

The final key component of hypnosis and self-hypnosis is a suggestion (or a set of suggestions) that you give yourself while in a relaxed state. All such suggestions are simply statements in which you tell yourself that you must, can, and will be able to achieve a certain goal: for example, "I can and will stop smoking"; "I will feel no pain"; "I am able to relax myself and fall asleep whenever I need to"; "I am able to relax and reduce my blood pressure"; "I can control my drinking and will never ever take more than two drinks when I go out with friends."

For self-hypnotic suggestions to work, it is essential to give yourself these suggestions daily in order that you keep your attention focused on achieving your goal (for example, telling yourself that you can and will follow a certain diet in order to lose weight).

This phase assumes that what the mind causes, it can cure; or, as Caprio and Berger (1963) noted, it is based on the power of telling yourself

> I can—I must—I will achieve my goal—that I have the mind-power to accept and carry out certain self-given suggestions which will enable me to overcome almost any handicap, to improve my personality and acquire a healthier philosophy of life. [p. 34]

After giving yourself a hypnotic suggestion you can arouse yourself from the self-hypnotic trance by telling yourself that you will "come out" as you slowly count to ten. It is needless to worry that in the event of an emergency you will not be able to arouse yourself rapidly from the trance. Under hypnosis you are always able to arouse yourself immediately from the hypnotic state and are rapidly able to respond to the given emergency situation.

Caprio and Berger (1963) provided a number of case examples of hypnosis being successfully used. One involved a noted scientist in his seventies who was hesitant to address audiences because of stage fright. He generally declined invitations to speak. On one speaking engagement he became so frightened that he nearly fainted, and he experienced heart palpitations. This scientist was aware that his fear was largely caused by his thoughts and deduced that if he could learn to control his thoughts, he would in turn control his fear. He practiced a relaxation technique and repeatedly gave himself the following suggestions: "I have nothing to fear—I am going to concentrate on the message I wish to pass on to my audience and not on myself—I have confidence in the power of my mind" (p. 126). He reduced his fear with this approach and subsequently used this self-hypnosis approach before future lectures. He reportedly was able to deliver many talks with this approach and experienced little fear.

Hypnotic and self-hypnotic suggestions have been used for a wide variety of medical and psychological purposes:

- To control weight
- To alleviate emotional problems
- To reduce stress and anxiety
- To stop drinking or smoking
- To alleviate insomnia
- To improve one's sex life
- To treat sexual dysfunctions
- To alleviate pain
- To reduce tension
- To relax
- To alleviate depression
- To improve memory
- To increase self-confidence
- To improve interpersonal relationships
- To improve one's self-image
- To reduce fatigue
- To treat stress-related illnesses
- To reduce hostility and anger
- To reduce jealousy and guilt
- To overcome feelings of inferiority
- To conquer fears and phobias
- To treat migraine headaches, asthma, arthritis, backaches, bursitis, and allergies
- To treat gynecological problems
- To anesthetize

- To treat stuttering, by reducing anxiety and tension
- To alleviate pain during dentistry
- To treat hypertension

A more extensive review of the uses of hypnosis is contained in Caprio and Berger (1963), Freese (1976), and Lecron (1964).

Biofeedback[7]

Biofeedback is simply a mirror reflecting some aspect of your physiology. Learning takes place only when there is feedback. In the same way your eyes give you feedback when you throw a ball, a biofeedback machine gives you feedback about what you are doing with your body. This feedback is able to gauge levels of arousal or physical change that we usually do not become aware of until a markedly high level of arousal is reached. During an hour interview, for example, your hand temperature is apt to vary by 5 to 7 degrees. A higher hand temperature represents a more relaxed state, while a lower hand temperature indicates a higher level of tension or anxiety (when you are tense, blood flows inward, away from the skin, which lowers skin temperature). It is unlikely that you will be aware of these gradual changes, even though they are graphic indicators of your emotional state.

There are certain things biofeedback can and cannot do. Biofeedback does not alter one's physiological processes, nor does it solve personal or emotional problems, and it definitely does not reveal one's hidden thoughts or fantasies. What it does by meters, lights, or sounds is indicate what is happening in a person's body at that moment.

[7]This material on biofeedback is adapted from Charles Zastrow, "Biofeedback," in *Talk to Yourself: Using the Power of Self-Talk,* © 1979, pp. 204–210. Adapted by permission of Prentice-Hall, Inc., Englewood Cliffs, New Jersey.

There is a wide range of biofeedback measures. Some common ones that we generally do not associate with biofeedback are mirrors to reveal how we look, bathroom scales to measure our weight, tape measures to show our height, and fever thermometers to gauge our body temperature. A lie detector test is another common biofeedback machine that measures levels of arousal.

There are many clinical biofeedback measures:

- A thermometer to measure hand temperature
- Muscle feedback units to measure muscle tension and anxiety
- Equipment to measure pulse rate
- Galvanic skin response equipment to measure levels of arousal and anxiety
- Auditory feedback (using an amplified stethoscope) to measure peristaltic activity in the intestinal tract
- Equipment to measure blood pressure levels
- Electroencephalogram to measure brain wave activity
- Electrocardiograph to record changes in electrical potential occurring during the heartbeat

Basically, all of these devices are used to gauge stress (levels of anxiety or arousal) in various parts of the body. The problem that biofeedback training seeks to alleviate is stress and its long-term effects on our feelings, bodies, and thinking processes. Stress is an intense state of physical and emotional arousal that results from a person's perception of being threatened or endangered. The body prepares itself on the basis of the perception, not on whether the perception is realistic or unrealistic. If the perception is realistic, the physiological and emotional arousal prepares us better to handle the danger. If the perception is unrealistic, we needlessly expend our adaptive energy. Furthermore, prolonged stress is apt to play a key role in the development and severity of a wide variety of stress-related illnesses.

There are three basic ways to cope with high levels of stress and tension:

1. You can seek to change the events that contribute to your high stress level. For example, if you are dating someone and are feeling considerable anxiety over whether your partner is committed to the relationship, you can arrange a time to talk with your partner about commitment to the relationship. Often, however, events that cause your stress cannot be changed.

2. You can reassess whether you are realistically assessing situations. Doing a rational self-analysis (see Chapter 22) is an example of a structured way of examining the stress-producing self-talk, and of challenging irrational self-talk that generally is involved in prolonging high levels of stress.

3. You can get involved in meaningful activities that will stop you from thinking about the distressing event. Instead, you will think about the enjoyable and meaningful activity that you are involved in, which will reduce your stress level. There are many activities that can help to shift your mental focus: hobbies, exercising, going to a movie, relaxation techniques, meditation, hypnosis, biofeedback, and any other activity that you find enjoyable.

Conceptually, biofeedback is based on two basic principles: (1) Any biological function that can be monitored and amplified by electronic instrumentation and fed back to a person through one of his or her five senses can be regulated by that person. (2) "Every change in the physiological state is accompanied by an appropriate change in the mental emotional state, conscious or unconscious, and conversely, every change in the mental emotional state, conscious or unconscious, is accompanied by an appropriate change in the physiological state" (Pelletier, 1977, pp. 264–265).

Biofeedback research has demonstrated that many *autonomic* (that is, involuntary) nervous system processes can be brought under conscious control if a person obtains information about these processes. Such processes include heart rate, muscle tension, brain waves, body temperature, and stomach acidity level.

The following example described by Pelletier (1977) illustrates how it is possible to regulate heart rate via biofeedback.

> During the initial stages of electrocardiogram (ECG) or heart-rate feedback, patients are surprised to see how volatile their heart rates really are. At first the pattern seems random. . . . After a relatively short time the patient realizes that minor changes in his physical posture—even flexing an index finger, or changes in his breathing pattern—have a profound effect upon the heart. Breathing in a slow or regular manner or sitting in an upright posture helps to decelerate the heart rate, whereas slouching or breathing shallowly and quickly tends to accelerate it. . . . When thinking of a pleasant or relaxing vacation, he notes that his heart rate begins to decelerate. Conversely, when he thinks about a perplexing or stress-inducing situation, like his income tax or an argument with a close friend, heart rate accelerates. . . . Once this link between internal sensations and their effects upon the cardiovascular system is established, the individual has a means of regulating this critical autonomic function. [pp. 265–266]

The basic principles of learning how to regulate your heart rate, which are described in this example, provide a model of how biofeedback can be used to regulate practically all autonomic processes.

Brown (1977) provided another illustration of biofeedback:

> The average person can demonstrate to himself the biofeedback phenomenon by using an ordinary thermometer purchased from the drugstore or hardware store. One six to eight inches long and filled with fluid is best. He can tape the thermometer bulb to the fat pad of the middle finger with masking tape, making sure of good contact, but no constriction of circulation. After five or so minutes of quiet sitting, preferably with the eyes closed, note the temperature of the finger. Then, while still sitting quietly, repeat a few autosuggestion phrases to yourself slowly, such as, "I feel relaxed and warm," "My hands feel warm and relaxed," "I feel calm and relaxed." Repeat the phrases slowly, allowing the suggestion to take effect, then go on to the next one, and then repeat the series. Every five or ten minutes, take a reading of the finger temperature. Most people will show a rise in finger temperature three to five or even ten degrees, some only a degree. Only a few may not change or may even show a small fall in finger temperature. With repeated practice, everyone can learn to increase finger temperature by using mental activity. [pp. 4–5]

An increase in finger temperature indicates that a person is becoming more relaxed.

Clinical biofeedback can be integrated with other therapy techniques or used as a technique in and of itself. Clinical biofeedback has been successfully used in conjunction with traditional psychotherapy, rational therapy, behavior modification, hypnosis, meditation, and relaxation techniques. (Techniques such as relaxation approaches, meditation, and hypnosis are used at times together with biofeedback to help a person learn how to relax.)

Although biofeedback achieves the same relaxation response as meditation, hypnosis, and relaxation techniques, the essential difference is that biofeedback amplifies biological signals. Pelletier (1977) described an advantage of being able to amplify biological signals:

> An advantage of biofeedback over nonfeedback techniques is that the physiologi-

cal information tells an individual precisely how he is functioning. Interpreting the feedback, a person knows exactly how tense he is in certain muscles, and through trial and error he can discover the means of relaxing those muscles. When he is successful, the feedback lets him know immediately. [p. 260]

Most people are unaware when their body is under moderate stress. Only when they are highly anxious or highly aroused do they consciously become aware of their level of stress. Yet, moderately high levels of stress over extended periods can be damaging to physiological functioning and result in breakdown (that is, a stress-related illness). Biofeedback shows a person precisely his or her level of stress. It also provides immediate feedback when that level is increased or reduced. Since increases or decreases in stress are caused primarily by our thinking processes, biofeedback immediately provides feedback to a person on the kinds of thoughts that lead to a reduction in stress. Thus, through trial and error, with biofeedback, people can identify what kind of thinking (such as meditating or visualizing being in a relaxing place) will work for them in reducing stress.

Another advantage of biofeedback is that it provides instantaneous feedback on the particular area of affliction. An overall relaxation response usually induces all neurophysiological functions to move toward a state of deep relaxation. Yet the movement toward relaxation may vary considerably in various systems of the body. At times most systems become relaxed, while a few remain tensed. An additional advantage of biofeedback is that a specific physiological process (for example, high blood pressure of a hypertensive person) that needs to be corrected can be monitored, feeding information to the person to help evaluate progress in alleviating this dysfunction.

Brown (1977) described the therapeutic value of biofeedback:

There are more than fifty major medical and psychological problems in which biofeedback has been used with either greater success than conventional treatments or at least with equal benefits. The mind and body ailments that respond to biofeedback treatment span the entire spectrum of illnesses human beings suffer: emotional, psychosomatic, and physical disabilities. [pp. 3–4]

Biofeedback can be used to exert voluntary control over heart rate, skin temperature, blood pressure, muscle tension, brain waves, or any other internal biological function capable of being monitored. Biofeedback is radically altering the doctor-patient relationship in that it requires doctors to instruct patients in being active participants in the healing process.

Brown (1977) provided a summary of disorders that have been reported to respond to biofeedback: problems that are primarily emotional—anxiety, phobias, chronic headaches, tension headaches, hyperactivity, stage fright, insomnia, alcoholism, drug abuse, depression with anxiety; problems that are primarily psychosomatic—asthma, essential hypertension, bruxism (grinding of the teeth), menstrual distress, ulcers, colitis, functional diarrhea; and problems that are primarily physical—muscle spasms with pain, strokes, paralysis, spasticity, cerebral palsy, migraine headaches, and epilepsy.

Summary

This chapter presents a variety of treatment approaches for people with personal problems: milieu therapy, psychodrama, play therapy, parent effectiveness training, crisis intervention, task-centered practice, mediation, muscle relaxation approaches, deep-breathing relaxation, imagery relaxation, meditation, hypnosis, and biofeedback. These approaches were developed independently of a comprehensive theory of psychotherapy.

Parent effectiveness training has four techniques that anyone can use in improving interactions with others: active listening, I-messages, no-lose problem solving, and resolving collisions of values. Task-centered practice is a therapeutic approach that focuses on helping clients identify and carry out specific tasks that will help them resolve their problems.

Mediation is being used increasingly by a variety of professions to help resolve conflicts between two or more people. Social workers have used the following treatment approaches for a number of years: crisis intervention, milieu therapy, play therapy, and psychodrama.

Relaxation approaches, meditation, hypnosis, and biofeedback have been around a long time, but only recently have social workers begun to use these approaches. With the recognition that stress (and resulting stress-related problems) is our nation's number one health problem, social workers are using these approaches more and more to induce the relaxation response and thereby reduce anxiety and stress (among other objectives).

Exercises

1. Using I-messages

Goal: This exercise is designed to demonstrate how to phrase I-messages.

Step 1: Explain the goal of this exercise. Indicate I-messages are a nonblaming description of the effects a person is having on the sender of the message. I-messages do not involve giving a solution message or a put-down message.

Step 2: Ask the class how to formulate I-messages in a variety of situations. The following are examples:

a. Someone is smoking a cigarette near you and the smoke is bothering you.
b. You're riding in a car that a friend is driving dangerously fast.
c. Someone is playing a stereo loudly in a building, which is interfering with your studying.
d. A friend has just made another comment about your being overweight.
e. A person you're dating continues to write to someone he or she has dated in the past.

Step 3: Some of the responses given by students may well be you-messages. If that occurs, ask the class to indicate why the message is a you-message and not an I-message. If the class is having trouble in formulating I-messages, ask the students to discuss whether we are socialized in our society to use primarily you-messages.

2. Active listening

Goal: This exercise is designed to have students practice and further develop their active listening skills.

Step 1: Explain the purpose of the exercise and describe what active listening is and what it is designed to accomplish. Indicate that active listening involves using two types of statements: reflecting feelings and restating content.

Step 2: Have students pair off. (Participate if there is someone without a partner.) Have one member of each pair select a topic to discuss for about ten minutes. The topic may involve (a) a philosophical or moral issue such as abortion, (b) a problem with a friend or a relative, or (c) a problem at school.

Step 3: Ask the member who selected the topic to discuss it for about ten minutes. The listener should try to respond solely with active listening statements.

Step 4: After the discussion, ask the presenter to discuss with the listener the quality of the active listening statements. Did the listener make the mistake of making suggestions, asking questions, or beginning to talk about personal experiences? Did active listening motivate the presenter to continue talking? Did the presenter perceive the active listening statements as primarily "natural" or "artificial"?

Have the listener discuss with the presenter his or her thoughts and feelings about using active listening statements. Did the listener want to make other types of statements? If so, what?

Step 5: Reverse the roles and repeat the process.

Step 6: Ask the students to form a circle and discuss the merits and shortcomings of active listening. Were there some unique or unusual events that occurred?

3. Meditation and relaxation

Goal: This exercise is designed to demonstrate deep-breathing relaxation, meditation, imagery relaxation, and muscle relaxation to the class.

Step 1: Describe the goal of this exercise. Indicate that social workers are using meditation and relaxation approaches more and more to help clients handle stress more effectively. Describe the following approaches: deep-breathing relaxation, meditation, imagery relaxation, and muscle relaxation.

Step 2: State the following:

I will now lead you in a meditation exercise. The purpose is to show you that through meditating you can reduce stress and anxiety. You can do this exercise by yourself whenever you are anxious or want to relax. You can do it, for example, before giving a speech in class, before taking a crucial exam, or before going to bed at night.

Herbert Benson, who wrote the book *The Relaxation Response,* identified four key elements common to meditative approaches that help people relax. These four elements are (1) being in a quiet place; (2) getting in a comfortable position;

(3) having an object to dwell on, such as your breathing or thinking about your ideal relaxation place, or a neutral word or phrase that you can continually repeat silently to yourself; and (4) having a passive attitude in which you let go of your day-to-day concerns by no longer thinking about them. Having a passive attitude is the key element in helping you relax.

Now, I want you to form a circle. [*Wait until a circle is formed.*] I will lead you in three types of meditation. First, we will do a deep-breathing exercise. Then, we will move into repeating the word *relax* silently to ourselves. Third, I'll have you focus on visualizing your most relaxing place. We will move directly from the first to the second, and then from the second to the third without stopping. When we do this exercise, don't worry about anything unusual happening. There will be no tricks. Concentrate on what I'm telling you to focus on, while taking a passive attitude where you let go of your everyday thoughts and concerns. Everyday thoughts and concerns may occasionally enter your mind, but try to let go of them when they do.

Before we start, I want each of you to identify one of your most relaxing scenes. It may be lying in the sun on a beach or by a lake. It may be sitting in warm water in a bathtub reading a book. It may be sitting by a warm fireplace. Is there anyone who hasn't identified a relaxing scene? [*Wait until everyone has identified one.*]

OK, we're ready to start. [*If possible, dim the lights, or turn out some of them.*] First, I want you to close your eyes and keep them closed for the entire exercise. Next, get in a comfortable position. If you want, you can sit or lie on the floor. [*Take five or six minutes for each of the three meditative exercises. Speak softly and slowly. Pause frequently, sometimes for 20 seconds or more without saying anything. Feel free to add material to the following instructions.*]

First, I want you to focus only on your breathing. Breathe in and out slowly and deeply. . . . Breathe in and out slowly. . . . As you breathe out feel how relaxing it feels. . . . While exhaling, imagine your concerns are leaving you . . . as you're breathing in and out, feel how you're becoming more calm, more relaxed, more refreshed. . . . Just keep focusing on breathing slowly in and out. . . . Don't try to be in sync when I'm talking about breathing in and out. . . . Find a breathing rhythm that's comfortable for you. . . . Breathe in slowly and deeply, and then slowly breathe out. . . . You've got the power within you to get more and more relaxed. . . . All you have to do is focus on your breathing. . . . Breathe in slowly and deeply, and then slowly breathe out. . . . If other thoughts happen to enter your mind, just let them drift away as effortlessly as possible. . . . The key to becoming more relaxed is to let go of your day-to-day concerns. . . . To do this, all you need to do is simply focus on your breathing. . . . Breathe in slowly and deeply, and then breathe out.

Now, we will switch to repeating silently to yourself the word *relax*. Keep your eyes closed. . . . just keep repeating to yourself the word *relax*. . . . Keep repeating "relax" to yourself silently and slowly. . . . If day-to-day thoughts enter your mind, let them drift away. . . . Keep repeating "relax" to yourself. . . . All of us encounter daily stressors. . . . It is impossible to avoid daily stressors. . . . The important thing to remember about stress management is not to seek to avoid daily stressors but to find ways to relax when we are under high levels of stress. . . . An excellent and very simple way to learn to relax is to sit in a quiet place, in a comfortable position, and silently repeat to yourself the word *relax* . . . "relax" . . . "relax." . . . By simply repeating the word *relax* to yourself, you have the power within you to become more and more relaxed. . . . Find a nice comfortable pace for repeating the word *relax* to yourself. . . . The pace should be slow enough that you can relax. . . . But not be so slow that thoughts about your day-to-day concerns enter your mind. . . . Remember, the key to relaxing is letting go of your day-to-day concerns. . . . If such concerns begin to enter your mind, focus more of your attention on repeating "relax" silently and slowly to yourself. . . . By repeating "relax" to yourself, you will find it will appear to have magical powers for you, as you will find yourself becoming more and more relaxed and refreshed. . . . [*Have the students repeat "relax" for five or six minutes.*]

Now, we will switch to focusing on your most relaxing scene. Don't open your eyes. . . . Focus on being in your most relaxing place. . . . Feel how good and relaxing it feels. . . . Just dwell on how relaxing it feels. . . . Enjoy everything about how calm and relaxing this place is. . . . Feel yourself becoming calmer, more relaxed. . . . Enjoy the peacefulness of this place. . . . Feel yourself becoming more relaxed, more renewed and refreshed. . . . Enjoy all the sights and sounds of this special place for you. . . . Notice and cherish the pleasant smells and aromas. . . . Feel the warmth, peacefulness, and serenity of this very special place for you. . . . Whenever you want to become more relaxed, all you have to do is close your eyes, sit quietly, and visualize yourself in this very relaxing place. . . . The more you practice visualizing being in your relaxing place, the quicker you will find yourself becoming relaxed. . . . It will appear to you that your relaxing place has magical, relaxing powers for you, but in reality you are simply relaxing yourself by letting go of your day-to-day concerns and instead focusing on enjoying the peacefulness of your most relaxing place. . . . If you have to give a speech, or are facing some other stressful situation, you can learn to reduce your level of anxiety by simply closing your eyes for a short time and focusing your thoughts on being in your most relaxing place. . . . You always have the power within you to reduce your level of anxiety. . . . All you have to do is close your eyes and visualize being in your very special relaxing place. . . . Feel yourself becoming more relaxed, refreshed, and calm. . . . If you're feeling drowsy, that's fine. . . . Feeling drowsy is an indication that you're becoming more and more relaxed. . . . You're doing fine. . . . Just keep on visualizing being in your very relaxing place. . . . You will become more and more relaxed by simply letting go of your day-to-day concerns and by enjoying this very special relaxing place. . . . [*Continue this imagery relaxation exercise for five or six minutes.*]

Unfortunately, in a minute or so it will be time to return to this class. But there is no hurry. I will slowly count backward from five to one, and then ask you to open your eyes shortly after we reach one. . . . Five, enjoy how relaxed you feel. You may now feel warmer, drowsy, and so relaxed that you feel you don't want to move a muscle. . . . Enjoy this very special feeling. . . . It is healthy to become this relaxed as your immune system functions best when you are relaxed. . . . Four, slowly begin to return to this class. . . . There is no rush. . . . There is no hurry. . . . Take your time to become more alert. Any time you want to relax, all you need to do is use one of these three meditative approaches. With practice you will gradually get better at relaxing by using these approaches. . . . Three, you should now focus on returning in a short time to this class. . . . take your time . . . we still have a half-minute or so. . . . Examine whether you want to make a commitment to using relaxation exercises to reduce the daily stress you encounter. . . . Two, we are nearly at the time to return to this class. . . . You should now work toward becoming more and more alert. . . . One, slowly open your eyes. . . . There is no hurry. . . . Take your time to get oriented. A word of caution: If you have to drive some place soon, please walk around for several minutes before trying to drive a car, as you may be so relaxed now that you may not be alert enough to drive safely.

Step 3: Ask questions such as "What do you think of these three approaches? How relaxed did you get? Did any of you have trouble getting relaxed? If yes, why? Which of the three approaches did you like better and why?" (If the students feel very relaxed and drowsy, they may feel they do not have the energy to respond to these questions. Respect such a "mood" and do not pressure them to respond.) Note: As an additional relaxation technique, obtain and play a muscle relaxation tape, with the class going through the instructions to tense and relax different muscle groups. A variety of audiotapes containing muscle relaxation exercises are available from different sources. As an alternative to playing an audiotape, lead the class in a muscle relaxation exercise by reading the instructions presented earlier in this chapter.

Reality Therapy

The founder of reality therapy is William Glasser (1925–   ). Glasser is a psychiatrist who graduated from Western Reserve Medical School in Cleveland, Ohio, in 1953. In 1956 he became a consulting psychiatrist to the Ventura School for Girls, a California state institution for the treatment of delinquent girls.

Glasser had become skeptical of the value of orthodox psychoanalysis in which he had received training. At the Ventura School for Girls, he set up a treatment program based on the principles of a new approach, which he developed and named *reality therapy*. In developing this approach, he had been highly influenced by Dr. Helmuth Kaiser, an existential psychologist, and by Dr. G. L. Harrington, a psychiatrist who was his supervisor during his psychiatric residency at the University of California at Los Angeles. The reality therapy approach showed promise at Ventura; the girls began to enjoy and express enthusiasm for the program.

Glasser also applied this new approach in his work at a private outpatient clinic with patients having a variety of problems. In 1962 Dr. Harrington was placed in charge of a ward for psychotic patients at a Veterans Hospital in Los Angeles. Following a consultation with Glasser, Harrington successfully applied the reality therapy approach at this hospital, which led to dramatic increases in the discharge rate (Glasser & Zunin, 1979).

These successes led to the publication of this new approach, *Reality Therapy* (Glasser, 1965). In 1966 Glasser began consulting in the California school system and applied the concepts of reality therapy to education. His emphasis on the need for education to highlight involvement, relevance, and thinking is having a profound impact in changing the educational system. In 1969 he published *Schools Without Failure*, which presents suggestions for making education relevant for students, emphasizes developing the thinking capacities of students, and provides suggestions for getting students more involved and interested in getting a quality education.

In 1969 the Institute of Reality Therapy was formed, with Glasser as its first director. The basic principles of reality therapy are increasingly being adopted by counselors and therapists and are being used with clients having a wide variety of problems.

William Glasser: Theories of Personality Development and Psychopathology

Glasser has developed two different theories of personality development and psychopathology: an identity theory, which he developed in the 1960s, and a control theory, which he developed in the 1980s. Both are summarized here, as each has considerable merit in conceptualizing human behavior. We begin with the more recent theory.

Control Theory

Glasser (1984) developed a control theory explanation of human behavior. A major thrust of the theory is that we have pictures in our heads of what reality is like and pictures of how we would like the world to be. Glasser (1984, p. 32) asserted, "All our behavior is our constant attempt to reduce the difference between what we want (the pictures in our heads) and what we have (the way we see situations in the world)."

Some examples may help illustrate what Glasser is theorizing. Each of us has pictures in our head of the physical and personality characteristics of the kind of person we would like to date or form a relationship with; when we find someone who closely matches those characteristics, we seek to form a relationship. Each of us has pictures in our head of our favorite foods; when we are hungry, we select one of those pictures and seek to obtain that food. Each of us has pictures in our head of what we like to do with our leisure time; when we have leisure time, we select one of those pictures and seek to get involved in the activity we select.

How do we develop the pictures in our head that we believe will satisfy our needs? Glasser asserted that we begin to create our picture albums at an early age (perhaps even before birth) and that we spend our whole life enlarging these albums. Essentially, whenever what we do gets us something that satisfies a need, we store the picture of what satisfied us in our personal picture albums. Glasser (1984) gave the following example of this process by describing how a hungry child added chocolate-chip cookies to his picture album:

Suppose you had a grandson and your daughter left you in charge while he was taking a nap. She said she would be right back, because he would be ravenous when he awoke and she knew you had no idea what to feed an eleven-month-old child. She was right. As soon as she left, he awoke screaming his head off, obviously starved. You tried a bottle, but he rejected it—he had something more substantial in mind. But what? Being unused to a howling baby, and desperate, you tried a chocolate-chip cookie and it worked wonders. At first, he did not seem to know what it was, but he was a quick learner. He quickly polished off three cookies. She returned and almost polished you off for being so stupid as to give a baby chocolate. "Now," she said, "he will be yelling all day for those cookies." She was right. If he is like most of us, he will probably have chocolate on his mind for the rest of his life. [p. 19]

When this child learned how satisfying chocolate-chip cookies are, he placed the picture of these cookies in his personal picture album.

By the term *pictures*, Glasser meant *perceptions* from the five senses of sight, hearing, touch, smell, and taste. When we get hungry, or thirsty, or have some other needs or wants, we select one or more pictures from our albums and then try to obtain what that picture represents. For example, if we are really hungry, we may select a picture of a prime rib dinner (or lobster, or two hamburgers) from our album and then seek to obtain what our picture represents.

The pictures in our albums do not have to be rational. Anorexics have a picture that they are too fat and starve themselves to come closer to their irrational picture of unhealthy thinness. Alcoholics have a picture of themselves satisfying many of their needs through alcohol. Child molesters have pictures of satisfying their sexual needs through sexual activities with young children. Rapists have pictures of satisfying their power needs and perhaps sexual needs through sexual assault. To change a picture, we have to replace it with another that will at least reasonably satisfy the need in question. People who are unable to replace a picture may endure a lifetime of misery. Some battered women, for example, will endure brutal beatings and humiliations in marriage because they do not believe they can replace their husbands in their albums.

Glasser noted that whenever there is a difference between the picture we now see and the picture we want, a *signal* is generated by this difference that leads us to behave in a way to obtain the picture we want. We examine our behavioral systems and select from those behaviors one or more that we judge as being the best available behaviors to reduce this difference. These behaviors not only include straightforward problem-solving efforts but also such manipulative strategies as becoming angry, pouting, and trying to make others feel guilty. People who are acting irresponsibly or ineffectually have either failed to select responsible behaviors that they have in their behavioral repertoires or as yet have not learned responsible courses of action for the particular situation they are facing.

Glasser believed humans are driven by five basic, innate needs. As soon as one need is satisfied, another need (or perhaps more than one acting together) pushes for satisfaction. The first basic need is *to survive and reproduce*. Included in this need are such vital functions as breathing, digesting food, sweating, regulating blood pressure, and meeting the demands of hunger, thirst, and sex.

A second need is *to belong—to love, share, and cooperate*. The need is generally met through family, friends, pets, plans, and material possessions such as a beloved car or boat.

A third need is *power*. Glasser said this need involves getting others to obey us and to then receive the esteem and recognition that accompanies power. The drive for power is sometimes in conflict with the need to belong. For example, two people in a relationship may struggle to take control of the relationship, rather than seeking an equalitarian relationship.

A fourth need is *freedom*. People want the freedom to choose how they live their lives, to express themselves, to read and write what they choose, to associate with whom they select, and to worship or not worship as they believe.

A fifth need is *fun*. Glasser believed learning is often fun, which then is a great incentive to assimilate what we need to satisfy our needs. Classes without fun (those that are grim and boring) are major failings of our educational system. Laughing and humor help fulfill our needs for fun. Fun is such a vital part of living that most of us have trouble conceiving how life would be without it.

Glasser added there may be other (yet unidentified) needs in addition to these basic five. He also noted that there are differences among individuals in the intensity of each of these needs. Few people, for example, have such an intense need for power as Adolf Hitler, who wanted to control the world.

Glasser asserted that any theory that contends our behavior is solely a response to outside stimuli or events is wrong. He rejected behaviorism's stimulus-response (S-R) system. He asserted that people are in control of what they do. When a person is thirsty and seeks water (because a glass of water is a thirst-quenching picture in his or her head), the person's behavior is that of a well-functioning control system. An S-R theory, in contrast, would suggest a person would keep drinking (perhaps drinking himself to death) every time he was handed a glass of water.

Identity Theory

Glasser's earlier theory of personality development and psychopathology has been called identity theory. Reality therapy is based on the premise that there is a single basic psychological need faced by everyone: the need for an identity. Glasser and Zunin (1979, p. 302) defined the need for an identity as "the need to feel that each of us is somehow separate and distinct from every other living being on the face of this earth and that no other person thinks, looks, acts, and talks exactly as we do."

Although identity can be viewed from several viewpoints, Glasser believed that from a therapeutic vantage point it is most useful to conceptualize identity in terms of people who develop a *success identity* versus those who develop a *failure identity*.

People who develop a success identity do so through the pathways of *love* and *worth*. People who view themselves as a success must feel that at least one other person loves them, and that they also love at least one other person. They must also feel that at least one other person feels they are worthwhile, and they must feel they (themselves) are worthwhile.

To develop a success identity, a person must experience both love and worth. Glasser and Zunin (1979) stated:

> In reality therapy, we see *worth* and *love* as two very different elements; consider, for example, the extreme case of the "spoiled" child. One may fantasize that a child, if showered with "pure love," whose parents' "goal" was never to frustrate or stress or strain this child in any way, and when he was faced with a task or difficulty always had his parents to perform this task for him, this child always relieved of responsibility would develop into an individual who would feel loved but would not experience worth. Worth comes through accomplishing tasks and achieving success in the accomplishment of those tasks. [p. 312]

A person can also feel worthwhile through accomplishing tasks (for example, a successful businessperson), but believe she is unloved because she cannot name someone she loves and who loves her. Experiencing only one of these elements (worth or love) without the other can lead to a failure identity.

A failure identity is likely to develop when a child has received inadequate love or been made to feel worthless. People with failure identities express their sense of failure by becoming mentally ill, by delinquency, or by withdrawal. Almost everyone with a failure identity is lonely.

Why do some people become "mentally ill"? Glasser indicated that people who are labeled mentally ill are those who deny or distort reality. They change the world in their minds in order to feel important, significant, and meaningful. Having a failure identity is experienced by a person as being intensely discomforting, and changing reality through fantasizing is one way of dealing with this discomfort. Glasser and Zunin (1979) elaborated further:

> The person who is mentally ill has distorted the real world in his own fantasy to make himself feel more comfortable. He denies reality to protect himself from facing the feeling of being meaningless and insignificant in the world around him. For example, both the grandiose delusion and the persecutory delusion of the so-called schizophrenic provide support or solace for him. [p. 313]

Glasser (1976) described the *choice* aspect of those who decide to become "crazy":

> Crazy, psychotic, nuts, loony, bonkers, schizophrenic. There are a dozen popular, as well as pseudoscientific, words for this condition. I happen to prefer "crazy" because it is understandable; it doesn't have the pseudoscientific connotation of schizophrenia, it is not technical, and it emphasizes much better than any of the other terms *the choice aspect* of this category. Schizophrenia sounds so much like a disease that prominent scientists delude themselves into searching for its cure, when the "cure" is within each crazy person who has chosen it. If he can find love or worth he will give up the choice readily—a big "if," I will admit, but hundreds do each day as they are discharged from good hospitals and clinics. With adequate treatment they learn to become strong enough to stop choosing to be crazy. Becoming crazy is actually a fairly sensible choice of the weak because no one expects a crazy person to fulfill his needs in the real world for the obvious reason that he is no longer in it. He now lives in the world of his mind, and there within his own mind, crazy as it may be, he tries to find, and to some extent usually succeeds in finding, a substitute for the adequacy he can't find in reality. Within his own mind, within his own imagination, out of his own thought processes, he may be able to reduce the pain of his failure and find a little relief. For inadequacy he provides delusions of grandeur; for loneliness, hallucinations to keep him company. He may have a delusion that everybody loves him

or that he is an overwhelmingly omnipotent person, which does relieve his pain. Every mental hospital has one or two Jesus Christs, the acme of omnipotence and power. When all of this is created within a person's own mind we call it crazy, but it makes sense to him because it doesn't hurt as much as being lucid but miserably inadequate. [pp. 19–20]

Other individuals try to handle the discomfort of a failure identity through withdrawal or by ignoring reality, even though they are aware of the real world. Glasser and Zunin (1979, p. 313) described these people: "These individuals are referred to as delinquents, criminals, 'sociopaths,' 'personality disorders,' and so on. They are basically the anti-social individuals who choose to break the rules and regulations of society on a regular basis, thereby ignoring reality."

A success identity or a failure identity is not measured by finances or labels but rather in terms of how a person perceives herself or himself. It is possible for individuals to regard themselves as failures while others view them as being successful. Formation of a failure identity usually begins during the years when children first enroll in school. It is about this age (5 or 6) that children develop the social and verbal skills and the thinking capacities to define themselves as being either successful or unsuccessful. As they grow older, children then tend to associate with others having a similar identity; those with failure identities associate with others having a failure identity, and success identities associate with other successful people. As the years pass the two groups associate less and less with each other. Glasser and Zunin (1979, p. 312) noted, "for example, it is indeed rare for a person with a success identity to have, as a close and personal friend, someone who is a known criminal, felon, heroin addict, and so forth." People with success identities tend to compete constructively, meeting and seeking new challenges. Also, they tend to reinforce one another's successes. On the other hand, peo-

ple with failure identities find facing the real world to be uncomfortable and anxiety producing, and therefore choose either to withdraw, to distort reality, or to ignore reality.

Theory of Therapy

In counseling clients, reality therapy advances the following fourteen principles:

1. Encourage Responsible Behavior

The main goal of reality therapy is to help clients reject irresponsible behavior and to learn improved ways of functioning. A responsible person is one who has the ability to fulfill personal needs in a way that does not deprive others of the ability to fulfill their needs. (Glasser indicated that this description of a responsible person is also an excellent guide for determining whether actions are moral or immoral.)

One of the therapist's tasks is to confront clients with their cop-outs. Reality therapists do not excuse clients' irresponsible behavior through theoretical interpretations that blame personal problems on the past actions of parents or on other excuses. Responsibility is emphasized because for clients to feel worthwhile they must feel they are maintaining a satisfactory standard of behavior.

2. Recognize Mental Illness Labels as Destructive

Glasser agreed with Szasz (1961) that mental illness is a myth. Glasser (1965) presented his view:

In consonance with our emphasis on responsibility and irresponsibility, we who practice reality therapy advocate dispensing with the common psychiatric labels, such as neurosis and psychosis, which tend to categorize and stereotype people. Limiting our descriptions to the behavior which the patient manifests, we would, for example, describe a man who believes that

The film *One Flew Over the Cuckoo's Nest*, starring Jack Nicholson, vividly portrays life inside a mental hospital, where the primary objective of an authoritarian staff is to keep patients as docile and obedient as possible. Psychiatric institutions are depicted to be as controlling as jails.

he is President Johnson as irresponsible, followed by a brief description of his unrealistic behavior and thinking. Calling him psychotic or schizophrenic immediately places him in a mental illness category which separates him from most of us, the label thereby serving to compound his problem. Through our description it can immediately be understood that he is unsuccessful in fulfilling his needs. He has given up trying to do so as John Jones and is now trying as President Johnson, a logical delusion for a man who feels isolated and inadequate. The description *irresponsible* is much more precise, indicating our job is to help him to become more responsible so that he will be able to satisfy his needs as himself. [pp. 15–16]

Glasser urged that the word *irresponsible* be used in place of medical model labels of neurotic, psychotic, schizophrenic, and so on.

Glasser raised the question, If we relate to people who have emotional problems as if they are insane and lock them up in a mental institution, how can we expect them to learn to be responsible and productive? Those who adjust to the routine in a mental hospital are in no way learning how to make it in the real world, because a mental institution is an artificial environment in which dysfunctional behavior is expected and excused. Glasser asserted that labeling people as mentally ill sidetracks them onto dwelling on the erroneous notion that they have a "disease of the mind," which no one as yet knows how to treat. Instead, it would be far better to relate to people with emotional and behavioral problems as being people who have an excellent potential (like everyone) to improve and resolve their personal problems. It is well known that the way people are treated is the way they come to perceive themselves. If people are treated as mentally ill, they are apt to perceive themselves as being mentally ill, and they are apt to play that role (perhaps for the rest of their life). On the other hand, if people with emotional problems are related to as being sane, with a high potential to solve their problems, they are much more likely to become responsible and productive (see Exhibit 21.1).

3. **Foster Involved Relationships**

The identity we develop is largely dependent on our involvement with others. In therapy it is important for the therapist to help clients clarify and understand themselves, including their beliefs, values, opinions, and self-concepts.

For a therapist to become involved is also important, as every person at all times must have at least one person who cares about him or her. Cool detachment and aloofness are not considered helpful. Reality therapists seek to become involved through conveying warmth, understanding, and concern.

Reality therapists are *personal* in therapy; that is, they seek to present themselves as real people. They do not project an image of omnipotence but reveal themselves, including their strengths and frailties. When doing so is

Exhibit 21.1
Two approaches to mental illness

Much of the language relating to emotional disturbances has become a familiar part of everyday conversation. We use the following terms to express a judgment (often unfavorable) about unusual behavior or unusual emotions of another person: *crazy, psychotic, neurotic, having a nervous breakdown, insane, sick, uptight, mad.* Whatever term we use, we probably have only a vague idea of its meaning. Amazingly, we act as if the label accurately describes the person, and then we relate to the person as if the label were correct and all-encompassing. However, it is impossible to define these terms precisely—what, for example, are the specific characteristics that separate a "psychotic" from other persons? Can anyone give a precise answer?

There are two general approaches to diagnosing people who display emotional disturbances and abnormal behaviors: the medical model and the interactional model (which asserts that mental illness is a myth).

Medical Model

This model presents emotional and behavioral problems as illnesses, comparable to physical illness. The use of mental illness labels applies medical terminology (for example, schizophrenia, paranoia, psychosis, or insanity) to emotional problems. Adherents of the medical approach believe the disturbed person's mind is affected by some internal condition—usually unknown. That unknown internal condition, they assert, might result from genetic endowment, metabolic disorders, infectious diseases, internal conflicts, unconscious use of defense mechanisms, and traumatic early experiences that cause emotional fixations and prevent future psychological growth.

The medical model has a lengthy classification of mental disorders defined by the American Psychiatric Association. (See Chapter 1 for a summary of the numerous specific mental disorders that are classified in DSM-III-R [1987].)

The medical model approach arose in reaction to the historical notion that the emotionally disturbed were possessed by demons, were mad, and were to be blamed for their disturbances. These people were "treated" by being beaten, locked up, or killed. The medical model treated the disturbed as in need of help, stimulated research into the nature of emotional problems, and promoted the development of therapeutic approaches.

Interactional Model

Critics of the medical (mental illness) approach assert that medical labels have no diagnostic or treatment value and may actually have an adverse labeling effect. Thomas Szasz (1961) was one of the first authorities to assert that mental illness is a myth—that it does not exist. Szasz's theory is interactional; it focuses on the processes of everyday social interaction and the effects of labeling.

Beginning with the assumption that the term *mental illness* implies a "disease of the mind," Szasz categorized all so-called mental illnesses into three types of emotional disorders and discussed the inappropriateness of calling them "mental illnesses":

1. *Personal disabilities,* such as excessive anxiety, depression, fears, and feelings of inadequacy. (Another term for personal disabilities is "unwanted emotions.") Szasz said such so-called mental illnesses may be appropriately considered "mental" (in the sense that thinking and feeling are "mental" activities), but he asserts that they are not diseases.

2. *Antisocial acts,* such as bizarre homicides and other social deviations. (Homosexuality used to be listed in this category but was removed from the American Psychiatric Association's list of mental illnesses in 1974.) Szasz said such antisocial acts are actually social deviations, and not "mental" or "diseases."

3. *Deterioration of the brain with associated personality changes.* This category includes the "mental illnesses" in which personality changes result from brain deterioration caused by arteriosclerosis, chronic alcoholism, AIDS, general paresis, or serious brain injury. Common symptoms are loss of memory, listlessness, apathy, and deterioration of personal grooming habits. Szasz says these disorders can appropriately be considered "diseases," but are diseases of the *brain* rather than of the *mind.*

Szasz (1961) asserted that calling people with emotional problems "mentally ill" is as absurd as calling the emotionally disturbed "possessed":

The belief in mental illness as something other than man's trouble in getting along with his fellow man is the proper heir to the belief in demonology and witchcraft. Mental illness exists or is "real" in exactly the same sense in which witches existed or were "real." [p. 84]

In reality, there are three steps to being labeled "mentally ill": the person displays some deviant behavior, the behavior is not tolerated by the family or community, and the professional labeler, usually a psychiatrist, believes in the medical model and assigns a mental illness label. Thomas Scheff (1966) and David Mechanic (1962) offered evidence that family and community intolerance of deviant behavior and the professional labeler's belief in the medical model are more crucial than the behavior itself in determining whether someone will be labeled "mentally ill."

The point that Szasz and other authorities make is that people have emotional problems, not mystic "mental illnesses." They believed that the following terms are useful in describing behavior: depression, anxiety, obsession, compulsion, excessive fear, feelings of failure. These terms describe personal problems. Medical terms (for example, schizophrenia or psychosis) are not useful because no distinguishing symptom indicates whether a person has, or does not have, the "illness." In addition, Offer and Sabshin (1966) pointed out that there is considerable variation among cultures regarding what is defined as mental illness. Indeed, psychiatrists themselves frequently disagree about which "medical" diagnosis should be assigned to someone who is disturbed (Kolb, Bernard, & Dohrenwend, 1969).

In a dramatic study, psychologist David Rosenhan (1973) demonstrated that professional staff in mental hospitals could not distinguish between "sane" and "insane" people. Rosenhan and seven "normal" associates went to 12 mental hospitals in five different states and claimed to hear voices. After they were admitted, these pseudo-patients said they had stopped hearing the voices. Although they then began to behave completely normally, the hospital personnel were unable to recognize the difference between their sanity and the "insanity" of the other patients. The pseudo-patients were kept confined to the hospitals for an average of 19 days and were then discharged with a diagnosis of "schizophrenia in remission."

The use of such medical labels has several adverse labeling effects. The person labeled mentally ill (and frequently the therapist) believes that the person has a disease for which unfortunately there is no known "cure." The label gives the labeled person an excuse for not taking responsibility for his or her actions (for example, innocent by reason by insanity). Since there is no known "cure," the disturbed frequently idle away their time waiting for someone to discover a cure, rather than assuming responsibility for their behavior, examining the reasons that there are problems, and making efforts to improve. Other undesirable consequences of being labeled mentally ill are that those so labeled may lose some of their legal rights (Szasz, 1963); may be stigmatized in social interactions as being dangerous, unpredictable, untrustworthy, or of "weak" character (Phillips, 1963); and may find it more difficult to secure employment or receive a promotion (Lemert, 1951).

An even more harmful effect is the labeled person's tendency to view himself or herself as different—as "mentally ill"—and therefore to begin playing the role of the "sick" person. Everyone needs to evaluate feelings, opinions, and abilities. In the absence of any objective, nonsocial criteria, people rely on other people to gauge the validity of beliefs and feelings. If others define a person as mentally ill and react to that person accordingly, the person may begin to say, "I must be crazy, because other people treat me as if I were insane."

Authorities who adhere to the interactional model raise a key question, because expectations generally guide behavior: "If we relate to people with emotional problems as if they were mentally ill, how can we expect them to act in emotionally healthy and responsible ways?"

Compared to a physical illness, a diagnosis of mental illness carries a greater stigma. In 1972 Senator Thomas Eagleton was forced to withdraw his candidacy for vice-president on the Democratic ticket after it was revealed that he had received electroshock treatments for depression. The leaders of the Democratic party feared that the public would conclude that someone who had received psychiatric help would be too "unstable" and "dangerous" to be president. On the other hand, Franklin D. Roosevelt had a physical disability resulting from polio but was elected president four times.

(continued)

Exhibit 21.1
Two approaches to mental illness *(continued)*

Szasz (1967) also argued that the mental illness approach is used (perhaps unintentionally) as a means of control over people who do not conform to social expectations. The former Soviet Union had a long history of labeling dissenters (including poets, writers, and intellectuals who would be respected in this country) as mentally ill and sending them to concentration camps or to insane asylums. In the past, psychiatrists in Russia often concluded that people who did not accept Marxist-Leninist philosophy were psychologically impaired. Are some psychiatrists using the mental illness label to control the behavior of nonconformists in our country? Szasz (1967) asserted that they are. As an example, he cites the listing of homosexuality as a mental disorder by the American Psychiatric Association prior to 1974. As another example, Szasz (1963) quoted Dana L. Farnsworth, a Harvard psychiatrist and an authority on college psychiatric services:

Library vandalism, cheating and plagiarism, stealing in the college or community stores or in the dormitories, unacceptable or antisocial sexual practices (overt homosexuality, exhibitionism, promiscuity), and the unwise and unregulated use of harmful drugs are examples of behavior that suggest the presence of emotionally unstable persons. [p. 76]

Mental illness labels do have a "boundary" effect, defining what behaviors a society considers "sick" and pressuring citizens to avoid such behaviors. Szasz's point is that many nonconformists are adversely affected by the use of the medical model to control their behavior.

Labeling as the Primary Cause of Chronic "Mental Illness"

A legitimate question that is sometimes asked is "If mental illness does not exist, who do some people go through life as if they were mentally ill?" Scheff (1966) has developed a theory that provides an answer. His main hypothesis is that labeling is the most important determinant of chronic functional "mental illness." Scheff began by first arriving at a definition of *mental illness*.

One source of immediate embarrassment to any social theory of "mental illness" is that the terms used in referring to these phenomena in our society prejudge the issue. The medical metaphor "mental illness" suggests a determinant process which occurs within the individual: the unfolding and development of disease. In order to avoid this assumption, we will utilize sociological, rather than medical concepts to formulate the problem. [p. 31]

He stated that the symptoms of mental illness can be viewed as violations of social norms, and that for his purposes the term *mental illness* would be used to refer to those assigned such a label by professionals (usually psychiatrists).

Scheff indicated that literally thousands of studies have been conducted in recent years seeking to identify the origins of long-term mental disorders. Practically all of these studies have sought to identify the causes as being somewhere inside a person (for example, metabolic disorders, unconscious conflicts, heredity factors). These research efforts have been based on medical and psychological models of human behavior. Yet, amazingly, in spite of this extensive research, the determinants of chronic mental disorders (such as schizophrenia) are largely unknown.

Scheff suggested that researchers may well be looking in the wrong direction for determinants; instead of seeking causes inside a person, he suggested the major determinants are in social processes (that is, in interactions with others).

Scheff's theory is summarized here. Everyone, at times, violates social norms and commits acts that could be labeled symptoms of mental illness. For example, a person may on occasion angrily engage in fights with others, or experience intense depression or grief, or be highly anxious, or use drugs or alcohol to excess, or have a fetish, or be an exhibitionist, or commit a highly unusual and bizarre act.

Usually the person who has unwanted emotions or who commits deviant acts is not identified (labeled) as being mentally ill. In such cases, the unwanted emotions and deviant actions are usually not classified as symptoms of a mental illness but instead are ignored, unrecognized, or rationalized in some other manner.

Occasionally, however, such norm violations are perceived by others as being "abnormal." The offenders are then labeled mentally ill, and consequently related to as if they were mentally ill. When people are publicly labeled, they are highly suggestible to cues from others. They realize they have done something unusual and turn to others to obtain an assessment of who they really are. In the absence of objective measures of their sanity, they rely on others for this assessment. If others relate to them as if they are mentally ill, they begin to define and perceive themselves as being mentally ill.

Traditional stereotypes of mental illness define the mentally ill role, both for those who are labeled mentally ill and for people they interact with. Frequently people they interact with reward them for enacting the social role of being mentally ill. They are given such rewards as sympathy and attention, excused from being expected to hold a job, excused from fulfilling requirements of other roles, and excused from being held responsible for their wrongdoings.

In addition, people labeled mentally ill are punished for attempting to return to conventional roles. They are viewed with suspicion, implicitly considered to still be insane, and have considerable difficulty in obtaining employment or in receiving a job promotion.

Such pressures and interactions with others gradually lead to changes in their self-concept; they begin to view themselves as different, as being insane.

Often a vicious circle is created. The more they enact the role of being mentally ill, the more they are defined and treated as mentally ill; and the more explicitly they are defined as being mentally ill, the more they are related to as if they are mentally ill; and so on. Unless this vicious circle is interrupted, Scheff suggested it would lead to a career of long-term mental illness. Scheff concluded that with this process, labeling is the single most important determinant of chronic mental illness.

If labeling is an important determinant of chronic functional mental illness, significant changes are suggested in certain diagnostic and treatment practices. Mental health personnel are frequently faced with uncertainty in deciding whether a person has a mental disorder. An informal norm has been developed to handle this uncertainty; when in doubt, it is better to judge a well person ill than to judge an ill person well. This norm is based on two assumptions taken from treating physical illness: (1) a diagnosis of illness results in only minimal damage to the status and reputation of a person, and (2) unless the illness is treated, the illness will become progressively worse. However, both of these assumptions are questionable. Unlike medical treatment, psychiatric treatment can drastically change a person's status in the community; for example, it can remove rights that are difficult to regain. Furthermore, if Scheff is right that labeling is the key determinant in leading to long-term mental illness, the exact opposite norm should be established to handle uncertainty; namely, when in doubt, do not label a person mentally ill. This would be in accord with the legal approach that follows the norm, "When in doubt, acquit," or "a person is innocent until proven guilty."

If labeling is indeed a major determinant of mental illness, certain changes are also suggested in treating violators of social norms. One is to attempt to maintain people with problems in their local community without labeling them mentally ill or sending them to a mental hospital where their playing the role of the mentally ill is apt to be reinforced. In the past several years, the field of mental hygiene has been moving in this direction. Another outgrowth of Scheff's theory would be increasing public education efforts to inform the general public of the nature of emotional and behavioral problems, and the adverse effects that result from inappropriate labeling.

The adverse effects of labeling ultimately raise the issue of the value of labeling anyone mentally ill.

SOURCE: This material is adapted from the following articles: (1) Charles Zastrow, "When Labeled Mentally Ill," in *The Personal Problem Solver*, edited by Charles Zastrow and Dae H. Chang, © 1977, pp. 163–169. Adapted by permission of Prentice-Hall, Inc., Englewood Cliffs, New Jersey; (2) Charles Zastrow, "Understanding Deviant Behavior," in *Talk to Yourself: Using the Power of Self-Talk*, © 1979, pp. 117–124. Adapted by permission of Prentice-Hall, Inc., Englewood Cliffs, New Jersey.

appropriate and constructive, reality therapists will personalize the counseling by self-disclosing their own experiences.

Glasser and Zunin (1979) further elaborated on being personal and involved:

> The purpose of becoming personal in reality therapy is to help people become involved with someone who can help them understand that there is more to life than focusing on misery or symptoms or irresponsible behavior. However, it is an important part of the caring relationship to define the limits of involvement. It is not possible for a therapist to become deeply involved with everyone who comes for help. He becomes involved only within the context of the office. The therapist must be honest about this. . . .
>
> The therapist must define the situation so the patient understands exactly what the relationship is, where it is, and where it is going. [p. 317]

4. Focus on Present and Future

Reality therapists believe that what we want now and in the future, along with our motivation to achieve what we want, is more important than our past experiences in determining what our future will be. The past is fixed; it cannot be changed. All that can be changed is the present and the future. Past experiences brought us to the present but in no way should be used as justification for irresponsible behavior now and in the future. Permitting a person to dwell on the past is a waste of time. If the past is discussed, it is always related to current behavior. For example, if a person describes a broken romance that occurred several years ago, the therapist will ask how that event is related to the client's present behavior.

5. Focus on Behavior Rather Than on Feelings

Feelings and actions are considered to be interrelated and mutually reinforcing. Reality therapists assume that humans have only limited control over their feelings. Changing actions of clients is considered to be the most productive way to help them feel better. Glasser and Zunin (1979, p. 317) noted, "We cannot order ourselves to *feel* better but we can always order ourselves to *do* better, and so *doing better* makes us *feel better.*"

Reality therapists believe it is important for clients to become aware of what they are doing that is leading them into difficulty. If a client states, "I have really felt sad and miserable the last few weeks," a reality therapist will say, "What are you doing to make yourself depressed?" Or if a client indicates at some length that he is unhappily married, the reality therapist will ask such questions as "What are you doing that contributes to the unhappiness?" and "What are you planning to do about your unhappiness?"

6. Encourage Value Judgments

Reality therapists believe people need to learn to evaluate their own behavior and assess what they are doing to contribute to their failures before they can be assisted. This therapy is persistent in guiding clients to explore their actions for signs of irresponsible behavior. Therapists repeatedly ask clients what their current behavior is accomplishing and whether it is meeting their needs. Reality therapists believe people do not change irresponsible behavior unless they first understand what they are doing.

A major task for reality therapists is to help clients face the morality of their behavior. Reality therapists seek to help clients judge whether their behavior is irresponsible. Clients are assisted in seeing that their behavior is irresponsible whenever they are hurting themselves or hurting others—and this judgment is to be made by clients. Therapists generally do not make value judgments for clients as this would relieve them of the responsibility for their behavior.

By questioning *what* the person is doing now and *what* he or she can do differently, the therapist conveys a belief in the person's ability to behave responsibly.

7. Encourage Planning

Reality therapists seek to explore problems in depth with clients and then to explore alternative solutions and their consequences. If a client cannot develop a personal plan for future action, the therapist will help develop one. Once the plan is worked out, a contract is drawn up and signed by the client and the therapist. The plan is usually a realistic plan for behaving differently in matters in which the client admits to acting irresponsibly. If the contract is broken, a new one is designed and agreed on. Plans are also generally made for the contract to be reviewed periodically.

Commitment is a keystone in reality therapy. It is only from making and following through with plans that people gain a sense of self-worth and maturity.

8. Reject Excuses

Glasser realized that not all plans and commitments made by clients will be achieved. But he did not encourage searching for reasons to justify irresponsible behavior; to do so would support a belief that clients have acceptable reasons for not doing what they have agreed was within their capabilities. Excuses let people off the hook; they provide temporary relief, but they eventually lead to more failure and to a failure identity.

When a client fails to meet a commitment, the therapist simply asks, "Are you planning to meet your commitment?" If the answer is in the affirmative, the therapist asks, "When?" Or the therapist may suggest working together to develop a new contract.

In not accepting excuses, the therapist does not seek to deprecate or demean the client for failing, but seeks to convey that a reasonable plan for improvement is always possible.

9. Eliminate Punishment

Punishing persons when they fail to meet a commitment reinforces a failure identity. It also usually leads to more hostility without producing positive, lasting changes. It serves as only a temporary means of forcing different behavior. When clients no longer believe they are under surveillance, they will usually return to exhibiting irresponsible behavior.

Eliminating punishment is quite different, according to Glasser, from following through on the natural consequences of behavior involved in contractual planning.[1] For example, if a runaway youth contracts to receive shelter at a runaway center on the condition that she will remain drug free and then is caught smoking pot, the center must follow through on the consequences spelled out in the contract, which may include removal from the shelter. Not following through on such consequences would only reinforce the irresponsible behavior.

10. Do Not Offer Sympathy

Sympathy does little more than convey the therapist's lack of confidence in the client's ability to act more responsibly. Listening to long, sad stories about the client's past or sympathizing with a person's misery will do nothing to improve that person's ability to lead a responsible life.

11. Rarely Ask Why

Asking a client the reasons for irresponsible actions implies that such explanations make a difference. The reality therapist believes that irresponsible behavior is just that, regardless of the reasons. Listening to explanations for irresponsible behavior is not only time-consuming, it may also be counterproductive as it may lead the client to conclude that the irresponsible behavior can continue if he or she

---

[1]Glasser has a minor conceptual problem in this area, since learning theory defines following through on consequences as being a form of punishment.

Case Example

A reality therapy group

Several years ago when I was employed as a social worker at a maximum security hospital for the criminally insane, my supervisor requested that I develop and be a leader for a therapy group. When I asked such questions as "What should be the objectives of such a group?" and "Who shall be selected to join?" my supervisor indicated those decisions would be mine. He added that no one else was doing any group therapy at this hospital, and the hospital administration thought it would be desirable to develop group therapy programs for accountability reasons.

I was wary because I was newly employed and had never been a leader for a group before. I asked myself, "Who is in the greatest need of group therapy?" and "If the group members do not improve, or if they deteriorate, how will I be able to explain this—that is, cover my tracks?" I concluded that I should invite those identified as being the "sickest" (those labeled as chronic schizophrenic) to be members of the group. Those labeled as chronic schizophrenic are generally expected to show little improvement. With such an expectation, if they did not improve, I felt I would not be blamed. However, if they did improve, I thought it would be viewed as a substantial accomplishment. Having been trained in reality therapy in graduate school, I decided to use this approach with this group.

I first read the case records of all the residents (11) who were diagnosed as chronic schizophrenic. I then met individually with each of the residents to invite them to join the group. (To my surprise, each of the residents appeared to be very different from the impressions I received from reading the case records.) I explained the purpose of the group and the probable topics that would be covered. I then invited them to join; 8 of the 11 who were contacted decided to join. Some frankly stated they would join mainly because it would look good on their record and increase their chances for an early release.

At the first meeting, the purpose and the focus of the group was again presented and described. I explained that the purpose was not to review their past but to help them make their present life more enjoyable and meaningful and to help them plan for the future. Various topics would be covered including how to convince the hospital staff they no longer needed to be hospitalized; how to prepare themselves for returning to their home community (for example, learning an employable skill while at the institution); what to do when they felt depressed or had some other unwanted emotion; and, following their release, what they should do if and when they had an urge to do something that would get them into trouble again. I further explained that occasional films covering some of these topics would be shown and then discussed, and that the group would meet for about an hour each week for the next 12 weeks (until the fall when I had to return to school).

This focus on improving their current circumstances stimulated their interest, but soon they found it uncomfortable and anxiety producing to examine what the future might hold for them. The fact that they were informed they had some responsibility and some control of that future also created anxiety. They reacted to this discomfort by stating they were labeled mentally ill and therefore had some internal condition causing their strange behavior. Since a cure for schizophrenia had not yet been found, they stated they could do little to improve their situation.

They were informed their excuses were "garbage" (stronger terms were used), and we spent a few sessions getting them to understand that the label "chronic schizophrenic" was meaningless. I spent considerable time explaining that mental illness was a myth (that is, people do not have a "disease of the mind," even though they may have emotional problems). I went on to explain that what had gotten them locked up was their deviant behavior. I added that they held the key for getting released—that key was simply to act "sane."

The next set of excuses they tried was that their broken homes, or ghetto schools, or broken romances, or something else in their past had "messed them up," and therefore they could do little about their situation. They were informed such excuses were also "garbage." True, their past experiences were important in getting them here. But I emphasized that what they wanted out of the future, along with their motivation to do something about achieving their goals, was more important than their past experiences in determining what their future held.

Finally, after we had worked through a number of excuses we were able to focus on how they could better handle specific problems, such as how to handle being depressed, how to stop exhibiting behavior considered "strange," how to present themselves as being "sane" in order to increase their chances of an early release, how they would feel and adjust to returning to their home communities, what kind of work or career they desired on their release, and how they could prepare themselves by learning a skill or trade while at this institution. Another focus was to help them examine what they wanted out of the future and the specific steps they would have to take to achieve their goals.

The results of this approach were very encouraging. Instead of idly spending much of the time brooding about their situation, they became motivated to improve it. At the end of the 12 weeks (when I had to return to school), the 8 members of the group spontaneously stated that the meetings were making a positive change in their lives and requested that another social worker from the hospital be assigned to continue the group. This was arranged. Three years later on a return visit to the hospital I was told that 5 of the 8 group members had been released to their home communities; 2 were considered to have shown improvement; while the final group member's condition was described as "unchanged."

SOURCE: This case example is adapted from an illustration of a therapy group presented in Charles Zastrow's *Introduction to Social Welfare Institutions,* 2nd ed. (Pacific Grove, CA: Brooks/Cole, 1982), pp. 512–516.

continues to offer explanations (which are often contrived). By giving little attention to such explanations, the reality therapist conveys that responsible behavior is expected.

12. Praise Responsible Behavior
People need recognition for their positive accomplishments and for their positive efforts in *trying* to accomplish something even though they may not succeed. Reality therapists reinforce and praise such responsible behavior.

They also seek to convey that they believe people are capable of changing their irresponsible behavior. It is easier to do things well when others are encouraging and realistically optimistic.

13. Question Traditional Case Histories

Traditional case histories emphasize the failures, shortcomings, problems, and traumas that the client has to cope with. Such case histories are often tragic and notorious misrepresentations. They usually tell more about the theoretical orientation of the writer than about the client, as they try to reinterpret clients' behaviors and feelings in terms of diagnostic labels. Rarely do case histories provide an assessment of the person's successes and personality strengths, which are at least as important in understanding a person as that person's shortcomings and failures.

14. Foster Success Experiences

In helping clients develop plans to improve their circumstances, the reality therapist strives to help them achieve *realistic* goals and to understand and master the tasks (means) involved in accomplishing these goals. To counteract failure identities, clients need to begin to take risks and experience successes. Gradually such successes lead clients to perceive themselves more positively.

Evaluation

Reality therapy is a commonsense approach to therapy that is sensible and rational. It affirms a firm belief in the dignity of humans and their ability to improve their situations. The concept of personal responsibility for one's own behavior has broad applications. It is through a sense of individual responsibility that meaningful personal growth occurs. The goal of therapy is to help clients identify their irresponsible behavior and then learn to be more responsible. This goal provides a very useful focus for counseling people. Compared to other therapy approaches, the concepts of this approach are relatively simple to learn and apply, which is a distinct advantage.

Reality therapy differs substantially from psychoanalysis. Glasser (1965) discussed these differences, which are briefly summarized in Table 21.1.

Research studies have found reality therapy to be substantially more effective than psychoanalysis in producing positive therapeutic changes (Eysenck, 1965; Stuart, 1970).

Reality therapy has been successfully applied in a variety of settings, including corrections, mental health, education, unemployment, public welfare, and in treating delinquency.

Some criticisms of reality therapy can also be made:

1. Glasser asserted that the way to change unwanted emotions (such as depression, guilt) is by first changing the actions of clients. Although getting involved in meaningful activity may be one way of alleviating unwanted emotions, it is not the only way. Ellis (1962) demonstrated that all emotions, including unwanted emotions, are primarily caused by what people are thinking. Ellis has shown that changing clients' thoughts in a more positive and rational direction is also a very useful approach to alleviating unwanted emotions. (This concept will be further expanded in the next chapter when *rational therapy* is described.)

2. Glasser asserted that having a failure identity is a major determinant of having emotional problems and of becoming involved in irresponsible behavior. Yet, his theory fails to explain why some people become depressed while others become highly anxious, or explode in anger, or are shy, or experience guilt and shame. Also, his theory does not explain why some people behave irresponsibly by becoming involved in burglary while others commit murder, or rape, or extortion, or white-collar crimes, or neglect their children, and so on. Reality therapy, at best, provides only a partial explanation for the causes of emotional problems and irresponsible behavior.

Psychoanalysis	Reality Therapy
1. Mental illness exists.	1. The concept of mental illness is not accepted.
2. Therapist probes deep into client's past life.	2. Focus is on the present and the future.
3. Therapist should relate to patients as a neutral figure to further transference.	3. Therapist should relate as a genuine, real person.
4. Unconscious processes and conflicts are emphasized.	4. Unconscious processes and conflicts are deemphasized.
5. Patients are not responsible for their deviant behaviors, which are caused by unconscious motivations and/or mental illness.	5. Clients are responsible for their actions.
6. Patients will spontaneously learn better behavior through insight into the historical and unconscious sources of their problems.	6. Insight into problems will not of itself produce change; clients need to learn to act more responsibly.

Table 21.1
Psychoanalysis versus reality therapy

3. Glasser has advanced two theories of personality development and psychopathology. He first advanced an identity theory and in recent years has advanced a control theory. Glasser has not yet specified how these two theories relate to each other. It is unclear whether he is currently rejecting all or parts of his identity theory. If he now rejects the identity theory, it is unclear how such a rejection would affect reality therapy, as reality therapy was originally based on identity theory. In *Control Theory in the Practice of Reality Therapy: Case Studies,* Glasser (1989) made an effort to address this issue. However, he presented illustrations of the application of both control theory and identity theory to case studies, without providing an explanation of how these theories relate to each other.

Summary

The primary developer of reality therapy is William Glasser. Glasser has developed two theories of personality development and psychopathology—a control theory and an identity theory. Control theory asserts that all human behavior is an attempt to reduce the differences between the pictures in our head of what we want and the way we perceive situations in the world.

Identity theory asserts that the single, basic need that everyone has is the need for identity. People who develop a success identity do so through the pathways of love and worth. A failure identity is likely to develop when a child has received inadequate love or been made to feel worthless. People with failure identities express their discomfort in facing reality by distorting reality (becoming "mentally ill"), by withdrawal, or by ignoring reality (becoming involved in antisocial activities).

The main goal of reality therapy is to help clients reject irresponsible behavior and learn improved ways of functioning. Principles of reality therapy include the following: (1) mental illness is a myth; (2) the therapist should seek to be personal and involved in the therapy; (3) the focus in therapy should be on the present and the future, since the past cannot be changed; (4) the focus in therapy should be on behavior rather than on feelings; (5) clients should make value judgments about what they are doing that contributes to their failures; (6) clients are assisted in developing a plan to alter their irresponsible behavior; (7) excuses are not accepted when a client fails to meet a commitment; (8) the therapist does not punish a client for failing to meet a commitment; and (9) the therapist praises responsible behavior and seeks to help clients achieve realistic goals.

The question regarding whether mental illness exists is examined. Szasz (1961) and other authorities asserted that mental illness labels have no diagnostic or treatment value and may complicate therapy efforts due to labeling effects. These authorities assert that people certainly do have emotional and behavioral problems, but they do not have a disease of the mind as implied by the term *mental illness.*

Scheff's (1966) theory hypothesized that labeling is the single most important determinant of long-term mental illness. If the theory is accurate, significant changes are suggested in diagnostic and treatment practices—for example, attempting to maintain people with problems in their local community without labeling them mentally ill or sending them to a mental hospital.

Reality therapy is increasingly being used by social workers in a wide variety of settings. It is a commonsense approach to therapy that research has found to be effective.

Exercises

1. Counseling with reality therapy

Goal: This exercise is designed to have students practice using the concepts of reality therapy in counseling situations.

Step 1: Describe the purpose of this exercise. Summarize the 14 principles of reality therapy described in this chapter. Indicate that in summary form the basic format of reality therapy involves three phases:

a. Developing a relationship with clients.
b. Exploring problems in depth.
c. Exploring alternatives for resolving these problems.

(There is overlap among these three phases.)

Step 2: Have two volunteers make up a contrived problem that they jointly have. (For example, a husband wants to have children and to have his wife stay home to raise them, while the wife wants a career and does not want to have children.) Ask for two more volunteers to be "counselors" and to use the principles of reality therapy. Have the "counselors" counsel the "clients."

Step 3: Have the class discuss the merits of the counseling that was given and how well the "counselors" used the principles of reality therapy.

2. Does mental illness exist?

Goal: The purpose of this exercise is to have students examine whether mental illness exists.

Step 1: Explain the purpose of the exercise. Also explain that the medical approach assumes that mental illness is a disease of the mind. Adherents of the medical approach believe the disturbed person's mind is affected by some generally unknown internal condition. That unknown internal condition might be due to metabolic disorders, internal conflicts, genetic endowment, unconscious use of defense mechanisms, hormone deficiencies, or traumatic early experiences that cause emotional fixations and prevent future psychological growth.

Step 2: Explain the contrasting approach, first advocated by Thomas Szasz, that mental illness is a myth—that it does not exist. (This approach is described in this chapter.)

Step 3: Ask the students to form subgroups of five and have the subgroups discuss which approach they believe is most accurate. Also ask the subgroups to identify one or more symptoms that will enable professionals to distinguish who is "schizophrenic" or who is "mentally ill" from those who are "sane."

Step 4: Have the subgroups share their conclusions. A debate between subgroups may arise.

22

Rational Therapy

Albert Ellis (1913–   )

The founder of rational therapy is Albert Ellis (1913–   ). Ellis received a Ph.D. in clinical psychology at Columbia University in 1947, where he received training in psychoanalysis. During the late 1940s and early 1950s, he practiced psychoanalytic approaches to therapy but became disenchanted with the results and the approach. Ellis observed that even when patients achieved incredible insight into their childhood and unconscious processes, they continued to retain their emotional difficulties.

Ellis then began developing a new approach, which he named *rational therapy* (also called *rational-emotive therapy*), which seeks to treat clients by challenging and changing their irrational beliefs. Ellis first presented this new approach in 1957 at the annual convention of the American Psychological Association. Shortly afterward, Ellis (1957) was able to demonstrate significantly greater effectiveness with this new approach than with using psychoanalytic approaches.

In 1959 Ellis established the Institute for Rational Living in New York City, which provides adult education courses in rational living and a moderate-cost clinic for clients. In 1968 Ellis founded the Institute for Advanced Study in Rational Psychotherapy, which provides helping professionals with extensive training in rational therapy and also provides seminars and workshops throughout the country. Ellis is also recognized nationally as an authority on sexuality. In addition to running workshops and seminars and being a practicing psychotherapist, he has written nearly 40 books and 400 articles!

Considering its relative newness in the field of psychotherapy, rational therapy has made an enormous impact on both professionals and the public in recent years. Well over 100 books have been published by various authors applying the principles of rational therapy to such areas as assertiveness training, sexuality, adolescence, law and criminality, religion, executive leadership, children's literature, music, feminism, philosophy, personal problems, alcoholism, marriage and the family, and sex adjustment and therapy.

Recent writers on rational therapy (Dyer, 1976; Lembo, 1974; Maultsby, 1975; Zastrow, 1979, 1993b) have modified Ellis's theories of personality development, psychopathology, and therapy. Since these modifications make the approach easier to understand and to apply in therapy, this presentation of rational therapy will incorporate these revisions.

Albert Ellis: Theory of Personality Development and Psychopathology

Self-Talk Determines Our Feelings and Actions

Most people erroneously believe that our emotions and our actions are determined primarily by our experiences (that is, by events that happen to us). On the contrary, rational therapy asserts and has demonstrated (Ellis, 1979) that the primary cause of all our emotions and actions is what we tell ourselves about events that happen to us.

All feelings and actions occur according to the following format:

Events: (Or experiences)
↓
Self-talk: (Self-talk is the set of evaluating thoughts we give ourself about facts and events that happen to us.)
↓
Emotion: (May include remaining calm.)
↓
Actions

This basic principle is not new. The stoic philosopher Epictetus wrote in *The Enchiridion* in the first century A.D., "Men are disturbed not by things, but by the view which they take of them" (Ellis, 1979).

An example will illustrate this process:

Event: A husband unexpectedly arrives home early and on walking into his living rooms sees his wife and an acquaintance embracing.
↓
Self-talk: "My wife and this guy are having an affair—this is awful."
           "This guy is threatening my personal life."
           "This is morally wrong—the worst thing that could happen to me."
↓
           "This guy is violating my rights—I've got to forcefully protect my rights."
↓
Emotion: Anger, rage, and a vengeful feeling.
↓
Action: Running at the acquaintance and physically getting into a fight.

If, on the other hand, the husband remembers that his wife and the acquaintance are preparing to put on a romantic play at a nearby college, the following may occur:

Event: A husband unexpectedly arrives home early and on walking into his living room sees his wife and an acquaintance embracing.
↓
Self-talk: "Well, apparently they're only practicing for the play."
           "I'll watch closely, but I don't think there is anything romantic occurring."
           "There is no reason for me to get upset and make a fool of myself."
↓
Emotion: More emotionally relaxed and calm, although somewhat wary.
↓
Action: Casually making small talk with his wife and the acquaintance, while observing their interactions.

The most important point about this process is that our self-talk determines how we feel and act; by changing our self-talk, we can change how we feel and act. Generally we cannot control events that happen to us, but we have the power to think rationally and thereby change *all* of our unwanted emotions and ineffective actions.

Maultsby (1977) indicated thinking and behavior is rational if it

a. Is based on objective reality (that is, fits the facts).
b. Helps us to protect our lives.
c. Helps us to achieve our short- and long-term goals most quickly.
d. Helps us to avoid significant trouble with other people.
e. Helps us to feel the emotions we want to feel.

If our thoughts or our actions conflict with one or more of these criteria, they are considered to be irrational.

Frequently we do not have the power to control the events we encounter. However, we always have the capacity to tell ourselves rational thoughts about each of our experiences. John Lembo (1974, p. 9) notes:

> We can think rationally or irrationally about *the things that will happen to us* and insist that we will not be a failure if our boss fires us or that we will be a worthless no-account if we are dismissed from our job; that nothing catastrophic will happen if our parents die or that it will be horrible and unbearable if they do die.

Since we determine our feelings and our behaviors via self-talk, we are literally in control of our lives. If we are unhappy, unfulfilled, unsatisfied, frustrated, depressed, grief-stricken, or whatever, it is primarily our doing. Lembo (1974, p. 10) notes, "We have the ability to create a satisfying life for ourselves, and we will succeed in doing so if we rationally manage the thoughts we tell ourselves."

Personality Development and Self-Concept Formations.[1]

Webster's Ninth New Collegiate Dictionary (1983) defines personality as "the totality of an individual's behavioral and emotional characteristics."

According to this definition, our personality is composed of our emotions and our behaviors. Accepting such a definition leads to the conclusion that it is our self-talk that primarily controls our personality, as we have earlier seen that our self-talk determines our emotions and our behaviors.

[1]This section is adapted from Charles Zastrow, *Talk to Yourself: Using the Power of Self-Talk*, © 1979, pp. 85–88. Adapted by permission of Prentice-Hall, Inc., Englewood Cliffs, New Jersey.

Most personality theorists have focused on outside events in describing how our personality develops. Sigmund Freud, for example, focused on early traumatic childhood experiences, and on the nature of the relationships between parents and the child. Relatively few personality theorists have focused on the development of our thinking processes, which we have seen primarily determine our emotions and behaviors.

Our sense of identity (our sense of who and what we are) refers to the general, ongoing sets of self-talk related to the kind of person each of us is. (Other writers have referred to the sense of identity as being our self-concept, or our self-image.) Our sense of identity is *the* key element of our personality and refers to the usual sets of self-talk that control perhaps 90 percent of our emotions and actions.

The question of how our personality develops essentially involves how our self-concept develops. Identity development is a lifetime process. It begins during the early years and continues to change throughout our lifetime. During the early years, our sense of identity is largely determined by the reactions of others.

A long time ago, Cooley (1902) discussed this early labeling process as resulting in the "looking-glass self"; that is, persons develop their self-concept (sense of who and what they are) in terms of how they perceive that others relate to them, as if others were a looking-glass or mirror. For example, if a person receives respect from others and is praised for his positive qualities, that person is apt to feel good about himself, will gradually develop a positive sense of worth, will generally be happy, and will seek responsible and socially acceptable ways to continue to maintain the respect of others. On the other hand, if others relate to this person as if he is irresponsible, he is likely to begin to view himself as being irresponsible and gradually develop a negative self-concept; with such a view of himself, he decreases his efforts to act responsibly. In both these examples, the ways that others relate to a person (positively or negatively) become a self-fulfilling prophecy.

The labeling process undoubtedly has a substantial influence in shaping behavior. Yet, it fails to explain why children may be treated essentially the same and yet engage in very different behavior and develop substantially different self-concepts. We have all heard stories about children, raised essentially the same (in a ghetto or in an upper-class suburb) who develop vastly different lifestyles, with one becoming involved in a life of crime, while another becomes a law abiding, productive community leader. Why?

The following theory of self-concept development is adapted from the work of the Soviet psychologists Luria (1961) and Vygotsky (1962).

Phase I: Initially a child's behavior is determined by internal physical needs (such as hunger) and outside events (such as parental actions).

Phase II: The child begins to learn to control his or her behavior in line with the verbal instructions and reactions of external agents (such as parents).

Phase III: The verbal instructions and reactions of external people lead to the development of elementary beliefs. Based on these elementary beliefs, the child begins to regulate some of his or her own actions through self-talk.

Phase IV: Future behavior patterns are then developed through an interaction of events and self-talk about those events. Repeated sets of self-talk become covert (that is, go *underground,* to use Vygotsky's term) and become attitudes, beliefs, and values.

Phase V: These attitudes, beliefs, and values form our sense of who and what we are. Our self-talk (based on our beliefs, attitudes, and values) about events that happen to us then largely controls our emotions and actions.

The diagram in Exhibit 22.1 shows how events and self-talk interact to form our self-concepts and our personalities.

Given this theoretical material, let us return to the question of why, when two children have essentially the same experiences, they may develop very different personalities (that is, emotions and behaviors). The reason is that their self-talk about their experiences may vary.

For example, if an 8-year-old child is caught for shoplifting candy and is spanked by her parents, a wide range of self-talk is possible. If the child says, "I have done wrong. Stealing is wrong. Somehow I have got to restore my parent's trust in me," the child's inclinations to steal will be sharply reduced. However, if the child says the following to herself, shoplifting attempts are apt to continue: "Shoplifting is exciting. It's a way for me to get what I want. This is the first time I've been caught. Guess I was careless. I'll have to be more careful the next time." In a given situation, the self-talk of different people will vary because (1) the values, beliefs, attitudes, and desires on which self-talk is based will vary among individuals; and (2) each person has thousands of different values and beliefs, and in a particular situation, each person will somewhat haphazardly select only a few of these beliefs and values to base his or her self-talk on.

In summary, two components largely determine the personality of any individual: (1) the experiences that a person has, and (2) the self-talk that a person gives himself or herself about the experiences. Of these two components, self-talk is the key element in developing and perpetuating everyone's personality.

Additional Aspects of Self-Talk

With repeated occurrences of an event, a person's emotional reactions to that event become nearly automatic because the person rapidly gives himself or herself a set of self-

Exhibit 22.1
Formation of our self-concept and our personality

Events (experiences)
↓
Self-talk ⟶ Ongoing, repeated sets of self-talk be- ⟶ Self-talk (which is based on our atti-
come attitudes, values, and beliefs. tudes, beliefs, and needs) about our
(Beliefs about who and what we are experiences determines all of our
↓ form our *self-concept*.) emotions and behaviors (namely,
Immediate emotions our *personality*, which is composed
↓ of our emotions and behaviors).
Immediate actions

talk gradually acquired through past experiences. For example, a few years ago I counseled a woman who became intensely emotionally upset every time her husband (who had a drinking problem) came home intoxicated. In examining this situation, it became clear that because of repeated occurrences she would immediately give herself the following extensive set of self-talk on seeing him inebriated:

Self-talk: "He's foolishly spending the money we desperately need in this family."
"He is making a fool of himself and me in that condition."
"He's setting a terrible example for our children."
"One of these days while drunk he's going to get into a serious accident, become incapacitated, and then what will we do?"

Emotions: Anger, frustration, some depression, general unhappiness.

A person may be aware, or unaware, of the self-talk that he is giving himself about a fact or event. If a person is having a discomforting emotion and is unaware of the underlying self-talk, then the focus of counseling initially needs to be on discovering this self-talk. Several years ago I counseled a married woman who expressed a strong desire to want to continue having extramarital affairs but was afraid her husband would discover the affairs and end the marriage. Although she was fully aware of the emotional desire for having affairs, she was unaware of the self-talk generating this feeling. I probed into this area and got her to take a look (undoubtedly for the first time in her life) at the self-talk that was generating the emotional desire to have extramarital sex. After focusing her attention on this, she gradually expressed and became aware of the following underlying self-talk, "I enjoy the feeling of being able to seduce someone to whom I am attracted," "The people I seduce then feel somewhat obligated to me," and "The conquest of someone who is very attractive is three-quarters of the thrill."

Another aspect of self-talk has been labeled as *layering* in which the emotional reaction *(C)* becomes a new event *(A)* by a person giving himself or herself additional self-talk *(B)* about having the initial emotional reaction. Ellis (1973) described layering as follows:

Once the individual becomes emotionally upset—or, rather, upsets himself—another startling human thing frequently occurs. Most of the time, he *knows* that he is anxious, depressed, enraged, or otherwise agitated; and he also generally knows that his symptoms are undesirable and (in our culture) socially disapproved. For who approves or respects highly agitated or "crazy" people? He therefore makes his emotional Consequence *(C)* or symptom into another Activating Event *(A)*.

Thus, he originally starts with something like "*(A)* I did poorly on my job today; *(B)* Isn't that horrible! What a worm I am for failing!" and he winds up with *(C)* feelings of anxiety, worthlessness, and depression. He now starts all over: "*(A)* I feel anxious and depressed, and worthless. *(B)* Isn't *that* horrible! What a worm I am for feeling anxious, depressed, and worthless!" Now he winds up with *(C)* even greater feelings of anxiety, worthlessness, and depression. Or, in other words, once he becomes anxious, he frequently makes himself anxious about being anxious. Once he becomes depressed, he makes himself depressed about *being* depressed. Et cetera! He now has two consequences or symptoms for the price of one; and he often goes around and around in a vicious cycle of (1) condemning himself for doing poorly at some task; (2) feeling guilty or depressed because of his self-condemnation; (3) condemning himself for his feelings of guilt and depression; (4) condemning himself for condemning himself; (5) condemning himself for seeing that he condemns himself and for still not stopping condemning himself; (6) condemning himself for going for psychotherapeutic help and still not getting better; (7) condemning himself for being more disturbed than other individuals; (8) concluding that he is indubitably hopelessly disturbed and that nothing can be done about it; and so on, and so forth. [p. 178]

Self-talk is related to attitudes, beliefs, and values. Although self-talk is often based on our attitudes, beliefs, and values, self-talk is distinct from these terms. Self-talk has a here-and-now quality, since it represents those thoughts that we are giving ourselves at the present time. At any one point in time we hold thousands of beliefs, attitudes, and values, but our self-talk is based on only a fraction of our total set of attitudes and beliefs whenever we think about a fact or event. Our self-talk may also be generated by our needs, wants, desires, drives, and motives.

Understanding Deviant Behavior

Rational therapy maintains that *the reasons for any deviant act (including crime) can be determined by examining what the offender was telling himself or herself before and during the time the act was committed.*

The Charles Manson case will be used to illustrate this concept. On August 9, 1969, actress Sharon Tate was slain in her home, along with four other people. The next night Leno LaBianca (a wealthy president of a grocery chain) and his wife were brutally stabbed to death. In the weeks that followed, Charles Manson and several of his followers were arrested and later convicted of these murders. Charles Manson was head of a commune, "The Family," that lived in Death Valley, California.

Why did Manson and his followers commit these bizarre murders? The prosecuting attorney for the state of California, Vincent Bugliosi, was able to document the following reasons (Bugliosi & Gentry, 1974). Manson hoped that these brutal murders of the prominent and wealthy would create fear and panic among white people. Manson thought that whites, unable to determine who actually did the killing, would conclude these murders were committed by African Americans. He theorized that, out of fear, whites would go into the ghettos and start killing African Americans, causing a race war. Such a war, it was thought, would also lead to a split between liberals and conservatives, who would then begin killing each other. During this time Manson thought the "true black race" (at various times identified by Manson as the "Black Panthers" or the "Black Muslims"[2]) would go into hiding and would be unaffected. After almost all whites had perished, the "true black race" would come out and kill the remaining whites, except for

[2]The Black Panthers and Black Muslims were African American organizations that were active in the civil rights movement in the 1960s and 1970s. Sometimes these organizations advocated the use of physical force to achieve racial equality.

Manson and his followers who would be in hiding in Death Valley. Manson further thought the remaining African Americans would not have the capacities to govern the nation, and that after failing to govern they would turn to him to be the leader of the nation.

Thus, it appears this unrealistic belief system led Manson and his followers to murder seven people. Having an unrealistic belief system does not make a person "crazy." All the defendants in this case were judged by the court to be sane. While living together in isolation in a commune, the members apparently gave mutual support to each other for the accurateness of Manson's beliefs, probably partly because objective evidence was unavailable to refute Manson's interpretations. (Throughout history, various erroneous beliefs have been held at one time or another: the earth was believed to be flat until Columbus's voyage, blood-letting was thought to be therapeutic, thunder was thought to be a god with supernatural powers, people who committed bizarre or criminal acts were thought to be possessed by demons. Probably all of us presently hold certain beliefs that will one day be found to be erroneous.)

Theory of Therapy

The initial focus of therapy is to help clients become aware of the irrational and negative self-talk that is the primary source of their unwanted emotions and irresponsible behaviors. (Unwanted emotions are defined as those emotions that clients desire to change.) After clients become aware of their irrational self-talk, they are instructed and encouraged to challenge such irrational self-talk with a different set of self-talk that is more rational and positive. Developing rational self-challenges to irrational self-talk is done by the client, either through discussions with the therapist or by writing out a "Rational Self-Analysis."

Rational Self-Analysis[3]

Maultsby (1977) developed an approach entitled *Rational Self-Analysis* (RSA) that is very useful in alleviating any undesirable emotion. An RSA has six parts as shown in Exhibit 22.2.

The goal in doing an RSA is to change unwanted emotions (such as anger, guilt, depression, and shyness). An RSA is done by recording the event and self-talk on paper.

Under Part A (facts and events), simply state the facts or events that occurred.

Under Part B (self-talk), write all of your thoughts about A. Number each statement in order (1, 2, 3, 4, and so on). Also write either "good," "bad," or "neutral" after each self-talk statement to show yourself how you believed each B section statement reflected on you as a person. (The RSA example that soon follows illustrates the mechanics of this, and other components, of doing an RSA.)

Under Part C (emotional consequences), write simple statements describing your gut reactions/emotions stemming from your self-talk in B.

Part D(a) is to be written *only* after you have written sections A, B, and C, and *only* after you have reviewed the five questions for rational thinking (described earlier in this chapter). Part D(a) is a "camera check" of the A section. Reread the A section and ask yourself, "If I had taken a moving picture of what I wrote was happening, would the camera verify what I have written as facts?" A moving picture would probably have recorded the facts but not personal beliefs or opinions. Personal beliefs or opinions belong in the B section. A common example of a personal opinion mistaken as a fact is, "Karen made me look like a fool when she laughed at me while I was trying to make a serious point." Under D(a) (camera check of A), correct the opinion

[3]This description of Rational Self-Analysis is adapted from Charles Zastrow, *Talk to Yourself: Using the Power of Self-Talk,* © 1979, pp. 32–36. Adapted by permission of Prentice-Hall, Inc., Englewood Cliffs, New Jersey.

Exhibit 22.2
Format for RSA

A	D(a)
Facts and Events	Camera Check of A
B	D(b)
Self-Talk	Rational Debate of B
1. _____	1. _____
2. _____	2. _____
and so on	and so on
C	E
Emotional	Emotional Goals and
Consequences	Behavioral Goals for
of B	Similar Future Events

part of this statement by only writing the factual part: "I was attempting to make a serious point when Karen began laughing at what I was saying." Then add the personal opinion part of the statement to B (that is, "Karen made me look like a fool.").

Part D(b) is the section designed to challenge and change negative and irrational thinking. Take each B statement separately. Read B–1 first and ask yourself whether it is inconsistent with any of the five questions for rational thinking. It will be irrational if it does one or more of the following:

1. Is not based on objective reality.
2. Hampers you in protecting your life.
3. Hampers you in achieving your short- and long-term goals.
4. Causes significant trouble with other people.
5. Leads you to feel emotions that you do not want to feel.

If the self-talk statement is consistent with the five questions for rational thinking, merely write "that's rational." If, on the other hand, the self-talk statement meets one or more of the guidelines for irrational thinking, then think of an alternative "self-talk" to that B statement. This new self-talk statement is of crucial importance in changing your undesirable emotion, and needs to (1) be rational and (2) be a self-talk statement you are willing to accept as a new opinion for yourself. After

writing down this D(b–1) self-talk in the D(b) section, then consider B–2, B–3, and so on in the same way.

Under Part E, write down the new emotions you want to have in similar future A situations. In writing these new emotions that you desire, keep in mind that they will follow from your self-talk statements in your D(b) section. This section may also contain a description of certain actions you intend to take to help you achieve your emotional goals when you encounter future As.

Since irresponsible behavior (such as overeating, overdrinking, committing crimes, and sexual deviance) is also largely determined by our irrational thinking, rational self-challenges (including doing an RSA) can be effectively used to change irresponsible actions (Lembo, 1974; Maultsby, 1978; Zastrow, 1979). *Rational self-challenges will work only if the client actively practices using the rational self-challenges he or she develops.* They work best when they are used by the client every time he or she starts the original negative, irrational self-talk.

Therapy Is an Educational Process

Learning how to think rationally and to counter irrational and negative self-talk is an educational process. Clients can learn how to analyze and change irrational self-talk in a variety of ways: instruction by the therapist; viewing videotapes and films on rational therapy; reading books and pamphlets on rational therapy and attending workshops or seminars on rational therapy. Ellis has demonstrated that the basic principles of how to analyze irrational self-talk and to think rationally can be successfully taught to elementary and secondary school students.

In therapy, the therapist's role is to instruct clients on how to analyze the irrational self-talk underlying their unwanted emotions and irresponsible behavior. The therapist uses probes, confrontation, explanations, interpretations, humor, and suggestions to help clients discover their irrational thinking.

Case Example

Rational self-analysis: coping with a sexual affair

A 21-year-old woman, Cindy, sought counseling after she was informed by the person she was dating, Jim, that a few months earlier he had become sexually involved with another woman, Linda. Jim and Cindy had dated fairly steadily for the past two years. Both were attending the same college. Prior to their summer break, they were having frequent arguments and decided not to see each other during the summer. When they returned to college in the fall, they again felt strongly about each other and resumed their relationship. A few weeks later, Jim (after Cindy questioned him) informed her that he, on one evening, did become sexually involved with Linda.

Cindy told the counselor that she wanted to better handle the unwanted emotions she was having about this affair. After discussing her feelings in some depth, the counselor informed her that she could counter her undesirable emotions by doing a rational self-analysis (based on rational therapy). The following RSA was written by this coed:

A Facts and events	D(a) Camera check of A
My boyfriend, Jim, informed me that he had sexual relations with Linda, after a party at which they had both been drinking.	This is all factual. I know this because Jim told me himself. Jim and I are very close, and I know he would not lie to me.

B (Self-Talk)		D(b) Your rational debate of B	
B–1	It's not fair! How could Jim do such a thing to me? (bad)	D(b–1)	Jim had sex with Linda. I'll just have to accept that. Because people are human and fallible, it is a mistake to expect that I will always be treated with fairness by others. Besides, Jim and I had broken up, so I'm sure they didn't have me in mind when they did it. At the time they were sexually involved, neither Jim nor I had any commitment to each other. In truth I also considered getting sexually involved this summer and perhaps would have if I had met the right guy.
B–2	That creep just had sex with Linda because he wanted a piece of _____. (bad)	D(b–2)	Jim probably had sex with Linda for other reasons. I know he's not the type that "uses" a woman merely for relief of his sexual tensions. It is also a mistake to label him a creep. No one is a creep. People are

humans. If I mislabel him a creep, it may lead me to view him in terms of an inaccurate label.

B–3   Jim and Linda had no good reasons for doing what they did. They only did it because they were both drunk. What a couple of jerks! (bad)

D(b–3)   I do believe that alcohol had something to do with the fact that Jim and Linda had sex. I know for a fact that Jim becomes much less inhibited when he has had a few drinks. I don't know about Linda, though. The drinking can't be the only reason they had sex. Maybe they felt attracted to each other and wanted to have sex. I've got to remember that this summer Jim and I had no commitments to each other, and therefore I do not have the right to expect that he would be celibate to please me. Also, it is a mistake for me to refer to Jim or Linda as being a "jerk." People are people.

B–4.   Linda must be some kind of cheap tramp. Only a tramp would have sex with a guy she didn't love. (bad)

D(b–4)   I don't even know Linda so I shouldn't judge her like this. Furthermore, I have no way of knowing how Linda felt about Jim. Maybe she felt she loved him at the time. A woman isn't necessarily loose if she has sex with a guy.

B–5   Jim must think he's some kind of stud now. (bad)

D(b–5)   Jim has told me that he has had sex with only two women. My idea of a "stud" is a guy who thinks he can have sex with any woman who comes along. I know Jim better than that. He doesn't think he could, nor would he try to, conquer just any woman.

B–6   Jim and I will never again be able to have a good sexual relationship of our own now that he has someone else to compare me to. I just know that he'll be thinking of Linda from now on. (bad)

D(b–6)   Jim and I love each other. Jim told me that he does not love Linda. Just because Jim had sex with Linda does not mean our relationship will always be adversely affected. We can communicate easily during sex, and it has always been satisfying so far. It would be silly for Jim to compare our entire relationship to the one night he spent with Linda.

(continued)

Case Example

Rational Self-analysis: coping with a sexual affair *(continued)*

B–7   This is the worst thing that Jim could have done. (bad)

D(b–7)   This is not the worst thing that Jim could have done. What he did was not a crime, like murder or rape, which would have been worse. The situation would be worse if Jim had slept with Linda while he was still seeing me. I'm glad to know that he would never do that.

B–8   Now that I know Jim had sex with Linda, our whole relationship will be ruined. (bad)

D(b–8)   The fact that Jim had sex with Linda does not have to ruin our relationship. The event occurred in the past. It's over. Past sexual experiences should have no bearing on the future of our relationship. I want the relationship to continue, and I don't want to see it ruined.

B–9   I should never have broken up with Jim. Then he would never have slept with Linda. It's all my fault. (bad)

D(b–9)   It's not my fault at all. I broke up with Jim because I felt it was the best thing to do at the time. I know Jim would not have been unfaithful to me had we still been dating, but we weren't dating at the time this happened. I had no way of knowing he would some day go to bed with Linda, and knowing would not have changed my decision to break up with him. It's not my fault because I wasn't even involved.

B–10   From now on, whenever I hear Linda's name mentioned I'm going to have a fit! I won't be able to handle it! (bad)

D(b–10)   When I hear Linda's name mentioned, I don't have to respond by having a fit. I can handle my feelings by being calm and not letting the mention of her name bother me.

C *My emotions*	E *My emotional and behavior goals*
I feel guilty, hurt, angry, upset, and jealous. (very bad)	I want to get over my unwanted emotions that I have had about this affair. I want to put this affair in our past. At the time it happened, Jim and I had no commitments to each other. What is important to Jim and me is our present and future relationship and not what happened one evening when Jim and I had broken up.

Case Example
Using rational therapy to change irresponsible behavior

Dan Barber, age 4½, was taken to the emergency room of St. Mary's Hospital in a midwestern city. He was unconscious, severely bruised, and had a broken arm. Dan was brought in by neighbors after Mr. Barber had telephoned them. Dan had a concussion, sustained from what appeared to be several blows. Seven weeks earlier Dan had been rushed to the hospital for a broken leg. That time Mr. Barber stated Dan had fallen down a stairway. Protective services were contacted by the hospital, and in the initial interview Mr. Barber acknowledged that he had beaten Dan on both of these occasions. Why? The following is Mr. Barber's account of the thinking processes (self-talk) that led him to abuse his son.

Dan is my only son. I was married for nearly seven years, but got a divorce eight months ago. I'm an accountant and up until about a year ago I really thought I had it made. Mary was very attractive and we got along well. We had a nice house, and I had a good income—many days I worked 11 or 12 hours, getting overtime pay. Mary primarily took care of our son.

One day I arrived home and there was a note from my wife saying she was leaving me. I was shocked and couldn't believe it. A few weeks later I received papers indicating she had gotten a divorce in Mexico. Shortly afterward I heard she married a person from the same church I used to go to. I really don't understand how she could leave both Dan and me, without even talking about it. I guess I've been so involved with my work that I didn't realize how she felt.

As time went by after she left I discussed my problems with some of our neighbors. A few indicated that several men over the years visited with my wife during the day when I was at work. Apparently she has been having affairs for a long time.

My mother moved in after Mary left, to help take care of Dan.

In the past few months, I have been wondering if Dan is really my own son. (At this point Mr. Barber was asked to indicate what he was thinking during the last time he abused Dan. The events and self-talk are put into the format presented earlier.)

Event: That evening I came home from work feeling exhausted. I wanted just to relax and have a peaceful evening. My mother went grocery shopping, and I guess I was feeling sorry for myself. Dan was quite noisy, and I told him to stop making so much noise. But he continued.

Self-talk: "I can't take anymore of this."
"Here I have to take care of a kid who may not even be my own."
"This kid reminds me of the hurt that Mary has caused me. I have a right to even the score."
"This kid is willfully disobeying me—I've got to teach him a lesson."
"I can't stand this! I've got to shut this brat up!"
"My father beat me when I did wrong—that's the best way to show kids who's the boss."

Emotions: Anger, revenge, hostility, frustration.

↓

Actions: Hitting Dan with his hands, knocking him down several times. (Mr. Barber added, "Once I started hitting Dan, I thought I was evening the score with Mary, and didn't want to stop.")

At first, Mr. Barber indicated he could not understand how he could lose emotional control and abuse his son. He appeared to be remorseful and desirous of changing his actions. It was gradually explained and demonstrated that he (his thinking processes) controlled his emotions and actions and that he could change his unwanted emotions and actions by changing his self-talk. He realized he had severely hurt his son in the past and that he might lose his son if the abuse was not curbed.

Since Mr. Barber was concerned whether he really was Dan's father, blood tests were taken. It was explained to Mr. Barber that the blood tests, if different, would indicate that he was not the father, and if there was a match it would indicate that he probably was Dan's genetic father. The types matched, so Mr. Barber's concerns in this area were alleviated. Through rational therapy Mr. Barber learned how to challenge and change the self-talk that was leading to emotional outbursts of anger directed at Dan. Mr. Barber was also instructed to leave Dan in the care of his mother whenever he felt an urge to abuse Dan again. If an occasion arose when his mother was not available, Mr. Barber agreed to call the protective service worker to ventilate his feelings over the phone, rather than at Dan. Mr. Barber also received counseling about his feelings toward his wife and about the importance of focusing his thoughts and energies on the present and future, rather than wallowing in self-pity and dwelling on what happened in the past.

Once clients become aware of their irrational self-talk, a rational therapist uses a variety of techniques to help them change their unwanted emotions and irresponsible behavior.

An Eclectic Approach

For changing unwanted emotions, rational self-challenges (including writing an RSA) are often used. For certain unwanted emotions, such as depression, rational therapists may attempt to get clients involved in a meaningful or enjoyable activity (for example, playing golf, joining a social club). (Reality therapists, as described in Chapter 21, use this approach to change unwanted emo-

tions.) Rational therapists theorize that getting clients involved in enjoyable activities works because it switches their negative thinking (which is causing their unwanted emotions) to positive thoughts about the enjoyable activity, which then changes their emotions.

For people who are shy or prone to temper outbursts, rational therapists are apt to use assertiveness training techniques (described in Chapter 16). For clients who have drinking problems, rational therapists may supplement therapy by getting clients involved in Alcoholics Anonymous. For clients with sexual dysfunctions, rational therapists are apt to use such techniques as sensate focus and other techniques (see Chapter 18) developed by Masters and Johnson (Belliveau & Richter, 1970). Rational therapists use whatever approaches hold promise of helping change irrational self-talk. Ellis (1979, p. 186) noted, "The rational therapist uses role playing, assertion training, desensitization, humor, operant conditioning, suggestion, support, and a whole bag of other 'tricks.'"

Homework assignments are frequently given to clients. Shy clients, for example, might be given an assignment to try out assertive approaches that are practiced in therapy through role playing. Shy clients may also be given a homework assignment of writing an RSA in which they identify and challenge the negative and irrational self-talk that is leading them to feel shy. If a male client states he cannot stand to be rejected by the opposite sex, he might be assigned to ask three different females out on dates to test the hypothesis that he can indeed stand being rejected. A common homework assignment is to instruct clients to read books on rational therapy to help them learn and apply the basic concepts.

Rational therapists are willing to self-disclose some of their own foibles in order to dispute the client's irrational belief that anyone, even a therapist, can be more than human.

Common Irrational Beliefs

Rational therapy frequently seeks to refute clients' irrational beliefs. In therapy, clients are confronted with their irrational beliefs. The therapist asks questions such as "Show me where it is written that you must succeed at everything you try in order to feel good about yourself?" or "What evidence do you have that your girlfriend *must* treat you fairly?"

Several writers (Criddle, 1974; Ellis, 1958; Ellis & Harper, 1977b; Hauck, 1972; Raimy, 1977; Zastrow, 1979, 1993b) have identified common erroneous beliefs that frequently generate negative or irrational self-talk. In

counseling it is frequently found that such self-talk based on erroneous beliefs leads to unwanted emotions and ineffective actions. A number of these erroneous beliefs are summarized briefly:

1. The belief that it is a dire necessity to be loved or approved by everyone for everything you do. A more rational idea is to seek to do the things you want to do as long as you do not hinder others. No matter how hard you try, you will never get everyone to like you, since what will please one may displease another. Your opinion of yourself is much more important than others' views of you.

2. The belief that you should be thoroughly competent, skilled, and achieving in all possible respects if you are to consider yourself worthwhile. This idea represents a demand for perfection that is simply impossible to achieve. All humans are fallible. We all make mistakes. Achieving something does not make you a "better person." We all have intrinsic worth because we exist. If you fail at something, it does not make you a failure but only a person who has failed at something.

3. The belief that it is awful and catastrophic when things are not the way you would like them to be. In actuality, nothing is awful. Awful connotes that certain circumstances are more than "100 percent" negative. Events or circumstances are at times inconvenient, but they never are "awful." By telling ourselves that certain inconvenient events (such as a broken engagement) are awful, we are causing ourselves to overreact emotionally. In actuality we have limited control over events that happen to us. You can try to change reality, but you better stop *demanding* that it be as you say—there is a great deal of evidence that neither you nor I runs the world. Rational therapy seeks to "deawfulize" thinking.

4. The belief that there will be justice in the world and in interpersonal relationships. Since humans are fallible, injustices can be expected to occur. To expect justice in all interactions is unrealistic and will lead you to react with anger or frustration when an injustice occurs. Justice does not exist and it never did. A more rational philosophy is to seek to change conditions so they become more fair, but if you come to realize that it is impossible to change an "unfair" situation, you had better become resigned to its existence and stop telling yourself how awful it is.

5. The belief that human unhappiness (and happiness) is externally caused, and that you have little or no ability to control your unwanted emotions. The external environment can only cause you physical pain, never emotional pain. You cause all your emotions by your self-talk and thereby can control and relieve any uncomfortable emotion by changing your negative or irrational self-talk.

6. The belief that if something is or may be dangerous or fearsome, you should be terribly concerned about it and should keep dwelling on the possibility of its occurring. Worriers frequently believe the act of worrying has a "magical" value of preventing the worst from occurring. Of course, worrying has no magical power. Chronic worrying seldom achieves the results that calm deliberation and careful study do. Excessive worry often incapacitates a person to the point that the feared event is not avoided but often brought about. If you are a chronic worrier, analyze your self-talk to discover what is rational fear and what is irrational fear. Worriers will find most of their fears are irrational and can be countered with rational self-challenges.

7. The belief that you should depend on others and that you need someone stronger than yourself on whom to rely. Any time you enter into a dependent relationship, you become vulnerable to the whims of the person you are dependent on. It is usually far better to stand on your own feet and gain faith in yourself by doing what you can for yourself and for others. There is no guarantee that someone else's judgment is right—in fact, all humans are fallible. The only way you become efficient at acting on your own judgment is to practice risking it.

8. The belief that your past is an all-important determinant of your present behavior and that because something once strongly affected your life, it will indefinitely have a similar effect. In actuality, what you want out of life, now and in the future (along with your motivation to achieve what you want), is a much stronger determinant of what your life will be.

9. The belief that what other people do is vitally important to your existence and that you should make great efforts to change them in the direction you would like them to be. Forcing others to behave in a certain way frequently makes them rebel. In actuality, you have a right to live the way you want to as long as you do not hinder others in living the way they want to. You own your life and others own theirs, and you should respect their right to live the way they want to.

10. The belief that other people's problems are also yours and that you should become quite emotionally involved in other people's problems. You can do very little in controlling the emotions and behaviors of others, although you can do a great deal about controlling your own. When other people have problems, they *own* them; you don't. Becoming emotionally involved by psychologically taking on joint ownership usually is more destructive than helpful. The best way to help others is to recognize their problems are theirs and be an emotionally calm person who is available to help arrive at a sensible attack on the problems.

11. The belief that people with a stereotyped label (for example, ex-convict, men-

tally ill, mentally retarded, whore, juvenile delinquent, welfare mother) are somehow categorically different from "normal" people and should be viewed with suspicion and avoided. In actuality, such a label (at best) refers to only a small proportion of their past or present behavior. Every person is unique. Stereotypes that are based on labels are frequently myths without a factual base. We will get to know other people much more realistically if we interact with them as "unique persons" rather than in terms of expectations based on labels. The same approach is applicable to interacting with people having labels with more positive stereotypes, for example, priests, professors, executive directors, police officers, counselors, school principals, judges.

12. The belief that human happiness can be achieved by inaction. There is no magical way in which happiness is suddenly going to happen to you. We get out of life what we put into it. If you are bored or unhappy, there are two ways of counteracting these problems: challenging the irrational self-talk, or getting involved in meaningful activities. People are the happiest when they are fully absorbed in satisfying activities.

13. The belief that what you *want* are needs that *must* be fulfilled. In actuality, you have very few *needs*—you need food, water, and shelter to exist. The consequences of thinking in terms of needs are often self-defeating. Thinking in terms of needs implies life-and-death consequences. Faced with such consequences, you will tend to panic and think and behave irrationally, and thus self-defeatingly. Ellis (1973) coined the term *musterbation* for people who behave irrationally because they erroneously perceive their wants to be needs that *must* be fulfilled.

14. The belief that people and life *should* always be pleasing, and if they are not, they are awful and unbearable. This erroneous belief is operating when you give yourself the following self-talk about an unpleasant experience: "I *should* be treated in a totally satisfying way; it is *awful* when I'm not." But where is the evidence that people and life *should* treat anyone in a perfectly gratifying way? Everything in life is imperfect. Nothing completely lasts or fully satisfies. All people are fallible. Demanding "I should be treated in a certain way" requires that others act and events unfold according to your private wishes. You have neither the control over others, nor are you (or for that matter, anyone) such a superspecial person that the world *should* revolve around you.

Thinking psychologically in terms of "needs," "shoulds," "musts," "awful," and "unbearable" is a distortion of reality, and frequently leads us to overact. Instead of using "shoulds" and "musts" in our interactions with others, a more rational philosophy is "I would like to be treated reasonably well by people and life."

What Really Causes Psychotherapy Change?

Client-centered therapy, psychoanalysis, rational therapy, feminist intervention, behavior therapy, transactional analysis, reality therapy, hypnosis, meditation, and crisis intervention have all been used to treat a wide range of emotional and behavioral problems. Practically all of these approaches have been used to treat people who are depressed, or lonely, or have marital or other interpersonal relationship problems, or who have disabling fears and phobias, or are overly aggressive, or have drinking problems, or who suffer from grief, shame, or guilt. Each of these therapies differ substantially from every other in treatment techniques and in terms of explaining why therapeutic change occurs. Yet, each approach is used by various practitioners who are able to provide cases examples that the approaches lead to positive changes.

How can all these distinct and diverse psychotherapeutic approaches produce positive changes in clients?[4] What is it that produces positive changes in therapy? Is there a single explanation that will describe psychotherapy changes that are produced by diverse therapies? (The explanation presented here is advanced by rational therapists, but it has not been universally accepted.)

Earlier chapters described these approaches and presented the explanations advanced by each about why positive changes occur in counseling. Practically every theory postulates a different view for why positive changes occur. In reviewing this dilemma, Raimy (1977) stated:

Psychotherapists today are faced with an insistent, nagging problem: since widely diverse methods of treatment for similar problems have their successes as well as their failures, how can one defend a given set of treatment procedures as superior to others? Clearly, since quit different, even contradictory, methods of treatment produce similar results, explanations for the success of treatment must be sought outside the realm of method or technique. [p. 1]

What Causes Disturbing Emotions and Ineffective Actions?

Before attempting to provide an explanation of what produces positive changes in therapy, it would appear important to identify the primary determinants of emotional and behavior problems.

[4]This section tentatively assumes that all the above-mentioned therapies produce positive changes. Chapter 23 raises questions as to whether a few of these therapies (particularly psychoanalysis and client-centered therapy) do in fact produce positive changes. The reasons that reported negative changes may be occurring while the client is receiving psychoanalysis are discussed later in this section when psychoanalysis is reviewed.

As indicated earlier in this chapter, all feelings and actions occur according to the following format:

Events: (Or experiences.)
   ↓
Self-talk: (Self-talk is the set of evaluating thoughts we give ourselves about facts and events that happen to us.)
   ↓
Emotion: (May include remaining calm.)
   ↓
Actions

The most important point about this formula is that our self-talk determines how we feel and act; by changing our self-talk, we can change how we feel and act. Generally we cannot control events that happen to us, but we have the power to think rationally and thereby change *all* of our unwanted emotions and dysfunctional behaviors.

The formula shows that self-talk is the primary determinant of all actions and all emotions, including love, fear, anger, grief, depression, anxiety, shame, happiness, hate, and frustration. Zastrow (1979, 1993b) has also shown that self-talk is the primary determinant of our self-concept, sense of success, or sense of failure, our personality, and stress-related illnesses.

Could Restructuring Thinking Be the Key Psychotherapeutic Agent?

This conceptualization asserts that discomforting emotions and dysfunctional actions arise primarily from our self-talk, generally self-talk that is negative or irrational. If this conceptualization is accurate, an important corollary is that *any therapy technique that is successful in changing emotions or actions is effective primarily because it changes a person's thinking from self-talk that is negative or irrational to self-talk that is more rational* and *positive*. In other words, self-talk appears to me to be the key therapeutic agent in all approaches that produce positive changes in our emotions and our behaviors. Practically all the contemporary approaches to psychotherapy can be reinterpreted to be consistent with the basic therapeutic principle of producing psychotherapeutic change by restructuring thinking. A few examples are presented in the following paragraphs.

Psychoanalysis. Freud (1924) saw the basic goal of therapy as bringing disturbing, suppressed ideas and emotions to the conscious part of the mind so the ideas (now conscious) could be dealt with and the unconscious emotion (energy) could be expressed. Is not Freud, in essence, seeking to help clients become aware of their disturbing ideas (self-talk) so they can then change this disturbing self-talk? Once such disturbing self-talk is changed, the format presented here suggests that the unwanted emotions generated by the original self-talk (now changed) will be alleviated.[5]

Psychoanalysis asserts that these disturbing ideas are usually unconscious. Rational therapists partially agree, since it appears that clients occasionally may not be fully aware of the "disturbing ideas" that are getting them into trouble, and sometimes considerable probing is needed to identify such "self-talk."

Behavior therapy. Originally, behavior modification therapists conceptualized their

efforts as being S (stimulus) $\rightarrow$ R (response) in nature. Their efforts were focused on identifying and applying stimuli that would change unwanted responses (behaviors). In the past 30 years, there has been an increasingly large group of behavior therapists who emphasize the importance of changing cognitions to modify human behavior (Beck, 1976; Cautela & Upper, 1975; Craighead, Mahoney, & Kazdin, 1976; Goldfried & Merbaum, 1973; Lazarus, 1971; Mahoney, 1974; Meichenbaum, 1975). These authorities on behavior therapy are now calling themselves *cognitive behaviorists.* Their approach is focused on changing the person's thinking in order to change behavior. Instead of the old $S \rightarrow R$ conceptualization, they emphasize that behavior changes are best conceptualized as involving a change in a person's thinking, as illustrated in the following format: $S \rightarrow O$ (organism's thinking) $\rightarrow R$. Thought-stopping and reframing, which are described in Chapter 16, are good examples of techniques used to change irrational thoughts in order to alleviate unwanted emotions and to change dysfunctional behaviors.

One of the most popular applications of behavior therapy is assertiveness training. All of us are shy or timid in some situations, perhaps in arranging a date, or in talking to an authority figure, or in asking someone to put out a cigarette. Authorities on assertiveness training have pointed out that we are shy, or aggressive, because of what we tell ourselves about these situations and that it is necessary to change our cognitions to be able to express ourselves assertively (Alberti & Emmons, 1975).

Client-centered therapy. The goal of this approach is to help clients gain insight into the inconsistencies between their ideas about self and their experiences, so they can then reorganize their self-concept to be more consistent with what they experience. Isn't Carl Rogers saying that clients need to identify the

---

[5]Chapter 23 presents research suggesting that psychoanalysis, overall, appears to be less effective than receiving no treatment. How is this explainable? One explanation is that when the therapist uses such terms as *psychosis, Oedipal complex,* and *fixation at the oral stage of development,* the client is sidetracked from focusing his or her thinking on resolving real problems and instead develops irrational self-talk connected with worrying about having (and trying to resolve) mystical problems that do not exist. Such irrational self-talk, it is hypothesized, may then lead to deterioration.

thoughts (self-talk) about themselves that are inconsistent with reality, and then reorganize these thoughts to become more consistent with reality?

Other comprehensive therapy approaches. In *Misunderstandings of the Self*, Raimy (1977) proposed a theory to explain positive changes in counseling that is nearly identical to the self-talk approach presented here. Raimy's main hypothesis was "If those ideas or conceptions of a client or patient that are relevant to his psychological problems can be changed in the direction of greater accuracy where his reality is concerned, his maladjustments are likely to be eliminated." Raimy called his hypothesis the *misconception hypothesis* (Raimy, 1977, p. 7). He then provided a rationale that positive changes obtained through correcting "misconceptions" account for the changes in the following therapies: Adlerian, rational-emotive, psychoanalysis, transactional analysis, Gestalt therapy, client-centered therapy, and certain behavior modification techniques.

Nontraditional Psychotherapy Techniques

Zastrow (1979, 1993b) presented a rationale that changing self-talk primarily accounts for the positive changes produced with hypnosis, systematic desensitization, biofeedback, meditation, muscle relaxation, deep-breathing relaxation, imagery relaxation, in vivo desensitization, acupuncture, electroshock therapy, covert sensitization, sex therapy for sexual dysfunctions, assertiveness training, diet counseling, and therapy for alcoholics (Zastrow, 1979). The rationale for a few of these approaches is summarized as follows:

Meditation. Daniel Goleman (1977) summarized contemporary approaches to meditation and described how each attempts to accomplish its goal. Practically all the approaches seek to achieve a meditative state by having a person concentrate on an object or repeat a sound: a word, phrase, chant, spiritual value, image of an exquisite painting, and so forth. As described in Chapter 20, deep-breathing relaxation, imagery relaxation, and repeating the word *relax* are all forms of meditation.

Herbert Benson (1975) noted that the key element in inducing the relaxation response via meditation is having a passive attitude in which the meditator lets go of the thoughts underlying daily concerns. Maultsby (1975) showed that feelings of stress and anxiety arise primarily from negative and irrational self-talk about day-to-day problems. Meditation, it is hypothesized here, reduces the feelings of stress and anxiety by having the meditator switch his or her thinking from focusing on day-to-day problems to focusing on the mantra or meditative object. This process can be diagrammed as follows:

A. Event: Concentrating and repeating a mantra while great care is taken to prevent interruptions or distractions.

B. Self-talk: "This is relaxing." (At the same time the person stops thinking about day-to-day concerns.)

C. Emotion: Feeling of being relaxed.

Hypnosis. Hypnosis essentially involves two processes: (1) becoming relaxed so that a person goes into what is called a hypnotic trance; and (2) while in a trance, giving oneself hypnotic suggestions. The hypnotic trance state can be induced by a variety of relaxation techniques, including deep-breathing relaxation, imagery relaxation, and other forms of meditation. The hypnotic trance state can be best understood as a state of deep relaxation. As explained in the previous section on meditation, this relaxed state is induced by the meditator's letting go of thinking about everyday concerns.

The second process of hypnosis involves hypnotic suggestions. The therapeutic power of self-talk is dramatically demonstrated by hypnotic suggestions. While in a trance a person can be given a wide variety of instructions or suggestions, many of which are increasingly being used for therapeutic reasons. Nearly all of these hypnotic suggestions are, in actuality, self-talk statements, as the following illustrates:

> "I will feel no pain," for those with arthritis or undergoing surgery, for those with terminal cancer, for childbirth, and for practically any type of pain.
> "I will relax," for those who are very anxious or tense.
> "I will fall asleep after going to bed and counting to ten," for those suffering from insomnia.
> "My menstrual period will now be regular," for those with irregular periods.

Muscle relaxation. Deep muscle relaxation is a technique that people can use to become more relaxed when they are tense or anxious (Paul, 1966). The technique is learned by having a person first tighten and then relax a set of muscles. When relaxing the muscles, the person is instructed to think about the relaxed feeling, while noting that the muscles are more relaxed than before they were tensed. The following excerpt (Watson & Tharp, 1972) gives a brief illustration of the procedure.

> Make a fist with your dominant hand (usually right). Make a fist and tense the muscles of your (right) hand and forearm; tense it until it trembles. Feel the muscles pull across your fingers and the lower part of your forearm. . . . Hold this position for 5 to 7 seconds, then . . . relax. . . . Just let your hand go. Pay attention to the muscles of your (right) hand and forearm as they relax. Note how those muscles feel as relaxation flows through them (20 to 30 seconds). [pp. 182–183]

After a person learns to relax one set of muscles, he or she learns to relax other sets (for example, muscles of the arms, neck, shoulders, chest, stomach, lower back, hips, thighs, and so forth).

Applying the principles of *rational therapy*, it appears that self-talk is a key to achieving a relaxed state:

Event:	A person relaxes a set of muscles after having tensed the muscles.
Self-talk:	"This is relaxing." "Feels good." "This is calming."
Emotional consequence:	Relaxation.

Advocates of muscle relaxation point out that, with practice, a person can achieve deep relaxation without having to tense muscles— that is, by imagery (Watson & Tharp, 1972). Apparently the following is occurring:

Event:	I am imagining my arm (thigh, and so on) muscles first tensing and then becoming very relaxed.
Self-talk:	"This feels good, is relaxing."
Emotional consequence:	Relaxation.

Muscle relaxation, it is hypothesized here, also reduces the feelings of stress and anxiety by helping a person switch thinking from focusing on day-to-day problems to focusing on the relaxation exercises.

Consistent with the belief of a number of authorities, it is asserted that discomforting emotions and dysfunctional actions arise primarily from our self-talk, generally self-talk that is negative or irrational. If this conceptualization is accurate, an important corollary is that any therapy technique that is successful in changing emotions or actions is effective primarily because it changes a person's thinking from negative or irrational self-talk to more rational and positive self-talk.

At this point there is some support (although more research is needed) for the notion that changing negative or irrational self-talk is the key therapeutic agent in psychotherapy approaches. If accurate, the old argument of which therapy approaches are effective and which are not (Eysenck, 1952; Stuart, 1970) may be refocused to "Which therapy approaches are most effective in changing negative and irrational self-talk?" and "How can present therapy approaches be refined, and new approaches developed, to change negative and irrational self-talk more effectively?"

Explaining Mental Illness from a Rational Therapy Perspective

While working at a mental hospital, I was assigned a case of a 22-year-old male who decapitated his 17-year-old girlfriend. Why did he do it? Two psychiatrists diagnosed him as being schizophrenic and a court found him to be "innocent by reason of insanity." He was then committed to a mental hospital. Why did he do it? Labeling him as insane provides an explanation to the general public that he exhibited this strange behavior because he was "crazy." But does such a label explain why he killed this girl, rather than killing someone else, or doing something else that is bizarre? Does the label explain what would have prevented him from committing this slaying? Does the label suggest the kind of treatment that will cure him? The answer to all these questions is, of course, no.

In criminal trials where the defense pleads "innocent by reason of insanity," juries have to subjectively decide whether the defendant is insane. In 1991 Jeffrey Dahmer admitted to killing seventeen males; his victims were drugged, sexually assaulted, dismembered, and a few were partially cannibalized. In spite of these bizarre and shocking behaviors, Dahmer was judged to be sane by a jury.

What Is Schizophrenia?

A common definition of *schizophrenia* is a psychotic condition usually occurring during or shortly after adolescence and characterized by disorientation, loss of contact with reality, and disorganized patterns of thinking and feeling. Let us examine this definition. People who are intoxicated, or stoned on drugs, or who are asleep, or who have not slept for over a day experience a loss of contact with reality and their feelings and thinking patterns become disorganized. Are they schizophrenic? No. What about the severely and profoundly mentally retarded who have a mental age of less than 2? They have these symptoms but are not considered to be schizophrenic. What about people who go into a coma following a serious accident? They also fit the definition but are not considered schizophrenic. The 22-year-old male who committed the bizarre homicide knew the act was wrong, was aware of what he was doing, was in contact with reality, and told me the reasons for doing what he did.

Then why was he labeled schizophrenic? Could it be *that there is no definition of symptoms that separates people who have this "disease" from those who do not?* Chapter 21 presents the interactional model, which asserts that mental illness is a myth.

A Perspective from Rational Therapy

People are labeled mentally ill in our society because they are either displaying bizarre behavior or have serious discomforting emotions. Why do bizarre acts and discomforting emotions occur?

Rational therapy asserts that *any bizarre act can be understood by discovering the self-talk that led a person to do something "strange."* In almost all cases the reasons for the occurrence of any deviant act can be determined by examining what the offender was telling himself or herself before and during the time the deviant act was being committed. The reasons for the deviant act occurring (similar to any action) follow the formula postulated by rational therapy:

Events: (Experiences)
↓
Self-talk
↓
Emotion
↓
Actions: (In this case deviant actions)

Furthermore, identifying the self-talk that led a person to do something deviant will generally provide information on the kinds of services needed to prevent the deviant behavior from recurring (an example follows).

Committing a deviant act (or continuing to display deviant behavior) is not the only reason some people are labeled mentally ill. Mental illness labels are sometimes applied to people who have serious, discomforting emotions such as severe or chronic depression, anxiety, grief, or feelings of inferiority.

Discomforting emotions range on a continuum in severity from mild to extreme. Labelers who adhere to the medical model are forced to draw a line somewhere along this continuum to separate the "insane" from the "sane." All severe discomforting emotions, similar to any emotion, result from self-talk according to the following format:

Events or experiences
↓
Self-talk
↓
Emotion

Rational therapy asserts there is no need to attach a nondescript medical label (such as labeling a severe depression "psychotic") to a severe, discomforting emotion. Such medical labels have no diagnostic or treatment value and may well complicate therapy efforts due to labeling effects.

A Bizarre Murder

Let us return to the 22-year-old male who was labeled *schizophrenic* for murdering his girlfriend. A medical diagnosis should identify the general causes of the medical condition and suggest a treatment approach. In this case the label does not tell us why the murder occurred nor does it suggest what type of rehabilitation is needed. (Incidentally, this male was seen by a psychiatrist a few months before this slaying and was viewed as sane.)

However, after he described what happened, it was understandable (even though bizarre) why he did what he did, and his account also identified the specific problems he needed help with. He described himself as a very isolated person who, except for his girlfriend, had no close relatives or friends. He came from a broken home and was raised by a variety of relatives and foster parents. Because of frequent moves, he attended a number of different schools and made no lasting friends. At age 20 he met the victim and dated her periodically for two years. She provided the only real meaning that he had in life. He held the traditional vision of marrying her and living happily together thereafter.

However, a few months before the fatal day, he became very alarmed that he was going to "lose her." She encouraged him to date others, mentioned that she wanted to date others, and suggested that they no longer see as much of each other.

He thought intensely about how he could preserve the relationship. He also realized he had rather intense sexual tensions with no outlet. Putting the two together he naively concluded, "If I'm the first person to have sexual relations with her, she will forever feel tied to me." He therefore tried on several occasions to have coitus, but she always managed to dissuade him. Finally, one afternoon during the summer when he knew they would be alone together, he arrived at the following self-talk decision, "I *will* have sex with her this afternoon, even if I have to knock her unconscious." He stated he knew such action was wrong, but said, "It was my last hope of saving our relationship. Without her, life would not be worth living."

He again tried to have sexual relations with her that afternoon, but she continued to dissuade him. Being emotionally excited, he then took a soda bottle and knocked her unconscious. He again attempted to have coitus, but was still unsuccessful for reasons related to her physical structure. In an intense state of emotional and sexual excitement, he was unable rationally to consider the consequences of his actions. (All of us, at times, have acted dysfunctionally while angry or in a state of intense emotional excitement.) At this point he felt his whole world was caving in. When asked during an interview what he was thinking at this point, he stated, "I felt that if I couldn't have her, no one else would either." He sought and found a knife, became further carried away with emotions, and ended up slaying her. He knew it was wrong, and he was aware of what he was doing.

Conversations with this person (and identification of the self-talk before and during this bizarre murder) pinpoint certain factors that help explain why the murder took place, including his loneliness and isolation, his belief that continuing a romantic relationship with this young woman was the only source of meaning in his life, his naive thinking that a forced sexual relationship would lead this young woman to feel tied and attracted to him, his lack of any outlet for his sexual drives, and his jealous and possessive desires to go to extreme lengths to prevent this young woman from developing a romantic relationship with another man. Such reasons help explain why the bizarre behavior took place; the label *schizophrenia* does not.

If the above problems had been known before the murder, the slaying might have been prevented. What he needed was to find other sources of interest and other meaningful relationships in his life. Joining certain groups or developing hobbies may well have helped. An appropriate sexual outlet for his passions probably would have also been helpful. Better control of his passions and other sources of finding meaning might have prevented him from losing control of his emotions that afternoon. Reducing the intensity of his jealous and possessive feelings, along with developing more mature attitudes toward romance and sexuality, might also have been preventative. These specific problems are the areas that he needs help with while in a mental hospital, rather than with finding a cure for schizophrenia. In no way do I feel that he should be excused for his actions, as implied by the term *innocent by reason of insanity*. But he does need help for the specific problems identified. (In 10 or 15 years, he will probably be released and return to society.)

In summary, when a deviant act occurs, asserting that the behavior was due to a "mental illness" does not provide a useful explanation for why the behavior occurred. All such deviant behaviors are understandable, however, when viewed from the actor's perspective.

If the reader wonders how someone could arrive at a point of doing something as bizarre as taking the life of someone he loves, remember it is necessary to attempt to view the situation from the deviant person's perspective. To understand such a perspective, it is essential to try to consider all the circumstances, pressures, values, and belief systems of the deviant person. An unusual true example may help the reader become aware that practically anyone will do something bizarre when circumstances become desperate. Several years ago a passenger plane crashed in the Andes in the wintertime. A number of people were killed, but there were nearly 30 survivors. Rescue efforts initially failed to locate the survivors, who took shelter from the cold in the wreckage of the plane. The survivors were without food for over 40 days until they were finally rescued. During this time the survivors were faced with the choice of dying of starvation or cannibalism of those who died. It was a very desperate, difficult decision. (Psychologically, many people who commit a bizarre act feel they face a comparable decision.) In this situation, all but one of the initial plane crash survivors chose cannibalism. The one who refused died of starvation.

Evaluation

Since its formation in the 1950s, rational therapy has become one of the most widely used therapy approaches. DiGuiseppe, Miller, and Trexler (1977) summarized a wide number of outcome studies conducted on rational therapy and found over 90 percent of these studies supported its claims. Ellis (1989) noted:

> More than 200 outcome studies have been published, showing that RET [rational-emotive therapy] is effective in changing the thoughts, feelings, and behaviors of groups of individuals with various kinds of disturbances. [p. 223]

(Few other psychotherapy approaches have this kind of successful documentation.)

Rational therapy has been used successfully to treat clients with a wide range of problems, including unwanted emotions (depression, anxiety, fears and phobias, guilt, shame), sexual problems and sexual dysfunctions, worrying, marital problems, interaction problems, alcoholism, shyness, and such irresponsible actions as committing crimes, procrastination, and jealous actions. Its major hypotheses are also useful in child rearing, education, executive management, and social and political affairs.

By asserting that we primarily cause our unwanted emotions and irresponsible behaviors by what we think, the approach squarely puts the responsibility on us for improving our lives. We are in charge of our lives and have the power to alleviate unwanted emotions and change ineffective actions.

Zastrow (1979, 1993b) theorized that our self-talk has immense effects on our lives that we only now are beginning to understand. Self-talk, for example, plays a major part in leading people to experience chronic stress; and chronic stress causes a wide range of stress-related illnesses, including ulcers, migraine headaches, insomnia, diarrhea, heart problems, digestive problems, cancer, hypertension, and obesity. Zastrow suggested that changing the underlying irrational self-talk is a key to treating such problems. It is also hypothesized that success at any competitive game is substantially determined by the kind of self-talk we give ourselves.

Rational therapy has made a substantial contribution to psychotherapy. Yet there are some important unanswered questions:

1. *Physiology of self-talk and emotions.* As yet we do not precisely know the physiological components of thinking or of emotions. Our brain, of course, is important in enabling

us to think. But what precisely takes place in the brain that leads us to conceptualize every thought that we have? Are there other parts of the body involved in thinking? Thinking is related to memory. But what precisely is memory, and how do we "store" and "recall" experiences that we have? And how are memory and thinking physiologically related?

Rational therapy theorizes that our self-talk primarily causes our emotions. But, again, a number of physiological questions arise: What are the physiological processes involved in self-talk resulting in an emotion? What different physiological processes occur for such varied emotions as love, depression, grief, happiness, anger, frustration, sorrow, relaxation, hostility, fear, and so on? And, how, physiologically, do certain types of self-talk and certain kinds of emotional states influence our health? In a general fashion, we know certain kinds of self-talk lead to the stress reaction and that prolonged stress can cause stress-related illnesses. But what are the specific physiological processes involved?

2. *Separating the effects of self-talk from the effects of physiological factors.* For people with injuries or abnormal conditions in the brain, it is at times extremely difficult to separate the effects of their medical conditions from the effects of self-talk on their emotions and behaviors. Injuries of different areas of the brain will at times cause a change in the person's emotions and behaviors (White & Watt, 1973). Abnormal conditions of the brain can result from a wide range of factors, including brain tumors, disorders such as cerebral palsy, chronic alcoholic intoxication, Alzheimer's disease, general paresis, AIDS, and cerebral arteriosclerosis. Such medical conditions are a factor in causing confusion, incoherence, clouding of consciousness, loss of recent or past memory, reduction in reasoning capacities, listlessness, apathy, reduction in intel-lectual capacities, and sometimes perceptual changes. People with such medical conditions are at times fairly alert and at other times confused.

While these conditions tend to have permanent or long-lasting effects on thinking patterns and emotional reactions, there are also factors that can lead to temporary changes in mental activity—such as high fever, toxins or poisons, and the intake of drugs and alcohol.

Even with the presence of any of these factors, the self-talk that a person gives herself or himself about these conditions will also affect that person's emotions and behaviors. Separating which effects result from these other factors and which result from self-talk often is difficult.

3. *Nature versus nurture.* Nurture can be defined as the sum of the influences modifying the expression of the genetic potentialities of a person. The theory of human behavior presented in this chapter focuses on nurture determinants, as it states human behavior is determined by events and self-talk. This theory fails to include genetic factors, which obviously have some influence in determining human behavior.

4. *The importance of experiences or events themselves.* Some critics of rational therapy assert that experiences or events that happen to a person are as important (and perhaps even more important) in determining behavior than is the self-talk that people give themselves about such experiences. These critics point out that such events as poverty, discrimination, child abuse, overprotective parents, inadequate education, and being victimized by crime are major determinants of human behavior.

5. *Boundaries of self-talk.* Rational therapy theorizes that self-talk has immense effects on our lives, and many of these effects have been summarized in this chapter. But what are the limits of the effects of self-talk?

In reference to this question, Zastrow (1979) presented the following example:

A college student recently asked if her mother's long-time concern about giving birth to a child with a "dwarf" arm might have led to her youngest being born with a malformed arm.

The student mentioned that her mother had been mildly concerned for a number of years that she would give birth to a child with a malformed arm. This young woman and her older brother were born without having such a malformation. However, shortly after the mother became pregnant the third time, a neighbor woman gave birth to a child with a malformed arm. This led the mother to have intense concerns that the child she was carrying would be born with a "dwarf" arm. When the child was born, it in fact was born with a "dwarf" arm.

After I had given several lectures on the effects of self-talk in one of my classes, the student asked whether I thought this malformation was partly caused by self-talk or was just a matter of coincidence.

In truth, I answered I didn't know—and I still don't know. We know certain drugs (such as thalidomide and excessive drinking) can cause malformations. So can having certain illnesses, such as German measles, during the time when the mother is pregnant. There is also speculation that the mother's emotional state while pregnant can influence the emotional and physiological development of the unborn child (Ainsworth, 1966; Dunn, 1977). Is it possible that this mother's thoughts and fears about having a malformed child might have been a factor in the child's being born with a malformed arm? . . .

Daily I become aware of new ways in which my life, and that of others, is being influenced by self-talk. And, as I discuss the concept with others, the discussion usually ignites their relating to me specific incidents in which their self-talk has had a powerful effect on them.

At this point I frankly do not know what the boundaries are for the effects of self-talk. It may well be that we are only at the "tip of the iceberg" in understanding all its effects. [pp. 327–328]

Summary

Albert Ellis is acknowledged as the primary developer of rational therapy. Rational therapy asserts that the primary cause of all our emotions and actions is not our experiences but rather what we tell ourselves about events that happen to us. Generally we cannot control events that occur, but we have the power to think rationally and thereby change all of our unwanted emotions and dysfunctional actions. Self-talk has a here-and-now quality, since it represents those thoughts we are giving ourselves at the present time. Our self-talk is frequently based on our attitudes, beliefs, values, wants, needs, drives, and motives.

Rational therapy maintains that the reasons for any deviant act (including crime) can be determined by examining what the offender was telling himself or herself prior to and during the time the act was being committed.

The initial focus of therapy is to help clients become aware of the irrational and negative self-talk that is the primary source of their unwanted emotions and dysfunctional actions. Once the irrational self-talk is identified, a wide range of techniques is used to change the irrational self-talk, thereby alleviating unwanted emotions and changing irresponsible actions. A frequently used technique is to have the client develop (and practice using) rational self-challenges to counter the irrational self-talk. Often clients are asked to write out a rational self-analysis.

Learning how to think rationally and how to counter irrational and negative self-talk is an educational process. Rational therapy has a wide variety of applications in addition to changing unwanted emotions and dysfunctional actions. It can be used to reduce stress, change negative self-concepts, improve negative aspects of personalities, help clients become more assertive, and treat sexual dysfunctions.

The question "What really causes psychotherapy change?" is raised. I speculate that any therapy technique that is successful in changing emotions or actions is effective primarily because it changes a person's thinking from self-talk that is negative or irrational to self-talk that is more rational and positive.

Some unanswered questions still remain about rational therapy, including how does self-talk physiologically lead to emotions, and what are the limits of the effects of self-talk?

Exercises

1. Changing unwanted emotions

Goal: This exercise is designed to illustrate many of the principles of rational therapy and to demonstrate to students how to change unwanted emotions.

Step 1: Begin by asking students to think about the last time they were "sad" or "angry." Ask what made them sad or angry. List three or four responses on the chalkboard under each heading. The students in all probability will give you "events" as being the source of these emotions.

Step 2: Indicate to the students that what they told you was *not* the primary source of their emotions. Indicate instead that emotions are determined primarily by self-talk rather than events. For each "event" response given by a student, have the student tell you about personal self-talk that led to the emotion, or guess what the self-talk is. For example, if a student says, "I became sad because I received a speeding ticket," you might suggest the self-talk that led to being sad was something like "This is awful. I sure am stupid for driving so fast. Now my insurance rates will go up. Woe is me. I don't have enough money to pay for tickets and increased insurance payments. I'm a bad person for getting a ticket."

Step 3: Further demonstrate the principles of rational therapy by asking the students, "What would be your self-talk if the person you were dating for the past four years informed you that he or she no longer wanted to date you?" Write this event on the chalkboard. Ask students what would be their self-talk, and what would be the resulting emotions from each self-talk statement. Write these self-talk statements and the resulting emotions on the board. Using the five criteria for determining rational thinking, ask the students to identify which of the self-talk statements are irrational and to give the reasons they are irrational. For each irrational self-talk statement, ask the class to come up with rational self-challenges to challenge and change the irrational self-talk statement.

Step 4: Explain to students how to write a rational self-analysis. (Show them examples from this chapter or distribute a handout of a completed RSA.)

Step 5: Indicate that there are only three constructive ways to change an unwanted emotion:

  a. Challenging negative and irrational thinking with rational self-challenges.
  b. Getting involved in meaningful and enjoyable activities, which stops a person from thinking negatively and irrationally.
  c. Changing the distressing event(s); if you are successful, you are apt to feel better because you will then give yourself more positive self-talk.

Step 6: As a homework assignment, ask students to write a rational self-analysis on an unwanted emotion they have. Ask students their thoughts on the merits and shortcomings of rational therapy.

2. Positive affirmations

Goal: This exercise is designed to provide students with another approach to change negative and irrational thinking.

Step 1: Indicate that some people find writing a rational self-analysis too time-consuming and cumbersome. An alternative is to use positive affirmations. A positive affirmation is a positive assertion that helps in achieving emotional and behavioral goals. The process of writing a positive affirmation also enables a person to identify negative and irrational thinking that he or she may be unaware of.

Step 2: Instruct the students in the following process of writing a positive affirmation. Have each student select a realistic emotional or behavioral personal goal that he or she is currently struggling with. The following are examples:

"I believe I am a person of worth."
"I will no longer be depressed about _____."
"I will no longer get angry and aggressive when _____ occurs."
"I will lose fifteen pounds in two months."
"I will stop smoking today."
"I will limit my drinking of alcoholic beverages to two drinks when I go out."
"I will no longer feel guilty about _____."
"I believe I am an attractive person."
"I will assertively express myself when _____ occurs."

Step 3: Have each student start writing on a sheet of paper the selected positive affirmation. When negative thoughts enter their minds, have them record those thoughts and then continue writing the positive affirmation according to the following format:

Positive Affirmation	Negative Thoughts
"I will lose fifteen pounds in two months."	
"I will lose fifteen pounds in two months."	
"I will lose fifteen pounds in two months."	"I overeat when I'm bored, depressed or lonely."
"I will lose fifteen pounds in two months."	
"I will lose fifteen pounds in two months."	"I will need to develop an exercise program, which I hate to do."
"I will lose fifteen pounds in two months."	"One reason I'm fat is because I snack between meals."
"I will lose fifteen pounds in two months."	"I will have to limit the number of beers that I have when I go out—beer is putting a lot of weight on me."
"I will lose fifteen pounds in two months."	"I wonder if I really want to make all the changes that I will have to make to lose fifteen pounds."
"I will lose fifteen pounds in two months."	
"I will lose fifteen pounds in two months."	
"I will lose fifteen pounds in two months."	

Step 4: All the students to write for 10 to 15 minutes. Ask for volunteers to share what they wrote. Have the class discuss the merits and shortcomings of writing positive affirmations. One advantage of repeated writing of the affirmation is that it trains the mind to accept the positive affirmation more readily.

3. Assessing and changing dysfunctional behaviors

Goal: This exercise is designed to have students evaluate the merits and shortcomings of focusing on cognitions in assessing and changing dysfunctional behaviors.

Step 1: Explain the theory, described in this chapter, that thinking processes primarily determine behavior. The theory asserts that the reasons for unusual or dysfunctional behavior can always be identified by determining what the perpetrator was thinking before and during the time the act is being committed.

Step 2: Divide the class into several subgroups (ranging in size from three to six). Give each subgroup a different problematic or dysfunctional behavior. Examples include the following: (a) alcoholism, (b) child abuse, (c) bulimia, (d) date rape, (e) suicide attempt, and (f) compulsive gambling.

Step 3: Instruct each subgroup to (a) identify the *thinking processes* that would lead a person to engage in the dysfunctional behavior that is assigned to its group, and (b) identify the interventions that would be most effective in changing the thinking patterns of the perpetrator to "curb" the dysfunctional behavior. Instruct each subgroup to identify several intervention strategies or options, as (in one sense) social work practice involves "options planning." Give the subgroups ten or more minutes to arrive at their answers.

Step 4: Ask each subgroup to select a representative to share with the class what the subgroup arrived at for both thinking processes and interventions. Ask a representative to share what his or her subgroup arrived at. Then ask the class to discuss whether the representative identified thinking processes (as the exercise instructed) or focused on describing events and personality characteristics that the subgroup thought were related to the dysfunctional behavior. Also ask the class whether the subgroup may have overlooked some important intervention strategies and options. Continue this process for each subgroup: a representative of the group presents the group's findings, then the class discusses these.

Step 5: After the presentations and discussions end, ask the class for their thoughts on the merits, difficulties, and shortcomings of focusing on cognitions to assess and change dysfunctional behaviors.

CHAPTER

23

Analysis of Therapy Approaches

The preceding chapters in Part III of this text focused primarily on describing intervention techniques. This chapter will provide a critique of these approaches, organized under the following headings: comparison of counseling theories, insight versus resolution approaches, and how effective is counseling?

Comparison of Counseling Theories

This section compares and contrasts the comprehensive psychotherapy approaches presented earlier in the text: psychoanalysis, client-centered therapy, transactional analysis, behavior therapy, feminist intervention, reality therapy, and rational therapy.[1]

To begin with a hypothetical case example, let us assume that a 46-year-old woman seeks treatment for being fairly depressed. We will take a brief look at what the diagnostic and treatment focuses of the above-mentioned therapies would be. (The description given here has been simplified; a therapist with any

[1]There are other comprehensive psychotherapy theories (for example, see Corsini & Wedding, 1989, or Prochaska, 1979), but the theories reviewed in this text are the primary ones used by social workers. The neuro-linguistic programming approach is not reviewed here, because NLP is not designed to be a theoretical framework for assessing unwanted emotions or dysfunctional behavior.

of these treatment orientations would look at a broader range of possible causes and perhaps consider using a wider range of treatment approaches than contained in this summary.)

A psychoanalyst would consider the depression a symptom of a more serious underlying problem and would seek to identify unconscious processes (including defense mechanisms) that underlie the depression. Psychoanalysis would explore the possible causative factors such as unresolved, traumatic early childhood experiences that are probably sexual in nature. A psychoanalyst would use hypnosis, dream analysis, free association, and transference to identify the unresolved unconscious processes that are causing the depression. In treatment, a psychoanalyst would seek to bring the memory of the traumatic experiences to the conscious part of the patient's mind in order to release the pent-up emotions and to allow the patient to consciously work through the disturbing thoughts connected with the trauma. Once the pent-up emotions are released and once the patient gains insight into her disturbing thoughts, it is theorized that the patient's personality will be reorganized and the symptom of depression will disappear.

Client-centered therapy would consider the depression to be caused by incongruencies between the client's self-concept and her experiences. The focus of therapy would be to help the client become aware of these incongruencies. Once this insight is achieved, client-centered therapy postulates that the person's self-actualizing motive will foster a reorganization of the self-concept to be more congruent with experiences. Because client-centered therapy asserts that the self-actualizing motive is the best guide for directing the client, client-centered therapists are nondirective. In therapy, the therapist seeks to convey to the client empathy, positive regard, and genuineness or congruence. It is theorized that if a therapist conveys these three attitudes, the client will feel free to examine her incongruencies. During therapy the client-centered therapist would seek to help the client gain insight into her thoughts and feelings by using three types of statements: clarification or reflection of feeling, restatement of content, and simple acceptance.

Transactional analysis (TA) would view the causes of the depression as being due, potentially, to a variety of factors. The client may have a self-defeating life script or may be a victim of destructive psychological games that she or others are playing. Or, she may have communication or interaction difficulties. Or, she may be in an inappropriate ego state for what the circumstances warrant. TA would seek first to identify and make the client aware of the intrapsychic and interpersonal problems she has. These problems would be analyzed and interpreted to the client in terms of TA concepts (for example, in terms of psychological game concepts or of life script concepts). Once analyzed, the therapist would make a contract with the client that would specify courses of action to be taken by the client to alleviate the depression. For example, if the client is depressed because her husband has filed for divorce and has made it perfectly clear he wants a divorce, TA would help the client understand how defective communication and interaction patterns contributed to the divorce, and also help her examine possible games and life scripts that may have contributed to the divorce. The TA therapist would then make a contract for the client to take specific actions to improve the problematic areas and to make constructive plans for the future.

Behavior therapy would focus on identifying the stimuli that are eliciting the client's depression. The behavior therapist would seek to identify environmental pressures or stimuli rather than look "inside" the client for internal stimuli. Behavior therapists believe there are many possible environmental stimuli that may elicit the response of depression—a monotonous job, an unhappy relationship, pressure from relatives or in-laws, being taken advantage of by certain people, or losing money while gambling. The thera-

Deep muscle relaxation is often used in stress management classes.

pist would seek to identify as precisely as possible the stimuli associated with the response of depression. The therapist would then choose those techniques (from a variety of behavioral intervention techniques) that appear to have the best promise of breaking the stimulus-response connection. For example, if the client is being taken advantage of by a colleague at work, the client might be taught through role playing to be more assertive. If the client is in an unhappy marriage, the husband may be brought in and the client and her husband may be encouraged to develop contingency contracts by which each would seek to do specific things that please the other and would seek to stop doing the things that displease the other. If the client is depressed because she is unemployed, she might be given instruction on how to interview and look for jobs. Cognitive behavior therapists would seek to identify the cognitions that are leading the client to be depressed and then use such techniques as "thought stopping" and "reframing" to change these thoughts.

Feminist intervention views a woman's personal problems, such as depression, as being due to the constraints she experiences in attempting to survive in a politically, economically, and socially oppressive society. Feminist intervention maintains that what a woman experiences in her personal life is directly related to societal dynamics. There are an immense number of societal dynamics that negatively impact women. For example, a depressed female's distress may be related to oversubscription to sex-role stereotypes, which suggest that a woman should be docile, receptive, and dependent. The message is one of helplessness—she is unable to take care of herself and must depend on others for her well-being. Oversubscription to sex-role stereotypes engenders a state of powerlessness in which a woman is likely to become involved in situations where she becomes victimized. Because young girls are socialized to be helpless, when they become women they have a limited repertoire of resources when under stress. Oversubscription to sex-role stereotypes leads to a sense of diminished self-worth, which leads to depressive symptomology. Feminist intervention would first help the depressed client analyze how her problem is related to systematic difficulties experienced by women in a sexist, racist, and classist society. For example, is she in an abusive relationship? Or, is she being victimized by sex discrimination or sexual harassment at work? Or, is she so engrossed in providing care to others (such as her children or an elderly parent) that she has not been able to establish a positive sense of self? Or, is she an adult incest survivor? Once the nature of the personal and societal dynamics of the client's problems are analyzed, and she gains an understanding of them, the next stage is empowerment. This stage helps the client recognize that she does have choices or alternatives. The therapist and the client identify the alternatives together. During this stage, the client is encouraged to free herself from traditional gender-role expectations. Intervention focuses on identification and enhancement of the client's strengths rather than on her problems. She is encouraged to develop an independent, positive identity, to view other women as valuable, and to establish social support systems with other women. She is helped to express herself assertively. Once the client has selected some strategies to implement to improve her circumstances, she is given support by her therapist (perhaps through role playing, modeling, and other similar techniques) in implementing her courses of action. The client is also given support in taking responsibility for her personal change. The therapist may also encourage the client to become involved in social change efforts to combat oppression and discrimination in society.

Reality therapy would consider the depression as being related to the client's view of herself as a failure in some area of her life. A reality therapist would focus on the present and future, because the past cannot be changed. The therapist would seek to have the client understand that what she wants now and in the future, along with her motivation to achieve what she wants, is more important than her past experiences in determining what her future will be. In therapy, the therapist would seek to form a working relationship with the client, explore the nature of the depression in some depth, explore alternative actions that she could take to alleviate the depression, and finally make a contract with the client to take certain courses of action by specific deadlines. The reality therapist would seek to convey that the client is responsible for her behaviors through asking such questions as "What are you doing that contributes to the depression?" and "What do you intend to do to improve the situation?" For example, if the client is depressed because she is unhappily married, the therapist would ask such questions as "What are you doing to contribute to the unhappiness in the marriage?" and "What can you do to reduce your unhappiness?"

Rational therapy theorizes that the depression results primarily from the client's self-talk about events she is facing. The therapist would inform the client that unwanted emotions arise from negative and irrational self-talk rather than from events. The initial focus of therapy would be to help the client identify the irrational self-talk that is the primary source of her depression. The therapist would next inform the client of three different constructive approaches for resolving the depression: (1) seeking to change the events associated with her depression, (2) getting involved in meaningful activities (such as hobbies or jogging) that would shift her focus from problematic events to more gratifying events, and (3) countering the negative and irrational self-talk with rational self-challenges. The client would then be encouraged to make a verbal contract to try out one or more of these alternatives. If the third alternative is selected, the client would be instructed in how to write a rational self-analysis.

Insight Versus Resolution Approaches

A useful categorization of therapies is into approaches that emphasize "insight" and those that emphasize "resolution strategies." This categorization is based on a framework originally developed by London (1964). Insight approaches assert that clients will be able to resolve their problems through gaining an understanding or awareness of them. Resolution approaches assert that while it is helpful for clients to understand their problems, insight in and of itself will not resolve them; clients must also be taught or must learn specific ways of resolving their problems once insight is achieved. Another name that has been used for the resolution category is "learning approaches" (Eysenck, 1961).

These categories represent *ideal types*. Most therapy approaches do not really fit simply into one or the other of these two categories; they have some characteristics of both of these ideal types.

The characteristics of these two ideal types and the therapy approaches that adhere to these characteristics are listed in Table 23.1. In a nutshell, psychoanalysis and client-centered therapy are usually classified as being insight approaches. Reality therapy, rational therapy, transactional analysis, feminist intervention, and behavior therapy are usually classified as being resolution approaches. The purest therapy approach (the one that has nearly all the characteristics) in the insight category is psychoanalysis, while behavior therapy is perhaps the purest illustration in the resolution category. This material is presented to assist in analyzing and comparing the contemporary theories of psychotherapy.

Is Counseling Effective?

In the future some historian who is studying the 20th century may amusingly label it "The Age of Psychotherapy." Hundreds of thousands of people in our country are presently engaged in or seeking counseling or psychotherapy. Millions of dollars every year are being spent by our society to train therapists and to pay therapists for their services. The entertainment world—plays, television programs, movies, and novels—dramatically portrays the lives of many people who are receiving psychotherapy. Every year dozens of books are written on the different theories and techniques of psychotherapy. Certainly, many Americans now believe that receiving psychotherapy is a magical and effective way to change one's personality for the better, to relieve one's tensions, to resolve personal problems, and to lead a happier life. But is it really effective? Does it actually cause people to improve?

Most people, including many psychiatrists, social workers, and psychologists, think that this is an absurd question to ask. They point out that many people do improve after receiving psychotherapy. But is psychotherapy the cause of their improving, or is it just coincidentally connected with their improvement? Perhaps the people who improve while undergoing therapy would improve just as much without having therapy. The only way to discover the effects of psychotherapy is to study the process and the outcome of psychotherapy experimentally; ideally this would involve taking two matched groups of people with personal problems, treating one group by giving them therapy, and then testing both groups to see how

1. Behavior is viewed as being largely determined by internal underlying unconscious processes. Therapies adhering to this view seek to identify the cause of a person's actions by looking at internal factors. (Psychoanalysis, client-centered therapy.)	1. Behavior is viewed as being determined primarily by the environment. Therapies adhering to this view seek to identify the causes of a person's actions by looking at environmental or external factors. (Transactional analysis, reality therapy, behavior therapy, feminist intervention.)
2. The problematic behavior (for example, bed-wetting) is viewed as a *symptom* of an internal, unresolved, and unconscious conflict or fixation. (Psychoanalysis, client-centered therapy.)	2. The problematic behavior (for example, bed-wetting) is viewed as the problem needing to be resolved. (Transactional analysis, reality therapy, rational therapy, behavior therapy, feminist intervention.)
3. If only the symptoms are treated, it is postulated that the underlying conflicts will cause another symptom. (Psychoanalysis, client-centered therapy.)	3. If the problematic behavior is resolved, it is postulated that symptom substitution will not occur. (Transactional analysis, reality therapy, rational therapy, behavior therapy, feminist intervention.)
4. The goal in therapy is to resolve underlying conflicts or disturbing unconscious processes. (Psychoanalysis, client-centered therapy.)	4. The therapy goal is to eliminate the problematic behavior. (Transactional analysis, reality therapy, rational therapy, behavior therapy, feminist intervention.)
5. The medical model is used by labeling and interacting with counselees as patients. (Psychoanalysis.)	5. People with emotional and behavioral problems are viewed as being clients or consumers of services. (Practically all therapy approaches except psychoanalysis.)
6. To resolve the underlying conflict, it is necessary to probe deeply into patients' past. (Psychoanalysis.)	6. The "here-and-now" is important; it is not necessary to probe deeply into the clients' past. (Practically all therapy approaches except psychoanalysis.)

Table 23.1

Comparison of insight and resolution approaches to therapy

much they improved. If the therapy group improves more than the control group, then psychotherapy is probably effective; if both groups improve equally, then psychotherapy is probably ineffective.

At first thought, one would expect that therapists would have done many studies on the effectiveness of psychotherapy for several reasons. First, when psychotherapy was first introduced by Sigmund Freud and adopted shortly afterward by others, it received very strong criticism. The best way to have met this criticism would have been to do experimental studies to prove its effectiveness. Second, clinical psychologists, most of whom at least are part-time therapists, have strongly emphasized the necessity of doing research and have carried out many research studies. One would expect that at least this profession would have done many studies on psycho-

therapy. Third, since there are so many different theories and techniques on how to perform psychotherapy, the best way for a particular therapist to show that he or she has the most effective method would be to test the method experimentally. Fourth, since Americans are so interested in and spend so much money on psychotherapy, one would naturally expect that there would be good proof (by experimental studies) to show that therapy deserves its high position in our society.

However, when we examine the research literature on the effects of psychotherapy, we find that there have been few well-designed studies on this subject. There are numerous reasons for this lack. Many therapists are so convinced of the effectiveness of psychotherapy that they think there is no need to actually demonstrate that it is effective. In addition, it is very difficult to design and carry out

7. The goal of therapy is to bring the underlying conflict or the disturbing unconscious processes to the patients' awareness so (a) the unexpressed energy can be released and (b) the person can then consciously deal with the disabling ideas. (Psychoanalysis, client-centered therapy.)

8. Insight into problems is viewed as being curative in and of itself. (Psychoanalysis, client-centered therapy.)

9. Therapy is likely to last for a long time, often a year or more. (Psychoanalysis, client-centered therapy.)

10. The medical model is used, which asserts that mental illness exists. (Psychoanalysis, client-centered therapy, some advocates of transactional analysis, rational therapy, and behavior therapy.)

11. Mental illness is viewed as resulting from internal unconscious processes, such as conflicts, fixations, and use of defense mechanisms. (Psychoanalysis, client-centered therapy.)

12. The importance of unconscious processes in causing emotional and behavioral problems is emphasized. (Psychoanalysis, client-centered therapy.)

7. Once the therapist and client understand the problem, specific resolution approaches are explored, with the client selecting and contracting to try an approach. (Transactional analysis, reality therapy, rational therapy, behavior therapy, feminist intervention.)

8. Insight is not by itself viewed as being curative; once understanding of the problem is achieved, clients need to become aware of available resolution strategies and then select and try one or more. (Transactional analysis, reality therapy, rational therapy, behavior therapy, feminist intervention.)

9. Therapy is likely to be considerably shorter in duration. (Reality therapy, rational therapy, transactional analysis, behavior therapy, feminist intervention.)

10. The medical model is rejected and mental illness is viewed as being a myth. This concept was described in Chapter 21. (Reality therapy, some advocates of transactional analysis, rational therapy, and behavior therapy.)

11. A learning theory model is used that assumes behavior, including abnormal behavior, is learned. (Reality therapy, rational therapy, transactional analysis, behavior therapy.)

12. Focusing on unconscious processes in understanding human behavior is deemphasized. (Reality therapy, rational therapy, transactional analysis, behavior therapy, feminist intervention.)

studies on this subject. Discussing fully all the problems in designing outcome studies on psychotherapeutic approaches is beyond the scope of this chapter. An excellent discussion of these problems is found in Sundberg and Tyler (1962). A few of the problems are mentioned here to illustrate the difficulties involved in this type of research.

The first problem is to set up some sort of criteria to evaluate the success of treatment. One way to do this is simply to compare the clients' report of their problems when they first come in for help to their report of their problems after therapy has ended. But this is a very subjective method. One of the main difficulties of this method is what Hathaway (1948) has called the "Hello-Goodbye" effect; that is, when clients first ask for help, they try to convince the therapist that they have serious problems and need help; after therapy

has ended, they give the impression that they have been helped—perhaps because they think it is just common courtesy to say that they have been helped.

Another criterion that can be used is to have therapists rate the progress of each of their clients. Obviously, there is the danger of a strong bias operating here. Or, personality tests can be given before and after therapy to those clients for whom personality change is a goal of treatment. Here, however, one runs into the difficulty that the validity of most personality tests is low (Stuart, 1970). Perhaps the best way to solve the criterion problem is to use several different criteria to rate the improvement.

The second major problem is to set up an adequate control group. It is very difficult to match every person in the experimental group with another in the control group on variables that may influence therapeutic change, such as social status, age, intelligence, sex, motivation for improving, and problems they're having. Then there is the problem of trying to get rid of the *placebo effect*. (The placebo effect refers to the amazing fact that people actually do improve just because they believe they are being treated. For example, an injection of distilled water into some patients will produce the same positive effects that are being claimed for a drug.) Thus, the experimental group may show improvement over the control group, but this improvement may be entirely due to the placebo effect and not to psychotherapy at all.

There are many problems caused by the length of therapy—sometimes two or three years. To do research, including follow-ups, may take five years or longer. Such a long time means that many subjects will probably be lost—perhaps through dying or moving away. Losing subjects can easily lead to erroneous results. Also, it is hard to motivate researchers to want to do research on something that takes so long to obtain the results.

These problems in research on psychotherapy are indeed serious, but with ingenuity and perseverance they can be overcome. To show the kind of ingenuity that is needed, H. J. Eysenck (1961) described how to get around the ethical problem of withholding treatment from the control group when an experimental study is being designed:

There are several answers to this point. In the first place, the benefits are merely putative, and consequently nothing is being withheld which is known to be of assistance to the patient. The argument assumes that we have already proved what is in fact the point at issue. In the second place it is a universal practice in medicine, whenever a new method of treatment is put forward, that this new method must receive clinical trials, including a control group not treated by means of the new method. If this is ethically admissible in the whole of medicine, even when the

most serious disorders are involved and where the a priori probability of effectiveness in favour of the new cure may be rather high, then it is difficult to see why a different set of ethical ideals should apply in psychiatry where disorders are rather less serious. . . . In the third place it is quite untrue that psychotherapy would have to be withdrawn from certain people in order to provide a control group. Of all those who are said to be able to benefit from psychotherapy only a very small number have in fact received it. In the United States, at least, there is a high correlation between the income of the patient and the choice of therapy; middle-class patients by and large get psychotherapy, working-class patients get physical treatment. It would be very easy indeed to get together large groups of patients who would not in the normal way obtain psychotherapy and to form an experimental and control group from these patients. If this were done the outcome would not be that psychotherapy was withheld, because of the experiment, from people who might otherwise benefit from it; rather, the experiment would be instrumental in bringing psychotherapy to people who would not otherwise have received it. [p. 701]

In fact, some studies, because they were well designed and well executed, have proved that it is possible to do good outcome studies on psychotherapy. The Cambridge-Somerville Youth Study (Teuber & Powers, 1953) is a good example. For approximately eight years, from 1937 to 1945, this large-scale treatment effort was directed at the prevention of delinquency—by guidance, counseling, and therapy—in a group of over 600 delinquent boys. The surprising result of this study was that this treatment did not reduce the incidence of delinquency in the treatment group when compared to the control group. But what is important for our present purposes is that this study (1) used a control group that was properly chosen and had a large enough number of subjects in each group (control and experimental) to make the results statistically meaningful; (2) carried on the treatment and the follow-up over a long period to obtain meaningful results, (3) used objective criteria to evaluate the treatment, and (4) investigated the process of therapy in a properly controlled and unbiased fashion. Since this study was able to solve the problems of doing good outcome research on psychotherapy, it demonstrated that the effects of psychotherapy can be researched.

When we turn to studies on the effectiveness of psychotherapy, we find some very startling results!

In 1952 H. J. Eysenck first asked the question "Is psychotherapy effective?" Eysenck wanted to learn whether psychotherapy increased the rate of recovery from neurosis for adults over what might be expected if they received no psychotherapy. To set up his baseline of recovery from neurosis (the rate of recovery of those not receiving therapy), he used two sources of information: (1) Landis, in his study of New York State hospitals from 1917 to 1934, found that the recovery rate of the neurotic patients within these hospitals was 72 percent. This rate of recovery is probably even lower than the recovery rate of all neurotic people because only severe neurotics who have a poor chance of recovering are sent to state hospitals, and because at that time the patients in state hospitals received very little treatment besides custodial care. (2) Denker found that the rate of recovery of 500 disability claimants of the Equitable Life Assurance Society was also 72 percent. These 500 patients were under a physician's care but received no psychotherapy. Thus, Eysenck chose 72 percent as his baseline of recovery from neurosis.

Eysenck then examined the research literature on the effectiveness of psychotherapy and found 19 studies, covering over 7,000 cases, in which a wide variety of psychotherapeutic techniques had been used. The studies were divided according to whether the treatment was psychoanalytic or less intensive therapy. The percentage of cured or much improved by psychoanalysis was 44 percent if all cases are considered. (If only completed cases are used, the rate was 66 percent.) The percentage of cured or much improved for the other kinds of therapy was 66 percent. These percentages differ significantly from the baseline recovery rate of 72 percent for neurotic people without any therapy—but the differences are not in the predicted direction!

Eysenck (1952) summed up this study by stating:

> In general, certain conclusions are possible from these data. They fail to prove that psychotherapy, Freudian or otherwise, facilitates the recovery of neurotic patients. They show that roughly two-thirds of a group of neurotic patients will recover or improve to a marked extent within about two years of the onset of their illness, whether they are treated by means of psychotherapy or not. This figure appears to be remarkably stable from one investigation to another, regardless of type of patient treated, standard of recovery employed, or method of therapy used. From the point of view of the neurotic, these figures are encouraging: from the point of view of the psychotherapist, they can hardly be called very favourable to his claims. [p. 324]

These are, indeed, some very startling results. However, they were reaffirmed by E. E. Levitt in 1957, who summarized a large number of unpublished and published studies in which children were treated with psychotherapy. He concluded:

> The therapeutic eclecticism, the number of subjects, the results, and the conclusions of this paper are markedly similar to that of Eysenck's study. Two-thirds of the patients examined at close, and about three-quarters seen in follow-up have improved. Approximately the same percentages of improvement are found for comparable

groups of untreated children. . . . It now appears that Eysenck's conclusion concerning the data for adult psychotherapy is applicable to children as well; the results do not support the hypotheses that recovery from neurotic disorder is facilitated by psychotherapy. [p. 196]

When Eysenck's results were published in 1952, they stimulated more research on this subject. However, the increase in research was not as great as might have been expected from such startling results—perhaps therapists thought that Eysenck's results were so erroneous that many just ignored them, or maybe research in this area is so threatening to therapists that they do not want to research something that might show they are providing little or no useful service. Anyway, Eysenck in 1961 examined the studies in this area that had been done since 1952. He found only three studies showing an increase in the rate of recovery from neurosis for those receiving therapy that was higher than the 72 percent baseline recovery rate for those not receiving therapy. These three studies were done by J. Wolpe, Lakin Phillips, and Albert Ellis. All three of these therapists base their treatment on learning theory. Eysenck (1961) concluded:

With the single exception of the psychotherapeutic methods based on learning theory, results of published research with military and civilian neurotics, and with both adults and children, suggest that the therapeutic effects of psychotherapy are small or nonexistent, and do not in any demonstrable way add to the nonspecific effects of routine medical treatment, or to such events as occur in the patient's everyday experience.

The writer must admit to being somewhat surprised at the uniformly negative results issuing from all this work. In advancing his rather challenging conclusion in the 1952 report the main motive was one of stimulating better and more worthwhile

research in this important but somewhat neglected field; there was an underlying belief that while results to date had not disproved the null hypothesis, improved methods of research would undoubtedly do so. Such a belief does not seem to be tenable any longer in this easy optimistic form, and it would rather seem that psychologists and psychiatrists will have to acknowledge the fact that current psychotherapeutic procedures have not lived up to the hopes which greeted their emergence fifty years ago. [p. 720]

A little later in his summary, Eysenck (1961) went so far as to recommend the following:

It would appear advisable, therefore, to discard the psychoanalytic model, which both on the theoretical and practical plane fails to be useful in mediating verifiable predictions, and to adopt, provisionally at least, the learning theory model which, to date, appears to be much more promising theoretically and also with regard to application. [p. 721]

In 1965 Eysenck again reviewed all the studies conducted on psychotherapy and concluded:

Neurotic patients treated by means of psychotherapeutic procedures based on learning theory improve significantly more quickly than do patients treated by means of psychoanalytic or eclectic psychotherapy or not treated by psychotherapy at all.

Neurotic patients treated by psychoanalytic psychotherapy do not improve more quickly than patients treated by means of eclectic psychotherapy, and may improve less quickly when account is taken of the large proportion of patients breaking off treatment.

With the single exception of the psychotherapeutic methods based on learning theory, results of published research with military and civilian neurotics, and with both adults and children, suggest that the therapeutic effects of psychotherapy are small or nonexistent. [pp. 135–136]

A number of other authorities have reviewed the outcome studies conducted on psychotherapy and have arrived at similar conclusions. Stuart (1970), for example, concluded that only therapy approaches based on what we earlier categorized in this chapter as *resolution approaches* appear to be effective; outcome studies generally show that around 90 percent of clients treated by these approaches improve. Also, Stuart concluded that for clients treated by most insight approaches (such as client-centered therapy), the rate of improvement is about the same as for disturbed persons receiving no treatment.

Finally, for clients receiving therapy from the psychoanalytic approach, the rate of improvement is somewhat lower than for people with problems who receive no treatment. Stuart suggested that the reason for this deterioration is the assignment of nondescriptive medical labels (labels such as schizophrenia, unresolved Oedipus complex, psychosis) often by psychoanalysts, even though they do not know the causes of these supposed disorders and even though these labels do not describe specific behavior. Stuart suggested that such labels have a negative effect; they do not suggest a treatment approach and instead lead patients, and often those who interact with the patients, to try to resolve some unknown, nonexistent illness rather than focusing on resolving their personal problems. Also, such labels lead patients to view themselves as different, as having an illness, which leads them to lose their self-esteem and self-confidence and sidetracks them from seeking to be responsible and productive. (More material on the effects of mental illness labels is presented in Chapter 21.)

A recent review of outcome studies by Lambert, Shapiro, and Bergin (1986) concluded that there is now some evidence that some psychotherapies have beneficial results:

Many psychotherapies that have been subjected to empirical study have been shown to have demonstrable effects on a variety of clients. These effects are not only statistically significant but clinically meaningful. Psychotherapy facilitates the remission of symptoms. It not only speeds up the natural healing process but often provides additional coping strategies and methods for dealing with future problems. Psychologists, psychiatrists, social workers, and marriage and family therapists as well as patients can be assured that a broad range of therapies, when offered by skillful, wise, and stable therapists, are likely to result in appreciable gains for the client.... Behavior therapy, cognitive therapy, and eclectic mixtures of these show superior outcomes to traditional verbal therapies in several studies on specific disorders. [p. 201]

Behavior therapy and cognitive therapy (an example is rational therapy) are classified as resolution approaches to therapy.

Fischer (1973) asked the question, "Is casework effective?" He then reviewed all the outcome studies on casework that used both an experimental group and a control group— a total of 11 studies. The findings are similar to the findings of outcome studies on insight approaches to psychotherapy. Fischer (1973) reported:

Of all the controlled studies of the effectiveness of casework that could be located, nine out of eleven clearly showed that professional caseworkers were unable to bring about any positive, significant, measurable changes in their clients beyond those that would have occurred without the specific intervention program or that could have been induced by nonprofessionals dealing with similar clients, often in less intensive service programs. In the two additional studies, the results were obfuscated by deficiencies in the design or the statistical analysis. Thus not only has professional casework failed to demonstrate that it is effective, but lack of effectiveness appears to be the rule rather than the exception across several categories of clients, problems, situations, and types of casework. [pp. 13–14]

Fischer (1979) raised the question "Isn't casework effective yet?" and concluded (p. 245), "There is still no evidence that MSW-level social workers can produce better results with their clients than would occur with no treatment at all."

What do such research findings mean? I will provide my thoughts on the conclusions to be drawn from these reviews of outcome studies:

1. The effectiveness of casework, psychotherapy, and counseling can no longer be assumed. Additional research is definitely needed to determine which therapeutic approaches are effective, and why they are effective.

2. Available evidence suggests that the psychoanalytic approach should either be discarded or at least tested extensively to determine why patients have a lower rate of improvement than people with problems who receive no treatment.

3. Approaches that only seek to have clients gain insight into their problems appear to have no higher rate of improvement than people with problems who receive no treatment. (It appears that therapy techniques based on the insight model were largely used by caseworkers in the 11 studies reviewed by Fischer.) These research findings suggest that while insight into a problem may be useful, it is not in and of itself sufficient to bring about positive changes.

4. Therapies that are based on a learning theory approach to helping clients are generally being found to be effective in outcome studies. A crucial component of the learning model appears to be exploring resolution strategies and then having clients select and contract to use a specific resolution approach. Often clients need to be "taught" how to use the strategy (for example, doing a rational self-analysis) in their daily lives. Approaches that largely use the learning model include behavior therapy, transactional analysis, reality therapy, rational therapy, and feminist intervention.

5. Chapter 22 speculates that any therapeutic technique that is successful in changing unwanted emotions and dysfunctional actions is effective primarily because it changes a person's thinking from self-talk that is negative or irrational to self-talk that is more rational and positive. If changing negative or irrational self-talk is the key therapeutic agent in psychotherapy approaches, then the current controversy over which therapy approaches are effective and which are not may be refocused to address "Which therapy approaches are most effective in changing negative and irrational self-talk?" and "How can present therapy approaches be refined, and new approaches developed, to change negative and irrational self-talk more effectively?"

Summary

This chapter categorizes comprehensive psychotherapy theories in terms of whether they have characteristics of the insight approach or the resolution approach to therapy. *Insight approaches* assert that clients will be able to resolve their problems by gaining an understanding or awareness of their problems. *Resolution approaches* assert that clients must be taught, or must learn, specific ways of resolving their problems once insight is achieved. Psychoanalysis is the purest insight approach, and client-centered therapy adheres to most of the principles of the insight approach. Transactional analysis, rational therapy, reality therapy, feminist intervention, and behavior therapy adhere to most of the principles of the resolution approach.

It is difficult to design outcome studies on psychotherapeutic approaches for a variety of reasons. There are difficulties in setting up criteria to evaluate the success of treatment. Controlling for the "Hello-Goodbye" effect is difficult. Setting up an adequate control group is often problematic. Finally, doing follow-up research on clients who are in therapy for several years takes a lot of time and resources.

There have been few well-designed studies on the effectiveness of psychotherapy. The studies that have been conducted generally show that clients treated by insight approaches have no higher rate of improvement than people with problems who receive no treatment. Studies have shown that patients treated by psychoanalysis have a lower rate of improvement than people with problems who receive no treatment. Therapies that are based on a resolution or learning approach have generally been found to be effective in outcome studies.

A final word of caution is given in ending this chapter. Many of the therapy techniques described in this text (psychoanalysis, implosive therapy, intensive sex therapy, aversive techniques, hypnosis, covert sensitization, and systematic desensitization) should be used only by skilled therapists with extensive training because there is a danger that improper utilization may intensify the problematic behavior or create undesired side effects.

Exercises

1. What causes positive changes in therapy?

>*Goal:* This exercise is designed to have students discuss what the key psychotherapeutic element in counseling is.

>*Step 1:* Explain the purpose of the exercise. Indicate that at the present time there is no widely accepted theory about why such diverse therapies as behavior therapy, rational therapy, meditation, task-centered practice, reality therapy, hypnosis, transactional analysis, and feminist intervention are therapeutic.

>*Step 2:* Ask the class if they know of a key psychotherapeutic element that will explain why all these therapies lead to positive changes in clients. Indicate that this question is crucial because if such an element is identified, greater attention can be given in therapy to make certain this element is fully incorporated into the therapeutic process.

>*Step 3:* Indicate that the author of this text asserts that any therapy technique that is successful in changing emotions or actions is effective primarily because it changes a person's thinking from negative or irrational self-talk to self-talk that is more rational and positive. Give some examples (as described in Chapter 22) that such approaches as behavior therapy, psychoanalysis, client-centered therapy, and meditation can be "reinterpreted" to suggest that restructuring thinking is the key psychotherapeutic element in counseling.

>*Step 4:* Ask the students to discuss whether they believe restructuring thinking is the key psychotherapeutic element. Ask those who disagree what they believe the key psychotherapeutic element is.

2. Treating depression

Goal: This exercise is designed to help students identify the merits and shortcomings of therapeutic approaches that are used in treating depression.

Step 1: Prior to the class period in which this exercise is conducted, have the students read the section "Comparison of Counseling Theories" in this chapter. Divide the class into subgroups of three or four. Instruct each subgroup to rank, on a scale of 1 to 7 (based on their judgments), the following therapies' level of effectiveness in treating depression: psychoanalysis, client-centered therapy, transactional analysis, behavior therapy, feminist intervention, reality therapy, and rational therapy.

Step 2: Write the names of these seven therapy approaches on the chalkboard. After the subgroups complete this ranking process, ask a representative from each subgroup to write its ranking on the chalkboard. Ask each subgroup to explain the reasons for its ranking.

Step 3: Ask the class to discuss whether this exercise has been helpful in assisting them in making decisions about which therapeutic approach to use in treating depression.

IV

Taking Care of Self

24 Surviving and Enjoying Social Work

To be of help to others, helping professionals must first take care of themselves. Good emotional and physical health are internal resources that helping professionals need in order to help others.

The focus of this chapter is on how to survive and enjoy a career in social work. First, suggestions are presented for resolving common concerns of students receiving professional training in social work. Sections that follow then present material on how to avoid burnout, how to manage stress, and how to enjoy social work and life.

Students' Common Concerns

One of the surprises I found in teaching social work students is that although they have a number of common concerns, they believe their concerns are so unique and "secret" that they are reluctant to share and discuss them with others. In this section a number of these concerns are presented and some suggestions are given for resolving them.

Will I Be Able to Make It in Field Placement?

Associated with this concern are a number of more specific concerns. Will I be accepted and liked by the agency staff? Will I be accepted and liked by the clients who are assigned to me? Will I be able to help clients? Will the clothes I wear be acceptable? Will my shortcomings do me in? (*Every* student perceives a number of personal shortcomings—such as unusual tone of voice, inability to speak clearly, a low level of interviewing skills, questionable personal appearance, or inability to start and maintain a conversation, and so on; students by far are their own harshest critics.) Am I emotionally stable enough to handle field placement? Will I be able to speak on the telephone? Will I be able to learn to do all the paperwork? Will I be attacked by clients? Will my car hold up, or will I be able to get where I'm supposed to be? Will I become too anxious and get stage fright when I'm assigned certain tasks?

In 20 years of supervising students in field placement, I have heard these and many similar concerns from practically every student. The students I worry about in arranging field placements are those who deny having such concerns, since I have found they generally are not perceptive about themselves. If a person is not perceptive about personal concerns and emotions, it generally means he or she will not be perceptive about the thoughts and emotions of clients and therefore will not make a skillful counselor.

Practically every student will be anxious before field placement and during at least the first few weeks at placement. This anxiety is to be expected. Students will find in field placement that their moderate level of anxiety will drain their energy, and most will be exhausted when they leave in the evening.

Although such anxiety and concerns are normal, there are ways of reducing some of these concerns.

1. In many social work programs, students have considerable input in choosing their field placement setting. If you have a voice in selecting a placement, use this opportunity to visit the agency you are considering for a placement. You can meet with agency staff, receive a description of the agency's programs, and also discuss the ex-

pected tasks for student interns. Certain other concerns, such as expected dress code, can also be discussed. If after the visit you have serious reservations about taking a placement at that agency, discuss your reservations with the faculty at school who coordinate field placements. If your concerns are not reduced after such a discussion, many programs allow you to visit another agency to explore doing a field placement there.

2. Ask other students currently in field placement, or who have completed field placement, to share and discuss their experiences and concerns. This will give you a better idea of what placement is like and may also provide you with answers to some of your concerns. It is particularly useful to talk with students who have had a field placement at the agency where you want to go.

3. Discuss your concerns with faculty who coordinate field placements at your school. They will be able to answer some of your concerns and provide additional information about the agency where you want to be placed.

4. Volunteer in your classes to role-play simulated counseling situations. Particularly useful is to have these role playings videotaped and played back to you. This will enable you to assess and further develop your interviewing skills. Zastrow and Navarre (1979) have found that videotaped role playing of counseling situations also develops students' confidence in their counseling capacities.

5. These suggestions will reduce some, but certainly not all, of your concerns about whether you will make it in field placement. Therefore, it is normal to be anxious when you begin your placement. As the weeks pass, the vast majority of students receive feedback that they are doing well and become more and more relaxed.

While at your placement, express your concerns to your agency supervisor and ask any questions that you have about agency procedures and policies, and expectations for student interns. Also, if you are confused about how to carry out assigned tasks or have other questions related to your placement, talk to your agency supervisor. Open communication between you and your agency supervisor is an important key to making it in field placement.

Will I Conduct a Satisfactory Interview with My First Client?

Students have a number of specific concerns related to this question. How will I know what to say? How will I keep the conversation going? If I say the wrong thing, won't it be a calamity for the client? How will I introduce myself? Will the client discover that I am only a student and therefore feel he or she is being used as a guinea pig to train me? What if I become tongue-tied and am unable to say anything? Am I really ready to assume the awesome responsibility of counseling others? I've got personal problems that are unresolved—how can I possibly help others?

Some students become so concerned before seeing their first client that they are unable to sleep well the night before; others may develop a tension headache. A few have told me they have had such visceral reactions as being unable to eat, or developing diarrhea, or regurgitating. It happens. If you have such severe reactions, you are not alone. Furthermore, it is highly unlikely that you will "bomb" during your first interview; most anxious students report once the interview began they relaxed and the interview went fairly well.

Some suggestions follow for reducing some of the concerns:

1. Role-play simulated counseling situations, ideally playing the roles of both counselor and client. Videotaping and reviewing the tape is particularly helpful. Such role playing will give you practice in counseling.

2. Prepare for the interview by identifying what your objectives are, and by think-

ing about the kinds of questions you will need to ask to accomplish these objectives. Review the material in Chapters 4 and 5 on how to begin and end interviews, how to build a relationship, and how to begin to explore the client's problems.

3. Clients are much less fragile than beginning counselors believe they are. If you fail to cover something, you can probably do that at some future interview. If you fail to phrase a question properly, you won't cause a calamity in the client's life. It is irrational to expect that if you make some mistakes in this first interview that you will cause a disaster for the client—no one has that kind of power. Clients have been exposed to much more trauma and chaotic situations than talking to you; they survived those experiences, so they will definitely survive talking to you.

4. Review the interview with your agency supervisor or your faculty supervisor to identify the aspects you did well, and the aspects you need to improve. It is irrational to expect perfection in your first interview, or for that matter in any interview. Everyone is fallible, so mistakes will be made. In addition, the main purpose of field placement is *training*—helping you test and further develop your social work skills and techniques. Therefore, agency staff expect you to learn and grow and make some mistakes. Students who generally do best in placement are those who seek to test out and develop their social work skills. It is a serious mistake to "hang back" in field placement for fear of making mistakes. Focusing on making few errors to get a high grade usually leads the student intern to "hang back"—which then tends to result in a lower grade.

5. If you have specific questions prior to this first interview, ask your agency supervisor. For example, you may wonder whether you should inform the client that you are a student. Different agencies handle this question differently. In field placement your agency supervisor wants to hear your questions and concerns. Only through hearing your questions can your agency supervisor determine "where you are" and how to be most helpful to you. Agency supervisors were once in training themselves. They are aware of the pressures and anxieties of being in field placement and are committed to helping you. Many have told me that the questions students ask frequently add a fresh, new perspective to their practice, which leads them to make improvements in their counseling and interviewing approaches.

I'm Really Depressed, Because My Supervisor Is Able to Handle an Interview Much Better Than I—Will I Ever Be Able to Do That Well?
When student interns observe the interviewing and counseling skills of their agency or faculty supervisor, many become depressed because they realize their skills are not as highly developed. They tend to "awfulize" and erroneously conclude they never will do well at interviewing and counseling. It is simply irrational for a student to expect that his or her skills should be as highly developed as the supervisor's; the supervisor has had many more years of training and experience. With additional years of training and experience, most beginning counselors eventually develop skill levels that are comparable to those of their supervisors. "Rome was not built in a day." Rather than thinking negatively and "self-downing" oneself, it is much better to think positively and use your supervisors as role models in developing interviewing and counseling skills.

How Should I Separate the Role of Counselor from That of Friend?
Students generally have a small caseload in field placement, which allows them to spend considerable time with clients. It is not uncommon for clients to begin to become attracted to their worker as the sharing of personal concerns fosters an attachment.

Students are also generally young and physically attractive, which also fosters an attachment. A frequent question that students in field placement have is "Is this client beginning to see me as someone he wants to get socially involved with—and if so, how do I handle this?" There are a number of related questions. "This client has invited me to her home—should I go?" "This client has suggested we go have a soda (or a cup of coffee, or dinner) together—should I go?" "This client has suggested we go to a park (or play golf, or go to bar, or play cards)—should I go?"

There are no yes or no answers to these questions. Most agencies frown on, and some prohibit, fraternizing with clients. For example, if a probation officer were to socialize extensively with a probationee, problems might arise. The probationee might violate some conditions of probation and then try to use the friendship with the probation officer to avoid diverse consequences of the violations. In addition, other probationees and parolees are apt to become aware of the friendship relationship, and conclude they no longer have to rigidly adhere to the conditions of probation or of parole as the probation officer is "a nice guy" and "a soft touch." In addition, administrative officials are apt to see the friendship relationship as leading to a possible conflict of interest situation and may disapprove highly of such a relationship.

In addition, if you become socially involved with a client it is often more difficult to counsel that person effectively. The client, for example, may no longer be willing to accept suggestions from you as he may misinterpret the suggestions as being "put-downs." Counseling someone you are socially involved with brings forth the same personality clashes as when you try to teach a close member of your family how to drive a car.

On the other hand, the attraction of a client to a counselor can be a component of a helping relationship. This attraction can occasionally be used positively. For example, I've seen elderly, apathetic, depressed male clients in nursing homes become attracted to female student interns. These interns have then been able to use this attraction to motivate these elderly men to become involved in programs at the nursing homes (such as hobbies and craft activities). Once involved in such programs, they usually start to enjoy them, and as a result become more energetic, happier, and more active.

How then should a counselor decide whether to accept an invitation from a client to do something together? The guideline is simple. If the counselor believes doing something with a client will help develop a working relationship and be constructive for the client, then do it. For example, for some clients, going to a park and talking will help them relax and develop the kind of atmosphere in which they will feel free to share and discuss their secret personal concerns. On the other hand, if the counselor believes accepting an invitation has the potential for being destructive to the helping process, then don't do it. For example, if the counselor believes going to a park will lead the client to interpret that the counselor wants to become involved in a "dating" relationship, then it is best to tactfully decline the invitation. (Establishing professional boundaries with clients is discussed at greater length in Chapter 2.)

It may be useful for beginning workers to be aware of the essential difference between a friendship and a professional relationship. Friendship is both for *giving* and *receiving;* while a professional relationship involves the helping person *giving* and the client *receiving.*

Beginning counselors often wonder how, in practice, to separate the role of counselor from that of a friend. With experience, this problem gradually disappears. Apparently experienced counselors become more perceptive in determining the intent behind invitations from clients and more skillful in conveying the boundaries of the professional relationship. Experienced counselors also have more cases, which often reduces the amount of time spent per client, which reduces socializing opportunities.

How Can I Avoid Becoming Too Emotionally Involved with Clients' Problems?

Every counselor has, at one time or another, become overly emotionally involved in some cases.

I recently was a faculty supervisor for a student in a child welfare unit at a public welfare department. One of the cases assigned to this student was a 14-year-old girl who had been in a series of foster homes. The student, Linda H., became fairly attached to the girl, partly because she sympathized with the girl for having been placed in a series of foster homes since she was 3. This 14-year-old girl became interested in dating, which her conservative foster parents could not accept. Considerable friction developed, and the foster parents suggested to the agency that it would be best if the girl was placed in a different foster home. Linda H. arranged a meeting between the foster parents and the 14-year-old to try to work out a compromise, particularly because the girl was feeling rejected. The meeting didn't resolve any concerns. So Linda H., after considerable effort, found another foster home, and a trial visit was attempted. Linda H. indicated in describing this visit, "I felt like a nervous mother" about this visit. (Right away this statement led me to believe the student was becoming overly involved.) The trial visit went fairly well, but after a day of reflecting, these foster parents decided they did not want to take a foster child at this time. The girl felt rejected, unloved, and depressed. Linda H., being too emotionally involved, became so depressed that she had to take two days off from her placement. She sympathized, rather than empathized, with the girl. Fortunately she realized she was too emotionally involved at this point to search for another foster family. (She did ask the foster parents to keep the youth for a few more days until a new placement could be found, which they consented to do.)

As this case example indicates, when counselors become too emotionally involved, they have a reduced capacity to help clients discuss their problems and to explore alternative solutions objectively with clients.

There appear to be several types of irrational thinking that lead to overinvolvement. Table 24.1 lists these types of irrational thinking and presents rational self-challenges to counter them.

Beginning counselors are much more apt to become overly involved than experienced counselors, because with experience, counselors increasingly learn that clients own their problems, that clients are the primary problem solvers, and that to be of optimal assistance counselors need to remain objective rather than exaggerating the consequences of resolution approaches that don't work out. (The main reason counselors are less successful in counseling close friends and relatives is because they are too involved to be objective.)

Yet, even experienced counselors at times become too involved. I speak from experience. A few years ago I was asked by a high state official to provide professional help for a number of personal problems she faced— including burnout, grief over her husband's death, drinking problems, insomnia, depression, and lack of meaning in work or in living. This state official was highly respected. I realized I was giving myself the following irrational thinking that was leading to overinvolvement: "I must solve her problems. If she resigns her position this will be tragic, as several thousand people in the state will be adversely affected. If this person resigns, it will be awful." Through countering such irrational thinking with rational self-challenges, I was able to help her explore her problems, one at a time, and develop strategies to handle each.

Suggestions to counter emotional overinvolvement include the following:

1. When you feel emotionally involved in a case (for example, taking it home with you by thinking about it for several hours), discuss it with others, particularly your supervisor. Other people are often able to offer

Irrational Thinking	Rational Self-Challenges
1. "This client has shared his problems, and therefore I must help this client resolve these problems." (Such thinking leads to taking ownership of the client's problems.)	1. "Clients own their problems, and have the responsibility for resolving them. I do not have the power to resolve them. All I can do is help clients explore their problems, explore alternative solutions, and encourage clients to select a resolution approach."
2. "If things (events) don't work out for clients, I have failed. I am at fault for their problems. I am a failure."	2. "Everyone has ups and downs. We are all fallible, and we all have problems. If one resolution approach does not work out for a client, it only means that approach failed. It in no way means I am a failure. What the client and I need to do is to examine why that approach did not work out, explore other alternatives, select one, and try that."
3. "If things don't work out for clients, it is *awful, terrible, overwhelming, unbearable.*"	3. "As Ellis and Harper (1977b) pointed out, it is irrational to conclude that a problem is either awful, overwhelming, or unbearable. Adverse events are often inconvenient and problematic, but assigning labels such as *awful* only leads to unwanted emotions. Instead of viewing problems as being overwhelming, I need to take each problem one at a time, and in a step-by-step fashion develop strategies to deal with each."
4. "If I don't solve the client's problems, the consequences for the client, the client's family, and others close to the client will be tragic, unbearable." (Overly involved counselors often view the consequences as being more tragic than the clients themselves view the consequences.)	4. "Clients own their problems, and have the responsibility to resolve them. I am not God; I have no miracle power to resolve problems. All I can ever do is 'give it my best shot' in counseling. It is irrational and counterproductive to overexaggerate consequences. If the selected approach doesn't work, the client needs to select and try another."
5. "I've tried the only approach that there is, and that failed. There is no hope. Things are certainly bleak for this client. I feel overwhelmed—I give up!"	5. "There is always hope. Even though I am unaware of other alternatives, there may well be others. I need to talk to an authority in this area to learn about other alternatives."

Table 24.1
Irrational thinking leads to emotional overinvolvement, which can be changed by rational self-challenges

suggestions on alternatives and may be able to suggest ways to become more objective and less emotionally involved.

2. Do a rational self-analysis (described in Chapter 22) on your unwanted emotions about a case. A rational self-analysis will enable you to identify your irrational thinking and to counter it with rational self-challenges.

3. If you are intensely emotionally involved with a case, seriously consider transferring it to another worker. It is irrational to expect to be able to handle all cases optimally. You will be able to handle some cases better than your fellow workers, while your fellow workers will be able to handle other cases better than you. If you become intensely emotionally involved with a case for an extended period, this strongly suggests you will have difficulty in being objective and therefore transfer is indicated.

Do I Really Want a Career in Social Work?

Related specific concerns of students to this question are the following: Do I have the capacities to be a competent social worker? What area of social work (for example, mental health, corrections) should I pursue? Will a career in social work pay me enough money to live the way I want to live? What do I really want to do with my life? What will my parents, friends, and relatives think of me if I become a social worker? Is there a profession or vocation that I would find more enjoyable and gratifying?

Most of these questions only you can answer. As far as the money question goes, faculty members in your social work department will be able to tell you what the average starting salary is in your area for graduates of baccalaureate and master's programs in social work. Starting salaries vary considerably in different regions, and in different positions. Pay increases are largely determined by you—your skills, your efforts to obtain advanced degrees, and your efforts to seek administrative and supervisory positions that generally pay more than direct services. Some successful psychotherapists in private practice (who have an MSW degree and two or more years of counseling experience) are now earning over $100,000 per year. Skills at grant writing, consultation, public speaking, and developing new programs are also often financially rewarded.

But how do you determine whether social work is the right career for you, and which area of social work to pursue? Only you can make such decisions. The following are some suggestions:

1. Relax, don't be in a hurry to make a final career decision. Some social work students think they must make such decisions within a few weeks. They become so anxious over thinking about the pros and cons that they literally become overwhelmed and are unable to make any rational decision. In one sense you've got most of the rest of your life to make such career decisions.

Before, during, and after graduation, college students often ponder whether they chose the right career. Some occasionally change careers during their working years.

Many people have successfully started new careers in their forties, fifties, sixties, and even seventies.

2. Actively pursue a trial-and-error approach. If you try an area of social work that you find unsatisfying, try another. Skills learned in one area usually transfer to another. Perhaps you will find one area fulfilling for awhile, and then gradually find the position becoming more and more mundane, routine, and uninspiring. If that occurs, you may well want to try another area. If you really don't think you want a career in social work, fine; try something else— you may like it. Perhaps someday you'll change your mind and want to try social work again. No problem. You can take refresher or continuing education courses, or attend workshops to polish your skills, and to learn about newer techniques and revised procedures. We have students in our undergraduate courses in their forties, fifties, and sixties who are now pursuing a career in social work, and securing a position on graduation. It is a mistake to think that you have to make a *final* career decision. Times change, agencies change, and our interests and values change. With such changes we

may find it to our advantage at some point in future years to make career changes.

Now, I'm not suggesting that you should idly sit back and wait for some unknown force to make career decisions for you. That's the ostrich head-in-the-sand approach, which is totally unproductive. What I recommend is that you use a *trial-and-error* approach, trying those career opportunities you feel might be fulfilling, and moving on to other opportunities when you become disenchanted.

Burnout

Ron Pakenham is ten days behind in his paperwork. He has been a juvenile probation and parole officer for the past three and one-half years. Both the agency director and the juvenile judge are putting pressure on him to do his paperwork. Mr. Pakenham is also having problems at home. His mother has emphysema, and he and his wife are going through a divorce. While working on his paperwork he receives a call from a house-parent at a group home for adolescent youths, inquiring when high school is starting in fall. (Mr. Pakenham is supervising two teenage boys at this home.) Mr. Pakenham replies, "Hey, I don't know. You'll have to call the school system. I'm not your errand boy. Don't you know I have more important things to do than to hunt information for you?" After hanging up the phone, Mr. Pakenham considers his aggressive response. He also thinks about his family problems and about being behind in his work. Mr. Pakenham realizes he is nearing burnout.

Definitions and Symptoms of Burnout

Burnout is increasingly being recognized as a serious problem affecting many people, particularly professionals employed in human services. Pines and Aronson (1981) defined burnout as being

> a state of mind . . . accompanied by an array of symptoms that indicate a general

malaise: emotional, physical, and psychological fatigue; feelings of helplessness, hopelessness, and a lack of enthusiasm about work and even about life in general. [p. 3]

Maslach and Pines have studied burnout extensively among the following professionals: social workers, psychiatrists, psychologists, prison personnel, psychiatric nurses, legal aid attorneys, physicians, child care workers, teachers, ministers, and counselors. Maslach and Pines (1977) defined burnout and summarized a number of symptoms:

> Burnout involves the loss of concern for the people with whom one is working. In addition to physical exhaustion (and sometimes even illness), burnout is characterized by an emotional exhaustion in which the professional no longer has any positive feelings, sympathy, or respect for clients or patients. A very cynical and dehumanized perception of these people often develops, in which they are labeled in derogatory ways and treated accordingly. As a result of this dehumanizing process, these people are viewed as somehow deserving of their problems and are blamed for their own victimization, and thus there is a deterioration of the quality of care or service that they receive. The professional who burns out is unable to deal successfully with the overwhelming emotional stresses of the job, and this failure to cope can be manifested in a number of ways, ranging from impaired performance and absenteeism to various types of personal problems (such as alcohol and drug abuse, marital conflict, and mental illness). People who burn out often quit their jobs or even change professions, while some seek psychiatric treatment for what they believe to be their personal failings. [pp. 100–101]

Freudenberger (1977) described the symptoms of burnout as follows:

Briefly described, burnout includes such symptoms as cynicism and negativism and a tendency to be inflexible and almost rigid in thinking, which often leads to a closed mind about change or innovation. The worker may begin to discuss the client in intellectual and jargon terms and thereby distance himself from any emotional involvement. Along with this, a form of paranoia may set in whereby the worker feels that his peers and administration are out to make life more difficult. [pp. 90–91]

Burnout Is a Reaction to High Stress

The term *burnout* has been applied to many different situations. A student who has been writing a term paper for three hours may feel burned out with writing, but yet have plenty of energy to do something else. Individuals who abuse their spouse or children may attempt to explain their actions by claiming that they are under considerable stress and just burned out. People who become apathetic and cynical about a frustrating job may claim they are burned out. Some sport coaches (at the college and professional levels) claim the pressure to win is so extensive that after several seasons they feel burned out. A person in an unhappy romantic relationship may feel burned out.

The term *burned out* is closely related to, and has not been adequately differentiated from, the following terms: *alienated, indifferent, apathetic, cynical, discouraged, mentally or physically exhausted,* and *overwhelmed by stress.*

To better understand the nature of burnout, it is useful to conceptualize burnout as being one of the reactions to high levels of stress. The advantage of this conceptualization is that it suggests that stress management strategies can be used to prevent burnout and to treat burnout when it does occur.

Stress is a contributing causal factor in most illnesses, including heart attacks, migraine headaches, diabetes, allergies, colds, cancer, arthritis, insomnia, emphysema, hypertension, and alcoholism (McQuade & Aikman, 1974). Stress is also a contributing factor in numerous emotional and behavioral difficulties, including depression, anxiety, suicide attempts, spouse abuse, child abuse, physical assaults, irritability, and stuttering (Greenberg, 1980). Becoming skillful in reducing stress is now recognized as an effective way to prevent emotional and physical disorders, and is also an effective adjunct to treatment for emotional and physical disorders if they do develop (Pelletier, 1977).

Stress can be defined as the emotional and physiological reactions to stressors. A stressor is a demand, situation, or circumstance that disrupts a person's equilibrium and initiates the stress response. There are an infinite number of possible stressors: crowding, noise, death of a friend, excessive cold, loss of a job, toxic substances, arguments, and so on.

Hans Selye (1956), one of the foremost authorities on stress, has found that the body has a three-stage reaction to stress: the alarm stage, the resistance stage, and the exhaustion stage. Selye called this three-stage response the General Adaptation Syndrome.

In the alarm stage the body recognizes the stressor, such as an argument. The body reacts to the stressor by preparing for fight or flight. The body's reactions are complex and numerous, and will be summarized only briefly here (for an extended discussion, see Greenberg, 1980). The body sends messages from the brain (hypothalamus) to the pituitary gland to release its hormones. These hormones trigger the adrenal glands to release adrenaline. Adrenaline increases the rate of breathing and heartbeat, increases perspiration, raises blood sugar level, dilates the pupils, and slows digestion. The process results in a huge burst of energy, better hearing and vision, and greater muscular strength—all reactions that increase a person's capability to fight or flee. During the alarm stage, the body's immune system functions at a sharply reduced level. (The immune system fights germs, bacteria, and viruses, and facilitates healing within the body.)

In the second stage of resistance, the body becomes relaxed. The resistance stage is brought about by the person relaxing. When relaxed, a person's immune system functions at its optimal capacities. During this stage the body (and the immune system) repairs any damage caused during the alarm stage. Most stressors cause the body to go through only the stages of alarm and repair. During a lifetime a person goes through these two stages thousands of times.

Much stress is beneficial. Stress increases concentration and enhances capacities to accomplish physical tasks. A life without stress would be boring, and is in fact impossible, as even dreaming produces some stress.

The type of stress that causes long-term damage results when the body remains in a stage of high stress for an extended period. When this happens the body is unable to repair the damage and eventually the third stage of exhaustion occurs. This third stage is characterized by the person starting to develop one or more stress-related illnesses, such as an ulcer, hypertension, or arthritis.

A number of authorities on stress have noted there are two components of a stressor: the events or experiences that are encountered, and a person's thoughts and perceptions about these events. Exhibit 24.1 presents a conceptualization of stressors, stress, and stress-related illnesses, which suggests that there are two general approaches for reducing stress. People under stress can reduce stress either by changing the distressing events or by changing their thoughts and perceptions about the events.

As indicated earlier, burnout can be conceptualized as being one of the reactions to high-stress levels. Exhibit 24.2 summarizes this conceptualization. As suggested in Exhibit 24.2, *burnout is caused primarily by what people tell themselves about events or experiences they encounter.* Examples of this kind of thinking are "I've had it." "What's the use, whatever I try won't work." "I'm going to give up—am no longer going to make an effort." *Other people encountering the same events will not burn out if they do not give themselves the self-defeating thoughts characteristic of those who burn out. Conceptualized in this fashion, it follows that burnout will occur only when people give themselves the kind of self-defeating thoughts described here.*

Exhibit 24.1
Conceptualizing stressors, stress, and stress-related illnesses

Stressor
- Events or experiences (for example, backing into another car in a parking lot
- Certain kinds of thinking (for example, "What have I done! I'll probably get a ticket and maybe even get kicked out of my insurance company. What a hassle this is going to be!")

Stress
- Emotional reaction (such as tenseness, anxiety, worry, alarm)
- Physiological reactions (alarm stage of General Adaptation Syndrome) The body prepares for fight or flight. Adrenaline and other hormones increase heartbeat and rate of breathing, increase perspiration, raise blood sugar levels, dilate the pupils, and slow digestion. The process results in greater muscular strength, a huge burst of energy, and better vision and hearing. During the alarm stage, the body's immune system functions at a sharply reduced level.

Stress-related illness
- If the body remains at a high level of stress for a prolonged period, a stress-related disorder is apt to develop, such as an ulcer, insomnia, a heart problem, or a digestive problem.

Exhibit 24.2

Burnout is a reaction to high levels of stress

Stressors {
Events or experiences   (for example, extensive paperwork or considerable turmoil in family life)

↓

Certain kind of stressful thinking which leads to Burnout   (for example, "This is overwhelming. I've had it. Just leave me alone. This is more than I can take!"

Stress {
Emotions   (the emotions identified with burnout—anxiety, frustration, anger, apathy, and so on)

↓

Physiological reactions   (the alarm and exhaustion stages of the General Adaptation Syndrome.)

↓

Actions   (the actions characteristic of burnout; lack of respect for others; cynical toward life; less attention to work and family life; absenteeism, change of jobs, and so on)

} These thinking processes, emotions, physiological reactions, and actions constitute BURNOUT.

Structural Causes of Stress That May Lead to Burnout

As indicated in Exhibit 24.2, burnout is one of the possible reactions to or consequences of high stress levels. It therefore follows that those events or structural factors that are contributing causes of high-stress levels are also contributing factors to burnout.

Edelwich (1980) identified a number of structural factors associated with work that contribute to high stress levels and may lead to burnout:

- Too many work hours
- Career dead end
- Too much paperwork
- Not sufficiently trained for job
- Not appreciated by clients
- Not appreciated by supervisor
- Not paid enough money
- No support for important decisions
- Powerlessness
- System not responsive to clients' needs
- Bad office politics
- Sexism
- Too much travel
- Isolation from peers
- No social life

Edelwich added that people who seek a career in the helping professions are particularly vulnerable to burnout since many enter this field with unrealistic expectations. Such expectations include the beliefs that (1) the services they provide will decisively improve the lives of practically all their clients, (2) they will be highly appreciated by the employing agency and practically all clients, (3) they will be able to substantially change bureaucracies to be more responsive to clients' needs, and (4) there will be many opportunities for rapid advancement and high status. The frustrations experienced at work and the gradual recognition that many of these expectations are unrealistic are contributing factors to stress and to burnout.

Maslach (1976) found that high caseloads in the helping professions are a major cause of stress and may lead to burnout:

Burnout often becomes inevitable when the professional is forced to provide care for too many people. As the ratio increases, the result is higher and higher emotional overload until, like a wire that has too much electricity flowing through it, the worker just burns out and emotionally disconnects. [p. 19]

A lack of approved *time-outs* at work is another source of stress and may be a factor in leading to burnout. Time-outs are not merely short coffee breaks from work; they are opportunities for professionals having a stressful day to switch to less stressful tasks. Time-outs are possible in large agencies that have shared work responsibilities.

Additional causes of burnout include poor time management, inability to work effectively with other people, lack of purpose or undefined goals in life, and inability to handle effectively emergencies that arise (Pines & Aronson, 1981).

Clients are also a factor in determining staff burnout (Maslach, 1978). Certain types of clients are more apt to cause high levels of stress, particularly those whose problems are depressing or emotionally draining (such as terminally ill clients, belligerent clients, suicidal clients, obnoxious clients, incest cases, and severe abuse cases). Working with chronic clients who show no improvement (such as an alcoholic family in which the problem drinker denies a drinking problem) is also more apt to lead to frustration and high stress levels. Working with clients who remind workers of personal difficulties they are presently facing is also emotionally draining, such as providing marriage counseling services when workers are having marital difficulties at home.

Another important contributing factor to high stress and burnout at work is having extensive family responsibilities, such as taking care of a terminally ill parent. Extensive home responsibilities can drain a person's energy and may lead to burnout at home and at work.

In the helping professions another cause is taking "ownership" of client's problems. When a client tells a worker his or her innermost secrets and problems, there is a tendency to want to rescue and save that person. Helping professionals, especially in their early years of practice, are apt to fall victim to the rescue or savior fantasy. This fantasy involves the helping professional erroneously believing she or he has the power to make clients' lives better. When this fails, the helping professional is apt to feel emotionally drained and burned out. Realistically, clients are the chief problem solvers, and are the ones who decide whether they will put forth the effort to improve their lives.

Approaches to Manage Stress and Prevent Burnout

The following is a list and brief description of a number of approaches that are effective in reducing stress and preventing burnout. (Since burnout is one of the reactions to high levels of stress, it follows that stress management techniques are also useful in preventing burnout.) The following stress management techniques are a "smorgasbord" of approaches. It is up to each person to select the ones he or she believes are most needed and is most motivated to use. These approaches are similar to healthy diet plans—they *will* work for those who put forth effort to make them work. (The references provide expanded reading of these approaches.)

Goal Setting and Time Management

It is highly distressing and depressing to be uncertain of what you want out of life—for example, what career you want to pursue. Many people muddle through life without ever setting goals—and thereby generally feel unfulfilled, frustrated, bored, and dissatisfied. Realistic goal setting leads to increased self-confidence, improved decision making, a greater sense of purpose, and an improved sense of security. Have you set goals in your life, or are you a muddler?

Considerable stress also comes from the feeling of having "too much to do in too little time." Time is life. To waste time is to waste life.

Time management approaches help people set goals and use their time effectively in reaching their short-term and lifetime goals. Time management has users first set lifetime and short-term goals (Lakein, 1973). (Admittedly this is often a lengthy process. But failure to set such goals is almost a certain guarantee for feelings of being unfulfilled and dissatisfied.) For the high-priority goals (both short-term and lifetime goals), users write down tasks for accomplishing these goals. The tasks are then prioritized according to what is most important to do to accomplish each goal. Users are then instructed to do the high-priority tasks first, and urged to generally ignore doing the low-priority (low payoff) tasks. Low-priority tasks can bog down a person's time, and interfere with a high-priority task.

Positive Thinking

Everyone has a choice to take either a negative view of events that occur or to take a positive view. People who are prone to burnout tend to take a negative view and to tell themselves such things as "I've had it. I'm no longer going to try. I'm just going to go through the motions. I'm giving in." With such an attitude, they become cynical, apathetic, uncaring, and unproductive.

The positive thinking philosophy asserts that taking a positive view and positive action will lead to others' liking you, your being appreciated, your feeling worthwhile about yourself, your liking yourself, your being productive and creative, your having a pleasant disposition, and good things happening to you. (Positive thinking is discussed more fully later in this chapter.)

Closely related to positive thinking is having a philosophy of life that allows you to travel through life at a relaxed cruising speed. This philosophy also allows you to look at the scenery with enjoyment, to remain calm during crises and emergencies, to approach work thoughtfully in order to increase creativity, and to enjoy leisure in order to develop more fully as a person.

Changing the Thoughts That Produce Burnout

As indicated earlier, burnout is largely caused by a certain kind of thinking. Typical thinking processes that produce burnout are "I'm not going to try anymore. I've had it. I give up. I've failed so many times in the past.

Meditation can be helpful in relieving stress and avoiding burnout.

From now on I'm going to do as little as possible to get by."

Rational therapy (Chapter 22) has demonstrated that the primary cause of all our emotions and our actions is what we tell ourselves about our experiences. The emotions and actions associated with burnout are also primarily determined by our thinking processes.

Although we often cannot change events that happen to us, we always have the power to think rationally and positively, and thereby change *all* of our unwanted emotions and unproductive actions, including the emotions and actions associated with burnout. For example, burnout-producing thoughts can be challenged and changed by telling ourselves instead: "I'm not going to give up. To give up will only hurt me and other people. I've handled challenges in the past and I can and will be able to handle this. Instead of thinking negatively, I've got to work on things constructively, one step at a time. When the going gets tough, I get going."

The keys to changing burnout-producing thoughts are to (1) recognize when you are thinking burnout-producing thoughts, (2) select the kinds of positive thoughts that will challenge the burnout-producing thoughts, and (3) every time you start thinking the burnout-producing thoughts, replace them by telling yourself the positive thoughts.

Relaxation Techniques

People who burn out tend to maintain high levels of stress for prolonged periods. They have not learned to relax. Therefore, learning to relax is very helpful in preventing burnout. There are a number of relaxation techniques that induce the relaxation response: deep-breathing relaxation, imagery relaxation, progressive muscle relaxation, meditation, self-hypnosis, and biofeedback. (These relaxation techniques are described in Chapter 20.)

Exercise

Regular exercise will also help reduce stress and prevent burnout. An exercise program we enjoy (perhaps running, tennis, dancing, swimming, walking, softball, or golf) helps in a variety of ways. It helps keep us in physical shape, which makes us feel good about ourselves, and also gives us increased energy to meet crises and emergencies. It helps take our mind off negative aspects of our job and home life. A final advantage of exercising is that it directly reduces stress. As mentioned earlier, under stress the body prepares us to engage in large muscle activity, including fighting or fleeing. Through exercising we use up fuel in the blood, reduce our heart rate and blood pressure, and set off other physiological changes that reduce stress and induce the relaxation response (Greenberg, 1980).

In addition to exercising, there are several other components to taking care of our physical self: having a nutritious diet, getting suffi-cient sleep, and taking appropriate medical care of ourselves. Being in good physical condition helps us handle stresses and emergencies better and thereby decreases the chances of burnout.

Outside Activities

Getting involved in hobbies and attending entertainment events (concerts, movies, sporting events) will also help switch our thinking away from the negative aspects of our work and home life. Instead, we will be thinking positive thoughts about the outside activities we enjoy, thereby reducing stress and helping prevent burnout.

Research (Schafer, 1978) indicates that "stress reduces stress"; that is, an appropriate amount of stressful activities in one area (such as playing tennis) helps reduce excessive stress in others. Outside activities stop our negative thinking about our day-to-day concerns. (The key to reducing stress is to relax—we always will relax when we stop thinking negatively about our day-to-day concerns.)

Pleasurable Goodies

"Goodies" make us feel good; they change our pace and relieve stress; they are personal therapies. They add spice to life and serve as reminders that we have worth. Personal goodies vary among people. Possible goodies include traveling, listening to music, laughing, responsible sexual activity, being hugged, shopping, sitting in a tub of warm water, and having an exotic drink. Personal goodies help "recharge our batteries."

Goodies can also be used as rewards to ourselves for tasks done well. Most of us would not hesitate to compliment others for jobs done well; equally we should reward ourselves for successfully accomplishing tasks we take pride in.

Taking a mental health day is a goody that should not be overlooked. When under extended stress, take a day off and do only the things you want to do. (Some agencies now allow employees to take a certain number of mental health days with pay.) Mental health days help people who are wearing down from high stress recharge their batteries.

Social Support Systems

Developing trusting and mutually caring relationships at work will result in a "lifeline" support system, particularly during intense, exhausting days. Maslach (1976) noted:

> Our findings show that burnout rates are lower for those professionals who actively express, analyze and share their personal feelings with their colleagues. Not only do they consciously get things off their chest, but they have an opportunity to receive constructive feedback from other people and to develop new perspectives of their relationship with patients/clients. This process is greatly enhanced if the institution sets up some social outlets such as support groups, special staff meetings or workshops. [p. 19]

Social support groups (at work or outside work) allow people to let their hair down, to "kid around," to share their lives, to keep in touch, and to have a source of security and help when crises arise. There are a variety of possible support groups: co-workers, friends, sport or hobby groups, family, church groups, and community organizations such as Parents Without Partners. Support groups have several essential features: (1) the group meets regularly, (2) the same people attend, (3) a feeling of closeness has developed, and (4) there is an opportunity for spontaneity and informality (Greenberg, 1980).

Variety at Work

Doing the same thing, such as paperwork, for long periods becomes exhausting and mundane. Particularly important is to recognize that emotionally draining work (such as suicide counseling or hospice work) can be done only for limited periods or burnout will occur. Therefore it is important to attempt to structure a job to have a variety of job tasks during the week. "Variety is the spice of life." A useful way of adding variety, and also helping us grow as people, is to participate in workshops, conferences, continuing education courses, and in-service training programs.

Humor

Humor relaxes us, makes work more enjoyable, and takes the edge off intense emotional situations. Recognizing and using humor in our work and at home relieves stress and helps prevent burnout.

Changing or Adapting to Distressing Events

There are an infinite number of distressing events: an unfulfilling job, death of someone close, the end of a romantic relationship, unresolved religious questions, an unwanted pregnancy, and so on. When distressing events arise, it is important to confront them head-on to attempt to improve the situation.

For example, if you feel you are beginning to burn out at work, it is important to identify what you find frustrating and exhausting at work and then attempt to develop new approaches for handling these responsibilities. One worker, for instance, may find incest cases particularly exhausting, while another at the same agency may find working with the terminally ill to be more draining—perhaps they can exchange these cases.

If a worker is frustrated because program objectives and job expectations are unclear, these need to be discussed with the supervisor and efforts made to clarify such objectives and expectations.

Most distressing events can be improved by confronting them head-on and then taking positive action to change the event. Some events or situations cannot be changed. For example, you may not be able to change certain distasteful aspects of your job. If you cannot change these, the only constructive remaining alternative is to "bite the bullet" and accept them. It is counterproductive to get upset and to spend time complaining about a situation you cannot change.

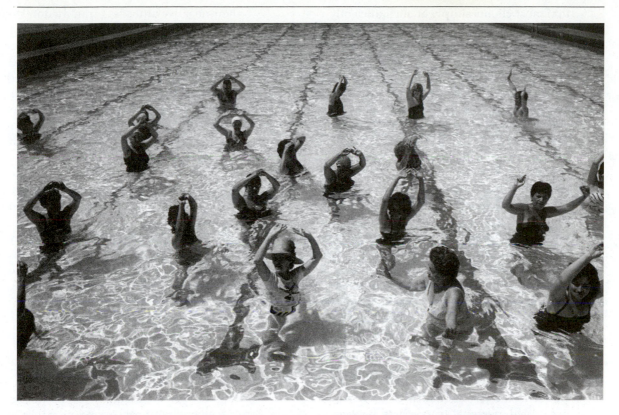

Exercise is an excellent way to reduce stress and also foster physical and emotional well-being.

Enjoying Social Work and Your Life

To gather material to write this section, I asked some friends who have practiced social work for several years to summarize their satisfactions and frustrations about pursuing a career in social work. The following is one of the replies.

It is difficult to find the right words to describe my satisfaction with having made a decision to be a social worker. I have worked in a protective services unit of a public welfare department for two years, as a probation and parole officer for three years, and now am a director of a group home for teenage males who have conflicts with their parents.

One of the satisfying aspects of social work is that there are a wide variety of areas where a person can work. When I found myself becoming stale as a probation officer, it was inspiring to look forward to moving on to something else. If this job becomes routine and no longer something I would look forward to doing, I would again move on to some other social work position.

I truly find it gratifying to work with people. If you don't like working with people, then certainly this is the wrong job to have. I know this sounds "naive," but when I feel I've been of some help in assisting someone to better handle a personal or social problem, it really makes me feel good. It should be noted I'm no longer as idealistic as I was when I was going to college and thought I would be able to help the vast majority of my clients. I've learned that most clients simply aren't sufficiently motivated to put forth the time and effort needed to improve their lives—it's like exercising; we all know exercising will improve our health and keep us trim, but only a few people are willing to put forth the time and effort.

Social work is a challenging profession. Every client's problem is unique. For that matter every client's personality is unique. Interacting with new people, and working out somewhat different treatment strategies with each client is a challenge. Through helping clients I also grow as a person, and learn more about myself. Also challenging, and often learning experiences, are speaking to groups in the community, and seeking to develop new services when a need arises. Also educational (and a way of seeing old friends) are in-service training sessions that are held at the agencies I've worked at.

I don't want to give an ever-glowing picture of social work. There are also frustrations. At every agency there seem to be occasional personality conflicts between staff. (Such conflicts are furthered by staff members being pitted against each other for merit increases, for desired task assignments, and for who will get to go to conferences.)

Another frustration is the amount of paperwork. At the three agencies I've worked at, ten to fifteen hours per week are spent on paperwork.

Some social workers complain this profession doesn't pay enough. I've found that in social work there are some jobs that pay a lot more than others. When I first started out, my annual salary was pretty low, but now that I'm a director of this group home I have no complaints.

Another thing that is frustrating is being aware that there are a few workers who are cynical, who always look at the negative side of things, and who really appear to be only interested in drawing their paycheck, rather than helping people. With their negative attitude, I frankly don't see how they can ever help anyone. If I was a client of theirs I would become even more discouraged and apathetic. To me, these social workers are "deadwood" and are on "welfare" themselves as they are drawing a check without doing anything productive. These people either burned out years ago, or were never "encouraging" persons who were motivated to help others.

All in all I really am delighted I chose a career in social work. I enjoy working with most clients (certainly not all of my clients as some I do find obnoxious) and with most of the other staff. I hope this information will be useful to you, and if you ever want someone to speak in your classes, give me a "jingle."

(Since this is only one social worker's response, the views expressed may or may not be representative of most social workers.)

One of the factors identified by this social worker is the importance of being an "encouraging" person. Chapter 5 noted this as a crucial characteristic of counselors if they are to motivate clients. Closely related to being an "encouraging" person is to be a positive thinker. Positive thinking is important not only in working with clients but also in being able to enjoy life.

The remainder of this chapter elaborates on three specific approaches for learning to enjoy social work and your life: becoming a positive thinker, developing an identity, and using rational challenges to develop a success identity.

Becoming a Positive Thinker

In *A Treasury of Success Unlimited,* W. Clement Stone (1966, pp. 9–10) presented some of the basic principles of positive thinking:

Your most precious, valued possessions and your greatest powers are invisible and intangible. No one can take them. You, and you alone, can give them. You will receive abundance for your giving. The more you give—the more you will have!

Give a smile to everyone you meet (smile with your eyes)—and you'll smile and receive smiles. . . .
Give a kind word (with a kindly thought behind the word)—you will be kind and receive kind words. . . .
Give appreciation (warmth from the heart)—you will appreciate and be appreciated. . . .
Give honor, credit and applause (the victor's wreath)—you will be honorable and receive credit and applause. . . .
Give time for a worthy cause (with eagerness)—you will be worthy and richly rewarded. . . .
Give hope (the magic ingredient for success)—you will have hope and be made hopeful. . . .
Give happiness (a most treasured state of mind)—you will be happy and be made happy. . . .
Give encouragement (the incentive to action)—you will have courage and be encouraged . . .
Give cheer (the verbal sunshine)—you'll be cheerful and cheered. . . .
Give a pleasant response (the neutralizer of irritants)—you will be pleasant and receive pleasant responses. . . .
Give good thoughts (nature's character builder)—you will be good and the world will have good thoughts for you. . . .

Few living Americans can write or speak on the power of positive thinking with more authority than W. Clement Stone. Beginning as a newsboy on the streets of Chicago, Mr. Stone applied the principles of positive thinking to amass, and share with others, a fortune that is in excess of $160 million (Mandino, 1966).

Harold Sherman (1966) in "The Surest Way in the World to Attract Success—or Failure" further elaborated on positive thinking:

"You might know this would happen to me!" Is this a comment you have made, not once, but many times, when things have gone wrong? . . . Certainly—you *knew* it was going to happen—and it did. Your *faith* in "things going wrong" caused the "power of TNT" [thinking negative thoughts] within you to work *against* you instead of for you. There is a great law of mind by which your thinking and your conduct should always be guided: "Like attracts like."

Think good thoughts; you will eventually attract good things. Think bad thoughts, you will ultimately attract bad things.

Simple—easy to remember—but also easy to forget. . . .

Get this point clearly in mind: you supply the material (by the nature of your thoughts) out of which your creative power builds your future. If the material is inferior, comprised of mental pictures of failure, despair, defeat and the like, you can readily see that only unhappy results can be materialized from them. . . .

Whatever conditions you are facing at the moment are the result of your past thinking—good and bad. These conditions cannot change until you have first changed your thinking. . . .

Things first happen in your mind before they can happen in this outer world. What are you picturing? Do you want it to happen? If not, you are the only one who can prevent it. Your future success or failure is in your hands—where it should be. [pp. 111–113]

There are a number of books on positive thinking philosophy (for example *Looking Out for No. 1* by Robert Ringer, 1977, and *Move Ahead with Possibility Thinking* by Robert Schuller, 1973). Positive thinking certainly has considerable merit. However, there is a potential danger. Every accomplishment requires certain abilities. For those who set goals above their capacities, positive thinking could create a false sense of hope. When people fail to achieve what they are seeking (particularly people suffering from emotional problems like anxiety or depression), they are going to realize what they have been taught doesn't work for them. After an initial period of hope, they are apt to become even more depressed.

On the other hand, positive thinking will usually get people started on a project. And, since many people do not realize their own potential, a bright outlook and positive action can help them achieve their goals as it enables them to use their capacities to the fullest.

You have the choice. You can think and act negatively about events that happen to you—which usually leads you to experience unwanted emotions and increases the chances that negative events will occur in the future. Or, you can think and act positively about events that happen to you—which usually leads you to experience pleasant emotions and increases the chances that positive events will occur in the future.

Positive thinking is an important aspect of enjoying your career (whatever it is) and your life. Another important part of enjoying life is knowing who you are and what you want out of life.

Developing an Identity[1]

What kind of a person are you? What do you want out of life? What kind of person do you want to be? Who are you? These questions are probably the most important you will have to face. Without answers, you will not be prepared to make such major decisions as selecting a career; deciding whether, when, or whom to marry; deciding whether to have children; deciding where to live; and deciding what to do with your leisure time. Unfor-

[1]This section is adapted from Charles Zastrow, "Who Am I? The Quest for Identity," in *The Personal Problem Solver*, edited by Charles Zastrow and Dae H. Chang, © 1977, pp. 365–370. Adapted by permission of Prentice-Hall, Inc., Englewood Cliffs, New Jersey.

tunately, many people muddle through life and never arrive at answers to these questions. Those who do not find answers are apt to be depressed, indecisive, anxious, and unfulfilled. All too often, their lives are carbon copies of Stan Sinclair's.

At age 18, Stan graduated from high school. Unable to find a job, he enlisted in the army for a three-year hitch. At 20, he started dating Julia Johnson while he was stationed in Illinois. He liked Julia. She became pregnant and they decided to get married. Money was tight and Julia wanted to live near her relatives. Two months after his discharge, Stan became a father. Needing a job in the area, he became a gas station attendant since it was the only employment he could find. Two and one-half years later, an opening occurred in an auto assembly plant. The pay was better, so Stan applied and was hired. The job was relatively easy but monotonous. Stan faithfully attached mufflers to new cars, over and over for 40 hours a week. During the next eight years, Stan and Julia had three more children. The pay and fringe benefits, combined with his family and financial responsibilities, locked Stan into this assembly line job until he retired at age 65. The morning after he retired, he looked into the mirror and began asking, finally, the key questions. Was it all worth it? Why did he feel empty and unfulfilled? What did he want out of the future? Never having in the past figured out what he wanted out of life, his only answer was a frown.

Identity is having a sense of who we are, a knowledge and a feeling of the ways in which we are separate, distinct persons.

Identity Development

Identity development is a lifelong process, and there are gradual changes in one's identity throughout one's lifetime. During the early years, our sense of who we are is largely determined by the reactions of others. Cooley (1902) a long time ago coined this labeling process as resulting in the *looking-glass self*; that is, persons develop their self-concept (who and what they are) in terms of how they perceive that others relate to them. For example, if a neighborhood identifies a male youth as being a "troublemaker" (a delinquent), the neighbors are apt to relate to the youth as if he were not to be trusted, may accuse him of delinquent acts, and will label his semidelinquent and aggressive behaviors as being *delinquent*. This labeling process, the youth begins to realize, also results in a type of prestige and status, at least from his peers. In the absence of objective ways to gauge whether he is, in fact, a delinquent, the youth will rely on the subjective evaluations of others. Thus, gradually, as the youth is related to as a delinquent, he is apt to begin to perceive himself in that way and will begin to enact the delinquent role.

Fortunately, since identity development is a lifetime process, positive changes are probable even for those who have a negative self-concept. In identity formation, a key principle to remember is that *although we cannot change the past, what we want out of the future, along with our motivation to achieve what we want, is more important (than our past experiences) in determining what our future will be.*

How to Determine Who You Are

Forming an identity essentially involves *thinking* about, and arriving at, answers to the following questions: (1) What do I want out of life? (2) What kind of person am I? (3) What kind of person do I want to be? (4) Who am I?

The most important decisions you make in your life may well be in arriving at answers to these questions. In answering them you are literally developing belief and attitudes about who you are and what you want out of life.

These questions are not easy to answer. They require considerable contemplation and trial and error. But if you are to lead a gratifying, fulfilling life, it is imperative to arrive at answers to give direction to your life and to help you have a chance of living the kind of life you find meaningful. Without answers, you are apt, like Stan Sinclair, to muddle

through life by being a passive responder to situations that arise, rather than a continual achiever of your life's goals.

To determine who you are, you need to arrive at answers to the following more specific questions:

1. What do I find satisfying/meaningful/enjoyable? (Only after you identify what is meaningful and gratifying will you be able to consciously seek involvement in activities that will make your life fulfilling, and avoid those activities that are meaningless or stifling.)

2. What is my moral code? (One possible code is to seek to fulfill your needs and to seek to do what you find enjoyable, doing so in a way that does not deprive others of the ability to fulfill their needs.)

3. What are my religious beliefs?

4. What kind of a career do I desire? (Ideally, you should see a career in which you find the work stimulating and satisfying, that you are skilled at, and that earns you enough money to support the lifestyle you want.)

5. What are my sexual mores? (All of us should develop a consistent code that we are comfortable with and that helps us to meet our needs without exploiting others. There is no one right code—what works for one may not work for another, because of differences in lifestyles, life goals, and personal values.)

6. Do I desire to marry? (If yes, to what type of person and when; how consistent are your answers here with your other life goals?)

7. Do I desire to have children? (If yes, how many, when, and how consistent are your answers here with your other life goals?)

8. What area of the country/world do I desire to live in? (Variables to be considered are climate, geography, type of dwelling, rural or urban setting, closeness to relatives or friends, and characteristics of the neighborhood.)

9. What do I enjoy doing with my leisure time?

10. What kind of image do I want to project to others? (Your image will be composed of your dressing style and grooming habits, your emotions, personality, degree of assertiveness, capacity to communicate, material possessions, moral code, physical features, and voice patterns. You need to assess your strengths and shortcomings honestly in this area, and seek to make improvements.)

11. What type of people do I enjoy being with and why?

12. Do I desire to improve the quality of my life and that of others? (If yes, in what ways, and how do you hope to achieve these goals?)

13. What types of relationships do I desire to have with relatives, friends, neighbors, with people I meet for the first time?

14. What are my thoughts about death and dying?

15. What do I hope to be doing 5 years from now, 10 years, 20 years?

To have a fairly well-developed sense of identity, you need to have answers to most, but not all, of these questions. Very few persons are able to arrive at rational, consistent answers to all the questions. Having answers to most of them will provide a reference for developing your views to the yet unanswered areas.

Honest, well-thought-out answers to these questions will go a long way toward defining who you are. Again, what you want out of life, along with your motivation to achieve these goals, will primarily determine your identity. These questions are simple to state, but arriving at answers is a complicated, ongoing process. In addition, expect some changes in your life goals as time goes on. Environmental influences change (for example, working conditions). Also, as personal growth occurs, changes are apt to occur in activities that you find enjoyable and also in your beliefs, attitudes, and values. Accept such changes, and if you have a fairly good idea of who you are, you will be prepared to make changes in your life goals in order to give continued direction to your life.

Your life is shaped by different events that are the results of decisions you make and decisions that are made for you. Without a sense of identity, you will not know what decisions are best for you, and your life will be unfulfilled. With a sense of identity, you will be able to direct your life toward goals you select and find personally meaningful.

Using Rational Challenges to Develop a Success Identity

While some people are muddling through life without a clear sense of what they want or who they are, a number of people wallow through life in self-pity, seeing themselves as failures. In another publication (Zastrow, 1979), I compared people who have a success identity with those who have a failure identity:

> Success identities are characterized by the following kinds of self-talk. "I have accomplished many of the things I have tried in the past." "I am a competent, worthwhile person." "I, similar to other people, have certain special talents." "Trying something new is challenging and stimulating." "I look forward to trying something more complicated that has the opportunity for substantial payoffs, and which will test and further develop my special talents." "Trying new things helps me grow as a person, and helps provide meaning to living." "I look forward to each new day with its opportunities for involvement in activities that will be gratifying and fulfilling."

Do you give yourself these types of positive self-talk, or do you give yourself the following negative kinds of self-talk, . . . characteristic of those with a "failure identity"?: "I can't accomplish anything I try." "I'm inferior to other people."

(continued on p. 664)

Case Example

Developing a positive self-concept

Since her early teenage years this individual had viewed herself as a failure. Her sense of being a failure was temporarily alleviated during her junior and senior years in high school when she steadily dated and became overly dependent on Tom.* However, her failure concept soon returned shortly after Tom left to attend the Air Force Academy. In this case example the student describes her deep sense of being a failure, and how she used rational self-challenges to develop a more positive self-concept.

An excerpt from my journal, August 10, 1975:

Breakfast at the airport appeared cheerful enough. His parents, full of optimistic talk of his future, kept the conversation light and promising. And I, my real feelings hidden by a facade of carefully planned cheerfulness, made attempts at bright small talk which seemed to add to the somehow phony color and splendor of the day.

At that point, after all of the months of waiting and preparation, all was ready. Every last detail had been checked and it was time. Tom was ready to embark on a new and challenging life style—without me!

Later, as I recall that first painful goodbye, our words edged with emotion, full of promises for the future, and yet our every thought charged with the upcoming agony of being apart from one another, I do not once remember thinking of how I was going to adjust to his absence. Tom was the most significant person in my life to that date, and yet I had not realized the powerful effect our new "separateness" would take in relation to my life from there on.

The sequence(s) of events and emotions that followed seemed to me to be normal or what I thought as being normal reactions for a person to feel when a loved one is away for a prolonged period of time. That is when I began my "Poor Me" syndrome!

It was summer and I was very lonely and didn't have enough to keep me busy. I worked at a local restaurant as much as I possibly could to pass the time, but it didn't seem to be enough—I still had those lonely nights to myself.

"Poor me," I'd say to myself. "I'm alone and no one cares enough to spend time with me, I must be worthless, boring, etc." This became repetitious with me to the point that whenever I felt a bit depressed, I would reinforce those feelings with other intense feelings of worthlessness. I could really bring myself down, you see, because I truly felt that I could never be happy, feel my personal worth, expand myself unless Tom was with me. I guess that was a rather natural feeling for me to have because while he was home, I allowed myself to be dependent upon him to fill my every need and whim. And gladly, he filled them. Call it "ego" or whatever, but it somehow filled a need in him to have me need him so desperately. It seemed to be a very workable arrangement while he was home with me. My belief was that we were "in love" and it was a very positive point to

(continued)

*Names and other identifying information in this case example have been changed.

Case Example
Developing a positive self-concept (*continued*)

"need" someone I loved. What I hadn't considered was how my dependency upon him was, in fact, setting me up for a lifetime of unhappiness. Time progressed and I felt myself more and more alone. I walled myself off from my "helpful friends," people who did in fact care for me and who wanted to include me in their activities. I did join them on occasion, but generally if I did, I'd begin to feel sorry for myself and bring out my tale of woe. Of course they listened, but one can listen to the same negative thoughts only so many times. I remember having feelings of bitterness and hostility toward these friends, people who had things going their way. I was jealous.

It seemed as though everything was going wrong. I began to drink more and to experience the effects of drugs. At times this seemed to be a haven for me, an escape from what seemed to be insurmountable problems.

I took an apartment with an acquaintance who was pregnant. (It created many problems.) I overextended myself financially, knowing full well that I was. I was enrolled in classes but had neither the motivation nor goal to attend all of them.

All around I began to see myself as a failure. Whenever I'd receive a poor grade on a test, paper, or quiz, I'd tell myself that I was stupid. If it came time to pay the bills and I did not have the money, I'd tell myself that I was a failure at supporting myself. Then, to pay those same bills for which I spent the money on extravagances, I'd have to work doubly hard.

Well, eventually I became tired of feeling negative all the time. After all, if I could feel good about myself when I was with Tom, then somehow I should be able to feel good about myself at other times. I had to—either that, suicide, or stay miserable. Neither of the latter two sounded too appealing, so I decided to make the best of it, and give myself a positive try. Many times, over tears on the telephone, I would explain to Tom my fears and anxieties and it would hurt him some, as he felt a bit responsible. He is a person whom I genuinely care for and I began to have my doubts as to what I should and shouldn't tell him. After all, I really don't intend to make those I care for feel responsible for my feelings and actions. I'm responsible for myself.

Fortunately, it was at this point in my life that I enrolled in a course on counseling, which exposed me to the concepts of rational therapy, and I proceeded to write the following rational self-analysis (RSA) on my personal concerns.

A Event	D^1 Camera check
In August of 1975 my boyfriend left for the Air Force Academy. At his leave-taking the two of us promised to wait until the end of his education and then to marry. I had little confidence in myself as a person to begin with. When he left I became less confident and began to discount myself as a person having no worth or value. As time progressed, I began to do poorly in several	This is all factual.

A Event	D¹ Camera check
aspects of life: poor grades, too much financial responsibility (too many extravagances), poor organization of my life's plans (work or school, which has priority?), hostile attitude toward friends, etc. I generally felt worthless and sad because Tom left.	

B Self-Talk	D² Rational Self-Challenges to the Self-Talk in Section B
1. "I am able to be happy only if Tom is with me." (bad)	1. False. If I hope to be a self-sufficient and satisfied person in my lifetime, I know that I must do it alone—for myself. Others may make it easier for me, but essentially, I have to make myself happy.
2. "I'm dependent upon Tom in all ways if I allow his leaving to affect me this way." (bad)	2. True. But I'm not allowing myself my own rights as a person. I realize that I could never mold my life around another's wants and likes. I've got to have my own identity.
3. "I'm a failure in my studies." (bad)	3. False. I'm not a failure and never have been. At my lowest point, I still received C's for grades. I received those C's with a minimal amount of effort; so if I really tried, I could do better.
4. "I'm worthless." (bad)	4. False. Every person has some worth. I do too. At times when I'm depressed I may like to tell myself I'm worthless, but I really know that I'm not. Every human being has some worth. I'm as valuable as any other person, just because I'm human.
5. "My friends won't like me if I react to them in a hostile manner." (bad)	5. True. My friends don't like to spend time with me when I react to them in a negative, hostile way. It doesn't do much for the friendship, which was built of positive, mutual concern to begin with. I really don't like to treat them in this way and from now on I will make a conscious effort to be more pleasant.
6. "I can't support myself sufficiently. I buy extravagant items." (bad)	6. False. In the past I've done quite well. It is when I take trips to visit Tom, or buy a new wardrobe that I feel depleted financially. At other times I manage quite well, and even if I overextend myself—I still work to pay for my expenses.
7. "Because Tom has left me, all things go wrong in my life." (bad)	7. False. Things do not go wrong because Tom left me, but because of circumstances or something I do to allow things to go wrong. Tom is away; there is no possible way he can control what happens to me here.

(continued)

Case Example
Developing a positive self-concept *(continued)*

B Self-Talk	D^2 Rational Self-Challenges to the Self-Talk in Section B
8. "The only thing I can look forward to is becoming Tom's wife and then I will hopefully feel better." (bad)	8. False. I intend to become a counselor if I really put forth an effort. If I do decide to become Tom's wife that will be a major event to look forward to—a life together, but that is not all I'm looking forward to. For two and a half years I've struggled with college—certainly not for nothing!
9. "Tom is responsible for my feeling so rotten. It's all his fault!" (bad)	9. False. Tom is away and has no control over my life. He never did. In the past I felt the way I wanted to, did what I liked because that is the power that I have as a person. When Tom left it was an unfortunate circumstance. I allowed myself to blame him for all the "wrongs" and unhappiness in my life when actually he had nothing to do with it. I'm the person living my life—choosing my own feelings, situations, etc., of which Tom has no control.

C My Emotions	E Emotional and Behavioral Goals
Depression, sadness, insecurity, inferiority, and loneliness. I had nine "bad." That doesn't say much for my ability to adjust well to a given situation.	In the future I'd like to try to build my self-image so that I will be capable of accepting and utilizing change in my life in a positive way. A way in which I can do this is through my self-talk—what I tell myself about occurrences. The given (A) situation is a continuing occurrence—it happens at least once every summer. Having worked on the problem since September, I've begun to realize what I need to do in this situation to make myself happy. I need to see myself happy. I need to see myself as a strong, self-sufficient, happily functioning person—with a "separate" life and identity from Tom. Since these qualities (strength, independence, self-sufficiency) have been hidden in me for some time, I've yet to cultivate them totally, but instead I'm working on them slowly. This, I expect, will make me a more satisfied person, and for others more pleasant and satisfying to be with.

(This young woman also wrote the following summary of the usefulness of this approach.)

I used Rational Therapy with the belief that I really did have the power to control my emotions and then, in turn, to control my life. I have always been a person of a negative nature—I had too much to say about all the "bads" and "wrongs" in my life that happened, and too little to say of the good.

I saw myself as a worthless, weak, submissive, and stupid person who really didn't matter in the course of this big world. There was one person who made me feel valuable, and when he left I allowed myself to feel useless again. This was followed by a succession of negative thoughts about myself, and fears.

A strong point of doing an RSA is what I found to be my ability to look at myself objectively on paper. What is written on paper looks factual and truthful. I found myself debating those facts and truths and actually finding out more of how I really felt inside. I had an outsider's view of myself on the objective side. This allowed me to weigh the pros and cons of my behavior, emotions, etc., and to take positive, realistic means to change what I didn't like.

Also doing a Rational Self-Analysis helped me to become, through my problem, more rational and realistic in regard to living my everyday life. In a world that is so disproportionate in itself, I find it easy to stretch many aspects of my personal life out of proportion. A rational self-analysis doesn't allow one to do that. A person must face the facts, debate the thoughts underlying his dysfunctional behaviors and unwanted emotions, and determine what he chooses to feel from there on. A rational self-analysis allows only honesty and a willingness to change those feelings that one is not comfortable with. A person who does his rational self-analysis dishonestly will get nowhere.

Ultimately, Rational Therapy taught me the power of control. A human person is a complex, highly intelligent organism. Then why should he not have the power of controlling what could turn out to be his own destiny in life?

An excerpt from my journal, December 1, 1977:

Inside myself, I guess that I'm really satisfied with the person I'm becoming. Sure, it can be a long, hard struggle at times, and often frustrating, but it is a part of my life. That is how things become important and significant in life—through the living of such experiences. Sometimes I'm amazed when I think that I was born a person in my own right, with potential emotional growth, strength, and abilities, to become what I choose to become.

SOURCE: This case example is reprinted from Charles Zastrow, *Talk to Yourself: Using the Power of Self-Talk*, © 1979, pp. 99–105. Reprinted by permission of Prentice-Hall, Inc., Englewood Cliffs, New Jersey.

"Why can't I be as competent, capable, or attractive as others?" "I'm a failure." "I can't afford to risk trying anything new as it will reveal my weaknesses to others." "I wish people would stop picking on me, and making cutting comments about my shortcomings." "I've got a number of personal problems that are overwhelming me, and draining my energy." "There just is no hope for a brighter tomorrow." "My problems are certainly more confusing and unresolvable than those that other people have." "Life is certainly the 'pits' and really not worth living." "I wish I was someone else." "I wonder why such and such hurt me so badly—I just can't stop thinking about it." "What did I do wrong to deserve all this misery?"

Such self-talk by people with failure orientations generates a variety of negative emotions, including excessive worry, fatigue, anxiety, boredom, depression, loneliness, and/or general feelings of misery. [pp. 92–93]

Merlin Manley (1977) also noted:

A sense of failure becomes a further problem since it limits the amount of risk-taking behavior in which we are willing to engage. If we feel that we are failures, we will feel threatened by any new behavior patterns that we perceive as risky. Accordingly, we will be very reluctant to try any such behaviors. This means that we will continue to operate as we have in the past, thereby creating somewhat of a "rut." To the degree that we follow this practice, we are precluded from growing psychologically or expanding our behavioral responses. We are stultifying ourselves from greater use of our potential and becoming a more complete individual. We learn and grow by our experiences. If we limit ourselves to only the "tried and true" modes of behavior, we are putting disabling constraints on ourselves and seriously limiting our growth potential. [p. 38]

To be an "encouraging" person in working with clients, and to feel good about yourself, it is essential to have a positive, success self-concept. There is a very simple formula for improving the lives of people who view themselves as failures; they need to shift their thinking from focusing on negative items to focusing on positive items.

One way of changing a failure identity into a success identity is to identify the failure self-talk, and then challenge this with rational self-talk (see Chapter 22 for how to write a rational self-analysis). A feeling of being a failure is an emotion. Similar to any other emotion, this feeling results mainly from a certain kind of self-talk, and the emotion can be changed by rational self-challenges.

Summary

To be of help to others, social workers must first take care of themselves. Good emotional and physical health are internal resources that social workers need to have to be of help to others. This chapter presents material on how to survive and enjoy social work and in a broader sense, on how to enjoy living.

Although social work students have a number of common concerns, they often are reluctant to share them with others. The following concerns are discussed, with suggestions given for resolving them: Will I be able to make it in field placement? Will I be able to handle my first interview with my first client? I'm really depressed, because my supervisor is able to handle an interview much better than I—will I ever be able to do that well? How should I separate the role of counselor from that of friend? How can I avoid becoming too emotionally involved with clients' problems? Do I really want to pursue a career in social work?

Burnout is increasingly being recognized as a major problem encountered by professionals, particularly professionals employed in human services. The symptoms and causes of burnout are discussed and suggestions given for reducing stress and preventing burnout. Since burnout is one of the reactions to high levels of stress, it follows that stress management techniques are also useful in preventing burnout.

The chapter ends with providing tips on how to enjoy social work and life. The value of positive thinking is described. Also, the importance of developing a sense of who you are and what you want out of life is discussed and suggestions are given for developing such an identity. Having a failure identity is contrasted with having a success identity, and a Rational Self-Analysis is presented as one approach that is useful in challenging and changing a failure identity.

Exercises

1. Common concerns of social work students

Goals: Practically every student has concerns about field placement and about pursuing social work as a career. This exercise is designed to help students realize their concerns are common and become more comfortable with their concerns.

Step 1: Describe the purposes of this exercise. Briefly indicate common concerns of students including the following:

a. Will I be able to make it in field placement?
b. I really wonder, will I be able to handle my first interview with my first client adequately?
c. I'm really depressed, because my supervisor is able to handle any interview much better than I—I doubt whether I'll ever be able to do that well.
d. How should I separate the role of being a counselor from that of being a friend?
e. How can I avoid becoming too emotionally involved with clients' problems?
f. Do I really want to have a career in social work?

Indicate that while students think their concerns are unique, these concerns are generally common to practically all students. Through analyzing and discussing concerns, information can generally be provided that will help students become more comfortable with them.

Step 2: Ask students to write on a note card or a sheet of paper a few concerns they have about field placement or about pursuing social work as a career. Indicate to students they should not place their names on what they write.

Step 3: Anonymously collect these concerns. Read each concern, and together with the class, seek to compile information that will provide at least partial answers to each concern. (Partial answers to a number of concerns are provided in the first section of this chapter.)

2. Reducing stress and preventing burnout

Goal: This exercise is designed to help students reduce stress and prevent burnout.

Step 1: Describe the purpose of this exercise. Using the material in this chapter, define stress and burnout. Indicate that burnout is one reaction to high stress levels. Also summarize a variety of strategies to reduce stress and prevent burnout. (These strategies are outlined in this chapter. It may be helpful to prepare and distribute a handout that identifies these strategies.)

Step 2: Ask students to write answers to the following questions on a sheet of paper:

a. A few problematic situations that are presently causing high levels of stress in my life are _____.
b. My current ways of handling these high levels of stress are _____.
c. Ways in which I could better handle these situations and become more relaxed are _____.

Step 3: Ask students to form subgroups of three and have them share what they wrote. Indicate that the subgroups may be able to offer additional suggestions on how to handle the stress-producing situations and on how to relax. Also indicate that each student has a right to privacy and is not expected to self-disclose what he or she wants to keep private.

Step 4: After the subgroups have concluded their discussions, ask whether there are questions or comments about what was discussed.

3. Establishing a sense of identity

Goal: This exercise is designed to help students establish a better sense of self and determine what they want out of life.

Step 1: Describe the purpose of this exercise. Indicate forming a sense of "who we are" is probably the most important psychological need we face. Indicate that while we cannot change the past, what we want out of the future, along with our motivation to achieve what we want, is more important (than our past experiences) in determining what our future will be.

Step 2: Indicate that one way to find out who we are and what we want out of life is to arrive at answers to the 15 questions listed on identity formation in this chapter. Distribute a questionnaire that lists these questions and has space for students to write their answers.

Step 3: Give the students 25 to 30 minutes to write down their answers. After this is completed, have the students form subgroups of three in which they share the questions they do not have answers to. Indicate that the subgroups may be able to offer additional ideas on how to arrive at answers to the unanswered questions. Also indicate that each student has a right to privacy and is not expected to share what he or she wants to keep private.

Step 4: After the subgroups have concluded their discussions, ask whether there are any questions or comments.

4. Positive and negative thinking become self-fulfilling prophecies

Goal: This exercise is designed to help students become aware that positive and negative thinking often become self-fulfilling prophecies.

Step 1: Indicate the purpose of the exercise. Indicate that we always have a choice of thinking either positively or negatively about events that happen to us. Also indicate that both positive and negative thinking frequently become self-fulfilling prophecies. For example, if we go for a job interview and think we have a good chance to get the job, we will be more relaxed and probably better able to sell ourselves. If we think negatively, we will be more anxious and probably less able to present ourselves with confidence. Give additional examples, if desired.

Step 2: Ask the students to write on a sheet of paper a situation in which positive thinking led to a self-fulfilling prophecy for themselves or for someone close to them. Also ask the students to write a situation in which negative thinking led to a self-fulfilling prophecy for themselves or for someone close to them.

Step 3: Ask for volunteers to share what they wrote. Also ask the class if they are aware of any situations where positive thinking led to undesirable results and negative thinking resulted in desirable consequences.

5. Ending the class

Goals: This exercise is designed to give the students a sense of closure for the class ending and to provide the instructor with suggestions on how to improve the course in the future.

Step 1: At the last (or near the last) class session, begin this closure exercise by administering the student course evaluation form (practically all college programs or departments have a form they use). Three useful questions are as follows:

a. The text for this course is one of the best that I have had in college.

1	2	3	4	5
Strongly disagree	Mildly disagree	Uncertain	Mildly agree	Strongly agree

b. This course is one of the best that I have had in college.

1	2	3	4	5
Strongly disagree	Mildly disagree	Uncertain	Mildly agree	Strongly agree

c. The instructor for this course is one of the best that I have had in college.

1	2	3	4	5
Strongly disagree	Mildly disagree	Uncertain	Mildly agree	Strongly agree

Step 2: Distribute sheets containing the following three questions, with room on the sheets for students to respond.

a. What are the strengths of this course?
b. What are the shortcomings of this course?
c. What suggestions do you have for changes in this course?

Note: For both steps 1 and 2, either leave the room while the students fill out the forms, or stay at the front of the class so you cannot see how students are responding. Give the completed forms for both steps 1 and 2 to a student volunteer, who returns the material to the department secretary in a sealed envelope.

Step 3: Ask the class to sit in a circle. Perhaps express a number of positive thoughts and feelings about the class, and mention a few memorable experiences. Ask the students questions similar to the following:

a. Is there anything that anyone wants to express before the class ends?
b. Is there unfinished business we should deal with?
c. What did you like about this course?
d. Do you have suggestions for improving the course?

Step 4: Starting from the left or right, ask students to express individually what they will most remember about this course, and/or what they believe they have learned from this course.

APPENDIX A
THE NASW CODE
OF ETHICS*

The National Association of Social Workers, Inc. (NASW), is the professional association that represents the social work profession in the United States. Its Code of Ethics summarizes important practice ethics for social workers and is presented as follows:

Preamble

This code is intended to serve as a guide to the everyday conduct of members of the social work profession and as a basis for the adjudication of issues in ethics when the conduct of social workers is alleged to deviate from the standards expressed or implied in this code. It represents standards of ethical behavior for social workers in professional relationships with those served, with colleagues, with employers, with other individuals and professions, and with the community and society as a whole. It also embodies standards of ethical behavior governing individual conduct to the extent that such conduct is associated with an individual's status and identity as a social worker.

This code is based on the fundamental values of the social work profession that in-

clude the worth, dignity, and uniqueness of all persons as well as their rights and opportunities. It is also based on the nature of social work, which fosters conditions that promote these values.

In subscribing to and abiding by this code, the social worker is expected to view ethical responsibility in as inclusive a context as each situation demands and within which ethical judgment is required. The social worker is expected to take into consideration all the principles in this code that have a bearing upon any situation in which ethical judgment is to be exercised and professional intervention or conduct is planned. The course of action that the social worker chooses is expected to be consistent with the spirit as well as the letter of this code.

In itself, this code does not represent a set of rules that will prescribe all the behaviors of social workers in all the complexities of professional life. Rather it offers general principles to guide conduct, and the judicious appraisal of conduct, in situations that have ethical implications. It provides the basis for making judgments about ethical actions before and after they occur. Frequently, the particular situation determines the ethical principles that apply and the manner of their application. In such cases, not only the particular ethical principles are taken into immediate consideration, but also the entire code and its spirit. Specific applications of ethical

*Reprinted by permission of the National Association of Social Workers, Inc.

I. The social worker's conduct and comportment as a social worker

  A. *Propriety.* The social worker should maintain high standards of personal conduct in the capacity or identity as social worker.

  B. *Competence and Professional Development.* The social worker should strive to become and remain proficient in professional practice and the performance of professional functions.

  C. *Service.* The social worker should regard as primary the service obligation of the social work profession.

  D. *Integrity.* The social worker should act in accordance with the highest standards of professional integrity.

  E. *Scholarship and Research.* The social worker engaged in study and research should be guided by the conventions for scholarly inquiry.

II. The social worker's ethical responsibility to clients

  F. *Primacy of Clients' Interests.* The social worker's primary responsibility is to clients.

  G. *Rights and Prerogatives of Clients.* The social worker should make every effort to foster maximum self-determination on the part of clients.

  H. *Confidentiality and Privacy.* The social worker should respect the privacy of clients and hold in confidence all information obtained in the course of professional service.

  I. *Fees.* When setting fees, the social worker should ensure that they are fair, reasonable, considerate, and commensurate with the service performed and with due regard for the clients' ability to pay.

III. The social worker's ethical responsibility to colleagues

  J. *Respect, Fairness, and Courtesy.* The social worker should treat colleagues with respect, courtesy, fairness, and good faith.

  K. *Dealing with Colleagues' Clients.* The social worker has the responsibility to relate to the clients of colleagues with full professional consideration.

IV. The social worker's ethical responsibility to employers and employing organizations

  L. *Commitments to Employing Organizations.* The social worker should adhere to commitments made to the employing organizations.

V. The social worker's ethical responsibility to the social work profession

  M. *Maintaining the Integrity of the Profession.* The social worker should uphold and advance the values, ethics, knowledge, and mission of the profession.

  N. *Community Service.* The social worker should assist the profession in making social services available to the general public.

  O. *Development of Knowledge.* The social worker should take responsibility for identifying, developing, and fully utilizing knowledge for professional practice.

VI. The social worker's ethical responsibility to society.

  P. *Promoting the General Welfare.* The social worker should promote the general welfare of society.

principles must be judged within the context in which they are being considered. Ethical behavior in a given situation must satisfy not only the judgment of the individual social worker, but also the judgment of an unbiased jury of professional peers.

This code should not be used as an instrument to deprive any social worker of the opportunity or freedom to practice with complete professional integrity; nor should any disciplinary action be taken on the basis of this code without maximum provision for safeguarding the rights of the social worker affected.

The ethical behavior of social workers results not from edict, but from a personal commitment of the individual. This code is offered to affirm the will and zeal of all social workers to be ethical and to act ethically in all that they do as social workers.

The following codified ethical principles should guide social workers in the various roles and relationships and at the various levels of responsibility in which they function professionally. These principles also serve as a basis for the adjudication by the National Association of Social Workers of issues in ethics.

In subscribing to this code, social workers are required to cooperate in its implementation and abide by any disciplinary rulings based on it. They should also take adequate measures to discourage, prevent, expose, and correct the unethical conduct of colleagues. Finally, social workers should be equally ready to defend and assist colleagues unjustly charged with unethical conduct.

I. **The social worker's conduct and comportment as a social worker.**
   A. **Propriety. The social worker should maintain high standards of personal conduct in the capacity or identity as social worker.**
      1. The private conduct of the social worker is a personal matter to the same degree as is any other person's, except when such conduct compromises the fulfillment of professional responsibilities.
      2. The social worker should not participate in, condone, or be associated with dishonesty, fraud, deceit, or misrepresentation.
      3. The social worker should distinguish clearly between statements and actions made as a private individual and as a representative of the social work profession or an organization or group.
   B. **Competence and professional development. The social worker should strive to become and remain proficient in professional practice and the performance of professional functions.**
      1. The social worker should accept responsibility or employment only on the basis of existing competence or the intention to acquire the necessary competence.
      2. The social worker should not misrepresent professional qualifications, education, experience, or affiliations.
      3. The social worker should not allow his or her own personal problems, psychosocial distress, substance abuse, or mental health difficulties to interfere with professional judgment and performance or jeopardize the best interests of those for whom the social worker has a professional responsibility.
      4. The social worker whose personal problems, psychosocial distress, substance abuse, or mental health difficulties interfere with professional judgment and performance should immediately seek consultation and take appropriate remedial action by seeking professional help, making adjustments in workload, terminating practice, or taking any other steps necessary to protect clients and others.
   C. **Service. The social worker should regard as primary the service obligation of the social work profession.**
      1. The social worker should retain ultimate responsibility for the quality and extent of the service that individual assumes, assigns, or performs.
      2. The social worker should act to prevent practices that are inhumane or discriminatory against any person or group of persons.
   D. **Integrity. The social worker should act in accordance with the highest standards of professional integrity and impartiality.**
      1. The social worker should be alert to and resist the influences and

pressures that interfere with the exercise of professional discretion and impartial judgment required for the performance of professional functions.

2. The social worker should not exploit professional relationships for personal gain.

E. **Scholarship and research. The social worker engaged in study and research should be guided by the conventions of scholarly inquiry.**

1. The social worker engaged in research should consider carefully its possible consequences for human beings.

2. The social worker engaged in research should ascertain that the consent of participants in the research is voluntary and informed, without any implied deprivation or penalty for refusal to participate, and with due regard for participants' privacy and dignity.

3. The social worker engaged in research should protect participants from unwarranted physical or mental discomfort, distress, harm, danger, or deprivation.

4. The social worker who engages in the evaluation of services or cases should discuss them only for professional purposes and only with persons directly and professionally concerned with them.

5. Information obtained about participants in research should be treated as confidential.

6. The social worker should take credit only for work actually done in connection with scholarly and research endeavors and credit contributions made by others.

II. **The social worker's ethical responsibility to clients.**

F. **Primacy of clients' interests. The social worker's primary responsibility is to clients.**

1. The social worker should serve clients with devotion, loyalty, determination, and the maximum application of professional skill and competence.

2. The social worker should not exploit relationships with clients for personal advantage.

3. The social worker should not practice, condone, facilitate, or collaborate with any form of discrimination on the basis of race, color, sex, sexual orientation, age, religion, national origin, marital status, political belief, mental or physical handicap, or any other preference or personal characteristic, condition, or status.

4. The social worker should not condone or engage in any dual or multiple relationships with clients or former clients in which there is a risk of exploitation of or potential harm to the client. The social worker is responsible for setting clear, appropriate, and culturally sensitive boundaries.

5. The social worker should under no circumstances engage in sexual activities with clients.

6. The social worker should provide clients with accurate and complete information regarding the extent and nature of the services available to them.

7. The social worker should apprise clients of their risks, rights, opportunities, and obligations associated with social service to them.

8. The social worker should seek advice and counsel of colleagues and supervisors whenever such consultation is in the best interest of clients.

9. The social worker should terminate service to clients, and professional relationships with them,

when such service and relationships are no longer required or no longer serve the clients' needs or interests.

10. The social worker should withdraw services precipitously only under unusual circumstances, giving careful consideration to all factors in the situation and taking care to minimize possible adverse effects.

11. The social worker who anticipates the termination or interruption of service to clients should notify clients promptly and seek the transfer, referral, or continuation of service in relation to the clients' needs and preferences.

G. Rights and prerogatives of clients. The social worker should make every effort to foster maximum self-determination on the part of clients.

1. When the social worker must act on behalf of a client who has been adjudged legally incompetent, the social worker should safeguard the interests and rights of that client.

2. When another individual has been legally authorized to act in behalf of a client, the social worker should deal with that person always with the client's best interest in mind.

3. The social worker should not engage in any action that violates or diminishes the civil or legal rights of clients.

H. Confidentiality and privacy. The social worker should respect the privacy of clients and hold in confidence all information obtained in the course of professional service.

1. The social worker should share with others confidences revealed by clients, without their consent, only for compelling professional reasons.

2. The social worker should inform clients fully about the limits of confidentiality in a given situation, the purposes for which information is obtained, and how it may be used.

3. The social worker should afford clients reasonable access to any official social work records concerning them.

4. When providing clients with access to records, the social worker should take due care to protect the confidences of others contained in those records.

5. The social worker should obtain informed consent of clients before taping, recording, or permitting third-party observation of their activities.

I. Fees. When setting fees, the social worker should ensure that they are fair, reasonable, considerate and commensurate with the service performed and with due regard for the clients' ability to pay.

1. The social worker should not divide a fee or accept or give anything of value for receiving or making a referral.

III. The social worker's ethical responsibility to colleagues.

J. Respect, fairness, and courtesy. The social worker should treat colleagues with respect, courtesy, fairness, and good faith.

1. The social worker should cooperate with colleagues to promote professional interests and concerns.

2. The social worker should respect confidences shared by colleagues in the course of their professional relationships and transactions.

3. The social worker should create and maintain conditions of

practice that facilitate ethical and competent professional performance by colleagues.

4. The social worker should treat with respect, and represent accurately and fairly, the qualifications, views, and findings of colleagues and use appropriate channels to express judgments on these matters.

5. The social worker who replaces or is replaced by a colleague in professional practice should act with consideration for the interest, character, and reputation of that colleague.

6. The social worker should not exploit a dispute between a colleague and employers to obtain a position or otherwise advance the social worker's interest.

7. The social worker should seek arbitration or mediation when conflicts with colleagues require resolution for compelling professional reasons.

8. The social worker should extend to colleagues of other professions the same respect and cooperation that is extended to social work colleagues.

9. The social worker who serves as an employer, supervisor, or mentor to colleagues should make orderly and explicit arrangements regarding the conditions of their continuing professional relationship.

10. The social worker who has the responsibility for employing and evaluating the performance of other staff members should fulfill such responsibility in a fair, considerate, and equitable manner, on the basis of clearly enunciated criteria.

11. The social worker who has the responsibility for evaluating the performance of employees, supervisees, or students should share evaluations with them.

12. The social worker should not use a professional position vested with power, such as that of employer, supervisor, teacher, or consultant, to his or her advantage or to exploit others.

13. The social worker who has direct knowledge of a social work colleague's impairment due to personal problems, psychosocial distress, substance abuse, or mental health difficulties should consult with that colleague and assist the colleague in taking remedial action.

K. **Dealing with colleagues' clients. The social worker has the responsibility to relate to the clients of colleagues with full professional consideration.**

1. The social worker should not assume professional responsibility for the clients of another agency or a colleague without appropriate communication with that agency or colleague.

2. The social worker who serves the clients of colleagues, during a temporary absence or emergency, should serve those clients with the same consideration as that afforded any client.

IV. **The social worker's ethical responsibility to employers and employing organizations.**

L. **Commitments to employing organizations. The social worker should adhere to commitments made to the employing organizations.**

1. The social worker should work to improve the employing agency's policies and procedures and the efficiency and effectiveness of its services.

2. The social worker should not accept employment or arrange student field placements in an organization which is currently under public sanction by NASW for violating personnel standards or imposing limitations on or penalties for professional actions on behalf of clients.

3. The social worker should act to prevent and eliminate discrimination in the employing organization's work assignments and in its employment policies and practices.

4. The social worker should use with scrupulous regard, and only for the purpose for which they are intended, the resources of the employing organization.

V. **The social worker's ethical responsibility to the social work profession.**

M. **Maintaining the integrity of the profession. The social worker should uphold and advance the values, ethics, knowledge, and mission of the profession.**

1. The social worker should protect and enhance the dignity and integrity of the profession and should be responsible and vigorous in discussion and criticism of the profession.

2. The social worker should take action through appropriate channels against unethical conduct by any other member of the profession.

3. The social worker should act to prevent the unauthorized and unqualified practice of social work.

4. The social worker should make no misrepresentation in advertising as to qualifications, competence, service, or results to be achieved.

N. **Community service. The social worker should assist the profes-**sion in making social services available to the general public.

1. The social worker should contribute time and professional expertise to activities that promote respect for the utility, the integrity, and the competence of the social work profession.

2. The social worker should support the formulation, development, enactment, and implementation of social policies of concern to the profession.

O. **Development of knowledge. The social worker should take responsibility for identifying, developing, and fully utilizing knowledge for professional practice.**

1. The social worker should base practice upon recognized knowledge relevant to social work.

2. The social worker should critically examine, and keep current with, emerging knowledge relevant to social work.

3. The social worker should contribute to the knowledge base of social work and share research knowledge and practice wisdom with colleagues.

VI. **The social worker's ethical responsibility to society.**

P. **Promoting the general welfare. The social worker should promote the general welfare of society.**

1. The social worker should act to prevent and eliminate discrimination against any person or group on the basis of race, color, sex, sexual orientation, age, religion, national origin, marital status, political belief, mental or physical handicap, or any other preference or personal characteristic, condition, or status.

2. The social worker should act to ensure that all persons have access to the resources, services,

and opportunities which they require.

3. The social worker should act to expand choice and opportunity for all persons, with special regard for disadvantaged or oppressed groups and persons.

4. The social worker should promote conditions that encourage respect for the diversity of cultures which constitute American society.

5. The social worker should provide appropriate professional services in public emergencies.

6. The social worker should advocate changes in policy and legislation to improve social conditions and to promote social justice.

7. The social worker should encourage informed participation by the public in shaping social policies and institutions.

APPENDIX B
CANADIAN ASSOCIATION
OF SOCIAL WORKERS'
CODE OF ETHICS*

Definitions

In this Code,
Best interest of client means

(a) that the wishes, desires, motivations, and plans of the client are taken by the social worker as the primary consideration in any intervention plan developed by the social worker subject to change only when the client's plans are documented to be unrealistic, unreasonable or potentially harmful to self or others or otherwise determined inappropriate when considered in relation to a mandated requirement,

(b) that all actions and interventions of the social worker are taken subject to the reasonable belief that the client will benefit from the action, and

(c) that the social worker will consider the client as an individual, a member of a family unit, a member of a community, a person with a distinct ancestry or culture and will consider those factors in any decision affecting the client.

*This *Social Work Code of Ethics,* adopted by the Board of Directors of the Canadian Association of Social Workers (CASW) is effective on January 1, 1994 and replaces the CASW *Code of Ethics* (1983). This Code is reprinted here with the permission of CASW. The copyright in the document has been registered with Consumer and Corporate Affairs Canada, Registration No. 427837.

Client[1] means

(a) a person, family, group of persons, incorporated body, association or community on whose behalf a social worker provides or agrees to provide a service
   (i) on request or with agreement[2] of the person, family, group of persons, incorporated body, associations or community, or
   (ii) as a result of a legislated responsibility, or

(b) a judge of a court of competent jurisdiction who orders the social worker to provide to the Court an assessment.[3]

Conduct unbecoming means behaviour or conduct that does not meet standard of care requirements and is therefore subject to discipline.[4]

Malpractice and negligence means behaviour that is included as "conduct unbecoming" and relates to social work practice behaviour within the parameters of the professional relationship that falls below the standard of practice and results in or aggravates an injury to a client. Without limiting the generality of the above,[5] it includes behaviour which results in assault, deceit, fraudulent misrepresentations, defamation of character, breach of contract, violation of human rights, malicious prosecution, false imprisonment or criminal conviction.

Practice of social work includes the assessment, remediation and prevention of social problems, and the enhancement of social functioning of individuals, families, groups and communities by means of

(a) the provision of direct counselling services within an established relationship between a social worker and client;

(b) the development, promotion and delivery of human service programs, including that done in collaboration with other professionals;

(c) the development and promotion of social policies aimed at improving social conditions and equality; and[6]

(d) any other activities approved by CASW.[7]

Social worker means a person who is duly registered to practice social work in a province or territory or where mandatory registration does not exist, a person practising social work who voluntarily agrees to be subject to this Code.

Standard of practice means the standard of care ordinarily expected of a competent social worker. It means that the public is assured that a social worker has the training, the skill and the diligence to provide them with professional social work services.

Preamble

Philosophy

The profession of social work is founded on humanitarian and egalitarian ideas. Social workers believe in the intrinsic worth and dignity of every human being and are committed to the values of acceptance, self-determination and respect of individuality. They believe in the obligation of all people, individually and collectively, to provide resources, services and opportunities for the overall benefit of humanity. The culture of individuals, families, groups, communities and nations has to be respected without prejudice.[8]

Social workers are dedicated to the welfare and self-realization of human beings; to the development and disciplined use of scientific knowledge regarding human and societal behaviours; to the development of resources to meet individual, group, national and international needs and aspirations; and to the achievement of social justice for all.

Professional Practice Conflicts

If a conflict arises in professional practice, the standards declared in this Code take precedence. Conflicts of interest may occur because of demands from the general public, workplace, organizations or clients. In all cases, if the ethical duties and obligations or ethical responsibilities of this Code would be compromised, the social worker must act in a manner consistent with this Code.

Nature of This Code

The first seven statements in this code establish ethical duties and obligations. These statements provide the basis of a social worker's relationship with a client and are based on the values of social work. A breach of any of these statements forms the basis of a disciplinary action. The remaining three statements are characterized as ethical responsibilities and are seen as being different from the ethical duties and obligations. These ethical responsibilities are not likely to form the basis of any disciplinary action if breached. However these sections may form the basis of inquiry. These ethical responsibilities may be used in conjunction with breaches of other sections of this code and may form the basis of necessary background information in any action for discipline. Of equal importance, these ethical responsibilities are desirable goals to be achieved by the social work profession which by its nature is driven by an adherence to the values that form the basis of these desirable ethical behaviours.

Social Work Code of Ethics

Ethical Duties and Obligations

1. A social worker shall maintain the best interest of the client as the primary professional obligation.
2. A social worker shall carry out her or his professional duties and obligations with integrity and objectivity.
3. A social worker shall have and maintain competence in the provision of a social work service to a client.
4. A social worker shall not exploit the relationship with a client for personal benefit, gain or gratification.
5. A social worker shall protect the confidentiality of all information acquired from the client or others regarding the client and the client's family during the professional relationship unless
   (a) the client authorizes in writing the release of specified information
   (b) the information is released under the authority of a statute or an order of a court of competent jurisdiction, or
   (c) otherwise authorized by this Code.
6. A social worker who engages in another profession, occupation, affiliation or calling shall not allow these outside interests to affect the social work relationship with the client.
7. A social worker in private practice shall not conduct the business of provision of social work services for a fee in a manner that discredits the profession or diminishes the public's trust in the profession.

Ethical Responsibilities

8. A social worker shall advocate for workplace conditions and policies that are consistent with the Code.
9. A social worker shall promote excellence in the social work profession.
10. A social worker shall advocate change
    (a) in the best interest of the client, and
    (b) for the overall benefit of society, the environment and the global community.

Primary Professional Obligation

1. A social worker shall maintain the best interest of the client as the primary professional obigation.

1.1 The social worker is to be guided primarily by this obligation. Any action which is substantially inconsistent with this obligation is an unethical action.

1.2 A social worker in the practice of social work shall not discriminate against any person on the basis of race, ethnic background, language, religion, marital status, sex, sexual orientation, age, abilities, socio-economic status, political affiliation or national ancestry.[9]

1.3 A social worker shall inform a client of the client's right to consult another professional at any time during the provision of social work services.

1.4 A social worker shall immediately inform the client of any factor, condition[10] or pressure that affects the social worker's ability to perform an acceptable level of service.

1.5 A social worker shall not become involved in a client's personal affairs that are not relevant to the service being provided.

1.6 A social worker shall not state an opinion, judgment or use a clinical diagnosis unless there is a documented assessment, observation or diagnosis to support the opinion, judgment or diagnosis.

1.7 Where possible, a social worker shall provide or secure social work services in the language chosen by the client.

Integrity and Objectivity

2. A social worker shall carry out his or her professional duties and obligations with integrity and objectivity.[11]

2.1 The social worker shall identify and describe education, training, experience, professional affiliations, competence, and nature of service in an honest and accurate manner.

2.2 The social worker shall explain to the client her or his education, experience, training, competence, nature of service and action at the request of the client.

2.3 A social worker shall cite an educational degree only after it has been received from the institution.

2.4 A social worker shall not claim formal social work education in an area of expertise or training solely by attending a lecture, demonstration, conference, panel discussion, workshop, seminar or other similar teaching presentation.[12]

2.5 The social worker shall not make a false, misleading or exaggerated claim of efficacy regarding past or anticipated achievement with respect to clients.

2.6 The social worker shall distinguish between actions and statements made as a private citizen and actions and statements made as a social worker.[13]

Competence in the Provision of Social Work Services

3. A social worker shall have and maintain competence in the provision of a social work service to a client.

3.1 The social worker shall not undertake a social work service unless the social worker has the competence to provide the serivce or the social worker can reasonably acquire the necessary competence without undue delay, risk or expense to the client.

3.2 Where a social worker cannot reasonably acquire the necessary competence in the provision of a service to a client, the social worker shall decline to provide the service to the client, advising the client of the reason and ensuring that the client is referred to another

professional person if the client agrees to the referral.

3.3 The social worker, with the agreement of the client, may obtain advice from other professionals in the provision of service to a client.

3.4 A social worker shall maintain an acceptable level of health and well-being in order to provide a competent level of service to a client.[14]

3.5 Where social worker has a physical or mental health problem, disability or illness that affects the ability of the social worker to provide competent service or that would threaten the health or well-being of the client, the social worker shall discontinue the provision of social work service to a client
  (a) advising the client of the reason and,[15]
  (b) ensuring that the client is referred to another professional person if the client agrees to the referral.

3.6 The social worker shall have, maintain and endeavor periodically to update an acceptable level of knowledge and skills to meet the standards of practice of the profession.

Limit on Professional Relationship

4. A social worker shall not exploit the relationship with a client for personal benefit, gain or gratification.

4.1 The social worker shall respect the client and act so that the dignity, individuality and rights of the person are protected.

4.2 The social worker shall assess and consider a client's motivation and physical and mental capacity in arranging for the provision of an appropriate service.

4.3 The social worker shall not have a sexual relationship with a client.

4.4 The social worker shall not have a business relationship with a client, borrow money from a client, or loan money to a client.[16]

4.5 The social worker shall not have a sexual relationship with a social work student assigned to the social worker.

4.6 The social worker shall not sexually harass any person.

Confidential Information

5. A social worker shall protect the confidentiality[17] of all information required from the client or others regarding the client and the client's family during the professional relationship[18] unless
    (a) the client authorizes in writing the release of specified information,[19]
    (b) the information is released under the authority of a statute or an order of a court of relevant jurisdiction, or
    (c) otherwise authorized under this Code.

5.1 The requirement of confidentiality also applies to social workers who work as
    (a) supervisors,
    (b) managers,
    (c) educators, or
    (d) administrators.

5.2 A social worker who works as a supervisor, manager or administrator shall establish policies and practices that protect the confidentiality of client information.

5.3 The social worker may disclose confidential information to other persons in the workplace who, by virtue of their responsibilities, have an identified need to know as determined by the social worker.

5.4 Clients shall be the initial or primary source of information about themselves and their problems unless the client is incapable or unwilling to give information or when corroborative reporting is required.

5.5 The social worker has the obligation to ensure that the client understands what is being asked, why and to what purpose the information will be used, and to understand the confidentiality policies and practices of the workplace setting.

5.6 Where information is required by law, the social worker shall explain to the client the consequences of refusing to provide the requested information.

5.7 Where information is required from other sources, the social worker
    (a) shall explain the requirement to the client, and
    (b) shall attempt to involve the client in selecting the sources to be used.

5.8 The social worker shall take reasonable care to safeguard the client's personal papers or property if the social worker agrees to keep the property at the request of the client.

Recording Information

5.9 The social worker shall maintain only one master file on each client.[20]

5.10 The social worker shall record all relevant information, and keep all relevant documents in the file.

5.11 The social worker shall not record in a client's file any characterization that is not based on clinical assessment or fact.

Accessibility of Records

5.12 The social worker who contracts for the delivery of social work services with a client is responsible to the client for maintaining the client record.

5.13 The social worker who is employed by a social agency that delivers social work services to clients is responsible
    (a) to the client for the maintaining of a client record, and
    (b) to the agency to maintain the records to facilitate the objectives of the agency.

5.14 A social worker is obligated to follow the provision of a statute that allows access to records by clients.

5.15 The social worker shall respect the client's right of access to a client record subject to the social worker's right to refuse access for just and reasonable cause.

5.16 Where a social worker refuses a client the right to access a file or part of a file, the social worker shall advise the client of the right to request a review of the decision in accordance with the relevant statute, workplace policy or other relevant procedure.

Disclosure

5.17 The social worker shall not disclose the identity of persons who have sought a social work service or disclose sources of information about clients unless compelled legally to do so.[21]

5.18 The obligation to maintain confidentiality continues indefinitely after the social worker has ceased contact with the client.

5.19 The social worker shall avoid unnecessary conversation regarding clients.

5.20 The social worker may divulge confidential information with consent of the client, preferably expressed in writing, where this is essential to a plan of care or treatment.

5.21 The social worker shall transfer information to another agency or individual, only with the informed consent of the client or guardian of the client and then only with the reasonable assurance that the receiving agency provides the same guarantee of confidentiality and respect for the right of privileged communication as provided by the sending agency.

5.22 The social worker shall explain to the client the disclosure of information requirements of the law or of the agency before the commencement of the provision of social work services.

5.23 The social worker in practice with groups and communities shall notify the participants of the likelihood that aspects of their private lives may be revealed in the course of their work together, and therefore require a commit-

ment from each member to respect the privileged and confidential nature of the communication between and among members of the client group.

5.24 Subject to section 5.26, the social worker shall not disclose information acquired from one client to a member of the client's family without the informed consent of the client who provided the information.

5.25 A social worker shall disclose information acquired from one client to a member of the client's family where
 (a) the information involves a threat of harm to self or others,[22]
 (b) the information was acquired from a child of tender years and the social worker determines that its disclosure is in the best interests of the child.[23]

5.26 A social worker shall disclose information acquired from a client to a person or a police officer where the information involves a threat of harm to that person.

5.27 A social worker may release confidential information as part of a discipline hearing of a social worker as directed by the tribunal or disciplinary body.

5.28 When disclosure is required by order of a court, the social worker shall not divulge more information than is reasonably required and shall where possible notify the client of this requirement.

5.29 The social worker shall not use confidential information for the purpose of teaching, public education or research except with the informed consent of the client.

5.30 The social worker may use non-identifying information for the purpose of teaching, public education or research.

Retention and Disposition of Information

5.31 Where the social worker's documentation is stored in a place or computer maintained and operated by an employer, the social worker shall advocate for the responsible retention and disposition of information contained in the file.

Outside Interest

6. A social worker who engages in another profession, occupation, affiliation or calling shall not allow these outside interests to affect the social work relationship with the client.

6.1 A social worker shall declare to the client any outside interests that would affect the social work relationship with the client.

6.2 A social worker shall not allow an outside interest:
   (a) to affect the social worker's ability to practise social work;
   (b) to present to the client or to the community that the social worker's ability to practise social work is affected; or
   (c) to bring the profession of social work into disrepute.[24]

Limit on Private Practice

7. A social worker in private practice shall not conduct the business of provision of social work services for a fee in a manner that discredits the profession or diminishes the public's trust in the profession.

7.1 A social worker shall not use the social work relationship within an agency to obtain clients for his or her private practice.

7.2 Subject to section 7.3, a social worker who enters into a contract for service with a client
   (a) shall disclose at the outset of the relationship, the fee schedule for the social work services,
   (b) shall not charge a fee that is greater than that agreed to and disclosed to the client, and

   (c) shall not charge for hours of service other than the reasonable hours of client services, research, consultation and administrative work directly connected to the case.

7.3 A social worker in private practice may charge differential fees for services except where an increased fee is charged based on race, ethnic background, language, religion, marital status, sex, sexual orientation, age, abilities, socio-economic status, political affiliation or national ancestry.

7.4 A social worker in private practice shall maintain adequate malpractice, defamation and liability insurance.

7.5 A social worker in private practice may charge a rate of interest on delinquent accounts as is allowed by law.[25]

7.6 Notwithstanding section 5.17 a social worker in private practice may pursue civil remedies to ensure payment for services to a client where the social worker has advised the client of this possibility at the outset of the social work service.

Ethical Responsibilities to the Workplace

8. A social worker shall advocate for workplace conditions and policies that are consistent with the Code.

8.1 Where the responsibilities to an employer are in conflict with the social worker's obligations to the client, the social worker shall document the issue in writing and shall bring the situation to the attention of the employer.

8.2 Where a serious ethical conflict continues to exist after the issue has been brought to the attention of the employer, the social worker shall bring the issue to the attention of the Association or regulatory body.[26]

8.3 A social worker shall follow the principles in the Code when dealing with
   (a) a social worker under the supervision of the social worker,

(b) an employee under the supervision of the social worker, and

(c) a social work student under the supervision of the social worker.

Ethical Responsibilities to the Profession

9. A social worker shall promote excellence in the social work profession.

9.1 A social worker shall report to the appropriate association or regulatory body any breach of this Code by another social worker which adversely affects or harms a client or prevents the effective delivery of a social service.

9.2 A social worker shall report to the association or regulatory body any unqualified or unlicensed person who is practising social work.

9.3 A social worker shall not intervene in the professional relationship of a social worker and client unless requested to do so by the client and unless convinced that the best interests and well-being of the client require such intervention.

9.4 Where a conflict arises between a social worker and other professionals, the social worker shall attempt to resolve the professional differences in ways that uphold the principles of this Code and the honour of the social work profession.

9.5 A social worker engaged in research shall ensure that the involvement of clients in the research is a result of informed consent.

Ethical Responsibilities for Social Change

10. A social worker shall advocate change
(a) in the best interest of the client, and
(b) for the overall benefit of society, the environment and the global community.

10.1 A social worker shall identify, document and advocate for the elimination of discrimination.

10.2 A social worker shall advocate for the equal distribution of resources to all persons.

10.3 A social worker shall advocate for the equal access of all persons to resources, services and opportunities.

10.4 A social worker shall advocate for a clean and healthy environment and shall advocate the development of environmental strategies consistent with social work principles.

10.5 A social worker shall provide reasonable professional services in a state of emergency.

10.6 A social worker shall promote social justice.

Notes

1. A client ceases to be a client 2 years after the termination of a social work service. It is advisable for this termination to be clearly documented on the case file.

2. This sub-paragraph identifies two situations where a person may be considered a voluntary client. The person who requests a social work service is clearly a voluntary client. A person also may originally be receiving services as a result of the actions of a court or other legally mandated entity. This person may receive a service beyond that originally mandated and therefore be able to terminate voluntarily that aspect of the service. A situation where a person is referred by another professional or family member clearly falls into this "voluntary service" relationship when that person agrees with the service to be provided. This type of social work relationship is clearly distinguishable from the relationship in sub-paragraph (ii) where the social worker does not seek or have agreement for the service to be provided.

3. In this situation, the social worker is providing an assessment, information or a professional opinion to a judge of competent jurisdiction to assist the judge in making a ruling or determination. In this situation, the relationship is with the judge and the person on whom the information, assessment or opinion is provided is not the client. The social worker still has some professional obligations towards that person, for example: competence and dignity.

4. In reaching a decision in *Re Matthews and the Board of Directors of Physiotherapy* (1986) 54 O.R. (2d) 375, Saunders J. makes three important statements regarding standards of practice and by implication Code of Ethics:

(i) Standards of practice are inherent characteristics of any profession.

(ii) Standards of practice may be written or unwritten.

(iii) Some conduct is clearly regarded as misconduct and need not be written down whereas other conduct may be the subject of dispute within a profession.

5. The importance of the collective opinion of the profession in establishing and ultimately modifying the Code of Ethics was established in a 1884 case involving the medical profession. Lord Esher, M.R. stated:

> "If it is shown that a medical man, in the pursuit of his profession, has done something with regard to it which would be reasonably regarded as disgraceful or dishonourable by his professional brethren of good repute and competency," then it is open to the General Medical Council to say that he has been guilty of "infamous conduct in a professional respect."

6. This definition except paragraph (d) has been taken from *An Act to Incorporate the New Brunswick Association of Social Workers,* chapter 78 of the Statutes of New Brunswick, 1988, section 2.

7. The procedure for adding activities under this paragraph will be established by a bylaw by the CASW Board of Directors.

8. Taken from: *Teaching and Learning about Human Rights; A Manual for School of Social Work and the Social Work Profession;* U.N. Centre for Human Rights, Co-operation with International Federation of Social Workers and International Association of Schools of Social Workers, United Nations, New York, 1992.

9. This obligation goes beyond grounds of discrimination stated in most *Human Rights Legislation* and therefore there is a greater professional obligation than that stated in provincial legislation.

10. The term condition means a physical, mental or psychological condition. There is an implied obligation that the social worker shall actively seek diagnosis and treatment for any signs or warnings of a condition. A disclosure under this section may be of a general nature. See also 3.4.

11. The term objectivity is taken from the Québec Code of Professional Conduct. See Division 2: Integrity and Objectivity (6.0 Québec) November 5, 1979 Vol. 2 No. 30. The term objectivity is stated in the following: 3.02.01. A social worker must discharge his professional duties with integrity and objectivity.

12. The provincial associations may regulate the areas of expertise to be stated or advertised by a social worker. This will vary in each province according to its enabling legislation. Where there is not sufficient legislative base for this regulation, the claim of an expertise without sufficient training may form the basis of a determination of unprofessional conduct.

13. Even with a distinction made under this section, a social worker's private actions or statements may be of such a nature that the social worker cannot avoid the responsibilities under this Code. See also 6.2 (c).

14. This section should be considered in relation to section 1.4 and involves proper maintenance, prevention and treatment of any type of risk to the health or well-being of the social worker.

15. It is not necessary in all circumstances to explain specifically the nature of the problem.

16. Where a social worker does keep money or assets belonging to a client, the social worker should hold this money or asset in a trust account or hold the money or asset in conjunction with an additional professional person.

17. Confidentiality means that information received or observed about a client by a social worker will be held in confidence and disclosed only when the social worker is properly authorized or obligated legally or professionally to do so. This also means that professionally acquired information may be treated as privileged communication and ordinarily only the client has the right to waive privilege.

Privileged communication means statements made within a protected relationship (i.e. husband–wife, professional–client) which the law protects against disclosure. The extent of the privilege is governed by law and not by this Code.

Maintaining confidentiality of privileged communication means that information about clients does not have to be transmitted in any oral, written or recorded form. Such information, for example, does not have to be disclosed to a supervisor, written into a workplace record, stored in a computer or microfilm data base, held on an audio or videotape or discussed orally. The right of privileged communication is respected by the social worker in the practice of social work notwithstanding that this right is not ordinarily granted in law.

The disclosure of confidential information in social work practice involves the obligation to share information professionally with others in the workplace of the social worker as part of a reasonable service to the client. Social workers recognize the need to obtain permission from clients before releasing information about them to sources outside their workplace; and to inform clients at the outset of their relationship that some information acquired may be shared with the officers and personnel of the agency who maintain the case record and who have a reasonable need for the information in the performance of their duties.

18. The social worker's relationship with a client can be characterized as a fiduciary relationship.

In *Fiduciary Duties in Canada* by Ellis, fiduciary duty is described as follows: . . . where one party has placed its "trust and confidence" in another and the latter has accepted—expressly or by operation of law—to act in a manner consistent with the reposing of such "trust and confidence," a fiduciary relationship has been established.

19. The "obligation of secrecy" was discussed by the Supreme Court of Canada in *Halls v. Mitchell*, (1928) S.C.R. 125, an action brought by a disabled CNR worker against a company doctor who had disclosed the employee's medical history, to the latter's detriment. Mr. Justice Duff reviewed the duty of confidentiality:

We are not required, for the purposes of this appeal, to attempt to state with any sort of precision the limits of the obligation of secrecy which rests upon the medical practitioner in relation to the professional secrets acquired by him in the course of his practice. Nobody would dispute that a secret so acquired is the secret of the patient, and, normally, is under his control, and not under that of the doctor. Prima facie, the patient has the right to require that the secret shall not be divulged; and that right is absolute, unless there is some paramount reason which overrides it.

Thus the right of secrecy / confidentiality rests squarely with the patient; the Court carefully provided that there is an "ownership" extant in the confidentiality of the personal information. Duff J. continued by allowing for "paramount" criteria which vitiates from the right:

Some reasons may arise, no doubt, from the existence of facts which bring into play overpowering considerations connected with public justice; and there may be cases in which reasons connected with the safety of individuals or of the public, physical or moral, would be sufficiently cogent to supersede or qualify the obligations prima facie imposed by the confidential relation.

Duff J. continued:
The general duty of medical men to observe secrecy, in relation to information acquired by them confidentially from their patients is subject, no doubt, to some exceptions, which have no operation in the case of solicitors; but the grounds of the legal, social or moral imperatives affecting physicians and surgeons, touching the inviolability of professional confidences, are not, any more than those affecting legal advisers, based exclusively upon the relationships between the parties as individuals.

20. The master file refers to all relevant documents pertaining to the client consisting of such information as demographics, case recordings, court documents, assessments, correspondence, treatment plans, bills, etc. This information is often collected through various means including electronic and computer-driven sources. However the client master file exists as one unit, inclusive of all information pertaining to the client, despite the various sources of the recording process. The description and ownership of the master file is most often defined by workplace standards or policies. The client's master file should be prepared keeping in mind that it may have to be revelaed to the client or disclosed in legal proceedings.

21. A social worker may be compelled to reveal information under the section when directly ordered by the court to do so. Before disclosing the information, the social worker shall advise the court of the professional obligations that exist under this section of the Code and where reasonably possible inform the client.

22. The case of *Tarasoff* v. *The Regents of the University of California et al.* (1976), 551 p.2d 334 (Cal. Supreme Court) focused on the obligation of a psychiatrist to maintain the confidentiality of his patients' statements in their discussions. In that case the patient told the psychiatrist that the

patient had an intention to kill a certain woman. When the patient actually did kill this woman, her parents brought suit alleging that the psychiatrist owed a duty to tell the woman of the danger to her.

It was held that the psychiatrist did have a duty to tell the woman of the threat. The court recognized that the psychiatrist owed a duty to the patient to keep in confidence the statements the patient made in therapy sessions, but held there was also a duty to care to anyone whom the psychiatrist knew might be endangered by the patient. At a certain point the obligation of confidentiality would be overriden by the obligation to this third person. The psychiatrist's knowledge itself gave rise to a duty of care. What conduct would be sufficient to fulfil the duty to this third person would depend on the circumstances, but it might be necessary to give a warning that would reveal what the patient had said about the third party. The court in this case held that the psychiatrist had a duty to warn the woman about the patient's stated intention to kill her, and having failed to warn her the psychiatrist was liable in negligence. Moreover, the court stated that the principle of this duty of care belonged not just to a psychiatrist but also to a psychologist performing therapy. It would follow that the principle would also apply to social workers performing therapy.

23. For the purpose of this Code, a child of tender years shall usually be determined to be a child under the age of seven years subject to a determination by a social worker considering the child's social, physical, intellectual, emotional or psychological development.

24. This section brings the social worker's outside interest and personal actions in line with the professional duties and obligations as set out in this Code.

25. This rate shall be stated on all invoices or bills sent to the client.

26. In this situation the professional obligations outweigh any obligations to a workplace.

APPENDIX C
SUGGESTED COUNSELOR'S RESPONSES TO CLIENT'S STATEMENTS

The following is a suggested response to each of the client's statements in Exercise 3, Chapter 5:

1. "I sense that you feel strongly about this, and that you've given this a lot of thought. I'd like to explore this further with you, as I care very much about you as a person. It makes me uncomfortable if you think that the only reason I meet with you is because I'm getting paid. Working with you and with the other clients I have is personally very gratifying to me. Perhaps I have miscommunicated with you, verbally or nonverbally. I'd like to hear more about why you've reached the conclusion that I don't care about you as a person."

2. "You're really feeling as if you're caught in a dilemma. Obviously in this situation, as in many situations, you can't please everyone. But, are you aware that the most important person to please is yourself? You're the one who has to live with your decisions. I'm wondering what your feelings are toward Kent, and what your feelings are about getting married at this time in your life. I'm also wondering why your parents dislike Kent. Let's examine these one at a time. What are your feelings toward Kent?"

3. "Yes, I did. I took them two summers ago when I was vacationing in the Colorado Rockies. But we're here to talk about you and how your life is going. Let's begin by discussing how you're doing in school. For each class that you have, could you tell me what grade you received on your midterm report this past week?"

4. "I sense this is extremely difficult for you to reveal. You probably are feeling very vulnerable at this point. I'm pleased that you shared this with me, and rest assured that I have an open mind about sexual orientation. It took real courage for you to talk about this, and I now believe we are in a much better position for you to make some decisions about your future. Could you tell me more about this person you are involved with?"

5. "It is true that I am neither black, nor have I lived in a ghetto. But I'm interested in you and in working with you. Just because I'm white doesn't mean we can't work together. Everyone, including me, has personal problems. You, too, have some personal problems. By taking each one, one at a time, and examining them and then coming up with some realistic ways of resolving them, I firmly believe we can make progress. Just as a teacher does not have to be blind to teach students with a visual disability, a counselor does not need to have the same color of skin to work with people who have personal problems. Have I said or done anything to lead you to believe that I

am prejudiced against people who have a different color of skin?"

6. "I'm sorry you're still involved with drugs, especially since you were using drugs when you committed the offenses that resulted in you being sent here. I don't like to see you get into trouble, but I have no choice. I have to report this. I made it crystal clear to you at our first meeting that the consequences of drug involvement here would probably be an extension of the time you spend here. As you know we do have a drug treatment program. I suggest you seriously consider participating in this program. Participation in this program, now, may not only lead to an earlier release, but may also help you become drug free. Are you interested in participating in this program?"

REFERENCES

ABRAMS, A. I. 1974. "Paired Associate Learning and Recall." In *Scientific Research on Transcendental Meditation: Collected Papers,* eds. D. W. Orme-Johnson, L. H. Domash, & J. T. Fallow. Los Angeles: MIU Press.

ACKERMAN, N. W. 1966. *Treating the Troubled Family.* New York: Basic Books.

"Acquired Immune Deficiency Syndrome: 100 Questions and Answers." 1985. Albany, NY: AIDS Institute.

"Acquired Immune Deficiency Syndrome: An Annotated Bibliography." 1986. New York: Sex Information and Education Council of the U.S.

ADDAMS, J. 1959. *Twenty Years of Hull House.* New York: Macmillan (original publication, 1910).

ADMINISTRATION IN SOCIAL WORK 5, nos. 3 and 4. Fall/Winter 1981. Special issue devoted to computer applications in social work administration.

AGUILAR, I. 1972. "Initial Contacts with Mexican-American Families." *Social Work 17* (May), pp. 186–189.

AHN, H. N., & N. Gilbert. 1992. "Cultural Diversity and Sexual Abuse Prevention." *Social Science Review 66,* no. 3, pp. 410–427.

AINSWORTH, M. D. et al. 1966. *Deprivation of Maternal Care.* New York: Schocken Books.

ALBERTI, R. E., & M. L. Emmons. 1970. *Your Perfect Right: A Guide to Assertive Behavior.* San Luis Obispo, CA: Impact Publishers.

———. 1975. *Stand Up, Speak Out, Talk Back!* New York: Pocket Books.

ALEXANDER, C. A. 1982. "Professional Social Work and Political Responsibility." In *Practical Politics: Social Work and Political Responsibility,* eds. M. Mahaffey & J. W. Hanks. Silver Spring, MD: National Association of Social Workers.

ALEXANDER, K. 1993. "Changes in Delivery of Services for Students with Limited English." *The Advocate 1*(2), p. 1.

ALINSKY, S. D. 1972. *Rules for Radicals.* New York: Random House.

ALTER, C., & W. Evens. 1990. *Evaluating Your Practice: A Guide to Self-Assessment.* New York: Springer.

ALYSON, S., ed. 1990. *You Can Do Something About AIDS: New Edition.* Boston, MA: The Stop AIDS Project.

AMERICAN PSYCHIATRIC ASSOCIATION. 1987. *Diagnostic and Statistical Manual of Mental Disorders.* 3rd ed., rev. (DSM-III-R). Washington, DC: American Psychiatric Association.

ANANT, S. S. 1967. "A Note on the Treatment of Alcoholics by a Verbal Aversion Technique." *Canadian Psychologist 8,* pp. 19–22.

———. 1968. "Verbal Aversion Therapy with a Promiscuous Girl: Case Report." *Psychological Reports 22,* pp. 795–796.

ANDERSON, G., ed. 1990. *Courage to Care.* Washington, DC: Child Welfare League of America.

ANDERSON, J. 1981. *Social Work Methods and Processes.* Belmont, CA: Wadsworth.

ANDREASEN, N. 1985. *The Broken Brain.* New York: Harper & Row.

ANNON, J. S. 1975. *Behavioral Treatment of Sexual Problems.* Vol. 2, *Intensive Therapy.* Honolulu: Enabling Systems.

———. 1976. *Behavioral Treatment of Sexual Problems, Brief Therapy.* New York: Harper & Row.

ARLOW, J. A. 1989. "Psychoanalysis." In *Current Psychotherapies,* 4th ed., eds. R. J. Corsini & D. Wedding, pp. 18–59. Itasca, IL: Peacock.

ASCH, S. E. 1955. "Opinions and Social Pressure." *Scientific American 193,* no. 5, pp. 31–35.

ASHEM, B., & L. Donner. 1968. "Covert Sensitization with Alcoholics: A Controlled Replication." *Behaviour Research and Therapy 6,* pp. 7–12.

AXLINE, V. 1947. *Play Therapy.* New York: Ballantine Books.

BAER, B. L. 1979. "Developing a New Curriculum for Social Work Education." In *The Pursuit of Competence in Social Work,* eds. F. Clark & M. Arkava, pp. 96–109. San Francisco: Jossey-Bass.

BAER, B. L., & R. Federico. 1978. *Educating the Baccalaureate Social Worker.* Cambridge, MA: Ballinger Publishing.

BAKER, F. 1977. "The Interface between Professional and Natural Support Systems." *Clinical Social Work Journal 5* (Summer), pp. 139–148.

BALES, R. F. 1950. *Interaction Process Analysis: A Method for the Study of Small Groups.* Reading, MA: Addison-Wesley.

BANCROFT, J. H., Jr., H. G. Jones, & B. R. Pullan. 1966. "A Simple Transducer for Measuring Penile Erection, with Comments on Its Use in the Treatment of Sexual Disorders." *Behaviour Research and Therapy 4,* pp. 239–241.

BANDLER, R., & J. Grinder. 1975. *The Structure of Magic,* vol. 1. Palo Alto, CA: Science and Behavior Books.

———. 1976(a). *The Structure of Magic*, vol. 2. Palo Alto, CA: Science and Behavior Books.

———. 1976(b). *Patterns of the Hypnotic Techniques of Milton H. Erickson, M.D.*, vol. 1. Cupertino, CA: Meta Publications.

———. 1979. *Frogs into Princes*. Moab, UT: Real People Press.

———. 1982. *Reframing*. Moab, UT: Real People Press.

BANDLER, R., J. Grinder, & V. Satir. 1976. *Changing with Families*, vol. 1. Palo Alto, CA: Science and Behavior Books.

BARBACH, L. G. 1975. *For Yourself: The Fulfillment of Female Sexuality*. New York: New American Library.

———. 1982. *For Each Other: Sharing Sexual Intimacy*. Garden City, NY: Doubleday Publishing.

———. 1984. *Pleasures*. New York: Harper & Row.

BARKER, R. L. 1991. *The Social Work Dictionary*. 2nd ed. Silver Spring, MD: National Association of Social Workers.

BARLOW, D. H., & M. Hersen. 1984. *Single Case Experimental Designs*. 2nd ed. Elmsford, NY: Pergamon Press.

BARLOW, D. H., S. C. Hayes, & R. O. Nelson. 1984. *The Scientist Practitioner*. Elmsford, NY: Pergamon Press.

BAROCAS, H. A. 1972. "Psychodrama Techniques in Training Police in Family Crisis Intervention." *Group Psychotherapy and Psychodrama 25*, pp. 30–31.

BARTLESS, H. M. 1970. *The Common Base of Social Work Practice*. New York: National Association of Social Workers.

BASS, E., & L. Davis. 1988. *The Courage to Heal*. New York: Harper & Row.

BATESON, G., D. Jackson, J. Haley, & J. Weakland. 1956. "Toward a Communication Theory of Schizophrenia." *Behavior Science*. Reprinted in *Communication, Family and Marriage* I, ed. D. Jackson. Palo Alto, CA: Science and Behavior Books, 1968.

BECK, A. T. 1976. *Cognitive Theory and the Emotional Disorders*. New York: International Universities Press.

BECK, A. T., & M. E. Weishaar. 1989. "Cognitive Therapy." In *Current Psychotherapies*. 4th ed., eds. R. J. Corsini & D. Wedding, pp. 284–320. Itasca, IL: Peacock.

BECKER, D. G. 1968. "Social Welfare Leaders as Spokesmen for the Poor." *Social Casework 49*, no. 2 (Feb.), p. 85.

BELLACK, A. S., & M. Hersen, eds. 1988. *Behavioral Assessment*. Elmsford, NY: Pergamon Press.

BELLIVEAU, F., & L. Richter. 1970. *Understanding Human Sexual Inadequacy*. New York: Bantam Books.

BEMNER, R. M. 1962. "The Rediscovery of Pauperism," *Current Issues in Social Work Seen in Historical Perspective*. New York: Council on Social Work Education.

BENJAMIN, A. 1974. *The Helping Interview*. 2nd ed. Boston: Houghton Mifflin.

BENSON, H. 1975. *The Relaxation Response*. New York: Morrow.

BENSON, H., B. A. Rosner, & B. R. Marzetta. 1973. "Decreased Systolic Blood Pressure in Hypertensive Subjects Who Practice Meditation." *Journal of Clinical Investigation 52*, p. 80.

BERGER, R. 1982. "The Unseen Minority: Older Gays and Lesbians." *Social Work 27*, no. 3 (May), pp. 236–242.

———. 1983. "What Is a Homosexual? A Definitional Model." *Social Work 28*, no. 2 (March–April), pp. 132–135.

———. 1987. "Homosexuality: Gay Men." *The Encyclopedia of Social Work*, pp. 795–805. Silver Spring, MD: National Association of Social Workers.

BERGMAN, A. 1989. "Informal Support Systems for Pregnant Teenagers." *Social Casework 70*, no. 9, pp. 526–533.

BERLIN, S. B. 1976. "Better Work with Women Clients." *Social Work 21* (Nov.), pp. 492–497.

BERNANOS, G. 1970. As quoted in J. C. DeBoer, *Let's Plan: A Guide to the Planning Process for Voluntary Organizations*. New York: United Church Press.

BERNE, E. 1964. *Games People Play*. New York: Grove Press.

———. 1966. *Principles of Group Treatment*. New York: Oxford University Press.

BERNSTEIN, B. E. 1975. "The Social Worker as a Courtroom Witness." *Social Casework 56*, no. 9 (Nov.), pp. 521–525.

BERNSTEIN, D., & T. Borkovec. 1973. *Progressive Relaxation Training: A Manual for the Helping Professions*. Champaign, IL: Research Press.

BERTCHER, J. H., & F. Maple. 1974. "Elements and Issues in Group Composition." In *Individual Change through Small Groups*, by P. Glasser, R. Sarri, & R. Vinter, pp. 186–208. New York: Free Press.

BERWICK, D. 1980. "Nonorganic Failure to Thrive." *Pediatrics in Review 1*, pp. 265–270.

BIDDLE, W. W., & L. J. Biddle. 1965. *The Community Development Process*. New York: Holt, Rinehart & Winston.

BLACK, B. J. 1977. "Milieu Therapy." In *Encyclopedia of Social Work*. 17th ed., pp. 919–927. New York: National Association of Social Workers.

BLACKMAN, D. K., C. Gehle, & E. M. Pinkston. 1979. "Modifying Eating Habits of the Institutionalized Elderly." *Social Work Research and Abstracts 15*, no. 3 (Fall), pp. 18–24.

BLADES, J. 1985. *Mediate Your Divorce*. Englewood Cliffs, NY: Prentice-Hall.

BLAIRE, F. D. 1979. "Women in the Labor Force: An Overview." In *Women: A Feminist Perspective*. ed. J. Freeman. Palo Alto, CA: Mayfield.

BLASDELL, K. 1974. "The Effect of Transcendental Meditation upon a Complex Perceptual Motor Test. In *Scientific Research on Transcendental Meditation: Collected Papers*, eds. D. W. Orme-Johnson, L. H. Domash, & J. T. Farrow. Los Angeles: MIU Press.

BLASSINGAME, J. 1972. *The Slave Community*. New York: Oxford University Press.

BLOOM, M. 1975. *The Paradox of Helping: Introduction to the Philosophy of Scientific Practice*. New York: Wiley.

———. 1983. "Empirically Based Clnical Research." In *Handbook of Clinical Social Work*, ed. A. Rosenblatt & D. Waldfogel, pp. 560–582. San Francisco: Jossey-Bass.

BLOOM, M., & J. Fischer. 1982. *Evaluating Practice: Guidelines for the Accountable Professional*. Englewood Cliffs, NJ: Prentice-Hall.

BLOOMFIELD, H., M. Cain, & R. Jaffe. 1975. *TM: Discovering Inner Energy and Overcoming Stress*. New York: Delacorte Press.

BLYTHE, B. J., & T. Tripodi. 1989. *Measurement in Direct Practice*. Newbury Park, CA: Sage.

BOUDREAU, L. 1972. "Transcendental Meditation and Yoga as Reciprocal Inhibitors." *Journal of Behavior Therapy and Experimental Psychiatry 3*, pp. 97–98.

BOULETTE, T. R. 1975. "Group Therapy with Low Income Mexican Americans." *Social Work 20* (Sept.), pp. 403–405.

BOYTE, H. C. 1989. "People Power Transforms a St. Louis Housing Project." *Occasional Papers* (Jan.). Chicago: Community Renewable Society, pp. 1–5.

BRAWLEY, E. A. 1983. *Mass Media and Human Services: Getting the Message Across*. Beverly Hills, CA: Sage.

BRECHER, E. M. 1984. *Love, Sex and Aging*. Boston: Little, Brown.

BREUER, J., & S. Freud. 1895. *Studies in Hysteria*. London: Hogarth Press.

BRIAR, S. 1973. "Effective Social Work Intervention in Direct Practice: Implications for Education" in *Facing the Challenge*. Plenary session papers from the 19th Annual Program Meeting of the Council on Social Work Education. New York: Council on Social Work Education.

BRIELAND, D., L. B. Costin, & C. R. Atherton. 1985. *Contemporary Social Work: An Introduction to Social Work and Social Welfare*. 3rd ed. New York: McGraw-Hill.

BROWN, B. B. 1977. *Stress and the Art of Biofeedback*. New York: Bantam Books.

BROWN, C. R., & M. L. Hellinger. 1975. "Therapists' Attitudes Toward Woman." *Social Work* 20 (July), pp. 266–270.

BROWN, E. G. 1978. "Minority Content in the First Year Practice Course." In *The Dual Perspective*, Dolores Norton, pp. 23–30. New York: Council on Social Work Education.

BUBER, M. 1958. *I and Thou*. New York: Scribner.

BUCHANAN, R. L., Jr., & M. A. Cummings. 1975. *Individual Differences: An Experience in Human Relations for Children*. Madison, WI: Madison Public Schools.

BUGLIOSI, V., & C. Gentry. 1974. *Helter Skelter*. New York: Norton.

BUREAU OF THE CENSUS. 1992. *Statistical Abstract of the United States, 1992*. Washington, DC: Government Printing Office.

BURGESS, A. W., A. N. Groth, L. L. Holmstrom, & S. M. Sgroi, eds. 1984. *Sexual Assault of Children and Adolescents*. Lexington, MA: Lexington Books.

BURGEST, D. R. 1973. "Racism in Everyday Speech and Social Work Jargon." *Social Work* 18 (July), pp. 20–25.

BURGEST, M. D. R. 1983. "Education and Skills for Multi-Racial and Multi-Ethnic Direct Practice." Presented at the Annual Program Meeting, Council on Social Work Education, New York.

BURGHARDT, S., & M. Fabricant. 1987. *Working Under the Safety Net: Policy and Practice with the New American Poor*. Beverly Hills, CA: Sage.

BUROS, O. K. ed. 1978. *The Eighth Mental Measurements Yearbook*. 2 vols. Highland Park, NJ: Gryphon Press.

BUXTON, E. 1976. "Delivering Social Services in Rural Areas." In *Social Work in Rural Communities* by Leon Ginsberg, pp. 28–38. New York: Council on Social Work Education.

CAMPBELL, J. A. 1988. "Client Acceptance of Single-System Evaluation Procedures." *Social Work Research & Abstracts* 24, pp. 21–22.

———. 1990. "Ability of Practitioners to Estimate Client Acceptance of Single-Subject Evaluation Procedures." *Social Work* 35, pp. 9–14.

CANADIAN ASSOCIATION OF SOCIAL WORKERS. 1994 and 1983. *Social Work Code of Ethics*. Ottawa: Canadian Association of Social Workers.

CAPRIO, F. S., & J. R. Berger. 1963. *Helping Yourself with Self-Hypnosis*. Englewood Cliffs, NJ: Prentice-Hall.

CARRERA, M. 1981. *Sex: The Facts, the Acts and Your Feelings*. New York: Crown Publishers.

CARTWRIGHT, T. J. 1973. "Problems, Solutions, and Strategies: A Contribution to the Theory and Practice of Planning." *AIP Examination Readings*. Washington, DC: American Institute of Planners.

CAUTELA, J. R. 1967. "Covert Sensitization." *Psychological Reports* 20, pp. 459–468.

CAUTELA, J. R., & D. Upper. 1975. "The Process of Individual Behavior Therapy." In *Progress in Behavior Modifica-*

tion, eds. M. Hersen, R. M. Eisler, & R. M. Miller, pp. 276–306. New York: Academic Press.

CENTER FOR SOCIAL RESEARCH AND DEVELOPMENT. 1974. *Analysis and Synthesis of Needs Assessment Research in the Field of Human Services*. Denver: University of Denver.

CHAGNON, N. A. 1967. "Yanomamö Social Organization and Warfare." In *War*, eds. M. Fried., M. Harris, & R. Murphy, pp. 109–150. Garden City, NY: Natural History Press.

———. 1968. "Yanomamö, The Fierce People." In *Case Studies in Cultural Anthropology*, eds. G. Spindler & L. Spindler. Chicago: University of Chicago Press.

CHAMBLESS, D. L., & A. J. Goldstein. 1979. "Behavioral Psychotherapy." In *Current Psychotherapies*, 2d ed., ed. R. Corsini. Itasca, IL: Peacock.

CHARLESWORTH, E. A., & R. G. Nathan. 1984. *Stress Management*. New York: Ballantine Books.

CHRISTIE, R., & F. Geis. 1970. *Studies in Machiavellianism*. New York: Academic Press.

CHURCH, D. 1980. *It's Time to Tell: A Media Handbook for Human Services Personnel*. Washington, DC: US Department of Health and Human Services.

CIMINERO, A. R., K. S. Calhoun, & H. E. Adams, eds. 1977. *Handbook of Behavioral Assessment*. New York: Wiley.

———. 1986. *Handbook of Behavioral Assessment*. 2nd ed. New York: Wiley.

CLARK, F. W., & C. R. Horejsi. 1979. "Mastering Specific Skills." In *The Pursuit of Competence in Social Work*, eds. F. Clark & M. Arkava, pp. 29–46. San Francisco: Jossey-Bass.

CLELAND, D., & W. King. 1972. *Management: A Systems Approach*. New York: McGraw-Hill.

CLIFTON, R. L., & A. M. Dahms. 1980. *Grassroots Administration: A Handbook for Staff and Directors of Small Community-Based Social-Service Agencies*. Belmont, CA: Wadsworth.

COHEN, N. E. 1958. *Social Work in the American Tradition*. Hinsdale, IL: Dryden Press.

COLEMAN, J. W., & D. R. Cressey, 1990. *Social Problems*. 4th ed. New York: Harper & Row.

COLLIER, H. V. 1982. *Counseling Women: A Guide for Therapists*. New York: Free Press.

COMFORT, A. 1978. *Sexual Consequences of Disability*. Philadelphia: Stickley.

COMMISSION ON ACCREDITATION. 1988. "Curriculum Policy for the Master's Degree and Baccalaureate Degree Program in Social Work Education." In *Handbook of Standards and Procedures, 1988*. Washington, DC: Council on Social Work Education.

COMPTON, B. R., & B. Galaway. 1975. *Social Work Processes*. Pacific Grove, CA: Brooks/Cole.

"CONCEPTUAL FRAMEWORKS II." 1981. *Social Work* 26 (Jan.), pp. 1–96.

COOK, T. D., & D. T. Campbell. 1979. *Quasi-Experimentation: Design and Analysis Issues for Field Settings*. Chicago: Rand McNally.

COOLEY, C. H. 1902. *Human Nature and the Social Order*. New York: Scribner.

COOPER, M. 1990. "Treatment of a Client with Obsessive-Compulsive Disorder." *Social Work Research & Abstracts* 26, pp. 26–32.

COOPERSMITH, S. 1967. *The Antecedents of Self-Esteem*. San Francisco: Freeman.

CORCORAN, K., & J. Fischer. 1987. *Measures for Clinical Practice: A Sourcebook*. New York: Free Press.

———. 1993. *Measures for Clinical Practice: A Sourcebook*. 2nd ed. New York: Free Press.

CORCORAN, K., & W. J. Gingerich. In press. "Practice Evaluation in the Context of Managed Care: Case Recording Methods for Quality Assurance Review." *Research in Social Work Practice.*

COREY, G., & M. S. Corey. 1977. *Groups: Process and Practice.* Belmont, CA: Wadsworth.

CORMIER, W. H., & L. S. Cormier. 1991. *Interviewing Strategies for Helpers.* Pacific Grove, CA: Brooks/Cole.

CORSINI, R. J., ed. 1979. *Current Psychotherapies.* 2nd ed. Itasca, IL: Peacock.

CORSINI, R. J., & D. Wedding, eds. 1989. *Current Psychotherapies.* 4th ed. Itasca, IL: Peacock.

CORTE, H. E., M. M. Wolf, & B. J. Locke. 1971. "A Comparison of Procedures for Eliminating Self-Injurious Behavior of Retarded Adolescents." *Journal of Applied Behavior Analysis 4,* pp. 201–215.

CORYELL, W., J. Endicott, N. C. Andreasen, et al. 1988. *American Journal of Psychiatry 145,* pp. 293–300.

COUNCIL ON SOCIAL WORK EDUCATION. 1968. *Working with the Poor: Cultural Differences—Worker and Community.* New York: Council on Social Work Education.

———. 1976. *TEaching for Competence in the Delivery of Direct Services.* New York: Council on Social Work Education.

———. 1982. "Curriculum Policy for the Master's Degree & Baccalaureate Degree Programs in Social Work Education." 1982. New York: Council on Social Work Education, adopted May 24.

———. 1992a. *Curriculum Policy Statement for Baccalaureate Degree Programs in Social Work Education.* Alexandria, VA: Council on Social Work Education.

———. 1992b. *Curriculum Policy Statement for Master's Degree Programs in Social Work Education.* Alexandria, VA: Council on Social Work Education.

CRAIGHEAD, W. E., M. J. Mahoney, & A. R. Kazdin. 1976. *Behavior Modification: Principles, Issues and Applications.* Boston: Houghton Mifflin.

CRIDDLE, W. D. 1974. "Guidelines for Challenging Irrational Beliefs." *Rational Living* (Spring), pp. 8–13.

CUMMINGS, M. 1977. "How to Handle Incidents of Racial Discrimination." In *The Personal Problem Solver,* eds. C. Zastrow & D. H. Chang. Englewood Cliffs, NJ: Prentice-Hall.

CWIKEL, J. G., & R. A. Cnaan. 1991. "Ethical Dilemmas in Applying Second-Wave Information Technology to Social Work Practice." *Social Work 36,* pp. 114–120.

DAVENPORT, J., & J. Davenport, III. 1982. "Utilizing the Social Network in Rural Communities." *Social Casework 63* (Feb.), pp. 106–112.

DAVENPORT, J., & N. Reims. 1978. "Theoretical Orientation and Attitudes toward Women." *Social Work 23* (July), pp. 306–309.

DAVIE, J. S., & A. P. Hare. 1956. "Button-Down Collar Culture: A Study of Undergraduate Life at a Men's College." *Human Organization 14,* pp. 13–20.

DAVIES, J. F. 1977. "The Country Mouse Comes into Her Own." In *Human Services in the Rural Environment Reader,* by David Bast, (June 1976–May 1977), pp. 16–20. Madison: University of Wisconsin-Extension.

DAVIS, K., & J. W. Newstrom. 1989. *Human Behavior at Work.* 8th ed. New York: McGraw-Hill.

DAVIS, L. E. 1979. "Racial Composition of Groups." *Social Work 24* (May), pp. 208–213.

DEBOER, J. C. 1970. *Let's Plan: A Guide to the Planning Process for Voluntary Organizations.* New York: United Church Press.

DeCRESCENZO, T. A. 1985. "Homophobia: A Study of the Attitudes of Mental Health Professionals Toward Homosexuality." In *With Compassion Toward Some: Homosexuality and Social Work in America,* by R. Schoenberg and R. S. Goldberg, with D. A. Shod. New York: Harrington Park Press.

DEITEL, H. M., & B. Deitel. 1985. *Computers and Data Processing.* Orlando, FL: Academic Press.

DELBECQ, A. L., & A. Van de Ven. 1971. "A Group Process Model for Problem Identification and Program Planning." *Journal of Applied Behavioral Science* (July–Aug.).

DELGADO, M., & D. Humm-Delgado. 1982. "Natural Support Systems: Source of Strength in Hispanic Communities." *Social Work 27,* no. 1 (Jan.), pp. 83–89.

DeMELLO, A. 1978. *Sadhana: A Way to God.* Garden City, NY: Image Books.

DeMOYA, A., D. DeMoya, M. E. Lewis, & H. R. Lewis. 1983. *Sex and Health.* New York: Stein & Day.

DEUTSCH, M. 1949. "A Theory of Cooperation and Competition." *Human Relations 2,* pp. 129–152.

DEVORE, W., & E. G. Schlesinger. 1981. *Ethnic-Sensitive Social Work Practice.* St. Louis: Mosby.

DiGIUSEPPE, R., N. Miller, & L. Trexler. 1977. "A Review of Rational Emotive Psychotherapy Outcome Studies." *Counseling Psychologist 7,* no. 1.

DILTS, R., L. Cameron-Bandler, R. Bandler, J. Grinder, & J. DeLozier. 1980. *Neuro-Linguistic Programming,* vol. 1. Cupertino, CA: Meta Publications.

DOLGOFF, R., & D. Feldstein. 1980. *Understanding Social Welfare.* New York: Harper & Row.

DREIKURS, R. 1964. *Children: The Challenge.* New York: Hawthorn Books.

DRUCKER, P. F. 1954. *The Practice of Management.* New York: Harper.

DUMONT, M. 1968. *The Absurd Healer.* New York: Viking Press.

DUNN, J. 1977. *Distress and Comfort.* Cambridge, MA: Harvard University Press.

DUSAY, J. M., & K. M. Dusay. 1979. "Transactional Analysis." In *Current Psychotherapies,* 2nd ed., ed. R. Corsini. Itasca, IL: Peacock.

———. 1984. "Transactional Analysis." In *Current Psychotherapies,* 3rd ed., ed. R. Corsini. Itasca, IL: Peacock.

———. 1989. "Transactional Analysis." In *Current Psychotherapies,* 4th ed., ed. R. Corsini & D. Wedding. Itasca, IL: Peacock.

DYER, W. W. 1976. *Your Erroneous Zones.* New York: Funk & Wagnalls.

EDELWICH, J. 1980. *Burn-Out.* New York: Human Sciences Press.

EDISON, T., ed. 1993. *The AIDS Caregiver's Handbook.* New York: St. Martin's Press.

EGAN, G. 1982. *The Skilled Helper: Model, Skills, and Methods for Effective Helping.* 2nd ed. Pacific Grove, CA: Brooks/Cole.

———. 1985. *Change Agent Skills in Helping and Human Service Settings.* Pacific Grove, CA: Brooks/Cole.

ELLIS, A. 1957. "Outcome of Employing Three Techniques of Psychotherapy." *Journal of Clinical Psychology 13,* pp. 344–350.

———. 1958. "Rational Psychotherapy." *Journal of General Psychology 58* (Jan.), pp. 35–49.

———. 1962. *Reason and Emotion in Psychotherapy*. New York: Lyle Stuart.

———. 1968. What *Really* Causes Psychotherapeutic Change?" *Voices: Art and Science of Psychotherapy 4*, no. 2 (Summer), pp. 90–97.

———. 1973. "Rational-Emotive Therapy." In *Current Psychotherapies*, ed. R. Corsini, pp. 167–206. Itasca, IL: Peacock.

———. 1979. "Rational-Emotive Therapy." In *Current Psychotherapies*, 2d ed., ed. R. Corsini, pp. 185–229. Itasca, IL: Peacock.

———. 1989. "Rational-Emotive Therapy. In *Current Psychotherapies*, 4th ed., ed. R. Corsini & D. Wedding, pp. 196–238. Itasca, IL: Peacock.

ELLIS, A., & R. Harper. 1977a. *A Guide to Successful Marriage*. North Hollywood, CA: Wilshire Books.

———. 1977b. *A New Guide to Rational Living*. North Hollywood, CA: Wilshire Books.

ERIKSEN, K. 1979. *Communication Skills for the Human Services*. Reston, VA: Reston Publishing.

ERIKSON, E. 1963. *Childhood and Society*, 2nd ed. New York: Norton.

ETZIONI, A. 1964. *Modern Organizations*. Englewood Cliffs: NJ: Prentice-Hall.

EUSTER, G. L. 1975. "Services to Groups." In *Contemporary Social work*, ed. D. Brieland et al., pp. 218–235. New York: McGraw-Hill.

EYSENCK, H. J. 1952. "The Effects of Psychotherapy: An Evaluation." *Journal of Consulting Psychology 11*, pp. 319–324.

———. 1961. "The Effects of Psychotherapy." In *Handbook of Abnormal Psychology*. New York: Basic Books, pp. 697–725.

———. 1965. "The Effects of Psychotherapy." *International Journal of Psychiatry 1*, pp. 97–144.

FALCK, H. E. 1966. "Integrating the Rural Welfare Department into the Community." In *Can Welfare Keep Pace?*, ed. M. Morton. New York: Columbia University Press.

FEATHERMAN, D. L., & R. M. Hauser. 1976. "Changes in the Socioeconomic Stratification of the Races, 1962–73." *American Journal of Sociology 82* (Nov.) pp. 621–651.

FEDERICO, R. 1973. *The Social Welfare Institution*. Lexington, MA: Heath.

FELLIN, P. 1987. *The Social Worker and the Community*. Itasca, IL: Peacock.

FENSTERHEIM, H., & J. Baer. 1975. *Don't Say Yes When You Want to Say No*. New York: Dell.

FERGUSON, P. C., & J. Gowan. 1974. "The Influence of Transcendental Meditation on Anxiety, Depression, Aggression, Neuroticism and Self-Actualization." *Journal of Humanistic Psychology*, pp. 51–60.

FERRIS, C. C., & L. S. Ferris. 1976. "Indian Children: The Struggle for Survival." *Social Work 21* (Sept.) pp. 386–389.

FICHTER, J. H., & V. K. Mills. 1972. "The Status of Women in American Churches." *Church and Society* (Sept.–Oct.).

FINDLAY, S. 1991. "AIDS: The Second Decade." *U.S. News & World Report* (June 17), p. 66.

FINE, L. J. 1979. "Psychodrama." In *Current Psychotherapies*, 2nd ed., ed. R. J. Corsini. Itasca, IL: Peacock.

FINKELHOR, D. 1979. *Sexually Abused Children*. New York: Free Press.

———. 1984. *Child Sexual Abuse*. New York: Free Press.

FISCHER, J. 1973. "Is Casework Effective? A Review." *Social Work 18* (Jan.), pp. 5–20.

———. 1978. *Effective Casework Practice*. New York: McGraw-Hill.

———. 1979. "Isn't Casework Effective Yet?" *Social Work 24* (May), pp. 245–247.

FISCHER, J. L., & A. Fischer. 1963. "The New Englanders of Orchard Town, U.S.A." In *Six Cultures, Studies of Child Rearing*, ed. B. B. Whiting. New York: Wiley.

FLANAGAN, J. 1977. *The Grass Roots Fundraising Book: How to Raise Money in Your Community*. Chicago: Swallow Press.

FORD, J., D. Young, B. Perez, R. Obermeyer, & D. Rohmer. 1992. "Needs Assessment for Persons with Severe Mental Illness: What Services Are Needed for Successful Community Living?" *Community Mental Health Journal 28*, no. 6, pp. 491–503.

FRANK, J. D. 1973. *Persuasion and Healing*. 2nd ed. Baltimore: John Hopkins University Press.

FREEDMAN, N., & R. Sherman. 1987. *Handbook of Measurements for Marriage and Family Therapy*. New York: Brunner/Mazel.

FREESE, A. S. 1976. *How Hypnosis Can Help You*. New York: Popular Library.

FRENCH, J. R. P., & B. Raven. 1968. "The Bases of Social Power." In *Group Dynamics: Research and Theory*, 3rd ed., eds. D. Cartwright & A. Zander. New York: Harper & Row.

FREUD, S. 1924. *A General Introduction to Psychoanalysis*. New York: Boni & Liveright.

FREUDENBERGER, H. J. 1974. "Staff Burn-Out." *Journal of Social Issues 30*, pp. 159–165.

———. 1977. "Burn-Out: Occupational Hazard of the Child Care Worker." *Child Care Quarterly 6*, pp. 90–99.

FREW, D. R. 1974. "Transcendental Meditation and Productivity." *Academy of Management Journal 17*, no. 2 (June), p. 362–368.

FREY, G. A. 1990. "A Framework for Promoting Organizational Change." *Families in Society 71*, no. 3, pp. 142–147.

FRIEDAN, B. 1963. *The Feminine Mystique*. New York: Dell.

FRIEDLANDER, W. A. 1968. *Introduction to Social Welfare*. 3rd ed. Englewood Cliffs: NJ: Prentice-Hall.

———. 1974. *Introduction to Social Welfare*. 4th ed. Englewood Cliffs, NJ: Prentice-Hall.

GALPER, J. H. 1975. *The Politics of Social Services*. Englewood Cliffs, NJ: Prentice-Hall.

———. 1980. *Social Work Practice: A Radical Perspective*. Englewood Cliffs, NJ: Prentice-Hall.

GARLAND, J. A., & L. A. Frey. 1973. "Application of Stages of Group Development to Groups in Psychiatric Settings." In *Further Explorations in Group Work*, ed. S. Bernstein, pp. 1–33. Boston: Milford House.

GARLAND, J. A., H. Jones, & R. Kolodny. 1965. "A Model for Stages of Development in Social Work Groups." In *Explorations in Group Work*, ed. S. Bernstein. Boston: Milford House.

GARTNER, A., & F. Riessman. 1980. *Help: A Working Guide to Self-Help Groups*. New York: Franklin-Watts.

GARVIN, C., & F. Cox. 1987. "A History of Community Organizing Since the Civil War with Special Reference to Oppressed Communities." In *Strategies of Community Organization*, eds. F. M. Cox, J. L. Erlich, J. Rothman, & J. E. Tropman. Itasca, IL: Peacock.

GEISS, G. R., & N. Viswanathan, eds. 1986. *The Human Edge: Information Technology and Helping People*. New York: Haworth Press.

GERMAIN, C. B., & A. Gitterman. 1980. *The Life Model of Social Work Practice*. New York: Columbia University Press.

GHALI, S. B. 1982. "Understanding Puerto Rican Traditions." *Social Work 27*, no. 1 (Jan.), pp. 98–102.

GIBSON, G., & K. Ottenbacher. 1988. "Characteristics Influencing the Visual Analysis of Single-Subject Data: An Empirical Investigation." *Journal of Applied Behavioral Science 24*, pp. 298–314.

GILBERT, G. C. 1974. "Counseling Black Adolescent Parents." *Social Work 19* (Jan.), pp. 88–95.

GILLIGAN, C. 1982. *In a Different Voice: Psychological Theory and Women's Development*. Cambridge: Harvard University Press.

GINGERICH, W. J. 1978. "Measuring the Process." *Social Work 23*, pp. 251–252.

———. 1979. "Procedure for Evaluating Clinical Practice." *Health and Social Work 4*, pp. 105–130.

———. 1983a. "Generalizing Single-Case Evaluation from Classroom to Practice." *Journal of Education for Social Work 20*, pp. 78–84.

———. 1983b. "Significance Testing in Single-Case Research." In *Handbook of Clinical Social Work*, eds. A. Rosenblatt & D. Waldfogel, pp. 694–720. San Francisco: Jossey-Bass.

———. 1990a. "Expert Systems and Their Potential Uses in Social Work." *Families in Society 71*, pp. 220–228.

———. 1990b. "Rethinking Single-Case Evaluation." In *Advances in Clinical Social Work Research*, eds. L. Videka-Sherman & W. J. Reid. Silver Spring, MD: National Association of Social Workers.

GINGERICH, W. J., & W. H. Feyerherm. 1979. "The Celeration Line Technique for Assessing Client Change." *Journal of Social Service Research 3* (Fall), pp. 99–113.

GINOTT, H. G. 1965. *Between Parent and Child*. New York: Macmillan.

———. 1969. *Between Parent and Child*. 2nd ed. New York: Avon Books.

GINSBERG, L. H. 1976. "An Overview of Social Work Education for Rural Areas." In *Social Work in Rural Communities*. New York: Council on Social Work Education.

GLASSER, N., ed. 1989. *Control Theory in the Practice of Reality Therapy: Case Studies*. New York: HarperCollins.

GLASSER, W. 1965. *Reality Therapy*. New York: Harper & Row.

———. 1969. *Schools Without Failure*. New York: Harper & Row.

———. 1972. *The Identity Society*. New York: Harper & Row.

———. 1976. *Positive Addiction*. New York: Harper & Row.

———. 1984. *Control Theory*. New York: Harper & Row.

GLASSER, W., & L. Zunin. 1979. "Reality Therapy." In *Current Psychotherapies*, 2nd ed., ed. R. Corsini, pp. 302–339. Itasca, IL: Peacock.

GOLAN, N. 1979. "Crisis Theory." In *Social Work Treatment*, 2nd ed., ed. F. J. Turner, pp. 499–531. London: Free Press.

GOLDENBERG, I., & H. Goldenberg. 1991. *Family Therapy, An Overview*. 3rd ed. Pacific Grove, CA: Brooks/Cole.

GOLDFRIED, M. R., & A. P. Goldfried. 1975. "Cognitive Change Methods." In *Helping People Change*, eds. F. Kanfer & A. Goldstein, pp. 89–115. Elmsford, NY: Pergamon Press.

GOLDFRIED, M. R., & M. Merbaum, eds. 1973. *Behavior Change Through Self Control*. New York: Holt, Rinehart & Winston.

GOLEMAN, D. 1976a. "Meditation Helps Break the Stress Spiral." *Psychology Today 9* (Feb.), pp. 82–93.

———. 1976b. "Migraine and Tension Headaches: Why Your Temples Pound." *Psychology Today 10* (August), pp. 41–42.

———. 1977. "Meditation Without Mystery." *Psychology Today 10* (March), pp. 55–67.

GOOD TRACKS, J. G. 1973. "Native American Noninterference." *Social Work 18* (Nov.), pp. 30–34.

GOOGINS, B., V. A. Capoccia, & N. Kaufman. 1983. "The Interactional Dimension of Planning: A Framework for Practice." *Social Work 28* (July–Aug.), pp. 273–278.

GORDON, T. 1970. *Parent Effectiveness Training*. New York: Wyden.

GRAMICK, J. 1983. "Homophobia: A New Challenge." *Social Work 28*, no. 2 (March–April), pp. 137–141.

GREENBERG, H. M. 1980. *Coping with Job Stress*. Englewood Cliffs, NJ: Spectrum.

GREENE, L. J. 1969. *The Negro in Colonial New England*. New York: Atheneum.

GRIER, W. H., & P. M. Cobbs. 1968. *Black Rage*. New York: Basic Books.

GROSSER, C. F. 1973. *New Directions in Community Organization*. New York: Praeger.

GROTEVANT, H. D., & C. I. Carlson. 1987. "Family Interaction Coding Systems: A Descriptive Review." *Family Process 26*, p. 49.

GRUBB, D. L., & D. R. Zwick. 1976. *Fundraising in the Public Interest*. Washington, DC: Public Citizen.

GUTHRIE, E. R. 1935. *The Psychology of Learning*. New York: Harper & Row.

GUTMAN, H. G. 1976. *The Black Family in Slavery and Freedom: 1750–1925*. New York: Pantheon.

HAEBERLE, E. J. 1978. *The Sex Atlas*. New York: Seabury Press.

HALEY, J. 1963. *Strategies of Psychotherapy*. New York: Grune & Stratton.

———. 1973. *Uncommon Therapy*. New York: Norton.

———. 1976. *Problem-Solving Therapy: New Strategies for Effective Family Therapy*. San Francisco: Jossey-Bass.

HALL, C. S., & G. Lindzey. 1957. *Theories of Personality*. New York: Wiley.

HALL, E. T. 1959. *The Silent Language*. Greenwich, CT: Fawcett Books.

HANSEN, J. C., R. W. Warner, & E. M. Smith. 1976. *Group Counseling*. Skokie, IL: Rand McNally.

HARE, A. 1962. *Handbook of Small Group Research*. New York: Free Press.

HARRIS, T. 1969. *I'm OK—You're OK*. New York: Harper & Row.

HARTFORD, M. 1971. *Groups in Social Work*. New York: Columbia University Press.

HARTMAN, A. 1978. "Diagrammatic Assessment of Family Relationships." *Social Casework, 59* (Oct.), pp. 465–476.

———. 1989. "Still Between Client and Community." *Social Work 34*, no. 5, pp. 387–388.

HARTMAN, W. E., & M. A. Fithian. 1972. *Treatment of Sexual Dysfunction*. Long Beach: CA: Center for Marital and Sexual Studies.

HATHAWAY, S. R. 1948. "Some Considerations Relative to Nondirective Counseling as Therapy." *Journal of Clinical Psychology 4*, pp. 226–231.

HAUCK, P. A. 1972. *The Rational Management of Children*. New York: Libra Publishers.

HEARN, G. 1979. "General Systems Theory and Social Work." In *Social Work Treatment*, 2nd ed., ed. F. J. Turner, pp. 333–360. New York: Free Press.

HEATON, O. P., & D. W. Orme-Johnson. 1974. "Influence of Transcendental Meditation on Grade Point Average:

Initial Findings." In *Scientific Research on Transcendental Meditation: Collected Papers,* eds. D. W. Orme-Johnson, L. H. Domash, & J. T. Farrow. Los Angeles: MIU Press.

HEBB, D. O., R. Held, A. Riesen, & H. Teuber. 1961. "Sensory Deprivation: Facts in Search of a Theory." *Journal of Nervous and Mental Disorders 132,* pp. 17–43.

HEPWORTH, D. H., & J. Larsen. 1986. *Direct Social Work Practice: Theory and Skills.* 2nd ed. Pacific Grove, CA: Brooks/Cole.

HERBERT, M. D., & J. W. Mould. 1992. "The Advocacy Role in Public Child Welfare." *Child Welfare 71,* no. 2 (March/April), pp. 114–130.

HERSEN, M., & A. S. Bellack. 1981. *Behavioral Assessment: A Practical Handbook.* 2nd ed. Elmsford, NY: Pergamon Press.

———, eds. 1988. *Dictionary of Behavioral Assessment Techniques.* Elmsford, NY: Pergamon Press.

HERSEY, P., & K. Blanchard. 1977. *Management of Organizational Behavior: Utilizing Human Resources.* 3rd ed. Englewood Cliffs, NJ: Prentice-Hall.

HIDALGO, H., T. Peterson, & N. J. Woodman. 1985. *Lesbian and Gay Issues: A Resource Manual.* Silver Spring, MD: National Association of Social Workers.

HITE, S. 1976. *The Hite Report.* New York: Macmillan.

HOFER, A., & W. Polin. 1970. "Schizophrenia in the NAS-NRC Panel of 15,909 Twin Pairs." *Archives of General Psychiatry 23,* p. 469–477.

HOGAN, R. A., & J. H. Kirchner. 1967. "A Preliminary Report of the Extinction of Learned Fears via Short-Term Implosive Therapy." *Journal of Abnormal Psychology 72,* pp. 106–111.

HOGAN, R. 1986. "Gaining Community Support for Group Homes." *Community Mental Health Journal 22,* no. 2, pp. 117–126.

HOLLAND, G. 1973. "Transactional Analysis." In *Current Psychotherapies,* ed. R. Corsini, pp. 353–399. Itasca, IL: Peacock.

HOLLANDER, E. P. 1958. "Conformity, Status, and Idiosyncrasy Credit." *Psychological Review,* pp. 117–127.

HOLLIS, F. 1972. *Casework: A Psychosocial Theory.* New York: Random House.

HONSBERGER, R., & A. F. Wilson. 1973. "Transcendental Meditation in Treating Asthma." *Respiratory Therapy: The Journal of Inhalation Technology 3,* pp. 79–81.

HOOK, M. V. 1979. "Female Clients, Female Counselors: Combating Learned Helplessness." *Social Work 24* (Jan.), pp. 63–65.

HOPKINS, T. J. 1973. "The Role of the Agency in Supporting Black Manhood." *Social Work 18* (Jan.), pp. 53–58.

HOWARD, J. 1970. *Please Touch: A Guided Tour of the Human Potential Movement.* New York: McGraw-Hill.

HUDSON, W. W. 1978. "First Axioms of Treatment." *Social Work 23,* pp. 65–66.

———. 1982. *The Clinical Measurement Package: A Field Manual.* Pacific Grove, CA: Brooks/Cole.

HULL, C. L. 1943. *Principles of Behavior.* New York: Appleton-Century-Crofts.

HULL, G. H. 1978. "The Parents' Anonymous Sponsor: A Professional Helping Role." Paper presented at the Child Welfare League of America Regional Conference, Omaha.

HULL, G. H. 1990. *Social Work Internship Manual.* Eau Claire: University of Wisconsin–Eau Claire, Department of Social Work.

HUMPHREYS, G. E. 1983. "Inclusion of Content on Homosexuality in the Social Work Curriculum." *Journal of Education for Social Work 19* (Winter), pp. 55–60.

HYDE, J. S. 1979. *Understanding Human Sexuality.* New York: McGraw-Hill.

HYDE, J. S. 1990. *Understanding Human Sexuality.* 4th ed. New York: McGraw-Hill.

INGERSOLL, S. L., & S. O. Patton. 1990. *Treating Perpetrators of Sexual Abuse.* Lexington, MA: Lexington Books.

JACKSON, D. D. 1965. "The Study of the Family." *Family Process 4,* pp. 1–20.

JACOBSON, E. 1934. *You Must Relax: A Practical Method of Reducing the Stress of Modern Life.* New York: McGraw-Hill.

———. 1938a. *Progressive Relaxation.* 2nd ed. Chicago: University of Chicago Press.

———. 1938b. *You Can Sleep Well: The ABC's of Restful Sleep for the Average Person.* New York: McGraw-Hill.

———. 1959. *How to Relax and Have Your Baby: Scientific Relaxation in Childbirth.* New York: McGraw-Hill.

———. 1964. *Anxiety and Tension Control: A Physiologic Approach.* Philadelphia: Lippincott.

———. 1973. *Teaching and Learning New Methods for Old Arts.* Chicago: National Foundation for Progressive Relaxation.

JAMES, M., & D. Jongeward. 1971. *Born to Win; Transactional Analysis with Gestalt Experiments.* Reading, MA: Addison-Wesley.

JANIS, I. 1971. "Group Think." *Psychology Today 15,* no 6. (Nov.), pp. 43–46, 74–76.

———. 1972. *Victims of Groupthink.* Boston: Houghton Mifflin.

JAYARATNE, S., & R. L. Levy. 1979. *Empirical Clinical Practice.* New York: Columbia University Press.

JEHU, D. 1972. *Behavior Modification in Social Work.* New York: Wiley.

JOHNSON, D. W., & F. P. Johnson. 1975. *Joining Together.* Englewood Cliffs, NJ: Prentice-Hall.

———. 1987. *Joining Together.* 3rd ed. Englewood Cliffs, NJ: Prentice-Hall.

JOHNSON, E. H. 1973. *Social Problems of Urban Man.* Pacific Grove, CA: Brooks/Cole.

JOHNSON, L. C. 1986. *Social Work Practice: A Generalist Approach.* 2nd ed. Boston: Allyn & Bacon.

JONES, R. R., R. S. Vaught, & M. R. A. Weinrott. 1977. "Time-Series Analysis in Operant Research." *Journal of Applied Behavior Analysis 10,* pp. 151–166.

KADUSHIN. A. 1972. *The Social Work Interview.* New York: Columbia University Press.

———. 1980. *Child Welfare Services.* 3rd ed. New York: Macmillan.

———. 1983. *The Social Work Interview.* 2nd ed. New York: Columbia University Press.

———. 1990. *The Social Work Interview.* 3rd ed. New York: Columbia University Press.

KAHN, M., & B. Baker. 1968. "Desensitization with Minimal Therapist Contact." *Journal of Abnormal Psychology 73,* pp. 198–200.

KANFER, F. 1975. "Self-Management Methods." In *Helping People Change,* eds. F. H. Kanfer & A. P. Goldstein, pp. 309–355. Elmsford, NY: Pergamon Press.

KAPLAN, H. S. 1974. *The New Sex Therapy.* New York: Brunner/Mazel.

———. 1983. *The Evaluation of Sexual Disorders.* New York: Brunner/Mazel.

KATZ, A. H., & E. I. Bender. 1976. *The Strength in Us: Self-Help Groups in the Modern World.* New York: Franklin-Watts.

KAUFMAN, R., & S. Thomas. 1980. *Evaluation Without Fear.* New York: New Viewpoints.

KAZDIN, A. E. 1977a. "Assessing the Clinical or Applied

Importance of Behavior Change Through Social Valida-
tion." *Behavior Modification 1*, pp. 427–452.

———. 1977b. *The Token Economy*. New York: Plenum.

KEITH-LUCAS, A. 1972. *The Giving and Taking of Help*. Chapel
Hill: University of North Carolina Press.

KELLY, H. H., & A. J. Stahelski. 1970. "Social Interaction Basis
of Cooperators' and Competitors' Beliefs About Others."
Journal of Personality and Social Psychology 16, pp. 66–91.

KELMAN, H. C. 1965. "Manipulation of Human Behavior:
An Ethical Dilemma for the Social Scientist." *Journal of
Social Issues 21*, no. 2, pp. 31–46.

KERR, M. E., & M. Bowen. 1988. *Family Evaluation: An Approach Based on Bowen's Theory*. New York: Norton.

KETY, S. S. 1976. "The Biological Roots of Schizophrenia."
Harvard Magazine 78, pp. 20–26.

KING, S. W., & R. S. Meyers. 1981. "Developing Self-Help
Groups: Integrating Group Work and Community Organization Strategies." *Social Development Issues 5*, pp.
33–46.

KIRESUK, T. J., & S. H. Lund. 1978. "Goal Attainment Scaling." In *Evaluation of Human Service Programs*, eds. C. C.
Attkisson, W. A. Hargreaves, M. J. Horowitz, & J. E. So-
rensen, New York: Academic Press, pp. 341–370.

KIRST-ASHMAN, K. K., & G. H. Hull, Jr. 1993. *Understanding
Generalist Practice*. Chicago: Nelson-Hall.

KNOPF, R. 1979. *Surviving the BS (Bureaucratic System)*. Wilm-
ington, NC: Mandala Press.

KNOPP, F. H. 1984. *Retraining Adult Sex Offenders: Methods
and Models*. Syracuse, NY: Safer Society Press.

KOLB, L. C., V. Bernard, & B. P. Dohrenwend. 1969. "The
Problem of Validity in Field Studies of Psychological Disorder." In *Urban Challenges to Psychiatry*, eds. B. P. Dohrenwend & B. S. Dohrenwend, pp. 429–460. New York:
Wiley.

KONLE, C., & J. A. Piliavin. 1976. "Vocational Aspirations in
Kindergarten Children: Early Sex Differences." *Wisconsin
Sociologist 13*, no. 4 (Fall), pp. 119–124.

KOOP, J. 1988. "Self-Monitoring: A Literature Review of Research and Practice." *Social Work Research & Abstracts 24*,
pp. 8–20.

KRATOCHWILL, T. R., ed. 1978. *Single Subject Research: Strategies for Evaluating Change*. New York: Academic Press.

KRAVETZ, D. 1982. "An Overview of Content on Women for
the Social Work Curriculum." *Journal of Education for Social Work 18* (Winter), pp. 42–49.

KRECH, D., R. S. Crutchfield, & E. L. Ballachey. 1962. *Individual in Society*. New York: McGraw-Hill.

KÜBLER-ROSS, E. 1969. *On Death and Dying*. New York:
Macmillan.

LABORDE, G. 1984. *Influencing with Integrity*. Palo Alto, CA:
Syntony Publishing.

LAKEIN, A. 1973. *How to Get Control of Your Time and Your
Life*. New York: Signet.

LAMBERT, M. J., D. A. Shapiro, & A. E. Bergin. 1986. "The
Effectiveness of Psychotherapy." In *Handbook of Psycho-
therapy and Behavior Change*, 3rd ed., eds. S. L. Garfield &
A. E. Bergin, pp. 157–211. New York: Wiley.

LANDAU-STANTON, J., & C. D. Clements. 1993. *AIDS,
Health and Mental Health*. New York: Brunner/Mazel.

LANDERS, S. 1993. "AIDS Deepens Duty-to-Warn Dilemma." *NASW News* (Jan.), p. 3.

LANKTON, S. 1980. *Practical Magic*. Cupertino, CA: Meta
Publications.

LAZARUS, A. A. 1971. *Behavior Therapy and Beyond*. New
York: McGraw-Hill.

LEAGUE OF WOMEN VOTERS. 1972. *Know Your Community*. Washington, DC: League of Women Voters.

LEAVITT, J. E. 1974. *The Battered Child*. Morristown, NJ: General Learning Press.

LECRON, L. M. 1964. *Self-Hypnotism*. Englewood Cliffs, NJ:
Prentice-Hall.

LEIBERT, E. R., & B. E. Sheldon. 1972. *Handbook of Special
Events for Nonprofit Organizations: Tested Ideas for Fund
Raising and Public Relations*. Washington, DC: Taft Corp.

LEMBO, J. 1974. *Help Yourself*. Niles, IL: Argus Communications.

LEMERT, E. M. 1951. *Social Pathology*. New York: McGraw-
Hill.

LEUKENFIELD, C. G., & M. Fimbres, eds. 1987. *Responding to
AIDS: Psychosocial Initiatives*. Silver Spring, MD: National
Association of Social Workers.

LEVITT, E. E. 1957. "The Results of Psychotherapy with Children: An Evaluation." *Journal of Consulting Psychology 21*,
pp. 189–196.

LEWIN, K. 1952. "Group Decision and Social Change." In
Readings in Social Psychology, eds. G. E. Swanson, T. M.
Newcomb, & E. L. Hartley. New York: Holt, Rinehart &
Winston.

LEWIN, K., R. Lippitt, & R. K. White. 1939. "Patterns of Aggressive Behavior in Experimentally Created Social Cli-
mates." *Journal of Social Psychology 10*, pp. 271–299.

LEWIS, R. G., & M. Keung Ho. 1975. "Social Work with Native Americans." *Social Work 20* (Sept.), pp. 378–382.

LIEBERMAN, M. A., E. D. Yalom, & M. B. Miles. 1973. "Encounter: The Leader Makes the Difference." *Psychology
Today 6*, pp. 69–76.

LINDBLOM, C. 1959. "The Science of Muddling Through."
Public Administration Review, Spring, pp. 79–88.

LOCKLEAR, H. H. 1972. "American Indian Myths." *Social
Work 17* (May), pp. 72–80.

———. 1977. "American Indian Alcoholism: Program for
Treatment." *Social Work 22* (May), pp. 202–207.

LOEWENBERG, F. M. 1977. *Fundamentals of Social Intervention*. New York: Columbia University Press.

LOEWENSTEIN, S. 1980. "Understanding Lesbian Women."
Social Casework 61 (Jan.), p. 31.

LOGAN, S. 1990. "Black Families: Race Ethnicity, Culture, So-
cial Class, and Gender Issues." In *Social Work Practice with
Black Families*, eds. S. Logan, E. Freeman, & R. McRoy.
New York: Longman.

LONDON, P. 1964. *The Modes and Morals of Psychotherapy*.
New York: Holt, Rinehart & Winston.

LOOFT, W. R. 1971. "Sex Differences in the Expression of Vocational Aspirations by Elementary School Children."
Developmental Psychology 5, p. 366.

LoPICCOLO, J., & L. LoPiccolo, eds. 1978. *Handbook of Sex
Therapy*. New York: Plenum.

LOSONCY, L. 1977. *Turning People On*. Englewood Cliffs, NJ:
Prentice-Hall.

LOWENBERG, F., & R. Dolgoff. 1971. *Teaching of Practice Skills
in Undergraduate Programs in Social Welfare and Other Helping Services*. New York: Council on Social Work Education.

LURIA, A. 1961. *The Role of Speech in the Regulation of Normal
and Abnormal Behavior*. New York: Liveright Publishing.

McGRATH, R. J. 1991. "Sex-Offender Risk Assessment and
Disposition Planning: A Review of Empirical and

Clinical Findings," *International Journal of Offender Therapy and Comparative Criminology 35* (4), pp. 328–350.

McGREGOR, D. 1960. *The Human Side of Enterprise.* New York: McGraw-Hill.

McMAHON, F. B. 1971. *The Forty-Eight Item Counseling Evaluation Test: Revised.* Los Angeles: Western Psychological Services.

McQUADE, W., & A. Aikman. 1974. *Stress.* New York: Bantam.

MacSHANE, D. 1979. *Using the Media: How to Deal with the Press, Radio, Television.* London: Pluto.

MADDI, S. 1968. *Personality Theories.* Pacific Grove, CA: Brooks/Cole.

MAGNER, D. K. 1993. "Colleges Faulted for Not Considering Differences in Asian-American Groups," *Chronicle of Higher Education* (Feb. 10), pp. A33–34.

MAHONEY, M. J. 1973. "Clinical Issues in Self-Control Training." Paper presented at the meeting of the American Psychological Association, Montreal.

———. 1974. *Cognition and Behavior Modification.* Cambridge, MA: Ballinger.

MAIER, N. R. F. 1970. *Problem Solving and Creativity in Individuals and Groups.* Pacific Grove, CA: Brooks/Cole.

MALUCCIO, A. 1979. "Perspectives of Social Workers and Clients on Treatment Outcome." *Social Casework 60,* pp. 394–401.

MANDINO, O., ed. 1966. *A Treasury of Success Unlimited.* New York: Hawthorn Books.

MANLEY, M. J. 1977. "How to Cope with a Sense of Failure." In *The Personal Problem Solver,* eds. C. Zastrow & D. Chang. Englewood Cliffs, NJ: Prentice-Hall.

MARCH, J. G. 1956. "Influence Measurement in Experimental and Semi-Experimental Groups." *Sociometry 19,* no. 4 (Dec.), pp. 260–271.

MARTI-COSTA, S., & I. Serrano-Garcia. 1987. "Needs Assessment and Community Development: An Ideological Perspective." In *Strategies of Community Organization: Macro Practice,* eds. F. M. Cox, J. L. Erlich, J. Rothman, & J. Trotman. Itasca, IL: Peacock.

MARTINEZ-BRAWLEY, E., & J. Blundall. 1989. "Farm Families' Preference toward the Personal Social Services." *Social Work 34,* no. 6, pp. 513–522.

MASLACH, C. 1976. "Burned-Out." *Human Behavior 5,* (Sept.), pp. 16–22.

———. 1978. "The Client Role in Staff Burn-Out." *Journal of Social Issues 34,* pp. 11–24.

MASLACH, C., & A. Pines. 1977. "The Burn-Out Syndrome in the Day Care Setting." *Child Care Quarterly 6,* pp. 100–113.

MASTERS, W. H., & V. E. Johnson. 1966. *Human Sexual Response.* Boston: Little, Brown.

———. 1970. *Human Sexual Inadequacy.* Boston: Little, Brown.

MASTERS, W. H., V. E. Johnson, & R. C. Kolodny. 1986. *Masters and Johnson on Sex and Human Loving.* Boston: Little, Brown.

MAUKSCH, H. O. 1975. "The Organizational Context of Dying." In *Death: The Final Stage of Growth,* ed. E. Kübler-Ross, pp. 7–26. Englewood Cliffs, NJ: Prentice-Hall.

MAULTSBY, M. C., Jr. 1975. *Help Yourself to Happiness.* Boston: Herman Publishing.

———. 1977. "The ABC's of Better Emotional Self-Control." In *The Personal Problem Solver,* eds. C. Zastrow & D. Chang, pp. 3–18. Englewood Cliffs, NJ: Prentice-Hall.

———. 1978. *A Millon Dollars for Your Hangover.* Lexington, KY: Rational Self-Help Books.

MEAD, M. 1935. *Sex and Temperament in Three Primitive Societies.* New York: Morrow.

MEADOR, B. D., & C. Rogers. 1979. "Person-Centered Therapy." In *Current Psychotherapies,* 2nd ed., ed. R. J. Corsini. Itasca, IL: Peacock.

MECHANIC, D. 1962. "Some Factors in Identifying and Defining Mental Illness." *Mental Hygiene 46,* pp. 66–74.

MEDINA, C., & M. R. Reyes. 1976. "Dilemmas of Chicano Counselors." *Social Work 21* (Nov.), pp. 515–517.

MEHRABIAN, A. 1981. *Silent Messages.* 2nd ed. Belmont, CA: Wadsworth.

MEICHENBAUM, D. 1975. "Self-Instructional Methods." In *Helping People Change,* eds. F. H. Kanfer & A. P. Goldstein, pp. 357–392. Elmsford, NY: Pergamon Press.

MEISELMAN, K. C. 1978. *Incest.* San Francisco: Jossey-Bass.

MERKEL, W. 1975. "Controlled Research in Transactional Analysis." Unpublished manuscript. Kingston: University of Rhode Island.

MIDWEST THERAPY CENTER FOR PSYCHOTHERAPY AND SEX THERAPY. Handout. Madison, WI: Author.

MIGLER, B. 1968. "A Supplementary Note on Automated Self-Desensitization." *Behavior Research and Therapy 6,* p. 243.

MILGRAM, S. 1963. "Behavioral Study of Obedience." *Journal of Abnormal and Social Psychology,* pp. 371–378.

MILLER, H. G., C. F. Turner, & L. E. Moses, eds. 1990. *AIDS: The Second Decade.* Washington, DC: National Academy Press.

MILLS, G. 1973. "The Wisconsin Mutual Agreement Programming." Paper represented to the 103rd Congress of Corrections, Seattle, Aug.

MINUCHIN, S. 1974. *Families and Family Therapy.* Cambridge: Harvard University Press.

MINUCHIN, S., & H. C. Fishman. 1981. *Family Therapy Techniques.* Cambridge: Harvard University Press.

MITCHELL, J. V., ed. 1985. *The Ninth Mental Measurements Yearbook.* Lincoln: University of Nebraska Press.

MIZIO, E. 1972. "White Worker—Minority Client." *Social Work 17* (May), pp. 82–86.

MONEY, J. 1986. *Venuses Penises.* Buffalo, NY: Prometheus Books.

MONTIEL, M. 1973. "The Chicano Family: A Review of Research." *Social Work 18* (March), pp. 22–31.

MOORE, C. W. 1986. *The Mediation Process.* San Francisco: Jossey-Bass.

MORENO, J. L. 1946. *Psychodrama: Vol 1.* Boston: Beacon House.

MORRIS, R. 1975. "Fear Reduction Methods." In *Helping People Change,* eds. F. H. Kanfer & A. P. Goldstein, pp. 229–271. Elmsford, NY: Pergamon Press.

———. 1986. "Fear Reduction Methods." In *Helping People Change,* 3rd ed., eds. F. H. Kanfer & A. P. Goldstein, pp. 145–190. Elmsford, NY: Pergamon Press.

NATIONAL ASSOCIATION OF SOCIAL WORKERS. 1971. *Encyclopedia of Social Work.* New York: NASW.

———. 1973. *Standards for Social Service Manpower.* Washington, DC: NASW.

———. 1976. *Standards for the Regulation of Social Work Practice.* Washington, DC: NASW.

———. 1979. *Code of Ethics.* Revised and adopted by the 1979 Delegate Assembly of NASW.

———. 1981. *Classification Processes for Social Service Positions: Parts I–IV* Washington, DC: NASW.

———. 1982. *Standards for the Classification of Social Work Practice.* Washington, DC: NASW.

NASW NEWS. 1979. "Bottom Line for Social Work Licensing up in Air." Washington, DC: NASW Publications, April.

NASW PRACTICE DIGEST 6, no. 3 (Winter 1983). Special issue devoted to computers in social work practice.

NATIONAL INSTITUTE OF LAW ENFORCEMENT AND CRIMINAL JUSTICE. 1978. *Treatment Programs for Sex Offenders.* Washington, DC: U.S. Government Printing Office, January.

NETTING, F. E., P. M. Kettner, & S. L. McMurtry. 1993, *Social Work Macro Practice.* New York: Longman.

NICHOLS, A., & R. Schilit. 1988. "Telephone Support for Latchkey Children." *Child Welfare 67,* no. 1, pp. 49–59.

NORTON, D. G. 1978. "Incorporating Content on Minority Groups into Social Work Practice Courses." In *The Dual Perspective.* New York: Council on Social Work Education.

NURIUS, P. S., & W. W. Hudson. 1993. *Human Services Practice, Evaluation, and Computers.* Pacific Grove, CA: Brooks/Cole.

O'CONNOR, G. 1972. "Toward a New Policy in Adult Corrections." *Social Service Review 46* (Dec.), pp. 482–493.

OFFER, D., & M. Sabshin. 1966. *Normality: Theoretical and Clinical Concepts in Mental Health.* New York: Basic Books.

OKUN, B., & L. Rappaport. 1980. *Working with Families: An Introduction to Family Therapy.* North Scituate, MA: Duxbury Press.

OLMSTEAD, M. S. 1959. *The Small Group.* New York: Random House.

ORME-JOHNSON, D. W. 1973. "Autonomic Stability and Transcendental Meditation." *Psychosomatic Medicine 35,* no. 4 (July–Aug.), pp. 341–349.

ORNE, M. T., & P. H. Wender. 1968. "Anticipatory Socialization for Psychotherapy: Method and Rationale." *American Journal of Psychiatry 124,* pp. 1202–1212.

ORTIZ, L. 1993. "Bibliography: Culture and Spirituality." Paper presented at the CSWE Annual Program Meeting, New York, Feb.

OSBORN, A. F. 1963. *Applied Imagination: Principles and Procedures of Creative Problem Solving.* 3rd ed. New York: Scribner.

OUCHI, W. 1981. *Theory Z: How American Business Can Meet the Japanese Challenge.* Reading, MA: Addison-Wesley.

PALMER, B., & S. Pablo. 1978. "Community Development Possibilities for Effective Indian Reservation and Child Abuse and Neglect Efforts." In *Child Abuse and Neglect: Issues on Innovation and Implementation,* vol. 1, ed. M. Lauderdale, R. Anderson, & S. Cramer, pp. 111–115. Washington, DC: U.S. Department of Health, Education, and Welfare.

PARAD, H. J., ed. 1965. *Crisis Intervention: Selected Readings.* New York: Family Service Association of America.

PARSONS, T. 1958. "Social Structure and the Development of Personality." *Psychiatry 21,* pp. 321–340.

PARSONSON, B. S., & D. M. Baer. 1978. "The Analysis and Presentation of Graphic Data." In *Single Subject Research: Strategies for Evaluating Change,* ed. T. R. Kratochwill, pp. 101–165. New York: Academic Press.

PATTERSON, G. R. 1971. *Families.* Champaign, IL: Research Press Co.

PAUL, G. 1966. *Insight Versus Desensitization in Psychotherapy.* Stanford: Stanford University Press.

———. 1969. "Outcome of Systematic Desensitization." In *Behavior Therapy: Appraisal and Status,* pp. 63–159. New York: McGraw-Hill.

PECK, R. E. 1974. *The Miracle of Shock Treatment.* Jericho, NY: Exposition Press.

PELLETIER, K. R. 1974. "Altered Attention Deployment in Meditation." In *The Psychobiology of Transcendental Meditation,* eds. D. Kannellakos & J. Lucas. Hunter, NY: Benjamin.

———. 1977. *Mind as Healer, Mind as Slayer.* New York: Dell.

PFEIFFER, J. W., & J. E. Jones. 1976. "Role Functions in a Group." In *1976 Annual Handbook for Group Facilitators,* by J. W. Pfeiffer & J. E. Jones, pp. 136–138. La Jolla, CA: University Associates.

PHILLIPS, D. L. 1963. "Rejection: A Possible Consequence of Seeking Help for Mental Disorder." *American Sociological Review 28,* pp. 963–973.

PIERCE, D. 1993. "Developing a Framework for Social Work Practice with Lesbian Women and Gay Men." Paper presented at CSWE Annual Program Meeting, New York, Feb.

PIERS, E. V., & D. B. Harris. 1969. *The Piers-Harris Children's Self-Concept Scale.* Los Angeles: Western Psychological Services.

PINCUS, A., & A. Minahan. 1973. *Social Work Practice: Model and Method.* Itasca, IL: Peacock.

PINDERHUGHES, E. B. 1979. "Teaching Empathy in Cross Cultural Social Work." *Social Work 24* (July), pp. 312–316.

PINES, A., & E. Arsonson. 1981. *Burnout: From Tedium to Personal Growth.* New York: Free Press.

POSAVAC, E. J., & R. G. Carey. 1980. *Program Evaluation: Methods and Case Studies.* Englewood Cliffs, NJ: Prentice-Hall.

POWDERMAKER, H. 1933. *Life in Lesu.* New York: Norton.

POWELL, T. J. 1987. *Self-Help Organizations and Professional Practice.* Silver Spring, MD: National Association of Social Workers.

PROCHASKA, J. O. 1979. *Systems of Psychotherapy.* Pacific Grove, CA: Brooks/Cole.

PROCTOR, P. 1978. "The Big Resurgence of Positive Thinking." *Parade.* May 21, pp. 23–24.

PRUGER, R. 1978. "Bureaucratic Functioning as a Social Work Skill." In *Educating the Baccalaureate Social Worker: Report of the Undergraduate Social Work Curriculum Development Project,* by B. L. Baer & R. Federico, Cambridge, MA: Ballinger.

RAIMY, V. 1977. *Misunderstandings of the Self.* San Francisco: Jossey-Bass.

RAMEY, J. W. 1979. *SIECUS Report 7,* no. 5 (May).

RARDIN, M. 1969. "Treatment of a Phobia by Partial Self-Desensitization." *Journal of Consulting and Clinical Psychology 33,* pp. 125–126.

RASMUSSEN, S. A., & M. T. Tsuang. 1986. *American Journal of Psychiatry 143,* pp. 317–322.

RASPBERRY, W. 1970. *Washington Post,* Feb. 20.

RATHUS, S. A., & S. Boughn. 1993. *AIDS, What Every Student Needs to Know.* Fort Worth, TX: Harcourt Brace Jovanovich.

RAUCH, J. B. 1978. "Gender as a Factor in Practice." *Social Work 23* (Sept.), pp. 388–396.

REID, W., & L. Epstein. 1972. *Task-Centered Casework.* New York: Columbia University Press.

———. 1977. *Task-Centered Practice.* New York: Columbia University Press.

REID, W., & A. Shyne. 1969. *Brief and Extended Casework*. New York: Columbia University Press.

REIN, M., & R. Morris. 1962. "Goals, Structures, and Strategies of Community Change." In *Social Work Practice 1962*. New York: National Conference of Social Welfare.

REISS, I. R. 1986. *Journey into Sexuality*. Englewood Cliffs: NJ: Prentice-Hall.

RICE, P. L. 1987. *Stress and Health*. Pacific Grove, CA: Brooks/Cole.

RICHMOND, M. E. 1917. *Social Diagnosis*. New York: Russell Sage Foundation.

———. 1965. *Social Diagnosis*. New York: Free Press.

RIESSMAN, F. 1965. "The 'Helper Therapy' Principle." *Journal of Social Work* 10, no. 2 (April), pp. 27–34.

———. 1987. "Foreword." In T. J. Powell, *Self-Help Organizations and Professional Practice*. Silver Spring, MD: National Association of Social Workers.

RIMM, D., & J. Masters. 1974. *Behavior Therapy*. New York: Academic Press.

RINGER, R. J. 1977. *Looking Out for No. 1*. New York: Fawcett Books.

RIVERA, F. G., & J. L. Erlich. 1992. *Community Organizing in a Diverse Society*. Boston: Allyn & Bacon.

ROETHLISBERGER, F. J., & W. J. Dickson, 1939. *Management and the Worker*. Cambridge: Harvard University Press.

ROGERS, C. R. 1942. *Counseling and Psychotherapy*. Boston: Houghton Mifflin.

———. 1951. *Client-Centered Therapy*. Boston: Houghton Mifflin.

———. 1959. "A Theory of Therapy, Personality, and Interpersonal Relationships, as Developed in the Client-Centered Framework." In *Psychology: A Study of a Science*, ed. S. Koch, vol. 3, pp. 184–256. New York: McGraw-Hill.

———. 1961. "The Process Equation of Psychotherapy." *American Journal of Psychotherapy* 15 (Jan.), pp. 27–45.

———. 1965. Client-Centered Therapy, film no. 1. In *Three Approaches to Psychotherapy*, ed. E. Shostrom. (Three 16 mm. color motion pictures) Santa Ana, CA: Psychological Films.

———. 1970. *Carl Rogers on Encounter Groups*. New York: Harper & Row.

———. 1984. "A Historic Note–Gloria." In *Client-Centered Therapy and the Person-Centered Approach*, pp. 423–425. New York: Praeger.

ROMERO, D. P. 1977. "Biases in Gender-Role Research." *Social Work* 22 (May), pp. 214–218.

ROSENHAN, D. 1973. "On Being Sane in Insane Places." *Science* 179, pp. 250–257.

ROSS, M. G. 1967. *Community Organization*. 2nd ed. New York: Harper & Row.

ROSSI, P. H., H. E. Freeman, & S. R. Wright. 1979. *Evaluation: A Systematic Approach*. Newbury Park, CA: Sage.

ROTHMAN, J. 1968. "Three Models of Community Organization Practice." In *Social Work Practice*, pp. 16–47. New York: Columbia University Press.

———. 1979. "Three Models of Community Organization Practice, Their Mixing and Phasing." In *Strategies of Community Organization*, 3rd ed., eds. F. M. Cox, J. L. Erlich, J. Rothman, & J. E. Tropman. Itasca, IL: Peacock.

ROUNDS, K. A. 1988. "Responding to AIDS: Rural Community Strategies." *Social Casework* 69, no. 6, pp. 306–364.

RUBIN, H. J., & I. S. Rubin. 1992. *Community Organizing and Development*. New York: Macmillan.

RUOSS, M. 1970. As quoted in J. C. DeBoer. *Let's Plan: A Guide to the Planning Process for Voluntary Organizations*. Princeton, NJ: Pilgrim Press.

RYAN, W. 1971. *Blaming the Victim*. New York: Pantheon Books.

SAGER, C. J., T. L. Brayboy, & B. R. Waxenberg. 1970. *Black Ghetto Family in Therapy: A Laboratory Experience*. New York: Grove Press.

SALTER, A. C. 1988. *Treating Child Sex Offenders and Victims*. Newbury Park, CA: Sage.

SANDLER, J. 1975. "Aversion Methods." In *Helping People Change*, eds. F. H. Kanfer & A. P. Goldstein, pp. 273–307. Elmsford, NY: Pergamon Press.

———. 1986. "Aversion Methods." In *Helping People Change*, 3rd ed., eds. F. H. Kanfer & A. P. Goldstein, pp. 191–235. Elmsford, NY: Pergamon Press.

SATIR, V. 1967. *Conjoint Family Therapy*. Rev. ed. Palo Alto, CA: Science & Behavior Books.

———. 1972. *Peoplemaking*. Palo Alto, CA: Science & Behavior Books.

SATIR, V., J. Stachowiak, & H. A. Taschman. 1975. *Helping Families to Change*, eds. D. Tiffany, J. Cohen, and A. Robinson. New York: Aronson.

SCHACHTER, S. 1959. *The Psychology of Affiliation*. Stanford: Stanford University Press.

SCHAFER, W. 1978. *Stress, Distress and Growth*. Davis, CA: International Dialogue Press.

SCHEFF, T. 1966. *Being Mentally Ill*. Hawthorne, NY: Aldine.

SCHELLENBERG, J. A. 1970. *An Introduction to Social Psychology*. New York: Random House.

SCHINKA, J. A. 1985. *Personal Problems Checklist for Adolescents*. Odessa, FL: Psychological Assessment Resources.

SCHNARCH, D. M. 1991. *Constructing the Sexual Crucible*. New York: Norton.

SCHOECH, R. J. 1982. *Computer Use in Human Services*. New York: Human Science Press.

———. 1990. *Human Service Computing: Concepts and Applications*. New York: Haworth Press.

SHREIBER, F. R. 1973. *Sybil*. New York: Warner Books.

SCHULLER, R., II. 1973. *Move Ahead with Possibility Thinking*. Moonachie, NJ: Pyramid Publications.

SCHWARTZ, G. 1989. "Confidentiality Revisited." *Social Work* (May), pp. 223–226.

SCHWARTZ, M. D., ed. 1984. *Using Computers in Clinical Practice*. New York: Haworth Press.

SCHWARTZ, R., & B. Friedland. 1965. *Linear Systems*. New York: McGraw-Hill.

SEARS, R. R., L. Rau, & R. Alpert. 1965. *Identification and Child Rearing*. Stanford: Stanford University Press.

SELYE, H. 1956. *The Stress of Life*. New York: McGraw-Hill.

SGROI, S. M., ed. 1982. *Handbook of Clinical Intervention in Child Sexual Abuse*. Lexington, MA: Lexington Books.

SHAW, R., & D. Kolb. 1974. "One-Point Reaction Time Involving Mediators and Non-Mediators." In *Scientific Research on Transcendental Meditation: Collected Papers*, vol. 1, eds. D. W. Orme-Johnson, L. G. Domash, & J. T. Farrow. Los Angeles: MIU Press.

SHEAFOR, B. W., C. R. Horejsi, & C. A. Horejsi. 1988. *Techniques and Guidelines for Social Work Practice*. Boston: Allyn & Bacon.

SHELLY, M. W. 1973. *Sources of Satisfaction*. Lawrence: University of Kansas Press.

SHERIF, M. 1936. *The Psychology of Social Norms*. New York: Harper & Row.

SHERMAN, H. 1966. "The Surest Way in the World to Attract Success—or Failure." In *A Treasury of Success Unlimited,* ed. O. Mandino, pp. 111–113. New York: Hawthorn Books.

SHIMKUS, J. R., & J. P. Winship. 1977. *Human Service Development: Working Together in the Community.* Athens: University of Georgia Printing Department.

SHOEMAKER, J. S., & D. L. Tasto. 1975. "The Effects of Muscle Relaxation on Blood Pressure of Essential Hypertensives." *Behavior Research and Therapy* 13 (Feb.), pp. 29–43.

SHOSTROM, E. L. 1969. "Group Therapy: Let the Buyer Beware." *Psychology Today* 2, no. 12 (May), pp. 36–40.

SIMON, B. K. 1970. "Social Casework Theory: An Overview." In *Theories of Social Casework,* eds. R. Roberts & R. Nee, pp. 353–396. Chicago: University of Chicago Press.

SIMOS, B. G. 1977. "Grief Therapy to Facilitate Healthy Restitution." *Social Casework* (June), pp. 337–342.

SINCLAIR, L., & C. Zastrow, 1993. "Human Sexuality Variations, Sex Counseling, and Sex Therapy." In *Introduction to Social Work and Social Welfare,* 5th ed., by C. Zastrow, pp. 193–243. Pacific Grove, CA: Brooks/Cole.

SINDLER, A. P. 1978. *Bakke, DeFunis and Minority Admissions: The Quest for Equal Opportunity.* New York: Longmans, Green.

SKINNER, B. F. 1938. *The Behavior of Organisms.* New York: Appleton-Century-Crofts.

———. 1948. *Walden Two.* New York: Macmillan.

———. 1953. *Science and Human Behavior.* New York: Free Press.

SLAFF, J. I., & J. K. Brubacker. 1985. *The AIDS Epidemic: How You Can Protect Yourself and Your Family—Why You Must.* New York: Warner Books.

SLATER, P. E. 1958. "Contrasting Correlates of Group Size." *Sociometry* 21, no. 2 (June), pp. 129–139.

SLOANE, R. B., F. R. Staples, A. H. Cristol, N. J. Yorkston, & K. Whipple. 1975. *Psychotherapy Versus Behavior Therapy.* Cambridge: Harvard University Press.

SMITH, L. L. 1978. "A Review of Crisis Intervention Theory." *Social Casework* 59, no. 7 (July), pp. 396–405.

SOLOMON, B. 1987. "Human Development: Socio-cultural Perspectives." *The Encyclopedia of Social Work,* pp. 856–866. Silver Spring, MD: National Association of Social Workers.

SOLOMON, P., P. Kubzansky, P. Leiderman, J. Menderson, R. Trumbull, & D. Wexler, eds. 1961. *Sensory Deprivation.* Cambridge: Harvard University Press.

SOUTHERN REGIONAL EDUCATION BOARD. 1976. "Educational Assumptions for Rural Social Work." In *Social Work in Rural Communities* by Leon Ginsberg. New York: Council on Social Work Education.

SOUTHWESTERN COOPERATIVE EDUCATIONAL LABORATORY. 1968. *Ethno-Pedagogy: A Manual in Cultural Sensitivity with Techniques for Improving Cross-Cultural Teaching by Fitting Ethnic Patterns.* Albuquerque: Southwestern Cooperative Educational Laboratory.

"SPECIAL ISSUE ON CONCEPTUAL FRAMEWORKS." 1977. *Social Work* 22 (Sept.), pp. 338–444.

SPITZ, R. 1945. "Hospitalism: Genesis of Psychiatric Conditions in Early Childhood." *Psychoanalytic Study of the Child* 1, p. 53.

SPOCK, B. 1957. *The Common-Sense Book of Baby and Child Care.* New York: Duell, Sloan & Pierce.

SPRANGER, E. 1928. *Types of Men.* New York: Hafner.

STAMPFL, T. G., & D. J. Levis. 1967. "Essentials of Implosive Therapy: A Learning-Based Psychodynamic Behavioral Therapy." *Journal of Abnormal Psychology* 72, pp. 496–503.

STARKWEATHER, C. L., & S. M. Turner. 1975. "Parents Anonymous: Reflections on the Development of a Self-Help Group." In *Child Abuse Interventions and Treatment,* eds. N. C. Ebeling & D. A. Hill. Littleton, MA: PSG.

STEINER, C. 1974. *Scripts People Live.* New York: Grove Press.

STEPHENSON, M. M. 1983. "The Talking Circle: A Resource for Personal and Community Development." Paper presented at the Eighth Annual Institute on Social Work in Rural Areas, July, Cheney, WA.

STONE, R. 1989. *The Feminization of Poverty Among the Elderly.* Rockville, MD: National Center for Health Services Research and Health Care Technology Assessment.

STONE, W. C. 1966. "Be Generous." In *A Treasury of Success Unlimited,* ed. O. Mandino, pp. 9–10. New York: Hawthorn Books.

STRACHEY, J. 1962. *Sigmund Freud: Three Essays on the Theory of Sexuality.* New York: Basic Books.

STROUP, H. 1986. *Social Welfare Pioneers.* Chicago: Nelson-Hall.

STUART, R. B. 1970. *Trick or Treatment.* Champaign, IL: Research Press Co.

SUINN, R. M. 1976. "Body Thinking: Psychology for Olympic Champs." *Psychology Today* 10 (July), pp. 38–43.

SULLIVAN, T., K. Thompson, R. Wright, G. Gross, & D. Spady. 1980. *Social Problems.* New York: Wiley.

SUNDBERG, N. D., & L. E. Tyler. 1962. *Clinical Psychology.* New York: Appleton-Century-Crofts.

SUNDEL, M., & S. S. Sundel. 1975. *Behavior Modification in the Human Services.* New York: Wiley.

SZASZ, T. 1961. "The Myth of Mental Illness." In *Clinical Psychology in Transition,* comp. J. R. Braun. Cleveland: Howard Allen.

———. 1963. *Law, Liberty and Psychiatry.* New York: Macmillan.

———. 1967. "The Psychiatrist as Double Agent." *Trans-Action* 4, pp. 3–25.

TAYLOR, F. W. 1947. *Scientific Management.* New York: Harper & Row.

TEARE, R. J. 1979. "A Task Analysis for Public Welfare Practice and Educational Implications." In *The Pursuit of Competence in Social Work,* ed. Frank Clark and Morton Arkava, pp. 131–145. San Francisco: Jossey-Bass.

TEUBER, H. L., & E. Powers. 1953. "Evaluating Therapy in a Delinquency Prevention Program." *Psychiatric Treatment* 21, pp. 138–147.

THOMAS, A., & S. Sillen. 1972. *Racism and Psychiatry.* New York: Brunner/Mazel.

THOMAS, E. 1959. *The Harmless People.* New York: Knopf.

THOMAS, E. J. 1978. "Research and Service in Single-Case Experimentation: Conflicts and Choices." *Social Work Research and Abstracts* 14, pp. 20–31.

———. 1984. *Designing Interventions for the Helping Professions.* New York: Sage.

THOMAS, S. A. 1977. "Theory and Practice in Feminine Therapy." *Social Work* 22 (Nov.), pp. 447–454.

THOMPSON, G. 1972. "The Identification of Ego States." *Transactional Analysis Journal* 2, pp. 196–211.

THORNDIKE, E. L. 1913. *The Psychology of Learning.* New York: Teachers College Press.

THORPE, L. P., & B. Katz. 1948. *The Psychology of Abnormal*

Behavior. New York: Ronald Press.

TOCH, H. 1970. "The Care and Feeding of Typologies and Labels." *Federal Probation 34* (Sept.), pp. 46–57.

TOLMAN, E. C. 1932. *Purposive Behavior in Animals and Men*. New York: Appleton-Century-Crofts.

TOULIATOS, J., B. F. Perlmutter, & M. A. Straus, eds. 1990. *Handbook of Family Measurement Techniques*. Newbury Park, CA: Sage.

TRACY, E. M. 1990. "Identifying Social Support Resources of At-Risk Families." *Social Work 35*, no. 3, pp. 252–258.

TRUAX, C. 1966. "Reinforcement and Non-reinforcement in Rogerian Psychotherapy." *Journal of Abnormal Psychology 71*, pp. 11–19.

TRUAX, C., & K. M. Mitchell. 1971. "Research on Certain Therapists' Interpersonal Skills in Relation to Process and Outcome." In *Handbook of Psychotherapy and Behavior Change*, eds. A. E. Bergin & S. L. Garfield, pp. 299–344. New York: Wiley.

TUBBS, S. I., & J. W. Baird. 1976. *The Open Person*. Columbus, OH: Merrill.

TURNER, C., H. Miller, & L. Moses, eds. 1989. *AIDS: Sexual Behavior and Intravenous Drug Use*. Washington, DC: The National Academy Press.

TURNER, J. B. 1972. "Education for Practice with Minorities." *Social Work 17* (May), pp. 112–118.

UNIVERSITY OF PITTSBURGH LAW REVIEW. 1975. "Tarasoff v. Regents of University of California: *The Psychotherapist's Peril*" *37*, pp. 159–164.

VAFEAS, J. G. 1991. "Personal Computer Based Clinical Systems: A Goal Oriented Case Management Model." *Computers in Human Services 8*, no. 2, pp. 21–36.

VAN DE VEN, A., & A. L. Delbecq, 1971. "Nominal versus Interacting Group Processes for Committee Decision-Making Effectiveness." *Academy of Management Journal 14*, no. 2 (June), pp. 203–212.

VAN DEN BERGH, N. 1992. "Feminist Treatment for People with Depression." In *Structuring Change*, ed. K. Corcoran, pp. 95–110. Chicago: Lyceum Books.

VAN DEN BERGH, N., & L. B. Cooper. 1987. "Feminist Social Work." In *The Encyclopedia of Social Work*, pp. 610–618. Washington, DC: National Association of Social Workers.

VOGLER, R. E., S. E. Lunde, G. R. Johnson, & P. L. Martin. 1970. "Electrical Aversion Conditioning with Chronic Alcoholics." *Journal of Consulting and Clinical Psychology 34*, pp. 302–307.

VYGOTSKY, L. 1962. *Thoughts and Language*. Cambridge, MA: MIT Press.

WACHTEL, D. 1974. "Structures of Community and Strategies for Organization." In *Strategies of Community Organization—A Book of Readings*, eds. F. Cox et al. Itasca, IL: Peacock.

WALKER, R. S. 1992. *AIDS Today, Tomorrow*. Atlantic Highlands, NJ: Humanities Press.

WALLACE, R. K. 1970. "Physiological Effects of Transcendental Meditation." *Science 167*, pp. 1751–1754.

WALZ, T. H., & N. Blum. 1987. *Sexual Health in Later Life*. Lexington, MA: Lexington Books.

WASHINGTON, V. 1987. "Community Involvement in Recruiting Adoptive Homes for Black Children." *Child Welfare 66*, no. 1, pp. 57–67.

WATKINS, T. R., & R. Gonzales. 1982. "Outreach to Mexican-Americans." *Social Work 27*, no. 1 (Jan.), pp. 68–73.

WATSON, D. L., & R. G. Tharp. 1972. *Self-Directed Behavior: Self-Modification for Personal Adjustment*. Pacific Grove, CA: Brooks/Cole.

WATSON, G., & D. W. Johnson. 1972. *Social Psychology: Issues and Insight*. 2nd ed. Philadelphia: Lippincott.

WATSON, J. B., & R. Rayner. 1920. "Conditioned Emotional Reaction." *Journal of Experimental Psychology 3*, no. 1, pp. 1–14.

Webster's Ninth New Collegiate Dictionary. 1983. Springfield, MA: Merriam.

WEISS, C. H. 1972. *Evaluation Research*. Englewood Cliffs, NJ: Prentice-Hall.

WEISS, J. C. 1990. "Violence Motivated by Bigotry: Ethnoviolence." In *The Encyclopedia of Social Work*. 18th ed., 1990 supplement, pp. 307–319. Silver Spring, MD: National Association of Social Workers.

WEISSMAN, H. H., I. E. Epstein, & A. Savage. 1987. "Expanding the Role Repertoire of Clinicians." *Social Casework 68*, no. 3, pp. 150–155.

WELTNER, C. 1977. "The Model Cities Program: A Sobering Scorecard." *Policy Review* (Fall), pp. 73–87.

WENDER, P., & D. Klein. 1968. *Mind, Mood and Medicine*. New York: Meridian.

"What Everyone Should Know About AIDS." 1985. South Deerfield, MA: Channing L. Bete Co.

WHITE, R. W., & N. F. Watt. 1973. *The Abnormal Personality*. 4th ed. New York: Ronald Press.

WHITTAKER, J. K. 1974. *Social Treatment*. Hawthorne, NY: Aldine.

WIGMORE, J. H. 1961. *Evidence in Trials at Common Law*, vol. 8 (rev.), ed. J. T. McNaughton. Boston: Little, Brown.

WILENSKY, H., & C. Lebeaux. 1965. *Industrial Society & Social Welfare*. New York: Free Press.

WILEY, G. E. 1973. "Win/Lose Situations." In *1973 Annual Handbook of Group Facilitators*, by J. E. Jones & J. W. Pfeiffer, pp. 105–107. La Jolla, CA: University Associates.

WILLIAMS, D. A., T. Jackson, D. Weathers, N. Joseph, & M. Anderson. 1985. "Roots III: Souls on Ice: A Post–Civil Rights Generation Struggle for Identity." *Newsweek*, pp. 82–84.

WILSON, S. J. 1978. *Confidentiality in Social Work: Issues and Principles*. New York: Free Press.

WILSON, T. G. 1989. "Behavior Therapy." In *Current Psychotherapies*, 4th ed., eds. R. J. Corsini & D. Wedding, pp. 241–282. Itasca, IL: Peacock.

WISEMAN, R. S. 1975. "Crisis Theory and the Process of Divorce." *Social Casework 56*, no. 4 (April), pp. 205–212.

WOFFORD, J. 1979. "Ebonics: A Legitimate System of Oral Communication." *Journal of Black Studies 9*, pp. 367–382.

WOLPE, J. 1958. *Psychotherapy by Reciprocal Inhibition*. Stanford, CA: Stanford University Press.

———. 1969. *The Practice of Behavior Therapy*. Elmsford, NY: Pergamon Press.

WOODMAN, N. J. 1987. "Homosexuality: Lesbian Women." In *The Encyclopedia of Social Work*, pp. 805–812. Silver Spring, MD: National Association of Social Workers.

WOODS, N. F. 1979. *Human Sexuality in Health & Illness*. St. Louis: Mosby.

WRIGHT, B. J., & V. R. Isenstein. 1975. *Psychological Tests and Minorities*. Rockville, MD: National Institute of Mental Health.

WRIGHT, C., & M. Tate. 1973. *Economic Concepts and Systems Analysis: An Introduction for Public Managers*. Reading, MA: Addison-Wesley.

ZASTROW, C. 1973. "The Nominal Group: A New Approach to Designing Programs for Curbing Delinquency." *Canadian Journal of Criminology and Corrections* (Jan.), pp. 109–117.

———. 1977. "How to Counsel." In *The Personal Problem Solver,* eds. C. Zastrow & D. H. Chang, pp. 267–274. Englewood Cliffs: NJ: Prentice-Hall.

———. 1979. *Talk to Yourself: Using the Power of Self-Talk.* Englewood Cliffs, NJ: Prentice-Hall.

———. 1982. *Introduction to Social Welfare Institutions.* 2nd ed. Pacific Grove, CA: Brooks/Cole.

———. 1986. *Introduction to Social Welfare Institutions.* 3rd ed. Pacific Grove, CA: Brooks/Cole.

———. 1990a. "Social Workers and Salesworkers: Similarities and Differences." *Journal of Independent Social Work* 4, no. 3, pp. 7–16.

———. 1990b. "Starting and Leading Therapy Groups: A Beginner's Guide." *Journal of Independent Social Work 4*, no. 4, pp. 7–26.

———. 1993a. *Introduction to Social Work and Social Welfare,* 5th ed. Pacific Grove, CA: Brooks/Cole.

———. 1993b. *You Are What You Think: A Guide to Self-Realization.* Chicago: Nelson-Hall.

ZASTROW, C., & D. Chang, eds. 1977. *The Personal Problem Solver.* Englewood Cliffs, NJ: Prentice-Hall.

ZASTROW, C., & R. Navarre. 1977. "The Nominal Group: A New Tool for Making Social Work Education Relevant." *Journal of Education for Social Work* 13 (Winter), pp. 112–118.

———. 1979. "Using Videotaped Role Playing to Assess and Develop Competence." In *The Pursuit of Competence in Social Work,* eds. F. Clark & M. Arkava, pp. 193–204. San Francisco: Jossey-Bass.

ZASTROW, C., V. Dotson, & M. Koch. 1986. "The Neuro-Linguistic Programming Treatment Approach." *Journal of Independent Social Work 1* (Fall), pp. 29–38.

ZAUNER, P. 1974. "Mothers Anonymous: The Last Resort." In *The Battered Child,* ed. J. E. Leavitt. Morristown, NJ: General Learning Press.

ZILBERGELD, B. 1978. *Male Sexuality.* Boston: Little Brown.

INDEX

Photo Credits

TO THE OWNER OF THIS BOOK:

We hope that you have found *The Practice of Social Work*, fifth edition, useful. So that this book can be improved in a future edition, would you take the time to complete this sheet and return it? Thank you.

School and address: _____

Department: _____

Instructor's name: _____

1. What I like most about this book is: _____

_____

_____

2. What I like least about this book is: _____

_____

_____

3. My general reaction to this book is: _____

_____

4. The name of the course in which I used this book is: _____

_____

5. Were all of the chapters of the book assigned for you to read? _____

   If not, which ones weren't? _____

6. In the space below, or on a separate sheet of paper, please write specific suggestions for improving this book and anything else you'd care to share about your experience in using the book.

_____

_____

_____

_____

_____

Optional:

Your name: _____ Date: _____

May Brooks/Cole quote you, either in promotion for *The Practice of Social Work*, fifth edition, or in future publishing ventures?

Yes: _____ No: _____

Sincerely,

Charles Zastrow

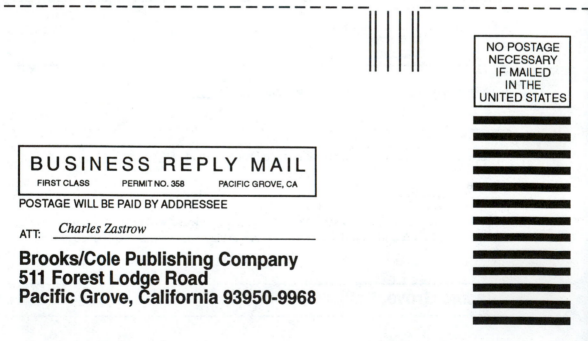

BUSINESS REPLY MAIL

FIRST CLASS   PERMIT NO. 358   PACIFIC GROVE, CA

POSTAGE WILL BE PAID BY ADDRESSEE

ATT: *Charles Zastrow* _____

**Brooks/Cole Publishing Company
511 Forest Lodge Road
Pacific Grove, California 93950-9968**

NO POSTAGE
NECESSARY
IF MAILED
IN THE
UNITED STATES

Brooks/Cole is dedicated to publishing quality publications for education in the human services fields. If you are interested in learning more about our publications, please fill in your name and address and request our latest catalogue, using this prepaid mailer.

Name: _____

Street Address: _____

City, State, and Zip: _____

FOLD HERE

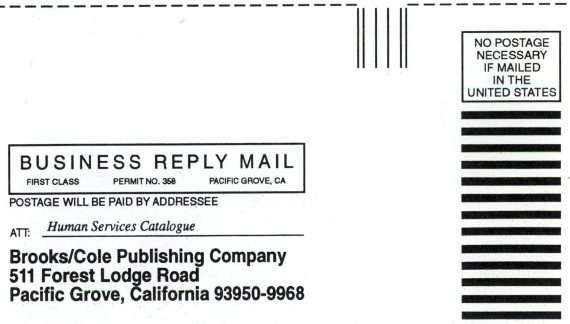

NO POSTAGE
NECESSARY
IF MAILED
IN THE
UNITED STATES

BUSINESS REPLY MAIL
FIRST CLASS   PERMIT NO. 358   PACIFIC GROVE, CA

POSTAGE WILL BE PAID BY ADDRESSEE

ATT: *Human Services Catalogue*

Brooks/Cole Publishing Company
511 Forest Lodge Road
Pacific Grove, California 93950-9968

FOLD HERE